Telecommunication Laws in Europe

Baker & McKenzie

Telecommunication Laws in Europe

Law and Regulation of Electronic Communications in Europe

Fifth edition

Edited by
Joachim Scherer
Baker & McKenzie LLP,
Frankfurt

Tottel
publishing

Tottel Publishing, Maxwelton House, 41–43 Boltro Road, Haywards Heath, West Sussex RH16 1BJ

© Tottel Publishing 2005

A CIP Catalogue record for this book is available from the British Library.

ISBN 1 84592 078 3

Typeset by Columns Design Ltd, Reading, Berkshire
Printed and bound in Great Britain by William Clowes Limited, Beccles, Suffolk

Foreword

The Commission's new initiative 'i2010: European Information Society 2010' is a comprehensive strategy for modernising and deploying EU policy and regulatory instruments to encourage the development of the digital economy. As the European Commissioner responsible for Information Society and Media, it is my task to ensure that an appropriate framework for the digital economy and for investment in ICT is in place. This is essential for delivering sustained growth and skilled jobs in Europe.

We need to put together all the tools and instruments available to the EU and the Member States to promote and accelerate a favourable development of the communications and media industries.

Today's regulatory framework for electronic communications builds on principles of competition law and technology neutrality. It takes account of the convergence of telecommunications, data transmission and broadcasting services, by dealing with all communications networks and services (fixed, mobile, satellite, broadcasting, etc) in a consistent way. The Directives are a thoughtful and well-considered attempt to provide a coherent framework for the delivery of different services which traditionally have been subject to different regulatory regimes.

Effective competition in these markets benefits consumers in terms of increased choice and lower prices. The framework provides a basis both to control the exercise of significant market power and the means to allow national regulators to take steps to allow self-sustaining competition to emerge. As markets become effectively competitive, the framework provides that sector-specific regulation will be removed. Thereafter, competitive markets will be subject only to competition law and consumer protection regulation.

The framework's flexibility, grounded in technology neutrality and competition law principles, has provided regulators with a solid basis for handling the challenges as existing services are delivered over new infrastructures or in new ways. Therefore, on the one hand, the framework combines a flexible approach allowing national authorities to deal with emerging services whilst maintaining a close focus on local circumstances. On the other hand, operators require a degree of legal certainty regarding the regulatory approach throughout the EU if they are to invest in the European Single Market. Operators need to know that a harmonised approach to regulatory legislation and practice will be adopted by the Member States and that there will be no fragmentation of the single market into a patchwork of differing national regulatory regimes. This allows companies to operate on a scale which only a European-wide market can provide. In order to meet these objectives, the regulatory framework establishes procedures strengthening collaboration among the national regulatory authorities of the Member States, and between the national regulatory authorities and the European Commission. In this way, a consistent approach is developed throughout the EU, while permitting at the same time a more flexible approach to deal with national conditions and markets where this is warranted.

Proper transposition into national law and speedy implementation of the regulatory framework are essential to stimulate competition, encourage lower prices and encourage investment. Today we know that, where the framework has been implemented consistently and effectively, these targets have been met. Yet – three years on – the implementation of the Directives is far from being complete in several European markets.

The Commission will review the functioning of the Directives, and report to the European Parliament and to the Council in 2006. The review is an opportunity to examine the functioning of the framework and to ensure that it remains valid for the period beyond 2010.

In the meantime, I trust that this collection of texts will be a very useful instrument for all those concerned with the application of Community law in the electronic communications sector and will facilitate the understanding by stakeholders, consumers and undertakings of the regulatory environment throughout the European Union.

Viviane Reding
European Commissioner for Information Society and Media

Preface

Only four years after the full liberalisation of the telecommunication network and service markets in the European Union, the EU adopted its 2002 Regulatory Package of legislative measures replacing the first generation of European telecommunication law which had been put in place in the 1990s.

The Regulatory Package has set ambitious objectives both for national legislators and for the national regulatory authorities (NRAs): National legislators had to transpose into national laws a complex and detailed set of rules aimed at a far-reaching harmonisation of the national provisions governing electronic communications. NRAs were to be given broad regulatory powers and a high degree of flexibility in applying the regulatory measures set forth in the laws. In order to achieve a balance of EU-wide harmonisation and national flexibility, procedural mechanisms and organisational structures were put in place allowing for consultation among national NRAs and ensuring 'co-regulation' by NRAs and the European Commission – with the Commission assuming the role of a European super-regulator.

The Regulatory Package should have been transposed into national law by July 2003, but it has taken some Member States two years longer to adapt their legislation to the requirements of the EU Regulatory Framework – and the effort is continuing. The NRAs are still struggling, under the Commission's watchful eye, with the requirement to analyse, for each Member State, 18 markets with a view to determining whether they are dominated by companies with significant market power and therefore require regulation.

As the implementation of the EU Regulatory Framework gains momentum, the objective of this book is to provide an overview of both the emerging pan-European legislative framework for electronic communications and its application at national level in the EU Member States and in seven non-EU Member States, some of which are candidates for accession.

The country chapters, all of which follow the EU Regulatory Framework's structure and use its legal categories as a frame of reference, highlight the common characteristics of national laws and regulation of electronic communications, as well as the differences which remain despite the EU's ongoing harmonisation efforts.

The contributions to the 5th edition of this book have again been prepared by Members of Baker & McKenzie's European Telecommunication Law Practice Group and by telecommunication law experts from correspondent law firms in Bulgaria, Cyprus, Denmark, Estonia, Finland, Greece, Ireland, Latvia, Lithuania, Luxembourg, Malta, Norway, Portugal, Romania, the Slovak Republic, Slovenia and Turkey.

The editor gratefully acknowledges the invaluable editorial assistance of Dr Toralf Noeding.

The law is as at 15 July 2005, save as otherwise stated.

Joachim Scherer, Frankfurt
17 August 2005

List of contributors

AUSTRIA

**Christoph Kerres and
  Peter Schludermann**
Baker & McKenzie–Kerres & Diwok
Rechtsanwälte GmbH
Schubertring 2
Vienna 1010
Austria

BELGIUM

Arne Gutermann and Els Janssens
Baker & McKenzie
Avenue Louise 149 Louizalaan
Eighth Floor
1050 Brussels
Belgium

BULGARIA

Violetta Kunze and Lilia Kisseva
Djingov, Gouginski, Kyutchukov &
  Velichkov
Untermainkai 71
60329 Frankfurt am Main
Germany

CYPRUS

Adamos Adamides
Adamos K. Adamides & Co, Lawyers
Eagle Star House, 1st floor
Thekla Lyssiotis 35
P.O.Box 51094
Limassol 3030
Cyprus

CZECH REPUBLIC

**Tomas Skoumal, Petra Ledvinkova
  and Patrik Kastner**
Baker & McKenzie
Klimentska 46
110 02 Prague 1
Czech Republic

DATA PROTECTION AND PRIVACY

Helen Kemmitt
Baker & McKenzie LLP
100 New Bridge Street
London EC4V 6JA
United Kingdom

Chris Mögelin
Baker & McKenzie LLP
Bethmannstraße 50-54
60311 Frankfurt am Main
Germany

DENMARK

Lise Engel and Henning Hansen
Philip & Partners
7 Vognmagergade
PO Box 2227
DK-1018 Copenhagen K
Denmark

ESTONIA

Pirkko-Liis Harkmaa
Advokaadibüroo Lepik & Luhaäär
LAWIN
Dunkri 7
10123 Tallinn
Estonia

EU COMPETITION LAW

Keith Jones
Baker & McKenzie LLP
100 New Bridge Street
London EC4V 6JA
United Kingdom

Fiona Carlin
Baker & McKenzie
Avenue Louise 149 Louizalaan
Eighth Floor
1050 Brussels
Belgium

EU ELECTRONIC COMMUNICATIONS LAW AND POLICY

Joachim Scherer
Baker & McKenzie LLP
Bethmannstraße 50-54
60311 Frankfurt am Main
Germany

FINLAND

Marko Vuorinen, Jalmari Sasi and Kaisa Fahllund
Hannes Snellman Attorneys at Law Ltd
P.O. Box 333 (Eteläranta 8)
FIN-00131 Helsinki
Finland

FRANCE

Valerie Kostrzewski-Pugnat
Baker & McKenzie
32 avenue Kléber
BP 2112
75771 Paris Cedex 16
France

GERMANY

Joachim Scherer
Baker & McKenzie LLP
Bethmannstraße 50-54
60311 Frankfurt am Main
Germany

GREECE

Alkistis Christofolu, Virginia Murray and Stelios Katevatis
IKRP Rokas & Partners
25 Boukourestiou St.
106 71 Athens
Greece

HUNGARY

Emese Szitasi and Ines Radmilovic
Baker & McKenzie
Andrássy-út 102
1062 Budapest
Hungary

IRELAND

Claire Waterson and John Handoll
William Fry Solicitors
Fitzwilton House
Wilton Place
Dublin 2
Ireland

ITALY

Raffaele Giarda, Valerio Bruno and Andrea Perotti
Baker & McKenzie
Viale di Villa Massimo, 57
00161 Rome
Italy

ITU/WTO

Joachim Scherer
Baker & McKenzie LLP
Bethmannstraße 50-54
60311 Frankfurt am Main
Germany

Sunwinder Mann
Baker & McKenzie LLP
100 New Bridge Street
London EC4V 6JA
United Kingdom

Hannes Schloemann
WTI Advisors Ltd (Oxford/Geneva)
29, quai du Mont-Blanc
CH-1201 Genève
Switzerland

LATVIA

Martins Gailis and Sanda Lace
Law offices of Klavins & Slaidins
Elizabetes 15,
Riga LV-1010
Latvia

LITHUANIA

**Jaunius Gumbis, Giedre Valentaite
and Agne Makanskaite**
Lideika, Petrauskas, Valiunas ir partneriai
LAWIN
Jogailos g. 9/1
LT-01116 Vilnius
Lithuania

LUXEMBOURG

**Sophie Wagner-Chartier and
Héloise Bock**
Arendt & Medernach
14, rue Erasme
B.P. 39
L-2010
Luxembourg

MALTA

Louis Cassar Pullicino
Ganado & Associates - Advocates
171, Old Bakery Street
Valletta VLT 09
Malta

NETHERLANDS

Serge Gijrath and Koen Parren
Baker & McKenzie
Leidseplein 29
1017 PS Amsterdam
The Netherlands

NORWAY

**Nicolai Stenersen, Knut Glad, Espen
Sandvik and Margarethe Stoltz**
Arntzen de Besche Advokatfirma AS
Bygdøy allé 2
0257 Oslo
Norway

POLAND

**Wojciech Bialik and Eligiusz
Krzesniak**
Baker & McKenzie
Focus Building
Al. Armii Ludowej 26
00-609 Warsaw
Poland

PORTUGAL

**António de Mendonça Raimundo
and João de Castro**
Albuquerque & Associados
Rua Victor Cordon, 21
1200-482 Lisboa
Portugal

ROMANIA

**Horatiu Dumitru and
Bogdan-Petru Mihai**
Musat & Asociatii
B-dul Aviatorilor Nr. 43, sect. 1
011853 Bukarest
Romania

RUSSIA

**Edward Bekeschenko, Sergei Nosov
and Max Gutbrod**
Baker & McKenzie
Sadovaya Plaza
11th Floor
7 Dolgorukovskaya Street
Moscow 127006
Russia

SLOVAK REPUBLIC

**Branislav Brocko and
Lubomir Marek**
Marek & Partners
Attorneys-at-Law
Palisady 36
811 06 Bratislava
Slovak Republic

SLOVENIA

**Sreco Jadek, Jure Levovnik and
  Ozbej Merc**
Jadek & Pensa
Tav_arjeva 6
1000 Ljubljana
Slovenija

SPAIN

**Maite Diez and José Antonio
  de la Calle**
Baker & McKenzie
Paseo de la Castellana 92
28046 Madrid
Spain

SWEDEN

**Stefan Brandt and Sara Elgstrand
  Johansson**
Baker & McKenzie Advokatbyrå KB
Linnégatan 18
Box 5719
SE-114 87 Stockholm
Sweden

SWITZERLAND

**Markus Berni and Corinne
  Casanova**
Baker & McKenzie
Zollikerstrasse 225
CH-8034 Zürich
Switzerland

TURKEY

**Dr. Mehmet Komurcu and
  Serdar Akcasu**
Birsel Law Offices
Inonu Cadsi 53
Ongan Apt, 4th Floor, Gumussuyu
80090 Istanbul
Turkey

UKRAINE

**Olexander Martinenko,
  Anna Yegupova and
  Vitaliy Radchenko**
Baker & McKenzie
Millennium Business Center
Fifth Floor
12a Volodymyrska Street
Kyiv 01025
Ukraine

UNITED KINGDOM

**Peter Strivens, Helen Kemmitt and
  Keith Jones**
Baker & McKenzie LLP
100 New Bridge Street
London EC4V 6JA
United Kingdom

Contents

Part III
Telecommunication Law in EU Member States

5   The Austrian Market for Electronic Communications

6   The Belgian Market for Electronic Communications

7   The Cyprus Market for Electronic Communications

Part IV
Telecommunication Law in Non-EU Member States

List of abbreviations

This list includes only general, communications-related abbreviations that are used throughout the work; for abbreviations that are specific to an individual country, please refer to the appropriate chapter, where the full term is set out where the abbreviation is first used.

3G	third generation
API	Application Programming Interface
CEPT	European Conference of Postal and Telecommunications Administrations
CFI	Court of First Instance
ECJ	European Court of Justice
ECMR	EC Merger Regulation
EPG	Electronic Program Guide
ERG	European Regulators Group for Electronic Communications Networks and Services
ETSI	European Telecommunications Standards Institute
GATS	General Agreement on Trade in Services
GATT	General Agreement on Tariffs and Trade
GTS	global telecommunications services
IRG	Independent Regulators Group
ISDN	Integrated Services Digital Network
ITR	International Telecommunication Regulations
ITU	International Telecommunication Union
MHP	Multimedia Home Platform
MNO	Mobile Network Operator
MVNO	Mobile Virtual Network Operator
NCA	National Competition Authority
NRA	National Regulatory Authority
ONP	open network provision
PABX	private automatic branch exchange
RPI	Retail Prices Index
SMP	significant market power
SMS	short message service
TO	telecommunication organisation
VoIP	Voice over Internet Protocol
WTO	World Trade Organisation

Key EU Directives

DIRECTIVE	FULL TITLE	OJ REFERENCE
Access Directive	Directive 2002/19/EC of the European Parliament and of the Council of 7 March 2002 on access to, and interconnection of, electronic communications networks and associated facilities	OJ L 108/7
Authorisation Directive	Directive 2002/20/EC of the European Parliament and of the Council of 7 March 2002 on the authorisation of electronic communications networks and services	OJ L 108/21
Framework Directive	Directive 2002/21/EC of the European Parliament and of the Council of 7 March 2002 on a common regulatory framework for electronic communications networks and services	OJ L 108/33
Universal Service Directive	Directive 2002/22/EC of the European Parliament and of the Council of 7 March 2002 on universal service and users' rights relating to electronic communications networks and services	OJ L 108/51
E-Privacy Directive	Directive 2002/58/EC of the European Parliament and of the Council of 12 July 2002 concerning the processing of personal data and the protection of privacy in the electronic communications sector	OJ L 201/37
Competition Directive	Commission Directive 2002/77/EC of 16 September 2002 on competition in the markets for electronic communications networks and services	OJ L 249/21

DIRECTIVE	FULL TITLE	OJ REFERENCE
Directive on electronic commerce	Directive 2000/31/EC of the European Parliament and of the Council of 8 June 2000 on certain legal aspects of information society services, in particular electronic commerce, in the Internal Market	OJ L 178/17
ONP Voice Telephony Directive (1998)	Directive 98/10/EC of the European Parliament and of the Council of 26 February 1998 on the application of open network provision (ONP) to voice telephony and on universal service for telecommunications in a competitive environment	OJ L 101/24
Distance Selling Directive	Directive 97/7/EC of the European Parliament and of the Council of 20 May 1997 on the protection of consumers in respect of distance contracts	OJ L 144/19
Interconnection Directive	Directive 97/33/EC on inter-connection in telecommunication	OJ L 199/32
ONP Framework Directive (1997)	Directive 97/51/EC of the European Parliament and of the Council of 6 October 1997 amending Council Directives 90/387/EEC and 92/44/EEC for the purpose of adaptation to a competitive environment in telecommunications	OJ L 295/23
Voice Telephony Directive (1995)	Directive 95/62/EC on the application of open network provision to voice telephony	OJ L 321/6
Leased Lines Directive (1992)	Council Directive 92/44/EEC on the application of open network provisions to leased lines	OJ L 165/27
ONP Framework Directive (1990)	Council Directive 90/387/EEC on the establishment of the internal market for telecommunications services through the implementation of open network provision	OJ L 192/1
Services Directive (1990)	Commission Directive 90/388/EEC, of 28 June 1990 on competition in the markets for telecommunications services	OJ L 192/10

Electronic Communication Law and Policy of the European Union[1]

Joachim Scherer
Baker & McKenzie, Frankfurt

INTRODUCTION

1.1   At the beginning of the twenty-first century, electronic communication plays a key role in the economic prosperity and development of all nations. Electronic communication networks are the backbone of the 'information society'.

1.2   In the early 1980s, the telecommunication sector in Europe was still characterised by exclusive rights of national telecommunication organisations ('TOs') in almost all Member States of the European Union ('EU') to provide telecommunication networks and services. In 1987, the Commission issued its Green Paper on the development of the common market for telecommunication services and equipment, and started a Europe-wide debate on the liberalisation and harmonisation of the telecommunication regulatory environment, with the objective of adapting it to the requirements of a single Community-wide market. In a remarkably short period of time, the EU then established a comprehensive and flexible regulatory system, culminating in the full liberalisation of telecommunication networks and services with effect from 1 January 1998. Only four years after this far-reaching liberalisation and the re-regulation of the European telecommunications markets that came with it,[2] and less than two years after the publication of the

---

1   Editing of this chapter closed on 19 July 2005. The author would like to thank Toralf Noeding for his valuable contribution in drafting this chapter.

2   The following legal instruments are counted among the most important legal instruments of re-regulation: Directive 97/51/EC of the European Parliament and of the Council of 6 October 1997 amending Council Directives 90/387/EEC and 92/44/EEC for the purpose of adaptation to a competitive environment in telecommunications, OJ L 295/23, 29.10.1997; Directive 97/13/EC of the European Parliament and of the Council of 10 April 1997 on a common framework for general authorisations and individual licences in the field of telecommunications services, OJ L 117/15, 07.05.1997; Directive 97/33/EC of the European Parliament and of the Council of 30 June 1997 on interconnection in telecommunications with regard to ensuring universal service and interoperability through application of the principles of Open Network Provision ('ONP'), OJ L 199/32, 26.07.1997; Directive 98/10/EC of the European Parliament and of the Council of 26 February 1998 on the application of open network provision (ONP) to voice telephony and on universal service for telecommunications in a competitive environment; OJ L 101/24, 01.04.1998.

'Communications Review 1999',[3] the European Union adopted a package of six Directives[4] and one Decision[5] constituting a new legal framework for electronic communications (the '2002 EU Regulatory Package').[6]

On that basis, the EU Member States are currently establishing and refining their new legal and regulatory frameworks for electronic communications.

1.3   The convergence of the telecommunications, media and information technology sectors creates new challenges for the regulatory framework. The borders between the once separate sectors of telecommunication, media and information technology become blurred, and market players are confronted with multiple layers of legislation addressing different aspects of the converging communications systems and services. The '2002 EU Regulatory Package' endeavours to meet the challenge of the technical convergence, ie the merging of transmission networks and services by providing a single legal framework not only for 'telecommunication networks' but for all 'electronic communication networks' including mobile networks, cable TV networks and even electricity cable systems if used for the transmission of signals. Electronic communication is, however, only one aspect of the entire phenomenon of the 'information society'. In addition to the 'conduit'-related rules governing electronic communications networks and services, the policy and law of the EU have addressed and continue to address 'content'-related issues such as the regulation of trans-border television services[7] and the regulatory challenges presented by the internet, eg the question of responsibility for contents

---

3   Communication from the Commission to the European Parliament, the Council, the Economic and Social Committee and the Committee of the Regions: Towards a new framework for Electronic Communications infrastructure and associated services, The 1999 Communications Review, COM(1999) 539 final, 10.11.1999.

4   Directive 2002/21/EC of the European Parliament and of the Council of 7 March 2002 on a common regulatory framework for electronic communications networks and services ('Framework Directive'), OJ L 108/33, 24.04.2002; Directive 2002/19/EC of the European Parliament and of the Council of 7 March 2002 on access to, and interconnection of, electronic communications networks and associated facilities ('Access Directive'), OJ L 108/7, 24.04.2002; Directive 2002/20/EC of the European Parliament and of the Council of 7 March 2002 on the authorisation of electronic communications networks and services ('Authorisation Directive'), OJ L 108/21, 24.04.2002; Directive 2002/22/EC of the European Parliament and of the Council of 7 March 2002 on universal service and users' rights relating to electronic communications networks and services ('Universal Service Directive'), OJ L 108/51, 24.04.2002; Directive 2002/58/EC of the European Parliament and of the Council of 12 July 2002 concerning the processing of personal data and the protection of privacy in the electronic communications sector ('E-Privacy Directive'), OJ L 201/37, 31.07.2002; Commission Directive 2002/77/EC of 16 September 2002 on competition in the markets for electronic communications networks and services, OJ L 249/21, 17.09.2002.

5   Commission Decision of 26 July 2002 establishing a Radio Spectrum Policy Group, OJ L 198/49, 27.07.2002.

6   See *Bondroit/Cheffert et al*, Vers un nouveau cadre réglementaire européen des réseaux et services de communications électroniques: Réflexions à mi-chemin, La Revue Ubiquité 2001, 41 et seq; *Nikolinakos*, The new European regulatory regime for electronic communications networks and associated services, ECLR 2001, 93 et seq; *Scherer*, Die Umgestaltung des europäischen und deutschen Telekommunikationsrechts durch das EU-Richtlinienpaket, Kommunikation und Recht 2002, 273 et seq, 329 et seq, 385 et seq; *Sinclair*, A new European communications services regulatory package: an overview, CTLR 2001, issue 6, 156.

7   Council Directive 89/552/EEC of 3 October 1989 on the co-ordination of certain provisions laid down by law, regulation or administrative action in Member States concerning the pursuit of television broadcasting activities ('Television without Frontiers'), OJ L 298/23, 17.10.1989; amended by Directive 97/36/EC of the European Parliament and of the Council of 30 June

on the internet,[8] domain names[9] and copyright protection.[10] Moreover, the Community is active in assuring the safety of electronic commerce by fostering electronic signatures,[11] means of electronic payment[12] and consumer protection.[13]

This chapter deals mainly with the 'core' regulatory aspects of electronic communication in the EU, covering only in a non-exhaustive way the related areas of media and information technology regulation. The application of the competition rules to electronic communications is dealt with in Chapter 2.

FUNDAMENTALS OF EU TELECOMMUNICATION LAW

Legislative Powers of the European Union in the Field of Telecommunications

1.4   The European Community ('EC'), being the supranational 'first pillar' of the EU, acts mainly on the basis of the Treaty of Rome of 1957 ('EC Treaty'). It has legislative powers only in those fields for which the EC Treaty specifically establishes such powers. Legislative activities in the field of telecommunications can be based either on article 95 (ex article 100a), aimed at creating a genuine internal market for the free movement of people, goods and services in the EU, or on article 86 (ex article 90), which provides for the abolition of special or exclusive rights granted to undertakings. In 1993, the Maastricht Treaty introduced explicit

---

1997, OJ L 202/60, 30.07.1997. Currently the Commission is undertaking a public consultation on the impact of recent technological and market developments on the implementation of the 'Television without Frontiers' Directive, see Fourth Report from the Commission to the Council, The European Parliament, the European Economic and Social Committee and the Committee of the Regions on the application of Directive 89/552/EEC 'Television without Frontiers', COM(2002) 778 final, 06.01.2003.

8   Decision No 276/1999/EC of the European Parliament and of the Council of 25 January 1999 adopting a multi-annual Community action plan on promoting safer use of the internet by combating illegal and harmful content on global networks, OJ L 33/1, 06.02.1999; Council Decision of 29 May 2000 to combat child pornography on the internet, OJ L 138/1, 09.06.2000.

9   Council Resolution of 3 October 2000 on the organisation and management of the internet, OJ C 293/3, 14.10.2000; Regulation (EC) No 733/2002 of the European Parliament and of the Council of 22 April 2002 on the implementation of the .eu Top Level Domain, OJ L 113/1, 30.04.2002.

10   Directive 2001/29/EC of the European Parliament and of the Council of 22 May 2001 on the harmonisation of certain aspects of copyright and related rights in the information society, OJ L 167/10, 22.06.2001.

11   Directive 1999/93/EC of the European Parliament and of the Council of 13 December 1999 on a Community framework for electronic signatures, OJ L 13/12, 19.01.2000.

12   Commission Recommendation 97/489/EC of 30 July 1997 concerning transactions by electronic payment instruments and in particular the relationship between issuer and holder, OJ L 208/52, 02.08.1997; Directive 2000/46/EC of the European Parliament and of the Council of 18 September 2000 on the taking up, pursuit of and prudential supervision of the business of electronic money institutions, OJ L 275/39, 27.10.2000.

13   Directive 97/7/EC of the European Parliament and of the Council of 20 May 1997 on the protection of consumers in respect of distance contracts, OJ L 144/19, 04.06.1997; Council Resolution of 19 January 1999 on the Consumer Dimension of the Information Society, OJ C 23/1, 28.01.1999; Directive 2002/65/EC of the European Parliament and of the Council of 23 September 2002 concerning the distance marketing of consumer financial services and amending Council Directive 90/619/EEC and Directives 97/7/EC and 98/27/EC, OJ L 271/16, 09.10.2002.

telecommunication policy goals: according to articles 154 to 156 EC Treaty (ex articles 129b to 129d) the Community shall contribute to the establishment and development of trans-European networks.[14] Moreover, article 157 EC Treaty (ex article 130) calls for action of the EC and the Member States to create a favourable and competitive environment for the Community's industry.

1.5 The Community has, since 1987, pursued a dual regulatory approach of liberalising the telecommunications sector and harmonising market conditions. This dual regulatory approach is a consequence of the distribution of the main regulatory powers between Commission and Council. The Commission is empowered by article 86(3) (ex article 90(3)) EC Treaty to dismantle monopoly rights, while the Council is entitled to adopt measures aimed at establishing the internal market under article 95 (ex article 100a).[15] This split between liberalisation and harmonisation powers has resulted in the adoption of two basic legislative acts under the 'old' regulatory framework: the Commission Directive on competition in markets for telecommunications services ('Services Directive'),[16] and the Council Directive on the establishment of the internal market for telecommunications services through the implementation of open network provision ('ONP Framework Directive (1990)'),[17] which have both been amended by other Directives over the years.[18] The dual regulatory approach is also reflected in the new regulatory framework: The Directives on the regulatory framework, access, authorisations, universal service and data protection are based on the Council's regulatory powers under article 95, while the Competition Directive was adopted by the Commission under article 86(3) EC Treaty.

Shaping EC Telecommunication Law: Basic Policy Decisions

1.6 The major policy decisions on the way towards full liberalisation of the European telecommunication markets and a harmonised regulatory framework have been brought about by a series of policy papers and resolutions. The policy papers, so-called 'Green Papers', which are prepared and published by the Commission, are consultative documents setting out basic policy goals for public debate. On that basis, the Council of Telecommunications Ministers and, in some cases, the European Parliament generally adopt resolutions, ie legally non-binding political decisions, establishing action plans and timetables for future legislative and other measures.

1.7 The Commission's 1987 Green Paper on the development of the common market for telecommunication services and equipment proposed the introduction of more competition in the telecommunication market combined with a higher degree of harmonisation. The Commission's policy proposals were broadly endorsed by

---

14   See Decision No 1376/2002/EC of the European Parliament and of the Council of 12 July 2002 amending Decision No 1336/97/EC on a series of guidelines for trans-European telecommunications networks, OJ L 200/1, 30.07.2002.

15   See para 1.4 above.

16   Commission Directive 90/388/EEC, of 28 June 1990 on competition in the markets for telecommunications services OJ L 192/10, 24.07.1990; see para 1.16 below.

17   Council Directive 90/387/EEC of 28 June 1990 on the establishment of the internal market for telecommunications services through the implementation of open network provision, OJ L 192/1, 24.07.1990; see para 1.22 below.

18   See paras 1.18–1.20 (amendments to the Services Directive) and paras 1.23–1.25 (amendments to the ONP Framework Directive) below.

the Council of Telecommunications Ministers, which passed a resolution giving its general support to the objectives of the Commission's planned actions. They included the following:

- rapid full opening of the terminal equipment market to full competition;
- full mutual recognition of type-approval for terminal equipment;
- progressive opening of the telecommunication markets to competition;
- clear separation of the regulatory and entrepreneurial functions in the Member States;
- establishment of open access conditions to networks and services through the Open Network Provision('ONP') concept; and
- enhancement of European standardisation through the establishment of the European Telecommunications Standards Institute ('ETSI').

1.8   After the Council's 1993 resolution[19] establishing a timetable for liberalisation actions to be taken, the Commission published in 1994 the Green Paper on a common approach to mobile and personal communications in the European Union ('Mobile Green Paper')[20] and the 1994/1995 Green Paper on the liberalisation of telecommunications infrastructure and cable television networks ('Infrastructure Green Paper').[21]

1.9   In 1995 the Commission adopted a Green Paper on a numbering policy for telecommunication services in Europe ('Numbering Green Paper').[22] The 'Green Paper on Radio Spectrum Policy'[23] published in 1998 aimed at the development of a consistent radio spectrum policy.

1.10   In 1997 the Commission started to prepare for the transition to the new regulatory framework by analysing the implications of convergence in the 'Convergence Green Paper'.[24] In June 2000 the Commission published its '1999 Review', exploring regulatory options for the new legal framework.[25]

The Regulatory Instruments

1.11   The most important, and most frequently used, legislative instrument in the processes of liberalisation and re-regulation of the various telecommunication sectors are Directives. In addition, the Community also uses Decisions[26] and – in

---

19   Council Resolution of 22 July 1993 on the review of the situation in the telecommunication sector and the need for further development in that market, OJ C 213/1, 06.08.1993.

20   COM(1994) 145 final, 27.04.1994.

21   Part I: Principle and Timetable, COM(1994) 440 final, 25.10.1994; Part II: A common approach to the provision of infrastructure in the European Union, COM(1994) 682 final, 25.01.1995.

22   Towards an European numbering environment – Green Paper on a numbering policy for telecommunications, COM(1996) 590 final, 20.11.1996.

23   Green Paper on radio spectrum policy in the context of European Community policies such as telecommunications, broadcasting, transport, and R&D, COM(1998) 596 final, 03.12.1998.

24   Green Paper on the convergence of the telecommunications, media and information technology sectors, and the implications for Regulation – Towards an information society approach, COM(1997) 623 final, 03.12.1998.

25   COM(1999) 539 final, 10.11.1999; for an analysis see *Scherer*, The 1999 Review – Towards a new regulatory framework, Camford info, the journal of policy, regulation and strategy for telecommunications information and media, Vol 2 No 3, 313 et seq.

26   Eg Commission Decision No 1376/2002/EC of the European Parliament and of the Council

one single case – a Regulation.[27] The new regulatory framework provides for the increased use of non-binding sector-specific measures, such as guidelines,[28] recommendations[29] and working papers.[30] These 'soft law' regulatory tools can be more easily and quickly agreed on than Directives or Regulations and can be adopted to changing technological and market conditions, which allows for a high degree of responsiveness to changing regulatory needs.[31] The price for this increased regulatory flexibility, however, is a loss of legal certainty.

1.12 Directives are addressed to, and binding upon, the Member States and require implementation by national laws (article 249(3) EC Treaty (ex article 189(3)). Regulations are directly applicable in all Member States and do not need implementation (article 249(2) EC Treaty (ex article 189(2)). Both Regulations and Directives can be issued by the Council together with the European Parliament, by the Council alone or by the Commission, depending upon the relevant provision EC Treaty on which the Directives are based. Directives in the telecommunication sector are mostly based either on article 95 (ex article 100a) or on article 86 (ex article 90).[32] The implications of these two legal bases are very different: article 95 provides for the adoption, by qualified majority, of Council Directives for the approximation of national laws in order to establish the Single European Market. It has served as the basis of various Council Directives.[33] As of 1 November 1993, Directives based on article 95 EC Treaty are adopted under the co-decision

---

of 12 July 2002 amending Decision No 1336/97/EC on a series of guidelines for trans-European telecommunications networks, OJ L 200/1, 30.07.2002; Commission Decision of 24 July 2003 on the minimum set of leased lines with harmonised characteristics and associated standards referred to in art 18 Universal Service Directive, OJ L 186/43, 25.07.2003;Commission Decision of 17 May 2005 pursuant to art 7(4) of Directive 2002/21/EC, Case DE/2005/0144: Call termination on individual public telephone networks provided at a fixed location.

27　Regulation (EC) No 2887/2000 of the European Parliament and of the Council of 18 December 2000 on unbundled access to the local loop, OJ L 336/4, 30.12.2000.

28　Eg Commission Guidelines on market analysis and the assessment of significant market power under the Community regulatory framework for electronic communications networks and services, OJ C 165/6, 11.07.2002 ('Commission Guidelines on market analysis').

29　Eg Commission Recommendation on relevant product and service markets within the electronic communications sector susceptible to ex ante regulation in accordance with Directive 2002/21/EC of the European Parliament and of the Council on a common regulatory framework for electronic communication networks and services, OJ C 114/45, 8.05.2003; Commission Recommendation on the processing of caller location information in electronic communication networks for the purpose of location-enhanced emergency call services, OJ L 189/49, 29.07.2003; Commission Recommendation of 23 July 2003 on notifications, time limits and consultations provided for in art 7 of Directive 2002/21/EC of the European Parliament and of the Council on a common regulatory framework for electronic communications networks and services, OJ L 190/13, 30.07.2003.

30　Eg European Commission, Working Document on 'Must-carry' obligations under the 2003 regulatory framework for electronic communications networks and services (22.07.2002); Open Network Provision Committee, Working document the implications for broadcasting of the 2003 regulatory framework for electronic communications (14.06.2002); Commission Staff Working Document on the treatment of Voice over Internet Protocol ('VoIP') under the EU Regulatory Framework, 14 June 2004.

31　COM(1999) 539, final, 10.11.1999, p 18; see *Scherer*, The 1999 Review – towards a new regulatory framework, Camford info, the journal of policy, regulation and strategy for telecommunications information and media, Vol 2 No 3, 313, 320.

32　See para 1.4 above.

33　Eg the ONP Framework Directive (1990) (see para 1.22 below), the Leased Lines Directive (1992) (see para 1.23 below), the Interconnection Directive (see para 1.27 below) and all

procedure introduced by the Maastricht Treaty and set out in article 251 EC Treaty (ex article 189b). This procedure strengthens the legislative powers of the European Parliament to the extent that the Parliament may prevent the entry into force of such a Directive. By contrast, the legislative procedure under article 86 (ex article 90(3)) does not provide for the involvement of the Council or the European Parliament.

1.13 Contrary to Regulations and Directives, Decisions are specifically addressed to natural persons, legal persons or Member States; they apply solely to their addressees (article 249(4) EC Treaty (ex article 189(4)). The Commission's power to issue Decisions can either be derived directly from Treaty provisions (see article 86(3), ex article 90(3)) or from powers conferred by the Council (article 211 4th indent EC Treaty, ex article 155 4th indent).[34]

Regulatory Authorities at European Level

1.14 The principal institutional actors at Community level in the regulation of the telecommunication sector are the Commission, the Council and, to a lesser extent, the European Parliament. Within the Commission, the Information Society Directorate General is responsible for telecommunication policy in general and the Directorate General for Competition, to which a major share of the liberalisation efforts must be credited, is responsible for the application of articles 81 and 82 EC Treaty (ex articles 85 and 86) as well as for the adoption and implementation of the liberalisation Directives under article 86 (ex article 90).

1.15 There is no central authority in charge of telecommunication issues at European level. Several proposals on the establishment and structure of such an authority have been discussed in recent years. Under article 22(2) Interconnection Directive, the Commission was obliged to investigate 'the added value of the setting up of a European Regulatory Authority'. The Commission therefore commissioned several studies on the topic[35] but finally came to the conclusion that the creation of a European Regulatory Authority would not provide sufficient added value to justify the likely costs.[36]

Under the 2002 EU Regulatory Framework, a network of organisational entities has been established, in lieu of a centralised European regulatory agency, with a view to advising the Commission on regulatory measures at EU level, to ensure cooperation among NRAs as well as between NRAs and the Commission, and to develop best regulatory practices at EU level and, beyond the boundaries of the European Union, at a pan-European level: The Communications Committee ('CoCom') and the Radio Spectrum Committee have been established on the basis

---

Directives of the '2002 EU Regulatory Package' with the exception of the Commission Directive on competition in the markets for electronic communications networks and services.

34   See art 18(3) Universal Service Directive.

35   Report on 'Issues associated with the creation of a European Regulatory Authority for Telecommunications', by NERA and Denton Hall for the European Commission (DG XIII) March 1997, ECSC-EC-EAEC, Brussels – Luxembourg, 1997, http://europa.eu.int/ISPO/infosoc/telecompolicy/en/Nera.htm; Final Report on possible added value of European Regulatory Authority for Telecommunications', by Eurostrategies/Cullen International for the European Commission October 1999, ECSC-EC-EAEC Brussels – Luxembourg 1999, http://europa.eu.int/ISPO/infosoc/telecompolicy/en/erafl12–99.pdf.

36   COM(1999) 539, final, 10.11.1999, p 9.

of article 22 Framework Directive and article 3 Spectrum Decision, respectively. They are committees with both advisory and decision-making functions in line with the Council's comitology rules.[37]

The European Regulators Group for Electronic Communications Networks and Services (ERG) is an advisory body of the independent national regulatory authorities on electronic communications networks and services, which was established by the Commission.[38] The ERG consists of the heads of the NRAs or their representatives; its role is to advise and assist the Commission in consolidating the internal market for electronic communications networks and services.

Similarly, the Commission has established an advisory group on radio spectrum policy, called the Radio Spectrum Policy Group, which is composed of one high-level government expert from each Member State and a high-level representative from the Commission.[39] The purpose of this Group is to assist and advise the Commission on radio spectrum policy, on coordination of policy approaches and, where appropriate, on harmonised conditions with regard to the availability and efficient use of radio spectrum necessary for the establishment and functioning of the internal market.

At a pan-European level – and without the involvement of the Commission, the NRAs established in 1997 the Independent Regulators Group (IRG) which currently consists of representatives of 31 NRAs. The purpose of this group is to share experience and viewpoints among its members on issues of common interest and to develop 'principles of implementation and best practice' (PIBs) on regulatory matters.

TELECOMMUNICATIONS REGULATION PRIOR TO THE 2002 EU REGULATORY PACKAGE

Liberalisation of the Telecommunication Markets

The 1988 Terminal Equipment Directive

1.16   One of the first landmarks in liberalising the telecommunication markets was the abolition of the TOs' national monopolies for terminal equipment on the basis of the Commission Directive on competition in the markets for telecommunication terminal equipment ('Terminal Equipment Directive').[40] According to the definition in article 1 of the Directive, terminal equipment includes telephone sets, private automatic branch exchanges (PABX), data transmission terminals, mobile telephones, as well as, after a 1994 amendment,[41] satellite earth station equipment. The Terminal Equipment Directive has abolished all exclusive rights for the

---

37   Council Decision of 28 June 1999 laying down the procedures for the exercise of implementing powers conferred on the Commission, OJ L 184/23, 17.07.1999; see also paras 1.62, 1.65, 1.85 and 1.194 et seq below.

38   Commission Decision of 29 July 2002 establishing the European Regulators Group for Electronic Communications Networks and Services, OJ L 200/38, 30.7.2002.

39   Cf. arts 1 and 3 Commission Decision of 26 July 2002 establishing a Radio Spectrum Policy Group, OJ L 198/49, 27.07.2002.

40   Directive 88/301/EEC, OJ L 131/73, 27.05.1988.

41   Commission Directive 94/46/EC of 13 October 1994 amending Directive 88/301/EEC and Directive 90/388/EEC in particular with regard to satellite communications, OJ L 268/15, 19.10.1994.

importation, marketing, connection, and bringing into service of telecommunication equipment and/or maintenance of such equipment (article 2). Furthermore, it ensures that economic operators (ie private suppliers) have the right to import, market, connect, bring into service and maintain terminal equipment (article 3).[42] Finally, the Terminal Equipment Directive ensures that users have access to new public network termination points (article 4). The Directive stays in force after the enactment of the 2002 EU Regulatory Package, although some provisions referring to satellite earth station equipment have been moved to the Directive on competition in the markets for electronic communications services (article 7).

The 1990 Services Directive

1.17   The Services Directive of 28 June 1990 required Member States to remove 'all special or exclusive rights' that had been granted to TOs 'for the supply of telecommunication services other than voice telephony' (article 2(1)).[43] Similar to the Terminal Equipment Directive it allowed Member States to impose licensing or notification requirements or other restrictions only in order to ensure compliance with narrowly defined 'essential requirements'. Furthermore, the Services Directive required Member States to separate regulatory tasks (the granting of licences, control of type approval, allocation of frequencies and surveillance of usage conditions) to an entity separate from their TOs. The Directive drew a definitional boundary line between 'voice telephony' and other telecommunication services, and allowed Member States to maintain 'special or exclusive rights' for the provision of voice telephony. Moreover, for the time being, it did not apply to telex, mobile radiotelephony, paging and satellite services (article 1(2)).

Sector-oriented amendments of the Services Directive

1.18   Following the 1990 Satellite Green Paper,[44] the Commission adopted, on 13 October 1994, Directive 94/46/EC[45] amending the Services Directive insofar as exclusive rights for the provision of satellite services and equipment were abolished by the end of 1994. Licensing and declaration procedures could only be justified by compliance with essential requirements, including interactive services such as tele-shopping services, tele-teaching services and on-line data services.

1.19   The Cable TV Directive[46] opened existing cable television networks throughout the EU for the carriage of all telecommunication services (with the possible

---

42   However, Member States may require private suppliers to possess certain technical qualifications: art 3 Terminal Equipment Directive.

43   See ECJ Judgment of 17 November 1992, Joined Cases C-271/90, C-281/90 and C-289/90, *Kingdom of Spain, Kingdom of Belgium and Republic of Italy v Commission of the European Communities* [1992] ECR I-5833, 5867, where the legality of the Services Directive was generally confirmed, although the provisions on 'special rights' were declared void; for details see 4th edition, para 1.19.

44   Toward Europe-wide systems and services – Green Paper on a common approach in the field of satellite communications in the European, COM(1990) 490 final, 14.11.1999.

45   Commission Directive 94/46/EC of 13 October 1994 amending Directive 88/301/EEC and Directive 90/388/EEC in particular with regard to satellite communications, OJ L 268/15, 19.10.1994.

46   Commission Directive 95/51/EC of 18 October 1995 amending Directive 90/388/EEC with regard to the abolition of the restrictions on the use of cable television networks for the provision of already liberalised telecommunications services, OJ L 256/49, 26.10.1995.

exception of voice telephony) as of 1 January 1996. As a consequence, Member States were no longer allowed to restrict the use of cable TV networks to the provision of conventional, one-way television broadcasting services. Rather, cable TV operators were entitled, under the amended Services Directive, to offer all liberalised telecommunication services. In cases where operators owned both telecommunications and cable TV networks, the Directive required a minimum level of accounting separation. However, after a review published in March 1998[47] the Commission adopted Directive 99/64/EC obliging Member States to ensure that no telecommunications organisation operates its cable TV network using the same legal entity as it uses for its public telecommunications network, when such organisation:

- is controlled by that Member State or benefits from special rights, and
- is dominant in a substantial part of the common market in the provision of public telecommunications networks and public voice telephony services, and
- operates a cable TV network established under a special or exclusive right in the same geographic area.

1.20   Following the publication of its Mobile Green Paper[48] the Commission adopted, on 16 January 1996, a Directive[49] requiring the removal of any remaining special and exclusive rights by February 1996. The Mobile and Personal Communications Directive obliges Member States to lift all restrictions on operators of mobile and personal communications systems with regard to the establishment of their own infrastructure, the use of infrastructures provided by third parties, and the sharing of infrastructure, other facilities and sites. The Directive also established a basic framework for the licensing of mobile and personal communication systems and for the allocation of frequencies, which has since been complemented by the 1997 Licensing Directive.[50]

The Full Competition Directive

1.21   The Commission's Full Competition Directive[51] of 13 March 1996 concluded the series of measures under article 86 (ex article 90) EC Treaty, opening segments of the telecommunication markets to competition. Based on the political consensus among the Member States to liberalise all telecommunication services – including voice telephony – and all telecommunication infrastructure as from 1 January 1998, the Full Competition Directive required the Member States to take the necessary steps to ensure that markets were fully open by 1 January 1998.[52] Besides these liberalisation-related provisions, the Directive established basic principles and procedural requirements for licensing new entrants to both the voice

---

47   Commission communication concerning the review under competition rules of the joint provision of telecommunications and cable TV networks by a single operator and the abolition of restrictions on the provision of cable TV capacity over telecommunications networks ('Cable Review'), OJ C 71/4, 07.03.1998.

48   COM(1994) 145 final, 27.04.1994; see para 1.8 above.

49   Commission Directive 96/2/EC of 16 January 1996 amending Directive 90/388/EEC with regard to mobile and personal communications, OJ L 20/59, 26.01.1996.

50   See para 1.28 below.

51   Commission Directive 96/19/EC of 13 March 1996 amending Directive 90/388/EEC with regard to the implementation of full competition in telecommunications markets, OJ L 74/13, 22.03.1996.

52   With the possibility of transitional periods of up to two years (for Member States with less developed networks) or up to five years (for Member States with very small networks).

telephony and the telecommunication infrastructure ('network') markets.[53] The Full Competition Directive also established basic rules on interconnection.[54]

Harmonisation of the Telecommunications Markets

The ONP Framework Directive 1990

1.22   The ONP Framework Directive (1990)[55] was intended to facilitate access by private companies to public telecommunication networks and to certain public telecommunication services. Moreover, the Directive's aim was to achieve harmonisation of technical interfaces and to eliminate discrepancies in conditions of use and tariffs, thus facilitating the provision of pan-European telecommunication services. To achieve these goals, the Directive defined sector-specific 'ONP conditions'. 'ONP conditions' had to comply with certain 'basic principles', such as that:

- the conditions had to be based on objective criteria;
- the conditions had to be transparent, and published in an appropriate manner; and
- the conditions had to guarantee equality of access and must be non-discriminatory, in accordance with EC law (article 3(1)).

Furthermore, the 'ONP conditions' were not allowed to restrict access to networks and services except for 'essential requirements', which were defined in the Directive.[56]

Sector-oriented amendments of the ONP Framework Directive

1.23   The ONP Framework Directive (1990) had established a timetable for further legislative measures to be adopted, the first of which was the 1992 Council Directive on the application of open network provisions to leased lines[57] ('Leased Lines Directive (1992)').[58] The Directive was designed to ensure the Community-wide availability of a minimum set of analogue and digital leased lines with harmonised technical characteristics. Thus, it prescribed Community-wide harmonised usage conditions and tariff principles and defined a harmonised set of leased

---

53   For details see 4th edition, paras 1.31 et seq.
54   For details see 4th edition, para 1.33.
55   Council Directive 90/387/EEC of 28 June 1990 on the establishment of the internal market for telecommunications services through the implementation of open network provision, OJ L 192/1, 24.07.1990.
56   For details see 4th edition, para 1.41.
57   Council Directive 92/44/EEC of 5 June 1992 on the application of open network provision to leased lines, OJ L 165/27, 19.06.1992. The Directive was challenged in a British case but upheld by a 1996 preliminary ruling of the ECJ, Judgment of 12 December 1996, Case C-302/94, *The Queen v Secretary of State for Trade and Industry, ex parte British Telecommunications plc* [1996] ECR-I 6417.
58   In the same year, the Council also adopted two recommendations on the sector-specific application of ONP: Council Recommendation 92/382/EEC of 5 June 1992 on the harmonised provision of a minimum set of packet-switched data services (PSDS) in accordance with open network provision (ONP) principles, OJ L 200/1, 18.07.1992 and Council Recommendation 92/383/EEC of 5 June 1992 on the provision of harmonised integrated services digital network (ISDN) access arrangements and a minimum set of ISDN offerings in accordance with open network provision (ONP) principles, OJ L 200/10, 18.07.1992.

lines with defined network termination points which was to be made available in all Member States for communications within a Member State and between Member States.[59]

1.24   The 1995 Directive on the application of open network provision to voice telephony ('Voice Telephony Directive (1995)')[60] was primarily aimed at assuring the availability of harmonised voice telephony service throughout the EU, but also included several universal service provisions and rules on special network access, tariffs and numbering.[61] The Directive ensured that users could obtain access to the fixed public telephone network and could connect their telecommunication terminal equipment; it addressed consumer protection issues, such as supply time and quality of service.[62]

1.25   In 1997, the Voice Telephony Directive (1995) was completely replaced by a new Directive of the European Parliament and of the Council 'on the application of open network provision (ONP) to voice telephony and on universal service for telecommunication in a competitive environment'.[63] The Directive continued to pursue the twofold aim of the preceding Directive to ensure the availability throughout the Community of good quality fixed public telephone services and to define – partially overlapping with the Interconnection Directive[64] – the set of services which all users should have access to in the context of universal service. It set out specific obligations for organisations that provide fixed and/or mobile public telephone networks and/or publicly available telephone services, including basic rules safeguarding the interests of users and subscribers. Furthermore, the Voice Telephony Directive (1997) established tariff and cost accounting principles and a range of procedural provisions designed to set up consultative mechanisms on issues of universal service as well as on national dispute resolution.

The ONP Framework Directive 1997

1.26   In July 1997, the ONP Framework Directive (1990) and the Leased Lines Directive (1992) were adapted to the 'competitive environment in telecommunications'. Different from the ONP Framework Directive (1990), the ONP Framework Directive (1997)[65] applied not only to the TOs, but to all organisations providing public telecommunication networks and/or services, taking into account an organisation's position in the relevant market. The Directive followed three main approaches for the safeguarding of effective competition in the internal market:

---

59   Furthermore, the Directive required the implementation of cost accounting systems by TOs and provided for a conciliation procedure to deal with disputes arising out of alleged infringements of its provisions; for details see 4th edition, paras 1.73 et seq.

60   Directive 95/62/EC of the European Parliament and of the Council of 13 December 1995 on the application of open network provision (ONP) to voice telephony, OJ L 321/6, 30.12.1995.

61   See 4th edition, paras 1.82 et seq and 1.137 et seq.

62   For details see 4th edition, para 1.45.

63   Directive 98/10/EC of the European Parliament and of the Council of 26 February 1998 on the application of open network provision (ONP) to voice telephony and on universal service for telecommunications in a competitive environment ('ONP Voice Telephony Directive (1998)'), OJ L 101/24, 01.04.1998.

64   See para 1.27 below.

65   Directive 97/51/EC of the European Parliament and of the Council of 6 October 1997 amending Council Directives 90/387/EEC and 92/44/EEC for the purpose of adaptation to a competitive environment in telecommunications ('ONP Framework Directive (1997)'), OJ L 295/23, 29.10.1997.

first, it set out the harmonised basic principles to be followed by ONP conditions; secondly, it encouraged technical harmonisation by market players on a voluntary basis by providing for the Commission to publish a list of technical European standards drawn up as a basis for harmonised technical interfaces and/or service features for ONP;[66] and, thirdly, the Directive ensured the effective structural separation of the NRAs from activities that were associated with ownership or control of telecommunication networks, services or equipment.

Regulation of interconnection and special network access

1.27 After a lengthy legislative process the European Parliament and the Council adopted, on 30 June 1997, the Directive on interconnection in telecommunication ('Interconnection Directive').[67] The Directive established obligations to grant and rights to obtain interconnection[68] and provided for regulatory measures and dispute resolution procedures at national level.[69] It promoted a high degree of standardisation and transparency of interconnection terms and prices.[70] It imposed additional obligations on TOs providing public telecommunication networks and systems which have significant market power, and in particular with regard to interconnection charges.[71]

Licensing

1.28 To ensure a Community-wide, harmonised framework for licensing and authorisations regimes which do not impose undue burdens on operators, the Community adopted in 1997 the Licensing Directive[72] which set out principles for the Member States to observe if they made the provision of a telecommunication service subject to an authorisation. Authorisations were only allowed to contain conditions listed in the Annex to the Directive, the Directive distinguishing between 'general authorisations' and 'individual licences'.[73] As regards the relationship between general authorisations and individual licences, Member States had to give priority to the less onerous general authorisation as opposed to individual licences. Nevertheless, considerable room existed for individual licences.[74]

Regulation of universal service

1.29 The Voice Telephony Directive (1997) provided that a 'connection to the fixed public telephone network at a fixed location, and access to fixed public

---

66 However, Commission or Council were entitled to make the implementation of such standards or specifications compulsory, if the voluntary approach had failed.

67 Directive 97/33/EC of the European Parliament and of the Council of 30 June 1997 on interconnection in telecommunications with regard to ensuring universal service and interoperability through application of the principles of Open Network Provision (ONP), OJ L 199/32, 26.07.1997.

68 For details see 4th edition, paras 1.98 et seq.

69 For details see 4th edition, paras 1.100 et seq.

70 For details see 4th edition, para 1.105.

71 For details see 4th edition, paras 1.106 et seq.

72 Directive 97/13/EC of the European Parliament and the Council of 10 April 1997 on a common framework for general authorisations and individual licences in the field of telecommunications services, OJ L 117/15, 07.05.1997.

73 For details see 4th edition, paras 1.142 et seq.

74 For details see 4th edition, para 1.144.

telephone services' must be ensured for all users in the Member States' territories, independent of geographical location and at an affordable price, allowing service delivery both via a fixed line or by wireless technology to 'bridge the last mile' to the user. The Interconnection Directive, which contained rules on the computation of universal service contributions, confirmed and defined, in some detail, the scope of this universal service. The universal service obligations under the Voice Telephony Directive (1997) also included directory services, a public pay telephone service, and imposed a general obligation on Member States to take specific measures to ensure access to and the affordability of fixed public telephone services for disabled users and users with special needs.[75]

1.30   According to the Voice Telephony Directive (1997), universal services had to be 'affordable', the design of the schemes to ensure affordability being left largely to the Member States themselves.[76]

The Voice Telephony Directive (1997), the Full Competition Directive and the Interconnection Directive prescribed rules to determine if, how and to what extent the financial burdens of universal service provision were to be shared between the market players. The Directives permitted Member States to make use of either a universal service fund, established at national level, or a system of supplementary charges to be paid by undertakings interconnecting with the universal service provider, to share the cost of universal service provision.[77]

Numbering

1.31   Numbering has always been seen as a crucial element for the development of the competitive environment in the telecommunications sector. The Voice Telephony Directive (1995) required Member States to control national telephone numbering plans and to apply the ONP principles to the allocation of numbers. The Full Competition Directive reiterated this requirement, and also required Member States to ensure, before 1 July 1997, that adequate numbers were available for all telecommunication services. In September 1996, a Council Resolution[78] based on the 'Numbering Green Paper'[79] then took a comprehensive approach toward the development of a Community-wide numbering policy, this approach later being implemented by the Interconnection Directive and by Directive 98/61/EC.[80] Member States had to ensure the provision of adequate numbers and numbering ranges for all publicly available telecommunication services, national numbering plans had to be controlled by the NRAs, and allocation procedures and the allocation itself had to be in line with the ONP principles of transparency and non-discrimination. Moreover, the Commission introduced number portability and required dominant carriers to allow carrier pre-selection.[81]

---

75   For details see 4th edition, paras 1.120 et seq.
76   For details see 4th edition, paras 1.126 et seq.
77   For details see 4th edition, paras 1.129 et seq.
78   Council Resolution of 22 September 1997 on the further development of a numbering policy for telecommunications services in the European Community, OJ C 303/1, 04.10.1997.
79   COM(1996) 590 final, 20.11.1996.
80   Directive 98/61/EC of the European Parliament and of the Council of 24 September 1998 amending Directive 97/33/EC with regard to number portability and carrier pre-selection, OJ L 268, 03.10.1998.
81   For details see 4th edition, paras 1.166 et seq.

Rights of way

1.32 In the interest of effective competition, the Services Directive (as amended by the Full Competition Directive) provided that Member States must not discriminate between providers of public telecommunication networks with regard to the granting of rights of way for the provision of such networks. Where the granting of additional rights of way to undertakings wishing to provide public telecommunication networks was not possible due to applicable essential requirements, Member States had to ensure that the undertakings have access to the existing facilities on reasonable terms.[82]

Consumer protection issues

1.33 As consumer protection is recognised, in article 129a EC Treaty, as one of the main public interest objectives to be pursued by the Community, several provisions of the Voice Telephony Directive (1997), as well as the Leased Lines Directive (1997), were aimed at the protection of telecommunication users, including consumers.[83] The NRAs were obliged to ensure that organisations providing access to both fixed and mobile public networks provide a contract, which had to fulfil certain requirements; the Directives also provided for a harmonised framework for procedures for the resolution of unresolved disputes at national level.[84] Moreover, there were provisions relating to the procedures in cases of non-payment of bills, itemised billing and the establishment and provision of directory services.[85] Besides, the Voice Telephony Directive (1997) provided for a system by which the quality of services could be monitored according to common criteria throughout the Community.[86]

Data protection

1.34 Data protection issues in the old regulatory framework were addressed by the 1995 Directive on the protection of individuals with regard to the processing of personal data and on the free movement of such data,[87] covering all kinds of data processing and by a 1997 sector-specific Directive dealing with data protection in the telecommunication sector.[88] The 1995 Directive established strict conditions, based on the individual's information and prior consent, for the processing and transfer of personal data both in the public and in the private sectors, while the 1997 sector-specific Directive specified the data protection rights of individual

---

82   Art 4(d) Services Directive.
83   For the distinction between 'consumer' and 'user' under the old regulatory framework, see 4th edition, para 1.170.
84   For details see 4th edition, para 1.172.
85   For details see 4th edition, paras 1.175 et seq.
86   For details see 4th edition, paras 1.180 et seq.
87   Council Directive 95/46/EC, OJ L 281/31, 23.11.1995; Directive 97/66/EC of the European Parliament and of the Council concerning the processing of personal data and the protection of privacy in the telecommunications sector, OJ L 24/1, 30.01.1998.
88   Directive 97/66/EC of the European Parliament and of the Council concerning the processing of personal data and the protection of privacy in the telecommunications sector, OJ L 24/1, 30.01.1998.

telecommunication service users, and awarded data protection to a lesser degree to legal persons which subscribe to telecommunication services.[89]

THE 2002 EU REGULATORY PACKAGE

Introduction

1.35   In response to the conclusions from both the Convergence Green Paper and the 1999 Review,[90] the Commission proposed in July 2000 five Draft Directives[91] and one draft Decision[92] for a new regulatory framework for electronic communications networks and services. Except for the E-Privacy Directive, all Directives and the Decision were adopted in the European Parliament's second reading in February 2002.[93] They were published on 24 April in the Official Journal,[94] entering in force the day following publication. Due to far-reaching amendments by the European Parliament, the adoption and publication of the E-Privacy Directive was delayed until July 2002.[95] In addition, the Commission proposed a Regulation for unbundled access to the local loop,[96] which was adopted in December 2000,[97] entering into force on 2 January 2001. Moreover, the Commission adopted a Directive on competition in the markets for electronic communications services,[98]

---

89   For details see 4th edition, paras 1.227 et seq.

90   See para 1.10 above.

91   Proposal for a Directive of the European Parliament and of the Council on a common regulatory framework for electronic communications networks and services, COM(2000) 393 final, 12.07.2000; Proposal for a Directive of the European Parliament and of the Council on the authorisation of electronic communications networks and services, COM(2000) 386 final, 12.07.2000; Proposal for a Directive of the European Parliament and of the Council on access to, and interconnection of, electronic communications networks and associated facilities, COM(2000) 384 final, 12.07.2000; Proposal for a Directive of the European Parliament and of the Council on universal service and users' rights relating to electronic communications networks and services, COM(2000) 392 final, 12.07.2000.

92   Proposal for a Decision of the European Parliament and of the Council on a regulatory framework for radio spectrum policy in the European Community, COM(2000) 407 final, 12.07.2000.

93   Framework Directive, European Parliament Decision (second reading) of 12 December 2001, OJ C 177 E/142, 25.07.2002; Access Directive, European Parliament Decision (second reading) of 12 December 2001, OJ C 177 E/152, 25.07.2002; Authorisation Directive, European Parliament Decision (second reading) of 12 December 2001, OJ C 177 E/155, 25.07.2002; Universal Service Directive, European Parliament Decision (second reading) of 12 December 2001, OJ C 177 E/157, 25.07.2002; Radio Spectrum Decision, European Parliament Decision (second reading) of 12 December 2001, OJ C 177 E/164, 25.07.2002.

94   See footnotes 3 and 4 above.

95   European Parliament Decision (second reading) of 30 May 2002, OJ C 187 E/103, 7.08.2003; Directive 2002/58/EC of the European Parliament and of the Council of 12 July 2002 concerning the processing of personal data and the protection of privacy in the electronic communications sector (Directive on privacy and electronic communications), OJ L 201/37, 31.07.2002.

96   Proposal for a Regulation of the European Parliament and of the Council on unbundled access to the local loop, COM(2000) 394 final, 12.07.2000.

97   OJ L 336/4, 30.12.2000.

98   Commission Directive 2002/77/EC of 16 September 2002 on competition in the markets for electronic communications networks and services, OJ L 249/21, 17.09.2002.

consolidating all relevant provisions of Directive 90/388 (and the sector-specific amendments) and replacing all existing 'liberalisation Directives'[99] in the telecommunications sector.

Regulatory Objectives

1.36 With its 2002 EU Regulatory Package, the European legislator pursues four main regulatory objectives, which were either explicitly addressed during the legislative process or mentioned in the Directives and their recitals. The 2002 EU Regulatory Package is aimed at:

- simplifying and consolidating the current legislation;[100]
- adapting the regulatory framework to 'the convergence of the telecommunications, media and information technology sectors';[101]
- a more flexible application of sector-specific regulation on the one hand and of the instruments of national and European competition law on the other hand;[102] and
- establishing the legal basis, in terms of substantive and procedural rules as well as with respect to the organisational structure, to allow for a more harmonised application of the regulatory framework throughout the Community.[103]

1.37 At first glance, it would seem that the 2002 EU Regulatory Package has achieved the objective of simplifying and consolidating the European regulatory framework: the number of legislative measures has been reduced from 20[104] to six Directives and one Decision.[105] This has not led, however, to a more transparent or user-friendly body of law for the electronic communications sector: The Framework Directive and the sector-specific Directives are characterised by a multitude of cross-references and contain numerous provisions allowing for the adoption of guidelines, recommendations and Decisions,[106] which are growing to become a regulatory jungle comparable to the previous regulatory framework.

1.38 The 2002 EU Regulatory Package responds to the convergence of the telecommunications, media and information technologies by creating 'a single regulatory framework' for all transmission networks and services.[107] This framework is, broadly speaking, limited to the regulation of 'transmission', which is separated, to a large extent, from the regulation of 'content'.[108] There are, however, limits to the establishment of a 'single regulatory framework' for the different communications network platforms which are subject to technical convergence.[109] Consequently, the 2002 EU Regulatory Package contains a number of provisions

---

99   See paras 1.16 et seq above.
100 Communications Review, COM(1999) 539, final, 10.11.1999, p 19.
101 Recital 5 Framework Directive.
102 See recitals 25 and 27 Framework Directive; see also Communications Review, COM(1999) 539, final, 10.11.1999, pp 7, 14, 57–59.
103 See art 1(1) and (2) Framework Directive; recital 16 Framework Directive.
104 Communications Review, COM(1999) 539, final, 10.11.1999, pp 16 et seq.
105 See para 1.35 above.
106 See para 1.11 above; para 1.66 below.
107 See recital 5 Framework Directive.
108 See para 1.50 below.
109 See para 1.3 above.

addressing the specificities of mobile and cable television networks and services;[110] it is to be expected that the scope of the 'Single Regulatory Framework' will be further refined and specified in accordance with the specificities of the various communications systems in the course of the market definition and market analysis procedures.[111]

1.39   In order to achieve the third regulatory objective (more flexible application of regulatory instruments), the Regulatory Framework establishes a new set of rules for the ex-ante regulation of undertakings deemed to have significant market power ('SMP'). The Directives establish a formalised procedure which is aimed at determining whether a given market is 'effectively competitive' or whether an undertaking shall be deemed to have SMP because, 'either individually or jointly with others, it enjoys a position equivalent to dominance'.[112] The decision on the existence or non-existence of SMP is taken by the National Regulatory Authorities ('NRAs'), based on Commission Guidelines and recommendations and subject to limited so-called veto rights of the Commission.[113] The NRAs have broad discretion in the selection of the regulatory remedies[114] to be imposed upon undertakings deemed to have SMP ('SMP undertakings').[115]

1.40   The 2002 EU Regulatory Package establishes both broad discretion of the NRAs in selecting reasonable and proportioned remedies[116] and new and strengthened Commission powers to monitor and harmonise national regulatory measures: The dual regulatory system, which has intertwined national and European regulation and has strengthened, on the basis of Community law, the NRAs powers, requires 'a counterbalance in the form of greater co-ordination of NRA decisions and positions at EU level'.[117]

The 2002 EU Regulatory Package: Overview

1.41   The Framework Directive[118] defines the scope of applicability of the 2002 EU Regulatory Package and defines its most important legal terms. It obliges the Member States to guarantee the independence of the NRAs and the effective structural separation of their regulatory functions from activities associated with ownership or control of undertakings providing electronic communications networks and/or services (article 3(2)). It further establishes policy objectives and regulatory principles for the NRAs' regulatory tasks and provides for a consolidation procedure under which the NRAs are obliged to 'contribute to the development of the internal market by cooperating with each other and the Commission in a transparent manner to ensure the consistent application, in all Member States', of

---

110   Eg art 18(1) Framework Directive; arts 4(2), 12(1)(g) Access Directive; arts 30(1), 31 Universal Service Directive.

111   See para 1.72 below.

112   Art 14(2) Framework Directive; further details below, paras 1.70 et seq.

113   See art 7 Framework Directive; further details below, paras 1.60 et seq. The Commission's veto power extends to a decision requiring a NRA to withdraw a draft measure, but not to replace a NRA's draft measure with a Commission measure.

114   Cf ERG Common Position on the approach to appropriate remedies in the new regulatory framework, ERG (03)30 of 1 April 2004.

115   See art 8(2) Access Directive and the discretionary powers of the NRAs under arts 9–13 Access Directive.

116   See para 1.59, 1.77 and 1.138 below.

117   Communications Review, COM(1999) 539, final, 10.11.1999, p 51.

118   Further details below, paras 1.48 et seq.

the Regulatory Framework (article 7(2) Framework Directive). Furthermore, the Framework Directive establishes rules on the management of scarce resources, eg radio frequencies, numbering, naming and addressing (articles 9, 10), for the granting of rights of way (article 11), co-location and facility sharing (article 12). With respect to the activities of undertakings providing public communications networks or publicly available electronic communications services which have special or exclusive rights for the provision of services in other sectors in the same or another Member State, the Directive obliges Member States to ensure accounting separation and 'structural separation' for the activities associated with the provision of electronic communications networks and services (article 13). At the core of the Framework Directive are rules regarding the determination of significant market power (article 14) on the basis of a market definition procedure (article 15) and a market analysis procedure (article 16) to be initiated and conducted by the respective NRA in accordance with Community law.

1.42 The Authorisation Directive[119] is aimed at simplifying and harmonising the authorisation rules and conditions for all electronic communications networks and services (article 1(1)). The provision of electronic communications networks or services may, in principle, only be subject to a general authorisation (article 3(2)); individual rights of use may only be granted where necessary for the use of radio frequencies or numbers (article 5). The Authorisation Directive establishes the rights and obligations of the addressees of the general authorisations, of the users of radio frequencies and of numbers (article 4, 6) and establishes far-reaching rights of the Member States to impose 'administrative charges' on undertakings providing a service or a network under the general authorisation or exercising a right of use (article 12).

1.43 The Access Directive[120] harmonises the way in which Member States regulate access to, and interconnection of, electronic communications networks and associated facilities (article 1(1)). The Directive creates a framework for the relationships between suppliers of networks and services, based on the principle of priority of commercial negotiations, but allowing for regulatory intervention by the NRAs at their own initiative or, in the absence of agreement between undertakings, at the request of either of the parties involved (article 5). The Directive establishes far-reaching regulatory powers of the NRAs with respect to undertakings designated as having SMP (article 8), as well as a number of regulatory powers to be exercised, irrespective of the existence of significant market power, with a view to ensure adequate access and interconnection and interoperability of services 'in a way that promotes efficiency, sustainable competition, and gives the maximum benefit to end-users' (article 5).

1.44 Whereas the Access Directive establishes a framework for the regulation of wholesale markets, the Universal Service Directive governs the provision of electronic communications networks and services to end-users (article 1(1)).[121] The Directive aims at ensuring the availability throughout the Community of good quality services publicly available through effective competition and deals with circumstances in which the needs of end-users are not satisfactorily met by the markets. To this end, the Directive establishes a minimum set of services of specified quality to which all end-users have access at an affordable price in the light of specific national conditions (articles 4 to 7). The Directive allows Member States

---

119 Further details below, paras 1.91 et seq.
120 Further details below, paras 1.122 et seq.
121 Further details below, paras 1.160 et seq.

to designate one or more undertakings to guarantee the provision of these universal services (article 8) and to establish mechanisms for the financing of universal service obligations (article 13). In addition, the Universal Service Directive establishes rules for the regulation of services provided by undertakings designated as having SMP to end-users, including the regulation of retail tariffs (articles 16 et seq), sector-specific consumer protection rules (articles 20 et seq), provisions regarding European emergency call numbers and telephone access codes (articles 26 et seq), number portability (article 30), and carrier selection and carrier pre-selection (article 19).

1.45   The Directive concerning the processing of personal data and the protection of privacy in the electronic communications sector[122] modernises the provisions of Directive 97/66.[123] Many of the provisions of the 1997 Directive are restated without major substantive changes. The Directive contains new provisions regarding the protection of location data (article 9) and extends the protection from unsolicited communications so as to apply to all types of electronic communications (article 13).

1.46   The Directive on competition in the markets for electronic communications services consolidates and simplifies the provisions of the existing liberalisation Directives[124] in one single piece of legislation. Apart from the clarification of certain provisions and terminological adjustments (eg 'telecommunications services', 'telecommunications networks') to the terms used in the other Directives of the 2002 EU Regulatory Package, the main provisions remain unaltered.

1.47   The Decision on a regulatory framework for radio spectrum policy in the European Community[125] establishes a procedure which allows the EU to pursue, largely independently of but in co-ordination with the European Conference of Postal and Telecommunications Administrations ('CEPT'), a Community radio spectrum policy. The Decision establishes a consultative body, the Radio Spectrum Committee, which assists the Commission in coordinating policy approaches and, where appropriate, developing harmonised conditions regarding the availability and efficient use of the radio spectrum (article 1).

---

122   Further details below, paras 1.191 et seq.

123   See para 1.34 above.

124   Commission Directive 90/388/EEC of 28 June 1990 on competition in the markets for telecommunications services, OJ L192/10, 24.07.1990 as amended by Commission Directive 94/46/EC of 13 October 1994 amending Directive 88/301/EEC and Directive 90/388/EEC in particular with regard to satellite communications, OJ L268/15, 19.10.1994; Commission Directive 95/51/EC of 18 October 1995 amending Directive 90/388/EEC with regard to the abolition of the restrictions on the use of cable television networks for the provision of already liberalised telecommunications services, OJ L 256/49, 26.10.1995; Commission Directive 96/2/EC of 16 January 1996 amending Directive 90/388/EEC with regard to mobile and personal communications, OJ L 20/59, 26.01.1996; Commission Directive 96/19/EC of 28 February 1996 amending Directive 90/388/EEC regarding the implementation of full competition in telecommunications markets, OJ L 74/13, 22.03.1996; Commission Directive 1999/64/EC of 23 June 1999 amending Directive 90/388/EEC in order to ensure that telecommunications networks and cable TV networks owned by a single operator are separate legal entities, OJ L 175/39, 10.07.1999.

125   Further details below, paras 1.191 et seq.

Regulatory Principles: the Framework Directive

Scope of regulation

1.48   The European legislator has reacted to the technical convergence of:

- mobile and satellite communications with the fixed network,
- cable television and telecommunications networks as well as power lines, and
- communications services on the basis of the internet protocol

by creating a single legal framework for all transmission networks.[126] To achieve this, the scope of applicability of the traditional European telecommunications law has been expanded by replacing the terms 'public telecommunications network' and 'telecommunications services'[127] with the new, broader terms 'electronic communications network' and 'electronic communications service'.

1.49   The term 'electronic communications network', as defined in article 2(a) Framework Directive, means 'transmission systems and, where applicable, switching or routing equipment and other resources which permit the conveyance of signals by wire, by radio, by optical or by other electromagnetic means'. By way of example, the Directive mentions satellite networks, fixed (circuit- and packet-switched, including internet) and mobile terrestrial networks, electricity cable systems, to the extent that they are used for the purpose of transmitting signals,[128] networks used for radio and television broadcasting, and cable television networks, irrespective of the type of information conveyed. This non-inclusive enumeration leaves room for future technological developments, including the emerging Voice over Internet Protocol ('VoIP') services.[129]

1.50   'Electronic communications service' is defined in article 2(c) Framework Directive as 'a service normally provided for remuneration which consists wholly or mainly in the conveyance of signals on electronic communications networks' .This definition is specified in two ways: the provision makes clear that electronic communication services comprise, but are not limited to, telecommunications services and transmission services and networks used for broadcasting, but that they exclude services 'providing, or exercising editorial control over, content transmitted using electronic communications networks and services' as well as 'information society services',[130] which do not consist wholly or mainly in the conveyance of signals on electronic communications networks. Ultimately, none of these boundary lines allow for a clear-cut separation of the scope of applicability of the various legislative measures. Rather, NRAs (and the Commission, see article 7 Framework

---

126   See paras 1.3 and 1.38 above.
127   See statutory definitions in art 1(1) Services Directive and in art 2 No 3, 4 ONP Framework Directive 1990.
128   Cf European Commission, Recommendation on broadband communication through power-lines, L 93/42, 12.04.2005 2005/292/EC.
129   VoIP is a generic term for the conveyance of voice, fax and related services partially or wholly over packet-switched IP-based networks, cf European Regulators Group, ERG Common Statement for VoIP regulatory approaches, ERG (05) 12, part 1; for a categorisation of various classes of VoIP offerings see Commission Staff Working Document on the treatment of Voice over Internet Protocol (VoIP) under the EU Regulatory Framework, 14 06 2004, p 6.
130   See statutory definition in art 1 Directive 98/34/EC as amended by Directive 98/48/EC of the European Parliament and the Council of 20 July 1998: 'any service normally provided for remuneration, at a distance, by electronic means and at the individual request of a recipient of services', OJ L 217/18, 05.08.1998.

Directive) will also in the future be called upon to decide, on occasion, whether or not a given service is an 'electronic communications service' or a 'content'-related service. The 'content transmitted using electronic communications networks and services' is governed by other provisions of Community law.[131] There are undoubtedly legal interfaces between 'transmission infrastructures' and 'content' if and when regulatory decisions regarding the transmission infrastructure have a direct or indirect effect on 'content'. The 'regulation of transmission infrastructures' and the 'regulation of content' are explicitly intertwined in article 8(1) para 3 Framework Directive which allows the NRAs to 'contribute within their competencies to ensuring the implementation of policies aimed at the promotion of cultural and linguistic diversity, as well as media pluralism'.[132]

1.51   The scope of applicability of the Directives (and, as a consequence, the regulatory powers of the NRAs, see article 8(2) Access Directive) is expanded by the inclusion of 'associated facilities'. These are 'those facilities associated with an electronic communications network and/or an electronic communications service which enable and/or support the provision of services via that network and/or service' (article 2(e) Framework Directive); this includes, among other things, conditional access systems and electronic programme guides.

National Regulatory Authorities: Organisation, Regulatory Objectives, Competencies and Procedural Rules

1.52   The Member States are obliged to ensure that their national regulatory authorities 'are legally distinct from and functionally independent of all organisations providing electronic communications networks, equipment or services' (article 3(2) Framework Directive). Most Member States still retain ownership or control of undertakings providing electronic communications networks and/or services;[133] they are obliged to ensure effective structural separation of the regulatory function from activities associated with ownership and control. The Member States also have to ensure that NRAs exercise their powers 'impartially and transparently' (article 3(3) Framework Directive).

1.53   Article 8 Framework Directive obliges the Member States to ensure that the NRAs pursue certain policy objectives and abide by the regulatory principles established by Community law. The NRAs have to take all 'reasonable' measures which are aimed at achieving a number of regulatory objectives which are set out in three categories: Promotion of competition, development of the internal market, and promotion of the interests of the citizens of the European Union. Each of

---

131   See Council Directive 89/552/EEC of 3 October 1989 on the coordination of certain provisions laid down by Law, Regulation or Administrative Action in Member States concerning the pursuit of television broadcasting activities, OJ L 298/23, 17.10.1989 as amended by Directive 97/36/EC of the European Parliament and of the Council of 30 June 1997 on the coordination of certain provisions laid down by law, regulation or administrative action in Member States concerning the pursuit of television broadcasting activities, OJ L 202/60, 30.07.1997; Directive 2000/31/EC of the European Parliament and of the Council of 8 June 2000 on certain legal aspects of information society services, in particular electronic commerce, in the Internal Market ('Directive on electronic commerce'), OJ L 178/17, 17.07.2000.

132   Other content-related provisions can be found in: art 5(1) sub-para 2(b) Access Directive; art 6(4) Authorisation Directive; art 31 Universal Service Directive.

133   At the end of 2003, only Denmark and the United Kingdom had completely privatised their formerly publicly owned telecommunications companies.

these overarching, primary regulatory objectives is specified by a broad variety of non-inclusive secondary objectives. In taking regulatory measures, the NRAs have to abide by the principle of proportionality (article 8(1) para 1 Framework Directive).

The primary policy objective to promote competition and the provision of electronic communications networks and services means, among other things, that the national regulatory authorities shall:

• ensure that users, including disabled users, derive maximum benefit in terms of choice, price and quality;
• ensure that there is no distortional restriction of competition in the electronic communications sector;
• encourage efficient investment in infrastructure, and promote innovation; and
• encourage efficient use and ensure the effective management of radio frequencies and numbering resources (article 8(2) Framework Directive).

The colourful patchwork of the secondary objectives set out in article 8(2) and (4) Framework Directive is complemented by the regulatory objectives established in the Specific Directives.[134] When balancing the various regulatory objectives, the NRAs will need to consider their relative importance, which is expressed, to a certain extent, by subtle differences in the wording ('ensure', 'encourage', 'promote', 'contribute', 'address').

An additional, albeit not mandatory, requirement for the NRAs' regulatory decisions is that they should be technologically neutral: Member States are obliged to ensure that NRAs 'take the utmost account of the desirability of making regulations technologically neutral'.

The obligation of NRAs to contribute to the achievement of content-related regulatory objectives is even weaker, which is hardly surprising given the 'content neutrality' of the 2002 EU Regulatory Package.[135] NRAs 'may contribute within their competencies' to ensuring the implementation of policies that are aimed at the promotion of cultural and linguistic diversity as well as media pluralism. This provision does not prevent a Member State from precluding its NRA, either on the basis of its constitutional law or through other statutory provisions, from pursuing the objectives of cultural and linguistic diversity or media pluralism and assigning theses tasks to other governmental authorities.

1.54 Article 5(1) Framework Directive obliges the Member States to ensure that NRAs may request, from undertakings providing electronic communications networks and services, all the information, including financial information, that is necessary to ensure conformity with the provisions of the Framework Directive and the Specific Directives. Such information is to be provided 'promptly on request and to the time scales and level of detail required by the national regulatory authority'. The information request needs to comply with the principle of proportionality and the NRA shall provide the reasons justifying the request for information.

1.55 The Framework Directive establishes a number of procedural rules which pertain, in part, to the regulatory procedures of the NRAs and, in part, to the cooperation between NRAs and Commission. These procedural rules include:

---

134 Art 1(1) and (2) Access Directive, art 1(1) and (2) Universal Service Directive, art 1(1) Authorisation Directive.
135 See art 1(3) Framework Directive and paras 1.51 above and 1.63 below.

- obligations to publish information,[136]
- obligations to conduct public hearings or consultations,[137] and
- obligations to cooperate.[138]

The consultation procedure under article 6 Framework Directive is particularly important: Member States shall ensure that, where NRAs intend to take measures in accordance with the Framework Directive or the Specific Directives 'which have a significant impact on the relevant market', a consultation procedure is conducted.[139] The Directive does not specify how 'a significant impact on the relevant market' is to be assessed. The Directive also fails to provide detailed guidance for conducting the consultation procedure: the NRAs are obliged to 'give interested parties the opportunity to comment on the draft measure within a reasonable period'. This leaves open the question as to who is to be included among the 'interested parties'.[140] It would seem, from the wording of other provisions of secondary Community law, that 'interested parties' are 'third parties whose interests may be affected'; this means that the consultation procedure is not open to anybody, but only to parties who can show a sufficient interest in the decision at hand.[141]

More generally, article 3(4) Framework Directive obliges the Member States to ensure 'consultation and cooperation' between the NRAs of the various Member States and between the NRAs and national authorities entrusted with the implementation of competition law and consumer law 'on matters of common interest'. This general cooperation obligation is further specified in article 3(5) Framework Directive, which obliges NRAs and national competition authorities to provide each other 'with the information necessary for the application of the provisions of [the Framework Directive] and the Specific Directives'.

1.56   Article 20 Framework Directive establishes the Community law framework for the establishment of dispute resolution procedures to be conducted by the NRAs for the speedy, non-judicial resolution of controversies between undertakings in a given Member State. Under this provision, the NRA shall, at the request of one of the parties to a controversy, issue a binding decision on any dispute 'arising in connection with obligations arising under [the Framework Directive] or the Specific Directives between undertakings providing electronic communications networks or services in a Member State'. This binding decision shall be rendered 'in the shortest possible time frame'.[142] By way of example, the recitals of the

---

136   Art 5(4) Framework Directive: obligation to publish such information as would contribute to an open and competitive market; art 10(3) Framework Directive: obligation to publish the national numbering plans; art 24(1) Framework Directive: obligation to publish up-to-date information pertaining to the application of the Directives.

137   Art 6 Framework Directive: see below; art 12(2) Framework Directive: obligation to hold a public consultation with all 'interested parties' prior to imposing the sharing of facilities or property.

138   See paras 1.160 et seq below.

139   See arts 7(6), 20 and 21 for exceptions.

140   See *Nikolinakos*, ECLR 2001, 93, 99.

141   Cf Recital 32, art 17(1) sub-para 3, art 27(4), 33(2) Council Regulation (EC) No 1/2003 of 16 December 2002 on the implementation of the rules on competition laid down in art 81 and art 82 of the Treaty, OJ L 1/1, 04.01.2003; for a clear distinction between parties showing 'a sufficient interest' and 'other third parties' see also recital 6, and in particular art 9 Commission Regulation (EC) No 2842/98 of 22 December 1998 on the hearing of parties in certain proceedings under art 85 and art 86 of the EC Treaty, OJ L 354/18, 13.12.1998.

142   Within four months, except in exceptional circumstances.

Framework Directive[143] mention disputes 'relating to obligations for access and interconnection or to the means of transferring subscriber lines'. The dispute resolution procedure does not preclude either party from bringing an action before the courts (article 20(4) Framework Directive).

With respect to cross-border disputes arising under the Framework Directive or the Specific Directives between parties in different Member States where the dispute lies within the competence of NRAs for more than one Member State, the Framework Directive provides for a co-ordinated dispute resolution procedure at the request of one of the parties. The Member States may make provision for NRAs jointly to decline to resolve a dispute 'where other mechanisms, including mediation, exist and would better contribute to resolution of the dispute in a timely manner' (article 21(3) para 1 Framework Directive). If, however, after four months the dispute is not resolved, if the dispute has not been brought before the court by the parties seeking regress, and if either party requests it, the NRAs are obliged to 'coordinate their efforts in order to bring about the resolution of the dispute' (article 21(3) Framework Directive).

Right of appeal against NRA's decisions

1.57   Article 4(1) sentence 1 Framework Directive provides that any user or undertaking providing electronic communications networks and/or services who is affected by a decision of an NRA has the right of appeal against the decision to an 'appeal body' that is independent of the parties involved. This independent appeal body may be a court (article 4(1) sentence 2). Pending the outcome of any appeal, the decision of the NRA shall stand 'unless the appeal body decides otherwise' (article 4(1) sentence 1).

1.58   Article 4(1) sentence 1 Framework Directive does not establish an obligation of national legislators, under EU law, to allow a user or undertaking providing electronic networks and/or services to appeal against decisions of an NRA by which they are somehow 'affected'. This follows, in particular, from recital 12 Framework Directive which states that 'any party who *is the subject of a decision* by a national regulatory authority should have the right to appeal to a body that is independent of the parties involved' [emphasis added]. It follows from this recital that, from a Community law perspective, only the addressees and others that are directly affected ('the subject') of a regulatory decision shall have a right to appeal. National legislators are not prevented, however, by article 4(1) Framework Directive, from extending the right of appeal to other third parties that have an interest in the outcome of the controversy.

The Commission's powers of control and harmonisation

1.59   The European legislator has delegated broad regulatory powers to the NRAs and has strengthened the NRAs' discretion to select the appropriate regulatory remedies;[144] these regulatory powers at national level are counterbalanced, however, by increased requirements for co-ordination of NRA decisions and positions at EU level.[145] This co-ordination is achieved in the first instance by obliging the NRAs to

---

143   Recital 32 Framework Directive.
144   See para 1.40 above and paras 1.77 and 1.138 below.
145   Communications Review, COM(1999) 539, final, 10.11.1999, p 51.

cooperate and to consult with each other and with the Commission (article 7(2), (3))[146] and, at an organisational level, through the establishment of the CoCom.[147] In addition, the legislator considered it to be necessary to back up such consensus building 'by the possibility to give decisions [of the Commission] legal force'.[148] To this end, powers of control and harmonisation have been granted to the Commission, including a right to veto certain decisions of the NRAs.

The consolidation procedure

1.60 Under the heading '*Consolidating the Internal Market for Electronic Communications*', the Framework Directive establishes in article 7 a cooperation obligation under which the NRAs have to cooperate with each other and with the Commission 'in a transparent manner' in order to ensure 'the consistent application, in all Member States, of the [Framework] Directive and the Specific Directives' (article 7(2) Framework Directive). The provision further establishes a two-tiered 'consolidation procedure', the structure of which was, during the legislative process, controversial between the Council and the Commission[149] and was finalised only during the second reading in parliament (article 7(3)–(5) Framework Directive).[150]

1.61 The NRAs are obliged to notify the Commission and the NRAs in other Member States and to conduct a consultation procedure (article 7(3)) before taking a measure which:

● falls within the scope of article 15 or 16 of the Framework Directive,[151] article 5 or 8 Access Directive[152] or article 16 Universal Service Directive,[153] and

● would affect trade between Member States.

The Commission has adopted detailed rules for the notification process in a recommendation.[154] The NRA makes the draft measure accessible to the Commission and the other national regulatory authorities, together with the reasons on

---

146 See paras 1.61 et seq below.

147 See para 1.15 above.

148 Communications Review, COM(1999) 539, final, 10.11.1999, p 51.

149 See Amendment 33, European Parliament Opinion (first reading) of 1 March 2001, OJ C 277/91, 01.10.2001; amended proposal for a Directive of the European Parliament and of the Council on a common regulatory framework for electronic communications networks and services, COM(2001) 380 final, 04.07.2001, pp 3 et seq; Common Position EC No 38/2001 adopted by the Council on 17 September 2001, OJ C 337/34, 30.11.2001, pp 52 et seq.

150 Communication from the Commission to the European Parliament concerning the common position of the Council, SEC(2001) 1365 final, pp 4 and 6; amendment 23, Recommendation for second reading of 4 December 2001, Committee on Industry, External Trade, Research and Energy, A5–0435/2001 PE 309.058, p 25.

151 Measures of the NRA in the context of the market definition procedure or the market analysis procedure – see paras 1.76 below.

152 Measures concerning access and interconnection (art 5 Access Directive) and measures concerning undertakings designated to have SMP (art 8 Access Directive); see paras 1.135 and 1.137 below.

153 Market analysis procedures to determine whether to maintain, amend or withdraw obligations relating to retail markets (art 16(3) Universal Service Directive); see paras 1.171 et seq below.

154 Commission Recommendation of 23 July 2003 on notifications, time limits and consultations provided for in art 7 of Directive 2002/21/EC of the European Parliament and of the Council on a common regulatory framework for electronic communications networks and services, OJ L 190/13, 30.07.2003.

which the measure is based. The NRAs in other Member States and the Commission then have one month[155] to comment on the draft measure.[156] Once the comment period has ended, the NRA may adopt the draft measure, taking 'the utmost account of comments of other national regulatory authorities and the Commission' (article 7(5) Framework Directive); this means that the measure may be adopted despite objections raised by other NRAs and/or the Commission.

1.62 When a measure that an NRA intends to take aims to:

- define a relevant market which differs from those defined in the relevant Commission recommendation[157] or
- decide whether or not to designate an undertaking as having, either individually or jointly with others, significant market power,[158]

the one-month consultation period is followed by the veto procedure under article 7(4)[159] if the measure would affect trade between the Member States and the Commission has indicated to the NRA that:

- it considers that the draft measure would create a barrier to the single market, or
- it has serious doubts as to its compatibility with Community law and, in particular, the objectives referred to in article 8 Framework Directive.

In this case, the NRA is prevented from adopting the measure for a further two months. During this two-month period, the Commission may take a decision requiring the NRA concerned to withdraw the draft measure (article 7(4) sentence 3). This decision must be accompanied by a detailed and objective analysis of why the Commission considers that the draft measure should not be adopted, together with specific proposals for adopting the draft measure (article 7(4) sentence 5);[160] the Commission does not have the right to replace the proposed measure of the NRA with a measure of its own. The Commission's decision requiring the NRA to withdraw its draft measure is preceded by the advisory procedure in accordance with the Council's comitology Decision.[161]

As of 31 January 2005, the Commission had received 140 notifications from 12 NRAs and had sent out 80 so-called Phase I letters, ie letters with comments (in 56

---

155 Or more than one month, in cases concerning art 6 Framework Directive (art 7(3) sentence 2).

156 The one-month period cannot be extended (art 7(3) sentence 3 Framework Directive).

157 See para 1.75 below.

158 See para 1.77 below.

159 NRAs may in exceptional circumstances derogate from the consolidation procedure and adopt provisional measures (art 7(6) Framework Directive); see para 1.64 below.

160 See Commission Recommendation of 23 July 2003 on notifications, time limits and consultations provided for in art 7 of Directive 2002/21/EC of the European Parliament and of the Council on a common regulatory framework for electronic communications networks and services, OJ L 190/13, 30.07.2003.

161 Council Decision of 28 June 1999 laying down the procedures for the exercise of implementing powers conferred on the Commission, OJ L 184/23, 17.07.1999.

cases) or no comments (in 24 cases) on the proposed measures (article 7(3) Framework Directive).[162] To date (June 2005), the Commission has taken four veto Decisions.[163]

1.63   The assessment as to whether the proposed measure 'would affect trade between Member States' is based on the same standard as the comparable assessment under articles 81(1) and 82 sentence 2 EC Treaty. This means that it must be possible to foresee with a sufficient degree of probability on the basis of a set of objective factors of law or of fact that the measure in question may have an influence, direct or indirect, actual or potential, on the pattern of trade between Member States.[164] The same applies to the prognosis that a proposed measure of an NRA 'would create a barrier to the single market'. The alternatively existing threshold of 'serious doubts as to [the draft measure's] compatibility with Community law' would appear to be more difficult to overcome, whereas the further requirement of 'serious doubts as to its compatibility with … the objectives referred to in article 8' can very easily be met, given both the vagueness and the multitude of the objectives set out in article 8[165] Framework Directive. In its veto Decisions, to date, the Commission has held that a draft measure designating or not designating an undertaking with SMP and the regulatory obligations that may or may not be imposed in one Member State on the provision of a given service 'may have an influence, direct or indirect, actual or potential, on the ability of undertakings established in other Member States to provide such electronic communications services'.[166]

1.64   The consultation procedure as well as, in particular, the veto procedure can lead to delays of the regulatory procedures at national level;[167] the NRAs can avoid the veto procedure, however, by taking the Commission's objections into account during the consultation procedure.

The veto procedure is the quid pro quo for the flexible and procedure-oriented regulatory approach established by the 2002 EU Regulatory Package, under which ex-ante obligations can only be imposed on undertakings which have been designated, in the course of a complex, multi-tiered market definition and market analysis procedure as undertakings with significant market power.[168]

The Commission's veto Decisions, to date, relate to proposed NRA measures which were aimed at deciding whether or not to designate an undertaking as having significant market power (article 7(4) lit b Framework Directive). Specifically, the Commission held that:

- the Finnish regulator had failed to provide sufficient evidence to support its finding of the absence of SMP in the markets for (retail) publicly available

---

162   Cf Commission Report to the European Regulators Group, Notifications received under art 7 Framework Directive, ERG (04) 40, 25.11.2004; see also European Commission, Communications Committee Working Document, Update on Art 7 Procedures, COCOM 04–51, 30.06.2004.

163   Commission Decisions of 20.02.2004, C (2004) 527 final; 20.02.2004, C (2004) 527 final; 5.10.2004, C (2004) 3682 final; 20.10.2004, C (2004) 4070 final; 17.05.2005, C (2005) 1442 final; for details see para 1.64 below.

164   ECJ Judgment of 30 June 1966, Case 56–65, *Société Technique Minière v Maschinenbau Ulm GmbH* [1966] ECR 282.

165   See para 1.53 above.

166   Cf Commission Decision of 20.02.2004, C (2004) 527 final, para 14.

167   See *Nikolinakos*, ECLR 2001, 93, 99.

168   See para 1.59 above and paras 1.76 et seq below.

international telephone services provided at fixed locations for residential customers and for non-residential customers,[169]

- the Finnish regulator had failed to provide sufficient evidence to support its finding of the existence of SMP in the market for access and call origination on public mobile telephone networks,[170]
- the Austrian regulator had failed to provide sufficient evidence to support its finding of the absence of SMP on the market for transit services in the fixed public telephone network,[171] and
- the German regulator had failed to provide sufficient evidence to support its finding that the alternative fixed telephone network operators in Germany, ʻdespite having a market share of 100 per cent with respect to their respective networks, did not have SMP in the market for call termination on individual public telephone networks at a fixed location.[172]

While emphasising that the NRAs are accorded discretionary powers correlative to the complex character of the economic, factual and legal situations that need to be assessed, the Commission has included, in each of its veto Decisions, detailed ʻproposalsʻ for amending the draft measures. It remains to be seen whether the Commission will refrain from micro-managing and prejudicing the NRAs' market analyses and limit itself to monitoring abuses of the NRAs' discretion instead.

An NRA may only ʻin exceptional circumstancesʼ adopt provisional measures by way of derogation from the consultation and veto procedures where it considers that there is an urgent need to act in order to safeguard competition and protect the interests of users. In this case, the NRA shall, without delay, communicate its provisional measures, with full reasons, to the Commission and the other NRAs (article 7(6) Framework Directive).

The Commission's power to stipulate standards and specifications

1.65 The Commission's powers to ensure the harmonised application of the Regulatory Framework have been expanded[173] to include the initiation of standardisation procedures and the power to make technical standards or specifications compulsory if these standards or specifications have not been adequately implemented so that interoperability of services in one or more Member States cannot be ensured (article 17(3) Framework Directive).[174] The Commission's ʻnoticeʼ by which specifications or standards are made compulsory is prepared in a regulatory procedure under article 5 of the Council's comitology Decision;[175] from a legal view point, the ʻnoticeʼ is a Decision within the meaning of article 249(4) EC Treaty.

---

169 Commission Decision of 20.02.2004, C (2004) 527 final, paras 15 et seq.

170 Commission Decision of 05.10. 2004, C (2004) 3682 final, paras 11 et seq.

171 Commission Decision of 20.10.2004, C (2004) 4070 final, paras 15 et seq.

172 Commission Decision of 17.05.2005, C (2005) 1442 final., paras 17 et seq.

173 See, previously, art 5 ONP Framework Directive.

174 An interim issue of the list of standards and/or specifications for electronic communications networks, services and associated facilities was published by the Commission in December 2002, OJ C 331/32, 31.12.2002. In February 2005 the Communication Committee's Expert Group on Standardisation launched a guidance paper proposing criteria to be used for revising the interim list of standards.

175 See arts 17(4) and 22(3) Framework Directive and arts 5 and 7 Council Decision of 28 June 1999 laying down the procedures for the exercise of implementing powers conferred on the Commission, OJ L 184/23, 17.07.1999.

The Commission's power to issue recommendations

1.66   In addition to the recommendations[176] and guidelines[177] which are aimed at harmonising the market definition and market analysis procedures, the Commission has the power, under article 19 Framework Directive, to issue 'recommendations to Member States on the harmonised application of the provisions in this [Framework] Directive and the Specific Directives in order to further the achievement of the objectives set out in article 8 [Framework Directive]'.[178] These recommendations are issued on the basis of the advisory procedure (article 22(2) Framework Directive). These – legally non-binding – recommendations (article 249(5) EC Treaty) appear to have a specific 'soft law' quality: Member States are obliged to ensure that the NRAs 'take the utmost account of those recommendations in carrying out their tasks' (article 19(1) sentence 1 Framework Directive). Where a national regulatory authority chooses not to follow a recommendation, it is obliged to inform the Commission, giving the reasons for its position (article 19(1) sentence 2 Framework Directive).

Safeguarding the Commission's powers of control and harmonisation

1.67   In order to exercise their control and harmonisation powers in the most effective manner, the NRAs need to cooperate closely with the Commission (article 7(2) Framework Directive) and the Commission needs to receive, from Member States and NRAs, all information that is necessary for the exercise of its duties. To this end, article 5(2) Framework Directive establishes a right of the Commission to obtain from Member States all information 'necessary for it to carry out its tasks under the Treaty'. In addition, the 2002 EU Regulatory Package establishes a number of specific information and cooperation obligations:

Provision	Obligation
Article 19(1) Framework Directive	**Obligation of the Member States to take utmost account of the Commission's Recommendations on the harmonised application of the Directives.**
Article 24(2) Framework Directive	**Obligation of the Member States to provide to the Commission up-to-date information pertaining to the application of the Directives.**
Article 8(5) Access Directive	**Obligation of the NRAs to notify the Commission of decisions to impose, amend or withdraw obligations on market players not designated as having SMP in order to comply with international commitments.**

---

176   Art 15(1) Framework Directive; see para 1.75 below.

177   Art 15(2) Framework Directive; see para 1.72 below.

178   The recommendations which have been issued by the Commission include: Commission Recommendation on the processing of caller location information in electronic communication networks for the purpose of location-enhanced emergency call services, OJ L 189/49, 29.07.2003; Commission Recommendation on the provision of leased lines in the European Union (Part 1 – Major supply conditions for wholesale leased lines), OJ L 24/39, 27.01.2005; Commission Recommendation 2005/268/EC of 29.03.2005 on the provision of leased lines in the European Union (Part 2 – Pricing aspects of wholesale leased lines part circuits), OJ L 83/52, 01.04.2005; Commission Recommendation 2005/292/EC of 06.04.2005 on broadband electronic communications through powerlines, OJ L 93/42, 12.04.2005.

Provision	Obligation
Article 15(2) Access Directive	Obligation of the Member States to provide to the Commission information on the specific obligations imposed on undertakings under the Access Directive.
Article 16 sentence 2 Authorisation Directive	Obligation of the Member States to supply at the Commission's request information on the functioning of the national authorisation systems.
Article 17(3) Universal Service Directive	Obligation of the NRAs to supply at the Commission's request information concerning the retail controls applied and, where appropriate, the cost accounting systems used by undertakings concerned according to article 17(1) Universal Service Directive.
Article 36(1) and (2) Universal Service Directive	Obligation of the NRAs to notify the Commission of the names of undertakings designated as having universal service obligations under article 8 Universal Service Directive.

'Significant Market Power' as fundamental prerequisite of regulation

1.68 The Framework Directive and the Specific Directives establish a number of regulatory powers of the NRAs with respect to the providers of electronic communications networks and services.[179] The majority of these regulatory powers are aimed at undertakings designated as having SMP.[180] In order to achieve public interest objectives other than the promotion of competition (cultural and linguistic diversity, media pluralism, etc) – including the objectives of interoperability and of 'end-to-end' communications – the Directives also provide for regulatory powers regardless of the regulated enterprise's market position.[181]

The following regulatory measures apply exclusively to undertakings designated as having significant market power:

- transparency obligations in conjunction with access and interconnection (article 9 Access Directive),
- obligation of non-discrimination regarding access and interconnection (article 10 Access Directive),
- obligation of accounting separation (article 11 Access Directive),
- obligations of access to, and use of, specific network facilities (article 12 Access Directive),
- price control and cost accounting obligations (article 13 Access Directive, article 18(1) sentence 2 in conjunction with No 2 Annex II Universal Service Directive),
- regulatory controls on retail services (article 17 Universal Service Directive),
- regulatory controls on the minimum set of leased lines (article 18(1) sentence 2 in conjunction with No 1, 3 Annex II Universal Service Directive), and

---

179 For the regulatory powers of the NRAs, see paras 1.79, 1.133 and 1.173 below. Cf ERG Common Position on the approach to appropriate remedies in the new regulatory framework, ERG (03)30 of 1 April 2004.

180 See para 1.133 below.

181 Eg arts 5 and 6 Access Directive, art 12(2) Framework Directive, arts 29, 30, 31 Universal Service Directive.

- obligations regarding carrier selection and carrier pre-selection (article 19 Universal Service Directive).

REASONS FOR THE REVISION OF THE CONCEPT OF SIGNIFICANT MARKET POWER

1.69   The legislative reasons that are provided for the re-definition of the regulatory concept of 'significant market power' are fairly vague: Recital 25 Framework Directive merely states that the previous definition of significant market power in Directive 97/33/EC,[182] which provided for a rebuttable presumption of significant market power in cases of market shares of more than 25%, 'needs to be adapted to suit more complex and dynamic markets'. By transposing the competition law concept of 'dominant market power' into the 2002 EU Regulatory Package, the legislator takes a first, important step toward the replacement of sector-specific regulation by competition law.[183] The predictability of regulatory measures which had been ensured by the 25% threshold under the previous regulatory framework is now replaced by a 'more flexible' threshold for regulatory measures; the flexibility is, however, limited by the procedural rules of secondary Community law governing the determination of SMP undertakings, and by recommendations.

SIGNIFICANT MARKET POWER – ASSESSMENT CRITERIA

1.70   The Framework Directive replaces, as mentioned above, the rebuttable presumption which was set out in several Directives of the previous regulatory framework under which significant market power was presumed to exist if an organisation had 'a share of more than 25% of a particular telecommunications market in the geographical area in a Member State within which it is authorised to operate'.[184] This presumption is replaced by a new definition of significant market power, which follows closely the definition established, in the case law of the European Court of Justice, for a 'dominant market position'.[185] According to article 14(2) Framework Directive, an undertaking 'shall be deemed to have significant market power if, either individually or jointly with others, it enjoys a position equivalent to dominance, that is to say a position of economic strength affording it the power to behave to an appreciable extent independently of competitors, customers and ultimately consumers'. The Directive adopts the concept of collective dominance, which has not yet been fully developed in the jurisprudence of the European Court of Justice.[186] In particular, the existence of structural links among the undertakings concerned is not a prerequisite for a finding of collective dominance.[187] If there are fringe competitors, collective dominance can only be assumed if these competitors are not able to counteract the results expected from

---

182   OJ L 199/32, 26.07.1997 as amended by Directive 98/61/EC, OJ L 268/37, 03.10.1998, see art 4(3).

183   Communications Review, COM(1999) 539, final, 10.11.1999, p vi.

184   Art 4(3) Interconnection Directive (as amended by Directive 98/61/EC); see also art 2(3) Leased Lines Directive (as amended by ONP Framework Directive (1997); art 2(2)(i) Voice Telephony Directive (1998) and art 7(1)(d) in conjunction with art 2(2) Directive 97/13/EC.

185   See the European Court of Justice's definition as provided in ECJ Judgment of 14 February 1978, Case 27/76, *United Brands v Commission* [1978] ECR 207, 286.

186   See ECJ Judgment of 16 March 2000, Joined Cases C-395/96 P and C- 396/96 P, *Compagnie Maritime Belge et al v Commission* [2000] ECR-I 1365, 1387 et seq and ECJ Judgment of the Court of First Instance, Case T-102/96, *Gencor v Commission* [1999] ECR-II 753, 815 et seq; for details see also Commission Guidelines on market analysis, paras 86 et seq.

187   Commission Guidelines on market analysis, paras 87, 90–94.

the common position; important criteria to be considered in this context are the existence of high barriers to entry, differences in cost structures and demand elasticities.[188]

1.71   The regulation of vertically integrated providers of networks and/or services is facilitated by article 14(3) Framework Directive which provides that, where an undertaking has SMP on a specific market, 'it may also be deemed to have significant market power on a closely related market, where the links between the two markets are such as to allow the market power held in one market to be leveraged into the other market, thereby strengthening the market power of the undertaking'.[189] However, if an undertaking has been designated as having SMP on an upstream wholesale or access market, the NRAs will normally be in a position to prevent likely spill-over or leverage effects downstream into the retail or services market by imposing on that undertaking specific obligations provided for in the Directives to avoid such effects. 'Therefore, it is only where the imposition of ex-ante obligations on an undertaking which is dominant in the (access) upstream market would not result in effective competition on the (retail) downstream market that NRAs should examine whether article 14(3) may apply'.[190]

1.72   The concept of significant market power is specified in the Commission's 'Guidelines' which were adopted on the basis of article 15(2) Framework Directive.[191] Under the Guidelines, the main criteria for defining the relevant market are demand-side substitutability and supply-side substitutability:

(1)   Demand-side substitutability can be used to measure the extent to which consumers are prepared to substitute other services or products for the service or product in question.[192]

(2)   Supply-side substitutability indicates whether suppliers other than those offering the product or services in question would switch in the immediate to short term their line of production or offer the relevant product or services without incurring significant additional costs.[193]

One possible way for the NRAs to assess the existence of demand- and supply-side substitution is to apply the so-called 'hypothetical monopolist test'. Under this test, an NRA assesses what would happen if there were a small but significant, lasting increase in the price of a given product or service, assuming the prices of all other products or services remain constant.[194] The Commission acknowledges that the significance of a price increase will depend on each individual case but expects that

---

188   European Regulators Group, Working paper on the SMP concept for the new regulatory framework (May 2003), pp 8 et seq.

189   See ECJ Judgment of 14 November 1996, Case C-333/94P, *Tetra Pak v Commission* [1996] ECR-I 5951, 6008 et seq; ECJ Judgment of 3 October 1985, Case 311/84, *Centre Belge d'Etudes de Marche SA v Compagnie Luxembourgeoise de Telediffusion SA* [1985] ECR-I 3261, 3278; ECJ Judgment of 13 December 1991, Case 18/88, *Régie des Télégraphes et des Téléphones v GB-Inno-BM* [1991] ECR-I, 5941, 5979 et seq; see also *Koenig/Kühlings/ Braun*, Die Interpendenz von Märkten in der Telekommunikation, Computer und Recht 2001, 745, 825; *Polster/Brandl*, The new concept of market dominance in the proposed EU telecommunications framework, Computer and Telecommunications Law Review 2001, 216, 218.

190   Commission Guidelines on market analysis, para 84.

191   Commission Guidelines on market analysis and the assessment of significant market power under the Community regulatory framework for electronic communications networks and services, OJ C 165/6, 11.07.2002.

192   Commission Guidelines on market analysis, para 39.

193   Commission Guidelines on market analysis, para 39.

194   Commission Guidelines on market analysis, para 40.

NRAs should normally consider customers' reactions to a permanent price increase of between 5 and 10%. The Commission believes that the responses by consumers or undertakings concerned will aid in determining whether substitutable products do exist and, if so, where the boundaries of the relevant product markets should be delineated.[195] The Commission believes that product substitutability between different electronic communication services will arise increasingly through the convergence of various technologies. 'In order, therefore, to complete the market-definition analysis, an NRA, in addition to considering products or services whose objective characteristics, prices and intended use make them sufficiently interchangeable, should also examine, where necessary, the prevailing conditions of demand and supply substitution by applying the hypothetical monopolist test'.[196]

As regards the definition of the geographic market, the Guidelines make reference to the well-established case law of the European Court of Justice according to which the relevant geographic market comprises an area in which the undertakings concerned are involved in the supply and demand of the relevant products and services, in which area the conditions of competition are similar or sufficiently homogenous and which can be distinguished from neighbouring areas in which the prevailing conditions of competition are appreciably different.[197] The Commission emphasises that market definition is not a mechanical or abstract process but 'requires an analysis of any available evidence of past market behaviour and an overall understanding of the mechanics of a given sector'. Therefore, 'a dynamic rather than a static approach is required when carrying out a prospective, or forward-looking, market analysis'.[198] Annex I to the Framework Directive sets out a list of markets to be included in the initial Commission Recommendation on relevant product and service markets.[199]

1.73   In assessing whether or not an undertaking has significant market power, the NRAs have to ensure that their decisions are in accordance with the Commission's practice and the relevant jurisprudence of the European Court of Justice and the Court of First Instance.[200] Although the Framework Directive has aligned the definition of SMP with the court's definition of dominance within the meaning of article 82 (ex article 86) EC Treaty, the application of the new definition of SMP by the NRAs requires 'certain methodological adjustments ... regarding the way market power is assessed'.[201] These adjustments result from the fact that competition authorities apply article 82 EC Treaty ex post, whereas the NRAs have to apply the definition of SMP ex ante and are therefore required to base their market analysis on a prognostic assessment.

The ex-ante assessment of SMP is, in essence, measured by reference to the power of the undertaking concerned to raise prices by restricting output without incurring

---

195   Commission Guidelines on market analysis, para 40.
196   Commission Guidelines on market analysis, para 48.
197   Commission Guidelines on market analysis, para 56, see also ECJ Judgment of 14 February 1978, Case 27/76, *United Brands v Commission* [1978] ECR 207, 284.
198   Commission Guidelines on market analysis, para 35.
199   Some of the markets defined in Annex I Framework Directive have been derived from market definitions used in the regulatory framework prior to the 2002 EU Regulatory Package, see *European Commission*, Determination of Organisations with Significant Market Power (SMP) for Implementation of the ONP Directives, Explanatory Note, March 1999, see below, para 1.75.
200   Commission Guidelines on market analysis, para 70.
201   Commission Guidelines on market analysis, para 70.

a significant loss of sales or revenues.[202] In addition to the market share of an undertaking, the criteria upon which the forward-looking market analysis can be based include amongst others:

- the overall size of the undertaking,
- control of infrastructure not easily duplicated,
- technological advantages or superiority,
- absence of or low countervailing buying power,
- easy or privileged access to capital markets/financial resources,
- product/services diversification (e g bundled products or services),
- economies of scale or economies of scope,
- vertical integration,
- a highly developed distribution and sales network,
- absence of potential competition, and
- barriers to extension.[203]

A dominant position can derive from a combination of these and other criteria, which become more relevant as indicators of significant market power where an undertaking's market share is lower than 50%. Following established case law, very large market shares – in excess of 50% – are in themselves, save in exceptional circumstances, evidence of the existence of a dominant position;[204] undertakings with market shares of between 25 and 50% are likely to enjoy a dominant position if additional criteria confirm that the undertaking can behave to an appreciable extent independently of its competitors, customers and consumers. On the other hand, undertakings with market shares of no more than 25% are not likely to enjoy a dominant position on their market.[205] In general, the development of market shares will be more meaningful than a snapshot picture of market shares at a given time: The persistence of high market shares over time may indicate dominance, while declining shares might be a sign of increasing competition; on the other hand, fluctuating market shares over time may be indicative of a lack of market power in the relevant market.[206]

SIGNIFICANT MARKET POWER – PROCEDURES

1.74 The NRAs decide whether the relevant market is effectively competitive (article 16(3) Framework Directive) or not effectively competitive but dominated by an undertaking which, either individually or jointly with others, enjoys significant market power (article 16(4) Framework Directive).

This decision is prepared in the course of two distinct procedures: the market definition procedure (article 15 Framework Directive); and the market analysis procedure (article 16 Framework Directive). Both of these procedures require the involvement of the Commission and the NRAs.

1.75 The market definition procedure is initiated at the European level: The Commission has adopted, after public consultation and consultation with the

---

202 Commission Guidelines on market analysis, para 73.
203 Commission Guidelines on market analysis, para 78; for further criteria see also European Regulators Group, Working paper on the SMP concept for the new regulatory framework (May 2003), pp 3 et seq.
204 Commission Guidelines on market analysis, para 75; see also Commission Decision of 20.02.2004, C (2004)527 final, paras 16 et seq; Decision of 17.05.2005, C (2005) 14442 final, paras 17 et seq.
205 Commission Guidelines on market analysis, para 75.
206 Commission Guidelines on market analysis, para 75.

NRAs, a recommendation on relevant product and service markets which identifies those product and service markets within the electronic communication sector, the characteristics of which 'may be such as to justify the imposition of regulatory obligations'.[207] The legal basis of and substantive criteria for this recommendation are set out in Annex I to the Framework Directive which establishes, on the basis of previous EU Directives,[208] a list of those markets which are to be included in the initial Commission Recommendation.[209] The recommendation shall be regularly reviewed by the Commission; the first review was scheduled, by the Commission, for no later than 30 June 2004.[210] For its future recommendations, the Commission will not be bound by the list of markets in Annex I to the Framework Directive, which applies only to 'the initial Commission Recommendation'.

The initial Recommendation[211] defines 18 markets 'in which ex ante regulation may be warranted'.[212] They include seven retail-level markets and eleven wholesale-level markets. The retail-level markets include markets for network access, markets for local and/or national telephone services, and markets for international telephone services and distinguish between residential and non-residential customers (markets No 1 to 6). At wholesale level, the Recommendation defines a market for 'wholesale broadband access' (market No 12) which covers 'bit-stream' access that permits the transmission of broadband data in both directions and other wholesale access provided over other infrastructures, if and when they offer facilities equivalent to bit-stream access.[213] In contrast to the previous Directives,[214] the Recommendation divides the wholesale-level market for leased lines into a market for 'wholesale terminating segments of leased lines' (market No 13) and 'wholesale trunk segments of leased lines' (market No 14). The Recommendation also defines, at wholesale level, three separate mobile communications markets, namely:

---

207   Commission Recommendation on relevant product and service markets within the electronic communications sector susceptible to ex ante regulation in accordance with Directive 2002/21/EC of the European Parliament and of the Council on a common regulatory framework for electronic communication networks and services ('Commission Recommendation on relevant markets'), OJ C 114/45, 08.05.2003.

208   See footnote 199 above.

209   Annex I Framework Directive includes markets for the provision of connection to and use of the public telephone network at fixed locations, for the provision of leased lines to end users, for call origination in the fixed public telephone network, for call termination in the fixed public telephone network, for transit services in the fixed public telephone network, for call origination on public mobile telephone networks, for call termination of public mobile telephone networks, for leased line interconnection, for access to the fixed public telephone network, for access to public mobile telephone networks, for wholesale provision of leased line capacity to other suppliers of electronic communications networks or services, for services provided over unbundled loops and the national market for international roaming services on public mobile telephone networks.

210   Commission Recommendation on relevant markets, para 21.

211   See *Krüger*, Marktabgrenzung im Telekommunikationssektor und die Definition von beträchtlicher Marktmacht (SMP), Kommunikation & Recht-Beilage 1/2003, p 9.

212   Commission Recommendation on relevant markets, para 2.

213   See *Holznagel*, Breitbandiger Internetzugang durch Bitstromzugang, Multimedia und Recht Beilage 3/2003, 37 et seq; *Kurth*, Bitstromzugang in Deutschland, Multimedia und Recht Beilage 20/2003, 3. See also ERG Common Position on Bitstream Access, ERG (03)33 of 2 April 2004 as amended on 25 May 2005, launching a public consultation on 'Bitstream Access'. For a summary of the results of the consultation see ERG Document (03) 34.

214   Annex II Leased Lines Directive (1992); Annex III Leased Lines Directive (1992) as amended by ONP Framework Directive (1997); see also European Commission, Determination of Organisations with Significant Market Power (SMP) for Implementation of the ONP Directives, Explanatory Note, March 1999, pp 4 et seq.

- the market for access and call origination on public mobile telephone networks (market No 15),
- the market for voice call termination on individual mobile networks (market No 16), and
- the wholesale national market for international roaming on public networks (market No 17).[215]

The definition provided for market No 16 (voice call termination on *individual* mobile networks) paves the way for sector-specific regulation of the mobile termination markets, as this market definition implies that each mobile network operator is a single supplier on each market. However, the Commission emphasises that 'whether every operator then has market power still depends on whether there is any countervailing buyer power, which would render any non-transitory price increase unprofitable'.[216]

The Commission is considering the impact of VoIP-based services[217] on the markets identified in its Recommendation.[218]

1.76 The market definition procedure continues at the national level: The NRAs are obliged to define relevant markets 'appropriate to national circumstances'. In defining the relevant markets, the NRAs are not only bound by 'the principles of competition law' but shall also take 'the utmost account of the recommendation and the guidelines' (article 15(3) Framework Directive). Although this unusually worded obligation alters neither the non-binding nature of the recommendation nor of the guidelines (article 249(5) EC Treaty), it does force the NRAs to justify their market definition. The need to justify national market definitions is further strengthened by procedural rules: If an NRA intends to deviate from the market definitions set out in the Commission Recommendation on relevant markets, it has to give interested parties the opportunity to comment (article 6) and, in addition, has to follow the consultation procedure under article 7 (article 15(3) sentence 2 Framework Directive). If the Commission is of the view that the definition of a relevant market which differs from those defined in the Recommendation on relevant markets would affect trade between Member States or if it has serious doubts as to its compatibility with Community law, the Commission can take a decision requiring the NRA to withdraw the proposed market definition in accordance with article 7(4) Framework Directive.[219] Transnational markets can be defined, by the Commission, after consultation with the NRAs in accordance with the procedure set out in article 22(3) Framework Directive.

1.77 The market definition procedure is followed by the market analysis procedure, which is to be conducted by the NRAs 'as soon as possible after the adoption of the Recommendation or any updating thereof' (article 16(1) Framework Directive). The market analysis is aimed at determining whether a relevant market is 'effectively competitive' (article 16(3) Framework Directive) or, where the NRA determines that a relevant market is not effectively competitive, which 'appropriate

---

215 Cf ERG Common position on the coordinated analysis of the markets for wholesale international roaming, ERG (05)20.

216 Explanatory memorandum to Commission Recommendation on relevant markets, p 34. Cf IRG Decision of 1 April 2004, Principles of implementation and best practice on the application of remedies in the mobile voice call termination market, which is intended to give guidance to the NRAs for a common approach towards the use of remedies in this market.

217 See para 1.49 above.

218 Cf Commission Staff Working Document on the treatment of Voice over Internet Protocol (VoIP) services under the EU Regulatory Framework, 14.06.2004, p 3.

219 See paras 1.62 et seq above.

specific regulatory obligations' shall be imposed upon the identified SMP undertakings (article 16(4) Framework Directive). In the course of the market analysis, the NRAs are again obliged to take 'the utmost account of the [Commission's] Guidelines' (article 16(1) sentence 1 Framework Directive). The Framework Directive specifically distinguishes three procedural alternatives:

- *Alternative 1:* The NRA concludes that the relevant market is 'effectively competitive'. In this case, it shall not impose or maintain any specific regulatory obligations and, in cases where sector-specific regulatory obligations already exist, such obligations placed on undertakings in that relevant market shall be withdrawn. The 'parties affected', which will include the competitors on the relevant market, shall be given 'an appropriate period of notice' prior to the withdrawal of the obligations (article 16(3) Framework Directive).

- *Alternative 2:* The NRA determines that a relevant market is not effectively competitive. In this case it has to identify undertakings with significant market power on that market, and impose on such undertakings 'appropriate specific regulatory obligations' in accordance with article 16(2) Framework Directive to maintain or amend such obligations where they already exist (article 16(4) Framework Directive).

- It should be noted that neither alternative 1 nor alternative 2 allows for any discretion of the NRA in deciding whether or not to impose sector-specific obligations ('remedies'). If the market is 'effectively competitive', the NRA cannot impose sector-specific regulatory obligations; if, however, a relevant market is not effectively competitive, the NRA is obliged to impose 'appropriate specific regulatory obligations' upon the undertakings designated as having SMP. The NRA's discretion relates (only) to the selection of the appropriate remedy.

- *Alternative 3:* In the case of transnational markets which have been identified by a Commission Decision (article 15(4) Framework Directive), the NRAs concerned have to jointly conduct the market analysis 'taking the utmost account of the guidelines' and decide 'in a concerted fashion' on any imposition, maintenance, amendment or withdrawal of regulatory obligations.

1.78   All three procedural alternatives are subject to the provisions regarding the consultation procedure (article 6 Framework Directive) and the consolidation procedure (article 7 Framework Directive). As a consequence, all 'interested parties' must be given the opportunity to comment on draft measures to impose, maintain, amend or withdraw SMP obligations. Furthermore, the NRAs of other Member States as well as the Commission need to be consulted. In all three procedural alternatives, the Commission has a right of veto if it is of the opinion that an intended decision, by the NRA, to designate or not to designate an undertaking as having, either individually or jointly with others, significant market power would affect trade between Member States, and provided that the Commission has indicated to the NRA that it considers that the proposed decision 'would create a barrier to the single market or it has serious doubts as to its compatibility with Community law' and, in particular, the regulatory objectives referred to in article 8 Framework Directive (article 7(4)(b) Framework Directive).[220]

---

220   See para 1.62 above.

NRAs' regulatory duties

MANAGEMENT OF RADIO FREQUENCIES FOR ELECTRONIC COMMUNICATION SERVICES

1.79   The Framework Directive establishes principles for the management of radio frequencies for electronic communications services; in particular, Member States shall ensure that the allocation and assignment of radio frequencies by NRAs are based on objective, transparent, non-discriminatory and proportionate criteria (article 9(1) Framework Directive). The regulatory objective to encourage efficient use and to ensure the effective management of radio frequencies, which is set out in article 8(2)(d) Framework Directive, is complemented by the other regulatory objectives set out in article 8 through a cross-reference in article 9(1) Framework Directive. Article 9(2) Framework Directive establishes an obligation on Member States to promote the harmonisation of use of radio frequencies in accordance with the Radio Spectrum Decision.[221]

1.80   Article 9(3) Framework Directive allows Member States to 'make provision for undertakings to transfer rights to use radio frequencies with other undertakings'. The legislator sees frequency trading (the 'transfer of radio frequencies') as a potentially 'effective means of increasing efficient use of spectrum, as long as there are sufficient safeguards in place to protect the public interest'.[222] Spectrum trading might lessen the risk in entering markets for new entrants; it allows enterprises to grow their business by acquiring spectrum as their demand increases in a shorter time frame than they currently do.[223] If a Member State opts for the introduction of frequency trading, it is obliged to ensure that an undertaking's intention to transfer rights to use radio frequencies is notified to the NRA responsible for spectrum assignment (article 9(4) Framework Directive). Any transfer of rights to use radio frequencies must take place in accordance with procedures to be laid down by the NRAs. The NRAs are obliged to ensure transparency and to prevent distortions of competition. Where radio frequency use has been harmonised through the application of the Radio Spectrum Decision[224] or other Community measures, any transfer of rights to use radio frequencies shall not result in a change of use of that radio frequency.

1.81   Whereas article 9 Framework Directive establishes the regulatory objectives and sets out basic procedural rules, the Authorisation Directive[225] establishes substantive provisions in relation to the rights of use for radio frequencies, and the Radio Spectrum Decision is aimed at the Community-wide harmonisation of the use of radio frequencies.[226]

---

221   Decision No 676/2002/EC of the European Parliament and of the Council of 7 March 2002 on a regulatory framework for radio spectrum policy in the European Community ('Radio Spectrum Decision'), OJ L 108/1, 24.04.2002, see paras 1.191 et seq below.
222   See recital 19 Framework Directive.
223   Oftel's response to the Independent Spectrum Review of Radio Spectrum Management, Statement issued by the Direction General of Telecommunications 28 September 2001, para 3.9.
224   See paras 1.191 et seq below.
225   See paras 1.91 et seq below.
226   See para 1.191 below.

MANAGEMENT OF NATIONAL NUMBERING RESOURCES

1.82   The 2002 EU Regulatory Package contains rules relating to numbering, naming and addressing in the Framework Directive (article 10) and in the Authorisation Directive (articles 5–7, 10–15). Whereas the Framework Directive defines the duties of the NRAs in relation to the assignment of national numbering resources and the management of the national numbering plans (article 10(1) sentence 1 Framework Directive) as well as basic principles for the allocation of numbers, the Authorisation Directive defines the rights of use in relation to numbers and the corresponding obligations that may be imposed upon providers of electronic communications networks and services.[227]

1.83   Among the duties of the NRAs which already existed under the regulatory framework prior to the 2002 EU Regulatory Package[228] are the allocation of numbering resources and the administration of the national numbering plans (article 10(1) sentence 1 Framework Directive). The allocation of national numbering resources is governed, as under the now repealed Directives,[229] by the principles of objectivity, transparency and non-discrimination (article 10(1) sentence 2 Framework Directive).

1.84   The principle of non-discrimination (equal treatment) is specified in article 10(2) sentence 1 Framework Directive with respect to numbering plans and procedures and applies also with respect to third parties: Member States are obliged to ensure that an undertaking allocated a range of numbers does not discriminate against other providers of electronic communications services as regards the number sequences used to give access to their services; this non-discrimination obligation applies regardless of the market position of the undertaking concerned (article 10(2) Framework Directive). The transparency obligation (article 10(1) Framework Directive) is further specified by an obligation to publish national numbering plans and all subsequent additions or amendments thereto (article 10(3) Framework Directive).

1.85   In order to ensure harmonisation of the use of numbering resources both within the Community and beyond the Community's borders, article 10(4) and (5) Framework Directive establishes co-operation and co-ordination obligations. In order to harmonise numbering resources within the Community with a view to supporting the development of pan-European services, the Commission may take appropriate 'technical implementing measures' on the basis of the regulatory procedure in accordance with the Council's comitology Decision.[230] This harmonisation power is complemented by article 19(2) Framework Directive which also allows the Commission to take 'the appropriate technical implementing measures' if it finds that divergence at national level with respect to national provisions regarding the harmonisation of numbering resources creates a barrier to the single market.

---

227   See paras 1.106 et seq below.
228   Art 21(1) and (2) Voice Telephony Directive (1995), art 12(3) sentence 1 Interconnection Directive.
229   Art 3 b Services Directive (1990) (as amended by the Full Competition Directive), art 21(1) sentence 2 Voice Telephony Directive (1995) and art 12(3) sentence 2 Interconnection Directive.
230   Council Decision of 28 June 1999 laying down the procedures for the exercise of implementing powers conferred on the Commission, OJ L 184/23, 17.07.1999.

RIGHTS OF WAY

1.86 Article 11 Framework Directive establishes principles for the granting of rights of way, ie of 'rights to install facilities on, over or under public or private property' (article 11(1) sentence 1 Framework Directive). According to the Commission's findings in one of its reports on the implementation of the regulatory framework prior to the adoption of the 2002 EU Regulatory Package, there have been problems arising from the multiplicity of local and regional authorities with powers in this area.[231]

1.87 The Directive distinguishes between rights of way for undertakings authorised to provide public electronic communications networks and undertakings authorised to provide electronic communications networks other than to the public, and allows Member States to establish differing procedures depending on whether the applicant is providing public communications networks or not. In both cases, however, the procedures for the granting of rights to install the relevant facilities must be covered by the same administrative principles – the procedures must be transparent, publicly available and apply without discrimination and without delay (article 11(1) sentence 1 indent 3 Framework Directive). It is unclear whether the Directive provides that undertakings which are authorised to provide electronic communications networks other than to the public should also be able to obtain, upon application, a right to install facilities on, over or under public property, or whether the Directive merely provides that the administrative principles set out in article 11(1) sentence 2 Framework Directive should apply only if national law allows for the granting of such rights. The latter interpretation would seem to be preferable since it reflects the principle of neutrality with regard to the rules of Member States governing the system of property ownership (article 295 EC Treaty), which are specifically mentioned in recital 22 Framework Directive. Since the Directive is 'without prejudice to national provisions governing the expropriation or use of property', it cannot be assumed that the Directive obliges Member States to create new, extended rights of way.

1.88 Article 11(2) Framework Directive obliges Member States to ensure that, where public or local authorities retain ownership or control of undertakings operating electronic communications networks and/or services, there is effective 'structural separation' of the function responsible for granting the rights of way from activities associated with ownership or control. In addition, article 11(3) Framework Directive requires Member States to ensure that effective mechanisms exist to allow undertakings to appeal against decisions on the granting of rights to install facilities to a body that is independent of the parties involved.

CO-LOCATION AND FACILITY SHARING

1.89 Similar to provisions of the regulatory framework prior to the 2002 EU Regulatory Package,[232] article 12(1) Framework Directive obliges the NRAs to encourage the sharing of facilities or property on the basis of voluntary agreements,[233] and empowers Member States to impose the sharing of facilities or property (including physical collocation) on undertakings operating electronic communications networks. Because of the benefit for town planning, public health

---

231 Commission of the European Communities, Seventh Report on the Implementation of the Telecommunications Regulatory Package, COM(2001) 706 final, 26.11.2001, para 4.2.10.
232 Art 11 Interconnection Directive.
233 See recital 23 Framework Directive.

or environmental reasons, compulsory facility or property sharing obligations may be appropriate 'where undertakings are deprived of access to viable alternatives'. The facilities for which sharing or co-ordination arrangements may be appropriate include, inter alia, ducts, buildings, masts, and antennae or antenna systems.[234]

Transitional measures

1.90   The transition from the previous telecommunications Directives to the new regulatory framework is governed by article 27 Framework Directive. It provides that the Member States shall maintain all obligations under national law in relation to access and universal service, which are based on the relevant 'old' Directives, until such time as the determination is made in respect of those obligations by a national regulatory authority following the market analysis procedure.[235] The obligations that shall be maintained on the basis of article 7 Access Directive are the following:

- obligations to negotiate interconnection and to meet reasonable requests for access (article 4 Interconnection Directive),
- obligations to adhere to the principle of non-discrimination and transparency (article 6 Interconnection Directive),
- obligations to follow the principles of transparency and cost orientation in relation to interconnection charges (article 7 Interconnection Directive),
- obligations to keep separate accounts (article 8 Interconnection Directive),
- obligations relating to facility and/or property sharing arrangements (article 11 Interconnection Directive) and obligations concerning number portability (article 12 Interconnection Directive),
- obligations to publish up-to-date information concerning interconnection issues (article 14 Interconnection Directive),
- obligations to grant special network access (article 16 Voice Telephony Directive (1998)), and
- obligations concerning the provision of a minimum set of leased lines (article 7 and 8 Leased Lines Directive).

The universal service obligations under article 16 Universal Service Directive, which are to be maintained for the transitional period, are:

- obligations concerning tariff principles for the provision of voice telephony services according to article 17 Voice Telephony Directive (1998),
- obligations relating to carrier selection and pre-selection according to article 12(6) Interconnection Directive as amended by Directive 98/61/EC, and
- obligations concerning leased lines (articles 3, 4, 6, 7, 8 and 10 Leased Lines Directive).

Article 27 Framework Directive does not establish a precise deadline by which the market analysis procedure and the related 'determination' regarding these various obligations has to be completed. Article 16(1) Framework Directive merely provides somewhat weakly that the market analysis procedures should be carried out 'as soon as possible' after the adoption of the Commission's initial recommendation on relevant product and service markets.[236]

---

234 Cf recital 23 Framework Directive.

235 A special transitional provision applies to existing authorisations, cf art 17 Authorisation Directive; see para 1.121 below.

236 On 8 October 2003, the Commission opened infringement proceedings against eight Member

Regulation of Market Entry: the Authorisation Directive

Objectives and scope of regulation

1.91   The aim of the Authorisation Directive is to (further) harmonise and simplify the authorisation rules and conditions with a view to implement an internal market in electronic communications networks and services (article 1(1) Authorisation Directive). The Directive obliges the Member States to ensure the freedom to provide electronic communications networks and services (article 3(1) sentence 1 Authorisation Directive). This freedom may only be limited by the conditions specifically set out in the Authorisation Directive (article 3(1) sentence 1 Authorisation Directive). The Directive provides that the provision of electronic communications networks or services may, in principle, only be subject to a 'general authorisation' (article 3(2) sentence 1 Authorisation Directive).[237]

1.92   The replacement of individual telecommunications licences, which provided, in many of the EU Member States, the legal basis for the assignment of rights to use frequencies and numbers,[238] requires the installation of a new regulatory regime regarding the granting of such usage rights.[239] In order to ensure compliance with the conditions of the general authorisations or the usage rights, the Authorisation Directive establishes harmonised enforcement powers for the NRAs. The 'administrative charges' which may be imposed on undertakings providing a service or a network under the general authorisations or exercising a right of use, as well as the fees for rights of use and rights to install facilities, have been redefined and further harmonised.[240] With respect to existing authorisations, the Directive establishes transitional rules, which have to be interpreted and applied in conjunction with the transitional provisions of both the Access Directive and the Universal Service Directive.[241]

States (Belgium, Germany, Greece, Spain, France, Luxembourg, the Netherlands and Portugal) for failure to notify transposition measures concerning the transposition of the main provisions of the 2002 EU Regulatory Package, see IP/03/1365. The Commission issued Reasoned Opinions to seven of those Member States (Belgium, Germany, Greece, France, Luxembourg, the Netherlands and Portugal) on 17 December 2003, see IP/03/1750. In April 2004, the Commission brought the matter before the European Court of Justice under art 226(2) EC Treaty as far as Belgium, Germany, Greece, France, Luxembourg, the Netherlands were concerned, see IP/04/510. In April 2005 the Commission opened another batch of infringement proceedings against 10 Member States (Germany, Italy, Latvia, the Netherlands, Austria, Poland, Portugal, Slovakia) concerning specific defects in the way the 2002 EU Regulatory Package has been transposed in those Member States, see IP/05/430.

237   See paras 1.93 et seq below.
238   See 4th edition, paras 1.144 et seq; Communication from the Commission to the European Parliament, the Council, the Economic and Social Committee and the Committee of the Regions: Fifth Report on the Implementation of the Telecommunications Regulatory Package, pp 12 et seq and pp 163 et seq.
239   See paras 1.101, 1.106 below.
240   See paras 1.117 et seq below.
241   See para 1.121 below; see art 7 Access Directive and art 16 Universal Service Directive, and paras 1.159, 1.190 below.

Transition to a regime of general authorisations

1.93   Despite the 'priority' given to general authorisations under article 3(3) Licensing Directive 1997,[242] many Member States have in the past availed themselves of the option to make access subject to individual licences. In the course of the 1999 Communications Review, it became clear that the majority of market participants perceived general authorisations as the most appropriate tool for authorising the provision of services, specific authorisations merely being justified for the use of radio spectrum.[243] The Authorisation Directive therefore aims to abolish barriers to market entry and ensure the freedom to provide electronic communications networks and services.

PROCEDURAL RULES

1.94   The Member States may make the provision of electronic communications networks or services subject to general authorisations, more specifically: subject to the conditions set out in the general authorisations (articles 6(1), 10 Authorisation Directive). In addition, Member States may establish a notification requirement; this notification shall not, however, 'entail more than a declaration by a legal or natural person to the national regulatory authority of the intention to commence the provision of electronic communications networks or services and the submission of a minimum of information which is required to allow the NRA to keep a register of providers of electronic communications networks and services' (article 3(3) Authorisation Directive). The notification shall not be combined with any form of 'explicit decision' or any other administrative act by the NRA before the freedom to provide electronic communications networks and services may be exercised (article 6(2) sentence 2 Authorisation Directive); rather, the undertaking concerned may begin its activity immediately upon notification (article 3(2) sentence 3 Authorisation Directive), subject only to provisions regarding the rights of use for radio frequencies or numbers (articles 5, 6 and 7 Authorisation Directive).

1.95   Under article 9 Authorisation Directive, NRAs are obliged, at the request of an undertaking, to issue within one week a standardised declaration 'confirming, where applicable, that the undertaking has submitted a notification under article 3(2) and detailing under what circumstances any undertaking providing electronic communications networks or services under the general authorisation has the right to apply for rights to install facilities, negotiate a connection and/or obtain access or interconnection'. The purpose of this standardised declaration is to facilitate the exercise of those rights in relation to other governmental entities or other undertakings.

CONTENT OF GENERAL AUTHORISATIONS

1.96   The 'general authorisation' is 'a legal framework established by the Member State ensuring rights for the provision of electronic communications networks or services and laying down sector-specific obligations that may apply to all or to specific types of electronic communications networks and services' (article 2(2)(a) Authorisation Directive).

---

242   See para 1.28 above.
243   Communication of the Commission: The results of the public consultation on the 1999 Communications Review and orientations for the new regulatory framework, COM(2000) 239 final, 02.06.2000, p 8.

1.97   From the general authorisation, a 'minimum' number of rights, set out in article 4 Authorisation Directive, is derived, namely:

- the right to provide electronic communications networks and services,
- the right to have applications for the necessary rights to install facilities considered of article 4(1)(a) and (b) Authorisation Directive,

and, in the case of undertakings providing electronic communications networks or services to the public

- the right to negotiate interconnection with and where applicable obtain access to or interconnection from other providers of publicly available communications networks and services covered by a general authorisation anywhere in the Community, and
- the right to be given an opportunity to be designated to provide different elements of an universal service and/or to cover different parts of the national territory in accordance with the Universal Service Directive (article 4 (2)(a) and (b) Authorisation Directive).

1.98   The Directive does not define, in detail, the manner in which Member States have to establish the 'legal framework' which constitutes 'general authorisations' (article 2(2)(a) Authorisation Directive); in particular, the Directive leaves to Member States the decision as to whether general authorisations should be granted on the basis of governmental ordinances or in the form of 'class licences'.[244] The use of the term 'general authorisation' (in German 'Allgemeingenehmigung', in French 'autorisation générale', in Italian 'autorizzazione generale', in Spanish 'autorización general') would seem to indicate that the 'legal framework' shall be established by the executive branch of the national governments.

CONDITIONS ATTACHED TO GENERAL AUTHORISATIONS

1.99   The general authorisations may be subject only to those conditions that are listed in the Annex to the Authorisation Directive. Part A of the Annex establishes what is called a 'maximum' list of conditions, which is considerably more precise than the conditions set out in the 1997 Licensing Directive.[245] The conditions may be attached to general authorisations, but only if they are objectively justified in relation to the network or service concerned, non-discriminatory, proportionate and transparent (article 6(1) sentence 2 Authorisation Directive). The general authorisation shall only contain conditions which are 'specific for that sector … and shall not duplicate conditions which are applicable to undertakings by virtue of other national legislation' (article 6(3) Authorisation Directive).

1.100   The specific obligations which may be imposed on providers of electronic communications networks and services in the course of the ex-ante regulation of undertakings designated as having SMP or on the basis of the Universal Service Directive[246] must be 'legally separate' from the rights and obligations under the general authorisation. In order to ensure regulatory transparency, the criteria and procedures for imposing such specific obligations on individual undertakings shall be set out in the general authorisation (article 6(2) Authorisation Directive).

---

244 See, on class licences, *Bratby/Strivens*, Telecommunication Law in the United Kingdom, in Scherer (ed), Telecommunication Laws in Europe, 4th ed, paras 16. 22 et seq; see also paras 29.75 et seq below.

245 See Annex, paras 1–3.6 Licensing Directive.

246 Obligations according to arts 5(1) and (2), 6 and 8 Access Directive; arts 16–19 Universal Service Directive.

Rights of use for radio frequencies

GENERAL AUTHORISATIONS AND GRANTING OF INDIVIDUAL RIGHTS

1.101   The principle that 'the least onerous authorisation system possible should be used'[247] also applies to the granting of use for radio frequencies: Article 5(1) provides that Member States shall, 'where possible, in particular where the risk of harmful interference is negligible',[248] include the conditions for usage of such radio frequencies in the general authorisations. The granting of individual rights of use is therefore the exception, rather than the rule. Where it is necessary to grant individual rights of use for radio frequencies, Member States are obliged to grant such rights, upon request, to any undertaking providing or using network services under a general authorisation. Both the general authorisation as well as the individual granting of a right of use may be subject to conditions.[249]

1.102   The Directive provides, similar to the preceding Directives,[250] that the procedures for the granting of frequency usage rights shall be open, transparent and non-discriminatory (article 5(2) sentence 2 Authorisation Directive). The recitals clarify that Member States may, as part of the application procedure for granting rights to use a radio frequency, 'verify whether the applicant will be able to comply with the conditions attached to such rights'; if the applicant cannot prove this ability, the application for the right to use a radio frequency may be rejected.[251] Where a Member State has made provision for undertakings to transfer rights to use radio frequencies (article 9(3) Framework Directive),[252] the individual granting of the rights of use has to specify whether those rights can be transferred at the initiative of the right holder, and under which conditions (article 5(2) sentence 3 Access Directive). Decisions on the vesting of rights of use must be taken 'as soon as possible after receipt of the complete application'; they must be communicated to the applicant and made public. In the case of radio frequencies that have been allocated for specific purposes within the national frequency plan, the decision must be taken within six weeks after receipt of the complete application (article 5(3) Authorisation Directive).

ADMISSIBLE CONDITIONS

1.103   Usage rights for radio frequencies may be granted for a limited period of time, provided that the duration is 'appropriate for the service concerned' (article 5(2) sentence 4 Authorisation Directive). Furthermore, the granting of frequency usage rights can be subject only to the conditions specified in Part B of the Annex to the Authorisation Directive, which includes, inter alia, 'any commitments, which the undertaking obtaining the usage right has made in the course of a

---

247   Recital 7 Authorisation Directive.
248   According to art 2(2)(b) 'harmful interference' is an 'interference which endangers the functioning of a radio navigation service or of other safety services or which otherwise seriously degrades, obstructs or repeatedly interrupts a radio communications service operating in accordance with the applicable Community or national regulations'.
249   See para 1.103 below.
250   See art 3 a Services Directive (as amended by the Mobile Communications Directive).
251   Recital 13 Authorisation Directive.
252   See paras 1.80 et seq above.

competitive or comparative selection procedure'. This may include network build-out obligations, obligations regarding geographical coverage as well as the obligation to pay fees for the right of use of the radio frequencies.[253]

LIMITATION OF THE NUMBER OF RIGHTS OF USE TO BE GRANTED

1.104 According to article 5(5) Authorisation Directive, the number of rights of use for radio frequencies can be limited 'where this is necessary to ensure the efficient use of radio frequencies'. The substantive and procedural rules regarding such limitations are set out in article 7: The decision to limit the number of rights of use to be granted for radio frequencies is to be prepared by giving all interested parties, including users and consumers, the opportunity to be heard. The decision must 'give due weight to the need to maximise benefits for users and to facilitate the development of competition' (article 7(1)(a) Authorisation Directive). The decision, including its reasons, must be published and must be reviewed 'at reasonable intervals or at the reasonable request of affected undertakings' (article 7(1)(e) Authorisation Directive). Where the granting of rights of use for radio frequencies has been limited, Member States may grant such rights on the basis of competitive or comparative selection procedures (article 7(4) Authorisation Directive); the Directive does not grant preference to one of these two selection procedures.

HARMONISED ASSIGNMENT OF RADIO FREQUENCIES

1.105 Where the usage of radio frequencies has been harmonised, access conditions and procedures have been agreed on, and undertakings to which the radio frequencies shall be assigned have been selected in accordance with international agreements and Community rules, Member States are obliged to grant the right of use for such radio frequencies in accordance therewith and without imposing any further conditions, additional criteria or procedures which would restrict, alter or delay the correct implementation of the common assignment of such radio frequencies (article 8 Authorisation Directive). This provision, which is aimed at promoting the coordinated introduction of electronic communications services at Community level, could in future become the basis for the implementation of harmonised conditions for the availability and efficient use of radio spectrum on the basis of the Radio Spectrum Decision.[254]

Rights of use for numbers

GENERAL AUTHORISATIONS AND GRANTING OF INDIVIDUAL RIGHTS

1.106 The provisions in the Authorisation Directive in relation to rights of use for numbers follow broadly those regarding rights of use for radio frequencies. With respect to the granting of rights of use for numbers, the Directive provides, as in the case of radio frequencies, that individual rights of use shall be granted by Member States to any undertaking upon request, providing or using networks or services under a general authorisation. It follows from article 5(1) Authorisation Directive, which establishes the priority of general authorisations, that rights of use for numbers should be granted on an individual basis. The recitals indicate that rights

---

253 Annex, Part B, No 6; see also art 13 Authorisation Directive and paras 1.117 et seq below.
254 See paras 1.191 et seq below and art 1(2)(b) Radio Spectrum Decision.

to numbers may also be allocated from a European numbering plan.[255] Member States may, but are not obliged to, grant rights of use for numbers to undertakings other than providers of telecommunications networks or services.[256]

1.107   Decisions on rights of use for numbers shall also be taken 'as soon as possible' after receipt of the complete application and must be communicated and published. In the case of numbers that have been allocated for specific purposes within the national numbering plan, allocation decisions shall be taken within three weeks (article 5(3) Authorisation Directive).

ADMISSIBLE CONDITIONS

1.108   Rights of use for numbers may be granted for a limited period of time[257] provided that the duration is 'appropriate for the service concerned' (article 5(4) sentence 4 Authorisation Directive). The regulatory approach regarding the conditions that may be attached to the rights of use for numbers is identical to the approach regarding radio frequencies: Part C of the Annex to the Authorisation Directive sets out an inclusive list of conditions which may be attached to rights of use for numbers. They include, inter alia, conditions for the effective and efficient use of numbers, the obligation to provide public directories subscriber information for the purposes of articles 5 and 25 Universal Service Directive, and the obligation to pay usage fees in accordance with article 13 Authorisation Directive.[258] Member States may determine whether or not rights of use for numbers can be transferred to other undertakings,[259] to the extent that number portability is not governed by Community law.[260]

LIMITATION OF THE NUMBER OF RIGHTS OF USE TO BE GRANTED

1.109   Member States may, after giving all interested parties the opportunity to comment, determine that rights of use for numbers of exceptional economic value can be granted through competitive or comparative selection procedures (article 5(4) Authorisation Directive). The Directive does not, however, provide for detailed procedural rules as in the case of selection procedures regarding radio frequencies (article 7 Authorisation Directive).

The NRAs' enforcement powers

1.110   In order to monitor whether or not undertakings comply with the conditions established in the general authorisations or with the conditions attached to rights of use granted to undertakings, NRAs need to obtain, from the undertakings, relevant information. To this end, the Authorisation Directive establishes far-reaching powers of the NRAs to obtain information (article 11).[261] The

---

255   Recital 11 Authorisation Directive.
256   See recital 14 Authorisation Directive.
257   See Annex, Part C, No 5 Authorisation Directive.
258   Annex, Part C, No 7 and art 13 Authorisation Directive.
259   See art 9(3) Framework Directive for the transfer of rights of use for frequencies; see also paras 1.80 et seq above. See art 5(2) sentence 3 alternative 1 for the transfer of rights of use for numbers.
260   See art 30 Universal Service Directive.
261   See para 1.111 below.

Directive also establishes both procedural and substantive rules to ensure compliance with the conditions of the general authorisations or rights of use and with respect to the 'specific obligations' which are imposed on undertakings designated as having SMP (article 10).[262]

POWERS TO REQUEST INFORMATION

1.111   In exercising their information powers with respect to undertakings operating under general authorisations, rights of use for frequencies or numbers or fulfilling 'specific obligations' which have been imposed on the basis of article 6(2) Authorisation Directive,[263] the NRAs are bound by the principle of proportionality. They may only request information that is proportionate and objectively justified to achieve specific objectives (article 11(1) sentence 1 Authorisation Directive) and are obliged to inform the undertakings of the specific purpose for which the information is to be used (article 11(2) Authorisation Directive). The purposes for which information may be required by the NRAs include the 'systematic or case-by-case verification of compliance with' conditions attached to general authorisations regarding financial contributions to the funding of universal services (Annex, Part A, No 1) or administrative charges in accordance with article 12 Authorisation Directive (Annex, Part A, No 2), and with conditions attached to rights of use for radio frequencies or numbers regarding usage fees in accordance with article 13 Authorisations Directive (Annex, Part B, No 6 and Annex, Part C, No 7). Moreover, NRAs may require information to verify compliance with obligations imposed on providers of electronic communications networks and services under articles 5(1), 5(2), 6, 8 Access Directive and articles 16–19 Universal Service Directive or with obligations imposed under the Universal Service Directive on undertakings designated to provide universal services. In addition, the NRA may engage in the case-by-case verification of compliance with any of the conditions set out in the Annex to the Authorisation Directive, where a complaint has been received or where the NRA has other reasons to believe that the condition is not being complied with or in the case of an investigation by the NRA upon its own initiative (article 11(1)(b) Authorisation Directive). Furthermore, the NRA may require information for comparative overviews of quality and price of services and for market analysis.[264]

1.112   If an undertaking fails to provide information, inter alia, in conjunction with the verification of compliance with conditions of general authorisations within reasonable periods stipulated by the NRA, the NRA may impose financial penalties on the basis of national laws (article 10(4) Authorisation Directive).

POWERS TO ENSURE COMPLIANCE WITH THE CONDITIONS OF THE AUTHORISATIONS

1.113   Article 10 Authorisation Directive establishes a tiered procedure for the enforcement of the conditions of the general authorisations of rights of use and the 'specific obligations' of SMP enterprises, and sets out the measures that the NRAs may take: where an NRA finds that an undertaking is not complying with one or more of the conditions of the general authorisation, of rights of use or with the specific obligations imposed on SMP undertakings, it shall notify the undertaking

---

262   See paras 1.113 et seq below.
263   See para 1.100 above.
264   According to arts 6(3), 7(3), 8(2), 13(1) Access Directive or arts 16(3), 17(1)(a), 18(1) and (2), 19(2) Universal Service Directive.

of those findings and give the undertaking a reasonable opportunity to state its view or remedy any breaches within a certain deadline, for which the Directive establishes three options: remedial action shall be taken:

- within one month after notification, or
- within a shorter period 'agreed by the undertaking' or, in the case of repeated breaches, stipulated by the NRA, or
- within a longer period decided by the NRA (article 10(2) Authorisation Directive).

1.114   If the relevant undertaking does not remedy the breaches within the established period, the NRA shall 'take appropriate and proportionate measures aimed at ensuring compliance'. The Directive does not specify these measures, but makes it clear that they may include financial penalties. The measures, and the reasons on which they are based, must be communicated to the undertaking concerned within one week of their adoption, and the NRAs are obliged to stipulate a reasonable period for the undertaking to comply with the measure (article 10(3) Authorisation Directive).

1.115   Only in cases of 'serious and repeated breaches' of relevant conditions, and where measures aimed at ensuring compliance have failed, may NRAs prevent an undertaking from continuing to provide electronic communications networks or services or suspend or withdraw rights of use (article 10(5) Authorisation Directive).

1.116   Urgent interim measures are permissible if the relevant authority 'has evidence' of a breach of the conditions of the general authorisation, rights of use or specific obligations of the SMP undertaking representing an 'immediate and serious threat to public safety, public security or public health' or likely to create serious economic or operational problems for other providers or users of electronic communications networks or services (article 10(6) Authorisation Directive). In transposing the concepts of 'public safety', 'public security' and 'public health' into national laws and in applying these concepts, national legislators and regulators will have to be mindful of the jurisprudence of the European Court of Justice in relation to the identical terms used in article 30 EC Treaty.[265]

Administrative charges and fees for rights of use

ADMINISTRATIVE CHARGES

1.117   Article 12 Authorisation Directive introduces an important innovation to European telecommunications law: under this provision, Member States may impose on undertakings providing a service or a network under the general authorisation, or to whom a right of use has been granted, certain administrative charges. Despite the comforting wording that these administrative charges shall

---

265   See, with regard to 'public order', ECJ Judgment of 23 November 1978, Case 7/78, *Thompson* [1978] ECR 2247, 2275; ECJ Judgment of 22 June 1994, Case C-426/92, *Deutsches Milchkonto* [1994] ECR 2757, 2782; ECJ Judgment of 4 December 1974,Case 41/74, *van Duyn v Home Office* [1974] ECR 1337. For 'public safety', see ECJ Judgment of 10 July 1984, Case 72/83, *Campus Oil* [1984] ECR 2727, 2751; ECJ Judgment of 17 June 1987, Case 154/85, *Commission v Italy* [1987] ECR 2717. For 'health protection', see ECJ Judgment of 8 July 1975,Case 4/75, *Rewe* [1975] ECR 843, 859; ECJ Judgment of 12 March 1987, Case 178/84, *Commission v Germany* [1987] ECR 1227.

cover 'only' the administrative costs 'which will be incurred in the management, control and enforcement of the general authorisation scheme and of rights of use and of specific obligations as referred to in article 6(2)' (article 12(1)(a) Authorisation Directive), it is clear that the administrative charges may cover the costs of the entirety of the NRAs' operations. Specifically, article 12(1)(a) states in its second part that the administrative costs 'may include costs for international cooperation, harmonisation and standardisation, market analysis, monitoring compliance and other market control, as well as regulatory work in all its preparation and enforcement of secondary legislation and administrative decisions, such as decisions on access and interconnection'.

On this basis, there will hardly be any administrative task of an NRA the cost of which may not be defrayed by way of the administrative charge.

1.118 By way of limitation, article 12(1)(b) Authorisation Directive provides that the administrative charges shall be imposed upon the individual undertakings in an objective, transparent and proportionate manner which minimises additional administrative costs and attendant charges. The recitals mention, as an example of a fair, simple and transparent alternative for these 'charge attribution criteria', a turnover-related distribution key.[266] The principle of proportionality is specified in the recitals by the caveat that the system for administrative charges should not distort competition or create barriers for entry into the market.[267]

As a procedural safeguard for the principle of proportionality, article 12(2) provides that, where NRAs impose administrative charges, they shall publish a yearly overview of their administrative costs and of the total sum of the charges collected. Taking account of the difference between the total sum of the charges and the administrative costs, appropriate adjustments must be made (article 12(2) Authorisation Directive).

1.119 The Commission's proposal for a Directive provided that 'administrative charges and fees imposed on operators shall only cover the administrative costs incurred in the issue, management, control and enforcement of the applicable authorisation and licensing schemes'.[268]

Member States' fiscal desires have led, on the basis of the common position adopted by the Council, to the provision as adopted. The reason provided for by the Council simply stated that the scope of the administrative costs which may be recovered through charges was extended to maintain 'the financial independence' of the NRAs.[269]

It should be noted that the Directive does not establish an *obligation* of Member States to impose administrative charges and that the attribution basis for the charge does not need to include all of the administrative costs set out in article 12(1)(a) Authorisation Directive.

---

266 Recital 31 sentence 4 Authorisation Directive.
267 Recital 31 sentence 1 Authorisation Directive.
268 Commission Proposal of 12 July 2000, COM(2000) 386 final.
269 Common Position (EC) No 37/2001 of 17 September 2001 adopted by the Council, OJ C 337/18, 30.11.2001, p 32.

FEES FOR RIGHTS OF USE

1.120   Notwithstanding the administrative charges and, as the recitals explicitly state, 'in addition' to them,[270] 'Member States may allow the relevant authority to impose fees for the rights of use for radio frequencies or numbers or rights to install facilities on, over or under public or private property ...'. These fees shall 'reflect the need to ensure the optimal use of the resources' (article 13 sentence 1 Authorisation Directive). The proposal of the European Parliament and of the Commission to apply the public consultation procedure under article 7 Framework Directive to all national measures relating to fees for rights of use was not accepted by the Council.[271]

Transitional regulations for existing authorisations

1.121   The Authorisation Directive contains transition provisions for those authorisations which were already in existence on the date of entry into force of the Directive (24 April 2002). These authorisations had to be brought into line with the provisions of the Directive by 25 July 2003 at the latest (article 17(1) Authorisation Directive).[272] Only where the application of this rule results in a reduction of the rights or in the extension of the obligations under an authorisation already in existence are Member States allowed to extend the validity of those rights and obligations for a maximum of nine months beyond 25 July 2003, provided that the rights of other undertakings under Community law are not affected thereby (article 17(2) Authorisation Directive). In specific cases, where a Member State can prove that the abolition of an authorisation regarding access to electronic communications networks, which was in force before the date of entry into force of the Authorisation Directive (25 July 2003), creates 'excessive difficulties' for undertakings that have benefited from mandated access to another network, and where it is not possible for these undertakings to negotiate the agreements on reasonable commercial terms before July 2003, Member States may request a temporary prolongation of the relevant conditions. The Commission is obliged to decide upon applications for such prolongations within six months after receipt of the application (article 17(3) Authorisation Directive).

---

270   Recital 32 Authorisation Directive.

271   Communication from the Commission to the European Parliament pursuant to the second subparagraph of art 251(2) of the EC Treaty concerning the common position of the Council on the adoption of a Directive of the European Parliament and of the Council on the authorisation of electronic communications networks and service, 18.09.2001, SEC/2001/1411 final: 'There is considerable risk of further variation in levels of charges between the Member States. There is less certainty that systems for charges will be simple, pro-competitive and in line with the basic principles of a general authorisation system'.

272   On 5 December 2003, the Commission launched infringement proceedings against nine Member States (Belgium, Germany, Greece, France, Luxembourg, the Netherlands, Portugal, Finland and Sweden) for failure to notify transposition measures concerning the implementation of the E-Privacy Directive, see IP/03/1663. The Commission issued Reasoned Opinions to all of those Member States except for Sweden on 1 April 2004, see IP/04/435.

Regulation of Network Access and Interconnection: the Access Directive

Objectives and scope of regulation

1.122   The Access Directive harmonises the way in which Member States regulate access to, and interconnection of, electronic communications networks and associated facilities. The objective of the Directive is to establish a regulatory framework, in accordance with internal market principles, for the relationships between suppliers of networks and services that will result in sustainable competition, interoperability of electronic communications services as well as consumer benefits (article 1 sentence 2 Authorisation Directive).

1.123   The Directive defines the legal concept of access more broadly and in more detail than the previous Directive.[273] It establishes the general principles for access and interconnection, the rights and obligations of undertakings – in particular the principles that agreements on a commercial basis shall have priority over regulatory decisions – as well as powers and responsibilities of the NRAs.[274] With respect to these regulatory powers, the Directive sets out both regulatory powers which exist irrespective of the market position of undertakings[275] and regulatory powers which exist with respect to SMP undertakings;[276] specific access obligations exist with regard to digital television and radio broadcasting services.[277] The Directive establishes specific transitional provisions which allow for the adaptation of existing access rights and obligations to the new regulatory framework.[278]

1.124   The Access Directive applies to operators[279] of public communications networks[280] and to undertakings seeking interconnection and/or access to their networks or associated facilities. Non-public networks are not subject to the Directive, unless they benefit from access to public networks.[281] In accordance with the principle of content neutrality, which governs the entire 2002 EU Regulatory Package,[282] the Access Directive does not apply to services providing content.[283]

---

273   See para 1.125 below.
274   See paras 1.127 et seq below.
275   See paras 1.135 et seq below.
276   See paras 1.137 et seq below.
277   See paras 1.154 et seq below.
278   See para 1.159 below.
279   An operator may own the relevant infrastructure facilities or may rent some or all of them; cf art 2(c) Access Directive and recital 3 sentence 2.
280   Art 1(2) sentence 1 is unclear in this respect; art 4(1) Access Directive is more specific; see art 2(d) Framework Directive for a statutory definition and para 1.49 above; see also recital 1 sentence 3 Access Directive: 'The provisions of this Directive apply to those networks that are used for the provision of publicly available electronic communications services'.
281   Cf recital 1 Access Directive.
282   Art 1(3) Framework Directive and see paras 1.38, 1.50 above.
283   Recital 2 specifically mentions, as an example of 'services providing content', the offer for sale of a package of sound or television broadcasting content.

Fundamental terms of regulation

1.125   Whereas the previous telecommunications Directives refrained from defining the term 'access' and addressed only the access to telecommunications networks,[284] the new Access Directive defines access broadly as 'the making available of facilities and/or services, to another undertaking, on either an exclusive or non-exclusive basis, for the purpose of providing electronic communications services'. This definition is further illustrated by a non-inclusive list of examples, according to which 'access' includes access to:

- network elements and associated facilities, which may involve the connection of equipment, by fixed or non-fixed means,[285]
- physical infrastructure including buildings, ducts and masts,
- relevant software systems including operational support systems,
- number translation or systems offering equivalent functionality,
- fixed and mobile networks, in particular for roaming,
- conditional access systems for digital television services, and
- virtual network services.

The Directive specifically excludes, from its scope of applicability, access by end-users, which is governed by the Universal Service Directive.[286]

1.126   'Interconnection' is defined, in article 2(b) sentence 2 Access Directive, as 'a specific type of access implemented between public network operators'. It is further described as the physical and logical linking of public communications networks used by the same or a different undertaking in order to allow the users of an undertaking to communicate with users of the same or another undertaking, or to access services provided by another undertaking; services of the (interconnected) public communications networks may be provided by the parties involved in the interconnection or by other parties who have access to the network.[287]

Regulatory Principles

FREEDOM OF ACCESS

1.127   The Member States are obliged to ensure that undertakings are not prevented from negotiating between themselves agreements on technical and commercial arrangements for access and/or interconnection either in the same Member States or in different Member States. In particular, undertakings requesting access

---

284   Cf art 4(2) Directive 97/33/EC and art 16(1) Directive 98/10/EC.

285   This includes access to the local loop and to facilities and services that are necessary to provide services over the local loop; cf the definition of 'local loop' in art 2(d) Access Directive and the specific and more narrow rules in Regulation (EC) No 2887/2000 of the European Parliament and the Council of 18 December 2000 on unbundled access to the local loop, OJ L 33/4, 30.12.2000.

286   Art 2(b) sentence 1 Access Directive; similarly art 2(1)(a) Directive 97/33/EC; cf *Scherer/ Bartsch*, Telecommunication Law and Policy of the European Union, in: *Scherer* (ed), Telecommunication Laws in Europe, 4th ed, paras 1.96 et seq.
Cf Art 1(2) sentence 3 Access Directive; see also paras 1.160 et seq below.

287   Art 2(b) sentence 1 Access Directive; similarly art 2(1)(a) Directive 97/33/EC; cf *Scherer/ Bartsch*, Telecommunication Law and Policy of the European Union, in: Scherer (ed), Telecommunication Laws in Europe, 4th ed, paras 1.96 et seq.

or interconnection shall not be required to obtain an authorisation to operate in the Member State where access or interconnection is requested.[288]

PRIORITY OF COMMERCIAL NEGOTIATIONS

1.128 The principle that commercial negotiation takes priority over regulatory intervention, which was already enshrined in the previous Directives,[289] follows from the regulatory approach of articles 3 and 4 Access Directive on the one hand, and article 5(1) Access Directive on the other hand, as well as from the explicit provision obliging Member States to 'ensure that the national regulatory authority is empowered to intervene at its own initiative ... in the absence of agreement between undertakings, at the request of either of the parties involved' (article 5(4) Access Directive). The principle of priority of commercial negotiations is also emphasised in the recitals which stipulate that 'undertakings which receive requests for access or interconnection should in principle conclude such agreements on a commercial basis, and negotiate in good faith'; NRAs should have the power to secure 'where commercial negotiation fails' adequate access and interconnection and interoperability of services in the interest of end-users.[290]

1.129 To that effect, article 4(1) sentence 1 Access Directive establishes a right of operators of public communications networks 'to negotiate interconnection with each other'. At the request of another authorised undertaking, operators of public communications networks are obliged to negotiate interconnection. The purpose of the right and obligation to negotiate is 'to ensure provision and interoperability of services throughout the Community'; this does not mean that the obligation to negotiate exists only in the case of cross-border interconnection. This follows both from the definition of 'interconnection' in article 2(b) Access Directive, which is not limited to cross-border interconnection, and from the Directive's justification set out in a recital which explains that there should be no restrictions that prevent undertakings from negotiating access and interconnection arrangements between themselves, 'in particular', but not only, 'on cross-border agreements'.[291]

1.130 Whereas the obligation to negotiate refers only to interconnection,[292] the obligation of operators to submit offers refers to both access and interconnection. This obligation to contract does not apply, however, to all operators of public communication networks, but only to those upon which the NRA has imposed specific 'obligations'.[293] Only those operators upon which the NRA has imposed obligations pursuant to articles 5, 6, 7 and 8 Access Directive are obliged to offer access and interconnection to other undertakings 'on terms and conditions consistent with' the obligations imposed.

---

288   Art 3(1) sentence 1 Access Directive.
289   Art 4(1) in conjunction with Annex II Directive 97/33/EC.
290   Recital 5 sentence 2 and recital 6 Access Directive; but see also art 5(4) Framework Directive on the authorisation of the NRA to take action ex-officio in reasonable cases.
291   Recital 5 Access Directive.
292   The Commission did not follow a suggestion of the Committee of Industry, External Trade, Research and Energy to expand the obligation to negotiate on the granting of access (cf Report of the Committee of 14 February 2001, A5–0061/2001 PE 297.116, pp 13 et seq as well as the opinion of the European Parliament of 1 March 2001, amendment 12, OJ C 277/72, 01.10.2001, pp 75 et seq; cf European Commission, COM(2001) 369 final, 04.07.2001, p 12).
293   According to art 5 (see paras 1.135 et seq below), art 6 (see paras 1.155 et seq below), art 7 (see para 1.159 below) and art 8 (see paras 1.137 et seq below).

1.131   Article 4(2) Access Directive establishes specific access obligations which reflect the Community's policy decision to introduce wide-screen television services: Public electronic communications networks established for the distribution of digital television services must be capable of distributing wide-screen television services and programs. Network operators that receive and re-distribute wide-screen television services or programs are obliged to maintain the wide-screen format.[294]

1.132   Undertakings which acquire information from another undertaking before, during or after the process of negotiating access or interconnection arrangements may use that information solely for the purpose for which it was supplied. Member States are obliged to ensure the effectiveness of this confidentiality obligation which applies with respect to 'any other party', including 'other departments, subsidiaries or partners' of the undertaking (article 4(3) Access Directive).

OVERVIEW OF THE NRAS' REGULATORY POWERS UNDER THE ACCESS DIRECTIVE

1.133   The Access Directive sets out general objectives to be pursued by the NRAs exercising their responsibilities with respect to access and interconnection (article 5(1) sub-para 1), distinguishes between general regulatory powers and those existing with respect to SMP undertakings (article 5(1) sub-para 2), specifying the former (article 5(1) sub-para 1(a) and (b)), and empowers the NRAs to adopt technical and operational conditions for the access to the network of SMP undertakings (article 5(2)). In the exercise of all of their regulatory powers, the NRAs are bound by the principles of objectivity, transparency, proportionality and non-discrimination; all obligations and conditions imposed on the basis of article 5 Access Directive are subject to the consultation procedure according to article 6 Framework Directive and the consolidation procedure under article 7 Framework Directive.[295]

1.134   Article 5(1) sub-para 1 Access Directive establishes three specific tasks of the NRAs: They are obliged to encourage and, where appropriate, ensure:

- adequate access,
- adequate interconnection, and
- interoperability of services.

These specific obligations are to be fulfilled in pursuit of the more general objectives set out in article 8 Framework Directive.[296] In exercising their responsibilities, the NRAs are obliged to promote efficiency, sustainable competition and provide the maximum benefit to end-users. The multitude and variety of regulatory objectives which are encapsulated in article 5(1) sub-para 1 Access Directive allow for an extraordinarily broad discretion of the NRAs in their selection of the appropriate regulatory measures, both when regulating undertakings regardless of their market position[297] and when regulating SMP undertakings.[298]

---

294 For an analysis of access obligations in connection with radio broadcasting services, see paras 1.154 et seq below.
295 See paras 1.55 and 1.60 et seq above; on the corresponding requirements with respect to access related regulatory powers towards SMP undertakings, see art 8(4) Access Directive.
296 See para 1.53 below.
297 See paras 1.135 et seq below.
298 See paras 1.137 et seq below.

Regulatory powers applicable to all market participants

THE BASIC REGULATORY POWER UNDER ARTICLE 5(1)(A)

1.135 Member States may grant, to their NRAs, regulatory powers with respect to operators regardless of their market position; article 5 Access Directive specifies the purpose and the scope of these regulatory powers 'in particular' with respect to specific market segments,[299] which seems to indicate that additional, more far-reaching national regulation remains permissible. Under article 5(1) sub-para 1 (a) Access Directive, NRAs may, 'to the extent that it is necessary to ensure end-to-end connectivity, [impose] obligations on undertakings that control access to end-users'. This provision, which was not contained in the original Commission proposal, but was introduced at a later stage by the Common position adopted by the Council, is aimed at ensuring 'the end-to-end connectivity of the networks'.[300]

IMPOSING OTHER OBLIGATIONS

1.136 The Access Directive does not explicitly state other 'obligations' which NRAs may impose upon undertakings that control access to end-users, regardless of their market position, in order to ensure end-to-end connectivity. According to the cross-reference to article 5(1) Access Directive contained in article 8(3) first indent, NRAs shall not impose the obligations set out in articles 9 to 13 Access Directive on operators that have not been designated as SMP undertakings, 'without prejudice' to article 5(1) Access Directive. It follows, on the contrary, that the obligations set out in articles 9 to 13 Access Directive may, under exceptional circumstances, be imposed upon operators that have not been designated as SMP undertakings 'to the extent that is necessary to ensure end-to-end connectivity', if and when such undertakings 'control access to end-users'. The Directive again does not specify the permissible regulatory measures, and seems to rely on the consolidation procedure to bring about a Community-wide harmonisation of the measures taken under article 5(1) Access Directive.

Regulatory powers only applicable to market participants designated as having SMP

1.137 With respect to the regulation of access and interconnection for SMP undertakings, article 8(1) Access Directive obliges the Member States to ensure that NRAs are empowered to impose the obligations set out in articles 9 to 13. These obligations are:

- obligations of transparency (article 9),
- obligations of non-discrimination (article 10),
- obligations of accounting separation (article 11),
- obligations of access to, and use of, specific network facilities (article 12), and
- obligations relating to price control and cost accounting (article 13).

REGULATORY PRINCIPLES

1.138 If an undertaking has been designated as having significant market power on a specific market, the NRA is obliged to impose the obligations set out in the

---

299 On regulatory powers with regard to the access to digital radio and television broadcasting services, see paras 1.154 et seq below.

300 See Common Position (EC) No 36/2001 adopted by the Council of 17 September 2001, OJ C 337/1, 30.11.2001, p 16.

Access Directive 'as appropriate'. This means that the NRA has discretion in the selection of the regulatory remedies to be imposed upon undertakings ('as appropriate'), but no discretion in deciding whether or not to impose remedies.[301] By selecting remedies, the NRAs are obliged to take into account 'the nature of the problem identified' and the objectives set out in article 8 Framework Directive (article 8(4) Access Directive). The Access Directive's reference to regulatory objectives set out in article 8 Framework Directive broadens the NRAs' discretion. Limitations result, in particular, from the principle of proportionality, which is specifically mentioned in article 8(4) sentence 1 Access Directive, and from the procedural requirement that obligations shall only be imposed following consultation in accordance with articles 6 and 7 Framework Directive.[302]

1.139   When an NRA intends to impose upon an operator with significant market power other obligations for access or interconnection than those set out in articles 9 to 13 Access Directive, specific procedural safeguards apply. In this case, the NRA has to submit its request to the Commission which decides on the basis of an advisory procedure, ie following consultation with the Communications Committee.[303]

OBLIGATIONS OF TRANSPARENCY

1.140   According to article 9(1) Access Directive, NRAs may impose, upon SMP undertakings, 'obligations for transparency in relation to interconnection and/or access'; these obligations serve, in particular, to speed up negotiation, avoid disputes and give confidence to market players that a service is not being provided on discriminatory terms.[304] The object of transparency obligations can be information in relation to access (article 2(a) Access Directive) or interconnection of public communications networks (article 2(b) Access Directive). The Directive mentions, in a non-inclusive list ('such as'), accounting information, technical specifications, network characteristics, terms and conditions for supply and use, and prices.[305]

1.141   The NRAs' discretion extends not only to the objects of the transparency obligation, but also to the modalities of bringing about transparency. The NRAs may 'specify the precise information to be made available, the level of detail required and the manner of publication' (article 9(3) Access Directive); this includes a determination as to whether or not the information has to be provided free of charge.[306]

---

301   Cf art 8(2) Access Directive: '... the [NRA] shall impose the obligation ... as appropriate'. The Commission did not follow the European Parliament's proposal to grant to the NRA discretion in deciding whether or not to impose obligations on undertakings (cf amendment 26 Report of the Committee on Industry, External Trade, Research and Energy of 14 February 2001, A5–0061/2001 PE 297.116, pp 25 et seq, as well as the opinion of the European Parliament of 1 March 2001, OJ C 277/72, 01.10.2001, p 81); cf European Commission, COM(2001) 369 final, 04.07.2001, pp 2 et seq.
302   See paras 1.55 and 1.60 et seq below.
303   Art 8(3) sub-para 2 Access Directive in conjunction with art 14(2) Framework Directive; art 3 Council Decision 1999/468/EC of 28 June 1999 laying down the procedures for the exercise of implementing powers conferred on the Commission, OJ L 184/23, 17.07.1999; see para 1.62 above.
304   Cf recital 16 Access Directive.
305   See also the Commission's Directive Proposal, COM(2000) 384 final, 12.07.2000, p 7, mentioning 'access, interconnection and interoperability conditions' as further examples.
306   Recital 16 Access Directive.

1.142   Specific means to ensure transparency are reference offers, the publication of which may be required by NRAs (article 9(2) Access Directive). The NRAs' power to require the publication of a reference offer exists 'in particular', but not only, where an operator has obligations of non-discrimination.[307] The reference offers must comply with the unbundling obligation, which means that they must be sufficiently unbundled to ensure that undertakings are not required to pay for facilities which are not necessary for the service requested and must be broken down into components according to market needs and provide the associated terms and conditions including prices.

1.143   Specific   unbundling   requirements   apply   on   the   basis   of Regulation 2887/2000 of 18 December 2000[308] with respect to the unbundled access to the local loop with (physical) twisted metallic pair (circuit): Under article 9(4) Access Directive, NRAs are obliged to ensure the publication of a reference offer by operators which are obliged to provide unbundled access to the twisted metallic pair local loop; this reference offer shall contain at least the elements set out in Annex II to the Access Directive, which correspond to the requirements set out in Regulation 2887/2000. This (somewhat opaque) system of legislative cross-references ensures that the reference offers which had to be published by SMP undertakings under Regulation 2887/2000 may also be imposed upon SMP undertakings in the future.

OBLIGATIONS OF NON-DISCRIMINATION

1.144   In order to ensure 'in particular' that SMP undertakings, specifically vertically integrated undertakings,[309] apply equivalent conditions in equivalent circumstances to other undertakings providing equivalent services and information to others under the same conditions and of the same quality as they provide for their own services or those of their subsidiaries or partners, the NRAs may impose obligations of non-discrimination in relation to interconnection and/or access (article 10(2) Access Directive).[310] The scope of applicability of these obligations is quite broad: The Directive merely requires that the non-discrimination obligations pertain to 'interconnection and/or access' and serve the objectives set out in article 8 Access Directive.

SPECIFIC OBLIGATIONS OF ACCESS

1.145   Whereas the obligations of transparency, non-discrimination and accounting separation are secondary obligations which are aimed at ensuring fair access and interconnection, article 12 Access Directive is aimed at the granting of access as such. Under this provision, the NRAs are empowered to impose obligations on SMP undertakings to meet reasonable requests for access to, and use of, specific network elements and associated facilities. In deciding on the imposition of access obligations, as in the case of the obligations under articles 9 to 13 Access Directive, NRAs have to take into account the regulatory objectives of article 8 Framework Directive (cf article 8(4) Access Directive). Obligations of access to, and use of,

---

307   See para 1.144 below.
308   Regulation (EC) No 2887/2000 of the European Parliament and the Council of 18 December 2000 on the unbundled access to local loops, OJ L 336/4, 30.12.2000; see also recital 12 sentence 2 Access Directive.
309   Recital 17 Access Directive.
310   See also art 6 and 9 Directive 97/33/EC.

specific network facilities should be considered by NRAs in particular (but not only) in situations where the NRA considers that denial of access or unreasonable terms and conditions having a similar effect would hinder the emergence of a sustainable competitive market at the retail level, or would not be in the end-user's interest (article 12(1) sub-para 1 Access Directive).

1.146   Among the specific obligations which NRAs may impose upon SMP undertakings are the following:

- the obligation to give third parties access to specified network elements and/or facilities, including unbundled access to the local loop,
- the obligation to negotiate in good faith with undertakings requesting access,
- the obligation to provide specified services on a wholesale basis for resale by third parties,
- the obligation to grant open access to technical interfaces, protocols or other key technologies that are indispensable for the interoperability of services or virtual network services,
- the obligation to provide co-location or other forms of facility sharing, including ducts, building or mast sharing, and
- the obligation to interconnect networks or network facilities.

These and other specific obligations are set out in a non-inclusive catalogue in article 12(1) sub-para 2 Access Directive.

When imposing these access obligations, the NRAs may attach conditions ensuring 'fairness, reasonableness and timeliness' (article 12(1) sub-para 3 Access Directive).

1.147   Article 8(4) Access Directive repeats and article 12(2) Access Directive re-iterates that regulatory decisions regarding the imposition of access obligations shall be justified in the light of the objectives laid down in article 8 Framework Directive and must comply with the principle of proportionality (article 8(1) Framework Directive)[311] which applies to all regulatory decisions. Article 12(2) Access Directive specifies the principle of proportionality by providing a non-inclusive list of 'factors' which shall be taken into account when assessing whether access obligations would be proportionate to the objectives set out in article 8 Framework Directive; these factors – many of which are based on the 'essential facilities' case law of the Commission and the European Court of Justice[312] – include:

- the technical and economic viability of using or installing competing facilities, in the light of the rate of market development, taking into account the nature and type of interconnection and access involved,
- the feasibility of providing the access proposed, in relation to the capacity available,
- the initial investment by the facility owner, bearing in mind the risks involved in making the investment,
- the need to safeguard competition in the long term, and
- the provision of pan-European services.

---

311 See para 1.53 above.

312 Cf in particular European Commission: Decision (IV 34.174- *B& I Line PLC v Ceiling Harbours Ltd*) Bull EC No 6, 1992, para 1.3.30; Decision 94/19/EC of 21 December 1993 (IV/34.689 – *Sea Containers v Stena Sealink – Interim measures*), OJ L 15/8, 18.01.1994; Decision 94/119/EC of 21 December 1993, *Port of Rødby*, OJ L 55/52, 26.02.1994. See also ECJ Judgment of 6 April 1995, Joined Cases C-241/91 P and C-242/91, *Magill* [1995] ECR I-743.

The recitals point out that mandating access to network infrastructures can be justified as 'a means of increasing competition', but that the imposition by NRAs of mandated access that increases competition in the short term should not reduce incentives for competitors to invest in alternative facilities that will secure more competition in the long term.[313] Neither this description of the conflicting interests of infrastructure providers and service providers nor the Commission's notice on the application of the competition rules to access agreements in the telecommunications sector, which is specifically mentioned in the recitals,[314] replace the need to balance, in each individual case, the rights of an infrastructure owner to exploit its infrastructure for its own benefit, and the rights of other service providers to access facilities that are essential for the provision of competing services.

PRICE CONTROL AND COST ACCOUNTING OBLIGATIONS

1.148 The obligations which NRAs may impose upon SMP undertakings include obligations relating to cost recovery and price controls, including obligations for cost orientation of prices in relation to the provision of specific types of interconnection and/or access (article 13(1) sentence 1 Access Directive). These price control measures are predicated on indications, based on a market analysis under article 16 Framework Directive, 'that the operator concerned might sustain prices at an excessively high level, or apply a price squeeze, to the detriment of end-users'. The Directive does not require proof of excessive prices or of price squeezing; rather, a mere 'indication' that a lack of effective competition might lead to these results is sufficient.

1.149 Whereas the threshold for regulatory intervention by the NRAs is low, article 13(1) Access Directive provides for a broad variety of regulatory measures, ranging, as the recitals specifically state,[315] from relatively light measures, such as an obligation that prices for carrier selection shall be reasonable,[316] to relatively stringent measures, such as the obligation that the prices must be cost-oriented,[317] culminating in the ex-ante regulation of prices.

1.150 In determining cost-oriented prices, the NRAs have to take into account the investment made by the operator and allow him a reasonable rate of return on adequate capital employed, taking into account the risks involved (article 13(1) sentence 2 Access Directive). The burden of proof that charges are derived from costs including a reasonable rate of return on investment lies with the regulated undertaking (article 13(3) sentence 1 Access Directive); furthermore, the undertaking is obliged to provide, at the NRAs' request, 'full justification' for its prices and, where necessary, to adjust such prices (article 13(3) sentence 3 Access Directive). The Directive specifically states that cost-orientation of prices means 'cost of efficient provision of services' and allows NRAs to use cost-accounting methods

---

313 Recital 19 Access Directive.
314 Cf reference in recital 19 Access Directive to Commission's notice on the application of the competition rules to access agreements in the telecommunications sector – framework, relevant markets and principles, OJ C 265/2, 22.08.1998. On the requirement to balance the rights of the infrastructure owner and the rights of other service providers, see recital 19 Access Directive.
315 See also recital 20 Access Directive.
316 Cf art 7(3) in conjunction with Annex IV Directive 97/33/EC.
317 Cf Common Position (EC) No 36/2001, OJ C 337/1, 30.11.2001.

independent of those used by the undertaking in order to calculate the cost of efficient provision of services (article 13(3) Access Directive).[318]

1.151   When regulating cost recovery mechanisms or pricing methodologies, the NRAs are bound by the triple objectives of efficiency, promoting sustainable competition and maximising consumer benefits (article 13(2) sentence 1 Access Directive). In pursuing these objectives, the NRAs may also 'take account' of prices available in comparable competitive markets (article 13(2) sentence 2 Access Directive). It would seem to follow, from the reference of this somewhat vague wording ('may also take account'), which is based on the Council's Common Position,[319] to the power to 'mandate' cost recovery mechanisms or pricing methodologies, that the NRAs may use comparative market studies also when examining the cost-orientation of prices. If an NRA mandates the implementation of a specific cost-accounting system in order to support price controls, the description of the cost-accounting system must be made publicly available, showing at least the main categories under which costs are grouped and the rules used for the allocation of costs (article 13(4) sentence 1 Access Directive). In compliance with the cost-accounting system imposed upon an SMP undertaking, it must be verified by a 'qualified independent body', which may either be the NRA or an independent third party;[320] the results of the review shall be published.

OBLIGATION OF ACCOUNTING SEPARATION

1.152   The Access Directive establishes broad powers to impose obligations for accounting separation 'in relation to specified activities related to interconnection and/or access' (article 11(1) sub-para 1) and empowers NRAs to request, in particular, vertically integrated companies to make transparent their wholesale prices and their internal transfer prices (article 11(1) sub-para 2). The main purpose of this specific accounting obligation is to ensure compliance with non-discrimination obligations under article 10 Access Directive and to prevent unfair cross-subsidisation practices. The NRAs are empowered to specify the format and the accounting methodology to be used.[321]

1.153   In order to facilitate the verification of compliance with both transparency obligations and non-discrimination obligations, the NRAs may – above and beyond their information powers under article 5 Framework Directive[322] – require that accounting records, including data on revenues received from third parties, are provided on request. This information may be published, subject to national and Community rules and commercial confidentiality, provided that the publication 'would contribute to an open and competitive market' (article 11(2) sentence 2 Access Directive).

---

318   Cf ERG Opinion on proposed changes to Commission Recommendation of 1998 on Accounting separation and cost accounting, ERG (04)15; see also Working Document of the Communications Committee, Draft Commission Recommendation on regulatory accounting systems applied by notified operators in the electronic communications markets, 1 December 2004.

319   Common Position (EC) No 36/2001, OJ C 337/1, 30.11.2001.

320   See clarification in recital 21 Access Directive.

321   Cf ERG Opinion on proposed changes to Commission Recommendation of 1998 on Accounting separation and cost accounting, ERG (04)15; also see Working Document of the Communications Committee, Draft Commission Recommendation on regulatory accounting systems applied by notified operators in the electronic communications markets, 1 December 2004.

322   See para 1.54 above.

Access to digital radio and television broadcasting services

OBLIGATIONS TO PROVIDE ACCESS ON FAIR, REASONABLE AND
NON-DISCRIMINATORY TERMS

1.154 The specific issues of access to digital radio and television broadcasting services[323] are governed by article 5(1) sentence 2(b) Access Directive. Under this provision, Member States may grant to their NRAs the powers to impose, regardless of an undertaking's market position, fair, reasonable and non-discriminatory terms of access to Application Programming Interfaces (API)[324] and Electronic Program Guides (EPG). This provision is to be read in conjunction with article 6(1) and Part I of Annex I to the Access Directive, which transposes the provisions of the Television Standards Directive 95/47/EC on conditional access systems[325] into the new regulatory framework. The Council took the position that the mere adoption of the provisions of the Television Standards Directive 95/47/EC would not be sufficient. Rather, the Member States should be given, from the outset, the option to establish conditions for technical access to API and EPG.[326]

OBLIGATIONS CONCERNING CONDITIONAL ACCESS SYSTEMS

1.155 Article 6(1) Access Directive restates, as mentioned above, the obligations that were set out in the Television Standards Directive, and which are now contained in Part I of Annex I to the Access Directive. According to this set of conditions for access to digital television and radio services, conditional access systems operated on the market in the Community are to have the necessary technical capability for cost-effective transcontrol allowing the possibility for full control by network operators at local or regional level of the services using such conditional access systems.[327] Operators of conditional access services who provide access services to digital television and radio services and whose access services broadcasters depend upon to reach any group of potential viewers or listeners are obliged to offer their services on fair, reasonable and non-discriminatory terms.[328] The owners of industrial property rights to conditional access products and systems shall not subject the granting of licences to conditions prohibiting, deterring or discouraging the inclusion in the same product of a common interface allowing connection with several other access systems.[329]

---

323 The terminology of the Access Directive is inconsistent: Art 5(1)(b) mentions 'radio and television broadcasting services', art 6(1) and (3) sub-para 2(b)(i) mentions 'television and radio broadcasting services'; art 31(1) sentence 1 Universal Service Directive mentions 'radio or television broadcasts'.

324 According to art 2(p) Framework Directive 'Application programming interfaces (API)' means 'the software interfaces between applications, made available by broadcasters or service providers, and the resources in the enhanced digital television equipment for digital television and radio services'.

325 Directive 95/47/EC of the European Parliament and the Council of 24 October 1995 on the use of standards for the transmission of television signals, OJ L 281/51, 23.11.1995; the Directive has been repealed by art 26 Framework Directive.

326 Cf Common Position (EC) No 36/2001 adopted by the Council of 17 September, OJ C 337/1, 30.11.2001, p 16.

327 Annex I, Part I (a) Access Directive.

328 Annex I, Part I (b) Access Directive.

329 Annex I, Part I (c) Access Directive.

1.156   A new feature of the obligations and conditions for access to digital television and radio services is that they can be adapted to economic and technical developments under the regulatory procedure set out in the comitology Decision[330] (article 6(2) Access Directive).

1.157   Member States may allow the NRAs to conduct a market analysis in accordance with article 16(1) Framework Directive 'as soon as possible' after the entry into force of the 2002 EU Regulatory Package in order to ascertain whether to maintain, amend or withdraw the conditions for access to digital television and radio services.[331] If an NRA concludes, as a result of this market analysis, that one or more operators do not have significant market power on the relevant market, it may amend or withdraw the conditions imposed on the basis of article 16 and Annex I. Whereas article 16(3) Framework Directive provides that the NRA is obliged to withdraw obligations imposed on undertakings if the market is effectively competitive,[332] the Access Directive allows for NRA discretion in the case of operators of access systems or services ('[NRA] may amend or withdraw'). If the NRA decides to amend or withdraw the access conditions, it is bound by the provisions of article 6(3) sub-para 2(a) and (b) Access Directive: neither the accessibility for end-users to radio and television broadcasts and broadcasting channels and services specified in the 'must carry' provision under article 31 Universal Service Directive, nor the prospects for effective competition in the markets for retail digital television and radio broadcasting services and for conditional access systems in other associated services, must be adversely affected by the amendment or withdrawal of access obligations.[333]

OBLIGATIONS CONCERNING THE INTEROPERABILITY OF DIGITAL INTERACTIVE TELEVISION SERVICES

1.158   The regulatory powers of the NRAs are complemented by a regulatory competence of the Commission which was inserted into the Framework Directive by the European Parliament during the second reading.[334] In the interest of the speedy creation of 'open' APIs, article 18(1) Framework Directive obliges the Member States to encourage providers of digital interactive television services and providers of enhanced digital television equipment to use and to comply with APIs. If this encouragement does not lead to interoperability and freedom of choice for users within one year after the transposition of the Directive, the Commission is empowered to impose the mandatory use of an open API which complies with the standards and specifications adopted by the European standardisation bodies. One possible standard is the Multimedia Home Platform ('MHP') standard which has been adopted by the European Telecommunications Standards Institute (ETSI) and which is aimed at the creation of harmonised network architecture for interactive

---

330   Council Decision 1999/468/EC of 28 June 1999 laying down the procedures for the exercise of implementing powers conferred on the Commission, OJ L 184/23,17.07.1999; see para 1.62 above.

331   See paras 1.76 et seq above.

332   See para 1.77 above.

333   Cf art 6(3) sub-para 2(b)(i) Access Directive.

334   Amendment 30, Recommendation for the second reading of 4 December 2001, Committee on Industry, External Trade, Research and Energy, A5–0435/2001 PE 309.058, pp 29 et seq; Legislative Decision of the Commission, COM(2002) 78 final, 12.12.2001, pp 3 et seq. For further details see European Commission's Report on the development of the market for digital television in the European Union, COM(1999) 540, 10.11.1999.

television services.[335] In a Communication of June 2004, the Commission concluded that there is no clear case for mandating standards at present and that the
issue should be reviewed in 2005; it proposed a range of promotional actions to
promote the deployment of interactive digital services using the MHP standard
instead.[336]

Transitional regulations

1.159   In order to ensure the transition from access and interconnection rules that
were adopted under the previous regulatory regime[337] to the new Regulatory
Framework which provides for individualised, market-specific access and interconnection obligations on the basis of regulatory decisions with respect to individual
SMP undertakings,[338] article 7 Access Directive provides for detailed transitional
rules which complement the general transitional measures set out in article 27
Framework Directive: according to article 7 Access Directive, Member States shall
maintain all obligations regarding access and interconnection that were in force
prior to the date of entering into force of the Access Directive until such time as
these obligations have been reviewed and a determination has been made, on the
basis of a market analysis, whether to maintain, amend or withdraw these obligations with respect to SMP undertakings.

Regulation of Universal Services and Users' Rights: the Universal Service Directive

Objectives and scope of regulation

1.160   The Universal Service Directive is aimed at ensuring the availability
throughout the Community of good quality, publicly available services through
effective competition and choice; in addition, it provides for regulatory measures in
those cases of market failure 'in which the needs of end-users are not satisfactorily
met by the market' (article 1(1)).

1.161   The new regulatory framework regarding the scope, imposition and financing of universal service obligations reflects the universal service regime of the
previous EU framework, which was spread out over a number of Directives[339] and
specifies them. The Directive establishes, in accordance with the universal service

---

335 Art 18(3) Framework Directive and on that see recital 31. On the MHP-Standard see the
     Digital Video Broadcasting Project's (DVB) website, www.mhp.org; on ETSI-standard TS 101
     812 see ETSI's homepage, www.etsi.org/.
336 Communication from the Commission to the European Parliament, the Council, the Eco-
     nomic and Social Committee and the Committee of the Regions on interoperability of digital
     interactive television services, COM(2004) 28 final, 22.01.2004.
337 See paras 1.22 et seq above.
338 See paras 1.137 et seq above.
339 See in particular art 3 and 4 c Directive 90/388/EEC of 28 June 1990 (in the version of
     Directive 96/19/EC of 13 March 1996, OJ L 74/13, 22.03.1996) on competition in the markets
     for telecommunications services, OJ L 192/10, 24.07.1990; art 5 Directive 97/33/EC of 30 June
     1997 (in the version of Directive 98/61/EC of 24 September 1998, OJ L 268/37, 03.10.1988) on
     interconnection in telecommunications with regards to ensuring universal service and the
     interoperability through application of the principles of Open Network Provision (ONP),
     OJ L 199/23, 26.07.1997 and art 4 Directive 98/10/EC of 26 February 1998 on the application

regime of the previous Directives, a minimum set of services of specified quality to which all end users shall have access, at an affordable price in the light of specific national conditions, without distorting competition. Furthermore, the Directive allows, with reference to the Framework Directive,[340] the regulation of SMP undertakings in end-user markets, thus complementing the Access Directive which is aimed at wholesale markets[341] (articles 16–19).[342] Under the heading 'end-user interests and rights', the Directive establishes consumer rights, obligations of network operators and service providers and allows for regulatory measures in the interest of consumer protection (articles 20–31).[343]

Regulation of universal service obligations

SCOPE OF UNIVERSAL SERVICE OBLIGATIONS

1.162 The Member States are obliged to ensure that the services described in articles 4–7 Universal Service Directive are made available to all end-users in their respective territory 'independently of geographical location, and, in the light of specific national conditions, at an affordable price' (article 3(1) Universal Service Directive). The nature of the 'specific national conditions'[344] is neither defined in the provisions of the Directives nor in its recitals. Recital 7 merely confirms what already follows from article 3(1), namely that the 'specific national conditions' are relevant only for the determination of the 'affordable price'. In establishing the universal service obligation, the Universal Service Directive refers back to the definition set out in article 2(j) Framework Directive which, in turn, refers to the Universal Service Directive for the definition of the 'minimum set of services' which comprise the 'universal service'. The Directive allows the Member States, to a large degree, to determine 'the most efficient and appropriate approach' to ensure the provision of universal services. They have to respect the principles of objectivity, transparency, non-discrimination and proportionality and are obliged to minimise market distortions, 'in particular the provision of services at prices or subject to other terms and conditions which depart from normal commercial conditions whilst safeguarding the public interest'.[345]

1.163 Despite numerous demands to extend the catalogue of universal services,[346] the EU legislators left the list of universal service obligations largely unchanged. As under the previous Directives, they include:

- the connection at a fixed location to the public telephone network including access to publicly available telephone services at a fixed location (article 4(1)),[347] whereby the connection provided shall be capable of allowing end-users to make and receive in addition to local, national and international

---

of open network provision (ONP) to voice telephony and on universal service for telecommunications in a competitive environment, OJ L 101/24, 01.04.1998.

340 See paras 1.48 et seq above.
341 See paras 1.122 et seq above.
342 See paras 1.171 et seq below.
343 See paras 1.178 et seq below.
344 See also art 3(1) Directive 98/10/EC.
345 Cf also art 3(1) Directive 98/10/EC.
346 See, on the discussion regarding the proposed inclusion of broadband services in the catalogue of universal services, Commission's Communication Review 1999, pp 45 et seq.
347 See also art 5 Directive 98/10/EC.

telephone calls, facsimile communications and data communications. The data rates must be sufficient to permit 'functional internet access' (article 4(2)),

- the provision of at least one comprehensive directory to be provided to end-users either in printed or electronic form or both and to be updated at least once a year (article 5(1)(a)),[348]
- the provision of a comprehensive telephone directory enquiry service for end-users (article 5(1)(b)),[349] and
- the provision of public pay telephones (article 6(1)) including the possibility to make emergency calls from public pay telephones using the single European emergency call number and other national emergency numbers free of charge (article 6(3)).[350]

With respect to the special measures for disabled users set out in article 7 Universal Service Directive, Member States are granted a large degree of discretion. They should, where appropriate, take suitable measures in order to guarantee access to and affordability of all publicly available telephone services at a fixed location for disabled users and users with special social needs; such specific measures could include, for example, making available accessible public telephones, public text telephones or equivalent measures for deaf or speech-impaired people, and providing services such as directory enquiry services or equivalent measures free of charge for blind or partially sighted people.[351] The Directive neither specifies the measures to be taken nor does it make their imposition mandatory ('Member States *may* take specific measures').

The list of universal services is inclusive. The Directive provides that the Commission shall 'periodically' review the scope of universal service, starting in July 2005 and subsequently every three years. In the course of this review, the Commission has to take into account social, economic and technological developments in accordance with article 15(2) and a methodology which is set out in Annex V of the Universal Service Directive. In the first of those reviews, having analysed the mobile and broadband markets, the Commission concluded in May 2005 that the scope of universal service should remain unchanged.[352] The Directive makes it clear that any change of the scope of universal services should be subject to the twin test of services that become available to a substantial majority of the population, with a consequent risk of social exclusion for those who cannot afford them.[353] The 'twin test' is to be conducted at Community level; consequently, Member States are not permitted to expand, on their own, the scope of universal service obligations or to impose on market players 'financial contributions which relate to measures which are not part of universal service obligations'.[354] Outside the scope of universal service obligations, however, Member States remain free to impose special measures (including 'mandatory services') and finance them in conformity with Community

---

348 Also in this respect there are only minor changes compared to the law previously in force.

349 See the predecessor provision: art 6(2)(c) Directive 98/10/EC.

350 See the predecessor provision: arts 7(1) and (2) as well as art 8 Directive 98/10/EC.

351 See recital 13 Universal Service Directive; see also the predecessor provision art 8 Directive 98/10/EC.

352 Communication from the Commission to the Council, the European Parliament, the European Economic and Social Committee and the Committee of the Regions: On the Review of the Scope of Universal Service in accordance with art 15 of Directive 2002/22/EC, COM(2005) 5203 final, 24.05.2005.

353 Recital 25 as well as art 15 Universal Service Directive; on the criteria of review see Annex V Universal Service Directive.

354 Cf recital 25 Universal Service Directive.

law, but not by means of contributions from market players (article 32 Universal Service Directive).[355] This provision is aimed at opening, to Member States, a broad spectrum of possible measures,[356] which are not, however, specified in the Directive.

The Commission has announced that it intends to address the impact of Voice over Internet Protocol services on universal service in the context of its universal service review.[357]

PROCEDURE FOR THE DESIGNATION OF UNDERTAKINGS OBLIGED TO PROVIDE UNIVERSAL SERVICES

1.164 The regulatory options for Member States in determining 'the most efficient and appropriate approach' to ensure the provision of universal services (article 3(1) Universal Service Directive) include the 'designation' of one or more undertakings which are obliged to provide different elements of universal service and/or to cover different parts of the national territory. It follows from article 8(2) sentence 2 Universal Service Directive that this 'designation' is a legally binding regulatory measure that is aimed to ensure, among other things, 'that universal service is provided in a cost-effective manner'. The designation procedure shall be efficient, objective, transparent and non-discriminatory and shall not exclude any undertaking *a priori* from being designated (article 8(2) sentence 1 Universal Service Directive).

Undertakings with a universal service obligation may use whatever technology is appropriate to meet their obligations as long as they comply with the quality requirements established under the Universal Service Directive and national legislation; this could include the use of VoIP technology.[358]

REGULATION OF RETAIL TARIFFS, USERS' EXPENDITURES AND QUALITY OF SERVICE

1.165 In order to ensure that the end-user tariffs for the provision of universal services are affordable, article 9(1) Universal Service Directive obliges the NRAs to monitor the evolution and level of retail tariffs 'in particular in relation to national consumer prices and income'. The objective of this monitoring duty is to ensure that the services are provided 'at an affordable price' (article 3(1) Universal Service Directive); it would seem to follow, from this objective, that Member States are not only empowered to 'monitor' but also to regulate end-user tariffs in order to achieve 'affordability'.

1.166 With respect to the regulation of end-user tariffs, the Universal Service Directive provides for a number of regulatory options. Member States may:

- require that designated undertakings provide tariff options or packages to consumers which depart from those provided under normal commercial conditions, eg to ensure that those on low incomes or with special social needs are not prevented from accessing or using the publicly available telephone service (article 9(2)),

---

355 Cf recital 25 Universal Service Directive.
356 COM(2001) 503 final, OJ C 332 E/292, 27.11.2001, p 298.
357 Cf para 1.49 above; see Commission Staff Working Document on the treatment of Voice over Internet Protocol (VoIP) under the EU Regulatory Framework, 14.06.2004, p 10.
358 Cf Commission Staff Working Document on the treatment of Voice over Internet Protocol (VoIP) under the EU Regulatory Framework, 14.06.2004, p 11.

- in addition to tariff regulation, ensure that support is provided to consumers identified as having low incomes or special social needs (article 9(3)), and
- require undertakings with universal service obligations to apply common tariffs, including geographical averaging, throughout the territory, in the light of national conditions or to comply with price caps (article 9(4)).

The NRAs have to ensure that, where a designated undertaking is obliged to provide special tariff options, common tariffs, including geographical averaging, or to comply with price caps, the conditions are fully transparent and are published and applied in accordance with the principle of non-discrimination.[359]

1.167 In order to allow subscribers to control their expenditures for universal services, the Universal Service Directive provides, on the one hand, that designated undertakings have to establish terms and conditions in such a way that the subscriber is not obliged to pay for facilities or services which are not necessary or not required for the service requested.[360] On the other hand, article 10(2) Universal Service Directive obliges the Member States to ensure that the designated undertakings provide specific facilities and services, which are specified in Part A of Annex I, allowing subscribers to monitor and control expenditure and avoid unwarranted disconnection of service. These facilities and services include, among others, itemised billing, selective call barring for outgoing calls (free of charge), prepayment systems for the provision of access to the public telephone network and the use of publicly available telephone services.[361] These broad obligations are limited by article 10(3) Universal Service Directive which obliges Member States to ensure that the relevant authority will waive the requirements to provide the facilities or services mentioned 'if it is satisfied that the facility is widely available'.

1.168 The Universal Service Directive establishes partly broadened and partly new regulatory powers of the NRAs to establish quality standards and monitor compliance with performance targets in relation to universal services. Article 11 Universal Service Directive obliges NRAs, as under the previous Directive, to obtain information concerning the undertaking's performance in the provision of universal service (article 11(1)) and to establish quality of service standards (article 11(2)).[362] In addition, NRAs are now able to monitor compliance with performance targets by designated undertakings (article 11(5)). If an undertaking persistently fails to meet performance targets, the NRA may take 'specific measures' on the basis of the Authorisation Directive, which may include a prohibition to provide services (article 10(5) Authorisation Directive).[363] In order to ensure the accuracy and comparability of the data made available by undertakings with universal service obligations, NRAs may order independent audits or similar reviews of the performance data at the expense of the undertaking concerned (article 11(6) sentence 2 Universal Service Directive).

---

359   See also art 3(1) Directive 98/10/EC.

360   See also art 17(4) Directive 98/10/EC.

361   The provision of these facilities and services according to Annex I, Part A is not a universal service obligation. This follows from the separation between art 10(2) Universal Service Directive and the 'catalogue' of universal service obligations in arts 4–7 Universal Service Directive.

362   Art 11(1) and (4) Universal Service Directive; cf art 12(1), (2) and (3) Directive 98/10/EC.

363   See art 11(6) sentence 1 Universal Service Directive.

COST CALCULATION AND FINANCING OF UNIVERSAL SERVICES

1.169 The Universal Service Directive obliges Member States, more clearly than the previous Directives,[364] to ensure, upon request from a designated undertaking, the establishment of a financing mechanism if the undertaking is found to be 'subject to an unfair burden' (article 13(1) Universal Service Directive). The Directive establishes rules for the determination of the net cost of the universal service provision: the NRAs may determine the net cost of the universal service obligation in accordance with article 12(1) Universal Service Directive; in this case, they have to follow the calculation rules set out in Part A of Annex IV. Alternatively, the NRAs may base their calculation on the net costs of providing universal service identified by a 'designation mechanism' in accordance with article 8(2) Universal Service Directive.

1.170 The compensation of the undertakings that have been designated for the provision of universal services can be based on a mechanism that ensures compensation of the net cost from public funds (article 13(1)(a) Universal Service Directive)[365] and/or on a sharing of the net cost of universal service obligations between providers of electronic communications networks and services (article 13(1)(b) Universal Service Directive); these may include providers of VoIP-based services.[366] Contrary to the previous framework,[367] universal services can no longer be financed by 'a supplementary charge added to the interconnection charge'.[368] The cost sharing (article 13(1)(b) Universal Service Directive) has to be supervised by the NRA or another body independent from the beneficiaries under the NRA's supervision; the sharing mechanism must comply with the principles of transparency, minimal market distortion, non-discrimination and proportionality.[369] The Member States have the right not to require contributions from undertakings whose national turnover is less than a set limit. An assumption applies to undertakings that are not providing services in the territory of the Member State that has established a sharing mechanism: These undertakings may not be subject to charges related to the sharing of the cost of universal service obligations (article 13(3) sentence 2 Universal Service Directive).

Regulation of retail markets

MARKET ANALYSIS

1.171 Regulation of retail services is based on a market analysis which NRAs have to undertake 'as soon as possible' after the coming into force of the Universal Service Directive on the basis of the Recommendation on relevant product and service markets[370] and the Commission Decision identifying trans-national markets (article 15(4) Framework Directive).[371]

---

364 Art 5(1) Directive 97/33/EC.
365 The predecessor provision (art 5 Directive 97/33/EC) did not provide this possibility.
366 Cf Commission Staff Working Document on the treatment of Voice over Internet Protocol (VoIP) under the EU Regulatory Framework, 14.06.2004, p 11.
367 See art 5(2) Directive 97/33/EC.
368 Art 5(2) Directive 97/33/EC.
369 Art 13(3) in conjunction with Annex IV, Part B Universal Service Directive.
370 See para 1.75 above.
371 See para 1.77 above.

PREREQUISITES FOR THE REGULATION OF RETAIL MARKETS

1.172 On the basis of its market analysis, an NRA has to impose 'appropriate regulatory obligations on undertakings identified as having significant market power'. This obligation to regulate, which leaves no room for discretion, applies only if:

- the NRA has determined as a result of its market analysis[372] that a given retail market[373] is not effectively competitive (article 17(1)(a) Universal Service Directive), and
- the NRA has further concluded that obligations imposed under the Access Directive or obligations to allow for call-by-call carrier selection or carrier pre-selection[374] would not result in the achievement of the objectives set out in article 8 Framework Directive[375] (article 17(1(b) Universal Service Directive).

Article 17(5) Universal Service Directive mirrors article 17(1)(a) Universal Service Directive and clarifies that NRAs shall not apply retail control mechanisms to geographical or user markets where they are satisfied that there is effective competition.[376]

The principle that regulation of retail services is permissible only if regulation at the wholesale level does not achieve the regulatory objectives had been suggested by the Parliamentary Committee of Legal Affairs and the Internal Market, but was not accepted by the Commission.[377] The final version of article 17(1)(b) Universal Service Directive is based on the Council's Common Position. By establishing a requirement to first consider whether a remedy under the Access Directive might not be more effective, the Council intended 'to guard against over-regulation'.[378] This more restrictive approach to imposing regulatory controls on retail services has been somewhat diluted, however, by allowing for NRA discretion ('where the national regulatory authority concludes that').

REGULATORY POWERS

1.173 If the NRA has determined that a given retail market is not effectively competitive and that regulation at wholesale level would not achieve the regulatory objectives, it is obliged to 'impose appropriate regulatory obligations' on those undertakings that have been identified as having significant market power (article 17(1) Universal Service Directive). The Commission's Draft Directive did not provide for this broad discretion regarding the appropriate regulatory remedies: The corresponding provision in the Commission's proposal (article 16(3) merely empowered the NRAs 'to apply appropriate retail price cap measures ... in order to protect user and consumer interests'.

---

372 See para 1.77above and also art 16(3) Framework Directive.
373 See para 1.75 above.
374 Cf art 19 Universal Service Directive and para 1.177 below.
375 See para 1.53 above.
376 Measures of tariff regulation under art 9(2) Universal Service Directive, requiring SMP undertakings to provide special tariff options or tariff bundles, remain unaffected.
377 COM(2001) 503 final, 27.11.2001.
378 OJ C 53 E/195, 28.02.2002.

The expansion of the permissible regulatory remedies was first proposed in the report of the Committee on Legal Affairs and Internal Market,[379] but not accepted by the Commission.[380] It was the Council's Common Position that brought about the provision in its current form.

1.174   The NRAs' broad discretion in selecting regulatory remedies is somewhat mitigated by the regulatory objectives set out in article 8 Framework Directive[381] and the principle of proportionality. The regulatory discretion is further limited by the non-inclusive list of possible ex-ante obligations which NRAs may impose upon SMP undertakings. They include, but are not limited to, the requirements that the identified undertakings do not:

- charge excessive prices,
- inhibit market entry or restrict competition by setting predatory prices, or
- show undue preference to specific end-users or unreasonably bundle services.

1.175   Furthermore, NRAs may regulate end-user tariffs in order to protect end-user interests whilst promoting effective competition. Article 17(2) sentence 3 Universal Service Directive provides for three different types of tariff regulation: first, the NRAs may apply to SMP undertakings 'appropriate retail price cap measures'; secondly, they may take 'measures to control individual tariffs'; and, thirdly, NRAs can take measures 'to orient tariffs towards costs or prices on comparable markets'. This list of possible regulatory measures, which may be taken 'as a last resort and after due consideration',[382] is non-inclusive: The recitals specifically state that NRAs may use 'price cap regulation, geographical averaging *or similar instruments*' to achieve the twin objectives of promoting effective competition whilst pursuing public interests needs.[383]

The provisions allowing for end-user tariff regulation are complemented by mandatory rules regarding the implementation of cost accounting systems. Where an SMP undertaking is subject to retail tariff regulation or other relevant retail controls, the NRAs are obliged to ensure that 'the necessary and appropriate cost accounting systems are implemented'.[384] The NRAs may specify the format and accounting methodology to be used.[385] Compliance with the cost accounting system is to be verified by a qualified independent body;[386] this may also be the NRA itself.[387] The NRAs have to ensure that the statement concerning compliance with the cost accounting requirements is published annually.[388]

IMPOSITION OF OBLIGATIONS CONCERNING THE PROVISION OF A MINIMUM SET OF LEASED LINES

1.176   Similar to the previous regulatory framework,[389] the Universal Service Directive empowers NRAs to impose obligations regarding the provision of a

---

379 Amendment 25, A5–0202/2001 PE 294.936.
380 COM(2001) 503 final, 27.11.2001.
381 See para 1.53 above.
382 Recital 26 sentence 8 Universal Service Directive.
383 Recital 26 sentence 8 Universal Service Directive (emphasis added).
384 Art 17(4) sentence 1 Universal Service Directive.
385 Art 17(4) sentence 2 Universal Service Directive.
386 Art 17(4) sentence 3 Universal Service Directive; cf also art 14(4) sentence 1 Access Directive.
387 Cf the clarification in recital 27 Universal Service Directive.
388 Art 17(4) sentence 4 Universal Service Directive; see also art 13(4) sentence 3 Access Directive.
389 Cf art 4(2) Universal Service Directive and Council Directive 92/44/EEC of 5 June 1992 on

minimum set of leased lines.[390] The scope of this minimum offering is published by the Commission in accordance with article 17 Framework Directive as part of the list of standards for the harmonised provision of electronic communications networks and services.[391] This publication, which is not a legally binding decision (article 249 EC Treaty), has a mere indicative function. The NRA has to determine, in the course of a market analysis in accordance with article 16(3) Universal Service Directive, whether or not the market for the provision of part or all of the minimum set of leased lines is 'effectively competitive'. If it is determined that the market is not effectively competitive, the NRA has to identify undertakings with significant market power in the provision of those specific elements of the minimum set of leased lines services and impose obligations regarding the provision of the minimum set of leased lines (article 18(1) Universal Service Directive). The market analysis has to be carried out at periodic intervals.[392] If the NRA finds, as a result of such market analysis, that a relevant market for the provision of leased lines is effectively competitive, it shall withdraw the regulatory obligations in relation to this specific leased line market (article 18(2) Universal Service Directive). Annex VII Universal Service Directive specifies the conditions which may be imposed on SMP undertakings that are obliged to provide the minimum set of leased lines. These conditions are designed to ensure compliance with the basic principles of non-discrimination, cost orientation and transparency. Specifically, NRAs have to ensure that regulated SMP undertakings:

- apply similar conditions in similar circumstances ... and are to provide leased lines to others under the same conditions and of the same quality as they provide for their own services, or those of their subsidiaries or partners (Annex VII, No 1),
- establish tariffs that follow the principles of cost orientation (Annex VII, No 2), and
- publish technical characteristics, tariffs and supply conditions in respect of the minimum set of leased lines in an easily accessible form (Annex VII, No 3.1, 3.2). Where a Member State considers that the performance achieved for the provision of the minimum set of leased lines does not meet users' needs, it may define appropriate targets for the supply conditions including the delivery period and the typical repair time.[393]

---

the application of open network provision to leased lines, OJ L 65/27, 19.06.1992 (in the version of Directive 97/51/EC), there in particular arts 7 and 10.

390 In terms of content the provisions of art 18 and Annex VII Universal Service Directive correspond to the predecessor provisions of Directive 92/44/EEC (Council Directive 92/44/EEC of 5 June 1992 on the application of open network provision to leased lines, OJ L 165/27, 19.06.1992). An important difference lies however in the fact that the NRA will be able to refrain from imposing leased line specific obligations in the future in case that the market analysis on the relevant market determines the functioning of competition. Cf in contrast to that art 1(2) and (3) Directive 92/44/EEC (in the version of Directive 97/51/EC). The authority of the NRA contained in Annex VII, No 3.3 Universal Service Directive to 'define appropriate targets for the supply conditions' is also new.

391 See Commission Decision of 24 July 2003 on the minimum set of leased lines with harmonised characteristics and associated standards referred to in art 18 Universal Service Directive, OJ L 186/43, 25.07.2003; see also para 1.65 above.

392 Cf art 16(3) Universal Service Directive.

393 Annex VII, No 3.3.

IMPOSITION OF OBLIGATIONS CONCERNING CARRIER (PRE-)SELECTION

1.177   Article 19 Universal Service Directive provides that undertakings which have significant market power for the provision of connection to and use of the public telephone network at a fixed location have to enable their subscribers to access the services of any interconnected provider of public telephone services, both on a call-by-call basis by dialling a carrier selection code and by means of pre-selection. Contrary to its predecessor provision,[394] article 19 Universal Service Directive no longer provides for exceptions and transitional rules. Recital 29 makes it clear that NRAs may also require mobile operators with significant market power to enable their subscribers to access the services of interconnected providers on a call-by-call basis or by means of pre-selection.[395]

End-user rights

Chapter IV of the Universal Service Directive establishes under the heading 'end-user interests and rights' a number of rights of 'consumers' and 'end-users',[396] which correspond to obligations of the providers of specific communications networks and services.

CONTRACTS: OBLIGATION TO CONTRACT AND MINIMUM STANDARDS

1.178   Any consumer, ie any natural person who uses or requests the publicly available electronic communications service for purposes which are outside his or her trade, business or profession (article 2(i) Framework Directive) has a right to enter into a contract with operators providing connection and/or access to the public telephone network (article 20(2) Universal Service Directive). The undertakings that are obliged to enter into such contracts include mobile communications providers.[397]

1.179   In the interest of 'transparency of information and legal security',[398] article 20(2) Universal Service Directive establishes a number of minimum requirements for the contracts with undertakings providing connection and/or access to the public telephone network. These minimum requirements go well beyond those that were established in article 10 Directive 98/10/EC[399] and complement the Community's consumer protection rules, including the Directive on unfair terms in

---

394   Art 10(7), art 20(2) sentence 1 Directive 97/33/EC, as amended by Directive 98/61.
395   Cf art 20(2) sentence 1 Directive 97/33/EC.
396   See art 2(i) and (n) Framework Directive: ' "Consumer" means any natural person who uses or requests a publicly available electronic communications service for purpose which are outside his or her trade, business or profession; "end-user" means any user not providing public communications networks or publicly available electronic communications services'. The difference lies in the purpose of use.
397   This results from the definition of 'public telephone network' set out in art 2(b) Universal Service Directive: 'an electronic communications network which is used to provide publicly available telephone service' and 'supports the transfer between network termination points of speech communications ...'. The Directive no longer requires the *direct* transmission of speech between network termination points, thereby making it clear that mobile services are now covered by the definition, cf European Commission, Green Paper on a common approach in the field of mobile and personal communications in the European Union COM(1994) 145 final, 27.04.1994, p 172.
398   Cf recital 30 Universal Service Directive.
399   The indication of 'particulars of prices and tariffs and the means by which up-to-date

consumer contracts[400] and the Directive on the protection of consumers in respect of distance contracts[401] (article 20(1) Universal Service Directive). The minimum requirements include:

- definition of the services provided,
- specification of the service quality levels offered, including the time for the initial connection, and
- specification of the types of maintenance services offered.[402]

These minimum requirements may be extended, by a Member State, to other 'end-users', ie beyond the 'consumers' (article 20(2) Universal Service Directive).

According to article 20(3) Universal Service Directive, the minimum requirements apply also to contracts between consumers and electronic communications services providers other than those providing connections and/or access to the public telephone network. These other service providers, however, are not under an obligation to enter into contracts with consumers or end-users.

1.180   Subscribers (including consumers and end-users) have a right to withdraw from their contracts without penalty, upon notice of proposed modifications in the contractual conditions. They must be given adequate notice of such proposed modifications, which shall be not shorter than one month ahead of any modification (article 20(4) Universal Service Directive).

TRANSPARENCY OBLIGATIONS

1.181   Member States are obliged to publish 'transparent and up-to-date information' on applicable prices, tariffs and standard terms and conditions regarding access to and use of publicly available telephone services; this includes, among other things, information regarding the standard tariffs, compensation and refund policies, the type of maintenance service offered, the standard contract conditions, including any minimum contractual period, and dispute settlement mechanisms.[403]

1.182   Furthermore, Member States have to ensure that NRAs are able to require undertakings that provide publicly available electronic communication services to publish 'comparable, adequate and up-to-date information for end-users on the quality of their services'.[404] The Directive allows for broad discretion of the NRAs

---

information on all applicable tariffs and maintenance charges may be obtained' (art 20(2)(d) Universal Service Directive) is a new requirement.

400   Council Directive 93/13/EEC of 5 April 1993 on unfair terms in consumer contracts, OJ L 95/29, 21.04.1993.

401   Directive 97/7/EC of the European Parliament and of the Council of 20 May 1997 on the protection of consumers in respect of distance contracts ('Distance Selling Directive'), OJ L 144/19, 04.06.1997.

402   In addition, the contract must specify the identity and address of the supplier, particulars of prices and tariffs and the means by which up-to-date information on all applicable tariffs and maintenance charges may be obtained, the duration of the contract, the conditions for renewal and termination of services and of the contract, any compensation and refund arrangements which apply if contracted service quality levels are not met, and the method of initiating procedures for the settlement of disputes.

403   Cf art 21 Universal Service Directive and Annex II. See also the predecessor provision, art 11 Directive 98/10/EC, which established less stringent requirements regarding scope and level of detail of the information to be published.

404   Art 22(1) Universal Service Directive. Cf also art 12(2) Directive 98/10/EC. The predecessor provision obliged only organisations with significant market power and named organisations

with respect to the detailed requirements: the Member States may specify, for example, the quality of service parameters to be measured, and the content, form and manner of information to be published. To achieve the regulatory goal that end-users have access to comprehensive, comparable and user-friendly information, NRAs may also use the parameters, definitions and measurement methods set out in Annex III of the Universal Service Directive. They include the supply time for initial connection, fault rate per access line, fault repair time, unsuccessful call ratio, call set-up time and other parameters.[405]

REGULATORY MEASURES CONCERNING THE INTEGRITY OF THE NETWORK

1.183   The Member States are obliged to ensure the integrity of the public telephone network at fixed locations and, in the event of catastrophic network breakdown or in cases of *force majeure*, the availability of the public telephone network and publicly available telephone services at fixed locations. To this end, undertakings providing publicly available telephone services at fixed locations have to take all reasonable steps to ensure uninterrupted access to emergency services.[406]

OPERATOR ASSISTANCE AND DIRECTORY ENQUIRY SERVICES

1.184   Subject to applicable data protection provisions,[407] subscribers to publicly available telephone services have 05the right to have an entry in the publicly available directory.[408] Undertakings which assign telephone numbers to subscribers have to meet all reasonable requests to make available, for the purposes of the provision of publicly available directory inquiry services and directories, the relevant information in an agreed format on 'fair, objective, cost-oriented and non-discriminatory' terms.[409]

All end-users that are provided with a connection to the public telephone network have a right to access operator assistance services and directory enquiry services.[410] Regulatory restrictions preventing end-users in one Member State from accessing directly the directory enquiry services in another Member State must be abolished.

according to art 5 Directive 98/10/EC. Furthermore, it provided only for the provision of information to the NRA which then had to ensure publication.

405   For these parameters, the European Standardisation Organisation (ETSI) has established definitions and measurement methods, cf art 12(1) and Annex III Directive 98/10/EC.

406   Art 23 Universal Service Directive. The provision was inserted at the Proposal of the Committee of Industry, External Trade, Research and Energy of the European Parliament, amendment 37, A5–0202/2001 PE 294.936. Cf also art 13(2)(b) Directive 98/10/EC.

407   See art 25(5) Universal Service Directive, which refers particularly to art 11 of Directive 97/66/EC of the European Parliament and of the Council of 15 December 1997 concerning the processing of personal data and the protection of privacy in the telecommunications sector, OJ L 24/1, 30.01.1998.

408   Art 25(1) Universal Service Directive in conjunction with art 5(1)(a) Universal Service Directive.

409   Art 25(1) Universal Service Directive. Cf also art 6(1), (2)(a) and (b) and (3) Directive 98/10/EC.

410   Art 25 (1) Universal Service Directive. Cf also art 6(2)(c) Directive 98/10/EC.

EUROPEAN EMERGENCY CALL NUMBER

1.185 The rules which were formerly set out in Decision 91/396/EC[411] regarding access to the single European emergency call number 112 are now set out in article 26 Universal Service Directive. The Directive provides that users must be able to call the emergency services free of charge.[412] Furthermore, the Directive deviates from Decision 91/396/EC by establishing an obligation on operators of public telephone networks to make caller location information available to authorities handling emergencies 'to the extent technically feasible'.[413] Article 26(4) Universal Service Directive obliges Member States to ensure that citizens are 'adequately informed' about the existence and use of the single European emergency call number.

Both the Commission and the ERG are considering the provision of access to emergency services by VoIP service providers. The problems in providing access to emergency services are mainly related to the nomadic use of VoIP and the fact that a user can access the network at any access point in any country and the VoIP service provider can be located in any country. This raises practical questions of routing the emergency call to the nearest emergency centre or to a specific emergency services answering point and on the transmission of information on the caller's location.[414]

EUROPEAN TELEPHONE ACCESS CODES

1.186 Member States are obliged to ensure that the '00' code continues[415] to be the standard international access code. For calls between adjacent locations across borders between Member States, special arrangements may be established or continued. Undertakings providing public telephone networks shall handle all calls to the European telephone numbering space.[416]

NON-GEOGRAPHIC NUMBERS

1.187 End-users from one Member State must be able to access non-geographic numbers (eg numbers for free phone or premium rate services) in other Member States where this is technically and economically feasible, except where a called subscriber has chosen for commercial reasons to limit access by calling parties located in specific geographical areas. The recitals make it clear that tariffs charged to parties calling from outside the Member State concerned need not be the same as for those parties calling from inside that Member State.[417]

---

411 Council Decision 91/396/EEC of 29 July 1991 on the introduction of a single European emergency call number, OJ L 217/31, 06.08.1991.

412 Cf art 7(2) Directive 98/10/EC providing for emergency calls free of charge from public pay telephones.

413 See Commission Recommendation of 25 July 2003 on the processing of caller location information in electronic communication networks for the purpose of location-enhanced emergency call services, OJ L 189/49, 29.07.2003.

414 Cf European Regulators Group, ERG Common Statement for VoIP regulatory approaches, ERG (05) 12, part 4; see also Commission Staff Working Document on the treatment of Voice over Internet Protocol (VoIP) under the EU Regulatory Framework, 14.06.2004, pp 13 et seq.

415 Cf Council Decision 92/264/EEC of 11 May 1992 on the introduction of a standard international telephone access code in the Community, OJ L 137/21, 20.05.1992.

416 Art 27(2) Framework Directive.

417 Art 28 Universal Service Directive and recital 38.

OBLIGATIONS TO PROVIDE ADDITIONAL FACILITIES

1.188   Member States shall ensure that NRAs are able to require all undertakings operating public telephone networks to make available to end-users, subject to technical feasibility and economic viability, phone dialling, or dual tone multi-frequency operation and calling-line identification.[418] Member States are not required to impose obligations to provide these facilities: the obligation may be waived by a Member State for all or part of its territory if it considers, after public consultation, that there is already 'sufficient access' to these facilities. Member States are free to impose obligations limiting the right to disconnect a subscriber from the network, which applies to universal services[419] as a general requirement on all undertakings.[420]

Obligations to ensure number portability

1.189   The European legislator considers number portability, ie the ability of end-users to retain their numbers independently of the undertaking providing the service, as 'a key facilitator of consumer choice and effective competition in a competitive telecommunications environment'.[421] Accordingly, article 30 Universal Service Directive allows all subscribers to publicly available telephone services, including mobile services, who so request, to retain their numbers independently of the undertaking providing the service as follows: in the case of geographic numbers, the numbers can be retained at a specific location, whereas in the case of non-geographic numbers, they can be retained at any location. In order to safeguard tariff transparency, the Directive does not provide for the transfer of numbers between networks providing services at a fixed location and mobile networks;[422] the recitals specifically state, however, that Member States are free to allow for the transfer of numbers between fixed and mobile networks.[423]

The number portability requirements in relation to VoIP service providers are currently in flux. The Commission and the European Regulators Group are considering whether or not VoIP service providers should be allowed to use geographic numbers for nomadic use and whether number portability should be allowed for all services (including VoIP services) inside each range of services or beyond service categories.[424]

The NRAs have to ensure that pricing for interconnection related to the provision of number portability is cost oriented, and that direct charges to subscribers do not act as a disincentive for the use of these facilities.[425]

---

418   Art 29(1) Universal Service Directive in conjunction with Annex I, Part B; see also arts 14(1) and 15(1) Directive 98/10/EC.
419   For details see Annex I, Part A (e) Universal Service Directive.
420   Art 29(3) Universal Service Directive.
421   Recital 40 Universal Service Directive.
422   European Commission, Commission Report 1999, p 55.
423   Recital 40 sentence 3 Universal Service Directive.
424   Cf European Regulators Group, ERG Common Statement for VoIP regulatory approaches, ERG (05) 12, Annex 1; see also Commission Staff Working Document on the treatment of Voice over Internet Protocol (VoIP) under the EU Regulatory Framework, 14.06.2004, pp 18 et seq.
425   Art 30(2) Universal Service Directive. See also art 12(7) sub-para 2 Interconnection Directive (in the version of Directive 98/61/EC).

Transitional provisions

1.190   On the basis of the market analysis in accordance with article 16(3),[426] the NRAs have to determine whether or not to maintain, amend or withdraw existing obligations relating to retail markets; measures taken as a consequence of the market analysis are subject to the consolidation procedure under article 7 Framework Directive.[427] Until the market analysis has been carried out and the measures to be taken have been determined, Member States shall maintain the retail obligations that are specified in article 16(1) Universal Service Directive. They relate to:

- retail tariffs for the provision of access to and use of the public telephone network imposed under article 17 Directive 98/10/EC,
- carrier selection or pre-selection, imposed under Directive 97/33/EC, and
- provision of leased lines under articles 3, 4, 6, 7, 8, and 10 Directive 92/44/EEC.

Regulation of the Use of Radio Spectrum: the Radio Spectrum Decision

Regulatory approach

1.191   Prior to the 2002 reform, the focus of the European Union's radio spectrum policy was on the harmonisation of radio spectrum allocations for the Community-wide provision of certain telecommunications services. In order to achieve this objective, the number of regulatory instruments, including Directives, Decisions of the European Parliament and the Council and (legally non-binding) Council resolutions were used.[428] The radio spectrum requirements of other, important policy sectors of the Community, such as broadcasting or transport, were not subject to these fragmented regulatory measures. In its attempts to influence the spectrum policy of the International Telecommunications Union (ITU) and the European Conference of Postal and Telecommunications Administrations (CEPT), the Commission was often restrained by institutional limitations.

---

426   See paras 1.76 et seq above.
427   See paras 1.60 et seq above.
428   Eg Council Directive 87/372/EEC of 25 June 1987 on the frequency bands to be reserved for the coordinated introduction of public pan-European cellular digital land-based mobile communications in the Community, OJ L 196/85, 16.09.1987; Council Resolution of 28 June 1990 on the strengthening of the Europe-wide cooperation on radio frequencies, in particular with regard to services with a pan-European dimension, OJ C 166/4, 07.07.1990; Council Directive 90/544/EEC of 9 October 1990 on the frequency bands designated for the coordinated introduction of pan-European land-based public radio paging in the Community, OJ L 310/28, 09.11.1990; Council Directive 91/287/EEC of 3 June 1991 on the frequency band to be designated for the coordinated introduction of digital European cordless telecommunications (DECT) into the Community, OJ L 144/45, 08.06.1991; Council Resolution of 19 November 1992 on the implementation in the Community of the European Radiocommunications Committee Decisions, OJ C 318/1, 04.12.1992; Decision No 710/97/EC of the European Parliament and of the Council of 24 March 1997 on a coordinated authorisation approach in the field of satellite personal-communication services in the Community, OJ L 105/4, 23.04.1997; Decision No 128/1999/EC of the European Parliament and of the Council of 14 December 1998 on the coordinated introduction of a third-generation mobile and wireless communications system (UMTS) in the Community, OJ L 171/1, 22.01.1999.

1.192   The Commission's Green Paper on Radio Spectrum Policy[429] was aimed at establishing a Community spectrum policy, independent from CEPT. As services using the radio spectrum converge and the demand for harmonised radio spectrum increases, it becomes more important to take into account the interests of all radio spectrum users in the strategic planning of spectrum allocation.[430]

1.193   The Commission's Radio Spectrum Decision[431] replaces the fragmented approach towards the planning of frequency uses and harmonisation of spectrum allocation and assignment by a technology-neutral regulatory framework, which allows for the Community-wide harmonisation of frequency uses on the basis of a legally binding Community Spectrum Policy.[432]

Installation of the Radio Spectrum Committee

1.194   The Radio Spectrum Decision does not provide for harmonisation measures; rather, it establishes a generally applicable procedure under which harmonisation measures will be adopted with a view to ensuring the effective implementation of a radio spectrum policy in the Community and to ensuring harmonised conditions for the availability and efficient use of radio spectrum. To this end, the Commission is assisted by a newly established Radio Spectrum Committee (article 3(1) Radio Spectrum Decision), which consists of representatives of the Member States.[433]

1.195   Depending upon the type of harmonisation measure envisaged, the Radio Spectrum Committee has either a merely consultative function (advisory procedure, article 4(2) Radio Spectrum Decision) or it is in a position to instruct the Commission to submit a proposed measure to the Council for its decision (regulatory procedure, article 4(3), (4) and (6) Radio Spectrum Decision).

Procedures

1.196   The Commission is empowered to adopt appropriate 'technical implementing measures' with a view to ensuring harmonised conditions for the availability and efficient use of radio spectrum, as well as the availability of information related to the use of radio spectrum (article 4(1) Radio Spectrum Decision). Different adoption procedures apply to measures which fall within the remit of the CEPT and other measures.

---

429   European Commission, Green Paper on radio spectrum policy in the context of European Community policies such as telecommunications, broadcasting, transport, and research and development, COM(1998) 596 final, 03.12.1998.

430   Communication from the Commission to the Council, the European Parliament, the Economic and Social Committee and the Committee of the Regions – Next steps in radio spectrum policy – Results of the public consultation on the Green Paper, COM(1999) 538 final, 10.11.1999, p 11.

431   Decision No 676/2002/EC of the European Parliament and of the Council of 7 March 2002 on a regulatory framework for radio spectrum policy in the European Community (Radio Spectrum Decision), OJ L 108/1, 14.04.2002.

432   Cf the Commission's Explanatory Memorandum to the proposal for the Radio Spectrum Decision: 'The proper implementation of Community policies which require radio spectrum may be put at risk if spectrum availability has not been fully considered. This cannot be decided ... in entities which are external to the Community such as CEPT or ITU/WRC'.

433   Art 3(1) Council Decision 1999/468/EC of 28 June 1999 laying down the procedures for the exercise of implementing powers conferred on the Commission, OJ L 184/23, 17.07.1999.

1.197 In the case of measures falling within the remit of CEPT, the Commission issues 'mandates' to CEPT. This means that the Commission communicates to CEPT which harmonisation measures it envisages, the tasks to be performed and the timetable therefor (article 4(2) Radio Spectrum Decision). In this case, the Commission cooperates with the Radio Spectrum Committee in accordance with the advisory procedure. If the CEPT completes its work in a timely fashion, the Commission decides, on the basis of the regulatory procedure,[434] whether the results of the work carried out pursuant to the Commission mandate shall apply in the Community and on the deadline for their implementation by the Member States. These decisions are published in the Official Journal (article 4(3) Radio Spectrum Decision). If the Commission or any Member State considers, however, that the work carried out by CEPT on the basis of a mandate is not progressing satisfactorily, ie in a timely manner, or if the results of the mandate are not acceptable, the Commission may, at its discretion, adopt appropriate measures to achieve the objectives of the mandate; in this case, the regulatory procedure applies (article 4(4) Radio Spectrum Decision).

1.198 If the Commission intends, at its discretion, to adopt harmonisation measures which do not fall within the remit of the CEPT, it has to act in accordance with the regulatory procedure (article 4(6) Radio Spectrum Decision). This provision also allows for technical implementing measures with respect to sectors other than the communications sector.

1.199 The procedures for the adoption of technical implementing measures to ensure harmonised conditions for the availability and use of radio spectrum allow, on the one hand, for the continued cooperation between the Community and CEPT,[435] with a view to adopting harmonisation measures beyond the Community borders in all 44 member countries of CEPT while transforming those CEPT measures that comply with the Community's spectrum policy objectives, with the force of law. On the other hand, the Community retains the freedom to accelerate CEPT procedures, which have sometimes been exceedingly slow in the past, to reject measures proposed by CEPT, where necessary, and to adopt Community measures outside the remit of CEPT.

Co-operation with third countries and international organisations

1.200 The Radio Spectrum Decision is aimed at the international representation of the Community, for example in the context of ITU World Radio Communication Conferences. To this end, article 6(2) Radio Spectrum Decision establishes a broad duty on Member States to inform the Commission of 'any difficulties created, de jure or de facto, by third countries or international organisations' for the implementation of the Radio Spectrum Decision. The Commission is obliged to monitor developments regarding radio spectrum in third countries and in international organisations and to report to the European Parliament and the Council. Where necessary, 'common policy objectives' shall be agreed to ensure Community coordination among Member States (article 6(3) Radio Spectrum Decision).

---

434 See para 1.195 above. The Radio Spectrum Committee does not only attend in an advisory capacity but can, in case of disputes, enforce an ultimate decision of the Council.

435 Cf recital 13 Radio Spectrum Decision on the need for harmonising the use of radio spectrum, particularly at the Community's borders.

Obligations concerning the availability of information

1.201   A precondition for the development of a Community radio spectrum policy is the availability of information regarding the national radio frequency allocation and information regarding the availability and use of radio spectrum in the Community. Article 5 Radio Spectrum Decision obliges Member States to publish this information in a user-friendly manner,[436] taking into account confidentiality requirements (article 8 Radio Spectrum Decision).

---

436   Cf recital 14 Radio Spectrum Decision.

EU Competition Law in the Electronic Communications Sector[1]

Keith Jones and Fiona Carlin
Baker & McKenzie, London/Brussels

INTRODUCTION

2.1 Competition law is now firmly at the heart of the legal framework for the electronic communications sector.[2] The European Commission sees the new regulatory framework as a means of further liberalising the sector and competition law concepts are central to this, reflected by then Competition Commissioner Mario Monti: 'The aim of regulatory remedies should be to allow antitrust remedies to be the only ones needed in the long term. While for those parts of the industry which can be characterised as natural monopolies, this may be difficult to achieve, as technology develops regulatory intervention will increasingly play a smaller role'.[3]

2.2 At the same time, the Commission has increasingly used competition law to attack abusive practices in the telecoms sector, in addition to reviewing strategic alliances and arrangements under the merger control rules and article 81. Recent examples include fining Wanadoo Interactive, a subsidiary of France Telecom, €10.35 million and Deutsche Telekom €12 million for abuse of dominance due to their pricing strategies. It is clear therefore that an understanding of competition law and its underlying concepts is now of fundamental importance to the sector.

---

1   Chapter up to date as of 15 June 2005. Although this chapter is focused on the 'telecommunications' sector, the development of the law cannot be seen in isolation, and cases in the communications sector in general (as well as more widely) should also be taken into account.
2   See also Chapter 1.
3   See 'Remarks at the European Regulators Group Hearing on Remedies', 26 January 2004 (SPEECH/04/37).

EU COMPETITION LAW – BASIC LEGISLATION AND NOTICES

2.3   There are three main limbs to competition law[4] for present purposes: article 81, article 82 and EC merger control law, known as the EC Merger Regulation or 'ECMR'.[5]

Article 81 – Restrictive Agreements

2.4   Article 81 prohibits agreements and concerted practices between undertakings that have as their object or effect the prevention, restriction or distortion of competition. Intra-group agreements are generally not caught, as they are part of one and the same 'undertaking'. Further, only agreements that give rise to an *appreciable* restriction of competition are caught by article 81(1) (a mere contractual restriction is not enough). The Commission's 'de minimis notice',[6] for example, provides guidance on this. In order to determine whether there is an appreciable restriction of competition, the impact of the agreement in the relevant market must be considered. The Commission's guidelines on the application of article 81(3)[7] include a summary of how the Commission sees article 81(1) operating in practice. This deals with restrictions of competition 'by object' (those that by their very nature have the potential of restricting competition) and restrictions by effect.

2.5   Article 81 can apply to all commercial agreements and arrangements. If any agreement gives rise to a restriction of competition, it is void and unenforceable pursuant to article 81(2) unless the article 81(3) criteria are satisfied. Article 81(3) is satisfied if the restrictive agreement:

- contributes to improving the production or distribution of goods or services and promotes technical or economic progress;
- allows consumers a fair share of the resulting benefit;
- contains only indispensable restrictions; and
- does not afford the possibility of eliminating competition.

2.6   There are a number of pieces of legislation under article 81(3), generally known as 'block exemption' regulations,[8] that provide 'safe harbours' for particular types of agreements, including certain technology transfer agreements (eg licensing of intellectual property rights, know-how etc), vertical agreements and various horizontal cooperation agreements (including research and development and specialisation).[9]

---

4   A detailed analysis of the basic concepts underlying competition law, such as 'undertaking' and 'agreement' is outside the scope of this work. See *Whish* Competition Law (5th ed, 2003), chs 3–5 and 21 for more details.

5   Council Regulation No 139/2004 on the control of concentrations between undertakings, OJ L 24/1, 29.01.2004.

6   Commission Notice on agreements of minor importance which do not appreciably restrict competition under art 81(1) of the Treaty, OJ C 368/13, 22.12.2001.

7   Commission Notice: Guidelines on the application of Article 81(3) of the Treaty, OJ C 101/97, 06.04.2004.

8   Although this phrase is now out of date following the modernisation of the competition enforcement rules.

9   Commission Regulation No 772/2004 on the application of Article 81(3) of the Treaty to categories of technology transfer agreements, OJ L 123/11, 27.04.2004; Commission Regulation No 2790/1999 on the application of Article 81(3) of the Treaty to categories of vertical agreements and concerted practices, OJ L 336/21, 29.12.1999; Commission Regulation

2.7   In considering the application of article 81, one must be very aware of the 'hardcore' restrictions that are likely to breach article 81(1) and will have little prospect of benefiting from article 81(3). Such restrictions include price-fixing, market sharing and customer allocation between actual or potential competitors (cartels, for example, will almost never be exempted). Further, agreements that restrict or inhibit the creation of a single market through preventing parallel imports are serious infringements. The treatment of such restrictions is not sector specific.

2.8   Although article 81, as with article 82, only applies if there is an appreciable effect on trade between Member States, this is not likely to be a significant distinction given that relevant national competition law is now aligned with EC competition law.[10]

Article 82 – the Abuse of Market Power

2.9   Article 82 prohibits the abuse of a dominant position. 'Dominance' is explained in Chapter 1.[11] It is essentially the ability to act independently (to a certain degree) from competitors and customers on the market. In substance, this is the same as 'SMP' under the new regulatory framework and underlies the notion of a 'notified operator' under the LLU regulation.[12] While the text of article 82 gives some examples of what constitutes an abuse of dominance, this is largely established through judgments of the European Court of Justice ('ECJ'). Broadly speaking, the various types of abuse can be described as 'exploitative' or 'anticompetitive' practices. Examples of the former include excessive pricing and tying, ie exploiting the dominant position by reaping the excess profit or by using it to gain an advantage in a related market. Examples of the latter (largely focused on protecting the dominant position or otherwise acting unfairly) include predation (pricing below cost), loyalty rebates, margin (or price) squeeze and refusals to deal. Other abuses include refusal to give access to an 'essential facility'[13] and discrimination.[14] While it seems unlikely that an 'essential facility' abuse case will be brought in the telecoms sector given the remedies now available under the new

---

No 2659/2000 on the application of Article 81(3) to categories of research and development agreements, OJ L 304/07, 05.12.2000 and Commission Regulation No 2658/2000 on the application of Article 81(3) to categories of specialisation agreements, OJ L 304/03, 05.12.2000.

10   The policy aim of creating a single market may be one possible difference.

11   See also *Whish* Competition Law (5th ed, 2003), pp 178–191.

12   Regulation No 2887/2000 of the European Parliament and of the Council of 18 December 2000 on unbundled access to the local loop, OJ L 336/04, 30.12.2000.

13   For a discussion of the notion of essential facilities, see *Whish*, Competition Law (5th ed, 2003), pp 667–677. For a slightly different view, see *Koenig, Bartosch and Braun*, EC Competition and Telecommunications Law (1st ed, 2002), Ch 4. Note, however, that the author appears to argue that a significant factor in considering the judgment of the ECJ in *Oscar Bronner v Mediaprint Zeitungs- und Zeitschriftenverlag* ([1998] ECR 1–7791) is that it relates to Austrian competition law rather than art 82. This would, at best, seem to be a very conservative view. Most commentators, such as *Whish*, consider that the ECJ has now explicitly approved, albeit in limited circumstances, the doctrine of essential facilities under competition law in general.

14   For further information on abuse of dominance, see *Whish* Competition Law (5th ed, 2003), chs 5, 17–18.

regulatory framework, the fact that the telecoms sector is generally characterised by former State monopolies/incumbents means that the application of article 82 is particularly important.[15]

2.10   There are significant consequences for breach of either article 81 or article 82. Fines of up to 10% of worldwide turnover can be imposed and, while generally short of this maximum, have been increasing in size. Further, in addition to relevant agreements or parts of them being void and unenforceable, third parties may claim damages to compensate for any loss suffered as a result of the infringement. Such claims are becoming increasingly common.

The ECMR

2.11   The ECMR provides the framework for assessing mergers and certain joint ventures/strategic alliances which constitute 'concentrations' with a 'Community dimension' within the meaning of the ECMR. If the ECMR applies, national merger control does not (subject to the ability to make referrals of transactions to and from Member States). The merger control legislation was recently revised. This modified the previous system both in terms of the substantive test to apply as well as in relation to certain jurisdictional and procedural matters.

Notices and Guidelines

2.12   The specific application of each of these aspects of competition law in the telecoms sector is described in more detail below.[16] The Commission has published numerous notices and guidelines in relation to article 81 and the ECMR, which should also be considered.[17] Of particular importance are the Access Notice, the Guidelines accompanying the block exemptions[18] as well as the Commission guidelines on market analysis.[19] Many of these, including several of the block exemptions, have recently been revised due to the root and branch review of article 81. Further, a number of notices have been issued to facilitate the modernisation of EC competition law enforcement.[20] Similarly, the ECMR has been revised with new legislation and guidelines effective from 1 May 2004. In contrast, the

---

15   The 'Notice on the application of the competition rules to access agreements in the telecommunications sector – framework, relevant markets and principles', OJ C 265/02, 22.08.1998 (the 'Access Notice') remains relevant in considering what constitutes an abuse of dominance in the sector, although it must be read in the light of developments in the case law.

16   See paras 2.17–2.53 and 2.82–2.89 below. Article 86 EC, State aid and the public procurement rules, which can also be relevant, are not within the scope of this chapter. For an alternative discussion which attempts to analyse the application of EU competition law to the telecoms sector, see *Koenig, Bartosch and Braun*, EC Competition and Telecommunications Law (1st ed, 2002), Ch 6.

17   Relevant notices are found on the website of DG Competition (www.europa.eu.int/comm/ competition/index-en.html).

18   Commission Notice: Guidelines on Vertical Restraints, OJ C 291/01, 13.10.2000; Commission Notice: Guidelines on the application of Article 81 of the EC Treaty to technology transfer agreements, OJ C 101/2, 27.04.2004 and Commission Notice: Guidelines on the applicability of Article 81 of the EC Treaty to horizontal cooperation agreements, OJ C 3/2, 06.01.2001.

19   Guidelines on market analysis and the assessment of significant market power under the Community regulatory framework for electronic communications networks and services, OJ C 165/6, 11.07.2002, see paras 1.70 et seq above.

20   See paras 2.13–2.15 below.

application of article 82 is currently unreformed, although it is subject to an internal review by the Commission which is expected to result in new guidelines. Such a review throws up a number of issues and it may be that there will be no significant change of policy as it is difficult to reform the law relating to article 82 without a change to the EC Treaty; furthermore, the law is derived from judgments of the ECJ, which cannot be overturned. Even if the substance of the law cannot be reformed, it is possible that the enforcement policy of the Commission may well change to reflect different priorities going forward as a result of any new guidelines. Nevertheless, the telecoms sector is still likely to remain a centre of attention.

MODERNISATION OF THE ENFORCEMENT OF EU COMPETITION LAW

2.13 With the enlargement of the EU, the Commission considered it necessary to modernise competition law enforcement. As a result, the EU adopted the 'Modernisation Regulation'[21] which came into play on 1 May 2004 to coincide with enlargement. This Regulation radically reforms the framework for enforcement throughout the EU. Detailed guidelines[22] dealing with the functioning of the new rules were also issued.

2.14 The Modernisation Regulation has brought about a number of fundamental changes to the previous system, including:

- *the abolition of the mandatory notification system under article 81(3).* Prior to 1 May 2004 only the Commission could grant an exemption under article 81(3). Now 'self-assessment' is key, ie firms undertake their own analysis.
- *the decentralised enforcement of the EC rules.* National courts and competition authorities can and must now apply EC competition law, including article 81(3), and must cooperate in doing so.
- *enhancement of powers of investigation.* The Commission now has greater powers of evidence gathering, including the power to visit homes.

2.15 These changes are likely to give rise to an increased need to consider strategic issues. For example, telecom companies wishing to complain about an anti-competitive practice will need to consider which of the various authorities is best placed/most likely to take action. This will often involve an analysis of whether the Commission, the National Competition Authority ('NCA')/National Regulatory Authority ('NRA') should be approached or, indeed, whether direct action through the courts should be taken. A review of the 'Notice on cooperation'[23] indicates that the authority complained to will generally continue with the investigation but other factors will be considered. These include which authority can best gather evidence as well as impose or enforce any remedies required. The interventionist nature of the particular authority as well as other factors (including costs) will need to be considered.

2.16 While the Modernisation Regulation provides for the consistent and uniform application of competition law, it seems likely that there will be tensions and

---

21 Council Regulation No 1/2003 on the implementation of the rules on competition laid down in Articles 81 and 82 of the Treaty, OJ L 01/01, 04.01.2003.

22 The new guidelines are designed to provide details on how the Commission foresees the new enforcement rules working in practice. The guidelines cover both substantive issues, such as guidance on self-assessment, and procedural issues, such as the handling of complaints.

23 Commission Notice on cooperation within the Network of Competition Authorities, OJ C 101/43, 27.04.2004.

inconsistencies particularly as certain authorities will develop the law on certain issues.[24] This may result in a reference to the ECJ to determine key issues, which can be a lengthy process.[25] Harmonising the approach and ensuring consistency throughout the EU will be a key task for the Commission and may lead to increased referrals, although it is hoped that this will be avoided. In any event, the fact that national authorities are applying articles 81 and 82 means that the body of competition law decisions in the telecoms sector is likely to increase.

APPLICATION OF ARTICLE 81 IN THE COMMUNICATIONS SECTOR

Application in the Traditional Telecoms Sector

2.17   The basic law on article 81 has been described above. The basic method for defining the relevant market has been set out in Chapter 1.[26] However, despite numerous cases on its general application, there have been relatively few Commission decisions in the telecoms sector under article 81.

2.18   Of the existing decisions under article 81,[27] a number have related to strategic alliances falling outside the ECMR including *BT/MCI,*[28] *Atlas,*[29] *Iridium,*[30] *Phoenix/GlobalOne,*[31] *Uniworld,*[32] *Unisource*[33] and *Cégétel and Télécom Developpement*[34] where the Commission granted negative clearance and/or individual exemption.[35] It also approved the *GSM MoU Standard International Roaming Agreement,*[36] which enables GSM mobile telephone users in one country to use networks in another country.[37]

---

24   One current example relates to the Commission's decision in Case COMP/38.233 – *Wanadoo Interactive*, not yet published (IP/03/1025, 16 July 2003). The UK telecoms regulator, the Office of Communications, took a decision on a substantially similar issue but applied its own principles/methodology rather than adopting the Commission's approach. Both decisions are on appeal.

25   It can take several years for the ECJ to render judgment.

26   See paras 1.75 et seq above. The methodology for defining the market is essentially the same for both arts 81 and 82 and establishing SMP although there are potentially some differences given the different aims involved.

27   There have been no 'cartel' decisions (although there have been 'dawn raids' – i e investigations by the Commission at the premises of undertakings *suspected* of infringing competition law). This could change in the future as the Commission has placed increased emphasis on pursuing cartels.

28   Case COMP/34.857, OJ L 223/36, 27.08.1994.

29   Case COMP/35.337, OJ L 239/23, 19.09.1996.

30   Case COMP/35.518, OJ L 16/87, 18.01.1997.

31   Case COMP/36.617, OJ L 239/57, 19.09.1996.

32   Case COMP/35.738, OJ L 318/24, 20.11.1997.

33   Case COMP/35.830, OJ L 318/1, 20.11.1997, this exemption decision was subsequently revoked and replaced with negative clearance due to changes in the market: see IP/01/1, 3 January 2001.

34   Case COMP/36.581 – *Télécom Developpement*, OJ L 218/24, 18.08.1999.

35   For a discussion of these cases, see *Scherer* (ed) Telecommunication Laws in Europe (4th ed, 1998), pp 45–49.

36   See Commission's XXVIIth *Annual Report on Competition Policy* (1997), point 75 and pp 139–140.

37   See also Access Notice, paras 131–143 for an indication of clauses in access agreements that may raise competition issues.

2.19   More recently, the Commission has assessed 3G network infrastructure-sharing agreements in the UK and Germany.[38] In 2003, the Commission concluded that the UK arrangements between O$_2$ and T-Mobile fell outside the scope of article 81(1) in part and otherwise benefited from article 81(3).[39] Similar findings were reached for Germany.[40] These decisions provide useful guidance as to the structuring and acceptability of such arrangements.

2.20   The Commission's investigation into the UK agreement (which had two main parts) found that the agreement on site sharing did not restrict competition because the coverage of the agreement was restricted to sharing basic network infrastructure such as masts, power supply, racking and cooling. The Commission was aware of the background to the agreement, noting that infrastructure sharing was widely promoted at both national and EU level for environmental and health reasons. The Commission also noted that network sharing involved varying degrees of cooperation, depending upon the amount of infrastructure shared:

- First level – the shared use of sites, ranging from individual mast sites to sharing of the grid.
- Second level – radio access network sharing, ie the sharing of initial transmission equipment.
- Third level – sharing the core network, including mobile switching centres and various databases, also referred to as the 'intelligent part' of the network.
- Fourth level – the sharing of radio frequencies.

2.21   The deeper the level of network sharing, the more significant the concern. In assessing the UK agreement, the Commission took the view that while site sharing can raise issues, in particular by reducing network competition, denying competitors access to necessary sites and site infrastructure and, in some cases, facilitating collusive behaviour, access to sites in this case was unlikely to be an issue. There were a number of reasons for this including the regulatory remedy available under article 12 Framework Directive. This allows Member States to impose the sharing of facilities as a remedy even if there is no dominance/SMP.[41] The Commission also took account of the fact that the parties were sharing a limited number of passive components of the access network. They retained independent control of their networks and the ability to differentiate services downstream. Further, the level of common costs[42] brought about by the site sharing was not significant. As a result, article 81(1) did not apply.

2.22   The analysis was different for the roaming arrangements. They were considered to restrict competition as they limited network-based competition with respect to coverage, retail prices, quality and transmission speeds. Nevertheless, the conditions of article 81(3) were satisfied. The agreement enabled the parties to have a greater density of coverage and a more extended footprint than they would have individually. Given that the parties compete with three other operators as well as MVNOs at the retail level, the agreement would lead to better and quicker 3G service coverage, with coverage accelerated in rural areas. National roaming in rural areas was therefore exempted until the end of 2008. The Commission also recognised the benefits of roaming in urban areas so long as it was limited to a short

---

38   O$_2$ and T-Mobile entered into agreements to share 3G site infrastructure and to roam on their networks in the UK and Germany.

39   Case COMP/38.370 – *O$_2$ UK Limited/T-Mobile UK Limited*, OJ L 200/59, 07.08.2003.

40   Case COMP/38.369 – *T-Mobile Deutschland/O$_2$ Germany*, OJ L 75/32, 12.03.2004.

41   For a more complete discussion, see para 1.89 above.

42   Often a factor in assessing the likelihood of coordination.

start-up period and helps new and innovative services to be available earlier to customers. Therefore reciprocal roaming in urban areas was exempted until the end of 2007.[43]

2.23   While the Commission's decision sets the parameters for assessing such 3G alliances, it is also a useful general guide to assessing infrastructure arrangements. The Commission sought to balance infrastructure competition and the immediate consumer benefits (faster roll-out). Nevertheless, the fact that the case related to 3G was an important policy consideration. The Commission's desire to promote 3G is also reflected in the fact that it granted clearance to a set of agreements aimed at giving 3G mobile equipment manufacturers better access to patents.[44]

2.24   Of some interest going forward is how national courts will apply article 81(3). As is highlighted by the above, the Commission has on many occasions entered into detailed discussions with the parties and then decided to close the case subject to significant amendments or granted an exemption subjects to conditions/ for a limited period. A court, on the other hand, may not be able to enter such discussions as it is required to assess the arrangement as presented. As such, an agreement which may have been valid in a slightly modified form, if discussed with the Commission in advance, may possibly be found by a court to infringe article 81. Alternatively, courts may be less interventionist than the Commission, seeking to preserve commercial arrangements in their entirety if possible.

Application in the Wider Communications Sector

2.25   While this chapter is focused on telecommunications, rather than broadcasting and interactive services, it is important to be aware of the approach adopted in such cases, whether under article 81, article 82 or the ECMR.

2.26   In terms of article 81, the Commission has examined issues raised by telecommunications operators seeking to expand into other areas in a number of cases, such as *British Interactive Broadcasting/Open*.[45] The case involved a joint venture between BT, BSkyB (the dominant pay-TV operator), HSBC and Matsushita. The aim of the JV was to provide digital interactive television services so that banks and retail shops could interact directly with customers. There would also be interactive television programmes and internet services. The case, which could easily have fallen within the scope of the ECMR (and also article 82), raised a number of issues, in particular the loss of competition in the supply of interactive digital services and in pay-TV. There were also concern over bottlenecks in the delivery of programme material. An exemption was granted on the basis of detailed conditions and obligations, including:

- restrictions on the ability of retailers to bundle BSkyB's pay-TV offering with the interactive set-top box;
- the disposal of BT's cable franchise;
- restrictions on the ability to cross-subsidise the price of the set-top box;
- conditions designed to protect the distributors of programme channels who use other platforms; and
- obligations to make set-top box interface information available to third parties in a timely manner.

---

43   This coincides with a condition of the 3G licence which requires the 3G network roll-out by each licensee to be such as to cover 80% of the population by the end of 2007.
44   IP/02/1651, 12 November 2002.
45   Case IV/36.539 – *British Interactive Broadcasting/Open*, OJ L 312/1, 6.12.1999.

2.27 Another key factor for electronic communications is content. Ensuring a level playing field as regards access to communication infrastructures is regarded by the Commission as a necessary condition for the development of competitive broadband services. However, the Commission recognises that this is not sufficient to guarantee that the potential of such services will be fully exploited to the benefit of consumers.

2.28 The Commission has noted that premium sport, feature films and music are generally regarded as classic examples of content which could boost the growth of innovative services through the internet and that premium sport seems also to be particularly well suited for distribution via 3G mobile services.

2.29 However, the Commission also notes that media rights-holders for popular sports events such as football are often reluctant to grant licences to new media operators since they fear that this could undermine the value of their TV rights.[46] In some instances the Commission notes that they have applied restrictions in the form of holdbacks, embargoes or bundling of TV rights with internet and/or UMTS rights, with (in the Commission's view) appreciable foreclosure effects. The Commission has had such factors in mind when examining a number of 'content' cases under article 81.

2.30 In *UEFA Champions League*,[47] the Commission challenged for the first time a joint selling scheme affecting competition on both the upstream market for the acquisition of football media rights and the downstream markets for the distribution of such a content via traditional media – TV and radio – and new platforms – UMTS and internet. An exemption decision was adopted in July 2003, following a settlement whereby UEFA undertook, *inter alia*, to make its rights available for internet operators and 3G mobile services, also allowing individual clubs to retail club-focused products through new media services. This example demonstrates the importance the Commission attaches to opening up equally for new media the access to premium content, which the Commission regards as a prerequisite for successful commercial development of broadband as well as 3G.

Similarly, in *DFB*,[48] the German Football League gave commitments to liberalise the joint selling of Bundesliga media rights. These were made legally binding by a Commission decision in January 2005. The commitments given by the German Football League ('Ligaverband') related to the central marketing of the media rights of the Bundesliga and the 2. Bundesliga until June 2009. They were rendered legally binding by a formal decision adopted by the Commission, the first ever so-called 'commitment decision' under the new procedures under Regulation 1/2003 that entered into effect on 1 May 2004. The commitments liberalise the central marketing arrangements and maximise the rights for television and new media (UMTS, internet) available to football fans. The Commission had been concerned that the exclusive selling of commercial broadcasting rights by the 'Ligaverband' may have violated article 81 but has now closed the case in the light of the 'Ligaverband' commitments.[49]

---

46 This has led to a sectoral inquiry into 3G content: see http://europa.eu.int/comm/competition/antitrust/others/sector_inquiries/new_media/3g/.

47 COMP/C.2–37.398 – *Joint selling of the commercial rights of the UEFA Champions League*, OJ L 291/25, 8.11.2003.

48 Case COMP/C.2/37.214 – *Joint selling of the media rights to the German Bundesliga*, OJ L 134/46, 19.1.2005.

49 For earlier cases, see, for example, *Screensport* (OJ L 63/32, 1999) and *EBU/Eurovision System* (Case IV/32.150, OJ L 179/23, 11.6.1993). The latter exemption decision was quashed by the

APPLICATION OF ARTICLE 82 IN THE COMMUNICATIONS SECTOR

Application in the Traditional Telecoms Sector

2.31   Chapter 1[50] sets out the method for assessing a dominant position/SMP. The Commission guidelines on market analysis are a detailed and informative guide to market definition, single firm dominance and collective dominance in the light of previous cases relevant to the telecoms sector.

2.32   In terms of Commission decisions, there has been a significant escalation of enforcement policy under article 82 in the telecoms sector, illustrated by *Wanadoo*[51] and *Deutsche Telekom*[52] in 2003, where the Commission issued the first infringement decisions in the telecoms sector for over 20 years. Perhaps surprisingly, given the Access Notice[53] and the nature of telecoms networks, there has been no abuse case in the telecoms sector relying on the doctrine of essential facilities that has resulted in a decision[54] (and there is not likely to be one in the future given the remedies available under the new regulatory framework). The notion of an essential facility has, however, been referred to in merger cases, such as *WorldCom/MCI (II)*.[55]

2.33   The previous abuse case was in 1982 against BT[56] when it was still a State monopoly: the Commission held that BT breached article 82 with regard to the restrictions it imposed on message-forwarding agencies in the UK. The case

---

CFI on appeal in *Metropole Television v Commission* ([1996] ECR II-649). The system was then re-notified resulting in a further exemption decision (Case IV/32.150, OJ L 151/18, 10.5.2000). The Commission reasoned that the joint acquisition of broadcasting rights, the sharing of products amongst the members of the European Broadcasting Union within the Eurovision System as well as the exchange of the Eurovision signal fell within article 81(1) but deserved an exemption under article 81(3).

50   See para 1.73 above.

51   Case COMP/38.233 – *Wanadoo Interactive,* not yet published (IP/03/1025, 16 July 2003). This is on appeal to the CFI, Case T-340/03.

52   Case COMP/37.451 – *Deutsche Telekom* AG, OJ L 263/9, 14.10.2003. This is on appeal to the CFI, Case T-271/03.

53   At paras 49–53 and 87–98.

54   There are numerous articles considering the notion in the light of *Oscar Bronner*. cf *Nikoliakos* 'Access Agreements in the Telecommunications Sector – Refusal to Supply and the Essential Facilities Doctrine under EC Competition Law' (1999) 20 ECLR 399 and *Scherer* 'Das Bronner-Urteil des EuGH und die Essential facilities-Doktrin im TK-Sektor' [1999] MMR 315–321.

55   Case IV/M.1069 – *WorldCom/MCI (II)*, OJ L 116/1, 4.5.1999, para 126, where the Commission reasoned: 'Because of the specific features of network competition and the existence of network externalities which make it valuable for customers to have access to the largest network, MCI WorldCom's position can hardly be challenged once it has obtained a dominant position. The more its network grows, the less need it has to interconnect with competitors and the more need they have to interconnect with the merged entity. Furthermore, the larger its network becomes, the greater is its ability to control a significant element of the costs of any new entrant. It can achieve this by denying such entrants the opportunity to peer and insisting that they remain as customers and pay a margin accordingly for all the services they want to offer. The merger could thus have the effect of raising entry barriers still higher. Indeed, it could be argued that, as a result of the merger, the MCI WorldCom network would constitute, either immediately or in a relatively short time thereafter, an essential facility, to which all other ISPs would have no choice but to interconnect (directly or indirectly) in order to offer a credible internet access service.'

56   Case COMP/29.877 – *British Telecommunications*, OJ L 360/36, 21.12.1982.

concerned BT's attempts to comply with the regulations of the International Telecommunication Union ('ITU'). With reference to recommendations issued by the International Telegraph and Telephone Consultative Committee, one of the permanent organs of the ITU, BT further developed its 'Scheme' restricting the ability of message-forwarding agencies to offer their services as an intermediary where a message originating outside the UK was being sent on to a non-UK destination. This Scheme was supported by a written request from BT to the message-forwarding agencies requiring that they provide a written assurance that they would refrain from offering such services. The Commission found that BT's practices prejudiced customers located in other Member States, placed message-forwarding agencies in the UK at a competitive disadvantage vis-à-vis their counterparts in other Member States, limited the development of new markets and new technology and restricted trade between Member States. No fine was imposed due to the circumstances of the case, including the pressure exerted upon BT by other national telecommunication authorities. (The appeal of this decision in *Italy v Commission*[57] arguably acted as the catalyst for the subsequent liberalisation of the sector by the Commission.)

2.34 The Commission's decisions need to be seen in context. One of the driving forces behind the increased activity is the Commission's desire to see a competitive market in broadband. It is also concerned by the failure of 'local loop' unbundling.[58] More generally, the Commission's decisions can be seen as a 'push', alongside the new regulatory framework, to ensure that the sector is fully liberalised *and* that competition law is in practice acting as the 'punishment' for infringements.

2.35 Much of the focus has been on pricing abuses. *Wanadoo* and *Deutsche Telekom* illustrate the determination of the Commission to address pricing issues even in a sector subject to ex-ante regulation and where the Member States play an important role in the setting of prices. The Commission sees these cases as particularly significant because the communications infrastructure is often owned and controlled by the former State monopolist that is also active in the relevant downstream (often retail) market. There is therefore significant scope for pricing abuse by way of predation or margin squeeze.

2.36 In *Deutsche Telekom*, the Commission held that Deutsche Telekom ('DT') was engaging in a margin squeeze by charging new entrants higher fees for wholesale access to the local loop than that which subscribers had to pay for retail lines. This discouraged new entry and reduced the choice of suppliers of services as well as price competition. The Commission found an abusive margin squeeze because the difference between DT's retail and wholesale prices was either negative or slightly positive, but in any case insufficient to cover DT's costs of providing its

---

57 ECJ Judgment of 20 March 1985, Case 41/83, *Italian Republic v Commission* [1985] ECR 873, see in particular para. 20 and 22. The fact that BT was a statutory monopoly did not prevent the application of the competition rules.

58 This is despite the Commission's communication of September 2000 on 'Unbundled access to the local loop: enabling the competitive provision of a full range of electronic communication services, including broadband multimedia and high-speed internet' OJ C 272/55, 23.9.2000. See in particular, section 3.2 and section 4. Section 4 sets out the duty of the dominant operator under competition rules to grant access to the local loop and indicates the possible abuses that may occur if not (refusal to deal, discrimination and limitation of production, markets or technical development to the prejudice of consumers).

own retail services. The Commission's review[59] revealed that from 1998 to 2000, DT charged competitors more for unbundled access at the wholesale level than it charged its own subscribers for access at the retail level. The Commission rejected DT's argument that the prices were set by the German regulator ('RegTP'), and hence it was not responsible.[60] It considered DT had sufficient freedom of choice in the setting of its prices to avoid the margin squeeze.

2.37   Notably, the Commission seems to have examined the issue of abuse on the basis of total costs, not just incremental costs, without needing further evidence of adverse impact on the market/anti-competitive intent. Generally, in predatory pricing cases, the Commission has looked at variable costs/incremental costs[61] as well as total costs in order to establish an abuse. It is only if pricing is below average variable/incremental cost that an abuse is clearly established; if above variable but below total costs, evidence of anti-competitive intent is needed (the '*AKZO* test').[62] In *Deutsche Telekom*, the Commission appears to have said that if there is pricing below cost (possibly even total costs but above incremental cost) in a margin squeeze situation, this is sufficient to establish a material adverse effect on competition and hence an abuse.

2.38   While some (no doubt including DT)[63] will consider this an unmeritorious *per se* application of the competition rules that ignores economic effects, the Commission's approach is perhaps justifiable, at least in this case. A margin squeeze can be profitable for the vertically integrated firm indefinitely but yet produce anti-competitive effects in the longer term. As such, it may be legitimate in vertical margin squeeze cases to put the burden on the dominant firm to show that there is an objective justification for its pricing below total cost. If not, it could set the price at a level that raises no immediate issues but which, over time, will distort and hinder competition.

2.39   DT settled a subsequent Commission investigation into an alleged abuse of dominance by making commitments as to its future behaviour.[64] The investigation had been triggered by a complaint from a German provider, QSC. QSC complained that DT was imposing a margin squeeze between its retail tariffs for ADSL broadband internet connections and the corresponding wholesale tariffs for line sharing, allowing DT to become a quasi-monopolist for ADSL services in Germany. The Commission accepted DT's commitment to significantly reduce line-sharing fees and closed the investigation.

2.40   In *Wanadoo*, the Commission fined Wanadoo €10.35 million for predatory pricing. The decision, which is on appeal, is of importance in that it clarifies how

---

59   The Commission compared the tariffs for wholesale access to the local loop with those of a number of different retail offers (analogue, ISDN and ADSL) by using a weighted approach, taking into account the number of customers.

60   This is an argument often raised by dominant firms. However, the State compulsion defence (or State defence doctrine), as it is known, rarely succeeds in competition cases. There have been no decisions to date where the defence has been successful (although this reflects, to a limited degree, the enforcement practice where the defence is successful).

61   The Commission looks at incremental costs in the telecommunications sector as it considers that a price which equates to the variable cost of a service may be substantially lower than the price the operator needs in order to cover the cost of providing the service: see Access Notice, para 114.

62   See ECJ Judgment of 3 July 1991, Case C-62/86, *Akzo Chemie BV v Commission* [1991] ECR I-3359.

63   Indeed, Deutsche Telekom is appealing the decision (see Case T-271/03).

64   IP/04/281, 1 March 2004.

the *AKZO* test for predatory pricing is to be applied in emerging market cases. The decision states that the *AKZO* test applies in full, subject to the acquisition costs and revenue for new customers being spread over the lifetime of the subscriber acquired. This is highly significant for incumbents considering pricing strategies in emerging markets. Furthermore, the Commission appears to reject in principle certain economic methodologies for the assessment of pricing abuses (in particular, 'discounted cash-flow' models) as they can conceal periods of predatory pricing. The Commission also rejected various justifications advanced for Wanadoo's pricing below cost, such as a desire to grow the market, 'learning by doing' and future economies of scale.[65]

2.41   The relationship between the various types of possible price abuse (cross-subsidy, margin squeeze, discrimination, predation and excessive pricing) is complicated as, indeed, is the precise nature of the legal tests. Various possibilities exist. One can argue that a cross-subsidy is at most only an abuse in the limited circumstances set down by the Court of First Instance.[66] In terms of the relationship between margin squeeze and predation, some may argue that a margin squeeze is a particular form of predation that can be exercised by a vertically integrated dominant firm. If so, the analysis and outcome should be the same as if *AKZO* and *Wanadoo* were applied direct. Others would argue that they are distinct, but related abuses – with margin squeeze being a more long-term pricing strategy – hence they should be assessed separately. If so, there are a number of possible grounds of distinction, including:

- margin squeeze is appropriate where the downstream business is 100% owned,[67] and
- a margin squeeze exists only where there is an 'essential input' either in the sense of essential for certain competitors or an 'essential facility'.

2.42   There are also additional issues, such as what is the relevant cost floor for assessing a margin squeeze? As indicated above, one can argue that, for vertically integrated dominant firms, pricing below total costs is presumed to be abusive[68] given that a margin squeeze can be a long term, profitable strategy to drive out competitors. Some would say that the test for margin squeeze is, or should be based upon, the costs of the reasonably efficient competitor, while others argue that this is impractical and one must look at the dominant firm's own costs.[69] Some even argue that both the costs of the dominant firm and the reasonably efficient operator must be looked at.[70] The law in this area is unclear. It is possible that one of the current appeals, whether at national or EU level, may give some clarity.

---

65   A similar case is also before the UK national authorities (*Wanadoo UK plc v The Office of Communications*).

66   Namely, where there has been the acquisition of something where the funds used were derived from excessive or discriminatory prices or from other unfair practices in a reserved market by the undertaking holding the monopoly (CFI Judgment of 20 March 2002, Case T-175/99, *UPS Europe v Commission*, [2002] ECR II-1915, paras 61 to 64); cf *Whish*, Competition Law, (5th ed, 2003), p 710.

67   This implies that in all other ownership structures, even if there is sole control as in *Wanadoo*, the appropriate analysis is one of predation.

68   Deutsche Telekom, para 179.

69   See also Access Notice, paras 117–119.

70   See *Grout*, Defining a Price Squeeze in Competition Law, in The Pros and Cons of Low Prices, (Swedish Competition Authority, 2003), p 85.

2.43   The Commission has also taken enforcement action against Telia Sonera (Sweden) for having abused a dominant position in the provision of high-speed internet access.[71] This relates to infrastructure competition rather than retail competition. The matter concerns a contract for the construction and operation of a fibre-optic broadband network on behalf of a regional housing association. The Commission took the view that Telia Sonera's bid for the contract was intentionally set below cost and did not allow the operator to recover the investments and expenses claimed for the provision of infrastructures and services contained in the contract. In so doing, Telia Sonera prevented the development of alternative infrastructure and the entry of competing service providers, thereby strengthening its dominant position in the markets for the provision of local broadband infrastructure and the provision of high-speed internet access. While no decision has yet been reached, the case illustrates the importance of broadband to the Commission on a policy level – it is taking action in seemingly local cases to pursue its wider objective of promoting competitive broadband.

2.44   Call termination on the mobile network is also an important issue. The Commission issued a statement of objections against KPN in March 2002[72] alleging that KPN abused its dominant position regarding the termination of telephone calls on the KPN mobile network through discriminatory or otherwise unfair behaviour. Studies showed that fixed to mobile termination rates in Europe could be ten times higher than the average charge for fixed to fixed interconnection. The Commission considered that this results in undue barriers for newcomers to the market and high prices for consumers. It therefore decided to take action.

2.45   The KPN case followed the Commission's identification of the mobile call termination market as a source of concern. However, the Commission is often willing to take a pragmatic view. No action was taken in the German call termination market, for example, due to a 50% reduction in rates by the German operators.[73]

2.46   More recently, the Commission has challenged UK international roaming rates. In July 2004, the Commission announced that it had sent two statements of objections to the mobile network operators O$_2$ and Vodafone under article 82. The objections relate to the rates that both O$_2$ and Vodafone charged other Mobile Network Operators ('MNOs') for international roaming services at the wholesale level. Other MNOs needed to roam on O$_2$'s and Vodafone's UK networks in order to enable their own subscribers to use their mobile phones in the UK. The Commission's investigation revealed that Vodafone, since 1997 through to at least the end of September 2003, exploited its dominant position in the UK market for the provision of international roaming services at the wholesale level on its own network (otherwise known as 'inter-operator tariffs' or IOTs). The abuse consisted of charging unfair and excessive prices to European MNOs.[74]

---

71   Case COMP/37.663 – *B2/Telia* (IP/03/1797, 19 December 2003).

72   Case COMP/37.704 – *MCI/Mobile Termination Rates* (IP/02/483, 27 March 2002).

73   In Sweden, where there was also a complaint, the national authority dealt with the case. In contrast, the UK dealt with similar issues under the licensing provisions by way of an inquiry by the Competition Commission. This resulted in a price cap but no fine.

74   The Commission concluded that each individual network constituted a separate market. The level of IOTs was high particularly compared to the prices charged for similar calls made on their networks by UK subscribers of Independent Service Providers to whom both O$_2$ and Vodafone had supplied wholesale airtime access. Vodafone and O$_2$ now have a chance to respond. See IP/04/994, 26 July 2004.

2.47   Since 1 May 2004, NCAs have been obliged to apply article 82 EC Treaty whenever they apply national competition law to any abuse prohibited by article 82 (the position is similar under article 81 EC Treaty). NCAs have started to utilise these powers. For example, the UK's Office of Communications ('OFCOM') has issued a Statement of Objections against BT for an alleged pricing abuse.[75] Likewise, the Swedish Competition Authority has filed suit against TeliaSonera for allegedly carrying out a margin squeeze on ADSL high-speed internet connections.[76] The Italian Antitrust Authority ('IAA') opened an investigation on 23 February 2005 in relation to Telecom Italia Mobile ('TIM'), Vodafone Omnitel ('Vodafone') and Wind Telecommunicazioni ('Wind') to ascertain whether they had violated articles 81 and 82. The case is particularly interesting in that it raises the issue of abuse of a collective dominant position. The IAA is considering the following:[77]

- whether TIM, Vodafone and Wind, which together hold a dominant position over network infrastructure, abused their collective dominance by refusing to negotiate access agreements with the aim of preventing entry to the mobile communications services retail market by any alternative operators, including MVNOs (Mobile Virtual Network Operators), ESPs (Enhanced Service Providers) and Resellers. The IAA is also considering whether such conduct, performed homogeneously and simultaneously by all three mobile telephony operators against all the applicant operators, might also evidence/constitute an anti-competitive agreement.
- whether TIM, Vodafone and Wind, each of which has a dominant position over their own mobile networks, may have abused that position by allegedly charging their competitors higher prices for their landline-mobile termination services than those charged to their own business customers for the whole integrated landline-mobile service. More specifically, TIM, Vodafone and Wind are alleged to offer favourable financial or technical terms and conditions to their own commercial divisions for the sale of terminal services, designed to exclude competitors from the business customer integrated services market, in violation of article 82.
- whether the three mobile operators have engaged in commercial practices designed to prevent telecommunications operators from using business contracts to re-sell services to their end customers, thereby preventing any kind of competition on the mobile services retail market, in violation of article 81.
- whether the fact that TIM and Vodafone charge almost identical prices for certain commercial offerings to their business customers also constitutes a violation of article 81.

2.48   Decisions of the NCAs will need to be monitored both for developments in the law and as an early sign of possible similar cases elsewhere, given the network of authorities that exists.[78] It may be that some issues previously considered by the

---

75   See OFCOM press release of 1 September 2004.
76   See Swedish Competition Authority press release of 15 December 2004.
77   See press release, A357, Tele2/TIM-Vodafone-Wind, 1 March 2005.
78   See also the IAA's decision to fine Telecom Italia €152 million for abuse of dominance under national legislation (IAA press release, Case A351, Telecom Italia, 19 November 2004). This has apparently been quashed by the Tribunale Amministrativo Regionale del Lazio (20 May 2005) although is likely to be appealed by the IAA. The Spanish competition authority has also fined Telefonica for abusing a dominant position. The Spanish Competition Tribunal

Commission but not pursued (such as SIM locking, which arguably could only be a problem in terms of abuse of dominance) may be re-examined by NCAs.[79]

Application in the Wider Communications Sector

2.49   The recent *Microsoft* case[80] is likely to be influential in the analysis of tying. The Commission found that Microsoft had tied its Windows Media Player to the Windows operating system. By offering the two as a package there was no incentive for competitors to develop alternative media players. Capturing this market also enabled Microsoft to control related markets in the digital media sector. As well as being heavily fined, Microsoft has been obliged to offer manufacturers a version of the Windows PC operating system without the Windows Media Player attached as a result.[81]

2.50   Microsoft has been a significant source of decisions and actions under article 82. Following an investigation under the ECMR into its proposed acquisition of joint control of Telewest, the UK cable franchise (subsequently aborted) the Commission used article 82 to look at other Microsoft investments. As a result, Microsoft agreed not to influence the technology decisions of European digital cable operators.[82] The Commission's comments on the settlement are informative and reflect the Commission's desire to use competition law to avoid or negate bottlenecks in emerging markets. The Commission stated that it recognised that digital TV is expected to become the most widespread means for consumers to access entertainment, education, news and e-commerce as well as digital TV programmes. In this respect, the Commission expected that cable operators will offer consumers a full range of advanced broadband communications services considered vital for the development of the Information Society in Europe. The investigation aimed to ensure that the technology decisions of cable operators were made on merit and that suppliers of set-top box technology could compete with Microsoft on equal terms. The Commission closed the investigation on the basis that Microsoft and its strategic allies agreed to abolish or change their so-called 'Technology Boards' so that the recommendations were no longer binding.

2.51   The investigation flowed from the previous year's Microsoft/Telewest investigation. This concerned Microsoft's strategic investments in other leading European broadband cable operators: Dutch-based UPC, NTL of Britain and TV Cabo of Portugal. These operators provide a wide range of services to businesses and consumers, including digital television, interactive services and high-speed internet access. In addition, NTL and UPC also offer cable telephony services. In two of these companies (UPC and NTL), the investment was accompanied by the setting up of a joint 'Technology Board' that made binding recommendations as to the technology decisions of the cable company.

---

fined Telefónica de España SA €57 million for abuse of its dominant position in the telecoms market. The fine, publicised on 13 April, is the largest the Tribunal has imposed. This is in fact Telefónica's tenth fine from the Tribunal.

79   The Commission did previously issues a press release on SIM locking in the mid 1990's but did not specify the legal basis for its concerns.

80   Case COMP/37.792 – *Microsoft/ W2000* (IP/04/382, 24 March 2004).

81   The CFI rejected Microsoft's application for suspension of the remedies imposed by the Commission on 22 December 2004, MEMO/04/305. The main action for annulment by Microsoft still awaits judgment – see Case T-201/04 R, *Microsoft v Commission*, Order of the President of the CFI, available on the Court's website.

82   See Commission press release IP/01/569, 18 April 2001. The press release does not specify the legal basis for the investigation but it is likely to have been under article 82.

2.52 In order to avoid discussions on the status and powers of these 'Technology Boards', Microsoft agreed with one cable operator to abolish the Technology Board completely and with the other to change the Technology Board into an Industry Technology Forum that was equally open for competing suppliers of set-top box technology.

2.53 The Commission accepted these modifications. The Commission stated that it did not want to prevent the companies from buying the new Microsoft products for digital interactive television, only to make sure that new technologies are brought to the consumers on fair and equal terms, referring to the need in emerging markets to ensure that there are no supply bottlenecks. The Commission reasoned that, as final consumers cannot decide on the software and the digital services that are delivered to their homes via the set-top boxes, it is of the utmost importance that cable operators are able to make technology decisions on the basis of fair and equal competition.

SECTORAL ENQUIRIES

2.54 The Commission also has power to launch sectoral investigations. While rarely used prior to the recent decision to launch investigations into energy, insurance and banks, this power was utilised in 1999 when the Commission launched an inquiry in the telecoms sector.[83] This concerned three issues: leased lines, mobile roaming services and the local loop. It was only the third occasion on which the Commission had initiated an investigation under the provision.[84] The leased line investigation ended in 2002, as a result of substantial price decreases.[85] The *Wanadoo* case arose out of the Commission's sectoral inquiry into the unbundling of the local loop.

2.55 As illustrated by its recent decision to launch a number of investigations, the power to conduct sectoral enquiries is likely to be used by the Commission more regularly going forward across all sectors as the Commission has recognised that there are certain aspects of markets that may not work effectively. The Modernisation Regulation provides a basis for sectoral enquiries and the Commission has indicated it may make greater use of such powers. However, given the new regulatory framework, it may be that the Commission will also look to the market reviews to identify and consider issues in the communications sector. Nevertheless, its current inquiry into 3G media content demonstrates that they will still have relevance.[86] The preliminary issues paper[87] identified two scenarios of undesirable market practices arising as a result of certain commercial practices, namely:

- *Scenario 1* – a situation in which all 3G operators find it difficult to obtain competitive access to 3G sports rights, and hence cannot develop an attractive sports content offering. This may hinder the development of 3G as a whole.

---

83 Under article 12 of the old Regulation 17/62.

84 See the Commission's XXIXth *Report on Competition Policy* (1999), points 74–76; see further the XXXth Report (2000), points 157–160 and XXXIst Report (2001), points 125–131; speech by Sauter 'The Sector Inquiries into Leased Lines and Mobile Roaming: Findings and follow-up of the competition law investigations' 17 September 2001, available at http://europa.eu.int/comm/competition/speeches/text/sp2001_016_en.pdf.

85 See IP/02/1852, 11 December 2002; details of the leased line inquiries can be found at: http://europa.eu.int/comm/competition/antitrust/others/sector_inquiries/leased_lines/.

86 See Commission press release IP/04/134, 30.1.2004. Commissioner Kroes has also signalled that a sectoral investigation will occur in the future.

87 May 2005.

- *Scenario 2* – a situation in which only one or a few mobile operators obtain a strong market position that will be reinforced as 3G develops further, thus making it increasingly difficult for other mobile operators to enter the market or compete successfully. This situation can be described as a lack of development of competition within the 3G New Media platform.

2.56   The Commission's analysis of the data collected indicated that these undesirable outcomes are arising in practice, due to:

- lack of access to sports content for mobile operators (given that sports content is one of the main drivers for new platforms);
- exclusive access to premium content – exclusive access can, if the content is a sufficiently strong driver of demand, contribute to operators obtaining or protecting positions of significant market power in the retail markets;
- cross-platform bundling of rights – likely to prevent mobile operators from purchasing rights, as the value of the TV rights is likely to be several times higher;
- the effects of collective selling – collective selling has been associated with concerns raised by mobile operators, although other factors, such as the degree of vertical integration, have played an additional role;
- pricing practices for mobile rights – e g rights sold on a fixed rate (lump sum) basis or excessive pricing. These could distort competition between mobile operators and cause competitive harm to 3G and other distribution platforms; and
- coverage restrictions – restrictions with regard to timing (leading to deferred transmission) are regarded as disproportionate given that there is little evidence of direct substitution between TV rights and mobile rights.

2.57   The inquiry is ongoing, with a public presentation having been held on 27 May 2005.

RELATIONSHIP OF COMPETITION LAW WITH THE NEW REGULATORY FRAMEWORK

2.58   A significant issue going forward is the interrelationship between competition law and the new regulatory framework. There is clear scope for overlap and many points of interaction. Indeed, some authorities with dual powers may consider they are taking a decision within the regulatory regime but yet reach a decision under the competition rules. Set out below are a number of factors in considering the relationship between the two.

Impact of the New Regulatory Framework on Conditions of Competition

2.59   The new regulatory framework will impact on the assessment of the conditions of competition. The 3G network sharing cases[88] demonstrate that the new regulatory framework, including the availability of remedies thereunder, will be taken into account in assessing whether any competition issue arises.

---

88   See paras 2.19–2.23 above.

Relationship of Underlying Objectives

2.60   The new regulatory framework and competition law have different aims. A clear understanding of this is vital given the similar concepts used. Article 8 Framework Directive sets out the policy objectives and regulatory principles that NRAs must take the 'utmost account of' (article 7(1)) in carrying out their tasks.[89] Article 8(2) states that NRAs 'shall promote competition' by, inter alia:

- ensuring that users derive maximum benefit in terms of choice, price and quality,
- ensuring that there is no distortion or restriction of competition,
- encouraging efficient investment in infrastructure and promoting innovation, and
- encouraging efficient use and ensuring the effective management of radio frequencies and numbering resources.

2.61   As previously stated, 'competition' is the central theme. However, the key difference is that the NRAs under the new regulatory framework have wide latitude to *promote* competition, not just see that there are no restrictive agreements or abusive practices as in the competition law field. In other words, competition law seeks to restrain dominant firms and anti-competitive practices; the new regulatory framework seeks to eliminate dominance or at least reduce the ability of the dominant firm to exercise its market power. This is, in effect, a continuation of the underlying policy of telecoms liberalisation (including the old regulatory framework), namely, a desire to tip the market in favour of new entrants and other operators as opposed to the incumbents, but it is much more explicit.

Consistency of Concepts

2.62   Given the general alignment of concepts, a mechanism to try and ensure consistency was necessary. Just before the new regulatory framework was transposed, the then Commissioners Liikanen and Monti said that the new consultation proceedings under article 7 Framework Directive (the 'article 7 mechanism') will 'take the best of both competition law and sector specific legislation. National regulators will apply the resulting principles in a coherent manner aimed at stimulating the growth and development of a wide variety of electronic communications'. The Commission also stated that it attributes great importance to the article 7 mechanism and DG Competition and DG Information Society will 'jointly enjoy and exercise the review power vis-à-vis regulator's regulatory measures given to the Commission'.[90]

2.63   More generally, the Commission envisages that the new regulatory framework will roll back ex-ante regulation as competition becomes effective. This is perhaps a reflection of the fact that regulation in the sector has become a patchwork of often piece-meal remedies that are not based on sound economic analysis (in replacing these with a coherent system, the new regulatory framework should also in theory create a more level playing field across the EU). In seeking to roll-back regulation and rely on competition law, the Commission recognises that there is a need for consistency of interpretation in both areas. An operator will in general be subject to relevant regulatory obligations only if it is designated as

---

89   For a more in-depth discussion of the Framework Directive, see paras 1.48–1.90 above.
90   IP/03/1012, 14 July 2003.

having SMP.[91] An operator is deemed to have SMP if it is in a dominant position (article 14(2) Framework Directive). Whether operators are faced with ex-ante regulation or find themselves involved in ex-post antitrust proceedings they should have the legal certainty that issues such as 'relevant market' and 'market power' will have the same meaning irrespective of whether the proceedings in question are initiated by national regulators or competition authorities. Such consistency is provided for in article 15 Framework Directive.[92]

Tensions

2.64 Notwithstanding the proposed consistency of concepts, there are a number of tensions and issues that could arise. One such issue relates to the 'recommended markets' that have been identified in the EU regulatory framework.[93] Under competition law and the new regulatory framework, the definition of the relevant market rests on the same economic principles. By setting out a list of 'recommended markets' (Annex 1 Framework Directive) there is a danger that these will become the 'default' market definition even though they may not align with the true economic markets (although this would breach the Directive). If so, this would result in either false positives – ie a finding of SMP and hence a remedy where there is in fact no dominance – or false negatives – ie too wide a market definition and hence no finding of SMP even though it actually exists. While some NRAs have closely followed the recommended markets, others, such as the UK's Ofcom, have readily departed, albeit generating comment from the Commission. This is illustrated by the letter from the Commission to Ofcom, dated 5 February 2004, pursuant to article 7(3) Framework Directive,[94] where the Commission criticised Ofcom's definition of the market relating to wholesale broadband, in particular, its reliance on indirect pricing constraints. The Commission did not veto the measure as Ofcom found SMP to exist in any event.

'Precedent Value' of Market Reviews?

2.65 The definition(s) adopted in the market reviews under the new regulatory framework will be likely adopted under any subsequent competition investigations, notwithstanding comments that the market definition may differ on an ex-ante and ex-post basis. While competition authorities are legally required to examine the issue of market definition afresh in every case,[95] it is perhaps natural that the conclusion reached in the market reviews under the new regulatory framework will heavily influence the definition used in subsequent competition cases. In the UK, for example, Oftel/Ofcom has already adopted decisions that are based on relevant markets determined in its market reviews.

2.66 This view is supported by the Commission's announcement of concern over, for example, the Austrian market review of transit services in the fixed public

---

91 Certain others will of course apply in any event. For a more detailed consideration of the concept of SMP in the regulatory framework, see paras 1.68–1.78 above.
92 Many NRAs may need some time to adapt to this way of thinking.
93 For a fuller explanation of 'recommended markets' under the Framework Directive, see para 1.75 above.
94 In cases UK/2003/0032–34.
95 CFI Judgment of 22 March 2000, Joined Cases T-125/97 and T-127/97, *The Coca-Cola Company and Coca-Cola Enterprises Inc v Commission* [2000] ECR II-1733, para 82.

telephone network.[96] The Commission expressed serious doubts about the evidence used to define the market and the Austrian authority's conclusions on SMP. A second phase investigation was opened into the compatibility of the market review with articles 7 and 8 Framework Directive.[97] This case, as well as the Commission's veto of certain reviews by the Finnish NRA, clearly illustrates the seriousness with which market reviews are being treated. A significant recent case is the Commission's veto of the decision by the German regulator (RegTP) on call termination in fixed telephone networks. The RegTP concluded that the alternative fixed network operators did not have SMP despite having 100% of the market (essentially, relating to own infrastructure/customers) because of the countervailing bargaining power of Deutsche Telekom. However, the Commission considered that the RegTP had not provided sufficient evidence to rebut the presumption of dominance, given the high market share, particularly given that the Commission is very concerned about termination rates.[98]

Roll-back of Ex-ante Regulation

2.67 If effective, the sector-specific legislation would ultimately lead to further deregulation, limiting the scope of ex-ante regulation to an area where competition law instruments cannot be effectively applied. This is the logical consequence of the changed definition of 'SMP' under the old and new regulatory frameworks (see also discussion on remedies below).[99] However, many consider that this is some way off and could cite the likely imposition of SMP remedies on the alternative fixed network operators in Germany as an example (although the Commission has pointed out that the RegTP had been de facto imposing regulation by way of dispute resolution even without finding SMP).

Relationship of Antitrust and Regulatory Remedies

2.68 Another issue is the relationship between regulatory remedies and remedies under antitrust enforcement. As indicated above, regulatory remedies are relevant for assessing competition issues. In terms of the remedies themselves, the regulatory remedies have a wider remit due to the nature of article 8, ie the *promotion* of competition not just preventing restrictions etc. The previous Competition Commissioner, Mario Monti, has already indicated what he perceives as the key distinction, namely:

- Regulation is, by definition, an ex-ante type of intervention. Remedies imposed under regulatory intervention have the specific remit to allow competition to develop, and to increase the competitive conditions in any market in a self-sustaining manner. Their aim is, or should be, creating a pro-competitive environment in the long term, while at the same time providing, in the shorter term, the benefits to end users which the market would offer if it were effectively competitive.
- Antitrust remedies, on the other hand, have purely the objective of punishing forms of behaviour which have occurred in the past, and which are seen as

---

96   Invitation to comment, published 25 August 2004.
97   The Commission has twice previously vetoed draft measures, each time in cases notified by the Finnish NRA.
98   See Commission press release IP/05/564, 17 May 2005 and MEMO/05/162.
99   See paras 254–258.

detrimental for the welfare of citizens/users. They assume that competitive conditions are already developed and that market structures would not be automatically conducive to their degradation.

2.69   Monti noted that there are, however, specific areas in antitrust enforcement which are closer to regulation in relation to the nature of the remedies imposed. Remedies under merger control are, for example, ex-ante by definition, and offer a wider range of types of intervention than conventional antitrust, including divestiture. Similarly, access remedies under the doctrine of essential facilities[100] (developed under article 82) may be seen as closer to regulation. (It seems unlikely that future essential facilities cases in the telecoms sector would be brought under the antitrust rules, as opposed to being dealt with under the new regulatory framework, given the straightforward nature of the remedy available under article 12 Framework Directive.)

2.70   From the Commission's perspective, the relationship between antitrust and regulatory remedies is particularly significant because it informs policy decisions. In a way, the aim of regulatory remedies should be to allow antitrust remedies to be the only ones needed in the long term. For those parts of the industry which can be characterised as natural monopolies, this may be difficult to achieve. However, as technology develops, the Commission (or at least DG Competition) considers that regulatory intervention should increasingly play a smaller role.

2.71   In considering such matters, the Commission recognises that there is a balance to be found between short-term needs and longer-term considerations (this is one of the reasons why the issue of regulatory remedies under the new regulatory framework sparked heated discussions). An obvious example is the debate between those who advocate a facilities-based model of competition (referred to in article 8(2)(6) Framework Directive), and those who advocate a model of competition based on access. However, there is not necessarily a contradiction between access-based and facilities-based competition. Access services are essential in the opening up of previously monopolistic market structures. Competition would never be able to develop, in the short term, if entrants were not able to gain access to the incumbent operator's network to start offering services. In fact, the 'liberalisation' of network industries, vigorously pursued by the Commission in a number of areas, would never take place without access obligations.

2.72   Nevertheless, there is a valid concern about providing the right incentives to new entrants. In the longer term, the Commission recognises that in accordance with article 8 Framework Directive, the regulatory framework should privilege operators which base their competitive advantage on building their own infrastructure as such operators are more likely to improve the competitive conditions of the market by changing its structure. In order to reconcile access-based and facilities-based competition, the Commission is of the view that the time dimension must be considered. NRAs should provide incentives for competitors to seek access from the incumbent in the shorter term, and to rely increasingly more on building their own infrastructure in the longer term.[101] Whether this happens in practice remains to be seen.

---

100   For a discussion of this, see *Whish*, Competition Law (5th ed, 2003), pp 667–677.

101   See Commissioner Monti, 'Remarks at the European Regulators Group Hearing on Remedies', 26 January 2004, SPEECH/04/37, available at: http://europa.eu.int/comm/competition/speeches/index_2001.html.

THE APPLICATION OF THE ECMR IN THE COMMUNICATIONS SECTOR

A Brief Outline of the ECMR

2.73   There are a vast number (around 200) EC merger control decisions related to the telecoms sector. A detailed consideration of these is not possible in this chapter. However, telecoms companies contemplating an acquisition, merger or joint venture need to understand the basic framework and policy as well as the recent changes to the ECMR.[102] Several key changes, including a revised substantive test and reforms to the procedural rules, were introduced in 2004.

(a)   Jurisdiction

2.74   If a particular transaction constitutes a 'Concentration'[103] with a 'Community dimension' it falls within the scope of the ECMR. Notification is mandatory and the transaction cannot, in general, be completed before a decision is reached. The concept of a 'Community dimension' is founded upon turnover thresholds (not adjusted in the recent review). This is a somewhat crude test. Some cases that would be best dealt with at Commission level may not have a 'Community dimension' as defined; similarly, some transactions which meet the relevant thresholds would be best examined at national level. The old ECMR had some flexibility to address this problem in that a referral of all or part of a merger to a Member State could be made post-notification if there were sufficient substantive concerns. However, this was not considered sufficient.[104]

2.75   Hence, although the basic jurisdictional test remains unchanged, the revised ECMR introduces more flexibility to address the concern that certain mergers and joint ventures etc were not being dealt with at the appropriate level, (ie Commission or national).[105] This is by way of both pre-notification referrals, a wholly new concept, and increased flexibility on post-notification referrals. The position now is that merging parties, *prior to notification*, can provide a 'reasoned submission' requesting the Commission to take jurisdiction over a case where the turnover thresholds are not satisfied but which could otherwise be notified in three or more Member States.[106] Such an application will not necessarily succeed – some national authorities may be reluctant to lose jurisdiction in any particular case and can easily veto an application, although there have been relatively few veto decisions to date.

---

102   Council Regulation No 139/2004 on the control of concentrations between undertakings, OJ L 24/1, 29.01.2004. This came into force on 1 May 2004.

103   Covering mergers, some joint ventures (if 'full function') and even some other contracts.

104   There was also a mechanism for referring mergers that fell within national merger control law to the Commission, although this was rarely used.

105   This is a further watering down of the notion of 'one stop shop'. The concept originally meant that if the Commission had jurisdiction, it would examine the merger in the vast majority of cases. This was once fundamental but has been gradually watered down over time as the notion of subsidiarity has become more prominent (or at least that the Commission trusted the Member States more). The recent changes can be seen as an example of this.

106   The Commission will refuse to examine a case if any of the Member States that would otherwise have jurisdiction object within 15 working days of receiving a copy of the reasoned submission. Silence, however, will be construed as agreement with the Commission's proposal to take over a case.

The parties may also request that the Commission refer a case that satisfies the turnover thresholds to one or more Member States on the basis of merely national or local impact.[107]

2.76   The existing system of post-notification referrals from the Commission to one or more national competition authorities or vice-versa remains in place subject to a number of amendments designed to promote the effectiveness of the mechanism.

2.77   There are also a number of other procedural reforms. The rule that parties must notify within one week from signing a binding agreement has been abandoned. Merging parties can now notify where they can demonstrate a 'good faith intention to conclude an agreement' (a signed letter of intent or a memorandum of understanding between the parties will suffice). All deadlines are expressed to be in working days rather than months and weeks (but continue to exclude Commission holidays). Phase I investigations have been extended from one month to 25 working days, or from six weeks to 35 working days if the merging parties offer commitments or a national authority has requested the referral of a case. The additional four-month in-depth investigation period (Phase II) remains, although it is now expressed as 90 working days. This deadline may be extended by a further 20 working days. If the parties offer commitments 55 working days or more after the start of Phase II proceedings, there is an automatic extension of 15 working days. The Commission's powers of investigation have also been enhanced to bring them largely into line with Regulation 1/2003. The new powers include the ability to inspect and seal business premises and the ability to conduct interviews (with the consent of the interviewee). The scope and significance of fines has also increased. Fines are now up to 1% of aggregate annual turnover in the preceding financial year for supplying incorrect, misleading or incomplete information to the Commission or failing to submit to an inspection. Daily penalty payments have increased to up to 5% of daily aggregate turnover for any failure to comply with a Commission request for information or documents.

(b)   Substantive test

2.78   Previously, the substantive test was whether or not the concentration created or strengthened a dominant position. The position has now changed. Although the 'dominance' test worked well, it generated a degree of uncertainty and debate as to whether it dealt with non-collusive oligopoly situations where there is a risk that, below a dominance threshold, the merging firms may be able to successfully raise prices to the detriment of consumers, without having to rely on the coordinated response of other members of the oligopoly. In order to close this perceived gap, the new test is whether the concentration *'would significantly impede effective competition, in the common market or a substantial part of it, in particular as a result of the creation or strengthening of a dominant position'* (inverting the old test).

2.79   Officially, the new wording does not signal any shift in the level of the Commission's intervention in merger investigations.[108] The dominance test will continue to be applied in most scenarios. Even so, the change could be significant in the telecoms sector. For example, if a merger of two of the main mobile telephony

---

107   This decision must be taken within 25 days from the Commission's receipt of the reasoned submission.
108   See Recital 26.

operators occurred, such that the main players were reduced from five to four (or even four to three), it may be[109] that while neither single firm nor collective dominance would be created or strengthened, the merger could significantly impede effective competition.

2.80   The new ECMR is accompanied by a number of flanking measures. In considering substantive issues, the most significant are the guidelines that describe the approach the Commission takes when assessing horizontal mergers (the Horizontal Merger Guidelines).[110] Although the Commission will look at market shares and market concentration levels, the focus is on competitive harm, including:

- *non-coordinated* (*or unilateral*) *effects* leading to single firm dominance or to a reduction of competitive pressure from non-merging firms if, as a result of the merger, the latter find it profitable to increase their prices even in the absence of coordination between them, and
- *coordinated effects* resulting in collective dominance where competitors are able to coordinate their behaviour and raise prices even without entering into an agreement to do so.

2.81   Other factors may counterbalance the potential anti-competitive effects. These include countervailing buyer power, ease of market entry, the failing firm defence and efficiencies. Efficiency claims will only be accepted when they are sufficiently substantiated so as to convince the Commission that the efficiencies will benefit consumers, are merger-specific and are verifiable. The level of information required to support efficiency claims has increased substantially in recent years.

ECMR Decisions in the Telecoms Sector

2.82   For any particular merger, the proposed transaction will need to be assessed in the light of its likely impact on conditions of competition in the relevant market to determine whether or not it is likely to raise substantive issues. Relevant factors include market shares, barriers to entry, countervailing bargaining power etc. A study of previous cases can be beneficial. Liberalisation has led to many joint ventures designed to exploit the resulting opportunities (some undertakings have been particularly active such as BT, Vodafone and France Telecom). Of particular interest is *Telia/Telenor*[111] in which the Commission granted conditional clearance following a Phase II investigation to a proposed concentration between the telecom incumbents of Sweden and Norway. The decision indicates that access to infrastructure can be as constraining on potential competition as access to intellectual property. Post merger, the parties would have been in a position to prevent competition by denying access to the 'local loop'. Prior to the merger, neither party had been so well equipped to prevent entry into their respective 'captive home markets' as they both needed access to each other's market to provide a number of services to their own countries. They therefore had an incentive to allow each other entry on mutually beneficial terms. However, by merging to become a single operator in the Nordic region, this gave complete control over the local access network in the home markets. The merger, subsequently abandoned for commercial reasons, was allowed only after the parties gave undertakings as to access for

---

109 The circumstances would, of course, have to be examined. It may be that such a transaction would be approved.

110 Guidelines on the assessment of horizontal mergers under the Council Regulation on the control of concentrations between undertakings, OJ C 31/05, 05.02.2004.

111 Case COMP/M.1439, OJ L 40/1, 9.02.2001.

competitors. The Commission later gave conditional clearance in *Telia/Sonera*,[112] the merger of the incumbent operators of Sweden and Finland and this merger was consummated in December 2002.

2.83   *Telia/Sonera* stated that an international roaming network may establish a vertical link between networks in different countries. The Commission analysed this point when considering the acquisition of Orange's Danish mobile operations by TeliaSonera.[113] However, it found TeliaSonera's position in Sweden and Finland did not mean that any such vertical effects would be created in the Danish market as a result of the acquisition.

2.84   The number of merger cases arising in the telecoms sector and dealt with by the Commission continues to increase. For example, the Commission recently cleared Slovak Telecom's acquisition of sole control over EuroTel's mobile phone business from its joint venture partner American West.[114] The Commission found that the change in control would not result in an increment in EuroTel's market share. The fact that Slovak Telecom was already EuroTel's majority shareholder, and so capable of determining its competitive behaviour, meant that the transaction raised no new competition concerns. The Commission also continues to have a number of cases involving the former State monopolist expanding into other areas through acquisition, such as BT's acquisition of Infonet. The Commission investigated the competitive effects of the proposed transaction on the possible markets for global telecommunications services ('GTS') that are provided to multinational corporations. It found that the transaction would not significantly change the market conditions either on a global, or on a European, scale as Infonet brings only a minimal incremental market share to BT. The combined BT/Infonet will continue to face a number of competitors that are present in these markets. In addition, customers have indicated that they will still have the possibility to switch competitively to alternative GTS suppliers. Furthermore, the Commission continues to look at alliances or arrangements between the 'incumbents', such as the proposed joint venture between Belgacom and Swisscom for international telecommunication carrier services, which the Commission cleared notwithstanding Belgacom's strong position in several markets.[115]

2.85   The internet is giving rise to a number of issues. The Commission granted conditional clearance, following a Phase II investigation, to *Worldcom/MCI*[116] in 2000. However, it prohibited the proposed concentration in *MCI WorldCom/ Sprint*,[117] which, in its view, would either have created a dominant position for the merged entity or would have reinforced the dominant position of MCI WorldCom in the provision of 'top-level' or universal interconnectivity on the internet. This decision has been annulled by the CFI on a technicality. The CFI considered that the Commission should have found itself without the power to adopt a decision

---

112 Case COMP/M.2803, OJ C 201/19, 24.08.2002.
113 Case COMP/M.3530, *TeliaSonera AB/ Orange AS*, OJ C 263/7, 26.10.2004.
114 Case COMP/M.3561, *DT/ EuroTel*, cleared on 15 December 2004 (decisions available on DG Competition website) (IP/04/1492).
115 See Commission press release IP/05/582, 20 May 2005.
116 Case COMP/M.1069, OJ L 116/1, 04.05.1999.
117 Case COMP/M.1741, OJ L 300/01, 18.11.2003 – annulled by the CFI on appeal (Case T-310/00 *WorldCom v Commission*). The CFI considered that the Commission should have found itself without the power to adopt a decision when the parties withdrew their notification. The CFI added that the parties were entitled to expect their letter to the Commission withdrawing notification of the merger to close the file.

when the parties withdrew their notification, since the parties were entitled to expect their letter to the Commission withdrawing the notification of the merger to close the file.

2.86 In *Vivendi/Canal +Seagram*,[118] 2000, the Commission found that Vivendi's acquisition of Seagram, and through Seagram, Universal, threatened to create a dominant position on the market for internet portals for Vivendi's subsidiary Vizzavi if the latter were allowed exclusive access to Universal's music libraries. Universal offered not to discriminate in favour of Vizzavi in the supply of music for downloading or streaming on the internet to its subscribers in the EU for a period of two years. This undertaking, however, was found to be inadequate. The Commission held that it was behavioural with no structural effect, and the duration was too short. Consequently, Vivendi undertook to provide for access to Universal's music content on a non-discriminatory basis as regards pricing and terms and conditions. It also undertook to provide for an arbitration procedure in case of any dispute concerning the access conditions. The undertaking was for five years, with the possibility of revision after three. This revised commitment was accepted by the Commission.

2.87 At the time of writing, the latest Commission merger decisions in the sector related to the Czech Republic. The first was the clearance of the acquisition of Clearwave, a holding company with mobile telecommunications subsidiaries in the Czech Republic (Oskar Mobil) and Romania (Mobilfon), by Vodafone.[119] Prior to the acquisition, Vodafone neither had a mobile telephony network nor offered mobile telephony services directly in the Czech Republic. Hence, there were no direct overlaps in the EEA. The investigation therefore focused on whether the proposed acquisition would have any significant effects on the provision of pan-European mobile telephony services and whether it could have any significant impact on the markets for international wholesale roaming services. In relation to the former, the Commission's analysis showed that the provision of advance seamless pan-European services encompasses permanent roaming on a pan-European basis for customers seeking pan-European mobile voice and data/internet services as there was an increasing demand of such services, in particular from business travellers and multi-national companies. At the time of the decision, most of these services were still country-specific in terms of price, contractual terms and legislation. In any case, the Commission reasoned, even from a pan-European perspective, the acquisition does not significantly increase Vodafone's European footprint. The Commission also considered that no issues arise as a result of the transaction in relation to the markets for international wholesale roaming services. Although, following the transaction, Vodafone will send more traffic to Oskar Mobil whilst Oskar Mobil will be able to participate in the Vodafone group discount negotiations, the Commission considered that this will not significantly impede competition. Oskar Mobil's purchases of wholesale international roaming services are insignificant, and so the impact of Oskar Mobil's purchases of international roaming in the Vodafone group will be negligible. Further, Vodafone will also continue to face a number of actual and potential competitors for the provision of roaming services both in the Czech Republic and in other EU countries where Vodafone is active.

---

118 Case COMP/M.2050, OJ C 311/03, 31.10.2000.
119 IP/05/607, 25 May 2005.

2.88 On 10 June 2005, the Commission approved the proposed acquisition of Cĕskí Telecom by Téléfonica.[120] The transaction, illustrative of the consolidation in the sector, raised no issues as there were no horizontal overlaps and no vertical concerns in the Spanish and Czech markets for wholesale international roaming and fixed and mobile telecommunications. As regards Téléfonica's intention to integrate Eurotel in FreeMove, the recently formed international alliance for the provision of pan-European advanced mobile telecommunication services, the Commission concluded that, in spite of the fact that another Czech mobile operator (T-Mobile) is also a member of FreeMove, the rules governing this alliance will ensure that effective competition will be maintained following the transaction.

ECMR Decisions in the Wider Communications Sector

2.89 As indicated above, there are a number of decisions in the wider communications sector that are of interest. In addition to the internet cases, some of the more significant cases relate to the Commission's concern regarding vertical integration. These include:

- *Bertelsmann/Kirch Premiere*[121] – a prohibition decision in order to check market power in the German digital pay-TV market. The proposals would have lead to bottlenecks in the provision of pay-TV and similar services and would have strengthened Kirch's dominant position;
- *BSkyB/Kirch*[122] – clearance was given after concessions were made by Kirch concerning access to Premiere's pay-TV technical platform. The Commission, inter alia, was concerned about the increased potential of Kirch to leverage from the dominant position in pay-TV into the neighbouring market for digital interactive services. Kirch would have been the only undertaking in Germany able, at the time of the merger and in the foreseeable future, to offer pay-TV in combination with digital interactive television services, so that Kirch's 'd-box' would have become the standard decoder for digital services, as it already was for pay-TV. As the d-box was a closed decoder, a third party service provider wishing to reach customers via the d-box would have been dependent on its competitor. The parties offered commitments with regard to the technical platform for pay-TV which counter-balanced the increase in barriers to entry on the pay-TV market and also prevented KirchPayTV from leveraging its dominance.[123]

---

120 10 June 2005.
121 Case IV/M.993, OJ L 53/1, 27.2.1999.
122 Case COMP/JV.37 – *BSkyB/KirchPayTV*. IP/00/279, 21.3.2000.
123 In essence, two sets of undertakings were offered. The first enabled providers of digital interactive television services to establish their own technical platform and to compete with Kirch by giving them access to Kirch's pay-TV services. They also made it possible to manufacture decoder boxes using Kirch's conditional access system in combination with other conditional access systems. The second set of undertakings enabled providers of digital interactive services to run their services more easily on Kirch's technical platform via both the implementation of the DVB Multimedia Home Platform (MHP), which enabled operators to develop interactive applications for Kirch's d-box, and a commitment facilitating the negotiation of Simulcrypt arrangements.

- *Microsoft/Liberty Media/Telewest* – the transaction was abandoned after the Commission opened a Phase II ECMR investigation into Microsoft and Liberty's proposed acquisition of joint control of Telewest.[124] The Commission's concerns centred on the potential for Microsoft to foreclose competitors from supplying software to Telewest for use in set-top boxes. There was also concern that the acquisition could increase incentives for writers of application software to tailor their offerings to a Microsoft-based platform.

- *Time-Warner/AOL*[125] – where the Commission investigated a merger between Time-Warner, one of the world's largest media and entertainment companies, and AOL, the only internet access provider with a pan-European presence. The main concern was that the vertically-integrated merged entity would have dominated the market for internet music delivery: AOL would have been the gatekeeper, dictating the conditions for distribution over the internet. The transaction was cleared after commitments were given in Phase II to severe links with Bertelsmann, another media and entertainment company, with which AOL had an unrelated European joint venture, giving AOL access to Bertelsmann's music libraries.

- *Newscorp/Telepiu*[126] – where the Commission considered vertical issues arising out of the merger of two Italian pay-TV platforms, Telepiu and Stream. The transaction resulted in a near monopoly in the Italian pay-TV market, but the Commission took the view that authorising the merger, subject to appropriate conditions, would be more beneficial to consumers than the disruption that would have been caused by the likely closure of Stream, the smaller and weaker of the two existing operators.[127]

CONCLUSION

2.90 An understanding of competition law is now fundamental for any telecoms undertaking considering its legal position and obligations. Arguments based on competition law are relevant to the market reviews and possible obligations that arise thereunder. They also determine many of the obligations of operators in any particular market and impact on any joint venture, strategic alliance or other arrangement that it wants to enter into, including distribution arrangements. Given the Commission's renewed enthusiasm for bringing competition cases against telecoms operators, mirrored by many NCAs, operators need to be aware of the possible 'punishment' for perceived anti-competitive activity, as well as the opportunities that exist in using competition law as a means of attacking the anti-competitive practices of incumbents or competitors.

---

124 Case COMP/JV.27. See Commission press release IP/00/287, 22.3.2000 and para 2.50 above. See also *UGC/Liberty Media* (Case COMP/M.2222, OJ L 172/20, 16.6.2001) where the Commission examined the vertical issues arising in connection with the acquisition by UGC of Liberty Media, a company active in cable television and pay-TV that held shares in News Corporation, which produced television programmes and operated pay-TV channels. Any adverse effects were excluded since News Corp's content did not match UGC's needs so any foreclosure effect would be insignificant.

125 Case COMP/M.1845, OJ L 268/28, 9.10.2001.

126 Case COMP/M.2876, OJ, L 110/73, 16.4.2004.

127 Other media cases include *RTL/Vernoica/Endemol*, (Case IV/M.553, OJ L 134/32, 1996, a prohibition decision); *Nordic Satellite Distribution* (Case IV/M.490, OJ L 53/20, 1996); *MSG Media Service* (Case IV/M.469, OJ L 364/1, 31.12.1994).

Data Protection and Privacy[1]

Helen Kemmitt and Chris Mögelin
Baker & McKenzie, London and Frankfurt

INTRODUCTION – HISTORY AND PURPOSE

3.1 It is now ten years since the Directive on the protection of individuals with regard to the processing of personal data (the 'Data Protection Directive')[2] came into force. This Directive sets out the basic provisions for protecting the fundamental rights of individuals with respect to processing of their personal data in Europe.[3] A further Directive dealt with the particular issues which were raised by new advanced technologies being introduced into public telecommunications networks – the Directive on the processing of personal data and the protection of privacy in the telecommunications sector (the 'Telecommunications Privacy Directive').[4] The Telecommunications Privacy Directive complemented the Data Protection Directive. Its ambit was, however, wider. Notably, it provided protection for subscribers who were legal persons, as opposed to only individuals.

3.2 In 2002, as part of the 2002 EU Regulatory Package, the European Parliament and the Council adopted a further Directive on privacy and electronic communications (the 'E-Privacy Directive').[5] The E-Privacy Directive replaced the Telecommunications Privacy Directive. The Commission's aim was to ensure that people could be confident that their privacy would be respected when they used electronic communications networks and services of all kinds, and that network and

---

1   Editing of this chapter closed on 1 July 2005. With thanks to the editorial assistance of Dr Ian Walden, consultant to Baker & McKenzie and Head of the Institute of Computer and Communications Law Unit at the Centre for Commercial Law Studies, Queen Mary, University of London.

2   Directive 95/46/EC of the European Parliament and of the Council of 24 October 1995 on the protection of individuals with regard to the processing of personal data and on the free movement of such data, OJ L 281/31, 23.11.1995.

3   The rights in this Directive gave substance to the rights contained in the Council of Europe Convention of 28 January 1981 for the Protection of Individuals with regard to the Automatic Processing of Personal Data.

4   Directive 97/66/EC of the European Parliament of 15 December 1997 concerning the processing of personal data and the protection of privacy in the telecommunications sector, OJ L 24/1, 30.1.1998.

5   Directive 2002/58/EC of the European Parliament and of the Council of 12 July 2002 concerning the processing of personal data and the protection of privacy in the electronic communications sector, OJ L 201/37, 31.7.2002.

service providers have a clear framework in which to operate. As with the Telecommunications Privacy Directive, its provisions complement those of the Data Protection Directive. It carries over much of the previous regime, but there are some important changes; and some grey areas, such as the applicability of the rules on sending unsolicited communications by e-mail, are clarified.

The E-Privacy Directive was due for implementation by Member States by 31 October 2003.

SCOPE OF APPLICATION

3.3   The E-Privacy Directive is intended to be technology neutral. The Commission wanted to provide an equal level of protection and privacy for users of publicly available electronic communications services regardless of the technologies used.

It covers the processing of personal data in connection with the provision of publicly available electronic communication networks and services in the Community. It is therefore concerned with *public* networks and services only. It does not apply to closed or private networks. (However, any personal data processing on closed or private networks would be subject to the general Data Protection Directive. In addition, national implementing regulations may be applicable to private networks.)

3.4   The E-Privacy Directive is primarily concerned with the regulation of the transmission of communications and not the content of those communications. The definition of an electronic communications service[6] clearly excludes the provision of content. It provides that an electronic communications service is:

'a service normally provided for remuneration which consists wholly or mainly in the conveyance of signals on electronic communications networks … but excludes services providing, or exercising editorial control over, content transmitted using electronic communications networks and services …'

This definition is based on the idea of the conveyance of signals on electronic communications networks. This means that providers who, for example, provide content to a website would not be covered by the E-Privacy Directive (although they will still be covered by the Data Protection Directive in so far as they process personal data).

3.5   The Data Protection Directive is concerned with the rights and freedoms of individuals, that is natural persons. The E-Privacy Directive is wider than this and, for example, requires Member States to take measures to protect corporate subscribers. It also distinguishes between subscribers and users. Subscribers are defined as:

'any natural person or legal entity who or which is a party to a contract with the provider of publicly available electronic communications services for the supply of such services'.[7]

It is clear from this that a subscriber can be a natural or a legal person. It is also clear from the Directive that the contractual relationship between the subscriber

---

6   Art 2 Framework Directive; see para 1.50 above.
7   Art 2(k) Framework Directive.

and the service provider may entail a periodic or one-off payment and that pre-paid cards are also considered to be a contract.

A user is defined as:

> 'any natural person using a publicly available electronic communication service, for private or business purposes, without necessarily having sub-scribed to this service'.[8]

3.6   The intention is clearly to distinguish between those who have a contract for the provision of relevant services and those individuals who have access to the services, even though they do not have a contract with a service provider, but who, nevertheless, may have rights which require protection, eg members of the same family. The rights and protections given to users and subscribers are not always identical.

CONFIDENTIALITY OF COMMUNICATIONS

3.7   As mentioned above, the E-Privacy Directive aims to guarantee the confiden-tiality of communications and related traffic data by means of public communica-tions networks.[9] Member States are obliged to prohibit in particular the listening, tapping, storing or surveillance of communications (and the related traffic data) by persons other than users, unless the user has given his consent.

3.8   There are a number of exceptions to this, including for reasons of national and public safety, defence and the prevention, detection and prosecution of criminal offences. There is also an exception which permits the recording of communications (and related traffic data) which is carried out in the course of lawful business practice for the purpose of providing evidence of a commercial transaction or any other business communication,[10] provided that confidentiality is ensured. This exception is subject to the following conditions:

- the parties to the communications should be informed prior to the recording about the fact of the recording, its purpose and for how long it is to be stored, and
- the recording must be erased as soon as possible and at the latest by the end of the period during which the transaction can be lawfully challenged.[11]

3.9   The Directive places special emphasis on the protection of information stored on a user's terminal equipment. The Directive is trying to control the use of software programs which monitor users' internet usage. The information collected can then be used for marketing or other purposes. The Directive specifically refers to 'spyware', 'web bugs' and 'cookies'.[12]

Cookies are software sent to and stored in the terminal of a user by a service provider, often without the knowledge of the user. The device then acts as a marker or identifier that can be recognised automatically by the service provider. Cookies are used for a wide range of purposes and can provide benefits to the user, for example by facilitating internet shopping by remembering a user's preferences and

---

8   Art 2(a) E-Privacy Directive.
9   Art 15(1) E-Privacy Directive.
10   Art 5(2) E-Privacy Directive.
11   Recital 23 E-Privacy Directive.
12   Recitals 24 and 25 E-Privacy Directive.

saving the user time when he returns to a website. Nevertheless, they can contain very sensitive information and many users are completely unaware of them. Other technologies, such as spyware,[13] can be equally invasive.

3.10   The Directive recognises that these devices can be used for legitimate purposes and attempts to reach a middle ground by providing that they can be used without the consent of the subscriber or user but only for legitimate purposes and with the knowledge of the subscriber or user. The Directive does not define what is a legitimate purpose but it does state that it would include the provision of information society services.[14]

3.11   Essentially, the Directive requires that website operators must provide users and subscribers with:

- clear and comprehensive information in accordance with the Data Protection Directive[15] about the purposes of processing, and
- the right to refuse such processing.[16]

The methods that the website operators use for complying with these requirements must be as user friendly as possible.[17]

These obligations do not apply if the device is used for the sole purpose of carrying out or facilitating the transmission of a communication or are strictly necessary in order to provide an information society service explicitly requested by the subscriber or user.

Access to specific website content can still be made conditional on the acceptance of cookies or similar device if the cookie is used for a legitimate purpose.[18]

3.12   Network and service providers are required to work together, if necessary, to safeguard the security of the network. The providers of publicly available electronic communications services are required to take appropriate technical and organisational measures to safeguard the security of their services.[19] If there are particular risks of a breach of the security of the network, the service provider must fully inform subscribers and users about the risks, any possible remedies and the likely costs involved.[20] The service provider must fulfil its information obligation even if the existing security risk is outside the scope of possible remedies by the service provider. Service providers who offer services over the internet (such as e-mail

---

13   Spyware programs can capture data on which websites the user visits or even what a user types, potentially enabling the spyware to record user names and passwords for certain websites.

14   The term 'information society' services is defined in the E-Commerce Directive 98/48/EC. It covers any service normally provided for remuneration at a distance by means of electronic equipment for the processing and storage of data and at the individual request of a recipient of a service.

15   It is assumed that this reference to the Data Protection Directive is a reference to the information requirements under the first data protection principle which requires that personal data must be processed fairly and lawfully.

16   Art 5(3) E-Privacy Directive.

17   Recital 25 E-Privacy Directive.

18   Recital 25 E-Privacy Directive.

19   Art 4(1) E-Privacy Directive.

20   Art 4(2) E-Privacy Directive.

services) should therefore inform subscribers and users about measures they can take to protect the security of their communications, for example by using encryption technologies.[21]

TRAFFIC DATA

3.13   The E-Privacy Directive regulates the use and retention of traffic data. 'Traffic data' is defined as:

> 'data processed for the purpose of the conveyance of a communication on an electronic communications network or for the billing thereof'.[22]

This definition replaces the term 'traffic and billing data' formerly used under the Telecommunications Privacy Directive.[23] It is much broader than the previous definition, which only encompassed data relating to subscribers and users that was processed to 'establish calls' and stored by the provider. Under the new definition, traffic data includes data regarding all electronic communications[24] and not only telephone calls. Traffic data includes data referring to routing, duration, volume or time of a call. It also includes the format in which the communication is conveyed by the network. It may include location data, such as the location of the terminal equipment of the sender and the recipient, and it may also include navigation data such as URLs.[25] The term 'location data' is separately defined. The definitions of traffic data and location data are not, however, mutually exclusive, and it is possible for certain data to fall within both definitions.

3.14   The basic rule is that when traffic data is no longer required for transmission purposes it must be erased or modified so that it is no longer personal data.[26]

The exact moment of the completion of the transmission of a communication will depend on the type of electronic communications service and may vary from case to case. For example, for a voice telephony call the transmission will be completed as soon as either of the users terminates the connection. For e-mail, the transmission is completed as soon as the addressee collects the message, typically from the server of his service provider.[27]

The service provider may want to keep this information for longer for example for statistical purposes such as monitoring call duration. This is permissible if such data is first anonymised.

3.15   The basic rule is subject to four important exceptions:

● **First, for billing purposes:** If traffic data is necessary for the purposes of subscriber billing and interconnection payments it may be processed as long as the bill may lawfully be challenged or payment is pursued.[28] The service provider must inform the subscriber or user of the types of traffic data which

---

21   Recital 20 E-Privacy Directive.
22   Art 2(b) E-Privacy Directive.
23   Cf art 6 Telecommunications Privacy Directive.
24   Art 2(d) E-Privacy Directive.
25   The 'Uniform Resource Locator' is the global address of documents and other resources on the World Wide Web.
26   Art 6(1) E-Privacy Directive.
27   Recital 27 E-Privacy Directive.
28   Art 6(2) E-Privacy Directive.

are processed and of the duration of such processing.[29] In addition, only traffic data that are adequate, relevant and non-excessive for billing and interconnection purposes may be processed. Other traffic data must be deleted.

The Data Protection Working Party[30] has been concerned that divergences exist in practice between the electronic communications companies in the Member States with regards to storage periods of traffic data. It has recommended that there should be a routine storage period for billing of a maximum of three to six months, with the exception of particular cases of dispute where data may be processed for a longer period.[31]

• **Secondly, for marketing purposes:** Service providers may process traffic data for the purpose of marketing electronic communications services to the extent and for the duration necessary for such marketing. The service provider is allowed to market not only its own electronic communications services but also those of third parties. Under the Telecommunications Privacy Directive only billing data could be used for marketing purposes.

The use of traffic data for marketing purposes is only allowed if the subscriber or user has given his prior consent.[32] This means that the subscriber or user must freely give a specific and informed indication of his wishes[33] before the processing takes place. Prior to obtaining this consent the service provider must inform the subscriber or user of the types of traffic data which are processed and of the duration of such processing.[34] Subscribers or users must also be able to withdraw their consent at any time.

• **Thirdly, for the provision of value added services:** Traffic data may be processed for the provision of value added services, such as advice on least expensive tariff packages, route guidance, traffic information, weather forecasts and tourist information. The use of the data requires the explicit consent of the subscriber or user.[35] The term 'value added services' is defined as meaning any service which requires the processing of traffic data or location data beyond what is necessary for the transmission of a communication or billing thereof.[36]

In all of the above exceptions the processing of traffic data is restricted to persons acting under the authority of providers of the networks and services handling billing or traffic management, customer enquiries, fraud detection, marketing electronic communications services or providing a value added service.[37] Where the provider of a service subcontracts the processing of personal data to another entity, the requirements set out in the Data Protection Directive apply. In this case the subscriber or user should be fully informed of this forwarding before giving their consent for the processing of the data.

---

29 Art 6(4) E-Privacy Directive.
30 The Working Party was set up under art 29 Directive 95/46/EC. It is an independent European advisory body on data protection and privacy.
31 Art 29 Data Protection Working Party Opinion 1/2003 on the storage of traffic data for billing purposes, adopted 29 January 2003.
32 Art 6(3) E-Privacy Directive.
33 Recital 17, E-Privacy Directive in conjunction with art 2(h) Data Protection Directive.
34 Art 6(4) E-Privacy Directive.
35 Art 6(3) E-Privacy Directive.
36 Art 2(g) E-Privacy Directive.
37 Art 6(5) E-Privacy Directive.

- **Fourthly, for law enforcement purposes.**[38]

LOCATION DATA

3.16   New provisions are intended to allow service providers to offer value added services also based on location data. The term 'location data' is defined as:

> 'any data processed in an electronic communications network, indicating the geographic position of the terminal equipment of a user of a publicly available electronic communications service'.[39]

This includes data which refers to the latitude, longitude and altitude of the user's terminal equipment. Such data may also refer to the direction of transmission, the level of accuracy of the location information, the identification of the network cell in which the terminal equipment is located at a certain point in time and to the time the location information was recorded.[40] As mentioned above, some location data may also qualify as traffic data. Where data falls within both definitions, it is the traffic data provisions which will apply.[41]

3.17   An example of location data is the data processed by digital mobile networks which contain more precise information than is necessary for the transmission of communications. This information is potentially useful for providers of value added services, such as services providing individualised traffic information.

3.18   In so far as the data contains information which is not necessary for the mere transmission of communications, it will be location data, and service providers must comply with the following conditions:

- Location data may only be processed when made anonymous or with the subscriber's or user's consent and only to the extent and for the duration necessary for the provision of a value added service.[42]
- The service provider must inform subscribers or users prior to obtaining their consent of the type of location data which will be processed, of the purposes and duration of the processing and whether the data will be transmitted to a third party for the purpose of providing the value added service.
- Subscribers or users must be able to withdraw their consent at any time.[43] In addition, subscribers or users must have the possibility to temporarily refuse the processing of such data for each connection to the network or for each transmission of a communication by using simple means and free of charge.[44]
- In all cases, processing of location data must be restricted to persons acting under the authority of the service provider or the third party providing the value added service.

3.19   Only in exceptional cases can the service provider override a subscriber's or user's choice regarding the processing of location data. One exception aims to ensure that emergency services can carry out their tasks as effectively as possible. Member States may allow a service provider to override the temporary denial or

---

38   See para 3.33 below.
39   Art 2(c) E-Privacy Directive.
40   Recital 14 E-Privacy Directive.
41   Art 9(1) E-Privacy Directive.
42   Art 9(1) E-Privacy Directive.
43   Art 9(1) E-Privacy Directive.
44   Art 9(2) E-Privacy Directive.

absence of consent of a subscriber or user for the processing of location data on a per-line basis for organisations dealing with emergency calls, including law enforcement agencies, ambulance services and fire brigades, for the purpose of responding to such calls.[45] There must be transparent procedures governing the way it is exercised. There are other exceptions with regard to national security.[46]

UNSOLICITED COMMUNICATIONS

3.20   The E-Privacy Directive harmonises the conditions under which electronic communications can be used for direct marketing purposes. Spamming is the practice of sending unsolicited e-mails, usually of a commercial nature, in large numbers and repeatedly to individuals with whom the sender has had no previous contact.[47] The problems from the individual's point of view include: the collection of email addresses without consent, the receipt of unwanted advertising and the cost of connection time.

3.21   Traditionally, legislators have attempted to deal with the problem of unsolicited communications by setting up systems under which recipients can either 'opt in' to or 'opt out' of receiving such communications. The term 'opt in' means individuals have to take some action, eg signing up for the promotional material in question. Typically, customers are invited to sign up to receive promotional information about one or more categories of products or services. Those who sign up have 'opted in'. An 'opt out' assumes a general permission to send marketing messages to everyone who has not explicitly stated that they do not want to receive such information.

3.22   There is no definition of direct marketing in either the E-Privacy Directive or the Data Protection Directive. Although the Data Protection Directive does refer to direct marketing and provides that:

> 'Member States may similarly specify the conditions under which personal data may be disclosed to a third party for the purposes of marketing whether carried out commercially or by a charitable organisation or by any other association or foundation, of a political nature …'.[48]

The Data Protection Working Party has expressed the view that the term 'direct marketing' in the E-Privacy Directive covers any form of sales promotion by charities and political organisations (eg fund raising).

3.23   The E-Privacy Directive provides[49] that unsolicited communications in the form of e-mail, facsimile messages and automated calling systems may only be allowed with the prior consent of subscribers.

3.24   Facsimile machines and automated calling systems were covered in the predecessor to this Directive. Automated calling systems are systems which automatically deliver a recorded message. They operate without human intervention. It is not entirely clear but it seems that this would *not* cover power diallers. Power

---

45   Art 10(b) E-Privacy Directive.
46   See para 3.33 below.
47   See Communication from the Commission on unsolicited commercial communications or 'spam' Brussels, 22.01.2004 COM(2004) 28 Final, and the CNIL report on Electronic Mailing and Data Protection, October 1999.
48   Recital 30 Data Protection Directive.
49   Art 13(1) E-Privacy Directive.

diallers systems can dial hundreds of numbers but are designed to establish contact with a human operator rather than a pre-recorded message.[50] The definition of e-mail is new. The previous Directive had clearly been drafted with conventional voice and fax calls in mind, and it was not clear whether the restrictions on direct marketing activities applied to e-mails. In the E-Privacy Directive, e-mail is now defined as:

> 'Any text, voice, sound or image message sent over a public communications network which can be stored in the network or in the recipient's terminal equipment until it is collected by the recipient'.[51]

This is a broad definition. It covers any message by electronic communications where the simultaneous participation of the sender and the recipient is not required. This includes basic email, messages left on answering machines and also Short Message Services.

3.25   The requirements for prior consent are the same as under the Data Protection Directive, and therefore any consent will only be valid if it is a specific and informed indication of the subscriber's wishes.[52]

The actual method which must be used to obtain that consent has not been set down by the E-Privacy Directive. Although the Directive does provide[53] that consent can be given by any 'appropriate method enabling a freely given specific and informed indication of the user's wishes, including by ticking a box when visiting an Internet website'. The Data Protection Working Party has said that it would not be compatible with the Directive to simply send a general e-mail to recipients asking for their consent to receive marketing e-mails, as this would not satisfy the requirement that the purpose be legitimate, explicit and specific. Neither does it consider that pre-ticked boxes on a website would be sufficient.[54]

In addition, the identity of the sender on whose behalf the communication was sent and an address to which the recipient may send a request that such communication end must be included.[55]

The prior consent requirement for unsolicited direct marketing via automated calling systems, facsimiles and e-mails only applies to subscribers who are natural persons. Member States can extend the prior consent requirement to subscribers who are legal persons.[56] There seems to be a gap in the protection offered to users, ie persons who are not directly subscribers, for example members of the subscriber's family. It would seem to be against the general intention of the Directive if they did not receive the same protection against unsolicited direct marketing as subscribers who are natural persons; however, the wording of the relevant articles in the Directive clearly refers to subscribers only.

3.26   There is an exception from the requirement for prior consent.[57] This is referred to as the 'soft opt-in'. It provides that where there is an existing customer

---

50   Guidance to the Privacy and Electronic Communications (EC Directive) Regulation 2003 – Information Commissioner.

51   Art 2(h) E-Privacy Directive.

52   Recital 17 and art 2(f) E-Privacy Directive.

53   Recital 17 E-Privacy Directive.

54   Data Protection Working Party, Opinion 5/2004 on unsolicited communications for marketing purposes under Article 13 of Directive 2002/58/EC.

55   Art 13(4) E-Privacy Directive.

56   Art 13(5) E-Privacy Directive.

57   Art 13(2) E-Privacy Directive.

relationship, further direct marketing is permitted, provided certain conditions are met. This exception does leave some room for interpretation and some of the key terms, for example what is an existing customer relationship, are not defined. The Data Protection Working Party[58] has said that the exception must be interpreted restrictively.

The conditions for this soft opt-in to apply are:

- It must be the same natural or legal entity which collected the data that uses the customer's e-mail details for direct marketing. Subsidiaries or other companies in the same group would not fall within this.
- The direct marketing must be for that entity's own similar products/services. This is not defined. The Working Party noted that this concept is not an easy one to apply in practice and it justifies further attention. They felt that similarity should be judged from the objective perspective (reasonable expectations) of the recipient, rather than the perspective of the seller.
- Customers must be given a clear opportunity to object to the direct marketing, both initially and on each occasion of direct marketing (ie an ongoing opt-out).
- The collection of data initially must be in accordance with the Data Protection Directive.

3.27 For other forms of unsolicited communications, for example by telephone, for purposes of direct marketing, Member States must take appropriate measures to ensure that they are not allowed, either without the consent of subscribers or by subscribers who do not wish to receive such communications. Member States are, therefore, free to choose between an opt-in or an opt-out protection. Once again, it is only in respect of subscribers who are natural persons that Member States are required to take action.[59] The reason for the less stringent provisions as regards these other forms of communication is that they are more costly for the sender and impose no financial costs on subscribers and users.[60]

As highlighted above, Member States are required to ensure the legitimate interests of subscribers other than natural persons (eg corporate subscribers) are adequately protected.[61] The E-Privacy Directive has, however, left it to Member States to determine the level of protection to be provided.

ADDITIONAL SERVICES FEATURES

3.28 The E-Privacy Directive also covers a number of additional services, such as directories and automatic call forwarding. These were included in the Telecommunications Privacy Directive and in some cases remain unchanged. These provisions include the following rights for subscribers:

- The right to receive bills that are not itemised.[62]

---

58 Art 29 Data Protection Working Party, Opinion 5/2004 on unsolicited communications for marketing purposes under Article 13 of Directive 2002/58/EC adopted on 27 February 2004.
59 See footnote 50 above.
60 Recital 42 E-Privacy Directive.
61 Art 13(5) E-Privacy Directive
62 Art 7 E-Privacy Directive.

- The right to prevent calling line identification on outgoing or incoming calls (except in the case of emergency calls, or where necessary to trace malicious or nuisance calls).[63]
- The right to prevent automatic forwarding of calls.[64]
- The right not to appear in public directories (free of charge) and to determine what if any data can be included in such directories. Subscribers also have to be informed in advance as to the purposes of the directory.[65]

Itemised Billing

3.29   Subscribers have the right to receive non-itemised bills. This recognises that even though itemised bills can be useful in enabling subscribers to verify charges, such bills may jeopardise the right to privacy of users, for example where different users share the same telephone. The E-Privacy Directive does provide that Member States should ensure that implementing national legislation allows for sufficient methods that do allow subscribers to verify their bills, eg alternative payment facilities or service options.[66] The Directive also refers to the possibility of providing a different sort of bill where a certain number of digits of the called number are altered.

Calling and Connected Line Identification

3.30   Calling and connected line identification can be valuable services for users, and the widespread introduction of digital switching technology means that such customer information is available on almost all calls. These services do, however, raise serious privacy issues and require data protection safeguards. The E-Privacy Directive carries over from the Telecommunications Privacy Directive a basic set of privacy rights for users making and receiving calls.

The calling user has the right to:

- have a simple means (which must be free of charge) to prevent presentation of its number on the connected line. This option may be exercised on a per-call basis or on a more permanent basis by preventing the display on all calls made from a particular line.[67]

The called end user has the right to have:

- a simple means (which must be free of charge for reasonable use) to prevent the display of calling line identification information for incoming calls. This means that certain services, such as help lines, can offer anonymity to callers;[68]
- a simple means of rejecting incoming calls where the display of calling line identification information has been withheld by the caller.[69]

---

63   Art 8 E-Privacy Directive.
64   Art 11 E-Privacy Directive.
65   Art 12 E-Privacy Directive.
66   Recital 33 and art 7(2) E-Privacy Directive.
67   Art 8(1) E-Privacy Directive.
68   Art 8(2) E-Privacy Directive.
69   Art 8(3) E-Privacy Directive.

Where connected line identification is offered, end users must be able, using a simple means and free of charge, to prevent the display to the caller of the actual number to which an incoming call has been connected.[70]

The Directive provides that Member States can override the caller's general right to prevent the display of their calling line identification information to facilitate emergency calls or where authorities are investigating malicious or nuisance calls.

Automatic Call Forwarding

3.31   The provisions on automatic call forwarding have been carried over from the Telecommunications Privacy Directive.[71] Subscribers must have the right to stop, using a simple means and free of charge, any automatic call forwarding by a third party to its terminal equipment.[72]

Directories of Subscribers

3.32   The E-Privacy Directive introduces a number of changes to the rules on subscriber directories and addresses the issue of reverse or multi-criteria searching services which raise particular privacy issues.

The provision of directory information is recognised by the Commission as an essential access tool for publicly available telephone services, and certain operators are obliged to provide directory information as part of universal service obligations which aim to ensure that all end users have access to a defined minimum set of services at an affordable price.[73] However, the concept of a directory has changed over the past few years. Directories are now frequently in electronic format and contain the names, addresses and telephone numbers of millions of citizens of different Member States. One of the main innovations with electronic directories is the possibility of providing extended capabilities for the processing of the information contained in these directories. These multi-criteria search facilities go way beyond traditional search facilities and can provide, for example, the names and telephone numbers of all the persons in a particular street. In particular there have been concerns about the potential for individuals to inadvertently disclose their name and address when they hand out their telephone number. Although, there is some evidence from countries where the use of these facilities is common that, in practice, there may not be specific problems with this type of searching.[74]

The E-Privacy Directive provides that:

- Individuals must be informed, before they are included in the directory, of the purpose of a directory and how it might be used, including any further usage possibilities based on search facilities embedded in electronic versions of the directory.
- Individuals can no longer be charged a fee by operators to be excluded from a directory, to specify which of their data is to be included, or to verify, correct or withdraw such data.

---

70   Art 8(4) E-Privacy Directive.
71   Art 10 Telecommunications Privacy Directive.
72   Art 11 E-Privacy Directive.
73   Recital 4 Universal Services Directive.
74   Art 29 Data Protection Working Party Opinion 5/2000 on the Use of Public Directories for Reverse or Multi Criteria Searching Services (Reverse Directories), fn 1.

- Member States *may* impose separate consent requirements for inclusion in any directory including reverse search functions.[75]

These rights apply to subscribers who are natural persons but may be extended to legal persons at the discretion of Member States.

LEGITIMATE RESTRICTIONS BY VIRTUE OF NATIONAL SECURITY

3.33   The E-Privacy Directive explicitly provides that Member States may deviate from the provisions on confidentiality, traffic and location data and calling line identification[76] if it is necessary, appropriate and proportionate for reasons of national security, the prevention, investigation, detection and prosecution of criminal offences or of unauthorised use of the electronic communication system. The Directive specifically provides that to this end, Member States may adopt legislative measures providing for the retention of data for a limited period.[77]

3.34   Initially, proposals to include such a provision had been opposed by most members of the European Parliament. In July 2001, the European Parliament's Civil Liberties Committee approved a draft Directive with limited data retention. However, following the events of 11 September 2001, the political climate changed, and the European Parliament came under increasing pressure to change its position.

3.35   There are concerns that, although the data retention provision is supposed to constitute an exception to the general regime of data protection established by the Directive, the ability of governments to compel internet service providers and telecommunications companies to store all data about all of their subscribers can hardly be construed as an exception to be narrowly interpreted. In any event, a government's ability to compel internet service providers and other companies to do so is not uncontrolled and would be subject to the European Convention on Human Rights.[78]

ENFORCEMENT

3.36   The provisions of the Data Protection Directive on judicial remedies, liability and sanctions are applicable to the provisions of the E-Privacy Directive.[79] Member States must ensure that penalties and remedies are in place for infringements. This includes the right to receive compensation for an individual who has suffered damage as a result of any unlawful act.

---

75   Art 12(3) E-Privacy Directive.
76   Arts 5, 6, 8 and 9 E-Privacy Directive.
77   Art 15(1). Cf for such a proposal to deviate from the obligations: Data Protection Working Party Opinion 9/2004 on a draft Framework Decision on the storage of data processed and retained for the purpose of providing electronic public communications services or data available in public communications networks with a view to the prevention, investigation, detection and prosecution of criminal acts, including terrorism. Proposal presented by France, Ireland, Sweden and Great Britain (Document of the Council 8958/04 of 28 April 2004).
78   Convention for the Protection of Human Rights and Fundamental Freedoms as amended by protocol 11, Rome, 4.XI.1950, CETS No 005.
79   Art 15(2) E-Privacy Directive.

The Law of the International Telecommunication Union and the World Trade Organisation[1]

Joachim Scherer, Sunwinder Mann and Hannes Schloemann
Baker & McKenzie, Frankfurt/London and WTI Advisors Ltd

THE ITU

History

4.1 The International Telecommunication Union (ITU) was established on 9 December 1932. On 1 January 1949, it became the specialised UN agency for telecommunications by an agreement with the United Nations of 4 September/ 15 November 1947.[2]

The ITU dates back to the International Telegraph Union, which was founded by 19 European states in 1865.[3]

Following the patenting of the telephone in 1876 and the subsequent growth of the telephony market, the International Telegraph Union began, in 1885, to draw up the first provisions governing the international telephone service. With the invention in 1896 of wireless telegraphy and the growing utilisation of this new radiocommunication technology, it was decided to convene a preliminary radio conference in 1903 to study the question of international regulations for radio telegraph communications. The first International Radio Telegraph Conference was held in 1906 in Berlin and led to the first International Telegraph Convention (revised London 1912, Washington DC 1927). In 1924, the International Telephone Consultative Committee (CCIF) was set up; the International Telegraph Consultative Committee (CCIT) was established in 1925 and the International Radio Consultative Committee (CCIR) in 1927. These bodies were responsible for coordinating the technical studies, tests and measurements in the various fields of telecommunications and for drawing up international standards.

4.2 At the 1932 Madrid conference, the Union decided to combine the International Telegraph Convention of 1865 and the International Radio Telegraph

---

1   Editing of this chapter closed on 28 July 2005. Joachim Scherer is the author of the ITU subchapter; Sunwinder Mann and Hannes Schloemann are the authors of the WTO subchapter.
2   UNTS, Vol 30 no 175.
3   For a history of the ITU see *Tegge*, Die Internationale Telekommunikations-Union, Baden-Baden 1994, pp 28 et seq.

Convention of 1906 to form the International Telecommunication Convention. It was also decided to change the name of the Union to International Telecommunication Union.

After World War II the ITU became a UN specialised agency, as mentioned above, and the headquarters of the organisation were transferred in 1948 from Bern to Geneva. At the same time, the International Frequency Registration Board (IFRB) was established to coordinate the increasingly complex task of managing the radio frequency spectrum. The Table of Frequency Allocations, which had first been introduced in 1912, was declared mandatory.

In 1956, the two International Consultative Committees, CCIT and the CCIF, were merged to form the International Telegraph and Telephone Consultative Committee, with a view to respond more effectively to the requirements generated by the development of these two types of communication.

4.3   In 1989, the Plenipotentiary Conference held in Nice[4] established the Telecommunications Development Bureau (BDT) in order to promote the development of telecommunication technologies and infrastructures in the developing countries of the world. At the same time, the Nice Plenipotentiary Conference launched an in-depth review of the structure and functioning of the Union with a view to achieve greater cost effectiveness within and between the ITU organs and activities and to improve the Union's structure, organisation, finance, staff, procedure and coordination to ensure that the Union would respond more effectively to the needs of its members. In 1992, an additional Plenipotentiary Conference held in Geneva decided on a number of far-reaching organisational reform measures, including the establishment of three Sectors, corresponding to the ITU's three main areas of activity: the Telecommunication Standardisation Sector (ITU-T), the Radiocommunication Sector (ITU-R), and the Telecommunication Development Sector (ITU-D). For each sector, an advisory group was established, including representatives of Member States and representatives of industry, to review the priorities, programs, operations and strategies of the sectors and provide guidance for their operation.[5]

Legal Framework

4.4   The legal framework of the ITU comprises three legal instruments, which have international treaty status. They are:

- the Constitution of the International Telecommunication Union ('CS'), which is the 'basic instrument' of the Union,[6]
- the Convention of the International Telecommunication Union, and
- the Administrative Regulations, which complement the Constitution and Convention.

---

4   For a brief summary of the reform process initiated at the Nice Plenipotentiary Conference, see *Noll*, The International Telecommunication Union, in: MMR 8/1999, pp 465 et seq.

5   See paras 4.34, 4.43 and 4.50 below.

6   Art 4 no 29 CS; In the following, references to the Constitution (CS) and the Convention (CV) are to the versions as amended by the Plenipotentiary Conference Kiyoto, 1994, the Plenipotentiary Conference Minneapolis, 1998 and the Plenipotentiary Conference Marrakesh, 2002. References are to the articles and margin numbers of the Constitution. A consolidated version can be found in International Telecommunication Union, Collection of the basic text of the International Telecommunication Union adopted by the Plenipotentiary Conference, edition 2003.

4.5 The Constitution contains the basic provisions regarding the purposes of the Union, its composition, the rights and obligation of its members, its legal instruments and sets out the organisational structure of the Union, including its three Sectors, their working methods and overall provisions on the functioning of the Union. The Constitution also contains a number of general provisions relating to telecommunications, such as the right of the public to use the international telecommunications service (Art 33 CS), the principle of secrecy of telecommunications (Article 37 CS) and the principle of priority of telecommunications concerning safety of life (Article 40 CS). Furthermore, the CS contains basic substantive provisions regarding radio communications, such as the principles of effective use of the radio frequency spectrum and of the geostationary satellite and other satellite orbits (Article 44 CS), the obligation to avoid harmful interference (Article 45 CS), and the principle of priority for distress calls and messages (Article 46 CS).

4.6 The Convention establishes detailed rules on the functioning of the Union and its organs, contains specific provisions regarding conferences and assemblies, and sets out the details of a voluntary arbitration procedure which may be initiated by Member States to settle their disputes on questions relating to the interpretation or application of the Constitution, the Convention or of the Administrative Regulations.

4.7 The two basic legal instruments of the Union, the Constitution and Convention, are complemented by the Administrative Regulations, which regulate the use of telecommunications and which are binding on all Member States. These Administrative Regulations are:

- the International Telecommunication Regulations, and
- the Radio Regulations.[7]

The standards (Recommendations) which are adopted by ITU-R and ITU-T are not legally binding, unless they are specifically incorporated in the Regulations.

The Radio Regulations

4.8 The Radio Regulations are an international treaty governing the use of the radio frequency spectrum and the geostationary satellite and non-geostationary orbits. The provisions of the radio regulations are legally binding. Under the Radio Regulations, the radio frequency spectrum is divided into frequency bands which are allocated to some 40 radio services for radiocommunication on an exclusive or shared basis. The list of services and frequency bands allocated in different regions constitute the Table of Frequency Allocations, which is part of the Radio Regulations. The Radio Regulations are regularly amended by the World Radiocommunication Conference.[8]

---

7   The Radio Regulations were signed on 4 July 2003 with a majority of their provisions having entered into force on 1 January 2005.

8   See para 4.27 below.

International Telecommunication Regulations

4.9   The International Telecommunication Regulations ('ITR')[9] were adopted at the World Administrative Telegraph and Telephone Conference in Melbourne (1988) and have not been amended since. They are binding international instruments[10] subject to revision by the World Conference on International Telecommunications.[11]

4.10   The purpose of the ITR is to establish general principles relating to the provision and operation of international telecommunications services offered to the public as well as to the underlying international telecommunication transport means used to provide such services.[12] The ITR contains statements of principle and specific provisions regarding the routing of international traffic, as well as charging and accounting principles. The ITR obliges Member States to ensure that their telecommunications 'administrations' or recognised private operating agencies cooperate in the establishment, operation and maintenance of the international network to provide a satisfactory quality of service,[13] to promote the implementation of international telecommunication services and to endeavour to make such services generally available to the public international networks.[14] The ITR recognises the right of Member States to allow their administrations and telecommunications organisations to enter into special mutual arrangements provided that no technical harm is caused to the operation of the telecommunication facilities of third countries.[15]

4.11   The ITR establishes the principle that for each applicable telecommunication service, the telecommunications operators concerned shall 'by mutual agreement' establish and revise the accounting rates to be applied between them, ie the mutual compensation for receiving and terminating calls.[16] In 1997, the Federal Communications Commission of the United States issued a 'Benchmark Order' which took effect on 1 January 1998.[17] It obliged US carriers to negotiate cost-based accounting and settlement rates with corresponding foreign carriers according to a timetable established by the FCC. Where carriers were unable to do so, the FCC specified what rates American carriers may pay. Both this unilateral challenge to the ITU's accounting rate regime and the methodology applied by the FCC led to considerably controversy.[18] The unilateral enforcement of the FCC's Benchmark Order

---

9   International Telecommunication Union, Final Acts of the World's Administrative Telegraph and Telephone Conference Melbourne, 1988, International Telecommunication Regulations, Geneva, 1989.

10   Art 54 no 215 CS.

11   Art 25 no 146 CS.

12   Art 1.1 ITR.

13   Art 3.1 ITR.

14   Art 4.1 ITR.

15   Art 9.1 ITR.

16   Art 6.2.1; see also ITU Recommendation D.140 Accounting Principles for International Telephone Services, which established key principles for accounting rates, such as the principle of cost orientation and non-discrimination.

17   Federal Communications Commission, In the matter of International Settlement Rates – Report and Order, FCC 97/280, Docket, no 96–261, adopted 7 August 1997.

18   See *William J Drake*, Towards Sustainable Competition in Global Telecommunications: From Principle to Practice – Summary Report of the Third Aspen Institute Roundtable on International Telecommunications, Washington, 1999; see also *William J Drake*, The Rise and Decline of the International Telecommunications Regime, in: Christopher T Marsden (ed), Regulating the Global Information Society, London 2000, pp 124, 170 et seq.

forced the telecommunications operators in other ITU Member States to reduce the rates at which US carriers compensate them for terminating traffic and thus rendered the relevant provision of the ITR de facto irrelevant.[19]

4.12   Given that the ITR had not been changed for a decade, despite the dramatic changes in technology and market structure, the Plenipotentiary Conference (Minneapolis 1998) instructed the Secretary General to review to what extent the needs of Member States were still satisfied by the ITU instruments, especially the ITR.[20] An expert group reviewed the ITR but did not come to a consensus and instead presented four options: (1) to terminate the ITR by integrating their provisions into the Constitution, Convention or Recommendations, (2) to modify the ITR keeping them as a treaty level text, (3) to defer the determination of whether to modify the ITR, or (4) to examine proposals of new areas of regulations to a now further development of the ITR.[21]

The Plenipotentiary Conference (Marrakesh, 2002) resolved that the process of reviewing the ITR should be continued.[22] After three years of work, a Council working group, which was open to all Member States, again did not achieve consensus and reported that three views had been expressed by Member States, namely (1) to leave the ITR unchanged, (2) to amend the ITR, including adding new provisions, or (3) to terminate the ITR and transfer certain provisions to the Constitution, Convention and ITU-T Recommendations.[23]

Among the topics that were suggested for inclusion in a new set of internationally binding rules were provisions on unsolicited electronic communications ('spam'), on the misuse of numbering, on the quality of service, on information security, on internet governance, and on IP telephony.[24]

Membership

4.13   Membership of the ITU is open to governments as well as to private organisations (the 'Sector Members').[25] The ITU had 189 Member States and 632 Sector Members. The membership of states is based on the principle of universality: any state which is a Member State of the United Nations or any other state with the approval of two-thirds of the Member States of the Union[26] may accede to the Union. Withdrawal is possible at any time with a one-year denunciation period.[27] Each Member State has one vote at all Plenipotentiary Conferences, all World Conference and all Sector Assemblies and Study Group Meetings and, if it is a Member State of the Council, all sessions of the Council ('one country, one vote').[28]

---

19   See also *William J Drake*, in Christopher T Marsden (ed), Regulating the Global Information Society, London 2000, p 172.
20   Resolution 79.
21   Expert Group on the International Telecommunication Regulations, ITR/08, May 2000.
22   Resolution 121.
23   International Telecommunication Union, Working Group on the International Telecommunication Regulations, Report 3 rev 1, 11–13 May 2005.
24   International Telecommunication Union, Working Group on the International Telecommunication Regulations, Annex 2: Summary of Positions with respect to terminating, retaining, or transferring current ITR Provisions.
25   Art 2 no 20 CS.
26   Art 2 no 23 CV.
27   Art 57 CV.
28   Art 3 no 27 CV.

4.14   The Sector Members are recognised operating agencies (including carriers, telecommunication service providers, equipment manufacturers), scientific or industrial organisations and financial or development institutions which are approved by the Member States concerned, other entities dealing with telecommunication matters which are approved by the Member State concerned, regional and other international telecommunication, standardisation, financial or development organisations.[29] Sector Members may elect to join one ore more of the ITU's three Sectors, depending on their particular interests. They are entitled to participate fully in the activities of the Sector of which they are members and, in particular, may provide chairmen and vice chairmen of Sector Assemblies and meetings as well as World Telecommunication Development Conferences; they are entitled to take part in the adoption of questions and recommendations and in decisions relating to the working methods and procedures of the sector concerned. They do not participate, however, in the Plenipotentiary Conference nor in the Council. They are not entitled to vote on amendments of the Constitution or of the Convention which are the prerogative of the Plenipotentiary Conference[30] nor on the adoption or amendment of administrative regulations, which are the prerogative of the World Conference on International Telecommunications[31] and of the World Radiocommunications Conferences.[32] In an attempt to broaden the participation of industry in the Union's proceedings, the assemblies and conferences of the individual Sectors[33] have been granted the right to admit entities or organisations to participate as 'associates' in the work of a given Study Group or subgroup.[34]

Purposes and Principles of the ITU

4.15   The ITU is an intergovernmental organisation which is based, according to the preamble of the Constitution, on the recognition of 'the sovereign right of each state to regulate its telecommunication'. The Union has been established 'with the object of facilitating peaceful relations, international cooperation among peoples and economic and social development by means of efficient telecommunications services'.[35] To this end, the purposes of the Union are, inter alia:

- to maintain and extend international cooperation among all its Member States for the improvement and rational use of telecommunications of all kinds,

- to promote and enhance participation of entities and organisations in the activities of the Union and foster fruitful cooperation and partnership between them and Member States for the fulfilment of the overall objectives as embodied in the purposes of the Union,

- to promote and to offer technical assistance to developing countries in the field of telecommunications,

- to promote the development of technical facilities and their most efficient operation with a view to improving the efficiency of telecommunication services,

- to promote the extension of the benefits of the new telecommunication technologies to all the world's inhabitants,

---

29   Annex no 1001 b CS, art 19 no 228–231 CV.
30   Art 8 no 57 CS.
31   Art 25 no 146 CS.
32   Art 13 no 89 CS, art 7 no 114 CV.
33   See below, paras 4.27, 4.29, 4.39, 4.47.
34   Art 20 no 241 A – 241 E CV.
35   Preamble CS.

- to promote the use of telecommunications services with the objective of facilitating peaceful relations,
- to harmonise the actions of Member States and promote fruitful and constructive cooperation and partnership between Member States and Sector Members in the attainment of those ends, and
- to promote, at the international level, the adoption of a broader approach to the issues of telecommunications in the global information economy and society, by cooperating with other world and regional intergovernmental organisations and those intergovernmental organisations concerned with telecommunications.[36]

4.16 Among the particular purposes of the Union are:

- to allocate bands of the radio-frequency spectrum, allot radio frequencies and register radio-frequency assignments and, for space services, any associated orbital position in the geostationary-satellite orbit or any associated characteristics of satellites in other orbits, in order to avoid harmful interference between radio stations of different countries,
- to coordinate efforts to eliminate harmful interference between the radio stations of different countries and to improve the use made of the radio-frequency spectrum for radiocommunication services and of the geostationary-satellite and other satellite orbits,
- to facilitate the worldwide standardisation of telecommunications, with the satisfactory quality of service,
- to foster international cooperation and solidarity in the delivery of technically assistance to the developing countries,
- to coordinate efforts to harmonise the development of telecommunication facilities, notably those using space techniques,
- to foster collaboration among Member States and Sector Members with a view to establishing the lowest possible rates, and
- to undertake studies, make regulations, adopt resolutions, formulate recommendations and opinions, and collect and publish information concerning telecommunication matters.[37]

4.17 Member States have reserved the right to convene regional conferences, to make regional arrangements and to form regional organisations for settling telecommunications questions which are susceptible of being treated on a regional basis, as long as such arrangements are not in conflict with either the Constitution or the Convention.[38] Such arrangements include, for example, the Inter-American Radio Agreement (Washington 1949); the Regional Agreement for the European Broadcasting Area (Stockholm 1961), and the Regional Agreement for the African Broadcasting Area (Geneva 1963).

---

36   Art 1 no 2–9 CS.
37   Art 1 no 10–16, 18 CS.
38   Art 43 CS.

Organisational Structure of the Union

Overview

4.18   The ITU has three organs which convene periodically and five permanent organs.[39] The supreme organ of the Union is the Plenipotentiary Conference, which is composed of delegations representing the Member States and is normally convened every four years.[40] The Council, which is composed of Members States elected by the Plenipotentiary Conference, acts in the interval between Plenipotentiary Conferences as the governing body of the Union within the limits of the powers delegated to it by the Plenipotentiary Conference.[41]

The World Conference on International Telecommunications may partially, or in exceptional cases, completely revise the International Telecommunication Regulations[42] and may deal with any question of a worldwide character within its competences and related to its agenda; its decisions must in all circumstances be in conformity with the Constitution and Convention of the Union.[43]

The permanent organs of the Union are the General Secretariat, which is directed by the Secretary General,[44] and the three Sectors of the Union, ITU-R, ITU-T and ITU-D.[45]

Plenipotentiary Conference

4.19   The Plenipotentiary Conference determines the general policies of the Union, establishes its strategic plan and the basis for the Union's budget, provides general directives dealing with the staffing of the Union, and examines its account and approves it, if appropriate.[46] The Plenipotentiary is also empowered to elect the Member States which are to serve on the Council, the Secretary General, the Deputy Secretary General and the Directors of the Bureaus, as well as the members of the Radio Regulations Board.[47] At any of these elections, the Plenipotentiary Conference has to give due consideration to an equitable geographical distribution amongst the regions of the world. As the Union's supreme organ, the Plenipotentiary is generally empowered to 'deal with such other telecommunication questions as may be necessary'.[48]

The Council

4.20   The Council comprises a maximum of 25 % of the total number of Member States, which are elected by the Plenipotentiary Conference with due regard to the need for equitable distribution of the Council seats among the five world regions

---

39   Art 7 CS.
40   Art 8 no 47 CS.
41   Art 20 no 65, 68 CS.
42   See paras 4.9–4.12 above.
43   Art 25 no 146–147 CS.
44   Art 11 CS.
45   See paras 4.25 et seq below.
46   Art 8 no 49, 51, 52, 53 CS.
47   Art 8 no 54, 55, 56 CS.
48   Art 8 no 59 CS.

(Americas, Western Europe, Eastern Europe, Africa, Asia and Australasia). Currently, the Council is comprised of 46 Members.

4.21 In addition to its task to consider, in the interval between Plenipotentiary Conferences, broad telecommunication policy issues and its duty to prepare a report, for consideration by the Plenipotentiary, on the policy and strategic planning of the Union, the Council is also responsible for ensuring the day-to-day functioning of the Union and to exercise effective financial control over the General Secretariat and the three Sectors. Furthermore, the Council has to take all steps to facilitate the implementation by the Member States of the provisions of the ITU's Constitution, the Convention, the administrative regulations, the decisions of the Plenipotentiary Conference and, where appropriate, of the decisions of other conferences and meetings of the Union.[49]

The General Secretariat

4.22 The General Secretariat, which is headed by the Secretary General, is responsible for the overall management of the Union's resources, the coordination of the activities of the General Secretariat and the Sectors of the Union, the coordination of the implementation of the Union's Strategic Plan and for the annual preparation of a four-year rolling operational plan of activities to be undertaken by the staff of the General Secretariat consistent with the strategic plan.[50] Other tasks of the General Secretariat include the management of the administrative and financial aspects of the Union's activities, including the provision of conference services, information services, and corporate functions, e.g. legal advice, finance, personnel, communications and common services.[51]

4.23 In order to ensure proper coordination among the three Sectors of the Union, a Coordination Committee has been established consisting of the Secretary General, the Deputy Secretary General and the Directors of the three Sector Bureaus.[52] The Coordination Committee is presided over by the Secretary General and acts as an 'internal management team, which advises and gives the Secretary General practical assistance on all administrative, financial, information system and technical cooperation matters which do not fall under the exclusive competence of a particular sector or of the General Secretariat and on external relations and public information'.[53]

World Conference on International Telecommunications

4.24 World Conferences on International Telecommunications are held at the request at the Plenipotentiary Conference and have treaty making powers: They can revise the International Telecommunication Regulations[54] and may deal with 'any question of a worldwide character within its competence and related to its agenda'.[55]

---

49   Art 10 no 69–71 CS, see also art 4 CV.
50   Art 5, 84, 85, 86 A, 87 A.
51   Cf art 5 CV.
52   Art 26 no 148 CS.
53   Art 26 no 149 CS; see also art 6 CV.
54   See paras 4.9–4.13 above.
55   Art 25 no 146 CS.

Tasks, Structure and Functioning of the Radiocommunications Sector

4.25 The tasks of the ITU's Radiocommunications Sector (ITU-R) are:

- to determine the technical characteristics and the operational procedures for a broad range of wireless communications services,
- to manage, at global level, the frequency spectrum by allocating bands of the radio frequency spectrum, allotting radio frequencies and registering radio frequency assignments and any associated orbital position in the geostationary satellite orbit in order to avoid harmful interference between radio stations of different countries, and
- to coordinate efforts to eliminate harmful interference between radio stations of different countries and to improve the use made of radio frequencies and of the geostationary satellite orbit for radiocommunication services.[56]

Structure

4.26 The Radiocommunication Sector works through:

- World and Regional Radiocommunication Conferences,
- Radiocommunication Assemblies,
- the Radiocommunication Bureau, which is headed by the elected Director,
- Radiocommunication Study Groups,
- the Radiocommunication Advisory Group, and
- the Radio Regulations Board.[57]

World Radiocommunication Conferences

4.27 World Radiocommunication Conferences ('WRC') are normally convened every two to three years. The conferences are composed of delegations of the administrations of Member States. The task of the WRC is to review and to revise, in part or in full, the Radio Regulations. In addition, the WRC may consider any radiocommunication matter of a worldwide character; it may instruct the Radio Regulation Board and the Radiocommunication Bureau and reviews their activities. Furthermore, the WRC identifies topics to be studied by the Radiocommunication Assembly and the Radiocommunication Study Group in preparation for future Radiocommunication Conferences. The general scope of the WRC's agenda is established four to six years in advance with the final agenda being established by the Council, two years before the conference, with the concurrence of a majority of the Member States.[58]

Regional Radiocommunication Conferences

4.28 Regional Radiocommunication Conferences (RRCs) are conferences of either one of the ITU regions or of a group of countries with a mandate to develop an agreement concerning a radiocommunication service or a frequency band of a

---

56 See also the mission statement in Resolution 71, Annex, Part II, 4.1.
57 Art 12 no 80–85 CS.
58 Section 8 no 118 CV.

regional nature.[59] A regional conference cannot modify the Radio Regulations, unless the proposed modifications are approved by a WRC[60] and the 'Final Acts' of the regional conferences are binding only on those countries that are party to the agreement.[61]

Radiocommunication Assembly

4.29 Radiocommunication Assemblies (RAs) are normally convened every two or three years and may be associated in time and place with Radiocommunication Conferences.[62] Their task is to approve the program of Radiocommunication Study Groups, to establish or dissolve Study Groups according to need, to consider Study Group reports and to approve, modify or reject the draft ITU-R recommendations contained in those reports. The Assembly assigns conference preparatory work and other questions to the Study Groups, responds to requests from ITU conferences, and suggests suitable topics for the agenda of future WRCs.

The Radiocommunication Bureau

4.30 The Radiocommunication Bureau ('BR'), which is headed by a Director elected by the Plenipotentiary Conference, organises and coordinates the work of the Radiocommunications Sector.[63] As the executive arm of the Radiocommunication sector, the Radiocommunication Bureau:

- provides administrative and technical support to Radiocommunication Conferences, Assemblies and Study Groups,
- applies the provisions of the Radio Regulations and of the various regional agreements,
- records and registers frequency assignments and orbital characteristics of space services, and maintains the 'Master International Frequency Register',
- provides advice to Member States on the equitable, effective and economical use of the radio frequency spectrum and satellite orbits and investigates and assists in resolving cases of harmful interference,
- coordinates the preparation, editing and dispatch of circulars, documents, and publications developed within the sector, and
- provides technical information and seminars on national frequency management and radio communications.

4.31 The Bureau fulfils its role as global spectrum coordinator through its Space Services Department ('SSD') and its Terrestrial Services Department ('TSD'). The SSD handles the procedures involved in the coordination and registration of satellite systems and earth stations, including the capture, processing and publication of the relevant data and the review of the frequency assignment notices submitted by national administrations with a view either to their inclusion in the official coordination procedure or to their recording in the Master International Frequency Register.

---

59   Art 9 no 138 CV.
60   Art 13 no 92 CS.
61   Art 9 no 138 CV.
62   Art 13 no 91 CS.
63   Art 16 CS, art 12 no 161 CV.

The TSD fulfils technical and regulatory functions in relation to terrestrial radio communication services, including the processing of frequency assignment notices and the maintenance of the Master International Frequency Register, which is regularly updated in accordance with the requirements of the Radio Regulations and of the relevant regional agreements. This Register currently includes over 1.2 million terrestrial frequency assignments and more than 325,000 assignments servicing some 1,500 satellite networks.

Radiocommunication Study Groups

4.32   Radiocommunication Study Groups are expert groups set up by a Radio-communications Assembly.[64] Currently, more than 1,500 specialists from telecommunication organisations and administrations throughout the world participate in the work of the Study Groups which encompasses the drafting of the technical bases for Radiocommunication Conferences, the preparation of draft recommendations and the compilation of handbooks on frequency management and use.

4.33   At present, ITU-R has established seven Study Groups specialising in (1) spectrum management, (2) radio wave propagation, (3) fixed-satellite service, (4) broadcasting services, (5) science services, (6) mobile, radiodetermination, amateur and related satellite services, and (7) fixed service.[65] As with other ITU Recommendations, compliance with the ITU-R Recommendations is not mandatory. However, having been developed by recognised radio communication experts, they enjoy a high reputation and are implemented on a worldwide basis.

Radiocommunication Advisory Group

4.34   The Radiocommunication Advisory Group ('RAG') consists of representatives of administrations of Member States, representatives of Sector Members and the Chairman of the Study Groups and other groups. The RAG's tasks are

- to review the priorities and strategies adopted in the ITU-R sector, to monitor the progress of and to provide guidance for the work of the Study Groups, and
- to recommend measures for fostering cooperation and coordination with other organisations and with other ITU Sectors.

The RAG acts as an advisory body to the Director of the Radiocommunication Bureau and may receive specific mandates from the Radiocommunication Assemblies.[66]

---

64   Art 11 no 148 CV.
65   For a detailed description of the work program of these Study Groups see International Telecommunication Union, Radiocommunication Bureau, ITU-R Study Groups, Geneva 2005.
66   For specific matters assigned to the RAG see Resolution ITU-R 52.

The Radio Regulations Board

4.35 The Radio Regulations Board ('RRB') consists of 12 elected members who are qualified in the field of Radiocommunications and have practical experience in the assignment and utilisation of frequencies.[67]

The Board Members do not act as representatives of their respective Member States or regions, but as 'custodians of an international public trust'.[68] They perform their duties independently and on a part-time basis.

4.36 The RRB approves the 'Rules of Procedure', which are used by the Radio-communication Bureau in applying the provisions of the Radio Regulations and registering frequency assignments made by the Member States. These 'Rules of Procedure' clarify and interpret the provisions of the Radio Regulations, regional agreements and resolutions and recommendations of World and Regional Radio-communication Conferences. The RRB also addresses matters referred to it by the Bureau which cannot be resolved through application of the Radio Regulations and the Rules of Procedures and considers appeals against decisions made by the Radiocommunication Bureau regarding frequency assignments. Furthermore, the RRB considers reports of unresolved interference investigations which have been carried out by the Bureau at the request of one or more administrations and adopts recommendations. Decisions of the RRB may be brought before the World Radiocommunication Conference.[69]

Tasks, Structure and Functioning of the Standardisation Sector

4.37 The task of the Telecommunication Standardisation Sector (ITU-T) is to study technical, operating and tariff questions and to ensure the production of recommendations with a view to standardising telecommunications on a worldwide basis.[70]

On 31 December 2004, ITU-T had 357 Sector Members and 90 associates. At present (July 2005), more than 2,700 recommendations (standards) are in force; while ITU-T recommendations are legally non-binding, they are generally complied with by manufacturers, network operators and service providers alike.

4.38 The Telecommunications Standardisation Sector operates through:

- World Telecommunication Standardisation Assemblies ('WTSA'),
- Telecommunications Standardisation Study Groups ('SG'),
- Telecommunications Standardisation Bureau ('TSB'), and
- Telecommunications Standardisation Advisory Group ('TSAG').

World Telecommunication Standardisation Assembly

4.39 The WTSA takes place every four years. It brings together delegations of the Member States, representatives of Sector Members and observers of regional telecommunication organisations, other regional organisations or international organisations dealing with matters of interest to the Assembly, and specialised

---

67 Art 14 no 93, 93 A CS, see also art 10 CV.
68 Art 14 no 98 CS.
69 Art 7 no 116 CV.
70 Art 17 no 104 CS; for the mission statement of ITU-T see Resolution 71, Annex, Part II, 5.1.

agencies of the United Nations.[71] The WTSA defines the general policy of the Sector and adopts its working methods and procedures.[72] It considers the reports of Study Groups and approves, modifies or rejects draft recommendations. It also approves the work program and the organisation of the work of ITU-T for each four year study period, establishes the Study Groups and appoints the Study Group Chairman and Vice Chairman.[73]

Telecommunication Standardisation Study Groups

4.40   The Telecommunication Standardisation Study Groups and their Working Parties conduct the actual standardisation work. They study the questions set forth in the work program established by the WTSA and elaborate the Recommendations.

For the study period 2005–2008, ITU-T has established 13 Study Groups which cover a broad range of topics, such as operational aspects of service provision, network and performance (Study Group 2), protection against electromagnet environment affects (Study Group 5), integrated broadband cable networks and television and sound transmission (Study Group 9), performance and quality of service (Study Group 12), next generation networks (Study Group 13), multimedia terminals, systems and applications (Study Group 16), and mobile telecommunication networks (Study Group 19).

Telecommunication Standardisation Bureau

4.41   The Telecommunication Standardisation Bureau ('TSB'), which is led by the elected director, organises and coordinates the work of the Telecommunication Standardisation Sector.[74] It provides secretarial support for the work of the ITU sector and services for the participants in ITU-T work, including the coordination of the approval process for recommendations and ensuring the publication of the ITU-T recommendations, handbooks and guides.

4.42   The TSB also coordinates international numbering: Based on an ITU-T recommendation establishing the country codes, which are the basis for the structuring of the international numbering space,[75] TSB provides country code number assignments for telephone, data and other services. It also acts as registrar for Universal International Free Phone Numbers, which enable an international free phone service customer to be allocated a unique Free Phone Number that is the same throughout the world.[76] The TSB also provides administrative support for the regulation of alternative calling procedures (call-back): Under a resolution adopted by the World Telecommunication Standardisation Assembly 2004[77] on alternative calling procedures on international telecommunication networks, each country has the right to authorise, prohibit or regulate call-back practices. National regulatory measures regarding call-back must be respected by other countries within the limits

---

71   Art 25 no 295–298 f CV.
72   Art 13 no 184 a CV.
73   Art 13 no 188, 191 a, 181 b CV.
74   Art 15 no 198 CV.
75   ITU-T Recommendation E.164.
76   This function is based on ITU-T Recommendation E.169 and Recommendation E.152.
77   Resolution 29 WTSA – 04.

of their own legislation. To facilitate the required collaboration between the National Regulatory Authorities in the ITU Member States, a draft guideline has been prepared under which ITU is to collect information once a year on the positions adopted by each country regarding call-back practices and to disseminate the findings among administrations to enable them to take the necessary steps to prevent call-back practices from being supplied to countries which prohibit them.[78]

Telecommunication Standardisation Advisory Group

4.43 The Telecommunication Standardisation Advisory Group ('TSAG') consists of representatives of the administrations of Member States, representatives of Sector Members and the Chairman of the ITU-T Study Groups and other Groups.[79] Its main task is to review the priorities, programs, operations, financial matters and strategies for the ITU-T sector, to restructure and establish ITU Study Groups and to provide guidelines for their operation. The TSAG also elaborates recommendations on the work methods and procedures of the ITU-T Study Groups.[80]

Alternative Approval Process (AAP)

4.44 In response to long-standing criticism of ITU-T's slow and cumbersome standardisation procedures, WTSA 2000 adopted a fast-track approval process for technical standards, the 'Alternative Approval Process' ('AAP').

Whereas the Traditional Approval Process ('TAP'), which is still used for recommendations that are considered to have regulatory or policy implications, requires an approval of proposed standards at a Study Group meeting, with prior determination at a previous Study Group or working party meeting, and an announcement by circular before the approval meeting, which adds up to an approval time of six to nine months, the Alternative Approval Process allows for approval of a recommendation within six weeks. under the AAP, once the text of a draft AAP recommendation is mature, it is submitted for consent at a Study Group or working party meeting. The consent given by the Study Group signals the start of the Approval Process which requires that the mature text is posted on the ITU-T website and an announcement is made that the AAP is in progress. Comments can then be made during a four week period. If no comments are received, the recommendation is considered approved by the Study Group Chairman in consultation with TSP.[81] Currently, more than 95 % of draft new or revised recommendations are approved under the AAP within six weeks of the 'consent' given at a Study Group meeting.

Tasks, Structure and Functioning of the Telecommunication Development Sector

4.45 The Telecommunication Development Sector ('ITU-D'), which was established in 1989, is the youngest Sector of the Union.

---

78   See, in this context, International Telecommunication Union, Telecommunication Standardisation Bureau, TSB Circular 30 CUM 3/ST of 2 May 2005: Replies to the questionnaire on conditions for provision of 'call-back'.

79   Art 14 a no 197 a CV.

80   Art 14 a no 197 b – 197 i CV.

81   For a detailed description see Recommendation H 8.

4.46   Its objective is to discharge 'the Union's dual responsibility as a United Nations specialised agency and executing agency for implementing projects under the United Nations development system or other funding arrangements so it has to facilitate and enhance telecommunications development by offering, organising and coordinating technical cooperation and assistance activities'.[82] ITU-D is structured similarly to the two other Sectors. It comprises:

- World and Regional Telecommunication Development Conferences,
- Telecommunication Development Study Groups,
- the Telecommunication Development Bureau, and
- the Telecommunication Development Advisory Group.

As of July 2005, ITU-D has approximately 500 Sector Members.

World and Regional Telecommunication Development Conferences

4.47   Telecommunication Development Conferences are fora for the discussion and consideration of topics, projects and programs relevant to telecommunication development and for the provision of direction and guidance to the Telecommunication Development Bureau.[83] The Telecommunication Development Conferences do not produce Final Acts, rather, their conclusions take the form of resolutions, decisions, recommendations or reports.[84] At the Third World Telecommunication Development Conference ('WTDC-02') in Istanbul 2002, a work programme and priorities for narrowing the 'digital divide' were defined.[85]

They include regulatory reform, the development of e-strategies and e-service applications for developing countries, the development and implementation of financing policies and strategies with a view to fostering affordable access to innovative and sustainable services, and human capacity building.

Study Groups

4.48   The current ITU-D Study Groups address telecommunication development strategies and policies and the development and management of telecommunication services and networks.[86] They produce recommendations, guidelines, handbooks, manuals and reports such as best practice guidelines for the regulation of interconnection, studies on communications systems for remote areas, or studies on the introduction of digital technology in developing countries.[87]

The Telecommunication Development Bureau

4.49   The Telecommunication Development Bureau ('BDT') is the executive arm of the Telecommunication Development Sector. It is headed by an elected Director.

---

82   Art 21 no 118 CS.
83   Art 22 no 137 CS.
84   Art 22 no 142 CS.
85   Istanbul Action Plan, in: Final Report, World Telecommunication Development Conference, Istanbul 2002, ITU 2002, pp 22 et seq.
86   Resolution 3 (Rev Istanbul, 2002).
87   Cf Resolution 3 (Rev Istanbul 2003), Appendix 3; ITU-D Study Group 2, List of Questions to be studied (study period 2002–2006).

Its tasks include fostering telecommunication development in developing countries through policy advise, the provision of technical assistance, the mobilisation of resources and initiatives with a view to bridge the 'digital divide'. BDT also supervises regional and global projects launch by ITU-D to assist developing countries in modernising their telecommunications systems and regulatory frameworks.

Telecommunication Development Advisory Group

4.50 The Telecommunication Development Advisory Group is open to representatives of Member States, Sector Members and to Chairmen and Vice Chairmen of Study Groups; it meets once a year. Its mandate is to review priorities, programs, operations, financial measures and strategies for the activities in the ITU-D sector and to advise the Director of ITU-D accordingly.

ITU Reform

4.51 For the last three decades, the ITU has been engaged in a lengthy process of mainly incremental reforms of its structure, its procedures and its management. Many of the reforms were brought about by the transformation of the telecommunications sector which, in turn, has been a consequence of market liberalisation, the convergence of the telecommunications sector with the computing and broadcasting sectors, and the development of the Internet which is transforming the industry.

4.52 Following a debate of the need to adapt the Union's organisational structure to its changing environment, the 1989 Nice Plenipotentiary Conference established the High Level Committee ('HLC') with a mandate to carry out an in-depth review of the ITU's structure and functioning. Based on the HLC's report,[88] a special Plenipotentiary Conference in 1992 overhauled the structure of the Union by creating the ITU-T, ITU-R and ITU-D Sectors. Initiated by the Kiyoto Plenipotentiary Conference of 1994,[89] a task force known as ITU-2000 conducted another in-depth review of the Union's structure and submitted a series of recommendations,[90] including recommendations on enhanced cooperation with the private sector through Sector Members and the membership status termed 'associate',[91] the acceleration of the ITU's standardisation process, and recommendations to improve the ITU's financial situation.

4.53 The Plenipotentiary Conference Minneapolis 1998 approved the streamlined standardisation process[92] and broadened the private sector's rights in the standardisation process. The Plenipotentiary renewed its commitment to organisational reform by establishing a new 'Working Group for Reform' ('WGR') with the mandate to review the management, functioning and structure of the Union as well as the rights and obligations of Member States and Sector Members. The WGR's

---

88 Report of the High Level Committee to review the structure and functioning of the International Telecommunication Union, Tomorrow's ITU: The Challenges of Change, Geneva 1991.
89 See Resolution 15, Resolution 39.
90 ITU-2000 Recommendations, RAG 98–1/6-E.
91 See para 4.14 above.
92 See para 4.44 above.

final report[93] contained forty recommendations for the improvement of the Union's budgetary system, the effectiveness of its overall management and of the effectiveness of several of its organs, including the Plenipotentiary Conference, the General Secretariat, the Council, the World Radiocommunications and Development Conferences and the Council.

4.54   At the Plenipotentiary Conference in Marrakesh in 2002, only modest steps were made towards increased rights for industry in the standardisation process; the Plenipotentiary instructed the Council to establish a 'Group of Specialists' ('GoS'), composed of five individuals, one from each administrative region, with a mandate to review the management of the Union.[94] In its report, which was submitted in May 2003, the GoS submitted 21 'near term', 'mid term' and 'long term' recommendations, including recommendations on the Council's oversight role, the Union's system of budgets, financial management control mechanisms and cost accounting, the need for decentralisation of authority and for comprehensive review of ITU's plans and budgets.[95]

4.55   As the debate on ITU reform has focused more on more on narrow and detailed issues of the ITU's management, more basic, structural issues seem to have disappeared from the reform agenda.[96] They include:

- the allocation of functions between the ITU Sectors, in particular ITU-R and ITU-T, and
- an adaptation of the Sectors' organisational structures and their procedural rules to their respective functions.

4.56   The development of telecommunications technology, the privatisation of state-owned communications entities and the liberalisation of telecommunications markets has led, in many Member States of the Union, to a separation of regulatory and operational functions.[97] As part of this functional separation, the preparation and adoption of technical standards, including standards in the telecommunications field, has largely been entrusted to private standardisation bodies.[98]

4.57   Regulatory functions include:

- regulation of market entry and/or supervision of market behaviour,
- regulation of enterprises with significant market power,
- regulation of access and interconnection,
- frequency planning and management including the allocation of frequency bands to specific radio services,
- management of the numbering space, including the allocation of country codes,
- regulation of universal service provision,

---

93   Document C 2001/25–1 of 1 May 2001.
94   Decision 7 (Marrakesh 2002).
95   See Review of the management of the Union, Report of Group of Specialists (GoS) to review the management of the Union to the ITU Council, C 03/32 (Rev 1)-E; for the implementation of the GoS Recommendations, see Council Resolution 1216 of 16 June 2004.
96   See Note by the Secretary General, Report by the Chairman of the Working Group on Structure – Review of the ITU Structure, Document C 05/34-E, 14 April 2005.
97   For Europe see art 3 para 2 Framework Directive; see para 1.52 above.
98   For an analysis of telecommunication standardisation in Europe as a system of 'regulated self-regulation', see Kerstin Schultheiss, Europäische Telekommunikationsstandardisierung, Münster 2004, pp 245 et seq.

- consumer protection, and
- protection of telecommunications secrecy and data protection.

4.58 The ITU has not adapted its organisational structure and its allocation of functions among ITU-R and ITU-T to this universally accepted structural separation: While ITU-R currently discharges mainly regulatory functions with respect to spectrum allocation and frequency management, it also engages in standardisation activity in the radiocommunications field. On the other hand, ITU-T, while predominantly entrusted with standardisation in the Telecommunications Sector, has traditionally also been engaged in certain regulatory functions, such as, in particular, the administration of the international numbering space.

4.59 Separating regulatory from standardisation functions and allocating them to ITU-R and ITU-T respectively, could have benefits for all stakeholders concerned: The standardisation process could be further streamlined and the role of Sector Members with respect to the adoption of standards could be strengthened. To the extent that technical standards have regulatory implications, ITU-R could be empowered to validate the relevant standards and/or to 'mandate' ITU-T to elaborate certain standards with regulatory implications.

On the other hand, ITU-R, as a 'regulatory' sector could streamline its organisational structure and its procedures and include the national regulatory authorities in its decision making structure.[99]

4.60 On the basis of a clear allocation of regulatory and non-regulatory (standardisation) functions, the Union would be well positioned to overcome what appears to be one of the major obstacles to its organisational efficiency, namely the Union's 'one size fits all' approach in organising its three Sectors. It has been noted[100] that for historical and political reasons, the three Sectors of the Union have been structured in a broadly identical fashion, despite their completely diverging purposes and objectives; this has led to radical reform proposals to re-organise ITU by establishing three differently structured organisational entities (a regulatory body, a standardisation body and a development agency) under its roof.

4.61 A less radical restructuring of the ITUs sectors along the lines of regulatory and operational (standardisation) functions would pave the way for a rational discussion of new, additional 'regulatory' tasks to be discharged by ITU-R at international level: they could include, for example, international cooperation to combat spam and the misuse of numbering, the coordination of measures to enhance information security and data protection and contributions to Internet governance, which is currently high on the agenda of communications policy makers in preparation of the 'World Summit on the Information Society in Tunis 2005'.[101]

---

99   To date, the NRAs participate in ITU activities mainly through conferences and regulator.

100 *Don McLean*, Sovereign Right and the Dynamics of Power in the ITU: Lessons in the Quest for Inclusive Global Governance, Manuscript, 2003.

101 For a summary of ITU's activities to date see ITU, ITU and its Activities Related to Internet Protocol (IP) Networks, April 2004; see also Working Group on Internet Governance, Report of the Working Group on Internet Governance, June 2005.

THE WTO

The WTO in a Nutshell

4.62   The World Trade Organisation ('WTO') is an international, intergovernmental organisation. There are currently 148 Members,[102] including all major trading nations. Key exceptions include Russia, Saudi Arabia, Iran, Ukraine and Vietnam, most of which are currently negotiating their accession to the organisation. The WTO thus enjoys near-global coverage.

4.63   The WTO came into being on 1 December 1995 as result of the 'Uruguay Round' of multilateral trade negotiations launched in 1986 by Members of the General Agreement on Tariffs and Trade ('GATT') of 1947. For the first time in the history of successive trade rounds, the agenda covered not only trade in goods but also, inter alia, trade in services and the protection of trade-related intellectual property rights. The round resulted in the Agreement establishing the World Trade Organisation ('WTO Agreement'), concluded in 1994 in Marrakesh, which contained under its umbrella not only the revised GATT with multiple sub-agreements but also, among other things, a new General Agreement on Trade in Services ('GATS') as well as the Agreement on Trade-Related Intellectual Property Rights ('TRIPS') – the three 'pillars' of the WTO system.

4.64   There are numerous other so-called WTO Covered Agreements that, depending upon the subject matter, may or may not be relevant to telecommunications services and products. Other Covered Agreements include:

- Agreement on Technical Barriers to Trade,
- Agreement on Trade-Related Investment Measures,
- Anti-Dumping Agreement,
- Agreement on Customs Valuation,
- Agreement on Pre-shipment Inspection,
- Agreement on Rules of Origin,
- Agreement on Import Licensing,
- Agreement on Subsidies and Countervailing Measures,
- Safeguards Agreement, and
- Government Procurement Agreement.

4.65   While the GATS is the most important of the Covered Agreements for telecommunications, GATT and TRIPS are also of significance to the sector. The GATS provides a framework of rules for the international trade in telecommunications services of all kinds. Specific market access commitments undertaken by WTO Members under the GATS include specific access rights for telecommunication services and service providers in a number of so-called 'modes of supply' (see below). In addition, in the landmark 1997 'Fourth Protocol to the GATS'[103] countries undertook a set of commitments on regulatory disciplines in the basic telecommunications sector by subscribing to the so-called 'Reference Paper'.[104] The GATT, in turn, governs the regulation of international trade in telecommunications-related goods, as well as trade in goods sold via telecommunication means, including the 'physical side' of virtually all forms of e-commerce. The TRIPS establishes a high level of protection of trade-related intellectual property

---

102   Status in August 2005.
103   Fourth Protocol to the General Agreement on Trade in Services, S/L/20, adopted 30 April 1996, entered into force on 5 February 1998.
104   See paras 4.110 et seq below.

rights ('IPRs'). These include IPRs specifically relevant to telecommunications operators such as patents, trademarks, copyrights, integrated circuits, and business secrets.

4.66 Apart from the substantive rules set out in the Covered Agreements, there is also the Dispute Settlement Understanding ('DSU'), establishing a very effective dispute settlement system, as well as a Trade Policy Review Mechanism ('TPRM') which provides for a regular comprehensive review of every Member's policies relating to the WTO agreements.[105]

The Relevance of WTO Rules to Private Companies

4.67 As the WTO is an intergovernmental organisation, it may be asked why WTO law may be of relevance to private persons. As the WTO system has only been in existence for ten years, businesses have yet to realise the full potential of how the WTO forum and its rules can be of assistance. In developing commercial strategy, a company must take on board important questions of market access, preferential tariffs, licensing requirements, entry tests and recognition of standards. A company can waste significant amounts of time and effort if it has not adequately considered the basic trade and investment framework of a target market. However, where a company keeps abreast of WTO rules and is attuned to their local implementation, it can reduce both trade and investment risks. There are at least three areas where companies will interface with the WTO, namely (i) in domestic litigation, (ii) in international dispute settlement and (iii) in domestic and international rule-making processes.

4.68 In certain jurisdictions, private persons can rely directly on the WTO obligations of their country in private actions before national courts. However, most systems (including the EC, the US and Japan) generally refuse to recognise the direct effect of WTO obligations within their domestic systems. Notwithstanding this, many courts adhere to a doctrine of consistent interpretation, whereby courts interpret domestic law to be consistent with the relevant country's obligations pursuant to public international law, which will include WTO law. WTO law can, therefore, be a useful mechanism to assist a private person to influence a national court to adopt a certain interpretation of domestic law.

4.69 Even though the WTO Dispute Settlement Mechanism is purely intergovernmental (with no rights for private persons to commence actions),[106] private persons can play a key role in initiating a dispute. It is often private companies that bring to the attention of their government the fact that they are having difficulty penetrating an overseas market and that accordingly an overseas country may be violating its

---

105 A useful text providing an overview of WTO law is *The World Trade Organization, Law, Practice, and Policy* (The Oxford International Law Library), Matsushita, Schoenbaum and Mavroidis. A number of articles have also been written addressing the impact of the WTO system on the telecommunications industry. See, for example, Luff, *Telecommunications and Audio-visual Services: Considerations for a Convergence Policy at the World Trade Organization*, Journal of World Trade 38(6), 2004, 1059 – 1086 and also Zhao, *Further Liberalization of Telecommunications Services in the Framework of the WTO in the 21st Century*, International Journal of Communications Law and Policy, Issue 8, Winter 2003/4.

106 There is the possibility for private persons to submit *amicus curiae* briefs (or so-called friend of the court letter) to WTO panels or the Appellate Body. However, past practice indicates that there is a reluctance to take on board the views of private companies in dispute settlement cases unless the brief is formally adopted by one of the governmental parties to the dispute.

WTO obligations. The company can assist its government to investigate a possible violation by another country by providing trade data and other relevant commercial information. Companies could also be the driving force behind the dispute by funding the legal costs associated with WTO dispute proceedings. A private person can also play a crucial role in monitoring compliance with dispute settlement rulings that are eventually handed down.

4.70   Finally, and perhaps most importantly, companies can also use WTO rules as part of policy advocacy or lobbying initiatives before both national and international fora. At the national level, this may involve, for example, private companies arguing that, in order to ensure compliance with WTO obligations, a national telecommunications regulator must take certain action against dominant telecommunications undertakings to prevent anti-competitive behaviour. At the international level, this could entail companies lobbying their national delegation to the ITU, for example, to argue against relevant ITU policy initiatives in case they could result in a conflict between the ITU and WTO regimes. Therefore, WTO rules can assist companies to play a pivotal role in influencing the rule-making process at both the domestic and international level.

Telecommunications at the WTO – A Brief Historical Overview

4.71   At the start of the Uruguay Round in 1986, telecommunications services around the globe were still largely in the hands of state-owned national monopolies. At the time, the United States had just experienced the break-up of AT&T. A year later, in 1987, the European Commission made its first proposals for a partial liberalisation of telecommunications services in the European Community.[107]

4.72   Sectoral talks on telecommunications services began in 1989. The negotiations, however, encountered several specific difficulties. The Members agreed to extend sectoral negotiations on basic telecommunications until 1996.[108] These continued negotiations first resulted in a breakdown in 1996 when the United States pulled out, claiming a lack of a critical mass of commitments from other Members. The negotiations ultimately resulted in a significant package of specific commitments in basic telecommunications services undertaken by 69 countries. In addition to specific market access commitments, all but two of these countries undertook to adhere to a 'Reference Paper' that includes regulatory disciplines.

4.73   In the recent landmark dispute settlement case of *Mexico – Measures Affecting Telecommunication Services* (hereinafter: *'Telmex'*), the WTO dispute settlement panel found Mexico to be in violation of, inter alia, obligations relating to interconnection and to the prevention of anti-competitive practices, both sets of obligations emanating from the 'Reference Paper'.[109]

'Rule of Law': Dispute Settlement at the WTO

4.74   In contrast to the former GATT system, the WTO emerged as a strictly rules-based system. While a dispute settlement system had in fact gradually evolved

---

107   See European Commission, Green Paper on the Development of the Common Market for Telecommunications Services and Equipment, COM (87) 290 Final (Brussels, June 30, 1987).

108   Decision on Negotiations on Basic Telecommunications, attached to the WTO Agreement.

109   The relevant findings of the Panel are discussed below in the context of the respective rules and commitments.

under the GATT over the 47 years of its operation, it remained largely a forum for diplomatic, rather than law-based, solutions. Under the previous GATT system, the final adoption of panel verdicts, or 'reports', required the consensus of GATT contracting parties. The reports could, therefore, be – and commonly were – blocked by the losing party. GATT obligations were, therefore, seen as something less than hard law due to the ability to block reports.

4.75 The WTO, in marked contrast, benefits from a two-instance, compulsory and rather expedient dispute settlement procedure under the Dispute Settlement Understanding (DSU), another multilateral agreement that forms part of the 'single undertaking' of all WTO Members. Disputes between WTO Members over alleged violations of the WTO Covered Agreements (eg the GATT, the GATS and the TRIPS) can be brought before a dispute settlement panel. The panel's verdict is issued in the form of a 'report'.[110] The parties to a dispute may then appeal a panel report, in which case the WTO Appellate Body will review the decision. The appeals review process is limited to issues of law.

4.76 The procedure is governed by detailed rules and a fixed timetable. The DSU provides that the time from the request for the establishment of a panel until the adoption of its report should be no longer than 9 months and, in the case of an appeal, no longer than 12 months. While these deadlines are sometimes missed, WTO dispute settlement proceedings are still, nonetheless, faster than many domestic judicial proceedings.

4.77 Most importantly, the DSU no longer allows the losing party to block the adoption of the ruling of the panel. Instead of the 'positive consensus' required under the old GATT 1947, which gave each country a veto, the DSU provides for a 'negative consensus' rule, under which a consensus will be required amongst Members to block a panel report.

4.78 The outcome, 'the report', is a legally binding decision, which obliges the state to comply with it. In the vast majority of cases, WTO Members comply with panel or Appellate Body rulings without further enforcement. However, the DSU permits two sanctions if the rulings of the panel or the Appellate Body are not implemented within a reasonable period. The first is compensation payable by the losing party, which may typically consist of additional trade concessions, usually in related economic areas to the dispute, that are acceptable to the winning party as a substitute for maintaining the trade barriers in dispute. Compensation is a voluntary remedy in that it requires the agreement of both parties to the dispute. The second sanction is retaliation (suspension of concessions) against the losing party. Retaliation must be authorised by the Dispute Settlement Body and it must match the level of the impairment suffered by the winning party.

4.79 In the ten years since its inception, the WTO dispute settlement system has handled more than 300 cases, more than its predecessor GATT in 47 years. In the recent *Telmex* case – the first WTO dispute to be resolved solely under the GATS – the United States successfully challenged certain regulations of Mexico's telecommunications law. The United States had, in particular, complained that Mexico

---

110 A semantic concession to GATT history. WTO panel or Appellate Body reports are de facto binding judgments.

failed to ensure that its dominant provider 'Telmex' provided interconnection to US telecom suppliers on reasonable terms and that Mexico failed to prevent Telmex's anti-competitive practices.[111]

THE GATS

Structure

4.80   The GATS aims to cover, in principle, all international trade in services between WTO Members. Broadly modelled on the GATT, the GATS is built on the principles of market access, non-discrimination, transparency, the rule of law, and, more generally, predictability and reliability in relation to national regulations affecting trade in services.

4.81   Unlike the GATT, however, the GATS itself does not provide for absolute market access rights. Such rights are exclusively contained in the specific national commitments embodied in the so-called schedules.

Principles

Four Modes of Supply

4.82   Article I (2) of the GATS defines four 'modes of supply' of services in international trade, namely:

(a)   services supplied from the territory of one Member into the territory of another Member (cross-border supply, also called 'mode 1');

(b)   services supplied in the territory of one Member to the service consumer of another Member (consumption abroad, also called 'mode 2');

(c)   services supplied by a service supplier of one Member through commercial presence in the territory of another Member (commercial presence, also called 'mode 3'); and

(d)   services supplied by a service supplier of one Member through the presence of natural persons of a Member in the territory of another Member (presence of natural persons, also called 'mode 4').

4.83   These four modes aim to cover any situation where a service is traded internationally. The most important, both generally and for telecommunications services, are modes 1 and 3. Under mode 1, the service itself, but not the service provider, crosses national borders. It, therefore, resembles to some extent trade in goods. Under mode 3, service suppliers establish themselves in the territory of another Member. This includes the establishment of a subsidiary or branch as well as the investment in existing service suppliers of that Member. Mode 3, in other words, covers investment in services sectors.

The modes of supply are of crucial relevance for the scheduling of specific market access commitments.[112]

4.84   The classification of a specific provision of a service into the system of the four modes of supply can be difficult. While, for example, mode 1 clearly applies if

---

111   We discuss the details of the case below in the respective context of the relevant legal provisions.

112   See para 4.94 below.

a lawyer provides legal advice via telephone to a client in another country, the panel in the *Telmex* case had to deal with an argument put forward by Mexico that the cross-border supply of voice telephony pre-supposed that the service provider was using its own lines on both sides of the border. The panel rejected that interpretation and held that a call from the United States into Mexico constituted the cross-border supply of voice telephony services, irrespective of whether the call was carried through on owned or leased network capacity.[113]

Most-Favoured Nation

4.85   Article II GATS provides in para 1:

'With respect to any measure covered by this Agreement, each Member shall accord immediately and unconditionally to services and service suppliers of any other Member treatment no less favourable than that it accords to like services and service suppliers of any other country.'

It should be noted that the Most-Favoured Nation Principle applies independently of whether the respective Member has made specific market access commitments in the respective sector. To the extent that it allows a service provider from any country (not only another WTO Member) to provide a service under any of the four modes of supply, it must grant the same access to services and service suppliers of other WTO Members. It should further be noted that, as under Article I GATT, the Most-Favoured Nation Principle applies unconditionally, ie it is not subject to reciprocity.

4.86   Members of the WTO had the one-time chance to schedule, ie reserve, exceptions to this Most-Favoured Nation Principle at the time when they scheduled their specific market access commitments. For the original Members of the WTO, this was at the time of the conclusion of the Uruguay Round. For Members who have acceded to the WTO after that date, their 'Article II Exemptions' had to be scheduled at the time of accession.

Market Access and National Treatment

4.87   Article XVI GATS is the provision that links the so-called 'Schedules' of specific commitments relating to market access to the GATS itself. Article XVI incorporates the individual schedules of WTO Members as integral parts into the GATS. The specific commitments included in a Member's schedule thereby become enforceable WTO law vis-à-vis any other Member.

4.88   Article XVII GATS provides that within scheduled/committed services sectors and modes of supply, a Member has to grant national treatment to services and service suppliers from other WTO Members. This means that they enjoy treatment no less favourable than corresponding national services or service suppliers of that Member.

4.89   The restriction of national treatment to scheduled services is a marked departure from the GATT model. Whereas under Article III GATT, goods generally enjoy national treatment (once they have cleared the border), national treatment under the GATS is firmly restricted to scheduled sectors and modes of supply.

---

113 *Mexico – Measures Affecting Telecommunication Services*, Report of the Panel, WT/DS 204/R, para 7.45 (2 April 2004).

This means that outside of such scheduled coverage, service suppliers can only demand Most-Favoured Nation treatment, ie equal treatment with other third country suppliers. They have no right to national treatment unless the services are scheduled. The nature and structure of schedules is further discussed below.

Transparency and Domestic Regulation

4.90 Article III (1) GATS provides that a Member must publish 'all relevant measures of general application which pertain to or affect the operation of this Agreement' promptly, which means at the latest by the time of their entry into force, except in emergency situations. Further, a Member must notify such measures to the WTO[114] (para 3). Most importantly, a Member is obliged to maintain so-called 'anchor points' where other Members can obtain relevant information.

Domestic Regulation

4.91 While the preamble of the GATS explicitly recognises the right of WTO Members to regulate services, Article VI of the Agreement provides for certain disciplines on such domestic regulation. In sectors where a Member has undertaken specific commitments, it is bound to 'ensure that all measures of general application affecting trade and services are administered in a reasonable, objective and impartial manner'.[115] In addition, Members have to provide for an objective and impartial review of administrative decisions relating to trade and services through judicial, arbitral or administrative tribunals or procedures.[116] A Member is further bound to provide for speedy and transparent authorisation procedures.[117] Qualification requirements and procedures, technical standards and licensing requirements should not constitute unnecessary barriers to trade in services. The requirements applied should be based on objective and transparent criteria, should not be more burdensome than necessary to ensure quality and, in the case of licensing procedures, should not in themselves constitute restrictions on the supply of the service.[118]

Exceptions

4.92 A number of exceptions apply to the coverage of general GATS rules. The Most-Favoured Nation and National Treatment Principles, as well as specific scheduled commitments, do not apply to government procurement. WTO Members thereby remain free to discriminate against, and not procure from, foreign service suppliers.[119]

4.93 Similar to Article XX GATT, Article XIV contains 'general exceptions' for measures necessary for the advancement of non-trade-related policy goals such as

---

114 Council for Trade and Services.
115 Article VI (1) GATS.
116 Article VI (2) (a) GATS.
117 Article VI (3) GATS.
118 These criteria apply directly in sectors where a Member has made specific commitments, see Article VI (5) GATS. In other sectors, guidelines are provided for further disciplines to be developed under the auspices of the Council for Trade and Services ((Article VI) (4) GATS).
119 Article XIII (1) GATS. Paragraph 2 of the provision provides for negotiations on disciplines on such government procurement. However, no results have been achieved until now.

the protection of public morals, the maintenance of public order or the protection of human, animal or plant life or health. Such measures are consistent with the GATS if they 'are not applied in a manner which could constitute a means of arbitrary or unjustifiable discrimination between countries where like conditions prevail, or a disguised restriction on trade and services'. Article XIV bis furthermore provides for security exceptions.

Schedules of Specific Commitments

4.94 GATS schedules are relatively complex documents.[120] They usually contain two major sections on horizontal commitments (applying to all scheduled services sectors) and vertical, or sector-specific, commitments (applying specifically to a listed services sector or sub-sector). Both are contained in tables consisting of four columns.

4.95 The first column names and, where necessary, further describes those service sectors or sub-sectors for which commitments are undertaken.[121] Listing sectors or sub-sectors in the first column opens up these sectors for services and service suppliers from other WTO Members under any of the four modes of supply, unless the second column specifies restrictions. The second column, therefore, usually contains a number of specific limitations, specified with respect to each mode of supply with respect to each scheduled sector. Typical market access limitations include, for example, maximum percentages of foreign shareholdings in national service supply companies (commercial presence, mode of supply 3).

4.96 Because Article XVII GATS provides in principle for the extension of national treatment to all scheduled services, the third column must contain all limitations on national treatment that the respective WTO Member wants to maintain in these sectors. Any limitation on national treatment not listed in this column would be contrary to WTO law. The fourth column finally contains any additional commitments WTO Members may want to schedule. By way of example, the parties to the Fourth Protocol to the GATS of 1997 included their commitment to the 'Reference Paper' in this column.

4.97 By way of example, the section of the United States' schedule covering basic telecommunications[122] – a relatively simple schedule – looks as follows:

---

120 For background information on schedules und scheduling see Guidelines for the Scheduling of Specific Commitments under the General Agreement on Trade in Services (GATS), S/L/92, 28 March 2001.

121 In the horizontal commitments section this entry usually reads 'All sectors included in this schedule,' referring to the specific sectors listed further below in the schedule.

122 GATS/SC/90/Suppl. 2, as agreed under the Fourth Protocol to the GATS of 11 April 1997.

UNITED STATES – SCHEDULE OF SPECIFIC COMMITMENTS (Excerpt)

Modes of supply: 1) Cross-border supply 2) Consumption abroad 3) Commercial presence 4) Presence of natural persons

Sector or Sub-sector	Limitations on Market Access	Limitations on National Treatment	Additional Commitments
2.C. TELECOMMUNICATIONS SERVICES:*			
2.C.a. Voice services 2.C.b. Packet-switched data transmission services 2.C.c. Circuit-switched data transmission services 2.C.d. Telex services 2.C.e. Telegraph services 2.C.f. Facsimile services 2.C.g. Private leased circuit services 2.C.o. Other Mobile Services Analogue/Digital cellular services PCS (Personal Communications services) Paging services Mobile data services * Excluding one-way satellite transmissions of DTH and DBS television services and of digital audio services	(1) None (2) None (3) None, other than - Comsat has exclusive rights to links with Intelsat and Inmarsat. - Ownership of a common carrier radio license: **Indirect: None** **Direct: May not be granted to or held by** (a) foreign government or the representative thereof (b) non-US citizen or the representative of any non-US citizen (c) any corporation not organized under the laws of the United States or (d) US corporation of which more than 20% of the capital stock is owned or voted by a foreign government or its representative, non-US citizens or their representatives or a corporation not organized under the laws of the United States. (4) Unbound except as indicated by horizontal commitments	(1) None (2) None (3) None (4) Unbound except as indicated by horizontal commitments.	The United States undertakes the obligations contained in the Reference Paper attached hereto.

4.98   It should be noted that in the language of GATS scheduling, 'none' indicates 'no limitations', ie full commitments, whereas 'unbound' indicates the opposite, namely 'no commitments'.

Specific Commitments and Rules Relating to Telecommunications under the GATS

Categories of Telecommunications services and the Distinction between Basic and Value-Added Telecommunications

4.99   The GATS Services Sectoral Classification List[123] used by most Members in the Uruguay Round negotiations breaks down telecommunications into 14 sub-sectors (a. – n.) and one 'other' (o.) category. The list did not differentiate between basic and value added telecommunications services. That distinction was introduced into the GATS framework by the United States, reflecting US regulatory categories used to delineate the powers of the FCC.[124] The exact delineation between the two categories is a matter of varying interpretations by Members.[125] US law defines basic services as 'the offering of transmission capacity for the movement of information' while value-added, or enhanced, services are defined as 'any offering over the telecommunications network that is more than a basic transmission service'.[126]

4.100   The distinction played a role not so much in designing schedules, where Members make use of the said 15 categories, but in the negotiations and in particular in the decision to split negotiations in two when it became clear that Members were too far away from an agreement on commitments on basic telecommunications at the end of the Uruguay Round. While Members did make commitments in value-added services at that time, they decided to leave basic telecommunications on the table. The Decision on Negotiations on Basic Telecommunications annexed to the WTO Agreement required further negotiations that eventually resulted in the Fourth Protocol to the GATS of 1997.[127] The Decision defines basic telecommunications simply as 'trade in telecommunications transport networks and services'.[128] The categories used in the negotiations leading to the 'Fourth Protocol' included a. voice telephone, b. packet-switched data transmission, c. circuit-switched data transmission, d. telex, e. telegraph, f. telefax, g. private-leased circuit and o. 'other' services, including, inter alia, mobile phone, paging and teleconferencing services.[129]

---

123   MTN.GNS/W/120. Use of the list was not obligatory. Members were free to use other categorisations if they saw fit. However, most Members' schedules make extensive use of the list.

124   See Marco Bronckers & Pierre Larouche, Telecommunications Services (2005), p 996.

125   See Telecommunications Services, Background Note by the WTO Secretariat, S/C/W/74, 8 December 1998, para 7.

126   The definitions stem from the FCC's 'Computer Inquiries', see Marco Bronckers & Pierre Larouche, Telecommunications Services, p 996 (2005).

127   See para 4.107 below.

128   Decision on Negotiations on Basic Telecommunications, para 1.

129   Use of the 'other' category in relation to the distinction is not uniform.

4.101   The distinction between basic and value-added services, however, does play an important role with respect to the 'Reference Paper', which defines its scope as being solely related to 'principles and definitions on the regulatory framework for the basic telecommunications services'.[130]

The Annex on Telecommunications

4.102   The Annex on Telecommunications[131] (the 'Annex') provides for additional, specific disciplines beyond the GATS on 'measures of a Member that affect access to and use of public telecommunications transport networks and services'.[132] The preamble to the Annex emphasises 'the dual role [of telecommunications] as a distinct sector of economic activity and as the underlying transport means for other economic activities'. The Annex, consequently, contains disciplines to ensure that other sectors do not suffer indirectly from insufficient commitments in telecommunications.[133] The Annex thereby comes as a 'bonus'[134] to service suppliers that benefit from scheduled commitments.

ACCESS TO AND USE OF NETWORKS

4.103   Paragraph 5 (a) of the Annex states that:

'[e]ach Member shall ensure that any service supplier of any other Member is accorded access to and use of public telecommunications transport networks and services on reasonable and non-discriminatory terms and conditions, for the supply of a service included in its Schedule.'[135]

4.104   These access rights are further specified in some detail.[136] The panel in *Telmex* interpreted 'reasonable terms' to include requirements akin to, even if not as far-reaching as, 'cost-orientation' as required by Section 2.1 (b) Reference Paper.[137] It, therefore, found Mexico's termination rates for incoming international calls in violation of the above provision (in addition to a violation of the Reference Paper) because they were significantly above costs.

RESERVED RIGHTS OF MEMBERS

4.105   Members retain the right to take measures necessary to ensure the security and confidentiality of messages as long as these measures are not discriminating.[138] They also retain the right to impose conditions necessary to safeguard suppliers'

---

130   Reference Paper, annexed to the Fourth Protocol to the GATS, see para 4.110 below.
131   'Integral part' of the GATS, see article XXIX GATS.
132   See para 1 of the Annex.
133   Bronckers and Larouche, para 4.99, note 124 above, p 998, call it 'an insurance policy for suppliers of other services.'
134   Bronckers and Larouche, para 4.99, note 124 above, at p 999.
135   Section 5 (a) of the Annex.
136   Subparagraph (b) specifies that such service suppliers should be allowed to:
137   purchase or lease and attach terminal or other equipment which interface with the network and which is necessary to supply a supplier's services;
138   interconnect private leased or owned circuits with public telecommunications transport networks and services; or with other privately owned or leased circuits; and

public services responsibilities, to protect the technical integrity of public networks and services or to enforce the limitations of services commitments made.[139]

TRANSPARENCY

4.106 Extending the transparency obligations of article III of the GATS, the Annex requires Members to ensure that

> 'relevant information on conditions affecting access to and use of public telecommunications transport networks and services is publicly available, including: tariffs and other terms and conditions of service; specifications of technical interfaces with such networks and services; information on bodies responsible for the preparation and adoption of standards affecting such access and use; conditions applying to attachment of terminal or other equipment; and notifications, registration or licensing requirements, if any.'[140]

The Fourth Protocol to the GATS

4.107 The Fourth Protocol,[141] at the time of its conclusion in 1997 also referred to as the 'Agreement on Basic Telecommunications,' brought two major developments.

4.108 First, it contained as annexes supplements to 55 GATS schedules covering 69 states[142] containing in large part significant market access commitments in basic telecommunications services, including commitments relating to commercial presence – ie total or partial equity investment in local telecoms operators – from 56 countries covering roughly 97% of total revenue from basic telecoms worldwide.[143]

4.109 Second, remarkably all but two[144] signatories to the Fourth Protocol agreed to undertake significant additional commitments on regulatory principles in the area of basic telecommunications contained in the so-called Reference Paper.[145]

The 'Reference Paper'

4.110 The Reference Paper contains a set of rules, or principles, to be applied in the national regulation of telecommunications services by WTO Members in

---

139 use operating protocols of the service supplier's choice in the supply of any service, other than as necessary to ensure the availability of telecommunications transport networks and services to the public generally.

140 paragraph (c) spells out the right of foreign service suppliers to use public telecommunications transport networks for the movement of information within and across borders, including for intra-corporate communications.

141 *Telmex,* Panel Report, para 4.84 above, at paras 7.310–7.344; see, in particular, para 7.344.

142 Section 5 (d) of the Annex.

143 Section 5 (e) of the Annex. Section 5 (f) contains examples of such conditions, such as restrictions on resale or shared use of services or technical requirements.

144 additional exception applies to developing countries. Section 5 (g) entitles them to 'place reasonable conditions on access to and use of public ... networks and services necessary to strengthen [their] domestic telecommunications infrastructure and service capacity and to increase [their] participation in international trade telecommunications services. However, this only applies if the conditions are contained in the Members schedule – which was not the case for Mexico in *Telmex*. See Panel Report, para 4.84 above, at paras 7.386–7.389.

145 Section 4 of the Annex.

relation to foreign services and service providers. The document has two primary purposes. The first is to provide an effective framework of domestic competitive safeguards for foreign telecommunications service providers, in most cases faced with an entrenched national industry, often dominated by the incumbent former monopolist. The second key purpose is to make such disciplines legally enforceable before the WTO Dispute Settlement Body.

4.111   Both purposes appear to have been put to effect in the recent *Telmex* case. The panel, largely following the complaints brought forward by the United States, found the Mexican law and practice relating to incoming calls – which the panel identified as price cartels and market sharing – to constitute anti-competitive practices in violation of Mexico's commitments, inter alia, under the Reference Paper.

THE NATURE OF THE REFERENCE PAPER: A SET OF ADDITIONAL COMMITMENTS

4.112   The Reference Paper is a very brief (2 ½ page) minimum standard set of pro-competitive regulatory principles for the regulation of basic telecommunications. As the name indicates, it became applicable to those Members who agreed to it by being incorporated by reference in, and annexed to, their respective schedules of specific GATS commitments. The Reference Paper can, in effect, be called a piece of industry-specific competition legislation.

SPECIFIC DISCIPLINES RELATING TO 'MAJOR SUPPLIERS'

4.113   Given the industry's history of monopoly structures it is not surprising that the Reference Paper takes as its point of reference the concept of the 'major supplier', which the Reference Paper, evidently basing itself on established competition law concepts of market dominance, defines as 'a supplier which has the ability to materially affect the terms of participation (having regard to price and supply) in the relevant market for basic telecommunications services as a result of (a) control over essential facilities;[146] or (b) use of its position in the market'. The panel in *Telmex* had little difficulty in finding that Telmex was such a 'major supplier'.[147]

The 'major supplier' is the specific addressee for two sets of disciplines, to be enforced by the WTO Member concerned, namely competitive safeguards and interconnection obligations.

COMPETITIVE SAFEGUARDS

4.114   Section 1.1 of the Reference Paper provides that '[a]ppropriate measures shall be maintained [to prevent] suppliers who, alone or together, are a major supplier from engaging in or continuing anti-competitive practices'. The onus is thus on the Member to ensure, by whatever appropriate means, adequate behaviour by 'major suppliers' within its jurisdiction.

4.115   The question of what is included in the notion of anti-competitive practices is a matter of fierce debate. Section 1.2 Reference Paper notes that it shall 'include in particular' anti-competitive cross-subsidisation, using information obtained from competitors with anti-competitive results and the refusal to provide information

---

146   See para 4.65 above.
147   The European Communities submitted a single schedule for their (then) 15 Member States.

about essential facilities and commercially relevant information to other service suppliers. While the examples and the starting point ('major supplier') may suggest that the relevant behaviour must be related to an abuse of dominance, the Panel in *Telmex* applied a more expansive interpretation of the concept to include price fixing cartels and market sharing arrangements. This has been heavily criticised by some[148] and defended by others.[149]

4.116 In the case at hand, the Mexican international long distance rules provided that uniform rates for the termination of international calls into Mexico were to be negotiated by the supplier who had the biggest market share of *outgoing* traffic from Mexico in the preceding six months (which was invariably Telmex). The rules further provided that incoming calls were to be distributed among Mexican international gateway providers in proportion to their respective share of outgoing calls in the preceding month. The Panel found that these practices amounted to price fixing and market sharing arrangements, which the Panel found to be 'anti-competitive practices' in the sense of Section 1.1 of the Reference Paper.[150] The fact that Mexican law in fact mandated the actions did not change the finding, as the Reference Paper obligation incumbent on Mexico to prevent such behaviour remained unaffected.[151]

4.117 With only one dispute ruled on to-date, the jurisprudence is yet novel and will clearly evolve as more disputes are brought before the Dispute Settlement Body. It is possible that future panels might not apply concepts and case references from national competition laws as freely as this one did. However, generally speaking, regulators and dominant operators should expect to be judged against high standards.

INTERCONNECTION

4.118 Section 2 of the Reference Paper imposes obligations on 'major suppliers' relating to interconnection with foreign service providers who enjoy market access under specific scheduled commitments. Section 2.2[152] requires that interconnection be ensured at any technically feasible point in the following manner:

---

148 See the very useful unofficial compilation of commitments under the Protocol prepared by the WTO Secretariat, available at www.wto.org/english/tratop_e/serv_e/recap_e.xls (last visited 15 August 2005); the compilation also contains Members recently acceded to the WTO and other Members not signatories to the Protocol who undertook similar commitments. See also Bronckers and Larouche, para 4.99, note 124 above, at 1000 for summaries.

149 Ecuador and Tunisia.

150 While most participants adopted the Reference Paper unmodified, some Members (Bolivia, India, Malaysia, Morocco, Pakistan, the Philippines, Turkey and Venezuela) deleted individual commitments. Others (Bangladesh, Brazil, Mauritius and Thailand) committed to introducing the Reference Paper at a later point in time.

151 The Reference Paper defines 'essential facilities' as 'facilities of a public telecommunications transport network or service that (a) are exclusively or predominantly provided by a single or limited number of suppliers; and (b) cannot feasibly be economically or technically substituted in order to provide a service. For a discussion the 'essential facilities' concept and its counterpart in competition law see Marco Bronckers, *The WTO Reference Paper on Telecommunications: A Model for WTO Competition Law?*, in: NEW DIRECTIONS IN INTERNATIONAL ECONOMIC LAW 371, 385–386 (Bronckers and Quick eds. 2000).

152 *Telmex*, Panel Report, para 4.84 above, at paras 7.146–7.159. In the course of doing so, the panel made an interesting finding on the 'relevant market' in the case. While Mexico had argued that the relevant market would have to include incoming *and* outgoing international calls, as Mexico was not providing termination services but was completing international calls

- under non-discriminatory terms …;
- in a timely fashion, on terms, conditions … and cost-oriented rates that are transparent, reasonable, having regard to economic feasibility, and sufficiently unbundled …; and
- upon request at additional termination points, subject to charges.

4.119   The provision contains a number of terms, like 'cost-oriented', 'sufficiently unbundled', 'reasonable', that are rather broad and for which clear definitions are yet to be developed.[153] It will be the task of the Dispute Settlement Mechanism to bring some clarification of the used terms and, thus, strengthen the impact of this provision.

4.120   The Panel in *Telmex* did some first steps in this regard. It found that the interconnection rates offered to US operators under the Mexican ILD rules were significantly above costs,[154] elaborating on the interpretation of 'cost-oriented rates'.[155] The Panel also clarified that relevant costs in the context of international interconnection under the Reference Paper must be those that relate to the actual, attributable cost of providing the service (in this case termination),[156] but may be calculated on the basis of incremental cost methodologies.[157]

4.121   It further clarified that guidance for the qualifying phrase 'having regard to economic feasibility' could be drawn from the EC Interconnection Directive, in the context of which, the phrase is understood to mean that operators must be allowed a reasonable rate of return on investment.[158]

4.122   Sections 2.3 and 2.4 of the Reference Paper oblige the major supplier to make publicly available its procedures for interconnection negotiations and either its interconnection agreements or a reference interconnection offer. Section 2.5 finally requires that a fast-track independent review procedure is available to suppliers requesting interconnection with a 'major supplier'.

4.123   Based on the *Telmex* experience, it can be said that the interconnection obligations under the Reference Paper are significant. To aggrieved providers, they offer good chances to gain access or reduce disproportionate costs.

UNIVERSAL SERVICE

4.124   An important exemption applies to the benefit of universal service provision. Section 3 of the Reference Paper allows for the implementation of a universal service obligation. These obligations 'will not be regarded as anti-competitive per se, provided they are administered in a transparent, non-discriminatory and competitively neutral manner and are not more burdensome than necessary for the kind of universal service defined by the Member'.

---

on a shared revenue basis (accounting rates), the United States had argued that a 'demand substitution' analysis suggested the opposite. The Panel followed this latter approach.

153   Marsden, WTO Decides Its First Competition – With Disappointing Results, 16 Competition Law Insight 3, 8 (May 2004). See also George, WTO panel condemns anti-competitive behaviour in international telecoms case, International Trade Law and Regulation, 2004, 10(5), p 106.

154   Bronckers and Larouche, para 4.99, note 124 above.

155   *Telmex,* Panel Report, para 4.84 above, at para 7.238.

156   *Telmex,* Panel Report, para 4.84 above, at paras 7.239–7.245.

157   The full text of section 2.2 reads:

158   Interconnection to be ensured

4.125   In the negotiations leading to the Reference Paper the issue of universal service obligations was subject to much debate. While it is generally accepted that the provision of universal service needs some kind of regulatory protection, it was disputed how far reaching this protection should be. It was argued that universal service exemptions significantly impede market access and are rather used to protect domestic service providers than to enable the provision of universal service.[159] Section 3 Reference Paper, however, makes it clear that every Member retains the right to define the kind of universal service obligation it wishes to maintain, ie which services are to be offered universally and what conditions shall apply.

4.126   Measures under this provision must not be 'more burdensome than necessary'.[160] It remains to be seen whether a reasonably strict necessity test, such as the one applied to measures under the 'general exceptions' provisions of article XX GATT, will take hold in the interpretation of this exemption.

Licensing disciplines

4.127   Where licensing applies, all criteria and time periods normally required as well as terms and conditions of individual licenses must be made public. Reasons must be given in case of denial of a license.[161]

Critics have voiced dissatisfaction with the limited scope of this provision, as important issues regarding licensing remain unaddressed.[162]

Independent Regulators

4.128   Section 5 of the Reference Paper demands an impartial regulatory body that is 'separate from, and not accountable to, any supplier of basic telecommunications services'. While this straightforward rule of the separation of operator and regulator is laudable, issues remain. Unlike in EC Law[163] there is no provision for the structural separation of regulator and (state) owner when a telecoms operator is state-owned or state-controlled,[164] so that conflicts of interests and undue pressures may not be fully excluded.

---

159   nterconnection with a major supplier will be ensured at any technically feasible point in the network. Such interconnection is provided

160   a) under non-discriminatory terms, conditions (including technical standards and specifications) and rates and of a quality no less favourable than that provided for its own like services or for like services of non-affiliated service suppliers or for its subsidiaries or other affiliates;

161   b) in a timely fashion, on terms, conditions (including technical standards and specifications) and cost-oriented rates that are transparent, reasonable, having regard to economic feasibility, and sufficiently unbundled so that the supplier need not pay for network components or facilities that it does not require for the service to be provided; and

162   c) upon request, at points in addition to the network termination points offered to the majority of users, subject to charges that reflect the cost of construction of necessary additional facilities.

163   Some terms, however, have their origin in US or EU law, so that recourse to EU/US interpretation is possible, eg: 'transparency and cost-orientation', 'sufficiently unbundled' in art. 7 of the former EC interconnection Directive 97/33; 'technical feasible points' in sec 251(c)(2)(B) of the US Telecommunications Act.

164   The Panel followed the United States' analysis. The United States had provided 4 comparisons by proxy, including comparisons with national termination rates that were supposed by law to cover costs. In all four comparisons, the international termination rates were significantly higher. See *Telmex*, Panel Report, 7.186–7.216.

ALLOCATION OF RESOURCES

4.129   Section 6 of the Reference Paper provides for the objective, timely and non-discriminatory allocation of scarce resources, such as frequencies.

THE GATT

4.130   Whilst the focus of this section has been on the GATS, it is, nonetheless, worth referring to the key obligations of the General Agreement on Tariffs and Trade ('GATT'). The GATT governs the international trade between WTO Members of goods, including telecommunications-related equipment. We briefly address the three key sets of obligations that apply to the international trade in goods.

4.131   Article I GATT guarantees Most Favoured Nation treatment for the goods of the WTO Members. Under the terms of Article I, any advantage, favour, privilege or immunity granted by any WTO Member to any product originating in or destined for any other country shall be accorded immediately and unconditionally to the 'like product' originating in or destined for the territories of other WTO Members. There is a significant amount of jurisprudence from both the GATT and WTO systems on what constitutes a 'like product'. As the Most Favoured Nation treatment is only accorded to 'like products', whether products are in fact 'like' is always a keenly disputed issue before the panels and the Appellate Body.

4.132   Article III GATT ensures that goods imported from other WTO Members receive national treatment in respect of taxation and other regulations. More specifically, Article III:2 GATT prohibits WTO Members from applying, directly or indirectly, internal taxes or charges of any kind in excess of those applied to like domestic products. Article III:4 requires WTO Members to accord treatment no less favourable to products imported from the territories of other WTO Members than that accorded to like products of national origin 'in respect of all laws, regulations and requirements affecting their internal sale, offering for sale, purchase, transportation, distribution or use'. Once again, any disputes raising issues under Article III will inevitably result in arguments as to whether the relevant products are 'like'. The national treatment principle embodied within the GATT has played a significant role to bring down trade barriers. Unlike the GATS system, national treatment under the GATT applies unconditionally and does not depend upon WTO Members adhering to or specifying additional commitments.

4.133   Finally, Article XI:1 GATT provides for the general elimination and prohibition of quantitative restrictions relating to both imports and exports. This provision requires WTO Members to remove any and all prohibitions and restrictions, whether made effective through quotas, import or export licences or other measures, in relation to imports from, or exports to, the territory of another WTO Member.

4.134   As with the GATS, the GATT has an exceptions clause that provides a derogation from compliance with the substantive obligations referred to above. Under Article XX GATT, nothing in the GATT prevents the adoption or enforcement of measures that are, inter alia, necessary to protect public morals, necessary to protect human, animal or plant life or health or relating to the conservation of exhaustible natural resources. Article XX GATT is a commonly litigated provision. Any dispute in which a complainant Member establishes a prima facie violation of the GATT under Articles I, III or XI will typically then move to the defendant Member seeking to justify its conduct under Article XX.

4.135   There appear to be no cases under the WTO Dispute Settlement Mechanism involving breaches of the GATT in relation to the international trade in telecommunications equipment. Requests for formal consultations were made in *Japan – Measures Affecting the Purchase of Telecommunications Equipment*[165] and *Korea – Laws, Regulations and Practices in the Telecommunications Procurement Sector*[166]. Both disputes, however, appear to have been resolved bilaterally before any panel decision was handed down.

THE TRIPS

4.136   The Agreement on Trade-Related Intellectual Property Rights ('TRIPS') is another key Covered Agreement that is likely to be of relevance to operators within the telecommunications sector. It is intended to provide minimum guarantees of protection for those who hold intellectual property rights.

4.137   As with the GATS and the GATT, TRIPS provides for the following basic rights:

- under article 3 of the TRIPS, each WTO Member must accord to the nationals of other Members treatment no less favourable than that it accords to its own nationals with regard to the 'protection' of intellectual property rights (so-called national treatment); and
- under article 4 of the TRIPS, with regard to the 'protection' of intellectual property rights, any advantage, favour, privilege or immunity granted by a Member to the nationals of any other country shall be accorded immediately and unconditionally to the nationals of all other Members (so-called Most Favoured Nation treatment).

For the purposes of both articles 3 and 4 of the TRIPS, the term 'protection' is defined as including 'matters affecting the availability, acquisition, scope, maintenance and enforcement of intellectual property rights as well as those matters affecting the use of intellectual property rights specifically addressed in this Agreement'.

4.138   The TRIPS governs a broad array of intellectual property rights including the following:

- copyright and related rights;
- trademarks;
- geographical indications;
- industrial designs;
- patents;
- layout designs (topographies) of integrated circuits; and
- protection of undisclosed information.

4.139   Perhaps most importantly, the TRIPS provides for minimum enforcement procedures so as to permit effective action against any act of infringement of intellectual property rights covered by the agreement. Enforcement procedures are required to be fair and equitable and not unnecessarily complicated or costly (article 41(2) TRIPS). Further, pursuant to article 41(4), parties to proceedings should be afforded the opportunity to have administrative decisions judicially

---

165 See *Telmex*, Panel Report, 7.166–7.185.
166 See *Telmex*, Panel Report, 7.171. The Panel sought and found guidance, inter alia, in ITU T-series Recommendation 1.40 and 1.50.

reviewed. TRIPS also requires WTO Members to ensure that the following remedies are made available in relation to intellectual property infringement proceedings: injunctions (article 44 TRIPS), damages (article 45 TRIPS), indemnification (article 48 TRIPS) and provisional measures (article 50 TRIPS). In addition, article 61 TRIPS obliges Members to provide for criminal prosecutions, at least in relation to wilful trademark counterfeiting or copyright piracy on a commercial scale.

THE WTO AND THE ITU

4.140   As the WTO begins to venture into developing rules for subject matters traditionally falling under the auspices of other international and multilateral organisations, the risk for conflict between different international regimes increases. This risk has been most acute in relation to the overlap between the international trading regime, as set out under the WTO Covered Agreements, and multilateral environmental or health agreements. However, the possibility of conflict also exists as between the rules developed by the WTO and the ITU.

4.141   One problem area relates to the size of, and differences in, international settlement rates. The price of each international connection has conventionally been negotiated under the ITU by single operators in the country of origin and destination of the call. Prices could vary significantly and inevitably exceeded costs in developing countries. A so-called peace clause was developed, under which WTO Members accepted, by way of informal gentleman's agreement, that they would not challenge the application of settlement rates, as developed under the ITU regime, before the WTO's Dispute Settlement Mechanism.[167] However, the *Telmex* case challenges this understanding by confirming that, in so far as a WTO Member is bound by the requirements of the Reference Paper, then switched international services will be governed by the rules of the Reference Paper in relation to interconnection. This would suggest that there should be an alignment as between settlement rates and the costs of interconnection. However, this could raise political issues for developing countries, in particular, since they may depend on higher settlement rates in order to help build a more effective domestic telecommunications system. As one commentator notes, '[t]his ruling obviously interferes with ITU rates and poses the politically difficult question of whether the WTO or the ITU has the ultimate economic governance of international telecommunications'.[168]

4.142   Another issue is the extent to which the WTO's trading rules would allow Members to take into account non-trade objectives including, for example, universal and public service or ensuring the safety and development of networks. Whilst this issue was addressed to some extent in the *Telmex* case, further clarity will be required from future WTO case-law.[169]

OUTLOOK: RECENT, CURRENT AND FUTURE NEGOTIATIONS

4.143   Like other parts of WTO law, GATS law is in a state of current development through accession and multilateral negotiations. New specific commitments

---

167   See *Telmex*, Panel Report, 7.177.
168   See *Telmex*, Panel Report, 7.185.
169   See Markus Fredebeul-Klein/ Andreas Freytag, Telecommunications and WTO discipline, Telecommunications Policy [1997], 477, 482.

are scheduled by acceding countries at the time of their accession. Recent accessions have, as a rule, included a number of commitments in telecommunications services. Major trading nations now routinely request from accession candidates commitments in key service areas, including financial services and telecommunications services.

4.144   The so-called 'GATS 2000' negotiations mandated by article XIX(1) GATS were phased into the new comprehensive 'Doha Development Agenda' negotiations launched in November 2001 in the Qatari capital Doha. The negotiations, however, have run into intermittent deadlocks. While initial requests and some offers have been exchanged between WTO Members, it is too early to say whether, and to what extent, significant commitments in telecommunications services can be expected. Given the rapid development of the industry, however, there is an evident need for progressive development. It is hoped that WTO members will respond to this need by advancing and successfully concluding the negotiations. However, given the current political focus of WTO Members on other more sensitive aspects of WTO negotiations (in particular, agriculture), it is far from clear that the needs of the telecommunications industry will be met in the near, or even mid-term, future.

The Austrian Market for Electronic Communications[1]

Christoph Kerres & Peter Schludermann
Baker & McKenzie – Kerres & Diwok Rechtsanwälte GmbH, Vienna

LEGAL STRUCTURE

Basic Policy

5.1 The Austrian approach mainly aims to implement the EU Directives into national law and to learn from the experiences made so far in the telecommunications sector. Where the EU Directives provide sufficient flexibility to the Member States, the Austrian legislation tries to strengthen the national telecommunications market. This especially includes improving the effectiveness of the NRA's decisions, creating a modern electronic infrastructure, and establishing effective competition with equal opportunities for all national operators.

5.2 While the national market for fixed telephone connections is still heavily influenced by the former monopolist Telekom Austria AG, in the mobile communications sector there is competition between various national players with considerable influence.

Implementation of EU Directives

5.3 In Austria, all five EU Directives were transposed into the Telecommunications Act 2003 on 19 August 2003,[2] which is a federal act.

Legislation

5.4 The main legislative act concerning the implementation of the EU Directives is the *Telekommunikationsgesetz* 2003[3] ('TKG 2003'). Beside the TKG 2003 the *Bundesgesetz über Funkanlagen und Telekommunikationsendeinrichtungen* contains

---

1   Editing of this chapter closed 8 July 2005. The authors gratefully acknowledge the assistance of Mary B. Murrow in the preparation of this chapter.
2   Bundesgesetz, mit dem ein Telekommunikationsgesetz erlassen wird und das Bundesgesetz über die Verkehrsarbeitsinspektion und das KommAustria-Gesetz geändert warden: BGBl I No 70/2003.
3   BGBl I No 70/2003.

various rules on radio equipment and telecommunications terminal equipment. Although they pre-date the EU Directives, these rules are still in force. The TKG 2003 grants various national authorities the power to pass regulations regarding the integrity of networks, the interoperability and quality of services, number portability, the provision of value added services, the quality of the universal service, interconnection, the management of frequencies, numbers and payments therefor, telecommunications terminal equipment, the surveillance of communication, itemised billing and the calculation of fees. These regulations provide additional and more detailed rules on the afore-mentioned topics.

REGULATORY PRINCIPLES: IMPLEMENTATION OF THE FRAMEWORK DIRECTIVE

Scope of Regulation

5.5   The definitions of 'electronic communication networks' and 'associated facilities' in Section 3 TKG 2003 are essentially the same as those in the Framework Directive. The Austrian TKG 2003 defines 'electronic communication services' as a 'commercial'[4] service rather than simply referring to remuneration. Due to the technology-neutral approach, various services previously outside the scope of the telecommunications legislation, such as VoIP, that provide access to or from public switched telephone networks and Conditional Access Systems, are now governed by the new regulatory regime. Concerning the growing debate on VoIP services, the RTR-GmbH has issued a consultation procedure. All interested parties are invited to state their views on the topic.[5]

National Regulatory Authorities: Organisation, Regulatory Objectives, Competencies

5.6   There are numerous authorities in Austria vested with powers with respect to the telecommunication sector. These are divided into two branches: the Communication Authorities and the Regulatory Authorities. The Communication Authorities include the Minister[6] of Transport, Innovation, and Technology, the Communications Bureaux and the Bureau of Radio Communications and Telecommunications Terminal Equipment. The Regulatory Authorities are the *Rundfunk und Telekom Regulierungs-GmbH* ('RTR-GmbH'), *Telekom-Control-Kommission* ('TKK') and KommAustria.

5.7   The Minister of Transport, Innovation and Technology ('BMVIT') is the highest-ranking telecommunications authority. His sphere of influence includes the whole federal territory. He manages the frequency spectrum allotted to Austria as well as international contracts regarding these.[7] In addition, he may pass regulations regarding number portability, universal service provision, fees for the use of

---

4   S 1 (2) Gewerbeordnung 1994 states that a commercial service needs to be recurrent and must be provided independently. Furthermore, it must be intended to make profits.

5   See consultation of the RTR-GmbH, 25 April 2005.

6   Please note that, in Austria, administrative powers are vested in the Minister. The Ministry merely supports the Minister when exercising these powers. Therefore, Austrian laws always refer to the Minister himself and not to the Ministry.

7   S 51 TKG 2003.

communication parameters, terminal equipment, technical equipment for the surveillance of transmissions, quality of services, integrity of networks and, interoperability of services and interconnection.

5.8   Furthermore, the BMVIT hears appeals from decisions of the Communications Bureaux and the Bureau of Radio Communications and Telecommunications Terminal Equipment.[8]

5.9   The Communications Bureaux are set up in the cities of Graz,[9] Innsbruck,[10] Linz[11] and Vienna.[12] They are given 'subsidiary competence', meaning they have jurisdiction to handle all matters relating to TKG 2003 that are not explicitly assigned to another authority.[13]

5.10   The Bureau of Radio Communications and Telecommunications Terminal Equipment deals with the approval of radio equipment and telecommunications terminal equipment where this power is not explicitly given to KommAustria.

5.11   The RTR-GmbH has two major duties. First, it acts as an administrative bureau for the TKK and the KommAustria. In these matters, the RTR-GmbH is not independent and must follow instructions given to it by the TKK or KommAustria. Secondly, the RTR-GmbH is given authority in all matters that are assigned to the Regulatory Authorities but are not explicitly[14] assigned to either the TKK or KommAustria.[15] This especially includes the management of numbers, dispute resolution and the definition of relevant markets. The RTR-GmbH is responsible for the management of numbers. It develops a plan containing further specifications on the various types of numbers[16] and the prerequisites for an assignment. A special procedure for 'vanity numbers' does not exist.

5.12   The Telekom-Control-Kommission ('TKK') is an independent authority and consists of a council of three members all in all with one substitute member for each. One must be a judge, one must possess relevant technical knowledge, and the last one must possess relevant economic knowledge.[17] The substitute members must have the same qualifications.

5.13   The duties[18] of the TKK consist of:

- decisions regarding the sharing of facilities,
- decisions regarding the provision of data for enquiry services or directories,
- the objection to and approval of general terms and conditions,
- determination of which operator possesses SMP and which remedies to impose,
- the allocation of frequencies with a limited number of rights to be granted and changes regarding the allocation,
- decisions regarding spectrum trading,

---

8   S 112 TKG 2003.
9   For the provinces of Styria and Carinthia.
10   For the provinces of Tyrol and Vorarlberg.
11   For the provinces of Upper Austria and Salzburg.
12   For the provinces of Lower Austria, Burgenland and Vienna.
13   S 113 (3) TKG 2003.
14   S 117 and S 120 TKG 2003.
15   S 115 TKG 2003.
16   Various types of service may only be used in specific ranges of numbers, e g enquiry services or erotic services.
17   S 118 (1) TKG 2003.
18   S 117 TKG 2003.

- exercising enforcement powers as named in Section 91(3) and Section 91(4) TKG 2003, and
- various other duties.[19]

5.14   The TKK is subject to the general rules of procedure in administrative matters[20] with two exceptions. Firstly, after closing the administrative investigation the parties involved must not produce any new evidence. Secondly, dispute resolution procedures are compulsory in various matters,[21] including site-sharing, interconnection and the making available of data for directory enquiry services and directories.

5.15   KommAustria is a subsidiary[22] of the Federal Chancellery and thus not independent. It deals with all regulatory matters that concern radio and television broadcasting.[23]

5.16   Generally, the exchange of information between authorities is governed by article 22 Austrian Constitution. Concerning the telecommunications sector, Section 126 TKG 2003 provides further specifications. The regulatory authorities are entitled to give to the national competition authorities, and to regulatory authorities of other Member States any information those authorities need to fulfil their duties in matters of mutual interest. If the European Commission demands information via a written and well-founded request, the regulatory authorities have to provide such information.[24] Any information that the regulatory authorities receive from those authorities has to be treated confidentially if the sending authority has designated the information as confidential. Section 128 (1) TKG 2003 keeps close to article 6 Framework Directive. The BMVIT as well as all Regulatory Authorities have to give interested parties the opportunity to comment on draft measures within a reasonable period of time. Consultation procedures and their results have to be published except for confidential information. Any procedural time limits are inhibited for the period in which comments are allowed.[25] Regarding individual measures, during the time in which comments on it are allowed, only the cancellation of the application is admissible.[26]

5.17   If the national regulatory authority suspects that a violation of antitrust law may have occurred, it may (after further investigation) bring the matter to the attention of the Restrictive Practices Court.[27] In some cases, it even has the duty to do so.[28]

Right of Appeal against NRA's Decisions

5.18   There are numerous authorities in Austria which may hear appeals: the BMVIT hears appeals against decisions of the Communications Bureaux and the

---

19   Applications to the restrictive practices court, decisions with regards to number portability, non-discrimination, access, leased lines, carrier (pre-)selection, and interconnection, calculation of the amount that operators have to pay to the Universal Service Fund, and calculation of the financial compensation payable by the Universal Service Fund.
20   Allgemeines Verwaltungsverfahrensgesetz 1991.
21   S 121 (2) TKG 2003.
22   S 3 (3) KommAustria-Gesetz.
23   S 120 TKG 2003.
24   S 124 TKG 2003.
25   S 128 (2) TKG 2003.
26   S 128 (3) TKG 2003.
27   S 127 TKG 2003.
28   S 127 (2) TKG 2003.

Bureau of Radio Communications and Telecommunications Terminal Equipment; appeals against decisions of the TKK and the RTR-GmbH[29] may be brought before the Constitutional Court and the Administrative Court;[30] and appeals against KommAustria's decisions are heard by the Federal Communications Senate (or the Independent Administration Senate when concerning 'administrative penalties').

The NRA's Obligations to Co-operate with the Commission

5.19　In implementing the consolidation procedure, the TKG 2003 keeps close to the wording of article 7 Framework Directive.[31] However, carrier selection, carrier pre-selection, leased lines and end-user tariffs are not among the topics listed that require the national regulatory authority to co-operate with the European Commission.

'Significant Market Power' as a Fundamental Prerequisite of Regulation

Definition of SMP

5.20　The basic definition of 'significant market power' in Section 35 (1) TKG 2003 is essentially the same as in article 14(2) Framework Directive. The Commission Guidelines on market analysis, which further specify the definition of SMP,[32] have been transposed by the TKG 2003, although not with the same wording.

5.21　The Framework Directive's definition of SMP on closely related markets has been transposed to Austrian law in Section 35 (5) TKG 2003. By adding 'horizontally, vertically or geographically' it further specifies and clarifies the term 'closely related markets'.

Definition of relevant markets and SMP designation

5.22　The relevant markets are defined by the RTR-GmbH (or by the KommAustria concerning radio and television broadcasting).[33] Although they may define relevant markets other than those proposed in the Commission Recommendation on relevant markets, the RTR-GmbH until now has chosen not to do so. Prior to 2 May 2005 the market for wholesale broadband access (market No 12) had not yet been defined as a relevant market. KommAustria on the other hand strayed from the Recommendation and could only define the relevant markets after initiating the European veto-procedure.[34] If the Regulatory Authorities identify an undertaking as having significant market power, at least one remedy has to be imposed on it.

5.23　The TKK or KommAustria may impose remedies of non-discrimination, transparency, accounting separation, providing access, price control and cost

---

29　VfGH 28.11.2001, B 2271/00.
30　S 121 (5) TKG 2003.
31　S 129 TKG 2003.
32　See para 1.72 above.
33　S 36 TKG 2003.
34　See para 1.62 above.

accounting on non-SMP operators to a certain extent.[35] Since the TKK or KommAustria is not bound by further conditions, it lies in their discretion to actually impose those obligations on non-SMP operators.

5.24 Following the definition of the relevant markets by the RTR-GmbH, on 20 October 2003, the TKK initiated 15 proceedings[36] to further investigate the markets (with the exception of the national market for international roaming on public mobile networks) as defined by the RTR-GmbH.[37] On 2 May 2005 the RTR-GmbH defined the market of wholesale broadband access to be a relevant market regarding significant market power and initialised the analysis of said market.

5.25 The TKK came to the conclusion that Telekom Austria AG has significant market power on the following markets:

- access to the public telephone network at a fixed location for residential customers,
- access to the public telephone network at a fixed location for non-residential customers,
- national telephone services provided at a fixed location for residential customers,
- national telephone services provided at a fixed location for non-residential customers,
- call termination on the telephone network of Telekom Austria AG provided at a fixed location, and
- markets No 6, No 7, No 8, No 11 and No 13.[38]

Regarding the relatively strong influence of the former monopolist on said markets, the remedies of allowing carrier selection and carrier pre-selection, the obligation to provide various standard offers, non-discrimination, the approval of prices and price control, service descriptions and terms of business, accounting separation, obligations of access and interconnection, use of the 'Forward Looking Long Run Average Incremental Costs' Method ('FL-LRAIC'),[39] providing a minimum set of leased lines, as well as transparency, were imposed on Telekom Austria AG.

5.26 Concerning the markets for:

- international telephone services provided at a fixed location for residential customers,
- trunk segments of leased lines, and
- access and call origination in public mobile telephone networks,

the TKK decided that there was enough competition and therefore no provider was named as having significant market power.

---

35 The NRA may impose those remedies that an operator agreed to when he was assigned frequencies during the procedure in Section 55 TKG 2003, technical conditions that are necessary for the network to remain operational, and remedies that are needed to fulfil international obligations.

36 M 1/03, M 2/03, M 3/03, M 4/03, M 5/03, M 6/03, M 7/03, M 8a/03, M 8b-k/03, M 10/03, M 11/03, M 12/03, M 13/03, M 14/03, M 15a-e/03.

37 S 117 (6) TKG 2003.

38 As defined in the Annex to the Commission Recommendation on relevant markets of 11 February 2003.

39 The FL-LRAIC Method simulates a competitive market by using either a bottom-up model or a top-down model and calculates the prices on it.

5.27   On the market for call termination provided at a fixed location on telephone networks run by operators other than Telekom Austria AG, the TKK found Informations-Technologie Austria GmbH, Colt Telecom Austria GmbH, Tele.ring Telekom Service GmbH, Telekabel Wien GmbH, eTel Austria AG, Equant Austria Telekommunikationsdienste GmbH, UTA Telekom AG and LIWEST Kabelmedien GmbH each to have SMP with respect to their own network. The TKK imposed price control obligations[40] on each of them.[41]

5.28   Moreover, the TKK came to the conclusion that on the market for call termination on individual mobile networks, Mobilkom Austria AG & Co KG, T-Mobile Austria GmbH, One GmbH, tele.ring Telekom Service GmbH and Hutchison 3 G Austria GmbH each had SMP in respect of their own mobile network. The TKK imposed the remedies of price control[42] and non-discrimination[43] on each of the operators.

NRA's Regulatory Duties concerning Rights of Way, Co-location and Facility Sharing

Rights of way

5.29   The right of way is defined in Section 5 (1) TKG 2003 and may include the following privileges, subject to the decision of the Communications Bureaux or an agreement between the parties involved:

- the construction and maintenance of communication lines above or below the earth, as well as ancillary equipment,
- setting up cable lines in buildings and other structures,
- the right to operate all of the above mentioned, and
- the right to lop single or multiple[44] trees.

The entering of buildings is, with the exception of emergencies, only allowed during daytime and following prior notification.

5.30   Operators of electronic communication networks, whether public or private, are entitled to rights of way concerning public property, including streets, paths, public plazas and the airspace above. Public waters, however, are not included.

5.31   Operators of public electronic communication networks are entitled to rights of way concerning private property on the following conditions:[45]

- the right of way does not oppose public interests,
- the utilisation of the real estate is not (or, at most, only slightly) restricted, and
- no communication line or facility yet exists on the real estate or an already existing facility is to be expanded, or
- a communication line or facility owned by a third party already exists on the

---

40   See para 5.60 below.
41   The price the Telekom Austria is charging for its service of regional call termination serves as a benchmark.
42   Prices have to be calculated using the 'LRAIC-Method'.
43   See para 5.60 below.
44   Cutting clearings into woods is prohibited, unless it is the sole possible way of constructing a specific communication line and there is no danger to the preservation of the wood.
45   S 5 (4) TKG 2003.

real estate but sharing this line or facility is not possible technically or economically, or the owner of the line or facility is not obliged to share his line or facility.

Undertakings that want to obtain rights of way regarding private property have to engage in negotiations with the owner of the real estate. If the negotiations remain fruitless for six weeks, either party may call upon the Communications Bureaux to solve the dispute.

Co-location and facility sharing

5.32   Co-location and facility sharing are governed by Sections 7 and 8 TKG 2003. This allows operators to make use of other lines and facilities (e g electric power lines) when setting up communication lines,[46] if by doing so no further restrictions are imposed on the real estate. Section 8 TKG 2003 obliges operators to share existing communication lines and facilities provided that this is technically possible and economically reasonable and the use of public property is impossible or unreasonable. Antennae or power line poles have to be shared with providers of publicly available communication networks, fire departments, ambulance and police, if it is technically possible.

5.33   When asked to do so, operators who possess any rights as mentioned in Section 8 (1) TKG 2003 have to make an offer for the sharing of lines and facilities including aerial masts. If the parties cannot agree within six weeks, the TKK can be called upon to decide the matter.[47]

Expropriation

5.34   The expropriation of property for compensation is possible if the construction of a communication line is of public interest, and the granting of rights of way, co-location and facility sharing cannot serve this objective.[48] The construction of communication lines or public terminals by operators of public electronic communication networks is always to be seen as being of public interest.

REGULATION OF MARKET ENTRY: IMPLEMENTATION OF THE AUTHORISATION DIRECTIVE

The General Authorisation of Electronic Communications

5.35   The TKG 2003 allows any person or entity to provide electronic communication networks or services[49] subject only to prior notification.[50] Notification in written form is required in advance and has to contain the name of the operator, the legal form of the undertaking, a short description of the network or the service, and the anticipated date of beginning. Failure to do so is punishable by a fine of up to €58,000.

---

46   S 7 TKG 2003.
47   S 9 TKG 2003.
48   S 13 TKG 2003.
49   S 14 TKG 2003.
50   S 15 TKG 2003.

5.36   Within one week after receipt of the notification, the RTR-GmbH has to confirm the receipt. If it has reason to suspect that no electronic communication network or service is being operating, it has to engage in further investigations within one week. If it comes to the conclusion that the designated operator does not actually operate an electronic communication network or service, the RTR-GmbH has to communicate these findings in an official notification within four weeks, if the operator demands such notification. All notifications or confirmations of the RTR-GmbH have to be made available to the public.[51]

Rights of Use for Radio Frequencies

General authorisations and granting of individual rights

5.37   The BMVIT is responsible for the 'overall management' of frequencies in Austria.[52] However, various authorities may assign frequencies, depending on the type of the frequency concerned. These may be assigned for a limited time[53] only. Operators may lose their rights of use granted to them if they do not use the frequency in accordance with the assignment for a period of six months.[54] If a certain frequency is to be used only in connection with radio communications equipment that falls under the general licence[55] of the BMVIT, then no further assignment is needed.

5.38   If an undertaking decides to apply for a specific frequency, it has to submit an application to the appropriate authority, ie the TKK, the Communications Bureau or KommAustria. Rights of use for radio frequencies that are destined to be used for radio or television broadcasting are granted by the KommAustria. This is usually done in the form of a 'beauty contest'.[56] If KommAustria wants to assign any frequency that is not intended to be used for radio and television broadcasting, the approval of the BMVIT is needed. KommAustria has to decide on the allocation within six weeks after receipt of the application. This period may be extended by eight months if KommAustria is applying a selection procedure.[57]

Admissible conditions

5.39   In order to fulfil the objectives of the TKG 2003 and the European Directives the granting of rights to use frequencies may contain various conditions:[58]

- the declaration of the intended use of the frequency, the type of network and technology used, including exclusive uses of frequencies,
- conditions that are necessary to ensure the effective and efficient use of frequencies, including coverage and start of operation,

---

51   S 15 (5) TKG 2003.
52   See para 5.7 above.
53   The period of time has to be reasonable, see S 54 (11) TKG 2003.
54   S 54 (12) TKG 2003.
55   Verordnung des Bundesministers für Verkehr, Innovation und Technologie, mit der generelle Bewilligungen erteilt werden (BGBl II No 542/2003).
56   S 10 ff Private Radio Act and s 12 ff Private Television Act.
57   S 54 (5) TKG 2003.
58   S 55 (10) TKG 2003.

- temporal limitations,
- conditions regarding spectrum trading, and
- conditions described under No 3, 7 and 8 of Annex B Authorisation Directive.

Limitation of number of rights of use to be granted

5.40   The BMVIT may decide[59] for certain frequencies to limit the number of rights of use to be granted[60] and has done so on various occasions. Those frequencies are named in the Frequency Usage Ordinance (*Frequenznutzungsverordnung*).[61] Rights to these may be granted by the TKK.[62]

5.41   After public notification has been made by the TKK regarding the availability of a frequency band, the rights to it are then awarded via auction. All undertakings whose applications are incomplete or differing from the conditions set out by the TKK for the auction will be excluded from the auction by the TKK. The TKK then assigns the frequencies in question to that operator who is able to comply with the general prerequisites[63] set out by the TKK and who is best able to make efficient use of that particular frequency. The most efficient use of the frequency concerned is decided on the basis of the operators' bids. The auction has to be fair, non-discriminatory and economic.

5.42   Rights to frequencies that have not been named in the Frequency Usage Ordinance and that are not radio frequencies are granted by the Communications Bureaux. Whoever first applies for a frequency is awarded the right of use.[64]

Spectrum trading

5.43   Spectrum trading regarding frequencies assigned by the TKK or KommAustria[65] is possible in Austria but, in order to do so, the prior approval of the NRA is required.[66] Both the technical impact as well as the effect on competition have to be considered by the NRA. The request of the operator and the decision of the NRA have to be made available to the public.

5.44   Furthermore, the TKK has to approve any substantial restructuring regarding the ownership of undertakings that were given rights to frequencies according to Section 55 TKG 2003.

Rights of Use for Numbers

General authorisations and granting of individual rights

5.45   Numbers may be assigned to operators, in blocks of several thousand units, or to users by the RTR-GmbH after formal application. The RTR-GmbH has to

---

59   It lies in the discretion of the BMVIT to decide which frequencies should be affected by the limitation and whether or not they are to be handed down to the TKK for assignment.
60   S 52 (3) TKG 2003 and s 4a Frequenznutzungsverordnung.
61   BGBl II No 457/2003 amended last in BGBl II No 134/2004.
62   All previous and future auctions can be found on the website of the RTR-GmbH, www.rtr.at.
63   S 55 (2) and (10) TKG 2003.
64   S 74 and s 81 TKG 2003.
65   Depending on the type of frequency, either the TKK or the KommAustria would be competent.
66   S 56 TKG 2003.

decide on the application within three weeks after its receipt. It is then at the discretion of the operator to see to the further administration of these blocks. However, the assignees must comply with any conditions[67] imposed on them by the RTR-GmbH and by the TKG 2003. Failing to do so may result in the loss of the right of use.

5.46   Operators and users that are assigned numbers by the RTR-GmbH obtain the right to use these numbers. They do not, however, gain any property rights from this assignment.[68]

Admissible conditions

5.47   When granting rights to use numbers, the RTR-GmbH may impose the following conditions:[69]

- The naming of the type of service for which the assigned numbers may be used,
- time limits,
- conditions that are necessary in order to maintain the effective and efficient use of numbers, and
- conditions that are necessary in order to comply with international obligations.

5.48   Undertakings with significant market power have to provide the possibility of carrier selection and carrier pre-selection for their subscribers. Remuneration for these services has to be cost-oriented. Obligations to provide carrier selection and carrier pre-selection with regard to other networks than public communications networks at fixed locations may be imposed on the same conditions as granting access and interconnection.[70]

5.49   Operators of fixed and mobile networks are obliged to provide number portability to their subscribers.[71] The specific type of use of the number may not be altered, however. Location portability of geographical numbers is possible only within the area for which the number was first assigned. Operators are prohibited from charging 'deterrent fees' when providing number portability.

Limitation of numbers of rights of use to be granted

5.50   Numbers of rights of use regarding numbers and other communication parameters cannot be limited like numbers of rights of use for frequencies.

The NRA's Enforcement Powers

5.51   Section 90 TKG 2003 grants the RTR-GmbH, the TKK, KommAustria and the BMVIT the power to demand information from operators of communication

---

67   This mainly includes conditions to guarantee the effective and efficient use and conditions that are needed to comply with international agreements.
68   S 66 TKG 2003.
69   S 65 (4) TKG 2003.
70   S 46 (3) and s 41 TKG 2003.
71   On the basis of s 23 (3) TKG 2003 the BMVIT made further specifications on mobile number portability in the Nummernübertragungsverordnung.

networks or services. They are allowed to gather information that is needed in order to monitor compliance with the TKG 2003 and they may obtain information for statistical purposes. In addition, operators of electronic communication services are further obliged to provide administrative authorities with specific information[72] on their subscribers if those subscribers are under suspicion of having committed any administrative crimes by means of a public telecommunications network.

5.52   If the TKK or KommAustria finds an undertaking in violation of the TKG 2003 or of legal notices and regulations based on it, they notify the undertaking and give it an opportunity to remedy the shortcomings or provide a reply within a certain period of time.[73] If the undertaking fails to comply, the NRA orders it to do so via official notice. If the undertaking does not comply with the notice either, the NRA may suspend the right to provide communication networks or services or revoke any rights of use for frequencies or numbers. If the failure of compliance by the undertaking poses a serious threat to public safety, security or health or causes serious economic or operational problems for other operators or users of communication networks or services, the TKK or KommAustria may issue an injunction.[74]

5.53   The Communications Bureaux monitor the infrastructure[75] used by operators. In order to do so, they may enter buildings, and conduct searches. Furthermore, the Communications Bureaux may execute any measures necessary to protect any telecommunications equipment from interferences caused by other telecommunication equipment. These measures have to avoid unnecessary costs and need to be appropriate with respect to the circumstances concerned.[76] Any telecommunications equipment that is being operated without authorisation may be put out of operation by the Communications Bureaux without prior warning. Telecommunications equipment that violates the TKG 2003 in any other way may only be put out of operation if this is necessary in order to maintain or restore the unhindered traffic of communications.

Administrative Charges and Fees for Rights of Use

5.54   Undertakings that are granted rights of use for radio frequencies have to pay a monthly fee ('*Frequenznutzungsgebühr*') for this permit.[77] Furthermore, the undertaking usually has to pay a remuneration ('*Frequenznutzungsentgelt*') as proposed in its application for the frequency. If rights of use for frequencies are allocated without any remuneration the undertaking has to pay a non-recurring fee ('*Zuteilungsgebühr*').

5.55   The BMVIT is authorised[78] to set fees for the allocation of numbers. Until now, he has not chosen to do so.

---

72   This information is limited to name, surname, academic title, address, subscriber number and other contact information, information on the contract with the subscriber and his financial soundness.

73   S 91 TKG 2003.

74   S 91 (4) TKG 2003.

75   This includes, but is not limited to, networks, radio equipment and telecommunications terminal equipment. See s 86 et seq TKG 2003.

76   S 88 (1) TKG 2003.

77   S 82 TKG 2003.

78   S 67 TKG 2003.

REGULATION OF NETWORK ACCESS AND INTERCONNECTION: IMPLEMENTATION OF THE ACCESS DIRECTIVE

Objectives and Scope of Access Regulation

5.56   Access and interconnection are seen by the Austrian legislator as a way to stimulate competition and help the smooth functioning of the Austrian telecommunications market. Technical standards and the interests of users have to be taken into consideration as well.

5.57   While various obligations concerning the access to electronic communication networks may only be imposed on operators with significant market power, all operators of public communication networks are obliged to engage in negotiations concerning interconnection.[79]

Basic Regulatory Concepts

5.58   The definitions of 'access' and 'interconnection' are essentially the same as in Article 2 Access Directive. For the definition of interconnection, the term 'operators' has been used instead of 'parties'.

5.59   If two or more operators of publicly available communication networks desire interconnections between their networks, they have to try to come to a solution via negotiation.[80] If negotiations between operators remain fruitless for six weeks, each of them may turn to the TKK or KommAustria for a decision. The TKK or KommAustria themselves may start proceedings without prior call from the operators in well-founded situations.[81] This gives the NRA some discretion regarding the imposition of remedies.

Access and Interconnection-related Obligations with Respect to SMP Undertakings

5.60   After one or more undertakings have been identified as having significant market power, the TKK or KommAustria may impose such obligations on them as are defined in articles 9 to 13 Access Directive at its own discretion.[82] These are obligations relating to:

- transparency,
- non-discrimination,
- accounting separation,
- access to and use of specific network facilities, and
- price control and cost accounting.

5.61   In order to maintain transparency, an undertaking with significant market power may be ordered to provide information on its accounting, technical specifications, characteristics of its network, conditions of use and tariffs.[83]

---

79   S 48 TKG 2003.
80   S 48 TKG 2003.
81   S 50 (2) TKG 2003.
82   See para 5.22 above.
83   S 39 TKG 2003.

5.62 Non-discrimination may be achieved by ordering the undertaking to provide its services under the same conditions to other undertakings that provide similar services.[84] Furthermore, an undertaking with significant market power may be ordered to issue a standard offer regarding its services.

5.63 Regarding access to networks and their facilities, the regulatory authority may order the undertaking to provide access to its network and permission to use its facilities for other undertakings.[85] This also includes the interconnection of networks and network facilities.

5.64 When issuing price control, the regulatory authority may order the undertaking to provide cost-oriented prices, taking into account an adequate rate of return.[86] In addition, the regulatory authority may issue conditions regarding the method of cost accounting.

5.65 In order to achieve accounting separation, the regulatory authority may determine the accounting method and its format used by an undertaking with significant market power.[87]

5.66 Various of these obligations have been imposed on undertakings with significant market power by the TKK.[88] For various markets[89] Telekom Austria AG was ordered by the TKK to offer its services under the same conditions and with the same quality to itself, to joint undertakings and to all undertakings that provide similar services on the same market. This also included the provision of various standard offers with a specific minimum content. In order to prevent unauthorised cross-subsidisation, Telekom Austria AG was obliged to keep records of the costs and profits for each market separately from its other products.

Related Regulatory Powers with Respect to SMP Undertakings

5.67 Undertakings with significant market power have to provide the possibility of carrier selection and carrier pre-selection for their subscribers. Remuneration for these services has to be cost-oriented. The RTR-GmbH may impose the obligation to provide carrier selection and carrier pre-selection with regard to other networks than public communications networks at fixed locations on the same conditions as granting access and interconnection.[90]

5.68 In order to comply with Annex VII Universal Service Directive, section 44 (1) TKG 2003 prescribes the general principles of non-discrimination, cost-orientation and transparency[91] for the provision of leased lines by an undertaking with significant market power. Tariffs and general terms and conditions of such undertakings regarding leased lines have to be approved by the TKK.

---

84   S 38 TKG 2003.
85   S 41 TKG 2003.
86   S 42 TKG 2003.
87   S 40 TKG 2003.
88   See decisions of the TKK: M1/03, M2/03, M3/03, M6/03, M7/03, M8a/03, M8b-k/03, M10/03, M12/03, M13/03 and M15a-e/03.
89   See decisions of the TKK: M1/03, M2/03, M7/03, M8a/03, M10/03, M12/03 and M13/03.
90   S 46 (3) and s 41 TKG 2003.
91   These terms have to be interpreted with the help of Annex VII Universal Service Directive.

5.69   The TKK or KommAustria have the power to impose other remedies regarding access than those named in the TKG 2003 on an operator with significant market power.[92] However, they have to ask for the Commission's permission first.

Regulatory Powers Applicable to All Market Participants

5.70   The TKK or KommAustria may impose remedies of non-discrimination, transparency, accounting separation, providing access, price control and cost accounting on non-SMP operators to a certain extent. The NRA may impose those remedies that an operator agreed to when he was assigned frequencies during the procedure of Section 55 TKG 2003; technical conditions that are necessary for the network to remain operational and remedies that are needed to fulfil international obligations can also be imposed. Section 47 (2) TKG 2003 does not name any further prerequisites, hence it lies in the NRA's discretion to actually impose those obligations on non-SMP operators. However, the NRA still has to regard the consolidation procedure where applicable.

REGULATION OF UNIVERSAL SERVICES AND USERS' RIGHTS: THE UNIVERSAL SERVICE DIRECTIVE

Regulation of Universal Service Obligations

Scope of universal service obligations

5.71   Section 26 TKG 2003 defines the scope of obligations that are imposed on the Universal service provider.[93] They are essentially the same as the ones named in the Universal Service Directive[94] with minor differences: The access to emergency numbers for end-users is not mentioned among the provisions. Since every end-user must have access to emergency numbers, the Austrian legislator did not mention this provision in Section 26 TKG 2003 but made it an obligation for all operators.[95] Special services for disabled users as stated in Article 7 Universal Service Directive are not mentioned in the TKG 2003 either. However, the Universal Service Ordinance (*Universaldienst-Verordnung* – 'UVD') provides further specifications concerning the obligations of Universal service providers.[96]

5.72   The regulatory authorities have no discretion regarding the imposition of these obligations on universal service providers. Universal service providers are required by law to abide by them.

Designation of undertakings obliged to provide universal services

5.73   At least every 10 years, the BMVIT with the help of the RTR-GmbH has to invite operators to tender offers for becoming universal service provider. The

---

92   S 47 (1) TKG 2003.
93   See para 5.73 below.
94   See para 1.163 above.
95   S 20 TKG 2003.
96   It requires universal service providers to comply with the standards 1600 and 1601 of the Austrian Standards Institute when setting up publicly available telephone equipment. These standards contain conditions for the building of structures regarding their accessibility for disabled persons.

BMVIT then has to choose the operator that needs the smallest contribution to provide the universal services.[97] If only one operator fulfils the operational conditions required to become universal service provider and most likely is able to provide the universal services, then the BMVIT chooses that operator without prior invitation to tender offers. If no operator makes an offer for providing the universal services, then the BMVIT may choose the operator most suited for the task.

5.74   Until now, the former monopolist Telekom Austria remains the universal service provider. The BMVIT is obliged to review at least every five years whether or not the prerequisites for an invitation to tender are met.[98]

Regulation of retail tariffs, users' expenditures and quality of services

5.75   The obligations for universal service providers in Annex I Part A Universal Service Directive have been transposed into Austrian law with some differences. The free selective barring for outgoing calls[99] and the obligation to provide itemised billing are not limited to universal service providers alone; they are imposed on all operators of telecommunication services.[100] In addition, all bills have to contain information on the possibility of reviewing the bill and on how to contact the operator. At the request of the subscriber, itemised billing has to be provided in writing. Therefore, it is seen as sufficient to provide itemised billing by electronic means, ie the internet, unless the subscriber wishes otherwise. The RTR-GmbH is given authority to provide further details on which information is required on bills.

5.76   Furthermore, all prices and general terms and conditions of universal service providers for universal services have to be approved[101] by the TKK.

5.77   If a subscriber fails to pay the bill by the due date, operators of telecommunication services may not interrupt the service[102] unless they have sent a reminder in which they inform the subscriber about the possible penalties[103] for his or her non-payment and have given him or her at least two weeks to comply. Universal service providers have to follow even stricter rules. In addition, they may not interrupt the universal service because of a delay in payment in respect of other contractual relationships with the same subscriber.

5.78   The quality of the universal services is specified in Section 27 TKG 2003. The BMVIT is granted authority to further specify the details mentioned there. The BMVIT may even suspend the obligation to provide publicly available telecommunication devices.[104]

5.79   Universal service providers are required to publish information on their performance regarding the provision of universal service once a year. The RTR-GmbH is allowed to review the performance of the universal service providers and compare it to the information provided.

---

97   S 30 (1) TKG 2003.
98   S 133 (9) TKG 2003.
99   S 29 (2) TKG 2003.
100   S 100 TKG 2003.
101   S 26 (3) TKG 2003.
102   S 70 TKG 2003.
103   Ie the interruption of the service.
104   S 27 (2) TKG 2003.

5.80   If a universal service provider 'severely' fails to comply with the provisions concerning the quality of the service,[105] the TKK or KommAustria may use its powers[106] as described in Section 91 TKG 2003. However, the TKG 2003 makes no mention of what 'severe' means in this connection.

Cost calculation and financing of universal services

5.81   Effective costs relating to universal services may be refunded upon request if they could not have been avoided and are considered an undue burden.[107] If the universal service provider's market share of the relevant market exceeds 80 per cent, the request for a refund is not permissible.

5.82   If deemed necessary,[108] the RTR-GmbH may establish a Universal Services Fund[109] to compensate universal service providers. All operators of telecommunication services whose annual turnover exceeds €5 million would have to pay a certain amount to the Universal Services Fund depending on their market share. To date, no Universal Service Fund has been created.

Regulation of Retail Markets

Prerequisites for the regulation of retail markets

5.83   Section 43 TKG 2003 implements the principle that regulation of retail services is permissible only if regulation at wholesale level does not achieve the regulatory objectives. Except for the market of international telephone services provided at a fixed location for residential customers, the former monopolist Telekom Austria has significant market power on all retail markets and, therefore, various remedies were imposed on it.

5.84   Obligations that may be imposed on undertakings with significant market power include the prohibition to demand excessive prices, to hinder the entry of new competitors on the market, to engage in predatory pricing, to unduly favour groups of end-users and to bundle services without justification. Furthermore, the regulatory authority may impose appropriate measures to maintain upper limits for end-user prices or to control certain tariffs. Format and type of the cost accounting system of the undertaking may be determined and inspected by the regulatory authority. The TKK has imposed such obligations on various occasions.[110] As an undertaking with significant market power, Telekom Austria AG is obliged to submit its general terms and conditions to the TKK for prior approval. Furthermore, Telekom Austria AG's subscriber tariffs have to be cost oriented.

End User Rights

Contracts

5.85   Operators of telecommunication networks or services are obliged to use general terms and conditions which provide specific information on the operator, its

---

105   S 27 (5) TKG 2003.
106   See para 5.52 above.
107   S 31 TKG 2003.
108   Ie if one or more universal service providers apply for refunds.
109   'Universaldienstfonds'.
110   See decisions of the TKK: M1/03, M2/03, M3/03 and M6/03.

services, the duration of the contract, the means of dispute resolution, rules regarding compensation, the intervals of billing, the European emergency number and details on the prices.[111] Operators of television or radio networks or operators that are transmitting radio or television signals have to provide only limited information in their general terms and conditions.[112] Universal service providers, however, have to provide more.[113] The general terms and conditions, as well as any changes to them have to be brought to the subscribers' and the TKK's attention. Within eight weeks of the announcement of the general terms, the TKK may object to general terms and conditions that do not comply with any provision of the TKG 2003, Sections 6 and 9 Consumer Protection Act or Sections 864a and 879 (3) Civil Code. Universal service providers need the TKK's approval before being allowed to use new general terms and conditions.[114] The same obligation can be imposed on operators with significant market power. Regarding the general terms and conditions of other operators the TKK only has the right of objection as mentioned above.

5.86 If the changes made to the general terms and conditions do not solely benefit the subscriber, he or she has to be notified at least one month in advance before the changes can come into effect. During this time the subscriber has the right to terminate the contract free of charge.[115]

5.87 Operators of public telecommunication services are obliged to conclude contracts with subscribers concerning their services. However, they only need to do so under their own general terms and conditions.[116] That way, operators could still be able to exclude individuals from telecommunication services by means of implementing a check of credit-worthiness in their general terms and conditions.

5.88 Besides filing a complaint at court, users and operators as well as entities that represent their interests may take disputes regarding in particular the quality of services, payment or alleged violations of the TKG 2003 to the regulatory authority, ie KommAustria in matters concerning radio and television broadcasting or the RTR-GmbH otherwise.[117] Operators are required to co-operate in the process of dispute resolution and provide the regulatory authority with all information and documents it requires to assess the dispute and provide a solution.

5.89 The regulatory authority will try to work out a solution that both parties agree on. If the parties cannot agree to an amicable solution, the regulatory authority will offer a recommendation on how to solve the dispute, which, however, is not binding on the parties. It is possible for the parties to file a complaint after or even during the dispute resolution procedure.

5.90 The dispute resolution mechanism regarding the correction of bills consists of two steps.[118] If a subscriber doubts the correctness of a bill, he or she may request the operator to re-inspect it. The operator then has to issue a written confirmation or change the incorrect bill accordingly.

---

111   S 25 TKG 2003.
112   S 25 (8) TKG 2003.
113   S 26 (4) TKG 2003.
114   S 26 (3) TKG 2003.
115   S 25 (3) TKG 2003.
116   S 69 (1) TKG 2003.
117   S 122 TKG 2003.
118   S 71 TKG 2003.

5.91   If the operator and the subscriber cannot come to an agreement, either party may involve the RTR-GmbH. The disputed amount will not be due until the dispute resolution procedure is finished. The parties are not bound by the RTR-GmbH's decision, as either one can appeal to the court. If the RTR-GmbH decides that the disputed bill was correct from the beginning, then the operator may demand the subscriber to pay interest for the period of time the due date was postponed.

Transparency obligations

5.92   Beside the obligation to use general terms and conditions with the contents mentioned above, other rules in the TKG 2003 aim to accomplish transparency. Section 17 (1) TKG 2003 compels operators of public telecommunication services (the transmission of radio signals is exempt from this rule) to provide comparable, adequate and up-to-date information regarding the quality of their services. The BMVIT may provide more detailed rules on the exact type of information and the means of its publication. The RTR-GmbH is given authority to inspect the provided information.

5.93   Section 24 TKG 2003 grants the RTR-GmbH authority concerning the transparency of tariffs. It lies in the RTR-GmbH's discretion to publish rules on numbers of value added services, their prices, the method of calculation and the means of informing the subscribers of the tariff.[119] The RTR-GmbH has to provide rules that allow the adequate protection of users and the transparent provision of value-added services. Section 24 (2) TKG 2003 names the control of access regarding specific groups of users, the provision of time limits, rules on dialler programmes and rules on advertisement as examples of measures the RTR-GmbH may take. Furthermore, names and addresses of operators of value added services have to be kept in a public register by the RTR-GmbH.

DATA PROTECTION: IMPLEMENTATION OF THE E-PRIVACY DIRECTIVE

Confidentiality of Communications

5.94   Under Section 95 (1) TKG 2003 providers of publicly available electronic communication services are obliged to take measures as described in Section 14 Data Protection Act ('DSG') to ensure the safety of personal data. These measures have to prevent the processed data from being destroyed illegally or accidentally, and ensure that processed data is safe from accidental loss as well as unauthorised access.

5.95   Whenever there is a particular risk of a breach of confidentiality,[120] subscribers of publicly available electronic communication services have to be informed of it by the provider. Where the risk lies outside the scope of the measures to be taken by the provider, the subscriber has to be informed of possible remedies and the costs involved as well.

---

119 S 24 (1) TKG 2003.
120 The TKG 2003 chooses not to use the term 'breach of security of the network', but uses 'breach of confidentiality' instead.

5.96 Traffic data, location data and content data, including such data regarding unsuccessful connections, are to be kept confidential by providers and all individuals that assist in the provider's operation.[121] Interception, recording and any other surveillance of communication and the traffic, or location data connected to it, are generally prohibited, unless the TKG 2003 explicitly grants the right to process specific kinds of data.[122]

5.97 Exceptions are granted under Section 93 (3) TKG 2003 concerning the storage and tracing of emergency calls, investigations concerning harassing calls,[123] the technical storage necessary to transmit communication and the consent of all users involved. In addition, providers of publicly available communication services have to provide[124] the technical means that allow the surveillance of telecommunications[125] under the Rules on Criminal Procedure ('StPO').

5.98 Communications that have been intercepted unintentionally must be deleted or destroyed by other means,[126] any other use is prohibited.

Traffic Data and Location Data

5.99 The definitions of the terms 'traffic data' and 'location data'[127] are the same as in the E-Privacy Directive.[128]

5.100 Generally, the storage of traffic data is prohibited unless stated otherwise.[129] Any traffic data has to be deleted or anonymised by the provider immediately after the termination of the connection.

5.101 However, traffic data that serves the purpose of subscriber billing and the payment of interconnection fees has to be stored by the provider as long as the bill may be lawfully challenged, payment pursued, or for the period of any proceedings in which the bill is disputed. In this case, operators have to provide the decision-making entity with all the necessary traffic data.

5.102 When transposing Article 6(5) E-Privacy Directive, the TKG 2003 adds the 'removal of interference' to the list of activities that may be pursued when processing traffic data.[130] This was deemed necessary to provide a secure service and let the operator fulfil his contractual obligations. The Austrian legislator had particularly in mind the log files of internet access providers, since often specific information relating to connection is required in order to resolve connectivity problems.

---

121 S 93 TKG 2003.
122 This mainly applies to operators who need to process various types of data regarding their subscribers in order to provide their services.
123 S 106 TKG 2003.
124 S 94 TKG 2003.
125 Under the StPO, the surveillance of telecommunications requires an order from a criminal court.
126 S 93 (4) TKG 2003.
127 S 92 (3)(4) and 92 (3)(6) TKG 2003.
128 See Art 2(b) and (c) E-Privacy Directive.
129 S 99 (1) TKG 2003.
130 S 99 (3) TKG 2003.

5.103   Generally, location data other than traffic data may not be processed unless it is anonymised or the user or subscriber has given his consent[131] to the processing. The consent may be withdrawn at any time by the user or subscriber. In addition, providers of emergency call services may process and demand such location data of providers in case of emergency.[132]

5.104   The TKG 2003 does not mention the specific obligations of operators to inform users and subscribers on the processing of location data as provided for in Article 9 (1) E-Privacy Directive. However, all providers of publicly available communication services are obliged to inform their users and subscribers of the personal data they process, the reason and means of the processing as well as how long the personal data will be stored.[133]

Itemised Billing

5.105   Operators have to provide itemised billing as long as the subscriber does not object.[134] If requested by the subscriber, itemised billing has to be supplied in writing. Called party numbers are to be anonymised except where the complete number is needed to determine the tariff or the subscriber agrees in writing to inform all present and future users thereof. The RTR-GmbH may issue regulations on the exact form and detail of the bill.

Calling and Connected Line Identification

5.106   Users of publicly available communication services are granted the same rights[135] regarding the presentation and restriction of calling and connected line identification as provided in Article 8(1)–(4) E-Privacy Directive. The restriction of the identification of the calling party must be possible generally, or for each call individually. However, emergency calls must be identifiable at all times. The operator has to provide all necessary information on the availability and use of the presentation and restriction of line identifications in its general terms and conditions.

Automatic Call Forwarding

5.107   Subscribers must be given the opportunity to suppress automatic call forwarding from third parties to their terminal free of charge.[136]

Directories of Subscribers

5.108   Subscribers have to be given the opportunity to decide whether or not their personal data is included in a publicly available directory.[137] Furthermore, they

---

131   S 102 (1) TKG 2003.
132   S 98 TKG 2003.
133   S 96 (3) TKG 2003.
134   S 100 TKG 2003.
135   S 104 TKG 2003.
136   S 105 TKG 2003.
137   S 69 TKG 2003.

must be allowed to verify, correct or delete their entry. The option of not entering a subscriber's personal data, as well as entering name, academic title, address, subscriber number and profession, in a directory has to remain free of charge. Other information may be entered, if the subscriber wishes to do so, albeit not free of charge. Moreover, subscribers may opt out of being entered into electronic directories that allow a more detailed search than just by name.

5.109   Providers may use the information on subscribers provided in this way solely for the use of publicly available telephone services.[138] In particular, the creation of electronic profiles or the sorting of subscribers into categories by the provider, unless categories are necessary for the publication of the directory, are prohibited. In addition, all providers are obliged to take measures designed to prevent the duplication of their electronic directories.

Unsolicited Communications

5.110   Section 107 TKG 2003 provides rules regarding unsolicited communications. Advertising via telephone calls[139] or via fax is prohibited unless the recipient has previously agreed to it. Once given, the recipient's consent may be withdrawn at any time. Electronic mail – including SMS – that was sent for the purpose of direct marketing or that was sent to more than 50 recipients needs the prior consent of the addressee if sent to a consumer.[140] However, the prior consent of the consumer is not necessary if the sender had acquired the contact information of the consumer from a prior sale or provision of a service, the sender is now advertising for similar products or services and the customer was made aware during the initial inquiry for his or her contact information and on the electronic message that he or she may refuse further messages.

5.111   The sending of electronic mail to anyone who is not a consumer is allowed without prior consent of the recipient. However, they must be given the opportunity in the received mail to refuse further messages.[141]

5.112   The sending of an advertisement via electronic mail is prohibited if the sender of the message cannot be determined or if no authentic address is provided to which the refusal of further messages can be directed.[142] Any violation of Section 107 TKG 2003 is punishable with fines of up to €37,000.

---

138   S 103 (1) TKG 2003.
139   Either automatic calls or calls made by humans.
140   S 107 (2) TKG 2003.
141   S 107 (4) TKG 2003.
142   S 107 (5) TKG 2003.

The Belgian Market for Electronic Communications[1]

Arne Gutermann and Els Janssens
Baker & McKenzie Brussels

LEGAL STRUCTURE

6.1 Belgium is a federal state divided into three economic areas and three cultural areas. The economic areas (the 'Regions') are the Flemish, Walloon and Brussels-Capital Regions. The three cultural areas (the 'Communities') are the Flemish, French and German-language Communities. At federal, regional land community level, there are legislative authorities. A description of the Belgian telecommunication regulatory regime is complex because some aspects of telecommunications law in Belgium are organised at federal and others at community level.

Basic Policy

Regulatory approach and market conditions

6.2 Prior to 1998, the Belgian telecommunications market was almost entirely in the hands of Belgacom, the former incumbent. In January 1998,[2] the Belgian telecom market was liberalised along the lines of European legislation. Despite this liberalisation, the Belgian telecom market remains, however, one of the least competitive in Europe. Belgacom continues to control the lion's share of the market, but pressure on its dominant position is increasing now that saturation of the market has almost been reached. Particularly in the mobile telephony and broadband markets, and some segments of the fixed telephony market, fierce competition has developed.[3]

---

1   Editing of this chapter closed on 26 July 2005.
2   The Act of 19 December 1997 modifying the Act of 21 March 1991 on the Reform of Certain Public Enterprises in order to make the regulatory framework compliant with the obligations of free competition and harmonisation of the telecom market as laid down in decisions of the European Union.
3   Market information derived from: BIPT Annual Reports of 2003 and 2004, available at www.bipt.be; the European Commission's 10th report on the implementation of the regulatory framework in the member states, COM (2004) 759, final 02.12.2004; Fortis report 'The dynamics of the Belgian Telecom Market' of 29 November 2004 and presentation 'Status of the Belgian Telecom Market' of Bert Broens, journalist with De Tijd, at the annual Belgian Telecom Top of 8 June 2005.

6.3   *Fixed telephony*: While the markets for business and long-distance calls[4] have become highly competitive, Belgacom has managed to retain its leadership position in fixed telephony with a market share still estimated at 90%, in terms of access, and 61%, in terms of time, at the end of 2004. Belgacom's most important competitor in this market is Telenet (although only active in the Flemish part of the country), which offers telecommunication services in Flanders via its CATV-cable network.

6.4   *Mobile telephony*: After considerable delay in the 1990s, mobile penetration has significantly increased in recent years. Today, the penetration rate is estimated at 77%, which is, however, still below the European average of 87%. The market share of the leading cell phone operator, Belgacom's subsidiary Proximus,[5] amounts to 51%. Its competitors are Mobistar and Base.

6.5   *Broadband and internet*: The Belgian broadband market is atypical, in that the penetration rate in 2004 was around 14%, which is amongst the highest in Europe. The market is characterised by strong competition between Telenet and Belgacom. Other players are Versatel, Tiscali and Scarlet. This competition has resulted in low prices for broadband internet access.

Regulatory objectives

6.6   The Belgian legislator has expressed the wish that the market's regulation be carried out smoothly, that it be adapted to specific situations and that it be technologically neutral but favourable to innovative investments and the emergence of new markets. At the same time, it wishes to pay particular attention to the interests of consumers. The Belgian government is particularly keen to maintain and strengthen Belgium's leadership position with particular respect to broadband technology. Initiatives are, however, necessary to catch up in other domains.

Implementation of EU Directives

6.7   Belgium is one of the countries that did not meet the 24 July 2003 deadline for the implementation of the six European Directives and one Decision constituting the Regulatory Package.[6] As a consequence, the European Commission initiated legal proceedings against Belgium for not having prepared the necessary legislation on time. Belgium already faced one penalty[7] with respect to the Privacy Directive; proceedings with respect to the other Directives are still pending.

6.8   The delay in transposing the new EU regulatory framework was caused not only by specific political circumstances but also by the particularities of the Belgian legislative system providing for exclusive competences at the federal level and the level of the three Communities.[8] Currently, the Communities are competent for 'radio broadcasting and television, including all technical aspects related thereto',[9] while telecommunication is one of the residual competences of the federal authorities. Since the Regulatory Package relates to all forms of electronic communication,

---

4   As opposed to the market for residential and local calls.
5   Belgacom's subsidiary is incorporated under the name Belgacom Mobile SA, but renders its services under the trade name Proximus.
6   See para 1.2 above.
7   Judgment of the European Court of Justice dated 28 April 2005 (2005/C 143/20)
8   Being the Flemish, French and German Communities.
9   See article 4, 6° Special Act dated 8 August 1980 on the Reform of the Institutions ('SAHI').

it covers at the same time matters which should be enacted by the Communities (broadcasting) and others which should be adopted at federal level (telecommunications). Moreover, since Brussels does not form part of any of the three Communities, the federal legislator must take a separate legislative initiative for broadcasting in Brussels.

6.9   This multi-level implementation requirement can be explained by a difference in approach between the European and Belgian legislators: the new regulatory framework is horizontally oriented, ie a difference is made between the transmission of signals on the one hand and the content of such signals on the other hand; whereas the Belgian competences are divided vertically, ie a difference is made between telecommunication and broadcasting, and each of them covers both content and transmission.[10]

6.10   At the time of writing, the implementation process of the Regulatory Package in Belgium is finally making progress. The Act on Electronic Communications of 13 June 2005 ('Federal Act') has found its way through parliament and was published in the Belgian Official Gazette on 20 June 2005. It entered into force on 30 June 2005. Also, the Flemish and French Communities have adopted a new framework for broadcasting.[11] Only the German-language Community and the federal legislator are still working on a framework document to regulate broadcasting in the German-language Community and the Brussels area.

Legislation

6.11   With regard to telecommunications, the Federal Act implements the bulk of the new regulatory framework. It replaces or amends most parts of the former regulatory regime.[12] This Federal Act, however, is a framework document only, needing further implementation by means of Royal and Ministerial Decrees.

6.12   The broadcasting aspects of the regulatory framework are to be found in Community decrees of the Flemish, French and German-language Communities. As referred to above,[13] the Decree of the French Community of 27 February 2003 related to Radio Broadcasting (the 'French Broadcasting Decree') and the Decree of the Flemish Community of 7 May 2004 modifying some of the Provisions of the Decrees on Radio Broadcasting and Television, coordinated on 25 January 1995 and of some other Provisions on Radio Broadcasting and Television (the 'Flemish Broadcasting Decree') are already in force. The draft Decree of the German-language Community regarding Radio and Cinematography (the 'German Broadcasting Decree') will probably be adopted in the not-too-distant future. Also, the federal government has tabled a bill on broadcasting in Brussels. It is, however, unknown when it will become law. Similar to the Federal Act, this Community broadcasting legislation only forms a framework, requiring further implementation through governmental and ministerial decrees at Community level. Throughout this chapter the above-mentioned decrees will be collectively referred to as the 'Broadcasting Decrees'. Since the German Broadcasting Decree and the broadcasting act

---

10   Stevens, D., Uyttendaele, C. and Valcke, P., 'De implementatie van de communicatierichtlijnen in België: kwintet of kakofonie?'
11   See para 6.12 below.
12   The current regime is laid down in the Act of 21 March 1991 on the Reform of Certain Public Enterprises, and amended by the Act of 19 December 1997.
13   See para 6.10 above.

for the Brussels area are still subject to changes, this chapter will mainly focus on the legislation of the Flemish and French Community as far as broadcasting is concerned.

6.13   Apart from the legislation implementing the new regime, there are still two other legislative acts related to telecommunications, of which the most important one is the Act of 17 January 2003 on the statute of the regulator of the Belgian post and telecommunications sector (the 'BIPT Act'). The BIPT Act establishes and governs the organisation, competencies and procedural rules of the Belgian Institute for Post and Telecommunications ('BIPT') and sets out its regulatory objectives. The other act,[14] which was adopted on the same day, relates to remedies against BIPT decisions and the settlement of certain disputes between operators.

6.14   Finally, the sector is also regulated through decisions, resolutions and recommendations of BIPT, as far as telecom is concerned, and by recommendations and rules of the broadcasting authorities with regard to radio and television broadcasting.

REGULATORY PRINCIPLES: IMPLEMENTATION OF THE FRAMEWORK DIRECTIVE

Scope of Regulation

6.15   The new legislative acts at federal and Community level will together cover the entirety of electronic communications services and networks as referred to in the Framework Directive. However, due to the exclusive competences at federal and Community level as explained above, the scope of the Federal Act is limited to telecommunications, while the Broadcasting Decrees of the Communities exclusively deal with broadcasting aspects.

6.16   Such exclusive competences are also reflected in the wording of the definitions of 'electronic communications network' and 'electronic communication service' in the Federal Act, which are substantially similar[15] to the definitions in the Framework Directive but explicitly exclude any use of such networks or services for the transmission of broadcasting signals.

Regulatory Authorities: Organisation, Regulatory Objectives, Competencies

Telecommunications

REGULATORY BODY AND INDEPENDENCE

6.17   The regulatory authority in Belgium for telecommunications is BIPT. Until the adoption of the BIPT Act, BIPT was a government-dependent 'parastatal' body. The BIPT Act radically changed the status of the regulator to make it a

---

14   The Act of 17 January 2003 on Remedies and Dispute Settlement, with reference to the Act of 17 January 2003 on the Statute of the Regulator of the Belgian Post and Telecommunications Sector.

15   Notwithstanding some minor differences in the wording, the definitions have the same meaning as the definitions in the Framework Directive.

unique public interest body, based on the model of the financial and energy regulators in Belgium. Notwithstanding this change, concerns as to its independence still remain. These concerns are in summary based upon article 15 BIPT Act, which provides that the Council of Ministers has the right to suspend a decision of BIPT on certain matters to be determined by Royal Decree which the Council considers to be illegal or against the public interest. Although to date the Council has not yet exercised this right, conflicting interests might occur as the Belgian state still owns 50% plus one of the shares of Belgacom, the former incumbent. Therefore, the industry as well as the European Commission would welcome some further guarantees as to the independence of BIPT.

TASKS AND COMPETENCIES

6.18   Under the BIPT Act and the new Federal Act, BIPT's tasks are essentially:[16]

- to ensure that all legislation and regulations regarding telecommunications are observed;
- to advise the Minister regarding the policy the federal government wishes to pursue in telecommunications;
- to assist the Minister in the preparation of legislation regarding telecommunications;
- to manage the national numbering space and radio frequency spectrum; and
- to resolve conflicts between providers of networks, services and equipment, specifically with respect to interconnection, special access and shared use.

6.19   To this end, BIPT has been entrusted with powers to impose sanctions upon offenders and to take administrative decisions (such as the approval of interconnection tariffs) in the exercise of which it has some discretion. It is hoped that the transposition of the Regulatory Package will further increase this inclination.

6.20   Just like every other Belgian administrative body, BIPT is subject to the rules with respect to the formal motivation (ie justification) of administrative acts,[17] the public nature of administration,[18] and confidentiality.[19] Also, article 19 BIPT Act offers every person directly and personally involved in a decision of BIPT the possibility to be heard in advance. However, no specific rules are yet provided in this respect. In practice, BIPT will send a draft of the decision to the persons involved, with an invitation to communicate any comments by a specified date. Such persons may also be invited to formulate comments during a meeting. Decisions of BIPT are published on its website.

CONSULTATION PROCEDURES

6.21   To help it with its tasks, BIPT is entitled to request from any interested person all useful information and may organise any type of inquiry or public consultation. This right is set out in the BIPT Act[20] and is confirmed by the Federal Act.[21]

---

16   Article 14 § 1 BIPT Act.
17   Act of 29 July 1991 on the formal motivation of administrative acts.
18   Act of 11 April 1994 on the public nature of the administration.
19   Article 23 § 3 BIPT Act in conjunction with Article 6 §1 7° Act of 11 April 1994 on the public nature of the administration.
20   Article 14 § 2, 2° BIPT Act.
21   Articles 137 and 139 Federal Act.

6.22 With respect to individual enquiries, the Federal Act further specifies that BIPT's requests for information should be justified and proportionate to the performance of its tasks. The requests should also mention the timeframe for the submission of the requested information. The Minister is yet to define more detailed rules for the exchange of information. Meanwhile, BIPT's requests for information take into account the guarantees set out above.[22]

6.23 If and when BIPT intends to adopt a decision that may have a significant impact on the relevant market, it is obliged to organise a public consultation.[23] The consultation procedure should take place within a maximum time frame of two months, and the results should be made available to the public without prejudice to the confidential nature of certain business information. A Royal Decree with specific rules for the conduct of public consultations and the publication of the results is yet to be adopted. However, the lack of specific rules has not prevented BIPT from conducting public consultations. In practice, BIPT has drawn up questionnaires for several topics over the past years.

RELATIONSHIP WITH NATIONAL COMPETITION AUTHORITY

6.24 Although article 14 § 2, 3° BIPT Act imposes the obligation on BIPT to cooperate with other regulatory bodies, including the national competition authorities, cooperation between the Competition Council[24] and BIPT is reported as not going very smoothly. The main reason appears to be the lack of specific rules and procedures for cooperation. These are still to be defined in a Royal Decree after the completion of a consultation procedure with all the authorities involved. However, this could still be a difficult exercise, since the wording in the BIPT Act is somewhat unclear as to when exactly cooperation is required.

6.25 The new Federal Act does not bring much clarification either. The general obligation to work closely with the national competition authorities has been recaptured in article 7 without any further specification. The only concrete example of cooperation between the two regulators can be found in article 138 Federal Act, where it is stipulated that BIPT should give effect to any justified request for information of any other regulator in Belgium including the Competition Council.

DISPUTE RESOLUTION POWERS

6.26 In the event of disputes between operators of telecommunications networks, services or equipment, the disputing parties may request BIPT to work out proposals to reconcile the position between the parties within one month from the date of the request. A Royal Decree, which is yet to be adopted, should further specify the rules for this procedure.

6.27 Furthermore, the Competition Council has been made responsible for the settlement of disputes between operators in relation to interconnection, leased lines, special access, full unbundling and shared access.[25] BIPT is also involved in this procedure to the extent that it must assist the Competition Council in the investigation of the dispute. BIPT is equally entrusted with enforcing the decisions of the Competition Council for this type of dispute. The Competition Council must

---

22 See para 6.20 above.
23 Article 140 Federal Act.
24 'De Raad voor Mededinging' / 'Le Conseil de la Concurrence'.
25 Article 4 Act of 17 January 2003 on Legal Remedies and Disputes Settlement.

render its decision within a period of four months, it being understood that, where the parties are involved in a reconciliation procedure under the direction of BIPT, the procedure before the Competition Council is suspended.

Broadcasting

6.28   With the adoption of the new regulatory framework, the regulators of the Communities are responsible for supervising the market of broadcasting services.

6.29   The watchdog of the Flemish broadcasting market is the Flemish Commissioner's Office for Media (*Vlaams Commissariaat voor de Media* – 'VCM'). This body existed prior to 2004 but has been officially appointed as the Flemish regulatory authority – for broadcasting only – by the Flemish Broadcasting Decree. Its main tasks are to issue licences for broadcasting and to ensure observance of the regulatory framework.[26] To this end, it has received powers to impose fines or other sanctions. VCM is also responsible for conducting the market analysis on the broadcasting market under the new EU framework. Unlike BIPT, VCM does not have any advisory task: this competence is assigned to the Flemish Council for Media (*Vlaamse Raad voor Media*), a body within the Ministry of the Flemish Community.

6.30   The High Council for the Audiovisual Sector of the French Community (*Conseil Supérieur de l'audiovisuel de la Communauté Française* – 'CSAC') is the broadcasting regulator of the French Community. This body also existed prior to the adoption of the Broadcasting Decree. CSAC is composed of two colleges: the Advisory College, and the Licence and Supervision College ('LSC'). While the Advisory College is responsible for advising the government, LSC has substantially the same role as VCM in Flanders.

6.31   Following the adoption of the German Broadcasting Decree the Media Council ('Medienrat') will become the broadcasting regulator of the German-language Community. The regulator will have the same overall powers and tasks as its fellow regulators of the other Communities.

6.32   The federal state structure requires that a separate broadcasting regulator be appointed for the 19 municipalities of the Brussels-capital district. In order to avoid any further disintegration the federal legislator intends to entrust BIPT with the supervision of the Brussels broadcasting market.

Convergence

6.33   The Belgian Constitutional Court[27] ('*Arbitragehof* / '*Cour d'Arbitrage*') resolved that any mixed infrastructure, ie networks which can be used for both telecommunication and broadcasting services, requires cooperation between the

---

26   The settlement of certain types of dispute and the observance of some of the provisions of the Flemish Broadcasting Decree are, however, entrusted to the Flemish Disputes Council for Radio and Television and the Flemish Watching and Listening Council for Radio and Television, which exist alongside VCM. To simplify this rather complex structure a draft bill has recently been tabled to merge VCM with these two councils to form one external independent agency. This agency would take over the regulatory tasks of the current VCM. It is not known when this draft text will become law.

27   Decision of the Constitutional Court of 14 July 2004.

federal state and the Communities. By the end of 2005, the necessary mechanisms should be in place. To this effect, the federal government and the Communities are working out an agreement in principle within the Consultation Committee of the Belgian Governments. Once this agreement is adopted by the respective parliaments, it will call into existence a conference of regulators; where a regulator intends to adopt a decision involving mixed infrastructure, it will first have to submit a draft to the other regulators, who may decide to pass on such decision to the conference of regulators. In such a case, the conference will take a decision instead of the regulator in question. Apart from the cooperation between the regulators, the agreement also provides for a consultation procedure in respect of new legislation.

Right of Appeal against NRA's Decisions

6.34   The Act of 17 January 2003 on Legal Remedies and Dispute Settlement introduced a right of appeal against BIPT's decisions before the Court of Appeal in Brussels. Any person affected by a decision of BIPT (including the Minister of Telecommunications) may lodge an appeal. Such an appeal does not suspend the effect of BIPT's decision. The procedure takes the form of summary proceedings but, unlike in short proceedings where only temporary measures are attended to, the Court of Appeal delivers a judgment on the merits of the case. The competence of the Court of Appeal in Brussels for this type of dispute is exclusive. This means that an appeal against BIPT decisions cannot be brought in the highest administrative tribunal, the State Council ('*Raad van State*' / '*Conseil d'Etat*') in parallel with or after an appeal to the Brussels Court of Appeal.

6.35   At Community level no special appeal procedures have been introduced so far. Like any administrative decision for which no special appeal procedure exists, the decisions of the Community regulators can be challenged before the State Council by any person directly and personally affected by such a decision. The State Council has the possibility to annul such a decision. Also, any legal action related to acts of BIPT which do not qualify as a decision (such as advices etc) can be brought before the State Council.

6.36   The former incumbent appeals against almost every decision of BIPT. The numerous appeals, unfortunately, jeopardise the legal certainty since some of the disputes remain unresolved for extended periods of time. It is, therefore, hoped that, with the full implementation of the new regulatory framework, there will be fewer grounds for appeal.

The NRA's Obligations to Cooperate with the Commission

Consolidation procedure

6.37   The general principles of the consolidation procedure (article 7 Framework Agreement) for telecommunications are described in articles 141 to 143 Federal Act.

6.38   Whenever BIPT intends to take measures regarding market definitions and analysis, access and interconnection, obligations for SMP operators or exceptionally non-SMP operators,[28] which may affect trade between member states, it will consult with the European Commission and the other NRAs by submitting a draft text. BIPT must take into account the comments made by the Commission or the NRAs within a period of time still to be defined. The final decisions shall be communicated to the European Commission and the NRAs.

6.39   If the European Commission so requests within the initial period, BIPT must wait an additional two months before adopting its decision provided that the contemplated decision:

- identifies a market different from the markets already identified by the European Commission; or
- designates an operator which, solely or collectively with others, holds a strong dominant position.

These decisions of BIPT require the approval of the European Commission in accordance with article 7 Framework Directive.

6.40   Further rules for the consultation procedures, including the time frame for communicating comments on the draft decision, should be defined by Royal Decree.

6.41   Temporary measures within the meaning of article 20 BIPT Act are exempted from the consolidation procedure. This provision envisages any urgent temporary[29] measures taken by BIPT where there is a risk of serious irreparable damage.

6.42   The general principle of the consolidation procedure has also been set out in the Broadcasting Decrees, but only in connection with decisions regarding market definition and analysis as well as obligations for SMP operators. Whilst all of the Broadcasting Decrees still require further implementation to set the specific rules of procedure, a difference in approach has already been noticed between the Communities: where the French Community has clearly opted to provide a framework for the consolidation procedure in its Broadcasting Decree,[30] the Flemish government has simply (and somewhat confusingly) referred to the consolidation procedure as a possibility. It may, therefore, be hoped that further rules for consultation will shed light on the precise scope of the obligations to consult with the European Commission and the other NRAs.

'Significant Market Power' as a Fundamental Prerequisite of Regulation

Definition of SMP

6.43   The Federal Act defines 'Significant Market Power' as a position equivalent to dominance, which is a position of economic strength affording an undertaking the power to behave to an appreciable extent independently of competitors,

---

28   Obligations can only be imposed on non-SMP market players in order to comply with international obligations and to ensure end-to-end connections.
29   The decisions must not be effective beyond a period of two months.
30   Comparable to the framework provided in the Federal Act.

customers, and, ultimately, consumers. SMP may refer to individual or collective dominance. Undertakings with SMP on one market may also be deemed to have SMP on closely related markets where links between the two markets allow leveraging of market power.[31]

6.44 The Broadcasting Decrees define SMP in the same way as the Federal Act without, however, mentioning that undertakings with SMP on one market may also be deemed to have SMP on closely related markets. This can only be partially explained by the fact that, unlike BIPT,[32] the Community regulators are only responsible for conducting market analysis on one single market, i e the market of broadcasting services, because, even within that market, there can exist several sub-markets.

Definition of relevant markets and market analysis

6.45 Pursuant to articles 54 and 56 Federal Act, BIPT must define and analyse the relevant markets, taking into account the Commission's guidelines on market analysis, its recommendation on relevant markets, as well as the principles of competition. The public consultation and consolidation procedures[33] are applicable.

6.46 If, on the basis of the market analysis, it would appear that a market is not effectively competitive, BIPT must identify the SMP undertakings in that market and impose appropriate regulatory obligations or maintain existing obligations. Exceptionally, BIPT may also impose obligations on undertakings which do not have a significant market position within the meaning of the Act.

6.47 BIPT is responsible for conducting market analyses on all of the electronic communications markets except market 18, Broadcasting, which falls within the exclusive competence of the Communities. While the Belgian legislator was still fully occupied with the transposition of the Regulatory Package, BIPT has already taken a number of steps for its concrete implementation. It has clustered the 17 markets into 4 related market areas,[34] sent out questionnaires to operators since 2003 and appointed external consultants to assist with the analyses. The results are expected in the course of 2005. These preparatory steps were possible, even before the transposition of the EU Directives was completed, through an amendment to the BIPT Act.[35] However, imposing measures with a view to stimulating competition on the markets remains difficult for as long as the new regulatory framework is not fully implemented. This also implies the entry into force of the cooperation agreement for mixed infrastructure since, upon the request of the Communities, BIPT has agreed not to take any decisions until such date. As a consequence, no measures should be expected before the end of 2005[36] but it will probably take even longer to catch up on the delay. There is no doubt that the delays incurred have had a restraining effect on the development of competition in the market place and probably helped Belgacom to retain market control.

---

31 Article 55 § 3 Federal Act.
32 BIPT is responsible for market analyses on the other 17 markets defined by the European Commission.
33 See paras 6.23 and 6.37–6.40 above, respectively.
34 Namely (1) mobile telephony, (2) fixed telephony, (3) leased lines, and (4) broadband markets.
35 Article 443 Program Act of 22 December 2003 has added a subsection (5) to the list of powers and competencies of the BIPT, set out in Article 14 § 1 BIPT Act.
36 See newspaper article of Bert Broens '*BIPT deelt macht met controle-instanties media*' in De Tijd of 21 April 2005.

6.48   Market definition and analysis with respect to the broadcasting market has been reserved to the Communities' broadcasting regulators. The general principles to this end are laid down in the respective Broadcasting Decrees.[37] Specific rules are still to be adopted by all of the Communities for the consultation procedure, being part of the market analysis. As a consequence, none of the Communities has yet initiated the procedure for the analysis; it is expected that, once the analyses are completed, the respective regulators will probably impose obligations on the cable companies, as the majority of them have significant market power in their respective local territories.

NRA's Regulatory Duties concerning Rights of Way, Co-location and Facility Sharing

Rights of way

6.49   In Belgium, the granting of rights of way to network providers has been the subject of extensive constitutional debate as to the respective and diverging competences of the Belgian federal government (telecommunications) and the Communities (broadcasting) on the one hand, and the Regions (public domain) on the other hand. This is caused by the fact that rights of way relate to the use of public land on which the networks are installed, and 'public land' is the exclusive competence of the Regions. Hence, all of the federal government, the Communities and the Regions claim (partial) competence for the granting of rights of way.

6.50   The result of this debate was that the provisions related to the installation of telecom networks (including rights of way) were left out of the Federal Act to pave the way for further negotiations between the federal government, the Communities and the Regions. Until a cooperation agreement is reached, the old regime of the Act of 1 March 1991 on the Reform of Certain Public Enterprises continues to apply. This regime, which provides for the use of public land free of charge, appears to be conflicting with legislation of the Flemish government, which requires payment of a fee of €1 per metre of cable for the use of regional routes. For that reason the federal government has commenced an action against the Flemish government before the State Council.

6.51   Notwithstanding the ongoing debate, rights of way have been regulated in the Flemish[38] and French[39] Broadcasting Decrees.[40] On the basis of these decrees providers of cable networks have the right to install cables and relevant equipment on public land if they comply with the laws and decrees regarding the public domain, and respect its purpose. Prior to exercising their right, the cable companies have to submit information with respect to the location and the cable planning to the authority responsible for the public land. In general this will be a municipality. In Flanders this authority has to decide within two months of the request whether it will authorise the contemplated works. Municipalities in the French Community have an extra month to answer. The relevant authority may also propose amendments to the planning. In addition, the providers of cable networks have the right to

---

37   Articles 90–93 French Broadcasting Decree; Articles 122–125 Flemish Broadcasting Decree; and Articles 65–69 draft German Broadcasting Decree.
38   Article 132 Flemish Broadcasting Decree.
39   Article 98 French Broadcasting Decree.
40   At this stage, it is unclear whether the German Community will include provisions in this respect.

affix cramps and braces on façades and to install cables over open land or without fixings on private property. In such an event, the works cannot be started until the owners of the property and the tenants are notified. The cable company is responsible for ensuring the competent installation and maintenance of its network. Any damage caused by the installation and exploitation of the cable networks should be compensated by the provider.

6.52   A few years ago, some of the municipalities started to impose fees in the form of taxes on networks developed in their respective territories in order to compensate for decreasing revenues. To avoid escalation of this practice within the 19 Brussels municipalities, the Brussels region has issued a circular specifying tariff conditions.[41]

Co-location and facility sharing

6.53   Article 25 Federal Act provides that, as far as possible, operators have to install antennae on existing sites. Operators who own an antenna site should allow the use of such site by other operators in a reasonable and non-discriminating manner, for which they are entitled to receive compensation to be approved by BIPT. A database of antennae sites will be created, with all relevant information to facilitate the evaluation of antennae sites for the purpose of shared use.[42] Shared use of sites other than antennae sites will be regulated by a Royal Decree after consultation with BIPT. BIPT is bound to organise a public consultation prior to giving its advice to the Minister of Telecommunications.

6.54   The Broadcasting Decrees remain completely silent on the issue of co-location and facility sharing.

REGULATION OF MARKET ENTRY: IMPLEMENTATION OF THE AUTHORISATION DIRECTIVE

The General Authorisation of Electronic Communications

6.55   Under the Federal Act the conditions for undertakings to enter the telecommunications[43] market are significantly simplified. Where, in the past, a licence was necessary to provide telecommunications networks or telecommunications services, it now suffices to notify BIPT. Notification must be done by registered letter mentioning the full details of the applicant, its contact person, a succinct description of the network or service offered and the intended commencement date of the activities. BIPT subsequently confirms the notification and enters the notifying party in a public register. It also informs the operator that it has the right to make an application for the installation of facilities and to negotiate and receive access.

---

41   Circular of the Brussels Region dated 9 October 2002.
42   Article 27 Federal Act.
43   The Federal Act actually mentions 'electronic' networks and services but, due to the exclusive competence of the Communities for broadcasting, 'electronic' must be read as 'telecommunications'.

6.56   Only in exceptional circumstances (eg public security, public health, public order and state defence) can a Royal Decree restrict or even prohibit for a certain period of time the right[44] to provide telecommunications networks and services.[45]

6.57   However, the fact that the provision of networks and services is in principle free does not mean that market entry is not subject to any conditions.[46] The Belgian legislator has in this respect opted to follow the same approach as the Authorisation Directive, and adopted conditions along the lines of that Directive.

6.58   The Broadcasting Decrees mainly focus on the free provision of cable networks[47] subject to the conditions set out in the Decrees. Prior notification is required both under the Flemish and the French Broadcasting Decree; in Flanders, a cable company is required only to notify VCM; a cable network provider in the French Community should notify LSC and also the Community government.

Rights of Use for Radio Frequencies

Granting of individual rights

6.59   BIPT is responsible for management of the radio spectrum in Belgium. This task covers both the daily management of frequency allocations, as well as coordination and long-term policy on frequency and readjustment plans. While BIPT is not in charge of planning broadcasting frequencies, its frequency department does handle day-to-day coordination requests and the application of international agreements that distribute frequencies at international level.[48] This task is particularly important and complicated considering Belgium's small size and the associated issues of overlapping frequencies.[49]

6.60   Because the spectrum is considered a scarce resource, the use of radio frequencies in Belgium continues to be subject to the grant of individual user rights rather than being governed by a system of general authorisations. For the purpose of allocating radio frequencies, BIPT establishes a national frequency plan. Within this national frequency plan, a block of radio frequencies is reserved for broadcasting. The further planning of these broadcasting frequencies is entrusted to the respective Communities, which establish their own frequency plan. Applications for the use of radio frequencies for broadcasting must be addressed to the regulators of the Communities. In the Flemish Community it is the government that grants a right to use a radio frequency as part of the decision to grant a licence for broadcasting. Such decision will be taken upon consultation with VCM. In the French Community radio frequencies are allocated by LSC.

6.61   Applications[50] for purposes other than the transmission of broadcasting signals are handled by BIPT. As long as no new Royal Decree is adopted on the basis of the Federal Act, the application procedures for the use of radio frequencies

---

44   Article 3 Federal Act.
45   Article 4 Federal Act.
46   Article 3 Federal Act.
47   Article 97 French Broadcasting Decree and Article 126 Flemish Broadcasting Decree.
48   See BIPT annual report of 2003, p 23.
49   As a point of interest, it should be noted that, in Belgium, no single point is more than 60 km away from the border with a neighbouring country.
50   Such as frequencies used by transport companies, taxis, security services, intervention teams etc.

with BIPT remain subject to the provisions of the Act of 30 July 1979 on radio communications and its implementing orders. Applications must first pass through the licensing department of BIPT before being analysed by the frequency department from a technical perspective.

6.62   In accordance with EU legislation the Communities have put in place transparent and non-discriminatory procedures for the granting of individual rights for the use of radio frequencies, including public tenders. Such procedures do not, however, apply to the respective incumbents (such as VRT and RTBF), to which a special regime applies.

Admissible conditions

6.63   The conditions for obtaining and exercising individual user rights are still to be fixed by Royal Decree after completion of a consultation procedure, which requires the involvement of BIPT. These conditions can only relate to:

- the service, network or technology for which user rights are granted;
- the effective and efficient use of radio frequencies;
- the technical and operational conditions to prevent interference with other networks and exposure to electromagnetic fields;
- the maximum duration, subject to modifications of the national frequency plan;
- the transfer of rights at the holder's initiative;
- user fees;
- commitments made by the holder of user rights during the selection procedure; and
- obligations ensuing from international agreements regarding the use of radio frequencies.

6.64   The Communities set the technical and other conditions for the use of radio frequencies for broadcasting purposes independently from BIPT. The French Community, for instance, has imposed the payment of an annual fee for the use of a radio frequency.[51]

Limitation of number of rights of use to be granted

6.65   Article 20 Federal Act prohibits BIPT from limiting the number of rights of use that can be granted unless such limitation is necessary to prevent harmful interference caused by insufficient availability on the spectrum or to guarantee efficient and rational use of the radio frequencies. Any limitation to prevent interference should in addition be proportionate. The procedure that should be followed by BIPT in the case of limiting the number of user rights is still to be determined. The general principles, however, are set out in the Federal Act and reflect the guarantees required under the Authorisation Directive.

6.66   The respective Communities are responsible for limiting the number of user rights within the block of frequencies that is reserved for broadcasting purposes. This competence is not in so many words set forth in the Broadcasting Decrees but is considered to form part of their legal mission to establish a frequency plan for broadcasting.

---

51   Article 100 French Broadcasting Decree.

Frequency trading

6.67   Frequency trading is allowed in Belgium if radio frequencies are entirely or partially used for public telecommunication services. Any operator in Belgium who wishes to transfer such user rights for frequencies has to notify BIPT, which will authorise the frequency transfer if such transfer is not likely to distort competition and if it is in accordance with the requirements of effective and efficient management of the spectrum. More specific rules for the transfer are still to be adopted.

6.68   In Flanders, the transfer of rights to use frequencies for broadcasting services requires the authorisation of VCM. VCM is stated to approve the transfer only under very exceptional circumstances on a case-by-case basis. The transfer of frequency rights will be part of the transfer of the broadcasting permit, which also includes compliance with technical conditions for equipment etc. The French Broadcasting Decree simply prohibits the transfer of the rights of use of radio frequencies.

Rights of Use for Numbers

General authorisations and granting of individual rights

6.69   Like radio frequencies, telephone numbering is considered a scarce resource. Not only must the allocation of numbers be fair in terms of quantity (there must be enough numbers available to develop a clientele), but also in terms of quality (a number cannot contain too many digits). The national telecom regulator BIPT has, therefore, been charged with the general management of the national numbering plan.[52]

6.70   BIPT assigns the right to use numbers on an individual basis upon request. Assignment takes place within three weeks from receipt of the complete application.[53] BIPT publishes on its website model forms for applications.

Admissible conditions

6.71   The conditions for obtaining and exercising the rights to use numbers are still to be adopted by Ministerial Decree. In accordance with Article 11 § 3 Federal Act these conditions can only relate to:

- the indication of the service for which the number shall be used, together with the requirements connected to that service;
- the effective and efficient use of the numbers granted;
- compliance with the requirements with respect to number portability;
- providing information to subscribers entered into telephone directories and information services;
- the maximum duration, subject to modifications of the national numbering plan;
- user fees;
- commitments made by the holder of user rights during the selection procedure; and

---

52   Information derived from BIPT Annual Report 2003, available at www.bipt.be.
53   Article 11 § 4 Federal Act.

- obligations ensuing from international agreements regarding the use of numbers.

6.72   In addition, Article 11 § 7 Federal Act provides for an obligation on operators of public telephone services to offer the facility of number portability to their subscribers. Specific rules regarding number portability, the methodology for the calculation of the costs of this facility, and the sharing of the costs between the parties involved, will be set by a Royal Decree following consultation with BIPT.

6.73   In practice, however, BIPT has already had in place mechanisms for number portability since 1998, which at present operate as a matter of routine. For instance, BIPT has created two platforms, namely the Number Portability Task Force Fixed Networks and the Number Portability Task Force Mobile Numbers, which bring operators together under the chairmanship of BIPT to discuss various issues related to number portability. Also, BIPT monitors a non-profit association entrusted with the task of managing a central database for number portability.

Limitation of number of rights of use to be granted

6.74   Article 11 § 5 Federal Act provides that BIPT, after having carried out a public consultation, can decide to assign numbers with an exceptional economic value through a comparative or competition-based selection procedure. Such procedure shall not take longer than six weeks. Until now, BIPT has granted such numbers on a 'first come, first served' basis. Notwithstanding article 11 § 5 and until further rules are established, BIPT will continue to grant numbers with an exceptional economic value on the basis of the current method.

The NRA's Enforcement Powers

6.75   BIPT enforcement powers can mainly be found in the BIPT Act.

6.76   As mentioned above, BIPT is entitled to request information from any person at any time to the extent that this is reasonably necessary for the fulfilment of its tasks.[54] Moreover, in case of urgency (imminent risk of irreparable damage), BIPT can take all interim measures it deems appropriate. However, such measures must remain temporary, not exceeding a period of two months.[55]

6.77   Where BIPT identifies a failure to comply, it will notify the offender and ask him to stop the infringement within the period stipulated. If the offender does not act upon this request within the imposed timeframe, BIPT can impose an administrative fine of up to €5,000 for natural persons or, for legal entities, between 0.5% and 5% of the last annual turnover in the relevant market, up to a maximum of €12.5 million. If the infringement nonetheless continues, the partial or entire suspension of the exploitation of the network or telecom service[56] can be ordered. The European Commission reports that, in practice, BIPT has been rather reluctant to impose administrative fines and penalties, especially on Belgacom, the incumbent operator.

6.78   Some special enforcement powers of BIPT are set out in the Federal Act. An example is Article 18 § 3, stating that BIPT can cancel a frequency usage right if not brought into service within a reasonable period.

---

54   See paras 6.21 and 6.22 above.
55   Article 20 BIPT Act.
56   Article 21 BIPT Act.

6.79   The broadcasting regulators in the different Communities have similar powers to BIPT to ensure compliance with the broadcasting regulations. VCM and LSC can send warnings, impose administrative fines, suspend licences etc. In Flanders, administrative fines range between €1,250 and €125,000. The French Community has set the minimum fine at €250, up to a maximum of 3% of annual turnover, or even 5% in the case of repeated offending.

Administrative Charges and Fees for Rights of Use

6.80   The Federal Act only sets out the general framework regarding administrative charges and fees for rights of use, leaving the further regulation of amounts and specific conditions to the federal government. The general principles of the Federal Act basically mirror those of Articles 12 and 13 Authorisation Directive. Consequently, administrative charges are allowed only to the extent that they cover the costs incurred by BIPT in carrying out its tasks, and fees for rights of use can be levied to ensure optimal use of frequencies and numbers. BIPT is responsible for the collection of all fees and charges. It is worth noting that the federal legislator did not (and could not) use the possibility offered by Article 13 Authorisation Directive to levy fees for the rights to install facilities (including rights of way), in essence because the Regions are competent for this matter. Thus, fees for rights to install facilities will be addressed separately in a cooperation agreement between the federal government, the Communities and the Regions.[57]

6.81   BIPT levies fees for the use of numbers, the communication of access codes and general information on international and national signalling point codes. Fees include a once-only handling charge and an annual fee, and can be consulted on the BIPT website.

6.82   The once-only handling charge to be paid to VCM when applying for a radio broadcasting licence can also be seen as an administrative charge. This charge aims to cover the expenses of VCM in connection with frequency analysis and administration of the application file.[58] In addition, the Flemish government has introduced an annual fee for the use of radio frequencies, the amount of which depends on the broadcasting scale and the market share of the radio broadcasting company.

6.83   Article 100 § 2 French Broadcasting Decree equally confirms the principle of an annual fee for the use of broadcasting frequencies. The amount is, theoretically, to be determined by the government; however, further on in the text of the Decree,[59] some fees are already fixed. For example, a radio station which covers the whole of the French Community and the Brussels area has to pay a fee of €50,000 (subject to indexation) per year. Other radio networks and independent radio stations pay either €1,250 or €600 (subject to indexation) per frequency, depending on their advertising revenues.

---

57   See para 6.50 above.
58   Articles 16 ter, 17 ter and 18 bis Order of the Flemish government regarding the procedure before the Flemish Commissioner's Office for Media and the additional qualification criteria and conditions for the licence of private radio broadcasting companies.
59   Article 108 French Broadcasting Decree.

REGULATION OF NETWORK ACCESS AND INTERCONNECTION: IMPLEMENTATION OF THE ACCESS DIRECTIVE

Objectives and Scope of Access Regulation

6.84   BIPT's mission is to ensure access, interconnection and interoperability of services in such a way as to promote sustainable competition and innovation. The ultimate goal of its policy is to obtain maximum benefit for end-users.[60]

6.85   The rules of the Access Directive are transposed into Belgian law through Title III of the Federal Act. Title III is subdivided in three chapters: Chapter 1 applies to all operators irrespective of their market position; it lays down the principle of freedom of access and provides a general framework for the commercial negotiations between operators regarding access and interconnection; Chapter 2 contains the provisions with respect to the market analyses to be conducted by BIPT; and, finally, Chapter 3 sets out the special obligations that exist for SMP operators with respect to access and interconnection.

6.86   Some of the provisions of the Access Directive are also relevant for the transmission of broadcasting signals and are thus implemented in the Broadcasting Decrees. They aim to ensure interoperability of services[61] and provide the possibility for the regulator to impose special obligations on SMP undertakings.[62] Especially in Flanders, which is heavily cabled, this is a crucial factor for competition.

Basic Regulatory Concepts

6.87   In the Federal Act, 'access' is defined as 'the making available of network elements, associated facilities or electronic communication services in order to allow such operator to offer electronic communication networks and services'.

6.88   The first obvious difference is that the Belgian definition is shorter than its European equivalent. In particular, it does not refer either to the express conditions under which the network elements, associated facilities or electronic communication services are made available, or to the exclusive or non-exclusive basis of the access. Also, the Federal Act does not list the examples of access, as is the case in the Access Directive. A second difference is that the definition of 'access' in the Federal Act refers to 'operator' where the Access Directive mentions 'undertaking'. However, this difference is meaningless in the sense that an 'operator' under the Federal Act is defined as a person that has notified BIPT of its activities, a prerequisite to start providing electronic communication networks and services. Lastly, the definition of the Belgian legislator is broader than the European definition of 'access' to the extent that the operator to which such access is made available can use this access not only to provide electronic communication services but also networks.

6.89   'Interconnection' is defined as 'a specific type of access consisting of the physical or logical linking of public communication networks used by the same or a different operator in order to allow users to communicate with each other, or to have access to services provided by another operator'. The definition of interconnection in the Federal Act is substantially the same as that in the Access Directive.

---

60   See BIPT annual report of 2004, p 23, and Articles 5 to 8 Federal Act.
61   Article 124 Flemish Broadcasting Decree and Article 93 French Broadcasting Decree.
62   Article 125 Flemish Broadcasting Decree and Article 96 French Broadcasting Decree.

6.90   The Broadcasting Decrees do not contain definitions of 'access' and 'interconnection'.

Access- and Interconnection-related Obligations with Respect to SMP Undertakings

Telecom

OVERVIEW

6.91   Articles 58 to 65 Federal Act list the access and interconnection-related obligations that BIPT can impose upon telecom operators designated as having SMP. In summary they are:

*   transparency (Article 59),
*   non-discrimination (Article 58),
*   access to and use of specific network facilities (Article 61),
*   price control and cost accounting obligations (Article 62), and
*   accounting separation (Article 60).

6.92   BIPT is entitled to impose these obligations as it considers appropriate.[63] However, this does not mean that the powers of BIPT are unconditional. Obligations must be objective, transparent, proportionate and non-discriminatory. They should be tailored to the specific situation, taking into account the nature of the problem identified.[64] Notwithstanding such limitations, BIPT still enjoys a considerable level of discretion with respect to the choice of obligations it imposes on SMP operators.

TRANSPARENCY OBLIGATIONS

6.93   BIPT can oblige SMP operators to disclose certain access-related information. If and when it decides to do so, BIPT will specify the precise information to be made public, as well as the level of detail required and the manner in which the information should be made available.

6.94   BIPT can also require the publication of a reference offer for interconnection, unbundled access to the local loop, bitstream access or any other type of access, which the SMP operator involved should allow. Such reference offer must specify, for each type of access, the terms and conditions to gain access, including applicable tariffs. Before being published, the offer should be approved by BIPT.

6.95   Since the liberalisation of the fixed telephony market, Belgacom has been continuously identified as an SMP operator and, therefore, been made subject to regulation and monitoring of the conditions under which it allows access to its infrastructure. At present, Belgacom publishes three reference offers under the supervision of BIPT, namely: BRIO (Belgacom Reference Interconnect Offer), BRUO (Belgacom Reference Unbundling Offer) and BROBA (Belgacom Reference Offer Bitstream Access). These reference offers aim to establish for one year at what tariffs and under which conditions Belgacom grants alternative operators access to its network. The procedure is identical for the three offers: Belgacom submits a

---

63   Article 55 § 3 Federal Act.
64   Article 5 Federal Act.

proposal to BIPT; the market is then consulted and offered the possibility to express its remarks, after which BIPT takes a decision; once approved, the reference offer is published on the websites of BIPT and Belgacom and serves as a reference for the following year.[65]

NON-DISCRIMINATION OBLIGATIONS

6.96 Article 58 gives no further indications as to what must be understood by 'obligations of non-discrimination'. This leaves BIPT a large degree of freedom as to its choice of measures. However, in accordance with Article 10 Access Directive, the obligations imposed by BIPT should in any event aim to ensure that SMP undertakings apply equivalent conditions in equivalent circumstances to other undertakings providing equivalent services, and that in general they treat such undertakings as they treat their subsidiaries or partners.[66]

SPECIFIC ACCESS OBLIGATIONS

6.97 BIPT is authorised to require SMP operators to grant reasonable requests for access to and use of specific network elements and associated facilities, to be designated by BIPT. Article 61 Federal Act basically echoes the provisions of Article 12 Access Directive.

PRICE CONTROL AND COST ACCOUNTING OBLIGATIONS

6.98 Finally, BIPT can also impose certain obligations relating to cost accounting and price control. In accordance with Article 13 Access Directive, BIPT can only impose such measures if market analysis has indicated that the operator concerned might sustain prices at an excessively high level, or apply a price squeeze to the detriment of end-users.

6.99 Even before the entry into force of the Federal Act, BIPT identified two SMP operators in the mobile telephony market (Proximus and Mobistar) and imposed on them the obligation to apply cost-oriented prices with respect to charges for 'call termination'. To permit full and fair competition, it is of utmost importance that SMP mobile operators offer this termination service to other operators under transparent, non-discriminatory and cost-oriented conditions. Given the excessive tariffs for termination services applied by the SMP operators, BIPT has established schedules for the gradual lowering of tariffs by both Proximus (since 2001) and Mobistar (since 2003). These schedules are regularly revised to take into account any new trends.

6.100 However, in light of the new Regulatory Package, BIPT now intends to have a generic cost model adopted for the three mobile operators. This is basically because, under the new European rules, every operator is considered to have SMP status as far as the termination of calls on their network is concerned.[67]

ACCOUNTING SEPARATION OBLIGATIONS

6.101 On the basis of Article 60 Federal Act, BIPT can require that separate books be kept with respect to all access-related activities for which an operator has

---

65 See BIPT annual report of 2004, p 23.
66 See para 1.144 above.
67 See BIPT annual report of 2004, pp 26 and 27.

a significant market position. The accounting methodology and the format to be used will be specified in a Royal Decree, following completion of a consultation procedure with BIPT.

6.102   When it deems it necessary, BIPT can also request submission of accounting records, including data on revenues received from third parties. Such a request must be justified.

Broadcasting

6.103   While VCM is authorised to impose the same kind of obligations on SMP broadcasting operators in the Flemish Community as BIPT can impose on SMP telecom operators,[68] the French Broadcasting Decree has surprisingly not included specific access obligations, accounting separation, cost accounting and price control in the list of obligations that can be imposed on broadcasting operators in the French Community.

Regulatory Powers with Respect to SMP Undertakings

Carrier (pre-)selection

6.104   Article 63 Federal Act contains the obligation for undertakings identified as SMP operators to make both carrier selection and carrier pre-selection services accessible to their subscribers.

6.105   This obligation is actually not imposed by BIPT, but applies by operation of law to any operator designated as having SMP on the market for the provision of connection to and use of the public telephone network at fixed location. However, if justified by the interests of users, BIPT can impose some additional obligations on SMP operators.

6.106   The tariffs applicable between SMP operators of fixed telephone networks and CPS operators have to be cost oriented. As a matter of fact, such tariffs are contained in the BRIO, approved by BIPT on a yearly basis.

Leased lines

6.107   Article 65 Federal Act empowers BIPT to impose certain obligations for the provision of part or all of the minimum set of leased lines on operators identified as having SMP on the relevant market. In line with the other SMP obligations, they are designed to comply with the basic principles of non-discrimination, cost orientation and transparency.

---

68   See para 6.91 above.

Regulatory Powers Applicable to All Market Participants

Obligations to ensure end-to-end connectivity

6.108   Insofar as necessary to ensure end-to-end connectivity, BIPT can impose obligations on operators who, with or without SMP, control the access to end-users[69] ('last mile'). BIPT may thus determine the conditions for access, as it deems appropriate. Ensuring end-to-end connectivity may also imply the obligation for operators to establish interconnection of their networks where this would not yet be the case.

Access to digital radio and television broadcasting services

6.109   The Communities are exclusively competent to transpose the provisions of the Framework and Access Directives in relation to digital radio and television broadcasting services.

6.110   In Flanders, digital radio and television broadcasting is governed by the rules set out in articles 145 to 156 Flemish Broadcasting Decree. These rules become increasingly important for the Flemish broadcasting landscape as, at the time of writing, both Telenet and Belgacom are about to launch digital interactive television services.

6.111   Articles 154 and 155 Flemish Broadcasting Decree authorise the Flemish Government to impose obligations on providers of Application Programming Interfaces ('API')[70] and Electronic Program Guides ('EPG'), regardless of their market position. These obligations can relate to the use of an open API in accordance with the minimum requirements of the relevant standards and specifications, and to the installation, access and presentation of the EPG. In addition, the Flemish government can also oblige the owners of API to supply all information necessary to allow other providers of digital interactive television to offer their services using the same interface.

6.112   The rules for conditional access systems (e g pay television) are laid down in articles 150 to 153 Flemish Broadcasting Decree. The text basically echoes the provisions of article 6(1) Access Directive and the obligations contained in Annex I Part I of that Directive. However, some minor differences are noted: first, the scope of the rules with respect to conditional access systems appears to be somewhat broader in the Flemish Broadcasting Decree than in the Access Directive – the Flemish Broadcasting Decree indeed imposes obligations on all providers of conditional access systems without any further specification, while the Access Directive still adds 'which provide services for access to digital television and radio services', thus limiting the number of providers to which the obligations apply; secondly, where the Access Directive refers to 'cost effective' transcontrol, the Flemish Broadcasting Decree speaks about 'cheap' transcontrol; and, lastly, the Flemish Broadcasting Decree, contrary to the Access Directive, does not specify that offers for conditional access systems should be compatible with European competition rules. However, in practice this does not mean that such offers should not be compliant with European and Belgian competition rules.

6.113   The French Community has equally adopted the necessary rules to transpose articles 5(1) and 6(1) Access Directive into its legislation. The relevant

---

69   Article 51 § 2 Federal Act.
70   See para 1.154 above for further information on API.

provisions are to be found in articles 123 to 129 French Broadcasting Decree. The French Broadcasting Decree remains most of the time close to the text of the Access Directive. However, some differences are worth noting: first, like the Flemish Broadcasting Decree, the French Broadcasting Decree also refers to 'cheap' transcontrol instead of 'cost effective' transcontrol; and, secondly, the French Broadcasting Decree requires separate accounting 'for the provision of services of conditional access' instead of 'for the activities as provider of conditional access systems', as provided by the Access Directive. The different wording may cause misperception, as the terms chosen do not necessarily cover the same activities.

6.114   Furthermore, the French Broadcasting Decree offers some more detail with respect to the conditions, which can be imposed on providers of EPG (with or without SMP). These conditions can imply the following obligations: (1) the installation of an EPG, which has the technical capability to search a service amongst other services without discrimination; (2) the maintenance of a sufficient degree of competition in connection with access to EPG for broadcasters; and (3) the respect of the principles of pluralism and non-discrimination in relation to the presentation of available services through EPG.

REGULATION OF UNIVERSAL SERVICES AND USERS' RIGHTS: THE UNIVERSAL SERVICE DIRECTIVE

Regulation of Universal Service Obligations

Scope of universal service obligations

6.115   Article 68 Federal Act lists the services that are considered part of the universal service. The list corresponds to the catalogue contained in the Universal Service Directive and comprises several parts, namely:

- the fixed geographic element of the universal service (including access to the network and the basic telephone voice service, the free routing of emergency calls and the provision of a helpdesk);
- the application of social tariffs, and special measures in the case of non-payment of phone bills;
- the provision of public telephone booths across the country;
- the provision of a directory enquiries service for subscribers; and
- the annual publication of a directory.

6.116   These services must be available to all end-users, independently of geographic location, at an affordable price and of a specified quality.

6.117   An important novelty of the Federal Act relates to social tariffs. These tariffs used to be applied by Belgacom only, in its capacity as provider of the universal service. Today, a person who is entitled to such tariffs may go to any operator of his choice. As further explained below, a separate fund for social tariffs will be set up to compensate providers who serve a considerable number of customers who are entitled to social tariffs. Another change under the new legislation is that the number of public telephone booths will gradually be reduced as a consequence of increased mobile penetration.

Designation of undertakings obliged to provide universal services

6.118   The Belgian legislator has taken the approach of splitting the universal service into different components (as listed above), allowing it to adopt separate rules in terms of appointment and compensation of providers for each of the components.

6.119   Except for social tariffs, for which a person may go to any operator of his choice, the different components of the universal service will each be entrusted to one (or possibly more) providers. These providers will be appointed through a designation procedure, the rules of which are yet to be adopted by Royal Decree on the basis of proposals from BIPT. Notwithstanding the possibility of appointing a different provider for each of the components of the universal service, Belgacom will probably continue to be designated as the undertaking that is obliged to provide all elements of the minimum set of services of the universal service, it being understood that social tariffs from now on are applied by all operators. The selection of Belgacom may be inspired by the ease of having one operator meeting the national coverage requirement.

Regulation of retail tariffs, users' expenditures and quality of service

6.120   Rules with respect to permissible end-user tariffs[71] for the services which form part of the universal service, as well as requirements regarding the quality of such universal services, are set out in an annex to the Federal Act (the 'Annex'). By virtue of article 34 Annex, end-users should have access to publicly available telephone services at a fixed location at prices which are 'affordable'. To ensure that prices are affordable, the Belgian legislator introduced a mathematical formula for the calculation of retail tariffs.[72]

6.121   Article 38 Annex sets out the minimum discounts which should be granted to the beneficiaries of social tariffs. To be eligible, customers must fulfil certain conditions with respect to age, invalidity or income.[73] More specifically, requests for social tariffs will only be granted if submitted by persons who:

- are at least 65 years of age;
- are at least 66% handicapped and at least 18 years of age;
- are entitled to government support with regard to minimum subsistence;
- have impaired hearing;
- have had a laryngectomy; or
- became blind while on active service in wartime.

6.122   To allow customers to control expenditure, a series of payment facilities (including call barring, pre-payment, phased payment and selective call barring for outgoing calls) has been provided in articles 117 to 120 Federal Act. These provisions are merely a confirmation of the general principles. More detailed rules are yet to be adopted by the minister of telecommunications.

6.123   BIPT has the task of monitoring universal service obligations, including control on tariffs and quality levels.[74] To this end, BIPT performs field checks and submits each year a report to the minister of telecommunications. Where BIPT has

---

71   Articles 34 to 39 Annex.
72   Article 35 Annex.
73   Article 22 Annex.
74   Article 103 Federal Act.

identified a failure to comply, the minister of telecommunications can impose an administrative fine on the provider involved, which shall not exceed an amount equal to 1% of the turnover of the universal service provider in the relevant year.[75]

Cost calculation and financing of universal services

6.124   A 'Universal Service Fund' is established for the compensation of undertakings that have been designated to provide universal services.[76] All established providers must contribute to the fund in proportion to their turnover. The Federal Act remains silent as to the right to exempt undertakings whose national turnover is less than a set limit. BIPT does, however, not exclude that undertakings with a national turnover of less than 12,395,000 € still be exempted.

6.125   For each component of the universal service (except the application of social tariffs), the designated provider is entitled to compensation. The amount of the compensation depends on the way the provider was designated. If designation happened through an open selection procedure, the amount will be equal to the sum determined at the end of the procedure. However, if the provider was appointed ex-officio, compensation will be calculated on the basis of the net costs of providing the universal service and in accordance with the calculation rules set out in the Annex.[77] The Federal Act did not introduce the concept of the unfair burden as a condition to compensation, a fact that is much regretted by alternative operators.

6.126   A separate fund will be created for social tariffs. Operators serving more social customers than the number corresponding to their market share receive compensation; in the opposite case, operators have to contribute. Specific rules for the functioning of the fund are yet to be adopted.

Regulation of Retail Markets

Prerequisites for the regulation of retail markets

6.127   Article 64 Federal Act sets out the obligations that BIPT may impose upon undertakings with SMP on retail markets. However, regulation of retail services on the basis of article 64 is permissible only if regulation at wholesale level does not achieve the regulatory objectives established by the federal legislator.

6.128   Currently, no operator is identified as having SMP on the retail market; however, it cannot be excluded that, upon completion of the market analyses, Belgacom will be identified by BIPT as an operator with SMP on the retail market.

Regulatory powers

6.129   The obligations which BIPT can impose on SMP undertakings on the retail market aim to prohibit any:

- charging of excessively high prices;
- inhibiting of market entry;

---

75   Article 104 Federal Act.
76   Article 92 Federal Act.
77   Articles 40 to 44 Annex.

- setting of predatory prices which restrict competition;
- showing of undue preference to specific end-users; and
- unreasonable bundling of services.

6.130   Article 64 furthermore provides that BIPT, if and when it wishes to control end-users tariffs, can determine the necessary and appropriate cost-accounting systems that the targeted undertaking must apply.

End User Rights

Contracts

6.131   Any contract between a subscriber and a telecom operator for connection or access to the public telephone network must contain at least the following minimum information:[78]

- the identity and address of the operator;
- the definition of the services provided;
- the waiting time for the initial connection;
- the specification of the service quality levels offered;
- the types of maintenance services offered;
- the particulars of tariffs;
- the means by which up-to-date information on all applicable and maintenance charges can be obtained;
- the duration of the contract;
- the conditions for renewal of services and contract;
- the conditions for termination of services and contract;
- any compensation and refund arrangements which apply if contracted service quality levels are not met; and
- the dispute mechanisms, including the possibility of appeal to the mediation service for telecommunications.

6.132   The operator must supply such information to the subscriber at the latest when entering into the contract. The information can be laid down in the operator's general terms and conditions. The contract between the operator and the subscriber should be provided to the latter in writing.

6.133   If an operator wishes to change the contractual conditions that govern his relationship with a subscriber, he will give the subscriber at least one month's notice of any such proposed modifications and inform him of his right to terminate the contract without penalty until the last day of the month following the effective date of the modifications.[79] Where the proposed modifications relate to a tariff increase, such right of withdrawal continues to exist until the last day of the month following the receipt of the first invoice after the tariff increase has become effective.

6.134   By using the term 'subscriber', Belgium has seized the opportunity offered by article 20 Universal Directive to extend the above minimum information requirements to all end-users, ie beyond 'consumers' as referred to in the Directive.

---

78   Article 108 Federal Act.
79   Article 108 § 2 Federal Act.

Transparency obligations

6.135 In the interests of transparency of information and legal security, the standard terms and conditions and contract templates with respect to electronic communication services should be published on the operator's website after having obtained the advice of both the mediation service and the advisory committee for telecommunications.[80] Information on tariffs should be sufficiently detailed for the benefit of consumers.[81]

6.136 In addition, operators should make available comparative, adequate and up-to-date information regarding access to and use of their networks and services. BIPT will establish a set of guidelines with respect to the details of information to be provided and the requirements for publication.[82] The information must be communicated to BIPT at least one month prior to publication.

6.137 To allow end-users to benefit from the best price offer tailored to their needs, operators have to inform their subscribers at least once a year of the most advantageous tariff plan, taking into account the subscriber's past usage.[83] To the same end, BIPT has to put a tariff simulator on its website. Specific rules in this respect are yet to be adopted by Ministerial Decree.

Other obligations

6.138 *Network integrity:*[84] providers of publicly available telephone services have to take all reasonable[85] technical and organisational steps to ensure the safety of their services. To guarantee uninterrupted access of emergency services, operators must, in case of defect, give priority to emergency services, hospitals, physicians etc for the repair of such defect, including a back-up service.

6.139 *Helpdesk:* Article 116 Federal Act contains the obligation for operators to create a helpdesk to assist end-users. Such helpdesk can no longer be offered through expensive '0900' numbers but should be accessible via a geographical number or any other number representing an equivalent cost to the customer.

6.140 *Provision of additional facilities:* Article 121 Federal Act provides the possibility for BIPT to require that operators of public telecommunication networks offer the additional facilities of calling-line identification and tone dialling. However, these obligations can be waived for all or part of the territory if the federal government, following consultation with the advisory committee for telecommunications and BIPT, considers that there is already sufficient access to these facilities.

6.141 *Telephone directory:* subject to applicable data protection provisions, subscribers to publicly available telephone services have the right to be listed in a telephone directory or registered with a directory enquiry service. A standard entry must be free of charge. To include a subscriber in a telephone directory or in a directory enquiry service, his permission is required.

---

80   Article 108 § 3 Federal Act.
81   Article 109 Federal Act.
82   Article 111 Federal Act.
83   Article 110 § 4 Federal Act.
84   Articles 114 and 115 Federal Act.
85   Taking into account the state of technology and realisation costs.

DATA PROTECTION: IMPLEMENTATION OF THE DIRECTIVE ON PRIVACY AND ELECTRONIC COMMUNICATIONS

Overview

6.142   The E-Privacy Directive has been implemented into Belgian law by the Federal Act. The new provisions complement the existing framework under the Act of 11 March 2003 relating to certain legal aspects of Electronic Services ('Electronic Services Act') and the Data Protection Act of 8 December 1992 ('Data Protection Act').

Confidentiality of Communications

6.143   Except with the authorisation of all persons directly or indirectly concerned, no-one can:[86]

- intentionally acquire knowledge of the existence of information of any kind transmitted by means of electronic communication which is not personally directed to him;
- intentionally identify the persons concerned with the transmission of the information and its content;
- intentionally acquire knowledge of electronic communications data relating to another person; or
- modify, delete, disclose, store or make any use of the information, its identification or the data itself, whether or not intentionally obtained.

6.144   Exceptions, however, apply:

- where the law allows or requires the afore-mentioned acts;
- where those acts are carried out for the exclusive purpose of verifying the good running of the network and to ensure the good working of the electronic communications service;
- where those acts are carried out in order to allow the intervention of the emergency services, in response to requests for assistance;
- where those acts are carried out by BIPT within the scope of its legal duty of control; or
- where those acts are carried out for the sole purpose of providing services to the end user which consist of preventing receipt of undesirable electronic communications, provided the end user has given its consent.

6.145   Without prejudice to the Data Protection Act, the recording of electronic communications and the related traffic data, carried out in the course of lawful business practice or other professional communication, is authorised provided that all parties to that communication are informed beforehand of the recording, the precise purposes thereof and the period of time for which the recording will be stored.

---

86   Article 124 Federal Act.

Traffic Data and Location Data

6.146 The definitions of 'traffic data' and 'location data' are identical to those in the E-Privacy Directive. The main principle[87] is that traffic data relating to subscribers and users, processed and stored by the providers of a public communications network or publicly available electronic communications service, must be erased or made anonymous when it is no longer needed for the purpose of the transmission of a communication. The following exceptions, however, apply:

- providers can store and process traffic data necessary for the purposes of subscriber billing and interconnection payment. Such processing is permissible only up to the end of the period during which the bill can lawfully be challenged or payment pursued;
- providers can process traffic data for the purpose of marketing electronic communications services or services with traffic or location data, to the extent and for the duration necessary for such services or marketing, if the subscriber or user to whom the data relates has given his/her consent. Users or subscribers shall be given the possibility to withdraw their consent for the processing of traffic data at any time; and
- traffic data can be processed to detect fraud, and must be transferred to the competent authorities in case of crime or offence.

6.147 The service providers must inform the subscriber or user of the types of traffic data which are processed and of the duration of such processing for the purposes mentioned under the first item above – and, prior to obtaining consent, for the purposes mentioned under the second item above.

6.148 Location data other than traffic data, relating to users or subscribers, may only be processed if it has been anonymised or if the processing is part of a service concerning traffic or location data, provided the user's consent has been obtained. The consent is only valid if the provider has informed the user or subscriber of the types of location data processed, the purposes and duration of the processing, and third parties to whom the data may be disclosed. This consent can be withdrawn at any time.[88]

Itemised Billing[89]

6.149 Providers send to subscribers, free of charge, a basic itemised invoice, the level of detail of which is determined by the minister of telecommunications, after consultation with BIPT. If the basic invoice is challenged, subscribers can obtain, free of charge and on request, an itemised bill.

6.150 Free calls, calls to emergency numbers, as well as calls to certain numbers to be determined by the King (ie the federal government) after consultation with BIPT, are not mentioned on the invoice.

6.151 At least once a year, the provider must indicate on the invoice for its subscribers the most advantageous tariff plan for the subscriber on the basis of its usage profile.[90]

---

87   Article 122 Federal Act.
88   Article 123 Federal Act.
89   Article 110 Federal Act.
90   See para 6.137 above.

Calling and Connected Line Identification[91]

6.152   Where calling line identification is offered as a service, the service provider of the calling user must offer the calling user, free of charge and on request, the possibility of preventing the calling line identification on a per-call basis. Also, the service provider of the called subscriber must offer the called subscriber the possibility, free of charge and on request, to prevent the calling line identification of incoming calls. However, the obligation to provide this service free of charge does not apply when used in an unreasonable way by the subscriber.

6.153   If the calling line identification is displayed prior to the call being established, the service provider of the called subscriber must offer the latter the possibility of rejecting the incoming call, on mere request, where the calling line identification has been prevented on request by the calling user or subscriber.

6.154   Providers of publicly available electronic communications services must inform the public if and when calling and/or connected line identification is offered, and of the possibilities relating thereto as described above.

6.155   More detailed rules will be set by Royal Decree, after consultation with the Privacy Commission and BIPT.

Automatic Call Forwarding[92]

6.156   Providers of public electronic communications services must offer the possibility to their users and subscribers, free of charge and on mere request, of stopping automatic call forwarding by a third party to the subscriber's terminal, provided it is technically and operationally feasible for the provider.

Directories of Subscribers[93]

6.157   Providers of a telephone service accessible to the public must inform their subscribers, free of charge and before they are included in a directory or in a directory enquiry service, about the purposes of such directory or enquiry service, free inclusion in the directory, and any further usage other than the search of personal data based on the name or residence of the subscriber.[94]

6.158   The subscribers must be asked whether or not they wish their personal data to be included in a public directory and, if so, in which directory. Subscribers have the right to verify, correct or withdraw such data from the directory, free of charge.

6.159   Separate and specific consent from the subscribers is required for any purpose of a public directory other than the search of personal data of persons on the basis of their name and, as the case may arise, residence.

Unsolicited Communications

6.160   Under Belgian law, the sending of unsolicited e-mails ('spam') is subject to the Electronic Services Act and the Royal Decree of 4 April 2003 with respect to

---

91   Article 130 Federal Act.
92   Article 131 Federal Act.
93   Article 133 Federal Act.
94   See para 6.141 above.

advertising by electronic mail. These legislative acts establish an 'opt-in' system whereby the prior consent of the recipients is required to proceed with the sending of unsolicited e-mails.

6.161 However, there are a number of exceptions to this general 'opt-in' rule. As a matter of law, the sending of unsolicited e-mail is allowed:

- to the sender's own clients if the following conditions are cumulatively met:
  - the contact details were collected directly from the recipient upon the selling of goods or services and the collection is done in accordance with Belgian privacy regulations; and
  - the contact details are used for the exclusive purpose of promoting goods or services similar to those initially sold to the recipient, and the goods or services are offered by the entity which collected the data; and
  - upon collection of his data, the recipient can, easily and free of charge, object to the processing of his data for this purpose; or
- to public or private corporations provided that the following conditions are cumulatively met:
  - the recipient's e-mail address is impersonal (eg 'info@corp.com' or 'reception@justice.gov'); and
  - the promoted services or goods are intended for the recipients' activities.

6.162 The sending of unsolicited e-mails that does not comply with the above-mentioned rules amounts to a criminal offence.

The Cyprus Market for Electronic Communications[1]

A. K. Adamides
Adamos K. Adamides & Co, Lawyers, Limassol, Cyprus

LEGAL STRUCTURE

Basic Policy

7.1   The core regulatory objective is the welfare of the consumer.

7.2   The main part of the regulatory activity in the electronic communications and postal sector has been carried out by the Cyprus Telecommunications Authority ('CYTA') which, prior to liberalisation,[2] being a state-owned public utility entity, had a monopoly across the whole spectrum of electronic communications. The Commissioner of Electronic Communications and Postal Regulation ('ComECPR') declared, in the second quarter of 2003, that CYTA had significant market power (SMP) and proceeded to impose regulatory obligations.[3]

7.3   CYTA dominates in the field. The Electricity Authority of Cyprus has been developing a fibre-optic network which is leased to electronic communications providers. Although a number of new providers have entered the domestic market since 2003, their penetration is still low.[4]

Implementation of EU Directives, Legislation

7.4   Cyprus proceeded with the transposition and implementation of the 1998–2000 European telecommunications-related regulation in 2002 and 2003; a number of regulatory obligations were imposed on the incumbent. Full transposition of the 2002 EU Regulatory Package has now been achieved and all harmonised measures have been notified to the EU.

---

1   Editing of this chapter closed on 24 June 2005. The author is grateful to the Office of the Commissioner of Electronic Communications and Postal Regulation and the Department of Electronic Communications of the Ministry of Communications and Works for their valuable assistance.
2   First quarter of 2003 for fixed telephony, third quarter of 2004 for mobile telephony.
3   IAD 415/2003, L112(I)/2004 s 161; cf art 27 Framework Directive.
4   Apart from CYTA there are five operators in fixed telephony and one operator in mobile telephony. Their penetration is about 4% in fixed and 4% in mobile.

7.5   The following measures constitute the national electronic communications regulation legal framework.[5]

- Law ('L') 112(I)/2004 Electronic Communications and Postal Regulation Law of 2004 ('the Law'),
- Public Instrument ('PI') 849/2004 Administrative Fees (Electronic Communications) Order of 2004,
- PI 850/2004 Numbering (Electronic Communications) Order of 2004,
- PI 851/2004 Licensing (Electronic Communications) Order of 2004,
- PI 14/2005 Interconnection Agreements (Electronic Communications) Order of 2005,
- PI 15/2005 Procedures of the amendment of Reference Interconnection Offer and Reference Unbundling Offer (Electronic Communications) Order of 2005,
- PI 16/2005 Interconnection Fees (Electronic Communications) Order of 2005,
- PI 17/2005 LLU of Provision (Electronic Communications) Order of 2005,
- PI 18/2005 LLU Calculation Net Cost and Fees (Electronic Communications) Order of 2005,
- PI 137/2005 Definition of Criteria for the Selection of Universal Service Provider (Electronic Communications) Decision of 2005,
- PI 138/2005 Definition of Field of Universal Service (Electronic Communications) Decision of 2005,
- PI 140/2005 Calculation of the Nest Cost of Universal Telecommunications Service (Electronic Communications) Order of 2005,
- PI 141/2005 Financing the Universal Service Fund (Electronic Communications) Order of 2005,
- PI 142/2005 Definition of Specific Net Facilities (Electronic Communications) Order of 2005,
- Individual Administrative Decision ('IAD') 258/2005 Definition of CYTA as Universal Service Provider (Electronic Communications) Decision of 2005,
- PI 74/2005 Quality of Service (Electronic Communications) Order of 2005,
- PI 139/2005 Consumer Protection (Electronic Communications) Order of 2005,
- PI 34/2005 Legal Entities (Unsolicited Communications) (Electronic Communications) Order of 2005,
- PI 35/2005 Legal Entities (Public Directories) (Electronic Communications) Order of 2005,
- PI 143/2005 Public Hearings (Electronic Communications) Order of 2005,
- PI 144/2005 Public Consultations (Electronic Communications) Order of 2005,
- PI 147/2005 Procedures for Market Analysis (Electronic Communications) Order of 2005,
- PI 148/2005 Methodology for Market definition (Electronic Communications) Decision of 2005,
- Decision ('D') 2/2005 Retail Prices (Electronic Communications) Decision of 2005.

7.6   The following measures were issued prior to the 2002 EU Regulatory Package and continue to apply after the enactment of L112(I)/2004:

- PI 565/2003 The Number Portability Decree of 2003,
- PI 564/2003 The National Roaming Decree of 2003,

---

5   For frequency regulation see para 7.38 below.

- PI 331/2003 The Leased Lines Regulations of 2003,
- PI 1/2003 Designation of Operator with Significant Market Power,
- PI 332/2003 The Telecommunications Terminal Equipment of 2003,
- PI 328/2003 The Collection of Information and Imposition of Administrative Fines Regulations of 2003,
- PI 566/2003 The Collocation and Facilities Sharing Order of 2003,
- IAD 415/2003 Designation of Operator with Significant Market Power.[6]

REGULATORY PRINCIPLES: IMPLEMENTATION OF THE FRAMEWORK DIRECTIVE

Scope of Regulation

7.7   The legislation applies to the regulation of electronic communications networks and services and related facilities required for the implementation of a harmonised regulatory framework within the EU with a view to facilitating convergence of the telecommunications, information technology and electronic media sectors.[7]

The definitions of 'electronic communications network', 'electronic communications service' and 'associated facilities' in the Law[8] are identical to those in article 2 Framework Directive.

National Regulatory Authorities: Organisation, Regulatory Objectives, Competencies

7.8   Electronic communications network and services are regulated by ComECPR whereas spectrum management is carried out by the Department of Electronic Communications of the Ministry of Communications and Works.[9]

7.9   ComECPR shall act in such a way as to promote the provision of electronic communications services for the public as a whole, the interest of consumers, with particular reference to price, the introduction of effective competition, and the capability to provide or dispose of a wide range of electronic communications equipment and services.[10]

7.10   ComECPR acts by imposing ex-ante regulation in the field of electronic communications, whereas the Commission for the Protection of Competition ('CompA') acts by imposing ex-post regulation. ComECPR consults CompA when conducting market analysis;[11] on examination by CompA of anti-competitive behaviour, ComECPR may provide relevant information and technical support.

7.11   ComECPR is an independent regulatory authority. It has its own budget, approved by the House of Representatives, and carries out its own recruitment procedures. ComECPR and the Deputy Commissioner are appointed by the Council of Ministers, after consultation with the Committee of European Affairs of

---

6   ComECPR's Order 1/2003 – Sixth Appendix, Part II, Gazette No 3707.
7   S 2(1) L112(I)/2004.
8   S 4 L112(I)/2004.
9   See para 7.38 below.
10   S 18 L112(I)/2004.
11   See paras 7.20 et seq below.

the House of Representatives, for a term of six years. ComECPR's discretion, though implementing government policy guidelines, is not subject to government approval.

The same applies to CompA, whose members are appointed for a five-year term.

7.12   The powers and duties of both authorities are consistent with the Directives of the 2002 EU Regulatory Package and include the power to demand information.[12]

7.13   ComECPR is both empowered and obliged to obtain information, to consult with interested parties and to initiate dispute resolution procedures and public hearings.[13] Consultations may refer to measures to be taken and may contain a description of the issues and specific questions. Draft measures are published on ComECPR's website and in daily newspapers, are available in printed form and specify the period in which responses may be made which, as a rule, is 28 days. The results of consultations and the positions taken by the participants, except in confidential matters, are made publicly available.[14]

Right of Appeal against NRA's Decisions

7.14   Any act or decision of ComECPR is subject to judicial review by recourse to the Supreme Court pursuant to Article 146 of the Constitution.[15] The jurisdiction of the Supreme Court in reviewing administrative acts and decisions, though confined to either annulling or confirming the measure, is widely exercised.

The NRA's Obligations to Cooperate with the Commission

7.15   In the performance of its obligations, ComECPR shall cooperate and consult with the European Commission with a view to providing the European Commission with sufficient information so that it can effectively perform the supervisory role required of it under Community law, including:

- the communication of draft measures to the European Commission, allowing it sufficient time in which to make its views on the draft measures known to ComECPR,
- the communication of information to the European Commission in the event that the European Commission has serious doubts as to the compatibility of the draft measure with Community law,
- the communication of information to the European Commission in the event that the European Commission requests clarifications of market data or analyses conducted by ComECPR in the performance of its functions,
- the notification to the European Commission of a final decision taken in connection with any of the functions performed by ComECPR, including the names of undertakings designated as having significant market power and the

---

12   Part 6 L112(I)/2004.
13   Ss 25, 26 and 33 et seq L112(I)/2004; PI143/2005.
14   PI144/2005.
15   S 158 L112(I)/2004.

obligations imposed on them, in accordance with the requirements of article 36(2) Universal Service Directive and articles 15(2) and 16(2) Access Directive. The manner and form of cooperation and consultation under this section is prescribed by Order.[16]

7.16 The Commission's powers of standardisation and harmonisation as provided by articles 17 and 19 Framework Directive are reflected in sections 39 and 50 L112(I)/2004.

'Significant Market Power' as a Fundamental Prerequisite of Regulation

Definition of SMP

7.17 An undertaking shall be deemed to have SMP if, either individually or jointly with others, it enjoys a position equivalent to dominance under Community jurisprudence. Dominance is understood to be a position of economic strength affording an undertaking or undertakings the power to behave to an appreciable extent independently of competitors, customers and ultimately consumers.[17]

7.18 'Joint dominant position' refers to those cases where two or more providers function in a market, the structure of which is considered to be conducive to coordinated effects, ie it encourages parallel or aligned anti-competitive behaviour. Correct interpretation of the term should be sought by reference to the Court of Justice of the European Communities case law and the practice of the Commission.[18]

7.19 Where an undertaking has SMP on a specific market, it may also be deemed to have SMP on a closely related market, where the links between the two markets in question are such as to allow the market power held in one market to be leveraged into the other market, thereby strengthening the market power of the undertaking in question.[19]

Definition of relevant market and SMP designation

7.20 By virtue of the law and the relevant orders issued thereunder,[20] market definition and market analysis shall be carried out within the following framework: ComECPR shall, taking the utmost account of Community law, define by order or decision relevant markets in accordance with the principles of competition law. In the event that ComECPR intends to define markets that differ from those listed in the current Commission Recommendation it shall adhere to the procedures set out in articles 6 and 7 Framework Directive.

The procedures shall be designed to ensure that the prescribed consultation and transparency mechanism is respected wherever ComECPR intends to adopt a decision which will have a significant impact on a relevant market. They must further provide interested parties with the opportunity to comment on such a

---

16 S 50(2) L112(I)/2004.
17 S 48(3) L112(I)/2004, see also PI148/2005.
18 Reg 2 PI148/2005.
19 S 48(4) L112(I)/2004.
20 Ss 47, 48 L112(I)/2004; PI147/2005, PI148/2005.

decision at the draft stage, ensure that a centralised information point exists through which all consultations can be accessed, and that the results are made publicly available, subject to the right of interested parties to have their confidential information protected.

7.21   Markets defined for the purposes of imposing regulatory obligations under the Law shall be without prejudice to markets defined in specific cases under competition law.

7.22   After completion of the definition of relevant markets, ComECPR shall conduct an analysis of the effectiveness of competition in such markets, in accordance with Community law and where, as a result of the analysis of competition in a specific market, the market is found not to be effectively competitive, it shall designate an undertaking or undertakings as possessing SMP in that market.[21] Where, as a result of its analysis of the level of competition in a specific relevant market, ComECPR concludes that the market is effectively competitive, it must not impose or maintain any remedial measures and must withdraw existing obligations from that relevant market. An appropriate period of notice shall be given to parties affected by any such withdrawal of regulatory obligations.

7.23   Under the old regulatory regime, CYTA was designated as having SMP. No market analysis procedure or market definition has been concluded yet. It is expected that the first relevant decisions in respect of four markets will be taken during 2005.

NRA's Regulatory Duties concerning Rights of Way, Co-location and Facility Sharing

Rights of way

7.24   Public telecommunication network providers may acquire immovable property for the purposes of their activities. Property which cannot be acquired by agreement may be acquired under the provisions of the law for compulsory acquisition.[22]

7.25   Duly authorised public telecommunication network providers may[23] for the purpose of survey, examination and/or investigation, preliminary or incidental to the exercise of any of the functions of a licensed network provider, at all reasonable times, enter upon any land – privately or publicly owned – and, subject to providing 24 hours' prior notice in writing to its occupier, upon any premises.

7.26   For the purpose of carrying out work in connection with any electronic communication network, with the consent of the occupier of immovable property, or by agreement and the payment of an agreed sum of money, after giving 24 hours' prior notice to the occupier of the immovable property, the network provider may enter the property and carry out all necessary works and installations and may, in the course thereof, cut and/or lop trees, remove vegetation, hedges, drywalls and/or other things, as may be necessary for the purpose. In the event that no consent is granted or no agreement is concluded between the network provider and the occupier concerning entry and/or the amount to be paid, the provider has the right

---

21   See paras 7.17–7.19 above.
22   S 89(1) L112(I)/2004.
23   S 89 L112(I)/2004.

to apply to the court which, after considering and weighing the prejudice on the one hand and the benefit accruing to the parties involved on the other, shall decide whether or not to allow entry and the amount of compensation in the particular case.

7.27   An electronic communication network provider may, subject to reasonable notice, execute works upon any street and at all reasonable times enter upon any land, houses and/or buildings in which installations and/or machinery have been, are or will be installed.[24] Prior to executing any work, providers shall make sure that all necessary rights and permissions have been obtained.[25] Streets damaged and/or opened shall be reinstated to their previous condition with all reasonable speed. An electronic communication network installation shall not interrupt, obstruct and/or interfere with the passage along the street.[26]

7.28   The procedures for obtaining permits from local authorities are not yet harmonised.

Co-location and facility sharing

7.29   Public providers of electronic communication networks and/or services shall have the right to negotiate agreements for the use and/or access to their facilities and installations by any other organisation for co-location and/or facility sharing, and such agreements shall be a matter for commercial and technical agreement between the parties concerned.

7.30   ComECPR may, within the exercise of its competences, after public consultations, impose terms in relation to such an agreement, including conditions for the apportionment of the costs of facility sharing. ComECPR may, following a referral from any party to a dispute in relation to such an agreement, take measures to resolve the dispute. The aforesaid agreement shall be deemed to be an interconnection agreement for this purpose.[27]

REGULATION OF MARKET ENTRY: IMPLEMENTATION OF THE AUTHORISATION DIRECTIVE

The General Authorisation of Electronic Communications

7.31   Any undertaking may provide electronic communication networks and/or services in Cyprus subject to a general authorisation or, in exceptional circumstances, to an individual right of use relating to the use of radio frequencies or numbers.[28] General authorisation (other than general authorisation relating to the use of radio frequencies)[29] and the granting of an individual right of use of numbers are within the powers of ComECPR.

7.32   An undertaking seeking to provide electronic communication networks and/or services pursuant to a general authorisation can commence activities

---

24   S 90 L112(I)/2004.
25   S 96 L112(I)/2004.
26   S 89(9)L112(I)/2004.
27   S 62 L112(I)/2004. See also PI566/2003.
28   Ss 37(1), 38 L112(I)/2004. The authorisation regime is described in detail in PI851/2004.
29   The authorities lie with the Department of Electronic Communications of the Ministry of Communications and Works; see para 7.38 below.

immediately after filing formal notification with ComECPR. Permits from competent authorities are necessary for carrying out construction works.

7.33 On grounds of public order, safety or health, ComECPR may prohibit or limit the ability of a specific undertaking to provide electronic communication networks or services.

7.34 Any person who intends to provide an electronic communication network or an electronic communications service shall notify ComECPR in advance, and any changes to the information must be notified within 30 days.

7.35 An undertaking operating pursuant to a general authorisation may[30] provide electronic communication networks or services, as described in its notification, and apply for the necessary rights to install facilities on, over or under public or private property for the purposes of providing communications networks. Where an authorised undertaking is providing an electronic communication network or service to the public, the general authorisation also gives it the right to negotiate interconnection and obtain access to or interconnection from another undertaking authorised in Cyprus or in another Member State.

7.36 ComECPR shall, within one week of receiving a request from an authorised undertaking, issue a standardised declaration confirming, where applicable, that the undertaking has submitted a notification and detailing the terms and prerequisites applicable to the exercise of rights by the undertaking. The same declaration may be issued in response to the notification.

7.37 ComECPR shall specify the obligations of a provider operating pursuant to a general authorisation in the declaration[31] and may further specify that certain conditions shall not apply to undertakings of a class or type. The conditions set out in Part A of the Annex to the Authorisation Directive have been adopted. General authorisations may set out criteria and procedures for the imposition of specific obligations in respect of interconnection, end users' rights and universal service, where applicable.

Rights of Use for Radio Frequencies

General authorisation and granting of individual rights

7.38 Frequency regulation is governed by the Radiocommunications Law[32] as amended. The Minister of Communication and Works ('the Minister') is responsible for the overall policy on all radio matters, and the Director of the Department of Electronic Communications[33] ('the Director') is responsible for the management of the radio spectrum and advises the Minister on radio spectrum policy issues. The Director develops and maintains the National Frequency Plan, authorises use of the radio spectrum (including the assignment of frequencies to broadcasting stations) and monitors spectrum usage.

---

30   Ss 40 and 41L112(I)/2004.
31   S 39 L112(I)/2004.
32   L146(I)/2002 which was enacted to harmonise national law with Directives 87/372/EEC, 90/544/EEC, 91/287/EEC, 710/97/EC, 97/13/EC, 99/128/EC and 1999/5/EC.
33   A department of the Ministry of Communications and Works.

7.39   The legal framework fully adopts the relevant EU legislation: Rights of use for frequencies are[34] either granted by way of general authorisations or individual rights of use. The Minister may prescribe categories of radio frequencies and frequency bands that are not subject to an individual authorisation. Such order issued[35] includes all frequency bands for which CEPT/ECC Decisions[36] provide for exception from individual licensing.

7.40   Rights of use for frequencies allow the use as described in, and in accordance with, the conditions, restrictions and prerequisites contained in the respective authorisation. They do not confer on the licensee any right of ownership or to sell, auction, lease, transfer or control, and they do not discharge him of the obligation to apply for and acquire any other permit necessary under any other law.

Admissible conditions

7.41   A right of use may be issued under such terms, conditions and limitations as the Director may deem fit, in respect of the matters set out in the Law[37] adopting Part B of the Annex to the Authorisation Directive. For the GSM-900 MHz, GSM-1800 MHz and the 3G bands there are only geographical roll-out obligations. The Radio LAN bands (2.4 GHz and 5 GHz) are subject to a general authorisation with the technical requirements prescribed in the relevant CEPT/ECC Decisions.

Limitation of number of rights of use to be granted

7.42   There is no limit on the number of authorisations, except to the extent required to ensure the efficient use of radio frequencies.[38]

7.43   To optimise the use of frequency spectrum the Minister may decide whether auctions or invitations for submission of tenders are to be declared, where the total demand is not satisfied or it is anticipated that in the near future such a demand shall not be satisfied.[39] Auctions are planned for Fixed Wireless Access, Terrestrial Digital Television and TETRA networks. For the same purpose the Minister may decide as to the cases where applications for individual licences shall be made by way of submission of tenders.[40] Where a public auction or the invitation of tenders or a negotiation procedure is intended, or where the individual authorisation to be issued will be used for establishing a public telecommunications network or/and the provision of public telecommunications services, the Minister and ComECPR act jointly.[41]

---

34   S 18 L146(I)/2002.
35   PI355/2004.
36   ECC/DEC/(03)04, ECC/DEC/(02)08, ECC/DEC/(02)11, ERC/DEC/(01)01 to ERC/DEC/ (01)06, ERC/DEC/(01)08 to ERC/DEC/(01)18, ERC/DEC/(00)03 to ERC/DEC/(00)05, ERC/ DEC/(99)02, ERC/DEC/(99)03, ERC/DEC/(98)22, ERC/DEC/(98)23, ERC/DEC/(98)26, ERC/DEC/(98)27, ERC/DEC/(95)01.
37   S 28 L146(I)/2002.
38   S 19 L146(I)/2002.
39   S 23 L146(I)/2002.
40   S 24 L146(I)/2002.
41   S 3(6) L146(I)/2002.

7.44   Regulations are issued following a procedure safeguarding transparency and giving interested parties the opportunity to express views.[42]

7.45   Charges for spectrum[43] are levied, in relation to an individual right of use, for the application, operating, renewal and amendment; and, in relation to a general authorisation, charges are levied for registration, operating, renewal and amendment.

Frequency trading

7.46   Spectrum trading is not currently allowed. The Minister may, however, define the framework for authorised entities to sell, auction, lease or transfer the use of any part of the radio frequency spectrum.[44]

Rights of Use for Numbers

General authorisations and granting of individual rights

7.47   Individual rights to use numbers from the Numbering Plan are granted by a decision of ComECPR according to prescribed open, transparent and non-discriminatory procedures.[45] Rights of use for numbers and/or a series of numbers are issued to providers for their own use and for further allocation to their subscribers.[46] The procedures shall be published, open, transparent and non-discriminatory. ComECPR may impose fees for the right to use numbers.

Admissible conditions

7.48   ComECPR may impose one or more of the obligations set out in the Law which has adopted Part C of the Annex to the Authorisation Directive.[47]

7.49   An undertaking providing a publicly available telephone service, including a mobile service, shall ensure that a subscriber to such service can, upon request, retain his number irrespective of the undertaking providing the service, in the case of geographic numbers at a specific location, and, in the case of non-geographic numbers, at any location. It does not apply to the transfer of numbers between networks providing services at a fixed location and mobile networks.[48]

Limitation of number of rights of use to be granted

7.50   At reasonable intervals or at the reasonable request of affected undertakings, ComECPR may review the limitation on the number of rights of use by withdrawing any limitation or increasing or decreasing the relevant number. If it is found that

---

42   S 14 L146(I)/2002.
43   S 20 L146(I)/2002.
44   S 16(5) L146(I)/2002 as amended by s 10 L180(I)/2004.
45   See PI850/2004.
46   S 41L112(I)/2004.
47   S 41(3) L112(I)/2004.
48   S 75 L112(I)/2004.

it is possible to expand the scope of the relevant rights of use to include additional numbers, ComECPR shall amend its decision and will determine the type of procedure to be followed for such amendment.[49]

7.51   Competitive or comparative selection procedures for rights of use of numbers are provided for by the Law.[50]

The NRA's Enforcement Powers

7.52   ComECPR is empowered to demand and receive information and order any person accordingly,[51] and to conduct consultations with commercial and consumer organisations and with representatives of the government.[52] It is further authorised, inter alia: to supervise compliance with the terms and conditions set out in authorisations; to impose penalties in the form of administrative fines on any public or non-public provider; to summon and enforce the attendance of witnesses at inquiries; and to issue decisions necessary to secure compliance with the Law and Orders, upon its own motion or following a complaint, to hold an enquiry and summon and compel attendance of witnesses and parties and to examine them personally or through lawyers.[53] Failure to comply, without reasonable cause, with an order or decision constitutes a criminal offence.[54]

7.53   ComECPR is also empowered to issue interim decisions and/or orders,[55] upon evidence of a breach of the conditions of a general authorisation or right of use that represents an immediate and serious threat to public safety, public security or public health, or that will create serious economic or operational problems for other providers or users of electronic communication networks or services[56] and that requires urgent action in order to safeguard competition and protect the interests of users.[57]

Administrative Charges and Fees for Rights of Use

7.54   All authorised organisations have to pay the appropriate charges and fees.[58]

7.55   ComECPR prescribes and regulates the structure of charges, which may include minimum and/or maximum price levels required to ensure legitimate and healthy competition, and the principles of transparency and cost orientation of any provider designated as universal service provider or who has been determined as holding a position of SMP in a relevant market.[59]

---

49   S 41(9) L112(I)/2004.
50   S 41 L112(I)/2004.
51   S 25 L112(I)/2004.
52   S 26 L112(I)/2004.
53   Ss 27, 28 and 30 L112(I)/2004.
54   S 29 L112(I)/2004.
55   S 20 (o) L112(I)/2004.
56   S 42(7)L112(I)/2004.
57   Ss 33(2)(a), 49(7), 50(4)L112(I)/2004.
58   Cf for spectrum PI464/2004, for numbers PI464/2004 and, for rights of way, paras 7.24 et seq above.
59   S 20(q) L112(I)/2004 and relevant PIs, as set out in para 7.5 above.

REGULATION OF NETWORK ACCESS AND INTERCONNECTION: IMPLEMENTATION OF THE ACCESS DIRECTIVE

Objectives and Scope of Access Regulation

7.56   ComECPR may confer rights and impose obligations on undertakings in relation to access to, and/or interconnection of, electronic communication networks and services and associated facilities in order to achieve the interoperability of electronic communications services and produce sustainable competition on the merits between undertakings.[60]

Basic Regulatory Concepts

7.57   Where commercial negotiations between parties for access or interconnection fail, ComECPR may secure adequate access and interconnection and interoperability of services in the interest of end-users, by imposing on those undertakings with SMP in a relevant market one or more obligations relating to transparency, non-discrimination, accounting separation, access, and price control including cost orientation as well as other appropriate remedies.[61]

7.58   Obligations and conditions imposed shall be based on objective, transparent, proportionate and non-discriminatory criteria.[62]

7.59   'Access' means the making available of facilities and/or services to another undertaking, under defined conditions, on either an exclusive or non-exclusive basis, for the purpose of providing electronic communications services. It covers inter alia: access to network elements and associated facilities; access to physical infrastructure; access to relevant software systems; access to number translation or systems offering equivalent functionality; access to fixed and mobile networks; access to conditional access systems for digital television services; and access to virtual network services.

7.60   'Interconnection' is defined in the Law in identical terms to the Access Directive.[63]

7.61   The general authorisation also gives undertakings the right to negotiate interconnection and obtain access to or interconnection from another undertaking. An undertaking requesting access or interconnection within Cyprus does not require prior authorisation to operate in Cyprus.

7.62   ComECPR will intervene where appropriate agreement cannot be reached between the undertakings.[64]

---

60   S 51 L112(I)/2004.
61   S 49 L112(I)/2004.
62   S 53(4) L112(I)/2004.
63   S 4 L112(I)/2004.
64   Ss 53(5) and 51(3) L112(I)/2004.

Access- and Interconnection-related Obligations with Respect to SMP Undertakings

Overview

7.63   ComECPR may impose obligations on operators designated as having SMP in a relevant market[65] in respect of transparency, non-discrimination, accounting separation, access to and use of specific network facilities, price control and cost accounting.[66] In exceptional circumstances, further obligations may be imposed, provided that they are submitted to the European Commission for prior approval.[67]

Transparency obligations

7.64   Transparency obligations may require operators to make public or available to ComECPR specified information such as accounting information, technical specifications, network characteristics, terms and conditions for supply and use, and prices. The requirement may be in respect of reference interconnection offers, and ComECPR may, inter alia, impose changes.[68]

Non-discrimination obligations

7.65   Non-discrimination obligations shall ensure, in particular, that the undertaking subject to the obligation shall apply equivalent conditions in equivalent circumstances, and shall provide services and information to others under the same conditions and of the same quality as it provide for its own services, or those of its subsidiaries or partners.[69]

Specific access obligations

7.66   ComECPR may impose obligations on operators to meet reasonable requests for access to, and use of, specific network elements and associated facilities, inter alia, where development of a sustainable competitive market may be hindered at the retail level or the end-users' interests are not served. Such obligations may, inter alia, require that operators provide or do not withdraw access, negotiate in good faith, provide specified services on a wholesale basis for resale, grant open access to technical interfaces, and provide co-location or other forms of facility sharing. In assessing the imposition of obligations, ComECPR will take into account viability in the light of market development, feasibility of providing the access proposed in relation to the capacity available, the initial investment by the facility owner, the need to safeguard competition in the long term, any intellectual property rights, and the provision of pan-European services.[70]

7.67   In the mobile telephony market the incumbent has to offer interconnection, including carrier selection (cost-oriented pricing as derived from the incumbent's LRIC system audit) and national roaming.

---

65   S 55 L112(I)/2004.
66   Ss 55(1) and 56–60 L112(I)/2004.
67   Ss 55(3), 56–57 L112(I)/2004. See also reference interconnection offer as amended.
68   S 56 L112(I)/2004, PI15/2005.
69   S 57 L112(I)/2004.
70   S 59 L112(I)/2004.

Price control obligations

7.68   The costing system of the incumbent is reviewed on an annual basis by external auditors to evaluate the input data, the allocation factors used and the results generated. The operating costs and the cost of capital are the cost elements put into the system.

7.69   Data put into the system are financial data from the general ledger and the fixed asset register, and actual data relating to the number of customers, traffic volume (minutes) and number of customer applications and allocation bases. An audit carried out by ComECPR has confirmed that the incumbent's costing system is reliable.

7.70   The regulatory measures have adopted reference interconnection offers and reference unbundling offers. Modifications include immediate access for local loop unbundling to all network nodes of the incumbent, and full and shared access pricing. Leased line wholesale price regulation has also been imposed by PI331/2003.

Accounting separation obligations

7.71   ComECPR may impose obligations for accounting separation and, in particular, may require a vertically integrated company to make transparent its wholesale prices and its internal transfer prices, inter alia, to ensure compliance where there is a requirement for non-discrimination and to prevent unfair cross-subsidies. Further, it may require the submission of accounting records, including data on revenues received from third parties.[71]

Related Regulatory Powers with Respect to SMP Undertakings

7.72   Where, as a result of market analysis, ComECPR determines that the market for the provision of part or all of the minimum set of leased lines is not effectively competitive, it will identify those undertakings with SMP in the provision of those specific elements of the minimum set of leased lines services in all or part of Cyprus, including international leased lines terminating or originating in Cyprus. It shall impose obligations regarding the provision of the minimum set of leased lines, as identified in the list of standards published in the Official Journal of the European Communities, in relation to those specific leased line markets. It shall withdraw the obligations referred to in the Law in relation to a specific leased-lines market where, as a result of market analysis, it determines that a relevant market for the provision of the minimum set of leased lines is effectively competitive.[72]

7.73   Undertakings notified as having SMP for the provision of connection to and use of the public telephone network at a fixed location will enable their subscribers to access the services of any interconnected provider of publicly available telephone services on a call-by-call basis by dialling a carrier selection code and by means of pre-selection, with a facility to override any pre-selected choice on a call-by-call basis by dialling a carrier selection code. ComECPR shall ensure that pricing for

---

71   S 58 L112(I)/2004.
72   S 66 L112(I)/2004.

access and interconnection related to the provision of the said facilities is cost oriented, and that direct charges to subscribers, if any, do not act as a disincentive for the use of these facilities.[73]

Regulatory Powers Applicable to All Market Participants

7.74   Irrespective of any measures taken with respect to undertakings found to hold SMP, ComECPR may impose:[74]

- to the extent that it is necessary to ensure end-to-end connectivity, obligations on undertakings that control access to end-users, including in justified cases the obligation to interconnect networks which are not already interconnected,
- to the extent that it is necessary to ensure accessibility for end-users to digital radio and television broadcasting services in Cyprus, obligations on operators to provide access on fair, reasonable and non-discriminatory terms to the following facilities:
  - Application Program Interfaces (APIs), and
  - Electronic Program Guides (EPGs).

Transitional Provisions

7.75   All obligations on undertakings providing public communications networks and/or services concerning access and interconnection that were in force prior to the date of entry into force of L112(I)/2004 shall be maintained until such time as these obligations are reviewed and a determination is made accordingly.[75]

REGULATION OF UNIVERSAL SERVICES AND USERS' RIGHTS: THE UNIVERSAL SERVICE DIRECTIVE

Regulation of Universal Service Obligations

Scope of universal service obligations

7.76   ComECPR ensures that the a minimum set of services is made available at the level of quality specified to all end users, independent of their geographic location and, in the light of specific national conditions, at what is considered to be an affordable price.[76]

7.77   By a decision of ComECPR[77] the universal service has been defined as including connection on a permanent basis to the public telephone network and access to the relevant telephone services, information service by way of telephone directory and provision of the subscriber list in printed and electronic formats, provision of public telephones, services or facilities for individuals with special needs, low income and/or with special social needs and free access to emergency services.

---

73   S 67 L112(I)/2004.
74   S 53(2) L112(I)/2004.
75   S 161(1) L112(I)/2004.
76   S 108(1) L112(I)/2004.
77   PI 138/2005.

Designation of undertakings obliged to provide universal services

7.78   ComECPR designates the undertakings to provide a universal service for such period as may be specified, so that such universal service may be made available across the whole of the geographic territory of the Republic of Cyprus.[78]

7.79   By a decision of ComECPR, the Cyprus Telecommunications Authority (CYTA) has been designated as universal service provider for three years.[79] The same decision provides, inter alia, for the criteria and the procedure concerning the designation of universal service providers. These criteria include the prerequisite of prior authorisation of the candidate for fixed network and fixed telephony, the percentage of coverage of the territory and the population by the candidate's network, the quality of the service as specified from time to time by relevant orders, and the financial and operational viability of the candidate.

The provider of a universal service is obliged to provide, inter alia, access to the public fixed network upon reasonable request by any person, at affordable prices and according to transparent and non-discriminatory procedures.

Regulation of retail tariffs, users' expenditures and quality of service

7.80   Specific facilities including price control provisions and specific services, e g itemised billing and call barring, that should be provided by the universal service operator are defined in sections 108–113 L112(I)/2004, properly implementing the provisions of the Universal Service Directive; details are covered by a relevant order.[80]

7.81   Retail tariffs for all end-users are also regulated.[81]

7.82   Operators are required to collect, maintain and deliver to ComECPR information in particular as to quality of their services which are compared to published quality indices. ComECPR is empowered to impose administrative sanctions in case of breach of this obligation.[82]

Cost calculation and financing of universal services

7.83   Universal services are financed through the universal service fund according to specified procedures.[83] Contributors to the fund are all and any of those undertakings providing services or electronic communications within the territory of the Republic of Cyprus, with the exception of any categories of authorised persons that ComECPR has exempted by a duly reasoned decision. Exemptions may be granted for providers otherwise entitled,[84] or providers whose annual gross income does not exceed Cyprus Pounds 250,000 (approx €436,000).[85]

---

78   S 109 L112(I)/2004.
79   PI 137/2005 (18 March). It also provides, inter alia, for the criteria and procedure for designation.
80   PI142/2005.
81   D2/2005.
82   S 70 PI74/2005 L112(I)2005.
83   PI141/2005.
84   As defined in reg 2 PI141/2005.
85   Reg 7 PI141/2005.

7.84   The costs of the universal services obligations are calculated according to described methodology and procedure.[86] For this purpose, ComECPR has developed a LRAIC costing model.

Regulation of Retail Markets

Prerequisites for the regulation of retail markets

7.85   ComECPR may impose appropriate regulatory obligations on undertakings identified as having SMP on a given retail market if, as a result of a market analysis, a given retail market is not effectively competitive, and obligations imposed on the wholesale markets are assessed as not resulting in the achievement of the objectives set out in the Law.[87]

Regulatory powers

7.86   From 1 June 2005 retail price regulation is limited to a single basket of fixed network services comprising PSTN Line connection, monthly rental with a sub cap, calls originating from the fixed network and terminating in the fixed network, calls originating from the fixed network and terminating at an ISP connection on the fixed network. The incumbent's revenue from this basket is required to be cost oriented towards gradual rebalancing of monthly rental, PSTN connection and call pricing.

End User Rights

Contracts

7.87   An undertaking that provides end users with connection and/or access to the public telephone network shall do so in accordance with a written contract, which shall specify, inter alia, the details set out in art 20(2) Universal Service Directive.[88] The same applies where a contract is agreed between an end user and a provider of electronic communications services, other than one providing connection and/or access to the public telephone network.[89]

Transparency obligations

7.88   ComECPR ensures that transparent and current information on applicable prices and tariffs, and on standard terms and conditions, is made available to end-users and consumers in respect of access to and the use of publicly available telephone services.[90]

7.89   Operators are required, inter alia, to supply competition comparatives, information as to invoicing, details as discount offers and premium rates and

---

86   PI140/2005.
87   S 65(1) L112(I)/2004
88   S 69(1),(2) L112(I)2004.
89   S 69 L112(I)2004, PI139/2005, PI74/2005.
90   S 70 L112(I)/2004, PI139/2005.

annual reports. To this end, they must make available specified procedures securing correct information to end users/consumers, in particular, to the effect that: subscribers are informed of price increases prior to their implementation; printed invoices and operators' websites are duly updated; and personnel in charge, their resellers and their associates are effectively trained to supply correct and comprehensible information to end users in respect of the provision of electronic services.[91]

DATA PROTECTION: IMPLEMENTATION OF THE E-PRIVACY DIRECTIVE

Confidentiality of Communications

7.90   Public providers shall take all necessary technical and administrative measures in order to safeguard the security of their networks and services.[92]

7.91   No person, other than users communicating between themselves, shall be allowed to listen to, tap, store, intercept and/or undertake any other form of surveillance of communications without the consent of the users concerned, except interceptions of communications in circumstances provided for by law and with the authorisation of a court.[93] Legally authorised recording of electronic communications in the course of lawful business practice, for the purpose of providing evidence of a commercial transaction and/or of any other business communication, is permitted.

7.92   The use of electronic communication networks to store information or to gain access to information stored in the terminal equipment of a subscriber or user is only allowed on condition that the subscriber or user concerned is provided with clear and comprehensive information, inter alia, about the purposes of processing, and is offered the right to refuse such processing by the data controller.[94]

Traffic Data and Location Data

7.93   'Traffic data' is defined as any data processed for the purpose of the conveyance of a communication on an electronic communication network or for the billing thereof, and 'location data' as any data processed in an electronic communication network, indicating the geographic position of the terminal equipment of a user of a publicly available electronic communications service.[95]

7.94   Traffic data concerning subscribers and users which are submitted to processing so as to establish communications and which are stored by organisations

---

91   Reg 14 PI139/2005.
92   S 98 L112(I)/2004.
93   S 8 L92(I)/96. The application to the court is in writing, is made by or on behalf of the Attorney General of the Republic and is supported by affidavit sworn by an appropriate person. The court may allow interception if it is satisfied, inter alia, that there is reasonable suspicion that a person is committing, has committed or is about to commit an offence, that the private communication is connected with the offence, that usual investigating methods have been adopted without success, that there is reasonable suspicion that the apparatus which is to be intercepted is being or is to be or has been used in respect of such an offence, and that it is in the interest of justice for the order applied for to be issued.
94   S 99 L112(I)/2004.
95   S 4 L112(I)/2004.

shall be erased or made anonymous at the end of a call, except for the purpose of subscriber billing and interconnection payments processing and only up to the end of the period in which a bill may be lawfully challenged and/or the payment pursued, and provided that the subscriber or user consents that such data may be processed for the purpose of commercial promotion of the services of electronic communications or for the provision of added value services. The consent may be withdrawn at any time.[96]

7.95   Location data may only be processed when they are made anonymous, or with the consent of the user or subscriber, to the extent and for the duration necessary for the provision of a value added service. The consent may be withdrawn at any time.[97]

Itemised Billing

7.96   Subscribers shall have the right to receive non-itemised bills. ComECPR, after consultation with the Commissioner for the Protection of Personal Data, shall by order prescribe the alternative methods of communication among the associated users and called subscribers, in order to reconcile their respective rights to privacy.[98]

Calling and Connected Line Identification

7.97   Where the presentation of calling-line identification is offered, the calling user shall be able, via simple means and free of charge, to eliminate this function on a per-call basis and, likewise, the called subscriber for the reasonable use of this function, to prevent the presentation of the calling line identification of incoming calls. Where the calling-line identification is presented prior to the call being established, the called subscriber shall be able by a simple means to reject incoming calls where the presentation of the calling line identification has been eliminated by the calling user or subscriber. The called subscriber shall have the possibility, via simple means and free of charge, to eliminate the presentation of the connected line identification to the calling user.[99]

7.98   Through transparent procedures a provider may override the elimination of the presentation of calling line identification on a temporary basis, upon application by a subscriber and on a per-line basis, for recognised organisations dealing with emergency calls including law enforcement agencies, ambulance services and fire brigades, for the purpose of answering such calls.[100]

Automatic Call Forwarding

7.99   Subscribers shall be provided, free of charge and via simple means, with the possibility of stopping automatic call forwarding by a third party to the subscriber's terminal equipment.[101]

---

96   S 100 L112(I)/2004.
97   S 101 L112(I)/2004.
98   S 100(3) L112(I)/2004.
99   S 102 L112(I)/2004.
100   S 103 L112(I)/2004.
101   S 104 L112(I)/2004.

Directories of Subscribers

7.100   Personal data contained in printed or electronic directories of subscribers, available to the public and/or obtainable through directory enquiry services, shall be limited to what is necessary to identify a particular subscriber, unless the subscriber has given his unambiguous consent. The providers of directory inquiry services shall provide their subscribers with the possibility of an entry free of charge, and the choice as to which aspects of their personal data will be included in publicly available directories. Subscribers may request and obtain, free of charge, the verification, correction or withdrawal of their personal data from directories.[102]

Unsolicited Communications

7.101   The use of automated calling systems without human intervention may only be allowed with respect to subscribers who have given their prior consent. Unsolicited communications for the purposes of direct marketing, by means other those mentioned, are not permissible without the consent of the subscribers concerned. Rights conferred shall apply to subscribers who are natural persons.[103]

7.102   ComECPR, following consultation with the Commissioner for the Protection of Personal Data, shall by order ensure that the legitimate interests of subscribers other than natural persons, with regard to unsolicited communications, are sufficiently protected.

---

102   S 105 L112(I)/2004.
103   S 106 L112(I)/2004.

The Czech Market for Electronic Communications[1]

Tomas Skoumal & Petra Ledvinkova & Patrik Kastner
Baker & McKenzie, v.o.s.

LEGAL STRUCTURE

Basic Policy

8.1   The Czech voice telephony market was first opened to competition in 2001. Liberalisation continued with the introduction of carrier selection, carrier pre-selection services and fixed number portability in 2002, together with local loop unbundling in 2003. Mobile number portability is expected to be launched at the beginning of 2006.

8.2   Liberalisation of the telecommunications market has led to greater competition in both fixed line and mobile services. Cesky Telecom, a.s. ('Cesky Telecom'), the incumbent operator with more than 3.4 million customers, keeps its leading position in the fixed line market. Other significant operators in the fixed market are GTS Novera, a.s., Contactel, s.r.o., TELE2, a.s., Ceske radiokomunikace, a.s., Tiscalli, s.r.o., and Czech Online, a.s. The mobile market represents 2.5% of the GDP of the Czech Republic. Mobile penetration has exceeded 100% and is close to saturation. There are three nationwide mobile operators – Eurotel Praha, a.s., T-Mobile, a.s. and Oskar Mobil, a.s.

8.3   The overall policy objectives of the Ministry of Information Technologies[2] ('Ministry of IT') is to place the Czech Republic among the more advanced EU member states and to contribute to the EU Lisbon 2010 objective.[3]

Implementation of EU Directives

8.4   The Czech Republic was one of the last member states to transpose the 2002 EU Regulatory Package; this transposition was carried out by the adoption of one

---

1   Editing of this chapter closed on 17 June 2005.
2   'State Policy in the Field of Information and Communications,' 24 March 2004.
3   Accessible and secure communications services, education of the population in information technologies, modern public online services and a dynamic business environment are the priorities set by the Ministry of IT.

single act: Act No 127/2005 Coll., on Electronic Communications ('Act on EC'),[4] which became effective as of 1 May 2005.

8.5   The Act on EC provides a legal basis for the new electronic communications regime and sets out a framework in which the Czech Telecommunications Office ('CTO') regulates the market.

Legislation

8.6   The recently adopted Act on EC replaced the previous Act on Telecommunications, No 151/2000 Coll. ('Old Telecom Act'). The Act on EC provides for a transition period, during which the obligations imposed on telecommunications providers with significant market power ('SMP') under the Old Telecom Act remain in place. Also, the validity of the provisions issued by the regulator under the Old Telecom Act, including its price decisions, is prolonged by 12 months while the Act on EC takes effect.[5] The frequency and numbering plans issued by the regulator under the Old Telecom Act also remain in place, until they are replaced by new provisions.[6]

8.7   The regulator is entitled to issue general provisions regarding various issues specified in the Act on EC. Until new general provisions and/or price decisions are issued by the CTO, the respective provisions issued under the Old Telecom Act will remain in place.[7]

8.8   Generally, the CTO's decisions have had a significant influence on the telecommunications market. The CTO has so far held a relatively strong, impartial and independent position in regulation, and has shown an apparent effort to support competition in telecommunications for the benefit of end users.

REGULATORY PRINCIPLES: IMPLEMENTATION OF THE FRAMEWORK DIRECTIVE

Scope of Regulation

8.9   The Act on EC fully implements the Framework Directive and constitutes an overall legal regulation of electronic communications services, including the state administration.

8.10   The definitions of 'electronic communications network', 'electronic communications service' and 'associated facilities' in the Act on EC are identical to those in the Framework Directive.[8] Voice over IP (VoIP) services are covered by the definition of electronic communications services. The provisions of the Act on EC do not apply to content transmitted through the electronic communications networks.

---

4   Published in the Collection of Laws on 31 March 2005.
5   S 142 Act on EC.
6   S 136 Act on EC.
7   The CTO's rulings remaining in place during the transition period are: OU – 4/S/2000, OU – 6/S/2000, OU – 1/S/2004, 03/VNS/2000, 01/PROP/2002, 07/PROP/2002, 08/PROP/2002, 09/PROP/2002, 01/2003, 01/PROP/2003, 02/PROP/2003, 03/PROP/2003, 04/PROP/2003, 05/PROP/2003, 06/PROP/2003, 07/PROP/2003, 03/PROP/2004, 01/PROP/2005, 02/PROP/2005, 03/PROP/2005, 04/PROP/2005, 05/PROP/2005 and 01/2005.
8   S 2 Act on EC.

National Regulatory Authorities: Organisation, Regulatory Objectives, Competencies

8.11   The Act on EC defines the powers of the two principal regulators – the CTO and the Ministry of IT. The regulatory objectives of the regulators are to promote competition in the communications market; to contribute to the development of the EU internal market; and to promote the interests of end users.[9]

8.12   The Ministry of IT is primarily responsible for an overall telecommunications policy of the Czech Republic, international cooperation and the fulfilment of international obligations by the Czech Republic in the telecommunications sector.[10]

8.13   The principal regulator of telecommunications activities in the Czech Republic is the CTO. The CTO is an independent body, headed by a chairman of a council. Members of the council are appointed by the government.[11] The CTO is not directly subordinated to the Ministry of IT. It is responsible for ensuring compliance with obligations regarding the provision of and access to electronic communications services and networks. The CTO issues general authorisations, administers the frequency spectrum and numbers, carries out market analysis, imposes obligations on the service providers with significant market power and on other operators, issues price decisions, resolves disputes between operators, and brings prosecutions. It is also entitled to request information in order to monitor compliance with the Act on EC.[12]

8.14   The CTO is obliged to cooperate closely with the Office for Protection of Competition ('OPC')[13] and the Council for Radio and Television Broadcasting ('CRTB'), by exchanging information and other forms of collaboration.[14] The CTO must undertake a public consultation process if it intends to issue a general provision, or a price decision or other decision which could have a significant impact on the market of electronic communications.[15]

8.15   The chairman of the CTO is entitled to resolve disputes between electronic communications service providers.[16] Any party can initiate proceedings and the CTO is obliged to issue its decision within four months. Only in exceptional circumstances may the deadline for issue of a decision be prolonged. The CTO's decisions must be reasoned and published. The CTO may also decide not to initiate proceedings if, in its view, there are other more effective means of resolution available to the dispute.[17] The Act on EC also stipulates a procedure to deal with customer complaints against providers of public communications services.[18] If a dispute also falls within the jurisdiction of a regulator from another state, the CTO cooperates with the involved regulator.

---

9   S 4 Act on EC.
10   S 105 Act on EC.
11   S 107 Act on EC.
12   S 108 Act on EC.
13   S 111 Act on EC.
14   S 112 Act on EC.
15   S 130 Act on EC.
16   S 127 Act on EC.
17   S 128 Act on EC.
18   S 129 Act on EC.

Right of Appeal against NRA's Decisions

8.16   Any party to proceedings may lodge an appeal against a decision of the chairman of the CTO or the CTO itself.[19] Appeals must be submitted within 15 days from delivery of the contested decision, in writing, to the CTO.

8.17   Appeals against the chairman's decisions are heard by a five-person permanent Council of the CTO.[20] The Council may examine witnesses, enforce their attendance and compel the production of documents.[21]

8.18   The decision of the Council is final, conclusive and cannot be further appealed.[22] Their determination must contain reasoning, is delivered to the parties and published. The parties have the right to file a court action against the Council's decision.

The NRA's Obligations to Cooperate with the Commission

8.19   The Consultation Procedure has been implemented fully in accordance with the article 6 Framework Directive.[23] The Act on EC also fully implements the 'consolidation procedure' (including the 'veto procedure') as defined in article 7 Framework Directive.

8.20   An undertaking that provides electronic communications networks or services must use standards and specifications for the provision of its services, determination of technical interfaces and network functions, which list is published by the Official Journal of the European Union.[24] The CTO drafts and publishes network plans based on the standards and specifications issued by the Commission, which are binding for all operators and electronic service providers.

'Significant Market Power' as a Fundamental Prerequisite of Regulation

Definition of SMP

8.21   The definition of an SMP undertaking contained in section 53 Act on EC does not deviate from the 'SMP undertaking' definition in article 14 Framework Directive.

Definition of relevant markets and SMP designation

8.22   The CTO determines the relevant markets in electronic communications in a general provision on the basis of the Commission's decisions, recommendations and instructions, taking into account public consultations and consolidation procedures.

---

19   S 123 Act on EC.
20   S 107 Act on EC.
21   The rules of the proceedings are stipulated in S 122 Act on EC and in the Act No 500/2004 Coll., on Administrative Proceedings.
22   S 123 Act on EC.
23   S 131 Act on EC.
24   S 62 Act on EC.

CTO also takes into consideration the opinion of the OPC.[25] Since the Act on EC was adopted very recently, the CTO has not determined any SMP undertakings according to the new regime.

The Act on EC provides transition periods during which the current determination of SMP undertakings remains in place.[26]

8.23   The CTO will determine an SMP operator based on the outcomes of market analyses. In its decision, the CTO will impose on an SMP operator one or more access-related obligations.[27] With the consent of the Commission, the CTO is also entitled to impose on an SMP operator other access-related obligations than those specified in the Act on EC. The CTO can also impose access[28] or co-location[29] obligations on non-SMP operators or electronic communications service providers.

The NRA's Regulatory Duties concerning Rights of Way, Co-location and Facility Sharing

Rights of way

8.24   Any provider of a public electronic communications network is in the public interest and, in accordance with a permit granted by the building authority, entitled to establish and operate its network on or in another owner's land, based on a written agreement on right of way with the land owner.[30] The right of way is established for a lump sum compensation based on a written agreement with the land owner. If no agreement is reached, or if the land owner is unknown or inactive or inaccessible, the building authority may establish a right of way by its decision. Such right of way may be granted under the conditions stipulated in Act No. 50/1976 Coll., Building Act.[31] Such a decision can be appealed to the building authority at the district level. An administrative decision on the appeal is subject to judicial review. The Czech law does not distinguish between rights of way over public and private property.

8.25   The communications line of a public communications network may cross various types of lines, areas or zones.[32]

8.26   The provider of a public communications network is, after prior notification to the owner of the property, entitled to the extent necessary to enter the other

---

25   S 52 Act on EC.
26   In its provision No 1/S/2004 dated 26 April 2004, the CTO has identified the following SMP undertakings: Cesky Telecom (fixed telephony service, lease of circuits, data transmission); and Eurotel and T-Mobile (mobile telephony services and networks operation).
27   S 51 Act on EC; see paras 8.56 et seq below.
28   S 79 Act on EC.
29   S 84 Act on EC; see para 8.27 below.
30   S 104 Act on EC.
31   The conditions are the following: the establishment of the right of way is in the public interest; the aim of the establishment of the right of way cannot be reached otherwise; the establishment of the right of way is not in contradiction to the aims of the decision about the area management; and the rights of the land owner are injured only to the minimum necessary extent, and compensation is paid to the land owner.
32   Electricity, water, sewage and other lines, natural water reservoirs, territories protected under special legal regulations, railway tracks, public roads, water management structures or any other such schemes, including their protective zones.

owner's property in order to maintain, build or repair the network or electronic communications equipment or to cut or lop trees.[33]

Co-location and facility sharing

8.27   The CTO is entitled to impose on SMP operators an obligation to meet the reasonable requirements of another undertaking in terms of use of and access to its specific network elements and associated facilities.[34] These obligations include provision of co-location or any other form of sharing equipment in compliance with article 12 Framework Directive.

REGULATION OF MARKET ENTRY: IMPLEMENTATION OF THE AUTHORISATION DIRECTIVE

The General Authorisation of Electronic Communications

8.28   The general authorisation regime has replaced the licensing system that was previously in use. The Act on EC provides that the CTO issues general authorisations as a general provision, in which it sets out conditions applicable to all or some electronic communications services and networks and the operation of equipment.[35] The provisions of Czech law regarding general authorisations are in compliance with the provisions of the Authorisation Directive. Operators are obliged to notify the CTO in advance of their intention to provide a network or service.[36]

8.29   No notification is required by undertakings applying for access to or interconnection of networks, if they do not provide electronic communications services on the territory of the Czech Republic.

8.30   If an operator meets all legal requirements, the CTO is obliged to issue a confirmation of the notification within one week from delivery of the notification form and the related documentation.[37] Providers are allowed to start service once they have fulfilled their notification obligation.

8.31   Authorised operators have a wide range of rights, the most important being:

- the right to provide electronic communications services or networks,
- the right to apply for assignment of frequencies[38] and number allocation,[39]
- the right to negotiate and request interconnection with public electronic communications networks of other operators,[40] and
- the right to build communications lines in accordance with a permit issued by the building authority.

---

33   S 104 Act on EC.
34   S 84 Act on EC.
35   S 9 Act on EC.
36   S 13 Act on EC.
37   S 14 Act on EC.
38   S 17 Act on EC.
39   S 30 Act on EC.
40   S 79 Act on EC.

8.32   In compliance with the Authorisation Directive, the CTO is entitled to issue a general authorisation and therein specify conditions for the provision of electronic communications services or operation of communications networks. These conditions may relate to issues specified in the Act on EC.[41] The list of such conditions is in conformity with Part A of the Annex to the Authorisation Directive. With the Act on EC being adopted just recently, no general authorisations have so far been issued.

Rights of Use of Radio Frequencies

General authorisations and the granting of individual rights

8.33   The CTO manages the radio frequency spectrum.[42] In order to fulfil this obligation, it, inter alia, drafts a plan of frequency bands allocation, grants individual authorisations for use of radio frequencies, assigns radio frequencies and gives consent to the transfer of radio frequencies.

8.34   Radio frequencies may be used, based on individual authorisations for the use of radio frequencies or based on general authorisations if the issue of an individual authorisation is not necessary. The CTO has discretion to decide when the issue of an individual authorisation is not necessary, but no such decision has been taken so far. Any authorised operator, or user of an electronic communications network or any other person, may acquire an individual authorisation for the use of radio frequency, based on a written application. The CTO is obliged to decide about the application as soon as possible. If there are more applicants requesting permission for use of the same frequencies, the CTO will issue its decisions based on the sequence of applications.[43] If frequencies for broadcasting radio or television signals are requested, the CTO may issue such individual authorisation only to holders of licences issued by the CRTB or with the prior consent of the CRTB.

8.35   The CTO may refuse to grant an individual authorisation for use of radio frequencies, based on the reasons specified in the Act on EC.[44]

Admissible Conditions

8.36   In the individual authorisation, the CTO may impose additional conditions regarding protection from harmful interference and radiation, or regarding obligations arising from international treaties which are binding on the Czech Republic.[45] The list of additional conditions conforms with the conditions contained in Annex B to the Authorisation Directive. Special conditions may be imposed in the permit for use of radio frequencies, if these frequencies were allocated to an operator based on a public tender.[46]

---

41   S 10 Act on EC.
42   S 15 Act on EC.
43   S 17 Act on EC.
44   S 17 Act on EC
45   S 18 Act on EC.
46   S 22 Act on EC.

Limitation of number of rights of use to be granted

8.37   The CTO may limit the number of rights for use of radio frequencies, compared to the scheduled number, in order to ensure that the radio frequencies are used effectively.[47] The intention of the CTO to limit the number of rights to use radio frequencies is subject to the requirement for prior public consultations. In compliance with article 7 Authorisation Directive, the CTO has to carry out a tender for granting frequencies, where the number is limited.[48] The Act on EC does not mention the possibility of carrying out auctions for frequency assignments.

8.38   The Act on EC specifies annual fees for use of radio frequencies. The individual fees depend on the service provided and the frequency assigned.[49]

Frequency Trading

8.39   Frequency trading is allowed only with the prior consent of the CTO.[50] The CTO is authorised to issue a general provision, in which it will lay down the generally applicable conditions and procedures for transfer of the frequencies. No such general provision has yet been adopted.

Rights of Use for Numbers

General authorisation and granting of individual rights

8.40   To ensure that numbers, number series and codes, addresses and names, except internet addresses, are effectively managed and reasonably utilised, the CTO is responsible for the administration of numbers in compliance with the Community's harmonisation objectives.[51] The CTO arranges the numbering plans, draws up rules for creating addresses and names, and grants, amends or withdraws authorisations to utilise numbers.

8.41   Numbers in the numbering plan may only be used based on an individual authorisation.[52] Provisions of Czech law regarding the use of numbers do not deviate from those contained in article 7 Authorisation Directive. The transfer of allocated numbers to another undertaking is admissible only with the prior consent of the CTO.

8.42   The CTO may, after a public consultation process, decide to announce a tender for the issue of authorisations to utilise numbers with special economic value ('golden numbers'). The criteria for evaluation of bids are set by the CTO.

8.43   Numbers cannot be subject to ownership rights; they constitute non-proprietary data and no person may claim ownership of the assigned numbers.

---

47   S 20 Act on EC.
48   S 22 Act on EC.
49   S 24 Act on EC.
50   S 23 Act on EC.
51   S 28 Act on EC.
52   S 30 Act on EC.

8.44   The CTO may, in the authorisation to use numbers, impose conditions. The list of such conditions is similar to the conditions contained in Part C of the Annex to the Authorisation Directive.[53]

8.45   Any provider of a public telephony service must ensure full number portability both in fixed and mobile networks.[54] In the case of geographical numbers, number portability is offered only in a given location. The obligation of number portability does not apply to telephone number portability between public fixed and public mobile telephony networks.

8.46   The CTO may impose carrier selection and carrier pre-selection obligations on an operator designated as having SMP in the market of connection of end-users to a public telephony network.[55]

The NRA's Enforcement Powers

8.47   The CTO may request information from electronic communications network operators or service providers, including information which is considered to be a business secret, in order to verify compliance with the obligations set out by the Act on EC, the CTO's decisions, general authorisations or individual authorisations for frequency and number use.[56]

8.48   If the CTO learns that a liable person or an entity has failed to comply with the conditions or obligations specified in the general authorisation, authorisation to use radio frequencies, or authorisation to use numbers, or other obligations set out in the Act on EC or in the CTO's decision, the CTO has the right to request an operator to correct the identified irregularities within one month. The CTO is entitled to issue a decision on preliminary injunction to remedy the situation, if there is an imminent danger threatening public interests or third persons.[57]

8.49   The CTO may also impose sanctions for breaches of obligations specified in the Act.[58] The maximum penalty which can be imposed is up to 10% of the annual turnover of the offender, the maximum limit being CZK 10,000,000 (€33,000). In determining the amount of the penalty to be imposed, the CTO has to take into account the relevance of the offence, including but not limited to the manner in which the breach was committed, its consequences, duration, and the circumstances under which it was committed. The CTO's power to request that irregularities are corrected and the power to impose sanctions may be exercised simultaneously or separately.

Administrative Charges and Fees for Rights of Use

8.50   The Act on Administrative Charges[59] contains provisions regarding the following fees:

---

53   The conditions regarding number portability requirements and the provision of public directory subscriber information are excluded.
54   S 34 Act on EC.
55   S 70 Act on EC.
56   S 115 Act on EC.
57   S 114 Act on EC.
58   S 118 Act on EC.
59   No 368/1992 Coll.

- for the issue of a confirmation of the notification under general authorisation, of CZK 1,000 (€33);
- for the issue of an authorisation to use numbers, of CZK 5,000 (€167) per authorisation, and
- for the issue of an authorisation to use frequencies, from CZK 3,000 (€100) up to CZK 7,000 (€233) per authorisation.

8.51 In addition, the Act on EC provides that the holder of an individual authorisation for use of frequencies (or numbers) is obliged to pay an annual fee for the allocated frequencies (or numbers).[60]

Transitional Regulations for Existing Authorisations

8.52 Telecommunications licences, frequency allocations and registrations under general licences issued under the old regime of the Old Telecom Act remain valid during a transition period as set out by the Act on EC. The CTO is obliged to issue general authorisations within five months from the date of effectiveness of the Act on EC. Electronic communications service providers or network operators are obliged to notify the CTO, under the respective general authorisation, within one month from its issue. The CTO is obliged to allocate to the operators the same frequencies that were allocated to them under the old regime within three months from the date of effectiveness of the Act on EC.[61]

REGULATION OF NETWORK ACCESS AND INTERCONNECTION: IMPLEMENTATION OF THE ACCESS DIRECTIVE

Objectives and Scope of Access Regulation

8.53 Effective competition belongs among the principal objectives of the new regulatory regime.[62] The CTO, therefore, through its regulatory powers, is mandated to ensure that access to networks and interconnection effectively enables the entry of competitors to the market for the benefit of end users. Provisions regarding access to networks and interconnection apply to operators designated to have SMP, to other public communications network operators and to authorised undertakings seeking interconnection or access to these networks.

Basic Regulatory Concepts

8.54 Although wordings of the definitions of 'access' and 'interconnection'[63] are slightly different from the ones in the Access Directive, they have the same meaning as those in the Directive.

8.55 Any authorised operator is entitled to negotiate mutual access to or interconnection with networks of an undertaking providing a public communications

---

60   S 24 Act on EC.
61   S 136 Act on EC.
62   S 4 Act on EC.
63   S 78 Act on EC.

network in order to facilitate publicly accessible services of electronic communications on the whole territory of the Czech Republic.[64] If no agreement is reached within two months from commencement of the negotiations, any of the involved parties may request the CTO to issue a decision substituting conclusion of an access or interconnection agreement.

Access- and Interconnection-related Obligations with Respect to SMP Undertakings

Overview

8.56   Based on the outcomes of the market analyses, which the CTO carries out every one to three years, the CTO may impose on an SMP undertaking access- and interconnection-related obligations specified in the Act on EC.[65] Such obligations may be imposed only in the event that the relevant markets are not effectively competitive. Access- and interconnection-related obligations which are not listed in the Act on EC may be imposed only with the previous consent of the Commission.

8.57   Since the Act on EC was adopted very recently, no market analyses have been finalised yet. The CTO has not yet determined operators having SMP nor imposed any obligations on such operators under the new regime. Until the obligations under the new regime are imposed on SMP operators, the previous obligations under the old regime remain in place.

Transparency obligations

8.58   The transparency obligation under the Act on EC encompasses, in accordance with the Access Directive, the obligation to publish specified accounting information, technical specifications, network characteristics, contractual conditions and pricing conditions. The CTO may also oblige the SMP operator to publish its reference offer regarding access and interconnection and is also entitled to implement changes to it.[66]

Non-discrimination obligations

8.59   Provisions of the Act on EC regarding non-discrimination obligations do not deviate from the respective provisions of the Access Directive.

Specific access obligations

8.60   Local loop unbundling was introduced into Czech law during the second half of 2003 by an amendment to the Old Telecom Act. Currently, Cesky Telecom is obliged to enable access by other operators to its local loop under the old regime. The Act on EC provides that the CTO may impose the obligation of local loop

---

64   S 79 Act on EC.
65   S 51 Act on EC.
66   S 82 Act on EC.

unbundling on an SMP operator.[67] In addition, the CTO may impose the obligations of access to or use of facilities on an SMP operator. The provisions of Czech law do not deviate from those regarding access obligations contained in the Access Directive.

Price control obligations

8.61 The CTO may issue a price decision setting out the maximum prices or method of price calculation for specified electronic communications services if, according to the outcome of market analyses, the market is not effectively competitive and other measures of the CTO have not remedied the situation.[68] The CTO can define a price based on prices in comparable markets.[69]

Accounting separation obligations

8.62 The CTO may also impose accounting separation obligations.[70] These do not deviate from the accounting separation obligations as contained in the Access Directive.

Related Regulatory Powers with Respect to SMP Undertakings

8.63 Based on the outcome of market analyses, the CTO is entitled to impose carrier selection and carrier pre-selection obligations on an operator with SMP, for the provision of connection to and use of the public telephone network and use of it at a fixed location.[71]

8.64 The CTO is also entitled to impose an obligation to provide the lease of telecommunications lines service (lease of capacity between end points of electronic communications networks) on an SMP operator in the relevant market. Such operator must provide a minimum set of leased lines on a non-discriminatory basis, and is obliged to publish the general terms and conditions applicable to provision of these services.[72] The CTO is entitled, in justified cases, to change the general terms and conditions of an SMP operator regarding supply of leased line services.

8.65 Prices for leased line services must be independent of the mode of use of the leased lines. Prices for the installation and lease of circuits must be set separately. The wholesale prices for leased line services must be cost oriented.

---

67   S 85 Act on EC.
68   S 57 Act on EC.
69   Based on the CTO's price decision issued under the old regime, the following telecommunications prices for wholesale services are regulated: interconnection charges for both mobile and fixed termination; carrier selection and pre-selection services; local loop unbundling; interconnection charges for the use of virtual mobile operators services; interconnection charges for ADSL wholesale services; and interconnection charges for dial-up internet services.
70   S 86 Act on EC.
71   S 70 Act on EC.
72   S 76 Act on EC

Regulatory Powers Applicable to All Market Participants

Obligations to ensure end-to-end connectivity

8.66   The CTO is entitled, upon consultation, to issue a decision to impose obligations enabling connection of an end point with another end point, including, in justified cases, interconnection of networks on an undertaking which controls access to end users.[73]

8.67   The CTO may, upon its own initiative or on the initiative of any of the interested parties, enter into the negotiations between undertakings about interconnection or access agreements. It may also issue its opinion about the disputed part of the draft agreement. If no agreement is reached within two months of the beginning of negotiations, the CTO may issue its decision completing the interconnection or access agreement.

Access to digital and television broadcasting services

8.68   The CTO is also entitled to impose an obligation to provide access to Application Programming Interfaces (APIs) or Electronic Program Guides (EPGs) on an operator under equitable, fair, reasonable and non-discriminatory conditions.[74]

Transitional Provisions

8.69   The access and interconnection obligations imposed under the old regime will remain in place until market analyses are finalised and new obligations under the Act on EC are imposed. The CTO is obliged to reconsider and/or redefine the current obligations of SMP operators within 12 months from the date of effectiveness of the Act on EC.[75] Price-related decisions of the CTO issued under the old Telecommunications Act are valid until new price decisions regarding specified services are issued, within a deadline of 12 months from the date of effectiveness of the Act on EC.[76]

REGULATION OF UNIVERSAL SERVICES AND USERS' RIGHTS: THE UNIVERSAL SERVICE DIRECTIVE

Regulation of Universal Service Obligations

Scope of universal service obligations

8.70   The scope of the universal service obligation under Czech law is similar to the one contained in the Universal Service Directive.[77] The Czech universal service definition additionally covers supplemental services such as phased payment of

---

73   S 79 Act on EC.
74   S 79 Act on EC.
75   S 137 Act on EC.
76   S 142 Act on EC.
77   S 38 Act on EC.

price for connection to the public telephone network for consumers, selective barring of outgoing calls and itemised billing.

8.71 Since the Act on EC was adopted very recently, the CTO has not yet imposed any universal service obligation under the new regime.

Designation of undertakings obliged to provide universal service

8.72 The CTO must carry out a consultation process before imposing a universal service obligation on any operator. Such obligation, or some of the obligations comprised in the universal service, can be imposed on an undertaking based on a public tender carried out by the CTO or by the CTO's decision on an operator designated as having SMP on the relevant market. If there is no undertaking with SMP on the relevant market, the universal service obligation may be imposed on an undertaking best meeting the selection criteria.[78]

8.73 Currently, Cesky Telecom is the only operator designated under the old regime as having an obligation to provide universal service.

Regulation of retail tariffs, users' expenditures and quality of service

8.74 In its Price decision No 01/2005,[79] the CTO has set out maximum retail prices for specified services provided by Cesky Telecom within the scope of universal service obligation.[80]

8.75 Users may control their expenditure through using the following additional free of charge services: selective call barring service, itemised billing service, and the service of phased payment of the price for connection to the public telephone network.

8.76 The Act on EC obliges the universal service provider to provide special (lower) tariffs to persons with low income or with special social needs, or the disabled.[81]

8.77 A universal service provider must comply with the quality parameter levels and mandatory performance targets of the individual universal services set out by a general provision issued by the CTO.[82]

Cost calculation and financing of universal services

8.78 The CTO calculates net costs of provision of the universal service obligation based on information supplied by the provider of the universal service. A universal service provider is entitled to compensation for the costs incurred in connection with provision of the universal service obligation, if the amount of these costs represents an unfair burden to the operator. Compensation is paid from the universal service fund, to which other authorised providers of public electronic

---

78   S 39 Act on EC.
79   Issued on 25 April 2005.
80   Price caps are set for the establishment or transfer of end users telephony station, tariffs for telephone calls originating in fixed networks, and monthly line rental.
81   S 38 Act on EC.
82   S 47 Act on EC.

communications services contribute. If an obligation to provide supplemental services (phased payment of price for connection to the public telephone network for consumers, selective barring of outgoing calls and itemised billing) is imposed within the universal service obligation on an operator, costs for these services would also be compensated from the universal service fund. This is in contradiction with the Universal Service Directive.[83]

Regulation of Retail Markets

Prerequisites for the regulation of retail markets

8.79   Regulation of retail services is permissible only if regulation at a wholesale level does not achieve the regulatory objectives.[84] Such regulation may be implemented if a given retail market is not effectively competitive.

Regulatory powers

8.80   Based on the outcomes of the market analyses, the CTO may impose carrier selection or pre-selection obligations or a leased line obligation on an SMP operator.[85]

8.81   The CTO may, by its decision, also change the general terms and conditions of a public electronic communications service, if these are in contradiction to the law or secondary legislation.[86] In addition, the CTO may oblige an undertaking providing a public electronic communications service to publish an overview of its current prices, quality and conditions of services provided, in a form which enables the end users to compare the data with information provided by other electronic communications service providers.[87]

8.82   The CTO is also entitled to apply price regulation to services provided by an SMP undertaking in the relevant market.[88] The CTO may issue a price decision if competition in the relevant market is limited, because the negotiated prices are unreasonably high or unreasonably low to the detriment of end users,[89] or if the charges for carrier selection or pre-selection services or number portability services discourage subscribers from using such services.

End User Rights

Contracts

8.83   The scope of the minimum terms of a contract on provision of publicly accessible services of electronic communications contained in the Act on EC[90] is in

---

83   S 49 Act on EC.
84   S 57 Act on EC.
85   See paras 8.65–8.67 above.
86   S 63 Act on EC.
87   S 71 Act on EC.
88   S 56 Act on EC.
89   S 57 Act on EC.
90   S 63 Act on EC.

conformity with the list of these terms set out in article 20(2) Universal Service Directive. Some minimum terms are in addition to those in the Universal Service Directive.[91] The CTO is entitled to change the general terms and conditions of an operator if these are in contradiction to the law or secondary legislation.

Transparency obligations

8.84   Any provider of public electronic communications services is obliged to prepare a draft contract regarding provision of the offered services, which must also contain obligations specified in the Act on EC. The draft contract, together with general terms and conditions of the services provided, must be published in the premises of the operator and on its websites.

Dispute resolution

8.85   The Act on EC provides that a customer may file a complaint regarding charges for communications services provided by an operator within two months of receipt of a statement of account. The operator is obliged to handle the complaint within one month after its delivery. If the customer does not agree with the result of the complaint procedure, he/she can apply to the CTO to resolve the dispute.[92]

Other obligations

8.86   Providers of public electronic communications services have to provide their services uninterrupted each day of the year to a quality specified in the Act on EC. They are also obliged to maintain an updated database of their customers. Uninterrupted access to emergency numbers must be secured.[93]

8.87   End-users have a right to have their number or address information excluded from telephone directories and a right to request identification of the telephone number from which malicious or annoying calls originated.

8.88   Providers of public electronic communications services must ensure that it is possible to carry out all international calls to the European Telephone Numbering Area.

Transitional Provisions

8.89   A provider of a universal service designated under the old regime must continue to provide these services until the CTO issues its decision concerning which operator or operators will be obliged to provide a universal service under the new regime. Such decision must be issued by the CTO within nine months after the date of effectiveness of the Act on EC.[94]

---

91   The following terms are added: information about the dates and methods of billing and payment; conventional fines for failure to fulfil contractual obligations; and information about how the customer will be informed of any change to contractual conditions.
92   S 64 Act on EC.
93   S 61 Act on EC.
94   S 137 Act on EC.

DATA PROTECTION: IMPLEMENTATION OF THE E-PRIVACY DIRECTIVE

Confidentiality of Communications

8.90   The operators of a public communications network and providers of publicly available electronic communications services are obliged to take appropriate technical and organisational measures in order to safeguard the security of their services, especially in relation to personal data protection of natural persons (users), protection of traffic data and location data and privacy of communication of natural persons and legal entities. The rights and obligations relating to the protection of personal data, which are not specifically regulated in the Act on EC, shall be governed by Act No 101/2000 Coll.,[95] which implemented the provisions of Directive 95/46/EC.[96]

8.91   In particular, operators and service providers shall prevent listening, tapping, storage or other kinds of interception or surveillance of communications and related traffic data by persons other than users, without the consent of the users concerned.

8.92   However, this shall not prevent technical storage, which is necessary for the conveyance of a communication without prejudice to the principle of confidentiality. Moreover, Act No 141/1961 Coll. defines exceptions to the general confidentiality rule in the case of criminal proceedings concerning a serious criminal offence or other malicious criminal offences which must be prosecuted according to a promulgated international agreement.[97]

8.93   The measures adopted by service providers, in order to ensure security protection, shall include elaboration of an internal technical and organisational statute, which may be reviewed, upon request, by CTO.

8.94   The measures to be taken in the case of a particular risk of a breach of network security are identical to those stipulated in the E-Privacy Directive. The provider of a publicly available electronic communications service must inform the subscribers of such risk and, where a risk exceeds the scope of measures taken by the service provider, of any possible remedies, including an indication of the likely costs involved.

Traffic Data and Location Data

8.95   The wording of the definitions concerning traffic data and location data set out in sections 90 and 91 Act on EC is in compliance with the E-Privacy Directive. Traffic data is defined as 'any data processed for the purpose of transmission of a message via the electronic communications network or for the billing thereof'; location data is defined as 'any data processed within the electronic communications network which defines the geographical location of terminal equipment of a user of a publicly available electronic communications service'.

---

95   Act No. 101/2000 Coll. on Protection of Personal Data and Amendments to Certain other Laws.
96   Directive 95/46/EC of the European Parliament and of the Council of 24 October 1995 on the protection of individuals with regard to the processing of personal data and on the free movement of such data.
97   S 88 Act No 141/1961 Coll. on Criminal Court Procedure.

8.96   If the operator of a public communications network or the provider of a publicly available electronic communications service performs processing of traffic data, including the relevant location data related to subscribers and users, it must be deleted or made anonymous when it is no longer needed for the purpose of transmission of a communication, unless it is necessary for the purposes of subscriber billing, interconnection payments, or marketing of electronic communications services or the provision of value added services.

8.97   Traffic data necessary for the purposes of subscriber billing and interconnection payments may be processed only until the end of the period during which the bill may be lawfully challenged or payment pursued. For the purposes of marketing of electronic communications services or for the provision of value added services, data may be processed to the extent and for the duration necessary for such services or marketing if the subscriber or user to whom the data relates has given his/her consent. The consent for processing of the traffic data may be withdrawn at any time.[98]

8.98   Location data other than traffic data, relating to users or subscribers of public communications networks or publicly available electronic communications services, may only be processed when it is made anonymous, or with the consent of users or subscribers to the extent and for the duration necessary for provision of a value added service.[99] Users or subscribers must be allowed to withdraw their consent to, or temporarily refuse, using simple means and free of charge, the processing of location data other than traffic data at any time.[100]

8.99   Processing of location data other than traffic data by an operator of a communications network provider of a publicly available communications service and the provider of a value added service must only be conducted by persons empowered and authorised for processing by the statute (see para 8.95 above), and the processing must be restricted to the extent necessary for the purpose of providing the respective services.[101]

Itemised Billing

8.100   The provider of a publicly available electronic communications service, provided via a public telephone network, shall provide free of charge, either electronically or in printed form, either:

- a bill itemised by the type of service provided, or
- a summary bill, indicating one total item,

as the subscriber or user may choose.[102]

8.101   The bill shall not contain items regarding calls for which the subscriber is not supposed to pay, including calls to numbers identified as free call numbers.[103]

8.102   A provider that submits a bill containing an itemised list of individual calls shall also offer, for consideration, a suitable alternative to the bill, if so requested by

---

98   S 90 Act on EC.
99   S 91 Act on EC.
100   S 91 Act on EC.
101   S 91 Act on EC.
102   S 64 Act on EC.
103   S 64 Act on EC.

the subscriber, in order to provide increased protection of the subscriber's privacy. Such an alternative may consist, inter alia, in non-indication of a certain part (ie digits) of the dialled numbers in the bill.[104]

Calling and Connected Line Identification

8.103   The provider of a publicly available telephone service is obliged, where presentation is offered of:

- the calling line identification,
  - to offer the calling user the possibility, using a simple means and free of charge, of preventing the presentation of the calling line identification on a per-call basis. The calling subscriber must have this possibility on a per-line basis,
  - to offer the called subscriber the possibility, using a simple means and free of charge, for the reasonable use of this function (eg in crisis centres, hot lines), of preventing presentation of the calling line identification of incoming calls,
- the calling line identification and where the calling line identification is presented prior to the call being established, to offer the called subscriber the possibility, using a simple means, of rejecting incoming calls where presentation of the calling line identification has been prevented by the calling user or subscriber, and
- the called subscriber identification, to offer the called subscriber the possibility, using a simple means and free of charge, of preventing the presentation of the called line identification.[105]

8.104   The provisions stipulated in the first bullet point in para 8.103 above also apply to calls to third countries originating in the Community, and the provisions in the second and third bullet points also apply to incoming calls originating in third countries.

8.105   The operator of a public communications network or provider of a publicly available electronic communications service is entitled to cancel the prevention of presentation of the calling line identification under the terms and for the period stipulated in Act on EC.[106] The information must be communicated to the public, by means allowing for remote access, about the procedures regarding these measures.

Automatic Call Forwarding

8.106   The operator of a public communications network or provider of a publicly available electronic communications service shall ensure that every subscriber has the possibility, using simple means and free of charge, of stopping automatic call forwarding by a third party to the subscriber's terminal.[107]

8.107   In the event that, during provision of a publicly available electronic communications service, calls are automatically or disguisedly forwarded to another

---

104   S 64 Act on EC.
105   S 92 Act on EC.
106   S 92 Act on EC.
107   S 94 Act on EC.

service or to a service provided by another operator, or a new connection is realised and, thus, raises the price to be charged, an operator must notify the user free of charge about this fact and allow him to stop the call before it is forwarded or a new connection is established.[108]

Directories of Subscribers

8.108   Anyone gathering a subscriber's personal data in order to issue a directory of subscribers has to inform the subscribers about, and obtain prior consent of the subscribers to, inclusion of their data in the directory and its publication according to the terms stipulated in the Act on EC.[109]

8.109   Non-inclusion in a public directory of subscribers, verifications, corrections and removals of information from the directory and information about the subscriber's preference not to be contacted for marketing purposes shall be free of charge.

8.110   No one is allowed to offer, via a public communications network or a publicly available electronic communications service, any marketing, advertising or other method of offering goods or services to subscribers who have stated in a public directory that they do not wish to be contacted for such purposes. The provider of an information service, regarding subscribers' numbers or other information, is not allowed to provide information about subscribers that is not included in a public directory. The provisions in this paragraph apply, mutatis mutandis, to information about subscribers who are legal persons.

Unsolicited Communications

8.111   The promotion and advertising of products and services is regulated primarily in Act No 40/1995 Coll.[110] According to this Act, the dissemination of unsolicited advertising that causes expense on the part of the addressee or is viewed by the addressee as annoying is prohibited. The Act further stipulates that advertising is considered annoying where it is addressed to a particular addressee who has previously expressed that he does not wish to receive such advertising.

8.112   In addition to the general restrictions set out in Act No 40/1995 Coll., there is an Act No 480/2004 Coll.[111] on Certain Services of Information Society (so called 'anti-spam law'), which regulates the dissemination of advertising in electronic form. This anti-spam law implements the provisions of the Directive on electronic commerce and the E-Privacy Directive, and it restricts the sending of electronic commercial messages without the prior consent of the addressee (ie it applies the opt-in principle).

---

108 S 94 Act on EC.
109 S 95 Act on EC.
110 Act No 40/1995 Coll. on Regulation of Advertising and on Amendment to Act No 468/1991 Coll. on Radio and Television Broadcasting.
111 Act No 480/2004 Coll. on Certain Services of Information Society.

The Danish Market for Electronic Communications[1]

Henning Hansen and Lise Engel
Philip & Partners, Copenhagen

LEGAL STRUCTURE

Basic Policy

9.1   The Danish electronic communications market underwent complete liberali-sation during the 1990s following almost a century of virtual state monopoly. All relevant European directives pre-dating 1999 were implemented as part of the liberalisation process.[2]

9.2   Planning and regulation of the telecommunications sector during the decade 2000–2010 is outlined in a second political framework agreement dating from 1999 (the '1999 Agreement').[3] The regulatory emphasis is changed from sector regulation to competition-based regulation with a gradual phasing-out of parts of the regulatory framework that become redundant because of increasing competition. The number of applicable acts has been reduced considerably, as has the number of contradictory provisions, whilst the regulatory flexibility has increased.

9.3   A flexible approach has been adopted for the implementation of the 2002 EU Regulatory Package, whereby a limited number of framework acts state the broad outline and principles underlying the regulations and contain extensive delegation of power to issue detailed regulations to either the Minister for Science, Technology and Innovation ('the Minister') or in some cases directly to the Agency.[4] The Minister and the Agency issue detailed regulation by means of Ministerial Orders (*'bekendtgørelser'*) and other secondary legislation,[5] thereby reducing the need to amend the acts as local market conditions increase the level of competition.[6]

---

1   Editing of this chapter closed on 7 June 2005.
2   See paras 4.1–4.14, 4th edn, 1998.
3   Dated 8 September 1999, subject to continuing revision and updating.
4   See para 9.11 below.
5   Regulating e g interconnection, requirements of infrastructure owners and service providers with a strong market position, in detail.
6   Eg where increased competition leads to redundancy and abolition of specific requirements imposed on former SMP undertakings whose market shares decrease.

9.4 Overall market conditions in Denmark are such that the former telecommunications monopoly[7] continues to hold a strong position, particularly in infrastructure ownership and access to end-users in fixed networks markets, whereas the mobile communication sector is characterised by a stronger competitive edge.

Implementation of EU Directives

9.5 Denmark had implemented the entire 2002 EU Regulatory Package by July 2003.

Legislation

9.6 The key parts of the legislative framework in relation to the 2002 EU Regulatory Package are:

Acts and promulgation orders

- Consolidated Act no 679 of 23 June 2004 ('L679'),[8]
- Consolidated Act no 680 of 23 June 2004 ('L680'),[9]
- Consolidated Act no 662 of 10 July 2003 ('L662'),[10]
- Consolidated Act no 681 of 23 June 2004 ('L681'),[11] and
- Consolidated Act no 664 of 10 July 2003 ('L664').[12]

Ministerial orders

- Ministerial Order no 638 of 23 June 2005 ('MO638'),[13]
- Ministerial Order no 930 of 19 November 2002 ('MO930'),[14]
- Ministerial Order no 1254 of 14 December 2004 ('MO1254'),[15]
- Ministerial Order no 653 of 3 July 2003 ('MO653'),[16]
- Ministerial Order no 668 of 10 July 2003 ('MO668'),[17]
- Ministerial Order no 569 of 18 June 2004 ('MO569').[18]

---

7   *TDC*
8   Concerning Competitive Conditions and Consumer Interests in the Telecommunications Market (*Lov om konkurrence- og forbrugerforhold på telemarkedet*).
9   Concerning Radio Frequencies (*Lov om radiofrekvenser*).
10   Concerning Cable Laying Access and Expropriation etc for Telecommunications Purposes (*Lov om graveadgang og ekspropriation m.v. til telekommunikationsformål*).
11   Concerning the Establishment and Joint Utilisation of Masts for Radio Communication Purposes etc (*Lov om etablering og fælles udnyttelse af master til radiokommunikationsformål m.v.*).
12   Concerning Standards for the Broadcasting of Television Signals, etc (*Lov om standarder for transmission af TV-signaler, m.v.*).
13   Concerning Provision of Telecommunications Networks and Telecommunications Services (*Bekendtgørelse om udbud af elektroniske kommunikationsnet- og tjenester*).
14   Concerning Interconnection, etc (*Bekendtgørelse om samtrafik, m.v.*).
15   Concerning USO Services (*Bekendtgørelse om forsyningspligt ydelser*).
16   Concerning the Overall Danish Numbering Plan (*Bekendtgørelse om den samlede danske nummerplan*).
17   Concerning Consultation Procedures and Cross-border Conflict Resolution in the Interconnection Area, etc (*Bekendtgørelse om høringsprocedurer og grænseoverskridende konfliktløsning på samtrafikområdet m.v*).
18   Concerning the Activities of the Telecommunications Complaints Board (*Bekendtgørelse om Teleklagenævnets virksomhed*).

- Ministerial Order no 1078/2003 of 11 December 2003 ('MO1078'),[19] and
- Ministerial Order no 1266 of 10 December 2004 ('MO1266').[20]

9.7   The emphasis is on individual decisions, primarily by the Agency, based on findings resulting from market analyses. A basic premise of the regulatory approach is that commercial agreements take priority over regulatory intervention.[21]

REGULATORY PRINCIPLES: IMPLEMENTATION OF THE FRAMEWORK DIRECTIVE

Scope of Regulation

9.8   Definitions of the two key terms 'electronic communications network' and 'electronic communications service' contained in L679 determine the scope of its applicability. Electronic communication networks are defined as '... any form of radio or cable-based telecommunications infrastructure used for handling electronic communications services ... between network termination points ...'.[22] Electronic communication services are defined as '... services that consist wholly or partly in electronic conveyance of communications ... by means of radio or telecommunications techniques, between network termination points ...'.[23]

9.9   'Associated facilities' are not defined separately, but is likely to be interpreted as defined by Article 8(2) Access Directive. A reference is included in the opening paragraph of L679 giving its purpose as '... to promote the establishment of a well-functioning, competitive market for provision of electronic communication networks or services *and associated facilities* ...'.[24] No interpretational assistance is provided by the current practice of the Agency.

9.10   Voice over Internet Protocol Services ('VoIP') are covered by the same regulatory framework as other electronic communications.

National Regulatory Authorities: Organisation, Regulatory Objectives, Competencies

9.11   The National IT and Telecom Agency[25] ('the Agency') is responsible for administration of all telecommunication laws in Denmark. The Agency's tasks include supervision, ensuring compliance with legislation, decision making, conciliation, promotion of competition, and consumer protection. The Agency is a part of the Ministry for Science, Technology and Innovation ('the Ministry'). All telecommunications-related issues fall within the jurisdiction of the Ministry. The

---

19   Concerning Digital Radio and Television Services, etc (*Bekendtgørelse om digitale radio og TV-tjenester, m.v.*).
20   Concerning Use of Radio Frequencies without a Licence (*Bekendtgørelse om anvendelse af radiofrekvenser uden tilladelse, m.v.*).
21   Expressed e g in L679 s 41(1).
22   L679 s 3(1).
23   L679 s 3(2).
24   Emphasis added.
25   *IT- og Telestyrelsen.*

Agency is charged with overseeing all aspects of the telecommunications regulations save for certain competition-related issues.[26]

9.12   The Minister is authorised to define by regulation what decisions by the Agency may be subjected to extended consultation procedures and the conduct of such procedures. MO668 contains the resulting detailed regulations. The Agency is specifically required to apply the procedures outlined in Articles 6 and 7 Framework Directive as part of the extended consultation procedure. Other Directive requirements relating to consultation procedures have also been implemented by L679 (notably Articles 3(4) and 3(5) Framework Directive).

9.13   The Competition Authority,[27] and in particular the Competition Council,[28] interacts with the Agency as part of a range of consultative measures in matters involving competition issues. The Agency must consult and obtain binding opinions from the Competition Council on issues involving the Competition Act.[29] The Agency and the Competition Authority/Competition Council are independent of one another, the Competition Authority being responsible for the administration of Danish competition and merger policies.[30] The Competition Authority is part of the Danish Ministry for Economic and Business Affairs.

9.14   The powers and duties of the Agency and the Competition Authority are consistent with the requirements of the 2002 EU Regulatory Package and EU competition regulation. Both are vested with powers to demand information from undertakings in certain defined circumstances. The Agency can impose fines for failure to comply with statutory requirements for provision of information.[31]

9.15   The Agency has a duty to publish information concerning telecommunication sector issues, e g comparisons of prices charged by service providers. Comparative studies of this kind are published regularly and are available on the Agency website as well as in print.[32]

9.16   The Agency has sweeping powers to conduct market analyses and consultations that must be conducted in co-operation with the Competition Authority where appropriate and expedient.

9.17   L679, Part 18, governs 'supervision, mediation and specification of interconnection prices etc', granting the Agency powers to decide in such matters. The Telecommunications Consumer Board ('TCB')[33] is charged with supervising the resolution of certain types of disputes.[34] These include e g the Agency's decisions concerning compliance by universal service providers with their duties.

---

26   See para 9.13 below.
27   '*Konkurrencestyrelsen*'.
28   '*Konkurrencerådet*'.
29   Eg L679 s 19 and s 79.
30   Eg the Danish Competition Act and EU-based regulations concerning public offerings and governmental subsidies.
31   L679 s 112.
32   L679 s 74 (2).
33   '*Telebrugernævnet*'.
34   L679 s 96.

Right of Appeal against NRA's Decisions

9.18   Decisions by the Agency are subject to administrative review either by the TCB or the Telecommunications Complaints Board ('TCCB'),[35] depending on the nature of the decision concerned. Decisions by the TCB and TCCB may be challenged before a court of law. The TCB and TCCB hold extensive powers to demand information deemed necessary to discharge their duties and to facilitate their handling of specific complaints. The duties of the TCCB include reviewing complaints about the Agency's decision-making. Part 27 of L679 sets out these duties, and the detailed rules for dispute resolution are contained in MO569.

The NRA's Obligation to Cooperate with the Commission

9.19   The consolidation procedure provided for by Article 7 Framework Directive has not been directly restated in Danish law. L679 provides for a consultation procedure in matters involving the imposition of obligations (other than provided for by L679 s. 51) on SMP undertakings for which the consent of the Commission is required.[36] The Agency must take account of the Commission Recommendations on relevant markets and is also required to take account of the Commission Guidelines on market[37] analyses when assessing questions of dominant position.[38]

9.20   The telecommunications legislation include specific provisions reflecting the Commission's power to issue standards and specifications as is apparent in L662 and L681.[39] Both impose obligations on the Agency to notify relevant authorities about the Commission's specifications issued pursuant to Article 19 Framework Directive. L679 s. 50 provides that technical or operational conditions imposed by the Agency must comply with standardisation rules referred to in Article 17 Framework Directive.

'Significant Market Power' as a Fundamental Prerequisite to Regulation

Definition of SMP

9.21   Significant market power is defined in the same terms as in the Access Directive.[40]

9.22   Determination of whether an undertaking has SMP status requires a market analysis by the Agency, leading to the identification of relevant markets appropriate to Danish circumstances. L679 contains detailed provisions governing these procedures, including s. 84 d (3) pursuant to which the assessment of whether two or more undertakings are in a joint dominant position in a particular market or closely related markets must be made in accordance with Community law, taking into account the Commission Guidelines on market analysis and the assessment of significant market power as well as Annex II Framework Directive.

---

35   'Teleklagenævnet'.
36   L679 s 96.
37   L679, part 20b – dealing with market analyses and competition law issues.
38   L679 a. 84a and s 84b.
39   See para 9.6 above.
40   L679 s 84d (2).

Definition of relevant markets and SMP designation

9.23   At regular intervals the Agency must carry out market analyses to facilitate decisions involving the regulation of SMP undertakings.[41]

9.24   Determination of what are the relevant markets may be carried out in cooperation with the NRAs of other Member States where the Commission has identified a transnational market.[42]

9.25   The delineation of relevant markets should follow the Commission Recommendation on relevant markets[43] and include criteria outlined in the Commission Guidelines on market analysis.

9.26   A detailed report on competition in the Danish telecommunications market was published by the Agency in 2003. The report is based on extensive consultations with market players and identifies a number of barriers to efficient competition. Further consultations with operators have led to the identification of 18 different markets, 17 of which are currently under investigation by the Agency. These include markets identified by the European Commission.

9.27   A collation of data across the telecommunications industry was completed in April 2004. The Agency is still analysing the information collated and will conduct consultations with the industry in due course, to be followed by consultations with the Danish Competition Authority. Once the consultations have been completed draft decisions concerning eg SMP status in specific markets will be prepared. The process has not led to in any specific regulatory initiatives by the Agency so far.

9.28   Only the former monopoly provider, TDC, is deemed to have SMP status in certain markets. No other service providers have been found to have SMP status in specific markets, but competition in certain cellular networks is considered insufficient.

9.29   The Agency has the authority to impose specific remedies on SMP undertakings if considered necessary. The remedies relate to eg pricing, access to markets or prohibition of competition limiting measures, retail pricing and control of fee levels.[44] Similar powers are available vis-à-vis undertakings that are not found to have SMP status in certain circumstances, eg providers who control access to end users.[45]

NRA's Regulatory Duties concerning Rights of Way, Co-location and Facility Sharing

Rights of way

9.30   Anyone providing or operating public electronic communications networks is entitled to:

- *Open or use public roads to establish infrastructure:* The relevant road authority must be notified four weeks in advance of commencing such work,

---

41   L679 s 84a.
42   See para 1.76 above.
43   See paras 1.72 and 1.76 above.
44   See paras 9.57–9.66 below and L679 s21a.
45   L679 s 51 and s 44; see para 9.70 below.

regardless of whether it is an overground or underground structure, construction or maintenance of infrastructure under or along public roads or railway sites.[46] Consent of the relevant road authority is required.[47] Cables or other infrastructure facilities installed must be registered with the Land Register.[48] The operator must pay compensation to the landowner concerned and cover the cost of repairs or reinstatement of the road concerned.[49]

- *Relocation of infrastructure:* Anyone undertaking work to carry out construction or digging work that may disturb or damage underground cables must notify the cable owners no later than 8 days before commencing works that may affect the cable.[50] Costs associated with relocation of infrastructure are generally payable by the infrastructure owner.[51]

Co-location and facility sharing

9.31

L681 provides for a particular form of right of way involving joint utilisation of masts erected for radio (including mobile) communications purposes and the mounting of antenna systems on masts, buildings and other high structures. Owners have a statutory duty to accommodate requests for joint utilisation. This includes joint use of associated buildings, but only to the extent that joint utilisation is possible and there are no technical obstacles to the same. The rules apply if the property is not already being fully utilised. Authority to impose obligations on owners, leaseholders or those who hold rights of use rest with the local municipal authorities who may issue an order for access to joint utilisation. Initial installation of antenna systems etc will require permission from the local municipal council.

Expropriation

9.32   Expropriation is also available to facilitate installation of telecommunications networks. The Agency has power to initiate compulsory expropriation of land in accordance with the Danish Expropriations Act when 'required for the public good' to facilitate the construction, expansion and/or alteration of public electronic communications networks.[52] The Agency has power to initiate expropriation at the request of providers of public electronic communications networks. Expropriation should, however, only take place where no other options are open to establish underground cables as part of such networks, and the cables must be of significant importance to the provision of networks or services. Where no exceptional circumstances exist, network providers must negotiate a mutually satisfactory agreement with the landowners concerned, whether public or private.

9.33   The Expropriations Commission may impose obligations on network providers concerning alignment or securing of cables if the landowner demonstrates

---

46   L682 s 1(7).
47   L671 of 19 August 1999, (L671) concerning Public Roads, s 101, and L670 of 19 August 1999, (L670) s 50–51.
48   L662 s 6.
49   L662 s 7.
50   L662 s 5.
51   L671 s 106 and L670 s 52.
52   L662, s.1.

that it is necessary to permit him to commence construction work or to allow him the proper use of his property. Network providers shall be entitled to access to reside in public or private areas to the extent required for the laying of cables or performance of services or repairs, subject to paying compensation for any inconvenience or damage caused.

9.34   L681[53] contains similar provisions concerning expropriation as L662.[54] Expropriation under L681 is only available to licensed operators of radio based telecommunications infrastructure as part of public electronic telecommunications networks or services or providing national radio or television coverage through terrestrial networks.

REGULATION OF MARKET ENTRY: IMPLEMENTATION OF THE AUTHORISATION DIRECTIVE

The General Authorisation of Electronic Communications

9.35   No individual licence or authorisation is required to provide telecommunication networks and services or to establish and operate fixed or mobile networks. Networks and services may be provided on the terms set out in MO638.[55] A service provider is does not need a licence to provide or establish services or infrastructure covered by MO638. No action need be taken, no decision from the Agency need be awaited prior to launching a service, and no specific payment is required. Operators of mobile communications services must, however, obtain authorisation to use the (radio) frequencies concerned prior to commencing operations. No notifications are required.

Rights of Use for Radio Frequencies

General authorisation and granting of individual rights

9.36   The authorisation regime applicable to the use of radio frequencies is governed by L680. The Minister must issue a spectrum policy framework mandate containing guidelines for the general prioritisation of frequencies in Denmark. The most recent one was issued in 2004.[56] The mandate is renewed annually. The Agency prepares a nationwide frequency plan based on the mandate and international and EU frequency co-operation.

9.37   The use of radio frequencies requires a licence issued by the Agency save where express exemption is available, e g under MO1266.[57] Acquiring the right to use a particular radio frequency requires an application to be made to the Agency. The Agency will either issue licences on a 'first come first serve' basis or successively, provided sufficient spectrum is available within the relevant frequency band to satisfy requirements. If, on the other hand, there is a frequency scarcity, licences

---

53   L681, part 4.
54   See para 9.32 above.
55   General obligations include access to: the national emergency number; service providers' text phone service and related emergency numbers; at least one national call based directory enquiry service and a call based charge information facility.
56   MO no 142 of 3 March 2004.
57   See para 9.6 above.

may either be issued following the implementation of a public tender procedure or, alternatively, based on an auction of licences.[58]

Admissible conditions

9.38   The terms and conditions the Agency may specify for the use of a frequency licence may include[59] requirements:

- relating to radio engineering,
- aimed at avoiding interference,
- aimed at realising international and EU frequency co-operation,
- restricting the geographical extension of the application area of the licence, and
- aimed at meeting broader societal needs.

9.39   Licences for the use of radio frequencies will generally be limited in time.[60] Licences become effective on the day they are issued. On expiry of a licence, the licensee will be obliged to apply for a new licence. An annual fee (calculated on an individual basis for each type of licence) for the use radio of frequencies is payable by the licensee.

9.40   Licences have thus far been granted for the following wave band communication types:

- TETRA – Terrestrial Truncated Radio,[61]
- FWA – Fixed Wireless Access,[62]
- GSM – Global System for Mobile Communication,
- DCS1800 – Digital Cellular System,[63]
- POCSAG – Post Office Code Standardisation Advisory Group,[64] and
- 3G – Third Generation Mobile network.

Limitation of number of rights of use to be granted

9.41   The number of rights of use to be granted may be limited by the Agency in case of an existing or imminent frequency scarcity. L680 authorises the Minister to determine whether to initiate public tenders or auctions as the basis for issuing licences where a shortage is deemed to prevail. Auctions are conducted by the Agency.[65] Following a decision to initiate an auction or public tender the Minister must issue detailed rules in each case.

9.42   Only one auction has been held to date (for 3G frequencies) for which a separate act was passed. An auction of a regional FWA licence in 2003/2004 was a renewed auction of a licence originally awarded in 2000 that was returned to the Agency in October 2002. A re-auction of a 3G licence planned for May 2005 is still pending.

---

58   L680 s 6.
59   Time limits are fixed either as applied for, or to the application year plus five years or ten years L680 part 4, particularly s 11.
60   L680 s 16.
61   A public digital network for specific emergency and relief work.
62   A public wireless subscriber network.
63   Pan-European system, based on second generation GSM technology.
64   Public paging system.
65   L680 s 6–8.

Frequency trading

9.43   The transfer of licences to others is permitted, provided always that the licensee must obtain the approval of the Agency prior to the actual transfer. So-called indirect transfers (e g transfer of shares, stock or other ownership interests that involve a change of control over the licensee) will also require prior approval by the Agency.[66] Changes to the number of frequencies or the number of facilities covered by a licence will require a renewed application to the Agency.

Rights of Use for Numbers

9.44   The administration and allocation of Danish numbering resources is managed by the Agency and governed by L679 and secondary legislation. Rights of use for numbers are granted by the Agency in accordance with part 3 of MO653. Numbers may only be used in accordance with the National Numbering Plan.[67]

9.45   The Agency grants numbers and number series upon application. It is not possible to reserve specific numbers or number series. Operators obtain the rights specified in their individual authorisation. The agency may lay down specific terms for the allocation of numbers, eg

- specify what services the numbers may be used for and requirements associated with such services,
- actual, effective and efficient use must be made of the numbers concerned,
- fix a deadline for commencing use of numbers, and
- specify maximum validity of the numbers allocated.

9.46   Numbers and number series cannot be assigned or transferred to other providers without prior approval by the Agency. The Agency may withdraw or replace numbers or number series in certain circumstances, and providers may return number resources to the Agency. To retain ownership of numbers or number series, the title holder must pay an annual fee to the Agency. The undertaking that acquired the rights of use remains liable for the payment of the annual fee to the Agency.

9.47   All obligations relating to number portability and carrier pre-selection/ indirect access required by article 18(3) Authorisation Directive referring to the Universal Service Directive have been incorporated into L679 in virtually identical terms.[68]

The NRA's Enforcement Powers

9.48   The Agency has extensive powers to demand, from all undertakings whose activities are governed (in full or in part) by L679, such information as the Agency deems relevant to enable it to discharge its duties as national regulatory authority.

9.49   The Agency has authority to obtain court orders and initiate searches of physical premises as part of its technical investigations to obtain information in specific cases, or as part of its supervision of compliance with rules on consumer and universal service aspects, or as part of random checks, either of its own volition

---

66   L680 s 18.
67   Numbers are divided into three segments.
68   L679, part 9, s 35–37.

or at the request of eg the TCB. The Agency may ultimately impose fines, revoke appointments and/or licences, and issue orders and revoke status as universal service providers.[69]

9.50   The Agency may set a time limit for compliance with orders issued, impose terms and conditions for the grant of licences, either directly or through one of the complaints boards responsible for overseeing specific areas of the telecommunications sector. Furthermore, the Agency may impose interim measures either as part of a dispute resolution procedure[70] or in connection with temporary measures relating to eg interconnection agreements where the parties have been unable to reach agreement on all pertinent terms.[71] The Agency's interim measures or decisions remain in force until such time as the Agency makes its final decision in the matter. The tiered enforcement procedure provided for by article 10 Authorisation Directive has thus been incorporated into Danish law.[72]

Administrative Charges and Fees for Rights of Use

9.51   Revenues collected from licences for use of radio frequencies and allocated numbers contribute towards the costs of operating the Agency, being its primary source of funding. All applicable fees are fixed annually as part of the Finance Act and published by way of Ministerial Order, ensuring a transparent fee structure. The charges are collected by the Agency and are generally payable at the beginning of each year. No general administrative fees apply at present.

REGULATION OF NETWORK ACCESS AND INTERCONNECTION: IMPLEMENTATION OF THE ACCESS DIRECTIVE

Objectives and Scope of Access Regulation

9.52   The opening section of L679 outlines the objectives for the activities of the Agency's regulation of access and interconnection.[73] It is a basic principle that interconnection agreements must be concluded on commercial terms.[74] The obligation to negotiate relates only to interconnection, whereas the obligation of operators to submit offers relates to both access and interconnection. It is, however, only operators of public communications networks on whom the Agency has imposed specific obligations concerning interconnection who have a duty to offer access and interconnection contracts to other undertakings on terms and conditions consistent with the obligations imposed.[75]

---

69   L679, s 111.
70   Eg mediation under part 18 of L679.
71   Eg in relation to terms and conditions, pricing issues etc.
72   L680.
73   Ensuring all providers of electronic communications networks or services real and non-discriminatory opportunities to negotiate agreements eg concerning interconnection; permitting number portability; ensuring correct routing; ensuring non-SMP undertakings may obtain a real competitive margin through price regulation and lack of prize squeezing; and ensuring balanced competition between service and infrastructure providers.
74   L679 s 41(1).
75   See paras 9.57–9.66 below.

9.53   Access and interconnection related provisions of L679 apply to operators of public communications networks and services and to undertakings seeking interconnection and/or access to their networks or associated facilities. Danish regulation of SMP undertakings applies equally to operators in the fixed and mobile markets.

Basic Regulatory Concepts

9.54   The Agency's extensive regulatory powers in matters involving access and interconnection are primarily enshrined in L679. The Agency is authorised to intervene either on its own initiative or at the request of the parties, where commercial negotiations have failed and necessary agreement has not been reached. Overall, the Agency is charged with overseeing and regulating, where necessary, all issues relating to interconnection.[76]

9.55   Even though L679 does not contain a specific definition of interconnection, it operates on the basis of the same definitions of access and interconnection as the Access Directive. L679 s. 40 (implementing articles 2 and 12 Access Directive) outlines various types of interconnection products subject to regulation. L679 treats interconnection products as wholesale products being traded between service providers. The Agency determines the scope of each interconnection product as part of its determination of the possible imposition of universal service obligations under L679 s. 51.[77]

9.56   Access is not, strictly speaking, defined by L679 either, but as part of the determination of the scope of the provisions governing interconnection, s. 40(1) refers to 'access to or the making available of, facilities or services for another provider for the purpose of providing electronic communications services'.

Access- and Interconnection-related Obligations with Respect to SMP Undertakings

Overview

9.57   On identification of an SMP undertaking the Agency has a duty to impose one or more of the obligations detailed below.[78] Determination of precisely what obligation(s) to impose is left to the discretion of the Agency. Obligations thus imposed will remain in force until such time as the Agency withdraws them. This will only occur when SMP status no longer prevails.

9.58   The Agency operates on terms which are virtually identical to those described in articles 9–13 Access Directive and the reasons given in the recitals to the directive.[79] There are few respects in which it differs from the Access Directive.

---

76   See paras 9.57–9.66 below.
77   Interconnection products include eg: Access to and linking of network elements (eg unbundled access to local loop) and associated facilities; physical infrastructure; fixed and mobile communications networks (including roaming); virtual network access; wholesale purchase of services for resale purposes, and open access to indispensable interoperability services and services indispensable for the interoperability of the above services.
78   See paras 9.62–9.66 below.
79   See paras 1.137–1.155 above.

Where this is the case, the Danish regulations and the powers granted to the Agency are more extensive than required by the Access Directive.[80]

9.59   Obligations imposed must be appropriate and proportionate to the specific problem identified.[81] The Agency may impose one or more of the obligations described below on SMP undertakings.[82]

9.60   The Agency is furthermore authorised to impose other obligations on SMP undertakings in exceptional circumstances but only following consultations with and approval from the European Commission of such measures.[83]

9.61   The emphasis of the regulatory scheme is on individual decisions based on findings resulting from market analyses. Market analyses are in some cases still ongoing or hardly completed. So far, the Agency has imposed obligations on TDC, the only designated SMP undertaking in the fixed networks market. A proposal relating to termination markets requiring five non-SMP undertakings to grant access to their markets is pending.

9.62   Where an obligation to accommodate reasonable requests for access to interconnection has been imposed, requests may only be refused if the feasibility of technical interconnection or a special need to preserve the integrity of a network is deemed to exist. A refusal can be referred to the Agency for review. Similarly, the reasonableness of an applicant's request for specific types of access may be referred to the Agency by the SMP undertaking.

Transparency obligations and accounting separation obligations

9.63   Includes a duty to publish pertinent information and prepare separate accounts for each specific activity that forms part of interconnection. The transparency and accounting separation obligations are identical to those contained in articles 9 and 11(1) Access Directive.

Non-discrimination obligations and reference offers

9.64   The non-discrimination obligations the Agency may apply are identical to those described in the EU chapter,[84] eg a duty to grant competitors the same terms as those applied to the undertaking itself or its subsidiaries. The Agency may also impose an obligation to publish reference offers to ensure that they do not contain requirements for services to be rendered in return for executing or modifying agreements. The latter remedy is over and above those provided for by the Access Directive. It serves to ensure availability of access to unbundled services and that parties on whom obligations have been imposed do not shift the onus of the obligations to a party requesting access.

Specific access obligations

9.65   Involves a duty to accommodate reasonable requests for access to interconnection, including access to interconnection product(s), negotiate agreements in good faith and maintain access to the facilities concerned.

---

80   See e g para 9.64 below.
81   L679 s 51(4).
82   L679 s 51 (3) and s 51a-51g. See paras 9.62–9.66 below.
83   L679 s 76a.
84   See para 1.144 above.

Price control obligations and accounting obligations

9.66   Involves a duty to ensure cost based pricing[85] and a duty to use specific cost accounting systems to support price controls. The price control and cost accounting obligations have both been incorporated in Danish law in virtually identical terms.

Related Regulatory Powers with Respect to SMP Undertakings

9.67   The Agency has a duty to impose obligations on SMP providers of the minimum set of leased lines provided for by article 18 Universal Services Directive. The Danish regulatory framework[86] is identical to the Universal Service Directive[87] and Exhibit II to the 1992 ONP Directive.[88]

9.68   Carrier pre-selection obligations may be imposed only on undertakings with SMP status in the markets for provision of connection to and use of public telephone networks and from a fixed location. The Danish regulations are identical in terms and scope to article 19 Universal Services Directive.[89]

9.69   Mobile operators with SMP status may be required to enable the subscribers to access the services of interconnected providers, either on a call-by-call basis or by means of pre-selection, provided the Agency determines that it is necessary to impose such a duty. In case of a fixed network operator the duty to provide free carrier (pre-)selection follows automatically from its SMP status.

Regulatory Powers Applicable to All Market Participants

Obligations to ensure end-to-end connectivity

9.70   To ensure end-to-end connectivity, the Agency may impose obligations on providers/operators who control access to end-users similar to those that may be imposed on SMP undertakings in relation to interconnection agreements, including in exceptional circumstances an obligation to connect their networks. Article 5(1)(a) Access Directive is implemented by L679 s. 44 specifying the nature of the obligations that may be imposed on such service providers by a blanket reference to L679 s. 51.

Access to digital radio and television broadcasting services

9.71   Part 20a of L679 implements Access Directive requirements[90] concerning access to digital broadcasting services. The obligations that may be imposed on multiplex operators, regardless of their market power, are regulated by MO1078[91]

---

85   Art 13 Access Directive.
86   L679, s.21 a and s.21b.
87   See para 1.176 above.
88   Exhibit II to Directive 1992/44, as amended and Exhibit VII to the Access Directive.
89   See para 1.177 above.
90   Arts 4(2), 5(1)(b), 6(1), 7(3)(b)(i) and Annex 1 to Access Directive.
91   Pursuant to L679 s 83 b; see paras 9.80–9.82 below.

as envisaged by L679 s 83 b. Additional regulation is contained in L664.[92] The Agency is may impose additional obligations on SMP undertakings.[93]

9.72   Rules issued by the Agency governing conditional access systems must be based on article 6(1) and Part 1 Annex 1 Access Directive (and subsequent amendments).

9.73   The Agency has discretionary powers to initiate market analyses in the broadcasting and conditional access sectors. Previously imposed obligations may only be amended or withdrawn where this will not adversely affect effective competition in the relevant market or accessibility for end-users.

9.74   The Agency may issue orders to multiplex operators, providers of conditional access systems and services and holders of industrial property rights to bring conditions into conformity with the Agency's rules for such activities where a breach is found to have occurred.[94]

REGULATION OF UNIVERSAL SERVICES AND USERS' RIGHTS: THE UNIVERSAL SERVICE DIRECTIVE

Regulation of Universal Service Obligations

Scope of universal service obligations

9.75   The purpose of appointing universal service providers is designated as '... ensuring end-users access to basic electronic communications services on reasonable terms and at reasonable prices'.[95] Universal service obligations include the provision of:

- Basic voice telephony services,[96]
- ISDN services or other electronic communications service capable of providing at least the same basic functions,[97]
- Leased lines (expressly exempting broadband networks),[98]
- Special universal service obligations to designated groups of disabled people,[99]
- An exhaustive national number directory, a national directory enquiry service and a comprehensive directory enquiry service for international numbers,[100]
- Emergency and security communication via public radio based maritime emergency and security services covering Denmark and Greenland.[101]

9.76   Appointed universal service providers have a duty to supply or offer all of the above services to anyone applying for them, at prices that do not exceed certain tariff levels fixed by the Agency (this may include obligations to provide services free of charge), and on the terms imposed by Agency.

---

92   Concerning standards for broadcasting of television signals, etc.
93   Over and above those available pursuant to L679 s 83a.
94   L679 s 83 d.
95   L679 s 16.
96   MO1254 s 2 and Exhibit 1.
97   MO1254 s 3
98   MO1254 s 4.
99   MO1254 s 5–7.
100   MO1254 s 8 and L679 s 34.
101   MO1254 s 9.

Designation of undertakings obliged to provide universal services

9.77   The designation procedures[102] authorise the Agency to determine whether providers need be appointed universal service providers, and if so, what obligations need be imposed. It has been left to the discretion of the Agency to fix the terms on which the appointed universal service providers must undertake their obligations.

9.78   The Minister may issue detailed regulations governing the Agency's handling of the appointment and applicable terms (e g by public tender). These include the terms of an appointment; the basis on which the Agency may fix such terms; and content requirements for the terms designated.[103] MO1254 s. 11–13 provides the framework for the appointment of universal service providers.

9.79   TDC is the only undertaking whose status as SMP undertaking has currently been established. Five others are being considered for SMP undertaking status in different markets at the moment. This will not likely affect the universal service obligations of TDC.

Regulation of retail tariffs, users' expenditures and quality of service

9.80   The Agency determines tariff regulation based on proposals from the universal service provider concerned. The proposals are not binding on the Agency. In fixing the maximum tariffs the Agency may not impose obligations that do not permit overall coverage of the costs incurred in supplying the services. The Minister may issue detailed rules governing maximum tariffs, setting the framework for the Agency's determination of the tariffs and the universal service provider's preparation of the underlying proposals. When drafting such rules, the Minister may include other considerations that closely reflect the contents and requirements of articles 9 and 10 Universal Services Directive.[104]

9.81   When fixing the maximum tariffs the Agency may obtain the opinion of the Competition Council concerning whether the proposals prepared by the service provider comply with competition law requirements. The opinion will be binding on the Agency.[105]

9.82   Universal service providers are entitled to coverage of any overall losses incurred as a result of the obligation to offer the universal service, subject to providing satisfactory proof of such losses.[106] The proof is assessed by the Agency. The Agency's decision may trigger an obligation for networks and service providers[107] to jointly contribute towards the financing of universal service providers' losses. The Agency's powers include authority to fix and collect such contributions. A universal service provider must also contribute towards the losses, provided he is also a provider of other universal services. Rules governing calculation of contributions towards losses are fixed as part of the Finance Act and published by the Agency. The Agency may determine to initiate a public tender process with a view to appointing one or more universal service providers.

---

102   L679 s 17.
103   Eg quality requirements; assessment procedures and publication of their findings, etc.
104   See paras 1.165–1.168 above.
105   The opinion must be given within one month of request.
106   L679 s 20.
107   Of public electronic communications services and networks.

Regulation of Retail Markets

Prerequisites for the regulation of retail markets

9.83   The Universal Service Directive principle that regulation of retail services is only permissible if regulation at wholesale level does not achieve the regulatory objectives is enshrined in L679 s. 21a. Identification of an undertaking as an SMP undertaking means that the Agency may impose obligations relating to retail markets on the undertaking only if the Agency takes the view that obligations to provide free carrier selection[108] and interconnection[109] are insufficient to ensure compliance with the underlying objectives of L679.

Regulatory powers

9.84   L 679 s. 22–24 specify the supervisory duties of the Agency and specific remedies against failure by a universal service provider to comply with applicable rules, prescribed terms and obligations imposed by the Agency.

9.85   L679 contains several provisions authorising the Agency to take action that mirrors the powers provided for by article 17 Authorisation Directive. The Agency may issue orders requiring service providers to comply with existing rules, prescribed terms, maximum prices, obligations imposed, etc, or modify existing contract and subscription terms or require a provider to comply with contract and subscription terms. The Agency may impose fines the levels of which may vary according to the nature of the infringement.[110]

9.86   Obligations relating to control of individual tariffs, including requirements that tariffs be oriented towards costs or prices in comparable markets[111] may be imposed, and the Agency must impose obligations on providers of the minimum set of leased lines, provided the undertaking in question has been found to have SMP status. The obligations imposed must reflect the requirements of article 18(1) Universal Service Directive.

End User Rights

Contracts

9.87   Service providers have a duty to enter into end user contracts.[112] Minimum requirements for services provided by electronic communications networks and service providers include a basic requirement entitling end-users to a contract that meets specific minimum requirements.[113] This ensures consumer protection. The statutory rights are detailed in MO638 ensuring that a contract must include the minimum information outlined in article 20(2) Universal Services Directive. There is no statutory requirement that such contracts need to be in writing, although in practice they tend to be.

---

108   L679 s 35.
109   L679, part IV.
110   L679 s 112.
111   L679 s 51f.
112   S 10(2) L679 and article 20 Universal Service Directive.
113   L679 s 10 and MO638.

9.88   Disputes relating to billing complaints must be addressed to the service provider initially. Complaints must be dealt with and findings notified to the customer within three months of the initial complaint. The service provider's decision can be referred to the Agency for resolution of the complaint. If the Agency's findings do not satisfy the end-user, the matter may be referred to the TCCB. The complainant must pay a nominal fee.

9.89   Complaints concerning other matters may be lodged with the Agency.[114] The findings of the Agency in such matters may be referred to the TCCB for administrative review. This will involve payment of a nominal fee.

9.90   Undertakings have a statutory duty provide to information on tariffs, terms and quality of service specified in article 21, Annex 2 Universal Service Directive to end users.[115] The Agency may require providers of electronic communications networks or services and others to provide information that the Agency deems relevant to discharge its supervisory duties under L679. The Agency must prepare and publish at regular intervals statistics and documentation concerning issues that the Agency deems relevant.[116]

Other obligations

9.91   The additional obligations described in Articles 23 and 25–29 Universal Service Directive[117] have all been implemented in Danish law, primarily in L679.

DATA PROTECTION: IMPLEMENTATION OF THE E-PRIVACY DIRECTIVE

Confidentiality of Communications

9.92   Service and network providers are required to ensure the confidentiality of communications by taking appropriate technical and organisational precautions to safeguard the security of their services (if necessary in conjunction with the relevant network operators). The obligations are described in detail below.[118]

9.93   An exception to the generally applicable principle of prohibition on interception or surveillance of communications is included in L679 s. 15. This exception provides that the police must be allowed access to interception and surveillance of communications for investigatory purposes, provided the requirements of the Danish Administration of Justice Act[119] are complied with. Storage to convey communications is also excepted, without prejudice to the principle of confidentiality.

---

114   Includes complaints about non-compliance by SMP Undertakings or universal service providers, insufficient information from a service provider, or a universal service provider's failure to deliver as required.
115   MO638 s 5.
116   L679 s 107a.
117   See paras 1.183–1.188 above.
118   See paras 9.99, 9.101 and 9.103 below.
119   Act no 961 of 21 September 2004 ('*Retsplejeloven*') and the European Convention on Mutual Assistance in Criminal matters between Member States of the European Union, 2000/197.

9.94 Access to or storage of information on a subscriber's/user's terminal equipment and the processing of such information require express consent.[120] The information to be provided based on which the consent is to be given must be clear and comprehensive. It is an offence to use an electronic communications network to store information or gain access to information stored in a user's terminal equipment (eg by means of 'cookies') without first providing clear and comprehensive information regarding the intention, scope and purpose of processing. An exception to this prohibition is for technical storage or access for the sole purpose of transmitting a communication or providing services expressly requested by the subscriber/user.

Traffic Data and Location Data

9.95 The definitions of 'traffic data' and 'location data' are in identical terms to those contained in the E-Privacy Directive.[121]

9.96 Subscribers must always be advised of the types of data processed and the duration of such processing.

9.97 Service providers are permitted to store and process traffic data for the purpose of billing subscribers and invoicing for interconnection.[122] Such data may only be retained for the period of time during which the bill may be lawfully challenged and payment pursued (or the completion of any legal proceedings initiated during that time).

9.98 Traffic data must be erased or anonymised when it is no longer required for the purpose of transmitting communications. Subject to obtaining consent, operators may process data for the purpose of marketing electronic communications services or providing value added services. Consent may be withdrawn at any time.

9.99 Location data may only be processed by service providers if the subscriber's/user's consent has been obtained or the data have been anonymised[123] and only to the extent and for the period required to deliver a value added service. Consent may be withdrawn at any time.

9.100 Service providers must offer to provide, free of charge, either itemised bills[124] or tariff specific invoices.[125] Specified bills prepared in connection with complaints must always be offered free of charge.

Calling and Connected Line Identification

9.101 Service providers offering calling line identification services must permit users to withhold their numbers on a per-call and per-line basis, free of charge. The same applies to facilitating the blocking of numbers of incoming calls and rejecting

---

120 Act no 429 of 31 May 2000 ('*Persondataloven*') ('L429'), the Act on Processing of Personal Data, s 6.
121 MO638, s 2(3) and 2(4).
122 MO638, s 28(2).
123 MO638, s 29(1).
124 MO638, s 24.
125 MO638, s 19.

incoming calls automatically where the caller has withheld identification.[126] The service may be suspended temporarily during a police investigation of suspected malicious or nuisance calls. Calls to emergency services and law enforcement agencies are exempt.[127]

Automatic Call Forwarding

9.102   No later than six months after supply of services has commenced, service providers must offer their customers the right to request free of charge that automatically forwarded calls resulting from third party actions be discontinued.[128]

Directories of Subscribers

9.103   Anyone has the right to request not to be included in the telephone directory. Inclusion in the directory requires express consent from the individual concerned in relation not only to inclusion but also in relation to the nature of the personal data included.

Unsolicited Communications

9.104   Unsolicited communications are not covered by the telecommunications regulatory framework, but such communications are regulated by the marketing practices regulation.[129] The applicable rules apply to other forms of unsolicited communications besides e-mail.[130] A business that has obtained the electronic address of a customer in connection with sale of goods or services may market its own products or services in a similar manner. Customers must, however, be allowed to opt out in a simple manner free of charge. The trade association known as 'The Telecommunications industry in Denmark'[131] have not entered into any specific agreements among themselves or with the Agency concerning unsolicited communications. A set of voluntary guidelines *'Guidelines concerning good marketing practices in the telecommunications sector'*[132] came into force on 1 April 2005.

---

126   MO638, s 25 and 26.
127   MO638, s 27.
128   MO638, s 14 and 24.
129   Act no 699 of 17 July 2000 ('The Marketing Practices Act'), 'L699'.
130   Eg automatic call systems and telefax, L699 s 6a.
131   *'Telekommunikationsindustrien i Danmark'*.
132   *'Retningslinier om god markedsføringsskik på teleområdet'*.

The Estonian Market for Electronic Communications[1]

Attorney-at-law Pirkko-Liis Harkmaa
Law Office of Lepik & Luhaäär LAWIN

LEGAL STRUCTURE

Basic Policy

10.1 Estonia has a stable and well-developed electronic communications sector. Since regaining independence in the early 1990s, electronic communications have played a central role in the country's economic development. The lack of long-lasting traditions of trade and law that usually have a tendency to slow down innovation has contributed to the rapid spread of electronic and mobile communication in all fields of life, governance and business.

10.2 The telecoms market has been open to competition since 2001, when the exclusive rights of the incumbent national operator, Estonian Telecom (Eesti Telekom), expired. Unbundling is fully implemented and detailed regulation of access to telecoms networks is in place. Conditions have been created for the successful roll-out of 3G services and licences have already been issued to three national mobile operators.

10.3 The latest policy documents are 'The Basic Principles of the Estonian Information Policy for the years 2004–2006' with the sub-title 'Estonian IT Policy: Towards a More Service-Centered and Citizen-Friendly State' approved by the Government in May 2004 and 'The Information Policy Action Plan for 2005' developed by the Ministry of Economic Affairs and Communications and as approved by the Government in June 2004. As the Estonian information policy follows the objectives set out in the eEurope 2005 action plan and in other strategic documents of Europe, the priority fields of Estonian information policy are similar to those reflected in the eEurope 2005 action plan.

Implementation of EU Directives

10.4 By 1 May 2004 Estonia had transposed the main elements of the 1998 EU Regulatory Package into the Estonian Telecommunications Act that entered into

---

1   Editing of this chapter closed on 11 July 2005.

force in March 2000. Since 1 January 2005, the telecom market has been regulated by the new Electronic Communications Act ('ECA')[2] transposing the 2002 EU Regulatory Package.

Legislation

10.5   The main legislative act regulating the telecoms sector is the ECA that also requires the adoption of secondary legislation. Some secondary acts have been already adopted,[3] but a substantial amount is still in preparation. Pursuant to the ECA, however, the secondary acts adopted under the previous Telecommunications Act will remain in force until annulled, provided that they do not contradict the principles of the ECA. The main legal principles concerning the regulation of the telecoms market are contained in the ECA, and the secondary acts only describe certain requirements and procedures set out in the ECA in more detail.

10.6   The national regulatory agency – the Estonian National Communications Board ('ENCB') – has the right to issue individual administrative acts for performance of the duties provided under the ECA.[4] These acts could take the form of either administrative requests or decisions.

10.7   The ENCB however lacks the legal capacity to issue general executive acts that it would be required to issue under the Framework Directive to define the relevant markets in the field of telecoms, since these acts constitute a 'general act' within the meaning of the Estonian legal system, and these can only be issued by the institutions on or above the ministerial level. Therefore the ECA contains the list of certain pre-defined markets which can be changed only on the statutory level.

REGULATORY PRINCIPLES: IMPLEMENTATION OF THE FRAMEWORK DIRECTIVE

Scope of Regulation

10.8   After the enforcement of the ECA, regulation is not solely focused on 'telecoms networks and services', but on 'electronic communications networks and services' in general. As far as infrastructure and networks, as well as the technicalities of provision of respective services, are concerned, telecoms, IT and media in the sense of broadcasting all fall under the scope of the general regulatory framework set out in the ECA. The general regulatory framework of the ECA also covers VoIP services and does not make any specific reference to these in any respect.

10.9   The definition of the term 'electronic communications networks'[5] is identical to the definition in the Framework Directive. However, the definition of 'electronic communications service'[6] is slightly different, although the overall meaning remains the same as in Framework Directive. 'Associated facilities' are not separately

2   Riigi Teataja I ('RTI') 2004, 87, 593.
3   Eg Estonian Number Plan Riigi Teataja ('RTL') 2005, 41, 581, Estonian Frequency Plan RTL 2005, 21, 280, Technical Requirements of Number Portability upon Provision of Telephony and Mobile Telephony Services RTL 2005, 14, 131, Terms and Conditions for Booking Numbers RTL 2005, 48, 668.
4   Art 145 ECA.
5   Art 2(8) ECA.
6   Art 2(6) ECA.

defined, but are described in the context of provision of access as facilities and services necessary to provide services over the local loop.

10.10   Content is regulated separately under the Broadcasting Act[7] (which also regulates broadcasting licensing), as well as under the Information Society Services Act[8] and the Technical Regulations and Standards Act.[9]

The National Regulatory Authorities: Organisation, Regulatory Objectives, Competencies

10.11   The ENCB is the sole independent regulator, in the sense of the Framework Directive, to which have been attributed all respective rights and duties. In addition, state supervision in the electronic communications sector is also performed by the Competition Board, Data Protection Authority and Consumer Protection Board within the scope of their relevant competencies. The Ministry of Economic Affairs and Communications also has certain tasks in the electronic communications sector, but these relate mostly to strategic planning and policy making.

10.12   The ENCB is a governmental agency in the administrative field of the Ministry of Economic Affairs and Communications subordinated to the Government of the Republic. The ENCB has its own statutes and its own budget that is financed from the state budget. The ENCB has a director general, who is appointed and discharged by the Minister of Economic Affairs and Communications on the proposal by the Chancellor of the Minister.

10.13   Although the Ministry of Economic Affairs and Communications exercises certain supervisory control over the ENCB, it is sufficiently independent of the government and makes its own decisions. There is also sufficient independence of the ENCB from the network operators and service providers, as the state shareholding in the holding company holding 100% of shares in the fixed and mobile incumbents is administered by the Ministry of Finance.

10.14   The national regulatory objectives of the ENCB are listed in article 134 ECA and mirror those listed in article 8 Framework Directive. The ENCB has the right to request information for performance of the duties assigned thereto from undertakings providing electronic communications and networks and other persons.[10] The description of the tasks of the ENCB is published on its website. In addition, the ENCB makes available on its website other information related to its regulatory activities.[11] Public consultations are held by the ENCB prior to performing an act, assigning an obligation or application of a measure, and prior to establishing legislation which significantly affects the relevant electronic communications market, or the rights of end-users and consumers, in which case a notice is published on the ENCB's website.[12]

---

7   RTI 1994, 42, 680 (as amended from time to time).
8   RTI 2004, 29, 191.
9   RTI 1999, 29, 398 (as amended from time to time).
10   Art 148 ECA.
11   Art 151 ECA (ie decisions on declaring undertakings as undertakings with SMP, concerning assignment of obligations to undertakings or defining of electronic communications markets, decisions made in disputes between undertakings, etc).
12   Art 152 ECA.

10.15   The ENCB has to carry out supervisory control over competition on electronic communication markets in cooperation with the Competition Board and, if necessary, to exchange information concerning the situation on electronic communications markets, including confidential business-related information, with the Competition Board. An important element of such cooperation is to guarantee uniform and consistent understanding of the competition situation and to avoid making contradictory decisions in similar cases.

10.16   The ENCB is entitled to settle disputes in circumstances envisaged by the ECA (eg disputes related to access or interconnection[13] or line facilities).[14] In order to initiate dispute resolution procedures a party to the dispute should submit a written petition. The dispute should be resolved by the ENCB without undue delay but within no more than four months after the receipt of the petition. If the dispute is particularly complicated, the ENCB is not required to observe the four-month term and must explain why the dispute is considered to be particularly complicated and communicate the term for settlement of the dispute. The ENCB settles a dispute by passing a resolution granting or denying the petition, and depending on the circumstances such resolution is prepared in the form of either a decision or an administrative request. If the petitioner so desires, the ENCB may participate in the dispute as the conciliator but in such case, the ENCB cannot make a binding resolution. The ENCB does not settle private law disputes between end-users and communications undertakings, or consumers' complaints against undertakings providing electronic communications networks or services.[15]

Right of Appeal against NRA's Decisions

10.17   Administrative requests and decisions of the ENCB as administrative acts can be challenged pursuant to the procedures set out in the Administrative Procedures Act.[16] A challenge may be filed with the ENCB, by a person who finds that his or her rights are violated or his or her freedoms are restricted by an administrative act or in the course of administrative proceedings, within 30 days of the date when the person becomes or should become aware of the challenged administrative act or measure. A person whose challenge is dismissed or whose rights are violated in the course of the challenge proceedings has the right within 30 days to file an action with an administrative court under the conditions and pursuant to the procedure provided by the Code of Administrative Court Procedure.[17]

The NRA's Obligations to Cooperate with the Commission

10.18   The consolidation procedure has been implemented into article 48 ECA in full consistency with the relevant provisions of article 7 Framework Directive.

---

13   Art 68 ECA.
14   Art 120 ECA.
15   Art 149 ECA.
16   RTI 2001, 58, 354 (as amended from time to time).
17   RTI 1999, 31, 425 (as amended from time to time).

10.19   The ECA does not make a direct reference to article 19 Framework Directive and the obligation of the ENCB to take utmost account of the Commission's recommendations; however, article 133(3) ECA sets out that, upon performing the duties and carrying out the supervision proceeding from the ECA, guidance should also be taken from EU laws, including regulations, directives, decisions and recommendations.

10.20   The Commission's power to stipulate standards and specifications[18] is reflected in article 124 ECA.

'Significant Market Power' as a Fundamental Prerequisite of Regulation

Definition of SMP

10.21   The definition of significant market power in the ECA is similar to the definition set out in article 14 Framework Directive, ie the ENCB designates an undertaking as having significant market power in the specific electronic communications service market and in the region where the services are provided if, individually or together with other undertakings, the undertaking has significant market power which enables the undertaking to operate to an appreciable extent independently of competitors, parties and end-users.[19]

The ENCB may designate one or several SMP undertakings provided that it has established that competition is not present in the respective electronic communications service market and the undertaking(s) meet(s) the SMP criteria. The ENCB may also find that several undertakings have a joint dominant position in a specific communications service market and may designate an undertaking having SMP in one electronic communications service market as also having SMP in a closely related market.[20]

Definition of relevant markets

10.22   The rules for the determination and identification of the relevant markets do not differ from the relevant provisions of the Framework Directive in most part, except for the peculiarity of Estonian law requiring the list of the pre-defined relevant markets to be set out under primary law, ie the ECA. All the other procedures related to market definition are similar to those of the Framework Directive. The ENCB is obliged to conduct analysis of the competitive situation in the relevant markets listed in the ECA[21] regularly, but at least every three years. The ENCB also has an obligation to conduct an immediate market analysis if circumstances which may significantly affect the competitive situation become evident.

10.23   The list of the relevant markets in the ECA corresponds to the relevant markets identified in Annex 1 to the Framework Directive. In principle the markets listed in the ECA are the only markets where sector-specific regulation is allowed. If the European Commission changes or amends the recommendations on which the

---

18   Art 17 Framework Directive.
19   Art 45 (2) ECA.
20   Art 45 (4), (5) ECA.
21   Art 42 ECA.

list of the relevant markets is based or if the competitive situation requires amendments to the list of markets, then the ENCB through the Minister of Economic Affairs and Communications proposes that the Government of the Republic should initiate amendment of the ECA in order to change or amend the list of relevant markets, and any market added to the list must be approved by the European Commission in the course of the consolidation procedure.

10.24   The first market analysis conducted by the ENCB on the basis of the new procedures established under the ECA is presently on-going. In assessing market power, the ENCB takes guidance from EU competition law principles and the relevant guidelines and recommendations of the Commission.

10.25   At the moment no SMP designation has yet been made on the basis of the ECA. The SMP designations prior to the entry into force of the ECA pursuant to the previous Telecommunications Act, and the duties of designated SMP undertakings arising from the Telecommunications Act will be valid until 31 December 2005. For the year 2005 the ENCB designated the fixed incumbent Elioni Ettevõtted AS as an SMP undertaking on the telephone services market, the leased line services market and the interconnection services market, and the mobile incumbent AS EMT as an SMP undertaking on the mobile telephony services market.

NRA's Regulatory Duties concerning Rights of Way, Co-location and Facility Sharing

Rights of way

10.26   As regards the regulation of rights of way, the ECA itself only contains provisions concerning line facilities[22] and the restrictions applied to activities carried out in the exclusivity zones thereof.[23] Rights of way are regulated under the Law of Property Act,[24] the Act on Implementation of the Law of Property Act[25] and the Building Act.[26]

10.27   As a rule the owner of an immovable, regardless of whether it is in private or public property, is obliged to permit line facilities to be built on his or her immovable if these cannot be built without using the immovable or if the building

---

22   Art 2(24) ECA defines 'line' as a set of technical facilities which connects the termination point with the connection point of terminal equipment. Art 2(25) ECA defines "line facility" as a part of an electronic communications network permanently attached to subsoil, which includes an underground cable, cable in the bottom of a body of water, cable conduit or duct, a set of cables or wires installed on buildings and poles together with switching devices, distribution equipment and cable termination equipment, regenerator, equipment container and a radio mast, as well as utility networks and constructions within the meaning of the Building Act (RTI 2002, 47, 297; as amended from time to time) and the Law of Property Act Implementation Act (RTI 1993, 72/73, 1021; as amended from time to time).

23   Art 117 ECA defines the protective zone of a line facility as an area where any activity likely to damage or harm the line facility is permitted only with the permission of the owner of the line facility.

24   RTI 1999, 44, 509 (consolidated text, as amended from time to time).

25   RTI 1993, 72/73, 1021(as amended from time to time).

26   RTI 2002, 47, 297 (as amended from time to time).

thereof at another location would cause excessive expense. The owner is not subject to such an obligation if the line facility does not enable the immovable to be used in the manner intended.[27]

10.28   Line facilities located on an immovable belonging to another person are not essential parts of the immovable.[28] Encumbrance of the immovable with a corresponding private easement or personal right of use is required for the erection of line facilities on the immovable of another person. For the erection of line facilities on land not entered in the land register or land in state or local government ownership (eg public roads), unattested or notarised agreement of the land owner is sufficient.[29]

10.29   The owner of an immovable may refuse to establish a private easement or personal right of use if the continued location of the line facility on the immovable materially hinders the use of the immovable, and the damage caused by the line facility to the owner is higher than the cost of relocating the line facility to another location, and also if the owner bears all the costs of relocating the line facility and provides the owner of the line facility with sufficient security beforehand.[30]

10.30   The owner of an immovable has the right to demand payment for tolerating a line facility erected on the immovable of the owner regardless of whether the obligation to tolerate arises from law, the encumbrance of the immovable with private easement or personal right of use. The size of the payment shall equal the amount of the land tax corresponding to the area of the exclusivity zone of the line facility multiplied by the factor prescribed for the intended purpose of the land.[31]

10.31   Under the ECA the ENCB has been given the power to resolve disputes concerning line facilities.[32]

Co-location and facility sharing

10.32   The ENCB may also impose on an undertaking operating an electronic communications network an obligation to share or co-locate network equipment or other property used for the provision of electronic communications services, including line facilities.[33] The ENCB may impose the facility sharing or co-location obligations particularly if other providers of electronic communications services or networks do not have alternative possibilities for access due to environmental, health protection or building and planning requirements. The facility sharing or co-location obligation may mean that the respective undertaking must incur a proportional share of the costs relating to facility sharing or co-location or tolerate that line facilities, equipment or other property are used by another undertaking.

---

27   Art 14 Building Act.
28   Art 158 Law of Property Act.
29   Art 15^2 (2) Act on Implementation of the Law of Property Act.
30   Art 15^3 (1) Act on Implementation of the Law of Property Act.
31   Art 15^4 Act on Implementation of the Law of Property Act.
32   Art 120 ECA.
33   Art 63(3) ECA.

REGULATION OF MARKET ENTRY: IMPLEMENTATION OF THE AUTHORISATION DIRECTIVE

The General Authorisation of Electronic Communications

10.33   The ECA sets out a general authorisation for commencing the provision of all public electronic communication services, including fixed, mobile and satellite services.[34] The pre-condition for provision of electronic communications services is having an undertaking or a branch office registered in the Estonian Commercial Register.[35] This is also consistent with the Commercial Code[36] where it is stipulated that if a foreign undertaking wishes to permanently offer its products and services in Estonia under its own name, such foreign undertaking should establish a branch office in Estonia and register it in the Commercial Register. The undertaking or the branch office wishing to start provision of electronic communications services has to submit a respective written notice to the ENCB prior to commencing activities.[37]

10.34   Upon written request from the service provider, the ENCB issues within seven days of receiving the request a written confirmation of receiving the notice and, if the service provider so requests, an overview of the respective rights and obligations of the service provider arising from the ECA.

10.35   Conditions for the provision of public electronic communications are set out in the ECA or respective governmental regulations. In general, service providers should guarantee the security, integrity and interoperability of networks, secure the protection of transmitted or saved information, observe health-related and environmental requirements, guarantee the quality of services, avoid harmful interferences, secure public order and national security, and avoid any activities harming free competition.

Rights of Use for Radio Frequencies

General authorisations and granting of individual rights

10.36   Use of radio frequencies requires a frequency permit issued by a decision of the ENCB on the basis of an application submitted by the electronic communication service provider. A frequency permit is issued by the ENCB within six weeks of receiving the application, provided that the use of the respective frequency does not require international coordination, and within eight months where use of the respective frequency requires international coordination.[38] On written request from the holder of the frequency permit the ENCB submits to the applicant a written confirmation of the rights and obligations under the frequency permit within three working days of receipt of the application. The period of validity of the frequency permit is one year unless the applicant requests a shorter period of validity. The frequency permit is extendable.

---

34   Art 3(1) ECA.
35   Art 3(2) ECA.
36   RTI 1998, 91/93, 1500 (consolidated text; as amended).
37   Art 4(1) ECA.
38   Art 13(1) ECA.

10.37 In addition, pursuant to the Public Health Act[39] the approval of the Health Protection Inspectorate should be obtained for the conditions of use of radio frequencies on the basis of a frequency permit.

10.38 The Minister of Economic Affairs and Communications may also determine that certain frequencies may be used without a frequency permit, provided that the respective requirements established for the use of such frequencies are observed.

Admissible Conditions

10.39 The explicit terms and conditions that may be set out under a frequency permit listed in the ECA contain almost all of the terms and conditions set out in Part B of the Annex to the Authorisation Directive, except the terms and conditions referred to in items 6 and 7 of Part B of the said Annex.

10.40 The ECA does not contain any specific provisions related to 3G services, the initial roll-out of which started on the basis of the previous Telecommunications Act under which also the specific UMTS licence conditions were set out (including coverage requirements, data transfer rate, and validity period of the licence).

Limitation of number of rights of use to be granted

10.41 Where several persons have simultaneously submitted an application for the use of the same radio frequency, the ENCB will organise an auction for issuing the frequency permit. There are also certain frequencies set out in the frequency plan which have to be allocated through public tender.

Frequency trading

10.42 In principle, article 17 ECA allows trading of the licence spectrum, provided that the right to trade the respective frequencies has been envisaged in the Estonian frequency plan and that the transfer of frequencies would not result in distortion of competition. In order to trade the radio frequencies, an application should be submitted to the ENCB. Spectrum trading, however, will only be possible with effect from 31 December 2006.

Rights of Use for Numbers

General authorisations and granting of individual rights

10.43 In order to be granted rights of use for numbers an applicant should submit an application to the ENCB to obtain a number permit. Number permits are issued within 10 business days of receiving the application, provided that the applicant has paid the relevant state duties charged for issuing number permits. Number permits cannot be transferred or traded. The number permit is valid for one year and is extendable.

---

39   RTI 1995, 57, 978 (as amended).

10.44   The user of numbers does not acquire property rights in the numbers. Intellectual property issues can, however, arise in connection with certain short numbers. For instance, short numbers '1188' and '1184' are parts of trademarks registered by providers of directory and general information services.

Admissible conditions

10.45   A number permit grants the holder of the permit the right to reserve numbers, as a result of which a right to use a particular number is granted. Such reservation is not limited in time and the reservation for a particular portable number is transferred to another operator if the customer decides to change the service provider.

10.46   The holder of the number permit has the right to use geographical and other non-geographical numbers (telephone numbers) or mobile telephone numbers and grant these to their subscribers/clients for their own use or for using as service numbers for the provision of other services rendered by means of an electronic communications service.

10.47   In addition to the conditions for the use of numbering contained in the ECA, the Minister of Economic Affairs and Communications may establish certain other conditions; however; these conditions differ somewhat from those set out in Part C of the Annex to the Authorisation Directive. For example, the Minister may establish conditions for reserving numbers, as well as conditions for using numbers in order to ensure public order and national security.[40] The admissible conditions under the ECA also do not contain conditions referred to under items 2, 3, 7 and 8 of Part C of the Annex.

10.48   The client has the right to retain a number belonging to the Estonian Numbering Plan, and granted for his/her use by a telephone or mobile telephone service provider, upon changing to another telephone or mobile telephone service provider or upon changing the geographical location of the connection point.[41]

10.49   Undertakings designated as having SMP in the market of access to the public telephone network at a fixed location for residential customers may be subject to the obligation to enable its end-users to access the services of any interconnected provider of publicly available telephone services by dialling a carrier selection code and by means of pre-selection, with a facility to override any pre-selected choice on a call-by-call basis by dialling a carrier selection code.[42]

Limitation of number of rights of use to be granted

10.50   If several persons have submitted applications for number permits for the use of the same short number or identification code and the applicants cannot be granted joint use of the short number or identification code, the ENCB will organise an auction for the issue of the number permit.[43]

---

40   Art 29(2) ECA.
41   Art 89(1) ECA.
42   Art 56 ECA.
43   Art 39(1) ECA.

The NRA's Enforcement Powers

10.51   The ENCB supervises the fulfilment of the requirements set out in the ECA. If violations are detected the ENCB, depending on the circumstances, may:

- issue an administrative request for elimination of the violation or for the performance of certain acts together with the right to use a coercive measure, in the form of a penalty payment of up to EEK 150,000 (approx €9,600) if a request of an administrative authority is not voluntarily complied with by the deadline given,[44]
- suspend a frequency permit if the ENCB has notified the holder of the permit of a detected violation and the holder of the permit has failed to eliminate the violation within one month after receipt of the ENCB's respective notice,[45]
- revoke a frequency permit, for example where use of the rights granted by the frequency permit has not commenced within six months after the grant of the frequency permit, the holder of the frequency permit has materially or repeatedly violated the conditions of the frequency permit, use of the radio frequencies is suspended and the user of the radio frequencies has not eliminated the circumstances on which the suspension is based within one month of the date on which the decision on suspension is made,[46]
- restrict the rights of the holder of the number permit if the holder of the number permit has violated the established requirements and has failed to eliminate the violation within the prescribed term,[47] or
- carry out extra-judicial proceedings of handling misdemeanours and impose sanctions in the form of fines according to the procedures set out in the General Part of the Penal Code[48] and the Code of Misdemeanour Procedure,[49] which in the case of natural persons can be three to 300 penalty units, where one penalty unit is EEK 60 (approx €4), and in the case of legal persons EEK 500 (approx €32) up to EEK 50,000 (approx €3,200).[50]

Administrative Charges and Fees for Rights of Use

10.52   Submission of the notice of commencing the provision of electronic communications services is not subject to any fee. There is no general charge or fee for undertakings benefiting from general authorisations without having obtained rights of use for frequencies or numbers, except the universal service fee.[51]

10.53   The granting and extension of frequency permits and number permits is subject to the payment of state duties by the applicant. The amount of the said state duty varies. In the case of frequency permits the exact amount depends on the type of frequencies used and the nature and purpose of such use, and in the case of number permits on the type of numbers used. The detailed rates of state duties are listed in the Act on State Duties.[52]

---

44   Art 146(1) ECA.
45   Art 18(1) ECA.
46   Art 18(3) ECA.
47   Art 37 ECA.
48   RTI 2002, 86, 504 (consolidated text; as amended from time to time).
49   RTI 2002, 50, 313 (as amended from time to time).
50   Art 188(3) ECA.
51   See para 10.77 below.
52   RTI 2001, 55, 331 (consolidated text; as amended).

REGULATION OF NETWORK ACCESS AND INTERCONNECTION: IMPLEMENTATION OF THE ACCESS DIRECTIVE

Objectives and Scope of Access Regulation

10.54   The basic principles of access and interconnection as embodied in the ECA are derived from the Access Directive. The purpose of regulating access and interconnection is to ensure competition, the interoperability of communications services and protection of the interests of end-users.[53] General access- and interconnection-related provisions of the ECA, eg the obligation to enter into interconnection negotiations and to disclose information necessary for interconnection, apply to all electronic communications service providers. With regard to SMP undertakings the ENCB can impose additional, more specific obligations.

Basic Regulatory Concepts

10.55   'Access' is defined as the making available of networks, line facilities and network facilities or services provided by one communications undertaking to another undertaking for the purpose of providing communications services.[54] 'Interconnection' is defined as a special type of access which means the technical and logical linking of two or more communications networks in a manner which enables provision of communications services to the subscribers of the connected communications networks.[55] The principle of the 'freedom of access' as set out in article 3 (1) Access Directive is expressly stipulated in the ECA, entitling communications undertakings to agree freely on the technical and commercial conditions for access and interconnection, taking account of the facility sharing and co-location obligations and the possible SMP obligations imposed on communications undertakings.[56]

10.56   An undertaking providing electronic communications network services is required, at the request of another communications undertaking, to negotiate the interconnection in good faith if this is necessary for the provision of electronic communications services. An undertaking may terminate pre-contractual negotiations and refuse to enter into an access or interconnection agreement if the creation of technical conditions for interconnection or access is unreasonably burdensome or the interconnection or access damages the integrity of its network. The ENCB will become involved if a complaint is submitted with regard to access or interconnection.

Access- and Interconnection-Related Obligations with Respect to SMP Undertakings

10.57   The obligations that can be imposed on SMP undertakings are identical to those listed in articles 9–13 Access Directive. However, the ENCB has not yet issued any decisions imposing obligations under the ECA.

---

53   Art 59 ECA.
54   Art 60(1) ECA.
55   Art 61(1)ECA.
56   Art 62 ECA.

Transparency obligations

10.58   The ENCB may impose on SMP undertakings an obligation to publish information in relation to access and interconnection which concerns accounting information, technical specifications, network characteristics, terms and conditions for provision of services, and prices, as well as obligations to publish a reference offer regarding a specific access or interconnection service which should contain the conditions for provision of the corresponding service.[57] The ECA also sets out a detailed list of conditions that should be contained in a reference offer.[58]

Non-discrimination obligations

10.59   The ENCB may impose on SMP undertakings an obligation of non-discrimination which should ensure that SMP undertakings – and, in particular, vertically integrated SMP undertakings which provide services to undertakings with which they compete at the retail level – apply equivalent conditions in equivalent circumstances to other undertakings providing equivalent services, and provide services and information to others under the same conditions and of the same quality as they provide for their own services, or those of their subsidiaries or partners.[59]

Specific access obligations

10.60   The ENCB may impose on SMP undertakings an obligation to meet reasonable requests of other providers of electronic communications services or networks for access to, and use of, specific network elements and associated facilities, if denial of access or unreasonable terms and conditions having a similar effect would hinder the emergence of a sustainable competitive market at the retail level, or would not be in the end-users' interests.[60]

Price controls

10.61   The ENCB may impose on SMP undertakings an obligation relating to the recovery of costs for access or interconnection and price controls and obligations for cost orientation of prices and obligations concerning cost-accounting systems.[61]

Accounting separation

10.62   The ENCB may impose on SMP undertakings an obligation to maintain separate records of activities related to interconnection or access in connection with which the ENCB may require a vertically integrated undertaking to make transparent its wholesale prices and its internal transfer prices.[62]

---

57   Art 50 (1) [1], [2] ECA.
58   Art 53 ECA.
59   Art 50 (1) [3] ECA.
60   Art. 50 (1) [5] ECA.
61   Art 50 (1) [7] ECA.
62   Art 50 (1) [4] ECA.

Related Regulatory Powers with Respect to SMP Undertakings

10.63   If the ENCB finds as a result of a market analysis conducted in the market of leased line services that the market is not competitive, it may impose on an SMP undertaking in that market one or several obligations necessary to ensure competition in offering services which belong to the minimum set of leased line services and comply with the standards published in the Commission Decision 2003/548/EC on the minimum set of leased lines with harmonised characteristics and associated standards referred to in article 18 Universal Service Directive. SMP undertakings in the market of leased line services also have an obligation to comply with the requirements of non-discrimination, cost orientation and transparency.[63]

10.64   The ENCB imposes on SMP undertakings in the market of access to the public telephone network at a fixed location for residential customers, and in the market of access to the public telephone network at a fixed location for non-residential customers, the obligation to enable its end-users to access the services of any interconnected provider of publicly available telephone services by dialling a carrier selection code and by means of pre-selection, with a facility to override any pre-selected choice on a call-by-call basis by dialling a carrier selection code.[64] SMP undertakings may demand a cost-oriented price including a reasonable rate of return for performance of such an obligation, whereas charges to subscribers cannot act as a disincentive for the use of the said facilities.

Regulatory Powers Applicable to All Market Participants

Obligations to ensure end-to-end connectivity

10.65   The ENCB may impose on an undertaking providing electronic communications networks and controlling access to end-users any obligations necessary for ensuring end-to-end connectivity, including obligations for the interconnection of networks.[65] However, the ENCB has not yet issued any relevant decisions under the ECA.

Access to digital radio and television broadcasting services

10.66   The ENCB may impose the obligation to ensure access to application program interfaces (APIs) and electronic programme guides (EPGs) on fair, reasonable and non-discriminatory terms if that is necessary to ensure accessibility for end-users to specified digital radio and television broadcasting programmes, as well as facility sharing or co-location obligations.[66]

10.67   An undertaking which provides conditional access systems is required to ensure that the conditional access systems allow the technical conduct of cost-oriented cross-checks of services provided by other communications undertakings by means of conditional access systems.[67]

10.68   An undertaking which provides services of conditional access to digital television and radio services, and if the access of broadcasters to the potential

---

63   Art 55 ECA.
64   Art 56 ECA.
65   Art 63(1) ECA.
66   Art 63(2) ECA.
67   Art 67(1) ECA.

viewers and listeners depends on the access services, is required to offer to all broadcasters, on a fair, reasonable and non-discriminatory basis, technical services enabling the broadcasters' digitally transmitted services to be received by viewers or listeners authorised by means of decoders and to keep separate accounts of its activities as provider of conditional access services.[68]

REGULATION OF UNIVERSAL SERVICE AND USERS' RIGHTS: THE UNIVERSAL SERVICE DIRECTIVE

Regulation of Universal Service Obligations

Scope of universal service obligations

10.69   A universal service is a set of services which conforms with the technical and quality requirements established by the EU law, which is of specified quality and available to all end-users requesting it, independently of their geographical location, uniformly and at an affordable price.[69] Article 69 ECA defines the scope of universal services to include the connection to the public telephone network, the availability of a public pay-phone service and the accessibility of an electronic Public Number Directory and directory enquiry services.

Designation of undertakings obliged to provide universal services

10.70   The provider of universal services is chosen by means of a public tender or according to the procedures set out for state procurements. If a public tender or a public procurement fails, the Ministry of Economic Affairs and Communications may impose the obligation to provide universal services on a communications undertaking with special or exclusive rights or in control of essential facilities.[70] The basis for the provision of universal services is a universal service contract between the State and the relevant designated undertaking setting out the relevant details of the provision of universal service.

10.71   The obligation to provide universal services currently lies with the fixed incumbent Elioni Ettevõtted AS and this obligation remains valid under the conditions applicable before the entry into force of ECA until a new universal service provider is appointed pursuant to ECA, but in any event no longer than until 31 December 2006.

Regulation of retail tariffs, user expenditures and quality of service

10.72   The affordable price charged for the universal service to end-users by the provider of universal service is included in the conditions of the public tender or the tender documents relating to the public procurement and will be also fixed in the universal service contract. The affordable price is suggested by the ENCB and established by the Minister of Economic Affairs and Communications.[71]

---

68   Art 67(2) ECA.
69   Art 69 ECA.
70   Art 73(2) ECA.
71   Art 74(2) ECA.

10.73   Upon provision of universal service, the universal service provider should provide the end-users with several possibilities to control expenditure relating to the universal service (eg itemised bills, call barring, access on pre-paid terms, deferred payment of connection charges).[72]

10.74   In order to enable the monitoring of its service of quality the universal service provider has to make available to the public and submit to the ENCB at least the information listed in Annex III to the Universal Service Directive concerning the provision of universal services pursuant to the concepts and methods of measurement provided for in the Estonian standard EVS 874:2003.[73]

Cost calculation and financing of universal services

10.75   Upon determining the additional costs of and revenue involved in the provision of the universal service, the universal service provider should take into account only the costs necessary for performance of the universal service obligation, whereas the costs which the universal service provider would incur also without the universal service obligation (ordinary business expenses), and costs which have been incurred before the beginning of the calendar year of submission of the tender shall not be taken into account.[74]

10.76   A universal service provider may submit an application to the ENCB for compensation of the unfairly burdensome costs relating to the performance of the universal service obligation. The ENCB may decide to compensate for the costs related to the universal service obligation to the extent to which the price charged from end-users does not cover the costs related to performance of the universal service obligation or ensuring reasonable profit.[75]

10.77   The universal service is financed by means of a separate universal service fee payable into the state budget by all electronic communication service providers whose annual turnover from the provision of electronic communication services exceeds EEK 6 million (approx €363,636). The obligation to pay the said fee will however arise only as of 2007. The rate of the fee is 0.01–1% and it will be calculated on the basis of the turnover of the previous financial year. The exact rate of the fee is established by the Minister of Economic Affairs and Communications for each calendar year.

Regulation of Retail Markets

Prerequisites for the regulation of retail markets

10.78   Retail markets can only be regulated where the ENCB ascertains in the course of market analysis that the competition on a retail market is ineffective, and effective competition cannot be secured by the means of wholesale remedies. In such a case the ENCB designates an SMP undertaking on the relevant retail market and imposes relevant obligations on the said SMP undertaking.[76]

---

72   Art 79 ECA.
73   Art 78 ECA.
74   Art 76(2) ECA.
75   Art 75(4) ECA.
76   Art 54(1) ECA.

Regulatory powers

10.79   The ENCB may, inter alia, demand an SMP undertaking to avoid:

- sustaining prices at an excessively high level,
- prevention of competitors from entering a market or limitation of competition by applying excessively low prices,
- showing undue preference to certain end-users, and
- undue bundling of services.[77]

The ENCB may impose other obligations upon receiving appropriate permission from the European Commission[78] although no such permission requirement is set out in the Universal Service Directive.

10.80   Where obligations are imposed on an SMP undertaking, it is obliged to use the necessary and appropriate methodology of cost accounting, whereas the ENCB has the right to determine the methodology of cost accounting.[79]

End User Rights

Contracts

10.81   Electronic communications services are provided to end-users on the basis of electronic communications service contracts. As a rule, undertakings providing electronic communications services and end-users are free to agree on the conditions of an electronic communications service contract. However, any condition of an electronic communications service contract which restricts the rights of the end-user, as compared to the rights provided by the ECA, is null and void.[80]

10.82   The ECA sets out an exhaustive list of grounds for the refusal to enter into a subscription contract by the electronic communications service provider.[81] If there is no such ground, the service provider is obliged to enter into the contract.

10.83   The ECA also lists the mandatory terms and conditions of an electronic communications service contract entered into with the end-user.[82] The said terms and conditions are consistent with article 20(2) Universal Service Directive.

10.84   A consumer has the right to cancel an electronic communications service contract at any time without prior notice by informing the undertaking providing the electronic communication services.[83]

Transparency obligations

10.85   The electronic communications service provider is obliged to publish the mandatory terms and conditions of its end-user contracts, as well as any other

---

77   Art 54(2) ECA.
78   Art 54(3) ECA.
79   Art 54(4) ECA.
80   Art 92(2) ECA.
81   Art 93(2) ECA.
82   Art 96(1), (2) ECA.
83   Art 100(1) ECA.

general conditions applied to such contracts, on its website or make these available in any other reasonable way in the absence of a website.[84]

DATA PROTECTION: IMPLEMENTATION OF THE DIRECTIVE ON PRIVACY AND ELECTRONIC COMMUNICATIONS

Confidentiality of Communications

10.86 An undertaking providing electronic communications services is required to maintain the confidentiality of all information which becomes known to it in the process of providing electronic communications services and which concerns sub- scribers and other persons using electronic communications services with the consent of the subscriber. Such information may be disclosed only to the relevant subscriber and, with the consent of the subscriber, to third persons, and a subscriber has the right to withdraw his or her consent at any time. An electronic communications service provider must guarantee the security of a communications network and prevent third persons from accessing such information without legal grounds.[85]

10.87 The ECA sets out the obligation of electronic communication service providers to release certain information to respective governmental surveillance agencies or enable these agencies access to their network.

10.88 An undertaking providing electronic communications services may process the information if the undertaking notifies the subscriber, in a clear and unambigu- ous manner, of the purposes of processing the information, and gives the subscriber an opportunity to refuse the processing. Such an obligation does not however restrict the right to collect and process, without the consent of a subscriber, information which must be processed for the purposes of recording the transactions carried out in the conduct of business activities and for other business-related exchange of information, as well as the right to store or process data without the consent of a subscriber if the sole purpose of such activity is the provision of services through the communications network, or if such activity is necessary for the provision of the information society services which are directly requested by the subscriber.[86]

10.89 If an electronic communications service provider wishes to process, with the subscriber's consent, the information for marketing purposes, the service provider is required to inform the subscriber, prior to obtaining the consent, of the type of information needed for such purposes and the duration of the intended use of such information.

Traffic Data and Location Data

10.90 The ECA does not contain definitions for 'traffic data' or 'location data'. Electronic communications service providers have the right to process subscribers' location data only if such data is rendered anonymous prior to processing.[87] In

---

84   Art 96(3) ECA.
85   Arts 101, 102 ECA.
86   Art 102(4) ECA.
87   Art 105(1) ECA.

order to provide other services in the process of using the electronic communications services, service providers also have the right to process, with the consent of the subscribers, location data to an extent and during the term necessary for processing and without rendering the data anonymous. A subscriber has the right to withdraw his or her consent at any time. A subscriber who has granted consent for the processing of the location data must have easy opportunity to temporarily prohibit, free of charge, the processing of the data in the part of establishment of the connection or transmission of the information indicated thereby.[88]

Itemised Billing

10.91   A subscriber has the right to request that a bill presented to the subscriber would not reflect the details of provision of the service.

Calling and Connected Line Identification

10.92   Where presentation of calling-line identification is offered the service provider should provide users with a possibility via a simple means, free of charge, to eliminate the presentation of the calling-line identification and, where technically possible, provide such opportunity with respect to each separate call and number. A service provider is required to guarantee that the identity and telephone number of the caller is not disclosed to the person receiving the call even after the call is terminated.[89]

Automatic Call Forwarding

10.93   An undertaking providing electronic communications services is required to provide, where technical capability for such a function exists, the end-user with a possibility via a simple means, free of charge, to eliminate automatic routing of calls by third persons to the terminal equipment of the subscriber.[90]

Directories of Subscribers

10.94   Undertakings which wish to publish data on subscribers in telephone directories or through telephone enquiries are required, prior to publication of data on subscribers in telephone directories or through telephone enquiries, to provide the subscribers with free information concerning the purposes of the databases of the telephone directories or telephone enquiries.[91] They are also required to provide subscribers with an opportunity to decide on whether and to what extent they wish such data to be made public, whereas subscribers should also have the opportunity to verify and amend the data which concerns them, and to terminate the publication of such data.[92]

---

88   Art 105(2), (3), (4) ECA.
89   Art 108 ECA.
90   Art 109 ECA.
91   Art 107(1) ECA.
92   Art 107(2) ECA.

Unsolicited Communications

10.95   Unsolicited communications are regulated by the Information Society Services Act[93] that regulates the sending of commercial communications, ie any form of communication the intention of which is to promote on behalf of a respective service provider, either directly or indirectly, the goods or services offered by such service provider or enhance the reputation of such service provider. Unsolicited communications are prohibited.

10.96   As a general rule a service provider may send digital commercial communications to a private person by means of a public data communication network only if the addressee:

- has given his or her prior consent,
- is informed clearly and in a comprehensible way how to refuse any further commercial communications, and
- is guaranteed the possibility to exercise his or her right of refusal by the means of the public data communication network.

This prohibition concerns commercial communications sent only to private persons and not to legal entities.

---

93   RTI 2004, 29, 191.

The Finnish Market for Electronic Communications[1]

Kaisa Fahllund, Jalmari Sasi & Marko Vuorinen
Hannes Snellman Attorneys at Law Ltd

LEGAL STRUCTURE

Basic Policy

11.1   The Finnish telecommunications market is governed by the new Communications Market Act[2] ('CMA'). The objectives of the CMA are to promote the provision and use of services within communications networks and to ensure that communications networks and communications services are available to all telecommunications operators and users throughout the country under reasonable conditions. An additional objective of the CMA is to ensure that the opportunities available for telecommunications in Finland are in accordance with the reasonable needs of users and that they are competitive, technologically advanced, of high quality, reliable, safe, and inexpensive.

11.2   Due to historical reasons, the telecommunications market in Finland is characterised by its fragmentation into exceptionally small local markets. Today there are altogether over 40 local telecommunications operators in Finland. Each such operator, in practice, is also the sole operator in the related municipalities for the provision of a fixed telecommunications network and its services.

Legislation and Implementation of EU Directives

11.3   Most of the contents of the 2002 EU Regulatory Package have been implemented in the CMA. In connection with the enacting of the CMA, changes have been made also to other related Acts, such as the Act on Television and Radio Operations[3] and the Radio Act.[4] The view of the Finnish Government is that all applicable EU legislation has been sufficiently implemented with these legislative measures.

---

1   Editing of this chapter closed on 7 June 2005.
2   Viestintämarkkinalaki 23.5.2003/393.
3   Laki televisio- ja radiotoiminnasta 9.10.1998/744.
4   Laki radiotaajuuksista ja telelaitteista 16.11.2001/1015.

REGULATORY PRINCIPLES: IMPLEMENTATION OF THE FRAMEWORK DIRECTIVE

Scope of Regulation

11.4   The CMA applies to all communications markets (markets of network services, communications services and related services)[5] unless specifically provided otherwise. Under the CMA, a 'communications network' is a system comprising cables and equipment joined to each other for the purpose of transmitting or distributing messages by wire, radio waves, optically or by other electromagnetic means.[6] This general definition includes telephone networks, mass communications networks and other communications networks.

11.5   Network services and communications service are defined in articles 2(1)(17) and 2(1)(19) CMA through the definition of the provider of the service: 'network operator' means an operator that provides a communications network in its ownership or for other reasons in its possession for the purposes of transmitting, distributing or providing messages, while 'service operator' means an operator that transmits messages over a communications network in its possession or obtained for use from a network operator, or distributes or provides messages in a mass communications network.

11.6   The CMA applies to traditional telecommunications companies as well as to internet service providers and to television operators. Television and radio network providers as well as television and radio broadcasters are considered to be telecommunications operators. Furthermore, the CMA applies to different public authority networks.[7] Even voice over internet protocol (VoIP) services are partly covered by the definition of electronic communication services depending on how the service operates (ie whether the service resembles a traditional telephone network, so the CMA and other regulations can be applied).

11.7   The CMA only applies to the infrastructure of communications and service activities that are indispensable for communications. The operation of content production is excluded from the scope of the CMA. The content of messages transmitted in a communications network is regulated in other special laws.[8]

National Regulatory Authorities: Organisation, Regulatory Objectives, Competencies

11.8   According to article 119 CMA, the Ministry of Transport and Communications ('MTC') is responsible for general telecommunications guidance and development, while the Finnish Communications Regulatory Authority ('FICORA') supervises compliance with the CMA and provisions issued under it. The MTC is assisted by the Communications Administration Advisory Board, which monitors the activities of communications administration, prepares initiatives for developing communications administration and issues opinions.

---

5   Art 3 CMA.
6   Art 2(1)(1) CMA.
7   Public authority networks are networks built for the needs of public order and security, rescue activities or civil defence, Art 2(1)(9) CMA.
8   Act on the Protection of Privacy in Electronic Communications, Act on the Provision of Information Society Services.

11.9   The MTC and FICORA, in discharging duties under the CMA, shall work in cooperation with the competition authorities and the consumer authorities wherever necessary.[9] This cooperation includes the exchange of information between authorities, coordination of official comments given by the authorities and joint negotiations with telecommunications operators in connection with dispute resolution. The MTC and FICORA also have the right to provide the Finnish Competition Authority with confidential documents that they have received or drawn up in the course of discharging the duties prescribed in article 113 CMA if this is essential for the competition authority to manage its duties. A corresponding right to provide FICORA with confidential information is given to the Finnish Competition Authority in the Act on Restrictions of Competition.[10]

11.10   The obligation of cooperation between authorities also means that sanctions imposed by one authority for an act or omission should, when possible, be taken into account by another authority when determining sanctions for the same act or omission.

11.11   In carrying out their duties, the MTC and FICORA have certain powers to demand information. Telecommunications operator shall, upon request of the MTC or FICORA, be obliged to collect and, notwithstanding business and professional secrecy, supply to the MTC and FICORA any information necessary for the guidance and supervision of telecommunications. The obligation to collect and supply information may also apply to other companies than telecommunications operators.[11] In addition to the power to require information, FICORA has under article 124 CMA certain powers to conduct technical and financial inspections of a telecommunications operator.

11.12   According to the Act on Publicity in Authority Functions,[12] the main rule is that all documents of public authorities are public. In addition, some of the decisions that are to be published according to the EU directives are given in the form of legal acts and regulations in Finland. These are all public information and they have to be published in accordance with the Act on the Statutes of Finland[13] and the Act on the Compilation of Ministry and Other Authority Regulations.[14] Under article 117 CMA, FICORA shall publish certain decisions imposing obligations on telecommunications operators, decisions on the division into telecommunications areas, numbering decisions and decisions on disputes between telecommunications operators in a way that ensures that they are available to telecommunications operators and user groups. The Council of State (in practice the MTC) shall in the same manner publish licence application announcements and licence decisions.

11.13   According to article 118 CMA parties representing telecommunications operators and users shall be reserved an opportunity to present their views on licence application announcements, decisions on telecommunications areas and numbering decisions that significantly affect the communications market before the application announcement is published or the decision issued. Also, the licence holder and parties representing telecommunications operators and users shall be reserved an opportunity to present their views on any amendment to the licence

---

9   Art 120 CMA.
10   Laki kilpailunrajoituksista 27.5.1992/480. Art 10a.
11   Art 112 CMA.
12   Laki viranomaisten toiminnan julkisuudesta 21.5.1999/621.
13   Laki Suomen säädöskokoelmasta 25.2.2000/188.
14   Laki ministeriöiden ja valtion muiden viranomaisten määräyskokoelmista 25.2.2000/189.

terms or the cancellation of a licence. Furthermore, if in certain cases a decision of FICORA has a significant effect on the communications market, FICORA shall reserve the parties representing telecommunications operators and users an opportunity to present their views on the proposed decision. Other provisions on consultation obligations regarding public authorities are issued in the Administrative Procedure Act.[15]

11.14   According to the Governmental Bill, a telecommunications operator may present its views both in its capacity as a party in the case at hand and in its capacity as an acquirer of communications services from another telecommunications operator. The term 'users', in this context, means all acquirers of services who do not sell these services further, but use them themselves.[16] If a decision has an impact on appliance producers, the views of the representatives of these producers also have to be heard.

11.15   FICORA is granted specific dispute resolution powers by article 126 CMA. The CMA states that if a telecommunications operator or a person whose right or benefit is affected by the matter considers that someone is acting in violation of the CMA and the provisions issued under it, the telecommunications operator or person may refer the matter for examination by FICORA. FICORA may also, on its own initiative, take up the matter for examination.

11.16   Article 126 CMA also contains provisions on dispute resolution through mediation. However, FICORA does not have the power to decide on purely contractual disputes between telecommunications operators or other parties. This authority belongs to the regular public courts.

Right of Appeal against NRA's Decisions

11.17   Appeals against decisions of the MTC or FICORA made under the CMA are to be made by appealing to the Administrative Court.[17] However, appeals against decisions regarding market definition, SMP of a telecommunications operator or obligations imposed on an operator (with or without SMP) or on an operator on the retail market, as well as decisions made by FICORA following failed mediation attempts, shall be made by appealing directly to the Supreme Administrative Court.[18]

11.18   Any decision made under the CMA by the relevant authorities can be appealed, except for decisions regarding market definition, which cannot be separately appealed.[19] The person at whom the decision is directed always has the right to appeal. Furthermore, all such persons whose rights, duties or interests are immediately affected by the decision have the right to appeal.

---

15   Hallintolaki 6.6.2003/434.
16   A particular user group consists of consumers, who are represented by the Consumer Ombudsman and consumer organisations. Interest groups of the disabled are also mentioned as representatives of a specified group of users.
17   Art 127 CMA.
18   Art 127 CMA.
19   A market definition decision by FICORA or the MTC is, in itself, non-appealable. This means that an appeal against a market definition decision can be made only in connection with an appeal against a decision regarding SMP.

The NRA's Obligations to Cooperate with the Commission

11.19   According to article 21 CMA, FICORA shall reserve an opportunity for the Commission and the regulatory authorities of the EEA States to present a statement of their views within a period of one month before any of the following actions affecting trade between EEA States are taken:

- a market definition that deviates from the Commission Recommendation on relevant markets,
- a market analysis,
- a decision concerning SMP, or
- a decision concerning obligations imposed on telecommunications operators.

11.20   Requirements of article 7 (3–5) Framework Directive on consolidating the internal market for electronic communications are implemented in article 21 CMA. Requirements of article 7(6) Framework Directive are implemented in article 22 CMA.

11.21   The CMA further regulates the cooperation and exchange of information between the Commission and the regulatory authorities of the EEA States. According to article 115 CMA, the MTC and FICORA have an obligation to supply any information necessary for communications market supervision at the request of the Commission or the regulatory authority of another EEA State. The MTC and FICORA also have the right to supply a confidential document and to disclose confidential information to the Commission or the telecommunications regulatory authorities of other EEA States if this is necessary for communications market supervision. The MTC or FICORA may use a confidential document that has been obtained from a foreign public authority only for the purpose for which it was given.[20]

11.22   The provisions of articles 17 and 19 Framework Directive concerning the Commission's power to stipulate standards and specifications did not require any implementation in to the Finnish legislation. However, these provisions are taken into consideration through the practice of FICORA. In general, telecommunications standards are usually executed in Finland through regulations issued by FICORA.

'Significant Market Power' as Fundamental Prerequisite of Regulation

Definition of SMP

11.23   According to article 17 CMA FICORA shall declare a telecommunications operator to be an SMP operator if, on the basis of a market analysis, it is seen on a particular market to exert an economic influence alone or with others that allows it to operate to a considerable extent independently of competitors, consumers or other users. If a telecommunications operator has SMP on a particular market, it may be considered to have the same position on closely related markets if it is also able to strengthen its market power on those markets.

11.24   The essential criteria when evaluating whether an operator has SMP or not are the economic influence of the operator and its independence of other actors on

---

20   Art 114 CMA.

the market and users. The fact that an operator has a large market share on a particular market is seen as an indication that the operator may have SMP, but the information on the market share alone is not enough to make the final decision. The evaluation of SMP has to be made case-specifically.

Definition of relevant markets and SMP designation

11.25   FICORA shall issue decisions at regular intervals defining the relevant communications markets.[21] FICORA identifies relevant markets in cooperation with the MTC and the Finnish Competition Authority and in accordance with the principles of competition law, as stipulated by the Framework Directive. FICORA shall also take into consideration the Commission Recommendation on relevant markets as well as the Commission Guidelines on market analysis when identifying the relevant markets.[22]

11.26   FICORA, at regular intervals, performs a market analysis of relevant wholesale and retail markets, in order to establish the competitive situation.[23] When conducting its market analysis, FICORA evaluates the way that supply-side and demand-side substitutability limits the competitive behaviour of companies on a certain relevant market. Supply-side and demand-side substitutability shall be taken into account in the evaluation of both the product and service specific dimension and the geographical dimension of the market.

11.27   FICORA has identified 18 product and service markets that correspond with the Commission Recommendation with the following exceptions. Market 3 is divided into two submarkets for (a) local telephone services (market 3A) and (b) national telephone services (market 3B), and market 5 which is divided into two submarkets for (a) local telephone services (market 5A) and (b) national telephone services (market 5B). No separate VoIP market is planned at the present time. There is 1 SMP operator on market 18,[24] 4 SMP operators on market 16,[25] 15 SMP operators on market 15,[26] 42 SMP operators on markets 1,[27] 2,[28] 3A,[29] 5A[30] and 7,[31] 43 SMP operators on markets 14,[32] 15[33] and 16,[34] 45 SMP operators on market 8[35] and 49 SMP operators on market 9.[36] There are no SMP operators on markets 3B,[37] 5B,[38] 14[39] and 15.[40] No decisions on markets 6[41] and 17[42] have been made yet.

---

21   Art 16 CMA.
22   See paras 1.70–1.76 above.
23   Art 17 CMA.
24   Final decision given by FICORA 3 September 2004.
25   Final decisions given by FICORA 6 February 2004.
26   Final decision given by FICORA 28 September 2004.
27   Final decisions given by FICORA 5 March 2004.
28   Final decisions given by FICORA 5 March 2004.
29   Final decisions given by FICORA 5 March 2004.
30   Final decisions given by FICORA 5 March 2004.
31   Final decision given by FICORA 28 September 2004.
32   Final decisions given by FICORA 6 February 2004.
33   Final decision given by FICORA 30 September 2004.
34   Final decision given by FICORA 30 September 2004.
35   Final decisions given by FICORA 6 February 2004.
36   Final decisions given by FICORA 6 February 2004.
37   Final decision given by FICORA 5 March 2004.
38   Final decision given by FICORA 5 March 2004.
39   Final decision given by FICORA 28 September 2004.

11.28   When FICORA identifies an undertaking as having SMP on a certain market, it shall impose on the SMP operator one or more SMP obligations that are needed to eliminate barriers to competition or to promote competition.[43]

11.29   FICORA has the right to impose obligations on non-SMP undertakings as well.[44] However, whereas the list of obligations that may be imposed on SMP undertakings comprises 18 different measures, only 7 of these may be imposed on non-SMP undertakings. Also, the prerequisites for imposing obligations on non-SMP undertakings are significantly different from the prerequisites for imposing obligations on SMP undertakings.[45]

NRA's Regulatory Duties Concerning Rights of Way, Co-location and Facility Sharing

Rights of way

11.30   Provisions on the right of a telecommunications operator to install a telecommunications cable and related equipment, minor structures or poles in an area owned or controlled by a third party are given in articles 100–111 CMA and article 161 Land Use and Building Act.[46] According to the Land Use and Building Act, the owner or the holder of the property must allow the placement of such cable and the above-mentioned related structures, provided that the placement of the cable benefits a community or a real estate. If the cable does not benefit a community or a real estate directly, the telecommunications operator shall first draw up a plan for the installation of the telecommunications cable.[47]

11.31   The CMA encourage the parties to make an agreement in regard to the placement. However, if such an agreement is not possible, the municipal building supervision authority will make the relevant resolution in regard to the placement of the cable, e g by validating the cable route plan, provided always, however, that the placement cannot otherwise be accomplished in a satisfactory manner and with reasonable costs.[48]

11.32   If more extensive rights to third parties' property are needed in installing and maintaining telecommunications cables, the telecommunications operator may possibly redeem real property and specific rights in accordance with the Act on the Redemption of Immoveable Property and Special Rights.[49]

11.33   A telecommunications cable shall, if possible, be installed in a public or highway area and regard shall be had to existing zoning and other land-use

---

40   Final decision given by FICORA 13 October 2004.
41   FICORA has given draft decisions to the Commission, according to which there is no SMP operator on this market. The Commission has in its decision of 20 February 2004 required that the draft decisions are annulled, and that further market analysis is carried out before new decisions are made.
42   Market analysis is currently being done.
43   Art 18 CMA.
44   Art 19 CMA.
45   See paras 11.81–11.82 below.
46   Maankäyttö- ja rakennuslaki 5.2.1999/132.
47   Art 102 CMA.
48   Art 106 CMA.
49   Laki kiinteän omaisuuden ja erityisten oikeuksien lunastuksesta 29.7.1977/603.

planning, to landscape and environmental considerations and to avoidance of unnecessary hindrance or damage. In addition, the property owner and holder are entitled to receive full compensation for any hindrance and damage caused by such measures.[50] Furthermore, after a telecommunications operator has carried out work which is necessary for the implementation of a confirmed cable route plan, such as felling trees, affixing equipment to structures and buildings or undertaking construction work, the operator has a specific obligation to restore the condition of the area.[51]

Co-location and Facility Sharing

11.34   Article 110 CMA imposes on the municipality an obligation to supervise that the objectives in the CMA for the installation of telecommunications cables are fulfilled when routing cables. Article 110 CMA also stipulates that cable routing shall, when needed, be coordinated by the municipality so that the said objectives are fulfilled also when more than one telecommunications operator performs building or maintenance operations relating to cable routing within the municipality. There is no strict duty to always oblige telecommunications operators to co-locate and share facilities, but the promotion of co-location and facility sharing provided for by article 12(1) Framework Directive is implemented in practice through the decisions of relevant municipality organs.

11.35   According to article 26 CMA, FICORA may oblige an SMP telecommunications operator to lease out a radio mast antenna site or part of a cable duct to other telecommunications operators and thus promote co-location and facility sharing. FICORA may impose the same obligation on a non-SMP telecommunications operator, where undertakings are deprived of access due to reasons similar to those in article 12(2) Framework Directive.

REGULATION OF MARKET ENTRY: IMPLEMENTATION OF THE AUTHORISATION DIRECTIVE

The General Authorisation of Electronic Communications

11.36   The entire CMA and related lower-level regulations function as the general authorisation, encompassing all forms of public telecommunications falling under the general authorisation regime. In other words, telecommunications operators operating under the general authorisation regime have all the rights and obligations described in the CMA and in decrees, decisions and regulations issued by the MTC or FICORA under the CMA.

11.37   Written telecommunications notification of the intention to operate public telecommunications[52] shall be submitted to FICORA before the operation begins.[53] The notification duty does not apply to public telecommunications that are of a temporary nature, aimed at a small audience or otherwise of minor importance.

---

50   Art 108 CMA.
51   Art 107 CMA.
52   Public telecommunications means the provision of a network service or communications service to a set of users that is not subject to any prior restriction. Art 2(1)(23) CMA.
53   Art 13 CMA.

According to a decree given by the Council of State,[54] public telecommunications are seen to be of minor importance if operations consist of the provision of network or communications services in a communications network of less than 500 subscriber connections, or if turnover from telecommunications operations is less than €300,000.

11.38   Even though each operator of public telecommunications is obliged to submit a telecommunications notification to FICORA, the notification in itself does not create any legal rights or obligations. The purpose of the notification is solely to aid FICORA in its supervision of the telecommunications markets. Thus, a telecommunications operator has the rights and obligations described in the CMA whether it has fulfilled its notification duty or not. On a separate request of the telecommunications operator, FICORA shall send a confirmation notice to the operator that has submitted the notification. This confirmation notice shall indicate the rights and obligations of a telecommunications operator in Finland under the CMA.

Rights of Use for Radio Frequencies

General Authorisations and Granting of Individual Rights

11.39   According to article 4 CMA, a licence is required for the provision of a network service that uses radio frequencies in a digital terrestrial mass communications network or in a mobile network practising public communications. This applies also to a mobile network that functions as a public authority network and operates in more than one municipality.

11.40   When appropriate frequencies become available for the above-mentioned network services, the Council of State shall announce that a licence is available for application. Such an announcement shall be made in accordance with the frequency band utilisation plan.[55] The Council of State may grant a licence for up to 20 years.

11.41   A licence is granted if the applicant has sufficient economic resources to meet the network operators obligations and if the licensing authority has no justifiable reason to suspect the applicant will violate the provisions of CMA, the Radio Act, the Act on the Protection of Privacy and Data Security in Telecommunications[56] ('E-Privacy Act') or any other act relating to telecommunications operations.[57] In addition to these requirements, the granting of a licence for the provision of a network service in a public authority network requires that the applicant has the necessary ability and professional skills in regard to the special nature of the operation.

Admissible Conditions

11.42   According to article 10(1) CMA, the geographical operating area of the telecommunications operator shall be defined in the licence. In addition, provisions concerning quality and compatibility requirements as well as requirements concerning the technical characteristics of communications networks or the efficient use of

---

54   Valtioneuvoston asetus merkitykseltään vähäisestä teletoiminnasta 3.7.2003/675.
55   Art 5 CMA.
56   Sähköisen viestinnän tietosuojalaki 16.6.2004/516.
57   Art 9 CMA.

frequencies may be incorporated into a licence. The licence terms shall comply with the objectives of the CMA.[58] These provisions are in accordance with article 6 and Part B of the Annex to the Authorisations Directive.

11.43   A licence for the provision of network service in a terrestrial mass communications network may only be granted if the licence holder for his part ensures that the Finnish Broadcasting Company Ltd and a programming licence holder in accordance with the Act on Television and Radio Operations and the Provincial Act on Broadcasting Operations are able to obtain the necessary capacity at a cost-oriented price for their television and radio operations.[59]

11.44   Additional terms may be incorporated into a licence that concern the amount of capacity reserved for a programming licence holder or the cooperation between programming licence holders in questions relating to capacity distribution or electronic programme guides. Terms concerning broadcasting technology may also be incorporated into a licence.[60]

11.45   Radio permits do not add any significant additional requirements for a radio transmitter or a telecommunications operator with a licence.

Limitation of the number of rights of use to be granted

11.46   If the scarcity of radio frequencies prevents that all applicants are granted a licence, the licence(s) shall be granted to the applicant(s) whose operation best promotes the objectives of the CMA.[61] A similar scheme has been implemented in regard to radio permits in accordance with the Radio Act.

11.47   Due to the fact that licences are granted through beauty contests, no auctions are to be expected in regard to Finnish licences that are to be granted in accordance with the CMA.

Frequency Trading

11.48   According to article 12(2) CMA, as a general rule, a licence is non-transferable and the Council of State may cancel a licence if the effective control in respect of the holder of the licence changes. Any such change of control must be notified immediately to the licensing authority, which shall decide on whether to cancel the licence within two months of the notification.

Rights of Use for Numbers

General Authorisations and Granting of Individual Rights

11.49   The numbers and identifiers issued for the use of telecommunications operators and persons are decided by FICORA.[62] FICORA's regulations specify the type of numbers and identifiers that may be used in telecommunications and for

---

58   Art 10(2) CMA.
59   Art 10(3) CMA.
60   Art 10(4) CMA.
61   Art 9 CMA.
62   Art 48 CMA.

what purpose they are to be used. FICORA's regulation on numbering also specifies the geographical area of use for numbers and identifiers. No separate area code for VoIP services is planned. VoIP services are granted three different numbers: (i) geographic numbers, (ii) national company numbers, and (iii) numbers reserved for personal reaching services.

11.50   In the distribution procedure of the numbers and identifiers the telecommunications operators and other persons shall be treated as fairly as possible, taking into consideration the nature and extent of the operation.[63] The issuing of a number or identifier occurs, in most cases, through negotiations with telecommunications operators and other persons. If needed the numbers and identifiers may also be issued, for instance, by drawing lots.

11.51   Numbers of exceptional economic value are not auctioned or sold, but FICORA makes its numbering decisions based on a comparison of the applications, taking into account its obligation to treat applicants fairly and equally as well as the aim of a clear and efficient numbering allocation, while having regard to the nature and extent of the operation. If appropriate, lots may be drawn regarding numbers of exceptional value.

Admissible Conditions

11.52   FICORA may in its numbering decision order that the number is used to offer a specified service and may impose other conditions on the use of the number necessary to ensure the clarity and efficiency of numbering or the benefits to users.[64] The permissible conditions in accordance with the Authorisation Directive, which are listed in part C of its Annex, are incorporated in general in the numbering provisions of the CMA and the regulations given by FICORA.[65]

11.53   A telecommunications operator in a telephone network has an obligation to provide number portability free of charge to its users when they change a fixed-connection to another fixed-connection telecommunications operator in the same telecommunications area or a mobile-connection to another mobile-connection telecommunications operator.[66] Both telecommunications operators are responsible for meeting half of any per-call costs incurred from the transfer of the number. If the VoIP service is considered to be similar to traditional telephone network, the number transfer for the services is permissible and mandatory. Currently, FICORA is drafting guidelines on VoIP.

11.54   Only SMP telecommunications operators in a fixed telephone network have an obligation to provide carrier pre-selection and indirect access to other carriers' services. By a decision FICORA may impose the said obligation in respect of international calls on an operator with SMP operating in a mobile network.[67]

---

63   Art 48 CMA.
64   Art 48 CMA.
65   However, no mention is made regarding condition number 8. Furthermore, with regard to condition number 6, the transfer or rights on the initiative of the holder of the right is not allowed as such, but would require the cancellation of the right of use by the transferor and a new application by the transferee. In connection with mergers or transfer of business, notification to FICORA is required.
66   Art 51 CMA.
67   Art 62 CMA.

Limitation of Number of Rights of Use to be Granted

11.55 The selection procedure is comparative: the numbers and identifiers shall be distributed by FICORA in a manner that treats telecommunications operators and other persons as fairly as possible while having regard to the nature and extent of the operation. Hence the sufficiency and uniformity of the numbers can be assured.

The NRA's Enforcement Powers

11.56 If a telecommunications operator, another actor on the telecommunications market or a user violates the CMA or provisions issued under it, and fails to rectify its actions, FICORA may order the defaulter to make right the error or omission. A conditional fine or a threat of terminating the operation of or completing the incomplete action at the defaulter's expense may be imposed as a sanction in support of the obligation.[68]

11.57 A telecommunications operator that acts in violation of an individual obligation may be ordered to pay a penalty charge if it fails to rectify its actions.[69] The amount of the penalty is a minimum of €1,000 and a maximum of €1,000,000. If the act or omission has especially significant effects on the market, the stated amount may be exceeded.

11.58 If a telecommunications operator seriously and significantly breaches or fails to comply with the provisions of the CMA or regulations issued under it, and does not rectify its conduct, FICORA may prohibit the telecommunications operator from engaging in telecommunications in full or in part.[70]

11.59 A licence may be cancelled by the Council of State if the telecommunications operator has repeatedly and seriously violated the provisions of any act on telecommunications or the licence terms, or if the telecommunications operator no longer has sufficient economic resources to meet its obligations and if the telecommunications operator, despite being requested to do so, fails to rectify its conduct or replenish its economic resources to a sufficient level.[71]

11.60   FICORA may revoke the right to use a number or identifier if the holder of the right fails to pay the numbering fee, if the number is used in contravention of the numbering decision, if the number or identifier has not been taken into use within a reasonable period or its use has been discontinued, or if there is another similar, very weighty reason.[72]

11.61 In practice, interim measures and sanctions are very seldom ordered. Usually, FICORA simply orders the defaulter to correct its behaviour and to provide FICORA with evidence of such correction. Because the subjects generally comply with the order, there has been no need for stronger measures.

---

68   Art 121 CMA.
69   Art 122 CMA.
70   Art 123 CMA.
71   Art 12 CMA.
72   Art 50 CMA.

Administrative Charges and Fees for Rights of Use

11.62   According to article 7 CMA, a licence applicant[73] is required to pay to the State an application fee of €1,000 for the application. No application fee is needed for a licence application concerning a public authority network.

11.63   The common charge, which shall be paid by all telecommunications operators engaging in telecommunications subject to notification or licence, is the annual telecommunications market fee collected by FICORA. The telecommunications market fee corresponds to the costs of FICORA fulfilling its duties under the CMA regarding telecommunications operators,[74] except for the tasks of numbering administration and supervision, which is covered by a separate numbering fee. The telecommunications market fee can be collected without a judgement or decision in the same way as taxes. Unless the fee is paid on the due date, a penalty interest or a late fee is added to the amount.

11.64   Fees for the right to hold and use radio transmitters are collected in accordance with the MTC Decree on the Fees of FICORA.[75] Provisions on the fees for the right of use of numbers are found in the CMA and in the MTC Decree on the Fees of FICORA. Anyone who has obtained a number or identifier has an obligation to pay to FICORA a fixed numbering fee to cover the costs incurred in numbering management and supervision.[76]

Transitional Regulations for Existing Authorisations

11.65   A network licence valid at the time of entry into force of the CMA is valid until the end of the licence period. An operator providing a network service in a public authority network in operation before the CMA's entry into force, however, was to apply for a network licence in accordance with the CMA within two months from its entry into force.

11.66   Operators, who operated under the general authorisation regime when the CMA entered into force, were obligated to submit a telecommunications notification to FICORA according to the CMA within two months from its entry into force.

REGULATION OF NETWORK ACCESS AND INTERCONNECTION: THE IMPLEMENTATION OF THE ACCESS DIRECTIVE

Objectives and Scope of Access Regulation

11.67   FICORA and the MTC shall act in accordance with the objectives of the CMA.[77] Both SMP[78] and non-SMP[79] telecommunications operators can be subject to access and interconnection obligations. However, the list of access obligations that may be imposed on non-SMP operators is significantly shorter than that of

---

73   See para 11.39 above.
74   Art 15a CMA.
75   Liikenne- ja viestintäministeriön asetus Viestintäviraston maksuista 11.12.2002/1126.
76   Art 49 CMA.
77   See para 11.1 above.
78   Art 18 CMA.
79   Art 19 CMA.

SMP operators. The criteria for imposing an access or interconnection obligation on a non-SMP operator are also quite different from the criteria for imposing the same obligation on an operator with SMP.[80]

Basic Regulatory Concepts

11.68   When imposing access and interconnection obligations on SMP operators, the obligations shall be proportionate and FICORA shall, according to article 18 CMA, have special regard to the following:

- the appropriateness of access rights in technical and economic terms, having regard to the degree of development of the market and the type of access rights,
- the feasibility of access rights, having regard to available capacity,
- the requirements concerning protection of privacy and information security,
- the investment made and risks taken by the operator with SMP,
- the need to safeguard a competitive environment in the long term,
- relevant industrial property rights and copyrights, and
- the provision of services at European level.[81]

11.69   The term 'access' is not defined as such in the CMA. The CMA uses both the Finnish translation of the term from the Access Directive, which in Finnish means 'right to use', and, when access to physical locations or equipment is discussed, the CMA uses the term 'lease'. The term interconnection, on the other hand, is defined in article 2(1)(13) CMA. According to the definition interconnection means 'the physical and functional connecting of different communications networks and communications services to ensure that users can access other telecommunications operators communications networks and communications services'.

11.70   A telecommunications operator has an obligation to negotiate on interconnection with other telecommunications operators.[82] Unlike certain other obligations considered in this chapter, which require a decision of FICORA to be effective, this particular obligation is directly stated in the CMA. Also in cases where FICORA has to impose an interconnection obligation on an operator, which can be either an SMP or a non-SMP operator, agreements between operators have priority over most of the CMA provisions on interconnection.

11.71   The specific obligations that may be imposed on an operator with SMP are listed in article 18 CMA. Since the structure of the CMA differs from the structure of the four telecommunications directives, obligations from both the Access and the Universal Service Directive are included in the same list and handled in the same manner. The content of the access obligations corresponds largely with the obligations provided for by the EU Directives.

---

80   See paras 11.81–11.82 below.
81   The list is not exhaustive.
82   Art 39 CMA.

Access and Interconnection-related Obligations with Respect to SMP Undertakings

Transparency obligations

11.72 FICORA may impose an obligation on an operator to publish information, which is important in regard to access or interconnection obligations, such as information on service delivery conditions, tariff information and agreements made, excluding, however, business secrets and other confidential information.[83] Such obligations may be imposed on an SMP operator even if no access obligation is imposed on the operator.

Non-discrimination obligations

11.73 The non-discrimination requirement means that operators that are in similar situations shall be treated equally. If an operator uses a certain service itself or provides that service to a subsidiary or another similar party, it shall also offer an equivalent service on equivalent conditions to any competing operator.[84] A competitor may not be put in a different situation with regard to, for example, delivery terms or the standard of the service provided.

Specific Access Obligations

11.74 FICORA may, among others, impose the following access obligations on an SMP operator, obliging the operator to:

- relinquish access rights to a mobile network,
- lease out part of a local loop and equipment facilities,
- provide line rental of a leased line,
- lease out part of a terrestrial mass communications network,
- relinquish capacity in a terrestrial mass communications network,
- organise national roaming, and
- organise international roaming.[85]

11.75 As stated above, both SMP or non-SMP operator have an obligation to negotiate on interconnection with another telecommunications operator even without a decision by FICORA. When this is not enough, FICORA may impose an obligation on an SMP operator to connect a communications network or service to the communications network or service of another operator.[86]

Price control obligations

11.76 FICORA may impose an obligation on an operator to ensure that the prices to be charged for relinquishing access rights, roaming or interconnection are

---

83 Art 33 CMA.
84 Art 84(2) CMA.
85 In addition, the following obligations may be imposed: obligation to lease out an antenna site and part of a cable duct, obligation to relinquish cable television network capacity, obligation to relinquish access rights to smart card capacity, obligations to relinquish access rights to an electronic programme guide, and obligation to relinquish access rights to a programming interface for a television or radio system. As no separate VoIP market is planned at present, no separate obligations can be set.
86 Art 39 CMA.

either cost-oriented, non-discriminatory or both, and that non-discriminatory conditions are otherwise applied. FICORA is also authorised to impose on an operator a maximum price that may be charged for leasing out part of a local loop and equipment facilities, and for line rental of a leased line.[87] FICORA may impose pricing obligations on an SMP operator even if no access or interconnection obligation is imposed on the operator.[88] According to article 40 CMA, the charge for the use of the telephone network of the telecommunications operator requesting the interconnection that is collected from the telecommunications operator with the obligation to establish interconnection shall not be unreasonable.

11.77 A cost-oriented price means a price that is reasonable taking into account the costs incurred and the efficiency of the operation, as well as a reasonable return on capital.[89] Consequently, a cost-oriented price is higher than only the costs for the service produced. Investments made by the operator and related risks have to be taken into account. Costs shall relate to the service produced. According to the Government Bill,[90] the efficiency of the operation is measured by comparing costs incurred for producing the service with costs that are incurred by other operators operating under similar conditions when producing similar services. Only when there is reason to believe that operations are inefficient there is reason to examine the relation between pricing and operations efficiency.

Accounting separation obligations

11.78 In order to facilitate monitoring of price-control obligations, FICORA has the right to impose obligations on an SMP operator to implement cost-accounting procedures[91] and/or to separate in its accounts the functions related to access and interconnection.[92] The choice of which cost-accounting procedures to use, however, remains with the telecommunications operator.

11.79 The most common obligations imposed on SMP operators are the obligations to publish delivery conditions and tariff information, to provide interconnection and to use non-discriminatory delivery terms. On most markets some operators have also been imposed with the obligations to use cost-oriented pricing and to implement cost-accounting procedures and accounting separation.

Related Regulatory Powers with Respect to SMP Undertakings

11.80 FICORA may impose an obligation on a telecommunications operator with SMP to rent a leased line to telecommunication operators and users. In the decision FICORA may define the transmission capacity of a leased line and in defining the capacity FICORA shall have regard to the provisions of the EU on the

---

87　In addition, FICORA is entitled, while assessing the cost-orientation of the price charged under art 84 CMA, also in individual cases to determine the maximum amount of the price: art 86(3) CMA.
88　Art 37 CMA.
89　Art 84(1) CMA.
90　Hallituksen esitys Eduskunnalle viestintämarkkinoita koskevan lainsäädännön muuttamisesta 112/2002.
91　Art 87 CMA.
92　Art 89 CMA.

minimum choice of leased lines.[93] Moreover, obligations regarding carrier pre-selection and indirect access can be imposed.[94]

Regulatory Powers Applicable to All Market Participants

11.81   FICORA may impose the following obligations on a non-SMP operator:[95]

- lease out part of a local loop and equipment facilities;
- lease out antenna site and part of a cable duct;
- relinquish access rights to an electronic programme guide;
- relinquish access rights to a programming interface for a television or radio system;
- publish delivery terms and tariff information;
- comply with the provisions concerning pricing and other terms; and
- join a communications network to another communications network.

11.82   In addition to above, the obligation to lease out part of a local loop and equipment facilities can also be imposed on a non-SMP operator. However, these obligations can be imposed only if the operator controls user connections to the communications network and if the imposition of the obligation is necessary to ensure the benefit to users.[96]

11.83   The provisions in article 5 Access Directive on access to digital radio and television broadcasting services have been implemented in CMA.[97] In addition, the CMA contains provisions regarding the 'must carry' obligation for network service providers in a cable television network. Furthermore, FICORA has issued a regulation[98] on technical characteristics of television receivers, decoding systems and wide screen television networks.

REGULATION OF UNIVERSAL SERVICES AND USERS' RIGHTS: THE UNIVERSAL SERVICE DIRECTIVE

Regulation of Universal Service Obligations

Scope of Universal Service Obligations

11.84   The CMA imposes on operators with SMP within a certain operating area the obligation to provide connection to the fixed telephone network in its operating area at the user's fixed location. If there is no SMP operator, the obligation rests with the operator with the largest market share in the area in question.[99]

---

93   Art 25 CMA.
94   See para 11.54 above. For SMP obligations regarding universal services, see paras 11.84–11.86 below.
95   Art 19 CMA.
96   Art 24 CMA.
97   Art 18, art19, art 24, art 31, art 32, art 39, and art 119 CMA.
98   FICORA 36 A/2003 M; Regulation on technical characteristics on television receivers, decoding systems and wide-screen television networks.
99   Art 59 CMA.

11.85   The obligation to provide a comprehensive directory to end-users is also enacted directly in the CMA.[100] The obligation rests with all operators that provide subscriber connections in a fixed or mobile telephone network. All operators in a telephone network also have the obligation to ensure that users have access to a generally available and comprehensive directory enquiry service.[101]

11.86   No regulation on the provision of public pay phones has been implemented in Finland. The implementation of article 7 Universal Service Directive has not required new legislative implementation measures, because existing telecommunications services for disabled end-users were seen to be sufficient and guaranteed by legislation on services for the handicapped.

Designation of Undertakings Obliged to Provide Universal Services

11.87   Article 8 Universal Service Directive has not been implemented in Finland.

Regulation of Retail Tariffs, Users' Expenditures and Quality of Service

11.88   Retail tariffs of universal services are monitored by FICORA to ensure that they stay within the reasonable range required by the CMA. Article 9(2) Universal Service Directive[102] has not been implemented in Finland. Telephone expenses are included in the costs covered by the Finnish income support legislation, which ensures that low income and special need users can afford reasonable telecommunication services.

Cost calculation and financing of universal services

11.89   Due to the choice not to implement the designated undertaking regime, articles 10, 11, 12, 13 and 14 Universal Service Directive have not been implemented in Finnish legislation. However, the CMA contains quality and transparency requirements that apply to all telecommunications operators.[103]

Regulation of Retail Markets

11.90   If FICORA finds that no competition exists on a defined retail market and that the obligations imposed on SMP operators on the wholesale markets do not sufficiently promote competition on the retail market, FICORA shall impose one or more necessary additional obligations.[104] As additional obligations FICORA may forbid the SMP operator on the market from:

- charging unreasonable prices,
- preventing access to the market or restricting competition by unjustifiably low pricing,
- favouring certain service recipients in an unwarranted manner, and

---

100   Art 57 CMA.
101   Art 56 CMA.
102   See para 1.166 above.
103   Art 66, art 82 art 128, art 129 CMA.
104   Art 20 CMA.

- tying a specific product or service to other products or services.

11.91 It is evident that regulation of retail markets may be considered only when wholesale market regulation fails. In the SMP decisions regarding retail markets that FICORA has issued, none of the supplemental retail market obligations have been imposed. In its decisions FICORA has merely reiterated the universal service obligations that are, according to the CMA, directly applicable to SMP operators.

End User Rights

Contracts

11.92 The CMA contains provisions on the formal requirements as well as the minimum required substance of telephone network subscriber connection agreements and other communications service agreements.[105] The agreement may not restrict the users' right to select a content service provider[106] and the agreement shall mention the right of the consumer to refer a dispute regarding the agreement to the Consumer Complaint Board to be decided.[107]

11.93 In addition, a telecommunications operator may amend the agreement in accordance with article 71 CMA. Further, the user has the right to give notice of termination with immediate effect if the operator notifies of any amendment to the agreed terms.

Transparency Obligations

11.94 A telecommunications operator has an obligation to draw up standard agreement terms for agreements on telephone network subscriber connections and to use them when making agreements with consumers.[108] The operator shall publish standard agreement terms and tariff information on services and ensure that they are easily available to users without charge. Furthermore, the Consumer Ombudsman and FICORA have to be notified of the standard agreement terms and tariff information.[109]

11.95 By decision, FICORA may impose an obligation on an operator to publish comparable and up-to-date information on the quality of the services it offers. The information to be published may, among other things, concern the delivery time of a subscriber connection, the number of faults per subscriber connection and the fault repair time.[110]

Other Obligations

11.96 The CMA imposes several other obligations relating to end user rights, such as supplying tone dialling and calling line identification and providing itemised

---

105 Art 67 CMA.
106 Art 68 CMA.
107 In case a dispute arises between a consumer and an operator, the consumer has, according to the Consumer Protection Act, the right to bring proceedings against the operator in the public court of the consumer's place of residence. Any arbitration agreement that is entered into before a dispute arises is invalid with respect to a consumer.
108 Art 66 CMA.
109 Art 66 CMA.
110 Art 82 CMA.

bills. In contrast to the situation in most other European countries, article 70 CMA includes a prohibition on tie-in sales with regard to mobile network terminal equipment and related items. This means that the price of mobile phones may not be dependent on whether the user also acquires a subscriber connection from the seller. This helps consumers to compare separately the prices of subscriber connections and terminal equipment. The end user fees for VoIP services are not regulated, nor has any minimum price been set.

DATA PROTECTION: IMPLEMENTATION OF THE DIRECTIVE ON PRIVACY AND ELECTRONIC COMMUNICATIONS

Confidentiality of Communications

11.97   Service providers and network providers are defined in the E-Privacy Act as 'telecommunications operators'.[111] The right to confidential communications is based on the constitution of Finland and violations are criminalised by the Penal Code. The E-Privacy Act contains a general provision on confidentiality of messages, identification data and location data[112] and a general obligation of secrecy and non-exploitation provision.[113] In addition, the telecommunications operator is required to take applicable administrative and technical measures to maintain the information security of its services.[114]

11.98   The E-Privacy Act contains provision on guidance and supervision authorities' right of access to information[115] and on the right of authorities to receive emergency announcements.[116] The right of authorities to receive identification data for the purposes of preventing, investigating and uncovering crimes are based on the E-Privacy Act,[117] the Police Act,[118] the Customs Act[119] and the Coercive Measures Act.[120]

11.99   The provision of the E-Privacy Act[121] on saving data on the use of a service in the user's terminal device and the use of such data are in line with the provisions of article 5(3) E-Privacy Directive. Among other obligations the service provider has an obligation to provide information, users have right to prohibit the usage of their data, there are exceptions regarding transmission of messages and services requested by users, and the privacy of users may not be encroached any more than necessary.

---

111   Art 2(1)(4) Act on the Protection of Privacy and Data Security in Telecommunications (Sähköisen viestinnän tietosuojalaki 16.6.2004/516).
112   Art 4 E-Privacy Act.
113   Art 5 E-Privacy Act.
114   Art 19 E-Privacy Act.
115   FICORA and the Data Protection Ombudsman. Art 33 E-Privacy Act.
116   Art 35 E-Privacy Act.
117   Art 36 E-Privacy Act.
118   Poliisilaki 7.4.1995/493.
119   Tullilaki 29.12.1994/1466.
120   Pakkokeinolaki 30.4.1987/450.
121   Art 7 E-Privacy Act.

Traffic Data and Location Data

11.100   The E-Privacy Act defines traffic data as identification data, which can be associated with a subscriber or user and which is processed in communications networks for the purposes of transmitting, distributing or providing messages.[122] Location data is defined as data which shows the geographic location of a subscriber connection or terminal device and which is used for a purpose other than the provision of a network service or communication service.[123]

11.101   Telecommunications providers may process traffic data:

- for the purpose of the provisions and use of a network service, communications service and value added service and for the purpose of ensuring information security in these services,[124]
- if necessary, for defining fees between themselves and/or value added service providers and for billing purposes,[125]
- for the purpose of marketing communications services or value added services, to such extent and for such a period of time as the marketing requires,[126]
- for the purpose of technical development of services,[127]
- if necessary, to detect, prevent, investigate and commit to pre-trial investigation any non-paying use of fee-based network services, communications services or value added services, of any similar case on misuse,[128] and
- for the purpose of detecting a technical fault or error in the transmission of communications.[129]

11.102   To process traffic data under the first three bullets above, telecommunications operators are liable to inform subscribers or users on what traffic data is being processed and how long the processing will last.[130] Processing for marketing purposes requires that the subscriber or user to whom the data applies has given his consent thereto and he must have the opportunity to cancel his consent.[131]

11.103   Telecommunications operators may process location data for the purpose of providing and using value added services[132] if the subscriber has not forbidden it. The telecommunications operator must ensure that the subscriber can easily and at no separate charge prohibit processing of location data and that the subscriber has easy and continuous access to information on the precision of the location data

---

122   Art 2(1)(8) E-Privacy Act.
123   Art 2(1)(9) E-Privacy Act.
124   Art 9(1) E-Privacy Act.
125   Art 10(1) E-Privacy Act.
126   Art 11(1) E-Privacy Act. Please note that the E-Privacy Act contains separate provisions on direct marketing.
127   Art 12(1) E-Privacy Act.
128   Art 13 E-Privacy Act.
129   Art 14 E-Privacy Act.
130   Arts 10(6), 11(2) and 12(2) E-Privacy Act.
131   Art 11(2) and (3) E-Privacy Act. Please note that the E-Privacy Act contains separate provisions on direct marketing. In addition, the E-Privacy Act contain provisions on persons to whom traffic data may be disclosed, who may actually process the data, for which period of time the data must be stored, and saving information on processing.
132   'Value added service' has been defined as a service based on the processing of identification (ie traffic) data or location data for a purpose other than the provision of a network service or communication service, art 2(1)(7) E-Privacy Act.

processed, the purpose of the processing and on whether location data can be disclosed to a third party for the purpose of providing value added services.[133]

Itemised Billing

11.104   The telecommunications operator shall provide itemised bills on the use of the telephone network subscriber connection at no charge and, provided the bill is more than €50, without being separately requested to do so.[134] The bill shall conveniently present at least the following bill items:

- local calls and the network charges collected for calls referred to in bullets 2–4 below,
- long distance calls,
- international calls,
- mobile network calls,
- subscriber connection rates,
- text messages, picture messages and other messages, and
- data transfer services.

11.105   Irrespective of the size of the bill, the telecommunications operator must itemise the fees for services other than communications services without being requested to do so. The user[135] has the right to obtain a non-itemised bill on request.[136]

11.106   The telecommunications operator is obliged to release the call itemisation of a bill if the subscriber[137] so requests. Such an itemisation must be provided in a form where the last three digits of the phone number are obscured or the itemisation otherwise rendered so that the other party to the communication cannot be identified.[138]

11.107   Telecommunications operator must, if the user[139] so requests, release the call itemisation of a bill with the complete phone numbers or other communications service identification data of the parties to the communication.[140]

Calling and Connected Line Identification

11.108   Telecommunications operator operating in a telephone network is obliged to provide a user with a calling line identification service.[141] In addition, operator must offer the subscriber an easy way of barring:

---

133 Art 17 E-Privacy Act.
134 Art 80 CMA.
135 Art 2(1)(24) CMA defines a user as 'a person who uses the services provided by a telecommunications operator for purposes other than telecommunications'.
136 Art 80 CMA.
137 Art 2(1)(10) E-Privacy Act defines a subscriber as 'a legal person or natural person who has entered into an agreement concerning the provision of a communications service or a value added service'.
138 Art 24(2) E-Privacy Act.
139 Art 2(1)(12) E-Privacy Act defines a user as 'a natural person who uses a communications service or value added service without necessarily being a subscriber to the service'.
140 Art 24(3) E-Privacy Act.
141 Art 64 CMA.

- identification of any or all of his subscriber connections,
- identification of the subscriber connections of incoming calls,
- reception of calls whose subscriber connection identification is barred if this is technically possible without undue cost, and
- identification of the subscriber connection to which incoming calls have been transferred.[142]

The service referred to in bullets 1, 2 and 4 above must be free of charge to the subscriber.

11.109   In addition, such operator must offer the user an easy way of barring identification of his subscriber connection separately for each outgoing call, at no charge. The telecommunications operator is obliged to notify subscribers and users of the abovementioned services.[143]

Automatic Call Forwarding

11.110   If a user so requests, the telecommunications operator must, at no charge, remove any automatic call transfer to the user's subscriber connection that has been placed by a third party.[144]

Directories of Subscribers

11.111   A service provider providing a telephone directory, other subscriber directory or a directory inquiry service is entitled to process personal data for the purpose of creating and providing directory service or a directory inquiry service.[145] Under the CMA a telecommunications operator or value added service provider is obliged to disclose contact information to other service providers for the purpose of preparing a telephone directory or providing a directory inquiry service.[146]

11.112   A telecommunications operator is obliged to notify any subscriber who is a natural person about the purpose and use of any telephone directory or other subscriber directory that is publicly available or usable through a directory service, or any directory inquiry service. Such notification must be given at no charge before the subscriber's information is entered in the subscriber directory or directory inquiry service.

11.113   A telecommunications operator must give any subscriber, who is a natural person, the opportunity to prohibit, at no charge, the inclusion of any part or all of his contact information in a telephone directory, other subscriber directory or directory inquiry service. Any telecommunications operator that has received the subscriber's contact information under CMA must, if any subscriber who is a natural person so request, remove and amend incorrect information at no charge. The subscriber's right of access is stipulated in the Personal Data Act. In addition to the above, any subscriber, who is a natural person, has the right to prohibit, at no charge, the disclosure of his contact information.

---

142   Art 80 CMA.
143   Art 22 E-Privacy Act.
144   Art 23 E-Privacy Act.
145   Art 25 E-Privacy Act.
146   Art 58 CMA.

11.114   A telecommunications operator must allow companies and other organisations entered into a telephone directory, other subscriber directory or directory inquiry service the right to have their contact information inspected and removed, and incorrect contact information amended.

Unsolicited Communications

11.115   The E-Privacy Act regulates unsolicited communications through automated calling systems, facsimile machines, or e-mail, text, voice, sound or image messages.[147] Direct marketing by such means may only be directed at natural persons who have given their prior consent. Direct marketing other than referred to above is allowed if it has not been specifically prohibited. A natural person must be able easily and at no charge to prohibit direct marketing.[148] If the service provider or a seller obtains from a customer his contact information for e-mail, text, voice, sound or image messages in context of sale of a product or service, such contact information may be used for direct marketing of the products within the same product group and for other similar products or services by the service provider or seller.[149] Direct marketing to legal persons is allowed if the recipient has not specifically prohibited it.[150]

11.116   In addition to legislation, forms of self-regulation issued by the marketing associations exist. The Finnish Consumer Ombudsman has also given separate marketing guidelines. Collection, storing, use and assignments of personal data are guided and supervised by the Data Protection Ombudsman.

---

147   Art 26(1) E-Privacy Act.
148   Art 26(1) and (2) E-Privacy Act.
149   Art 26(3) E-Privacy Act.
150   Art 27 E-Privacy Act.

The French Market for Electronic Communications[1]

Valerie Kostrzewski-Pugnat
Baker & McKenzie

LEGAL STRUCTURE

Basic Policy

12.1   The French telecommunications sector has experienced important changes since 1 January 1998, when telecommunications services were opened to competition.

12.2   The implementation of the 2002 EU Regulatory Package and the taking into account of the purposes and procedures defined at Community level led to a revision due to changes in the markets' needs and obligations, and the desire to relax certain rules in the interests of promoting effective competition. The main purposes of the French legislator were as follows:

- to promote effective and fair competition for the benefit of users: competition is not the only purpose, it shall provide consumers with a better quality service, at better prices and with many service offerings meeting their requirements and needs,
- to control the supply and financing of all components of the public telecommunications service,
- to control the development of employment, innovation and competitiveness in the electronic communications sector: competition is useful only if it is a factor in the development of the market and the economy, and
- to take into account the interest of territories and users concerning access to services and equipment: city planning remains a central concern.

12.3   The legislative reform that occurred in Summer 2004 is marked by four major considerations:

- freedom to exercise electronic communication activities and reinforcement of competitiveness in a simplified regulatory context,
- reinforcement of the role of the legislator,
- city planning and the widening of powers of local authorities, and
- modernisation and simplification of the rules governing the freedom of communication.

---

1   Editing of this chapter closed 30 June 2005.

While France Telecom, the incumbent operator, is still very powerful on most markets, competition is gradually making its way into the sector.

Implementation of EU Directives, Legislation

12.4   The Directives of the 2002 EU Regulatory Package were properly implemented by the French legislator: the main implementation acts were adopted more than a year late. Many decrees relating to the application of the legislation had not been published one year after the adoption of the texts, which in practice makes the legal framework incomplete.

Three acts were adopted by the French Parliament to implement the 2002 EU Regulatory Package and reform the entire electronic communications sector and complete the existing Act No 96–659. All these texts are codified in the Code for Post and Electronic Communications ('CPCE'):

- Act No 2003–1365[2] relating to the obligations of telecommunications public service and France Telecom. It includes the regulatory modifications resulting from the implementation of the Universal Service Directive,
- Act No 2004–575[3] on confidence in the digital economy, specifying the terms and conditions to exercise specific telecommunications activities such as satellite services, and
- Act No 2004–669[4] relating to electronic communications and audiovisual communications services. This act, implementing the most important part of the EU Directives, was passed according to an emergency procedure in order to avoid the parliamentary discussions slowing down the process.

12.5   Numerous implementing decrees are to be adopted in order to complete the legislative texts. While the acts and decrees establish the new framework and are binding upon the French Regulatory Authority (*Autorité de Régulation des Communications Electroniques et des Postes* – 'ARCEP'), the latter's decisions also play a significant role in shaping the telecommunications policy of the country. As a matter of fact, ARCEP's role is to apply the dispositions of the legislative texts.

REGULATORY PRINCIPLES: IMPLEMENTATION OF THE FRAMEWORK DIRECTIVE

Scope of Regulation

12.6   The implementation of the 2002 EU Regulatory Package resulted in a revision of the CPCE and other legal instruments. The Government intended to modify the regulatory framework specific to the audiovisual sector as well, because of the need to coordinate the rules of audiovisual broadcasting between the multiple available platforms: under the current French system, convergence is taken into account not only in the networks and services but also in the contents.

12.7   The French legislator did not implement strictly the definitions contained in the Directives but it kept their spirit. Thus, 'electronic communications network' is

---

2   Act No 2003–1365, dated 31 December 2003.
3   Act No 2004–575, dated 21 June 2004.
4   Act No 2004–669, dated 9 July 2004.

defined as 'any installation or group of installations of transport or broadcasting as well as, if necessary, the other means ensuring the routing of electronic communications, in particular switching and routing means'.[5] The following networks are considered as electronic communications networks: satellite networks, mobile and terrestrial networks, systems using the electric network if they are used to route electronic communications, and networks ensuring the broadcasting or used for the distribution of audiovisual communication services. There is no reference to the difference between fixed networks and mobile networks since both networks are subject to the same development and operating conditions, subject to the frequency granting conditions. The legislator also deleted the reference to cable networks whose system is now in line with the system of the other electronic communications networks.

12.8 'Electronic communications services' are defined as 'services consisting, totally or mainly, in the provision of electronic communications. The services aiming at editing or distributing communications services to the public electronically are excluded'.[6] Contrary to the definition in article 2(c) Framework Directive, there is no reference to the fact that a fee will be charged for the service.

12.9 Numerous definitions contained in the Framework Directive have not been included under French law: notions of associated resources, conditional access systems or application program interfaces are not defined under French law.

National Regulatory Authorities: Organisation, Regulatory Objectives, Competencies

Overview

12.10 Regulation of the electronic communications sector is ensured by the Minister for Electronic Communications and ARCEP under their respective attributions[7] with one exception: the Prime minister manages and grants frequencies to ARCEP and the Superior Audiovisual Board ('CSA') who are in charge of frequency management.[8]

The Competition Council is also an important authority for the telecommunications sector.

The Minister for Electronic Communications

12.11 The Minister for Electronic Communications holds numerous exclusive subject-matter competencies. The main ones concern:

- the appointment of operators in charge of providing components of the universal service,[9] and
- the departure from the obligation on ARCEP to cooperate with the European Commission.

---

5   Art L32(2) CPCE.
6   Art L32(6).
7   Art L32(1) CPCE.
8   Art L41 CPCE.
9   Art L35(2) CPCE.

The Telecommunications Regulation Authority

STATUS AND COMPOSITION

12.12   ARCEP (formerly 'ART'), an independent administrative authority created under the act dated 26 July 1996,[10] was implemented as from 1 January 1997. Originally, ARCEP had a sectoral regulation role whereby it resolved interconnection disputes and regulated tariffs. Its powers have been increased through the implementation of the 2002 EU Regulatory Package. Its seven members[11] hold an irrevocable and non-renewable term of office of six years.

12.13   To ensure the independence of ARCEP as provided for in article 3(3) Framework Directive, article L.36(2) CPCE provides that the function of membership of ARCEP is not compatible with any other professional activity, national electoral office, public employment or the holding of interests in the electronic communications, postal, audiovisual sectors, and members shall not communicate their opinion publicly concerning any subject matter of a decision of ARCEP.

REGULATORY POWERS OF ARCEP

12.14   The new legal framework maintains the competencies of ARCEP concerning the allocation of rare resources (frequencies or numbers that are necessary for the operators' activity).[12]

12.15   ARCEP holds the power to settle disputes[13] between operators in three fields:

- refusal of interconnection, or the conclusion and execution of agreements of interconnection and conditions of access to a telecommunications network,
- adjustment of agreements including clauses excluding or limiting, from a legal or technical viewpoint, the provision of telecommunications services over cabled networks, and
- possibilities and conditions for shared use of the existing installations located on the public domain or on private property.

ARCEP shall also ensure the settlement of cross-border disputes.

The new legal framework imposes on ARCEP four months to make a decision. Under exceptional circumstances, this period may be increased to six months. Common law courts settle consumer/provider disputes.[14]

12.16   ARCEP defines the rules concerning:

- rights and obligations relating to the operation of the various categories of networks and services,
- requirements applicable to the technical and financial conditions of interconnection and access, and the technical and financial conditions of local roaming, and
- conditions of use of frequencies and frequency bands.

---

10   Act No 96–659, dated 26 July 1996 for the regulation of telecommunications.
11   Five members are appointed by the Government and the others are appointed by the Presidents of the parliamentary chambers.
12   Arts L42(1) and L44 CPCE.
13   Art L36(8) CPCE.
14   Art 8(2)(b) Framework Directive.

Contrary to article 3 Framework Directive, the CPCE does not contain any reference to the promotion of cultural diversity and media, or disputes between providers and consumers.

ARCEP's POWER TO DEMAND INFORMATION

12.17   Pursuant to article 5 Framework Directive, ARCEP has a right of information and powers of investigation, jointly exercised with the Minister for Electronic Communications.[15] Transparency is guaranteed, subject to compliance with business confidentiality.

The obligation of information, incumbent on operators, set out in article 5(1) Framework Directive is included in the various articles relating to the services for which such information is necessary to enable ARCEP to carry out its functions.[16]

12.18   ARCEP is also entitled to request the communication of:

• interconnection and access agreements concluded between operators,[17] and
• agreements concerning local roaming.[18]

Pursuant to article L.32(4) CPCE, ARCEP has investigation powers which permit its agents to enter premises, and to demand and copy documents relevant to the investigation.

12.19   ARCEP, during the preparation of its annual report, may prepare expert reports, studies, collect data, and carry out any action required to obtain information regarding the electronic communications sector. In this context, operators have to provide ARCEP with statistics about the use, area of coverage, and conditions of access to their service.

In other respects, under its contentious powers, ARCEP performs 'investigations and expertises'.[19]

COOPERATION WITH THE OTHER AUTHORITIES

12.20   The President of ARCEP may refer to the Competition Council any anti-competitive practices implemented in the electronic communications sector.[20] The Competition Council can be consulted on any matter falling within its jurisdiction and, typically, in the scope of relevant markets analysis.

12.21   ARCEP shall consult the CSA (Superior Audiovisual Board) before taking any decision that may have an impact on radio and television broadcasting, whether it is concerning interconnection and access,[21] dispute settlement[22] or relevant market analysis.[23]

---

15   Art L32(4) CPCE.
16   Arts L32(4), L36(13), L38, L39(4).
17   Art L34(8) CPCE.
18   Art L34(8)(1) CPCE.
19   Art L36(11)(2) CPCE.
20   Art L36(10) CPCE.
21   Art L36(6) CPCE.
22   Art L36(8) CPCE.
23   Art L37(1) CPCE.

12.22   In the event of cross-border disputes,[24] French law provides that ARCEP shall coordinate its action with the authorities which the case is referred to.[25] The procedure rules applicable to national disputes are applicable, except those relating to time limits.

To allow a comparison between the regulatory measures taken by other NRAs, article L.36(14) CPCE requires ARCEP to analyse, in its annual report, the main decisions made by the electronic communications regulation authorities of the member states of the European Union during the past year. When a dispute is also referred to an NRA of another member state, ARCEP shall coordinate the NRA of such state.[26] Finally, markets analysis must be notified to other member states' NRAs.

Transparency and Consultations

12.23   Pursuant to article 6 Framework Directive, article L.32(1) CPCE imposes on ARCEP an obligation to make public its consultations. The ARCEP website publishes all such information.[27]

12.24   Article L.36(14) CPCE imposes on ARCEP the obligation to prepare, every year, a public report concerning its activity and the enforcement of the legal and regulatory provisions relating to electronic communications. It includes in the report an analysis of the main decisions reached by its European counterparts in order to make a comparison between the different types of control performed and their consequences on the markets. This report is sent to the Government and the Parliament as well as to the Superior Commission of the Public Service of Post and Electronic Communications. ARCEP may suggest, in the report, any legal or regulatory modification deemed relevant to take into account changes in the electronic communications sector and the development of competition. ARCEP shall also report its activities to the parliamentary standing committees for the telecommunications sector.

Right of Appeal against NRA's Decisions

12.25   The decisions of ARCEP[28] may be cancelled or modified on appeal to the Court of Appeal in Paris within one month from their notification to the parties. Only the parties to the dispute may institute an appeal against ARCEP's decisions. The remedy does not suspend the decision.[29] The suspension of the decision may be ordered if it is likely to result in excessive consequences or if new, extremely serious events occurred after its notification. Interim measures granted by ARCEP may be the subject of a remedy before the same court within 10 days from their notification. In such a case, the Court shall examine the remedy within one month. Finally, the decision of the Court of Appeal in Paris may be referred to the French Supreme Court of Appeal (Cour de Cassation) within one month from the notification of the appeal decision. The sanctions taken pursuant to article L.36(11) CPCE may be the subject of a remedy before the French Administrative Supreme Court (Conseil d'Etat).

---

24   Art 21 Framework Directive.
25   Art L36(8)(V) CPCE.
26   Art L36(8)(V) CPCE.
27   www.art-telecom.fr.
28   Art L36(8) CPCE.
29   Art L36(8) CPCE.

The NRA's Obligations to Cooperate with the Commission

12.26   Cooperation with the Commission occurs mainly in relation to definition of the relevant markets and proposals for remedies.

12.27   The CPCE requires ARCEP to cooperate with the European Commission in two respects: ARCEP shall notify any measure relating to conditions of access and interconnection;[30] and it shall notify draft decisions relating to analysis of the relevant markets.[31]

12.28   The draft decisions on analysis of the markets are notified to the European Commission, which holds a 'right of veto' concerning the definition of relevant markets and the designation of the main operators.[32] Other member states' NRAs are also notified of the decision as part of an information and coordination process. Article L.37(3) CPCE provides that, under exceptional circumstances, it is possible to depart from the notification 'for a limited term'. The conditions of application of this article will be specified in a decree which has not yet been published.

12.29   Concerning the measures adopted in the interconnection sector, ARCEP shall have a public consultation and notify the measures to the relevant authorities of the member states concerned and the European Commission.[33]

12.30   ARCEP promotes respect for standards set by European and international authorities. The CPCE[34] describes the procedure for evaluating conformity in France. During dispute resolutions, ARCEP may issue recommendations on conformity. Although there is no formal provision that ARCEP may cooperate with the Commission on conformity matters, the latter's advice could be sought.

'Significant Market Power' as a Fundamental Prerequisite of Regulation

Definition of SMP

12.31   Article L.37(1) CPCE sets out a definition that is nearly identical to the Framework Directive's definition, even though the French legislator preferred the words 'significant influence' to 'significant power'. French law, while mentioning[35] that an operator exercising a significant influence may also be deemed as exercising such an influence on an associated market, does not define the notion of associated market. The same provision also stresses that significant influence may be exercised jointly.[36] ARCEP imposes obligations on operators exercising significant influence.[37] These obligations are described in the CPCE.[38]

---

30   Art L34(8) CPCE.
31   Art L37(3)(2) CPCE.
32   Art L37(3)(1) CPCE.
33   Art L34(8)(I) CPCE.
34   Art L34(9) CPCE.
35   Art L37(1) CPCE.
36   Art L37(1) CPCE.
37   Art L37(2)(2) CPCE.
38   Art L38 CPCE.

Definition of relevant markets and SMP designation

12.32   The conditions of enforcement of article L.37(1) CPCE concerning the definition of SMP will be the subject matter of a decree defining, inter alia, the conditions of renewal and the minimum frequency of the market analysis.

12.33   One of the main functions of ARCEP is to ensure that competition is effective over the 18 relevant markets identified by the Commission. At the end of its analysis, ARCEP shall identify the SMP operators on these markets and impose on them, if any, obligations justified, adjusted and based on the nature of the competitive problem that may be identified. The French texts did not necessarily implement all provisions of the EU Directives but it is stated in articles D.301 and D.302 CPCE that ARCEP will follow the instructions and recommendations of the Commission when analysing markets.

12.34   The different steps of the market analysis process followed by ARCEP are compliant with the procedure described in article 16 Framework Directive.

12.35   In order to collect the information it considers as 'necessary to assess the power of operators on any market',[39] ARCEP published in July 2003 quality and quantity questionnaires to which the parties concerned were invited to reply before 30 September 2003.

12.36   Pursuant to article 16(6) and article 6 Framework Directive, ARCEP started the first public consultation on 16 April 2004 concerning the analysis of the wholesale market of the voice call termination on mobile networks. It noted the obstacles to effective competition, and specified operators likely to exercise a significant power pursuant to article 14 Framework Directive. It then proposed remedies to the competition problems.

Several public consultations have been launched since then, and all the markets identified by the Commission are now under the market analysis process. At the end of each public consultation, and after having taken into account the comments it received on its analysis, ARCEP sends it to the Competition Council to obtain its opinion concerning definition of the markets and designation of the important operators.[40]

12.37   After this internal process, pursuant to article 7 Framework Directive, ARCEP submits the corresponding draft decisions to the Commission and the NRAs of the other member states. ARCEP shall take into account the comments made by the Commission and other NRAs in the draft decision that it will eventually adopt. The decision can, however, be dropped if the Commission vetoes it. Article L.37(3) CPCE provides that, in exceptional circumstances, if the electronic communications minister or ARCEP considers that it is urgent to act in order to preserve competition and protect the interests of users, appropriate measures, applicable for a limited term, may be adopted without consulting the Commission and the other NRAs.

12.38   ARCEP has identified in France the 18 markets listed by the Commission. Of the 14 markets already analysed by ARCEP, France Telecom was found to hold SMP on 13 of them. On the mobile telephony market, its subsidiary Orange was held to be jointly dominant with the other two mobile operators SFR and Bouygues

---

39   Commission Guidelines on the definition of the relevant markets, point 121.
40   Art L37(1) CPCE.

Telecom.[41] It should be noted however that ARCEP decided to withdraw its findings after the Commission did not approve its analysis and preferred to monitor this market for the time being. On the market for call termination on the alternative fixed telephone networks, a separate market was identified for each network and each operator has been held to enjoy a monopoly.

NRA's Regulatory Duties concerning Rights of Way, Co-location and Facility Sharing

Rights of way

RIGHTS OF WAY ON THE PUBLIC DOMAIN

12.39   The CPCE distinguishes between rights of way on the public domain and easements on private properties. Article L.45(1) CPCE distinguishes between the rights of way of *'operators of public networks open to the public'* and those of *'operators of electronic communications networks'*: only *'operators of networks open to the public'* benefit from a right of way on the public road domain whereas the possibilities to access the public domain with the exception of carriageways are extended to all *'operators of electronic communications networks'*.

12.40   For the public road domain, public networks operators benefit from a right of way, pursuant to articles L.45(1) and L.46 CPCE. Such occupancy is subject to an authorisation issued by the relevant authorities, according to the nature of the road, under the conditions defined by the Road System Code (*Code de la voirie routière*).[42] The authorities delivering the authorisation shall make a decision within two months following the application for authorisation.

12.41   Rights of way may only be impeded in order to ensure compliance with the essential requirements of conformity with standards,[43] environmental protection and compliance with the rules of city planning.

12.42   Following authorisation, fees must be paid to the public authorities according to the principle of equality between all operators. Thus, to avoid any discrimination, the maximum annual amount of these fees is set by decree. In the case of dispute concerning the fees for public domain occupancy, the administrative courts have jurisdiction.

12.43   The works necessary for the installation and maintenance of networks are carried out pursuant to the road regulations.

Concerning the public road domain, with the exception of carriageways, no right of access has been granted to telecommunications operators by the legislator; the managing authorities having a discretionary power to allow access to this domain.

When the authorities authorise this access, they shall do it under an occupancy agreement, subject to open and non-discriminatory conditions. The occupancy shall be compatible with the allocation of the public domain or with the available capacities of the managing or concessionary authorities of the public domain.

---

41   Decision dated 31 May 2005.
42   Art L113(3) *Code de la Voirie Routière*; arts L46, L47 CPCE.
43   Art L32(12) CPCE.

12.44 Article L.45(1) CPCE provides that the fees payable by operators of networks for the occupancy of non-road public domain shall be reasonable and in proportion to the effective use of the domain and in compliance with the principle of equality between all operators.

EASEMENTS ON PRIVATE PROPERTY

12.45 Operators authorised to establish public networks benefit from easements on private property in order to allow the installation and operation of network equipment:

- in parts of collective buildings and allotments allocated to a common use,
- on soil and subsoil of open property, and
- above private property insofar as the operator only uses the installation of a third party benefiting from easements without hindering, if applicable, the function of public service assigned to this third party.[44]

12.46 The implementation of easements is subject to an authorisation issued in the name of the state by the Mayor. Prior to the authorisation, concerned parties – landlords or, in the case of co-ownership, the managing agent of its union – are given justifications and explanations on the easement, on which they can comment within three months. The works may not start before the expiry of such time period. In case of dispute, the chief judge of the district court determines the terms of implementation of the easement.

Co-location and facility sharing

PUBLIC DOMAIN

12.47 In order to rationalise occupancy of the public domain and to limit civil engineering works, the relevant authorities may encourage or impose on an operator obligations to share existing infrastructures.[45]

12.48 So that the right of way of the operator may be ensured, under the same conditions as an authorised occupant, through the use of existing facilities and if such use does not compromise the public service function of such occupant, the relevant authorities may invite the concerned parties to meet in order to determine the technical and financial conditions of shared use of the facilities in question.

PRIVATE PROPERTY

12.49 Article L.48 CPCE provides that, if infrastructure sharing does not impede the exercise of the public service functioning of the beneficiary of the easement, the mayor acting in the name of the state may invite both parties to meet in order to define the technical and financial conditions of the shared use of the concerned facilities. In this case, except as otherwise agreed, the facilities' landlord receiving the authorised operator shall be liable, within the limits of the agreement concluded between the parties, for the maintenance of the infrastructure and equipment located in its facilities and placed under its liability, against the payment of compensation negotiated with the operator.

---

44   Art L48 CPCE.
45   Art L47 CPCE.

12.50   ARCEP may settle disputes arising between operators relating to the possibilities and conditions of the shared use of existing infrastructures located on the public domain or on private property. ARCEP shall carry out a public consultation of all the parties concerned prior to any decision requiring the shared use of existing facilities.

REGULATION OF MARKET ENTRY: IMPLEMENTATION OF THE AUTHORISATION DIRECTIVE

The General Authorisation of Electronic Communications

12.51   According to article L.33(1) CPCE, there are no limitations on the development and operation of public networks and the provision to the public of electronic communications services, subject to prior notification to ARCEP. The new framework maintains the granting of individual authorisations for the allocation of scarce resources (e g frequencies or numbers).

12.52   Due to the implementation of a general authorisation system, ARCEP no longer reviews applications for individual authorisation and the electronic communications minister does not grant licences. However, operators shall provide ARCEP with a notification[46] and ARCEP shall issue a receipt allowing them to enforce their rights (interconnection, rights of way, etc) and to be aware of their obligations (taxes, participation in the financing of the universal service, etc).

12.53   Concerning the content of the applicant's file and the forms required for the declarations, the law refers to a decree published on 26 July 2005, the provisions of which are codified in articles D.98(1) to D.99(3) CPCE. An individual or entity, whose right to develop and operate a network open to the public or to provide the public with an electronic communications service has been withdrawn or suspended, or who has been the subject of a sanction as provided for in article L.39 of the CPCE in case of breach or violation of its obligations, may not make a new notification.[47]

12.54   Article L.33(1) CPCE lists the conditions which are imposed on public network operators and service providers providing electronic communications services to the public. These conditions are detailed in articles D.98(3) to D.98(12) CPCE. The French legislator globally implemented Part A of the Annex to the Authorisation Directive except for points 4, 6 and 10 (access to numbers by end users, must carry obligations, information to be mentioned in the declaration insofar as this information is communicated before the benefit of the general authorisation) and point 16 (security of public networks in the face of non-authorised access).

12.55   Article L.33(1) CPCE provides for additional obligations:

- confidentiality and neutrality conditions concerning the messages forwarded and information in connection with communications,
- provision of information necessary for the creation of a universal telephone directory and a universal inquiry service,
- conditions necessary to ensure equal treatment of international operators, and
- obligations imposed on the operator in order to allow its control by ARCEP and those which are necessary under article L.37(1) CPCE.

---

46   Art L33(1) CPCE.
47   Art L33(1) CPCE.

12.56   In addition to these obligations, article L.33(1)(II) provides that operators with a turnover in the electronic communications sector greater than a threshold determined in a decree yet to be published have to comply with an obligation of accounting separation.

Rights of Use for Radio Frequencies

General authorisations and granting of individual rights

12.57   The Prime Minister defines, after consultation with the CSA (Superior Audiovisual Board) and ARCEP, the frequencies or radio-electric frequency bands granted to administrations of the state and those which may be assigned by NRAs, namely CSA and ARCEP.[48]

12.58   Subject to the exceptions set out in article L.33(3) CPCE,[49] the use of frequencies to ensure the transmission and reception of electronic signals is subject to an individual administrative authorisation. The use of radio-electric frequencies is considered, under French law, as a private use of the public domain of the state.

12.59   ARCEP determines, for each frequency or frequency band which it is empowered to assign:

- the type of equipment, network or service for which the use of the frequency is reserved,
- the technical conditions for use of the frequency, and
- the cases in which the use of the frequency is subject to a general authorisation.

This implies, conversely, that the assignment of frequencies is generally subject to an individual licence.

12.60   ARCEP grants authorisations to use frequencies under objective, open and non-discriminatory conditions, taking into account city planning requirements. Frequency assignments may be refused only in the following cases:

- maintaining public order, or requirements of national defence or public security,
- improper use of frequencies,
- technical or financial incapacity of the applicant to meet durably the obligations resulting from the conditions of exercise of its activity, and
- criminal record of the applicant.

Admissible conditions

12.61   The authorisation specifies the conditions of use of the frequency. Article L.42(1)(II) CPCE repeats the content of Part B of the Annex to the Authorisation Directive. The maximum term of the authorisation is 20 years. The authorisation shall also mention the minimum time period during which the conditions of renewal and the grounds of a refusal to renew apply; this time shall be in proportion to the term of the authorisation and shall take into account the level of investment undertaken by the holder.

---

48   Art L41 CPCE.
49   Facilities that do not use frequencies specially assigned or radio-electric facilities making the sending or arrival of mobile communications inoperative in theatres and prisons.

12.62   The time limits within which the authorisations are granted and the conditions of their renewal, as well as the obligations imposed on holders of the authorisation in order to allow control of the conditions of use of frequencies by ARCEP, are set out in a decree.[50]

Limitation of number of rights of use to be granted

12.63   If necessary for the proper use of the frequencies, ARCEP may, after a public consultation, propose to limit the number of authorisations to ensure effective competition conditions.[51]

12.64   The electronic communications minister, upon a proposal of ARCEP, determines the conditions of allocation and modification of the authorisations of use corresponding to these frequencies.

12.65   The choice of the holders of these authorisations is made via an invitation to tender under objective, transparent and non-discriminatory conditions.

12.66   ARCEP shall control the selection procedure and allocate the corresponding frequencies. Article L.42(1) of the CPCE lists conditions which successful candidates must fulfil, such as the technical and financial capability to comply with its obligations and a clear criminal record. The candidate must not be a threat to public order and must be able to meet requirements of any international agreements concerning frequencies etc.[52] The possibility of a spectrum auction is not excluded since the minister may decide that fees could be a criterion in the selection procedure.[53]

12.67   When operators obtain an authorisation, they shall be liable for 'all fixing up costs necessary for the provision of frequencies granted to them'.[54] The conditions of any financial participation by the spectrum redevelopment funds will be defined in a decree yet to be published.

Frequency trading

12.68   The 'trading' of frequencies has been introduced under French law by Act No 2004–669. The frequencies or frequency bands that may be 'transferred' are determined by the minister.[55]

12.69   Any project of frequency transfer shall be notified to ARCEP. ARCEP 's consent is necessary when the project concerns a frequency granted under an invitation to tender. In other cases, the consent is not necessary. A decree, to be published, will determine:

- procedures of notification and approval,
- conditions under which ARCEP may refuse the assignment contemplated or provide for conditions aimed at ensuring compliance with the purposes mentioned in the CPCE or continuity of the public service, and

---

50   Art D98(7) CPCE Decree No 2000–902, Decree No 2005–399.
51   Art D98(8) CPCE.
52   Art L42(1) CPCE.
53   Art L42(2) CPCE.
54   Art L41(2) CPCE.
55   Art L42(3) CPCE.

- cases in which the assignment must be accompanied by the issue of a new authorisation to use and the withdrawal or modification of rights and obligations transferred to the transferee as well as those which may remain incumbent upon the transferor.

Rights of Use for Numbers

General authorisations and granting of individual rights

12.70 The national numbering plan is prepared by ARCEP and managed under its control. It grants, under objective, transparent and non-discriminatory conditions, prefixes and numbers or blocks of numbers, against the payment of a fee mentioned in a decree yet to be published, in order to cover the management expenses of the numbering plan and the control of its use.

12.71 ARCEP ensures the efficient use and management of number resources. The operators have the obligation of regularly reporting to ARCEP about how the numbers are being used, or if they are being used at all. If they are not being used, ARCEP can retrieve the numbers, so as not to waste any resources. This obligation is provided for in the individual authorisations granted to the operators.

12.72 Article L.44 CPCE states that the national numbering plan 'guarantees equal and simple access by users to all networks and electronic communications services and equivalent numbering formats'.

12.73 The same article further provides that, subject to technical and economic feasibility, users located in other member states of the European Community may access non-geographic numbers accessible on the whole national territory.

12.74 Article L.44(5) CPCE excludes any industrial or intellectual property rights on prefixes, numbers, blocks of numbers and codes allocated. It sets out that they may be transferred with the prior consent of ARCEP.

12.75 Blocks of numbers are generally allocated to operators who request them under the conditions specified by ARCEP and according to the category of number in question (geographic, non-geographic, etc). The operator in turn allocates numbers to its subscribers. These numbers will be returned to ARCEP if, for example, changes to the national numbering plan are made.

12.76 ARCEP applies specific tariffs for certain numbers, which are more attractive either because they are short numbers or attention grabbing. In France, specific numbers may be allocated through a draw since auctions are excluded as a selection procedure. As an example, enquiry services numbers were allocated by this method.

Admissible conditions

12.77 ARCEP's decision on allocation specifies the conditions of use of these prefixes, numbers or blocks of numbers concerning:

- the type of service for which the use of the resources granted is reserved,
- the requirements necessary to ensure the correct use of the resources allocated,
- the requirements, if any, relating to number portability, and
- the term of the allocation, which shall not exceed 20 years.

12.78   Operators shall give their subscribers, at a reasonable price, the option to keep their geographic number when they change their operator without changing their geographic location, and to keep their fixed or mobile non-geographic number when they change their operator while remaining in the metropolitan territory. Fixed-to-mobile and mobile-to-fixed portability is not currently possible. To implement number portability, operators have to include the necessary provisions in the access and interconnection agreements, at prices reflecting the corresponding costs.[56]

Limitation of number of rights of use to be granted

12.79   French law excludes the allocation of number resources by comparative or competitive procedures. Operators are free to choose the available prefixes, numbers or blocks of numbers from the national numbering plan. The numbers are allocated subject to availability on a 'first come first served' basis unless a draw is organised for the allocation. To this end, ARCEP publishes on its website the list of number resources available. The numbers are allocated through a transparent and non-discriminatory process and a fee is required from the operator for the resource.[57]

The NRA's Enforcement Powers

12.80   ARCEP can impose sanctions on operators that do not meet their obligations. It exercises this power ex officio or upon the request of the Minister for Electronic Communications, of a professional entity, an authorised users' association or any concerned individual or legal entity. It may take protective orders, order financial sanctions and finally suspend or withdraw the frequency or numbers.[58] If a breach is likely to result in serious damage for an operator or the entire market, the President of ARCEP may request the President of the litigation section of the French Administrative Supreme Court (Conseil d'Etat) for a ruling under summary proceedings to require the liable person to comply with the applicable rules and decisions and to remedy the consequences of the breach. Facts dating back more than three years may not be referred to ARCEP. Decisions relating to sanctions must be justified, and they may be the subject of a remedy before the French Administrative Supreme Court.

12.81   Pursuant to article L.36(11) CPCE, ARCEP may formally request compliance, within a time limit, with its regulatory decisions or CPCE provisions in case of breach by a network operator or service provider. If applicable, in a case of serious and immediate breach of these provisions, ARCEP may take interim measures.

12.82   ARCEP's power to impose sanctions may be exercised regardless of the fact that the operator is subject to a general authorisation or an individual authorisation.

12.83   Article L.36(11) CPCE lists the sanctions that ARCEP may order in the case of a breach:

- depending on the seriousness of the breach, total or partial suspension of the

---

56   Art L44(6) CPCE.
57   Art L44 CPCE.
58   Art L36(8) CPCE.

right to develop an electronic communications network/provide an electronic communications service for up to one month is possible; the right may be removed for up to three years;

- the allocation of frequencies or numbers may be partially/totally suspended for up to one month; frequencies or numbers may also be withdrawn or the allocation term may be reduced by up to one year; or

- a financial sanction proportionate to the breach is imposed for non-criminal offences. It cannot exceed 3% of the previous year's turnover. Upon re-occurrence of the offence, a 5% sanction is imposed.

Administrative Charges and Fees for Rights of Use

12.84   The general authorisation system excludes the payment of a fee upon the declaration: instead, operators shall pay an annual administrative tax. The amount of such tax is defined in the finance law.[59] All operators who provide an electronic service to the public or operate a network which is open to the public pay these charges.

In addition, the allocation of frequency and number resources is subject to the payment of fees. These fees are also determined in the finance law.[60]

REGULATION OF NETWORK ACCESS AND INTERCONNECTION: IMPLEMENTATION OF THE ACCESS DIRECTIVE

Objectives and Scope of Access Regulation

12.85   ARCEP is empowered to regulate interconnection and access. It ensures that the pricing and operational conditions of interconnection and access favour the development of fair and lasting competition and provide the possibility, for all users, to communicate freely.

12.86   In its reply to the public call for comments launched by the Government prior to the preparation of the electronic communications act, ARCEP submitted that the powers it held under the 1996 law were limited. Thus, ARCEP wished to have widened and appropriate powers in order to comply fully with its functions of control and surveillance.

12.87   The implementation of the Access Directive increased the powers of ARCEP. It defines the scope of its intervention by determining, inter alia, the obligations that ARCEP could impose on operators exercising a significant influence on a relevant market concerning their offers of interconnection and access.

12.88   All provisions relating to access and interconnection provided for in article L.34(8) CPCE are applicable to operators of public networks, including public service providers.

Basic Regulatory Concepts

12.89   Pursuant to article L.32(1)(II) CPCE, ARCEP defines the public network access and interconnection conditions which guarantee equal market conditions

---

59   Act No 2003–1312 dated 31 December 2003.
60   Act No 2003–1312 dated 31 December 2003.

and the possibility of unrestricted communication between users. Furthermore, ARCEP can impose access and interconnection conditions if needed.[61] It can also settle disputes concerning refusal to grant access or interconnection.[62]

12.90   As per article L.32(8) CPCE, 'access' shall mean 'any provision of means, hardware or software, or services, in order to allow the beneficiary to provide electronic communications services'. However, and contrary to the Access Directive which applies, in particular, to conditional access systems for digital TV, article L.32(8) CPCE excludes audiovisual communications services which are governed by specific regulations.[63] This exclusion is a consequence of the fact that the CPCE does not govern audiovisual communications: all provisions relating to audiovisual communications are included in Act No 86–1067 relating to the freedom of communication, reformed upon the implementation of the 2002 EU Regulatory Package.

12.91   Regarding the exclusion of audiovisual communications services, the French definition of access is quite similar to the European Community one. However, the French legislator decided not to include information aiming at illustrating the definition. To the words 'resources and/or services', French law preferred 'means, hardware or software, or services', ie a wider notion and consequently likely to apply regardless of the future technologic innovations the sector will experience.

12.92   Article L.32(9) CPCE defines interconnection and repeats more or less the definition from the Access Directive: to the word '*undertaking*' the legislator preferred the word '*operator*'. In other respects, the French text refers to '*the parties authorised to access the network*' whereas the Access Directive mentions the '*parties having access to the network*'. Nevertheless, the word '*authorised*' shall not be construed as a regulatory authorisation but as an operator fulfilling the conditions necessary to benefit from access.

12.93   French law provides that interconnection or access is freely negotiated between the parties and is subject to private law agreements. The non-discriminatory conditions the operators have to comply with are not specific to the electronic communications sector: article L.442(6) of the French Commercial Code prohibits discriminatory practices between professionals when they are not justified by any compensation and create an advantage or disadvantage in terms of competition.

Access- and Interconnection-related Obligations with Respect to SMP Undertakings

Overview of the NRA's regulatory powers

12.94   ARCEP has the power to impose obligations on undertakings held to have SMP, on the matters of interconnection and access. Article L.36(1) CPCE thus requires SMP operators to publish information concerning interconnection or

---

61   Art L34(8) CPCE.
62   Art L36(8) CPCE.
63   Act No 86–1067 dated 30 September 1986.

access. It also requires that interconnection and access be provided under transparent and non-discriminatory conditions, and that tariffs charged reflect the corresponding costs. Account separation is also required. A decree specifies the application of this article.[64]

Transparency obligations

12.95   The operator who has SMP must publish a detailed technical and price offer of interconnection or access.[65]

Non-discrimination obligations

12.96   The operator who has SMP must also provide interconnection or access services under non-discriminatory conditions.[66] It must offer equivalent conditions to its subsidiaries and other operators, in the same circumstances[67] and accept reasonable requests for access to elements of the network or means associated therewith.

Price-control obligations

12.97   SMP operators must also use interconnection tariffs which reflect costs and they must be able to prove this.[68] ARCEP can require them to justify their tariffs or modify them if need be.

Accounting separation obligations

12.98

SMP operators must furthermore distinguish, in their accounting system, interconnection or access activities, or hold an accounting system allowing the control of compliance with SMP cost orientation obligations. Compliance with the cost accounting system is verified, at the operator's expense, by an independent entity appointed by ARCEP. The operators must render their accounting methods public. ARCEP specifies the formats of the documents needed and the mechanism used for accounting systems.

12.99   These measures are not applicable on emergent markets, in particular those created by technological innovation, unless the purposes of article L.32(1) CPCE are not achieved. In this case, ARCEP may impose the obligations described above only via a decision justified by specifying, on a case-by-base basis, which purposes are not achieved and by justifying the adequacy of the obligations provided for.

12.100   The CPCE, unlike the Access Directive, makes a very subtle distinction at article L.38. Indeed, the CPCE first elaborates the obligations to be imposed on

---

64   Decree No 2004–1301 dated 26 November 2004.
65   Art L38(I)(2) CPCE.
66   Art L38(I)(2) CPCE.
67   Art D309 CPCE.
68   Art D311 CPCE.

SMP undertakings on any electronic communications market[69] and then enumerates the obligations for SMP undertakings on the connection market[70] and also on the retail market.[71] Article L.38(1) is to be applied if Article L.38(I) does not achieve its objectives. Concerning the obligations to be imposed on SMP undertakings, French law has very closely transposed the obligations detailed in the Access Directive.

Related Regulatory Powers with Respect to SMP Undertakings

Obligations concerning carrier (pre-)selection

12.101   Operators exercising a significant influence on the market of connection to fixed public telephone networks shall provide any operators with the necessary interconnection and access services in order for their subscribers to pre-select, at a reasonable price, the telephone service of this operator and cancel, on a call-by-call basis, any choice of pre-selection by dialling a short prefix. Prices of these services shall reflect the corresponding costs.

12.102   The methods of enforcement of all obligations described above have been specified in a decree dated 26 November 2004.[72]

12.103   Since France implemented the Community Directives late, and since ARCEP only started the analysis of the relevant markets in Spring 2004, the mechanisms developed by the Directives and implemented under national law are not firmly applied yet.

Obligations concerning the provision of leased lines

12.104   Article L.38(2) CPCE applies to operators exercising a significant influence on all or part of the market for the minimum provision of leased lines on the wholesale market. The terms and conditions for the use of leased lines and the technical characteristics, including physical and electrical ones, are determined by ARCEP. The latter defines specifications concerning the network termination point. French law specifies some practical elements, such as the time limits for the provision of leased lines to the user who requested it, or the repair of leased lines. Decree No 2004–1301 details these elements.[73]

12.105   The third paragraph of article L.37(3) provides for emergency intervention by ARCEP or the Minister for Electronic Communications: for the purpose of preserving competition or protecting the interests of users, they can adopt temporary decisions even if the European Commission does not agree on the matter.

Regulatory Powers Applicable to All Market Participants

Obligations to ensure end-to-end connectivity

12.106   As per article 4 Access Directive, operators of public networks, regardless of their influence on the market, are obliged to negotiate interconnection with other

---

69   Art L38(I) CPCE.
70   Art L38(II) CPCE.
71   Art L38(1) CPCE.
72   Decree No 2004–1301.
73   Arts D369–D371 CPCE.

operators of public networks, including those located in another member state of the Community or party to the EEA agreement.[74] However, it is specified in the CPCE that the application for interconnection may not be refused if it is justified considering the needs of the applicant and if the operator has the capacity to meet such an application.[75] Any interconnection refusal shall be justified and may be the subject of a remedy before ARCEP under the procedure of dispute settlement.

Access to digital radio and television broadcasting services

12.107   Article 95 of the Act relating to communication freedom repeats the requirements of article 6 and Annex I Access Directive.[76] The 1986 Act makes an additional specification by providing that access to any group of terminals of reception of TV or sound broadcasting services provided to the public via digital signals shall also be offered under 'equitable, reasonable and non-discriminatory conditions to any distributor or editor of TV or sound broadcasting services wishing to use it to provide the authorised public with its offer'.

12.108   Conditional access system operators are required to allow the distributors of bundled service offers to use conditional systems of their choice, at reasonable prices.

12.109   Finally, article 95 of the 1986 Act requires that 'the operators or providers of public conditional access digital TV or sound broadcasting shall hold a separate financial accounting showing their entire activity of operating or provision of these systems'.

REGULATION OF UNIVERSAL SERVICES AND USERS' RIGHTS: THE UNIVERSAL SERVICE DIRECTIVE

Regulation of Universal Service Obligations

Overview

12.110   Pursuant to article L.35(3) CPCE, ARCEP shall:

* determine principles and methods of the universal service,
* determine the amounts of participations in the financing of the obligations of the universal service, based on turnover made through these services (except interconnection),
* ensure the control of financing systems, and
* impose sanctions on any operator who fails to pay.

Scope of universal service obligations

12.111   The components of the French universal service obligations set out in article L.35(1) CPCE are identical to those provided for in the Universal Service Directive:

---

74   Art L34(8)(II) CPCE.
75   Art L34(8) CPCE.
76   Act No 86–1067 dated 30 September 1986.

- a quality telephone service at a reasonable price meeting the conditions set in article 4(2) Universal Service Directive; concerning internet access, the French authorities have held this to be the equivalent of a dial-up connection via the telephone line,
- an inquiry service and directory of subscribers, in printed and electronic format,
- access to public telephone booths installed on the public domain; nevertheless, considering the development in France of mobile telephony, this component may be modified soon,[77] and
- special measures in favour of disabled individuals.

12.112 Article R20(30) CPCE[78] specifies the conditions attached to the provision of the universal service: the universal service is also to be provided to the French overseas territories. Article L.35(2) further mentions that the provider of the universal service must ensure that calls can be made to and received from the overseas territories and other foreign countries. In addition, operators selected to provide the obligations of article L.35(1) and L.35(3) must offer preferential tariffs for connections to the French overseas territories at non-peak hours.

Designation of undertakings obliged to provide universal services

12.113 Any operator may be given the responsibility of providing the universal service as far as it accepts providing it nation-wide.

12.114 However, an operator may be designated to provide one or more components of the universal service only and not all of them.[79]

12.115 The operator(s) appointed to provide one or more components of the universal service are subject to the provisions of the CPCE and must comply with a statement of works ('*Cahier des charges*') in which their obligations under their function of universal service are listed.

12.116 After an invitation to tender concerning technical and price conditions and the net cost to provide these services, the electronic communications minister appoints operators to provide the different components of the universal service. If an invitation to tender proves to be unsuccessful the minister appoints an operator who can ensure the service in question throughout the whole French territory. Obviously the criteria for this decision are the financial and technical capacity of the selected operator to provide the service. The first invitation to tender was initiated on 16 December 2004 but the only response was from France Telecom.[80] By a decision dated 3 March 2005, the Ministry of Economy, Finance and Industry confirmed France Telecom as the official provider for all components of the universal service. The attempt to introduce competition into universal service thus failed. The main complaint by the other potential providers was that the obligation to provide a universal service to the totality of the territory is not economically viable.

---

77   Decree No 2004–1222 dated 17 November 2004.
78   Decree No 2004–1222 dated 17 November 2004.
79   Art L35(2) CPCE.
80   Decision of 3 March 2005 by the Ministry of Economy, Finance and Industry.

Regulation of retail tariffs, users' expenditures and quality of service

PRICE CONTROL PROVISIONS

12.117   The prices of offers for the provision of components of the universal service are defined by the operator so as to comply with the principles of transparency, non-discrimination and cost orientation, and do not depend on the nature and use of the service by users.[81] The prices of the universal service are established to avoid any discrimination based on geographic location. The legislator maintained the principle of price standardisation, subject to exceptional circumstances under which the operator may apply different prices which shall be published.[82]

12.118   Article L.35(2) CPCE provides for a decree, adopted in February 2005,[83] determining the conditions under which the universal service prices are controlled and specifying, inter alia, the cases in which these prices may be subject to a long-term control measure or a refusal or a prior consent of ARCEP. This decree, codified at article R.20(30–11) CPCE, provides that tariffs can be controlled by ARCEP over a number of years. Where this type of control is not carried out, the decree states that the tariffs are transmitted to the ARCEP together with elements allowing their appraisal, and ARCEP gives its opinion within three weeks.

12.119   The new legal system of price control applicable to the universal service waives the ex-ante price approval system under which the minister approved, after receiving notice from ARCEP, the prices of the universal service before their application.

USERS' EXPENDITURES

12.120   The operator providing the universal service component defined at article L.35(1)(1) CPCE is under an obligation to maintain a limited telephone service for one year to users who have not paid their bills or who are in debt with the operator. The operator must also provide itemised billing to its customers.

12.121   The operator providing the universal service offers barring for the following outgoing calls: international, national, national calls made to mobiles, calls to numbers of the national numbering plan which enable call reverse mechanisms so that it is the final recipient who pays for the communication.[84] Itemised billing is also provided.[85]

QUALITY OF SERVICE

12.122   The service quality obligations to be complied with by universal service operators are detailed in their respective statements of works. Operators publish the values resulting from the application of the quality indicators: these indicators

---

81   Art L35(3) CPCE.
82   Art L35(1) CPCE.
83   Decree No 2005–75.
84   Art R 20–30(1) Decree No 2004–1222 on the obligations of public service and the funding of Universal Service.
85   Art R 20–30(1) Decree No 2004–1222 on the obligations of public service and the funding of Universal Service.

include those mentioned in Annex III to the Universal Service Directive as well as the rights of users on networks and electronic communications services as listed in the Universal Service Directive.[86]

12.123   The conditions under which universal service quality is controlled are set out in decree No 2004–1222.[87] ARCEP has jurisdiction, pursuant to article L.36(11) CPCE, to impose sanctions on operators that do not comply with their obligations. Operators also have the obligation of informing their customers of the universal service offer, its tariffs and any potential modifications. A time limit of six months is set for any modification or termination the operator might bring about. ARCEP must be informed of any technical or tariff-related alterations.

Cost calculation and financing of universal services

12.124   Article L.35(3) CPCE provides that the net costs resulting from the universal service obligations are assessed on the basis of the accounts held by the operators designated to ensure these obligations and audited, at their own expense, by an independent entity appointed by ARCEP. As per article 12(1)(a) Universal Service Directive, the assessment of these net costs shall take into account the advantage obtained on the market by operators subject to universal service obligations, if any. The net costs likely to be offset under the universal service financing cannot exceed the commitments made by the operator under the invitations to tender in which it participated.

12.125   Contrary to article 13 Universal Service Directive, French law did not introduce a mechanism of participation in the financing of the universal service upon request from a designated undertaking, but set the rules relating to the participation of each operator in the financing of universal service obligations.

12.126   Thus, each operator shall participate in the financing of the universal services on a prorated basis considering its turnover, excluding turnover from interconnection and access services and other services provided or billed on behalf of third operators.

12.127   However, pursuant to article L.35(3) CPCE, operators whose turnover is below an amount determined in decree No 2004–1222 do not participate in the financing of the universal service.

12.128   When an operator agrees to provide universal services under the price and technical conditions suitable to some categories of users, the net cost resulting from this service is deducted from its contribution to the universal service fund.

12.129   An electronic communication universal service fund ensures the financing of the net costs of the universal service obligations.

A setting-off mechanism is in place, where the operator providing a universal service sets off the costs incurred in its activities, except where these costs are not excessive for the operator.[88]

France has chosen a setting-off system with exceptions, and not the Community system which requires the company to prove it incurred an unjustified charge.

---

86   Art 22 Universal Service Directive.
87   Art R20–30 (7) CPCE.
88   Art L35(3)(III) CPCE.

12.130   The amount of the net participations that the operators shall pay to the fund and the amounts due by the fund to the operators is determined by ARCEP[89] according to their turnover.

12.131   The accounting and financial management of the fund is ensured by the French Deposit and Consignment Office (*Caisse des Dépôts et Consignations*) on a specific account. The management costs incurred by the Office are charged to the fund.

12.132   In the case of non-payment by any operator of its contribution, ARCEP orders one of the sanctions provided for in article L.36(11) CPCE. In the case of repeated failure, it may prohibition the operator from operating a public network or providing the public with electronic communication services. If the amounts due are not paid within one year, they are charged to the fund during the next fiscal year.

12.133   Decree No 2004–1222 defines the enforcement conditions of article L.35(3) CPCE and specifies the allocation conditions, the assessment methods if the requirements of transparency and publicity are met, setting off and sharing of the net costs of the universal service, and the management methods of the electronic communications universal service fund. This decree determines the categories of activity for which, due to their nature, operators do not participate in the financing of the costs resulting from the universal service obligations. Hence, the turnover from interconnection and access agreements negotiated under Article L.34(8), and from the routing and broadcasting of television and radio services and the operation of collective antennas, are not taken into account when calculating the prorated contributions. Moreover, the methods of evaluation of the net costs of universal service obligations have also evolved with the new legal framework. ARCEP who carries out this evaluation takes into consideration the capital used for these obligations and looks at certain elements which will determine the compensation of the operator for the provision of the universal service: social tariffs, universal directory, public payphones and geographic adjustment.

Regulation of Retail Markets

Prerequisites for the regulation of retail markets

12.134   The general rule is that retail markets are not regulated, since both ARCEP and the Competition Council agree that regulation should only intervene on wholesale markets. The only retail market regulated in France is the one for the universal service, where prices are controlled by the authorities. It could happen eventually that ARCEP and Competition Council might decide to regulate a retail market if competition was seriously impeded on it.

Regulatory powers

12.135   According to article L.38 (1)(I) CPCE, the following obligations may be 'imposed' on a retail market:

- provision of retail services under non-discriminatory conditions and without abusively tying services,
- not to apply excessive or predatory prices on the markets concerned,

---

89   Art L35(3)(III) CPCE.

- to apply prices reflecting the corresponding costs,
- to comply with long-term control of prices as defined by ARCEP,
- to communicate the prices to ARCEP prior to their implementation, insofar as these prices are not controlled under the universal service; ARCEP may refuse the implementation of a price communicated to it by a justified decision setting out the (economic) analysis explaining its refusal, and
- to hold an accounting system allowing the control of compliance with the cost orientation obligations. Compliance with the cost accounting system is verified, at the operator's expense, by an independent entity appointed by ARCEP.

12.136   These different obligations are established, maintained or withdrawn according to market analysis. These obligations are not applicable on emergent markets, in particular those created by means of technologic innovation, unless the purposes of the CPCE are breached. In such a case, ARCEP may impose the obligations described above only through a justified decision, specifying, on a case-by-case basis, the purposes breached and justifying the adequacy of the obligations required.[90]

12.137   The offer of leased lines on both retail and wholesale markets falls within the scope of compulsory services included in the French public service, which consists of the universal service and compulsory services.[91] Leased lines, although not part of the universal service, are provided under the compulsory services.[92]

12.138   When any operator is considered as exercising a significant influence on all or part of the market of the provision of the minimum number of leased lines mentioned in article 18 Universal Service Directive, it shall provide these lines under technical and price conditions defined in a decree.[93]

End User Rights

Contracts

12.139   The provisions concerning agreements relating to electronic communications services concluded with consumers are included in the French Consumer Code and not in the CPCE. Article L.121(83) Consumer Code provides that any agreement concluded by a consumer with an electronic communications service provider shall include all information mentioned in article 20(2) Universal Service Directive, except point (c) concerning the types of maintenance offered which are not mentioned under French law.

12.140   For the modification of contractual conditions, article L.121(84) French Consumer Code implements article 20(4) Universal Service Directive by providing that the client may terminate the agreement without penalty within three months as from the communication of new conditions, unless it expressly accepted the new conditions notified.

---

90   Art L38(1) CPCE.
91   Art L35(5) CPCE.
92   Decree No 2004–1301 dated 26 November 2004.
93   Decree No 2004–1301 dated 26 November 2004.

Transparency obligations

12.141   The CPCE does not contain any explicit transparency obligations. How-ever, the provisions of the Consumer Code apply. Its article L.113(3) imposes on sellers and service providers general information obligations about prices, contrac-tual liability limitations, special general terms and conditions of sale and delivery time limits.

Other obligations

12.142   The transmission of emergency calls is free and all operators of public telephony must provide it.[94] Access to the European emergency number '112' must also be provided and operators need to take necessary measures for its availability.

DATA PROTECTION: IMPLEMENTATION OF THE E-PRIVACY DIRECTIVE

Confidentiality of Communications

12.143   When service and network providers notify their activity to ARCEP, their project is approved if they comply with certain rules as listed by the CPCE, one being the rules on confidentiality and neutrality of all communications.[95] Confiden-tiality is guaranteed by French law, but certain exceptions are provided for, in particular for billing purposes and public order reasons.[96] In order to comply with the law, operators must take the necessary measures to ensure confidentiality of content transmitted on their networks. Operators must not discriminate between messages transmitted, that is between voice or data, and they must ensure their integrity whatever their nature.

12.144   Act No 91–646[97] states that the secrecy of messages is guaranteed, except the state can intervene if the public interest is at stake. Indeed, messages can be intercepted if they concern information relevant to national security, the prevention of terrorism, organised delinquency or the safeguard of elements essential to the economic and security potential of France.[98]

Such interception must, however, be carried out within very strict conditions. The National Commission for the Control of Interceptions oversees the operation so that the law on the subject is respected. Authorisation to intercept is given in writing by the Prime Minister and needs to be thoroughly justified, at the request of the Minister for Defence, the Home Minister and the Customs Minister. Such an authorisation cannot exceed four months, and the records of the interception have to be destroyed within 10 days. The information gathered cannot be used for any other purpose that the one described in the authorisation.

12.145   Under the provisions of the CPCE,[99] data allowing the localisation of the user's terminal equipment cannot be used during the communication for any other

---

94   Art L33(1)(f) CPCE.
95   Art L33(1)(I)(b).
96   Act No 91–646 dated 10 July 1991.
97   Art 1 Act No 91–646 dated 10 July 1991.
98   Arts 3, 4 Act No 91–646.
99   Art L34(1) CPCE.

purpose than the transmission of the message. This information can however be used if it is required in judicial investigations and if the user is properly informed of how the data will be used, for how long and provided he can withdraw his consent at any time, free of charge.

Traffic Data and Location Data

12.146   The CPCE defines traffic data as all the data which is processed so as to transmit a communication through a communication network or to charge for this communication.[100] It is however questionable whether this definition is consistent with the new framework. Traffic data is rendered anonymous by providers of electronic communications. There are some provisions for exceptions to this requirement.

12.147   Traffic data can be processed under two exceptions:[101]

- if needed in criminal prosecutions by the judicial authorities, it can be stored for up to one year before being rendered anonymous; the National Commission for Information Technology and Liberties ('CNIL') oversees this operation and specifies which data can be stored and for how long, and
- for billing purposes, operators can store and use traffic data over the period where the bill can be legally challenged, that is one year. They can transmit this data to concerned third parties. This is all supervised by the CNIL. The operators can further process traffic data so as to market their own electronic communications services or to provide value added services if subscribers expressly give their consent.

12.148   Location data allows the localisation of the user's terminal equipment.[102]

12.149   Location data cannot be used during communication for any purpose other than the transmission of the communication. It can be stored and processed after the transmission only if the subscriber gives his consent after being properly informed about which data will be processed, for how long and that the data will not be transferred to third parties.[103] The subscriber must be able to withdraw his consent at any time, free of charge.

12.150   Traffic and location data that are stored and processed can only relate to the identification of users, the technical characteristics of the services provided by the operators and the localisation of terminal equipment. They cannot relate to the content of the information, irrespective of its form, consulted during those communications.

12.151   The conservation and processing of these data has to respect the provisions of Act No 78–17[104] 'relating to information technology, files and liberties'.

---

100   Art L32(18) CPCE.
101   Art L34(1)(II), (III), CPCE.
102   Art L34(1)(IV) CPCE.
103   Art L34(1)(IV) CPCE.
104   Act No 78–17 dated 6 January 1978.

Itemised Billing

12.152   CPCE provides that subscribers are entitled to receive itemised bills free of charge if they request it.[105] When such a request is made, the bills must contain sufficient details which permit the verification of the sums billed. It should not mention the calls that are free of charge for the user and it should not display the last four digits of dialled numbers unless the customer asked for it.[106]

12.153   The customer has a choice on the way in which dialled numbers are displayed on his bills: either the last four digits of the numbers are displayed or they are hidden. The operator must be able to provide both.[107]

Calling and Connected Line Identification

12.154   Art D.98(1)(2.4) CPCE asserts that the operator must inform subscribers that it offers calling and connected line identification. When calling line identification is offered, the operator must enable the subscriber to choose whether he wants the service or not through a simple, free of charge method. When connected line identification is offered, the operator must permit the user to prevent the identification of his line, either on a permanent or call-by-call basis. Furthermore, when calling line identification is offered and is indicated before the call is made, the user must be able to block access to non-identified incoming calls.

Automatic Call Forwarding

12.155   The operator must enable the user to whom calls are transferred to interrupt or have interrupted this service by a simple, free of charge method.[108]

Directories of Subscribers

12.156   The publication of subscriber lists is free but is subject to the protection of individual rights.[109] Every user can choose whether or not he appears in the directory. Users can also prevent certain personal data to be displayed in the directory.[110]

He can prohibit the use of his personal data in marketing operations and must be able to alter, update, withdraw or clarify his personal data, as provided for by Act No 78–17.[111]

Pre-paid subscribers who do not have any contractual relationship with their operator can still be included in the directory upon request to the operator.

---

105 Art D98(1)(2.1) CPCE.
106 Art D98(1)(2.2) CPCE.
107 Art D98(1)(2.2) CPCE.
108 Art D98(1)(2.5) CPCE.
109 Art L34 CPCE.
110 Art R10 CPCE.
111 Act No 78–17 dated 6 January 1978.

Mobile subscribers need to give their consent in order to be included in any directory being compiled by the operator or information service.[112]

The lists obtained for the compilation of a directory cannot be used for any other purpose, nor can they be sold.[113]

Unsolicited Communications

12.157 Act No 2004–575[114] has implemented new provisions concerning unsolicited communications into the CPCE. Under the new regime, unsolicited communications to a natural person, irrespective of their nature, are prohibited unless the addressee has given his prior and express consent. However, when it comes to unsolicited messages for legal entities, prior consent is not needed if the message is sent to a professional address. But if a professional's email address can allow his identification, then his prior consent must be sought.

12.158 French law also specifies that messages can be sent to a professional without his prior consent if the message is directly linked to his professional activity.

12.159 There exists one exception to the general prohibition: if a person has previously entered into a contract with an entity for similar products and services, the latter may contact him again for marketing purposes. Of course, the person must be given the possibility to prevent this eventuality at the time of the said transaction.[115]

---

112 Art L34 CPCE.
113 Art R10(4) CPCE.
114 Art 22 Act No 2004–575 dated 21 June 2004.
115 Art 22(II) Act No 2004–575 dated 21 June 2004.

The German Market for Electronic Communications[1]

Joachim Scherer,
Baker & McKenzie, Frankfurt

LEGAL STRUCTURE

Basic Policy

13.1 The German market for electronic communication services is characterised by increasing competition both between mobile and fixed network operators and among operators within the mobile and fixed communication markets. In 2004, the four mobile communications operators in Germany achieved 86.4% market penetration, increasing the number of users to approximately 78 million. The roll-out of UMTS networks is progressing with network coverage achieving 70% at the end of 2004. An increasing number of companies and consumers are using broadband services via DSL (6.7 million), cable television networks (155,000), power line (9,300) and via satellite (41,000). The market share held by the competitors to the incumbent operator, Deutsche Telekom AG, increased to 20% in 2004 from 11% in 2003.

Competition in the local loop is gradually getting stronger. The competitors to Deutsche Telekom AG provide their services mainly on the basis of (unbundled) access lines provided by Deutsche Telekom AG. Their number has increased to approximately 2 million in 2004, which represents 60% of all unbundled access lines in Europe.[2] Internet usage is increasing, with Deutsche Telekom AG providing broadband internet access to approximately 65% of 6.9 million customers and the competitors servicing 35% of the market.[3]

13.2 The national regulatory body was formerly known as the Regulatory Authority for Telecommunications and Post (*Regulierungsbehörde für Telekommunikation und Post* – 'RegTP'); it has been entrusted with the additional tasks of regulating the energy and railway sectors and was renamed, in July 2005, the Federal Network Agency for Electricity, Gas, Telecommunications, Post and Railways – Federal Network Agency (*Bundesnetzagentur für Elektrizität, Gas, Telekommunikation, Post und Eisenbahnen* – 'BNA'). BNA defines its regulatory objectives

---

1 Editing of this chapter closed on 18 July 2005.
2 For an overview and for further details cf Regulierungsbehörde für Telekommunikation und Post, Annual Report 2004, pp 34 et seq.
3 For further details cf RegTP, Annual Report 2004, pp 44 et seq.

with respect to the telecommunications sector annually in its Strategic Plan which is published, after public consultation, as part of the Agency's Annual Report.[4] BNA's strategic objectives 2005 include the definition and analysis of relevant telecommunication markets and the imposition of appropriate remedies upon SMP operators, a task which has not been completed yet as a consequence of the delayed implementation of the 2002 EU Regulatory Package.[5] Other strategic objectives include the adoption of regulatory policies with respect to Voice over Internet Protocol,[6] the adoption of more flexible frequency regulation procedures,[7] and the development of policies and procedures to ensure consistent tariff regulation.[8]

Implementation of EU Directives

13.3 The EU Regulatory Framework has been transposed into German law with the Telecommunications Act of 22 June 2004 (*Telekommunikationsgesetz* – 'TKG'),[9] which replaced the TKG of 1996[10] and entered into force on 26 June 2004, almost one year after the deadline that had been mandated by EU law.[11]

The TKG follows the regulatory approach of the 2002 EU Regulatory Package by granting broad decision-making powers to BNA. In a number of instances, however, the TKG limits BNA's regulatory discretion to impose appropriate remedies (eg with regard to tariff regulation);[12] this has led the Commission to initiate infringement procedures against Germany.[13]

Legislation

13.4 The TKG is the main legislative act governing electronic communications. It is complemented by a number of ordinances (*Rechtsverordnungen*), which have been or will be adopted by the executive branch of government on the basis of the TKG and have the force of law. To date, a number of ordinances has been adopted on the basis of the TKG or remained in force on the basis of the TKG of 1996,[14] while other ordinances are expected to be adopted in the course of 2005/06.[15]

---

4   The draft Strategic Plan 2005 is published in the Official Gazette of RegTP ('ABl RegTP') 2004, 2131.
5   See paras 13.23–13.25 below.
6   RegTP, Annual Report 2004, pp 137, 141; cf RegTP's consultation in April 2004 (ABl RegTP 2004, 399).
7   See paras 13.33 et seq below.
8   RegTP, Annual Report 2004, pp 138 et seq.
9   Federal Gazette (*Bundesgesetzblatt* – 'BGBl') I 2004, 1190, last amended BGBl I 2005, 1970.
10 BGBl I 1996, 120.
11 Art 28 Framework Directive, art 18 Access Directive, art 18 Authorisation Directive, art 38 Universal Service Directive.
12 Cf para 13.82 below.
13 Infringement Procedure No 2004/2221, Infringement Procedure No 2005/2067.
14 They include: Ordinance on Frequency Band Allocation, BGBl I 2004, 2499; Ordinance on the Establishment of the Frequency Usage Plan, BGBl I 2001, 827, BGBl I 2003, 2304. Ordinance on Frequency Charges, BGBl I 1999, 1226, BGBl I 2002, 4564, Ordinance on Charges to Secure Interference Free Use of Frequencies, BGBl I 2004, 958; Ordinance on Protection of Telecommunications Customers, BGBl I 1997, 141, BGBl I 2002, 3365; Ordinance on Charges for Telecommunications Numbers, BGBl I 1999, 1887, BGBl I 2004, 868; Telecommunications Surveillance Ordinance, BGBl I 2002, 458, BGBl I 2004, 3603.
15 Proposed telecommunications ordinances include ordinances on numbering, emergency calls,

REGULATORY PRINCIPLES: IMPLEMENTATION OF THE FRAMEWORK DIRECTIVE

Scope of Regulation

13.5   The TKG governs 'telecommunications', which is defined as the technical process of sending, transmitting and receiving signals by means of telecommunications systems.[16] Telecommunications systems are technical facilities or equipment capable of sending, transmitting, switching, receiving, steering or controlling electromagnetic or optical signals identifiable as messages.[17] Whereas the regulation of 'telecommunications' is under the authority of the Federal Government, most content-related regulation, particularly in the area of radio and television broadcasting, is governed by legislation of the Federal States. Media services (e g internet newspapers) are subject to the State Treaty on Media Services (*Mediendienstestaatsvertrag*)[18] and fall within the legislative competence of the Federal States. By contrast, tele-services (e g electronic shopping) are governed by the Tele Services Act (*Teledienstegesetz*), for which the legislative power rests with the Federal Government.[19]

The definitions of the terms 'telecommunications services' and 'telecommunications network' broadly correspond with the definitions set out in article 2(c) and (d) Framework Directive.[20]

National Regulatory Authority: Organisation, Regulatory Objectives, Competencies

Overview

13.6   BNA is a higher Federal Authority responsible to the Federal Ministry of Economics and Labour. It is the German regulatory body for the telecommunications and postal sectors and – as from 13 July 2005 – also for electricity and gas and railways.

---

telecommunications surveillance, telecommunications contribution charge and a comprehensive ordinance on telecommunications fees and charges.

16   S 3 no 22 TKG.
17   S 3 no 23 TKG.
18   As amended by the 8th State Treaty for the Amendment of State Treaties on Broadcasting.
19   BGBl 1997, 1870.
20   S 3 no 24 TKG defines telecommunications services as 'services normally provided for remuneration consisting in, or having as their principle feature, the conveyance of signals by means of telecommunications networks and includes transmission services in networks used for broadcasting'. The term 'telecommunications network' is defined as 'transmission systems and, where applicable, switching and routing equipment and other resources in their entirety which permit the conveyance of signals by wire, by radio, by optical or by other electromagnetic means, including satellite networks, fixed and mobile terrestrial networks, electricity cable systems, to the extent that they are used for the purpose of transmitting signals, networks used for radio and television broadcasting, and cable television networks, irrespective of the type of information conveyed'.

With respect to European and international telecommunications policy, in particular as regards participation in European and international institutions and organisations,[21] BNA acts on behalf of the Federal Ministry of Economics and Labour, which remains the governmental body representing the Federal Government in European and international organisations.[22]

13.7   Although BNA is part of the Federal Government and operates under the supervision of the Federal Ministry of Economics and Labour, the TKG aims to ensure a certain degree of independence of BNA from political influences. In particular, the Ministry is obliged to publish all directives which it issues in relation to BNA's regulatory tasks.[23]

13.8   BNA is run by a president who represents BNA in and out of court, and lays down the administration and order of business by rules of procedure which require confirmation by the Federal Ministry of Economics and Labour. The president and the two vice-presidents are nominated by the Federal Government upon the proposal of BNA's advisory council which, in turn, consists of 16 members of the German Bundestag and 16 representatives of the German Bundesrat.[24]

Regulatory objectives of BNA

13.9   BNA discharges the functions and exercises the powers that are assigned to it under the TKG. The aims of regulation, as stated in section 2 para 2 TKG, are broadly identical to those set out in article 8 Framework Directive. They are:

- to safeguard user, most notably consumer, interests in telecommunications and to safeguard telecommunications privacy,
- to secure fair competition and to promote telecommunications markets with sustainable competition in services and networks and in associated facilities and services, in rural areas as well,
- to encourage efficient investment in infrastructure and to promote innovation,
- to promote development of the internal market of the European Union,
- to ensure provision throughout the Federal Republic of Germany of basic telecommunications services (universal services) at affordable prices,
- to promote telecommunications services in public institutions,
- to secure efficient and interference-free use of frequencies, account also being taken of broadcasting interests,
- to secure efficient use of numbering resources, and
- to protect public safety interests.

Tasks and competences of BNA

13.10   The tasks and competences of BNA are defined in the TKG. Its main tasks include the definition of relevant telecommunications markets warranting regulation, conducting the market analysis with a view to determine whether there is

---

21   Including ITU.
22   S 140 TKG; see also Act on the Federal Network Agency for Electricity, Gas, Telecommunications, Post and Railways, BGBl I 2005, 2009 (the 'BNA Act').
23   S 117 TKG.
24   Ss 3, 5 BNA Act.

effective competition in the relevant market,[25] and the adoption of 'regulatory orders' (*Regulierungsverfügungen*) imposing remedies on operators with significant market power.

13.11   Other tasks include consumer protection in the telecommunications sector,[26] frequency management,[27] the management of numbering resources,[28] the granting of rights of way for telecommunications lines,[29] ensuring the provision of universal services,[30] dispute resolution[31] and the regulation of telecommunications privacy, data protection and the public safety of telecommunications.[32]

Powers of BNA

13.12   BNA has broad powers to ensure compliance with the provisions of TKG by taking remedial action. In the case of serious or repeated breaches of obligations by an undertaking or failure to comply with measures for remedial action ordered by BNA, the undertaking may be prohibited from operating its telecommunications network or providing telecommunications services.[33] BNA is empowered to impose fines for violations of specific provisions of the TKG.[34]

In addition, BNA may request, from network operators and service providers, the provision of any information that is required for the execution of the TKG. This includes information for the systematic or case-by-case verification of compliance with obligations ensuing from or by virtue of the TKG, the case-by-case verification of compliance with obligations when BNA has received a complaint or has other reasons to assume non-compliance with obligations or when it has opened investigations on its own initiative, information for the publication of comparative overviews, and information on quality and price of service for the benefit of end users, statistical purposes, market definition or market analysis procedures.[35]

Representatives of BNA are entitled to have access to the offices and business premises of undertakings and associations of undertakings during normal business or working hours; searches, however, may be carried out solely by order of the local court.[36]

BNA may conduct formal investigations and take evidence, including testimonies and expert opinions,[37] and it may seize objects which may be important as evidence in its investigations.[38]

13.13   BNA's decisions relating to market regulation as well as decisions regarding the assignment of frequencies in scarcity situations, decisions in frequency award

---

25   See paras 13.12 et seq below.
26   See paras 13.104 et seq below.
27   See paras 13.33 et seq below.
28   See paras 13.49 et seq below.
29   See para 13.27 below.
30   See paras 13.91 et seq below.
31   See para 13.16 below.
32   See paras 13.111 et seq below.
33   S 126(3) TKG; cf para 13.56 below.
34   S 115(2) TKG.
35   S 127(1) TKG.
36   S 127(6) TKG.
37   S 128 TKG.
38   S 129 TKG.

proceedings, on spectrum trading, and on the imposition of universal service obligations are made by BNA's Ruling Chambers. The Ruling Chambers are decision-making bodies which consist of a chairman and two assessors. The chairman and the assessors shall be qualified to hold office in the senior administrative grade of the civil service and at least one member of the Ruling Chamber shall be qualified to exercise the functions of a judge. The Ruling Chambers institute proceedings on their own initiative or upon a motion. Participants in the proceedings are the person presenting the motion, the network operators and service providers against whom the proceedings are directed and persons and associations of persons whose interests are likely to be affected by the decision and to whom BNA has sent a summons to attend proceedings in response to their request.[39] The Ruling Chamber takes its decisions on the basis of public oral proceedings; subject to the consent of the parties concerned, it can take its decisions without oral proceedings.[40] The parties concerned have a right to be heard and, where appropriate, the Ruling Chamber may give persons representing 'business circles affected by the proceedings', such as industry associations, the opportunity to state their views.[41]

Relationship between BNA and the Federal Cartel Office

13.14   BNA is obliged to cooperate with the Federal Cartel Office (*Bundeskartellamt* – 'BKartA') and with the State Media Authorities, ie the authorities, at state level, which are in charge of the regulation of radio and television broadcasting as well as media services.[42]

In relation to the definition of telecommunications markets, the market analysis,[43] decisions regarding the exclusion of an applicant from participation in frequency award proceedings and establishing the terms and conditions for frequency trading, BNA is obliged to take its decisions 'in agreement' with the BKartA. Where BNA takes decisions on specific remedies or on anti-competitive practices, it is obliged to give the BKartA the opportunity to state its views 'in good time before closure of the case'.[44]

The national consultation procedure

13.15   BNA is in charge of conducting the national consultation and consolidation procedures[45] in conjunction with the market definition, market analysis and the imposition of remedies. In accordance with article 6 Framework Directive, the TKG provides that a public consultation procedure shall also be conducted in the case of all measures 'having a significant impact on the relevant market'.[46]

Dispute resolution

13.16   In addition to its regulatory tasks, BNA also acts as a dispute resolution body. In the event of a dispute arising in connection with obligations under the

---

39   S 134 TKG.
40   S 135(3) TKG.
41   S 135(1), (2) TKG.
42   S 123 TKG.
43   See paras 13.23 et seq below.
44   S 123(1) sentence 1 TKG.
45   Ss 12 et seq TKG.
46   S 15 TKG.

TKG between undertakings operating public telecommunications networks or offering publicly available telecommunications services, BNA – acting through its Ruling Chambers[47] – is empowered to issue a binding decision to resolve the dispute at the request of either party and after consultation with the parties concerned. In the case of such a dispute, the Ruling Chamber is obliged to make its decision within a period not exceeding four months, from the date of the request from one of the parties concerned.[48] In the event of a dispute arising between undertakings and different Member States where a dispute falls within the competence of the NRAs of at least two Member States, any of the parties may refer the dispute to the NRA concerned. In this case, the Ruling Chamber is obliged to take its decision in consultation with the NRA concerned.[49]

Right of Appeal against NRA's Decisions

13.17   Decisions of BNA's Ruling Chambers are subject to judicial review by the administrative courts. In an attempt to accelerate the judicial review procedure, article 137 TKG provides that decisions of the administrative court of first instance are not, as are most decisions of the administrative courts, subject to appeal on issues of fact and law before the Superior Administrative Court, but merely subject to appeals on procedural issues before the Federal Administrative Court.

13.18   Administrative appeals and court actions against decisions of the Regulatory Authority do not have suspensory effect. In accordance with the general rules of the Code of Administrative Court Procedure, however, a suspension of BNA's decisions can be brought about by BNA or by the administrative court.

13.19   In accordance with the general rules of German administrative law and procedure, not only the decisions of BNA's Ruling Chambers, but any administrative act issued by BNA as well as any other BNA action which negatively affects an individual's or a company's right, are subject to court review.[50]

The NRA's Obligations to Cooperate with the Commission

13.20   The consolidation procedure set out in article 7 Framework Directive has been transposed into German law, which requires that this procedure shall take place prior to BNA's final decision on:

- the definition of a telecommunications market warranting regulation,
- the determination whether there is effective competition in the market being analysed and which undertaking is deemed to have significant market power,
- the imposition of remedies as a result of the market analysis,
- the imposition of remedies in the case of trans-national markets.[51]

---

47   See para 13.13 above.
48   S 133(1) TKG.
49   S 133(2) TKG.
50   For an overview see Quaas, Constitutional, Administrative and Public Business Law, in: Ruster (ed), Business Transactions in Germany, Looseleaf, § 7.05.
51   S 11 (2), (3) TKG.

The consolidation procedure is initiated by BNA making available its proposals to the Commission and to the NRAs of the other Member States. BNA is obliged not to give effect to its proposals prior to the expiry of the deadlines set out in article 7 para 3 Framework Directive.[52]

In taking its final decision, BNA is obliged to take the utmost account of the comments of the Commission and of the NRAs and to communicate the resulting draft to the Commission.

13.21   With respect to regulatory decisions which are subject to the Commission's veto powers,[53] detailed procedural rules apply, which reflect the provisions of article 7 para 4 Framework Directive. Where the Commission takes a decision requiring BNA to withdraw its draft, BNA is bound by such decision. It may again consult the parties concerned on the Commission's decision. Where BNA wishes to accept the amendments proposed by the Commission, it shall amend the draft in accordance with the Commission's decision and submit the amended draft to the Commission. Otherwise, it shall inform the Federal Ministry of Economics and Labour of the Commission's decision.[54] It is then up to the Ministry to decide whether or not to bring an action against the Commission's decision before the European Court of Justice.

'Significant Market Power' as a Fundamental Prerequisite of Regulation

Definition of SMP

13.22   The TKG defines, in line with article 16 para 2 Framework Directive, the existence of effective competition in terms of the market power of the enterprises that are active in the relevant market. Effective competition is deemed absent if one or more undertakings have significant market power in a relevant market.[55] The definition of SMP is almost identical to the terminology of article 16 para 4 Framework Directive. An undertaking is deemed to have significant market power if, either individually or jointly with others, it enjoys a position equivalent to dominance, ie a position of economic strength affording it the power to behave to an appreciable extent independently of competitors and end-users.[56]

Definition of relevant markets and SMP designation

13.23   The TKG's regulatory approach follows the concept of articles 15 and 16 Framework Directive. On the basis of a market definition and the subsequent market analysis, BNA defines those markets that are not effectively competitive and which are therefore subject to regulation. Those markets where effective competition exists are not subject to sector-specific regulation but rather to general competition law.[57]

---

52   See paras 1.60 et seq above.
53   See paras 1.62 et seq above.
54   S 12(2)(3) TKG.
55   S 11(1) sentence 2 TKG.
56   S 11(1) sentence 3 TKG.
57   S 2(3) TKG.

13.24   BNA is obliged to identify the relevant product and geographic telecommunications markets warranting regulation under the TKG. For the first time, this market definition has to occur 'without undue delay' after the entry into force of the TKG and subsequently at two-year intervals. The TKG establishes criteria for those markets that are subject to regulation.[58] They are markets:

- with high, non-transitory entry barriers of a structural or legal nature,
- which do not tend towards effective competition within the relevant time horizon, and
- in respect of which the application of competition law alone would not adequately address the market failure concerned.

In defining those markets, BNA has an administrative discretion which is subject to limited court review only.[59] In identifying the markets that are subject to regulation, BNA is obliged to 'take the utmost account' of the Commission Recommendation on relevant markets.[60]

13.25   To date, BNA has concluded its market analysis of a number of the markets identified in the Commission Recommendation on relevant markets[61] and has imposed preliminary measures or remedies with respect to several of these markets: With regard to the retail markets 1–6, BNA has imposed preliminary measures upon Deutsche Telekom AG, which has been identified as SMP operator. They include an obligation on Deutsche Telekom AG to provide information on its end-user tariffs. With respect to market 7 (retail market for leased lines), the market definition and analysis has commenced.

With respect to the wholesale level markets, the market analysis process regarding markets 12 (wholesale broadband access), 13–14 (wholesale terminating segments of leased lines, wholesale trunk segments of leased lines), 15 (access and call origination on public mobile networks), 17 (wholesale national market for international roaming and public mobile networks) and 18 (broadcasting transmission services) are still pending. With respect to BNA's market analysis of the call termination market (market 9), the Commission exercised its veto powers on the grounds that 'the evidence provided by the RegTP did not support its finding of an absence of SMP for alternative network operators'; The Commission did not question, however, BNA's finding of SMP of Deutsche Telekom AG on market 9.[62] With respect to the wholesale market for termination of leased lines (market 13) and for trunk segments of leased lines (market 14), preliminary measures have been imposed on Deutsche Telekom AG to provide access to certain types of leased line.

In the wholesale market for voice call termination on individual mobile services (market 16), the four German mobile telecommunications operators[63] have been identified as SMP undertakings. On markets 8–12 (call origination, call termination and transit services), Deutsche Telekom AG has been identified as SMP operator; to date, no remedies have been imposed. On the market for wholesale unbundled

---

58   S 10(2) TKG.
59   S 10(2) sentence 2 TKG.
60   S 10(2) sentence 3 TKG.
61   See para 1.75 above.
62   European Commission Decision of 17 May 2005 pursuant to art 7(4) of Directive 2002/21/EC, Case DE/2005/0144.
63   The four mobile operators are: T-Mobile Deutschland GmbH, Vodafone D 2 GmbH, E-Plus Mobilfunk GmbH & Co. KG and O2 Germany GmbH & Co. KG.

access to the local loop (market 11), the SMP operator Deutsche Telekom AG has been obliged to provide access to the customer access lines and co-location, and to publish a standard offer.[64]

13.26   The TKG provides that BNA is obliged to impose one or more suitable remedies on SMP enterprises. In selecting the appropriate remedies, BNA has administrative discretion, the scope of which is defined in the TKG's provisions on access regulation and on rate regulation,[65] in the Commission's view, however, the German legislator has, in a number of instances, restricted the regulatory authority's discretion in violation of the directives.[66]

Exceptionally, BNA may, in justified cases, impose obligations on network operators which do not have significant market power, provided that such network operator controls access to end-users. Upon request, the network operator can be obliged to interconnect its network with those of other public network operators, as far as may be necessary to secure user communication, the provision of services and service interoperability.[67] In addition, BNA may impose further access obligations on network operators controlling access to end users and not having SMP, as far as may be necessary to secure 'end-to-end connectivity'.

NRA's Regulatory Duties concerning Rights of Way, Co-location and Facility Sharing

Rights of way

13.27   The right to use traffic ways, including public ways, squares, bridges, and public waters, for telecommunications lines serving public purposes, lies with the German Federation.[68] The Federation, acting through BNA, transfers its right of use to public telecommunications network operators upon written application.[69] The applicant must be an operator of a public telecommunications network with proven specialist knowledge, reliability and efficiency to install telecommunications lines. The right of use will be granted for the duration of the public activity; BNA has to render its decision on complete applications within a period of six weeks.

13.28   The installation of new, and the modification of existing, telecommunications lines requires the written consent of the authorities responsible for the construction and maintenance of public ways. The TKG does not favour the installation of overhead lines and requires that, in this case, the interests of the authorities responsible for public ways, of the network operators and the requirements of town planning shall be weighed. Where the installation can be coordinated under a comprehensive building project to be carried out close in time to the application for consent, lines shall typically be installed underground. The authorities in charge of public ways may grant their consent subject to non-discriminatory conditions which may, however, make stipulations solely on the way in which a

---

64   RegTP decision BK 4–04-075/R, 20.04.2005.
65   See paras 13.62 et seq and 13.99 et seq below.
66   European Commission, Infringement Procedure No 2004/2221, Infringement Procedure No 2005/2067; for details see paras 13.71, 13.74 below.
67   See para 13.87 below.
68   S 68(1) TKG.
69   S 69(1) TKG.

telecommunications line is to be installed, the rules of engineering to be observed in doing so, the safety and ease of traffic, local documentation requirements, and traffic safety obligations.[70]

In using traffic ways for the installation of telecommunication lines, any hindrance to their maintenance and any temporary restriction of their use is to be avoided as far as possible; where maintenance is hindered, the party enjoying the right of use is obliged to reimburse the party liable for maintenance for costs arising from the hindrance. After completion of work on the telecommunication lines, the traffic way must be restored without undue delay at the expense of the party enjoying the right of use unless the party liable for maintenance has declared its willingness to undertake restoration itself. Any expenses incurred in the restoration must be reimbursed by the party enjoying the right of use.[71] Trees planted on and around traffic ways are to be protected as far as possible; lopping may be required only to the extent necessary to install the telecommunications line or to prevent interruption of service. The party enjoying the right of use is to set the tree owner an appropriate period within which to carry out lopping himself. Where lopping has not been carried out or has not been carried out sufficiently within the specified period, the party enjoying the right of use may bring about the lopping. The party enjoying the right of use is obliged to pay compensation for all damage to trees and repay the costs of all lopping carried out at its request.

13.29   The use of private property is subject to negotiation and private agreement, under Civil Law, between the network operator and the private landowner. A private landowner cannot prohibit the installation, operation or renewal of telecommunications lines on his property in so far as:

- an existing line or installation (e g an electricity line) that is secured by a right (either a contractual right or an easement) is used also for the installation, operation or renewal of a telecommunications line and the usability of the property is not thereby additionally restricted on a lasting basis, or
- the property is not, or is not significantly, affected by such use.[72]

Co-location and facility sharing

13.30   Section 70 TKG provides for a right of network operators to 'shared use' of installations intended for the accommodation of telecommunications cables. Where it is not possible, or is possible only at disproportionately high expense, to establish new telecommunication lines, other operators are obliged to acquiesce in the shared use of existing installations, provided that the shared use is economically reasonable and no major additional construction work is needed. In this case, the party enjoying the right of shared use is obliged to pay adequate compensation to the party obliged to grant shared use.

---

70   S 68(3) TKG.
71   S 71 TKG.
72   S 76(1) TKG.

REGULATION OF MARKET ENTRY: IMPLEMENTATION OF THE AUTHORISATION DIRECTIVE

The General Authorisation of Electronic Communications

13.31   In accordance with the provisions of the Authorisation Directive, the TKG no longer provides for a prior approval for the operation of telecommunications networks or the provision of telecommunications services.[73] Network operators and service providers are merely obliged to notify BNA without undue delay of beginning to provide services, of changing the service provision or ceasing to provide services as well as of any changes in their undertaking.[74] Upon request, BNA confirms within a period of one week that the notification is complete and certifies that the undertaking has the rights granted by or under the TKG.[75] At regular intervals, BNA publishes a list of notified undertakings. A failure to file a notification or the filing of a false, incomplete or otherwise wrongful notification, as well as the delayed filing of a notification, are administrative offences subject to a fine.

13.32   The TKG establishes a number of obligations which apply, by operation of law, to specific categories of operators: for example, all public telecommunications network operators and providers of publicly available telecommunications services are obliged to provide BNA, upon request, with all information that it requires to fulfil its reporting requirements in relation to the Commission and other international bodies.[76] All providers of publicly available telephone services are obliged to provide all users with access to emergency services by using, free of charge, the single European emergency call number '112' and additional national emergency call numbers set out in an ordinance. Operators of telecommunications networks used for publicly available telephone services are required to transmit to the local emergency service centre, without undue delay, emergency calls.[77]

Rights of Use for Radio Frequencies

Overview

13.33   Frequency management in Germany is based on the National Table of Frequency Allocations[78] and on the Frequency Usage Plan.[79] Whereas the National Table of Frequency Allocations is set out in an ordinance having the force of law, the Frequency Usage Plan, which is based on the National Table of Frequency Allocations, is drawn up, with the participation of the public, by BNA.

---

73   For the prior approval ('assignment') requirement with respect to frequencies, see paras 13.34 et seq below.
74   S 6(1) TKG.
75   S 6(3) TKG.
76   S 4 TKG, S 108 (1), sentence 2 TKG.
77   See para 13.95 below.
78   Cf BGBl I 2001, 781 et seq.
79   Official Gazette RegTP 23/2003 of 19 November 2003.

General authorisation and granting of individual rights

13.34   Each frequency usage requires a prior frequency assignment, unless otherwise provided in the TKG. The frequency assignment is the authorisation given by a public authority (generally BNA) or by operation of law to use particular frequencies under specified conditions.

Frequencies are assigned for a particular purpose on the basis of the Frequency Usage Plan. An assignment is not required where usage rights can be exercised by virtue of another statutory regulation.

13.35   Frequencies are assigned by administrative act, either ex-officio or upon application. Ex-officio assignments are 'general assignments' which allow for the use of particular frequencies by the general public or by a group of persons defined or capable of being defined by general characteristics (eg all operators of a specific type of radio installation). Such 'general assignments' are published in BNA's Official Gazette.[80] Where a general assignment is not possible, frequencies for particular usages are assigned by BNA to natural persons, legal entities and associations of persons upon written application ('individual assignments'). This applies in particular in cases where the risk of harmful interference cannot otherwise be ruled out or if an individual assignment is necessary in order to secure efficient frequency use.

13.36   Applications for individual assignments have to specify the area in which the frequencies are to be used. Furthermore, the applicant has to show that the subjective requirements for frequency assignment with regard to the efficient and interference-free use of frequencies and other conditions[81] are satisfied. BNA is obliged to take a decision on a complete application for an individual assignment within a period of six weeks.[82]

Frequencies are generally assigned subject to:

- their designation for the planned usage in the Frequency Usage Plan,
- their availability,
- their compatibility with other frequency usages, and
- their efficient and interference-free use by the applicant being secured.[83]

13.37   Applicants are not entitled to any particular frequency and are obliged to notify BNA without undue delay of the beginning and the cessation of frequency usage. They shall also notify BNA of any change of name, change of address, change in ownership structure and any identity-preserving transformations.

13.38   Changes in the frequency assignment are subject to BNA's prior approval.[84] Frequencies are typically assigned for a limited period, with the possibility of an extension; the time limit for the frequency usage must be appropriate to the service concerned.

13.39   A frequency assignment may be denied in full or in part where the use intended by the applicant is incompatible with the TKG's regulatory objectives.[85]

---

80   For BNA's regulatory principles, see Official Gazette RegTP 193/2003 of 16.07.2003, pp 767 et seq.
81   As specified in Part B of the Annex to the Authorisation Directive, cf para 1.103 above.
82   S 55(1) TKG.
83   S 55(5) TKG:
84   Cf s 55(7) TKG.
85   Cf para 13.09 above.

Where the interests of the Federal States relating to broadcasting within their jurisdiction are concerned, BNA is obliged to consult with the competent state authority.

Admissible conditions

13.40   Frequency assignments generally specify, in particular, the type and extent of the frequency usage as far as necessary to secure efficient and interference-free use of frequencies.

In order to secure the efficient and interference-free use of frequencies, frequency assignments may be made subject to specific conditions. Where, after assignment, it is established that usage is being significantly restricted on account of increased use of the radio spectrum or that considerable efficiency gains are possible on account of technological progress, the type and extent of the frequency usage may subsequently be modified.[86] The frequency assignment will generally contain references to the parameters for the receiving equipment on which BNA has based its specifications on the type and extent of the frequency usage.[87]

13.41   The TKG sets out special preconditions for the assignment of frequencies for broadcasting within the jurisdiction of the Federal States. In particular, BNA is obliged to consult with the relevant state authorities with respect to their coverage requirements and before using frequencies allocated to the broadcasting service for purposes other than broadcasting. Frequency usages of the Federal Ministry of Defence in the bands designated in the Frequency Usage Plan exclusively for military purposes do not require an assignment. Special conditions apply with regard to frequencies designated in the Frequency Usage Plan for public safety or radio communications.[88] The TKG allows for the assignment of frequencies to more than one party for shared use if frequency usage by one party alone is not expected to be efficient.[89]

13.42   Frequency assignments may be revoked where use of the assigned frequency for the intended purpose has not commenced within one year of the assignment or where the frequency has not been used for the intended purpose for more than one year.[90] Furthermore, frequency assignments may be revoked, inter alia, if an obligation arising from the assignment is repeatedly violated, has not been fulfilled despite repeated requests for fulfilment, if competition or the introduction of new spectrum-efficient technologies is prevented or unreasonably hindered as a result of a scarcity of frequencies arising after the assignment, or if a distortion of competition in the relevant product in geographic market is to be feared as a result of a change in ownership structure in the person of the assignee.[91] Furthermore, revocations are permissible in accordance with the general rules of the Administrative Procedure Act.[92]

---

86   S 60(2) TKG.
87   S 60(3) sentence 1 TKG.
88   S 57(4) TKG.
89   S 59 TKG.
90   S 63(1) TKG.
91   S 63(2) TKG.
92   Cf Quaas, in: Ruster (ed) Business Transactions in Germany, § 7.03 [2].

Limitation of number of rights of use to be granted

13.43 In situations of frequency scarcity, ie where frequencies are not available for assignment in sufficient numbers or where more than one application has been made for particular frequencies, BNA may order, following a public hearing, that the frequency assignment be preceded by award proceedings.[93] Where such an order has been issued, BNA may, after hearing the parties concerned, either conduct an auction or invite tenders for the relevant frequencies. Decisions on the choice of proceedings, and the determinations and rules for the conduct of the proceedings, are to be published by BNA. The TKG provides that, as a general rule, award proceedings shall be conducted in the form of an auction, except where such proceedings are not likely to secure the regulatory objectives set out in the TKG.[94] This may be the case, in particular, when frequencies have already been assigned, without a prior auction, in the relevant product and geographic market for which the radio frequencies may be used, or where an applicant can claim a legal right to preference for the frequencies to be assigned.

13.44 The objective of award proceedings (both auctions and tender proceedings) is to determine which of the applicants is or are best placed to make efficient use of the frequencies to be assigned. Prior to carrying out award proceedings, BNA is obliged to determine:

- the minimum specialist and other requirements to be met by applicants in order to qualify for the award proceedings,
- the relevant product and geographic market for which the frequencies to be assigned may be used in accordance with the Frequency Usage Plan,
- the basic spectrum package required for commencement of the telecommunications service, where necessary, and
- the frequency usage conditions, including the degree of coverage with the frequency usage and the time required to achieve such degree of coverage.[95]

13.45 If BNA decides to conduct an auction, it shall, prior to the award proceedings, detail the rules for conducting the auction; such rules must be objective, transparent and non-discriminatory and have regard to the interest of small and medium-sized enterprises. BNA is entitled to stipulate a minimum bid for participation in the auction.[96]

13.46 In the case of tender proceedings, BNA shall, prior to the award proceedings, determine the criteria against which tenderers' eligibility will be assessed. Such criteria include the tenderers' specialist knowledge and efficiency, the suitability of their plans for providing the telecommunications service for which the tender has been invited, and the promotion of sustainable competition in the market. Preference is to be given in the selection procedure to tenderers' ensuring a higher degree of coverage with the particular telecommunications service. Where the outcome of tendering shows several tenders to be equally well placed, the decision shall be made by drawing lots.[97]

Any commitment entered into by bidders in the course of an auction or by tenderers in the course of a tendering procedure becomes a constituent part of the frequency assignment.

---

93   S 55(9) TKG.
94   See para 13.9 above.
95   S 61(4) TKG.
96   S 61(5) TKG.
97   S 61(6) TKG.

13.47   BNA is empowered to charge fees and contributions for frequency assignments and usage. The exact charges are set out in the frequency fee ordinance[98] and in the Ordinance on Charges to Secure Interference-free Use of Frequencies.[99]

Frequency trading

13.48   BNA may, after a public hearing, release specific frequency bands for trading and stipulate the conditions of and the procedure for trading, provided that there is an interest in trading usage rights for the spectrum concerned.[100] The conditions of and the procedure for trading shall ensure in particular that spectrum efficiency is increased or maintained, that the original award proceedings do not preclude frequency assignment after spectrum trading, that no distortion of competition in the relevant product and geographic market is to be feared, that other legal conditions, in particular the conditions of use and international agreements on spectrum use, are complied with and, generally, that the regulatory objectives of the TKG are secured.[101] Decisions on the conditions of and the procedure for spectrum trading are to be published. The proceeds from spectrum trading, less the administrative costs incurred, are due to the party selling the usage rights.

Rights of Use for Numbers

Overview

13.49   BNA is responsible for structuring and configuring the numbering space and for the allocation of numbers to telecommunications network operators, service providers and end users. To implement international obligations and recommendations and to ensure sufficient availability of numbers, BNA may modify the structure and configuration of the numbering space and the national numbering plan. Proposed modifications need to be made known in good time prior to becoming effective.

13.50   The criteria and guidelines for the structuring, configuration and administration of numbering space, for the acquisition, the extent and the loss of rights to use numbers including the requirements for telecommunications-based services, and to transpose international recommendations and obligations into national legislation, are to be set out in an ordinance.[102]

General authorisations and granting of individual rights

13.51   The right to use numbers is subject to prior assignment. The assignment is either:

- a direct assignment by BNA of numbers for the assignee's own use, or
- an 'original assignment' by BNA to an operator of a telecommunications

---

98   BGBl I 1996, 1226, last amended by BGBl I 2002, 464.
99   BGBl I 2004, 958.
100   S 62(1) TKG.
101   S 62(2) TKG.
102   Draft Telecommunications Numbering Ordinance (May 2005).

network or a provider of telecommunication services for use of the numbers by the assignee for the purposes of a 'derived assignment', or

- by way of a 'derived assignment', whereby an operator of a telecommunications network or a provider of telecommunications services assigns a number for the assignee's own use, or
- exceptionally, by way of a general assignment issued by BNA.[103]

13.52 Both direct and original assignments are based on administrative acts issued by BNA upon request.

Only 'derived assignments' can be transferred on the basis of contractual arrangements; otherwise, the 'sale' of numbers is not permissible.[104]

Admissible conditions

13.53 The assignment of numbers may be limited in time and may be subject to conditions, including a deadline by which an assigned number needs to be used, as well as conditions for the procedure to assign numbers to end customers ('derived assignment'). A number assignment may be refused, at BNA's discretion, if BNA has reason to believe that an applicant will not be reachable in Germany, and that it will not be able to ensure the proper usage of the assigned numbers from a technical and organisational viewpoint.

13.54 In order to ensure number portability, BNA may oblige the providers of public telecommunications services to participate in automated data exchange procedures to ensure the portability of numbers.

Limitation of number of rights of use to be granted

13.55 German law does not provide for the granting of rights of use for numbers through 'competitive' or comparative selection procedures. The assignment of numbers is subject to procedural rules to be determined by BNA in accordance with the Ordinance on Numbering.[105] Decisions on assignments of numbers shall be taken on a 'first come, first served' basis, and, in the case of simultaneous receipt of several applications, by lot.[106] BNA is obliged to take its decision on the allocation of numbers as fast as possible and within three weeks at the latest.

The NRA's Enforcement Powers

13.56 BNA has broad powers to enforce the obligations of network operators and service providers under the TKG.

Where BNA finds that an undertaking is failing to meet its obligations by or under the TKG, it shall require the undertaking to state its views and to take remedial action within a given time limit.[107] If the undertaking fails to meet its obligations within the time limit set, BNA may order such measures as are necessary to secure

---

103   See Sec 3(2) Draft Telecommunications Numbering Ordinance (May 2005).
104   Sec 3(6) Draft Telecommunications Numbering Ordinance (May 2005).
105   See para 13.50 above.
106   Sec 4(2) Draft Telecommunications Numbering Ordinance (May 2005).
107   S 126(1) TKG.

compliance with the obligations concerned. Again, BNA has to set a reasonable time limit to allow the undertaking to comply with the measures. In the case of serious or repeated breaches of obligations by the undertaking or failure to comply with an order for remedial action, BNA may prohibit the undertaking from acting as a network operator or service provider.[108] BNA may take provisional measures where a breach of obligations constitutes a direct and serious threat to public safety and order, or where a violation of duties creates serious economic and operational problems for other providers or users of telecommunications networks or services. If provisional measures have been taken, BNA has to give the undertaking concerned the opportunity to state its views within a reasonable period and to decide whether the provisional measures shall be confirmed, withdrawn or modified.[109]

To enforce its orders against non-compliant undertakings, BNA may impose an administrative enforcement fine of up to €500,000.

Administrative Charges and Fees for Rights of Use

13.57   BNA is empowered to charge fees and expenses for a number of its regulatory measures, including:

- decisions on the grant of rights of use for frequencies,[110]
- decisions on the grant of rights of use for telephone numbers,[111]
- the processing of publications for the registration of diallers using premium rate numbers,
- the case-by-case coordination, advance publication, assignment and notification of satellite systems,
- measures to counteract violations of the TKG or of ordinances issued by virtue of the TKG, and
- decisions on the transfer of rights of way.

The chargeable acts and the level of fees are set out in specific ordinances.[112]

13.58   In addition to the fees and expenses for the granting of the right to use frequencies, BNA levies annual contribution charges to recover costs it incurs for the management, control and enforcement of general assignments and rights of use for spectrum and orbit usage.[113] This 'frequency usage contribution charge' is to be paid by all those who have been assigned frequencies.

13.59   The German legislator has availed itself of the possibility under article 12 Authorisation Directive to impose 'telecommunications contribution charges' to offset costs incurred by BNA to secure fair competition and to promote public telecommunications markets with sustainable competition and for the management, control and enforcement of rights and obligations under the TKG. The contribution charge may be imposed on public telecommunications network operators and providers of publicly available telecommunications services.

---

108   S 126(3) TKG.
109   S 126(5) TKG.
110   Cf Ordinance on Frequency Fees, BGBl I 1996, 1226, last amended by BGBl I 2002, 4564.
111   Cf Ordinance on Numbering Fees, BGBl I 1999, 1887, last amended by BGBl I 2004, 868.
112   Ordinance on Frequency Charges, BGBl I 1996, 1226, last amended by BGBl I 2002, 4564; Ordinance on Charges to Secure Interference Free Use of Frequencies, BGBl I 2004, 958; Ordinance on Charges for Telecommunications Numbers, BGBl I 2004, 868.
113   S 144 TKG; cf Ordinance on Contribution Charges for the Protection of Frequencies, BGBl I 2004, 958.

The charge is meant to offset the relevant costs incurred by BNA, unless such costs are otherwise covered by fees or contribution charges under the Act. The relevant costs shall be split in proportion among the contributing undertakings in accordance with their revenues from their activities as network or service providers. The charges will be levied by BNA on an annual basis.[114]

Transitional Regulations for Existing Authorisations

13.60   The notification requirement[115] does not apply to undertakings which have given notification under the previous Telecommunications Act of 1996 and to operators that have been licensed under the 1996 Act. Existing frequency assignments, number allocations and rights of way granted under the 1996 Act remain in effect.[116]

REGULATION OF NETWORK ACCESS AND INTERCONNECTION: IMPLEMENTATION OF THE ACCESS DIRECTIVE

Objectives and Scope of Access Regulation

13.61   The Access Directive has been transposed by sections 16–26 TKG. The provisions distinguish between interconnection[117] and access,[118] and empower BNA to impose access obligations on both network operators with and without SMP.

Basic Regulatory Concepts

13.62   The Act defines 'access' as 'the provision of services and/or the making available of facilities to another undertaking, under defined conditions, for the purpose of providing telecommunications services'.[119] The non-conclusive list of different types of access set out in article 2(a) Access Directive[120] has not been explicitly transposed into German law, but needs to be taken into consideration in interpreting the 'access' concept under the TKG. The definition of the term 'interconnection' is almost identical to the definition set out in article 2(b) Access Directive.[121]

13.63   All operators of public telecommunications networks are obliged to make an interconnection offer to other public telecommunications network operators upon their request in order to secure user communication, the provision of telecommunications services and service interoperability throughout the European Community.[122] In addition to this general obligation which applies to all network operators, regardless of their market position, the TKG allows for the imposition of

---

114   S 144(2) TKG.
115   See para 13.31 above.
116   S 150(2)–(4) TKG.
117   S 16 TKG.
118   S 18–22 TKG.
119   S 3 No 32 TKG.
120   See para 1.125 above.
121   Cf s 3 No 34 TKG.
122   S 16 TKG.

access- and interconnection-related obligations with respect to SMP undertakings[123] and network operators controlling access to end users and not having significant market power.[124] The access provisions of the Act are predicated on the principle that commercial negotiations shall have priority over access orders.

Access- and Interconnection-related Obligations with Respect to SMP Undertakings

Overview

13.64   BNA is empowered to impose access- and interconnection-related obligations on SMP operators on the basis of regulatory orders following a market analysis,[125] and by way of individual access orders as and when a regulated operator and another operator fail to conclude an access agreement.[126]

Transparency obligation

13.65   In order to ensure transparency of access conditions, BNA may impose on an SMP operator the obligation to publish, for the benefit of undertakings entitled to access, all such information as is required for use of the relevant access services and/or facilities, in particular accounting information, information on technical specifications, network characteristics, terms and conditions of supply and use, and the charges payable.[127]

Non-discrimination obligations

13.66   BNA may impose obligations on an SMP operator requiring access agreements to be based on objective criteria, to be transparent, to grant equally good access and to meet the requirements of fairness and reasonableness.[128] These obligations of non-discrimination shall ensure, in particular, that the operator applies equivalent conditions in the same circumstances to other undertakings providing like services, and provides services and information to others under the same conditions and of the same quality as it provides for its own services or those of its subsidiaries or partners.

Specific access obligations

13.67   BNA may also, upon request or on its own initiative, impose specific access obligations on network operators with SMP, including the obligation to provide unbundled access.[129]

---

123   See paras 13.65 et seq below.
124   See para 13.86 below.
125   S 13 TKG, cf para 13.26 above.
126   S 25 TKG.
127   S 20(1) TKG.
128   S 19(1) TKG.
129   S 21 TKG.

In exercising its discretion, BNA has to take into account, in particular, the following factors:

- the technical and economic viability, having regard to the pace of market development, of using or installing alternative facilities, bearing in mind the nature and type of interconnection access proposed,
- the feasibility of providing the access proposed, in relation to the capacity available,
- the initial investment by the facility owner, bearing in mind the risks involved in making the investment,
- the need to secure competition in public telecommunications networks and publicly available telecommunications services in the long term,
- industrial property rights and intellectual property rights,
- the provision of services that are available throughout Europe, and
- the already imposed obligations or non-mandated services available in and taken up by a large part of the market as sufficient to ensure the regulatory objectives.[130]

13.68 The TKG distinguishes between two types of access obligations: those that BNA may, at its discretion, impose on SMP operators; and those that it should impose, ie the latter being obligations which shall be imposed unless BNA has overriding reasons not to impose them.

Among the access obligations which BNA may impose, at its discretion, are the following:

- to grant access to specified network elements and/or facilities, including unbundled broadband access,
- to grant access on a wholesale basis to particular services offered by the operator as offered to end users, for the purpose of resale by third parties in their own name and for their own account,
- to create the necessary prerequisites for the interoperability of end-to-end communication, including the provision of facilities for intelligent network services and roaming, and
- to grant access to operational support systems or similar software systems required to secure fair competition in the provision of services, while ensuring the efficient use of existing facilities.[131]

These specific access obligations also include very detailed access provisions in relation to billing and collection services.

13.69 Whereas the list of specific access obligations which BNA 'may' impose is non-conclusive, the Act provides for four specific obligations which BNA 'should' impose on SMP operators, namely:

- the granting of fully unbundled access to the local loop and shared access to the local loop,
- the interconnection of telecommunications networks,
- the granting of open access to technical interfaces, protocols and other key technologies essential for service interoperability and virtual network services, and

---

130 S 21(1) TKG.
131 S 21(2) TKG.

- the provision of co-location and other forms of facility sharing, including building, duct and mast sharing, and the grant, to users or their agents, of access to these facilities at any time.[132]

13.70 Limitations on the imposition of access obligations exist where an operator shows that use of the facility would endanger the maintenance of network integrity or the safety of network operations. The maintenance of network integrity and the safety of network operations are to be judged on the basis of objective standards, and the burden of proof lies with the SMP operator.[133]

Price control obligations

13.71 The rates charged by an SMP public telecommunications network operator for access services and/or facilities mandated by way of an access order are subject to prior approval by BNA.[134] In derogation from this principle, BNA 'should' subject such rates to mere ex-post regulation when (1) the operator does not also, at the same time, have significant market power in the retail market in which he is active, (2) significant market power has been determined after the entry into force of the TKG without the operator having been designated by BNA as having dominance prior to the entering to force of the TKG, and (3) this measure is sufficient to achieve the regulatory objectives of the TKG. This exemption from the principle of ex-ante regulation is considered, by the Commission, as an unwarranted limitation of the administrative discretion which is to be granted to the NRA under articles 8, 13 Access Directive.[135]

13.72 Rates for access services in conjunction with the provision of billing and the first time collection of receivables are subject to ex-post regulation only.[136]

Accounting separation obligations

13.73 In order to ensure transparency of pricing, BNA may require an SMP operator to keep separate accounts for certain activities related to access services and facilities. In particular, BNA shall require, as a rule, a vertically integrated undertaking to make its wholesale prices and its internal transfer prices transparent in order to prevent a breach of the prohibition on discrimination and unlawful cross-subsidisation.[137]

Related Regulatory Powers with Respect to SMP Undertakings

13.74 Operators with significant market power regarding the provision of connection to and use of the public telephone network at fixed locations are obliged to allow for carrier selection on a call-by-call basis as well as carrier pre-selection.[138] The charges to end users for use of these services and facilities are subject to ex-post

---

132 S 21(3) TKG.
133 S 21(4) TKG.
134 S 30 in conjunction with S 31 TKG.
135 European Commission, Infringement Procedure No 2004–2221, pp 5 seq.
136 S 30(2) TKG.
137 S 24(1) TKG.
138 S 40 TKG.

regulation. Obligations to provide call-by-call carrier selection and pre-selection may also be imposed on other SMP undertakings provided that the regulatory aims of the TKG[139] would not otherwise be achieved. The Act provides that, as long as there is sustainable services competition in the retail mobile market, the carrier selection and pre-selection obligations will not be imposed on mobile operators.[140] The Commission believes that this limitation violates article 19 para 2 Universal Service Directive and has initiated an infringement procedure against the German government.[141]

13.75 BNA requires SMP undertakings in the provision of part or all of the leased lines market to provide the minimum set of leased lines as identified in the list of standards drawn up by the Commission on the basis of article 17 Framework Directive.[142] The undertakings have to publish the technical characteristics, tariffs and supply conditions set out in Annex VII to the Universal Service Directive,[143] BNA is empowered to set targets in respect of the supply conditions.

Regulatory Powers Applicable to All Market Participants

Obligations to ensure end-to-end connectivity

13.76 In order to ensure end-to-end connectivity, BNA may oblige both SMP operators[144] and non-SMP operators controlling access to end users to interconnect their networks with those of other telecommunications network operators.

Access to digital radio and television broadcasting services

13.77 Rights holders of application programming interfaces are obliged to provide on fair, reasonable and non-discriminatory terms and against appropriate remuneration, manufacturers of digital television receivers and third parties claiming legitimate interest with all such information as is necessary to provide all the services supported by the application programming interface in fully functional form.[145]

13.78 Providers of conditional access systems are obliged to ensure that these have the necessary technical capability for the cost-effective transfer of control functions, allowing the possibility for full control by public telecommunications network operators at local or regional level of the services using such conditional access systems.[146]

Holders of industrial property rights to conditional access systems are obliged to grant licences to manufacturers of digital television receivers or to third parties demonstrating a legitimate interest on fair, reasonable and non-discriminatory

---

139 See para 13.9 above.
140 S 40(2) sentence 2 TKG.
141 European Commission, Infringement Procedure No 2005/2067.
142 Commission Decision of 24 July 2003 on the minimum set of leased lines with harmonised characteristics and associated standards referred to in art 18 Universal Service Directive, OJ L 186/43, 25.07.2003; see para 1.176 above.
143 See para 1.176 above.
144 See paras 13.79 et seq above.
145 S 49(2) TKG.
146 S 50(1) TKG.

terms, if and when they decide to grant such licences. The licences may not be made subject to conditions hindering the installation of a common interface allowing connection with other conditional access systems or components specific to another conditional access system, for reasons of transaction security with regard to the content to be protected.[147]

Transitional Provisions

13.79   In order to ensure the transition from the access and interconnection regime of the 1996 Telecommunications Act to the new TKG, section 150 para 1 TKG provides that determinations of market dominance made by BNA prior to the entry into force of the new TKG, and the resulting obligations remain in effect until such time as they are replaced by new decisions, including decisions on access and interconnection, taken in accordance with the new TKG.

REGULATION OF UNIVERSAL SERVICES AND USERS' RIGHTS: THE UNIVERSAL SERVICE DIRECTIVE

Regulation of Universal Service Obligations

Scope of universal service obligations

13.80   The TKG defines universal services in almost identical terms to article 2(j) Framework Directive.[148]

The list of services that have been determined as universal services under German law is identical with the list set out in articles 4–6 Universal Service Directive. BNA may, after consulting the undertaking with universal service obligations (the 'designated universal service provider'), identify general demand for the universal services in terms of the needs of end users with regard to, in particular, geographical coverage, number of telephones, accessibility and quality of service. BNA also has the power to impose obligations on undertakings in order to secure provision of the service and of service features. It may choose not to impose such obligations for all or part of its territory if it is satisfied, after consulting the interested parties, that these service features or comparable services are deemed widely available.[149]

Designation of undertakings obliged to provide universal services

13.81   If a universal service is not being adequately or appropriately provided by the market or where there is reason to fear that such provision will not be secured, each provider operating in the relevant product market and achieving, within the area of application of the TKG, at least 4% of total sales in this market or having significant market power in the relevant geographic market is obliged to contribute to making possible the provision of the universal service.[150] This statutory obligation can result either in an obligation to provide the universal services as such or to contribute to the funding of universal service provision.

---

147 S 50(2) TKG.
148 Cf s 78(1) TKG.
149 S 78(4) TKG.
150 S 80 sentence 1 TKG.

13.82   If BNA finds that a universal service is not being adequately or appropriately provided, it announces its intention to impose universal service obligations, unless an undertaking declares itself willing, within a period of one month of the publication of notice, to provide such universal service without compensation.[151]

After consulting the undertakings likely to be concerned, BNA shall decide whether and to what extent to oblige one or more of these undertakings to provide the universal service.

Where an undertaking that is to be obliged to provide a universal service can demonstrate by prima facie evidence that, in the case of such obligation, financial compensation will be necessary, BNA is obliged to invite tenders for the provision of the universal service and award it to a qualified applicant requiring the least financial compensation for providing the universal service in compliance with the requirements of the Act.[152]

At present, universal services are provided by Deutsche Telekom AG. If Deutsche Telekom AG intends to stop providing universal services or to offer them under less favourable conditions, it is obliged to notify BNA of its intentions one year prior to their taking effect, to allow the regulator time to take the necessary measures under the Act.

Regulation of retail tariffs, users' expenditures and quality of service

13.83   The TKG requires, in accordance with the Universal Service Directive,[153] that universal services shall be provided at affordable prices. The price for providing a connection at a fixed location to a public telephone network and access to publicly available telephone services at a fixed location[154] is deemed affordable if it does not exceed the real price of the telephone services required on average by a household situated outside a town or city with a population of more than 100,000 on 1 January 1998. In its assessment of affordability, BNA shall take into account the quality of service levels, including supply times at that time and the rate of growth in productivity up to 31 December of the year prior to the previous one.[155]

All other universal services are deemed affordable if the rates are not abusive.[156]

13.84   BNA is empowered to monitor the provision of universal services, including their quality, and applies the parameters, definitions and measuring methods established by EU law.[157]

Cost calculation and financing of universal services

13.85   If BNA grants compensation for the provision of a universal service, each undertaking operating in the relevant product market and achieving, within the area of application of the TKG, at least 4% of total sales in this market or having

---

151 S 81(1) TKG.
152 S 81(3) TKG.
153 See para 1.162 above.
154 S 78(2) No 1 TKG; see also art 4(1) Universal Service Directive.
155 S 79(1) TKG.
156 Section 79(2) TKG in conjunction with S 28 TKG.
157 S 84 (3) TKG; cf Annex 3 to the Universal Service Directive, see paras 1.165 et seq above.

SMP[158] shall share, by means of a universal service contribution, in funding the compensation. The sharing mechanism is assessed on the basis of the proportion of the sales of the particular undertaking to the total sales of all those that are obliged to contribute to the funding.[159]

13.86   The compensation payable for the provision of a universal service is determined by calculating the difference between the cost for a designated undertaking of operating without the universal service obligation and the cost of operating in observance of the obligation. Benefits and proceeds accruing to the universal service provider, including intangible benefits, are to be taken into account.[160] To calculate the amount of compensation, BNA may ask the designated universal service provider for the necessary documentation. The results of the cost calculation and of the examination are to be published.

Regulation of Retail Markets

Prerequisites for the regulation of retail markets

13.87   Whereas article 17 Universal Service Directive obliges Member States to ensure that national regulatory authorities shall be empowered to 'impose appropriate regulatory obligations' on undertakings identified as having SMP on a given retail market, the TKG merely provides for BNA's power to regulate the rates charged by SMP undertakings for retail telecommunications services.[161] The Commission has initiated an infringement procedure against the German government for failure to provide for a range of regulatory tools in its national legislation on retail regulation. Under the TKG, the rates charged by an SMP undertaking for retail telecommunication services are subject to regulation only if facts warrant the assumption that the imposition of access-related obligations or the imposition of carrier selection and carrier pre-selection obligations would not result in the achievement of the regulatory objectives.[162]

Regulatory powers

13.88   The regulation of end-user tariffs may be subject to ex-ante approval or to ex-post regulation by BNA.

BNA is obliged to limit the prior approval requirement to those markets in which the sustainable competition is not expected to develop in the foreseeable future, unless exceptional circumstances prevail.[163] Rates which require prior approval are eligible for approval if they do not exceed the costs of efficient service provision.

These costs are derived from the long-run incremental costs of providing the service and an appropriate mark-up for volume-neutral common costs, including a reasonable return on capital employed.[164] In determining a reasonable return on capital employed, BNA takes into account, in particular:

---

158   See paras 13.22 et seq above.
159   S 83(1) TKG.
160   S 82(2) TKG.
161   S 39 TKG.
162   S 39(1) TKG.
163   S 39(1) TKG.
164   S 31(2) TKG.

- the capital structure of the regulating undertaking,
- the situation in the national or international capital markets and the rating of the regulated undertaking in these markets,
- the requirements concerning the return on equity capital employed, whereby the service-specific risks of equity capital employed may also be acknowledged, and
- the long-term stability of the economic environment, also with a view to the situation as regards competition in the telecommunications market.[165]

13.89 Rates for retail services supplied by an SMP operator which are not subject to prior approval are subject to ex-post regulation. Under the rules for ex-post regulation, BNA is obliged to open an investigation of rates if it becomes aware of facts warranting the assumption that the rates may be abusive.[166] Abuse is constituted, in particular, by the undertaking levying rates which:

- prevail solely as a result of it having significant market power in the particular telecommunications markets,
- considerably prejudice the competitive opportunities of other undertakings in a telecommunications market, or
- create advantages for particular users in relation to other users of the same or similar telecommunications services.[167]

In the two latter instances, the SMP operator is allowed to show that its conduct is objectively justified.

Abusive pricing is presumed where:

- the price for the service in question does not cover its long-run incremental costs, including a reasonable return on capital employed,
- the margin between the price that the SMP public telecommunications operator charges competitors for an access service of facility and the corresponding retail price is not enough to enable an efficient undertaking to achieve a reasonable return on capital employed in the retail markets (margin squeeze), or
- an undertaking bundles its products in an objectively unreasonable manner.[168]

13.90 BNA may oblige an SMP undertaking to inform it of proposed end user rates two months prior to their planned effective date. If BNA finds that the proposed rates might be abusive, it shall, within two weeks of receiving notice of the measure, prohibit the introduction of the proposed rates until such time as it has completed its examination.[169]

In order to ensure a level playing field for competitors, TKG provides that an undertaking with SMP in a retail market and obliged to grant access to a service and/or a facility which includes components that are likewise essential to a service offer in the retail market, is obliged to submit at the same time as its planned rates measure for the retail service an offer for the wholesale product which meets, in particular, the requirements of fair pricing. The purpose of this provision is to ensure that the SMP operator's competitors are able to provide competing service

---

165 S 31(4) TKG.
166 S 38(2) TKG.
167 S 28(1) TKG.
168 S 28(2) TKG.
169 S 38(1) sentences 1 and 2.

offerings, based on wholesale products to be provided by the SMP operator, at the same time as the SMP operator provides its retail services.[170]

13.91   Retail rates for the provision of leased lines are subject to the same rate regulation provisions as all other retail services.[171]

End User Rights

Contracts

13.92   The obligations regarding end-user contracts and the minimum requirements of contract terms are currently set out in the Telecommunications Customer Protection Ordinance (*Telekommunikations-Kundenschutzverordnung*) of 1997 which applies until new provisions on end-user rights have been adopted. Whereas the TKG originally contemplated that the end-user rights would be governed by an ordinance, the government currently intends to adopt an amendment to the Telecommunications Act addressing the requirements for end-user contracts.

Transparency obligations

13.93   Providers of publicly available telecommunications services are obliged to publish general information for end users and provide interested parties with easy access to this information, including information on access, conditions of use and supply, the customer's right to withhold consent wholly or in part to the entry in directories of their data, prices, and, with reference to voice telephony, information on certain quality parameters.[172] In addition, providers of access to fixed public telecommunications networks are obliged to publish the technical characteristics of interfaces and to provide three months' notice prior to the introduction of new interface specifications.

13.94   Customers may request their provider of publicly available voice communications services to include them in a generally accessible subscriber directory, free of charge, and may check and correct or have the entry deleted again. The subscriber directories shall state at least the number, name, first name and address of the network access holder. Subject to applicable data protection rules, the network access holder may request that co-users also be included in the directory, on payment of a fee.[173]

13.95   The provision of the possibility to make emergency calls from all public pay telephones free of charge, simply by the use of the number '112' and the national emergency call numbers determined in an ordinance, is part of the universal service obligations under the TKG.[174] In addition, any person offering publicly available telephone services is obliged to provide all users with access to emergency services by using, free of charge, the single European emergency call number '112' and the additional national emergency call numbers.[175] It is currently

---

170   S 39(4) TKG.
171   S 41(3) TKG, cf paras 13.100, 13.107 above.
172   S 27(1) Telecommunications Customer Ordinance.
173   S 21 Telecommunications Customer Ordinance.
174   S 78(2) no 5 TKG.
175   S 108(1) TKG.

an open question whether or not providers of 'Voice over Internet Protocol' services are to be subjected to the same emergency call obligations.

13.96   Public telephone network operators are obliged to enable subscribers to retain their telephone number, independently of the undertaking providing the telephone services, (1) in the case of geographic numbers, at a specific location, and (2) in the case of non-geographic numbers, at any location. This obligation to ensure number portability applies only within the numbering ranges and sub-ranges designated for a telephone service. The transfer of telephone numbers for telephone services provided at a fixed location to those not provided at a fixed location and vice versa is not permitted.[176] Furthermore, providers of publicly available telecommunications services are obliged to ensure that their end-users can retain telephone numbers allocated to them when changing to another provider of publicly available telecommunications services.[177]

13.97   In order to ensure Community-wide electronic communications, public telephone network operators are obliged to make provision in their networks for handling all calls to the European telephone numbering space.[178]

Transitional Provisions

13.98   At present, the German TKG is not yet fully adapted to the provisions in relation to end-user rights set out in articles 20 et seq Universal Service Directive. The current transitional provisions set out in the Telecommunications Customer Protection Ordinance of 1997[179] are expected to be replaced in 2005/2006 by an amendment to the TKG.

DATA PROTECTION: IMPLEMENTATION OF THE E-PRIVACY-DIRECTIVE

Confidentiality of Communications

13.99   The principle of telecommunications secrecy is enshrined in article 10 of the German Federal Constitution. On this basis, the TKG provides that the content and detailed circumstances of telecommunications, in particular the fact of whether or not a person is or was engaged in a telecommunications activity, is subject to telecommunications secrecy which also covers the detailed circumstances surrounding unsuccessful call attempts. Every service provider is obliged to maintain telecommunications secrecy; this obligation also applies after the end of the activity through which such commitment arose.[180]

13.100   The interception or surveillance of communications is permissible only on the basis of specific legislative acts and, in principle, subject to a court order. The operators of telecommunications systems by means of which publicly available telecommunications services are provided are obliged to provide, at their own

---

176   S 46(1) TKG.
177   S 46(2) TKG.
178   S 46(4) TKG.
179   See para 13.4 above.
180   S 88 TKG.

expense, the technical facilities which allow for the implementation of telecommunications interception measures provided for by law and to make organisational arrangements for the implementation of such measures.[181]

Traffic Data and Location Data

13.101   Traffic data, ie data collected, processed or used in the provision of a telecommunications service,[182] may only be collected and used to the extent required for purposes specifically set out in the TKG. This applies, in particular, to:

- the number or other identification of the lines in question or of the terminal, personal authorisation codes; additionally, the card number when customer cards are used, and the location data when mobile handsets are used,
- the beginning and end of the connection, indicated by date and time and, where relevant to the charges, the volume of data transmitted,
- the telecommunications service used by the user,
- the termination points of fixed connections, the beginning and end of their use, indicated by date and time and, where relevant to the charges, the volume of data transmitted, and
- any other traffic data required for set up and maintenance of the telecommunications connection and for billing purposes.

13.102   Stored traffic data may be used after the termination of a connection only where required to set up a further connection or for billing purposes, to prevent faults, malfunctions, or unlawful use of telecommunications systems. Otherwise, traffic data are to be erased by the service provider without undue delay following termination of the connection.[183]

13.103   Location data, ie data collected or used in a telecommunications network indicating the geographic position of the terminal equipment of an end-user of a publicly available telecommunications service,[184] may be processed only when they have been made anonymous or with the consent of the subscriber, to the extent and for the duration necessary for the provision of value added services. The subscriber shall inform his co-users of all such consent given and the consent may be withdrawn at any time.[185] In respect of calls to the emergency call number '112' and to telephones specifically determined by ordinance, the service provider shall ensure that the transmission of location data is not ruled out on a per-call or a per-line basis.

Itemised Billing

13.104   If a subscriber has requested, in text form, an itemised bill, he shall be informed of certain traffic data in relation to calls for which he is liable to pay.[186] In respect of residential lines, the disclosure of such information is permitted only if the subscriber has declared, in writing, that he has informed all co-users of the line, and will inform future co-users without undue delay, of the disclosure to him of the

---

181   S 110(1) TKG.
182   S 3 No 30 TKG.
183   S 96(2) TKG.
184   S 3 No 19 TKG.
185   S 98(1) TKG.
186   S 99(1) sentence 1 TKG.

traffic data underpinning the bill. In respect of lines in businesses and public authorities, the disclosure of such information is permitted only if the subscriber has declared, in writing, that the employees have been informed, new employees will be informed without undue delay and the works council or the staff representation has been involved in accordance with the statutory requirements, or that such involvement is not necessary.[187]

13.105   The itemised bill may not allow calls to persons, public authorities or organisations in the social or the church domain who or which offer anonymous counselling wholly or predominantly by telephone to callers in emotional or social distress and who or which themselves or whose employees therefore have a special duty not to disclose confidential information, to be identified. To this end, BNA keeps a register where such called lines are entered.[188]

Calling and Connected Line Identification

13.106   Service providers offering calling line identification shall ensure that the calling and the called parties have the possibility, using a simple means and free of charge, to prevent presentation of the telephone number on a per-line or a per-call basis. Called parties shall be given the possibility, using a simple means and free of charge, of rejecting incoming calls from a calling party that has prevented presentation of its telephone number. On application by the subscriber, service providers are obliged to provide lines on which presentation on the connected line of the telephone number of the calling line is ruled out, free of charge. With regard to calls to the emergency call number '112' and to telephone numbers specifically determined in an ordinance and to the telephone number '124124' the service provider is obliged to ensure that calling line identification presentation is not ruled out on a per-call or on a per-line basis.[189]

Automatic Call Forwarding

13.107   Service providers are obliged to give their subscribers the possibility, using a simple means and free of charge, of stopping calls being automatically forwarded to their terminal as a result of action taken by a third party, to the extent that this is technically feasible.[190]

Directories of Subscribers

13.108   Upon request, subscribers may have their name and address, and additional information such as occupation, branch and type of line, entered in public printed or electronic directories. They may specify what information is to be published in the directories. At the subscribers' request, co-users may also be entered, provided they agree.[191] Information on telephone numbers included in the directories may be provided; information on data published in subscriber directories other than telephone numbers may be provided only if the subscriber has given its

---

187 S 99(1) sentences 2 and 3 TKG.
188 S 99(2) TKG.
189 S 102 TKG.
190 S 103 TKG.
191 S 104 TKG.

consent to such additional data being passed on.[192] Information provided by means of a telephone system on the telephone numbers of subscribers may be given only if the subscribers have been suitably informed that they may withhold consent to their telephone number being passed on and have not exercised their right to withhold consent.[193]

Unsolicited Communications

13.109   The recipients of unsolicited electronic communications ('spam') can avail themselves of legal remedies under the Unfair Competition Law. In addition, BNA is empowered to take regulatory action against providers that use their telecommunications numbers for spamming via email, unsolicited telefax or SMS or so called 'ping' calls.[194] The regulatory measures taken by BNA in these cases include the blockage of the relevant numbers or administrative cease and desist orders.[195]

---

192   S 105(1) TKG.
193   S 105(2) sentence 1 TKG.
194   Ping calls are calls which consist in the mere transmission of a single signal or with a view to soliciting a return call.
195   S 67 TKG.

The Greek Market for Electronic Communications[1]

Alkistis Christofilou, Virginia Murray and Stelios Katevatis
I. K. Rokas & Partners, Athens

LEGAL STRUCTURE

Basic Policy

14.1 Greece did not start free competition in the voice telephony market until 2002; the benefits of opening up really began to show in 2004, with a further 6.6% increase in the overall market, including another 17% rise in the mobile market (with an estimated 93% population coverage) and a 46% increase in the business of alternative network providers, accompanied by an 8% drop in the turnover of the incumbent, Greek Telecommunications Organisation ('OTE').[2] However, OTE continues to hold a huge market share (over 85% of the overall market and 98% of local calls), and its activities have been subject to trenchant criticism by the national regulator, the National Telecommunications and Postal Services Authority ('EETT') and alternative providers, both for its relations with other providers and for the fairness of its advertising and promotional techniques. Less than 50% of OTE's shares now belong to the State and further divestment is planned, although it effectively remains state controlled; the government has announced that management will leave state control and a voluntary resignation scheme has been agreed to tackle acute overstaffing. Whilst broadband access has increased significantly in the last two years[3] the 10th annual Commission Report found Greece lagging way behind the rest of Europe in relation to broadband.[4] Over 46% of this market is provided by OTE, which also provides over 96% of the lines.

14.2 The lack of a strong cable provider in Greece and the failure of alternative providers to invest in last mile network has led to a reliance on OTE which it is alleged to exploit unfairly.

---

1. Editing of this chapter closed on 15 June 2005.
2. These figures are based on the Telecommunications and Postal Services Authority's 2004 Report.
3. The number of broadband subscribers increased fivefold in the first half of 2004 and doubled again in the second half of 2004.
4. 0.24% penetration as of July 2004.

14.3 Competition is fierce in mobile telephony with four players in the market. 3G licences were issued after a competitive tendering process in the summer of 2001. DCS frequencies were issued to existing providers and a mobile licence was granted to a new provider, Q Telecom.

14.4 In fixed telephony, the painful process of dismantling the wide-ranging effects of the incumbent OTE's huge market power has given rise to intense and repeated conflict between the regulator, OTE and the alternative providers who, for the time being, own limited grid of their own and almost no access network. These disputes have already been brought to court.

Implementation of EU Directives

14.5 Greece is one of the few member states that by May 2005 had not yet implemented the 2002 EU Regulatory Package. The implementing draft law on Electronic Communications (the 'Draft Law')[5] was presented on 25 May 2005 for public consultation ending on 6 June 2005. The law is expected to be passed within the course of the summer. In view of the scheduled publication timetable, the draft law has been discussed in this Chapter, while including the information on the existing primary and secondary legislation, and on the regulator's dispute resolution decisions. A significant part of this legislation is expected to remain in force after the new law is passed.

14.6 Greece has implemented the EU legal regime which preceded the 2002 EU Regulatory Package.

Legislation

14.7 The sources of law in the Hellenic Republic are laws, presidential decrees ('PD') and ministerial decisions ('MD') issued by the Minister of Transport and Communication (*Ypourgos Metaforon kai Epikoinonion* – 'YME'). These are supplemented by decisions of the regulator, EETT.

14.8 Law 2867/2000 (the 'Telecommunications Act 2000') is the principal legislation in the field of telecommunications, pending the implementation[6] of the fourth telecoms package into Greek national law.

14.9 Presidential Decrees mainly transpose EU Directives into Greek law, including PD 150/01 which implements Directive 99/93/EC of the European Parliament and of the Council of 13 December 1999 on a Community framework for electronic signatures; PD 165/99 implementing the Interconnection Directive and Directive 98/61/EC; PD 156/99 implementing the ONP Framework Directive (1997); and PD 44/2002 implementing Directive 99/5/EC of the European Parliament and of the Council of 9 March 1999 on Radio Equipment and Telecommunications Terminal Equipment and the Mutual Recognition of Conformity.

14.10 EETT has issued numerous decisions which regulate all other issues and procedures of the Greek telecommunications market, including the numbering

---

5   Downloadable at www.parliament.gr/ergasies.
6   See para 14.5 above.

plan,[7] regulations for the issue of general and special licences,[8] interconnection pricing principles,[9] SMP,[10] radio frequency fees[11] and universal service.[12]

REGULATORY PRINCIPLES: IMPLEMENTATION OF THE FRAMEWORK DIRECTIVE

Scope of Regulation

14.11 The current regulated area is limited to the ambit defined in the pre-Regulatory Package legislation. The Draft Law's scope of regulation refers to electronic communications networks, associated facilities and associated services, in accordance with the Framework Directive. It is important to mention that VoIP is, indeed, covered within the Draft Law's definition of 'electronic communication services'. Although EETT has not yet defined a separate market for these services, there are several electronic communications undertakings that currently hold licences for VoIP services.[13] The Draft Law excludes government electronic communication networks, amateur networks and radio-communication stations as well as amateur services via satellite, and networks used for experimental or research or for demonstration purposes. In line with the Regulatory Package, it further excludes regulation of any audiovisual content and related hardware, including digital TV equipment.

National Regulatory Authorities: Organisation, Regulatory Objectives, Competencies

14.12 The YME takes policy decisions for the telecommunications sector and introduces legislation. It regulates satellite orbits, allocates radio frequencies and issues the National Regulation for the Allocation of Frequency Bands. When it comes to assigning frequencies within the band allocated for the broadcasting and transmission of radio and television programmes, a joint decision is taken with the Minister of Press and Media.[14]

14.13 Radio and television broadcasting is governed principally by Law No. 2328/95. The licensing authority is the national broadcasting council (*Ethniko Symvoulio Radiotileorasis* – ESR).

14.14 Greece's independent telecommunications monitoring body, initially created by Law No 2075/92, is EETT, now regulated by the Telecommunications Act 2000. EETT is funded by the licence levies on telecommunications companies, whether public or private, and by the fines imposed on such companies by EETT or by the courts.[15]

---

7   EETT Decision 206/2/2001.
8   EETT Decisions 207/2/2001 and 207/3/2001.
9   EETT Decision 211/3/2001.
10   EETT Decision 248/68/2002.
11   EETT Decision 276/49/2003.
12   EETT Decisions 240/13/2001 (undertakings) and 255/83/2002 (contents of USO).
13   VoIP services are provided through a general licence.
14   Art 1(5) Law 2867/2000.
15   Art 13(8) Law 2867/2000.

14.15   EETT is an independent authority and enjoys administrative and economic independence. Pursuant to article 101A.1 of the Constitution, its members are designated by a 4/5 majority of the Conference of Chairs of the Greek Parliament and consequently appointed by the Minister for Transport and Communications. They must fulfil criteria such as scientific competence, social recognition and professional esteem in the technical, economic or legal area. Their term of service is five years and they can be appointed for only two terms. They enjoy personal and functional independence in the exercise of their duties.

14.16   Article 3 Telecommunications Act 2000 sets out EETT's responsibilities, which include: licensing, control of the national numbering plan and domain names ending in '.gr'; defining the identity and obligations of undertakings with significant market power; defining the conditions of open network provision and pricing principles for the access and use of the LLU, the leased lines and the internet; administering all matters concerning universal service including the determination of its funding scheme; administering the radio spectrum, including the national radio-spectrum regulations and maintaining the radio frequency registry and licensing antenna installation; supervising voice telephony and mobile communications interconnection and service agreements and generally protecting consumer/end-user interests. EETT also conveys all relevant or requested information to and cooperates with the European Commission, cooperates with international organisations and represents Greece in international telecommunication conferences.

14.17   Under the Draft Law, EETT's general powers and responsibilities remain largely the same; EETT in its comments to the Draft Law published during the consultation procedure attacks the law for transferring some of its powers to the Ministry of Transport and Communications by contrast to Community law.

14.18   EETT publishes information relating to telecommunications and conducts public hearings.[16] It is bound by obligations of confidentiality.[17] It does comply with the Framework Directive's public consultation requirements.[18] The Draft Law includes a requirement for public consultation.

14.19   EETT is independent, as shown by its record of protracted disputes, principally with the incumbent OTE and secondarily with independent providers, as well as from the distance it maintains from the Ministry of Transport and Communications.

14.20   In relation to matters of competition, EETT is entitled to supervise the standards of competition in the market and to either make findings on anti-competitive behaviour itself or to seek the cooperation of, or refer the case to, the national regulatory authority, the Competition Commission.[19] When EETT reserves the resolution of the matter for itself, it is entitled to apply the fines provided by Competition Law 703/1977.[20]

14.21   EETT is entitled to demand information and has the powers to obtain the information itself by conducting investigations to the full extent granted to the Competition Commission in accordance with EU competition law.

---

16   Art 3(17) Law 2867/2000.
17   Art 3(13) Law 2867/2000.
18   See para 14.16 above.
19   Art 3(14) (ιδδ) Law 2867/2000.
20   By virtue of art 12(2) Law 2867/2000.

14.22   EETT provides a dispute resolution facility for conflicts between market players[21] or between market players and their users or with the state. The designated procedure for the dispute resolution function of the EETT is provided in PD 388/2002. EETT is entitled to adjudicate on matters arising in relation to, inter alia, network installation, installation and operation of mobile telephone antennas and terminal equipment access, interconnection, universal service obligation, competition, and consumer protection.

14.23   A roster of arbitrators is drawn up annually, principally from members of the Athens Bar and the Chamber of Engineers with experience in telecommunications and/or competition. Decisions must be rendered within three months from the final hearing. Arbitrators' fees and other costs are proportionate to the value of the dispute. In practice, much of the dispute resolution function of EETT is managed by intervention without recourse to these procedures, following notification of problems to the regulator.

14.24   The Draft Law contains an extensive chapter on the dispute resolution facility of the EETT.[22] As drafted, it restricts EETT's competence to disputes between undertakings; unlike the present law, it does not include the state and users. Cross-border disputes are dealt with in a very vague manner in the Draft.[23] The section on Arbitration[24] describes the procedure. More strictly than the Framework Directive,[25] the law retains the existing requirement that the award be issued within three months from the last hearing.

Right of Appeal against NRA's Decisions

14.25   EETT issues administrative acts of a regulatory or individual nature. These acts are subject to appeal in the same manner as acts of public administrative bodies. The regulatory acts are subject to checks on their constitutionality and authority by the courts. Individual acts may be challenged before the Supreme Administrative Court (*Symvoulion tis Epikrateias, Conseil d' Etat*) by any person who has legal interest within 60 days from the day the person was informed of the act.[26]

14.26   The procedures before the court are of considerable length. The average time for the trial to conclude usually exceeds three years. It is for this reason that judicial protection is not considered adequate. Provisional measures are also available, within a reasonably efficient time frame.[27]

14.27   The Draft Law makes a considerable attempt to accelerate proceedings: The decisions of EETT are subject to challenge before the Athens Administrative Court of Appeal within 30 days from publication if they are of a regulatory nature or, in the case of decisions with individual character, from notification to the interested person.[28] There is strict monitoring of time limits for each consequent action, so that decisions are issued within six months at the latest from filing the

---

21   Art 3(16) Law 2867/2000.
22   Art 18 Draft Law on Dispute Resolution between Undertakings.
23   Art 19 Draft Law on Cross-border Disputes.
24   Art 20 Draft Law.
25   Art 20 Framework Directive.
26   Articles 46–47 PD 18/1989.
27   Estimate based on practice.
28   Art 67 Draft Law.

challenge. The decision is subject to appeal before the Conseil d' Etat, where the decision must be issued within seven months from filing.

The NRA's Obligation to Cooperate with the Commission

14.28   Greek law has not adopted the consolidation procedure provided in article 7 Framework Directive. Although a general obligation exists for EETT to cooperate with international organisations and to represent Greece in international telecommunication forums,[29] there has been no legislative move towards consolidating EETT's work with the Commission and other European NRAs. This, however, will be remedied by the Draft Law, which explicitly imposes the obligation upon EETT to cooperate with Community NRAs and to forward to them draft decisions for consultation[30] and thereby endorses the consolidation procedure.

14.29   In addition, the Draft Law implements the Commission's power[31] to stipulate standards and specifications in article 66.

Significant Market Power as a Fundamental Prerequisite of Regulation

Definition of SMP

14.30   Significant market power is defined in article 8(9) Telecommunications Act 2000. The test of 25% of market share in the geographic and service markets applies.

14.31   In implementing the 'old' law, EETT has determined the existence of SMPs in accordance with Commission guidelines. In a 2002 Decision,[32] EETT classified the incumbent OTE as an organisation with SMP in the leased lines market. In the public mobile network and services market, EETT has classified both COSMOTE and PANAFON as holding SMP.[33] According to article 39(14).7 Telecommunications Act 2000, EETT is empowered with the task of imposing specific obligations on undertakings with SMP.[34]

14.32   The Draft Law[35] refers to individual or collective dominance by applying the independent behaviour test of article 14(2) Framework Directive. Undertakings with SMP in one market may also be deemed to have SMP on a closely related market if there are links between the two as described in article 14(3) Framework Directive. EETT shall impose at least one regulatory obligation on SMP undertakings.[36]

---

29   Art 3(14) (κε) Law 2867/2000.
30   Art 12(ι) and (ια) Draft Law.
31   Cf arts 17 and 18 Framework Directive.
32   EETT Decision 251/77/2002.
33   EETT Decision 248/68/2002.
34   See para 14.89 below.
35   Art 35(1) Draft Law.
36   Art 35(3) Draft Law.

Definition of relevant markets and SMP designation

14.33   The whole territory of Greece has been defined as the relevant geographic market in leased lines[37] and in mobile telephony for both network and services.[38]

14.34   EETT has implemented public consultation procedures for the definition of Markets 8, 9 and 10 of the Commission Recommendation on relevant markets for the interconnection of public fixed networks.

14.35   In the mobile telephony market, networks and services have been viewed together, as the SMP undertakings own their own network through which they provide the service. In view of the implementation of the 2002 EU Regulatory Package, EETT has conducted a market analysis of the wholesale mobile voice call termination market,[39] in which it took the view that each of the four providers has SMP in the relevant market. The criteria it applied were market share, potential competition, countervailing buying power and historical anti-competitive practices of providers. The measures to be imposed are subject to implementation of the 2002 EU Regulatory Package.

14.36   The Draft Law[40] aligns the procedure and the tests for market analysis with those of the 2002 EU Regulatory package. In determining SMP undertakings, EETT must take into account Commission Recommendations on relevant markets and Commission Guidelines on market analysis and, where necessary, cooperate with the Competition Commission. The market review is repeated at least every two years.[41]

NRA's Regulatory Duties concerning Rights of Way, Co-location and Facility Sharing

Rights of Way

14.37   Greek law has had difficulties implementing legislation on rights of way. Until recently, such matters were resolved in accordance with articles 1029 and 1031 Greek Civil Code. OTE was not affected, as its rights of way had been established under earlier legislation for utilities. However, attempts to remedy the situation were made in article 8(4) Telecommunications Act 2000, which stipulates that telecommunication service providers with a special licence are entitled to rights of way over public property. The procedure by which they acquire such rights is by submitting an application to the relevant governmental body, which must respond to the application within 12 weeks. If no decision is made within this deadline, the application is deemed to have been approved. Governmental bodies receiving such applications are obliged to grant such rights but may impose conditions. Refusal to grant the rights is possible only for reasons of environmental protection, public health and protection of archaeological sites. Appeals against decisions of local authorities refusing access or applying inappropriate criteria cause significant delays.

14.38   Where the request is made concerning private property, telecommunication services providers enjoy the same privileges. The difference is that the requested

---

37   EETT Decision 251/77/2002.
38   EETT Decisions 248/68/2002 as supplemented by Decision 278/65/20.3.2003.
39   (Re)Notification of Draft Measures Pursuant to art 7(3) Framework Directive for Market 16.
40   Arts 35–37 Draft Law
41   Art 35(4) Draft Law.

rights of way shall be accompanied by reasonable compensation to the owner of the private property in question and it is the latter who grants such rights. The lack of a complete and centrally monitored land registry in order to identify the owner of private property and the requirement of all the joint owners of the property to agree (all the owners of flats in an apartment block, for example) frequently impedes the use of private property, including roofs and open areas.

14.39   Article 29 Draft Law provides for a three-month period within which all interested public bodies must submit their procedures to EETT and, following a further period of public consultation, the issue of a Ministerial Decision setting out unified procedures for granting rights of way over public property. The permission to grant rights of way to a public network provider must be granted within 30 days of submission of the appropriate application, extending to 60 days for private networks. The permission is deemed to have been given on expiry of the time limits unless a reasoned refusal is issued. Disputes over refusals will be heard by the Administrative Court of Appeal under the faster interim injunction procedure.

14.40   Once permission has been granted, there must be co-ordination with all other public or private organisations which intend to dig in the same area in the following six months to avoid repeated disturbance.

14.41   EETT will set the fees for rights of way, taking into account not only the need to ensure that the provider can complete his investment profitably, but also the local land values and the degree of inconvenience to be caused to the user.

Co-location and facility sharing

14.42   PD 165/99 allows co-location and facility sharing between undertakings providing telecommunication networks and services and having licences necessary for the use of public property. In case of dispute, the interested undertakings may apply to EETT to resolve that dispute.[42] There has been increased interest in co-location following a decision of the Ombudsman concerning the safety of antennae close to built-up areas, particularly in light of the higher number of antennae required for 3G services and the intervention of local authorities in the grant of antennae licences. Co-location has, however, remained plagued by disagreements between mobile telephony providers.

14.43   The Draft Law applies special rules requiring reduced emissions for antennae sited close to nurseries, schools, hospitals and nursing homes. There are also provisions governing the placing of mobile telephony masts in border zones where the availability of mobile telephony services are deemed to be a matter of national importance. Administrative disputes on permit applications for antennae are subject to an expedited procedure before the administrative court.

14.44   With the Draft Law, EETT will acquire the right to enforce co-location with existing permit holders in circumstances where a new installation permit is refused due to environmental, public health, planning or safety reasons. A public consultation will take place on this issue, including cost sharing issues, prior to the issue of EETT regulations.

---

42   Art 11(2) PD 165/1999.

REGULATION OF MARKET ENTRY: IMPLEMENTATION OF THE AUTHORISATION DIRECTIVE

The General Authorisation of Electronic Communications

14.45   Since the Greek Telecommunications legislation has not yet implemented the 2002 EU Regulatory Package, it retains the old legal framework with respect to authorisations.[43] According to that authorisations regime, there are two types of licences, the General Licence and the Special Licence.

14.46   General Licences are required for all commercial telecommunication activities for which a Special Licence is not required.[44]

14.47   To obtain a General Licence, the telecommunications undertaking must submit a Notice of Interest to the EETT,[45] in which it describes in detail the activity for which it requests a licence. Within 15 days from submission the undertaking can start the commercial activity without the need for a positive reaction by EETT.[46] Only if, exceptionally, EETT opposes in writing may the service be delayed or prohibited, usually where EETT is uncertain whether it falls within the current legal framework or where the undertaking has not disclosed all the required information.[47]

14.48   Special Licences are required only for the installation of telecommunication networks for which access to public or private property is necessary and for the provision of telecommunication services using scarce resources.

14.49   Depending on the availability and efficient utilisation of the scarce resource used, the number of licences may be limited by decision of the Minister of Transport and Communications, following EETT's recommendation and prior public consultation.[48] Limited licensing took place in mobile telephony, where the first two licences were issued in 1993, while the 3G and DCS licences were issued following a quasi-auction procedure in 2001.[49]

14.50   EETT must grant the licence within six weeks from submission of a completed application in the case of unlimited licences, and within four to eight months in the case of a limited number of licences.

14.51   Special Licences are granted for a period of 15 to 20 years[50] and can be renewed for the period for which they have been initially granted.[51] They may be conditional on terms consistent with EU competition law, subject to proportionality.[52] EETT may terminate them, subject to proportionality for breach of law[53] or licence terms.

---

43   The relevant provisions are found in arts 5 and 6 Law 2867/2000 and EETT Decisions 207/2 and 207/3 of 2001.

44   Art 5(1) Law 2867/2000.

45   Art 3(1) EETT Decision 207/3/2001.

46   Art 3(3) EETT Decision 207/3/2001.

47   Art 3(5) and (6) EETT Decision 207/3/2001.

48   Art 6(2) Law 2867/2000.

49   See para 14.3 above.

50   Art 10(1) EETT Decision 207/2/2001.

51   Art 13 EETT Decision 207/2/2001

52   Art 10(2) EETT Decision 207/2/2001.

53   Art. 15(1) EETT Decision 207/2/2001.

14.52   Under the Draft Law,[54] the provision of electronic communication networks and/or services is free subject to the status of a General Authorisation. Notification is necessary, but exercise of the rights deriving from the Authorisation does not require the prior issue of an express decision or other individual administrative act by EETT. EETT will issue a certificate of registration of the notification in the register of providers within a week of request.

14.53   EETT may intervene and restrict or ban the provision of the network or the service only to protect public order, health and safety.

14.54   EETT shall issue a Licensing Regulation which shall replace Regulations 207/1 and 207/2 of 2001. The Regulation shall cover the issues pertaining to rights of use of numbers and frequencies, the provider's solvency requirements, the special obligations for the use of frequencies and numbers, any additional special rights and obligations imposed on the licensee, regulatory controls on consumer rights and prices, and any other relevant matter. The Regulation shall have the legal nature of a 'regulatory administrative act', which is a governmental act with general application.

14.55   The general authorisation shall be subject to the conditions listed in Annex IX.A to the Draft Law, in compliance with the Annex to the Authorisation Directive.

14.56   There are activities which are not subject to notification, such as:

- simple resale of services to users, except for the commercial resale of services on the basis of a contract with a network or service provider, and
- own use of termination equipment with non-exclusive use of special frequencies for purposes not related to economic activity which does not constitute the provision of network and services in the sense of the law.

Rights of Use for Radio Frequencies

General authorisations and granting of individual rights

14.57   The grant of radio frequencies is made through EETT and according to a procedure specified by EETT Decision 210/2 of 2001. The procedure for granting radio frequencies does not constitute a special regulatory regime.

14.58   In terms of procedure, the applicant undertaking submits the relevant application to EETT, which must conduct a preliminary review of the application and respond within 15 days. The final decision by EETT with regard to the granting of the radio frequency must not exceed 40 days.[55] The Draft Law provides for the issue of rights within six weeks, or a maximum of eight months if a competitive or comparative procedure is to be used for scarce frequencies.

Admissible conditions

14.59   EETT must consider a number of factors before granting radio frequencies to applicant undertakings. Frequencies will only be granted to those with Special Licences (or a General Authorisation under the Draft Law). Provided that the radio

---

54   Arts 21 et seq Draft Law.
55   Art 4(8) EETT Decision 210/2/2001.

frequencies and equipment proposed which the applicant undertaking requests are available and suitable for the prospective service and the applicant undertaking does not exceed the threshold of 12 radio frequencies occupied per week,[56] EETT will make its decision based on the need for the frequency, quality standards, the risk of interference, and whether the broadcast frequency of the service is as prescribed by the ITU Radio Regulations.

14.60   The Draft Law provides a limited number of conditions which can be applied to applications for radio frequencies, reflecting those in Part B of the Annex to the Authorisation Directive.[57]

Limitation of number of rights of use to be granted

14.61   Under the Draft Law, the number of rights to be granted can only be limited on the basis of ensuring the efficiency of their use. Appropriate weight should be given in making the decision to the need to maximise benefits to users and the development of a competitive market.[58] EETT will hold a public consultation on the limitation of radio frequency rights, after which a reasoned decision on any limitation and the competitive procedure to be introduced will be issued by the YME. Additional obligations may be imposed on undertakings which obtain frequencies through competitive procedures.

14.62   Currently, EETT is entitled to alter the rights of use granted to an undertaking making use of radio frequencies, in order to ensure the rational, efficient and safe usage of the radio spectrum. EETT may also grant radio frequencies of different technical specifications to those requested by the undertaking.[59] EETT may also alter the rights of use already granted if there is a change of position, radio equipment or of any other technical apparatus for which the granting of radio frequencies was initially made.[60] The Draft Law provides for compensation for any loss caused by the alteration of allocated frequencies.

14.63   EETT issues the annual 'Regulation on the Determination of Levies for Using Radio Spectrum'. The determination of the levies for the use of radio spectrum is the result of a mathematical equation comprised of three factors:

- geographical and spectrum scarcity of the frequency;
- bandwidth; and
- technology used (digital or analogue).

In the determination of levies, the ratio of bandwidth is taken into account, so some spectrum bands are more expensive than others. However, there are no special conditions attached to some spectrum bands, as opposed to others, in the context of granting the radio frequencies.

14.64   The Greek regulatory framework as its stands does not provide for spectrum auctions but does provide for auctions of limited Special Licences[61] on

---

56   Art 4(3) (a) EETT Decision 210/2/2001.
57   Annex IX to the Draft Law.
58   Art 25 Draft Law.
59   Art 4(7) EETT Decision 210/2/2001.
60   Art 8 EETT Decision 210/2/2001.
61   For this type of Special Licence, see para 14.49 above.

decision of the Minister of Transport and Communications, taking into consideration the maximisation of efficient use and the facilitation of the further development of competition.[62] The procedure and terms of that auction are determined by EETT.[63] This procedure was followed for the issue of 3G mobile telephony licences.

Frequency trading

14.65   The current Greek regulatory regime does not allow spectrum-trading, but the Draft Law provides for transfer or subletting of frequency rights with the permission of EETT, principally on condition that the licensed use should not change.

Rights of Use for Numbers

General authorisations and granting of individual rights

14.66   Numbers are regulated by EETT in accordance with the National Numbering Plan ('ESA').[64] Significant alterations have been made in the Greek national numbering system to allow number portability.

14.67   The process of granting numbers is set out in EETT Regulatory Decision 207/6 of 2001. The regulations refer to the issue of primary and secondary numbers. The former are large groups of numbers granted by EETT to service providers, while the latter are individual or small groups of numbers granted by the service providers to either users or other service providers. EETT is principally concerned with the primary grant of numbers to service providers.

14.68   The procedure for primary number granting is initiated by an application. The interested undertaking applies to EETT for groups of 10,000 numbers.[65] Once the application is submitted, EETT considers the service to be provided and the numbers to be used, as well as applying the principles of non-discrimination, transparency and the objective of maintaining effective competition, together with the applicant's conformity with relevant international regulations and Community legislation.[66]

14.69   The processing of applications is conducted on a 'first come first served' basis by EETT, and the right of use of the numbers is granted for a period equal to the duration of the Special Licence.

14.70   There are also provisions for reserving a group of numbers of the undertaking's choice. The process of obtaining such groups of numbers resembles the one by which regular groups of numbers are granted. In particular, applicants for 'golden numbers' also have to possess a Special Licence.

---

62   Art 6(2) Law No 2867/2000.
63   Art 9(3b) EETT Decision No 207/2/2001.
64   Art 3(14) (a) and art 7 Law 2867/2000.
65   Exceptionally, groups of less than 10,000 numbers are granted in some cases. For instance, when a geographical area cannot support such large groups of numbers, or when the application relates to telephone services operated through cards.
66   Art 3(3) EETT Decision 207/6/2001.

14.71   Greek legislation specifies that no property rights are attached to the numbers provided.[67]

14.72   Telecommunications providers, particularly mobile operators, have questioned the level of fees charged by EETT for number allocation; they maintain that, now that the new numbering plan is in force, fees should no longer be set on the basis that numbers are a scarce resource.

Admissible conditions

14.73   The granting of the right of use for numbers is accompanied by certain obligations. Therefore, undertakings that have the right to use certain numbers are obliged, inter alia, to pay the relevant levies; to comply with the terms of use as these are specified by EETT, including the obligation to allow number portability and to provide the numbers for inclusion in directories; and to ensure that its customers are promptly informed of any alterations to their numbers.[68]

14.74   By EETT Decisions 254/70 and 254/71 of 2002, number portability and carrier pre-selection became available to Greek telecommunication consumers. With respect to carrier pre-selection, the relevant regulation obliges providers of telecommunication networks with SMP to afford their customers this option within seven days.[69] Providers without SMP are not obliged to provide a carrier pre-selection option, although they are allowed to do so. OTE has been accused of significant delay in processing applications (20 days on average) and allowing them to lapse without notice.

14.75   Similarly, EETT Regulatory Decision 254/71 obliges all providers of telecommunication networks to afford their customers a choice of number portability.[70] The more recent EETT Decisions on number portability (amending EETT Decision 254/71) impose on telecommunication networks providers the obligation to afford their subscribers with number portability in fixed, mobile and 'pay as you go' mobile subscriptions.[71] However, there is no obligation for number portability between fixed and mobile telephony. The first decision came into effect on 1 March 2004 and, according to EETT, within a month there were 3,000 applications made by consumers to transfer numbers between providers.

Limitation of number of rights of use to be granted

14.76   With respect to the process of granting rights for numbers, no provision for either a competitive or comparative selection procedure currently applies in Greek law. However, the Draft Law provides for competitive or comparative procedures for numbers characterised by a decision of EETT as being of particular commercial value; the entire procedure cannot take more than six weeks. Special conditions may be imposed on numbers granted under a competitive or comparative system.

---

67   Art 11(2) EETT Decision 207/6/2001.
68   Art 12 EETT Decision 207/6/2001, Annex IX to the Draft Law.
69   Art 3(1) EETT Decision 254/70/2002.
70   Art 4.1 EETT Decision 254/71/2002 as amended by EETT Decisions 300/22 and 351/75.
71   Art.2 EETT Decision 351/75.

The NRA's Enforcement Powers

14.77   EETT is empowered by the Telecommunications Act 2000 to enforce all the obligations that ensue from the relevant legislation with respect to telecommunications undertakings. In particular, article 12 Telecommunications Act 2000 stipulates that EETT shall have at its disposal a number of sanctions. These include cautioning, the imposition of fines and temporary or even permanent revocation of the licence.

14.78   EETT has full powers to obtain information including investigation powers, as the Competition Commission does, in conformity with EU law and also, if necessary, the powers of a public prosecutor.

14.79   EETT may impose such interim measures as it deems appropriate to protect the threatened public safety, public order and public health, or endangered legal rights of users or providers. EETT may proceed on its own initiative or following a complaint. The measures are imposed pursuant to the Regulation on Hearings.[72] Should the provider not remedy the breach, EETT may impose a fine of up to €100,000 per day of breach. EETT has already exercised these powers against OTE in connection with its Reference Interconnection Offer ('RIO') for 2004.

14.80   The Draft Law largely provides the same system of fines and interim measures. EETT must require the undertaking in breach to remedy the breach or attend a hearing to explain its position. The hearing is conducted in accordance with the existing EETT regulations.[73]

Administrative Charges and Fees for Rights of Use

14.81   Undertakings holding General or Special Licences are obliged to pay levies. These levies are specified by EETT and their level is determined by two factors, namely the cost of managing these resources and the level of scarcity. The levies are divided between lump sums payable on initial grant and annual levies.[74]

14.82   In accordance with articles 60 and 61 Draft Law, charges and fees must be applied in an objective, transparent and proportionate way. EETT may elect to apply a system based on percentages of turnover or a lump sum system per item charged or a combination of the two. Charges are reviewed annually.

REGULATION OF NETWORK ACCESS AND INTERCONNECTION: IMPLEMENTATION OF THE ACCESS DIRECTIVE

Objectives and Scope of Access Regulation

14.83   EETT has the task of ensuring the availability of both network access and interconnection to all telecommunication undertakings.[75] In this role, EETT's objectives are explicitly stated as guaranteeing the maximum economic outcome while ensuring the maximum possible benefit to end-users[76] and the general policy

---

72   PD 388/2002.
73   Art 63 Draft Law.
74   Art 10 EETT Decision 207/6/2001.
75   Art 8(1) Law 2867/2000.
76   Art 9(1) PD 165/99.

objectives and regulatory principles set out in the Draft Law, which mirror those in the Framework Directive. The terms 'access' and 'interconnection' are defined in the Draft Law in the same terms as the Access Directive.

14.84   By virtue of article 8(1) Telecommunications Act 2000 and the Draft Law, all telecommunication undertakings must provide interconnection to networks which control access to subscribers in order to ensure end-to-end connectivity, including in justified circumstances the obligation to connect their networks.

Basic Regulatory Concepts

14.85   The powers and obligations of EETT in regulating access and interconnection are set out in PD 165/99. EETT may pre-determine the terms of access and interconnection agreements between telecommunication organisations. In addition, it may intervene and impose terms on agreements already concluded. These terms may relate, inter alia, to matters of technical operation and operability as well as fees, conditions of offer and use and environmental protection.[77] The Draft Law provides for the issue of Regulations which will set out in detail the application of these principles.

14.86   Under the current law, EETT may also determine the time schedule within which interconnection agreements may be concluded, which may not exceed three months.[78] Finally, EETT may exercise its dispute resolution powers for disputes between undertakings.[79]

14.87   The principle of freedom of access exists in Greek law as it was enunciated in the Interconnection Directive. According to PD 165/99, only telecommunication organisations that possess Special Licences (network providers) may enter into interconnection agreements. Under the Draft Law, only a General Authorisation will be required, which will not be required for interconnection agreements for network providers from other member states provided that they do not provide a service in Greece.

14.88   The principle of the priority of commercial negotiations[80] has not been expressly implemented even in the Draft Law, which allows generally for the intervention of EETT in appropriate circumstances, and not only if commercial negotiations fail. EETT must apply objective, transparent, proportionate and non-discriminatory criteria.

Access- and Interconnection-related Obligations with Respect to SMP Undertakings

Overview

14.89   The access obligations imposed on organisations, and in particular SMP undertakings, are enunciated in the Draft Law. As well as OTE for the fixed network, EETT has designated all four mobile telephony operators as holding SMP

---

77   Art 9(3) Law 2867/2000.
78   Art 9(4) Law 2867/2000.
79   Art 9(7) Law 2867/2000.
80   Art 3(1) Access Directive.

in relation to termination of voice calls on their own networks.[81] Many complaints were made by alternative network providers in relation to charges for calls terminating on mobile networks; EETT has found that all three major mobile telephony providers (Cosmote, Vodafone and Tim) have failed to establish that prices for calls terminating on their networks are cost related.

Transparency obligations

14.90   All network providers must publish technical standards, accounting information and network characteristics, terms and prices. EETT may establish a list of information which must be published and indicate the means of publication. Network providers must also publish and submit to EETT an analytical sample services offer, which must adequately break down the prices offered. Those obliged to offer unbundled access to the twisted metallic pair local loop must submit a Reference Offer which contains the minimum contents in the same terms listed in Annex II to the Access Directive.[82]

Non-discrimination obligations

14.91   Network providers are not only required to provide access to their networks on non-discriminatory terms, but are also required to provide services and information to third parties on the same terms and to the same quality as that provided to their own services, affiliates or partners.

Specific access obligations

14.92   Under the Draft Law, all network providers, irrespective of market share, have obligations in respect of co-location, accounting separation, ETNS, international number codes and access to non-geographical numbers as well as number pre-selection. They are also bound by data protection provisions.

Price control obligations

14.93   The pricing for such provisions must reflect the real cost to the SMP. EETT by its decision of 20 December 2002 imposed a fine of €1,500,000 on OTE for not generating cost-oriented pricing for its leased lines.[83]

14.94   With respect to price control, the Draft Law provides that interconnection charges must adhere to the principles of non-discrimination, transparency and accounting separation.[84] The burden of proving that charges are cost oriented lies on the said organisations. In addition, organisations with SMP are obliged to submit a Reference Interconnection Offer to EETT, which retains the right to

81   EETT (Re) Notification of Draft Measures pursuant to art 7(3) Framework Directive for the market of Wholesale Mobile Voice Call termination following the Commission's Comments (EL/2004/0078).

82   Draft Law, Annex III.

83   EETT Press Release, dated 20 December 2002, available at www.eet.gr/gr_pages/dimosiotita/ deltia_typou/DT-18_12_02.htm.

84   Art 43 Draft Law.

amend it, and publishes it in the Government Gazette.[85] Numerous complaints have been made by alternative providers concerning the late publication of the annual 'RIO'. The RIO for 2002 was not finally published until August 2002, after OTE submitted its proposal to EETT late, and EETT demanded numerous amendments. The RIO for 2003 was also published late after an extended consultation period. EETT appoints an independent auditor each year to investigate OTE's pricing principles for unbundling of the local loop, and has referred OTE's pricing back to OTE for revision after it failed to establish its pricing on LRA-IC/CCA principles.[86]

14.95   New market entrants have complained about the level of interconnection charges, particularly in relation to local calls, which makes it practically impossible for any new player to compete with OTE in this sector.[87]

Accounting separation obligations

14.96   In terms of accounting separation, organisations with SMP are obliged to maintain separate accounts for, on the one hand, providing interconnection services and, on the other hand, other activities. The aim of this accounting separation is to illustrate clearly the elements of costs and revenues.[88]

Related Regulatory Powers with Respect to SMP Undertakings

14.97   There are a few further obligations imposed on organisations with SMP. These include the obligation to announce to EETT, prior to their application, any price discounts with respect to the leasing of lines,[89] and also to communicate to EETT reference offers for leased lines which shall pertain to both wholesale and retail leasing of their lines.[90] Moreover, organisations with SMP shall not differentiate between the contractual terms of wholesale and retail leased lines, thereby making the latter less profitable.[91]

14.98   Finally, obligations on organisations with SMP exist with respect to carrier pre-selection and number portability. In particular, organisations with SMP must provide their customers with the option of carrier pre-selection.[92] With respect to number portability, the obligation applies to all telecommunication providers irrespective of their market power.[93]

---

85   Art 8(3) Law 2867/2000.
86   EETT Decision 277/63 of 28 February 2003.
87   Results of Public Consultation on RIO 2002 and other issues related to the preparation of RIO 2003, EETT, of 21 February 2003.
88   Art 8(3) PD 165/99.
89   Art 3(4) EETT Decision 255/84/2002.
90   Art 3 EETT Decision 255/84/2002.
91   Art 10 EETT Decision 255/84/2002.
92   See para 14.92 above.
93   See para 14.92 above.

Regulatory Powers Applicable to All Market Participants

Obligations to ensure end-to-end connectivity

14.99   Under the current regime there are other general obligations directed to all market participants irrespective of their market power, for example the obligation to provide unlimited access to the local loop[94] (although, given OTE's huge dominance of this market, this is currently of more theoretical than real application), as well as general obligations to negotiate in good faith and avoid anticompetitive behaviour.[95] EETT must ensure[96] that interconnection agreements between organisations guarantee end-to-end connectivity. Moreover, the obligation to provide end-to-end connectivity of users of different networks is included within the 'essential requirements'.[97]

14.100   The Draft Law[98] foresees the option for EETT to impose on undertakings which control access to end users the obligation to interconnect, if this is necessary to ensure end-to-end connectivity. It may impose further proportionate and justified obligations[99] subject to, among others, public consultation[100] and data protection regulations, to the country's obligations deriving from international conventions, and to compliance with obligations imposed in connection with the grant of rights to frequencies in cases of restricted use.

Access to digital and television broadcasting services

14.101   Under the Draft Law,[101] networks established for the transmission of digital television signals must be able to transmit wide-screen services and programmes, and this format must be retained by network operators who retransmit the signal. Furthermore,[102] the Ministers responsible for Media and for Communications may issue a joint decision and impose on providers of networks used for the transmission of radio or television programmes to the public reasonable, proportionate and transparent obligations to transmit specific programmes, channels and services. Such obligations are only imposed to serve specific public interest purposes, in which case they must be regularly reviewed, or if these networks are used by a significant number of end users as the basic means for the receipt of radio and TV programmes.

---

94   Art 8(6) Law 2867/2000.
95   Art 10 MD 68141/95.
96   Art 9(1a) PD 165/99.
97   As listed in PD 165/99 Art 10(1)(γ), which implements the 1997 Interconnection Directive.
98   Art 42(1) Draft Law.
99   Art 42(6) Draft Law, subject to arts 30, 34, 50(2)(b), 50(4), 50(5), 59 Draft Law.
100   Art 42(7) Draft Law.
101   Art 41(5) Draft Law.
102   Art 58 Draft Law.

REGULATION OF UNIVERSAL SERVICES AND USERS' RIGHTS: THE UNIVERSAL SERVICE DIRECTIVE

Regulation of Universal Service Obligations

Scope of universal service obligations

14.102   PD 181/1999 and EETT Regulatory Decision 255/83/2002 govern universal services. The scope of the services is compliant with the Universal Service Directive. It includes:

- availability of good quality fixed and mobile public telephone, data and facsimile service to all end users of the network regardless of their geographical location, at a quality level of the standard primarily used by users to the extent this is technologically possible, and at an affordable price,[103]
- directory enquiry services available to end-users of both mobile and fixed telephony services,[104]
- the obligation to install or maintain public pay telephones capable of providing free access to emergency calls and access to directory services,[105] and
- measures accommodating the needs of disabled and senior end-users.[106]

Designation of undertakings obliged to provide universal services

14.103   EETT designates the undertakings obliged to provide universal services by issuing a Decision published in the Official Government Gazette.[107] The incumbent OTE is the designated provider until 31 December 2005.[108] The criteria applied by EETT for OTE's designation were its territorial expansion over the whole territory of Greece and the fact that there was no alternative access capability to the whole territory, which would not foreseeably change over the following two years. According to the Draft Law,[109] the criteria and procedures for the designation of providers in the future shall be set by a decision of the Minister of Transport and Communications following EETT's opinion, which shall be based on objectivity, transparency and non-discrimination. One or more undertakings may be designated for one or more of the USO services. The Draft Law organises all requirements in Chapter VI, including number portability.

Regulation of retail tariffs, user's expenditures and quality of service

14.104   Undertakings designated to provide universal services must issue analytical and itemised bills to their customers and are subject to quality control by EETT. EETT has formulated a Quality Indicators Chart and, at the end of every year, undertakings obliged to provide universal service submit a performance report based on that Chart. EETT retains the right to request such a report from the

---

103   Art. 4(1) PD 181/99 and art 3(1a) EETT Decision 255/83/2002.
104   Art 7 PD 181/99 and art 4 EETT Decision 255/83.
105   Art 8 PD 181/99 and art 5 EETT Decision 255/83.
106   Art 4(1) PD 181/1999.
107   Art 8(5) Law No 2867/2000.
108   EETT Decision 292/57/2003.
109   Art 46(3) Draft Law.

undertaking at any time during the year. A public consultation procedure shall take place to define the quality requirements for USO.

14.105   EETT is empowered to penalise universal service providers failing to observe their obligations. The law allows EETT to caution, impose fines, or revoke the undertaking's licence[110] temporarily or permanently.

Cost calculation and financing of universal services

14.106   With respect to the affordability of tariffs, EETT through a Regulatory Decision sets out the principles with which universal services providers must calculate costs, including areas which are not cost effective, and price their services accordingly. Transparency, objectivity and predictability are to be observed. The fully distributed cost (FDC) method[111] is compulsory for the calculation of costs.

14.107   Under the Draft Law, the compensation mechanism shall be determined by the Minister of Transport and Communications following EETT suggestions. Compensation shall be paid either from state funds or by the providers after an expense allocation procedure is defined, or by combination of the two. EETT's suggestion may be triggered by a provider complaining that it is unfairly burdened on the basis of net cost calculation.

Regulation of Retail Markets

14.108   Although Greek law, as it now stands, does not provide regulations for the retail market, EETT has taken measures to rectify anti-competitive behaviour. In May 2003 EETT applied to the court for an injunction against OTE for introducing an offer to charge all national calls at local rates on Sundays. The injunction was not finally granted by the court, but the proceedings do show an attempt on EETT's part to control the power of the company which still provides over 90% of all long-distance domestic calls.

14.109   The Draft Law[112] endorses the principle of article 17(1)(b) Universal Service Directive, that regulation of retail services is permissible if regulation at wholesale level does not achieve the regulatory objectives; it mentions indicative measures that can be taken, which are in compliance with the Universal Service Directive.

End User Rights

Contracts

14.110   End users are entitled by PD 181/1999 to full information on the terms on which the service is provided. In particular, undertakings providing telecommunication services are obliged not only to provide their customers with a contract but also to incorporate within it a minimum set of terms.[113]

---

110   Art 12(36) Draft Law.
111   Arts 4 and 5 EETT Decision 261/143/2002.
112   Art 38 Draft Law.
113   Art 10 PD 181/1999.

14.111 Any undertaking providing telecommunication services to consumers must submit their prospective standard customer contract to EETT for approval at least two months before it is used. EETT is entitled either to reject, or impose changes to, the proposed contract. The contract must contain the following minimum terms:

- description of the service, the terms and the conditions under which it is provided;
- the date on which the service starts;
- possible complementary maintenance services;
- terms and conditions for compensation of the consumer by the undertaking;
- thorough description of the quality level of the service provided; and
- description of dispute resolution procedures.[114]

14.112 The current regime satisfies the requirements of article 20(2) Universal Service Directive.

Transparency obligations

14.113 Undertakings providing telecommunication services are also obliged to distribute clear explanatory periodic invoices to their customers. These invoices must be itemised and specify the total balance, the total duration of all calls, the financial reductions and the deadline for payment.[115]

14.114 Under the Draft Law,[116] undertakings providing services to the public are also obliged to provide full, accurate and easy-to-use information on prices, tariffs, pre-defined contract terms and conditions for access and use of services. EETT shall issue a decision to determine the kind, detail, frequency and manner of publication of comparative data on the quality of services and other information.

Other obligations

14.115 The Telecommunications Act 2000 provides an array of general rights for users, which satisfy the requirements of article 20(2) Universal Service Directive, including:

- equal treatment by telecommunication providers,
- respect of their privacy rights,
- prompt initiation of service (in no more than two weeks), and
- full and prompt compensation where necessary.[117]

---

114   Art 10(2) and (3) 3PD 181/1999.
115   Art 9(3.2) EETT Decision 255/83/2002.
116   Art 57 Draft Law.
117   Art 9 Law 2867/2000.

DATA PROTECTION: IMPLEMENTATION OF THE E-PRIVACY DIRECTIVE

Confidentiality of Communications

14.116   The Hellenic Authority for Information and Communication Security and Privacy (ADAE)[118] has imposed on service providers the general obligation to ensure and protect the confidentiality of any communications, data and any other information pertaining to their subscribers.[119]

14.117   Under Law 2774/1999 on the Protection of Personal Data in Telecommunications, providers of public telecommunications services are prohibited from processing, or forwarding to third parties, personal data for other purposes and especially for promotional or market research purposes, without the prior specific and explicit consent of the subscriber or user. The providers are also prohibited from making the provision of their services dependent upon this consent.[120]

14.118   There are two exceptions to the ban on interception or surveillance of communications, namely for reasons of national security[121] and criminal investigations.[122] Both are stipulated within Law 2225/1994, but the prescribed procedure for lifting prohibition differs between the two. In the case of telephone tapping for reasons of national security, any judicial, political, military or law enforcement public authority may make a request to the appropriate public prosecutor, who must make a decision within 24 hours. In the case of criminal investigations, the public prosecutor must make a request to the judicial council of the Court of Appeal, which makes a decision within 24 hours.

Traffic Data and Location Data

14.119   Traffic data has been defined as the totality of information subjected to processing for the facilitation of communication through a telecommunication network or for its billing. Location data is defined as the totality of information subjected to processing within the telecommunication network and indicates the geographic location of the terminal equipment of a user of a publicly available telecommunications service.[123]

14.120   Service providers may process traffic and location data only if it is both necessary and for the purposes of subscriber billing and interconnection payments.[124] This processing is only allowed for the period during which the bill may be lawfully challenged or payment pursued. There is no need to obtain the user's consent for this type of processing. There is only the obligation on the part of service providers to delegate the processing of data to individuals who are under the direct supervision of public telecommunication service providers and who deal with the billing and payment processes.

---

118   Established by Law 3115/2003.
119   ADAE Regulatory Decisions, 629, 630, 631 and 632 of 26.1.2005 on Mobile Telephony, Fixed Telephony, Wireless Networks Communications and Internet Communications respectively.
120   Art 4(4) Law 2774/1999.
121   Art 3 Law 2225/1994.
122   Art 4 Law 2225/1994.
123   Art 2 ADAE Regulation 629a of 26.1.2005.
124   Art 5(2) Law 2774/1994.

Itemised Billing

14.121 Subscribers have the right to request the issue of itemised bills from their service providers. In cases where terminal equipment is used by several residents or in commercial establishments by several users, itemised billing is only allowed with the written confirmation of the subscriber that all the users have been duly informed.[125]

Calling and Connected Line Identification

14.122 Article 6 Law 2774/1994 on calling and connected line identification is identical to article 8 E-Privacy Directive.

Automatic Call Forwarding

14.123 Article 7 Law 2774/1994 is identical to article 11 E-Privacy Directive.

Directories of Subscribers

14.124 The provision pertaining to the directory of subscribers is found in Law 2774/1999[126] and is identical to that in the old Directive 97/66[127] concerning the processing of personal data and the protection of privacy in the telecommunications sector.

Unsolicited Communications

14.125 Unsolicited communications are regulated in article 9 of Law 2774/1999 on the Protection of Personal Data in Telecommunications. The said article allows the use of automated calls for promotional or commercial purposes only in cases where the subscriber has explicitly consented to such service. Nonetheless, in the case of subscribers who are legal entities, unsolicited communications are allowed unless their legal representatives declare to providers on behalf of the legal entity their opposition to such service.

14.126 The law regulates unsolicited communications applicable in all telecommunication services without specifying whether it covers e-mails.

---

125 Art 5(5) Law 2774/1994.
126 Art 8 Law 2774/1994.
127 Art 11 Law 2774/1994.

The Hungarian Market for Electronic Communications[1]

Emese Szitasi and Ines Radmilovic
Baker & McKenzie, Budapest

LEGAL STRUCTURE

Basic Policy

15.1 Hungary opened up its telecommunications market at the end of 2001 by allowing access to infrastructure, abolishing the previous licensing and exclusive licence regime and introducing universal services and stricter rules on SMP undertakings. However, the long-awaited opening up of the market still had room for improvement as real competition did not develop, interconnection fees were high, and the dispute resolution system and the NRA's activities were not providing the desired effect. Also, Hungary, with its accession to the EU, had to comply with the rules of the 2002 EU Regulatory Package. This led to the adoption of a new communications act, which harmonises Hungarian rules with those of the EU, and aims to provide a stronger and more successful NRA and real competition on the market. The aim of the new act is to further improve the electronic communications infrastructure of the information society, provide consumers with reliable and safe electronic communications services of proper quality at the lowest possible prices, and promote efficient competition in the electronic communications market regardless of the technology applied.[2]

Implementation of EU Directives

15.2 Hungary undertook to fully harmonise its laws with the applicable EU legislation by its accession on 1 May 2004. The Electronic Communications Act implementing the 2002 EU Regulatory Package's Directives is generally considered to be in line with EU legislation. Market players, however, argue that regulations relating to the role of the NRA or the regulations on termination fees have been not fully transposed.

Legislation

15.3 The communications rules are set out in Act 100 of 2003 on electronic communications (*elektronikus hírközlésröl szóló törvény*, 'EHT') which generally

---

1   Editing of this chapter closed on 8 July 2005.
2   Preamble of the Hungarian Electronic Communications Act.

came into force on 1 January 2004. The EHT provides an overall framework for market players; the detailed rules are set out in various implementing decrees adopted either by the Government or by the Communications Minister.[3] In addition, the National Communications Authority ('NCA') is empowered to carry out regulatory as well as supervisory tasks, including but not limited to the designation of SMP undertakings, imposing remedies, etc.

REGULATORY PRINCIPLES: IMPLEMENTATION OF THE FRAMEWORK DIRECTIVE

Scope of Regulation

15.4   The EHT applies to mobile and fixed telephony, cable television and the internet. Generally, it covers all electronic communications-related activities performed in, or directed to, the territory of Hungary together with all other activities where radio-frequency signals are generated. The EHT defines electronic communications activity as 'an activity in the course of which signals, signs, texts, images, voice or messages of any other nature and generated in any form (ie also VoIP) that can be interpreted, are transmitted via electronic communications networks to one or more users, including, in particular, electronic communications services, the operation of electronic communications networks and equipment, distribution of terminal equipment and related services'.[4] The terms electronic communications service[5] and electronic communications network[6] are given the same meaning as in the Framework Directive. Separate legislation[7] regulates radio and television activities, and content is also to be regulated separately.

National Regulatory Authorities: Organisation, Regulatory Objectives, Competencies

15.5   The EHT introduces new regulatory and supervisory bodies and reforms the previous regulatory structure. The Communications Minister's responsibility for the regulation of the communication market remains, but the NCA's tasks and responsibilities were widened and strengthened, to be able to comply with enlarged duties created by the 2002 EU Regulatory Package.

15.6   Regulatory authorities include not only the Government, the Communications Minister and the NCA, but also the Competition Office, the Consumer Protection Office, and the Commission together with other member states' NRAs.

15.7   The NCA is an independent, state administrative entity pursuing its own financial management, covering the expenditures incurred in the course of performing its duties from its own revenues. The regulatory objectives of the NCA include those set out in the Framework Directive.[8] Furthermore, the tasks of the NCA are to facilitate the smooth and successful operation and development of the electronic communications market, to protect the interests of entities both performing and

---

3   The most important decrees will be referred to throughout this document.
4   S 188 EHT.
5   S 188(13) EHT.
6   S 188(19) EHT.
7   Act 1 of 1996 on radio and television broadcasting.
8   See para 1.53 above.

using electronic communications activities, to promote the establishment and maintenance of fair and efficient competition in the electronic communications industry, and to supervise compliance with the applicable legislation.[9]

15.8   The powers and obligations of the NCA are consistent with the Framework Directive; however, as regards requesting information, the NCA is entrusted with wider possibilities mainly relating to evidence gathering, inspections and information requests. If information needs to be obtained from any third party to clarify the case, the relevant person or organisation is obliged to supply the necessary information and make available the documents associated with the matter.[10]

15.9   Under the EHT, the NCA's tasks are divided between the Council of the National Communications Authority ('Council') and the Authority of the National Communications Authority ('Authority').[11]

15.10   The Council has been appointed to regulate the market, whereas the Authority is involved in supervisory and market monitoring tasks. Under section 14 EHT, the main tasks of the Council include initiation of amendments to the communications legislation, market analysis, designation of SMP undertakings and imposing remedies. The Council assesses and continuously analyses the communications market and the IT market to pave the way for regulatory, market development and procurement decisions. The Council also approves reference offers, manages the Authority, supervises compliance with the remedies imposed on SMP undertakings, and acts in the event of violation thereof.[12] Furthermore, the Council acts in abusive pricing policy cases and in disputes, and adopts the annual market monitoring plan and supervises its execution.

15.11   The Authority, amongst others, assists the Council to fulfil its tasks, acts in cases which do not require action by the Council, deals with notifications and individual authorisations, record keeping, and acts as technical authority or reconciles matters with administrators in the case of establishing, interconnecting, developing and updating closed networks.[13]

15.12   To fulfil its tasks and objectives, the NCA co-operates with the Competition Office especially in cases relating to the definition of relevant markets and analysing competition thereon, to the identification of SMP undertakings, and to the prescription of remedies together with the procedures relating to abusive pricing policy.

15.13   The NCA is entrusted with market supervision and, as the EHT does not distinguish between the various service providers, the NCA's rights and actions focus on communications-related activities rather than on the service providers themselves. The NCA, in line with the applicable EU legislation, has to inform the entity subject to the investigation of the alleged infringement and the facts of the investigation so as to enable the service provider, or the relevant third party, to reflect on the allegations. The NCA's obligations with respect to publishing information, conducting public hearings and disclosing information, and cooperating with regulatory authorities, are consistent with the provisions of articles 3(4) and 3(5) Framework Directive.

---

9   S 9 EHT.
10   S 31 EHT.
11   For ease of reference, no distinction will be made between the Council and the Authority throughout this chapter and will be referred to as NCA, unless indicated otherwise.
12   Ss 14–16 EHT.
13   Ss 18–19 EHT.

15.14   The NCA is entitled, and in the case of recurrent violations it is obliged, to fine the entity involved in the investigation[14] and the executive officer of the entity.[15]

15.15   In addition to the above, the NCA, within the market supervisory investigation, can determine the conditions for carrying out an activity or prohibit the behaviour violating the law as interim measures to protect life and health, environment and public security, prevent bodily harm or any danger affecting a wide range of consumers or severely and directly threatening the management or operation of other service providers or users. The NCA withdraws the interim measures when the reason for their adoption has ceased; otherwise, they remain in force until the decision on the merits becomes final.

15.16   Section 72 EHT establishes the Permanent Arbitration Court for Communications Cases to act in communications-related matters. The Arbitration Court deals with cases in which a service provider's right or lawful interest related to electronic communications is violated by another service provider and the parties submit their dispute to the Arbitration Court. In addition to communications-related arbitration tasks, the Arbitration Court may also conduct mediation procedures.

Right of Appeal against NRA's Decisions

15.17   The right of appeal follows the division of tasks between the Council and the Authority. Any decision delivered by the Authority as a first instance regulatory authority can be challenged before the chairman of the Council, except for the violation of business secrets and certain cases relating to compliance with an information request. The chairman's decision can be appealed to the court, but such an appeal does not automatically suspend the chairman's order; the suspension thereto must be requested of the civil court. On the other hand, a decision delivered by the Council cannot be further appealed. However, in cases where the Council's decision, either on the merits of a case or in respect of the refusal to initiate a procedure, violates the rights or rightful interests of a party, such decision can be challenged by the related parties before the civil courts.[16]

The NRA's Obligations to Cooperate with the Commission

15.18   The EHT does not deviate from the Framework Directive relating to the consolidation procedure and the Commission's right to stipulate standards and specifications.[17]

'Significant Market Power' as a Fundamental Prerequisite of Regulation

Definition of SMP

15.19   The definition of significant market power ('SMP') follows the definition and the logic of that in the Framework Directive, namely it is based on the

---

14   Ss 31–32 EHT.
15   The latter fine can reach up to HUF 3m (€12,000).
16   Ss 37 and 46–48 EHT.
17   S 65 EHT. For further details see para 1.65 et seq above.

dominance test.[18] Furthermore, similarly to EU legislation, SMP may apply to individual or collective dominance. Collective dominance may arise particularly if there is no effective competition between two or more undertakings in the relevant market, or the same two or more undertakings are jointly in a dominant position against the other providers in the relevant market. Collective dominance may also exist without any structural or other relationship between the service providers if the relevant service providers operate in a market the structure of which facilitates the coordination of actions. Furthermore, an SMP undertaking on one market can be designated as an SMP undertaking on a closely related market if, as a result of the connection between the relevant market and the closely related market, the market power of the undertaking held in one market can be leveraged in the other market, thereby strengthening its market power.

Definition of relevant markets and SMP designation

15.20   The Council defines the relevant market on the basis of the guidelines issued by the Communications Minister and the so-called 'Methodology' issued by the NCA.[19] These documents, which describe the criteria for designating SMP undertakings, the way market definition should be handled and the procedure for designating of SMP undertakings, are in line with the Commission Guidelines on market analysis and EU case law. The Council has defined relevant markets in the majority of the 18 product and service markets; however, it is currently undertaking a number of reviews including analysing the markets for minimum set of leased lines and several of the wholesale market of leased lines, broadband access and international roaming.[20]

15.21   The Council is obliged to impose remedies on SMP undertakings which mirror the provisions of the Access and Universal Services Directives.[21] The Council, if justified by and most consistent with the restrictive practices revealed by the market analysis, can either impose individual remedies,[22] details of which are subject to deliberation or mandatory/determined remedies detailed by law,[23] in both cases keeping in mind the mandatory EU objectives of key importance set out in the Framework Directive determining the detailed conditions and procedures of imposing remedies.

15.22   In addition to the remedies imposed on SMP operators, the Council is also entitled to impose remedies on undertakings not designated as SMP undertakings. To achieve connection between subscriber access points, the subscriber access service provider can be required to interconnect its network with the network of

18   S 53 EHT.
19   S 52 EHT, Decree No 16/2004 of the Communications Minister, Communications Ministry Guidelines No 8001/2004 and the NCA's Methodology, 30 June 2004.
20   These markets are: markets 7, 11 to 14, together with markets 17 and 18 in the Commission Recommendation on relevant markets.
21   Part XII EHT.
22   Individual remedies can be: transparency, accounting separation, facility sharing and co-location, cost-based prices and controllability of prices, obligations related to access and interconnection or to subscriber services fees (in case of an SMP undertaking in a given retail market), including the prohibition on applying unjustified abusive pricing policies or the obligation to provide a minimum set of leased line services in respect of an SMP undertaking in the leased line market.
23   Mandatory remedies are: carrier selection; internet access offer and prohibition on price squeeze.

another service provider.[24] Furthermore, to the extent that is necessary to ensure accessibility for end-users to digital radio and television broadcasting services, the obligation to provide access to other service providers to the other facilities under fair, reasonable and non-discriminatory terms can also be imposed on these undertakings.[25]

NRA's Regulatory Duties concerning Rights of Way, Co-location and Facility Sharing

Rights of way

15.23   All service providers, both public and non-public,[26] have to use existing electronic communications structures, or must place their own structure(s) on public property, or use the facilities of a public utility service provider; or, in exceptional cases, they are also entitled to use private property. The developer of a structure is also entitled to use waterways, canals, natural lakes and the beds and channels thereof together with the airspace above the country for electronic communications purposes.

15.24   The NCA/local government, upon request, grants rights of way to the service provider.[27] If private property is to be used and provided that no agreement has been reached between the owner of the real estate and the builder, the NCA may restrict, in the interest of the public, the use of the property by its owner (manager or user) to enable the service provider to install the electronic communications structure on, above, below or within the property, structure or facility.[28] The owner of the relevant real property is entitled to indemnification and may exercise his rights in accordance with the provisions of the Civil Code.

15.25   Upon completion of the construction work, the builder (or the installer) of an electronic communications structure is generally obliged to restore the environment to its original condition; however, the parties can agree otherwise.

Co-location and facility sharing

15.26   The regulations concerning co-location and facility sharing fully implement article 12(1) Framework Directive with respect to compulsory facility sharing in the case of lack of access to viable alternatives, as well as to the encouragement of voluntary agreements about (possible) shared facilities.[29]

REGULATION OF MARKET ENTRY: IMPLEMENTATION OF THE AUTHORISATION DIRECTIVE

The General Authorisation of Electronic Communications

15.27   Hungarian legislation has moved from an individual licensing regime, which was applicable until the end of 2001, to a general authorisation regime.

---

24   See paras 15.53–15.54 below.
25   Communications Minister Decree No 11/2004, S 101 EHT.
26   Special rules described in Government Decree No. 50/1998 are applicable to services for a special purpose, e g governmental or national security.
27   Ss 94–96, 98 EHT.
28   S 95 EHT.
29   S 90 EHT.

Under the general authorisation regime, the rights and obligations derive from an act of law and are not subject to any approval from the NCA.[30] Individual licences are only required for using radio frequencies and identifiers, acquiring authorisation for the building of electronic communications structures[31] or using certain non-harmonised communications equipment. Further restrictions are, however, applicable to network operators if they desire to operate a program distribution network via cable.[32]

15.28 Any natural person, entity or organisation intending to provide electronic communications services or wanting to operate an electronic communication structure shall notify the authority of its intention to commence the provision of such service, as well as the planned date of commencement, together with some basic information, amongst others, on the person wanting to offer the services and a short description of the services to be offered.[33] If the service provider intends to offer retail services, it also has to submit the general terms and conditions of such services. The NCA registers the notifying entity, based on the data disclosed and confirms the fact of registration within eight days from the date of notification.[34] The NCA can only stop an operator from providing the services if the services endanger safety or public order, or if the NCA cannot identify, from the submitted data, either the service provider or the activities to be offered. In the latter case, simultaneously with the refusal, the NCA obliges the service provider to re-submit the notification within eight days. Failure to re-submit results in the imposition of a fine.[35] In addition to being responsible for the notification process, the NCA, together with the relevant building authorities, is also in charge of issuing an authorisation for the installation, occupancy, continuation, re-modelling and dismantling of electronic communications structures. Authorisation, however, is not required for construction works for non-public service providers.[36]

Rights of Use for Radio Frequencies

General authorisation and granting of individual rights

15.29 The rules for using radio frequencies and identifiers are generally laid down in the EHT[37] but detailed in various ministerial decrees.[38] The frequencies that can be used are set out in the national table of frequency allocation. Any natural or legal person, company or other organisation having no legal personality can request the use of the civilian-purpose frequency bands set out in the table. The operation of radio equipment for radio applications with a harmonised frequency or frequency band is not subject to an individual licence. On the other hand, to operate radio equipment, radio stations and radio electronic communications networks, an individual licence is required, and furthermore, the installation of these is also subject to a frequency assignment.

---

30   Ss 74 and 76 EHT, Act 93/1990 on duties; see para 15.28 below.
31   S 69 EHT.
32   S 75 EHT.
33   S 76(2) EHT.
34   S 76(3) EHT.
35   S 76(5)EHT.
36   S 83 (2) EHT.
37   Ss 69 and 84 EHT.
38   Communications Minister Decrees 35/2004 and 6/2004.

15.30   The NCA, which deals with frequencies allocated for civilian purposes, grants the civilian-purpose frequency assignments, radio licence or authorisation to use frequencies through the general administrative procedure or through auctions or tenders. Licensing and allocation are made on the basis of open, objective, transparent and non-discriminatory procedures.[39] Frequencies are allocated on a 'first come, first served' basis through individual licensing; however, certain frequencies, such as 1800 MHz or 3G were distributed through tenders or, in the case of 2.5 GHz, through auction. Frequency assignment licences, frequency reservations and radio licences are only transferable to a limited extent and, with certain exemptions, are not assignable to third parties.[40]

15.31   Operators are obliged to pay a one-time frequency reservation fee, but they are also subject to a regular frequency usage fee. The frequency usage fee must be established reflecting the need to ensure the optimal use of resources. The fees have to be objective, transparent, non-discriminatory and proportionate with respect to the goal to be achieved, and they should also serve the goals of frequency management.

Admissible conditions

15.32   The frequency use has to be in compliance with legislation concerning the national allocation of frequency bands and the rules for the utilisation of frequency bands, as well as regulations concerning public health and the emission of and protection against interference.

15.33   GSM 900 MHz, DCS 1800 MHz, WiFi and 2.5 GHz are already in use in Hungary, whereas 3G frequencies have just been recently allocated. As the majority of the frequencies were assigned under the old telecommunications regime, the operators only have to comply with obligations such as equal treatment and account separation.[41] As regards 3G frequencies, the licences only include general obligations to the encouragement of market entry and promotion of competition if a new market participant emerges.

Limitation of number of rights of use to be granted

15.34   The conditions and the number of rights of use to be granted depends on the legislation concerning the national allocation of frequency bands, the utilisation of frequency bands and the general provisions of Hungarian administrative procedure rules. Frequency auctions and tenders are prepared and organised by the NCA[42] and should be conducted according to Hungarian administrative procedure rules. Auctions and tenders are generally open to the public and so there are no limitations on the number of applicants. The auction/tender has to be conducted in the presence of all members of the auction committee to be established by the NCA. After the procedure, the committee determines the winner(s) of the auction/tender, enters the names into the final protocol and recommends to the NCA to declare the auction/tender as valid and successful. The tender for the 3G frequencies

---

39   S 84 EHT.
40   Communications Minister Decree No 35/2004.
41   Part III of Act 40 of 2001.
42   Government Decree No 11/2003.

has recently been conducted, with the result that the existing three mobile operators received the right to use the frequency and to provide UMTS services.

Frequency trading

15.35   As frequency assignments are not transferable,[43] spectrum trading is not authorised in Hungary.

Rights of Use for Numbers

General authorisations and granting of individual rights

15.36   Identifiers, save for IP addresses, e-mail addresses and domain names, can only be used based on assignment licences subject to prior reservation. Certain identifiers (e g area codes, special numbers and prefixes for carrier selections) are, however, not subject to the individual licensing regime, as these identifiers are generally allocated by law for the various tasks.[44] Furthermore, those service providers who have already received various identifiers for their services (e g mobile operators, previous local incumbent service providers) do not need a licence to use those identifiers which were already designated to them. The NCA, at the service provider's request, issues the identifier reservation and the assignment licences. The assignment of numbers is carried out on a 'first come, first served' basis and, once assigned, the numbers cannot be assigned to other service operators.[45] For the usage and reservation of identifiers, an identifier reservation and usage fee is payable. An identifier's allocation can be revoked if, amongst others, the assigned identifier cannot be used for the assigned purpose in the future, e g due to obligations arising from international agreements.

Admissible conditions

15.37   Conditions relating to the use of numbers include, amongst others, number portability and carrier pre-selection.[46] Other conditions such as the transfer of allocated numbers, the duration of the reservation and use of the number, or the obligation to provide public directory subscribers' information are set out in the EHT and in the various implementing regulations.[47]

15.38   Number portability is already available for both mobile and fixed line services. The service provider is obliged to enable the subscriber to retain his subscriber number for fixed line telephone services when the subscriber changes the service provider providing subscriber access. Furthermore, the service provider providing subscriber access and the recipient provider have to agree on number portability if an offer of interconnection is received from the recipient service provider.[48]

---

43   See para 15.35 above.
44   Government Decree No 72/2004.
45   Ss 70 and 89 and Government Decree No 75/2000.
46   Government Decree No 73/2004.
47   Ss 146–150; Government Decree No 75/2000.
48   S 150 EHT.

The NRA's Enforcement Powers

15.39   The NCA under its general tasks as a market supervisory authority also has to ensure compliance with the applicable rules in respect of the use of numbers, e g it has the right to revoke the various licences or impose sanctions on service providers for non-compliance, etc. For further information on the NCA's enforcement rights, see paras 15.13–15.15 above.

Administrative Charges and Fees for Rights of Use

15.40   The NCA's activities are subject to administrative charges payable for notification, for individual licences, for assignment of local loop, and in every case when a procedure is initiated. The administrative charge has to be paid in advance by the party initiating the procedure, as detailed in the legislation relating to the various procedures.[49] In addition to the administrative charges, service providers are obliged to pay an annual supervisory fee based on their turnover from the year preceding the year in question, together with an annual fee for the use of frequencies and identifiers.[50]

REGULATION OF NETWORK ACCESS AND INTERCONNECTION: IMPLEMENTATION OF THE ACCESS DIRECTIVE

Objectives and Scope of Access Regulation, Basic Regulatory Concepts

15.41   The EHT's provisions on access and interconnection are applicable to public and non-public network operators/service providers. The definitions of access and interconnection are in line with EU law, as the EHT[51] mirrors the definitions in the Access Directive. The EHT therefore bases the regulation of access and interconnection on the principles set out in the Access Directive.[52]

Access- and Interconnection-related Obligations with Respect to SMP Undertakings

Overview

15.42   The access- and interconnection-related obligations which may be imposed on SMP undertakings correspond to those set out in the Access Directive:

- transparency, including the obligation to provide a reference offer,
- equal treatment,
- accounting separation,
- obligations related to access and interconnection,
- joint use of facilities and co-location, and
- price control and cost-accounting obligations.

---

49   Communications Minister Decree Nos. 19/2001 or 8/1991 etc.
50   Ibis 49.
51   S 188 EHT.
52   See paras 1.127–1.132 above.

The various obligations are applicable both to mobile and fixed line service providers; the EHT does not make any distinction between the different types of operators.

15.43   When deciding on the applicable obligations, the NCA has to take into account factors such as investments made by efficient service providers, the related risks and fair return on capital invested, and the prices available on comparative competitive markets. The NCA can also consider criteria such as the prices applied by service providers who are in a situation similar to that of the SMP undertaking.[53]

Transparency obligations

15.44   For guaranteeing transparency, the NCA can require the SMP undertaking to disclose specific information, including accounting and technical information, network features, the terms and conditions of providing and using the service, prices or network contracts; or to draw up a reference offer and specify the range of data to be disclosed and also the method of their disclosure.[54]

Non-discrimination obligations

15.45   Under the non-discrimination obligation, SMP undertaking must apply substantially the same conditions and information, of the same quality to other service providers providing similar services as it applies to its own services and the services of any of its controlled service providers.[55]

Specific access obligations

15.46   Section 106 EHT implements the non-exhaustive list of article 12(1) sub-paras 1 and 2 of the Access Directive relating to the various obligations that the NCA may impose on an SMP undertaking and relating to the factors to be taken into account when prescribing these obligations.

Price control and cost accounting obligations

15.47   Section 108 EHT, reflecting the wording of article 13 of the Access Directive,[56] states that if, on the basis of the market analysis, it is established that the absence of efficient competition could result in the application of unjustifiably high fees or pricing methods by the service provider concerned, the NCA can impose various obligations (eg the application of cost-based fees, or a specific method of cost calculations) to promote efficiency and sustainable competition and to enforce consumer advantages.

15.48   Various obligations, amongst others, price control, have already been imposed on the national incumbent service provider, Magyar Telekom Rt (a

---

53   Ss 54 and 108 EHT.
54   Ss 102–103 EHT.
55   S 104 EHT.
56   See paras 1.150–1.152 above.

subsidiary of Deutsche Telecom AG), on the local incumbent service providers and on public mobile operators on the majority of the relevant markets that have already been identified.[57] In addition to fixed line incumbents, the obligations of transparency and equal treatment have also been imposed on Hungarian Telephone and Cable Corporation's and British Telecom's local subsidiaries on the call termination wholesale market.[58]

15.49   SMP undertakings in any of the markets concerned must determine the counter value of the network service provided in that market so it does not give rise to a price squeeze on the basis of the [must carry] subscriber services' prices. The Council ex officio, upon request or based on the initiative of the Communication Minister, the head of the Competition Office or the head of the Consumer Protection Authority, must investigate cases of alleged price squeeze. If, despite the fact that the existence of a price squeeze is established, the compensation for the network service is adjusted to the costs incurred in relation to the supply of the network service, the case should be referred to the Competition Office to establish whether the price setting for the service constitutes a violation of the Hungarian Competition Act. When, based on new circumstances that have come to the NCA's attention, it cannot be established that the compensation for the network service is adjusted to the magnitude of the costs incurred relating to the supply of the network service, a price reduction, changing of the reference offer or a suitable fine can be imposed by the NCA. The service provider must inform the NCA about the changed pricelist and it also has to publish such changes.

Accounting separation obligations

15.50   The EHT,[59] mirroring the wording of the Access Directive,[60] empowers the NRA to prescribe, inter alia, that an SMP undertaking should make its wholesale and transfer prices transparent. It can require the SMP undertaking to assume additional obligations either related to transparent operation and equal treatment or related to providing data required for checking the prohibition on unjustified pricing methods.

Related Regulatory Powers with Respect to SMP Undertakings

15.51   The EHT, in addition to the obligations set out above, can impose obligations relating to the spread of internet usage and the prohibition of any price squeeze on a service provider having SMP.

15.52   In order to promote use of the internet, the EHT requires an SMP undertaking identified on a given market for internet access via fixed public telephone networks to publish a reference offer either on the basis of a flat rate or at prices set on the basis of cost-orientation. Internet interconnection services can either be conducted through the call origination model[61] or through the number

---

57   DH 664–69/2005, DH 664–71/2005.

58   Market 9 in the Commission Recommendation on the relevant markets; DH-664–140/2005.

59   S 105 EHT.

60   See paras 1.145–1.146 above.

61   Under the call origination model, subscriber internet calls shall be transmitted to the internet
      service provider's network access point by the carrier service provider selected by the

translation model.[62] Furthermore, service providers must apply the principle of non-discrimination towards all of their customers, including entities controlled by them.

Regulatory Powers Applicable to All Market Participants

Obligations to ensure end-to-end connectivity

15.53   In addition to the above obligations, obligations ensuring end-to-end connectivity and providing access to digital radio and television broadcasting services can also be imposed. As at June 2005, none of these obligations had been imposed on service providers.

15.54   To ensure interconnection between subscriber access points, the NCA can oblige the service provider providing subscriber access to interconnect its network with the networks of other service providers. To achieve this, obligations on equal treatment, access and interconnection and co-location and facility sharing obligations could be imposed.

Access to digital radio and television broadcasting services

15.55   In order to enable end users to access digital radio and television broadcasts, the service provider shall guarantee access to the relevant facilities. The rules on digital television are set out in a ministerial decree.[63]

REGULATION OF UNIVERSAL SERVICES AND USERS' RIGHTS: THE UNIVERSAL SERVICE DIRECTIVE

Regulation of Universal Service Obligations

Scope of universal service obligations

15.56   The definition of universal service and the scope of the universal service obligations under the EHT are deemed to be in line with articles 3 to 7 Universal Service Directive.[64] At the beginning of July 2005, however, the Commission expressed concerns, in a letter of formal notice, about the fact that Hungarian law provides that only those undertakings capable of providing all components of the universal services basket can participate in the designation process. This could result in the exclusion of undertakings capable of providing only one or more element(s) of the set of universal services.

---

subscribers by way of the carrier service provider contracting voice transmission wholesale service over the internet, or flat-rate voice transmission wholesale service over the internet from the notified operator.

62   Under the number translation model, the notified operator – regardless of whether a carrier service provider has been selected – must turn over the call to the carrier service provider that is liable to transmit the subscribers' internet call to the internet service provider's network access point under contract with the internet service provider, and that is receiving regular and flat-rate voice transmission wholesale service over the internet from the notified operator.

63   Communications Minister's Decree No. 11/2004.

64   S 188(11) EHT; see paras 1.162 et seq above.

Designation of undertakings obliged to provide universal services

15.57   The Communications Minister has to designate the universal service provider, ensuring the coverage of the entire country with universal services, and the least distortion to competition in the market. Currently, the national and regional incumbent companies are appointed as universal service providers in respect of their own territories.

15.58   Universal services are to be provided by a service provider which is able to offer such services most efficiently and at the lowest net avoidable cost.[65] In designating the universal service provider and concluding the universal service contract, the Communications Minister also has to ensure that the price of the universal service remains affordable. Appointment of the universal services provider commences with the relevant announcement by the Communications Minister. Following the assessment of the submitted offers and the appointment of the chosen operator, the Communications Minister enters into a universal service contract with the designated service provider in which the parties agree on at least the provisions laid down by legislation. The Communications Minister publishes the universal contract. Currently, Magyar Telekom Rt, the former incumbent and subsidiary of Deutsche Telecom, is appointed as universal service provider.

Regulation of retail tariffs, users' expenditures and quality of service

15.59   The designated service provider has to provide national directory services, access to directory subscriber information, itemised bills, and call barring. Furthermore, it must operate at least one public telephone site per 1,000 inhabitants or in each settlement with a population of less than 1,000. At least 3% of the universal service provider's compulsory public telephone facilities must accommodate hearing-impaired and disabled persons, and the universal service provider also has to provide special packages and to subsidise low-income or disabled subscribers.[66]

15.60   The NCA supervises the universal service provider with regard to the execution of its activities and performance of the contract on an ongoing basis. The universal service provider is obliged to submit the data required for controlling compliance with its obligations to the NCA on an ongoing basis. The data providing evaluation on compliance with the obligations should be publicly available. The NCA has to notify the Communications Minister when it identifies any breach of the obligations undertaken in the contract. If the universal service provider fails to meet the service quality values specified in the contract for an extended period of time, the NCA can request an inspection by an independent expert. The NCA, of course, can also use its enforcement measures in case of non-compliance.[67]

Cost calculation and financing of universal services

15.61   The principles for calculating the net avoidable costs, and the detailed rules of compensation[68] for, and the distribution of the financial burden related to,

---

65   S 119 EHT.
66   S 117 EHT, Communications Minister Decree No 16/2003.
67   See paras 15.13–15.15 above.
68   Communications Minister Decree No 18/2004.

universal services together with the detailed conditions of the universal services and the designation procedure are set out in a decree.[69] The rules of such decree are all in compliance with the Universal Service Directive.

15.62   The universal service provider is entitled to compensation on the basis of calculation of the net costs and the unfair burden related to providing universal services. The extent of the subsidy, however, cannot exceed the net avoidable cost of providing the universal service. Furthermore, to mitigate the financial burden arising from providing the universal service, a universal electronic communications support fund has been established.

Regulation of Retail Markets

15.63   The EHT fully implements the principles and regulatory rules relating to the retail market under the applicable Directives. One notable difference is that although the Framework Directive allows Member States to choose from a non-inclusive list of possible ex-ante obligations which could be imposed on SMP undertakings, the EHT only lists the following obligations: SMP undertakings cannot charge excessive prices, inhibit market entry or restrict competition by setting predatory prices, they cannot show unjustifiable preference to specific end-users or unreasonably bundle services, together with the obligations relating to the minimum set of leased lines and carrier pre-selection.[70]

15.64   The Council may impose other obligations on SMP undertakings in respect of their activities on the retail market. These obligations relate to ensuring the minimum set of leased line services, providing carrier pre-selection and subscriber fees. These obligations are intended to be regulated in line with Chapter III of Universal Services Directives; however, the EHT does not include, as a general rule as set out in article 17 Universal Services Directive, that prior to imposing any obligations a market analysis on the relevant retail market has to be carried out and discrepancies need to be identified.

15.65   Section 109 EHT nevertheless states that, if the Council establishes that, based on its market analysis, competition is insufficiently effective on an identified retail service market and other obligations applicable to SMP undertakings or an instruction to apply carrier pre-selection would not achieve effective competition, it can restrict the SMP undertaking from applying, on the retail market, unjustifiably high fees, unjustifiably low prices impeding market entry or competition, unjustifiable discrimination against certain consumers, or unjustifiable bundling. An SMP undertaking could also be obliged to keep statements relating to cost calculations. Furthermore, the Council may also propose to the Communications Minister to set the maximum level of subscriber fees. As regards the minimum set of leased lines, detailed rules have not yet published. The EHT only states that obligations may be imposed and such obligations may contain provisions concerning transmission capacity and technical characteristics relating to the minimum set of leased line services.

---

69   Communications Minister Decree No 3/2004.
70   For further details, see paras 15.64–15.65 above.

End User Rights

Contracts

15.66   The subscriber contract consists of the general terms and conditions (eg detailing the terms of the services, the procedural rules for concluding the agreement, data necessary for providing the services, suspension of the services, customer services, etc) and the individual subscriber contract. The individual subscriber contract sets out the specifics of the services and the service provider, eg details of the parties, duration, fees, termination, etc.[71] Only the universal service provider is obliged to conclude a subscriber contract.

15.67   Pursuant to the individual subscriber contract, the subscriber will be entitled to connect electronic communications terminal equipment that complies with the essential requirements to the subscriber interface provided in the network and to make use of the given service at any time during the term of the contract. The service provider cannot unjustifiably tie their services to other services.[72]

15.68   The individual subscriber contract must include, in addition to the provisions set out in article 20(2) Universal Service Directive, further information, amongst others:

- details of the subscriber,
- the consent of the subscriber to handle his data,
- the place of installing the subscriber terminal equipment and the calling number of the subscriber,
- statements and data concerning the carrier service provider selected by pre-selection,
- a statement requesting an itemised bill, and
- accessibility to the general terms and conditions and the statement of the subscriber under which he accepts the provisions of the individual subscription contract.[73]

Transparency obligations

15.69   The service provider is obliged to inform its users about the content of the written general terms and conditions, and it also has to make them available to the customers at the service provider's customer service centre and on its website, free of charge. The general terms and conditions must be published and must also be sent to the NCA. The NCA regularly reviews and ensures compliance by the general terms and conditions with the applicable rules.

15.70   The general terms and conditions must contain at least the provisions set out in Annex II of the Universal Services Directive and the following issues:

- the period agreed for the installation of the subscriber access point and the commencement of its operation,
- terms of connecting the subscriber's terminal equipment,
- data protection,
- number portability rules, if applicable,

---

71   Ss 127–130 EHT.
72   S 128 EHT.
73   S 129 EHT.

- rules of carrier selection,
- details of the supervisory authority, and
- accessibility of the general terms and conditions.[74]

15.71 When legislation requires that a subscriber is notified of an event, the service provider can inform its subscriber by mail, by email or any other form of electronic communications or through public announcement. In order that consumers have adequate information on the quality of services, prices and fees and can compare individual services and make rational decisions, the NCA can require communications service providers to provide data on the quality, accessibility and price of the services provided by them to the authority or to disclose such data. The NCA publishes comparative data on the basis of information submitted by service providers.

Other obligations

15.72 Other obligations on the universal service provider, including obligations to provide access to emergency call numbers, and directory enquiry services, are also incorporated into the EHT on the basis of the Universal Service Directive.[75]

15.73 Under the applicable rules, end users can decide whether they wish to select their carrier through call-by-call prefix selection or by using pre-selection for all types of calls including VoIP calls. SMP undertakings have to ensure carrier selection, therefore, they cannot exclude or restrict carrier selection in their respective subscriber contracts. Service providers providing subscriber access and the recipient provider also have to agree on number portability if an offer on interconnection is received from the recipient service provider.[76]

DATA PROTECTION: IMPLEMENTATION OF THE E-PRIVACY DIRECTIVE

Confidentiality of Communications

15.74 Service providers can only process end-users' and subscribers' personal data to the extent required and necessary for their identification for the purpose of drawing up the relevant contracts, to define and amend the contents of these contracts, to monitor contractual performance, charges and fees as contracted and for enforcing any related claims together with personal data which is technically essential for providing the services. Furthermore, personal data can be processed in connection with charges for the services only for calculating and billing charges (in particular the data relating to the date, duration and place of service to which it pertains).[77]

15.75 Service providers must take appropriate technical and organisational measures – jointly with other service providers if necessary – to safeguard the security of their services. The technical and organisational measures must also be sufficient – with regard to best practices and the costs of the proposed measures – to afford a

---

74   S 131 EHT.
75   For further details see paras 1.183 et seq above.
76   S 111 EHT.
77   S 154 EHT.

level of security appropriate to the risk presented in connection with the services. Exact details of personal data processing and related rules must be set out in the service providers' data protection policy, which must be made available to the public at their customer services centre and on the internet.

15.76 Service providers are authorised to obtain and store communications transmitted on their network only to the extent absolutely necessary for the provision of services for technical reasons. Information obtained via electronic communications networks may be stored on electronic communication terminal equipment or accessed only with the end-users' or subscribers' prior consent granted in possession of clear and comprehensive information about the implications. However, national security agencies, investigating authorities and the NCA as frequency management authority may monitor, intercept and store communications or may otherwise intrude on communications for surveillance purposes.[78]

Traffic Data and Location Data

15.77 The EHT does not give a precise definition for traffic data and location data; however, it uses these expressions in line with the definition set out in the E-Privacy Directive.[79]

15.78 Service providers can only process traffic or location data with the prior consent of the subscribers or users to whom the data are related, and only to the extent and for the duration that is necessary for the provision of value added services. If providing value added services requires that traffic or location data are forwarded, the service provider must inform the subscribers or users concerning the type of data required, the purpose and duration of data processing, and whether or not the data is to be forwarded to third persons.[80]

Itemised Billing

15.79 Service providers have to provide an itemised billing statement, free of charge. In connection with such billing, service providers are entitled to process various data including personal data.[81]

Calling and Connection Line Identification

15.80 Service providers, upon the written request of the subscriber but without charge, must allow users to withhold their number on a per-call or per-line basis. Users must also be provided with the possibility to block the numbers of incoming call or to reject those incoming calls where the caller has withheld the caller identification. Withholding the caller identity can, however, be limited in case of emergency calls or in those institutions which are considered to be vital for the operation of the state.[82]

---

78   Ss 154–156 EHT.
79   Government Decree No 73/2004.
80   S 157 EHT.
81   Ss 142 and 157 EHT.
82   Government Decree No 226/2003.

Automatic Call Forwarding

15.81   Users have the right to request, without charge, the cancellation of automatic call forwarding if such cancellation is technically possible.[83]

Directories of Subscribers

15.82   Subscriber directories and address registers can only contain as much data relating to a subscriber as is essential for the identification thereof unless the relevant subscriber clearly approves, on a voluntary basis, to the publication of more of his/her data.[84]

Unsolicited Communications

15.83   Provisions relating to unsolicited communications are generally set out in data protection legislation (eg communications of the data protection commissioner), although the EHT states that no communication serving the purposes of direct marketing or information may be forwarded to a subscriber, by telephone or through other means of electronic communications, unless the subscriber agrees to such communications.[85]

---

83   Ibis 82.
84   S 160 EHT.
85   S 162 EHT.

The Irish Market for Electronic Communications[1]

John Handoll & Claire Waterson
William Fry Solicitors, Dublin

LEGAL STRUCTURE

Basic Policy

16.1 The Irish telecommunications market experienced fast growth in the 1990s as players were attracted to Ireland's economic boom, relatively low cost base, favourable taxation regime and skilled labour force. Governmental recognition of the information technology sector as an instrument to increase levels of employment and wealth and the subsequent adoption of flexible and responsive policies encouraged its growth. The telecommunications market was fully liberalised in December 1998.

16.2 The Irish telecommunications market is characterised by diverse market segments, such as large corporate customers with integrated data/voice requirements, a large number of SMEs increasingly demanding data products and domestic customers seeking inexpensive voice and broadband services.

16.3 The stated overall policy objectives of the Department of Communications, Marine and Natural Resources include placing Ireland in the top quartile of OECD economies in terms of key Internet and telecommunications benchmarks by creating a legislative framework providing for light handed regulation and by promoting increased Information Society inclusion at both regional and community level.[2] Once established by the Minister, policy is implemented on a day-to-day basis by the national communications regulator, ComReg.

Implementation of EU Directives

16.4 Ireland was one of eight Member States to transpose the 2002 EU Regulatory Package on time. The Framework, Authorisation, Universal Service and Access Directives were transposed into Irish law on 21 July 2003 and the Data Protection Directive on 6 November 2003.

---

1   Editing of this chapter closed on 7 July 2005. The authors gratefully acknowledge the assistance of Maria Ortiz-Vilela in preparing this chapter.
2   Dept. Communications Statement of Strategy 2003–2005.

16.5   Transposition into Irish law has been by Regulations[3] made under the European Communities Acts 1972–2002. The Regulations were adopted by the Minister for Communications, Marine and Natural Resources (the 'Minister') after a period of public consultation. They are:

- SI 307 of 2003, the European Communities (Electronic Communications Networks and Services)(Framework) Regulations 2003, transposing the Framework Directive,
- SI 306 of 2003, the European Communities (Electronic Communications Networks and Services)(Authorisation) Regulations 2003, transposing the Authorisation Directive,
- SI 308 of 2003, the European Communities (Electronic Communications Networks and Services)(Universal Service and Users Rights) Regulations 2003, transposing the Universal Service Directive,
- SI 305 of 2003, the European Communities (Electronic Communications Networks and Services)(Access) Regulations 2003, transposing the Access Directive and
- SI 535 of 2003, the European Communities (Electronic Communications Networks and Services)(Data Protection and Privacy) Regulations 2003, transposing the E-Privacy Directive.

16.6   The Regulations provide the legal basis for the new regime and set out the framework in which ComReg regulates the market on an ongoing basis.

Legislation

16.7   As well as the Regulations implementing the new regime, there are a number of legislative acts relating to telecommunications. The principal act is the Communications Regulation Act 2002 (the '2002 Act') which establishes and governs the operation of the regulator, together with some transferred functions contained in the Telecommunications (Miscellaneous Provisions) Act 1996. The former incumbent, eircom, was established under the Postal and Telecommunications Services Act 1983, which (as amended) also contains a number of provisions relating to interception. The regulation of spectrum and licensing of wireless telegraphy apparatus are governed by the Wireless Telegraphy Acts 1926–1988 and a number of statutory instruments.

REGULATORY PRINCIPLES: IMPLEMENTATION OF THE FRAMEWORK DIRECTIVE

Scope of Regulation

16.8   Irish legislation has adopted the technology-neutral approach of the Directives, with the result that some services not licensable under the old regime[4] have been brought within the scope of the regulatory framework. The definitions of 'electronic communications network' and 'electronic communications service' in Regulation 2 of the Framework Regulations are identical to those in the Framework Directive. The definition of 'associated facilities', although slightly different in wording, has the same meaning as in the Framework Directive.

---

3   In the form of Statutory Instruments, a form of delegated or secondary legislation.
4   Eg, re-seller services and community repeater services.

National Regulatory Authorities: Organisation, Regulatory Objectives, Competencies

16.9   The Irish communications regulator is the Commission for Communications Regulation ('ComReg'). ComReg is an independent[5] three-person commission established under the 2002 Act to replace the Office of the Director of Telecommunications Regulation. The Minister appoints the members of ComReg.

16.10   ComReg's objectives are established in Section 12 of the 2002 Act as:
- 'in relation to the provision of electronic communications networks, electronic communications services and associated facilities –
  - to promote competition,
  - to contribute to the development of the internal market, and
  - to promote the interests of users within the Community,
- to ensure the efficient management and use of the radio frequency spectrum and numbers from the national numbering scheme in the State in accordance with [Ministerial direction], and
- to promote the development of the postal sector ...'

16.11   ComReg is responsible for ensuring compliance with obligations regarding the supply of and access to electronic communications networks and services. While it manages spectrum and the national numbering resource and regulates the placing on the market of radio and communications equipment,[6] content is regulated separately under the Broadcasting Authority Acts 1960–2001. It is also charged with regulating the postal service.

16.12   ComReg has enforcement powers and may bring prosecutions.[7] It may also require the provision of information in order to monitor compliance.[8] ComReg's obligations to publish information, to conduct public hearings or consultations and to co-operate with other NRAs are contained in Regulations 17(11) and 19 of the Framework Regulations.

16.13   In exercising its duties, ComReg must follow directions given by the Minister.[9] Subject to certain specified exceptions, the Freedom of Information Acts 1997 and 2003 provide a right of public access to records held by ComReg.[10]

16.14   Consultation and co-operation between ComReg and the Competition Authority is guaranteed by a co-operation agreement.[11] This sets out procedures for the exchange of information and consultation and identifies situations in which one party may agree to forbear to perform any of its functions. ComReg has liaised with the Competition Authority with regard to market analysis and definition for the purposes of designating operators with SMP.

16.15   Regulation 18 of the Framework Regulations obliges ComReg to consult and co-operate with the Director of Consumer Affairs on matters of common interest.

---

5   Section 11 of the 2002 Act.
6   Section 10 of the 2002 Act. These functions are consistent with the NRA tasks identified in the Framework Directive.
7   Part 3 of the 2002 Act; Regulation 35 Framework Regulations.
8   Regulation 17 Framework Regulations.
9   Section 13 of the 2002 Act. However, the Minister may not give policy directions in respect of individual operators or the performance of ComReg's functions in relation to individuals.
10   See also ComReg guidelines on treatment of confidential information, document 05/24.
11   ComReg document 03/06.

16.16   In April 2004 ComReg and Northern Ireland's Communications Regulator (Ofcom) set up a Joint Working Group on cross-border issues.

16.17   Where ComReg intends to take a measure which has a significant impact on a market for electronic communications networks or services, it must undertake a public consultation process, procedures for which are set out in Regulation 19 of the Framework Regulations.

16.18   The Framework Regulations confer specific powers and duties on ComReg with regard to dispute resolution. The exercise of such functions must comply with Article 8 of the Framework Directive and Section 12(c)(ii) of the 2002 Act (obligation to ensure the availability of simple and inexpensive dispute resolution procedures).

16.19   Dispute resolution between undertakings is governed by Regulation 31 of the Framework Regulations and ComReg's published procedures.[12] Any party may initiate an investigation and ComReg is normally obliged to make a determination within four months. Decisions must be reasoned and published. ComReg's approach to dispute resolution is flexible: it may decide not to initiate an investigation where it is satisfied that other means are available, such as resolution through informal contacts or negotiation.

16.20   ComReg has established separate procedures to deal with consumer complaints.[13] Procedures are also provided for the resolution of cross-border disputes.[14]

Right of Appeal against NRA's Decisions

16.21   The right to appeal ComReg decisions[15] is set out in Part 2 of the Framework Regulations. Any user or undertaking affected by a decision may lodge an appeal on the basis that the decision is vitiated by errors of fact or law. Appeals must be made in writing to the Minister within 28 days of the contested decision.

16.22   Appeals are heard by a three-person Electronic Communications Appeal Panel, established by the Minister on an ad hoc basis. One member must be a practising lawyer, and the remaining members must have appropriate commercial, technical, economic, regulatory or financial experience. The Panel is independent and determines its own procedures.[16] It is not bound by the rules of evidence, and is required to act with as little formality as the circumstances of the case permit.[17] However, it can enforce the attendance of witnesses, examine them on oath and compel the production of documents.[18]

16.23   Each party (and interested third parties) has the right to be given a reasonable opportunity to present its case and to make submissions in relation to issues arising.[19] A party may appear without representation or be represented by an

---

12   ComReg document 03/89.
13   ComReg document 03/86.
14   Regulation 32 Framework Regulations.
15   'Decision' includes decision, designation, determination, specification, requirement, direction or any other act of an equivalent nature: Regulation 3(1) Framework Regulations.
16   Regulation 8.
17   Regulation 8(6) and (7).
18   Regulation 11(1).
19   Regulation 8(4).

agent.[20] A witness before a Panel has the same immunities and privileges as if he were before the High Court, including the privilege against self-incrimination.[21]

16.24   As far as practicable, appeals must be determined within four months of referral.[22] The Panel's determination is final and conclusive, although the right to seek judicial review of the decision is not affected. The determination will be notified to the parties and published.[23]

The NRA's Obligations to Co-operate with the Commission

16.25   Regulation 20 of the Framework Regulations implements the Consolidation Procedure.[24] This establishes the need to co-operate with NRAs of different EU Member States and with the European Commission, as well as the need to agree on the most appropriate types of instruments and remedies to address certain situations in the marketplace. The 'veto procedure' has been implemented in accordance with Article 7 of the Framework Directive.

16.26   The Commission's power to draw up and publish standards and specifications is recognised in Regulation 29 of the Framework Regulations. ComReg must encourage the use of standards and specifications published by the Commission for the provision of services, technical interfaces or network functions, to ensure interoperability of services and to improve users' freedom of choice. This obligation refers to published standards and those made compulsory in accordance with Article 17(4) of the Framework Directive. Regulation 30 establishes similar conditions in relation to harmonisation.

'Significant Market Power' as a Fundamental Prerequisite of Regulation

Definition of SMP

16.27   'Significant market power' (SMP) is a position equivalent to dominance, a position of economic strength affording an undertaking the power to behave to an appreciable extent independently of competitors, customers, and, ultimately, consumers. SMP may refer to individual or collective dominance. Undertakings with SMP on one market may also be deemed to have SMP on closely related markets where links between the two markets allow leveraging of market power.[25]

Definition of relevant markets and SMP designation

16.28   Under Regulation 26 of the Framework Regulations, ComReg must define relevant markets taking into account the Commission Guidelines on market analysis and the Commission Recommendation on relevant markets, as well as public consultation and consolidation procedures and the principles of competition.

---

20   Regulation 8(5).
21   Regulation 8(11).
22   Regulation 12(1).
23   Regulation 13.
24   Art 7 Framework Directive.
25   Regulation 25 Framework Regulations.

16.29   In the first designation under the new framework, ComReg designated RTÉ Transmission Network Limited (the transmission operating arm of the national broadcaster) as having SMP in the markets for radio and television broadcasting transmission services on analogue terrestrial networks. Obligations of transparency, non-discrimination and accounting separation have been imposed.[26]

16.30   eircom, the former incumbent, has been designated as having SMP in the markets for wholesale broadband access and for wholesale unbundled access (including shared access) to metallic loops and sub-loops. In both markets, obligations of reasonable access, non-discrimination, transparency, accounting separation and price control have been imposed.[27] It has also been designated as having SMP in the retail leased lines market, the wholesale trunk and wholesale termination segment markets,[28] the retail fixed narrowband access and retail fixed calls markets.[29]

16.31   The four licensed mobile operators (Vodafone, O_2, Meteor and 3) have been designated as having SMP in wholesale voice call termination on their individual mobile markets although the remedies to be imposed have not been finalised.[30] ComReg has also designated Vodafone and O_2 as jointly having SMP in the wholesale mobile access and call origination market. Remedies of access for Mobile Virtual Network Operators, non-discrimination, price control, accounting separation and cost accounting have been imposed.[31]

16.32   ComReg is undertaking a number of market reviews on interconnection,[32] retail fixed calls[33] and retail fixed narrowband access.[34] Until these have been completed, the obligations imposed on operators designated with SMP under the old regime continue.[35]

16.33   Operators designated as having SMP are subject to a number of obligations under the Access and Universal Service Regulations, which mirror the provisions of the Directives.

16.34   Under the old regime (and until designations are made under the new regime), designated SMP operators have been subject to obligations under national legislation transposing the Interconnection Directive, the ONP Framework Directive (1997) and the ONP Voice Telephony Directive (1998).[36] The principal obligation is to publish a Reference Interconnect Offer (RIO) defining the processes of interconnection to the operator's networks and associated prices. SMP operators must adhere to the principles of transparency and non-discrimination in providing access and interconnection.

16.35   ComReg may impose obligations on undertakings which have not been designated as having SMP.[37] In order to protect end-to-end connectivity, it may

---

26   ComReg documents 04/47 and 04/122.
27   ComReg documents 04/83, 04/113 and 04/70.
28   ComReg document 05/29.
29   ComReg document 05/25.
30   ComReg documents 04/82, 04/62 and 05/51.
31   ComReg documents 05/14 and 05/27. At the time of writing, this decision was under appeal.
32   ComReg document 05/37a.
33   ComReg document 05/26.
34   ComReg document 05/25.
35   eircom in the fixed network and services markets.
36   Transposed by SI 15 of 1998, SI 109 of 1998 and SI 71 of 1999.
37   Regulation 6 Access Regulations.

impose obligations on undertakings controlling access to end-users, including the obligation to interconnect. To ensure accessibility for end-users to digital radio and television broadcasting services, it may, after consultation with the Broadcasting Commission of Ireland, oblige operators to provide access to application programme interfaces and electronic programme guides on fair, reasonable and non-discriminatory terms.

NRA's Regulatory Duties concerning Rights of Way, Co-location and Facility Sharing

Rights of way

16.36   Any person who provides or operates an electronic communications network, whether public or private, is entitled to the following rights:

- *Opening of public road to establish underground infrastructure:*[38] consent of the relevant road authority is required and exempts the operator from the requirement to hold a licence under Section 254 of the Planning and Development Act 2000. Refusals to grant consent must be reasoned and may be appealed to the High Court. The local road authority may impose charges to cover administrative costs and costs incurred in repairing or reinstating a road following work by an operator.
- *Use of public road to establish overground infrastructure:*[39] the erection, construction or maintenance of overground infrastructure and associated physical infrastructure on, under or along a public road requires a licence from the local planning authority.[40] An operator will be responsible for all costs incurred in the reinstatement of a road to a satisfactory standard where it has opened a road to establish, maintain or repair overground infrastructure.
- *Lopping of trees:*[41] operators may lop or cut trees, shrubs or hedges which interfere with physical infrastructure (but not trees interfering with radio signals) on giving 28 days' notice to the landowner and may enter land at any reasonable time to do so.
- *Relocation of infrastructure due to road improvements:*[42] road authorities undertaking work to improve a road shall pay all reasonable costs incurred by an operator in relocating its infrastructure.

Co-location and facility sharing

16.37   Section 57 of the 2002 Act entitles network operators to negotiate infrastructure sharing agreements with other providers. Operators may serve notice on ComReg of such negotiations. If requested, or on its own initiative, ComReg will specify a timeframe within which negotiations shall be completed. If an agreement is not reached, ComReg will take steps necessary to resolve the dispute and may impose conditions for physical infrastructure sharing.

---

38   Section 53 of the 2002 Act.
39   Section 54 of the 2002 Act.
40   Section 254 of the Planning and Development Act 2000.
41   Section 58 of the 2002 Act.
42   Section 55 of the 2002 Act.

REGULATION OF MARKET ENTRY: IMPLEMENTATION OF THE AUTHORISATION DIRECTIVE

General Authorisation of Electronic Communications

16.38 The Authorisation Regulations abolish the requirement to apply for a licence to provide an electronic communications network or service. Any person may do so provided they comply with the conditions set out in a General Authorisation. Operators are required to notify ComReg in advance of their intention to provide a network or service. Failure to notify is an offence punishable by a fine of up to € 3,000. Where the proposed network and services are designed wholly for own use by an operator, including use by connected entities,[43] the operator is exempt from the requirement to make a notification and is deemed to be authorised, but must comply with the conditions of the General Authorisation.

16.39 Notification is made by submitting a completed notification form to ComReg. It may be submitted electronically but must also be submitted in hard copy. The form requests a minimal amount of information, such as contact details, description of network/service and estimated date of commencement of network or service. Notification need only be made once, but authorised undertakings have an ongoing obligation to inform ComReg of changes in their details. Where networks or services are provided by different group companies, a separate notification form should be completed by each legal entity. Details of notifying parties are entered onto a register of authorised undertakings on ComReg's website.[44]

16.40 Authorised undertakings may apply for consent to carry out road works and for a licence to establish overground infrastructure. In addition, undertakings providing services or networks to the public have the right to negotiate interconnection with and, where applicable, obtain access to or interconnection from another authorised undertaking and to be given an opportunity to be designated under the Universal Service Regulations.[45]

16.41 The Conditions for Authorisation have been specified by ComReg in accordance with Regulation 8 of the Authorisation Regulations.[46] ComReg is charged with monitoring compliance with the conditions, which are binding.

16.42 The general conditions for authorisation are:

- Provision of information to ComReg
- Compliance with decisions on emergency services and services during disasters
- Compliance with radiation emission standards
- Ensuring no harmful interference with other networks
- Compliance with decisions on maintenance of the integrity of public electronic communications networks
- Use of apparatus for wireless telegraphy in accordance with applicable conditions
- Having regard to issued notices or guidelines on the use of standards or specifications.

---

43   'Connected entities' are entities directly or indirectly owned by a common entity, and wholly owned subsidiaries: ComReg document 03/90.
44   www.comreg.ie
45   Section 7 Authorisation Regulations.
46   ComReg document 03/81.

16.43   Operators providing a network or service that is not wholly for their own use are also subject to conditions regarding:

- Universal service funding
- Administrative charges
- Interconnection
- Compliance with the National Numbering Conventions
- Co-location and facility sharing
- Misuse of data
- Consumer protection rules
- Security of public networks.

16.44   ComReg may impose additional obligations on operators designated as having SMP or as universal service providers.

Rights of Use for Radio Frequencies

General authorisation and granting of individual rights

16.45   ComReg is responsible for the effective management of radio frequencies for electronic communications services in accordance with Section 12 of the 2002 Act and Regulation 23 of the Framework Regulations.

16.46   Authorisations to use the spectrum are granted under the Wireless Telegraphy Acts, either by way of exemption order or in the form of a licence.[47] This exemption/licence is in addition to the requirements of the General Authorisation set out above.

16.47   Where the risk of harmful interference arising from the use of a class or description of apparatus for wireless telegraphy is negligible *and* the effective management of the radio spectrum would not be badly affected, ComReg will make an order under Section 3(6) of the Wireless Telegraphy Act 1926 exempting the apparatus from the licensing requirement. It may specify conditions for use for that class of equipment.

16.48   If the apparatus represents a risk of harmful interference, its use will be subject to a licence under Section 5 of the 1926 Act. This grants the licensee the right to install and use the apparatus, but grants no other interest or entitlement in the spectrum. The form and conditions attaching to licences are established by way of statutory instrument. On transposition of the new regime, these were amended to conform to the conditions set out in the Authorisation Regulations.

Limitation of numbers of rights of use to be granted

16.49   ComReg may limit the number of licences granted in respect of a particular class or description of apparatus, giving due weight to the need to maximise benefits for users and to facilitate the development of competition. It must undertake a public consultation and publish reasons for its decision. Licences must be granted on the basis of objective, transparent, non-discriminatory and proportionate selection criteria.[48]

---

47   Regulation 9 Authorisation Regulations.
48   Regulation 11 Authorisation Regulations.

Frequency trading

16.50   To date, there have been no spectrum auctions in Ireland, although in the case of mobile and 3G licences spectrum has been allocated through "beauty contests" (rights of use were granted to operators proposing to fulfil objectives in the most efficient manner). The introduction of spectrum auctions and the trading of spectrum rights are being considered in a consultation on spectrum management strategy.[49]

Rights of Use for Numbers

General authorisations and granting of individual rights

16.51   ComReg is responsible for the administration of the national telecommunications numbering resource.[50] It establishes National Numbering Conventions[51] setting out eligibility criteria, application procedures and conditions for allocation and use of numbers. It is a condition of the General Authorisation that operators comply with the Conventions.

16.52   Primary allocation of numbers is made to operators following application to ComReg, which should be done not more than 6 months before the planned activation date. In the case of numbers for which designations exist, ComReg will normally notify the applicant of its decision within 3 weeks of application. Refusal to make an allocation, or the attachment of conditions, may be appealed in accordance with the normal appeals procedure. Operators then make a secondary allocation of the numbers to end-users. A refusal to make an allocation, or the attachment of conditions to an allocation, may be appealed to ComReg.

16.53   ComReg may, after carrying out a public consultation, decide that rights of use of numbers with exceptional economic value will be granted through a competitive or comparative selection procedure.[52]

Admissible conditions

16.54   The Schedule to the Authorisation Regulations lists the conditions which may be attached to rights of use for numbers, repeating the conditions set out in the Authorisation Directive. General conditions of use and conditions for specific number types are set out in the National Numbering Conventions.

16.55   Operators have a right to use numbers allocated to them in accordance with the Conventions. No operator is entitled to ownership of or to any other interest in any number(s) allocated to that operator or to any customer. Numbers constitute non-proprietary data of which no particular organisation or institution or individual may claim ownership.

16.56   End-users have a right to use numbers allocated to them subject to directions set by the operator and/or ComReg. Their rights of use include the allocation of telephone numbers that are not subject to frequent mis-dialling, a

---

49   ComReg document 05/36.
50   Regulation 22 Framework Regulations.
51   ComReg document 04/35.
52   Regulation 13 Authorisation Regulations.

change of telephone number if an existing number is subject to unacceptable levels of nuisance or malicious calls and having numbers or address information excluded from telephone directories.

16.57   All fixed network operators (including mobile network operators) are obliged to offer full number portability to their customers. In the case of geographical numbers, an operator may also offer location portability, but only within the area for which the number was originally allocated.[53]

16.58   ComReg has designated a new non-geographic number range, based on the access code 076, for VoIP-based services and has issued a series of directions to eircom to allow access to the number range.[54]

The NRA's Enforcement Powers

16.59   ComReg's enforcement powers are set out in Regulations 16 to 26 of the Authorisation Regulations. These powers echo the powers of the NRA set out in the Authorisation Directive and apply to authorisations, licences for spectrum and rights to use of numbers. ComReg can require the provision of information in order to verify compliance with the conditions for authorisation or with any direction issued to an operator.[55] Where it identifies a failure to comply, ComReg will notify the operator and give it an opportunity to state its views. If ComReg believes that the person concerned has not complied with the condition or direction, it will apply to the High Court. The Court may make an order compelling compliance and stipulate a period within which the undertaking or person must comply.

16.60   ComReg may direct immediate compliance in the case of a breach representing an immediate and serious threat to public safety, security or health, or a breach which could in ComReg's opinion create serious economic or operational problems for undertakings or for end-users.

16.61   Offences under the Authorisation Regulations are punishable on summary conviction by a fine of up to € 3,000. Proceedings may be prosecuted by ComReg.

Administrative Charges and Fees for Rights of Use

16.62   There is no fee for notification. However, authorised operators providing a public network or service with a turnover of € 500,000 or more are subject to an annual levy of 0.2% of their turnover to meet ComReg's expenses in the discharge of its functions.[56]

16.63   Regulation 20 of the Authorisation Regulations empowers ComReg to impose fees in connection with wireless telegraphy licences. These fees vary according to the type of licence granted and the number and type of apparatus used.

16.64   Currently, 'no charge is made for the allocation of numbers, number blocks or codes although this may be introduced in the future.

---

53   Section 11.6 of the Conventions.
54   ComReg document 05/23.
55   Regulation 23 Authorisation Regulations.
56   SI 346 of 2003, Communications Regulation Act (Section 30) Levy Order 2003. A number of operators are exempt from this obligation, ie, providers of satellite, radio and television terrestrial transmission networks.

REGULATION OF NETWORK ACCESS AND INTERCONNECTION: IMPLEMENTATION OF THE ACCESS DIRECTIVE

Objectives and Scope of Access Regulations

16.65 ComReg is mandated to encourage and, where appropriate, ensure adequate access, interconnection and interoperability of services in such a way as to promote efficiency, promote sustainable competition and give maximum benefit to end-users.[57]

16.66 The Irish provisions on interconnection and access apply to operators of public communications networks and to authorised undertakings seeking interconnection or access to these networks or associated facilities.

Basic Regulatory Concepts

16.67 There are no major differences between the Access Directive and the implementing Regulations. 'Access' is defined as in the Access Directive, with the addition that 'access does not include, apply or refer to access by end users'. The definition of 'interconnection' is identical to that in the Directive.

16.68 Regulation 4(1) of the Access Regulations provides a framework within which an undertaking in Ireland or in any other Member State is entitled to negotiate access and/or interconnection in Ireland. An authorisation to operate in the State is not required if an undertaking is not providing services and does not operate a network in Ireland. ComReg must not maintain or impose measures obliging operators to offer different terms and conditions to different undertakings for equivalent services or to impose obligations unrelated to the actual access or interconnection services provided.

16.69 In accordance with the principle of priority of commercial negotiations, Regulation 6(5) of the Access Regulations states that ComReg may exercise its powers on its own initiative or, in the absence of agreement between undertakings, at the request of either of the parties involved.

Access- and Interconnection-related Obligations with Respect to SMP Undertakings

16.70 ComReg may impose such of the obligations identified in Regulations 10 to 14 of the Access Regulations on operators designated as having SMP as it considers appropriate. The obligations are as listed in Articles 9 to 13 Access Directive, namely:

- Transparency
- Non-discrimination
- Accounting separation
- Access to and use of specific network facilities
- Price control and cost accounting obligations.

16.71 Obligations must be objective, transparent, proportionate and non-discriminatory and may only be imposed following the appropriate consultation

---

57   Regulation 6 Access Regulations.

and consolidation procedures. Any proposal to impose obligations other than the above must be approved by the European Commission.

16.72   Combinations of the above obligations have been imposed on eircom, RTÉNL and the licensed mobile operators in different markets.[58]

16.73   Pending the outcome of ComReg's investigation into other markets, the obligations imposed on operators designated with SMP under the old regime continue.[59] An SMP operator is required to publish a RIO defining the processes of interconnection to its networks and associated prices. ComReg has reviewed eircom's RIO and is currently engaging in a consultation process aimed at establishing a definitive, transparent, non-discriminatory and compliant version of the RIO.[60]

Related Regulatory Powers with Respect to SMP Undertakings

16.74   Carrier pre-selection ('CPS') was introduced in Ireland in 2000 as a proxy for the level of competition in the market. ComReg has directed eircom to establish two products – wholesale line rental and agency rebilling – to enable CPS operators to provide a single bill for telephony rental, calls and ancillary services to their customers.[61]

16.75   eircom has been designated as having SMP in the retail leased lines market and the wholesale trunk and wholesale termination segment markets. ComReg has concluded that the Irish market for retail leased lines above 2Mb/s is effectively competitive and obligations previously applicable to eircom have been withdrawn. Obligations regarding international leased lines have also been withdrawn.[62] The Minister has directed ComReg to introduce wholesale line rental for voice and data services and to report monthly to the Minister on the commercial take-up of the rental product from June 2004. If sufficient progress is not evident, the Minister may direct ComReg to take line rental out of the present price cap.

16.76   eircom's RIO establishes a number of charges relating to wholesale line rental, including a charge for inter-operator testing, an order handling charge and the retail margin for wholesale rental of the line. Most of these charges have been established by agreement between ComReg and eircom. ComReg has directed eircom to set the charge in relation to wholesale line rental order handling on a retail minus basis.[63]

16.77   At ComReg's direction, a new wholesale version of leased lines known as Partial Private Circuits[64] was launched in July 2003. ComReg has also directed a price for Unbundled Metallic Paths (the price of a local loop)[65] and is consulting on the rental price for shared access.[66]

---

58   See paras 16.29–16.31 above.
59   Regulation 8 Access Regulations: see para 16.34 above.
60   ComReg document 03/140ar.
61   ComReg document 02/64.
62   ComReg documents 05/29 and 05/06.
63   ComReg document 04/32.
64   PPCs are an interconnection product allowing operators to provide point to point data services by availing of eircom's network together with elements of their own infrastructure to provide a service equivalent to eircom's wholesale leased line product.
65   ComReg document 04/110.
66   ComReg document 05/22.

16.78   ComReg monitors compliance with obligations imposed on SMP opera-tors, enforcing Regulation 18 of the Access Regulations. Where other operators experience difficulties obtaining access or interconnection, ComReg will intervene in accordance with the normal dispute resolution procedures.

16.79   ComReg has the power to impose obligations on all market participants to protect end-to-end connectivity and to ensure accessibility to digital radio and television broadcasting services.[67]

REGULATION OF UNIVERSAL SERVICES AND USERS' RIGHTS: THE UNIVERSAL SERVICE DIRECTIVE

Regulation of Universal Service Obligations

Scope of universal service obligations and designation of undertakings

16.80   Regulation 7 of the Universal Service Regulations states that one or more undertakings may be designated to comply with universal service obligations including provision of access at fixed locations, of public pay phones, directory enquiry facilities and services for disabled users. It also sets out the procedure for designation of undertakings to comply with these obligations.

16.81   Following a public consultation, eircom was designated as Universal Service Provider throughout the State for a period of three years from 25 July 2003, subject to the following obligations:[68]

- *The obligation to provide reasonable access*: it must propose criteria for assessing the reasonableness of requests for installation; publish factors that can affect network performance; publish standard terms on internet access; and develop a plan to address network performance issues.
- *The provision of directory enquiry services and directories*: it must provide users with a free printed phone book and offer directory enquiry services through-out the State. It will also be required to make a comprehensive directory available on CD format.
- *The provision of public pay telephones throughout the State to meet the reasonable needs of users, subject to agreed guidelines.*
- *The provision of specific measures to ensure that disabled users have access to services*: including a Code of Practice on the provision of services to disabled users and specified measures in respect of hearing, speech, mobility and sight impaired users.
- *Affordability for users by offering geographically averaged prices for its services to end-users.*
- *Regulation of retail tariffs, users' expenditures and quality of service:* it must offer a range of services to allow users to control expenditure including itemised billing, call barring, phased payment of connection fees and the publication of its disconnection policy.
- *Monitoring of quality of universal service:* it is required to publish information on its universal service performance based on the service parameters and measurement methods set out in Annex III to the Universal Service Directive. ComReg intends to develop performance targets following consultation with eircom and interested parties.

---

67   See para 16.35 above.
68   ComReg document 03/87.

- *Cost calculation and financing of universal services:* The onus is on the universal service operator to claim that the universal service obligation is an undue burden, in which case ComReg will determine how to share the costs among operators. This has not yet occurred.[69]

Regulation of Retail Markets

Prerequisites for the regulation of retail markets

16.82   The principle that regulation of retail services is permissible only if regulation at wholesale level does not achieve the regulatory objectives has been implemented by Regulation 14 of the Universal Service Regulations. No operator has been designated as having SMP in the retail market.

Regulatory powers

16.83   ComReg monitors compliance with the Universal Service Regulations with the exception of Regulations 20(3) and (5) (requirements regarding interface sockets in analogue and digital television sets sold). The procedure for notifying breach and compelling compliance is set out in Regulation 32 of the Regulations and is similar to the procedure set out in the Authorisation Regulations.[70] Regulations 20(3) and (5) are enforced by the Director of Consumer Affairs, who has similar powers to issue directions.

End User Rights

Contracts

16.84   Operators providing connection or access to the public telephone network must do so in accordance with a contract containing a minimum level of information specified in Regulation 17 of the Universal Service Regulations. Where providers of other electronic communications services conclude agreements with end users, these contracts must also include the information specified.

16.85   ComReg has issued a set of Guidelines setting out the level of detail to be included in contracts with end-users.[71] It may require operators to provide information in order to verify compliance with these obligations. Separate Guidelines have been issued for VoIP service providers on the treatment of consumers.[72]

16.86   In order for terms and conditions to be valid they must be brought to the attention of the end-users before any agreement is concluded. This may be done by providing a written contract or by indicating where written terms and conditions can be found. Standard terms and conditions should be published in a transparent and accessible manner and a paper copy should be provided if requested.

---

69   Regulations 11 and 12 Universal Service Regulations.
70   See paras 16.59–16.61 above.
71   ComReg document 03/129.
72   ComReg document 05/50.

Complaint handling procedures

16.87   Operators must establish a Code of Practice for handling customer complaints, including procedures, time frames and appropriate cases where
reimbursement/payments in settlement of losses will be made.[73] It must contain a
customer guarantee scheme setting out minimum service levels. The Code of
Practice must be clearly referred to in the customer contract, and must explain
ComReg's role in the resolution of disputes.

Transparency obligations

16.88   Details of prices and tariffs must be included in the customer contract,
including the types of charges, connection costs, rebates, peak and off-peak calling
times, billing frequency and billing and payment mechanisms.[74] A direct link must
be provided from the homepage of an operator's website to the tariff information
section.[75] ComReg has published a detailed Code of Practice for the presentation of
tariff information and proposes to develop an interactive tariff guide for consumers
to facilitate comparison of operators' rates.[76]

DATA PROTECTION: IMPLEMENTATION OF THE E-PRIVACY DIRECTIVE

Confidentiality of Communications

16.89   Operators providing publicly available electronic communications services
are obliged to take appropriate technical and organisational measures to safeguard
the security of their services (if necessary in conjunction with the relevant network
operators). Where there is a risk of security breach, subscribers must be informed
without delay of the risk and possible remedies (as well as cost implications).[77]

16.90   It is an offence to use an electronic communications network to store
information or to gain access to information stored in a user's terminal equipment
(eg, by way of 'cookies') without first providing clear and comprehensive information regarding the intention and purpose of processing and offering the user or
subscriber the opportunity to refuse processing. An exception to this prohibition
lies for technical storage or access for the sole purpose of transmitting the
communication or providing services explicitly requested by the subscriber/user.[78]

16.91   Section 98 of the Postal and Telecommunications Services Act 1983
contains a general prohibition on interception or surveillance of communications.
Exceptions exist for police investigations into suspected offences concerning
obscene or malicious calls, following a direction from the Minister or under other
lawful authority. Storage necessary for the conveyance of a communication is also
excepted, without prejudice to the principle of confidentiality.

---

73   Regulation 28 Universal Service Regulations.
74   ComReg document 03/129.
75   ComReg document 03/86.
76   ComReg document 04/86.
77   Regulation 4 E-Privacy Regulations.
78   Regulation 5.

Traffic Data and Location Data

16.92   The definitions of 'traffic data' and 'location data' are identical to those in the E-Privacy Directive.[79]

16.93   Service providers must inform subscribers of the types of data processed and the duration of such processing.

16.94   Traffic data processed for the purpose of transmitting communications must be erased or anonymised when it is no longer needed for that purpose. Operators may process data for the purposes of marketing electronic communications services or the provision of value added services, provided consent is obtained. Users must be allowed to withdraw their consent at any time.

16.95   Data necessary for the purpose of subscriber billing and interconnection payments may be retained only for the period during which the bill may be lawfully challenged and payment pursued (or the determination of proceedings if taken during that time).

16.96   Location data may only be processed if it has been made anonymous and the users' consent has been obtained to the extent and for the duration necessary for the provision of a value added service. This consent may be withdrawn at any time.

16.97   In an exception to the above rule, the Criminal Justice (Terrorist Offences) Act 2005 provides for the retention of communications data for the purpose of detection, prevention etc of crime (including terrorist offences). The Garda Commissioner may issue directions requesting service providers to retain data for a period of 3 years for such purposes.

Itemised Billing

16.98   Users have the right to request service providers *not* to provide itemised bills. As universal service provider, eircom has been directed to make a minimum level of itemised billing available to customers free of charge.

Calling and Connected Line Identification

16.99   Service providers offering calling line identification services must allow users to withhold their number on a per-call and per-line basis, using simple means and free of charge. Users must also have the facility to block the numbers of incoming calls and to reject incoming calls automatically in cases where the caller has withheld the caller identification.[80] This service may be eliminated temporarily during a police investigation into suspected malicious or nuisance calls. An exception also lies in respect of calls to emergency services and law enforcement agencies.

---

79   Regulation 2.
80   Regulation 8.

Automatic Call Forwarding

16.100   Users to whom calls have been automatically forwarded as a result of third party actions have the right, without charge, to request that these be ceased as soon as practicable after receipt of the request.[81]

Directories of Subscribers

16.101   The universal service operator and any other person making subscribers' data available for inclusion in a directory must inform all subscribers in advance of the purposes of the directory and any further usage possibilities based on search functions embedded in electronic versions of the directory. Subscribers must have the opportunity, without charge, to determine whether and to what extent their personal data is included in the directory and be given the opportunity to verify, correct or withdraw the data.[82]

Unsolicited Communications

16.102   The Data Protection Acts 1988 and 2003 govern the dispatch of unsolicited communications and the protection of personal data in Ireland. The E-Privacy Regulations contain special provisions in respect of the sending of unsolicited communications for direct marketing purposes by telephone, fax messages, e-mail, SMS, MMS, voicemail and sound.[83]

16.103   Generally speaking, an individual's express consent must be obtained before he or she may be contacted via fax, automatic calling machine or e-mail. An 'opt-out' system applies to unsolicited communications directed to business customers. Unsolicited telephone contact with subscribers (individuals and business customers) must not be made where the subscriber has indicated that it does not consent to the call, either individually or by joining the National Opt-Out Register.

16.104   A limited exception applies to the sending of unsolicited messages to existing customers by e-mail (including SMS and MMS messages) for direct marketing of a company's own similar products or services, provided an easy to use, free of charge opportunity is given to the customer to object to receiving future marketing messages, both when the contact details are initially collected and on the occasion of each message.

16.105   Breach of the rules set out in Regulation 13 is an offence punishable by a fine of up to €3,000. Offences may be prosecuted by the Data Protection Commissioner, who has general responsibility for enforcing Irish data protection legislation.

---

81   Regulation 11.
82   Regulation 12.
83   Regulation 13.

The Italian Market for Electronic Communications[1]

Raffaele Giarda, Valerio Bruno and Andrea Perotti
Baker & McKenzie Roma S.t.P

LEGAL STRUCTURE

Basic Policy

Regulatory approach and market conditions

17.1 As one of the founding member states of the European Community, Italy has followed the EC's regulatory approach in the telecommunications sector, thus liberalising the national telecommunications market[2] and adopting the Harmonisation Directives.[3]

17.2 In addition, and differently from other EU member states, throughout the years, Italy has privatised to a large extent the former Public Telecommunications Operator so that the Italian Treasury has now fully divested its participation in the corporate capital of the former incumbent, Telecom Italia. On the other hand, national and local utilities – directly or indirectly owned by the State – continue to hold interests in a number of players.

17.3 Telecom Italia still dominates the fixed telephony and leased line markets. At the same time, other competitors – both national and local – have increasing access to such markets, mostly in larger cities. The mobile, data services/internet and broadband markets are more competitive with numerous alternative providers, while the CATV market is still very small compared with the satellite and DTH services market.

Regulatory objectives

17.4 The main regulatory principles followed by the Italian policy-makers are the freedom to use electronic communications and the right of economic initiative in a competitive environment. The primary regulatory objective is the provision of

---

1   Editing of this chapter closed on 15 June 2005. The authors gratefully acknowledge the contribution of Rodolfo G. La Rosa.
2   See paras 1.16 et seq above.
3   See paras 1.22 et seq above.

communications networks and services: in addition to the regulatory objectives set out in the 2002 EU Regulatory Package,[4] under Italian law, the regulator must guarantee the right of information in accordance with article 19 UN Universal Declaration of Human Rights.[5]

Implementation of EU Directives

17.5 With the enactment of the Code of Electronic Communications ('CEC'),[6] which entered into force on 16 September 2003, Italy has implemented all the Directives of the 2002 EU Regulatory Package,[7] with the exception of the E-Privacy Directive, which was implemented by the Code of Personal Data Protection ('Privacy Act').[8]

17.6 The CEC and the Privacy Act implemented the above-mentioned EU Directives following the same structure and approach,[9] though maintaining some of the characteristics of the former national regulatory regime. These specific variations are examined in the following paragraphs.

Legislation

17.7 The CEC is the main piece of legislation on the regulation of electronic communications in Italy. The CEC abrogated or amended most parts of the former regulatory regime.[10] Accordingly, the entry into force of the CEC has simplified and consolidated the Italian sector-specific regulation, reducing significantly the number of legislative measures. At the same time, the CEC has maintained or only partially amended part of the previous legislative measures, thus giving rise to interpretation and harmonisation issues.

17.8 Apart from the CEC, the main legislative measures in the sector are the laws enacted before the adoption of the CEC and not abrogated by the latter, including legislative decrees and law decrees. The latter are considered statutes in the Italian legal system. In addition, other regulatory provisions are contained in ministerial decrees and regulations which, under Italian law, are secondary legislative measures to be adopted in compliance with the (higher-ranking) laws. Finally, the sector is also regulated through decisions, resolutions and recommendations of both the Ministry of Communications ('the Ministry') and the Italian Communications

---

4   Art 8 Framework Directive. For an analysis, see para 1.53 above.
5   Adopted by UN General Assembly Resolution 217 A (III) of 10 December 1948.
6   Legislative Decree no 259 of 1 August 2003, published in the Official Gazette no 214 of 15 September 2003.
7   See para 1.35 above.
8   Legislative Decree no 196 of 20 June 2003, which entered into force on 1 January 2004.
9   On 14 April 2005, the EU Commission launched infringements proceedings against Italy and other nine member states for defects in national laws and incorrect practical application of EU rules. In particular, for Italy, the EU Commission claimed that defects in the way the EU rules have been transposed handicap NRAs and prevent them from bringing the benefits of EU rules to the citizen.
10 Among others, the main legislative acts of the former regulatory regime which have not been abrogated, but only supplemented by the CEC, are the laws and decrees setting out the legal status, powers and duties of the Ministry of Communications and the Italian Communications Regulatory Authority. See fn 12 below for further details.

Regulatory Authority (*Autorità per le Garanzie nelle Comunicazioni* – 'AGCOM'), which are administrative provisions under Italian law.

REGULATORY PRINCIPLES: IMPLEMENTATION OF THE FRAMEWORK DIRECTIVE

Scope of Regulation

17.9   The following sectors and activities fall within the scope of the CEC:

- public electronic communications networks and services, including networks used for audio or video broadcasting and cable television networks,
- electronic communications activities for private use,
- protection of submarine electronic communications apparatus, and
- radio electrical services.

17.10   The CEC defines 'electronic communications networks', 'electronic communications services' and 'associated facilities' in exactly the same way as the Framework Directive.[11] The CEC does not expressly address VoIP services. Depending on the technical features offered by providers, these services could qualify as electronic communication services or as publicly available telephone services.

17.11   The CEC does not regulate the following:

- services which provide content transmitted through electronic communications networks and services, as well as services which provide editorial control over content,
- radio equipment and telecommunications terminal equipment except for the apparatus utilised by digital TV users, and
- electronic commerce and information society services which do not consist wholly or mainly in the conveyance of signals on electronic communications networks.

National Regulatory Authorities: Organisation, Regulatory Objectives, Competencies

Regulatory bodies and their independent status

17.12   In Italy, the regulatory powers and competences are split between the Ministry and AGCOM.[12] Such powers are consistent with the provisions set out in the EU regulatory framework. Specifically, the Ministry:

- issues general authorisations and manages, controls and applies the general authorisation regime for electronic communications services and the rights for use of radio frequencies and numbers,

---

11   For the relevant definitions, see paras 1.49, 1.50 and 1.51 above.

12   The Ministry has the regulatory powers set out by Legislative Decree no 300 of 30 July 1999, as amended by Law Decree no 217 of 12 June 2001 (as converted into Law no 317 of 3 August 2001), Law Decree no 5 of 2 January 2001 (as converted into Law no 66 of 20 March 2001), and Law no 3 of 16 January 2003. AGCOM has the regulatory powers set out under Laws no 481 of 14 November 1995 and no 249 of 31 July 1997, the latter as amended by Law Decree no 5 of 2 January 2001 (converted into Law no 66 of 20 March 2001) and by Law no 3 of 16 January 2003.

- monitors compliance with universal service obligations in the electronic communications sector,
- controls the allocation of national numbering resources and the management of the national numbering plan, and
- monitors radio frequencies so as to ensure compatibility with human health.

17.13   AGCOM is an independent body, whose members are appointed by the Parliament, responsible for implementing the legal framework in most regulatory areas as well as in press and audiovisual matters. More specifically, AGCOM:

- sets out and issues the national numbering plan and the procedures for the assignment of numbering resources,
- elaborates the frequency allocation plan,
- holds the public register of communications operators (*Registro degli Operatori di Comunicazione*),
- issues regulations regarding the general quality of service levels and oversees the application of quality service standards by communications operators,
- provides the European Commission with the list of operators with significant market power (SMP) and their obligations, and
- has dispute resolution powers in cases of disputes between providers as well as between providers and users.

17.14   The Ministry and AGCOM are legally and functionally independent from all telecommunications operators. AGCOM, in performing its tasks, takes its own decisions independently of the Government.

Coordination between regulators and with competition authority

17.15   The functions of the Ministry and AGCOM are complementary. Coordination issues may arise especially in the areas where the Ministry and AGCOM have complementary competences as set out above. Pursuant to article 8 CEC, the Ministry, AGCOM and the Italian Competition Authority (*Autorità Garante della Concorrenza e del Mercato* – 'ICA') exchange the necessary information for the application of the EU regulatory framework and are required to adopt, also through specific agreements, procedures for reciprocal consultation and cooperation in areas of common interest.[13]

17.16   Each of the Ministry, AGCOM and ICA have the power to request information from operators and undertakings. In particular, the CEC provides that the Ministry and AGCOM may do so in order to ensure that the operators comply with the provisions of the CEC or with decisions adopted pursuant to the CEC. The Ministry and AGCOM are to publish the relevant information to the extent it contributes to creating a free and competitive market, in compliance with European and national legislation on confidentiality.

Implementation of consultation procedure

17.17   When the Ministry and AGCOM intend to adopt a decision that may have a significant impact on the relevant market, they must allow interested parties to

---

13   To this end, on 28 January 2004, AGCOM and ICA entered into a collaboration agreement which covers market analysis procedures, the transfer of rights of use of radio frequencies and access to documents and confidential information.

submit their observations on the proposed decision within at least 30 days following the date of notification of the proposed decision.[14] In addition, the Ministry and AGCOM must publish information about the relevant consultation procedure on their websites and in their Official Bulletins.[15] In the case of confidential information, the right of access is granted to the extent necessary to guarantee the right of defence. All disclosable information regarding a decision to open a consultation procedure, the results of such consultation and the proposed final decision are promptly published on the websites and in the Official Bulletins of the Ministry and AGCOM.[16]

17.18 AGCOM must cooperate with other member states' NRAs and the European Commission in order to ensure that the provisions set out in the 2002 EU Regulatory Package are fully implemented in all member states. To this end, AGCOM must undertake activities in order to reach agreements with other member states' NRAs and the European Commission on the most appropriate means and solutions.[17]

Dispute resolution power

17.19 AGCOM has the power to resolve disputes between providers of electronic communications networks/services. AGCOM must adopt a binding decision within four months from submission of the claim. If the parties agreed to derogate from the competence of AGCOM by choosing to use an alternative dispute resolution method and the parties did not settle within four months from the beginning of the alternative proceedings, AGCOM must adopt a binding decision on the dispute within the following four months. The decision of AGCOM shall be published on AGCOM's website and in the Official Bulletin.[18]

17.20 AGCOM must administer transparent, simple and inexpensive procedures to resolve disputes between operators and users, in order to ensure a fair and prompt resolution of such disputes by providing a reimbursement and indemnification system when justified.[19]

17.21 AGCOM also has dispute resolution powers in cases of transnational disputes where one of the parties is established in another EU member state. In this case, AGCOM must coordinate with the NRA of the other EU member state in order to resolve the dispute. Again, if the parties agreed to derogate from the competence of NRAs by choosing to use an alternative dispute resolution method, and the parties did not settle within four months from the beginning of the

---

14   Art 11 CEC.
15   To this end, AGCOM, by Decision no 253/03, published in the Italian Official Gazette on 28 January 2004, adopted a specific regulation on the consultation procedure.
16   See para 17.29 below.
17   Cf art 12 CEC. To this end, by Decisions 2002/627/EC of 29 July 2002 and 2004/3445/EC of 14 September 2004, the EU Commission created the European Regulators Group, see para 1.59 above.
18   Art 23 CEC.
19   Art 84 CEC. In compliance with art 1 Law no 249 of 31 July 1997, AGCOM by Resolution no 182/02 published in the Italian Official Gazette on 18 July 2002 (as modified by Resolution 307/03 published in the Italian Official Gazette on 25 August 2003) adopted a regulation for the resolution of disputes between operators and users.

proceedings, AGCOM and the other EU state's NRA must adopt a binding decision on the dispute.[20] All such AGCOM decisions may be challenged as outlined in the following paragraph.

Right of Appeal against NRA's Decisions

17.22 All decisions and resolutions adopted by AGCOM and the Ministry pursuant to the CEC may be challenged before the administrative court (*Tribunale Amministrativo Regionale* – 'TAR' – of Lazio), based in Rome.[21] The TAR may grant temporary restraining orders and may rule on the merits of any such decision or resolution. The decisions of the TAR may be appealed before the Council of State (the highest administrative court). The Council of State may also reverse the decision and grant temporary restraining orders.

The NRA's Obligations to Cooperate with the Commission

Implementation of the consolidation procedure

17.23 AGCOM must cooperate in a transparent manner with the NRAs of the other member states in order to ensure full compliance with the EU regulatory framework as implemented by the CEC. To this end, AGCOM must endeavour to reach an agreement with the other NRAs as well as with the European Commission on the most appropriate instruments and solutions to be adopted.[22] Furthermore, and in addition to the consultation procedure,[23] whenever AGCOM intends to make a decision – regarding market definitions and analysis, access and interconnection as well as obligations for SMP operators – which affects trade between EU member states, it must make the draft decision available to the European Commission and the other NRAs. AGCOM may not adopt the draft decision within one month from the date of its communication to the European Commission and the other NRAs. If the European Commission so requests within the one-month period, AGCOM must wait an additional two months before adopting the draft decision and must amend the same, if:

- the draft decision identifies a market different from the markets identified in the relevant European Commission recommendations,[24] or
- the draft decision designates SMP operators, affects trade between member states, and the European Commission believes that it may create a barrier to the EU market or has doubts as to its compatibility with Community law or with the objectives of the EU regulatory framework.

17.24 AGCOM may derogate from the procedure set out above in urgent cases and when needed to protect competition and users' rights. In these cases, AGCOM may adopt appropriate temporary measures with immediate effect and must promptly inform the European Commission and the other NRAs. Any decision of AGCOM regarding the extension of the term of such temporary measures or their adoption as definitive decisions must follow the procedure set out above.

---

20   Art 24 CEC.
21   Art 9 CEC.
22   Art 12 CEC and para 17.18 above.
23   See para 17.17 above for further details.
24   Commission Recommendation on relevant markets, OJ C 114/45, 8 May 2003.

Implementation of powers of the Commission to stipulate standards and issue specifications

17.25 The CEC reflects the Commission's power to stipulate standards and issue specifications. In fact, the Ministry must monitor the use of technical provisions and specifications published in the Official Journal of the European Union for the harmonised provision of services, technical interfaces and network functions to the extent necessary to guarantee interoperability of services and improve the users' freedom of choice. Until the European Commission adopts such technical provisions and specifications, the Ministry must promote the application of technical specifications and provisions adopted by the European standardisation organisations.[25]

'Significant Market Power' as a Fundamental Prerequisite of Regulation

Definition of SMP

17.26 AGCOM determines whether an undertaking has significant market power by carrying out the market analysis procedure.[26] According to such provision, AGCOM – after consulting with the ICA and taking into account the recommendations and guidelines of the European Commission – carries out the first market analysis. Subsequently, AGCOM reviews the market analysis within 90 days from the date of publication of any update of the European Commission recommendations and, in any event, every 18 months. As regards the outcome of such market analysis procedure, the CEC reflects exactly the provisions set out in article 16 Framework Directive.[27] AGCOM has initiated the first market analysis on 15 markets.[28]

17.27 The CEC defines dominance with respect to closely related markets in exactly the same way as the Framework Directive.[29] When evaluating whether two or more undertakings are in a joint dominant position in a market, the CEC requires AGCOM to take into account the guidelines of the European Commission.[30]

Definition of relevant markets and SMP designation

17.28 AGCOM – taking into account the recommendations and guidelines of the European Commission – must define the relevant markets in accordance with the principles of competition law and on the basis of the structure and characteristics of the Italian market for electronic communications.[31] As said, before defining

---

25   Cf art 20 CEC.
26   Cf art 19 CEC.
27   Cf para 1.77 above.
28   See para 17.29 below.
29   For the definition of SMP as set out in the Framework Directive, see para 1.70 above.
30   Commission Guidelines on market analysis, OJ C 165/6, 11 July 2002.
31   Cf art 18 CEC.

markets in a manner different from the EU Commission Recommendation on relevant markets, AGCOM must follow the consultation and consolidation procedure outlined above.[32]

17.29 AGCOM has carried out public consultations in relation to the market analysis procedure on each market identified in the Commission Recommendation on relevant markets other than markets no 15, 17 and 18 of such Recommendation, and has proposed the following remedies vis-à-vis the following operators:

Telecom Italia, the former monopolist, is proposed to be designated as having SMP in the following markets:

- access to the public telephone network at a fixed location for residential and non-residential customers,
- publicly available local and/or national telephone services provided at a fixed location for residential and non-residential customers,
- publicly available international telephone services provided at a fixed location for residential and non-residential customers,
- the leased lines market with capacity up to 155 Mbits,
- call origination and termination (excluding internet termination) on the public telephone network provided at a fixed location. In the public consultation document the NRA stated that VoIP constitutes only an alternative technology for voice transportation and that it does not, therefore, impact on the definition of markets related to call origination, termination and transit on fixed networks,
- transit services in the fixed public telephone network,
- wholesale unbundled access (including shared access) to metallic loops and sub-loops for the purpose of providing broadband and voice services,
- wholesale broadband access, and
- wholesale terminating segments and wholesale trunk segments of leased lines.

Consequently, Telecom Italia would have to comply with non-discrimination, transparency, accounting separation and price control obligations.

17.30 TIM (Telecom Italia Mobile),[33] Vodafone Omnitel, Wind and H3G are proposed to be designated as having significant market power in the market of wholesale voice call termination on their individual mobile networks.

TIM and Vodafone could have to comply with price control (together with Wind) and accounting separation obligations. H3G will not be subject to price control obligations during the term of AGCOM's market analysis (18 months).

17.31 Further to completion of the above-mentioned public consultations, AGCOM will make the draft decisions on such markets available to the European Commission and the other NRAs in compliance with the consolidation procedure.[34]

Until the market analysis procedure is completed, public fixed network operators identified as SMP operators pursuant to the Interconnection Directive and the

---

32   Cf para 17.17 above.
33   Now merged into Telecom Italia.
34   See para 17.23 above.

ONP Voice Telephony Directive (1998) will continue to be considered as notified operators in accordance with EU Regulation 2887/2000 on unbundled access to the local loop.[35]

17.32   If, on the basis of the market analysis procedure, AGCOM determines that a market is not effectively competitive, it must identify the SMP undertakings in that market and impose appropriate specific regulatory obligations (remedies) or maintain or amend the existing obligations. AGCOM is also allowed to impose obligations on other undertakings not identified as having SMP, such as:[36]

- for providers controlling access to end-users, the obligation to interconnect their networks to the extent necessary to guarantee point-to-point interconnection,[37] and
- the obligation to provide access to Application Programming Interfaces (APIs) and Electronic Program Guides (EPGs) on fair, reasonable and non-discriminatory terms in order to ensure accessibility for end-users to digital radio and TV broadcasting services.[38]

NRA's Regulatory Duties concerning Rights of Way, Co-location and Facility Sharing

Rights of way

OVERVIEW

17.33   The CEC establishes the principles for the grant of rights of way.[39] Although expressly allowed under the Framework Directive, no distinctions are drawn between rights of way for undertakings authorised to provide public electronic communications networks and undertakings authorised to provide electronic communications networks other than to the public. Similar rules apply to the grant of rights of way in relation to electronic communications infrastructures used for radio electronic systems and civil infrastructures, digging works and the occupation of public land. In these cases, local governmental entities ('local entities') or the land owner concerned must grant the rights of way for the installation of the electronic communications infrastructures.

PROCEDURAL PRINCIPLES FOR GRANTING RIGHTS OF WAY FOR RADIO
ELECTRONIC SYSTEMS

17.34   The CEC also governs the grant of rights of way in relation to electronic communications infrastructures for radio electronic systems.[40] Such infrastructures include radio base stations for mobile GSM/UMTS communications networks and for point-to-multipoint broadband radio networks using ad hoc frequencies (WLL networks). Both an express and an implicit authorisation regime can apply. More specifically:

---

35   Art 19 CEC.
36   Art 42 CEC.
37   See para 17.102 below.
38   See para 17.103 below.
39   Art 86 CEC.
40   Art 87 CEC.

- Under the express authorisation regime, undertakings must file an application with the relevant local entity, giving evidence that the infrastructure is compatible with the electromagnetic fields exposure limits set out by applicable laws.[41] Once the competent administration bodies have confirmed the infrastructure's compatibility, the local entity may grant the rights of way. The application must be approved within 30 days. However, if there is a disagreement among the administrations involved in the processing, the time period may be extended.

  It is not necessary to file an application when the installation involves systems based on UMTS or other technologies with single antenna power not in excess of 20 Watts. In this case, a declaration describing the infrastructures to be installed is sufficient.

- Under the implicit authorisation regime, the application and the declaration are deemed as approved if the local entities do not reject them within 90 days from receipt of the relevant documents.

17.35 The operators are solely responsible for the costs related to the works and for restoring the site in accordance with the timeframe given by the local entities.

PROCEDURAL PRINCIPLES FOR GRANTING RIGHTS OF WAY FOR CIVIL
INFRASTRUCTURES, DIGGING WORKS AND OCCUPATION OF PUBLIC LAND

17.36 Authorisation is required to install civil infrastructures, carry out digging works or occupy public land. Such authorisation is granted by the local entities through an express or implicit authorisation regime similar to that provided for infrastructures for radio electronic systems highlighted above.[42] The period for the grant of the implicit authorisation is reduced from 90 to 30 days for digging works pertaining to crossroads and, in any event, for those relating to less than 200 metres.

17.37 The CEC contains a number of provisions aimed at facilitating the installation of electronic communications networks systems. Such provisions include the expropriation of real estate, and limitations on ownership rights and rights of easement.

EXPROPRIATION

17.38 A different regulation may apply to public and private networks depending on whether or not they qualify as 'public utility' infrastructures. In particular, public electronic communications networks automatically qualify as public utility infrastructures, while private electronic communications networks may be so qualified only through a decree of the Ministry.[43]

17.39 Undertakings authorised to install public or private networks qualified as public utility infrastructures are entitled to expropriate the necessary real estate. The expropriation, however, will be allowed only if it was impossible to reach an amicable agreement with the owner of the real estate concerned.

---

41   This matter is governed by Law no 36 of 22 February 2001 and implementing legislation (eg Prime Minister Decree dated 8 July 2003).
42   Art 88 CEC.
43   Art 90 CEC.

LIMITATIONS TO OWNERSHIP RIGHTS

17.40   Aerial wires or cables which are part of public or private networks may be placed above public or private properties as well as on those sides of the buildings where there are no windows.[44] Such installation may be effected without the owner's consent. Further, the owner may not object to the installation of antennas, masts or ducts, wires, or any other systems necessary to meet the service needs of other occupants of the same building. The service provider is also entitled to start legal action to restrict any behaviour which prevents or disturbs the installation of the above-mentioned infrastructures. The owner is not entitled to any indemnity.

EASEMENTS

17.41   The CEC expressly provides for the right to obtain easements for the deployment of wires, cables and apparatus (of public and private networks) on, over or below private or public land without the land owner's consent.[45] If the easements concern public land, they are subject to the conclusion of an ad hoc master agreement with the relevant local entities. The latter are entitled to an indemnity. Decisions on easements may be challenged before the administrative courts. Special rules apply in relation to easements on highways.[46]

STRUCTURAL SEPARATION

17.42   The CEC provides for a structural separation mechanism equivalent to that set out in the Framework Directive.[47]

Co-location and facility sharing

17.43   The CEC contains rules for co-location and facility sharing which mirror those set out in the Framework Directive.[48] The relevant provision of the Access Directive, however, refers to equivalent conditions to be applied to '*other undertakings*' while the corresponding rule of the CEC refers to '*other operators*'.[49] Also, if the installation of infrastructures requires digging works within inhabited areas, the operator must file a communication describing the relevant project to the Ministry. Within 30 days from such filing, operators interested in co-location or facility sharing may agree on a shared co-location or facility plan with the operator that filed the above-mentioned communication.

---

44   Art 91 CEC.
45   Art 92 CEC.
46   Art 94 CEC.
47   Art 86 CEC implements art 11(2) Framework Directive.
48   Art 89 CEC implements art 12 Framework Directive.
49   See para 17.91 below.

REGULATION OF MARKET ENTRY: IMPLEMENTATION OF THE AUTHORISATION DIRECTIVE

The General Authorisation of Electronic Communications

The general authorisation regime

17.44 The provision of electronic communications networks and services is subject only to a general authorisation.[50] This does not prevent the Ministry from supplementing such a 'general' authorisation by regulatory decisions with regard to specific obligations related to network access, interconnection, universal service and individual rights to use frequencies and/or numbers.

17.45 To obtain a general authorisation, the interested individual or, in the case of an entity, the legal representative must file a declaration with the Ministry, stating the intention to commence the provision of electronic communications networks or services. Such declaration is equivalent to the 'notification' set out in article 3(3) Authorisation Directive. The declaration must contain the information strictly necessary to allow the Ministry to keep an up-to-date register of electronic communications network and service providers.

17.46 After filing the declaration, the undertaking concerned may begin its activity immediately, subject to the specific provisions on rights to use frequencies or numbers. Within 60 days of the filing, the Ministry is to verify the compliance of the above-mentioned declaration with the necessary requirements. In case of non-compliance, the Ministry may order the undertaking concerned to cease its activity.

17.47 The general authorisation may be granted to individuals or entities of the European Union and individuals or entities of non-EU countries under condition of reciprocity (but particular limitations deriving from international treaties may apply).

17.48 The duration of the general authorisation may not exceed 20 years, but it may be renewed by filing a new declaration at least 60 days before its expiration.

17.49 General authorisations do not entail the issue of any paper permit. However, at the operator's request and within one week thereafter, the Ministry must issue a statement to confirm that the operator has filed a declaration under the above-mentioned rules,[51] indicating the conditions under which the operator is providing electronic communications networks or services. The ministerial statement is aimed at facilitating the exercise of the operator's rights to install facilities, negotiate interconnection agreements with, or obtain access from, other operators or governmental entities.

'Minimum' rights granted in the general authorisation

17.50 Authorised undertakings have the right to:[52]

● provide electronic communications networks and services to the public, and

---

50   Art 25 CEC.
51   See para 17.45 above.
52   Art 26 CEC.

- apply for specific authorisations, or file the necessary declarations, to exercise the rights to install facilities, in compliance with the provisions set out in the CEC.[53]

17.51   If the undertaking intends to provide electronic communications networks or services to the public, the general authorisation allows the undertaking to:

- negotiate interconnection with other authorised providers of publicly available electronic communications networks and services and, where applicable, obtain network access and interconnection anywhere in the European Union, subject to the access and interconnection conditions set out in the CEC,[54] and
- be designated as provider, in all or part of the national territory, of one or more services which fall within the obligations of universal service.

Conditions attached to general authorisations

17.52   The 'maximum' number of conditions which may be attached to the general authorisation are those listed in Part A of Annex 1 CEC, which, in essence, mirrors Part A of the Annex to the Authorisation Directive. Among these conditions, the CEC specifies that the general authorisation must always contain the specific obligation to enable legal interception by the relevant judicial authorities.[55] However, the general authorisation must not duplicate conditions that are applicable to undertakings by virtue of other national legislation.

17.53   In granting rights to use frequencies and numbers, the Ministry applies only the conditions listed in Parts B and C respectively of Annex 1 CEC, which again mirror those listed in Parts B and C of the Annex to the Authorisation Directive.

Separate conditions applicable to SMP providers and universal service providers

17.54   The specific obligations which may be imposed on providers of electronic communications networks and services designated as having significant market power or undertakings designated for the provision of universal service are separate from the rights and obligations attached to the general authorisation. However, in order to ensure transparency, the general authorisations for such undertakings must specify the additional obligations so imposed.

Rights of Use for Radio Frequencies

General authorisations and granting of individual rights

17.55   The provisions set out in article 5 Authorisation Directive on radio frequencies use have been transposed into article 27 CEC.

17.56   Where it is necessary to grant individual rights to use frequencies, the Ministry grants such rights, upon request, to any undertaking providing or using network services under a general authorisation.

---

53   Such provisions are arts 86, 87 and 88 CEC. See para 17.33 above.
54   See para 17.85 below.
55   Point 11, Part A, Annex 1 CEC.

Procedural requirements

17.57   Similar to the Authorisation Directive, the CEC[56] provides that, except for the specific regulation on the grant of rights to use frequencies to the providers of radio and video broadcasting contents, such rights of use are granted through public, transparent and non-discriminatory procedures. Further, with particular reference to the grant of rights to use frequencies, the Ministry specifies from time to time whether and under which conditions those rights may be transferred at the initiative of the relevant holder.[57]

17.58   The Ministry must adopt and publish its decisions on the rights to use frequencies immediately after receipt of the relevant application or, in the case of frequencies that have been allocated for specific purposes under the National Frequencies Allocation Plan ('NAFP'), within six weeks, without prejudice to the international agreements on frequencies coordination and satellite orbits.

17.59   Where the usage of radio frequencies has been harmonised, and subject to the other conditions set out in article 8 Authorisation Directive as transposed in article 30 CEC,[58] the Ministry must grant the right of use for such frequencies in accordance with said conditions, provided that the applicant has complied with all national requirements related to the rights to use frequencies. The Ministry may not impose any further conditions or procedure which would restrict, alter or delay the correct implementation of the common assignment of such radio frequencies.

Admissible conditions

17.60   The right to use radio frequencies may be granted for a limited period of time, provided that the duration is appropriate for the service concerned. As indicated above, the grant of rights to use frequencies may be subject only to the conditions listed in Part B of Annex 1 CEC.

17.61   Where the number of rights to use frequencies has been limited through competitive bidding procedures,[59] the undertaking must comply with all special commitments made in the course of the relevant competitive bidding procedure.[60]

17.62   There are no special conditions set out specifically for important spectrum bands. However, in Italy, the rights to use spectrum, concerning eg GSM, 3G or WLL, have always been granted through competitive selection procedures.

17.63   Examples of special conditions imposed during competitive selection procedures include the obligations:

- to start the service within the time indicated by AGCOM,
- to ensure certain territorial and population coverage,
- to comply with minimum service quality standards,[61] and
- to pay penalties in case of failure to fulfil the targets set out under the licence.

---

56   Art 27(5) CEC.
57   Art 27(5) CEC.
58   See para 1.105 above.
59   See paras 17.64–17.67 below.
60   See condition no 7, Part B of Annex 1 CEC.
61   See para 17.130 below.

Limitation of the number of rights of use to be granted

17.64   AGCOM is in charge of adopting all decisions on the limitation of the number of rights to use frequencies.

17.65   The relevant procedure as set out in article 29 CEC mirrors that indicated in article 7 Authorisation Directive.[62] The main difference is that the Italian legislature has deemed it appropriate to specify that AGCOM – in considering the possibility to limit the number of rights to use to be granted – must take into account not only the need to maximise users' benefits and the development of competition, but also the sustainability of investments in relation to market needs, pursuing the efficient and effective use of radio frequencies.

17.66   In the case of competitive selection procedures, the CEC requires the Ministry to administer the procedure and to grant the rights to use pursuant to rules that are established by AGCOM on the basis of objective, transparent, proportionate and non-discriminatory selection criteria, aimed at developing competition and pursuing efficient and effective use of radio frequencies. The awards are made within eight months, and usage fees can be levied under auction procedures, provided that such fees are proportionate and reflect the need to ensure optimal use of the radio spectrum. In all other cases, fees for rights to use for radio frequencies or numbers are defined by the Ministry on the basis of the criteria indicated below.[63]

17.67   In case of competitive selection procedures of particular national importance, AGCOM may propose to the Ministry and the Prime Minister that a Committee of Ministries be established in order to co-ordinate the procedure for the grant of individual rights of use.

17.68   In April 2004, AGCOM launched a public consultation regarding the grant of rights of use for GSM frequencies to current mobile operators or a new operator. In February 2005, the Ministry launched a competitive bidding procedure for the grant of rights to use 24.5–26.5 GHz and 27.5–29.5 GHz WLL frequencies not assigned through a WLL auction in 2002.

Frequency trading

17.69   Without prejudice to the specific radio and video broadcasting regulation, the rights to use frequencies with limited bandwidth availability which have been granted to a limited number of operators may be transferred against consideration between operators authorised to provide electronic networks based on similar technology.[64] Such transfer is allowed only with the express consent of the Ministry. The undertaking's intention to transfer rights to use radio frequencies must be notified to the Ministry and AGCOM. The Ministry must consent or object within 90 days from the relevant operator's notification. Based on the opinion issued by ICA that competition will not be distorted as a result of the envisaged transfer, the Ministry may make its consent subject to specific conditions. Any such transfer is made public and must not result in a change of use of those radio frequencies

---

62   See para 1.104 above.
63   See paras 17.82–17.83 below.
64   Art 14 CEC.

whose use has been harmonised through the application of the Radio Spectrum Decision[65] or other Community measures.

Rights of Use for Numbers

General authorisations and granting of individual rights

17.70   The Ministry assigns the rights to use numbers on an individual basis upon request by any undertaking which provides or uses networks or services under a general authorisation. The assignment is effected immediately after receipt of the relevant application or within three weeks in the case of numbers dedicated to specific purposes under the National Numbering Plan ('NNP').

17.71   The Ministry is responsible for the management of the NNP and is required to ensure that adequate numbering resources be allocated to all public electronic communications services. Further, the Ministry is to monitor the numbering resources to ensure that they are used pursuant to the types of services which such numbers are allocated to under the NNP.

17.72   AGCOM defines and publishes the NNP and all subsequent additions or amendments thereto as well as the procedures for the assignment of numbering resources. Such assignment is to be effected in compliance with the principles of objectivity, transparency and non-discrimination, in order to ensure that an undertaking that has been assigned a range of numbers does not discriminate against other providers of electronic communications services with respect to the numbering sequences to be used for access to their services. The undertaking that has been assigned the right to use numbers does not obtain property rights in such numbers.

Admissible conditions

17.73   Part C of Annex 1 CEC sets out an inclusive list of conditions which may be attached to rights of use for numbers. These include the effective and efficient use of numbers, the obligation to pay the relevant fees, and compliance with number portability rules.

17.74   In this respect, AGCOM ensures that all subscribers to public telephony services, including mobile services, may maintain their own number/s, regardless of the undertaking providing the service. There is no number portability between fixed and mobile services. AGCOM takes steps to ensure that interconnection charges related to number portability are cost-oriented and that the possible charges on end-users do not result in a disincentive to the demand for number portability.

Limitation of the number of rights of use to be granted

17.75   Whenever, after public consultation, AGCOM determines that rights of use for numbers of exceptional economic value must be granted through competitive selection procedures, the same procedural rules and principles as those described with reference to the limitation of rights to use radio frequencies apply.[66]

---

65   See paras 1.191 et seq above.
66   See paras 17.64–17.67 above.

The NRA's Enforcement Powers

17.76 Undertakings providing electronic communications services or networks under a general authorisation or which have been granted rights to use numbers or frequencies must provide the Ministry with the information necessary to verify compliance with the conditions attached to the general authorisation or the rights to use. Also, undertakings must provide AGCOM with the information necessary to verify compliance with the 'separate conditions' which are imposed on undertakings designated as having SMP.[67]

17.77 The Ministry and AGCOM may only request information that is proportionate and objectively justified and must inform the undertakings of the specific purpose for which the information is to be used.[68]

17.78 If an undertaking fails to provide information within the timeframe indicated by AGCOM, the latter may impose administrative fines ranging from €1,500 to €115,000.[69]

17.79 Where the Ministry or AGCOM finds that an undertaking has not complied with one or more conditions of the general authorisation or of the rights to use or with the specific obligations imposed on SMP undertakings, it must notify the undertaking of those findings and give the undertaking a reasonable opportunity to state its view and remedy any breaches within one month after notification. If the relevant undertaking does not remedy the breach within the one-month period, the Ministry or AGCOM must take appropriate and proportionate measures aimed at ensuring compliance and may impose administrative fines ranging from €12,000 to €250,000. Should the breaches concern specific obligations imposed on SMP undertakings, AGCOM may impose an administrative fine ranging from 2% to 5% of the defaulting undertaking's previous financial-year turnover in the market concerned.[70]

17.80 In cases of serious and repeated breaches in a five-year period, and if measures aimed at ensuring compliance have failed, the Ministry and AGCOM may prevent an undertaking from continuing to provide electronic communications networks or services or suspend or revoke the rights to use the relevant resources. In addition, should the repeated breaches entail the installation and provision of public electronic communications networks or the offer of public electronic communications services without general authorisation, the Ministry may impose an administrative fine of €250,000.[71]

17.81 The Ministry and AGCOM may take urgent temporary measures whenever they have evidence of a breach of the conditions of the general authorisation, rights to use or specific obligations of SMP undertakings which would entail an immediate and serious threat to public safety, public security or public health or are likely to create a barrier to criminal investigations or serious economic or operational problems for other providers or users of electronic communications networks or services.[72]

---

67   See art 32 CEC.
68   See art 11 Authorisation Directive, analysed in para 1.111 above.
69   See art 98 CEC.
70   See art 98 CEC.
71   See art 98 CEC.
72   See art 32 CEC.

Administrative Charges and Fees for Rights of Use

17.82   Administrative fees ranging from €600 (for each site where a switch is located) to €111,000, depending on the type of service and its geographical coverage, are imposed on undertakings providing a communication service or network under the general authorisation. These fees must cover only the administrative costs incurred in the management, control and enforcement of the general authorisation regime, the rights to use and the specific obligations attached (eg to SMP operators or service providers).[73]

17.83   Fees for the rights to use frequencies or numbers are defined by the Ministry on the basis of the criteria set out by AGCOM and are indicated in Annex 10 CEC. In essence, the relevant amounts depend on the frequencies and bandwidth used as well as on the number and type of apparatus utilised.

Transitional Regulations for Existing Authorisations

17.84   Individual licences and general authorisations for public telecommunications networks and services which were already in existence on the date of entry into force of the CEC continue to be valid until their natural expiration, and the provisions set out in the CEC apply. However, where application of this rule would result in a reduction of the rights or in an extension of the obligations under an authorisation already in existence, the Ministry, after consultation with AGCOM, may extend the validity of those rights and obligations for no more than nine months from the date of entry into force of the CEC.[74]

REGULATION OF NETWORK ACCESS AND INTERCONNECTION: IMPLEMENTATION OF THE ACCESS DIRECTIVE

Objectives and Scope of Access Regulation

17.85   The CEC specifies both the aim and objectives of access and interconnection regulation.[75]

17.86   In particular, the regulation of electronic communications networks and services must guarantee flexible rules on access and interconnection in relation to broadband electronic communications networks, in order to ensure a sustainable degree of competition, innovation and benefits for consumers.[76]

17.87   Also, the Ministry and AGCOM are to contribute to the development of the electronic communications market through the adoption of flexible regulation of access and interconnection.[77]

17.88   Access and interconnection rules apply to all undertakings authorised to provide electronic communications services and networks in Italy as well as operators similarly authorised in another EU member state. Such foreign operators

---

73   See arts 34 and 35 CEC.
74   Art 38 CEC.
75   See arts 4 and 13 CEC.
76   See art 4(3) CEC.
77   See art 13 CEC

do not need a general authorisation under Italian law in order to obtain access or interconnection if they do not manage a network or offer electronic communications services within the Italian territory.

Basic Regulatory Concepts

17.89   AGCOM must encourage and guarantee adequate access, interconnection and interoperability of services.[78] AGCOM must also exercise its responsibilities in order to promote economic efficiency, sustainable competition and provide maximum benefit to end-users.

17.90   AGCOM is empowered to apply ex ante regulatory obligations on SMP undertakings as well as on other market players irrespective of their market power. Unlike under the previous regulatory framework, these obligations include specific conditions on digital television and radio broadcasting services.[79] In the exercise of its regulatory powers, AGCOM must comply with the principles of objectivity, transparency, proportionality and non-discrimination. All obligations are subject to consultation procedures.[80]

17.91   Unlike the previous regulatory framework, the CEC contains a definition of 'access' which is almost identical to that contained in the Access Directive.[81] The only difference is that the Access Directive refers to any 'undertaking', while the CEC mentions any 'operator' which is defined as an 'undertaking authorised to provide a public communications network or an associated facility'. Although an identical definition of operator is contained in the Access Directive, the latter does not include such term in the definition of access. This difference entails interpretation issues because a literal reading of the definition of 'operator' could lead to the conclusion that access and interconnection regulation applies only to undertakings authorised to provide electronic communications networks while omitting undertakings offering electronic communications services.

17.92   The new definition of 'access' under the CEC contains a sweeping change in the Italian telecommunications law because it includes elements which were not included in the previous concept of access, such as access to conditional access systems for digital television services, access to physical infrastructures including buildings, ducts and masts, as well as access to private virtual network services.

17.93   'Interconnection' is defined almost in the same terms as in the Access Directive,[82] again with the difference based on the expression 'operator' (used by the CEC) as opposed to 'undertaking' (used by the Access Directive).

17.94   The principle of freedom of access as set out in article 3(1) Access Directive has been reproduced almost verbatim in the CEC.[83]

17.95   The principle that commercial negotiations take priority over regulatory intervention is set out in a number of provisions contained in the CEC,[84] which mirror article 3(1) as well as article 5(4) Access Directive. The CEC also regulates

---

78   Art 42 CEC.
79   See para 17.103 below.
80   Arts 11 and 12 CEC.
81   Art 1(1)(b) CEC.
82   Art 1(1)(m) CEC.
83   Art 40 CEC.
84   Arts 40, 41 and 42(5) CEC.

the confidentiality obligations applicable to access and interconnection agreement negotiations. The relevant provision[85] is identical to that set out in article 4(3) Access Directive.

Access- and Interconnection-related Obligations with Respect to SMP Undertakings

Overview

17.96   If an undertaking has been designated as having SMP in a specific market, AGCOM must, at its discretion, impose one of the obligations detailed under the following subheadings. Obligations imposed as indicated under these subheadings shall be based on the nature of the issues investigated, and they must be proportionate and justified in the light of the objectives laid down in article 13 CEC.[86]

Transparency obligations

Transparency obligations are regulated in the same manner as under article 9 Access Directive.[87]

Non-discrimination obligations

Non-discrimination obligations correspond to those contained in article 10 Access Directive.[88] The relevant provision of the Access Directive, however, refers to equivalent conditions to be applied to *'other undertakings'* while the corresponding rule of the CEC refers to *'other operators'* (the latter being a more restricted definition than the former).[89]

Specific access obligations

The CEC specifies the obligations for SMP operators regarding reasonable requests for access to, and use of, specific network elements and associated facilities.[90] The relevant provision is almost identical to article 12 Access Directive. The Italian text, however, slightly differs from the European rule with respect to some of the specific obligations. In particular, article 49 CEC refers to obligations to grant 'operators' access to specified network elements and facilities including local loop unbundling; and to negotiate in good faith with operators requesting access (as opposed to 'third parties' included in the corresponding European provision).

Also, the Italian text refers to an obligation to grant open access to technical interfaces, protocols and other technologies that are of the essence for the interoperability of services or virtual network services.

---

85   Art 41(3) CEC.
86   Art 45 CEC.
87   Art 46 CEC.
88   Art 47 CEC.
89   See para 17.91 above.
90   Art 49 CEC.

Price control obligations

The CEC contains certain obligations relating to cost recovery and price controls which correspond exactly to those set out in article 13 Access Directive.[91] In determining cost-oriented prices, AGCOM must take into account the investment made by the operator and allow a reasonable rate of return on the capital invested, taking into account the risks involved and the investments related to the development of innovative networks and services. This particular element – which is not contained in the corresponding provision of the Access Directive – seems to constitute an additional incentive for operators to invest in advanced infrastructures and technologies, such as broadband.

Accounting separation obligations

The CEC implements verbatim article 11 Access Directive.[92]

Obligations imposed on SMP operators in specific markets

17.97   Obligations related to access and interconnection in specific markets are contained in various sections of the CEC as well as in AGCOM resolutions which will be valid until completion of the analysis of the relevant markets to be carried out in accordance with article 19 CEC.[93] In particular, these obligations include the grant of reasonable access, non-discrimination, transparency, accounting separation and cost orientation on Telecom Italia, Wind Telecomunicazioni, and the licensed mobile operators Telecom Italia Mobile and Vodafone Omnitel in different markets.[94] Furthermore, legislative measures have been imposed on Telecom Italia and the two above-mentioned mobile operators to govern obligations related to the fixed-to-mobile calls market. AGCOM has fixed the maximum price that Telecom Italia – as SMP operator in the market of fixed telephony networks – may charge its customers for calls to be terminated on mobile networks (so-called 'retention charge') as well as the maximum price that Telecom Italia Mobile and Vodafone Omnitel – as SMP operators in the Italian markets of public mobile communications and interconnection – may charge for the termination of calls on their networks (so-called 'termination charge').[95]

17.98   AGCOM is in the process of completing the public consultations aimed at establishing whether or not, with respect to fixed operators, the new regime could result in a confirmation of interconnection, leased lines, and wholesale broadband access obligations upon Telecom Italia,[96] and in the imposition of transparency and

---

91   Art 50 CEC.
92   Art 48 CEC.
93   See para 17.28 above. The rule mirrors art 27(2) Framework Directive.
94   See paras 17.29–17.31 above.
95   AGCOM Resolution no 47/03/CONS fixed the 'retention' charge at €0.0485 per minute and the 'termination' charge at €0.1495 per minute. These charges have been applied since 1 June 2003.
96   Pursuant to AGCOM Resolution no 30/05/CONS, no operators were identified as having dominant position in the market of termination of Internet traffic. Should this finding be confirmed, AGCOM will revoke the obligations currently imposed on Wind Telecomunicazioni as an SMP operator in the wholesale interconnection market for Internet call termination.

non-discrimination obligations on each fixed network operator in relation to voice call termination on its respective fixed network.[97]

17.99   With respect to mobile operators, the public consultation procedure could result in the confirmation of interconnection obligations on Telecom Italia Mobile and Vodafone Omnitel as well as in the extension of regulatory obligations on Wind Telecomunicazioni and H3G in relation to voice call termination on their respective mobile networks.[98]

Related Regulatory Powers with Respect to SMP Undertakings

17.100   AGCOM is empowered to impose obligations for the provision of part or all of the minimum set of leased lines on undertakings notified as having SMP in the relevant market.

17.101   The CEC sets out carrier selection and carrier pre-selection obligations corresponding to those contained in article 19 Universal Service Directive.[99]

Regulatory Powers Applicable to All Market Participants

Obligations to ensure end-to-end connectivity

17.102   End-to-end connectivity obligations are set out in the CEC. These apply to all market players along the same lines as those contained in article 5(1)(a) Access Directive.[100] Such obligation can be imposed by AGCOM in order to encourage and, where appropriate, ensure adequate access and interconnection, and interoperability of services so as to promote efficiency, sustainable competition, and give the maximum benefit to end-users.

Access to digital radio and television broadcasting services

17.103   In addition to the 'traditional telecommunications' interconnection services, article 42 CEC also regulates access to digital radio and television broadcasting services. These obligations correspond to those set out in article 5(1)(b) Access Directive. Article 42 should be read in conjunction with article 43(1) and Annex 2, Part I, to the CEC, on conditional access systems, which reproduce article 6 Access Directive. Unlike the Access Directive, however, the CEC does expressly provide for the possibility to modify the list of conditions as set out in Annex 2, Part I, to the CEC.

---

97   Pursuant to AGCOM Resolution no 30/05/CONS, AGCOM proposed the identification of one relevant market for each fixed network and the identification of each fixed network operator as SMP operator in the identified markets.

98   Under AGCOM Resolution no 465/04/CONS, AGCOM proposed the identification of a relevant market for each mobile network for calls originated from both mobile and fixed networks and regardless of the technology used by the mobile operator (whether GSM or UMTS). AGCOM also proposed the identification of the four mobile operators currently active on the Italian mobile market (TIM, Wind, Vodafone and H3G) as SMP operators in the identified markets.

99   Art 69 CEC.

100   Art 42 CEC.

17.104   Nonetheless, AGCOM is to encourage providers of digital interactive television services and providers of enhanced digital television equipment to use and comply with Application Program Interfaces (APIs).[101]

Transitional provisions

17.105   The CEC contains a transitional provision on access and interconnection that reproduces almost verbatim article 7 Access Directive.[102]

REGULATION OF UNIVERSAL SERVICES AND USERS' RIGHTS: THE UNIVERSAL SERVICE DIRECTIVE

Regulation of Universal Service Obligations

Scope of universal service obligations

17.106   In line with article 3(1) Universal Service Directive, article 53 CEC requires that those services falling within the definition of universal service[103] be made available to all end-users on the Italian territory, at a specified quality, independent of the end-users' geographical location. AGCOM must establish the most effective and appropriate method to guarantee the provision of universal service at an affordable price.

17.107   The catalogue of universal services (which is largely the same as that established under the previous rules contained in article 3 of Presidential Decree no 318/97) follows the list set out in the Universal Service Directive with certain exceptions, as outlined below:

- In order to establish the type of 'connection at a fixed location to the public telephone network' to be provided by operators,[104] the CEC does not require 'taking into account prevailing technologies used by the majority of subscribers and technological feasibility' (differently from what is required by article 4(2) Universal Service Directive). This may be interpreted as a manner of maintaining the scope of 'fixed connection' as broad as possible in order to include (in the near future) broadband internet access within the universal service catalogue.
- The provision of at least one comprehensive directory to be provided to any end-user is limited to the urban network to which the end-user belongs.[105] It is worth noting that each operator must make all its directories (including directories of pre-paid mobile users as these are identified at the time of the first purchase) available to the Ministry of Internal Affairs so that judicial authorities may access the relevant data for investigation purposes.
- The provision of comprehensive telephone directory enquiry services falls

---

101   Art 21 CEC.
102   Art 70 CEC.
103   Mirroring the definition contained in art 2(j) Framework Directive, art 1(ll) CEC defines 'universal service' as a 'minimum set of services, of a specified quality, which is available to all users [not only end-users] regardless of their geographical location and offered, in the light of the specific national conditions, at an affordable price'.
104   See arts 54(1) and 54(2) CEC.
105   See art 55(1)(a) CEC.

outside the scope of the universal service because there are 'various offers in terms of availability, quality and affordable price' on the relevant market.[106] The Ministry may apply universal service obligations to directory enquiry services if in the future it will assess that said market conditions are no longer satisfied.

- The provision of public pay telephones may be excluded by decree of the Ministry in those locations where – after consultation with the interested parties – it is assessed that these facilities or comparable services are widely available.[107]

17.108   The catalogue no longer includes 'links and services for the general public interest, with specific reference to public security, public aid, national defence, justice, education and government' which were considered as part of the universal service obligations under the previous regime.[108]

17.109   The list of obligations falling within the universal service is inclusive. However, under article 65 CEC, the Ministry, after having consulted AGCOM, must review the scope of universal service on a periodical basis. Such review should have been carried out for the first time within one year after the entry into force of the CEC (ie by 16 September 2004) and every two years thereafter. The CEC contains no express reference to the 'twin test' set out in Annex V Universal Service Directive. Nonetheless, this test seems to be a mandatory reference in any event because the CEC requires the Ministry to review the universal service obligations on the basis, inter alia, of the guidelines of the European Commission.[109]

17.110   Also, the Ministry – after consultation with the so-called *Conferenza Unificata*[110] – may decide to make additional services publicly available on a mandatory basis, but outside the scope of the universal service. This means that the relevant costs may not be subject to sharing or compensation mechanisms such as the universal service fund.[111] Such decision on new mandatory services will likely need to be coordinated with the above-mentioned periodical review process.

Designation of undertakings obliged to provide universal services

17.111   The procedure for the designation of undertakings in charge of the universal service must be established by AGCOM according to principles, inter alia, of efficiency, objectivity, transparency and non-discrimination.[112] The procedure must not only ensure that the universal service is provided in a cost-effective manner, but it must also be capable of being used as a means to determine the net cost of universal service.

17.112   Until such designation is made, Telecom Italia continues to be the only universal service provider in the entire Italian territory.

---

106   See art 55(3) CEC.
107   See art 56(2) CEC.
108   This was set out in art 3(1)(f) Presidential Decree no 318/97.
109   See art 65 CEC.
110   This is a public body created by Legislative Decree no 281/97 with the mission to foster the cooperation between the State and local entities in all those matters where they share a common interest.
111   See para 17.120 below.
112   See art 58 CEC which mirrors almost verbatim art 8 Universal Service Directive.

Regulation of retail tariffs, users' expenditures and quality of service

17.113   AGCOM must monitor the evolution and level of retail tariffs for those services which fall within the scope of the universal service. The relevant provision of the CEC[113] captures the wording of the entire article 9 Universal Service Directive except for the third paragraph whereby member states may – besides any provision for designated undertakings to provide special tariff options or to comply with price caps, geographical averaging or other similar schemes – ensure that support be provided to consumers with low income or special social needs.

17.114   The reverse side of the affordability of tariffs is the possibility for subscribers to control their expenditures and avoid unwarranted disconnection of services in case of non-payment. To this end, article 10 Universal Service Directive has been imported into the CEC,[114] thus requiring designated undertakings to provide:

- itemised billing,
- selective call barring (free of charge for outgoing calls),
- pre-payment systems for the provision of access to the public telephone network and the use of publicly available telephone services, and
- phased payment of connection fees.

17.115   Also, the designated undertakings must satisfy certain (eg warning) obligations before disconnecting the services in the case of non-payment of bills.

17.116   One of the elements that characterises universal service obligations is the 'specified quality'. For this reason, AGCOM must not only obtain and publish information concerning the undertakings' performance in the provision of universal service,[115] but it must also set performance targets to be met by undertakings with universal service obligations.[116] As under the Universal Service Directive, AGCOM may adopt 'specific measures' in case of persistent failure by such undertakings to meet performance targets. These specific measures may go as far as prohibiting an undertaking from providing all or part of its networks or services.

Cost calculation and financing of universal services

17.117   If AGCOM considers that the provision of universal service may present an 'unfair burden' for the designated undertaking(s), then it must calculate the net cost of such provision so that this may be shared among operators.

17.118   The calculation is based on avoidable long-run incremental costs and revenues incurred and generated, respectively, in serving customers/areas (or providing services) that are 'non viable'[117] plus a reasonable return on the incremental

---

113   See art 59 CEC.
114   See art 60 CEC.
115   AGCOM must also specify the content, form and manner for such publication (see art 61(3) CEC).
116   In this respect, art 61(4) CEC somewhat tightens the corresponding provision of art 11(4) Universal Service Directive in that, under the latter, NRAs *'shall be able to* set performance targets' (emphasis added).
117   Under art 1 of Exhibit 11 to the CEC, a non-viable customer/area is a customer/area that would not be served if the undertaking was not subject to universal service obligations. Likewise, a non-viable service is a service whose incremental cost of provision is higher than the incremental revenue stemming thereof.

capital invested for the provision of the universal service. Additional elements – such as branding recognition, possibility to apply economies of scale, benefits stemming from the transformation of non-viable customers/areas into viable ones, the availability of market information, etc – must be taken into account in calculating the net cost. AGCOM must appoint an independent body to verify the calculation. The independent body's fees are included in the net cost of the universal service.

17.119   The net cost must be shared among undertakings that operate public communications networks, provide publicly available telephone services (in proportion to their usage of public communications networks) and/or provide mobile and personal communications services in the Italian territory. Undertakings that provide private communications networks, telephone services to closed user groups, data transmission, value added services (such as video conference or telephone banking), and internet access are not required to share such net cost. Furthermore, each year AGCOM may exempt from the cost sharing all those 'undertakings that do not exceed certain turnover thresholds and those that are new entrants, taking into account their financial situation and the competitive conditions of the market'.[118] The CEC does not contain a definition of new entrant, but since 1999 AGCOM has consistently applied a 1%-net-revenue threshold (on the total net revenues) to allow undertakings to benefit from the exemption.

17.120   Undertakings designated to provide the universal service may obtain reimbursement of the eligible net cost by drawing from a specific fund administered by the Ministry and funded from the contributions of the above-mentioned operators.

17.121   The amount of the contribution owed by each operator is based on a mathematical formula described in Exhibit 11 to the CEC which in essence takes into consideration the percentage of the costs and revenues of each operator required to contribute over the total costs and revenues of the other operators.[119]

Regulation of Retail Markets

Prerequisites for the regulation of retail markets

17.122   The CEC reproduces articles 16 and 17 Universal Service Directive on the re-examination of existing obligations related to retail tariffs for access services and the use of the public telephone network, leased lines and carrier selection and pre-selection services.[120]

17.123   Accordingly, the regulation of retail services is permissible if regulation at the wholesale level does not achieve the competition and regulatory objectives established by the Italian legislature. Regulatory measures will only be imposed at the retail market level on SMP undertakings. Currently, Telecom Italia is the only operator identified as having SMP on retail markets.

---

118   See art 63(3) CEC.
119   Pursuant to AGCOM Resolution no 16/04/CIR of 23 December 2004, the universal service net cost for the year 2002 that is eligible for funding is equal to €37.22 million. This is to be shared among Telecom Italia (35.4%), Telecom Italia Mobile (31.4%), Vodafone Omnitel (22.8%), and Wind Telecomunicazioni (10.4%).
120   Arts 66 and 67 CEC.

Regulatory Powers

17.124   In line with article 17(2) Universal Service Directive, AGCOM has a broad discretion in the application of regulatory measures in retail markets.[121]The non-inclusive list of tariff obligations which may be imposed on SMP undertakings in a given retail market, as set out in article 17(2) Universal Directive, has been adopted almost verbatim in the CEC. Slight differences exist as regards the conditions under which AGCOM may apply such measures. In fact, whereas the EU allows the application of such tariff measures 'in order to protect end-users' interests whilst promoting effective competition', article 67(2) CEC expressly states that tariff obligations are permitted if measures related to wholesale carrier selection or pre-selection services are not able to ensure effective competition and the public interest. The list of tariff regulations includes the application of appropriate retail price cap measures which currently apply to the retail voice telephony services offered by Telecom Italia.[122]

17.125   The provisions allowing for end-user tariff regulation are complemented by mandatory rules[123] regarding the implementation of cost accounting systems, as required by article 17(4) Universal Service Directive.

17.126   As to the regulatory control on the minimum set of leased lines, the CEC accurately reproduces article 18 Universal Service Directive.

End User Rights

Contracts

17.127   The CEC implements the principles set out in article 20 Universal Service Directive requiring that 'consumers[124] who subscribe to services which provide connection or access to the public telephone network have the right to enter into contracts with the relevant undertakings'.[125] These contracts must contain the same minimum information and details as those required under article 20(2) Universal Service Directive. While the obligation to enter into contracts applies to both fixed and mobile operators,[126] it does not seem to apply to traffic resellers, voice service providers through credit/debit cards or internet service providers to the extent that they do not provide said connection or access.[127] However, should these undertakings enter into contract with consumers,[128] then the relevant agreements would have to contain the same minimum information and details as those indicated above.

---

121   Art 67(2) CEC.

122   See AGCOM Resolution no 289/03/CONS of 23 July 2003.

123   See AGCOM Resolution no 152/02/CONS of 17 June 2002 and art 67(4) CEC.

124   'Consumer' is defined as an 'individual who utilises a publicly available electronic communi-cation service for purposes outside his/her business, trade or professional activity' (art 1(j) CEC).

125   See art 70 CEC.

126   This is due to the definitions of 'public telephone network' and 'publicly available telephone service' set out by art 1(bb) and (hh) CEC.

127   See W. Maxwell, *Electronic Communications: The New EU Framework*, Oceana Publica-tions Inc., 2002, 1.4.25.

128   Under art 70(3) CEC, electronic communication service providers other than those providing connections and/or access to the public telephone network do not seem to be under an obligation to enter into contracts with consumers.

17.128   AGCOM may also extend the applicability of such provisions to other end-users. In some instances, such an extension seems to have been made by AGCOM even before the CEC came into force.[129] The contractual terms and conditions may be changed only according to the same rules as those set out by article 20(4) Universal Service Directive.[130]

Transparency obligations

17.129   In terms of transparency and publication of information as well as quality of service, the CEC affords the same protection as that granted by articles 21 and 22 Universal Service Directive.[131]As to the quality of service, however, this is treated in the CEC as a parameter whose publication (in a complete, comparable and user-friendly manner) is designed to help end-users to exercise their right to choose. On the other hand, when quality is addressed within the context of universal service obligations,[132] it also becomes a technical specification to be met by universal service providers in compliance with those quality levels that may have been previously established by AGCOM.

17.130   The quality of services has been specifically regulated by AGCOM Resolution no 179/03/CSP of 24 July 2003. Under articles 10(2) and 3(8) of the Resolution, quality of service indicators and relevant general and specific standards must be reported in the so-called 'charter of services'. This is a manifesto that each operator must publish and whose mandatory nature has been established by the Directive of the Prime Minister of 27 January 1994[133] and then confirmed by, inter alia, Law no 481 of 14 November 1995.[134] The charter of services must be updated annually to ensure constant improvement of effectiveness and efficiency of services.

Other obligations

17.131   The regulatory measures concerning the integrity of the network, operator assistance and directory enquiry services, the European emergency call number ('112'), the European standard international access code ('00'), non-geographic numbers, additional facilities (tone dialling or DTMF and calling line identification) and number portability are the same as those set out in articles 23–30 Universal Service Directive.[135] VoIP operators could be obliged to offer emergency services free of charge, particularly if they qualify as operators offering publicly available telephone services.

---

129 See AGCOM Resolution no 179/03/CSP of 24 July 2003 in the context of the quality of service regulation.

130 See art 70(4) CEC.

131 See arts 71 and 72 CEC.

132 See art 61 CEC.

133 The 1994 Prime Minister Directive has established that all public services (such as electronic communications services) must be rendered according to principles of non discrimination, impartiality, efficiency, effectiveness, continuity, right to choose and right to participate in the decision making process. As to the quality and charter of services in the voice telephony sector, see AGCOM Resolution no 254/04/CSP of 10 November 2004.

134 Law no 481/95 is aimed at guaranteeing appropriate quality levels for all public interest services, ensuring their availability and diffusion in a homogeneous manner throughout the Italian territory, thus promoting the protection of users' and consumers' interests.

135 See arts 73 and 75–80 CEC.

17.132   With particular reference to number portability, the regulation in principle of such a facility had been introduced in Italy since 1997[136] and it has been extended to the mobile sector in 1998 and 1999, in connection with the public tenders for the award of the third and fourth GSM/DCS 1800 licences in Italy.[137] Since 2001, it has been clarified that mobile number portability must be available to all mobile service users, including pre-paid users, provided the latter can prove legitimate possession of the SIM card.[138]

Transitional Provisions

17.133   AGCOM must determine whether or not to maintain, amend or withdraw existing obligations relating to retail markets by carrying out market analysis pursuant to article 19 CEC.[139] The measures to be adopted by AGCOM further to such market analysis are subject to the consolidation procedure set out under the CEC.[140] Until the market analysis is carried out and the measures to be taken determined, AGCOM must maintain the existing obligations relating to the following:

- retail tariffs for the provision of access services and use of the public telephone network,
- carrier selection or pre-selection, and
- leased lines.

DATA PROTECTION: IMPLEMENTATION OF THE E-PRIVACY DIRECTIVE

Overview

17.134   The E-Privacy Directive has been implemented in Italy by the Privacy Act, which deals with the regulation of publicly available electronic communication services and networks.

Confidentiality of Communications

17.135   Electronic communications networks must not be used to obtain access to information stored in users' terminal equipment (eg by way of 'spyware', 'web bug' or 'cookies'), to store information or to monitor users' activities without first providing clear and comprehensive information regarding the intention and purpose of processing and storage.

---

136   See art 11(8) of Presidential Decree no 318/97.
137   See art 11(2) Resolution of the Prime Minister of 4 April 1998 and art 12(1) AGCOM Resolution no 69/99 of 9 June 1999. Specific rules for the introduction of this facility have been enacted, *inter alia*, by AGCOM Resolutions no 12/01/CIR of 7 June 2001, no 19/01/CIR of 7 August 2001, no 22/01/CIR of 10 October 2001, no 7/02/CIR of 28 March 2002, no 13/02/CIR of 28 November 2002, and no 9/03/CIR of 3 July 2003.
138   See art 9(5) AGCOM Resolution no 19/01/CIR of 7 August 2001.
139   See art 66 CEC and para 17.26 above.
140   See art 12 CEC and para 17.18 above.

Such activities may be carried out only for the time that is strictly necessary for the conveyance of the communication or, in the case of specific services explicitly requested by users or subscribers, with their express consent.[141]

17.136 Operators providing publicly available electronic communications services must inform subscribers and, if possible, users of situations which unintentionally may allow third parties to access the content of communications or conversations. Subscribers must inform users when third parties may have access to the content of communications or conversations due to the terminal equipment or transmission links used at subscribers' premises. Users must inform the other users when equipment used during the conversation allows third parties to hear the conversation.[142]

Traffic Data and Location Data

17.137 The definitions of 'traffic data' and 'location data' are identical to those in the E-Privacy Directive. Service providers must inform subscribers of the types of data processed and the duration of such processing.[143]

17.138 Storage of traffic data for invoicing or interconnection purposes is allowed for a maximum period of six months, although storage is permitted for longer periods in the case of litigation.[144] In addition, providers must store traffic data for 24 months for law enforcement purposes. After expiration of this period, providers must store traffic data for an additional 24 months only for law enforcement purposes against terrorism, organised crime as well as crimes against computer or telecommunications systems.[145]

17.139 Location data may be processed if it has been made anonymous and the user's consent has been obtained to the extent and for the duration necessary for the provision only of value added services. The consent may be withdrawn at any time. To obtain consent, the service providers must inform users and subscribers about the nature of location data subject to processing, the purposes and duration of such processing as well as the possibility that such data may be transferred to third parties for the provision of the value added service.[146]

Itemised Billing

17.140 Users have the right to obtain, free of charge, itemised bills from service providers. When invoicing subscribers, service providers must cancel the last three digits of the called numbers from the bills, unless subscribers request such three digits to appear for claims against specific bills and for limited periods of time.

17.141 Service providers must allow users to communicate and request services from any terminal equipment, using payment means alternative to billing, such as credit, debit or pre-paid cards.[147]

---

141 Art 122 Privacy Act.
142 Art 131 Privacy Act.
143 Art 123(4) Privacy Act.
144 Art 123(2) Privacy Act.
145 Art 132(1) and (2) Privacy Act.
146 Art 126 Privacy Act.
147 Art 124 Privacy Act.

Calling and Connected Line Identification

17.142   If calling line identification services are available, service providers must allow calling users and subscribers to withhold their numbers on a per-call and (in case of subscribers) per-line basis, through simple means and free of charge. Called subscribers must also have the possibility to block the numbers of incoming calls and to reject incoming calls automatically in cases where the caller has withheld the caller identification.

Automatic Call Forwarding

17.143   Service providers must adopt the necessary measures to allow users, to whom calls have been automatically forwarded as a result of third party actions, to request that these be stopped without charge and with simple means.[148]

Directories of Subscribers

17.144   The Italian Data Protection Authority, in cooperation with AGCOM, sets out the modalities for inclusion and use of subscribers' personal data in paper and electronic directories, also with reference to data already processed prior to the entry into force of the Privacy Act.

17.145   The Data Protection Authority, in cooperation with AGCOM, also sets out the modalities for subscribers' consent to the inclusion of their personal data in such directories, based on criteria of maximum simplification, and subscribers' right to verify, modify and cancel such data free of charge.[149]

Unsolicited Communications

17.146   The use of automatic calling systems for advertising, direct marketing, market polls or commercial communications is allowed only upon the user's consent. This provision applies also to email messages, faxes, short messages, multimedia messaging and any other electronic communications with the above-mentioned purposes.

17.147   If the data processor uses the email accounts of its customers for direct marketing purposes, it does not need to request consent for such direct marketing communications, provided that the marketed services or products are similar to those already sold and that the users/customers, adequately informed, do not refuse to receive such communications.[150]

---

148   Art 128 Privacy Act.
149   Art 129 Privacy Act.
150   Art 120 Privacy Act.

The Latvian Market for Electronic Communications[1]

Sanda Lace and Martins Gailis
Klavins & Slaidins, Riga, Latvia

LEGAL STRUCTURE

Basic Policy

18.1   As of 1 January 2003, a number of telecommunications service markets were opened to competition. After liberalisation of the Latvian telecommunications market the indices grew rapidly. Within six months of the market being opened to competition, the market share held by new participants in the market of leased lines services comprised approximately 23%. By the end of 2003, the Public Utilities Regulation Commission ('PURC') had issued 183 individual licences and registered 26 general authorisations.

18.2   In order to ensure unified regulation in the field of electronic communications, creating open and transparent relations, the regulatory approach is to achieve mutual cooperation between the PURC, the Ministry of Transport and Communications, the Competition Council, the Consumer Rights Protection Centre and the Electronic Communications Agency.

18.3   The PURC participates in the drafting of primary acts and regulations in the field of electronic communications, leaving the drafting and adoption of secondary acts and regulations to the Cabinet of Ministers and other subordinated state administration institutions.

18.4   The major service provider in the field of fixed telecommunications in Latvia, in terms of turnover and number of clients, is still SIA Lattelekom ('LTM'), the former monopoly company. In the market of mobile telecommunications services, SIA LMT and SIA Tele2 still hold dominant positions, being the largest mobile telecommunications network operators.

---

1   Editing of this chapter closed on 11 July 2005.

Implementation of EU Directives

18.5 Latvia has transposed all Directives of the 2002 EU Regulatory Package into the Electronic Communications Act ('2004 Act'),[2] and it is also continuing to harmonise existing Latvian acts and regulations with the requirements of the EU Directives.

Legislation

18.6 Latvian telecommunications-related acts and regulations consist of the acts, Regulations of the Cabinet of Ministers, regulations and decisions issued by the PURC and acts issued by other state authorities with respect to any particular field in the market of telecommunications services.

The most significant legal acts in the telecommunication sector as adopted by the Parliament of Latvia are: the 2004 Act; the Law on Regulators of Public Utilities;[3] and the Radio and Television Law.[4] The Cabinet of Ministers has adopted, inter alia, Regulations No 44, On the Procedures for Issuance of Permits for Use of Spectrum of Radio Frequencies[5] and Regulations No 496, On Installation and Construction of Telecommunication Networks.[6] The PURC has also adopted numerous legal acts applicable to participants in the telecommunications sector, including: Regulations regarding the procedure for submission of applications for the right to use radio frequency spectrum and numeration resources for the purpose of commercial activity,[7] Regulations of Universal Service in the Electronic Communications Sector,[8] On Special Requirements for Telecommunications Companies with Significant Market Power,[9] Regulations for General Permit,[10] and others.[11]

REGULATORY PRINCIPLES: IMPLEMENTATION OF THE FRAMEWORK DIRECTIVE

Scope of Regulation

18.7 The Latvian legislation has adopted the technology-neutral approach of the EU Directives. The definitions of 'electronic communications networks' and 'electronic communications are identical to those in the Framework Directive.

---

2   Electronic Communications Act, adopted on 28 October 2004 by Latvian Parliament, Vestnesis, 17.11.2004, Nr.183.
3   Adopted on 19 October 2000, Latvijas Vestnesis, 21.12.2004, Nr.203.
4   Adopted on 24 August 1995, Latvijas Vestnesis, 08.09.1995, Nr. 137.
5   Issued on 21 January 2003, Latvijas Vestnesis, 24.01.2003, Nr.13.
6   Issued on 4 November 2002 Latvijas Vestnesis, 08.11.2002, Nr. 163.
7   Adopted on 24 February 2005, Latvijas Vestnesis, 10.03.2005, Nr. 41.
8   Adopted on 1 December 2004, Latvijas Vestnesis, 03.12.2004, Nr. 192.
9   Adopted on 3 December 2002, Latvijas Vestnesis, 13.12.2002, Nr. 183.
10   Adopted on 25 May 2005, Latvijas Vestnesis, 08.06.2005, Nr. 90.
11   Regulations regarding the procedure for sending of notices on registration of electronic communications undertakings (Adopted on 16.02.2005, Latvijas Vestnesis, 03.03.2005, Nr. 37), On Methods of Determination and Calculation of Net Costs of Telecommunications Service (Adopted on 4 February 2004, Latvijas Vestnesis, 12.02.2004, Nr. 23), Methods of Calculation of Telecommunication Service Fees (Adopted on 26 July 2002, Latvijas Vestnesis, 03.09.2002, Nr. 124), Regulations regarding introduction of number retention service (Adopted on 11 March 2005, Latvijas Vestnesis, 17.03.2005, Nr. 45) e.o.

'Associated facilities' are defined as 'facilities and equipment associated with an electronic communications network or an electronic communications service which enable or support the provision of services by assistance of that electronic communications network or electronic communications service (including conditional access systems and electronic program guides)'.

National Regulatory Authorities: Organisation, Regulatory Objectives, Competences

18.8   The State administrative body in the field of electronic communications is the Ministry of Transport ('the Ministry').

The technical authority in the field of electronic communications is exercised by the Electronic Communications Agency ('the Agency'). According to the 2004 Act and the Public Utilities Regulators Act the electronic communications sector is regulated by the PURC. Data protection in the electronic communications sector is supervised by the Data State Inspection ('the Inspection').

18.9   The PURC has many different tasks assigned by the 2004 Act which could more generally be classified as regulation of the electronic communications market. These tasks are to promote the development of the electronic communications market, supervise and ensure compliance with the legislation, and promote competition in the sector so that undertakings providing electronic communications networks are treated equally to undertakings offering electronic communications services. The PURC also makes decisions and issues administrative acts that are binding upon undertakings and consumers of electronic communications.

18.10   While the PURC deals with market regulation, the Agency deals with the technical regulation of electronic communications networks. The main objectives of the Agency are to supervise the limited resources in practice, to make quality measurements of the electronic communications networks and services, and to issue the relevant administrative acts.[12]

18.11   The PURC has the primary role in matters involving questions of competition in the electronic communications sector.[13] In order to achieve open and transparent regulation, the PURC has to cooperate with the Competition Council in matters involving competition. This cooperation, however, has not been expressly defined in the 2004 Act or any other normative act thus far. The two instances are independent from each other.

18.12   The powers vested in and the duties imposed on the PURC and the Agency are consistent with the requirements of the Framework Directive.[14] The relevant powers and duties are also generally in compliance with the requirements set out in article 3 Framework Directive,[15] except for lack of legal framework for cooperation on matters involving questions of competition.

18.13   The PURC has a duty to secure transparency of its actions by making public its yearly reviews, and compiling and publishing information on the electronic communications sector. Such information and reviews are regularly published and are available on the PURC's website. Information on regulation in the

---

12   Art 6 2004 Act.
13   Electronic Communications sector policy guidelines for 2004–2008, adopted by decree of the Cabinet of Ministers Nr 154 on 09.03.2004, Latvijas Vestnesis 11.03.2004, Nr. 39.
14   See para 1.53 above.
15   See paras 1.54 and 1.55 above.

electronic communications sector can also be found on the Ministry's website. The cooperation requirement (with other domestic and foreign institutions as well as with EU institutions) is also expressly stated in Article 8 of the 2004 Act but in rather general terms.

On 30 March 2005, the PURC adopted Regulations on Consultation Procedure with Participants of the Market, implementing into Latvian law the provisions of Article 6 Framework Directive. According to the Regulations, the PURC drafts a consultation document and publishes it in the official magazine '*Latvijas Vestnesis*' and places a copy on the PURC website, and afterwards considers proposals lodged by the market participants.

18.14   Having explicit competence to regulate dispute resolution the PURC has issued Regulations on Dispute Resolution Procedures in the Electronic Communications Sector.[16] These include rules on dispute resolution between electronic communications undertakings as well as rules on dispute resolution between undertakings and consumers in the electronic communications sector. Any disputes between electronic communications undertakings and end-users shall be settled in accordance with the procedures set out in the agreement between the parties and the regulations on the use of services. In the event that the parties fail to agree, the PURC settles the dispute as the compulsory preliminary out-of-court authority. The PURC reviews disputes on the basis of written application. The decision of the PURC on settlement of a dispute can be appealed by the parties to the court within one month from the effective date thereof.[17] The PURC does not settle any disputes regarding debt collection.

Right of Appeal against NRA's Decisions

18.15   Decisions and administrative acts issued by the PURC and the Agency are subject to the appeal procedure in the Administrative Court. The 2004 Act does not directly state which persons have the right to appeal decisions and administrative acts issued by the PURC, whereas in accordance with the Latvian Administrative Procedure Law, persons against whom the administrative act is issued as well as third parties whose rights are infringed by the issued administrative act have the right of appeal. Appeals must be made in writing to the Administrative Court.[18]

The NRA's Obligations to Cooperate with the Commission

18.16   The consolidation procedure (article 7 Framework Directive) has not been directly or indirectly implemented in the Latvian telecommunications regulations.

'Significant Market Power' as a Fundamental Prerequisite of Regulation

Definition of SMP

18.17   Significant Market Power in the 2004 Act is defined as 'an undertaking's position in the market that is equivalent to dominance', if it individually or jointly

---

16   Adopted by the PURC decision No 208 on 11.08.2004.
17   11 August 2004 Regulations on Dispute Resolution Procedure in the Electronic Communications Sector.
18   Chapter 21 of Administrative Procedure Law, adopted by the Parliament of Latvia on 25 October 2001, Latvijas Vestnesis, 14.11.2001, Nr. 164.

with other electronic communications undertakings is in a position on this market which is equal to the dominant position, namely, in a position of economic power which allows it up to a certain point to act independently from the end users.[19]

18.18   The PURC determines the undertakings in the electronic communications sector that have significant market power.[20] In doing this, the PURC follows the Commission Guidelines on market analysis.[21] An undertaking can be deemed to have significant market power in closely related (associated) markets if the connection between those markets allows the undertaking to use its power in one market to strengthen its position in the related market.[22] These provisions are however quite general in their scope.[23]

Definition of relevant markets and SMP designation

18.19   The PURC in cooperation with the Competition Council, taking into consideration the Commission Recommendation on relevant markets and the geographical markets in the state territory, identifies the relevant markets. The PURC in cooperation with the Competition Council performs the analysis of the relevant market in accordance with the Commission Guidelines on market analysis. The PURC adopts decisions on the application, maintenance, amendment or cancellation of adequate and proportionate special obligations in respect of electronic communications undertakings, in accordance with its own procedures.

18.20   The PURC has so far identified three relevant markets in the telecommunications sector. These are:

- the fixed voice telephony services market,
- the leased line services market, and
- the interconnection services market.

In these markets, three undertakings have been found to have SMP. Based on the decision of the PURC,[24] LTM, the former incumbent, is recognised as having SMP in the market of fixed voice telephony services and leased line services in the territory of Latvia, while in the market of interconnection there are three companies – LTM, SIA LMT and SIA Tele2 – recognised as SMP undertakings.

18.21   If the PURC determines that there is no active competition in the market, it adopts a decision on the application of adequate and proportionate special obligations to the electronic communications undertakings.[25]

---

19   Art 29(2) 2004 Act.
20   Art 29(1) 2004 Act.
21   See paras1.74–1.78 above.
22   Art 29(3) 2004 Act.
23   The PURC on 16 May 2002 issued its own Regulations on Recognition of Telecommunications Undertakings with Significant Market Power; however, the Regulations were adopted prior the Electronic Communications Law and contain reference to the null and void law on Telecommunications. Since these Regulations follow the old assessment criteria, they are not applicable any more and until now there has been a certain vacuum in the detailed domestic regulations on determining whether undertakings have SMP.
24   Administrative decision Nr 136, adopted by the PURC on 27.11.2002.
25   Art 31(2) 2004 Act.

NRA's Regulatory Duties concerning Rights of Way, Co-location and Facility Sharing

18.22   According to Article 16 of the 2004 Act, public electronic communications network undertakings which provide or operate electronic communications networks have the right to install such networks on public, municipal and private property. In order to exercise this right the undertaking has to coordinate the project with the tenant. Article 18 of the 2004 Act states that a public electronic communications network operator has the right of use (servitude) to maintain and operate a public electronic communications network. The right of use is exercised by mutual agreement between the operator and the owner of the real estate. If the parties fail to agree, the dispute is reviewed by the court.

18.23   All undertakings, after pursuing activities of installation, exploitation or development of electronic communications networks, are under an obligation to repair any damages or unwarranted alterations caused to the property.

REGULATION OF MARKET ENTRY: IMPLEMENTATION OF THE AUTHORISATION DIRECTIVE

The General Authorisation of Electronic Communications

18.24   The PURC prepares and publishes a list of electronic communications services which are subject to the registration requirements of general authorisations.[26] Electronic communications undertakings are entitled to provide electronic communications networks or services, if they have sent the registration notification to the PURC.

18.25   General authorisations are applied to those service suppliers which do not need the allocation of limited national resources (e g numbers or radio frequencies) for the supply of telecommunication services.

18.26   In accordance with Article 34 of the 2004 Act, the provisions of the general authorisation may cover the following conditions in relation to:

- contribution to universal service financing,
- compatibility of services and network interconnections,
- terms of transmission of signals of radio or television programs whose broadcasting is mandatory,
- protection of user data,
- specific protection requirements for user rights,
- conditions for the use of systems in emergency cases,
- special requirements for SMP providers,
- public network integrity requirements,
- protection of networks against unauthorised access, and
- terms of use of the radio frequencies spectrum.

---

26   Art 32 2004 Act.

Rights of Use for Radio Frequencies

General authorisations and granting of individual rights

18.27   Natural or legal persons may apply for rights of use for radio frequencies.[27] Applications for rights of use for radio frequencies for commercial purposes shall be submitted to the PURC which issues a decision on the granting of rights of use. In cases where the Cabinet of Ministers has determined bands of radio frequencies whose use is limited, the PURC can organise an auction for rights of use of such radio frequencies.

Admissible conditions

18.28   The PURC may set the following specific terms and conditions for use of the radio frequencies spectrum:

- requirements in respect of services, networks or technologies,
- requirements in respect of efficient use of the radio frequencies spectrum and ensuring coverage,
- technical requirements in respect of assessing potentially harmful radio disturbances,
- the term of validity of the rights of use,
- the procedures for further transfer of the rights of use,
- the fee for the rights of use of the spectrum,
- obligations to be met if the rights of use are granted as a result of a tender or auction, and
- requirements resulting from international agreements on use of the radio frequencies spectrum.[28]

18.29   The radio frequency spectrum may be used for the operation of radio equipment after receipt of a radio frequency allotment permit from the Agency, or in accordance with the permit for use of joint use radio frequency allotment.

18.30   In accordance with the decision of the PURC dated 5 February 2003, no individual licences for the performance of commercial activity using 2.4 GHz range (except for inside premises) in the capital of Latvia, Riga, shall be issued until 31 December 2005.[29]

Limitation of number of rights of use to be granted

18.31   Article 47(5) 2004 Act delegates to the Cabinet of Ministers the right to define radio frequency spectrum bands, in which, for the purpose of efficient utilisation, it is necessary to limit granting of the rights to use radio frequency spectrum to businesses in the electronic communications sector. As at June 2005, such spectrum bands have still not been defined, and radio frequency spectrum bands are granted to persons on the basis of the National Radio Frequencies

---

27   Art 47(2) 2004 Act.
28   Art 47(7) 2004 Act.
29   This decision provides for the rearrangement of telecommunications networks working in the 2.4 GHz range for the work with Effective Isotropic Radiated Power (EIRP) not exceeding 100 mW during the transition period.

Allocation Plan[30] and the allocation of radio frequencies spectrum of the International Telecommunications Union (ITU) among radio communications types (services). However, the Cabinet of Ministers is currently reviewing the Draft Regulations Regarding Radio Frequency Spectrum Bands, in which, for the Purpose of Efficient Utilisation, it is Necessary to Limit Granting of the Rights to Use Radio Frequency Spectrum to Businesses in Electronic Communications Sector, and they presumably could be adopted by autumn 2005. According to these Draft Regulations,[31] particular bands would be defined, which are commercially favourable for provision of electronic services and the performance of large-scale business activity. The 410.0–420.0 MHz/420.0–430.0 MHz; 450.0–457.5 MHz/460.0–467.5 MHz; 880.0–890.0 MHz/925.0–935.0 MHz radio frequency bands can be mentioned as some examples of radio frequency bands in which the granting of the rights to use the radio frequency spectrum will be limited to businesses in the electronic communications sector. The Draft also stipulates that the 3600.0–3800.0 MHz radio frequency band, starting from 1 January 2008, is meant for the operation of the UMTS/IMT-2000 system.

In these bands the PURC will organise a tender or auction proceedings in a transparent manner and will grant the rights to use radio frequency spectrum to the winner of the tender or auction, respectively.[32]

Rights of Use for Numbers

18.32 Numbering resources are granted, reserved, annulled or withdrawn from circulation by the PURC. The procedures under which the PURC shall perform these activities are set out in the regulations of the Republic of Latvia Cabinet of Ministers.[33] The Cabinet of Ministers also approves the national numbering plan.

18.33 If the existing numbering resources are insufficient, the Cabinet of Ministers can adopt a decision on transition to the closed 'eight digit' numbering scheme, in accordance with the transition plan approved by the PURC and previously coordinated with market participants.

18.34 The right to use of numbers or number series is granted, based on an application to the PURC by a supplier of electronic communications services.

18.35 The PURC may determine specific terms and conditions in respect of the rights of use for numbers, including:

- requirements in respect of the services for supply of which the rights of use for numbers are granted,
- requirements in respect of services for the efficient use of numbering resources,
- ensuring availability of a list of subscribers,
- the maximum term of duration of the rights of use,
- the procedures for further transfer of the rights of use,
- terms in respect of payment for the rights of use,
- obligations to be met if the rights of use are granted as a result of tender or auction, and

---

30   Approved by Order No.40 of the Ministry of Communications, dated 25 February 2004.
31   Draft regulations are publicly available on the website of the Cabinet of Ministers: www.m-k.gov.lv.
32   Art 47(5) 2004 Act.
33   There are currently no regulations, and the Latvian government is working on it.

- requirements resulting from international agreements on the use of numbering resources.

The service of number portability is not currently available in Latvia. It is expected that it will be available at the end of 2005.

The NRA's Enforcement Powers

18.36   The PURC has the right to request and receive, within the time limit set, the information from undertakings which is necessary for performance of its functions.[34]

18.37   The PURC has the right, by giving prior notice, to visit the premises and buildings and gain access to the equipment which is used for the supply of electronic communications services or network operation and to request permits, certificates and other documents.[35]

18.38   Where the provisions of the general authorisation are violated the PURC may suspend the operations of the electronic communications undertaking in accordance with the procedures set by law.[36]

Administrative Charges and Fees for Rights of Use

18.39   All undertakings providing electronic communication services or networks shall pay an annual fee for regulation of public services in accordance with the Public Services Regulators Act.[37] The rate is determined by 1 October each year by the Cabinet of Ministers, and is based on the annual net turnover of publicly available services and costs of ensuring the activities of the regulator.[38] The annual rate shall not exceed 0.2 per cent of the net turnover of publicly available services supplied by the undertaking in the previous financial year.

REGULATION OF NETWORK ACCESS AND INTERCONNECTION: IMPLEMENTATION OF THE ACCESS DIRECTIVE

Objectives and Scope of Access Regulation

18.40   The objectives of access and interconnection regulation are to encourage competition on the market of electronic communications in respect of interconnections, joint use of network infrastructure and unbundled access to the local loop, while at the same time reducing service costs.[39] The PURC stimulates cooperation between electronic communications undertakings, the execution of agreements on interconnection of electronic communications networks which regulate how these networks will be connected, what electronic communications services the undertakings will render to each other and how much will they cost, and the joint use of

---

34   Art 9(1) 2004 Act.
35   Art 9(1) 2004 Act.
36   Art 11(1) 2004 Act.
37   Art 30(1) 2004 Act.
38   Art 31(1) 2004 Act.
39   Art 9 2004 Act.

electronic communications network infrastructure, at the same time facilitating the approximation of the rates of these services to the costs thereof.

18.41   The provisions of the 2004 Act regarding access and interconnections are binding on operators of public electronic communications networks and electronic communications undertakings who wish to obtain access or interconnection.[40]

Basic Regulatory Concepts

18.42   Access covers access to network elements and associated facilities by fixed or non-fixed means; this includes access to the local loop and to facilities and services necessary to provide services over the local loop, access to physical infrastructure (including buildings, cable lines and ducts and masts), access to relevant software systems (including operational support systems), access to number translation or systems offering equivalent functionality, access to electronic communications networks (in particular for roaming), access to conditional access systems for digital television services, and access to virtual network services.[41]

18.43   The definition of 'interconnection' as provided in Article 1 of the 2004 Act is identical to that in the Access Directive.

Interconnection is a specific type of access implemented between network operators.

18.44   The PURC is vested with broad regulatory powers in respect of access and interconnections, and has the right:

- to determine what terms and conditions shall be included in agreements on access, interconnection, joint use of equipment, disconnection of leased lines or local loops and the provisions,[42]
- to request the amendment of agreements, that have already been executed, on interconnection, access or joint use of equipment, if it is necessary to ensure active competition or maximum economic efficiency, or the interoperability of electronic communications networks or electronic communications services,[43]
- upon its own initiative or, if reasonably so requested by any of the parties, to set the date by which negotiations on the execution of access or interconnection agreements shall be concluded,[44] and
- to specify the access and interconnection obligations of SMP undertakings.[45]

As provided for in article 3(1) Access Directive, it is ensured that the undertakings can freely enter into mutual commercial negotiations on access and interconnection. The PURC exercises its rights in respect of the execution of interconnection agreements in those cases where negotiations between the undertakings have reached an impasse and the parties are unable to agree.[46]

---

40   Arts 36, 37 2004 Act.
41   Art 1 2004 Act.
42   Art 9(1) 2004 Act.
43   Art 9(1) 2004 Act.
44   Art 9(1) 2004 Act.
45   See para 18.45 below.
46   Art 8(1) 2004 Act

Access- and Interconnection-related Obligations with Respect to SMP Undertakings

18.45 With regard to the regulation of access and interconnection with respect to SMP undertakings, according to article 39(1) 2004 Act, based on the results of the market analysis, the PURC has the right to impose the obligations set out in articles 9–13 Access Directive,[47] namely:

- transparency,
- non-discrimination,
- accounting separation,
- access to and use of specific network facilities, and
- price control and cost accounting obligations.

18.46 The same regulatory regime applies to the operators of fixed and mobile networks. Any and all obligations and requirements shall be applied by the PURC on fair and non-discriminatory terms.

18.47 SMP undertakings in the market of fixed voice telephony services shall comply with the special requirements that could generally be imposed by the PURC regarding:

- approximation of rates with costs, based on the methodology of the PURC;
- providing access to the communication services of other suppliers of public telecommunications services connected to the telecommunications network;
- providing a universal telecommunications service;
- ensuring special technical conditions for the supply of telecommunications services to disabled persons; and
- ensuring disconnected access to access network and equipment related thereto.

18.48 SMP undertakings in the market of interconnection services shall comply with the special requirements that could generally be imposed by the PURC regarding:

- ensuring connection of own public telecommunications network to other public telecommunications networks;
- meeting the demands of suppliers of telecommunication services in respect of special access; and
- submitting information to the PURC on the basic offer of interconnection, the basic offer of commercial calls, and special access agreements.

18.49 The PURC may intervene in accordance with the dispute resolution procedures if other operators have difficulties obtaining access or interconnection from SMP undertakings.

Related Regulatory Powers with Respect to SMP Undertakings

18.50 The PURC has approved regulations in which it has determined the scope of minimum services of leased lines, and these regulations are applicable to SMP undertakings in the market of leased line services.

---

47   See paras 1.140–1.154 above.

Regulatory Powers Applicable to All Market Participants

18.51   The PURC has the power to impose special obligations and binding regulations on all market participants in respect of access and interconnection.

REGULATION OF UNIVERSAL SERVICES AND USERS' RIGHTS: THE UNIVERSAL SERVICE DIRECTIVE

Regulation of Universal Service Obligations

Scope of universal service obligations

18.52   The PURC has determined the scope of universal service obligations which is confined to services at a fixed location:[48]

- origination and receipt of national and international calls,
- data and electronic message transmission services with a speed of at least 9600 bit/s,
- access to at least one directory enquiry service,
- services of public payphones, providing access to the following telecommunications services:
  - voice telephony services
  - free of charge calls to emergency services
  - free of charge calls
  - calls to operator's helpdesk
  - calls to directory enquiry services.

Designation of undertakings obliged to provide universal services

18.53   The PURC by its decision specifies one or more undertakings which are obliged to supply universal services, determining the scope, territory, users and the term for the supply provisions of the universal telecommunications service.[49] Currently, the supplier of universal services, based on the decision of the PURC,[50] is the LTM, the former incumbent.

Regulation of retail tariffs, users' expenditures and quality of service

18.54   The PURC lays down the principles for the determination of acceptable prices for the provision of universal services, and these are binding on those electronic communications undertakings which by decision of the PURC perform the universal service obligations.[51]

18.55   Acceptable prices for universal services with regard to telephone line subscription are determined not more than once per calendar year, using the last available statistical information in respect of the full calendar year. The acceptable

---

48   Regulations of Universal Service in the Electronic Communications Sector, adopted by the PURC on 1 December 2004, Latvijas Vestnesis, 03.12.2004, Nr. 192.

49   Art 64(3) 2004 Act.

50   Decision No 341 of 17 December 2003 adopted by the PURC.

51   www.sprk.gov.lv.

price is stated as a percentage of the average household consumer costs obtained from the Latvian Central Board of Statistics.

The supplier of universal services shall provide at least one optional tariff package under which the subscription price for a telephone subscription line does not exceed the acceptable price.[52]

18.56   The supplier of universal services shall provide users with the possibility of receiving upon demand a detailed invoice for the services used.[53]

18.57   The PURC sets requirements for each supplier of the universal service in respect of quality parameters of voice telephony services. Quality measurements of public electronic communications services are performed by the Agency in accordance with the methodology developed by the PURC.

Cost calculation and financing of universal services

18.58   Article 66(1) of the 2004 Act states that, for the purpose of compensation of undertakings obliged to provide universal services, a universal service fund or another financing mechanism can be created. The financing mechanism and the procedure under which contributions are to be made are set by the Latvian Cabinet of Ministers. The contributions made shall be used only for the purpose of financing the universal service. The PURC ensures management of the financing mechanism of the universal service. Currently, the Cabinet of Ministers has still not issued a normative act which would regulate the mechanism and procedure of financing the universal service.

18.59   The costs of universal service obligations are calculated according to the methodology for calculation and determination of universal service obligations developed by the PURC.

Net costs of the universal telecommunications service shall be calculated as the total of net costs derived from the components of universal telecommunications service obligations, deducting intangible benefits.

Regulation of Retail Markets

18.60   The principle that regulation of retail services is permissible only if regulation at wholesale level does not achieve the regulatory objectives has been implemented in Chapter IX of the 2004 Act.

18.61   Permissible remedies in the retail market are regulated in Articles 38–44 of the 2004 Act. The PURC can impose obligations on SMP undertakings in respect of:

- ensuring access to elements and equipment of the electronic communications network, and
- providing specific wholesale services to third parties for the supply of electronic communications retail services.

---

52   www.sprk.gov.lv.
53   www.sprk.gov.lv.

End User Rights

Contracts

18.62 Operators providing connection and/or access to the public telephone network have an obligation to enter into a written agreement on electronic communications services with each consumer.[54]

18.63 An agreement on electronic communications services shall specify the information as provided in article 20(2) Universal Service Directive and contain at least the following information:

- quality requirements applicable to services; and
- information on permission to process the consumer's data, in order to publish and use them for commercial purposes.

18.64 Consumers have the right to terminate the contract without penalty if, upon receipt of notice of changes to terms and conditions in the agreement, they do not agree to the notified changes. End-users shall be informed of changes to terms and conditions in the agreement not less than one month prior to the actual modification.[55]

Transparency obligations and other obligations

18.65 Operators shall ensure that rates, rate plans and rate discounts of services that are supplied to consumers are publicised and made publicly available.[56]

18.66 Consumers have a right to receive invoices without detailed records of the services that they have used.[57]

18.67 The PURC sets requirements for a basic level of detail for invoices to enable the end-user to examine and control payments, supervise costs and thereby keep control over his or her invoices.[58]

18.68 Additional obligations as described in articles 23 to 26 Universal Service Directive[59] are all incorporated in the 2004 Act.

DATA PROTECTION: IMPLEMENTATION OF THE E-PRIVACY DIRECTIVE

Confidentiality of Communications

18.69 Both service and network providers have an obligation not to disclose data on users or subscribers, as well as information on electronic communications services or value added services received.[60]

---

54   Art 19(1) 2004 Act.
55   Art 23(3) 2004 Act.
56   Art 60 2004 Act.
57   Art 75 2004 Act.
58   Art 75(2) 2004 Act.
59   See paras 1.183–1.188 above.
60   Art 68 2004 Act.

18.70   Service providers are prohibited, without the written consent of users or subscribers, to disclose transmitted information.

18.71   Only where users or subscribers are the subject of operational activities (eg by the police or the prosecutor's office) in order to obtain information can a connection to the electronic communications network be granted, based on a decision issued by the court. The Cabinet of Ministers has approved regulations which stipulate the procedures by which a service provider can attach phone-tapping equipment to the electronic communications network.

18.72   There are no precise and direct references in legislation with respect to the storage of or access to information on the terminal equipment of a subscriber/user, leaving the service provider obliged to follow the instructions of Article 5(3) E-Privacy Directive.

Traffic Data and Location Data

18.73   The definitions of 'traffic data' and 'location data' are identical to those in Article 2 E-Privacy Directive.

18.74   Traffic data processing is permitted with the aim of distributing electronic communications services and providing value added services, if the user or sub-scriber has given written consent. The user or subscriber is entitled at any time to withdraw consent to the processing of traffic data.[61]

18.75   Traffic data are stored for the period of time within which the user or subscriber can dispute the invoice and make payments.[62]

18.76   Location data processing is permitted only in order to ensure the provision of electronic communications services. The processing of the said data for other purposes is permitted, upon written consent of the user or subscriber, within the period of time necessary for provision of value added services. The user or subscriber is entitled at any time to withdraw consent to the processing of location data for other purposes.[63]

Itemised Billing

18.77   Subscribers are entitled to receive bills without detailed description of services used. The PURC can set requirements in respect to the basic level of detail of bills, which the service provider is obliged to ensure for subscribers free of charge; however, there are currently no such requirements imposed on any operator.

Calling and Connected Line Identification

18.78   Service providers are obliged to inform users and subscribers of the cases in which calling and connected line identification is performed. Calling users are entitled free of charge to prohibit calling line identification. Called subscribers are entitled free of charge to reject calling line identification for incoming calls. Called

---

61   Art 70(4) 2004 Act.
62   Art 70(2) 2004 Act.
63   Art 71 2004 Act.

subscribers are entitled free of charge and automatically to reject those calls for which users or subscribers have prohibited calling line identification. Called subscribers are entitled free of charge to prohibit the connected line identification for the calling user.[64]

Automatic Call Forwarding

18.79   Subscribers are entitled free of charge to prohibit the forwarding of calls by third persons to the subscriber.

Directories of Subscribers

18.80   Personal data of subscribers may be included in a publicly available subscribers' directory only upon written consent of the subscribers. Before inclusion of data into a publicly available subscribers' directory, the subscribers are to be informed free of charge of the name of the publisher of the subscribers' directory, and the purpose of use of the subscribers' directory. Subscribers are entitled free of charge to state which personal data may be included in the publicly available subscribers' directory, as well as to verify, recall or amend his/her personal data.[65]

Unsolicited Communications

18.81   Article 13 E-Privacy Directive laying down provisions on unsolicited communications has been partly implemented in Latvian law as at June 2005. The Consumer Rights Protection Law[66] and the Law on Information Society Services[67] should be mentioned as the main national laws implementing the relevant provisions of the Directive.

18.82   Article 9 of the Law on Information Society Services prohibits sending via e-mail commercial statements where the recipient's prior consent has not been obtained, as well as any other notices disturbing a person. Article 1 of the Law defines 'commercial statement' as any notice in electronic form which aims to directly or indirectly advertise goods or services or also to advertise the image of a business person, organisation or individual who performs a business activity, economic activity or regulated professional activity.

Please note that, within the meaning of the Law, information providing the possibility of directly accessing general information on the service provider and its activities, based on the domain name or e-mail address included in the statement, shall not be regarded as 'commercial statement'.

18.83   According to Article 10(2) of the Consumer Rights Protection Law, facsimiles, automatic answering machines and distance communication techniques, utilisation of which involves individual contact with the consumer, may be utilised by a manufacturer, seller or service provider only if explicit consent from the

---

64   Art 72 2004 Act.
65   Art 74 2004 Act.
66   Adopted by the Latvian Parliament on 18 March 1999, Latvijas Vestnesis, No. 104/105, 1 April 1999.
67   Adopted by the Latvian Parliament on 4 November 2004, Latvijas Vestnesis, No 183, 17 November 2004.

consumer has been received. The Regulations Regarding Distance Contracts, adopted by the Cabinet of Ministers, contain more detailed regulation of distance contracts, ie agreement between the consumer and the seller or service provider, based on the proposal of the seller or the service provider via addressed or non-addressed printed material, standard form letter, catalogue, advertisement in the press, telephone, facsimile, internet, e-mail, television, radio or other means of sending and broadcasting information.[68]

---

68   Thus, for example, Article 4 of the Regulations prescribes an obligation on the seller or service provider at the beginning of the phone conversation to disclose his/her identity and to give information on the commercial purpose of the call.

The Lithuanian Market for Electronic Communications[1]

Jaunius Gumbis, Agnė Makauskaitė, Giedrė Valentaitė
Lideika, Petrauskas, Valiūnas ir partneriai LAWIN

LEGAL STRUCTURE

Basic Policy

19.1 The Lithuanian Communications Regulatory Authority ('CRA') is entrusted by law with the basic policy task of developing effective competition in the field of electronic communications, efficient use of electronic communications resources, such as radio frequencies and telephone numbers, and ensuring protection of the rights of consumers of electronic communications services. This is pursued through promotion of the development of the European Union's internal market and a harmonised regulation of electronic communications in the European Union, ensuring conditions necessary for effective competition in electronic communications markets, and ensuring simple and affordable dispute settlement procedures and promoting effective long-term investments.

19.2 The regulatory emphasis has been gradually shifting from regulation of the retail markets to the wholesale markets: the barriers for customers to change service providers were diminished (by introduction of carrier pre-selection and number portability provisions), and more lenient retail regulation was introduced.

19.3 The telecommunications market was liberalised on 1 January 2003. Currently, there are 23[2] new entrants that provide fixed telephone services;[3] however, so far they have managed to take from the incumbent only 6% of the market (based on the number of subscribers).

19.4 There are three major players in the public mobile telephony market, ie Omnitel, holding 41% of the market regarding the number of subscribers and 54% of the market in terms of revenue, Tele2 (35% and 20% respectively) and Bite GSM (23% and 24% respectively). There are only a few new entrants in the mobile market.

---

1 Editing of this chapter closed on 14 April 2005.
2 The source of all data in this section is CRA: Report on the Telecommunications Sector, 4th quarter, 2004.
3 CRA: International calls – 21, long distance calls – 9, local calls – 9 (Report on the Telecommunications Sector, 4th quarter, 2004).

19.5   Internet and multimedia industries in Lithuania were largely affected by liberalisation of the telecommunications market, as well as by the emergence of alternative service networks. Landmark developments were the separation of Voice over Internet Protocol (VoIP) from fixed telecommunications services, the introduction by the competitors of fixed monthly price plans instead of per-minute fees, and the emergence of mobile and wireless alternatives for the provision of internet services.

19.6   The use of the internet in Lithuania is rather low.[4] Cost is a hindrance to wider access. Quite a high degree of liberalisation of the broadcasting market is evidenced by the number of broadcasters (23 television broadcasters and 41 commercial radio services providers).

Implementation of EU Directives

19.7   The 1998 EU Regulatory Package for telecommunications was transposed into Lithuanian law through a revision of the Law on Telecommunications that came into force on 1 January 2003. This law also implemented parts of the 2002 EU Regulatory Package, such as the general authorisation system and some of the regulatory principles such as those of technological neutrality and proportionality. Moreover, requirements of unbundled local loop and carrier selection (for fixed telephony) were introduced.

19.8   As of 1 January 2004, the carrier pre-selection and number portability requirements were further enforced, including mobile-to-mobile number portability; restrictions for foreign companies were abolished.

19.9   On 1 May 2004 the new Law on Electronic Communications ('LEC')[5] came into force, which is meant to fully transpose the 2002 EU Regulatory Package.

Legislation

19.10   The main legislative act in the area of electronic communications is the afore-mentioned LEC. The next in legislative hierarchy are the resolutions of the Government such as resolutions concerning the strategy for assigning radio frequencies to broadcast and transmit radio and television programmes[6] or rules and price caps for universal services.[7] A number of legal acts are issued by the CRA, such as concerning co-ordination of the fees and the budget of the CRA[8] and rules for market analysis and dispute resolution between service providers.[9]

---

4   With 30% of households online (data as per 4th quarter of 2004, data source is CRA – Report on the Telecommunications Sector, 4th quarter, 2004).

5   Law on Electronic Communications of the Republic of Lithuania (Official Journal, 2004, no 69–2382).

6   Strategy for Assigning Radio Frequencies to Broadcast and Transmit Radio and Television Programmes, approved by the Resolution of the Government of 27 March 2003, no 376.

7   Rules on Provision of Universal Telecommunications Service, Price Caps of Universal Telecommunication Service, approved by the Resolution of the Government of 3 June 2003, no 699.

8   2 December 2004 order of the Director of the CRA no 1V-600 (Official Journal, 2004, no 178–6622).

9   20 December 2002 order of the Director of the CRA no 195 'On the Approval of the Rules for Market Analysis' (Official Journal, 2002, no 125–5702).

19.11   The regulatory policy is ultimately shaped by the CRA, which exercises both regulatory and law enforcement functions. Currently, the main sources of secondary legislation in this sector are being or have been amended or adopted by the CRA to implement the new LEC and there are no contradictions to the European Directives.

REGULATORY PRINCIPLES: IMPLEMENTATION OF THE FRAMEWORK DIRECTIVE

Scope of Regulation

19.12   The LEC, in line with the Framework Directive, establishes consistent regulation of all electronic communications networks and services regardless of their technological differences. It sets forth the principles of technological neutrality and functional parity, which require that legal rules are applied to the greatest possible extent without any regard to specific technology.

19.13   The LEC covers electronic communications services, networks and associated facilities, as well as the use of electronic communications resources, radio equipment, terminal equipment and electromagnetic compatibility.

19.14   Significantly broader definitions of electronic communications network, electronic communications service and associated facilities compared to the former regulatory framework are provided in the LEC.[10] The definition of 'electronic communications services' also covers services, provided on Voice over Internet Protocol (VoIP) services.

National Regulatory Authorities: Organisation, Regulatory Objectives, Competencies, Procedural Rules

Overview

19.15   The Government of the Republic of Lithuania or its authorised institution (which traditionally is the Ministry of Transport) is empowered to formulate the policies that would guarantee economic development and competitiveness of the electronic communications sector. The Government also regulates universal services and approves the national plan of radio frequencies.

19.16   All other regulatory functions related to electronic communications are exercised by the CRA, except for product safety issues, data protection and some other spheres of mixed competences (eg standardisation).[11] The CRA was established in 2000. It is an independent state institution. The Director of the CRA is appointed by the President of the Republic. The CRA has no direct subordination to the Government; formally, the latter has no power to repeal orders or decisions of the CRA or its Director. The CRA is financed from the national budget and a separate budget of its own, comprised of revenues from the fees for the work and services of the CRA.[12]

---

10   Art 3(14), (15) LEC.
11   Art 12(2), (3), (5), (7), (9) LEC.
12   See para 19.60 below.

Regulatory objectives of the NRA

19.17   Regulatory authorities must follow the objectives set forth in the 2002 EU Regulatory Package, including: promotion of competition in the markets for the electronic communications networks and services and associated facilities; ensuring protection of interests of the end users; and development of the internal market.[13]

Powers to request information

19.18   The CRA is entitled to request from electronic communications network and service providers any information necessary for the performance of its functions, including financial information, whether confidential or not. The requested information must be provided within reasonable time limits set by the CRA and must be detailed to the requested extent. When requesting information, however, the CRA must indicate the purpose of using the requested information and should request only such information as would be proportionate and objectively justified with regard to the indicated purpose. The CRA is obliged to protect confidential information.[14]

19.19   The powers of the CRA, similarly to the competition authorities, are not limited to the receipt of information. Subject to permission of the court, the CRA is entitled to enter and inspect the premises, territory and vehicles used by the undertaking, to review documents and receive copies and extracts, to obtain information kept in computers and on magnetic media, and to receive oral and written explanations from persons associated with the activities of undertakings under investigation.

Public consultations and co-operation

19.20   The CRA must make public all draft legal acts (including individual decisions), which may have a significant influence on a relevant market, and provide reasonable time limits for the interested persons, including end users, consumers, producers and providers of electronic communications network and/or services to present their comments. The CRA must also consult with interested parties before setting standards. Furthermore, public consultations must be held with regard to the CRA's decisions pertaining to the rights of end users. The CRA must make public the results of its consultations, except for confidential information supplied by undertakings. The appropriate cases and procedure of such public consultations are established by the CRA itself.[15]

19.21   Institutions responsible for the implementation of the LEC, including, inter alia, the CRA and the Competition Council, are under a direct obligation to co-operate with the EU and Member States' institutions, as provided for in the Framework Directive and inter-institutional cooperation agreements.[16] The CRA

---

13   Art 1(5) LEC.
14   Art 71 LEC.
15   The Rules of Public Consultations on the Decisions of the CRA approved by the order of the Director of the CRA of 16 September 2004, no 1V-295.
16   Mutual inter-institutional cooperation agreements might be signed by different Member States' institutions according to Art 13 LEC. So far, no international agreements have been signed. Only three national cooperation agreements have been signed by Lithuanian national

must provide information to the Commission and national regulatory authorities of Member States upon their reasonable request.[17]

19.22   In order to secure effective competition within the electronic communications sector, the CRA must co-operate with the national competition authority (Competition Council). Co-operation involves exchange of information, including confidential information, and consultations on competition matters. The CRA may ask for consultations from the Competition Council during market analysis and has an obligation to obtain the opinion of the Competition Council on the relevant market definition, if it differs from that recommended by the European Commission.[18]

Dispute resolution powers

19.23   Extrajudicial hearings held by the CRA are mandatory prior to any judicial dispute resolution, when the disputed issue falls within the scope of LEC and the dispute arises between undertakings providing electronic communications networks and/or services.[19] Decisions of the CRA on disputes (including procedural rulings) come into force and become binding as of the date they are made. The CRA must resolve any dispute within four months from the date of application, unless there are exceptional circumstances requiring a longer period. The LEC, however, does not elaborate on such 'exceptional circumstances' nor on the applicable time limits. The LEC specifies the filing rules, the procedures of dispute resolution, the rights of the parties during dispute resolution and the application of provisional measures.[20]

19.24   The CRA also holds extrajudicial hearings in cases of disputes between end users and electronic communication service providers prior to referring such disputes to a court. End users, however, are entitled to apply directly to the court. Dispute resolution procedures in this case are identical in substance to those described above.

Right of Appeal against NRA's Decisions

19.25   Procedural rulings (when the dispute is not yet resolved in essence by a final decision) of the CRA passed in the process of dispute resolution may be appealed to the Administrative District Court within seven days, whereas appeals against substantive decisions have to be filed within 30 days.

19.26   Other individual acts adopted by the CRA, or its omission to adopt such acts within the established time limits, may also be appealed to the court. Any

---

regulatory authorities: between CRA and State non Food Products Inspectorate, between CRA and Lithuanian Customs, and between CRA and the Department of Statistics of Lithuania.
17   Art 13 LEC.
18   Art 16(7) LEC.
19   Art 28(1) LEC.
20   CRA may, either at the request of any party to the dispute or an interested undertaking, or on its own initiative, resort to provisional measures, ie impose an obligation to refrain from certain actions or perform certain actions prior to a final dispute resolution (Art 28(10) LEC).

person, who considers his rights or legitimate interests infringed, has a standing to file an appeal. Filing does not suspend the validity of the appealed act, except when the court rules otherwise.[21]

The NRA's Obligations to Co-operate with the Commission

19.27   In line with the Framework Directive, article 13 LEC imposes an obligation on the CRA to co-operate with the European Commission and national regulatory authorities of other Member States in the implementation of regulatory measures. This obligation to cooperate applies both to the consultation procedure and the veto procedure of article 7 Framework Directive.[22]

19.28   The CRA, before adopting certain decisions,[23] must submit drafts of such decisions to the Commission and national regulatory authorities of other Member States. The Commission and national regulatory authorities of other Member States may present their comments within one month or a longer period set for public consultations. The CRA is expected to take into account the opinions expressed by the Commission and national regulatory authorities of other Member States, but it may make its decision at its own discretion, except for the cases subject to the veto procedure. The CRA must communicate its final decision to the Commission.

19.29   When the consultation relates to decisions intended for a different definition of a relevant market than that given in the Commission Recommendation on relevant markets, as well as the decisions relating to designation or non-designation of undertakings with significant market power in a relevant market (Art 16(11) LEC), and the Commission notifies that the anticipated decision would create a barrier to the single market or if a serious doubt is expressed whether or not such decision is compatible with Community law, the CRA must refrain from adopting such decision for at least two months from the receipt of such notice. If during this period the Commission directs the CRA not to adopt the decision, the CRA can not adopt it without taking into account the suggestions of the Commission regarding any amendments.

19.30   Only in exceptional cases, if needed to safeguard competition and protect the interests of end users, the CRA may immediately adopt proportionate interim measures without prior consultation. Such interim measures may not last longer than nine months. The CRA must without delay notify the Commission and the national regulatory authorities of other Member States about such measures.

---

21   Art 6(7) LEC.
22   Art 13, Art 16(10)–(14) LEC.
23   These are decisions relating to definition of a relevant product or service market, designation or non-designation of undertakings with significant market power in a relevant market, and imposition or non-imposition or withdrawal of any regulatory obligations stipulated in the LEC; cf Art 16(10) LEC.

'Significant Market Power' as Fundamental Prerequisite of Regulation

Definition of SMP

19.31 Most of the ex-ante obligations provided for in the LEC may only be imposed on undertakings with significant market power (SMP) in a relevant electronic communications market.

19.32 In exceptional cases only and in accordance with the principle of proportionality, the CRA may impose additional (other than those listed in LEC) access and interconnection obligations on SMP undertakings, if the listed obligations are insufficient to ensure effective competition. Such additional obligations are subject to approval by the European Commission.

19.33 Ex-ante obligations imposed on the incumbent AB Lietuvos Telekomas, designated to have SMP in the fixed telecommunications networks and services market as well as the interconnection and leased lines services markets, came into force before the LEC and remain valid until the CRA carries out a new market analysis and decides that they are no longer necessary or appropriate.[24]

19.34 The definition of SMP is principally identical to the one provided in article 14(2) Framework Directive.[25] The SMP definition includes the concept of joint dominance, although it does not provide any criteria for it. Further, the LEC deals with closely related markets establishing that, if an undertaking has SMP on a specific market, it may also be considered to have SMP on a closely related market, where the links between the two markets are such as to allow the market power held in one market to be leveraged into the other market, thereby strengthening the market power of the undertaking.[26]

19.35 Undertakings are designated to have SMP by an individual decision of the CRA, subject to a prior market analysis. The CRA may carry out market analysis at its own initiative or at the request of interested undertakings or state or municipal institutions. Market analysis must be completed within four months, which period does not include consultation and veto procedures.[27] The CRA may prolong the market analysis period, but must attempt to have the market analysis completed within the shortest time possible.

19.36 Currently there is only one SMP operator in Lithuania – the incumbent AB Lietuvos Telekomas, designated to have SMP in the fixed telecommunications networks and services market, and the interconnection and leased lines services markets. In September 2004, the CRA started a new market analysis in four markets: call termination on individual public telephone networks provided at a fixed location market; transit services in the fixed public telephone network market; voice call termination on the individual mobile networks market; and wholesale broadband access market. After a first market analysis, two more operators were designated as SMP operators: UAB Bite GSM (in the public mobile telephone networks and services market) and UAB Omnitel (in the public mobile telephone

---

24   AB Lietuvos Telekomas was designated to have SMP by the relevant orders of the Director of the CRA in 2002 and 2003.
25   Art 15 (1) LEC.
26   Art 15 (2) LEC.
27   See paras 19.28–19.30 above.

networks and services market and interconnection market). However, the Lithuanian administrative courts have withdrawn these CRA's decisions.

Definition of relevant markets and SMP designation

19.37   In the first stage of market analysis a relevant market is defined. Article 16 LEC does not provide any specific criteria or rules for the market definition, but obliges the CRA to follow the Commission Recommendation on relevant markets defining product and service markets. It is therefore reasonable to assume that, in defining relevant electronic communications networks and services markets, the CRA will rely primarily on the Commission Recommendation on market definition and on national competition law.[28] Currently, there is a new market analysis being carried out by the CRA in four markets: call termination on individual public telephone networks provided at a fixed location market; transit services in the fixed public telephone network market; voice call termination on the individual mobile networks market; and wholesale broadband access market. It should be also noted that VoIP services will be defined as a separate market or will be assigned to voice telephony services market depending on the outcome of the current market analysis of the CRA and depending on analysis of substitutability of these services with voice telephony.

19.38   If market analysis is carried out following the decision of the European Commission defining a transnational market, the CRA will conduct market analysis together with the national regulatory authorities of other Member States.

19.39   During the second stage of the market analysis, the CRA determines whether the competition in a relevant market is effective and, if not, it identifies SMP undertakings. Article 16 LEC does not contain specific rules for the market analysis, but points out that the CRA must conduct its market analysis in compliance with national laws and regulations, Community law and guidelines and recommendations of the European Commission.[29] It is therefore reasonable to assume that, in order to analyse the effectiveness of competition in relevant markets, the CRA will rely on the Commission Guidelines on market analysis and on national competition law.[30]

---

28   The National Competition Authority has approved guidelines for the definition of a relevant market. See the 24 February 2000 resolution no 17 of the Competition Council *On the Competition Council's Guidelines Concerning Definition of a Relevant Market*, Official Gazette, 2000, no 19–487 ('Council's Guidelines on Relevant Market').

29   Art 16(6) LEC.

30   The National Competition Authority has approved the guidelines for the establishment of a dominant position. See the 17 May 2000 Resolution no 52 of the Competition Council *On Explanations of the Competition Council Concerning Establishment of a Dominant Position*, Official Gazette, 2000, no 52–1516. These guidelines are not specifically approved for electronic communications markets, but define the main and common competition law principles and rules for the definition of dominant position in the market and do not contradict the Commission Guidelines on market analysis.

NRA's Regulatory Duties concerning Rights of Way, Co-location and Facility Sharing

Rights of way

19.40   Every natural person or legal entity who intends to provide or operate a public electronic communications network upon coordination with the state or municipal institutions is entitled to use state and municipal roads, squares, pipelines, waters and their coasts, bridges, viaducts, tunnels and other constructions for the construction of public communication networks. Such use is free of charge, however upon finalising the works, the roads and their constructions must be reinstated at the expense of the public communications network owner.[31]

19.41   If the provider of the public communications networks is not able to build his network either through joint effort with other persons, or through infrastructure sharing, and the negotiations with the owners of the property fail, the network provider is entitled to apply to the civil court for a servitude.[32] A servitude may be placed on either state, municipal or private property if the court considers that this would not constitute an undue burden on the owner of such property. The network provider must pay to the owner a reasonable price determined by the court for his right to use the property.

19.42   The strip of land along the wires and around other pieces of the public communications network infrastructure is considered to be a protected zone irrespective of its ownership. Prior consent of the network provider is necessary in order to change the type of activities for which it is designated, to carry out construction, digging, drilling, explosive and other works that may damage the communications infrastructure.[33] Employees of the network operator are entitled to maintain the communications infrastructure.

Co-location and facility sharing

19.43   Those persons who are building electronic communications networks must publicly announce the start of construction and the possibilities for other persons to jointly build the electronic communications network. The CRA, on the other hand, following a public consultation with the interested parties, may also place an obligation to allow joint construction of the network.

19.44   If a provider of public communications networks cannot realise the right to install the necessary electronic communications infrastructure, or the costs of realisation of such a right are disproportionately high, the CRA may request that any provider of electronic communications networks or another person controlling the relevant infrastructure should permit, on non-discriminatory terms, the sharing of the existing electronic communications infrastructure as well as of other relevant pipelines, cable ducts, collectors, towers, masts, buildings and other facilities or installation of electronic communications infrastructure where this is cost-efficient and does not require significant additional work. In this case, the CRA shall provide the public consultations.

---

31   Art 38 LEC.
32   Servitude on land may also be placed by the Government or by the governor of the County, depending on the size of the plot of land.
33   Art 41(1) LEC.

19.45   The procedure and conditions for usage of electronic communications infrastructure as well as other relevant pipelines, cable ducts, collectors, towers, masts, buildings and other facilities and for installing electronic communications infrastructure shall be stipulated in a contract. A person controlling the relevant infrastructure may not refuse to conclude such a contract with a provider of public communications networks, nor may he request that it should be amended or terminated if contractual obligations are being fulfilled, even on the grounds that there are no documents providing evidence of legitimate control of the electronic communications infrastructure. By agreement between the parties, the user of the infrastructure shall pay a proper fee to the person whose infrastructure is being used.

REGULATION OF MARKET ENTRY: IMPLEMENTATION OF THE AUTHORISATION DIRECTIVE

The General Authorisation of Electronic Communications

19.46   Electronic communications activities may be provided without any prior individual authorisation, subject to compliance with the law. The CRA is vested with the responsibility to approve general terms and conditions for the electronic communications activities, ie conditions which may be attached to a general authorisation. Those general terms and conditions must be objective, non-discriminatory, transparent and proportionate. The Article 30 LEC lists 18 conditions which may be contained in these general terms and conditions; the list basically corresponds to the list contained in Part A of the Annex to the Authorisation Directive.

19.47   Only a person who plans to engage in electronic communications activities, included in the abovementioned general terms and conditions, must notify the CRA prior to the start of such activities. So far, five activities are included in the list: provision of public fixed telecommunications network and services; provision of public mobile telecommunications network and services; and provision of leased lines. The CRA may only request to supply as much information to be included in the notice as is necessary to include the provider in the list of providers of electronic communications services and networks.[34]

19.48   Within seven days, the CRA confirms the receipt of notification, as well as its compliance with the general terms and conditions for the electronic communications activities. Upon request of the provider, the CRA issues a standardised declaration as provided in article 9 Authorisation Directive.[35]

---

34   Art 29(3), (4) LEC, General Terms and Conditions for Engaging in Telecommunications Activities, approved by 12 December 2002 order no 176 of the CRA Director.

35   Art 29(6) LEC.

Rights of Use for Radio Frequencies

General authorisations and granting of individual rights

19.49   Radio frequencies are managed by the CRA in accordance with the National Radio Frequency Allocation Table approved by the Government.[36] As a general rule, the rights of use for radio frequencies are granted by issuing an individual authorisation, unless the CRA determines otherwise. So far quite an extensive list of frequencies, established by the CRA, whose use does not require individual authorisation,[37] applies.[38]

Admissible conditions

19.50   Legal regulations and individual authorisations for the use of frequencies may only be subject to eight types of conditions which are listed in article 58(2) LEC. The said list basically corresponds to Part B of the Annex to the Authorisation Directive.

Limitation of number of rights of use to be granted

19.51   As a general rule, the number of authorisations for the use of radio frequencies is unlimited. However, the limitations may be imposed by the decision of the CRA when this is necessary to ensure the effective use of radio frequencies. The CRA must go through a public consultation and, after having published a reasoned decision, periodically review it.[39]

19.52   After a decision to limit the number of authorisations, the CRA may grant an authorisation to use spectrum through one of the following procedures:[40]

- direct allocation to the applicant,
- 'beauty contest', or
- auction.

Direct allocation is only possible if no other person has applied for the same frequencies during the time period provided for by the CRA. Otherwise, it is for the CRA to choose whether to use a 'beauty contest' or auction procedure.

Frequency trading

19.53   As a general rule, spectrum trading or any other type of transfer of the rights of use is prohibited, except in cases and subject to the terms and conditions determined by the CRA.[41] So far, the CRA has only permitted frequency transfer within an undertaking (ie among or between natural or legal persons comprising one undertaking).

---

36   Currently valid version was approved by the 3 February 2003 Government Resolution no 174.
37   13 March 2003 Decree no 1V-27.
38   GSM 900 terminal equipment (880,2–915 MHz (transmission) 935–960 MHz (receiving)); GSM 1800 terminal equipment (1710–1785 MHz (transmission) 1805–1880 MHz (receiving)); UMTS terminal equipment (1900–1980 MHz, 2010–2025 MHz, 2110–2170 MHz) etc.
39   Plan of the Use of Radio Frequencies approved by the order of the Director of the CRA of 16 December 2003, no 1V-167 (last amendment made on 11 November 2004).
40   Art 52 LEC.
41   Art 57 LEC.

Rights of Use for Numbers

General authorisations and granting of individual rights

19.54 Numbers are managed in accordance with the National Numbering Plan approved by the CRA.[42] Rights of use for numbers are granted by the CRA by issuing individual authorisations, although the CRA may also choose to grant them by means of auction or 'beauty contest'.[43] Providers of public fixed and mobile telecommunications networks and/or services may apply for the allocation of numbers. In general, rights of use are non-transferable, except in cases and subject to the terms and conditions prescribed by the CRA. Pursuant to the currently valid legal regulations,[44] an authorisation holder may allocate his numbers only to the other service providers using his network.

19.55 Service numbers and short numbers are considered to be of an exclusive economic value. Once the application to allocate such number is received, it is published. If an alternative applicant approaches the CRA and the existing numbering resources are not sufficient to satisfy the demand, an auction is held.[45] Short numbers are allocated one by one, service numbers are allocated in blocks of 10, 100 or 1000. It should also be mentioned that Lithuania's CRA is not intending to set up a separate area code for VoIP services – it is possible to use the current National Numbering Plan for the provision of these services.

Admissible conditions

19.56 The rules for the use of telephone numbers[46] and individual authorisations for the use of numbers may only be linked with special conditions that relate to nine items listed in LEC.[47] This list basically corresponds to Part C of the Annex to the Authorisation Directive.

19.57 Number portability must be ensured by every public communications network and/or service provider at its own expense, within the terms and subject to the conditions determined by the CRA.[48] They require ensuring fixed-to-fixed and mobile-to-mobile number portability. Until 1 July 2005 number portability is affected by call redirection. According to an agreement on administration of a central database, signed between the CRA and a private enterprise, chosen by public 'beauty contest', this central database shall be launched on 1 July 2005 and be operated until 30 June 2015. Pricing for number portability must be cost oriented and directly charged to subscribers, but should not deter from the use of these facilities; to this end the CRA is allowed to set a price cap.[49]

---

42 Currently valid version was approved by the 20 December 2002 order no 196 of the Director of CRA (last amendment made on 28 May 2004).

43 In the same manner as referred to in para 19.52.

44 20 December 2002 order no 198 of the Director of the CRA.

45 Art 53 LEC.

46 The Rules on Granting and Use of Telephone Communication Numbers, approved by the order of the Director of the CRA of 20 December 2002, no 198.

47 Art 58(3) LEC.

48 Such terms and conditions were approved on 16 October 2003 order no 1V-129 of the Director of the CRA.

49 Art 34(9) LEC.

Limitation of number of rights of use to be granted

19.58   As a general rule, the number of authorisations which may be issued for the use of numbers is unlimited. However, limitations may be imposed by decision of the CRA when they have exclusive economic value and/or there is a shortage, subject to the principle of proportionality.[50]

The NRA's Enforcement Powers

19.59   The CRA may use all its general law enforcement powers in order to enforce obligations under authorisations. The most significant is its power to impose economic sanctions in the amount of up to 3% of an undertaking's annual income from communications services, or where an annual income cannot be determined, the penalty may reach approx. EUR 87.000, if the provisions of the LEC are not followed. So far, the CRA has imposed only two economic sanctions for not complying with the LEC and those were on the incumbent AB Lietuvos Telekomas.

Administrative Charges and Fees for Rights of Use

19.60   The Director of the CRA approves the fees charged by the CRA,[51] including those for the rights of use. The fees are charged for: (i) the review of applications to use radio frequencies or telephone numbers; (ii) registration to public tenders and auctions for the rights of use; (iii) supervision of the rights of use; and (iv) other. The amount of the fee depends on the particular radio frequency or telephone number at issue.

19.61   Application and registration fees are paid at the moment the application is submitted. The fee for the supervision of the rights of use is paid monthly by the user of the particular resource.

Transitional Regulations for Existing Authorisations

19.62   Existing authorisations remain valid as far as they are in line with the new LEC.[52]

REGULATION OF NETWORK ACCESS AND INTERCONNECTION: IMPLEMENTATION OF THE ACCESS DIRECTIVE

Objectives and Scope of Access Regulation

19.63   Access regulation is put in place in order to foster effectiveness of the use of resources, ensure long-term competition and the utmost possible benefit to end users of the respective services.[53] It primarily focuses on the behaviour of the undertakings that are providing or have the right to provide public communications

---

50   Art 51(5) LEC.
51   Tariffs approved by 2 December 2004 Decree no 1V-600 apply.
52   Art 79(4) LEC.
53   Art 22(2) LEC.

networks and associated facilities. Access-related provisions also apply with respect to undertakings seeking access and interconnection.[54]

Basic Regulatory Concepts

19.64   In general, all basic regulatory concepts, including the definitions of 'access' and 'interconnection',[55] as well as the majority of other provisions, were transposed verbatim from the Access Directive to the LEC.

19.65   Following the Access Directive, 'freedom of access' is granted for all undertakings that are engaged in provision of electronic communications networks or services.[56] The definition of 'undertaking' used in the LEC does not limit itself to the national entities, thus the same freedom extends to foreign entities either engaging in electronic communications activities in Lithuania or performing activities that affect or may affect economic activities performed in Lithuania.

19.66   Generally, access and interconnection is the subject to commercial negotiations. Only where the parties are not able to reach agreement may either of the parties apply to the CRA with the request to resolve the dispute or for an order to grant access.

19.67   The CRA is vested with the task to promote and, when necessary, ensure adequate access and interconnection. A primary responsibility of the CRA is to deal with SMP undertakings and ensure that appropriate access obligations are imposed. The CRA has also some general powers to set forth procedural rules for implementing access obligations and to resolve disputes related to access.[57] In exercising these powers, the CRA must ensure its decisions are objective, transparent, proportionate and non-discriminatory.[58]

Access- and Interconnection-related Obligations with Respect to SMP Undertakings

Transparency obligations

19.68   In line with article 9(1) Access Directive, in order to ensure efficient access and interconnection, the CRA may oblige SMP operators to publish access-related information, including:

- accounting data,
- technical specifications,
- network characteristics,
- terms and conditions of provision and use of access, and
- prices for access and related services.

19.69   The CRA may also request SMP operators to publish a reference offer, broken down into components according to market needs, with the specific terms and conditions, including prices. Publication of the reference offer is mandatory in

---

54   Arts 21, 22 LEC.
55   Art 22 LEC.
56   Art 22(1) LEC.
57   Art 22(6) LEC.
58   Art 22(3) LEC.

all cases without any request of the CRA for the operators that are obliged to provide unbundled access to the local loop.

Non-discrimination obligations

19.70 Non-discrimination means a prohibition to apply, insofar as it relates to access, different conditions for provision of equivalent services in equivalent circumstances to different undertakings, and to provide services and information to other undertakings under conditions or with a quality different from those of the services provided by the SMP operator to itself or to its subsidiaries, divisions or any third undertaking.[59]

19.71 In addition to the above-mentioned general provision, Art 19(2) LEC provides that obligations of non-discrimination in all cases must be imposed by the CRA, if it is necessary to ensure that vertically integrated undertakings, controlled by the state or municipalities and having SMP in the relevant market, would not discriminate, when providing electronic communications networks established by utilising exclusive or special rights, against other undertakings, thereby giving advantage to their own activities.

Specific access obligations

19.72 In line with article 12(1) of the Access Directive, access obligations may take the following forms.[60] All obligations can be imposed by the CRA:

- obligation to provide access to specified network elements and facilities, including unbundled access to the local loop,
- obligation to negotiate in a good faith with the undertakings requesting to provide access,
- obligation not to withdraw access to facilities already granted,
- obligation to provide specified services with the purpose of their resale,
- obligation to provide open access to technical interfaces, protocols or other technologies, that are indispensable for interoperability of services or provision of virtual network services,
- obligation to provide co-location or other forms of sharing of electronic communications facilities,
- obligation to provide specified services that are necessary for ensuring provision of services to users,
- obligation to provide access to operational support systems or other similar software systems necessary to ensure fair competition in the provision of services, and
- obligation to interconnect networks or network facilities, including the possibility to interconnect networks at any technically available network point.

Price control obligations

19.73 The legal provisions on the obligation to offer cost-oriented prices and requirements for cost accounting systems are in line with article 13 Access Directive.

---

59   Art 19(1) LEC.
60   Art 21(1) LEC.

19.74   In the event the CRA requires an SMP operator to prove that its prices are cost-oriented and the operator fails to do this within a reasonable term set by the CRA, a presumption that the prices are not cost-oriented shall apply. The CRA is entitled to request an audit of the information presented by the operator as evidence of cost-orientation at the operator's expense. Until the operator substantiates the prices, the CRA may set a temporary price cap, based on the data about the costs obtained through indirect methods of evaluation including bench marks, taking into account the best practices of the EU Member States, Lithuania and similarly developed countries, as well as the ratio of respective wholesale and retail prices.

19.75   The CRA is empowered to impose a mandatory cost accounting system, method or model in order to support the price control measures. They apply to operators having SMP in the relevant market or to the specific operator separately.

Accounting separation obligations

19.76   The obligation of accounting separation is established in article 20 LEC in a very general manner, by stating only that the CRA has the right to oblige an operator having SMP in the relevant market to keep separate accounting of the activities in that market and activities related to access. Specific rules on accounting separation and related requirements have been approved by the CRA.[61]

Imposition of obligations in practice

19.77   So far, ex-ante obligations were imposed on the incumbent AB Lietuvos Telekomas, designated to have SMP in the fixed telecommunications networks and services market and also in the interconnection and leased lines services markets. Obligations of transparency, non-discrimination, accounting separation and cost orientation, price controls, access, interconnection, carrier (pre-)selection and provision of leased lines obligations were imposed.

Related Regulatory Powers with Respect to SMP Undertakings

19.78   In addition to the access and interconnection obligations, the CRA may impose on SMP undertakings carrier pre-selection obligations, obligations to provide leased lines at cost-oriented prices and obligations related to the provision of services to end-users.

19.79   Failure to comply with access and interconnection-related obligations would be treated as a violation of the law and may lead to the imposition of economic sanctions on the undertaking.[62]

19.80   Enabling of carrier pre-selection is mandatory for SMP undertakings in the market for access to public telephone communications networks used at fixed locations, but may also be imposed by the CRA on any other SMP undertaking

---

61   Rules for Cost Allocation and Requirements related to Cost Accounting, approved by 20 December 2002 order no 194 of the Director of the CRA.
62   See para 19.59 above.

(normally, along with access obligation).[63] The prices for the implementation of this right must be cost-oriented – for this purpose, the CRA is entitled to set the price caps.[64]

19.81   Undertakings having SMP on the relevant leased lines market are required to provide leased lines of the types specified by the CRA, and to observe the terms and conditions set by the CRA for provision of such services and fulfil obligations related to non-discrimination, cost-orientation (including implementation of cost accounting systems) and transparency. In order to ensure cost orientation, the CRA has a power to impose price caps.[65]

Regulatory Powers Applicable to All Market Participants

Obligations to ensure end-to-end connectivity

19.82   In line with article 5(1)(a) Access Directive, the CRA, in order to ensure end-to-end connectivity of users, may impose certain obligations for undertakings that control access to end users, including the obligation to interconnect networks.[66]

Access to digital radio and television broadcasting services

19.83   The CRA may also impose, to the extent it is necessary to ensure end users access to specified digital radio and television services, obligations on operators to ensure access to application programming interfaces and electronic program guides under fair, reasonable and non-discriminatory conditions.[67]

19.84   Conditional access systems and providers of conditional access to digital radio and television have the obligations defined identically to the wording of Annex I, Part I (a) and (b) Access Directive. More specific rules will be elaborated by the CRA.

19.85   The owners of application programme interfaces must disclose, against due remuneration and under fair, reasonable and non-discriminatory conditions, all the information which is necessary for the providers of digital television services to provide in a fully functional manner all the services supported by the interfaces.

---

63   Art 33 LEC. Undertakings having SMP for the provision of connection to and use of the public telephone network at a fixed location shall, in accordance with the procedure and conditions set forth by the CRA, enable on their own account their subscribers to access the services of any provider of publicly available telephone services. This obligation may be imposed by the CRA on any undertaking having SMP on the relevant market as well as in relation to the imposition of the obligation to provide access.
64   Art 33 LEC.
65   Art 35 LEC.
66   Art 22(2)1 LEC.
67   Art 22(2)2 LEC.

Transitional Provisions

19.86   Access obligations imposed on the incumbent AB Lietuvos Telekomas remain in force until the CRA carries out a new market analysis and decides that they are no longer necessary or appropriate.[68]

REGULATION OF UNIVERSAL SERVICES AND USERS' RIGHTS: THE UNIVERSAL SERVICE DIRECTIVE

Regulation of Universal Service Obligations

Scope of universal service obligations

19.87   The minimum services of a defined quality that have to be provided to all end users within the whole territory of Lithuania at an affordable price, ie universal services, include:[69]

- connection at a fixed location to the public telephone network, including access to public telephone services at a fixed location, whereby end-users must be able to make and receive local, national and international telephone calls, facsimile communications and data communications at a rate of not less than 3.1 kHz,
- provision of at least one comprehensive printed or electronic directory updated at least once every two years; and a comprehensive telephone directory enquiry service, directories for which have to be updated at least once a week,
- public pay telephones at the minimum density in cities of 2.2 pay phones per thousand inhabitants, and 0.5 pay phones per thousand inhabitants in other areas of the country,
- access to the above services for disabled users.

19.88   The Government has the power to impose any additional universal service obligations, as well as to define their scope, terms of provisions and quality requirements. However, the Government may not establish that the losses incurred in connection with the provision of such additional universal services are compensated from the funds of providers of electronic communications services.

Designation of undertakings obliged to provide universal services

19.89   Undertakings with SMP in a fixed telephony market within a particular territory are obliged to continue the provision of universal services within such geographical territory to the same extent, of the same quality and for the same prices as prior to the SMP designation. Currently, the incumbent AB Lietuvos Telekomas is obliged to provide universal services. Where there are territories with an unsatisfactory level of universal service, the CRA would announce a tender for the provision of universal services within such territories. If no response is received

---

68   See para 19.33 above.
69   Art 31(1) LEC; The Rules on Provision of Universal Telecommunications Services, approved by the Resolution of the Government of 3 June 2003, no 699.

within one month from the tender announcement, the undertaking designated as having SMP in the fixed telephony market would have an obligation to provide universal services in the territory.[70]

Regulation of retail tariffs, users' expenditures and quality of service

19.90   Designated undertakings are subject to price caps on the retail tariffs, approved by the Government.[71] The CRA must ensure that the terms and conditions of such undertakings are fully transparent, published and applied in accordance with the principle of non-discrimination.

19.91   The CRA must establish quality standards of universal services and monitor compliance with required performance levels.[72] The CRA may set up independent audits or similar reviews of the performance data at the expense of the undertaking concerned. If an undertaking fails persistently to meet the required performance level, the CRA may:

- set forth a grace period to rectify the situation,
- prohibit or suspend provision of the services up to three years, and
- impose economic sanctions.[73]

Cost calculation and financing of universal services

19.92   Designated undertakings may request financial assistance for universal services where such services can only be provided at a loss and would constitute an 'unfair burden'. Under the relevant resolution of the Government,[74] the calculation of the net cost of the universal service must be based upon the costs attributable to:

- the elements of the listed services, which can only be provided at a loss; in contrast to the Universal Services Directive this must not include costs of access to emergency telephone services, and
- specific end users or groups of end users who (taking into account the cost of providing the specified network and service, the revenue generated and price cap imposed) can only be served at a loss.

19.93   None of the above categories may include investment costs for the network modernisation incurred prior to 31 December 2002; where the designated undertaking holds an 80% or bigger share of the relevant market (in revenue terms), the provision of the universal services cannot be considered as being an 'unfair burden' under any circumstances.

19.94   Universal service providers may be compensated either by sharing the net cost of universal service obligations between all providers of electronic communications networks and services, or from public funds. As an additional measure, the

---

70   Pursuant to the Rules on Provision of Universal Telecommunications Services, cf fn 69 above.
71   Price caps have been approved by the Resolution of the Government of 3 June 2003, no 699.
72   Resolution of the Government of 6 December 2004, no 1593, On the Issue of Authorisations to Implement LEC.
73   See para 19.59 above.
74   Rules on Provision of Universal Telecommunications Services, approved by the Resolution of the Government of 3 June 2003, no 699.

Resolution allows reconsideration of the price caps, scope and the quality requirements of the universal services, as well as re-allocation or transfer of the universal services obligations to other service providers. The compensation mechanism must be shaped taking into account the efficiency of the proposed measure, its costs, and any factors that may have implications on its implementation and efficiency.

Regulation of Retail Markets

Prerequisites for the regulation of retail markets

19.95   Under the LEC, the CRA may impose on SMP undertakings certain obligations on the retail markets in addition to the 'traditional' SMP obligations (ie access, non-discrimination, transparency, accounting separation, price control and, when relevant, carrier pre-selection obligations), where the CRA considers these wholesale obligations to be insufficient. Market analysis is a prerequisite, and regulation of retail services is permissible only if regulation at wholesale level does not achieve the regulatory objectives.[75] Imposition of these obligations must be reasonable in the light of the particular problem, proportionate and justifiable by reference to the objectives sought.

Regulatory powers

19.96   In order to protect user and consumer interests and increase competition, the CRA may impose appropriate regulatory obligations on SMP undertakings. These include obligations foreseen in the Universal Services Directive:

- not to charge excessive prices,
- not to inhibit market entry or restrict competition by setting predatory retail prices, and
- not to show undue preference to specific end-users or unreasonably bundle services

as well as an obligation to ensure the quality of services specified by the CRA.

19.97   Furthermore, the CRA may regulate end-user tariffs in order to protect end-user interests whilst promoting effective competition by the same measures that are set forth in the Universal Services Directive:

- application of standard price caps to SMP undertakings,
- control of individual tariffs, and
- orientation of tariffs towards costs or prices on comparable markets.

These measures are complemented by mandatory rules regarding the implementation of cost accounting systems.[76]

19.98   SMP undertakings in the relevant retail leased lines market are required to provide the types of leased lines specified by the CRA,[77] and to observe the terms and conditions set by the CRA for the provision of such services and fulfil obligations related to non-discrimination, orientation of prices to costs (including

---

75   Art 32(1) LEC.
76   See paras 19.73–19.76 above.
77   The Rules on Provision of Leased Lines Service, approved by the order of the Director of the CRA of 10 December 2004, no 1V-645.

implementation and use of cost accounting systems) and transparency. The prices for the leased lines of the above-mentioned SMP undertakings have to be cost-oriented and may include a reasonable rate of return on investment. For this purpose the CRA is granted the right to establish the price caps.[78] It should also be mentioned that the CRA has not yet decided upon the regulation of end-user fees for VoIP services – it is awaiting the decision on the substitutability of these services with voice telephony services.

End User Rights

Contracts

19.99   Whereas the Universal Services Directive limits the right to enter into contracts with consumers, Lithuanian legal acts[79] extend this right to all end-users, both natural persons and legal entities and irrespective of the purpose of use – whether private consumption or commercial/professional needs. The obligation to contract extends to operators providing connection and/or access to the public telephone network, including mobile operators.[80]

19.100   Minimum requirements for contracts are established by the CRA[81] and go well beyond those contained in article 20(1) Universal Services Directive.

19.101   Subscribers have the right to terminate their contracts upon notice, except those with a fixed term, without penalty and without any cause. Fixed-term contracts can be terminated where a service provider increases the prices for the services or commits material breaches of the contract. Subscribers must be given adequate notice of proposed modifications, one month ahead of any modification.[82]

Transparency obligations

19.102   Service providers are obliged to publish transparent and up-to-date information on applicable prices, tariffs and standard terms and conditions of access to end users of publicly available telephone services, including the minimum contract period. There is a requirement to publish information on the quality of the services and on safe use of the services, which must not cause unreasonable expenditure.[83]

19.103   Rules for publishing the above-mentioned information must be set by the CRA, but have not been approved so far.

---

78   Temporary Price Caps on Leased Lines Service Provided by AB Lietuvos Telekomas and Allied Legal Persons, approved by the order of the Director of the CRA of 13 January 2003, no 6.
79   Cf art 34(1) LEC.
80   Art 34(1) LEC.
81   Rules on Provision of Public Telephone Communication Services approved by the order of the Director of the CRA of 31 October 2003, no IV-138.
82   Rules on Provision of Public Telephone Communication Services approved by the order of the Director of the CRA of 31 October 2003, no IV-138.
83   Art 34(2) LEC; Rules on Provision of Public Telephone Communication Services approved by the order of the Director of the CRA of 31 October 2003, no IV-138.

Other Obligations

19.104   In cases of force majeure or other extraordinary circumstances, the Government or an institution authorised by it may issue mandatory instructions, tasks and assignments to undertakings providing electronic communications networks and/or services, as well as to owners or users of equipment and devices in order to protect and maintain the relevant electronic communications networks and to interconnect them and, where necessary, restrict public use of electronic communications networks.[84] It should also be mentioned that VoIP service providers will also be obliged to offer free of charge emergency services where the CRA proves the substitutability of these services with voice telephony services.

19.105   Subject to applicable data protection provisions, subscribers to publicly available telephone services have the right to have an entry in the publicly available directory.[85] Undertakings which assign telephone numbers to subscribers have to meet all reasonable requests to make available, for the purposes of the provision of publicly available directory inquiry services and directories, the relevant information in an agreed format on fair, objective, cost-oriented and non-discriminatory terms. There are no regulatory restrictions preventing end-users in one Member State from accessing directly the directory enquiry services in another Member State.

Transitional Provisions

19.106   Universal service obligations imposed on AB Lietuvos Telekomas remain in force until the CRA carries out a new market analysis and decides that they are no longer necessary or appropriate.

DATA PROTECTION: IMPLEMENTATION OF THE E-PRIVACY DIRECTIVE

Confidentiality of Communications

19.107   Article 63 LEC requires that supervision over the processing of personal data in the field of electronic communications shall be exercised pursuant to regulations on processing of personal data and the protection of privacy. Service providers must implement appropriate technical and organisational measures to safeguard security of its services, if necessary in conjunction with network providers with respect to network security. These measures shall ensure a level of security appropriate to the risk presented. In case of a particular risk of a breach of the security of the electronic communications network, the service provider must inform subscribers.[86]

19.108   The law introduces a general prohibition on disclosing the content of information transmitted over electronic communications networks and/or related traffic data to persons that are not users of any electronic communications services

---

84   Art 78 LEC.
85   Art 67 LEC.
86   Art 62 LEC.

without the consent of the subscribers to the electronic communications services; similarly, creating conditions for gaining access to such information and/or related traffic data is prohibited.[87]

19.109   Service providers have the right to record and store technical data on electronic communications and their participants only to the extent that is necessary to ensure economic activities of the said undertakings.[88] The service providers must submit to operational investigation services, certain pre-trial investigation institutions, prosecutors, courts or judges any information which is available to them and which is necessary to prevent, investigate and detect criminal acts.[89] There is also an obligation for all persons taking part in such exchange of information to make necessary arrangements to ensure data security. Furthermore, where there is a reasoned court ruling, the service providers must provide operational investigation services and pre-trial investigation institutions with technical possibilities to exercise control over the content of information transmitted by electronic communications networks.[90]

Traffic Data and Location Data

19.110   Traffic data means any data processed for the purpose of the conveyance of a communication on an electronic communications network and/or for the billing thereof.[91]

19.111   Location data means any data processed in an electronic communications network, indicating the geographic position of the terminal equipment of an actual user of the electronic communications services.[92]

19.112   Traffic data necessary for the purposes of subscriber billing and electronic communications network interconnection payments may be processed only for a period of six months, except in cases where the bill is lawfully challenged or the data are necessary for the collection of payment.[93]

19.113   Furthermore LEC stipulates that traffic data may be processed for the purpose of marketing electronic communications services or for the provision of value added services, whereas location data other than traffic data may only be processed for the provision of value added services. The requirements and procedure established for such processing is principally the same as in the E-Privacy Directive.[94]

Itemised Billing

19.114   Itemised bills shall be presented only with the consent, or at the request, of the subscriber.[95] The State Data Protection Inspectorate will establish common requirements for itemised bills.

---

87   Art 63 LEC.
88   Art 64 LEC.
89   Art 64 LEC.
90   Art 77 LEC.
91   Art 3(52) LEC.
92   Art 3(76) LEC.
93   Art 64 LEC.
94   Arts 64 , 65 LEC.
95   Art 66 LEC.

Calling and Connected Line Identification

19.115   Article 70 LEC on presentation and restriction of calling and connected line identification basically repeats the regulation of the E-Privacy Directive. Furthermore, service providers and/or network providers may not impose the elimination of the presentation of calling line identification upon application of a subscriber requesting the tracing of malicious or nuisance calls, as well as in respect of specific lines operated by institutions dealing with emergency calls, such as law enforcement agencies, ambulance services, fire brigades and other emergency services for the purpose of responding to such calls by the subscriber or the actual user of electronic communications services.[96]

Automatic Call Forwarding

19.116   The service providers must ensure that any subscriber has the possibility, free of charge and using a simple means, of stopping automatic call forwarding by a third party to the subscriber's terminal equipment.[97]

Directories of Subscribers

19.117   Subscribers shall be informed, free of charge and before they are included in a printed or electronic directory of subscribers available to the public or obtainable through directory enquiry services, about the purpose of a subscriber directory in which their personal data can be included and of any further usage possibilities based on search functions embedded in electronic versions of the directory.

19.118   Subscribers shall have the right to decide whether their personal data are included in a public directory, and if so, which data is to be included to the extent that such data are relevant to the purpose of the directory as determined by the provider of the directory, and to verify, correct or withdraw such data. Not being included in a public subscriber directory, verifying, correcting or withdrawing of personal data is free of charge.[98]

19.119   For any purpose of a public directory other than the search of contact details of persons on the basis of their name, a subscriber's consent for the inclusion of personal data in such a directory shall be required.[99]

Unsolicited Communications

19.120   There are two laws regulating unsolicited communications issues in Lithuania: LEC and Law on Advertising.[100]

19.121   Article 68 LEC covers unsolicited electronic communications. It allows the use of electronic communications services, including electronic mail, for the purposes of direct marketing only in respect of subscribers who have given their

---

96   Art 70 LEC.
97   Art 69 LEC.
98   Art 67 LEC.
99   Art 67 LEC.
100   Law on Advertising of the Republic of Lithuania, Official Journal, 2000, no 64–1937.

prior consent. It also prohibits the practice of sending electronic mail for the purposes of direct marketing disguising or concealing the identity of the sender on whose behalf the communication is made, or without a valid address to which the recipient may send a request that such communications cease.

19.122   The Law on Advertising covers more than electronic communications advertising. According to Article 13 of the Law on Advertising, advertising by telephone, fax and electronic mail may only be supplied with the advertising consumer's agreement or in response to his request. It also prohibits direct advertising to a specific person if this person's disagreement has been clearly stated. There are not many issues of self-regulation, except for a number of non-governmental consumer protection organisations.

The Luxembourg Market for Electronic Communications[1]

Sophie Wagner-Chartier and Héloïse Bock
Arendt & Medernach, Luxembourg

LEGAL STRUCTURE

Basic Policy

20.1   Luxembourg did not implement any EU Directives relating to telecommunication until the adoption of the law of 21 March 1997 on Telecommunications ('1997 Law'),[2] amended by the law of 17 July 2001.[3] At that time, one of the reasons for non-implementation of the Directives was that the previous laws on telecommunications dated from the 19th century and it was necessary to fundamentally modify them to implement the Directives. The law of 20 February 1884 on telegraph and telephone services still served as the basis for telecommunication services, except in the matter of television and radio.

However, under this law, some regulations were adopted in 1990. These regulations concerned, in particular, telephone services, leased lines, and telex and facsimile services. They have been abrogated by a grand-ducal regulation dated 29 June 1993. The reason for this abrogation was that the regulations were not in accordance with the law of 10 August 1992 relating to the creation of the Enterprise of Post and Telecommunications (the '1992 Law').[4] The 1992 Law was adopted in order to comply with the principles of separation of regulatory and operational functions provided for by the European Community.

According to the Luxembourg Government, separation of the regulatory and operational entities was the first step towards adapting the relevant legislation. The second step was to enact new legislation relating to the telecommunications sector, namely the 1997 Law.

20.2   By the adoption of the 1997 Law, Luxembourg has implemented the various ONP Directives[5] and has created free and non-discriminatory access to telecommunications.

---

1   Editing of this chapter closed on 21 June 2005.
2   Mémorial A, no 18 of 27 March 1997 p 761.
3   Mémorial A, no 95 of 13 August 2001 p 1898.
4   Mémorial A, no 60 of 13 August 1992 p 2006.
5   See paras 1.22 et seq above.

20.3   The development of the electronic communications sector is, however, one of the priorities of the Luxembourg government, which has notably launched a program called *eLuxembourg.*[6]

Implementation of EU Directives and Legislation

20.4   Luxembourg's legal provisions on electronic communications matters are contained in four laws of 30 May 2005, in force from 1 July 2005 (the '2005 Laws').[7] The 2005 Laws implement the 2002 EU Regulatory Package and they each concern the following matters:

- the law concerning electronic communications networks and services (the 'E-Law'); it repeals the 1997 Law,
- the law concerning the organisation of the management of radio frequencies (the 'RF Law'),[8]
- the law concerning the organisation of the *Institut Luxembourgeois de Régulation* (ie the Luxembourg regulatory authority) (the 'ILR Law'),[9] and
- the law concerning specific provisions regarding the protection of privacy in relation to the processing of personal data in the electronic communications sector (the 'E-Privacy Law').[10]

20.5   In addition to the four laws implementing the 2002 EU Regulatory Package,[11] the Luxembourg legal framework on telecommunications includes the following laws:

- the law of 27 November 1996 approving the Convention for the establishment of the European Radiocommunications Office ('ERO'),[12] and
- the law of 8 April 1999 approving the Convention creating the European Telecommunications Office ('ETO').[13]

20.6   The Luxembourg legal framework is also composed of grand-ducal regulations implementing certain provisions of the 1997 Law. Some such grand-ducal regulations shall remain in force under the new regulatory regime laid down in the 2005 Laws, either on a temporary or on a permanent basis.

20.7   The Luxembourg regulatory authority (*Institut Luxembourgeois de Régulation* – 'ILR') shall regulate the market on the basis of the 2005 Laws as from 1 July 2005.

---

6   www.eluxembourg.lu. The eLuxembourg program was created during a government council meeting dated 30 June 2000.

7   Mémorial A, no 73 of 7 June 2005.

8   Mémorial A, no 73 of 7 June 2005 p 1159.

9   Mémorial A, no 73 of 7 June 2005 p 1162.

10   Mémorial A, no 73 of 7 June 2005 p 1168.

11   See para 20.4 above.

12   Mémorial A, no 87 of 12 December 1996 p 2468.

13   Mémorial A, no 38 of 16 April 2004 p 993. It should be noted that, in order to reduce overheads and increase efficiency, ETO was merged with ERO with effect from 1 January 2001, and ERO took over some of the functions previously carried out by ETO.

REGULATORY PRINCIPLES: IMPLEMENTATION OF THE FRAMEWORK DIRECTIVE

Scope of Regulation

20.8   The provisions of the E-Law provide for a technology-neutral approach. The definitions of 'electronic communications network', 'electronic communications service' and 'associated facilities'[14] are identical to those contained in the Framework Directive.

National Regulatory Authority: Organisation, Regulatory Objectives, Competencies

20.9   The Luxembourg regulatory authority is the ILR. It has been established under the 1997 Law. The ILR is an independent public authority placed under the authority of the competent Minister.[15] The management bodies of the ILR are a council and a board of managers.[16]

20.10   The Luxembourg legislator has deemed it preferable to define the framework, ie the status, organisation and operational rules of the ILR, in a separate law, given the fact that this regulatory authority is also competent in sectors[17] other than the electronic communications market.[18] This framework is contained in the ILR Law, whereas the other 2005 Laws define the ILR's missions with regard to the electronic communications market.

20.11   The ILR has administrative duties, according to which it is notably in charge of receiving notifications from undertakings who wish to operate or provide electronic communications networks and services.[19] The ILR keeps a register of such authorised undertakings[20] and checks compliance with the E-Law, in particular by analysing the information, including financial information, disclosed to it by authorised undertakings and ensuring enforcement.[21] The ILR allocates frequencies to users in conformity with the national frequency plan and manages the numbering resources.[22] The ILR monitors the placing on the market of radio and telecommunication equipment, in cooperation with other national authorities.[23]

20.12   The ILR monitors the application of competition rules, in close cooperation with the authority in charge of competition matters and, if necessary, with the authority in charge of the protection of consumer rights.[24] To this end, the ILR proceeds with market analyses in order to determine the level of competition and

---

14   Art 2(22), (25) and (26) E-Law.
15   Art 1 ILR Law.
16   Art 5 ILR Law.
17   ILR is also the regulatory authority in the sectors of gas, electricity and postal services.
18   Parliamentary Documents 5180, p 2.
19   Art 8(1) E-Law.
20   See para 20.55 below and fn 64.
21   Arts 14 and 15 E-Law.
22   Art 63 E-Law.
23   Grand-ducal regulation of 4 February 2000 on radio equipment and telecommunications terminal equipment and the mutual recognition of their conformity, which implements Directive 1999/5/EC of the European Parliament and of the Council of 9 March 1999.
24   Art 73 E-Law.

may publish information in order to promote a competitive market.[25] When they are solicited by the ILR, the above-mentioned authorities have one month in order to propose amendments to the planned measure of the ILR or to oppose its adoption. After the month has passed, the approval of the relevant authority is deemed to have been given to the ILR.[26]

20.13   The E-Law provides that the ILR may disclose any information collected in the context of the E-Law, including confidential information, to the competition law authority.[27]

20.14   The prior approval of the authority in charge of competition matters is required before the adoption by the ILR of measures concerning products' and services' markets, access and interconnection and the universal service.[28] In the case of formal opposition to a decision that is proposed by the ILR, it must renounce the adoption of the measure to the extent that opposition was based solely on competition law.[29]

20.15   The ILR periodically consults the industry and users.[30] Before adopting a measure that would have a significant impact on the market, the ILR must allow interested parties to present their observations on the planned measure within one month. To this end, the ILR sets up a consultation procedure which is published in the official gazette (*Mémorial*) and on the ILR's website, which also provides, unless it contains confidential information, information concerning the consultations already in progress and the results of past consultations.[31]

20.16   Where the ILR intends to take a decision concerning access or interconnection or which aims to modify obligations imposed on authorised undertakings and which would affect the exchanges between the member states, it shall include the European Commission and the regulatory authorities of the other EU member states in the consultation procedure. The measure finally adopted by the ILR is communicated to the European Commission.[32]

20.17   Pursuant to the E-Law, the ILR holds periodic consultations with authorised undertakings, manufacturers and consumers' and end-users' representatives on any questions related to the rights of end-users and consumers with regard to the electronic communications services accessible by the public, in particular when these questions have a significant impact on the market.[33]

20.18   It may also act in the context of dispute resolution.[34] The E-Law states that, without prejudice to an action before the courts, a dispute arising between authorised undertakings with regard to the obligations provided by the Law and its implementing regulations and decisions may be submitted to the ILR.[35] The dispute is brought before the ILR by one party's registered letter.[36] After having heard the

---

25   Art 74 E-Law.
26   Art 73(2) E-Law.
27   Art 74(3) E-Law.
28   Art 73(1) E-Law.
29   Art 73(2) E-Law.
30   Art 77 E-Law.
31   Art 75 E-Law.
32   Art 76(1) E-Law.
33   Art 77 E-Law.
34   Arts 77 and 79 E-Law.
35   Art 78(1) E-Law.
36   Art 78(2) E-Law.

observations of each party, the ILR's decision shall be issued within four months from the date of receipt of the request.[37] Such decision is made available to the public having regard to the requirements of business confidentiality.[38] The E-Law also provides for the resolution of disputes through mediation. The ILR may act as a mediator between authorised undertakings. To the extent that the parties to the mediation agree with the result of the mediation, they will be bound by the decision of the ILR acting as mediator, which may not be challenged on appeal.[39]

Right of Appeal against NRA's Decisions

20.19   The E-Law provides that the two usual distinct types of administrative appeals may be lodged against the ILR's decisions.[40]

An action in cancellation (*recours en annulation*) before the administrative court is, in principle, available in respect of all decisions of the ILR. However, decisions taken by the ILR on the basis of article 80 E-Law, which concern the administrative and disciplinary sanctions that may be imposed by the ILR, may only be challenged by an action in reversal (*recours en réformation*) before the administrative court.[41]

The NRA's Obligations to Cooperate with the Commission

20.20   The ILR must cooperate with the regulatory authorities of other member states and with the European Commission in the context of the consolidation procedure in accordance with article 7 Framework Directive.[42] The ILR may have to withdraw a decision which results in the definition of a market not retained by the Commission or which identifies an undertaking as having significant market power where the Commission expresses its doubt with regard to such qualification.[43]

20.21   The E-Law does not reflect the Commission's power to stipulate standards and specifications (article 17 Framework Directive) and to issue specifications (article 19 Framework Directive).

'Significant Market Power' as a Fundamental Prerequisite of Regulation

Definition of SMP

20.22   The definition in the E-Law[44] of an undertaking with significant market power is identical to the one contained in article 14 (2) and (3) Framework

---

37   Art 78(3) E-Law.
38   Art 78(4) E-Law.
39   Art 78(6) E-Law.
40   Art 6 E-Law.
41   An action in cancellation may only cancel the administrative decision, while the action in reversal does not cancel such administrative decision but amends it.
42   See para 20.16 above.
43   Art 76(2) E-Law.
44   Art 2(11) E-Law.

Directive. The E-Law provides that the ILR shall take into account the criteria set out in Annex II of the Framework Directive, which have been reproduced in article 19(2) E-Law.

Definition of relevant markets and SMP designation

20.23   If the ILR determines that, based on its analysis of a market in the electronic communications sector, such market is not competitive, it identifies the undertakings with significant market power in such market.[45] It then imposes specific and appropriate obligations on undertakings with significant market power in accordance with the provisions of the E-Law, or it maintains or modifies these obligations, if they already exist.[46]

20.24   Certain obligations that may be imposed by the ILR on undertakings with significant market power are detailed under the sections of the E-Law concerning access and interconnection and the universal service.[47] However, the ILR may require such undertakings with significant market power to comply with other 'additional' obligations that it deems appropriate.[48]

20.25   If a retail market is not competitive according to the ILR, and if the ILR concludes that the imposed access, interconnection or numbering obligations are not sufficient to ensure effective competition on such market, it may impose adequate obligations on undertakings having significant market power.[49]

NRA's Regulatory Duties concerning Rights of Way, Co-location and Facility Sharing

Rights of way

20.26   Pursuant to the E-Law, any authorised undertaking has a right of way on the public property of the State and of local authorities. This right allows access to technical infrastructures/facilities and equipment as well as their installation.[50] The installation of facilities and associated facilities must be carried out under the least detrimental conditions for the public property concerned, having due regard to the environment and the aesthetic quality of the locations.[51]

20.27   Where the relevant public property does not concern the road or railway networks, the authorities' managers grant access to such property by way of contract. Such contract may not contain provisions relating to the commercial conditions of the activity. A copy of the contract must be disclosed by the authorised undertaking to the ILR within one month from its date of coming into force.[52] The right of way over public property pertaining to roads and railways is

---

45   Art 19(1) E-Law.
46   Art 20 E-Law.
47   See para 20.65 below.
48   Art 21(1) Law. Please note that such appropriate obligations are not detailed in the Law.
49   Art 21 E-Law; see para 20.65 below.
50   Art 64(1) E-Law.
51   Art 64(2) E-Law.
52   Art 65(1) E-Law.

subject to an authorisation delivered by the competent authority.[53] No tax, fees, toll fee, remuneration or indemnity of any nature may be imposed for the passage through public property.[54]

20.28   The owner of a road or railway is under a duty to negotiate the terms of a contract with the authorised undertakings which shall use the right of way with regard to the same property.[55]

20.29   An authorised undertaking which intends to establish facilities and associated facilities on private property must enter into a written contract with the owner of the property that is to be used. The contract shall regulate the possibility of sharing facilities and associated facilities with another authorised undertaking.[56]

Co-location and facility sharing

20.30   Where the maximum capacities of occupation of a public property have been reached by the use made of it by one authorised undertaking only, the owner of a public property shall make the granting of rights conditional on the execution of works that will allow the subsequent sharing of the facilities. The terms and conditions of access to such facilities are disclosed by the owner to the ILR, which publishes them on its website.[57]

20.31   Where an authorised undertaking wishes to use land in order to install equipment on it, and if such land is already used by another authorised undertaking, the E-Law provides that the owner of the land shall oblige the two undertakings to negotiate the terms of a sharing contract for the existing facilities. The contract must contain provisions regarding the apportionment of maintenance costs of the shared equipment and facilities. Where no contract is found or in the case of a dispute, each of the parties concerned, including the owner, may request that the ILR take a decision in the context of its dispute resolution role.[58]

20.32   Where an undertaking has entered into a contract authorising it to install facilities or associated facilities on private property, and such installation is not exclusively used for the connection of such private property to the network, it must disclose a copy of this contract to the ILR within one month from the date of its coming into force. The ILR is authorised to disclose the provisions of such a contract to any authorised undertaking which requests it, allowing such undertaking to address a request for the sharing of facilities to the parties to such contracts.[59]

Transitional Provisions

20.33   Authorised undertakings which have significant market power, according to the ministerial decree of 21 June 2000 establishing a list of the important operators on the telecommunications market and notified as such, retain their

---

53   Art 65(2) E-Law.
54   Art 65(3) E-Law.
55   Art 66 E-Law.
56   Art 68 E-Law.
57   Art 69 E-Law.
58   Art 70 E-Law.
59   Art 71 E-Law.

status and the obligations that result from such status until a new classification concerning power on the markets is established by the ILR in accordance with the Law.[60]

20.34   Operators and authorised undertakings that provide communications networks must notify any contract entered into before the date of entry into force of the E-Law on 1 July 2005 which concerns the granting of rights of way, as provided for by the E-Law, before 1 July 2006.

REGULATION OF MARKET ENTRY: IMPLEMENTATION OF THE AUTHORISATION DIRECTIVE

The General Authorisation of Electronic Communications

20.35   Without prejudice to the provisions of other applicable legislation, the business of providing networks and electronic communication services is freely exercised, upon notification to the ILR.[61]

20.36   'General authorisation' is defined as the provisions put in place by the E-Law and its implementing regulations, which ensure rights for the provision of electronic communications networks and services and which lay down sector-specific obligations that may apply to all or specific types of electronic communications networks and services.[62]

20.37   Luxembourg opted in favour of the introduction of a notification system in accordance with article 3(2) Authorisation Directive. Thus, the only prior obligation imposed on companies that wish to operate electronic communications networks or provide electronic communications services is to make a prior notification to the ILR which has to be filed at least 20 days before the commencement date of the activities which fall under the provisions of the Law.[63] The notification must identify the contemplated activities and their expected launch date. Such information is recorded by the ILR in a register which is accessible electronically to the public. Upon request by the applicant, the ILR may deliver a certificate confirming that the notification has been filed. The purpose of the certificate is to facilitate the dealings of the authorised undertaking[64] with other regulatory authorities.

20.38   When the authorised undertaking offers electronic communications networks or services to the public, it has the right to negotiate interconnection with other providers of public communications networks and services and, if applicable, to obtain access to or interconnection with their networks on any part of the EU territory, in accordance with applicable legislation.[65]

---

60   Art 82(5) E-Law.

61   Art 7 E-Law.

62   Art 2(6) E-Law. Please note that the E-Law does not provide specific rules for Voice over Internet Protocol (VoIP) services which are encompassed in the definition of electronic communications provided for by art 2(26) E-Law, which is the same as the one provided for by the Framework Directive. Based on the 1997 Law, some Luxembourg companies already offered these services such as Coditel and Luxembourg Online.

63   Art 8 E-Law.

64   The term 'authorised undertaking' as used in this chapter is an undertaking that has filed a notification with ILR.

65   Art 9 E-Law.

Rights of Use for Radio Frequencies

20.39 The provisions on the organisation of the management of radio frequencies are contained in the RF Law. The RF Law provides that radio frequencies are scarce facilities whose management and use are reserved to the state.[66] A prior individual authorisation is required for any use of a radio frequency or channel on Luxembourg territory.[67]

20.40 The use, with specific assignment(s), of radio frequencies or channels, for both transmission and reception, is subject to a licence. The licence is personal and non transferable.[68] Such licence is granted by the competent minister on the basis of objective criteria and according to a transparent, non-discriminatory and proportional procedure. A grand-ducal regulation entitled 'frequency plan'[69] determines the plan of apportionment and distribution of radio frequencies.

20.41 If several candidates request a licence for the exclusive use of the same frequency, or if such a frequency must serve for the setting up of a network with the primary purpose of providing electronic communications services that are accessible to the public, such licence shall be granted through a procedure of public call for tenders, with either a competitive or a comparative selection.[70]

20.42 A grand-ducal regulation shall define and determine the conditions of use of parts of the spectrum of frequencies that may be used without specific assignment, for both transmission and reception.[71]

20.43 Frequency assignments are recorded in the Frequency Register, which also contains information about the obligations associated with the frequencies.[72]

20.44 The conditions attached to the right to use radio frequencies are identical to those listed under Annex B to the Authorisation Directive except for the fifth condition since, under Luxembourg law, a licence is personal and non-transferable.[73]

20.45 The fees that are payable for the making available of radio frequencies are set out in a grand-ducal regulation.[74]

Rights of Use for Numbers

20.46 Article 63 E-Law states that the ILR establishes a national numbering plan that is placed under its control, by taking into account the consumers' interest and by ensuring fair competition between authorised undertakings. The ILR sets out provisions regarding numbering, the modification of such numbering, the use and

---

66 Art 2(1) RF Law.
67 Art 3 RF Law.
68 Art 3(2) RF Law.
69 Grand-ducal regulation of 10 March 2001 determining the frequency allocation, attribution and assignment plan.
70 Art 6(2) RF Law.
71 Art 3(3) RF Law.
72 Art 5(2) RF Law.
73 Art 7 RF Law.
74 Grand-ducal regulation of 25 September 1988 on the amount and means of payment of the fees due for the establishment and the operation of telecommunications networks or services, as amended by the grand-ducal regulation of 4 December 2003.

the structure of the numbers, the allocation of numbers to each authorised undertaking and each electronic communications service, as well as regarding number portability.

20.47   The applicable conditions and the fees that are due for the use of numbers are published by the ILR.

20.48   The Law provides that the allocation of individual numbers and of series of numbers to authorised undertakings should be done by the ILR in an objective, proportional, transparent, non-discriminatory and expedient manner.

20.49   An authorised undertaking that uses series of numbers may not discriminate against other undertakings that provide electronic communications services with regard to the sequences of numbers that are used in order to gain access to their services.

20.50   No obligation exists under the E-Law to provide number portability, carrier pre-selection or indirect access.

The NRA's Enforcement Powers

20.51   The ILR may impose sanctions on an authorised undertaking that fails to comply with the provisions provided for by the E-Law.[75] Before doing so, the ILR informs it of the alleged infringement and allows the undertaking to express its views or to remedy the infringement within a certain timeframe set by the ILR, which may in principle not be less than one month.[76] If the undertaking concerned does not remedy the situation, the ILR may take appropriate and proportionate measures, as provided by article 80 E-Law.

20.52   The ILR may impose fines of up to €5,000 for a natural person and up to €25,000 for a legal entity. Such fines may be doubled in the case of a second offence. It may pronounce, either instead of or in addition to the fine, one or more of the following disciplinary punishments: warning, blame, prohibition on carrying out certain operations, or the temporary suspension of one or more leaders of the undertaking.

20.53   If an infringement represents an immediate threat to public safety, national security or public health, the competent authority may take urgent interim measures to remedy the situation. If such an infringement is liable to create serious economic damage or operational problems for other suppliers or users of electronic communications networks or services, the ILR is in charge of applying appropriate measures. Such interim measures may be maintained by the ILR or the competent authority for as long as the infringement has not ceased. The costs involved with the above-mentioned interim measures shall be borne by the infringing undertaking.

Administrative Charges and Fees for Rights of Use

20.54   The E-Law provides that the filing of a notification shall mean that the undertaking accepts the conditions of contributing to the costs incurred by the ILR

---

75   Art 15 E-Law.
76   A shorter timeframe may be applicable when the undertaking agrees to such shorter timeframe or in case of repeated breach. A longer timeframe may also be granted by ILR.

for the management of the sector.[77] The amount of such contribution is set annually by the ILR.[78] It will depend on the global administrative costs of the ILR arising from the regulation of the electronic communications sector and will be shared between the authorised undertakings by using an objective, open and proportionate method. The ILR publishes an annual balance sheet of its administrative costs and of the global amount of collected fees. The fees that are due for making radio frequencies available are set out in a grand-ducal regulation. The fees that are due for the use of numbers are published by the ILR.

Transitional Regulations for Existing Authorisations

20.55   Undertakings that were granted a licence under the 1997 Law, as well as undertakings that had filed a declaration under the 1997 Law, are considered as being authorised undertakings with respect to the E-Law, unless they file a declaration to the contrary with the ILR.[79] No further steps relating to authorisations are thus required for undertakings that were in compliance with the 1997 Law.

REGULATION OF NETWORK ACCESS AND INTERCONNECTION: IMPLEMENTATION OF THE ACCESS DIRECTIVE

Objectives and Scope of Access Regulation

20.56   The E-Law establishes rights and obligations for authorised undertakings and operators with regard to access or interconnection. The objectives of the E-Law are to ensure sustainable competition, interoperability of electronic communications services and consumer benefits. The gist of the regulation resides in the possibility or obligation, depending on the circumstances, to negotiate appropriate commercial contracts with regard to access or interconnection.

20.57   The provisions on access apply to authorised undertakings seeking access to facilities and/or services for the purpose of providing electronic communications services, whereas the provisions on interconnection apply to the physical and logical linking of public communications networks. Interconnection is a specific type of access implemented between public network operators.

Basic Regulatory Concepts

20.58   The definitions of the words 'access' and 'interconnection' contained in the E-Law are identical to those set out in the Access Directive.[80]

20.59   Any authorised undertaking may freely negotiate contracts establishing the technical and commercial aspects of access or interconnection with another authorised undertaking or with an undertaking authorised in another member state of the EU. An undertaking that does not provide electronic communications services and

---

77   Art 10 E-Law.
78   Until publication of the fees provided for by article 10(2) E-Law, the amounts fixed in the grand-ducal regulations of 25 September 1988 and 14 December 2001 shall continue to be due.
79   Art 82(1) and (2) E-Law.
80   Art 2(2) and (14) E-Law.

does not operate an electronic communications network in Luxembourg may not be required to notify its activities to the ILR before being able to request access or interconnection.[81]

20.60   Upon request by other authorised undertakings, operators have an obligation to negotiate a reciprocal interconnection to provide electronic communications services that are accessible to the public in order to guarantee the provision of services and their interoperability in the whole EU. Operators shall offer access and interconnection to other undertakings according to terms and conditions that are compatible with the obligations imposed upon them by the ILR in accordance with the provisions of the E-Law.[82]

20.61   The E-Law provides for the priority of commercial negotiations[83] in the sense that it is only in the case of failure of such negotiations that the ILR shall intervene.

20.62   According to article 26 E-Law, the ILR may impose the following obligations in order to ensure, as far as possible, adequate access and interconnection:

- on authorised undertakings that control access to end-users, to the extent necessary in order to ensure end-to-end connectivity: obligations of access and interconnection, including, where it is justified, the obligation to ensure interconnection of their networks where such interconnection has not yet been realised; and
- on operators, to the extent necessary in order to ensure access by end-users to services of specific digital radio and television broadcasts: obligations of access, under fair, reasonable and non-discriminatory conditions, to application program interfaces and to electronic programme guides.

20.63   Moreover, the ILR may also:

- set out a mandatory procedure with precise timeframes for the completion of the negotiation of any contract on access to the network(s), including on unbundled access to the local loop or on an interconnection contract,
- set out the terms and conditions of access or interconnection, including the financial terms and conditions, if no contract is entered into within the specified timeframe or in the event of failure of negotiations, and
- impose amendment to an existing contract, including of the relevant financial terms and conditions, in exceptional cases justified by requirements of interoperability of the services or accounting obligations imposed on one of the parties. The ILR may set a deadline for implementation of the amendment. After expiry of the deadline, the ILR may impose terms and conditions of access and interconnection, as set out above in this paragraph.[84]

---

81   Art 23(1) E-Law.
82   Art 23(2) E-Law.
83   Art 23 E-Law.
84   Art 29 E-Law.

Access- and Interconnection-related Obligations with Respect to SMP Undertakings

20.64   The access and interconnection obligations for SMP undertakings are identical to those of other authorised undertakings. However, the national regulatory authority may, under certain circumstances, impose supplementary obligations on SMP undertakings which go beyond the ILR's regulatory power with regard to non-SMP undertakings.

20.65   If the ILR considers, after having made a market analysis, that an operator has significant market power, it may impose obligations:

- of transparency in relation to access and/or interconnection, requiring operators to make public specified information,
- of non-discrimination,
- of accounting separation,
- of access to, and use of, specific network facilities (the non-exhaustive list of requirements that may be imposed on operators on this account and which is contained in article 12(1) Access Directive has been copied into the E-Law), or
- of price control and cost accounting.[85]

The Luxembourg legislator has copied the more detailed provisions of the Access Directive on the above-mentioned obligations.

Related Regulatory Powers with Respect to SMP Undertakings

20.66   Pursuant to article 25 E-Law, an undertaking with significant market power on the market for the provision of connection to and use of the public telephone network at a fixed location shall enable its subscribers to access the services of any interconnected undertaking providing publicly available telephone services:

- on a call-by-call basis, by dialling a carrier selection code, and
- by means of pre-selection, with a facility to override any pre-selected choice on a call-by-call basis by dialling a carrier selection code.

20.67   The E-Law specifies that pricing for access and interconnection related to the provision of the above-mentioned facilities is cost-oriented; and direct charges, if any, must not act as a disincentive for the use of such facilities.

20.68   Requests by end-users in order for the above-mentioned services to be put in place, with regard to other networks or by other means, are examined by the ILR in accordance with the market analysis procedure, and shall be imposed with regard to the consultation procedure.

20.69   If the ILR determines that the wholesale market for the supply of the minimum leased line network or part of such network is not competitive, the ILR shall identify the undertaking having SMP in the market of the supply of the specific elements of the minimum leased line network and shall impose obligations to provide the minimum leased lines on such identified undertakings.[86]

---

85   Art 30 E-Law.
86   Art 22 E-Law.

Transitional Provisions

20.70   Obligations in the matters of access, interconnection, the application of the open network provision and the local loop unbundling in the electronic communications sector that have been imposed on undertakings in the sector under earlier legislation (see below) are maintained until a re-examination of such obligations is made by the ILR in accordance with the relevant provisions of the E-Law. The earlier legislation (referred to above) comprises: the 1997 Law; the amended grand-ducal regulation of 22 December 1997 on the general conditions for the establishment and operation of fixed telecommunications networks and telephony services; the amended grand-ducal regulation of 22 December 1997 on the general conditions for the establishment and operation of fixed telecommunications networks; and the amended grand-ducal regulation of 2 July 1998 on the general conditions for the establishment and operation of telephony services.

REGULATION OF UNIVERSAL SERVICES AND USERS' RIGHTS: THE UNIVERSAL SERVICE DIRECTIVE

Regulation of Universal Service Obligations

Scope of universal service obligations

20.71   All end-users have a right to the universal service in the matter of electronic communications. The universal service encompasses the following:

- the provision of access at a fixed location,
- the making available of public pay telephones,
- the making available and publication of at least one telephone directory, and
- the provision of one telephone directory enquiry service.[87]

20.72   Article 40 E-Law provides that public pay telephones shall be available to meet the reasonable needs of users in terms of geographical coverage, numbers of telephones, quality of services and accessibility for disabled users.

20.73   Such public pay telephones may offer the possibility to call, free of charge, emergency numbers[88] and must advertise, at least by billposting, the tariffs of use, the terms and conditions of use, the telephone number for help services, of emergency services and enquiry services,[89] and the telephone number of the public pay telephone.[90]

20.74   At least one directory of information, including all subscribers to the publicly available telephone service, has to be published and made available, free of charge, to end users. Such directory shall be updated at least once a year.[91]

20.75   At least one telephone directory enquiry service is available to end-users, including users of public pay telephones.[92]

20.76   The E-Law provides that the universal service may be offered by one or several authorised undertakings or groups of authorised undertakings which

---

87   Art 37 E-Law.
88   Art 40(2) E-Law.
89   These services are free of charge.
90   Art 41(4) E-Law.
91   Art 43(5) E-Law.
92   Art 46 E-Law.

provide different parts of the universal service or which cover different parts of the national territory. The ILR ensures that the whole national territory is covered.[93]

Designation of undertakings obliged to provide universal services

20.77   If the ILR notices that all or part of the universal service is not ensured or is not sufficiently or adequately ensured, the ILR organises a call for tenders for the provision of the universal service.[94] If the function of providing the universal service cannot be attributed to an authorised undertaking pursuant to the call for tenders, the ILR may impose the obligation to contribute to the provision of the public service on any undertaking with significant market power.[95] According to article 58 E-Law, an authorised undertaking may be obliged, by decision of the Minister, upon advice of the ILR, to render electronic communications services, other than those regarding universal services obligations, accessible to the public.

20.78   The E-Law is based on the same principle as the formerly applicable 1997 Law: the services relating to the 'universal service' are ensured by the various undertakings on the entire territory under the conditions set out in the E-Law. The universal service has not been 'launched' yet, in the sense that no specific undertaking has been designated in order to provide the universal service. Only in the case of failure of this system, ie in the case of a lack of provision of the universal service, shall the ILR make a call for tenders or designate one or more undertakings with significant market power in order to ensure the provision of the universal service.[96]

Regulation of retail tariffs, user's expenditures and quality of service

20.79   Article 49 E-Law provides for the obligation on any undertaking providing universal service to comply with the obligations detailed in Part A of Annex 1 to the Universal Service Directive.[97]

20.80   The ILR shall specify the minimum quality criteria for the services. The undertaking providing a universal service communicates to the ILR, once a year, the data allowing verification in respect of the quality criteria established by the ILR.[98]

Cost calculation and financing of universal services

20.81   Article 56 E-Law provides for a fund for the maintenance of the universal service to be created. Such fund is managed by the ILR. The financial management of the fund is subject to dual control by an external auditor and by the *Cour des Comptes*.

Any authorised undertaking shall, if necessary, contribute to the funds for the maintenance of the universal service. The amount of contribution is determined by

---

93   Art 38 E-Law.
94   Art 52 E-Law.
95   Art 53 E-Law.
96   Parliamentary Documents 5178, pp 19 and 20.
97   Itemised billing, selective call barring for outgoing calls free of charge, pre-payment system, phased payment of connection fees, and terms of recovery of non-payment of bills.
98   Art 50 E-Law.

the ILR according to the proportion between the total sales generated by all notified companies and the sales of any authorised undertaking. Such contributions are defined separately for each authorised undertaking.

The amount of the contribution for each calendar year is determined, for each notified company, on the basis of sales in the previous year.[99]

When the ILR has decided to implement the mechanism of the funds for the maintenance of the universal service, it makes available to the public the principles of cost sharing and details regarding this mechanism.[100]

The ILR publishes an annual report indicating the cost of the obligations of universal service as calculated, setting out the contributions made by all the authorised undertakings and announcing the commercial advantages that the authorised undertaking has gained from providing the universal service.

End User Rights

Contracts

20.82   At the time of negotiating the Universal Service Directive, the Luxembourg delegation was opposed to a sector-specific consumer protection provision, such as the minimum provisions that must be contained in a written subscriber contract for connection and/or access to the public telephone network. It argued in favour of the application of a general contract and consumer protection law. The arguments of the Luxembourg delegation were not adopted, however, and the above-mentioned minimum provisions concerning sector-specific consumer protection have been implemented as such in the E-Law, except the provision on the method of initiating procedures for the settlement of disputes.[101]

Complaint handling procedures

20.83   With regard to the settlement of disputes, the Parliamentary Documents explain that, as the alternative dispute resolution procedures in Luxembourg, such as mediation, require the consent of both parties involved, undertakings who offer telephone services that are accessible to the public must accept recourse to such a dispute resolution method if the consumer requires it.[102]

Article 61 E-Law provides that the written contract must contain the agreement of the undertaking to submit any possible dispute to an extra-judicial procedure.

Transparency obligations

20.84   An undertaking that offers electronic communications services accessible to the public is under a duty to publish transparent and up-to-date information on the services that are offered, applicable prices and tariffs as well as on standard terms and conditions, in respect of the access to and use of publicly available telephone

---

99   Art 56(3) E-Law.
100   Art 57 E-Law.
101   Parliamentary Documents 5178, pp 75 and 76.
102   Parliamentary Documents 5178, p 76.

services, compensation options or reimbursement proposed, and dispute resolution mechanisms.[103] Such information shall be complete, comparable, and easy to read. The information is disclosed to the ILR before publication. The ILR determines the content and the form of the publication as well as the method of publication.

20.85   Article 60(2) E-Law states that the ILR must give to organisations representing end-users and consumers, upon request, the necessary information to make an independent evaluation of the cost of alternative usage patterns.

DATA PROTECTION: IMPLEMENTATION OF THE E-PRIVACY DIRECTIVE

Overview

20.86   The E-Privacy Law contains one major difference from the E-Privacy Directive: the definitions of 'user' and 'subscriber'[104] concern legal entities in addition to natural persons. Thus, data processing in connection with the provision of publicly available electronic communications networks and which concerns legal entities falls under the provisions of the E-Privacy Law. It should be noted that the Luxembourg legislator has previously opted for this approach. The law of 2 August 2002 relating to the protection of natural persons or legal entities with regard to the processing of personal data, which implemented Directive 1995/46/EC of the European Parliament and of the Council of 24 October 1995 on the protection of individuals with regard to the processing of personal data and on the free movement of such data, also applies to the processing of data regarding legal entities. The Luxembourg legislator considers that it is necessary to regulate the processing of data concerning legal entities because such data indirectly relates to natural persons.

Confidentiality of Communications

20.87   Article 4 E-Privacy Law sets out the fundamental principle of confidentiality of communications, as contained in article 5 E-Privacy Directive.

20.88   The E-Privacy Law distinguishes itself from the E-Privacy Directive by the list of authorised actions, which is longer than that of the E-Privacy Directive.

20.89   In conformity with the E-Privacy Directive, the E-Privacy Law contains provisions concerning:

- the data processing required for the conveyance of a communication,
- the data processing done in the course of business practice for the purpose of providing evidence of a commercial transaction or any other business communication,
- the processing of data, collected by the use of cookies or other similar techniques, with regard to information stored in the terminal equipment of a subscriber, user or end-user, and
- the data processing undertaken by the competent authorities with regard to the safeguarding of national security, defence, national safety, the prevention,

---

103   Art 60 E-Law.
104   Art 2(a) and (m) E-Privacy Law.

investigation, detection and prosecution of criminal offences (the E-Privacy Law specifies the authorities that are entitled to proceed with this type of data processing).[105]

20.90   However, the E-Privacy Law also contains provisions on the possibility of recording telephone conversations in the context of the provision of emergency or alert services.[106] The traffic data, including location data, shall be erased once help has been provided. The content of communications, which may be used to listen again to certain messages in the case of incomprehension or ambiguity, the documentation of false alerts or of abusive or menacing calls and the production of evidence in case of a dispute with regard to events concerning emergency interventions, must be erased within six months.

20.91   Failure to comply with the above-mentioned provisions of the E-Privacy Law bears a prison sentence of eight days to one year and/or a fine of €251 to €125,000.[107]

Traffic Data and Location Data

20.92   The definitions of 'traffic data'[108] and 'location data'[109] are identical to the definitions contained in the E-Privacy Directive.

20.93   Any service provider or operator which processes traffic data must keep such data for a period of 12 months for the purpose of investigation, detection and prosecution of criminal offences, and with the sole aim of allowing, if necessary, the making available of information to judicial authorities.[110] The E-Privacy Law further provides that the traffic data concerning subscribers or users must be erased or rendered anonymous after the expiry of the above-mentioned period of 12 months.[111]

20.94   During the period of retention of the traffic data, any service provider or operator must render access to the data impossible when such data is not required any more for the conveyance of a communication or for billing purposes. Access must, however, still be granted to certain competent official authorities acting in accordance with the provisions of the law, such as criminal prosecution authorities acting in the context of an investigation relating to a criminal offence.[112]

20.95   Traffic data that are necessary to establish subscribers' bills and for the purpose of interconnection payments may be processed. Such processing is only lawful up to the date until which the bill may lawfully be contested or until which legal proceedings for the payment of such bill may be brought, but may in any case not exceed a period of six months if the bill has been paid or is not the object of legal action or dispute.[113] Traffic data may also be processed in order to provide

---

105   Art 4(3) E-Privacy Law.
106   Art 4(3)(d) E-Privacy Law.
107   Art 4(4) E-Privacy Law.
108   Art 2(f) E-Privacy Law.
109   Art 2(g) E-Privacy Law.
110   Art 5(1)(a) E-Privacy Law.
111   Art 5(1)(b) E-Privacy Law.
112   Art 5(2) E-Privacy Law.
113   Art 5(3) E-Privacy Law.

value added services or for the marketing of electronic communications services in accordance with article 6(3) E-Privacy Directive, which has been implemented as such by the E-Privacy Law.[114]

20.96 The provisions of the E-Privacy Law on location data other than traffic data[115] are similar to the above-mentioned provisions on traffic data.

20.97 Infringement of the provisions on the processing of traffic data or location data contained in the E-Privacy Law bears a prison sentence of eight days to one year and/or a fine of €251 to €125,000.[116]

Itemised Billing

20.98 Every subscriber has the right to receive a non-itemised bill according to the E-Privacy Law.[117] Itemised bills shall not indicate any calls that are free of charge (including calls to the emergency services) and shall not contain any indication which would make it possible to identify the called person.[118]

Calling and Connected Line Identification

20.99 Article 7 E-Privacy Law contains provisions identical to the E-Privacy Directive with regard to the presentation and restriction of calling and connected line identification.

20.100 The Luxembourg legislator has specified that, with regard to calls to the unique European emergency number 112 and to other emergency numbers identified by the ILR, the identification of the calling line is always presented, even if the calling person has prevented it.[119]

20.101 With regard to the information of the public concerning rights relating to the presentation and restriction of calling and connected line identification by the service provider, the E-Privacy Law provides that such information shall take place by appropriate means and, at the latest, at the time a contract is entered into.[120]

20.102 A called subscriber claiming to be the victim of malicious anonymous calls may, in certain circumstances, ask for the identification of the calling or connected line.[121]

Automatic Call Forwarding

20.103 Where automatic call forwarding (or diversion) is offered as a service, the service provider must offer to any subscriber the possibility to stop the automatic call forwarding by a third party to the subscriber's terminal, using a simple means and free of charge, provided that the service provider may identify the origin of the

---

114 Art 5(4) E-Privacy Law.
115 Art 9 E-Privacy Law.
116 Arts 5(6) and 9(6) E-Privacy Law.
117 Art 6(1) E-Privacy Law.
118 Art 6(2) E-Privacy Law.
119 Art 7(5) E-Privacy Law.
120 Art 7(7) E-Privacy Law.
121 Art 7(8) E-Privacy Law.

forwarded calls. If applicable, the identification of such origin shall be done in cooperation with other service providers.[122]

Directories of Subscribers

20.104   Subscribers must be informed, free of charge and before they are included in the directory, about the purpose of a printed or electronic directory of subscribers available to the public or obtainable through directory enquiry services, in which their personal data can be included and of any further usage possibilities based on search functions embedded in electronic versions of the directory.[123]

20.105   Subscribers must be offered the possibility to decide which data, if any, concerning them is included in the directory; and they have a right to verify, correct and withdraw their data. Not being included in a public subscriber directory, verifying, correcting or withdrawing personal data from it is free of charge.[124]

Unsolicited Communications

20.106   Unsolicited communications are regulated by article 11 E-Privacy Law. Article 11 applies to automated calling systems without human intervention (automatic calling machines), facsimile machines or electronic mail. Pursuant to Art 11–1 E-Privacy Law, Luxembourg has an opt-in system, ie unsolicited communications are only allowed if the subscriber, a natural person, has given his prior consent. Any supplier which obtains from its customers their electronic contact details for electronic mail in the context of the sale of a product or service may use these electronic contact details for direct marketing of its own similar products or services, provided that the customer is clearly and expressly given the right to object, free of charge and in an easy manner, to such use of electronic contact details when they are collected and on the occasion of each message where the customer has not initially refused such use. When the customer is a natural person, unsolicited communications for the purposes of direct marketing in cases other than those referred to above are subject to an opt-in system.

20.107   The practice of sending electronic mail for the purposes of direct marketing disguising or concealing the identity of the sender on whose behalf the communication is made, or without a valid address to which the recipient may send a request that such communications cease, is prohibited.

20.108   Infringement of these provisions bears a prison sentence of eight days to one year and/or a fine of €251 to €125,000.[125]

---

122   Art 8 E-Privacy Law.
123   Art 10(1) E-Privacy Law.
124   Art 10(2) E-Privacy Law.
125   Art 11(6) E-Privacy Law.

Transitional provisions

20.109   A service provider offering a public directory before the entry into force of the E-Privacy Law must inform subscribers without delay, in accordance with the provisions of the E-Privacy Law, of the purpose of the data processing.[126]

---

126 Art 13 E-Privacy Law.

The Maltese Market for Electronic Communications[1]

Louis Cassar Pullicino (assisted by Paul Edgar Micallef, David Gonzi and Celia Falzon)
Ganado & Associates (Malta)

LEGAL STRUCTURE

Basic Policy

21.1   In December 1997 the Maltese Government started the process of liberalising the telecommunications market in Malta: it established a telecommunications regulator, and divested the incumbent Telemalta Corporation (now Maltacom plc) of the regulatory role which it had enjoyed until then, thereby paving the way for the gradual introduction of competition in the various telecommunications markets. In 2000 the Maltese Government approved a National Plan for the Reform of the Telecommunications Sector[2] detailing the process from the position at that time, and culminating in the full liberalisation of the various telecommunications markets in January 2003, whilst highlighting the impact on, and benefits for, the existing principal market players.

21.2   The overall policy objectives as reflected in the mission statement of the Malta Communications Authority ('MCA'), and the objectives as established at law, focus on achieving sustainable competition, enabling customer choice and value for money, whilst contributing to the development of an environment that is conducive to investment and continued social and economic growth. To some extent this has been attained in a number of the markets, notably mobile telephony, internet services and voice over the internet protocol.

Implementation of the EU Directives, Legislation

21.3   The 2002 EU Regulatory Package was transposed into Maltese law in two phases: on 3 August 2004 an Act of Parliament[3] was approved amending various

---

1   Editing of this chapter closed on 21 June 2005. Dr. Micallef, Ms. Falzon and Dr Gonzi assisted Ganado & Associates by preparing different sections of this contribution. All three are officers within the Malta Communications Authority.

2   This Plan was included as an annex to the Act XXVIII of 2000. This Act amended the Telecommunications (Regulation) Act, whilst enacting the Malta Communications Authority Act.

3   Act VII of 2004 entitled the 'Communications Laws (Amendment) Act, 2004'.

laws relating to communications with the purpose of implementing the high level norms as stated in the Framework Directive and, to a lesser degree, in the Access and Authorisation Directives; and, on 14 September 2004, regulations[4] were enacted by the Minister responsible for communications to implement the remaining provisions of the Framework, Authorisation, Universal Service and Access Directives.[5] The E-Privacy Directive was implemented by a separate legislative process following the enactment of two sets of regulations on 10 January 2003.[6]

21.4   Transposition into Maltese law has been by means of amendments to the following primary laws.[7]

- the Malta Communications Authority Act, Cap 418,
- the Telecommunications (Regulation) Act, Cap 399,
- the Utilities and Services (Regulation of Certain Works) Act, Cap 81,
- the Malta Maritime Authority Act, Cap 352,
- the Wireless Telegraphy Ordinance, Cap 49,[8] and
- the Broadcasting Authority Act, Cap 350.

Prior to the enactment of the amendments to the Malta Communications Authority Act (the 'MCA Act') and to the Electronic Communications (Regulation) Act (the 'ECR Act'), the Government issued a consultative public document with the proposed legislative changes in January 2004.[9]

21.5   Following the enactment of the above-mentioned amendments to primary legislation, the Minister responsible for communications after consultation with the MCA, by virtue of his powers to make regulations under the ECR Act, enacted the Electronic Communications Networks and Services (General) Regulations, 2004[10] ('Electronic Communications Regulations').

21.6   The Data Protection Directive was implemented following the enactment of two sets of regulations, namely the Processing of Personal Data (Electronic Communications Sector) Regulations and the Electronic Communications (Personal Data and Protection of Privacy) Regulations.[11]

21.7   The amendments to the MCA Act and to the ECR Act, coupled with the Regulations made under the latter Act, establish the legal basis for the new

---

4   The Electronic Communications Networks and Services (General) Regulations, 2004 enacted as per Legal Notice 412 of 2004.

5   The Minister was acting by virtue of the powers granted to him pursuant to the Act No VII of 2004 approved by Parliament earlier in 2004.

6   The applicable Maltese legislation to data protection is administered by two separate public authorities, the MCA and the Office of the Data Protection Commissioner. In the exercise of their respective functions these authorities are, where applicable, required to consult each other.

7   Other primary laws were amended; however, these are not included in the list as they do not relate to telecommunications but to other sectors – notably postal services and electronic commerce – which also fall within the remit of the MCA.

8   As a results of the amendments which came into force on 14 September 2004, this law was renamed the 'Radiocommunications Act'.

9   'A New Regulatory Framework for Electronic Communications Markets – A White Paper', January 2004.

10   As per Legal Notice 412 of 2004.

11   These Regulations were respectively enacted as per Legal Notice 16 of 2003 and Legal Notice 19 of 2003. The titles of the Regulations were amended to read respectively 'Processing of Personal Data (Electronic Communications Sector) Regulations' and 'Electronic Communications (Personal Data and Protection of Privacy) Regulations'.

regulatory regime whilst setting out the framework under which the MCA regulates the market and ensures compliance by undertakings with the applicable legislation and decisions.

REGULATORY PRINCIPLES: IMPLEMENTATION OF THE FRAMEWORK DIRECTIVE

Scope of Regulation

21.8   Maltese legislation has adopted the technology-neutral approach of the EU Directives. In doing so the Maltese legislator has used similar wording to that used in the Framework Directive in defining the key terms 'electronic communications network', 'electronic communications service' and 'associated facilities'.[12]

National Regulatory Authorities: Organisation, Regulatory Objectives, Competencies

21.9   The Maltese communications regulator is the MCA and started to operate as of 1 January 2001. The MCA was established following the enactment in 2000 of the MCA Act and of amendments to the Telecommunications (Regulation) Act, replacing the former Telecommunications Regulator.[13] The MCA is composed of a board consisting of a Chairman and four to six other members appointed by the Minister responsible for communications.

21.10   The objectives of the MCA in the exercise of its functions in relation to electronic communications include[14] the promotion of competition, contributing to the development of the internal market, promoting the interests of users within the European Communities, and ensuring, in so far as is practicable, that electronic communications services in Malta are provided to such an extent as to satisfy all reasonable demands for such services including emergency services, public call services and directory information services.

21.11   The MCA is responsible for ensuring compliance with obligations regarding the supply of and access to electronic communications networks and services, and for managing the national numbering resources. In accordance with its objectives at law and subject to the national radio frequency plan adopted by the Minister responsible for communications, the MCA is responsible for the effective management of the radio frequencies assigned to it under the aforesaid plan.

21.12   The MCA is empowered to require any person to provide it with any information, including financial information, which it considers to be necessary to ensure compliance with the laws it enforces and with any decisions or directives it may issue. The obligations on the MCA to publish information and to conduct consultations and to co-operate with other NRA's are dealt with under article 10 ECR Act and under regulation 5 Electronic Communications Regulations.

21.13   The Minister responsible for communications may, in relation to matters that appear to him to affect the public interest, give the MCA directions in writing

---

12   Art 2 ECR Act.
13   The Office of the Telecommunications Regulator was established when the Telecommunications (Regulation) Act was enacted in 1997.
14   Art 4 ECR Act.

of a general nature on the policy that the MCA must follow in carrying out its functions under the MCA Act. Such directions must not be inconsistent with the provisions of the said Act.[15]

21.14   The MCA and the Office of Fair Trading and the Director of Consumer Affairs are required to provide each other with such information as is necessary for the application of the provisions of the MCA Act. The MCA and the Office of Fair Trading have concluded a memorandum of understanding in relation to the co-operation and co-ordination of investigations between the two authorities particularly with regard to competition issues that may involve both authorities.[16] The MCA and the Data Protection Commissioner are, where appropriate, required to consult with each other in enforcing respectively the Processing of Personal Data (Electronic Communications Sector) Regulations, and the Electronic Communications (Personal Data and Protection of Privacy) Regulations.

21.15   If the MCA proposes to take a measure that has a significant impact on a market for electronic communications networks or services, it must first undertake a public consultation process in accordance with article 10 ECR Act.

21.16   Articles 24 to 26 ECR Act establish the procedure to be followed in dealing with disputes between undertakings, and with disputes between consumers and undertakings. In the case of disputes between undertakings, the MCA is required to determine the dispute within four months from when the dispute is notified to the MCA, unless there are circumstances which the MCA considers to be exceptional or if the MCA decides not to proceed because it is satisfied that there are other means of redress available to the parties for resolving the dispute in a timely manner. The MCA may of its own initiative investigate any dispute it becomes aware of.

21.17   Consumer complaints are dealt with by MCA under a similar though separate procedure. The consumer when referring a dispute to the MCA must allege that his or her complaint relates to an infringement of the ECR Act and that, *prima facie*, he or she has been affected by the said act or omission causing the said infringement. The procedure to be followed when dealing with such disputes is established by the MCA. The MCA must ensure that such a procedure is transparent, simple, inexpensive and conducive to a prompt and fair settlement. In resolving such disputes the MCA may issue directives to the undertaking concerned, requiring it to comply with any measures the MCA may specify, which measures may include an order to make compensation payments to the consumer affected.

21.18   Regulation 12 Electronic Communications Regulations establishes the procedure in the event of disputes between parties in different states, where the dispute lies within the competence of the MCA and the NRA of another state. The MCA in dealing with such disputes is required to co-ordinate with the other NRAs in accordance with the objectives stated in article 8 Framework Directive.

Right of Appeal against Decisions of the MCA

21.19   Part VIII of the MCA Act establishes the right of appeal to contest any decision or directive issued by the MCA. Any person, including an undertaking,

---

15   Art 6 MCA Act.
16   'Memorandum of Understanding between the Malta Communications Authority and the Consumer and Competition Division', May 2005.

aggrieved by a decision or directive of the MCA may, within 30 days from when notified of the decision, lodge an appeal before the Communications Appeals Board. In doing so the appellant must explain his or her juridical interest in contesting the decision or directive of the MCA. The MCA in turn has 20 days from the date when it is notified with the appeal application filed against it to reply to the appeal application.

21.20   The Communications Appeals Board is independent in the exercise of its functions, and a member may only be removed by the Prime Minister on grounds of gross negligence, conflict of interest or incompetence or acts or omissions unbecoming to a member of the Appeals Board.

21.21   The Appeals Board in the exercise of its functions has the same powers as the First Hall of the Civil Court and may, subject to any regulations that the Minister for communications establishes, regulate its own procedure.

21.22   The Appeals Board when determining an appeal may in whole or in part confirm or annul the decision appealed. In doing so the Appeals Board must in writing give the reasons for its decision, make the decision public and communicate it to the parties to the appeal.[17] All the parties to the proceedings before the Appeals Board can, on a point of law, contest the decision of the Appeals Board before the Court of Appeal (inferior jurisdiction).

21.23   Whilst proceedings are still pending before the Appeals Board or the Court of Appeal, the decision of the MCA stands and must be adhered to by all parties involved. Any party to the appeal may, however, apply to the Appeals Board or the Court of Appeal, as the case may be, to suspend the decision or directive of the MCA that is being contested pending the final outcome of the appeal.[18]

The NRA's Obligations to Cooperate with the Commission

21.24   The consolidation procedure[19] has been implemented into Maltese Law by Regulation 6 Electronic Communications Regulations. This regulation sets out the obligations of the MCA to make draft measures available to the NRAs of other Member States as well as to the Commission, and to take account of comments made by the Commission or by an NRA of another member state. Within the same framework the MCA is empowered to adopt provisional measures in exceptional circumstances to safeguard competition and protect the interest of users. The Commission also has veto powers in accordance with article 7 Framework Directive.

21.25   The powers of the European Commission and the obligations of the NRAs in relation to standards and specifications are reflected in condition 12 of the General Authorisation conditions applicable to undertakings providing electronic communications networks and services.[20] This condition requires undertakings to comply with any relevant compulsory standards adopted for the provision of services, technical interfaces or network functions, and to give due regard to any notices or guidelines that the MCA issues with respect to standards. Undertakings are also required to give due regard to any voluntary standards adopted by internationally recognised standardisation bodies.

---

17   Art 39 MCA Act.
18   Art 42 MCA Act.
19   Art 7 Framework Directive.
20   See condition 12 Twelfth Schedule Electronic Communications Regulations.

'Significant Market Power' as a Fundamental Prerequisite of Regulation

Definition of SMP

21.26 The definition of 'significant market power' under the ECR Act is similar to that used in the Framework Directive. SMP is defined as being a position equivalent to dominance, a position of economic strength affording an undertaking the power to behave to an appreciable extent independently of competitors, customers and, ultimately, consumers.[21] In October 2004, the MCA published a document entitled 'Market Review Methodology' detailing the manner in which significant market power is to be assessed.[22]

Definition of relevant markets and SMP designation

21.27 Article 9 ECR Act stipulates that the MCA must define relevant markets in accordance with the principles of competition law, taking the utmost account of any relevant recommendations and guidelines that the European Commission may issue.

21.28 The MCA is currently carrying out reviews of a number of markets. According to the timeframes stipulated in the MCA report 'Market Review Methodology' the majority of the market reviews are to be completed by the end of 2006.[23] It is expected that, whilst the MCA will define the markets similar to those markets listed in the Commission Recommendation on relevant markets,[24] the MCA may also – because of the small size of Malta and the particularities of the local markets – identify additional markets or extend recommended markets motivated in particular by the limited number of international gateways to Malta, the increasing use of Voice over IP for international calls, and the ubiquity of the cable network in Malta.

21.29 During the transitional period between the implementation of the measures under the new regulatory regime and the phasing out of those established under the previous regime, the ECR Act provides that the specific obligations imposed on operators designated as enjoying dominance under the former regime continue to apply.[25] These obligations include obligations relating to access and interconnection, tariffs for the provision of access to and use of public telephones, carrier selection or pre-selection, and the provision of leased lines.[26]

21.30 Where the MCA determines that a relevant market is not effectively competitive and designates undertakings with SMP, it is required to impose upon such undertakings the appropriate regulatory obligations and controls.[27] The remedies that may be imposed are delineated in the regulations published under the

21 Art 2 ECR Act, and see also reg 8 Electronic Communications Regulations.
22 Market Review Guidelines, Malta Communications Authority, 8 October 2004 (Market Review Guidelines 2004).
23 Market Review Guidelines 2004, p 43.
24 Melita Cable plc (C12715) u Video-On-Line Limited (C19013) vs Minister of Competitiveness and Communications and the Malta Communications Authority, First Hall Civil Court, App. no 443/2004 GCD.
25 Arts 38 to 40 ECR Act.
26 Art 39 ECR Act.
27 Art 9 ECR Act.

ECR Act.[28] These regulations implement faithfully the provisions of the 2002 EU Regulatory Package relating to the obligations of SMP operators.

21.31   Nonetheless, until the market reviews are carried out, specific obligations imposed under the former legal regime continue to be applicable vis-à-vis undertakings that were formerly designated as being dominant.

NRA's Regulatory Duties concerning Rights of Way, Co-location and Facility Sharing

Rights of way

21.32   The Malta Transport Authority (ADT) is empowered, under article 4 Utilities and Services (Regulation of Certain Works) Act, to grant rights of way to undertakings, over any property whether public or private including any road, path, building or water. Decisions of the ADT must be reasoned and are subject to the principles of transparency and non-discrimination, and the levy of fees must be proportionate. Decisions taken may be contested before the Communications Appeals Board established under the MCA Act. Responsibility for the reinstatement of roads rests with the undertaking enjoying the rights of way.

Co-location and facility sharing

21.33   The ADT is also empowered, under article 4 Utilities and Services (Regulation of Certain Works) Act, after consultation with the MCA, to impose co-location and facility sharing obligations. Planning permits are still required from the Malta Environment and Planning Authority and, where applicable, from the competent Maltese local authorities.

REGULATION OF MARKET ENTRY: IMPLEMENTATION OF THE AUTHORISATION DIRECTIVE

General Authorisation of Electronic Communications

The general authorisation regime

21.34   The ECR Act introduces the concept of a general authorisation regime, replacing the former regime that required undertakings to apply for a licence to provide electronic communications networks or services. The ECR Act expressly provides that no exclusive or special rights for the establishment or provision of networks and/or services shall be granted or maintained in force.

21.35   An undertaking is, in accordance with the provisions of the ECR Act and with the procedure under the Electronic Communications Regulations, entitled to provide electronic communications services or to establish, extend or provide electronic communications networks. In doing so, an undertaking is required to act in compliance with the applicable general authorisation conditions as established

---

28   Regs 15 to 24 Electronic Communications Regulations.

under the Electronic Communications Regulations, and in particular must first notify the MCA of its intention to provide the service and/or network.

21.36   The Electronic Communications Regulations establish different categories of authorisation based on the nature of the service offered rather than, as was previously the case, on the technology used to provide the service, reflecting the different rights and obligations applicable to these services. The categories of general authorisation are:

- public communications networks,
- publicly available telephone services,
- television and radio distribution services,
- other publicly available electronic communications services,
- non-public electronic communications services, and
- private electronic communications networks and/or services.[29]

21.37   A notification of a general authorisation is made by completing a notification form as provided by the MCA. An undertaking is required to inform the MCA if it ceases to provide the network or service as notified, or if there is any change to the information supplied. The MCA is required to maintain a register of those authorised undertakings that have notified it of their intention to provide a network or service. The register shall include such information as the MCA considers appropriate and which is not of a confidential nature.

21.38   Undertakings acting under a general authorisation have a right to provide the electronic communications networks and/or services as described in the notification made to the MCA.[30] In addition, such undertakings are entitled to:

- where applicable, have their applications for rights of use of numbers and radio frequencies considered in according with the ECR Act and with the Electronic Communications Regulations,[31]
- request the MCA to issue a declaration to facilitate the exercise of rights to install facilities and rights to interconnection,[32]
- have their applications for rights to install facilities considered in accordance with the applicable legislation,[33] and
- to refer a dispute to the MCA.[34]

Undertakings providing publicly available electronic communications networks and/or services enjoy additional rights to negotiate interconnection with and, where applicable, obtain access to or interconnection from another authorised undertaking and to be given an opportunity to be designated to carry out universal service obligations.[35]

21.39   General conditions for authorisation are established in the Twelfth Schedule to the Electronic Communications Regulations in accordance with article 17 ECR Act and with regulation 59 of the said regulations. Compliance with the conditions is monitored by the MCA.

---

29   Reg 54 Electronic Communications Regulations.
30   Reg 58 Electronic Communications Regulations.
31   Reg 58 Electronic Communications Regulations.
32   Reg 56 Electronic Communications Regulations.
33   Reg 58 Electronic Communications Regulations.
34   Reg 12 Electronic Communications Regulations.
35   Reg 58 Electronic Communications Regulations.

21.40   The MCA may impose additional obligations on undertakings designated as having SMP or as universal service providers. The MCA may amend the Twelfth Schedule to the Electronic Communications Regulations (and therefore the conditions of authorisation) with the approval of the Minister responsible for communications. This power is circumscribed by the maximum conditions set out in the Tenth Schedule to the Electronic Communications Regulations. The MCA may also establish that certain conditions do not apply to specific categories of undertakings. The powers of the MCA under this regulation are to be exercised in a non-discriminatory, proportionate and transparent manner, and any conditions applied and their exercise must be objectively justified.[36]

Rights of Use for Radio Frequencies

General authorisations and granting of individual rights

21.41   Article 30 ECR Act gives the MCA the responsibility for the effective management of radio frequencies assigned to it in the National Frequency Plan. The National Frequency Plan is drawn up and amended by the Minister responsible for communications after consultation with the MCA.[37]

21.42   Authorisations to use radio frequencies, with the exception of authorisation to use frequencies for broadcasting services and any other frequencies not assigned to the MCA under the National Frequency Plan, are granted by the MCA under article 32 ECR Act. Rights to use frequencies that have not been identified as licence exempt are granted in the form of an individual licence. Assignment of such licences must be conducted in accordance with open, transparent, and non-discriminatory procedures that are publicly available.[38]

21.43   The Minister responsible for communications may make regulations exempting the use of radio frequencies or equipment from the requirement of individual licences. Where the risk of harmful interference is negligible, the MCA is required under the Electronic Communications Regulations[39] to advise the Minister with respect to the need or otherwise to make the use of radio frequencies subject to an individual licence. The advice may also relate to conditions for use of such frequencies to be included in the general authorisation.

Admissible conditions

The conditions attached to individual rights of use are established by the MCA but cannot exceed the maximum conditions set out in the Tenth Schedule to the Electronic Communications Regulations.[40]

---

36   Reg 59 Electronic Communications Regulations.
37   Art 31 ECR Act.
38   Reg 61(3) Electronic Communications Regulations.
39   Reg 61 Electronic Communications Regulations.
40   Reg 64 Electronic Communications Regulations.

Limitation of numbers of rights of use to be granted

21.44   The MCA may limit the number of licences granted in respect of a particular radio frequency.[41] The charges that may be levied are established by the MCA and must be objectively justified and in accordance with the principles of transparency, non-discrimination.[42] To date, the MCA has not assigned any frequencies by auction, although it is empowered to do so. The MCA invited applications for participation in a 'beauty contest' for the assignment of rights of use of radio frequencies for Digital Terrestrial Television Networks and Services; however, the number of applications matched the number of frequencies available and these were therefore assigned directly. The same occurred with rights of use of frequencies for 3G. At the time of writing, the MCA is processing the applications received following a call for participation in a 'beauty contest' for the assignment of frequencies for Broadband Wireless Access.

Frequency trading

21.45   The MCA is required to indicate in the conditions attached to the right of use whether any of the rights granted may be transferred.[43] Assignments made to date have prohibited frequency trading.

Rights of Use for Numbers

General authorisations and granting of individual rights

21.46   The MCA is responsible for establishing and managing the national numbering plan for electronic communications services and for controlling the assignment of all national numbering resources.[44] It also has a statutory obligation to put in place procedures to ensure that the allocation of numbers is carried out in an objective, transparent, equitable, non-discriminatory and timely manner. Any undertaking or person may apply to the MCA to have numbering resources assigned in accordance with regulation 66 Electronic Communications Regulations. Undertakings have an explicit right to have their applications for numbering resources considered in accordance with ECR Act.[45]

21.47   Primary allocation of numbers is made to eligible undertakings following application to the MCA. The time limit between receipt of a properly completed application for primary allocation and the notification of the subsequent decision should normally not exceed three weeks, which period may be extended to a further three weeks in the case of numbers of exceptional economic value, where it decided that such numbers are to be allocated through a comparative or competitive selection process.[46]

Admissible conditions

21.48   The maximum conditions that may be imposed with respect to rights of use of numbering resources are set out in the Tenth Schedule to the Electronic

---

41   Reg 62 Electronic Communications Regulations.
42   Art 18(4) and (5) ECR Act.
43   Reg 64(2) Electronic Communications Regulations.
44   Art 11 ECR Act.
45   Reg 58 Electronic Communications Regulations.
46   Reg 66 Electronic Communications Regulations.

Communications Regulations, in line with Part C of the Annex to the Authorisation Directive. All undertakings providing publicly available telephone services (including mobile network operators and VoIP providers who qualify as publicly available telephone service providers under the Regulations)[47] are required to provide full number portability facilities to their subscribers in line with regulation 50 Electronic Communications Regulations.

21.49   Under the new regime, carrier pre-selection can only be imposed following a market analysis carried out in accordance with the ECR Act,[48] but obligations imposed prior to the coming into force of the new legislation remain in place until a market analysis has been carried out.[49]

21.50   Undertakings have a right to use numbers assigned to them, subject to compliance with the conditions attached to the right of use.

21.51   No specific end-user rights have been set out either at law or in the numbering conventions.

Limitation of number of rights of use to be granted

21.52   The MCA may, after public consultation, assign numbering resources deemed to have an exceptional economic value, by using a comparative or competitive selection process.

The NRA's Enforcement Powers

21.53   The enforcement powers of the MCA are primarily dealt with under Part VII of the MCA Act. In the majority of instances where there is non-compliance with a law enforced by the MCA or else with a decision or directive issued by the MCA, the MCA is empowered to impose administrative fines on the undertaking or person acting in breach of the law, decision or directive. Unless otherwise stated at law,[50] the MCA may impose a maximum administrative fine of Lm 100,000 and/or a daily fine not exceeding Lm 2,000 for each day of non-compliance. If the infringement committed by the undertaking has especially significant effects on the market to the detriment of other competing undertakings and/or consumers, the maximum limit of the administrative fine may be exceeded, provided this does not exceed 5% of the turnover of the undertaking in the calendar year immediately preceding the year when the infringement was committed. In deciding on the amount of the fine to be imposed the MCA is required to have regard to the nature and extent of the infringement, its duration and its impact on the market and on consumers.[51] The MCA is normally required, before deciding whether to impose an administrative fine, to give the undertaking or person concerned a minimum period of 30 days in which to rectify the infringement and/or make submissions thereto.

---

47   See definition in article 2 ECR Act.
48   Reg 39 Electronic Communications Regulations.
49   Art 40 ECR Act.
50   There are certain provisions that expressly establish the maximum administrative fine that can be imposed. If the specific provision does not state anything, the maximum limits stated in art 32 MCA Act apply.
51   Art 32 MCA Act.

21.54   If the alleged infringement constitutes an immediate and serious threat to public safety, public security or public health, or creates or may create serious economic or operational problems to other undertakings providing communications services or networks, or for consumers, then the MCA may take urgent interim measures to remedy the situation, which may also include the imposition of administrative fines. Even in such instances, the person against whom the measures are being contemplated must be afforded a reasonable opportunity to state his view and propose any remedies.[52]

Administrative Charges and Fees for Rights of Use

21.55   The general principles relating to administrative charges are established under article 18 ECR Act, which in substance mirrors the provisions of article 12 Authorisation Directive, and requires the levy of such fees as are necessary to cover the administrative costs of the MCA. No fee is charged when a person notifies the MCA that he intends to provide a network and/or service. However, authorised undertakings are required to pay an annual set fee depending on the category of network or service provided. In the case of publicly available telephone services, television and radio distribution services, other publicly available electronic communication services and non-public electronic communications services, undertakings must pay a percentage of their total gross revenues, which percentage varies according to the amount, decreasing as the revenue band increases.[53]

21.56   Undertakings are required to pay usage fees for radio frequencies on an annual basis; these fees include a fixed annual fee plus a percentage of the total gross revenue.[54]

21.57   Undertakings are required to pay usage fees for numbers on an annual basis; for geographic and mobile numbers, these fees are 15 cents for each individual number and Lm 100 for each block of 10,000 numbers; for carrier select or pre-select codes, there is a fee of Lm 1,000 for each code.[55]

REGULATION OF NETWORK ACCESS AND INTERCONNECTION: IMPLEMENTATION OF THE ACCESS DIRECTIVE

Objectives and Scope of Access Regulation

21.58   Article 13 ECR Act provides that the MCA shall ensure adequate access and interconnection and interoperability of services in such a way as to promote efficiency, promote sustainable competition and give the maximum benefit to end-users. No restrictions may be imposed that prevent undertakings from negotiating between themselves agreements on technical and commercial arrangements for access and/or interconnection, in accordance with Community law.[56] The manner in which the MCA may regulate access and interconnection in practice is further detailed in the Electronic Communications Regulations.[57]

---

52   Art 31(4) MCA Act.
53   Eleventh Schedule Part A Electronic Communications Regulations.
54   Eleventh Schedule Part B Electronic Communications Regulations.
55   Eleventh Schedule Part C Electronic Communications Regulations.
56   Article 14(1) ECR Act.
57   See regs 15 to 24 Electronic Communications Regulations.

21.59 The provisions dealing with access and interconnection apply to operators of public communications networks on whom access obligations may be imposed, and to authorised undertakings seeking access. The term 'operator' is defined as meaning an undertaking providing or authorised to provide a public communications network or an associated facility.[58]

Basic Regulatory Concepts

21.60 The powers of the MCA with respect to access and interconnection are clearly delineated by the Electronic Communications Regulations which reflect the provisions of the Access Directive. The MCA has the power to impose access obligations on undertakings identified as having significant market power following the market review process.[59] In addition, the MCA has the power to impose obligations on all undertakings to ensure end-to-end connectivity and accessibility for end-users to specified digital radio and television broadcasting services.[60]

21.61 The definitions of access and interconnection are identical to those in the Access Directive.[61]

21.62 An undertaking requesting access or interconnection does not require a general authorisation if it does not provide services and/or does not operate a network in Malta. Furthermore, no restrictions may be imposed that prevent undertakings in Malta, or undertakings in member states, from negotiating between themselves agreements on technical and commercial arrangements for access and/or interconnection, in accordance with Community law.[62]

21.63 Any undertaking infringing the above obligations may become liable to an administrative fine by the MCA not exceeding the sum of Lm 10,000 (€23,000) and/or Lm 200 (€460) for each day during which failure to comply persists.[63]

21.64 The MCA may intervene of its own initiative where justified or, in the absence of agreement between undertakings, at the request of either of the parties involved, in order to secure the policy objectives established under article 4 ECR Act.[64]

Access- and Interconnection-related Obligations with Respect to SMP Undertakings

Overview

21.65 The obligations that the MCA may impose reflect those in the Access Directive, namely transparency, non-discrimination, accounting separation, access to and use of specific network facilities, and price control and cost accounting obligations.[65] The MCA may also, in exceptional circumstances, impose additional

---

58   Art 2 ECR Act.
59   Reg 17 Electronic Communications Regulations.
60   Reg 15 Electronic Communications Regulations.
61   Art 2 ECR Act.
62   Art 14(1) ECR Act.
63   Art 14(7) ECR Act.
64   Reg 15(4) Electronic Communications Regulations.
65   See Regs 15 to 24 Electronic Communications Regulations.

access obligations on operators with significant market power. However, such obligations may be imposed only after the MCA has submitted a request to the European Commission for permission to impose such other obligations.[66] In all cases, any obligations imposed should be based on the nature of the problem identified, be proportionate and justified in the light of the objectives of ECR Act, and must then only be imposed following consultation.

Transparency obligations

The MCA may impose transparency obligations in relation to access requiring operators to make public specified information, such as accounting information, technical specifications, network characteristics, terms and conditions for supply and use, and prices.[67] Where an operator has an obligation of non-discrimination, that operator may be required to publish a reference offer, giving a description of relevant offerings broken down into components according to market needs, and providing relevant terms and conditions for the provision of those offerings including prices. Currently, dominant operators on the fixed and mobile markets provide such a reference interconnection offer. The MCA may specify precise information to be made available, the level of detail required and the manner of publication.

Non-discrimination obligations

With respect to the provision of access or interconnection, the MCA may also impose an obligation of non-discrimination to ensure that the SMP operator applies the same conditions in equivalent circumstances to other undertakings providing equivalent services. Such an obligation also requires that services and information are provided to others under the same conditions and of the same quality as the SMP operator provides for its own services, or for those of its subsidiaries or partners.[68]

Specific access obligations

If the MCA considers that denial of access hinders the emergence of a sustainable competitive market at the retail level, or is not in the end-users' interest, the MCA may impose an obligation on an SMP operator to meet reasonable requests for access to, and use of, specific network elements and associated facilities.[69] When considering whether to impose such an obligation, the MCA is required to take into account the technical and economic viability of using or installing competing facilities, available capacity and initial investment amongst other factors.

Price control obligations

Where lack of effective competition means that the operator concerned may sustain prices at an excessively high level, or apply a price squeeze, to the detriment of

---

66   Reg 17(3) Electronic Communications Regulations.
67   Reg 18 Electronic Communications Regulations.
68   Reg 19 Electronic Communications Regulations.
69   Reg 21 Electronic Communications Regulations.

end-users, the MCA may impose price controls in the provision of access, including an obligation that prices are cost-oriented whilst allowing for a reasonable return on capital employed.[70] The MCA is required to ensure that any cost recovery mechanism or pricing methodology that is mandated serves to promote efficiency and sustainable competition and maximise consumer benefits.

Accounting separation obligations

The MCA may also impose accounting separation obligations in relation to specified activities related to interconnection or access,[71] such as requiring a vertically integrated company to make transparent its wholesale prices and its internal transfer prices.

Related Regulatory Powers with Respect to SMP Undertakings

21.66   In May 2004, the MCA published its decision on 'Introduction of Carrier Selection and Carrier Pre-Selection in Malta'.[72] This decision provides that carrier selection and carrier pre-selection shall be available on fixed telephony services for both local and international calls. This obligation was not extended to mobile operators. According to this decision, the position may be revised during the market review process. In accordance with article 40 ECR Act, obligations relating to carrier selection or pre-selection shall be applicable until the market reviews are completed.

21.67   The MCA is required to ensure that at least one undertaking is obliged to provide leased lines to every point in Malta. In accordance with the provisions of regulations 3 and 4 Electronic Communications (Leased Lines) Regulations, the MCA in June 2003 determined[73] that Maltacom plc has a dominant market position as a leased lines provider with the attendant obligation of publishing information in respect of technical characteristics, tariffs and usage conditions for leased lines. This decision also required Maltacom plc to set tariffs for leased lines in adherence to the principles of cost orientation and transparency. It is relevant to note that article 40 ECR Act expressly provides that obligations under the applicable legislation relating to leased lines enacted under the former regime shall continue to apply until these regulations are amended or withdrawn following a market analysis by the MCA.

---

70   Reg 22 Electronic Communications Regulations.
71   Reg 20 Electronic Communications Regulations.
72   Report on Consultation and Decision, 'Introducing Carrier Selection and Carrier Pre-Selection in Malta', Malta Communications Authority, May 2004.
73   The decision was titled 'Dominant Market Position in the Leased Lines Market'.

Regulatory Powers Applicable to All Market Participants

Obligations to ensure end-to-end connectivity

21.68 In accordance with the provisions of the Access Directive, in exceptional circumstances, the MCA may also impose obligations on undertakings that have not been designated as having SMP.[74]

21.69 Thus, to the extent that is necessary to ensure end-to-end connectivity, the MCA may require undertakings that control access to end-users to provide access and interconnection to any interested third party. In all cases, any such obligation shall be objective, transparent, proportionate and non-discriminatory, and shall be notified to the Commission in a similar fashion as notifications for the conclusions of market analysis.[75] Currently, no such obligations have been imposed.

Access to digital radio and television broadcasting services

21.70 Similarly, access may be imposed on non-SMP operators to ensure accessibility for end-users to specified digital radio and television broadcasting services, subject to the pre-conditions of objectivity, transparency, proportionality and non-discrimination. At present no such obligations have been imposed on undertakings.

21.71 Operators of conditional access services who provide access services to digital television and radio services, and whose access services broadcasters depend on to reach any group of potential viewers or listeners, are required to offer to all broadcasters the technical services enabling transmissions to be received by means of decoders administered by the service operators.[76] This obligation may only be withdrawn by the MCA if, following a market review, it finds that particular operators of conditional access systems do not have SMP in the relevant market.[77]

Transitional Provisions

21.72 The MCA plans to finalise its market reviews by the end of 2006. Meanwhile, during the transitional period the ECR Act provides that obligations related to access and interconnection imposed on operators designated as enjoying dominance under the former regime continue to apply.[78] Under the former regime, undertakings enjoying a dominant position had to comply with the full range of SMP obligations including transparency, non-discrimination, accounting separation, access to and use of specific network facilities and price control and cost accounting obligations.

---

74 Reg 15 Electronic Communications Regulations.
75 See art 10 ECR Act and reg 6 Electronic Communications Regulations.
76 Third Schedule Part A Electronic Communications Regulations.
77 Reg 16(2) Electronic Communications Regulations.
78 Art 39 ECR Act.

REGULATION OF UNIVERSAL SERVICES AND USERS' RIGHTS: THE UNIVERSAL SERVICE DIRECTIVE

Regulation of Universal Service Obligations

Scope of universal service obligations

21.73   The MCA is required to ensure that universal services are made available at the quality specified to all end-users in Malta, independently of geographical location, and in the light of specific national conditions, at an affordable price.

21.74   The MCA may, in accordance with regulation 30 Electronic Communications Regulations, impose the following universal service obligations:

- the provision of access at a fixed location: this must include connections to the public telephone network and access to publicly available telephone services. Moreover, any connection provided by the designated undertaking must be capable of enabling end-users to make and receive local and international calls, facsimile communications and data communications at data rates sufficient to allow internet access,[79]
- the provision of directory enquiry and directories: the undertaking must ensure that a comprehensive directory of subscribers is available to all end-users in a form approved by the MCA whether printed or electronic or both as the MCA may determine, which must be updated at least once a year,[80]
- the provision of public pay telephones throughout Malta: this must meet the reasonable needs of end-users in terms of geographical coverage, number of telephones, the accessibility of such telephones to disabled users and the quality of services,[81] and
- specific measures for disabled end-users: these measures must ensure that such end-users can enjoy access to and affordability of publicly available telephone services, including access to emergency services, directory enquiry services and directories.[82]

Designation of undertakings obliged to provide universal services

21.75   The MCA may designate one or more undertakings to comply with universal service obligations. Part IV of the Electronic Communications Regulations also sets out the procedure for the designation of undertakings to comply with these obligations. The MCA in doing so may impose such obligations on one or more undertakings. It may also require different undertakings or sets of undertakings to provide different elements of universal service, and/or to cover different parts of the Maltese national territory.[83]

21.76   In designating an undertaking or undertakings the MCA is required to adopt efficient, objective, transparent and non-discriminatory designation mechanism whereby no undertaking is, *a priori*, excluded from being designated. The

---

79   Reg 26 Electronic Communications Regulations.
80   Reg 27 Electronic Communications Regulations.
81   Reg 28 Electronic Communications Regulations.
82   Reg 29 Electronic Communications Regulations.
83   Regs 30(1) and (2) Electronic Communications Regulations.

designation methods adopted must ensure that the universal service obligations are provided in a cost-effective manner and may be used as a means to determine the net cost of the said obligations.[84]

Regulation of retail tariffs, users' expenditures and quality of service

21.77   The MCA is empowered, in the light of national conditions, to specify requirements to be complied with by a designated undertaking to ensure that such an undertaking provides tariff options or packages to consumers that depart from those provided under normal commercial conditions, in particular to ensure that those on low incomes or with special needs are not prevented from accessing or using the publicly available telephone service.[85] A designated undertaking is required to publish adequate and updated information about its performance in providing universal service obligations, based on the quality of service parameters, definitions and measurements as stated in the Sixth Schedule[86] to the Electronic Communications Regulations. The MCA may issue directives to an undertaking to ensure compliance with performance targets. The MCA may then impose proportionate fines if the directive is not adhered to.

Cost calculation and financing of universal services

21.78   An undertaking may submit a written request to the MCA for funding of the net costs of meeting an universal service obligation imposed upon it. On the basis of the information submitted with the request, the MCA decides whether the universal service obligation represents an unfair burden on the undertaking concerned. If the MCA considers that the undertaking is subject to an unfair burden, the MCA may introduce a mechanism to compensate the undertaking for determined net costs under transparent conditions from public funds,[87] and/or share the net cost of the obligations between providers of electronic communications networks and services.

Regulation of Retail Markets

Prerequisites for the regulation of retail markets

21.79   The principle that regulation of retail services is permissible only if regulation at wholesale level does not achieve the regulatory objectives has been implemented by regulation 37 Electronic Communications Regulations. No market review related to the retail markets has yet been completed. The current retail obligations on undertakings imposed under the former legal framework shall remain in place until the relevant market reviews are completed.

Regulatory powers

21.80   In accordance with the Universal Service Directive, where there is a concern that an operator enjoying significant market power may charge excessive

---

84   Reg 30(3) Electronic Communications Regulations.
85   Reg 31(2) Electronic Communications Regulations.
86   This is identical to Annex III Universal Service Directive.
87   In which case the MCA also requires the consent of the Minister. See reg 35.

prices, inhibit market entry, restrict competition by setting predatory prices, show undue preference to specific end-users, or unreasonably bundle services, the MCA may impose obligations on retail markets to curtail such abuse. In particular the MCA may require appropriate retail price cap measures, measures to control individual tariffs, or measures to orient tariffs towards costs or prices on comparable markets, in order to protect end-user interests whilst promoting effective competition.[88]

21.81   Currently, no market review on the retail markets has been completed. Therefore, in accordance with the transitional provisions under the ECR Act, retail tariff regulation for the provision of access to and use of the public telephone access existing prior to the coming into force of the new regime shall continue to be applicable until such time as a market review is carried out.[89] Under the former regime, an operator providing telephony services having a dominant market position was required to apply cost-oriented tariffs. Such operators could not, without the approval of the MCA, bundle a number of services into a single tariff without also offering each of the constituent services under separate tariffs.[90] In accordance with the afore-mentioned transitional provisions, such obligations on former dominant operators will continue to apply until the market reviews are completed.

End User Rights

Contracts

21.82   An undertaking providing connection and/or access to the public telephone network is required to provide the person subscribing to the service with a written contract containing at least the information[91] stated in regulation 40 Electronic Communications Regulations.[92]

21.83   Before an undertaking makes modifications to any of the conditions in the contract it must, at least 30 days before the coming into effect of the proposed modifications, notify every subscriber to that service of the said modifications, informing him or her of the right to withdraw without penalty from such a contract if he or she does not accept the modification.

21.84   A term or condition for the provision of an electronic communications service, even if agreed to by the subscriber or user, is null and without effect to the extent that it is inconsistent with the ECR Act or any regulations made thereunder or with the terms or conditions of the authorisation on the basis of which the service is being provided.[93]

21.85   The MCA may require undertakings to prepare a code of practice that includes the minimum standards of service to be provided to end-users and gives guidance to the employees of such undertakings in their dealings with end-users.[94]

---

88   Reg 37(2) Electronic Communications Regulations.
89   Art 40 ECR Act.
90   Telecommunications Services (General) Regulations (LN 151 of 2000) as amended, reg 11.
91   Reg 40 Electronic Communications Regulations.
92   The minimum information is identical to that required under art 20(2) Universal Service Directive.
93   Art 23 ECR Act.
94   Reg 14 Electronic Communications Regulations.

Transparency obligations

21.86   In a contract made with a customer, an undertaking must include certain information, including particulars of prices and tariffs, how up-to-date information on applicable tariffs and maintenance charges can be obtained, the duration of the contract and conditions for renewal and termination, information about the method of initiating procedures for settlement of disputes, and information about compensation and refund arrangements which apply if the contracted service quality levels are not met.[95]

DATA PROTECTION: IMPLEMENTATION OF THE E-PRIVACY DIRECTIVE

Confidentiality of Communications

21.87   Data protection in electronic communications is regulated by two sets of regulations, administered respectively by the Data Protection Commissioner and the MCA. Regulation 5 Processing of Personal Data (Electronic Communications Sector) Regulations[96] prohibits any form of interception or surveillance of communications without the consent of the user concerned. This prohibition does not extend to the recording of communications as part of lawful business practice or for the purpose of providing evidence of a commercial transaction. This provision in its entirety is excluded from applicability with respect to measures taken in accordance with legislation for the following purposes:[97]

- national and public security and defence,
- the prevention, investigation, detection and prosecution of criminal or administrative offences or of breaches of ethics for regulated professions,
- important economic or financial interests, including monetary, budgetary and taxation matters, and
- the protection of the subscriber or user or of the rights and freedoms of others.

21.88   Undertakings providing publicly available electronic communications services are required to take appropriate technical and organisational measures to safeguard the security of the services they provide. Where, despite the taking of such measures, there is significant risk of a breach of security, service providers are required to inform subscribers of the risk, possible remedies and associated costs.[98]

21.89   Persons wishing to use electronic communications system to gain access to information stored in terminal equipment are required to inform the subscriber of the purposes of such processing. The subscriber or user is entitled to object to, or refuse, such processing at any time.[99]

21.90   The technical storage or access to information stored in terminal equipment for the sole purpose of carrying out or facilitating the transmission of a

---

95   Reg 40 Electronic Communications Regulations.
96   These regulations are enforced by the Data Protection Commissioner.
97   Reg 11 Processing of Personal Data (Electronic Communications Sector) Regulations.
98   Reg 4 Electronic Communications (Personal Data and Protection of Privacy) Regulations.
99   Reg 6 Processing of Personal Data (Electronic Communications Sector) Regulations.

communication or providing an information society service explicitly requested by the subscriber or user is not subject to the above-mentioned requirements.[100]

Traffic Data and Location Data

21.91   The definitions of 'traffic data' and 'location data' were transposed in accordance with the terminology used in the E-Privacy Directive.[101]

21.92   Undertakings are required to erase or render anonymous traffic data processed for the purpose of transmitting communications as soon as the data is no longer needed for that purpose. However, traffic data necessary for billing purposes, including interconnection payments, may be retained for the period during which the bill may be challenged at law. The processing of data for marketing purposes or for the provision of value added services is subject to the consent of the subscriber.

21.93   In the instances where data processing is permitted, the undertaking concerned is required to inform the subscriber or user of the data being processed and the duration of such processing.

21.94   The rules related to location data follow the same lines as those for traffic data. Such data may be processed if it has been rendered anonymous, or to the extent and for the duration necessary for the provision of a value added service. In the latter instance, such use is subject to the consent of the user. Specific rules apply about the information to be provided to the user prior to obtaining such consent.[102]

Itemised Billing

21.95   Maltacom plc, the incumbent fixed line operator is required to provide to its subscribers a minimum level of itemised billing, free of charge.[103] The itemised bill is provided on an 'opt-in' rather than 'opt-out' basis. Calls that are free of charge to the calling subscriber, including calls to helplines, are not included in itemised bills.

Calling and Connected Line Identification

21.96   The rules related to calling and connected line identification are established in the Electronic (Personal Data and Protection of Privacy) Regulations and are modelled on the provisions of the E-Privacy Directive.[104] These facilities may be overridden by the undertaking providing the public communications network for the purpose of tracing malicious or nuisance calls and during the period when such calls are taking place, provided that the data containing the identification of subscribers is stored and made available to the competent authority in accordance with relevant legislation. Requests for the activation of this rule must be in writing, except in cases of urgency.

---

100   Reg 6(3) Processing of Personal Data (Electronic Communications Sector) Regulations.
101   Reg 3 Processing of Personal Data (Electronic Communications Sector) Regulations.
102   Reg 8 Processing of Personal Data (Electronic Communications Sector) Regulations.
103   Decision 01/02, MCA.
104   Reg 8 Electronic Communications (Personal Data and Protection of Privacy) Regulations.

21.97 Undertakings providing publicly available electronic communications services are required to present calling line identification and location data for calls made to emergency access numbers. The application of this rule does not require the consent of the user or subscriber.

Automatic Call Forwarding

21.98 Undertakings providing publicly available electronic communication services are required, on request from a subscriber, to terminate calls being forwarded to that subscriber's line by a third party. This service must be provided free of charge. Service providers are required to cooperate with each other for the purpose of ensuring compliance with this rule.[105]

Directories of Subscribers

21.99 The Processing of Personal Data (Electronic Communications Sector) Regulations require any persons producing a directory of subscribers to inform all subscribers in advance of the purposes of the directory and any further usage possibilities based on search functions of any electronic versions of the directory. Data may only be included subject to the subscribers' consent. In giving their consent, subscribers may indicate which personal data is to be included in the directory. Subscribers who have given their consent must be given the opportunity to verify, correct or withdraw the data.[106] The personal data included in directories is required to be limited to the data necessary to identify the subscriber and his or her number. Any additional information is subject to a further consent, over and above that obtained for the inclusion of the basic data in the directory.

Unsolicited Communications

21.100 A person cannot use any publicly available telecommunications service to make unsolicited communications for the purpose of direct marketing by means of an automatic calling machine, by fax or electronic mail to a subscriber, unless the subscriber has given prior explicit consent in writing agreeing to receive such communications.[107]

---

105 Reg 10 Electronic Communications (Personal Data and Protection of Privacy) Regulations.
106 Reg 9 Processing of Personal Data (Electronic Communications Sector) Regulations.
107 Reg 10 Processing of Personal Data (Electronic Communications Sector) Regulations.

The Dutch Market for Electronic Communications[1]

Serge J.H. Gijrath & Koen Parren
Baker & McKenzie Amsterdam N.V.

LEGAL STRUCTURE

Basic Policy

22.1   The Dutch market for electronic communication services is highly dynamic. In particular, there have been many developments on the market for broadband (Internet) services. An increasing number of companies and consumers are utilising fast broadband services, mostly via DSL technology or the dense cable television network. On 1 July 2004, the Netherlands was amongst the countries with the highest broadband penetration rate in the EU of 14.7 lines per 100 persons. It has over 2.5 million broadband lines. 58% of these lines use DSL technology and 77% of these DSL lines are on offer from the fixed line incumbent operator, KPN. A rapid emergence of new technologies for telephony via the Internet shows that the distinction between the markets for classical telephony and data services is fading.[2]

22.2   In addition, an increasing number of consumers are replacing their fixed telephone connection with a mobile telephone, which has caused the total volume of fixed telephony traffic on KPN's fixed network to decline. Currently, the mobile penetration rate is just above EU average, at 84%. The leading mobile operator (KPN Mobile) has a 36% market share. The second operator (Vodafone) has a 24% market share, while the three other mobile operators (Orange, T-Mobile and Telfort) share the remaining 40% of the mobile market.[3]

Implementation of EU Directives

22.3   The new regulatory framework was transposed into the thoroughly revised Telecommunications Act (*Telecommunicatiewet* – 'Tw'), which replaced the 1998 Tw and entered into force in the Netherlands on 19 May 2004, after a 10-month delay. The Tw is drafted as a framework act, leaving many details to be laid down in secondary legislation by way of governmental and ministerial decrees. In February

---

1   Editing of this chapter closed on 31 May 2005.
2   See also OPTA Annual Report 2004, May 2005 available at www.opta.nl.
3   Figures derived from the Commission's 10th report on the implementation of the Regulatory Framework in the Members States, COM(2004) 759, final, 02.12.2004.

2004, through another legislative amendment, the national regulatory authority (*Onafhankelijke Post en Telecommunicatie Autoriteit* – 'OPTA') had already been given full powers to start market analysis procedures.[4]

REGULATORY PRINCIPLES: IMPLEMENTATION OF THE FRAMEWORK DIRECTIVE

Scope of Regulation

22.4   The Tw covers all electronic communications services and networks, including communications services in networks used for broadcasting. The provision of Voice over the Internet Protocol ('VoIP') is considered to fall under the definition, and the Dutch National Regulatory Authority ('NRA') is developing its policy in respect of VoIP. In line with article 2(c) Framework Directive,[5] services providing, or exercising editorial control over content transmitted using electronic communications networks and services, are excluded from the scope of the Tw, if these services do not consist wholly or mainly in the conveyance of signals on electronic communications networks. Such 'content services' are typically governed by, inter alia, the Dutch Media Act.

National Regulatory Authorities: Organisation, Regulatory Objectives, Competencies

Overview

22.5   OPTA is the Dutch regulator for the electronic communications and postal sector. OPTA was established on 1 August 1997 as successor to the Networks and Services Board of the Ministry of Transport, Public Works and Water Management. Some specific issues under the Tw remain under the authority of the Ministry of Economic Affairs, which is also registered as an NRA with the European Commission.[6]

Tasks and competences of OPTA

22.6   OPTA is an independent executive body (*zelfstandig bestuursorgaan*), a status that enables it to operate at a distance from the State, which still holds a 20% share and a golden share[7] in the fixed line incumbent operator, KPN (even though ongoing Commission infringement proceedings are aimed at the removal of that golden share).[8] The Minister of Economic Affairs, Directorate General Telecommunications and Post (DGTP) bears political responsibility for a number of OPTA's tasks, but has no influence on the decisions made by the independent OPTA Commission.

---

4   See paras 22.35–22.39 below.
5   See para 1.50 below.
6   See paras 22.12–22.13 below.
7   The 'golden share' entitles the State of the Netherlands to approve certain resolutions taken by KPN's general meeting of shareholders and/or KPN's Board of Management.
8   The European Commission takes the view that this 'golden share' could deter investors from other Member States from investing in the capital of KPN and is, therefore, contrary to the free movement of capital laid down in Article 56 of the EC Treaty and the right of establishment in Article 43. Therefore, on 30 June 2004, the Commission brought an action in the European Court of Justice against the Kingdom of the Netherlands (Case C-282/04).

22.7   The tasks and competence of OPTA are defined in the Tw and in the OPTA Act.[9] Under the new Tw, OPTA's most important tasks are to define markets, to identify parties on these markets with significant market power ('SMP'), and to determine the obligations to be assigned to these parties.

22.8   Another important task of OPTA is the settlement of disputes between providers regarding access to and interconnection between networks.[10] The new Tw includes shorter deadlines for dispute resolution, in line with the Directives: OPTA must render a decision within 17 weeks after receiving the request for dispute resolution, except in exceptional circumstances. In urgent matters, OPTA may render a provisional measure that shall bind the disputing parties until a final decision is made.[11]

22.9   Since the enactment of the Electronic Signatures Act (*Wet elektronische handtekeningen*)[12] in May 2003, OPTA is also responsible for registering and supervising Certification Service Providers authorised to issue electronic signatures.

22.10   Other tasks of OPTA include:

- approving or rejecting interconnection and end-user tariffs,
- issuing telephone numbers,
- protecting the privacy of consumers in the area of post and telecommunication,
- regulation of certification providers for electronic signatures, and
- safeguarding the legal minimum of services to be provided in the area of fixed telephony.

Tasks and competences of the Minister of Economic Affairs

22.11   One important task under the new Tw has not been assigned to OPTA, and remains the responsibility of the Minister of Economic Affairs: the management and allocation of radio spectrum (ie frequency planning, issuing licences for frequency use, and enforcement of frequency use). In practice, this task is carried out by the Netherlands Radiocommunications Agency (*Agentschap Telecom*), a government agency operating under the responsibility of the Minister of Economic Affairs.

22.12   In order to enforce regulation, the Minister of Economic Affairs is authorised, inter alia, to collect information from regulated market parties, to issue fines in the event of violations, as well as to issue threats of fines in order to force compliance with legal obligations. OPTA has the same powers.[13]

Relationship between OPTA and the Dutch Competition Authority

22.13   OPTA issues sector-specific ex ante regulatory decisions in order to promote competition in the electronic communications sector. The Dutch Competition Authority (*Nederlandse Mededingingsautoriteit* – 'NMa') enforces the prohibition

---

9   *Wet onafhankelijke post- en telecommunicatieautoriteit*, 5 July 1997, Bulletin of Acts and Decrees 1997, 320.
10   Arts 6.2, 12.2 Tw.
11   Art 12.5 Tw.
12   Wet elektronische handtekening, 8 May 2003, Bulletin of Acts and Decrees 2003, 199.
13   See paras 22.62–22.66 below.

against cartels or abuse of a position of economic power in all markets, and determines ex post whether a violation to the Competition Act has taken place. The NMa is competent to decide whether companies that submit an application will be allowed to merge. This is where the ex ante regulation tasks of the two organisations coincide and where the NMa and OPTA work closely together. In 1999, the two organisations developed a cooperation protocol.[14] In June 2004, the protocol was revised to reflect the amendments in the new Tw.[15]

22.14 It is envisaged that OPTA will eventually become a 'chamber' within the NMa. Before this happens, the NMa, which currently forms part of the Ministry of Economic Affairs, must obtain the status of an independent executive body. The bill to give effect to this change passed the Dutch Senate on 7 December 2004, and is expected to enter into force in 2005.[16]

The national consultation procedure

22.15 Where OPTA intends to take any measures based on article 6.2,[17] 6a.2,[18] 6a.3,[19] 6a.16[20] or 6a.18 Tw,[21] the 'extensive preparatory procedure' laid down in paragraph 3.5.6 General Administrative Law Act (*Algemene Wet Bestuursrecht – 'AWB'*)[22] shall apply. In short, this procedure includes the following steps:

- OPTA takes a draft measure, announces this in the Dutch Government Gazette (*Staatscourant*) and makes the draft decision available for inspection,
- OPTA consults, where appropriate, on the draft measure with the Dutch Competition Authority (NMa),
- OPTA shall give any party the opportunity to comment on the draft measure within one month after the announcement thereof, and
- OPTA publishes the results of the consultation procedure (usually on its website).

22.16 It should be noted that, under the AWB, the extensive preparatory procedure is open to anybody, not just to parties who can show a sufficient interest in the decision at hand. With the Act on Uniform Preparatory Procedures[23] having come into effect as of 1 July 2005, only 'interested parties' are allowed to comment on

---

14   *Samenwerkingsprotocol OPTA/NMa*, Dutch Government Gazette 1999, 2, p 5.
15   Herzien samenwerkingsprotocol OPTA/NMa over de wijze van samenwerking bij aangelegenheden van wederzijds belang, Dutch Government Gazette 2004, 121, p 34.
16   First Chamber, 2001–2002, 27 639, no 228.
17   Measures concerning access and interconnection.
18   Measures of OPTA in the context of the market definition procedure or the market analysis procedure.
19   Market analysis procedures to determine whether to maintain, amend or withdraw obligations relating to retail markets.
20   Measures concerning undertakings designated to have SMP on the market for the access to or use of public telephone services at a fixed location.
21   Measures concerning undertakings designated to have SMP on the market for the minimum set of leased lines.
22   *Algemene wet bestuursrecht*, 4 June 1992, Bulletin of Acts and Decrees 1992, 315, as amended from time to time.
23   *Wet uniforme openbare voorbereidingsprocedures*, 24 January 2002, Bulletin of Acts and Decrees 2002, 54.

draft measures.[24] Furthermore, it should be noted that the AWB provides for a one-month term for making comments, while paragraph 145 of the Commission Guidelines on market analysis considers that 'a period of two months would be reasonable for the public consultation' for decisions related to the existence and designation of undertakings with SMP.

22.17   If the intended measure does not have a 'significant impact on the relevant market', OPTA may refrain from conducting the national consultation procedure described above. The Tw does not specify how 'a significant impact on the relevant market' is to be assessed, so this leaves OPTA a certain amount of discretion in deciding whether or not to submit an intended measure to the national consultation procedure.

Right of Appeal against NRA's Decisions

22.18   The right of appeal of an electronic communications provider who is affected by a decision of OPTA is not regulated by the Tw, but by the AWB.

22.19   In deviation from the general rule of the AWB, under the new Tw providers are now able to appeal most OPTA decisions directly in court, instead of first having to object to the decision with OPTA itself. This does not apply to decisions by OPTA to impose fines, which can still be objected with OPTA. In addition, the Tw provides that most OPTA decisions can be appealed at one appellate body, the Trade and Industry Appeals Tribunal (*College van Beroep voor het Bedrijfsleven – 'CBB'*).[25] It is envisaged that this will substantially shorten the duration of the appellate proceedings. Again, this does not apply to fines, which should still be appealed first in the administrative court in Rotterdam.

22.20   It is hoped that, with OPTA's increased and clarified powers in the new Tw, there will be less ground for appeal on the basis of lack of OPTA's competence on certain issues. Currently, most regulated market parties, and KPN in particular, appeal against almost all decisions of OPTA. The high number of objections and appeals causes a great deal of legal uncertainty, as some important disputes have remained unresolved for extended periods, some for even a few years.

The NRA's Obligations to Cooperate with the Commission

The consolidation procedure

22.21   The consolidation procedure (article 7 Framework Directive) has been implemented into national law in chapter 6b of the Tw.

22.22   Where OPTA intends to take any of the measures listed in paragraph 22.15 above, and this intended measure would affect trade between Member States, OPTA is obliged to conduct a consultation procedure at EU level. This means that OPTA makes the draft measure accessible to the Commission and the other NRAs, together with the reasons on which the measure is based. The other NRAs and the Commission then have one month to comment on the draft measure. Once the comment period has ended, OPTA may adopt the draft measure taking into

---

24   *Wet uniforme openbare voorbereidingsprocedures*, 24 January 2002, Bulletin of Acts and Decrees 2002, 54.

25   Art 17.1 Tw.

account 'as much as possible' the comments of the other NRAs and the Commission.[26] This means that OPTA may adopt the measure despite objections raised by other NRAs and/or the Commission.

22.23   This is different when the Commission has indicated to OPTA that it considers that the draft measure would create a barrier to the single market, or it has serious doubts as to its compatibility with Community law and in particular the objectives referred to in article 8 Framework Directive. In such a case, OPTA is prevented from adopting the measure for a further two months. During this two-month period, the Commission may take a decision requiring OPTA to bring the draft measure in line with Community law, or to withdraw the draft measure.[27]

22.24   The Tw does not specify whether the international consultation procedure should be preceded by the national consultation procedure,[28] or whether both procedures can be held at the same time. The expectation is that OPTA will decide this on a case-by-case basis.

22.25   The first Dutch notification in the context of the international consultation procedure occurred in November 2003, even before the new Tw had entered into force.[29] The notification concerned a draft Interoperability Decree taken under a national measure transposing article 5(1)(a) Access Directive. The notified draft Decree imposed an obligation upon all providers of publicly available telephone services[30] and operators of the underlying networks to ensure that retail customers are able at all times to make calls to all other retail customers, regardless of whether they are on the same or different networks. The obligations imposed were limited to ensuring end-to-end connectivity; the Decree did not regulate the terms and conditions on which operators must interconnect.

22.26   The Commission considered that, given the limited scope of the proposed obligation (limited to ensuring end-to-end connectivity and limited to publicly available telephony services) and its relatively low impact on the providers concerned, the notified draft measure was proportional and justified.[31] The Dutch legislator subsequently enacted the draft measure on 19 May 2004, together with the enactment of the new Tw.[32]

22.27   The Commission further commented that, once OPTA has completed the market analysis process under articles 15 and 16 Framework Directive and the designation of provider(s) with universal service obligations under the Universal Services Directive, the Dutch legislator should consider whether the decree remains necessary and proportionate to avoid any severance of end-to-end connectivity in the Netherlands.

---

26   Art 6b.2(3) Tw.
27   Art 6b.2(5) Tw.
28   See paras 22.15 et seq above.
29   Case number NL/2003/0017.
30   Ie fixed and mobile voice calls. Carrier (pre-)selection services are excluded from the definition of publicly available telephone services.
31   Commission's comments pursuant to Article 7(3) of Directive 2002/21/EC (Case NL/2003/0017).
32   Case NL/2003/0017: draft Interoperability Decree, Commission's comments pursuant to Article 7(3) of Directive 2002/21/EC.

Derogation from consultation procedures

22.28   In exceptional circumstances, OPTA may adopt provisional measures (valid for a period of up to 26 weeks) without applying the national and international consultation procedures. OPTA may only do so if it considers that there is an urgent need to act in order to safeguard competition and protect the interests of users.[33]

22.29   In August 2004, the Dutch provider of broadband Internet services 'Wanadoo' requested OPTA, on the basis of article 6b.3 Tw, to refrain from applying the consultation procedures, and to take immediate appropriate measures to safeguard competition on the broadband market. Wanadoo claimed that KPN was causing irreparable damage to competition on the broadband market by applying consumer tariffs that were below cost, and wholesale tariffs for broadband providers that were significantly above cost. In its ruling of 31 January 2005,[34] OPTA rejected Wanadoo's request on the ground that the decision to derogate from the consultation procedures can only be taken after the market analysis procedure has been completed. OPTA argued that, as long as the market analysis procedure for wholesale broadband access has not been completed, OPTA is unable to ascertain whether competition on that market and the interests of users are being compromised.

'Significant Market Power' as a Fundamental Prerequisite of Regulation

Definition of SMP

22.30   The presumption of the 1998 Tw[35] that a provider with a market share of more than 25% had SMP is replaced by a new definition of SMP, which is identical to the definition of SMP in article 14(2) Framework Directive.[36] This definition follows closely the definition established, in the case law of the European Court of Justice, for a 'dominant market position'.[37]

Definition of relevant markets and SMP designation

22.31   The procedures for identifying relevant markets in the Netherlands have been implemented in chapter 6a Tw. Each market analysis comprises three elements:

- the demarcations of the relevant product market and geographical market,
- the assessment as to the presence of parties with SMP in the requisite market, and
- the determination of appropriate and proportional obligations to be imposed on parties with SMP.

22.32   OPTA is obligated to define the geographic scope of the 18 markets for products and services that the Commission considered eligible for ex ante regulation

---

33   Art 6b.3 Tw.
34   OPTA/IBT/2005/200046.
35   See *Telecommunication Laws in Europe*, fourth edition (1998), para 12.77.
36   Art 1.1(s) Tw.
37   See the European Court of Justice's definition as provided in ECJ Judgment of 14 February 1978, Case 27/76, *United Brands v Commission* [1978] ECR 207, 286.

in its Recommendation on relevant markets[38] and then analyse them. Moreover, based on the specific national circumstances, OPTA can also define markets other than those specified in the Recommendation. For the purpose of carrying out the market analysis, OPTA has clustered the 18 markets from the Commission Recommendation into five related market areas:

- mobile telephony,
- broadcasting,
- leased lines,
- broadband, and
- fixed telephony.

22.33   Article 6a.1(1) Tw provides that OPTA shall identify the relevant markets 'as soon as possible' after the enactment of the Commission Recommendation on relevant markets. However, the market analysis process was delayed substantially due to late implementation of the new Tw, which was needed to give OPTA the necessary powers to collect market data. Furthermore, the Dutch Parliament voted for an amendment to the Tw, which obliged OPTA to provide detailed reasoning for its regulatory decisions following the market analysis procedures. In practice, this led to extensive questionnaires being used in the data-gathering process. These questionnaires have been a considerable administrative burden for the regulated market parties and have led to more delays in the process.

22.34   OPTA's first draft decisions were taken on 17 March 2005.[39] They concerned the market for access and call origination on public mobile telephone networks (market No 15), and the market for voice call termination on individual mobile networks (market No 16). With respect to the latter market, OPTA concluded – as was expected – that each mobile network operator is a single supplier on each market and thus has SMP. OPTA's draft decision obliges these SMP operators of mobile telephone networks to gradually decrease their call termination tariffs over a period of three years. By July 2008, the call termination tariffs should be cost oriented. OPTA foresees that end-users will eventually save a minimum of €145 million on calls from fixed to mobile networks.

22.35   OPTA had indicated that the draft decisions for the other market clusters would be taken in mid-May 2005 (broadcasting) and May/June 2005 (leased lines, broadband and fixed telephony).[40] However, as at July 2005, no draft decisions had been taken for the other market clusters (leased lines, broadband and fixed telephony). The draft decision for broadcasting has also been postponed again, and no indications as to the final date have been given by OPTA.[41] Once the draft decisions have been taken, these will then be notified under Article 7 Framework Directive.

22.36   In order to get regular feedback from the regulated market parties regarding how both the approach to and progress with the market analyses are experienced, OPTA has set up a 'reference group'. Represented parties are allowed to give

---

38   See para 1.75 above.
39   Draft decision by OPTA on the market for access and call origination on public mobile telephone networks, 17 March 2005. Draft decision by OPTA on the market for voice call termination on individual mobile networks, 17 March 2005.
40   Letter from OPTA to market parties of 13 September 2004, concerning revised schedule for the OPTA Market Analyses (OPTA/EGM/2004/203434).
41   Letter from OPTA to market parties, concerning revised schedule for the OPTA Broadcasting Market Analysis (OPTA/EGM/2005/200840).

OPTA their view on the process side of the market analysis; they are not supposed to comment on the content of OPTA's findings. The five participating market parties (KPN, MCI, Tele-2, T-Mobile, UPC and Versatel) represent the five market clusters mentioned above.

NRA's Regulatory Duties concerning Rights of Way, Co-location and Facility Sharing

Rights of way

22.37   Any person or entity is obliged to tolerate the installation and maintenance, as well as the clearance, of cables for a public electronic communications network in and on public land.[42]

In the 1998 Tw, the obligation to allow the installation of cables in public or private land was restricted to cables that are actually used.[43] Under the new Tw, this obligation is extended to unused cables or empty 'ducts' that are to be filled with cables at a later stage.[44] The Tw provides for the right to compensation for landowners who are obliged to tolerate the installation of cables, though these compensation rights are rather restricted.[45]

22.38   The Dutch municipalities are responsible for coordinating the work carried out within their territories by providers of public electronic communications networks in connection with the installation and maintenance of cables.[46] The municipality may require separate providers to carry out the installation of cables under public roads at the same time, in order to reduce the inconvenience to users of the public roads. In any event, providers may only begin to perform digging on the municipality's land if they have notified the municipality concerned of their intention to do so, and if they have received permission from the municipal executive with regard to the time, place and method of carrying out the work.

22.39   If the landowner subject to the obligation to tolerate is a private party, the provider must try to reach an agreement with the landowner with respect to the time, place and method of carrying out the work. If the parties fail to reach an agreement, the landowner or the provider may request OPTA to give a decision.[47] OPTA must give this decision within eight weeks after the request is received. In the meanwhile, the provider may not commence the intended work.

22.40   In two rulings of 6 June 2003,[48] the Dutch Supreme Court ruled that an underground cable network qualifies as an immovable. This has important consequences for owners of electronic communications networks. For instance, underground networks should be registered with the land register (*kadaster*), and transfer of such an underground network must be carried out by notarial deed, for which transfer tax is due.

---

42   Art 5.1(1) Tw.
43   See *Telecommunication Laws in Europe*, fourth edition (1998), paras 12.129–12.131.
44   Art 1.1(z) Tw, art 5.1(1) Tw.
45   Art 5.4 Tw.
46   Art 5.2 Tw.
47   Art 5.3(2) Tw.
48   Dutch Supreme Court rulings of 6 June 2003, 36075 and 36076, *JOR* 2003, 222, vol. 52, issue 11, p 842–847.

Co-location and facility sharing

22.41   The holders of a licence for the use of sets of frequencies which are intended for the provision of electronic communications networks or services are reciprocally obliged to fulfil reasonable requests to share the use of aerial installation points (site sharing).[49] In the event that parties fail to reach an agreement, they may request OPTA to resolve their dispute. In the past, OPTA has also published guidelines on co-location of equipment in connection with access to the local loop.[50]

REGULATION OF MARKET ENTRY: IMPLEMENTATION OF THE AUTHORISATION DIRECTIVE

The General Authorisation of Electronic Communications

22.42   Any person or entity that wishes to provide electronic communications networks, electronic communications services, or associated facilities, is free to do so. The sole requirement is the obligation to notify OPTA.[51] Notification is carried out by completing a standard notification form. OPTA subsequently confirms the notification and enters the notified parties in a public register, which can be accessed though OPTA's website.[52]

22.43   Only where scarce resources are concerned, an exception is made to the basic rule that market entry should be subject to such a general authorisation: licences will be required for the use of specific frequencies,[53] and, in effect, for the use of numbers.[54]

Rights of Use for Radio Frequencies

General authorisations and granting of individual rights

22.44   Under the Authorisation Directive, the use of radio frequencies should be primarily governed by a system of general authorisations, rather than be made subject to the grant of individual rights of use. In practice, however, for the vast majority of the frequencies within the available spectrum, an individually granted licence is required in the Netherlands.

22.45   The National Frequency Plan, established periodically by the Minister of Economic Affairs, describes which frequency usages require a licence.[55] The contents of the Frequency Plan are predetermined to a large extent by arrangements made on an international level under the auspices of the International Telecommunications Union (ITU),[56] the European Conference of Postal and Telecommunications Administrations (CEPT) and the EU. The frequency policy as formulated in

---

49   Art 3.11 Tw.
50   OPTA guidelines 20 December (2000/OPTA/IBT/2000/203357).
51   Art 2.1(1) Tw.
52   www.opta.nl.
53   Art 3.3 Tw, see para 22.50 below.
54   Art 4.2 Tw see para 22.58 below.
55   Last revised in January 2005, available at the Radiocommunications Agency website, www.at-ez.nl.
56   See Chapter 2 above.

the National Frequency Plan is described in further detail in the Frequency Table, which indicates which frequencies can and may be used by which application.[57]

22.46   Only a very limited number of radio frequencies may be used without obtaining an individual licence. These licence-free frequencies are either frequencies that may be used by anyone, whether or not together with categories of radio transmission equipment to be designated by ministerial regulation[58] (eg mobile telephones, remote controls) or frequencies used by government bodies such as the armed forces and the police.[59]

22.47   The use of all other radio frequencies requires a licence.[60] Such licences are not granted by OPTA, but by the Minister of Economic Affairs, who is responsible for radio spectrum policy.[61] The Tw contains four different allocation methods for granting licences for the use of radio frequencies. Radio frequencies that are reserved for the performance of essential government tasks or for public broadcasting are granted with priority to the government bodies and public broadcasting organisations concerned. The granting of licences for other radio frequencies may take place: in the order of receipt of the applications ('first come, first served'); by means of a 'beauty contest' which may or may not include a financial bid, or by means of an auction.[62]

22.48   The Frequency Decree determines, to a certain extent, which of these allocation methods shall be applied for a certain radio frequency.[63] The 'first come, first served' method is only applied for frequencies that are not scarce (ie where demand does not exceed supply), and for non-commercial frequencies. For the economically most valuable frequencies (such as frequencies for GSM/UMTS and FM radio frequencies), the Minister of Economic Affairs has the choice between beauty contest or auction. Both the GSM and UMTS frequencies were auctioned off. A beauty contest, including a financial bid, was used to distribute commercial radio frequencies in 2003.

Admissible conditions

22.49   The Minister may also attach certain special conditions to the use of frequencies. Such conditions may include, for instance, financial obligations in the form of a one-time or recurring fee, obligations regarding the rollout of infrastructure, or obligations to provide a certain service to the public. The special conditions that are attached to the use of specific frequencies are laid down in the individual licence. For instance, the UMTS licences issued in 2000 included obligations for the licence holders to ensure that, before a certain date, specified areas of the Netherlands (such as major cities, airports and motorways) would have UMTS coverage.

22.50   The first frequencies that were auctioned in the Netherlands were the DCS 1800 frequencies in 1998. The auction allowed three new mobile operators (Telfort,

---

57   The Frequency table can be accessed through the Radiocommunications Agency website, www.at-ez.nl.
58   *Regeling gebruik van frequentieruimte zonder vergunning* (Decree on use of radio frequencies without licence), Dutch Government Gazette 2003, 211.
59   Art 3.4(1) Tw.
60   Art 3.3 Tw.
61   See para 22.12 above.
62   Art 3.3(2), 3.3(4) Tw.
63   *Frequentiebesluit* (Frequency Decree), Bulletin of Acts and Decrees 1998, 638.

Dutchtone (currently Orange) and Ben (currently T-Mobile) to enter the Dutch mobile market, in addition to the then-existing operators KPN and Libertel (currently Vodafone). The proceeds of the auction were approximately €830 million. In 2000, the Ministry auctioned the then-popular frequencies for UMTS. The five available UMTS licences went to KPN, Libertel (currently Vodafone), Dutchtone, Telfort and 3G-Blue (currently T-Mobile). The total proceeds for the Dutch government were almost €2.7 billion.

22.51 In 2003, the first two licences in the Netherlands for Wireless Local Loop (WLL) were granted. The two WLL licences attracted considerable interest. As there were more interested parties than available licences, the Ministry organised an auction. Five parties took part: Versatel acquired the licence for the 2.6 GHz band; the licence for the 3.5 GHz band went to Enertel. The WLL licences prescribe no obligatory services and exclusively contain conditions that are necessary to ensure efficient frequency usage. The WLL frequencies in the 26 GHz band were auctioned in March 2005. After one of the three participants in the auction withdrew at the last moment, KPN and T-Mobile were able to obtain WLL frequencies at very low costs.

Frequency trading

22.52 Frequency trading is allowed in the Netherlands, but requires the prior permission of the Minister of Economic Affairs.[64] The Minister may attach certain obligations and restrictions to this permission. The power to impose such restrictions may be used in the interest of a proper distribution of frequencies, as well as in the interests of an orderly and efficient use of frequencies.

Rights of Use for Numbers

General authorisations and granting of individual rights

22.53 The Minister of Economic Affairs, after consultation with OPTA, determines the designated use of (and ranges of) numbers in a so-called 'number plan'.[65] The numbers that are included in the number plan are assigned by OPTA upon application. Parties eligible to apply are providers of public electronic communications networks and/or services, as well as natural person or legal persons who require numbers for the use of an electronic communications service. OPTA must decide within three weeks of the application for the assignment.[66]

22.54 In the interest of an efficient assignment, certain conditions may be attached to an assignment of numbers.

22.55 The basic rule is that numbers are assigned on a 'first come, first served' basis.[67] In the event that OPTA receives, on the same day, several applications from applicants that have expressed an equal preference for the assignment of a certain

---

64 Art 3.8 Tw.
65 *Nummerplan telefoon- en ISDN-diensten,* Dutch Government Gazette 1999, 14. Last revised by Decree of 14 December 2004, *Wijziging Nummerplan Telefoon- en ISDN-diensten,* Dutch Government Gazette 2004, 247.
66 Art 4.2 Tw.
67 Art 4.2(9) Tw.

number, OPTA will allocate the number by drawing lots.[68] An exception applies to 'numbers of exceptional economic value'. These numbers are allocated by means of an auction.[69]

22.56   It is also possible for number applicants to request OPTA to reserve certain numbers.[70] This means that, for the duration of the reservation (which shall not exceed three years), the reserved numbers shall only be available for assignment to the relevant holder of that reservation. In order to be eligible for a reservation, the applicant must demonstrate that the intended use will be realised within three years or, if reservation is requested for a shorter period than three years, within the period requested by the applicant. OPTA keeps a publicly accessible number register, which shows all assignments and reservations.

Admissible conditions

22.57   Since 1999, article 4.10 Tw, in conjunction with the Decree on number portability,[71] has obliged providers of publicly available telephone services, including mobile services, to allow their subscribers to retain their numbers when switching to a different provider.[72] In October 2003, OPTA formulated new policy rules for number portability that lowered the obstacles for switching between mobile providers.[73] These new policy rules determined that mobile providers must ensure that their subscribers are able to switch to a different provider and transfer their numbers within 10 days, even if the end-user still has a contract with the former provider. However, the court did not share OPTA's view in this matter. In a dispute filed by KPN Mobile, the Rotterdam District Court determined that telephone companies could not be forced to cooperate in number portability during the course of a valid contract.[74] This view was confirmed on appeal by the Trade and Industry Appeals Tribunal.[75] This means that a mobile provider is not obliged towards its subscriber to cooperate, at the subscriber's request, in transferring the subscriber's mobile telephone numbers to another mobile provider, if the subscriber's current subscription agreement has not yet been rightfully terminated.

Number trading

22.58   Pursuant to Article 4.6 Tw, it is possible for the holder of a number or reservation to transfer that assignment or reservation to a third party, provided that the prior permission of OPTA is obtained.

The NRA's Enforcement Powers

22.59   The enforcement of the rules laid down in the Tw and underlying regulations is the responsibility of OPTA, except for the enforcement of the rules

---

68   Art 4.2(6) Tw.
69   Art 4.2(7) Tw.
70   Art 4.4 Tw.
71   *Besluit nummerportabiliteit*, Bulletin of Acts and Decrees 1998, 635.
72   The Tw does not provide for transferring numbers between fixed and mobile networks.
73   Aanpassing beleidsregels nummerportabiliteit mobiele telefonie, Government Gazette 2003, 50, p.21.
74   President district court Rotterdam, 18 December 2003 (VTELEC 04/493-RIP and TELEC 04/494-RIP, LJN AO7010).
75   Trade and Industry Appeals Tribunal, 8 December 2004, AWB 04/370.

regarding the management, allocation and protection of radio spectrum, which is the responsibility of the Minister of Economic Affairs.[76]

22.60   For the proper implementation of the provisions given by or pursuant to the Tw, OPTA and the Minister of Economic Affairs are authorised to demand information from anyone at any time insofar as this is reasonably necessary for the fulfilment of their tasks. Anyone from whom such information is demanded is obliged to provide the information and all further cooperation that can be reasonably demanded without delay, but in any case within the time limit stipulated by OPTA or the Minister.[77]

22.61   In the event that a provider fails to comply with the obligations laid down in the Tw, OPTA or the Minister of Economic Affairs (if the non-compliance concerns radio spectrum issues) may impose administrative sanctions on that provider. This means that OPTA or the Minister may take those measures needed to actually put an end to the situation of non-compliance. OPTA and the Minister may also impose financial fines of up to €450,000.[78] This maximum does not apply to providers that fail to live up to obligations that OPTA has imposed upon them as providers with SMP. In such a case, OPTA has the authority to impose fines of up to 10% of the relevant turnover of the provider in the Netherlands. The amount of the fine will in any case be geared to the gravity and duration of the violation, as well as to the extent to which the offender can be deemed to be at fault. On 7 November 2004, OPTA published guidelines regarding its authority to impose fines.[79] These guidelines provide an insight into the factors that determine the scale of a fine.

22.62   Although certain alternative operators are of the view that OPTA has not always used its enforcement powers under the 1998 Tw adequately, OPTA has performed various administrative enforcement activities over the last years, in which fines were imposed. In 2003, KPN was fined twice for violating the principle of non-discrimination.[80] In January 2005, OPTA imposed on KPN a penalty of €450,000 – the highest fine OPTA has imposed so far – for offering new business subscribers financial inducements without first obtaining OPTA's approval.[81]

22.63   OPTA and the Minister may prohibit a provider from offering its electronic communications networks or services for a certain period, if that provider has repeatedly and severely failed to comply with the applicable regulations, and the afore-mentioned measures of administrative sanctions or financial fines have failed.[82] To date, neither OPTA nor the Minister has used this measure.

---

76   See paras 22.47–22.55 above.
77   Art 18.7 Tw.
78   Art 15.4 Tw.
79   *OPTA Boetebeleidsregels*, Dutch Government Gazette 2004, 234.
80   12 OPTA/IBT/2003/201837, 11 March 2003 en OPTA/IBT/2003/204596, 19 December 2003.
81   KPN launched a marketing campaign in July 2004 offering to new clients up to €5,000 in exchange for signing up to a fixed-line business subscription. Being an operator with SMP on the market for fixed telephony, KPN is required to seek OPTA's prior permission before introducing such permanent discounts.
82   Art 15.2a(2) Tw.

Administrative Charges and Fees for Rights of Use

22.64   85% of OPTA's costs are covered by the regulated market parties, and 15% by the Ministry of Economic Affairs.[83] Parties for whose benefit OPTA has performed work or services under the provisions given by or pursuant to the Tw are under the obligation to reimburse OPTA's costs. The legal basis for such reimbursement is laid down in article 16.1 Tw, the Telecommunication Fees Decree,[84] as well as the Independent Post and Telecommunications Authority Act.[85]

22.65   The cost-covering tariffs to be charged to the market parties are approved each year by the Minister of Economic Affairs, and are published annually in the Dutch Government Gazette as the 'OPTA fees regulation'.[86] Market parties have to pay a non-recurring fee for their registration with OPTA as a provider, as well as an annually recurring fee to cover the costs of OPTA's task of supervising the electronic communications sector. The costs of individual objections and appeals are not charged to the providers, but are borne by the Ministry of Economic Affairs.

22.66   Pursuant to article 3.3a Tw, holders of frequency licences, including holders whose licence is or has been extended, can be charged a fee for the use of their frequencies. These fees, which may be non-recurring or periodical, are established by Ministerial decree and are based on the financial benefits that the licence holder is expected to obtain from the exploitation of the frequency.[87] Such fees were imposed, for instance, upon the licence holders that acquired frequencies for FM radio broadcasting.

REGULATION OF NETWORK ACCESS AND INTERCONNECTION: IMPLEMENTATION OF THE ACCESS DIRECTIVE

Objectives and Scope of Access Regulation

22.67   The Access Directive has been implemented mainly in Chapters 6 and 6a Tw. The rules laid down in these chapters regulate the relationships between suppliers of networks and services and are aimed at creating and/or maintaining sustainable competition, interoperability of electronic communications services, as well as consumer benefits.

22.68   Chapter 6 contains the rules that apply irrespective of the market position of undertakings, and is mainly aimed at ensuring interoperability of services. Chapter 6a contains the obligations that exist with respect to SMP undertakings. Specific access obligations with regard to digital television and radio broadcasting

---

83   *Visie op markttoezicht*, letter from the State Secretary to the Second Chamber, 5 November 2004 (EP/MW4066326).

84   *Besluit vergoedingen telecommunicatiewet*, 12 March 1999, Bulletin of Acts and Decrees 1999, 130, as amended from time to time.

85   *Wet onafhankelijke Post- en Telecommunicatieautoriteit*, 5 July 1997, Bulletin of Acts and Decrees 1997, 320, as amended from time to time.

86   The most recent fees regulation entered into force on 1 January 2005, *Regeling vergoedingen OPTA 2005*, Dutch Government Gazette 24 December 2004, 249.

87   See, for example, the Ministerial decree in which a non-recurring fee was established for the holders of a licence for nationwide commercial radio broadcasting, *Regeling vaststelling eenmalig bedrag landelijke commerciële radio-omroep 2003*, Dutch Government Gazette 2003, 151.

services are set out in chapter 8 Tw. Finally, chapter 18 contains specific transition provisions which allow for the adaptation of existing access rights and obligations to the new Tw.

Basic Regulatory Concepts

22.69 'Access' is broadly defined as 'the making available of network elements, associated facilities and/or services, to another undertaking, under express conditions on either an exclusive or non-exclusive basis, for the purpose of providing electronic communications services and/or distributing programmes to the public'.[88] Access does not only include access to physical infrastructure, or the connection of equipment, but also access to relevant software systems, access to number translation systems and access to virtual network services.

22.70 'Interconnection' is defined as 'a specific type of access implemented between public network operators, consisting of the physical and logical linking of public communications networks used by the same or a different undertaking in order to allow the users of an undertaking to communicate with users of the same or another undertaking, or to access services provided by another undertaking'.[89]

Access- and Interconnection-related Obligations with Respect to SMP Undertakings

Overview of the NRA's regulatory powers

22.71 Chapter 6a Tw lists the access- and interconnection-related obligations that OPTA may impose upon SMP undertakings. Logically, OPTA is not authorised to impose such obligations until it has completed the market analysis procedure, which entails delineating the relevant markets, determining whether the relevant markets are competitive and, for non-competitive markets, determining which parties have SMP.

22.72 With respect to the regulation of access and interconnection for SMP undertakings, OPTA is empowered to impose the following obligations:

- obligations of access to, and use of, specific network facilities (article 6a.6 Tw),
- obligations relating to price control and cost accounting (article 6a.7 Tw),
- obligations of non-discrimination (article 6a.8 Tw),
- obligations of transparency (article 6a.9 Tw) and
- obligations of accounting separation (article 6a.10 Tw).

22.73 If an undertaking has been designated as having SMP on a specific market, OPTA is obligated to impose the obligations set out above 'as appropriate'. A remedy shall be considered appropriate if it is proportional and justified, taken into account 'the nature of the problem identified' and the objectives set out in article 8 Framework Directive.[90] This leaves OPTA a considerable level of discretion with respect to the choice of the afore-mentioned access- and interconnection-related obligations.

---

88   Art 1.1(l) Tw.
89   Art 1.1(m) Tw
90   Art 6.1.2(3) Tw.

Transparency obligations

22.74   OPTA may oblige SMP undertakings to disclose information in relation to access to their public communications networks.[91] Such information may include tariffs and other terms and conditions for supply and use, as well as technical specifications and network characteristics. OPTA may specify the precise information to be made available and the level of detail required.

22.75   OPTA also has the authority to require the publication of reference offers, which shall include a description of those types of access designated by OPTA. For each type of access, the reference offer must separately mention the applicable tariffs and other terms and conditions. If the reference offer concerns unbundled access to the local loop, the reference offer must contain at least the elements set out in Annex II to the Access Directive, which correspond to the requirements set out in Regulation 2887/2000 of 18 December 2000 with respect to the unbundled access to the local loop with (physical) twisted metallic pair (circuit).

Non-discrimination obligations

22.76   OPTA may oblige SMP undertakings to provide certain types of access (to be designated by OPTA) under equivalent conditions in equivalent circumstances.[92] This entails that the SMP undertaking must apply to other undertakings the same conditions as it provides for its own services or those of its subsidiaries or partners.

Specific access obligations

22.77   Under Article 6.a.6 Tw, OPTA is authorised to impose obligations on SMP undertakings to meet reasonable requests for access to, and use of, specific network elements and associated facilities, to be designated by OPTA. OPTA may impose such access obligations, inter alia, in situations where OPTA considers that denial of access or unreasonable terms and conditions having a similar effect would hinder the emergence of a sustainable competitive market at the retail level, or would not be in the end-user's interest. Article 6a.6(2) Tw sets out a non-exhaustive catalogue of specific access obligations, which obligations are identical to the ones listed in article 12(1) and (2) Access Directive. When imposing such access obligations, OPTA may attach conditions ensuring fairness, reasonableness and timeliness.

Price control and cost accounting obligations

22.78   OPTA may impose upon SMP undertakings obligations relating to cost accounting and price controls in relation to the provision of specific types of interconnection and/or access, to be determined by OPTA.[93] OPTA may only impose these price control measures if a market analysis has indicated that the operator concerned might sustain prices at an excessively high level, or apply a price squeeze, to the detriment of end-users. Article 6a.7(2) Tw expressly mentions that the price control obligations imposed by OPTA may include the obligation to apply cost-oriented prices, which effectively amounts to the ex ante regulation of prices.

---

91   Art 6a.9 Tw.
92   Art 6a.8 Tw.
93   Art 6a.7 Tw.

In addition, the cost-accounting methods that SMP undertakings use may be made subject to OPTA's prior approval. The burden of proof that prices are cost-oriented lies with the SMP undertaking.

22.79   Under the 1998 Tw, OPTA has settled a vast amount of disputes between KPN and other licensed operators ('OLOs') concerning interconnection tariffs for both fixed and mobile networks and services. The disputes concerned various types of access, including originating access (the situation in which KPN delivers calls originating in the KPN network to the network of the OLO), as well as terminating access (the situation in which the OLO delivers calls originating in the OLO network to the network of KPN). The terminating tariffs applied by KPN are more closely regulated than the originating tariffs, because no competition is possible for call termination. For calculating cost-oriented originating tariffs, OPTA allows KPN to use its EDC[94] cost-allocation model. The EDC model uses the figures from KPN's own accounting records to calculate KPN's actual costs. For determining the level of cost-oriented terminating tariffs, on the other hand, OPTA calculates what the costs would be if KPN's network were operated in a sufficiently efficient manner under pressure from market mechanisms. This is known as the BULRIC[95] model. In this way, needlessly high or inefficient costs, whether inherited from the monopoly era or not, may not be charged to KPN's competitors.

These decisions given under the 1998 Tw remain of importance under the current Tw, as OPTA has indicated that it does not intend to amend its views in this respect.

Accounting separation obligations

22.80   Article 6a.10 Tw authorises OPTA to impose on SMP undertakings obligations for accounting separation in relation to specified types of access. OPTA is authorised to specify the accounting methodology to be used and the format of the accounting records to be provided to OPTA, including data on revenues received from third parties. Separated accounting records give OPTA an insight into the wholesale prices and internal transfer prices of SMP undertakings, allowing OPTA to ensure compliance with non-discrimination obligations and to prevent unfair cross-subsidisation practices.

Imposition of obligations in exceptional circumstances

22.81   In exceptional circumstances, OPTA may impose upon SMP undertakings other obligations for access or interconnection than those set out in articles 6.a.6 – 6.a.10 Tw, if appropriate.[96] However, before OPTA may impose any such additional obligations, the scope of such obligations, and the conditions in which they may be imposed, must be laid down in a Ministerial decree. So far, no such decree has been adopted. Therefore, OPTA currently has no authority to impose any such additional obligations.

---

94   Embedded Direct Costs.
95   Bottom Up Long Run Incremental Costs.
96   Art 6a.11 Tw.

Related Regulatory Powers with Respect to SMP Undertakings

Obligations concerning carrier (pre-)selection

22.82   Paragraph 6a.4 Tw contains obligations for SMP undertakings to make carrier (pre-)selection services accessible to their subscribers.

22.83   Pursuant to article 6a.16 in conjunction with article 6a.17 Tw, SMP undertakings on the market for the provision of connection to and use of the public telephone network at a fixed location have to enable their subscribers to access the services of any interconnected provider of public telephone services both on a call-by-call basis by dialling a carrier selection code and by means of pre-selection. In this context, the SMP undertakings are also obliged to grant reasonable requests for access to their fixed networks coming from carrier (pre-)selection providers. The tariffs applied by the SMP undertakings have to be cost-oriented.

22.84   The afore-mentioned obligations are not imposed by OPTA, but apply by operation of law to any undertaking designated as having SMP on the market for the provision of connection to and use of the public telephone network at a fixed location. This means that OPTA does not have to first determine whether the obligation is appropriate (as is the case with the obligations listed in articles 6a.6 – 6a.11 Tw).

Obligations concerning the provision of a minimum set of leased lines

22.85   Paragraph 6a.5 Tw contains obligations for undertakings with SMP to offer a certain minimum set of leased lines. The scope of this minimum offering is published by the European Commission in accordance with article 17 Framework Directive as part of the list of standards for the harmonised provision of electronic communications networks and services.[97]

22.86   If OPTA determines, in the course of a market analysis in accordance with article 6a.2(3) Tw, that an undertaking has SMP in the provision of one or more types of leased lines listed in the minimum set of leased lines, that undertaking is obliged to provide those types of leased lines to anyone who so requests.[98]

22.87   Certain additional conditions may be imposed on SMP undertakings that are obliged to provide the minimum set of leased lines. These conditions are designed to ensure compliance with the basic principles of non-discrimination, cost orientation and transparency. These conditions are not imposed by OPTA, but are laid down in a Ministerial decree, the 'Decree on minimum set of leased lines'.[99] The Decree obliges regulated SMP undertakings, inter alia, to apply similar conditions in similar circumstances, if appropriate, to establish tariffs that follow the principles of cost orientation, and to publish technical characteristics, tariffs and supply conditions in respect of the minimum set of leased lines in accordance with the detailed requirements set out in the Decree.

---

97   See para 1.176 above.
98   Art 6a.19(1) Tw.
99   *Regeling minimumpakket huurlijnen*, 10 May 2004, Dutch Government Gazette 2004, 92.

Regulatory Powers Applicable to All Market Participants

Obligations to ensure end-to-end connectivity

22.88   Article 6.1 Tw obliges all providers of public electronic communications networks or services, who control the access of end-users, to negotiate interconnection and other necessary measures for the purpose of end-to-end connectivity when requested to do so by another provider. This obligation applies to all providers of public electronic communications networks or services, regardless of their market position.

22.89   It should be noted that establishing such end-to-end connectivity usually involves interconnection, but may require further (technical and/or organisational) measures. Therefore, the negotiation obligation is not limited to interconnection agreements.[100]

22.90   Where negotiations fail to lead to an agreement between providers, article 6.2(1) Tw gives OPTA the authority to impose obligations, at the request of either of the providers, to ensure end-to-end connectivity between the providers involved. OPTA may also, on a case-by-case basis, impose such obligations of its own initiative. The Tw does not explicitly state the 'obligations' which OPTA may impose upon undertakings that control access to end-users, regardless of their market position, in order to ensure end-to-end connectivity. Article 6.2(2) Tw merely states that those obligations must be justified in the light of the policy objectives and regulatory principles of article 8 Framework Directive. In practice, the consolidation procedure[101] should make clear which regulatory measures are permissible and which are not.

22.91   The duty to negotiate set out in article 6.1. Tw seems to extend to providers of public electronic communications *services*, not just to network operators. Some fear that this will give service providers without a network the opportunity to force access to networks of non-SMP operators without the safeguards of a prior market analysis, in order to enhance the availability of their services.[102] In a dispute between the Dutch mobile network operator T-Mobile and the provider of text messaging services Yarosa, OPTA ordered T-Mobile to negotiate interconnection and other necessary measures with Yarosa, for the purpose of establishing end-to-end connectivity between both parties' end-users. In appeal proceedings, the CBB reversed OPTA's ruling, considering that a service provider may only invoke interoperability of services if intended for the purpose of enhancing its own end-users' possibilities to communicate or be accessible. According to the CBB, Yarosa's request for interoperability was primarily aimed at increasing its own revenues, by processing text messages originating in T-Mobile's network in Yarosa's network centre. The CBB reversed the duty to negotiate imposed by OPTA in first instance.[103]

---

100   Any (confidential) information acquired from the other undertaking before, during or after the process of negotiating may be used solely for the purpose for which it was supplied.
101   See para 1.60 above.
102   See, for instance, C.E. Schillemans, Interoperabiliteit: van toverwoord tot Trojaans paard-?,Mediaforum 2005, no. 2, p 38–43.
103   T-Mobile & Yarosa vs.OPTA, *College van Beroep voor het Bedrijfsleven*, 24 November 2004, Awb 04/651 and 04/727, *Mediaforum* 2005, no 2, pp 70–73.

22.92   Article 6.3 Tw allows the Minister of Economic Affairs, in the capacity of NRA, to designate by governmental decree certain categories of public electronic communications services, the providers of which shall be obliged to ensure end-to-end connectivity.

22.93   The Minister used this power in May 2004 by establishing the Interoperability Decree.[104] There, the Minister has designated publicly available telephone services as services referred to in article 6.3 Tw. This means that publicly available telephone services (mobile and fixed) are so important in the light of article 8 Framework Directive that an obligation for providers to ensure end-to-end connectivity is justified. For these categories of services, it is not sufficient to rely on commercial initiatives for realising end-to-end connectivity. Consequently, the providers of publicly available telephone services have a statutory obligation to ensure end-to-end connectivity.[105] In this context, it should be noted that carrier (pre-)selection services are not regarded by the Dutch legislator as publicly available telephone services, since these services only concern outgoing calls, and not incoming calls. Hence, providers of carrier (pre-)selection services are exempt from the obligation to ensure end-to-end connectivity between their networks and services.

22.94   In addition, the Interoperability Decree ensures access to the European telephony numbering space (implementing article 27(2) Universal Service Directive) and end-to-end connectivity of non-geographic telephone numbers on an international level (implementing article 28 Universal Service Directive).

22.95   OPTA may – on request – grant a dispensation from the obligation to ensure end-to-end connectivity under the Interoperability Decree, where end-to-end connectivity is technically not possible or economically not viable.[106]

Access to digital radio and television broadcasting services

22.96   Pursuant to article 8.6 Tw, the Minister of Economic Affairs has the authority to establish rules (by ministerial decree) regarding the access to digital radio and television broadcasting services. These rules may include obligations for providers of Application Programming Interfaces (APIs) and Electronic Program Guides (EPGs), regardless of their market position, to provide access to APIs and EPGs on fair, reasonable and non-discriminatory terms. The ministerial decree may also include obligations regarding transparency and accounting separation. So far, the Minister has not utilised his authority to establish such a ministerial decree.

22.97   The rules for conditional access systems are not laid down in the Tw, but in a ministerial decree, based on article 8.5 Tw: the Decree on conditional access.[107] This Decree implements the obligations that are set out in Annex I Part I Access Directive. These obligations apply to all providers of conditional access systems that provide access to digital television and radio services, regardless of their market position.

22.98   Providers of conditional access systems are obliged to offer broadcasters of digitally transmitted services those technical services which are necessary to enable

---

104   *Besluit Interoperabiliteit* (Interoperability Decree), 7 May 2004, Dutch Government Gazette 2004, 205.
105   Art 6.3 Tw.
106   Art 6.3(3) Tw.
107   *Besluit voorwaardelijke toegang*, 7 May 2004, Bulletin of Acts and Decrees 2004, 204.

the viewers or listeners 'behind the decoder' to receive the broadcasters' digitally transmitted services. Such technical services must be offered on a fair, reasonable and non-discriminatory basis compatible with Community competition law. Providers of conditional access systems must also keep separate financial accounts regarding their activity as conditional access providers.[108]

22.99 Furthermore, providers of conditional access systems must ensure that their systems have the necessary technical capability for cost-effective transfer of control. This means that network operators broadcasting services to the public should be enabled to have full control of the services using such conditional access systems.[109]

22.100 Another obligation included in the Decree applies to holders of industrial property rights to conditional access products and systems. When granting licences to manufacturers of consumer equipment, they must ensure that this is done on fair, reasonable and non-discriminatory terms. Taking into account technical and commercial factors, they are not allowed to subject the granting of licences to conditions prohibiting, deterring or discouraging the inclusion in the same product of a common interface allowing connection with several other access systems.[110]

Transitional Provisions

22.101 In order to ensure the transition, from asymmetric access and interconnection obligations imposed upon undertakings designated under the 1998 Tw as having SMP to the new Tw, chapter 19 provides for detailed transition rules.

22.102 Pursuant to article 19.5 Tw, OPTA shall maintain all obligations regarding access and interconnection that were in force prior to the entry into force of the revised Tw, until such time as these obligations have been reviewed (no later than 24 months after the revised Tw has entered into force) and a determination has been made, on the basis of a market analysis, whether to maintain, amend or withdraw these obligations with respect to SMP undertakings.

REGULATION OF UNIVERSAL SERVICES AND USERS' RIGHTS: THE UNIVERSAL SERVICE DIRECTIVE

Regulation of Universal Service Obligations

Scope of universal service obligations

22.103 Article 9.1 Tw lists the minimum set of services which together constitute the 'universal service'. The list is identical to the catalogue provided by the Universal Service Directive.

22.104 These services must be made available to all end-users, independently of geographical location, at an affordable price and to a specified quality.

Designation of undertakings obliged to provide universal services

22.105 Currently, KPN is and remains designated as the undertaking that is obliged to provide all elements of the minimum set of services that together

---

108 Art 2 Decree on conditional access.
109 Art 3 Decree on conditional access.
110 Art 4 Decree on conditional access.

comprise the 'universal service'. In deviation from the financing mechanism set out in article 9.3 Tw, KPN is not entitled to any remuneration of net costs involved in providing the universal service. Conversely, KPN is authorised to terminate unilaterally the universal service designation wholly or partially, subject to a one-year notice term.

22.106 Should KPN cease the provision of (one or more of) the universal services, and should this lead to a situation in which the availability, affordability or quality of one or more elements of the universal service cannot be guaranteed by normal market processes, the Minister may designate one or more undertakings which are obliged to provide different elements of the universal service and/or to cover different parts of the national territory. In order to ensure that universal service is provided in a cost-effective manner, the Minister shall, in principle, designate the undertaking that expects the lowest net costs for providing the specified universal services. Other undertakings may also apply for designation.

Regulation of retail tariffs, users' expenditures and quality of services

22.107 Rules regarding the permissible end-user tariffs for the afore-mentioned universal services, as well as requirements regarding the quality of such services, have been laid down in the Decree on universal services and end-user interests.[111] Pursuant to this Decree, consumers must have access to publicly available telephone services at a fixed location for tariffs that are 'no higher than reasonable'. According to the explanation to the Decree, an end-user tariff is reasonable if the scale of the tariff is in reasonable proportion to the economical value of the service rendered, plus a reasonable return. This is different from the principle of cost orientation.[112]

22.108 In addition, end-users who wish to use their fixed telephone connection mainly for the purpose of receiving calls, rather than making calls, must have access to a specific type of 'low budget' subscription with relatively low monthly fixed charges, and relatively high usage charges. The maximum scale of these charges has been specified in the Regulation on universal services and end-user interests.[113] The regulation also contains detailed rules on such issues as the compulsory provision of itemised billing and selective call barring for outgoing calls.

22.109 Furthermore, undertakings with universal service obligations are required to apply common tariffs throughout the territory where the services are provided. They may not oblige subscribers to pay for facilities or services which are not necessary or not required for the service requested.

22.110 The Dutch legislator has not (yet) adopted any specific measures for disabled users and users with special social needs (as set out in article 7 Universal Service Directive).

---

111 Besluit universele dienstverlening en eindgebruikersbelangen, 7 May 2004, Bulletin of Acts and Decrees 2004, 203.

112 OPTA may still impose cost-orientation obligations on providers of public telephone services at a fixed location that have been designated as SMP undertakings, on the basis of art 6.2 in conjunction with art 6a.13 Tw.

113 Regeling universele dienstverlening en eindgebruikersbelangen, 10 May 2004, Dutch Government Gazette 2004, 92.

Cost calculation and financing of universal services

22.111   The compensation for undertakings that have been designated for the provision of universal services is based on a sharing of the net cost of universal service obligations between providers of electronic communications networks and services.[114] Each provider that has realised an annual turnover of more than €7 million[115] by providing those services that fall within a specified category of universal services provided by the designated undertaking is required to contribute to the compensation of the designated undertaking. The amount of the contribution shall be proportional to the relevant turnover.

Regulation of Retail Markets

Prerequisites for the regulation of retail markets

22.112   Articles 6a.12 – 6a.15 Tw set out the obligations that OPTA may impose upon undertakings with SMP on retail markets. OPTA may impose such measures at the retail level only if the relevant retail market is not effectively competitive, and access-related obligations would not be sufficient to resolve the problems identified in the relevant retail market.

Regulatory powers

22.113   On the basis of article 6a.12 Tw, OPTA may prohibit SMP undertakings from discriminating between end-users (in order to prevent undue preference to specific end-users), and from unreasonably bundling end-user services. In addition, OPTA may require undertakings to announce specified information to end-users, such as pricing information, or the consumers' right to submit their dispute with the undertaking to the Telecommunications Dispute Committee.[116]

22.114   The most far-reaching authority that OPTA has in relation to end-user markets is the power to regulate end-user tariffs.[117] In order to prevent an SMP undertaking from charging excessively high prices, or from setting predatory prices, OPTA may set both a floor and a ceiling for the undertaking's end-user tariffs. Where OPTA regulates end-user tariffs, it must also impose mandatory rules regarding the implementation of cost-accounting systems. OPTA may specify the format and accounting methodology to be used. The SMP undertaking is further obliged to publish annually a statement concerning compliance with the cost-accounting requirements.

22.115   If OPTA has regulated an SMP undertaking's end-user tariffs once, OPTA may also prohibit the undertaking from implementing any new end-user

---

114 Art 9.4 Tw.
115 This amount is determined in article 2.6 of the Regulation on universal service and end-user interests and may be subject to change.
116 On the basis of art 12.1 Tw in conjunction with article 3.4 of the Decree on universal service and end-user interests, all providers of public telephone services, pager services (including ERMES), telex services and carrier services, are obliged to adhere to the Telecommunications Dispute Committee ('TDC') The TDC is an independent organisation that provides for alternative dispute resolution between providers of electronic communications and consumers.
117 Art 6a.13 Tw.

tariffs in the future.[118] OPTA has frequently used a similar power under the 1998 Tw to submit KPN's end-user tariffs to OPTA's prior approval.

End User Rights

Contracts

22.116   All providers of public electronic communication services are required, when entering into a contract with a consumer (ie any natural person that uses or requests the publicly available electronic communications service for purposes which are outside his or her trade, business or profession),[119] to provide at least the following information to the consumer:[120]

- the identity and address of the provider,
- the definition of the services provided, as well as the time for the initial connection,
- the specification of the service quality levels offered,
- the types of maintenance service offered,
- particulars of prices and tariffs and the means by which up-to-date information on all applicable tariffs and maintenance charges may be obtained,
- the duration of the contract, the conditions for renewal and termination of services and of the contract,
- any compensation and the refund arrangements which apply if contracted service quality levels are not met, and
- the method of initiating procedures for settlement of disputes by the Telecommunications Dispute Committee or OPTA.

22.117   The provider must supply the above information to the consumer before or at the moment of entering into the contract. The information may be laid down in the provider's general terms and conditions. In any event, the contract between the provider and the consumer must be made available to the consumer either in writing or on a durable electronic medium (implementing the Directive on the protection of consumers in respect of distance contracts).[121]

22.118   The minimum requirements above apply not only to providers of connection and/or access to the public telephone network, but to providers of all electronic communications services. None of these service providers, however, are under any obligation to enter into contracts with consumers (contrary to article 20(2) Universal Service Directive).

22.119   If a provider of public electronic communication services intends to modify the contractual conditions of existing contracts with subscribers (including consumers and end-users), the provider must give the subscribers adequate notice of such proposed modifications, at least four weeks ahead of any such modification. The subscribers must also be informed of their right to withdraw from their contracts without penalty upon such notice.[122]

---

118   Art 6a.14 Tw.
119   Art 1.1(q) Tw.
120   Art 7.1 Tw.
121   Art 5.1 Distance Selling Directive.
122   Art 7.2 Tw.

Transparency obligations

22.120   Providers of public telephone services are obliged to disclose to their potential end-users information regarding the standard tariffs, compensation and refund policies, the type of maintenance service offered, the standard contract conditions, including any minimum contractual period, and dispute settlement mechanisms.[123] This information must be disclosed 'in a satisfactory manner'. The Dutch legislator has pointed out that providing the information to the potential end-users in written form shall constitute disclosure 'in a satisfactory manner', but the mere publication of this information on a website does not.

22.121   Furthermore, providers of public telephone services at fixed locations or providers of public payphones that have been designated as providers of universal services, as well as any other provider of fixed public telephone services or public payphones that has been active on the Dutch market for more than one year, are obliged to publish an annual overview of the quality of their services, in accordance with Annex III Universal Service Directive.[124] The published information must include, inter alia, the supply time for initial connection, fault rate per access line, fault repair time, unsuccessful call ratio, call set-up time and other parameters.

Other obligations

OPERATOR ASSISTANCE AND DIRECTORY ENQUIRY SERVICES

22.122   Subject to applicable data protection provisions (chapter 11 Tw),[125] subscribers to publicly available telephone services have the right to be listed in the publicly available directory.[126] A standard entry must be provided free of charge for the subscriber and the telephone directory must be updated at least once per year. Upon obtaining the subscriber's personal data for the purpose of entering into a contract, the provider must request the subscriber's permission for the data to be included in the publicly available telephone directory.[127] Undertakings which assign telephone numbers to subscribers have to meet all reasonable requests to make available, for the purposes of the provision of publicly available directory inquiry services and directories, the relevant information in an agreed format on 'fair, objective, cost oriented and non-discriminatory' terms.[128]

22.123   All end-users that are provided with the connection to the public telephone network have a right to access operator assistance services and directory or enquiry services.[129]

EUROPEAN EMERGENCY CALL NUMBER

22.124   Providers of public telephone networks, public payphones or public telephone services must ensure that the users of their services shall have access to the single European emergency call number '112' free of charge, even in situations

---

123 Art 7.2 Tw, in conjunction with the Decree on universal service and end user interests.
124 Art 7.4 Tw.
125 See para 22.126 below.
126 Art 2.3 Decree on universal service and end-user interests.
127 Art 3.2 Decree on universal service and end-user interests
128 Art 3.1 Decree on universal service and end-user interests.
129 Art 7.6 Tw.

of network congestion.[130] Furthermore, if providers have calling line identification and/or caller location information, they are under the obligation to make that information available to the authorities handling the emergency calls.[131] The authorities may only use the received information for the purpose of providing aid in emergency situations, or combating abuse of the emergency call number '112'.

PACKET-SWITCHED SERVICES AND END-USER RIGHTS

22.125   In October 2004, OPTA published a consultation document regarding end-user rights in relation to packet-switched services. In the consultation document, OPTA expresses its vision on the applicability of the end-user rights set out in the Tw, to packet-switched communications services. OPTA considers that IP telephony and VoIP 'on top of' broadband services (eg 'Voice-over-DSL') qualify as a public telephone service and, therefore, are subject, inter alia, to the end-user rights discussed above. This has important implications for many Dutch broadband providers that offer voice services in a combined package with broadband services.

DATA PROTECTION: IMPLEMENTATION OF THE E-PRIVACY DIRECTIVE

Confidentiality of Communications

22.126   Without prejudice to the general Data Protection Act (*Wet bescherming persoonsgegevens* – 'WBP'),[132] operators providing publicly available electronic communications networks and/or services are obliged to take appropriate technical and organisational measures to safeguard the security of the networks and services they provide.[133] Taking account of the state of technology and the costs, the measures must guarantee a level of security which is proportionate to the risks involved. Where there is a risk of security breach, subscribers must be informed without delay of the risk and possible remedies, as well as cost implications.[134]

22.127   In addition, providers of publicly available telecommunications networks and/or services are obliged to allow lawful interception by police authorities of communications occurring over their networks or services. The provider shall receive no compensation for the costs of making the telecommunications network or service technically capable of being wiretapped. Only the administrative and personnel costs incurred by the provider as a direct result of carrying out an individual wiretapping order may be compensated by the State.[135]

22.128   The rules regarding cookies and spy-ware, set out in article 5(3) E-Privacy Directive, were implemented with some delay into the Decree on universal service and end-user interests. Anyone (not just providers of electronic communications networks or services) who wishes to use an electronic communications network to store information or to gain access to information stored in a user's terminal equipment (eg by way of cookies) must first provide clear and comprehensive information regarding the intention and purpose of processing and offer the user or

---

130   Art 7.7 Tw.
131   Art 11.10 Tw.
132   *Wet bescherming persoonsgegevens*, 6 July 2000, Bulletin of Acts and Decrees 200, 302.
133   Art 11.3(1) Tw.
134   Art 11.3(2) Tw.
135   See Chapter 13 Tw.

subscriber the opportunity to refuse processing. An exception to this prohibition applies to technical storage or access for the sole purpose of transmitting the communication or providing services explicitly requested by the subscriber/user.[136]

Traffic Data and Location Data

22.129   The definitions of 'traffic data' and 'location data' are identical to those in the E-Privacy Directive.[137] The main rule is that traffic data processed for the purpose of transmitting communications must be erased or anonymised when it is no longer needed for that purpose. Two exceptions apply: providers may retain traffic data if necessary for billing purposes, but only for the period during which the bill may be lawfully challenged and payment pursued, and providers may process traffic data for the purposes of marketing electronic communications services or the provision of value added services, provided consent is obtained. Users or subscribers must be allowed to withdraw their consent at any time. Providers must inform subscribers of the types of traffic data processed and the duration of such processing.[138]

22.130   Location data other than traffic data may only be processed if they have been anonymised or the user's consent has been obtained to the extent and for the duration necessary for the provision of a value added service. The consent is only valid if the provider has informed the user or subscriber of the types of location data processed, the purposes and duration of the processing, and the third parties to whom the data may be disclosed. This consent may be withdrawn at any time.[139]

Itemised Billing

22.131   At the request of a subscriber, the provider of a public electronic communications service is obliged to issue completely or partially non-itemised bills.[140] More detailed rules regarding the itemisation of bills for electronic communications services may be laid down in a ministerial decree. To date, the Minister has not issued such a ministerial decree.

Calling and Connected Line Identification

22.132   Providers offering calling line identification must allow every calling subscriber or user to block the provision of the calling number on a per-call and per-line basis, using simple means and free of charge. Users or subscribers must also have the facility to block the numbers of incoming calls and to reject incoming calls automatically in cases where the caller has withheld the caller identification.[141] More detailed rules, including rules regarding international line identification, have been laid down in the Regulation on universal services and end-user interests.[142]

---

136   Art 4.1 Decree on universal service and end-user interests.
137   Art 11.1(b), (d) Tw.
138   Art 11.5 Tw.
139   Art 11.5a Tw.
140   Art 11.4(1) Tw.
141   Art 11.9 Tw.
142   Regeling universele dienst en eindgebruikersbelangen, Dutch Government Gazette 14 May 2004, no. 92.

Automatic Call Forwarding

22.133 Providers of public electronic communications services are obliged to ensure that their subscribers have the possibility, free of charge and in a simple manner, to block automatic call forwarding from a third party to their terminal.[143]

Directories of Subscribers

22.134 The universal service operators and any other operator making subscribers data available for inclusion in a directory must inform all subscribers in advance of the purposes of the directory and any further usage possibilities based on search functions embedded in electronic versions of the directory. A subscriber's personal data may only be included in the directory if, and to the extent, the subscriber has given his consent thereto. Not being included in a public subscriber directory, and verifying, correcting or withdrawing personal data from it must be free of charge.[144]

Prohibition of Unsolicited Communications

22.135 The Tw provides for an opt-in system for unsolicited communications ('spam'). The use of automatic calling systems without human intervention, faxes or electronic messages (which is a wider concept than just e-mail, but also includes, for instance, text or video messages on mobile devices) for transmitting unsolicited communications to subscribers for commercial, idealistic or charitable purposes (which is broader than only direct marketing) will only be permitted if the sender can demonstrate that the subscriber concerned has given prior permission for this.[145]

22.136 An exception applies to the sender that has obtained from its existing customers their electronic contact details for electronic messages, in the context of a previous sale of a product or a service. This person or entity may use these electronic contact details for transmitting communications for commercial, idealistic or charitable purposes in connection with its own similar products or services, provided that customers clearly and distinctly are given the opportunity to object, free of charge and in an easy manner, to such use of electronic contact details when they are collected and on the occasion of each message in case the customer has not initially refused such use. This amounts to an opt-out system. The anti-spam rules protect only natural persons, and provide no protection for business e-mail addresses or phone numbers.

22.137 OPTA has a special website[146] where complaints can be submitted against violators of this spam prohibition. On 28 December 2004, OPTA imposed the first fines on distributors of spam: in this instance, the spam was distributed through e-mail and mobile text messages; and the highest fine imposed was €42,500. OPTA is also involved with NRAs from other EU member states in initiatives to combat spam.[147]

22.138 In addition to the statutory prohibition of spam in the Tw, various forms of self-regulation have emerged in the Netherlands. Since June 2004, there has been

---

143 Art 11.4(1) Tw.
144 Art 11.6 Tw.
145 Art 11.7 tw.
146 www.spamklacht.nl (only available in Dutch).
147 On the initiative of the European Commission, an informal group was created consisting of

a self-regulatory code on direct marketing, on the basis of which the participating companies make it clear they will not be involved in distributing spam. Direct marketing associations and the employers' association were involved in setting up this code, which also has the endorsement of the consumer association.

NRAs involved with the enforcement of Article 13 of the Privacy and Electronic Communication Directive 2002/58/EC called 'the Contact Network of Spam Authorities' (CNSA). In December 2004, the CNSA established a cooperation procedure aimed at facilitating the transmission of complaint information between NRAs.

The Polish Market for Electronic Communications[1]

Wojciech Bialik and Dr Eligiusz Jerzy Krześniak
Baker & McKenzie, Warsaw

LEGAL STRUCTURE

Basic Policy

23.1 Selected sectors of the Polish telecommunications market were opened up to private investors in the mid-1990s. The liberalisation process progressed through the 1990s and the early 2000s and included the successful two-stage privatisation of the incumbent operator – Telekomunikacja Polska S.A. ('TPSA') – as the key point. Full liberalisation of the market was completed by the end of 2003, when the last foreign ownership restrictions were lifted.

23.2 The most rapidly developing market in Poland is the mobile telephony sector, on which three operators are active: Polska Telefonia Cyfrowa Sp. z o.o., Polska Telefonia Komórkowa Centertel Sp. z o.o. and Polkomtel S.A., all of which are privately owned. All the operators provide their services in the GSM standard and hold licences for providing UMTS services, although the only one currently providing limited UMTS services is Polkomtel S.A., launched in early 2005. In May 2005 the Chairman of the Telecommunications and Post Regulation Office ('TPRO') closed the tender for additional frequencies for the UMTS standard. The winner of that tender was Netia Mobile, a subsidiary of Netia S.A., the private fixed-line operator active on the Warsaw market.

23.3 The largest operator on the fixed-line telephony market with a market share of over 90% is TPSA, which also dominates several other market segments. It may be expected that the consolidation processes, which started a few years ago, will continue over the upcoming years.

23.4 The overall policy objectives of the TPRO are stated in the Telecommunications Law of 16 July 2004 ('TL')[2] and include:

- the support of effective competition and equal rights with regard to the provision of telecommunications services,
- the development and support of modern telecommunications infrastructure,
- the assurance of proper management of numbering, frequencies and satellite resources,

---

1 Editing of this chapter closed on 11 June 2005.
2 Journal of Laws, No 171, item 1800.

- the assurance of maximum benefits in terms of diversity, price and quality of telecommunications services, and
- the assurance of technological neutrality.[3]

Implementation of EU Directives

23.5   The 2002 EU Regulatory Package was transposed into Polish law through the TL in July 2004 (which entered into force as of 3 September 2004) with only a three-month delay. In principle, the TL appropriately implements the 2002 Regulatory Package.

Legislation

23.6   The main sources of Polish telecommunication legislation are laws passed by the Parliament, supported by secondary regulations. The Polish telecommunications framework consists of:

- the Constitution of the Republic of Poland of 1997,[4]
- the TL,
- the Radio and Television Act of 29 December 1992, and[5]
- ordinances of the Minister of Infrastructure and the Chairman of the National Radio and Television Council ('NRTC').

REGULATORY PRINCIPLES: IMPLEMENTATION OF THE FRAMEWORK DIRECTIVE

Scope of Regulation

23.7   Polish legislation has adopted the technology-neutral approach of the Directives. The definition of a telecommunications network in the TL[6] has the same meaning as the term 'electronic communications network', as defined in article 2(a) Framework Directive. Telecommunications services, on the other hand, are defined as services 'which consist mainly in the conveyance of signals in a telecommunications network; electronic mail is not considered as such a service'[7] and differs from the definition of electronic communications services, as defined in article 2(c) Framework Directive by excluding the reference to remuneration and adding the express exclusion of electronic mail. The exclusion of electronic mail is clearly inconsistent with the Framework Directive. Even though this definition does not expressly refer to VoIP services, it may be assumed that such services are treated as telecommunications services. The provision as it is makes clear, however, that such services exclude services providing or exercising editorial control over transmitted content, just as is the case in the Framework Directive. The wording of the

---

3   Art 1.2(1)–(5) TL.
4   Constitution of the Republic of Poland of 2 April 1997, Journal of Laws No 78, item 483 as amended.
5   Journal of Laws No 253, item 2531 of 2004.
6   Art 2.35 TL.
7   Art 2.48 TL.

definition of 'associated facilities'[8] differs slightly from its equivalent in the Framework Directive, but the meaning is the same.

National Regulatory Authorities: Organisation, Regulatory Objectives and Competencies

23.8   The Polish regulator of the communications sector is the Chairman of the Telecommunications and Post Regulation Office (TRPO). TPRO is a one-person, independent governmental body with a wide range of competencies, situated at the highest level in the public administrative structure. The Chairman is appointed by the Prime Minister, upon the motion of the Minister of Infrastructure, for a period of five years. His term of office is thus longer than that of the Parliament. The Chairman may be recalled only in exceptional, strictly regulated cases.[9] The Minister of Infrastructure is also considered to be the regulatory authority.

23.9   The statutory objectives of both communications authorities (the Chairman of the TRPO and the Minister of Infrastructure)[10] are:

- to encourage competition in the provision of telecommunications networks, associated services or the provision of telecommunications services,
- to support the development of the domestic market,
- to promote the interests of the citizens of the European Union,
- to implement the policy of promoting cultural and language variety, as well as pluralism of the media, and
- to guarantee technological neutrality in the accepted legal standards.

23.10   The competencies of the Chairman of the TPRO are listed in the TL and include both regulatory and supervisory tasks. The main tasks are: intervening in matters regarding the functioning of the telecommunications services market and access to telecommunications infrastructure,[11] the settlement of disputes between telecommunications undertakings,[12] keeping telecommunications registers,[13] the coordination of frequency reservation,[14] preparing drafts of secondary regulations,[15] as well as initiation and support of scientific research related to telecommunications.[16]

23.11   Within the government itself, the Minister of Infrastructure is responsible for the telecommunications sector. His competencies, however, are limited to issuing secondary regulations to the TL. The Minister is thus not authorised to interfere with the day-to-day administration of the telecommunications sector, for which the Chairman of the TPRO is responsible.

23.12   The TL also gives the Chairman of the National Radio and Television Council ('NRTC') a range of powers within the telecommunications sector, such as the power to regulate the provision of conditional access systems, electronic programme guides, and the multiplexing of digital signals. The Chairman of the NRTC is also responsible for organising tenders for digital television frequencies.

---

8   Art 2.44 TL.
9   Art 190 TL.
10   Art 189.1 TL.
11   Art 192.5 TL.
12   Art 192.6 TL.
13   Art 192.10 TL.
14   Art 192.11 TL.
15   Art 192.4 TL.
16   Art 192.12 TL.

23.13   Consultation and co-operation between the Chairman of the TRPO and the Chairman of the Office for the Protection of Competition and Consumers ('the Competition Authority'), as well with the Chairman of the NRTC, is guaranteed in the TL, which sets out procedures for the exchange of information and consultation between those bodies.[17] The Chairman of the TRPO has already liaised with the Competition Authority with regard to market analysis and definition for the purposes of designating SMP operators.

23.14   The Chairman of the TRPO is entitled to request from undertakings providing telecommunications services any information that is necessary to enable the Chairman to perform his regulatory functions.[18]

23.15   When the Chairman of the TRPO takes decisions connected with market analysis and indication of an SMP or the repeal of a decision in this matter, imposing, withdrawing, maintaining or amending regulatory obligations in relation to SMPs as well as those relating to telecommunications access, he is obliged to allow interested parties to express in writing their positions on the proposed decision within a specific time limit.[19]

23.16   The Chairman of the TRPO is entrusted with certain dispute resolution powers. In particular, the Chairman conducts at the consumer's request, or at his own discretion, mediation proceedings with respect to disputes between consumers and providers of telecommunications services.[20] Furthermore, the Chairman settles disputes between undertakings if they cannot come to an agreement on access or interconnection.[21]

Right of Appeal against the NRA's Decisions

23.17   Decisions determining whether a given entity possesses significant market power or not and the imposition of regulatory duties and penalties are subject to appeal before one of the Provincial Courts in Warsaw – the Court for the Protection of Competition and Consumers. Other decisions cannot be directly appealed against in the first instance but the interested party may request the Chairman to re-examine the case. If the party is dissatisfied with a decision issued as a result of the review of the application for re-examination of the case, it may file a complaint with the administrative court requesting the decision to be overruled. The party should do so within 30 days from the delivery of the adjudication in the case.[22]

The NRA's Obligations to Cooperate with the Commission

23.18   The TL properly implements the requirements of article 7 Framework Directive regarding cooperation with the Commission. The Chairman of the TRPO is obliged to cooperate with NRAs of the EU Member States and with the European Commission. In particular, the Chairman of the TRPO grants other Member States' NRAs access to information gathered from telecommunications

---

17   Among others, arts 25.1, 116.6 and 117 TL.
18   Art 21.3 TL.
19   Art 15 TL.
20   Art 109 TL.
21   Art 28.1 TL, see para 23.50 below.
22   Art 53 of the Law on Proceedings before Administrative Courts, Journal of Laws of 2002, No 153, item 1270.

undertakings[23] and submits draft decisions together with their justifications to the Commission and the regulatory authorities of other EU Member States in cases where the decisions may influence commercial relations among the Member States.[24] The 'veto procedure' has been implemented in accordance with article 7 Framework Directive – when determining significant market power and the extent of the intention to define the relevant market as a market other than the markets specified in the Commission Recommendation on relevant markets, the Chairman of the TRPO as well as the Chairman of the NRTC must take into account the Commission's position. Should the Commission state that the proposed solution may hamper the development of 'the single European market' or would result in breach of Community law, the Chairman of the NRA or the Chairman of the NRTC delays issuance of the decision for a certain period of time and may then be forced to withdraw the draft decision during this period (following the demand from the European Commission) by discontinuing the proceedings in the case.[25]

'Significant Market Power' as a Fundamental Prerequisite of Regulation

Definition of SMP

23.19   Under the TL a telecommunications undertaking has significant market power if it has an economic position that reflects dominance on the relevant market, according to the provisions of EU law.[26] SMP may refer to individual or collective dominance, with the latter being applicable in the event that two or more undertakings hold a dominant economic position on the relevant market according to the provisions of EU law, even if there are no organisational connections or other relations between them.[27]

23.20   If a telecommunications undertaking possesses significant market power on the relevant market, it may be deemed an SMP undertaking on a related market where the links between the two markets are such as to allow the undertaking's market power to be transferred from the relevant market to the related market, thereby strengthening such an undertaking's power on the related market.[28]

23.21   Following the determination of relevant markets the Chairman of the TRPO initiates proceedings to establish whether there is effective competition on the relevant market. Should there be no effective competition, the regulatory authority initiates proceedings to determine which undertaking or undertakings have significant market power.[29] Such proceedings have not been yet been conducted in Poland.

Definition of relevant markets

23.22   A 'relevant market' is a market of goods and services considered by their purchasers to be substitutes because of their intended use, price or properties,

---

23   Art 8 TL. According to art 9.4 TL, the handover of documents may be limited by the obligation to keep commercial secrets.
24   Art 18 TL.
25   Art 19.2 TL.
26   Art 24.2 TL.
27   Art 24.4 TL.
28   Art 24.7 TL.
29   Arts 22–24 TL.

including quality, and which are offered in an area where there are similar competitive conditions because of the type and properties of the goods/services or because of hindered market access, consumer preferences, significant price differences, and transport costs.[30]

23.23   The Minister of Infrastructure has divided the markets in two groups: markets on the retail level, and markets on the wholesale level. Those markets are practically identical to those in the Commission Recommendation.

23.24   Operators that are designated to have SMP are subject to a number of obligations under the TL, which reflect the relevant provisions of the Directives. On 20 December 2004 the Chairman of the TRPO issued 18 decisions (ie with respect to all relevant markets) on the institution of proceedings aimed at determining whether there is actual competition on the relevant market. The proceedings are still ongoing and no decisions on the determination of the SMP have been issued so far.

NRA's Regulatory Duties concerning Rights of Way, Co-location and Facility Sharing

Rights of way

23.25   The owners or perpetual usufructuaries of real estate are obliged to allow operators and such entities as diplomatic and consular offices, military organisational units and security units to install telecommunications equipment on their real estate, by laying cable lines underneath or over their real estate.[31] These duties also apply where the real estate is the subject of an agreement of use, rental, lease or permanent management. The owner or usufructuary is obliged to fulfil the above duties provided that the fulfilment of those duties does not make the reasonable use of the real estate impossible.

23.26   The conditions for use of real estate by an operator are to be set out in the agreement between the landowner and the requesting operator which the parties should execute within 30 days from the day the operator makes his request for access. As a rule, the use of real estate is free of charge.[32] Access is subject to a fee if it is the property owner or user who requests that telecommunications services are provided and the line or telecommunications equipment is to be used for providing that services. This fee is freely negotiable. In practice, operators claim and request the access to be granted free of charge in most cases. Should the parties not agree on the content of the respective contract within the 30-day deadline, the operator may request the local administrative authority to issue a decision granting those access rights and specifying where lines or the equipment is the be installed. These procedures are not unique for telecommunications and are also used by undertakings in the energy and gas sector. Before access is granted, the requesting operator should attempt to negotiate in good faith the access rights with the land owners but it is possible to demonstrate this by presenting documents on negotiations held under the TL.

---

30   Art 21 TL refers in this instance to the definition of a relevant market contained in art 4.8 Act on competition and consumer protection of 15 December 2000, Journal of laws of 2003, No 86, item 804.

31   Art 140 TL.

32   Art 140.2 TL.

Co-location and Facility Sharing

23.27   The operator of a public telecommunications network is obliged to allow other public operators access to telecommunications buildings and infrastructure, and in particular the installation, operation, supervision and maintenance of telecommunications devices, if the fulfilment of these activities without access to the telecommunications buildings and infrastructure is impossible or is not recommended from the point of view of land planning, human health, or environmental protection, or there is no technical or financial justification for duplicating the existing telecommunications infrastructure. The conditions for providing access are to be specified in an agreement between both operators. If the parties cannot agree on the content of this agreement, the Chairman of the TRPO shall set out the conditions in an administrative decision.[33]

REGULATION OF MARKET ENTRY: IMPLEMENTATION OF THE AUTHORISATION DIRECTIVE

The General Authorisation of Electronic Communications

23.28   The pre-requisite for conducting telecommunications activities is now the entry into the register of telecommunications undertakings. Concessions or individual permits, which for many years governed the entire market, no longer exist. Individual authorisations are granted only for the use of radio equipment (radio permit) and scarce resources (frequencies and numbers).

23.29   A party intending to provide telecommunications services should complete a registration form and submit it to the Chairman of the NRTC (in the case of the supply of conditional access systems, electronic programme guides, and the multiplexing of signals) or to the Chairman of TRPO (in all other cases). Registration is evidenced by a registration certificate. The registration procedure is free of charge. Should the authority not enter the applicant within 14 days of the submission of a properly prepared application, the undertaking is authorised to provide telecommunications activities upon notification of the authority.

23.30   Upon registration, the applicant may start to provide telecommunications services. The failure to notify telecommunications services actually provided is an offence, punishable by a fine of up to a maximum of 3% of the annual income from the previous financial year of the relevant entity.[34]

Rights of Use for Radio Frequencies

General authorisations and granting of individual rights

23.31   An operator intending to use frequencies must apply for an individual decision (frequency reservation) to the Chairman of the TRPO or – in case of digital television – to the Chairman of the NRTC. Only a selected range of frequencies has been opened up to all interested entities without the need to apply for the reservation, i.e. those in the 2.4 GHz band. When assigning the frequencies, the Chairman must observe the National Frequency Designation Plan as well as

---

33   Art 191 TL.
34   Art 209 TL.

specific plans for the use of relevant frequencies. While the National Frequency Designation Plan is a very general document with limited information on the designated use of each frequency range, the specific plans are far more detailed and broad. On the other hand, the plans exist only for selected frequencies and the lack of the specific plan does not hinder the assignment of frequencies. Frequencies are assigned to all interested entities but if there are more applicants than the number of available frequencies, the Chairman of the TRPO should hold a tender prior to assigning the frequencies.[35]

23.32   While the Chairman of the TRPO is authorised to assign frequencies in almost every case, the authority which makes the reservation of frequencies for the purpose of digital broadcasting or transmitting of radio or television programs is the Chairman of the NRTC.

23.33   The use of radio equipment requires a radio permit,[36] except for selected radio equipment as listed in the TL itself[37] or in the Ordinance of the Minister of Infrastructure.[38]

Admissible conditions

23.34   The frequency reservation can regulate the conditions applicable to the use of the frequencies,[39] requirements regarding the prevention of harmful electromagnetic interference, the obligation to protect against electromagnetic radiation, and the arrangements arising from the tender proceedings or contest.

Limitation of the number of rights of use to be granted

23.35   Before assigning the frequencies, if it turns out that there is not enough frequencies in the particular band for all interested entities, the Chairman of the NRA will hold a tender (*przetarg*).[40] In the case of the frequencies to be used for the purpose of digital broadcasting or transmitting of radio or television programs the assigning of the frequencies is proceeded by a contest (*konkurs*), which the Chairman of the NRTC organises.[41] The main difference between a contest and a tender is the selection criteria – while the amount of the declared fee and the maintaining of competitive conditions are the main factors taken into account in the tender process, only the latter criteria (maintaining of competitive conditions) is taken into account in the case of the contest. Both tender and contest proceedings are preceded by consultation proceedings.

Frequency trading

23.36   Polish law allows for only limited trading in frequencies. Operators are not entitled to transfer the frequencies on their own but they are entitled to request the

---

35   Art 116 TL.
36   Art 143 TL.
37   Art 144 TL, which exempts, eg radio equipment used solely for receiving or such radio equipment which is used in the amateur radio-communications services.
38   Ordinance of the Minister of Infrastructure of 6 August 2002 on radio transmitters and transmitter receivers that may be used without a permit, Journal of Laws No 138, item 1162, which exempts eg radio equipment in the 2.4 GHz band.
39   Art 146.1 TL in conjunction with art 115.2, point 1 TL.
40   Art 116 TL.
41   Art 117 TL.

Chairman of the TRPO to do this. The Chairman of the TRPO may transfer the frequency reservation to another entity upon the motion of the operator already using these frequencies, but only if the decision on the frequency reservation allows for such transfer and the new operator meets the applicable legal requirements.[42] The conditions for the transfer of rights to frequencies are to be set out in the frequency reservation.[43]

Rights of Use for Numbers

General authorisations and granting of individual rights

23.37   The Chairman of the TRPO grants individual numbering resources to operators by way of an administrative decision issued upon the motion of operators. When granting those rights the Chairman must observe the limitations, as specified in the National Numbering Plan. The allocation of numbers gives the operator the right to use and allow access to the numbers. VoIP products now also use the geographic phone numbers.

Admissible conditions

23.38   The decision on the allocation of numbers may specify the conditions for using the numbers or for providing access to numbering, in particular the requirement for non-discriminatory access to telecommunications services using numbers assigned to other undertakings.[44] An entity that has received the numbers has to provide access to the assigned numbering to entities that interoperate with its telecommunications network and entities providing telecommunications services.[45]

23.39   All operators of public telephone networks (including mobile network operators) are obliged to offer number portability to their customers. In the case of geographical numbers, an operator is obligated to offer portability within the same geographical area only.

Limitation of the number of rights of use to be granted

23.40   In the case of insufficient numbering resources, undertakings to which numbers will be granted are selected by tender, the deciding criterion of which is the declared price.[46]

The NRA's Enforcement Powers

23.41   The Chairman of the TRPO is authorised to carry out reviews regarding adherence to the laws, decisions and regulations on telecommunications, frequency management, and the fulfilment of the requirements on electromagnetic compatibility of the equipment on the market. TRPO employees enjoy broad supervisory

---

42   Art. 122 TL.
43   Art 115.1, point 7 TL.
44   Art 126.7 TL.
45   Art 128.1 TL.
46   Art 126.6 TL.

powers.[47] Following the issuance of post-inspection recommendations, the Chairman of the TRPO may issue a decision ordering the elimination of the irregularities found while specifying measures for eliminating those irregularities, setting a deadline for doing this as well imposing an administrative fine on the inspected entity.

23.42   If the irregularities took place in the past and are serious and the inspected entity has not responded to such a decision, the Chairman of the NRA may prevent the entity from performing telecommunications activities, or change or withdraw the reservation of frequencies, satellite resources or numbering allocations.[48]

Administrative Charges and Fees for Rights of Use

23.43   The TL provides for the duty to pay an annual charge and charges (one-time and annual) for individual authorisations. The annual charge is to be paid by any undertaking that generated revenues from telecommunications activities in excess of four million zlotys (approx €1 million) during the financial year falling two years before the year in question. The undertaking starts to pay the charge after the first two years of conducting telecommunications activities. The amount of this annual charge has been specified in the secondary regulation to the TL.[49]

23.44   Undertakings that obtain rights of use for numbers pay annual fees for these rights. Entities that obtain rights of use for frequencies pay an annual charge for these rights. The fees are collected by the TRPO and constitute the state budget income. Interest is charged in arrears.[50]

Transitional Regulations for Existing Authorisations

23.45   Undertakings holding a telecommunications permit or which have reported their telecommunications activities under the previous telecoms regime – the Telecommunications Act of 21 July 2000[51] – are entered ex officio into the register of telecommunications undertakings by the Chairman of the TRPO.

23.46   Frequency reservations and allocations of numbers, including those contained in the telecommunications permits which were issued under the previous regulation, automatically became reservations and allocations under the TL.[52]

REGULATION OF NETWORK ACCESS AND INTERCONNECTION: IMPLEMENTATION OF THE ACCESS DIRECTIVE

Objectives and Scope of Access Regulation

23.47   The objective of regulating network access and interconnection (as with other provisions of the TL) is to support effective competition in the provision of

---

47   Art 201 TL.
48   Art 201.4 TL.
49   Ordinance of the Minister of Infrastructure on the amount, the mode of establishment, and the terms and manner of making payments of the annual telecommunications charge of 27 December 2004, Journal of Laws, of 2004, No 285, item 2857.
50   At the same level as for tax arrears, as defined by the Tax Ordinance of 29 August 1997, Journal of Laws No 137, item 926 as amended.
51   Journal of Laws No 73, item 852 as amended.
52   Art 227.1 TL.

telecommunications services on equal terms, as well as the assurance of maximum benefits to users as regards the diversity, price and quality of telecommunications services.[53]

23.48   The TL's regulations on telecommunications access apply to all telecommunications undertakings, including those that have not been identified as having significant market power.

Basic Regulatory Concepts

23.49   Telecommunications access is defined in the TL as the use of telecommunications facilities, associated facilities or services provided by another telecommunications undertaking, under defined conditions, for the purpose of providing telecommunications services.[54] This includes, among others:

* the connection of telecommunications equipment, in particular access to the local loop and to facilities and services necessary to provide services over the local loop,
* access to buildings and telecommunications infrastructure,
* access to relevant software systems including operational support systems,
* access to number translation or systems offering equivalent functionality,
* access to telecommunications networks, in particular for roaming,
* access to conditional access systems, and
* access to virtual network services.

23.50   The regulatory concept is based on the priority of commercial negotiations. Each operator of a public telecommunications network is obliged to negotiate the conclusion of a telecommunications access agreement at the request of another telecommunications undertaking for the purpose of providing publicly available telecommunications services and ensuring interoperability of services. Information obtained in connection with the negotiations may be used exclusively in accordance with the purpose for which it is collected, and must be kept confidential.[55] Only if the operators cannot agree on the content of the agreement is the Chairman of the TRPO authorised to intervene.

23.51   The freedom of access rule, as specified in article 3(1) Access Directive, has been implemented in the TL, according to the provisions of which the undertaking requesting access does not need to apply for entry into the register of telecommunications undertakings, if it is not providing services in Poland.[56]

Access- and Interconnection-related Obligations with Respect to SMP Undertakings

23.52   The TL provides for a number of remedies that the Chairman of TRPO can impose on an undertaking having significant market power.[57] These include

---

53   Art 1.2 TL.
54   Art 2.6 TL.
55   Art 26.1 TL.
56   Art 26.4 TL.
57   Arts 36–40 TL.

such duties as the duty to ensure equal treatment of telecommunications undertakings with respect to telecommunications access,[58] the duty to manage specific regulatory accounting,[59] or the duty to pay fees for telecommunications access based on the costs incurred.[60]

23.53   The Chairman of the TRPO is authorised to impose on an SMP undertaking the obligation to publish or make available the information regarding the issues of providing telecommunications access, related to accounting data, technical specifications of network and telecommunications equipment and network characteristics.[61]

23.54   The Chairman of the TRPO may also impose an obligation to treat other telecommunications undertakings equally in relation to the telecommunications access, in particular through offering equal conditions in comparable circumstances.[62]

23.55   The Chairman is also authorised to impose specific access obligations such as obligations to ensure the possibility of managing the end-user services and determine details concerning the provision of those services, grant access to interfaces, protocols and other technologies necessary for the interoperability of services, as well as provide other undertakings with systems which support operational activities and other software systems, including tariff systems, invoice issuance systems and collection systems for receivables.[63]

23.56   The Chairman of the TRPO may also impose the obligation to fix the fees for telecommunications access on the basis of costs incurred.[64]

23.57   The purpose of regulatory accounting is to separate and assign the assets, liabilities, incomes and costs of the telecommunications undertaking to given operations, as if each type of operation would be performed by an alternative telecommunications operator and the obligation to apply such accounting rules may be imposed on an SMP undertaking.[65] The Minister of Infrastructure has yet to issue an ordinance which will determine methods for assigning assets and liabilities, revenues and costs to the operations as well as methods of cost calculation and relevant procedures.[66]

23.58   As the proceedings aimed at determining whether there is actual competition on the relevant markets are not finished yet and no undertakings have been determined to have SMP, no remedies have been so far applied to such operators under the new legislative regime.

---

58   Art 36 TL.
59   Art 39.1.1 TL.
60   Art 39.1.2 TL.
61   Art 37 TL.
62   Art 36 TL.
63   Art 34.2 TL.
64   Art 40.1 TL.
65   Art 49.1 TL.
66   Art 51 TL.

Related Regulatory Powers with Respect to SMP Undertakings

23.59   A subscriber who is a party to an agreement with a service provider which ensures access to a fixed public telephony network of an SMP undertaking may choose any provider of publicly available telephone services whose services are available in interconnected networks.[67]

23.60   The Chairman of the TRPO is authorised to impose on an SMP undertaking an obligation to offer services on wholesale terms for the purpose of their future sale by another undertaking.[68] Another obligation that the Chairman of the TRPO may impose on an SMP undertaking is the obligation not to limit competition by fixing the price for services below the cost of their provision, as well as an obligation not to applying preferential treatment to particular end-users.[69]

Regulatory Powers Applicable to All Market Participants

Obligation to ensure end-to-end connectivity

23.61   The Chairman of the TRPO may, upon the written motion of any of the parties to the negotiations pertaining to the conclusion of a telecommunications access agreement or even ex officio (ie without any motion of a party), specify the end date of the negotiations for the conclusion of this agreement, which shall however not fall later than 90 days from the day of submission of the motion for the conclusion of the agreement. Further, in the case of negotiations not being started, the refusal to grant telecommunications access by the obliged party or the failure to conclude the agreement within the time limit specified above, either of the parties may file a motion with the Chairman of the TRPO for the issuance of a decision on any contentious issues or a decision determining the conditions for co-operation.[70] These rules follow from the duty to encourage and ensure access and interconnection, as specified in Art 5(1)(a) Access Directive.

Access to digital radio and television broadcasting services

23.62   The obligation to ensure access to the associated API and EPG facilities may be imposed on telecommunication undertakings in order to give an end user access to digital radio and television transmissions.[71] Telecommunications undertakings providing conditional access systems should offer technical services to broadcasters on equal and non-discriminatory terms, which enable the receipt of digital radio and television transmissions using decoders installed in the networks or at the subscriber's premises. Telecommunications undertakings providing conditional access systems are obliged to keep separate accounts for this activity.

Transitional Provisions

23.63   Any telecommunications undertaking that was an operator with significant market power or with respect to which a decision was issued determining significant

---

67   Art 72.1 TL.
68   Art 34.1(3) TL.
69   Art 46.2 TL.
70   Art 26 TL.
71   Art 136, item 1 TL.

market power before the date on which the TL became effective is now obliged to fulfil selected regulatory duties under the TL. Those obligations will remain until the relevant decisions on SMP undertakings issued under the new regulatory framework become final.[72] Since no undertakings having SMP have been identified so far, this provision of the TL is still of importance today.

REGULATION OF UNIVERSAL SERVICES AND USERS' RIGHTS: THE UNIVERSAL SERVICE DIRECTIVE

Regulation of Universal Service Obligations

Scope of universal service obligations

23.64   Universal services are defined as a set of telecommunications services provided by a designated telecommunications entity[73] that should be available to all end users of fixed-line public telephone networks on the territory of Poland and that should be of the required quality and offered at an affordable price.

23.65   Universal services include all services as prescribed in the Universal Service Directive. In case of specifically mentioned entities (schools, public libraries and universities), the provider of universal services shall also be obliged to offer an additional service in the form of broadband access to the internet.[74] The costs of this service shall be borne by the state budget.[75] The details regarding accessibility and quality shall be determined in a separate ordinance to be issued by the Minister of Infrastructure.[76]

Designation of undertakings obliged to provide universal services

23.66   The TL provides for two procedures for designation of undertakings obliged to provide universal services. Under the first procedure, to be applied initially, the undertaking is selected in a contest organised by the Chairman of the TPRO, in which any telecommunications undertaking may submit its offer. The selection is based on two criteria: the lowest cost of public telephony services, and on the quality of the services provided. In the event that no offer is submitted the Chairman of the TPRO, acting within the framework of the second procedure, designates a provider of telecommunications services that has significant market power on the retail market in the area specified by the authority to provide universal services. If no provider of publicly available telecommunications services in public fixed-line telephone networks has gained significant market power on the relevant market in the area indicated by the Chairman of the TPRO, the provider of fixed-line telecommunications services with the largest number of subscriber lines will be designated.[77]

23.67   Until the designation of the undertaking that will be providing universal telecommunications services has been made in accordance with the procedures set

---

72   Art 221 TL.
73   Art 81 TL.
74   Art 81.5 TL.
75   Art 100 TL.
76   Art 81.6 TL.
77   Art 81 TL.

out in the new TL, that role is fulfilled by the Polish incumbent, Telekomunikacja Polska S.A. The first contest aimed at the selection of the universal services provider shall be organised by the end of 2005.

Regulation of retail tariffs, user's expenditures and quality of service

23.68   The tariffs shall be determined by service providers on the basis of clear, objective and non-discriminatory criteria. The tariffs must be published and any increase notified to the subscribers in advance. The subscriber has the right to terminate the service agreement without any financial consequences in the event that the price increase is not accepted. Providers of public telecommunications services are also obliged to adhere to quality of services standards as determined by the Minister of Infrastructure in an Ordinance. The service providers have to publish data on the quality of their services. In case of non-compliance with the standards the provider may be fined; the fine being up to 3% of its income gained in the preceding year.

23.69   Other guarantees provided for in the TL include the power of the regulatory authority to review price lists and general terms and conditions of universal services. Furthermore, the provider of universal services is obliged to deliver itemised billing free of charge.

Cost calculation and financing of universal services

23.70   The provider of universal services sets the prices for such services based on reasonable costs, calculated in accordance with the Ordinance of the Minister of Infrastructure, taking into consideration economic situation of end users, including disabled persons.[78] The undertaking designated for the provision of universal services is also entitled to receive special compensation if the provision of such services turns out to be unprofitable.

23.71   The amount of that compensation is set by the Chairman of the TPRO who has to follow the instructions regarding the calculation of the respective figure, as provided by the Minister of Infrastructure in the Ordinance to be issued by that Minister. Such compensation is aimed at compensating the provider of universal services for losses (costs) incurred in connection with the provision of universal services. The calculation of the costs should include the costs directly incurred in connection with the provision of the universal services, revenues from the provision of such services, as well as other indirect benefits connected with the provision of universal services.[79] The reimbursement will be paid out of a special fund administered by the TPRO.[80] Contributions to this fund are to be made by those telecommunications undertakings whose revenues exceeded in a given year[81] PLN 4 million (approx €1 million). The maximum contribution shall not exceed 1% of the revenue of the contributing entity.[82]

---

78   Art 91 TL.
79   Art 95 TL.
80   Art 99 TL.
81   Art 97 TL.
82   Art 98 TL.

Regulation of Retail Markets

Prerequisites for the regulation of retail markets

23.72   Regulation of the market is admissible if it is determined that:

- there is no effective competition on the relevant retail market,
- the obligations relating to ensuring access to telecommunications on the wholesale market would not lead to the desired results,
- the obligations relating to carrier pre-selection have not led to the desired results in accordance with the provisions of the TL.[83]

Regulatory powers

23.73   The Chairman of the TRPO may impose the following obligations on undertakings with significant market power on retail markets:

- not to apply excessive pricing,[84]
- not to hinder market entry for other undertakings,[85]
- not to limit competition by setting prices of services below cost,[86]
- not to apply unjustified preferences for specific end users, except as provided for in the TL,[87] and
- not to unduly bundle services.[88]

23.74   The Chairman of the TPRO may oblige an undertaking with significant market power on the retail market for the provision of the whole or a part of the minimum set of leased lines to, among others, provide leased lines on transparent and non-discriminatory terms, to maintain regulatory accounts in accordance with the instruction approved by the Chairman of the TPRO, to calculate the costs of providing the whole or a part of the minimum set of leased lines in accordance with the description of the cost calculation approved by the Chairman of the TRPO, and to set their prices on the basis of reasonable costs incurred in connection with the provision of such services.[89]

End User Rights

Contracts

23.75   The designated undertaking cannot refuse to enter into an agreement regarding universal services or individual services making up the universal service or, in the case of so-called 'authorised entities', a network connection service to provide broadband internet access when the user satisfies the required conditions

---

83   Art 46 TL.
84   Art 46.2, item 1 TL.
85   Art 46.2, item 2 TL.
86   Art 46.2, item 3 TL.
87   Art 46.2, item 4 TL.
88   Art 46.2, item 5 TL.
89   Art 47.1 TL.

set out in the general terms and conditions for providing universal telecommunications services.[90] The agreement for the provision of the universal service shall be executed within 30 days of such a request being made. The agreement shall specify the date on which the provision of services shall commence.

23.76   The TL provides for mandatory elements of an agreement for the provision of telecommunications services.[91] In particular, the agreement shall regulate such issues as the quality of the service, scope of the services, prices, duration of the agreement and complaint procedure.

Transparency obligations

23.77   The TL imposes obligations connected with transparency on the providers of telecommunications services, such as the duty to make the price list for telecommunications services publicly available, to provide it to the subscriber free of charge and whenever requested by the subscriber. Every increase in the prices of telecommunications services needs to be announced one settlement period in advance. The provider is obliged to deliver the price list for review at the request of the regulatory authority. Furthermore, the provider is obliged to publish information on the quality of services offered. The Chairman of the TRPO publishes information on the rights and duties of end users in the Bulletin of the TRPO and on the authority's official website.[92]

Other obligations

According to the TL, the operator of a public telephone network is obliged to provide end users with the possibility of multi-frequency dialling (DTMF),[93] a directory enquiries service,[94] and lists of telephone subscribers, as well as to provide information on the location of a network termination from which a call was made to the 112 emergency number and other emergency numbers, in real time, as far as technically possible, on every request by the services officially appointed to provide assistance, in order that they can take immediate action.[95]

DATA PROTECTION: IMPLEMENTATION OF THE DIRECTIVE ON PRIVACY AND ELECTRONIC COMMUNICATIONS

Confidentiality of Communications

23.78   The TL defines the scope of confidentiality of communications and imposes several obligations on the providers of publicly available electronic communications in this respect. In particular the TL prohibits accessing, storage, transmitting or any other use of the content or data without the consent of the users

---

90   Art 86 TL.
91   Art 56.3 TL.
92   Art 62 TL.
93   Art 75 TL.
94   Art 66 TL.
95   Art 78 TL.

concerned[96] except when legally authorised to do so.[97] Entities involved in telecommunications activities are obliged to take all necessary precautions in order to safeguard the security of their services. In the case of a risk of a security breach, the operator must inform subscribers that the applied technical means do not guarantee the security of communications. The operator shall also inform the users about possible remedies that may be applied and the costs connected therewith.[98]

23.79 The use of an electronic communications network for the purpose of storing information or gaining access to information in a user's terminal equipment constitutes an offence (subject to monetary fines) if the user or the subscriber is not provided with easy to understand information regarding the purpose of the processing. The user or the subscriber must also be given the opportunity to refuse processing.[99]

Traffic Data and Location Data

23.80 Operators of publicly available telecommunications networks or providers of telecommunications services processing traffic data are obliged to store such data for the period of 12 months (due to certain obligations pertaining to state security and national defence). After that period the traffic data must be erased or made anonymous.[100]

23.81 The processing of traffic data which is necessary for the purpose of billing and interconnection payments is permitted, subject to the notification of the subscriber or user. Such processing is possible only up to the end of the period during which the bill may lawfully be challenged or payment pursued.[101] The providers of publicly available telecommunications services are obliged to inform the subscriber or user of the traffic data which will be processed for the purpose of marketing or for the purpose of providing value added services. The user or subscriber has the right to refuse to such processing.[102]

23.82 Location data can be processed only when such data are made anonymous or with the consent of the users or subscribers. Users or subscribers may withdraw their consent at any time. Before the processing of location data the user or subscriber must be informed of the type of location data subject to processing, the purpose and duration of the processing and whether the data will be transferred to another entity for the purpose of providing value added services.[103]

Itemised Billing

23.83 The provider of publicly available telecommunications services[104] is obliged to provide to the subscriber, free of charge, a specification of all services provided together with the invoice and information on the calls for which a charge was made,

---

96   Art 159.3 TL.
97   Art 159.4 TL.
98   Art 175 TL.
99   Art 173 TL.
100   Art 165.1 TL.
101   Art 165.2 TL.
102   Art 165 TL.
103   Art 166 TL.
104   Art 80 TL.

stating the number of billing units representing the value of call connections made by the subscriber. At the subscriber's request, the provider must supply a detailed specification of the telecommunications services for which a charge may be made at the rate specified in the price list.

Calling and Connected Line Identification

23.84   The operator of a publicly available telecommunications network is obliged to provide users with the capability of ID presentation of a network termination from which the call is originated, before answering the call.[105] At the same time the provider of services is obliged to notify subscribers that the network he uses allows for the presentation of the calling line ID and the called line ID.[106] If the subscriber chooses to cancel or restrict the call identification services the operator should do so free of charge.[107] A service provider may override the cancellation of the caller identification in the cases specified by law.

Automatic Call Forwarding

23.85   The provider of services in publicly available telecommunications networks that offer automatic call forwarding is obliged to provide the subscriber with the possibility of the easy restriction of automatic call forwarding by a third party to the subscriber's terminal equipment.[108]

Directories of Subscribers

23.86   The TL defines the scope of personal data that can be used for the preparation of telephone directories without obtaining consent from the subscriber. This includes: the subscriber's number or identification mark, his first and last name, the name of the city and street where the termination point made available to the subscriber is located (for fixed-line public telephone networks) and permanent registration (for mobile public telephone networks).[109] Before these data are included in the directory, subscribers must be informed free of charge about the purpose of the directory and further usage possibilities of the directory.

Unsolicited Communications

23.87   Polish law regulates the issue of unsolicited commercial information.[110] According to the law, it is forbidden to send unsolicited commercial information to a particular recipient by way of electronic communications means, and by way of electronic mail in particular.[111] A commercial information is considered as solicited if the recipient has agreed to receive such information and for that purpose has

---

105   Art 171.1 TL.
106   Art 171.5 TL.
107   Art 171.6 TL.
108   Art 171.4 TL.
109   Art 169 TL.
110   The Law on Provision of Services Electronically of 18 July 2002, Journal of Laws No 173, item 1808, with subsequent amendments ('EL').
111   Art 10.2 EL.

disclosed his electronic address which identifies the recipient.[112] Electronic communications means are defined as technical solutions, including telecommunications devices and supporting software, which allow communication by the use of data transmission between telecommunication systems, including e-mail in particular.[113]

23.88   The non-compliance with the above rules is considered an act of unfair competition within the meaning of the Polish unfair competition legislation.[114] The unsolicited sending of commercial information is also considered a misdemeanour and is subject to a monetary fine.[115]

---

112   Art 10.2 EL.
113   Art 2.5 EL.
114   The Law on Combating of Unfair Competition of 16 April 1997, Journal of Laws No 47, item 211 with subsequent amendments.
115   Art 24 EL.

The Portuguese Market for Electronic Communications[1]

António de Mendonça Raimundo and João de Castro[2]
Albuquerque & Associados – Law Firm, Lisbon

LEGAL STRUCTURE

Basic Policy

24.1 Progress in the telecommunication sector has forced the implementation of several changes in the ruling legal framework. Also, EU law has had an important effect on the Portuguese market, notably with regard to the liberalisation of the sector and its opening to competition.

24.2 The Portuguese telecommunications market was definitively liberalised in 2001. Portugal was the second last EU member to open the telecoms market. The end of the monopoly was completed with the unbundling of the local loop.

24.3 Portugal Telecom, the former incumbent, acquired ownership of the fixed terrestrial communications network in 2002, and has a position of significant market power (SMP) in almost all relevant markets. In the mobile sector, there is effective competition. This market sector is operated by TMN, which is owned by Portugal Telecom, and by two other operators.

24.4 The overall policy objectives stated by the Portuguese Government concerning the electronic communications sector in the Government Program[3] emphasise the development of the broadband connectivity sector, which has also been identified as a priority by the former Government, as a contribution to the competitiveness and productivity increase of the national economy.

Implementation of EU Directives

24.5 The status of implementation of the main EU Directives in Portugal is the following:

---

1   Editing of this chapter closed on 15 July 2005.
2   Rute Martins Santos, of Albuquerque & Associados, is the author of the subchapter on Data Protection.
3   Program of the XVII Constitutional Program for 2005–2009, presented to the Parliament – *Assembleia da República* – on 21 March 2005.

- The Law no 5/2004, of 10 February 2004, – Electronic Communications Law (*'Lei das Telecomunicações Electrónicas'*) has implemented the 2002 EU Regulatory Package except for the E-Privacy Directive,
- The E-Privacy Directive has been implemented by Law no 41/2004 of 18 August 2004, except for article 13, which has been implemented by the Decree-Law no 7/2004, of 7 January 2004, concerning electronic commerce.

Legislation

24.6   Law no 5/2004, of 10 February 2004 ('REGICOM'), establishes the legal regime applicable to the electronic communications networks and services, as well as associated services, and defines the responsibilities of the national regulatory authority – ICP-ANACOM. The provisions of REGICOM do not affect the application of provisions pursuant to Decree-Law no 192/2000, of 18 August 2000,[4] Decree-Law no 59/2000 of 19 April 2000,[5] Decree-Law no 151-A/2000 of 20 July 2000[6] and Decree-Law no 47/2000 of 24 March 2000.[7]

24.7   Additionally to the legislation implementing the 2002 EU Regulatory Package there are several Laws and Decree-laws applicable to telecommunication matters. ANACOM is governed by statutes (bylaws) approved by the Decree-law no 309/2001, of 7 December 2000.[8] The Decree-law no 31/2003, of 17 February 2003, provides for the bases of the telecommunications public service concession, which was granted therein to Portugal Telecom, the concessionaire and former incumbent. The Law no 91/97 of 1 August 1991 (Basic Telecommunications Law) was revoked.[9]

24.8   The regulatory decisions of ANACOM and the implementing of its measures are grounded in the REGICOM, specifically in article 5 on regulatory objectives.

REGULATORY PRINCIPLES: IMPLEMENTATION OF THE FRAMEWORK DIRECTIVE

Scope of Regulation

24.9   REGICOM covers electronic communications networks and services and associated facilities.[10] The definitions of 'electronic communications network', 'electronic communications service' and 'associated facilities' in article 3 REGICOM are identical to those in the Framework Directive.

---

4   The regime of free circulation, placing on the market and putting into service of radio equipment and telecommunications terminal equipment, as well as the regime of the respective conformity assessment and marking procedures.

5   The regime of installation of telecommunication infrastructures in buildings.

6   The regime applicable to radiocommunications networks and stations.

7   The regime applicable to the use of the Personal Radio Service – Citizen's Band (SRP-CB).

8   ICP – *Instituto de Comunicações de Portugal* – was established by the Decree-law no 188/81, of 2 July 1981; its designation was changed to ICP-ANACOM by the Decree-law no 309/2001, of 7 December 2001.

9   Revoked, except for art 12(2) and (3), which contains the elements of the legal notion of the basic telecommunications network.

10   REGICOM does not apply: to information society services, which do not consist wholly or mainly in the conveyance of signals on electronic communications networks; to services providing content transmitted using electronic communications networks and services; to the

24.10 Voice over Internet Protocol (VoIP) services are considered to be within the definition of electronic communications services, although the classification of the service and the definition of the market in which it is inserted are still subject to analysis by a commission within ANACOM and pending a decision on its regulatory aspects.

National Regulatory Authorities: Organisation, Regulatory Objectives, Competencies

24.11 The Portuguese national regulatory authority is 'Autoridade Nacional de Comunicações' ('ANACOM'), which succeeded the 'Instituto das Comunicações de Portugal' ('ICP'). ANACOM is a public corporation with administrative and financial autonomy and its own assets. It regulates and supervises the telecommunications sector and represents Portugal in supranational and international telecommunications organisations.

24.12 The Government appoints ANACOM's board of administration.[11] ANACOM should send to the Government an annual report on its regulatory activities, which is also to be submitted to Parliament. The chairman of the board of administration answers before Parliament, whenever so requested, to requests for hearing addressed by the appropriate committee of the Parliament.[12]

24.13 ANACOM is characterised as legal entity, functionally separated from the Government and from companies providing electronic communications networks, services and equipment, and provided with the necessary means to pursue its functions independently. The by-laws of ANACOM assure an effective separation[13] of the regulatory function of the Portuguese State from powers associated with the ownership or control of companies in the sector over which the state retains ownership or control.

24.14 The legal objectives of ANACOM are: to ensure and promote competition in the provision of electronic communications networks, electronic communications services and associated facilities and services; to contribute to the development of the internal market of the European Union; and to promote the interests of citizens by ensuring a high level of protection for consumers when dealing with suppliers.

24.15 The most important legal competencies of ANACOM are: to assist the Portuguese Government in the definition of strategic guidelines and general policies; to participate in setting strategies for communications development; to elaborate regulations; to assign spectral and numbering resources; and to co-ordinate the application of competition law to the communications field.

24.16 ANACOM acts as a supervisory entity, with competencies to apply penalties to the operators, and also to assist the Government. The nature of the matters associated with electronic commerce justified the creation of a Mission and Development for Electronic Commerce Unit ('*Unidade de Missão e Desenvolvimento para o Comércio Eléctronico*') within ANACOM.

---

private networks of the Ministry of National Defence and to the computer network of the Government, managed by the Government Computer Network Management Centre (CEGER).

11   Art 21 ANACOM's Bylaws (approved by the Decree-law no 309/2001, of 7 December 2000).
12   Art 51 ANACOM's Bylaws.
13   Art 4 ANACOM's Bylaws establishes the principle of independence of ANACOM.

24.17   Cooperation between ANACOM and other regulators (Consumer Institute and Competition Authority) in the area of consumer protection and competition is set out in article 7 REGICOM. Portugal implemented a dual system to assure effective competition, according to which ANACOM seeks to create the necessary regulation in order to avoid any harmful SMP situations, and the Competition Authority controls any possible mergers that may damage an effective competitive market.

24.18   Under the scope of the duty of cooperation, when ANACOM and other competent authorities provide each other information, both authorities are obliged to assure the same level of confidentiality that each one is originally obliged to.

24.19   REGICOM[14] provides for a general consultation procedure whenever ANACOM, in the exercise of its competencies, intends to take measures that have a significant impact on the relevant market. According to this procedure, ANACOM shall publish the draft measure to be adopted and give the interested parties the opportunity to comment on it within a period established for that purpose, which shall not be less than 20 days. Pursuant to this, ANACOM must publish the adopted consultation procedures.

24.20   As an exception to the above procedure, REGICOM establishes provisions for urgent measures in exceptional circumstances, to be applied where it considers that there is an urgent need to act in order to safeguard competition and protect the interests of users, within the terms of article 7(6) Framework Directive.

24.21   Articles 10 and 12 REGICOM implementing articles 20 and 21 Framework Directive provide for an administrative dispute resolution procedure whereby, at the request of any of the parties, ANACOM issues binding decisions to resolve any disputes in connection with obligations arising under REGICOM between undertakings, without prejudice to the possibility of either party bringing an action before the courts.

24.22   The request of the parties for the intervention of ANACOM should be made at the most within one year from the date of the beginning of the dispute. Under this procedure, ANACOM should issue its decision at the most within 4 months from the date of the request,[15] and notify the parties involved, together with a complete statement of the grounds on which it was based.

24.23   ANACOM may refuse dispute resolution requests made by undertakings only in the following cases: where the request does not concern compliance with obligations arising from REGICOM; where a period of more than a year has elapsed since the date of the beginning of the dispute; or where ANACOM deems that other mechanisms, including mediation, exist and would better contribute to the resolution of the dispute in a timely manner in accordance with ANACOM regulatory objectives. In case of cross-border disputes, the competent NRAs may jointly decide to refuse to resolve a dispute in accordance to article 21(3) Framework Directive.[16]

Right of Appeal against NRA's Decisions

24.24   Any user or undertaking providing electronic communications networks and/or services who is affected by any orders or decisions adopted by ANACOM

---

14   Art 8 REGICOM.
15   Under exceptional circumstances, there may be an extension.
16   Art 12(3) REGICOM.

within the framework of any proceedings resulting from violations (*contra-ordenação*) of the regulatory framework on electronic communications may appeal against such decision or measure to the Courts of Commerce.[17]

24.25   Whenever a user or an undertaking is affected by orders or decisions of ANACOM other than decisions on *contra-ordenações*, the user may appeal against such acts to the Administrative Courts. The trial of such an appeal has the compulsory intervention of three experts, one appointed by each party and the third by the court. The experts are bound to produce a report, but these reports and its conclusions are not binding, being deemed as evidence, which value may be freely appreciated by the Court.

24.26   Appeals to the Courts of Commerce against decisions issued by ANACOM which determine the application of fines or additional sanctions suspend the execution of ANACOM's decision (suspensive appeal). The appeals to Courts of Commerce against decisions of application of compulsory penalty payments, as well as other decisions, orders and further measures (which do not result in the application of fines or other sanctions), do not have a suspensive effect. Appeals to the Administrative Courts do not, as a general rule, have a suspensive effect.

24.27   ANACOM is entitled to lodge an appeal autonomously against decisions made in the proceedings contesting the validity of ANACOM's acts allowing appeal. Moreover, the decisions of the Courts of Commerce allowing appeal, pursuant to the general regime of *contra-ordenações*, may be contested at the Second Instance Court (*Tribunal da Relação*), which in this case is the court of last instance.

The NRA's Obligations to Cooperate with the Commission

24.28   The Consolidation Procedure[18] has been implemented by articles 6 and 57 REGICOM. This procedure establishes the need to cooperate with the Commission and other Member States' NRAs. Under the Consolidation Procedure, ANACOM must take the utmost account of the Commission recommendations on the harmonised application of the regulatory framework applicable to electronic communications and, where it chooses not to follow a recommendation, it should provide to the Commission the reasoning for its position.[19] The Commission veto procedure[20] has been implemented by article 57(5) REGICOM.

24.29   Article 29 REGICOM establishes that, without prejudice to rules made compulsory at EU level, ANACOM shall stimulate the use of standards and specifications, based on the list elaborated by the Commission, and published in the *Official Journal*, thus implementing article 17 Framework Directive into national law. Article 6(3) REGICOM implements article 19 Framework Directive, concerning recommendations on harmonisation procedures issued to Member States by the Commission.[21]

---

17   Commerce Courts are specialised Courts with their competence defined by Law 3/99, of 13 January 1999, to rule on commercial and competition matters.
18   See paras 1.60–1.64 above.
19   Art 6(3) REGICOM.
20   Art 7(4) Framework Directive.
21   See para 24.28 above.

'Significant Market Power' as a Fundamental Prerequisite of Regulation

Definition of SMP

24.30   Article 60 REGICOM provides a definition of 'significant market power' similar to the one used by the Framework Directive. Additionally, Portuguese law envisages that ANACOM may determine that two or more companies enjoy a 'joint dominance' situation where they operate in a market with a structure that leads to coordinated effects, even in the absence of structural or other links between them.

Definition of relevant markets and SMP designation

24.31   ANACOM adopts public consultation methods in order to define relevant markets and identify companies with SMP, and imposes the appropriate remedies. ANACOM has identified 18 markets as listed in the Commission Recommendation on relevant markets, having identified an additional (non-listed) market of telephone services destined to non-geographic numbers publicly available in a fixed location.

24.32   Where an undertaking has SMP on a particular market, it may also be deemed to have SMP on an adjacent market, where the links between the two markets allow the market power held in one market to be leveraged into the other market, thereby strengthening the market power of the undertaking.

24.33   Although ANACOM is not obliged by national law to impose regulatory obligations or remedies on undertakings identified as having SMP, ANACOM has the power to do so within the scope of its functions. ANACOM may also impose remedies on undertakings not identified as having SMP.

24.34   The definition of relevant markets for low bandwidth switched fixed services and the corresponding SMP assessment was approved. Portugal Telecom Group companies and all fixed network operators operating in the market for call termination in individual public telephone networks in a fixed location market were identified as having SMP.[22]

24.35   ANACOM has approved a decision regarding the wholesale-unbundled access market, and has identified companies of the Portugal Telecom Group as having SMP.[23] In the wholesale market of voice call termination on individual mobile networks, TMN, Vodafone Portugal, and Optimus were identified as having SMP.[24]

NRA's Regulatory Duties concerning Rights of Way, Co-location and Facility Sharing

Rights of way

24.36   Undertakings providing publicly available electronic communications networks and services have:

---

22   ANACOM determination of 8 July 2004, published at www.anacom.pt.
23   ANACOM determination of 30 March 2005, published at www.anacom.pt.
24   ANACOM determination of 25 February 2005, published at www.anacom.pt.

- the right to request, pursuant to general law, the expropriation and the constitution of public easements necessary for the installation, protection and maintenance of the respective systems, equipments and further resources, and
- the right to use public domain (land and facilities), in conditions of equality, for implanting, crossing or passing over necessary to the installation of systems, equipment and further resources.[25]

24.37   Undertakings providing electronic communications networks and services not available to the public are ensured the right to request the use of public domain necessary for the installation of systems, equipment and further resources.

24.38   Thus, according to REGICOM, the granting of rights of way over private property is achieved through an expropriation request (to compulsorily deprive a person of his property by the State).

24.39   The procedures for granting rights of way should be clear and duly published, applied without discrimination and without delay, and the conditions attached to any such rights shall follow the principles of transparency and non-discrimination.[26] All authorities with legal power over public domain[27] should elaborate and publish clear, swift and non-discriminatory procedures on the exercise of the right of use of public domain.

24.40   The rights and charges as regards implanting, crossing or passing over of systems, equipments and further resources of undertakings providing publicly available electronic communications networks and services, at a fixed location of a public or private municipal domain, may give rise to the establishment of a municipal fee for rights of way ('MFRW'), determined on the basis of a percentage on each bill issued by the undertaking, to all final clients of the corresponding municipality. These undertakings must explicitly include the amount due in the bills of end-clients of publicly available electronic communications at fixed locations.

Co-location and facility sharing

24.41   Undertakings providing publicly available electronic communications networks and services shall negotiate and promote between themselves the conclusion of agreements towards the sharing of property or facilities, already installed or to be installed. The conclusion of said agreements must be notified to ANACOM.[28]

24.42   If, for reasons of environmental protection, public health, public security, cultural heritage, country planning and to preserve town and country landscapes, there are no viable alternatives in specific situations regarding the installation of new infrastructure, ANACOM may impose obligations relating to the sharing of facilities, even if the owners thereof are undertakings providing electronic communications networks and services. Nevertheless, the referred determination may include rules for apportioning the costs thereof, and ANACOM may also force the adoption of measures limiting the function of the facilities to be installed, notably the reduction in the maximum transmitted power levels.[29]

---

25   Art 24(1) REGICOM.
26   Art 24(3) REGICOM.
27   The public domain is managed by the entities it is granted, notably Ministries of the Government, Public Institutes, etc.
28   Art 25(1) REGICOM.
29   Art 25(2), (3) and (4) REGICOM.

REGULATION OF MARKET ENTRY: IMPLEMENTATION OF THE AUTHORISATION DIRECTIVE

The General Authorisation of Electronic Communications

24.43 Undertakings that intend to provide electronic communications networks and services are bound to submit in advance to ANACOM a short description of the network or service they intend to begin and to notify an estimated date for starting the activity. They should also submit the minimal information required to allow their full identification, under terms and conditions to be defined by ANACOM.[30] These conditions are published by ANACOM on their website.[31]

24.44 Following notification, undertakings may begin their activity immediately, subject to the restrictions resulting from the allocation of rights of use of frequencies and numbers.[32] It is incumbent upon ANACOM, within five days from the receipt of notification, to issue a declaration confirming its submission. Undertakings terminating the provision of electronic communication networks or services shall immediately notify that fact to ANACOM.

24.45 Undertakings that provide publicly available electronic communications networks and services are entitled to the following rights: to negotiate interconnection with and obtain access to or interconnection from other providers of publicly available communications networks and services, and to be given an opportunity to be designated to provide different elements of a universal service and/or to cover different parts of the national territory in accordance with the provisions of REGICOM.[33]

24.46 The amendments to the conditions, rights and procedures concerning the provision of electronic communications networks and services, including the rights of use or rights to install facilities, are subject to a general consultation procedure.[34]

24.47 Undertakings providing publicly available electronic communications networks and services, regardless of SMP, may only be subject in the pursuit thereof to the general conditions referred in Annex A to the Authorisation Directive, implemented in article 27 REGICOM.

24.48 ANACOM should specify, among the conditions referred to above, those that are applicable to electronic communications networks and services, identifying categories for that purpose, if deemed convenient by ANACOM.

24.49 According to article 28 REGICOM, ANACOM can, without prejudice of the definition of conditions, determine the imposition of obligations regarding access and interconnection, regulatory control and universal service. Certain of these obligations are potentially applicable just to undertakings with SMP, and others are potentially applicable to all undertakings.

---

30 Art 21(1) REGICOM.
31 www.anacom.pt/template15.jsp?categoryId=113059.
32 Art 19(2) and (3), 21(4) REGICOM.
33 Art 22 REGICOM.
34 Except in exceptional circumstances, the consultation period shall be no less than 20 days.

Rights of Use for Radio Frequencies

General authorisations and granting of individual rights

24.50   ANACOM is responsible for the management of the spectrum, understood as the set of frequencies associated with radio waves.[35] ANACOM has the power to plan out, allocate and assign frequencies, publish annually the National Frequency Allocation Table ('NFAT'),[36] which shall comprise the frequency bands and number of channels already allocated to undertakings providing publicly available electronic communications networks and services, and the reserved frequency bands and those available in the following year, in the scope of electronic communications networks and services, as well as the frequencies whose rights of use are capable of being transferred.

24.51   The use of frequencies shall only be subject to the grant of individual rights of use where it is so provided for in NFAT.[37] The rights of use for frequencies may be granted to providers of electronic communication networks or services or to entities that use those networks or services.[38] The decision of granting rights of use shall be taken, communicated and made public within the following maximum period of 30 days from the appropriate request,[39] in the case of frequencies that have been allocated for specific purposes within the NFAT, without prejudice to any applicable international agreements relating to the use of radio frequencies or of orbital positions.

Admissible conditions

24.52   Without prejudice to the conditions attached to the general authorisation, article 32 REGICOM implements the list of conditions that may be attached by ANACOM to rights of use for radio frequencies as per Annex B of the Authorisation Directive.

Limitation of the number of rights of use to be granted

24.53   The limitation of the number of rights of use to be granted is only allowed where this is necessary to ensure the efficient use of radio frequencies.[40] When ANACOM is considering whether to limit the number of rights of use to be granted for frequencies, it should, notably, give due weight to the need to maximise benefits for users and to facilitate the development of competition.

24.54   ANACOM must undertake a public consultation and publish the reasons for a decision to limit the granting of rights of use, establishing at the same time the grant procedure, following the procedure pursuant to article 31 REGICOM. Although REGICOM provides for both comparative (public tenders) and competitive (spectrum auctions)[41] procedures, no spectrum auction has yet been conducted under REGICOM, and no such auctions are expected in the near future.

---

35   Art 15 REGICOM.
36   Art 16 REGICOM.
37   Art 30(1) REGICOM.
38   Art 30(2) REGICOM.
39   Art 35(2) REGICOM.
40   Art 31 REGICOM.
41   Art 35 REGICOM.

Frequency trading

24.55 The holders of rights of use for frequencies shall notify ANACOM, in advance, of their intention to trade those rights, as well as any conditions applicable to the transfer. ANACOM shall ensure that the frequencies are used effectively and efficiently, that the intended use of the frequencies is respected, and that the limits provided for in law are safeguarded.[42]

24.56 ANACOM may oppose the intended transfer of rights of use, or impose conditions necessary to ensure compliance with the rules mentioned above, on presentation of a duly substantiated decision. The transfer of rights of use cannot be completed where ANACOM opposes.

24.57 ANACOM must request prior advice from the Competition Authority, which shall be issued within 10 days from the respective request. The transfer of rights does not suspend or interrupt the time limit for which the rights of use have been granted pursuant to REGICOM, without prejudice to the renewal thereof.[43]

Rights of Use for Numbers

General authorisations and granting of individual rights

24.58 Article 17 REGICOM provides for ANACOM competences concerning the availability of numbering resources adequate for all publicly available electronics communications services. In this regard, it is incumbent upon ANACOM to define the guidelines and to manage the National Numbering Plan and to allocate numbering resources, among other competences.

24.59 According to article 33 REGICOM, the use of numbers depends on the grant of individual rights of use. These rights of use for numbers may be granted to providers of electronic communication networks or services or to entities that use those networks or services.

24.60 Rights of use for numbers should be granted by means of open, transparent and non-discriminatory procedures. Without prejudice to the previous considerations, ANACOM is entitled to decide, after the general consultation procedure, if rights for use of numbers of exceptional economic value are to be granted through tender or auction. The grant of rights of use for numbers depends on a request submitted to ANACOM, which shall include the necessary specifications to prove the applicant's ability to comply with the conditions attached to such a right.[44] The decision whether to grant those rights shall be taken, communicated and made public within the following maximum period of 15 days,[45] in the case of numbers that have been allocated for specific purposes within the National Numbering Plan.[46]

---

42   Art 37 REGICOM.
43   Art 36 REGICOM.
44   Art 35(1) REGICOM.
45   When the grant of rights of use is subject to competitive or comparative selection procedures, the period identified may be extended by an additional period of 15 days.
46   Art 35(2) REGICOM.

Admissible conditions

24.61   Without prejudice to the conditions attached to the general authorisation, article 34 REGICOM implements the list of conditions that may be attached by ANACOM to rights of use for radio frequencies as per Annex C of the Authorisation Directive.

24.62   According to article 54(5) REGICOM, it is incumbent upon ANACOM, following the general consultation procedure, to determine the rules necessary for the performance of number portability. Pursuant to this, ANACOM has approved a Draft Portability Regulation,[47] which establishes the principles and rules applicable to portability in the public telephone networks, being compulsory for all companies with portability obligations, thus giving the end-users the right to maintain its phone numbers regardless of their choice to change operators.

24.63   According to Article 38 REGICOM, the rights of use of numbers may be transferred by their respective holders, under the conditions to be implemented by ANACOM, which shall provide the instruments intended to safeguard, notably, the effective and efficient use of numbers and rights of users.

The NRA's Enforcement Powers

24.64   It is incumbent upon ANACOM to monitor compliance with the provisions of REGICOM and respective regulations,[48] set out in REGICOM, implementing articles 10 and 11 Authorisation Directive.

24.65   Undertakings subject to obligations[49] shall submit to ANACOM all information, including financial information concerning its activity, so that the regulator may pursue all assignments provided for in REGICOM. For such purposes the undertakings shall identify the information deemed confidential. The information requests made by ANACOM shall be proportionate and objectively justified for the purposes of article 11 Authorisation Directive.[50] Article 110 REGICOM implements article 10 Authorisation Directive regarding non-compliance issues.

24.66   The administrative offences foreseen in article 113 REGICOM are punishable with a fine of up to €5 million. Proceedings are carried out by ANACOM. Where the administrative offence results from the omission to comply with a legal duty or an order of ANACOM, the application of sanctions or the compliance therewith do not exempt the offender from complying with the duty or order, where such compliance is possible. In such cases, ANACOM may impose, where justified, a compulsory penalty payment[51] consisting of the payment of a pecuniary amount for each day exceeding the time limit set by ANACOM for compliance.

24.67   Where the significance of the infringement and the fault of the offender so justify, concerning certain offences ANACOM can apply additional sanctions such as the removal by the State of property, equipment and illicit devices, prohibition on carrying out the respective activity for a period of up to two years, or the cancellation of the right to participate in tenders or auctions promoted within the scope of REGICOM for a period of up to two years.

---

47   ANACOM determination of 11 March 2004.
48   Art 112 REGICOM.
49   Including conditions of the general authorisation or of rights of use and specific obligations.
50   Arts 108 and 109 REGICOM.
51   Art 116 REGICOM.

Administrative Charges and Fees for Rights of Use

24.68   Concerning administrative charges imposed on undertakings to which a right of use has been granted, the implementation provided by REGICOM[52] follows closely the wording of the Authorisation Directive. The amount of the fees covered by the Directive is to be determined by order of the member of the Government responsible for the electronics telecommunications sector. No such order has yet been issued.

24.69   The use of frequencies, whether or not comprising a right of use, is subject to the fees set out in another legal instrument.[53]

Transitional Regulations for Existing Authorisations

24.70   REGICOM provides for transitional provisions regarding the maintenance of obligations[54] and regularisation of registers and licences issued pursuant to prior law.[55]

REGULATION OF NETWORK ACCESS AND INTERCONNECTION: IMPLEMENTATION OF THE ACCESS DIRECTIVE

Objectives and Scope of Access Regulation

24.71   ANACOM shall encourage and, where appropriate, ensure adequate access and interconnection, as well as interoperability of services, aimed at promoting efficiency and sustainable competition, and at giving the maximum benefit to end-users.[56]

24.72   According to articles 66 and 77 REGICOM, access- and interconnection-related obligations apply to undertakings that provide electronic communications networks and services available to the public. Some obligations are applicable only to SMP undertakings[57] while other obligations are applicable to all undertakings, regardless of SMP.[58]

Basic Regulatory Concepts

24.73   Article 3(a) REGICOM implements in precise terms the definition of 'access' as found in article 2(a) Access Directive. The definition of 'interconnection' in article 3(j) REGICOM is the same as found in article 2(b) Access Directive.

24.74   According to article 62 REGICOM, undertakings providing electronic communications networks and services are entitled to negotiate and enter into technical and commercial agreements between themselves for access and intercon-nection.

---

52   Art 105 REGICOM.
53   Decree-Law no 151-A/2000 of 20 July 2000 (applicable to radio communication networks and stations).
54   Art 122 REGICOM.
55   Art 121 REGICOM.
56   Art 63(1) REGICOM.
57   See para 24.77 below.
58   See paras 24.83–24.86 below.

24.75   Operators shall have a right and, when requested by other undertakings, an obligation to negotiate interconnection with each other for the purpose of providing publicly available electronic communications services, in order to ensure provision and interoperability of services.[59]

24.76   ANACOM has the competence to impose obligations in matters of access and interconnection on undertakings providing electronic communications networks and services and to intervene at its own initiative where justified or, in the absence of agreement between undertakings, at the request of either of the parties involved, in order to secure the objectives established in accordance with the provisions of REGICOM.[60]

Access- and Interconnection-related Obligations with Respect to SMP Undertakings

24.77   According to article 66 REGICOM, ANACOM is competent to impose, maintain, amend or withdraw the following obligations applicable to undertakings with significant market power:

- obligations of transparency in relation to the publication of information, including reference offers,
- obligations of non-discrimination, in relation to access and interconnection provision and respective information provision,
- obligations for accounting separation in relation to specified activities related to access and interconnection,
- obligations to meet reasonable requests for access, and
- obligations of price control and cost accounting.

24.78   The implementation of these obligations by REGICOM follows very closely the wording in articles 9 to 13 Access Directive.

24.79   The transparency obligations consist of the requirement to publish information, such as accounting information, technical specifications, network characteristics, terms and conditions, including prices.[61] The obligation of non-discrimination consists namely of the requirement to apply equivalent conditions in equivalent circumstances to undertakings providing equivalent services.[62] The obligation of accounting separation consists, namely, of the requirement on operators, especially those that are vertically integrated, to make transparent their wholesale prices and internal prices to prevent unfair cross-subsidy.[63] The obligations to meet reasonable requests for access consist of the imposition on operators to meet reasonable requests for access to, and use of, specific network elements and associated facilities, namely where the denial of such requests within reasonable conditions would hinder a sustainable market at the retail level or the end-users' interests.[64] Obligations of price control and cost accounting may be imposed where

---

59   Art 64 (2) REGICOM.
60   Art 63 (2) REGICOM, see para 24.14 above.
61   Arts 67 to 69 REGICOM.
62   Art 70 REGICOM.
63   Art 71 REGICOM.
64   Art 72 REGICOM.

a market analysis indicates a lack of effective competition in which an operator might sustain prices at an excessive high level, or apply a price squeeze, to the detriment of end-users.[65]

24.80 The above obligations have been imposed in several markets on the PT Group and on mobile operators with SMP – namely TMN, Vodafone Portugal and Optimus.

24.81 ANACOM imposes the appropriate obligations, considering the nature of the issue identified, and such obligations shall be proportionate and justified with relation to ANACOM's regulatory objectives. In exceptional circumstances, and where appropriate, ANACOM can impose on operators with SMP other obligations than those specified in articles 9 to 13 Access Directive, provided it obtains prior authorisation from the European Commission, pursuant to article 7 Framework Directive.[66]

Related Regulatory Powers with Respect to SMP Undertakings

24.82 The obligations imposed by the rules implementing the 2002 EU Regulatory Package include obligations to provide leased lines,[67] and carrier pre-selection.[68] The provision of the minimum set of leased lines by undertakings identified as having SMP follows the basic principles of non-discrimination, cost orientation and transparency. Undertakings declared as having SMP for the provision of connection and use of the public telephone network at a fixed location shall enable their subscribers to access the services of any interconnected provider of publicly available telephone services.

Regulatory Powers Applicable to All Market Participants

Obligations to ensure end-to-end connectivity

24.83 ANACOM is empowered to impose access and interconnection obligations on any undertaking, to the extent that is considered necessary, regardless of whether it holds SMP or not, if the undertaking controls access to end-users, in particular those that operate cable networks, including in justified cases the obligation to interconnect their networks. The obligations imposed shall be objective, clear, proportionate and non-discriminatory.[69]

Access to digital and television broadcasting services

24.84 ANACOM can impose on non-SMP undertakings obligations to provide access to APIs and EPGs on fair, reasonable and non-discriminatory terms, in order to ensure accessibility for end-users to digital radio and television broadcasting services specified by the competent authorities under the law.[70]

---

65 Art 74 REGICOM.
66 Art 66(4) REGICOM.
67 Art 82 REGICOM.
68 Art 84 REGICOM.
69 Art 77 REGICOM.
70 Art 77 REGICOM.

24.85   All operators of conditional access services, irrespective of the means of transmission, which provide access services to digital television and radio services and whose access services broadcasters depending on reaching any group of potential viewers or listeners, are compelled by law: to offer to all broadcasters, on a fair, reasonable and non-discriminatory basis compatible with Community competition law, technical services enabling the broadcasters' digitally transmitted services to be received by viewers or listeners duly authorised by means of decoders administered by the service operators; to comply with Community competition law; and to keep separate financial accounts regarding their activity as conditional access providers.[71]

24.86   The offer conditions, including prices, disclosed by broadcasters of digital television must specify whether or not material related to conditional access is supplied. Operators of conditional access services must notify ANACOM of the technical procedures provided to ensure the interoperability of the different conditional access systems, within five days from the implementation thereof. For this purposes, ANACOM publishes the reference to the applicable technical specifications, through notice in the III Series of the Official Gazette (*'Diário da República'*), as well as in digital format on the internet.

Transitional Provisions

24.87   REGICOM provides for transitional provisions regarding the maintenance of access- and interconnection-related obligations.[72]

REGULATION OF UNIVERSAL SERVICES AND USERS' RIGHTS: THE UNIVERSAL SERVICE DIRECTIVE

Regulation of Universal Service Obligations

Scope of universal service obligations

24.88   Universal service obligations consist of the provision of a minimum set of services, with specified quality and made available to all end-users, regarding their geographical location, and at an affordable price. The scope of the universal service shall reflect the advances in technology, market developments and changes in user demand, being modified where such evolution so justifies it.

24.89   Universal services include:

- the connection at a fixed location to the public telephone network and access to publicly available telephone services at a fixed location,[73]
- availability of a comprehensive directory and of a comprehensive telephone directory enquiry service, and
- adequate provision of public pay telephones.

24.90   Universal service providers must make available specific services in order to ensure access for disabled end-users, equivalent to that enjoyed by other end-users,

---

71   Art 78 REGICOM.
72   Art 122 REGICOM.
73   Art 88 REGICOM.

to publicly available telephone services, including access to emergency services, directory enquiry services and list directories.[74]

Designation of undertakings obliged to provide universal services

24.91 Portugal Telecom, the former incumbent, as concessionaire of the telecommunications public service, maintained its position as Universal Services Provider. According to articles 124 and 121(3) REGICOM, all obligations pursuant to Decree-Law no 31/2003[75] remain in force, without prejudice to the enforcement of the new obligations arising from REGICOM, when a more demanding regime for the concessionaire results from the latter.

24.92 Although Portugal Telecom, the concessionaire of public telecommunications services, is designated by Decree-Law no 31/2003 as Universal Service Provider, article 99 REGICOM provides for the designation of undertakings. More than one undertaking may provide for the universal service in different geographic areas or with different obligations, without prejudice to the provision of universal services throughout the national territory.

24.93 It is incumbent upon the Government to designate the undertaking or undertakings responsible for the universal service provision following a public tender, in terms to be approved by the members of the Government with competence in the areas of finance and electronic communications. The designation process of providers must be efficient, objective, transparent and non-discriminatory, ensuring that no undertaking is a priori excluded from being designated.[76]

Regulation of retail tariffs, user's expenditures and quality of service

24.94 REGICOM provides for rules to ensure that universal service prices are affordable on the basis of national consumer prices and income,[77] as well as for the requirement of a minimum set of facilities and mechanisms imposed on undertakings permitting the control of expenditure by subscribers, including itemised billing, selective call barring for outgoing calls, pre-payment systems, publicly available telephone services and measures to cover non-payment of telephone bills.[78]

24.95 Article 92 REGICOM implements article 11 Universal Service Directive, concerning quality of service, setting obligations to Universal Service Providers, notably to provide information to end users and ANACOM on their performance, establishing ANACOM's competencies in this regard, including the ability to monitor compliance through independent audits and similar reviews of performance data. Non-compliance with these obligations or the opposition to the pursuance of the audit by undertakings are considered breaches, punishable by fines of up to €5 million.

---

74   Art 91 REGICOM.
75   Decree-Law no 31/2003 of 17 February 3003 on bases of the telecommunications public
      service concession.
76   Art 99 REGICOM.
77   Art 93 REGICOM.
78   Art 94 REGICOM.

Cost calculation and financing of universal services

24.96 Where ANACOM considers that the provision of universal service may represent an unfair burden on the respective providers, it should calculate the net costs of the universal service obligations according to the procedures set out in article 95 REGICOM, which mirrors article 12 Universal Services Directive. ANACOM has approved a decision on the net costs of the telecommunications universal service regarding the determination of 'unfair burden' and calculation of net costs.[79]

Regulation of Retail Markets

Prerequisites for the regulation of the retail markets

24.97 ANACOM has a duty[80] to impose adequate regulatory obligations on undertakings identified as having SMP in a given retail market, previously defined and analysed pursuant to the present law, where cumulatively:

- it determines that such retail market is not effectively competitive, and
- it concludes that the imposition of obligations laid down in the access and interconnection chapter would not result in the achievement of the regulatory objectives.

24.98 PTC and PT Prime, undertakings of the Portugal Telecom Group, have been identified as having SMP on the retail market for the minimum set of leased lines (which comprises the specified types of leased lines up to and including 2Mb/s as referenced in article 18 and Annex VII of the Universal Service Directive).[81]

Regulatory powers

24.99 The regulatory obligations imposed must be based on the nature of the problem identified, be proportionate and justified in the light of ANACOM's objectives, and may require in particular that the designated undertakings do not charge excessive prices, do not inhibit market entry or restrict competition by setting predatory prices, do not discriminate against end-users, and do not unreasonably bundle services.[82]

24.100 ANACOM may apply appropriate price cap measures, measures to control individual tariffs, or measures to orient tariffs towards costs or prices on comparable markets.[83] Undertakings subject to price regulation, as described above, or to relevant retail controls should implement cost accounting systems that are appropriate for the application of imposed measures.[84]

---

79   ANACOM determination of 21 August 2003, published at www.anacom.pt.
80   Art 85(1) REGICOM.
81   ANACOM deliberation March 2005.
82   Art 85(2) REGICOM.
83   Art 85(3) REGICOM.
84   Art 85(5) REGICOM.

24.101   ANACOM, or an independent body appointed, must undertake an annual audit of the cost accounting system as well as issuing and publishing the respective statement,[85] in order to support price controls, and verify compliance therewith.

24.102   ANACOM should, on request, submit information to the Commission concerning the retail controls applied and, where appropriate, the cost accounting systems used.[86]

End User Rights

Contracts

24.103   According to article 48(1) REGICOM, without prejudice to the rules on consumer protection, the offer of services providing connection and/or access to the public telephone network is subject to a contract that must specify the minimum requirements as defined by article 20(2) Universal Service Directive, as well as the conditions for the provision of itemised bills. The contract must also contain the subscriber's authorisation or non-authorisation for the inclusion of its personal data in a public directory, and for its disclosure through the directory enquiry service, whether or not the transfer thereof to third parties is involved, pursuant to legislation on the protection of personal data.

24.104   These provisions are also applicable to contracts concluded between consumers and undertakings providing electronic communications services other than those providing connection or access to the public telephone network.[87] According to article 46(6) REGICOM, the providers of universal services cannot refuse to enter into contracts with subscribers, regardless of whether such subscriber is indebted to the universal service provider.

24.105   Undertakings providing publicly available electronic communications networks and services must submit the respective accession contracts to ANACOM, who is responsible for the approval thereof, assessing specifically its compliance with REGICOM, following prior opinion of the Consumer Institute ('*Instituto do Consumidor*'). If ANACOM does not present its decision within 90 days, the submitted accession contract is deemed approved.[88]

Transparency obligations

24.106   Undertakings providing publicly available telephone networks and services are bound to make available to the public, especially to all consumers, transparent and up-to-date information on applicable prices, and on standard terms and conditions, in respect of access to and use of publicly available telephone services.[89] For the purposes of this set of obligations, such undertakings must publish and make available, in the form defined by ANACOM, the information

---

85   Art 85(6) REGICOM.
86   Art 85(7) REGICOM.
87   Art 48(2) REGICOM.
88   Art 39 REGICOM.
89   Art 47(1) REGICOM.

pursuant to Annex II Universal Service Directive The undertakings bound to publish and make available the information referred to shall notify them to ANACOM.[90]

Other obligations

24.107   Undertakings providing publicly available telephone networks and services must also provide for directory enquiry services and operator assistance services,[91] they shall ensure the integrity of the respective networks, the availability of networks and services in the event of emergency or in cases of force majeure and the uninterrupted access to emergency services.[92] Moreover, end-users must be granted access free of charge to the single European emergency call number 112.[93] Also, undertakings providing publicly available telephone networks and services must make available to end-users, subject to technical feasibility and economic viability, multi-frequency dialling(DTMF) and calling-line identification. It is incumbent upon ANACOM, following the general consultation procedure, to waive this obligation, in all or part of the national territory, where it considers that there is sufficient access to such facilities.[94]

Transitional Provisions

24.108   REGICOM provides for transitional rules concerning the maintenance of obligations and the regime applicable to the concessionaire of the telecommunications public service.[95]

DATA PROTECTION: IMPLEMENTATION OF THE E-PRIVACY DIRECTIVE[96]

Confidentiality of Communications

24.109   The E-Privacy Law complements and specifies the rules governing personal data protection matters[97] concerning the data processing in the context of networks and publicly available electronic communications.

24.110   Operators providing network and publicly available electronic communications services must ensure the confidentiality and inviolability of communications and related traffic data. The interception or surveillance of communications and related traffic data is permitted with the user's consent, or in exceptional situations envisaged by law, eg intercepting and recording telephone conversations is allowed where ordered or authorised by a judge, if the investigations concern certain crimes.[98] Recordings of communications conducted by and with public services intended to provide for emergency situations are authorised.

---

90   Art 47(2) and (3) REGICOM.
91   Art 50 REGICOM.
92   Art 49 REGICOM.
93   Art 51 REGICOM.
94   Art 53 REGICOM.
95   Arts 121, 124 and 125 REGICOM.
96   Sub-Chapter by Rute Martins Santos (Albuquerque & Associados).
97   Law no 67/98, of 26 October 1998.
98   Code of Criminal Process, article 187.

24.111   The storage of, or access to, information on the terminal equipment of a subscriber or a user is allowed only if the subscriber or user is provided with clear and comprehensive information, namely about the purposes of the processing, and the subscriber or user is offered the right to refuse such processing.

Traffic Data and Location Data

24.112   The definition of 'traffic data' and 'location data' is coincident with the E-Privacy Directive. The traffic data concerning subscribers or users must be eliminated or made anonymous once they become unnecessary to the communication transmission. However, its processing for the purposes of subscriber billing and interconnection payments is permitted,[99] up to the end of the period during which the bill may lawfully be challenged or the payment pursued.

24.113   The processing of traffic data for the purposes of marketing electronic communications services or for the provision of value added services is permitted, provided that the subscriber or user to whom the data relates has given his prior consent, which may be withdrawn at any time.

24.114   The processing of location data is permitted if the data is made anonymous, and also to the extent and for the duration necessary for the provision of a value added service provided the subscriber's or user's consent is obtained. The operators must provide information to subscribers and users regarding the types of traffic data which are processed, the purposes and the duration of such processing, as well as on a possible transmission to a third party for the purpose of providing the value added service, before obtaining their consent, which they can withdraw or refuse the processing for a period of time.

Itemised Billing

24.115   Under article 39 of REGICOM subscribers have the right to receive itemised bills upon request. The E-Privacy Law[100] also grants to subscribers the right to receive non-itemised bills. Calls free of charge are not to be identified in the calling subscriber's itemised bill.

Calling and Connected Line Identification

24.116   Where presentation of calling line identification is offered, operators should offer to users, on a per-line basis and on a per-call basis, the possibility of preventing the presentation of the calling line identification; and offer the called user the possibility of, free of charge, preventing the presentation of the connected line identification to the calling user and rejecting non-identified calls.

---

99   Under article 6 E-Privacy Law the processing of the following data is permitted: number or identification, address and type of station of the subscriber; total number of units to be charged for the accounting period, as well as the type, starting time and duration of the calls made and/or the data volume transmitted; date of the call or service and called number; and other information concerning payments such as advance payment, payments by instalments, disconnection and reminders.

100   Article 8 E-Privacy Law.

24.117   If a subscriber wants to determine the origin of non-identified calls that upset the peace of the family or its intimacy and presents a written substantiated request, the operator should cancel, for no more than 30 days, the elimination of the presentation of the calling line identification.[101] The calls to emergency services must be identified and the operators should record them and make available the location data.

Automatic Call Forwarding

24.118   Undertakings should offer any subscriber the possibility, free of charge, of stopping automatic call forwarding by a third party to the subscriber's terminal equipment.[102]

Directories of Subscribers

24.119   Before the data is included in printed or electronic directories available to the public or obtainable, subscribers must be informed of the purposes of the directories, and of any further usage possibilities based on search functions embedded in electronic versions of the directories. Subscribers must be given the opportunity to decide whether they wish their personal data to be included in a public directory, and if so, which, and also to verify, correct, alter or withdraw the data included in the referred directories, free of charge.[103]

Unsolicited Communications

24.120   The issue of unsolicited communications is governed by article 22 of Law no 7/2004, of 7 January 2004.

The above-mentioned rule applies to automatic messaging for the purposes of direct marketing through automatic calling machines, facsimile machines or electronic mail. It establishes the need for previous consent of individuals and a system of opt-out for legal entities. It is prohibited to send electronic mail for the purposes of direct marketing disguising or concealing the identity of the person on whose behalf the communication is made, and each unsolicited communication shall indicate an address and an electronic technical means, easy to identify and to use, that allow the recipient of the service to refuse future communications.

---

101   Article 10 E-Privacy Law.
102   Article 9 E-Privacy Law.
103   Article 13 E-Privacy Law.

The Slovak Market for Electronic Communications[1]

Branislav Brocko & Lubomir Marek
Marek & Partners, Bratislava

LEGAL STRUCTURE

Basic Policy

25.1 Over recent years, the Slovak telecommunications legislation has undergone significant changes required for its harmonisation with the applicable EU legislation. In the course of implementing the 2002 EU Regulatory Package, the Slovak Republic has adopted a whole new set of legislative acts forming an environment fully compatible with EU law in the area of electronic communications.

25.2 The overall objectives of the Slovak policy-makers were adjustment of the legal regulation of telecommunications to the changing market conditions, development of effective economic competition, and separation of the regulation of operation of electronic communications from the regulation of their content. The new regulatory framework liberalises and facilitates accessibility of market entry and promotes Information Society services and the common accessibility of the internet. Further, it strengthens the competencies and independence of the Telecommunications Office of the Slovak Republic ('STO').

Implementation of EU Directives

25.3 In the process of harmonising the Slovak electronic communications legislation with EU law, the Slovak Republic implemented the 2002 EU Regulatory Package into its legal system through adopting Act No 610/2003 Coll. on Electronic Communications ('ECA').[2]

---

1 Editing of this chapter closed on 10 June 2005.
2 The ECA came into effect on 1 January 2004, except for certain provisions coming into effect upon accession of the Slovak Republic to the European Union (ie on 1 May 2004), and was subsequently amended by Act No 716/2004 Coll, effective as of 28 December 2004, and Act No 69/2005 Coll effective as of 1 May 2005.

Legislation

25.4 The main legislative act in the area of electronic communications is the ECA.[3] The Slovak electronic communications legislation further includes implementing regulations issued by the Government of the Slovak Republic (the 'Cabinet') and the Ministry of Transportation, Posts and Telecommunications of the Slovak Republic (the 'Ministry'), as follows:

- Decree of the Cabinet setting out details on technical requirements and evaluating procedures in respect of the conformity of radio equipment and terminal telecommunications facilities,[4]
- Decree of the Cabinet setting out technical requirements for operability of terminal facilities designed for receiving digital television signal and operability of analogue television receivers and digital television receivers,[5]
- Regulation of the Ministry setting out details on organisation of telecommunications services in crisis periods,[6] and
- Regulation of the Ministry setting out details on the establishment and administration of special account of universal service.[7]

25.5 In addition, there have been several measures issued by the STO,[8] which has the power to issue generally binding regulations within the framework of the ECA.

REGULATORY PRINCIPLES: IMPLEMENTATION OF THE FRAMEWORK DIRECTIVE

Scope of Regulation

25.6 The ECA regulates the provision of networks and services, including universal service, the operation of radio facilities and use of the frequency spectrum and numbers.

25.7 The ECA's definitions of the terms 'electronic communications network'[9] and 'electronic communications service'[10] reflect the definitions of the said terms as contained in the Framework Directive.[11] The definition of electronic communications services also covers VoIP services.[12]

---

3   See para 25.3 above.
4   Decree No 443/2001 Coll.
5   Decree No 26/2005 Coll.
6   Regulation No 164/2003 Coll.
7   Regulation No 501/2004 Coll.
8   Eg Measure No O-5/2004 setting out details on quality of service parameters and performance targets; Measure No O-6/2004 setting out condition of conditional access to digital television and radio services; Measure No O-8/2004 setting out conditions of operability of public networks and services.
9   S 4(1) ECA.
10   S 5(1) ECA.
11   See paras 1.49 and 1.50 above.
12   There is no specific VoIP regime established by the ECA and implementing regulations. However, the specific regulation of the VoIP services is currently under development.

National Regulatory Authorities: Organisation, Regulatory Objectives, Competencies

25.8   The national regulatory authority in the Slovak Republic is the STO, an organisation financed from the state budget.

25.9   The powers of the STO set out in the ECA are laid down so as to transpose article 8 Framework Directive into Slovak legislation.

25.10   The STO is empowered, inter alia, to:[13]

- regulate activities in the field of electronic communications,
- administer the frequency spectrum,
- protect end-users' interests in respect of the quality and prices of services,
- promote competition, access to networks, operability of networks and services, and protect the freedom of choice of operators,
- conduct and publish comparative studies of quality and price of services,
- fulfil tasks relating to ownership right limitations, and
- perform supervision.

25.11   The STO may request, from undertakings or holders of rights to use frequencies or numbers, information necessary for applying the ECA and international treaties. In addition, the STO has the power to demand from undertakings information which is adequately and objectively required for verifying the compliance of such an undertaking with the applicable general authorisations, individual authorisations and obligations set out in the ECA, the assessment of applications for assignment of frequencies, identification characters or numbers, publication of comparative studies of quality and price of services, statistical purposes or analysis of relevant markets.[14]

25.12   The STO is the only national regulatory authority in the area of electronic communications. However, there are certain competencies lying with the Ministry. The tasks of the Ministry include, inter alia, drafting proposals of the national electronic communications policy and the national frequency spectrum table[15] and submitting them to the Cabinet for approval.

25.13   The STO is obliged to cooperate with the Antimonopoly Office of the Slovak Republic ('AMO') in determining and analysing the relevant electronic communications market and determining undertakings with significant market power. While exercising their competencies, the STO and the AMO are obliged to exchange information and documents.[16]

25.14   Article 3 Framework Directive[17] has been sufficiently transposed through the ECA into Slovak legislation to ensure the independence and efficient structural separation of the STO's regulatory powers from activities connected with ownership or control in the area of electronic communications.[18]

25.15   The STO is obliged to provide the undertakings concerned with the opportunity to comment on proposed measures which may have a significant

---

13   Cf s 6(3) ECA.
14   Cf s 38 ECA.
15   The STO and the Ministry cooperate in drafting proposals of the national frequency spectrum table; cf s 6(3)(c) ECA.
16   S 8(2) ECA.
17   See para 1.52 above.
18   S 6 ECA; s 7 ECA.

impact on the relevant market within the period of at least one month following the publication of the draft measure in the STO's bulletin ('Bulletin'). The STO is obliged to take into account the opinion of the undertakings concerned to the maximum possible extent.[19]

25.16 The ECA has established the powers of the STO to resolve disputes regarding end-users complaints,[20] as well as certain cross-border disputes between Slovak undertakings and parties from EU Member States.[21]

25.17 The STO is also empowered to solve disputes between undertakings, if the undertakings have not entered into a facility access agreement, facility interconnection agreement or facility co-location or sharing agreement within six weeks after the request of one of the undertakings to enter into such an agreement.[22] In such cases, the STO may either impose on the involved parties the obligation to enter into the relevant agreement or refuse the respective request. The STO must make a decision as soon as possible, but not later than within four months.

Right of Appeal against NRA's Decisions

25.18 Except for certain decisions exempted from the right of appeal,[23] the STO's decisions can be appealed by means of an administrative appeal under the Code of Administrative Procedure.[24] In general, administrative appeals must be submitted to the chairman of the STO within 15 days from delivery of the relevant contested decision. The Chairman decides upon appeals, based on proposals of a special committee established by him. The STO's decisions are further subject to revision by the Supreme Court of the Slovak Republic.

The NRA's Obligations to Cooperate with the Commission

25.19 The consolidation procedure[25] has been implemented by section 10 ECA. If a measure of the STO may have an impact on trade between EU Member States, the STO is obliged to consult on the draft measure with the European Commission and all EU Member States' NRAs and take the utmost account of their comments.[26] Section 10(5) ECA implements the 'veto procedure' in compliance with article 7 Framework Directive.[27]

---

19   S 10(2) ECA.
20   S 73 ECA.
21   S 74 ECA.
22   S 75 ECA.
23   Eg decisions relating to general authorisations, determination of relevant markets, determination of cost calculation methods, tenders for frequencies assignment, certificates of special professional qualification and non-judicial dispute resolutions; cf s 72(2) ECA.
24   Act No 71/1967 on Administrative Procedure (Code of Administrative Procedure), as amended.
25   Art 7 Framework Directive; see para 1.61 above.
26   S 10(3) and (4) ECA.
27   See para 1.62 above.

25.20 The STO observes the recommendations and guidelines of the European Commission, including technical standards and technical specifications for networks and services listed in the relevant list published by the European Commission.[28]

25.21 In exceptional cases, where the STO considers that there is an urgent need to act in order to protect competition and the interests of users, the STO may immediately and with no consultations, even if required, issue a preliminary measure or decision regarding definition of the relevant markets. The STO is obliged to deliver such a preliminary measure or decision together with its reasoning to the European Commission and all NRAs.[29]

'Significant Market Power' as a Fundamental Prerequisite of Regulation

Definition of SMP

25.22 The definition of an SMP undertaking contained in sections 16(3) and (5) ECA is based on the provisions of article 14(2) and (3) Framework Directive.[30]

Definition of relevant markets and SMP designation

25.23 The STO determines the relevant markets based on the Commission Recommendation on relevant markets and the Commission Guidelines on market analysis and in compliance with principles of ensuring a competitive environment, while considering specific national conditions.[31] The list of the relevant markets and amendments thereto are published in the Bulletin. Any determination of a relevant market that differs from those defined in the Commission Recommendation on relevant markets and the Commission Guidelines on market analysis must be consulted on with the European Commission and NRAs within the EU.[32]

25.24 On 28 January 2004, the STO issued its decision[33] providing for the list of relevant markets that defines the markets in accordance with the initial Commission Recommendation on relevant markets.[34] Under the said decision, from the geographical point of view, there is only one relevant market covering the entire territory of the Slovak Republic.

25.25 On 20 September 2002, the STO issued several decisions[35] determining the undertakings listed below as those having SMP in the relevant telecommunications markets:

---

28 S 11(2) ECA.
29 S 10(6) ECA.
30 See paras 1.70 and 1.71 above.
31 S 15 ECA.
32 See para 25.19 above.
33 The decision was published in the Bulletin on 5 February 2004.
34 See para 1.75 above.
35 Under s 76(8) ECA, the decisions are still effective until new decisions determining SMP undertakings issued by the STO under the ECA come into effect. To date, no such decisions have been published.

- Slovak Telecom, a.s. in the market of public telephone services provided via a public telecommunications network and in the market of public telecommunications leased lines,[36] and
- T-Mobile Slovensko, a.s. and Orange Slovensko, a.s. in the market of public telephone services provided via a public mobile telecommunications network.[37]

NRA's Regulatory Duties concerning Rights of Way, Co-location and Facility Sharing

Rights of way

25.26   Any public network operator is entitled, in the public interest and to the necessary extent, to benefit from the following rights of way:[38]

- to install and operate a public network and carry its lines over third parties' property (whether public or private),
- to enter upon third parties' property (whether public or private) for the purpose of establishing, operating, repairing and maintaining the lines, and
- to perform necessary modifications to the ground and its vesture for the purpose of ensuring safety and reliability of the lines, if such modifications are not performed by the relevant property owner or user upon the operator's request.

25.27   The rights of way are created by operation of law and registered with the Real Property Register. The operator is obliged to notify the owner or user of the property of commencement of the performance of the rights of way at least 15 days in advance.[39] The owner or user, who is restricted in a regular use of his property as a consequence of the operator's exercise of the rights of way, is entitled to reasonable compensation.

25.28   A public service operator may use third parties' internal distribution systems installed in the buildings or premises where the operator provides its services, provided that the operator compensates the owner of the building/ premises, on a pro-rata basis, for the costs incurred in connection with maintenance and repairs of such systems.[40]

Co-location and facility sharing

25.29   An operator who is unable to install new lines or facilities, or can do so only with unreasonable limits to use of third parties' property, because of the need to protect the environment, public health or public security or to meet the zone planning objectives, is entitled to request another operator to allow it to share/use

---

36   Decision No 8702/14/2002; Decision No 8703/14/2002.
37   Decision No 8699/14/2002; Decision No 8701/14/2002.
38   S 69(1) ECA.
39   In the case of a breakdown the operator may enter upon third parties' property without prior notification; however, such a notification must be made subsequently with undue delay; cf s 69(3) ECA.
40   S 69(9) ECA.

the existing infrastructure (including buildings, premises and parts of lines), provided that no significant additional works and costs are required.[41] The infrastructure sharing is provided under the terms and conditions agreed between the undertakings involved.[42] Entering into the agreement may be rejected only if the sharing is technically unfeasible.[43] If the undertakings fail to agree on the terms and conditions, any of them may request the STO to decide on the content of the agreement, including the rules of costs sharing.[44]

REGULATION OF MARKET ENTRY: IMPLEMENTATION OF THE AUTHORISATION DIRECTIVE

The General Authorisation of Electronic Communications

25.30   In compliance with the principles set out by the Authorisation Directive, the provision of networks or services is generally subject to a general authorisation.[45] However, should the provision of networks or services require an assignment of numbers or frequencies, an individual authorisation for the use of numbers, or individual authorisation for the use of frequencies and identification characters, must be obtained from the STO.[46]

25.31   A general authorisation sets out the rights and conditions for the provision of networks and services and the operation of radio facilities that can apply to all or some of them. Specific obligations, which may be imposed on SMP undertakings or universal service providers under the ECA, are not affected by the rights and obligations stipulated by the respective general authorisations.

25.32   The STO may only impose on general authorisations those conditions that are listed in section 13(2) ECA; the ECA's list of the admissible conditions corresponds to the list contained in Part A of the Annex to the Authorisation Directive. In accordance with the Authorisation Directive, the ECA permits the conditions to be attached to the general authorisation only if they are objectively justified in relation to the network or service concerned, and are non-discriminatory, proportionate and transparent.[47]

25.33   The STO has issued a number of general authorisations,[48] out of which the General Authorisation No 1/2004 for provision of electronic communications networks and electronic communications services ('general authorisation') is the most significant one.

25.34   An undertaking is authorised to provide networks or services under the general authorisation, if it complies with the conditions set out in the general authorisation and has properly fulfilled its notification obligation vis-à-vis the STO.

---

41   S 70(1) ECA.
42   The terms and conditions must be non-discriminatory; cf s 70(1) ECA.
43   S 70(2) ECA.
44   S 70(3) ECA and s 75 ECA; see para 25.17 above.
45   S 12(1) ECA.
46   S 12(1) ECA.
47   S 13(3) ECA.
48   Certain general authorisations have been issued by the STO prior to the effective date of the ECA; however, under the transitional provisions of the ECA, they remain effective and are deemed to be general authorisations issued under the ECA; cf s 76(4) and (5) ECA.

25.35 If the general authorisation so requires, an undertaking intending to provide networks or services is obliged to notify the STO of its intention before it commences to provide them.[49] The notification obligation also applies to changes or termination of the provision of networks or services. Upon delivery of the sufficient and complete notification, the STO shall register the undertaking as a network/service provider and publish such a registration on the internet. If the undertaking so requests, the STO is obliged to confirm to the undertaking the fulfilment of the notification obligation within one week after the delivery of the notification.[50] The notification obligation is deemed to be fulfilled on the date of submission of the sufficient and complete notification to the STO. With effect from that date, the undertaking may provide the respective networks or services.[51]

Rights of Use for Radio Frequencies

General authorisations and granting of individual rights

25.36 Rights of use for radio frequencies are granted based on authorisations to operate radio facilities. By such authorisations the STO authorises the operation of radio facilities through assignment of the frequencies or frequency band for operation of the facilities.[52] The authorisations may be issued as general authorisations to operate radio facilities, or in the form of individual authorisations for the use of frequencies and identification characters, if the provision of services or operation of networks requires the assignment of individual frequencies.

25.37 The STO assigns individual frequencies based on an application in accordance with the frequency spectrum use plan prepared by the STO. If an assignment of free frequencies under the frequency spectrum use plan is requested, the STO is obliged to issue the authorisation within six weeks after submission of the complete application.[53] In compliance with article 10(1) Authorisation Directive, the STO may request the applicant to submit the information necessary to verify the applicant's ability to comply with the conditions attached to the frequency usage right.

25.38 An individual authorisation to operate a radio facility can be issued for a period of up to 10 years.[54] The STO may repeatedly extend the term of the authorisation for further periods of 10 years. If it is justified by the period envisaged for return on investment, the STO may grant or extend the authorisation for more than 10 years.

---

49   For example, under the general authorisation an operator is not obliged to notify the STO of its intention to provide networks or services if the number of subscribers does not exceed 200 and the annual turnover from the provision of network/services does not exceed SKK 2 million (approx €52,500), or if the operator provides networks or services exclusively for its own purposes.

50   S 14(3) ECA.

51   S 13(7) ECA.

52   S 32(1) ECA.

53   The six-week period may be extended by the STO up to eight months, if it is necessary to ensure fair, proportionate, open and transparent procedures for all applicants; cf s 32(2) ECA.

54   S 32(19) ECA; the authorisations to operate radio facilities for radio or television broadcasting may not be granted for a period exceeding the term of the respective radio/television broadcasting licence.

25.39   The STO may refuse to grant the authorisation only for one of a limited number of reasons stipulated by the ECA (eg if it is necessary to comply with international treaties, assignment is not allowed under the frequency spectrum use plan, or a frequency is not available).

Admissible conditions

25.40   The authorisation granting rights of use for frequencies may be subject only to the conditions listed in section 32(17) ECA, which are consistent with the conditions set out in Part B of the Annex to the Authorisation Directive.[55]

Limitation of number of rights of use to be granted

25.41   Selected frequencies, which are harmonised for a certain type of service listed in the national frequency spectrum table and for which assignment conditions are specified in the frequency spectrum use plan, are assigned based on the results of a public tender organised by the STO.[56] In such a case, the frequencies are assigned to the bidders selected by the committee appointed by the STO's Chairman according to criteria specified in an invitation to participate in the tender. The STO issues the authorisations to the successful bidders in the order determined by the selection committee within four weeks after the bidders are selected.[57] The above regime does not apply to the assignment of frequencies for radio or television broadcasting.[58]

Frequency trading

25.42   The ECA expressly provides that an individual authorisation may not be transferred to another individual or legal entity. Moreover, the ECA does not allow transferring the authorisation within a sale of business or enforcement or bankruptcy proceedings.[59]

Rights of Use for Numbers

General authorisations and granting of individual rights

25.43   The STO manages the use of numbers by issuing the numbering plan and assigning numbers and number blocks pursuant to the issued numbering plan. The numbering plan provides for rules of setting and use of numbers and general conditions for their assignment. The STO publishes the numbering plan in the Bulletin and on the internet. The currently applicable numbering plan was issued on 11 June 2004.

---

55   See para 1.103 above.
56   S 32(5) ECA.
57   S 32(15) ECA.
58   Authorisations to operate radio facilities for radio or television broadcasting are issued by the STO to holders of a radio or television broadcasting licence or persons who entered into a service contract with the holder of such a licence; cf S 32(18) ECA.
59   S 32(20) ECA.

25.44   The rights of use for numbers are granted, and the numbers are assigned, based on an individual authorisation for the use of numbers issued by the STO. The individual authorisations are granted to public networks or public services operators upon their request within three weeks after submission of the complete application. The STO may refuse to assign the numbers only if the existing number plan does not allow the assignment of the requested numbers or where the applicant has not complied with the conditions for assignment.

Admissible conditions

25.45   The rights of use for numbers may be granted for a limited period of time. An individual authorisation for use of numbers may be subject only to the conditions listed in section 31(4) ECA. Such conditions generally correspond to the conditions set out in Part C of the Annex to the Authorisation Directive.[60]

25.46   Providers of publicly available telephone services must ensure number portability both in fixed and mobile networks under the conditions consistent with article 30 Universal Service Directive.[61] The number portability obligation does not apply to the transfer of numbers between fixed and mobile networks.

25.47   The STO may impose, on SMP undertakings in the market of fixed public telephone services, carrier selection and carrier pre-selection obligations.[62] The STO is further authorised to impose such obligations on SMP undertakings in other markets, if it is necessary to ensure effective competition.

Limitation of number of rights of use to be granted

25.48   Unlike article 5(4) Authorisation Directive, the ECA does not provide for the possibility of granting rights of use for numbers of exceptional economic value through a competitive or comparative selection procedure.

The NRA's Enforcement Powers

25.49   The ECA empowers the STO to request from undertakings the information necessary to verify undertakings' compliance with the conditions set out in the general authorisation or attached to rights for use of frequencies or numbers, or with specific obligations imposed on SMP undertakings under the ECA.[63] The principles that must be followed by the STO, when exercising its information powers, are consistent with the principles set out in article 11 Authorisation Directive.[64] Where an undertaking fails to provide the STO with the requested information, the STO may impose on such an undertaking a penalty of up to SKK 3 million (approx €79,000).

25.50   In compliance with article 10 Authorisation Directive, where the STO finds out that an undertaking has not complied with the conditions of the general or

---

60   See para 1.108 above.
61   See para 1.189 above.
62   See para 25.71 below.
63   S 38(2) ECA.
64   See para 1.111 above.

individual authorisations or with the specific obligations imposed on SMP undertakings under the ECA, the STO is obliged to notify the undertaking of such findings in writing and give the undertaking an opportunity to comment on the findings within the period determined by the STO. At the same time, the undertaking is obliged to remedy the breaches within one month after receipt of the written notification on the findings. If the STO so decides, the remedy period may be longer or, in case of repeated breaches, shorter than one month.[65] If the respective undertaking fails to remedy the breaches within the above period, the STO shall impose on the undertaking the obligation to perform measures aimed at ensuring compliance[66] and, at the same time, impose a penalty of up to SKK 20 million (approx €526,000).[67]

25.51   The STO may prevent an undertaking from providing networks or services under the general authorisation or cancel frequencies or numbers usage rights, only if the undertaking fails to perform the imposed measure aimed at ensuring compliance, and seriously and repeatedly breaches the ECA or the conditions set out in the general or individual authorisations.[68]

25.52   Under certain conditions,[69] the STO may take urgent interim measures consisting in the partial or complete cessation of supply, sale or operation of facilities of the relevant undertaking.

Administrative Charges and Fees for Rights of Use

25.53   In a general authorisation, the STO may impose on undertakings providing networks or services under such a general authorisation the obligation to pay administrative fees specified in the authorisation.[70]

25.54   Under section 31(12) ECA, undertakings that have been granted number usage rights are obliged to pay, in respect of each number used, an annual fee of up to SKK 20,000 (approx €525) according to the tariff issued by the STO.[71] Also, undertakings being granted frequencies usage rights are obliged to pay administrative fees consisting of a lump-sum amount for the allotment or assignment of frequencies, generally payable upon issue of the relevant individual authorisation, and recurring payments of up to SKK 1 million (approx €26,300)[72] for the use of each frequency and identification character, according to the tariff issued by the

---

65   S 37(4) ECA.
66   These measures are not further specified in the ECA.
67   S 71 ECA.
68   S 37(8) ECA.
69   S 37(6) ECA; the conditions generally correspond to those specified in art 10(6) Authorisation Directive; see para 1.116 above.
70   Eg under the general authorisation, an undertaking subject to the notification obligation must pay administrative fees consisting of a fixed annual amount, determined according to the population in the areas where the undertaking provides networks or services, and an amount of 0.05% of the turnover from the provision of networks or services.
71   The current applicable tariff for the use of numbers is laid down in Measure No O-3/2004 of 19 April 2004.
72   The maximum amount of the recurring payment is SKK 90,000 (approx €2,350) in the case of a radio broadcasting frequency and SKK 180,000 (approx €4,700) in the case of a television broadcasting frequency.

STO.[73] The STO is authorised to withdraw the relevant usage rights if the rights holder does not pay the respective fees within three months after their due date.[74]

Transitional Regulations for Existing Authorisations

25.55   The licences for telecommunication activities issued prior to 31 December 2003 are considered to be general authorisations under the ECA and proof of fulfilment of the notification obligation. The numbers and frequencies assigned under these licences are considered to be individual authorisations until expiry of their term. The rights and obligations arising from these licences remain valid, provided that the STO is obliged to modify these rights and obligations within nine months of the ECA's entry into force, if they do not comply with the applicable provisions of the ECA.[75]

REGULATION OF NETWORK ACCESS AND INTERCONNECTION: IMPLEMENTATION OF THE ACCESS DIRECTIVE

Objectives and Scope of Access Regulation

25.56   In compliance with the objectives set out in the Access Directive,[76] the ECA introduced certain regulatory powers of the STO with the objective of promoting effective competition and development of the internal market by preventing SMP undertakings from distorting effective competition in the end-user market or from acting against the interests of consumers through denying access or interconnection or imposing inappropriate conditions upon undertakings seeking access or interconnection to their networks or associated facilities.

25.57   The access- and interconnection-related provisions of the ECA apply in particular to SMP undertakings and undertakings seeking access and/or interconnection to the networks. Obligations relating to interconnection of networks apply to undertakings providing public networks, irrespective whether they are SMP undertakings or not.

Basic Regulatory Concepts

25.58   The ECA has established effective and relatively far-reaching competencies of the STO. Accordingly, if the STO finds out that there is no effective competition in a relevant market, it has the power to impose on the respective SMP undertakings one or more obligations stipulated by the ECA with the aim of facilitating access and interconnection, promoting the interoperability of networks and services, and enhancing competition in the relevant market and protecting consumer interests. These obligations must, however, be justified and appropriate with respect to the purpose and principles of regulation, ie the promotion of effective competition and internal market development.

---

73   The current applicable tariff for the use of frequencies is laid down in Measure No O-2/2004 of 19 April 2004.
74   S 31(9)(a) ECA; s 34(1)(d) ECA.
75   S 76(4) ECA.
76   See para 1.122 above.

25.59 The ECA's definitions of the terms 'access'[77] and 'interconnection'[78] reflect the definitions introduced by the Access Directive.[79]

25.60 The principle of freedom of access[80] has been implemented.[81] The ECA does not require that undertakings from other Member States seeking access or interconnection have to obtain an authorisation to operate in the Slovak Republic. Moreover, the ECA allows such undertakings to negotiate agreements with Slovak undertakings on technical and commercial terms of access and interconnection.

25.61 The principle of the priority of commercial negotiations[82] has been implemented as regards network interconnection. Under the ECA, a public network operator is entitled and, if requested by another undertaking providing a public network, obliged to negotiate the interconnection of networks and, if it is feasible, to interconnect its network with the network of the requesting undertaking on the basis of a contract.[83]

Access- and Interconnection-related Obligations with Respect to SMP Undertakings

Overview

25.62 In compliance with the Access Directive,[84] the STO has the power to impose on SMP undertakings the following obligations:

- transparency,
- non-discrimination,
- accounting separation,
- access to specific network facilities, and
- price control and cost accounting obligations.

25.63 Once the STO, based on a market analysis, finds out that there is no effective competition in the relevant market, the STO is obliged, after completion of the consultation procedure, to determine an SMP undertaking and, at the same time, to impose on such an SMP undertaking at least one of the above obligations. These obligations must be justified and appropriate with respect to the purpose and principles of regulation, ie the promotion of effective competition and internal market development.

---

77   S 4(9) ECA.
78   S 4(10) ECA.
79   See paras 1.125 and 1.126 above.
80   See para 1.127 above.
81   Cf s 28(2) ECA.
82   See para 1.128 above.
83   S 28(1) ECA.
84   See paras 1.137 – 1.153 above.

Transparency obligations

25.64 The STO is empowered to impose upon an SMP undertaking the obligation to publish specific information, such as accounting information, technical specifications, network characteristics, supply and use terms and conditions, including prices.[85]

25.65 Where non-discriminatory obligations[86] have been imposed upon an operator, the STO is obliged to impose upon such an operator the obligation to issue and publish a reference offer for access or interconnection.[87] SMP undertakings having the obligation to provide unbundled access to the local loop are automatically obliged to issue and publish a reference offer for unbundled access to the local loop containing the details specified in Annex 2 to the ECA.

Non-discrimination obligations

25.66 The STO may impose upon an SMP undertaking the non-discrimination obligation in relation to access or interconnection of networks to ensure the same objectives as set out in article 10(2) Access Directive.[88]

Specific access obligations

25.67 In compliance with article 12 Access Directive, the STO is authorised to impose upon an SMP undertaking the obligation to meet any reasonable and legitimate request for access to, and use of certain network elements and associated facilities and interconnection of networks.[89] The list of the access obligations that may be imposed[90] fully corresponds to that contained in article 12(1) Access Directive.[91] The STO may attach to the access obligations conditions ensuring fairness, reasonableness and timeliness.[92] When imposing the access obligations, the STO considers the factors corresponding to those listed in article 12(1) Access Directive.[93]

Price control obligations

25.68 If, based on a market analysis, the STO finds that a lack of effective competition allows an SMP undertaking to require inadequate prices, the STO may impose on the SMP undertaking the obligation to set the prices for the provision of specific types of access or interconnection so as to include only costs associated with the provision of access/interconnection and not to include the costs which are

---

85   S 18(1) ECA.
86   See para 25.66 below.
87   S 18(2) ECA; see para 1.143 above.
88   S 19 ECA; see para 1.144 above.
89   S 21 ECA; see para 1.145 above.
90   S 21(1) ECA.
91   See para 1.146 above; unlike the Access Directive, the list contained in s 21(1) ECA appears to be inclusive.
92   S 21(2) ECA.
93   See para 1.147 above.

not connected with such provision.[94] Such prices must be calculated based on the method determined by the STO.[95] When imposing the said obligation, the STO is obliged to take into account the extent of investments made by the SMP undertaking, an adequate rate of return on the investment, and associated risks. In authorising a cost recovery mechanism or pricing method, the STO must ensure the same objectives as provided for in article 13(2) Access Directive.[96] The STO may require an SMP undertaking to prove that its prices are set in compliance with the above conditions, provide full justification of the prices, and adjust the prices where appropriate.[97]

Accounting separation obligations

25.69   The scope of the accounting separation obligations that may be imposed by the STO under section 20 ECA, and related powers of the STO to request information, are established in consistency with article 11 Access Directive.[98]

Related Regulatory Powers with Respect to SMP Undertakings

25.70   The STO is authorised to impose on SMP undertakings the obligation to provide a minimum set of leased lines[99] in the relevant market, on a transparent, non-discriminatory and cost-oriented basis.[100] The SMP undertaking having the obligation to provide the leased lines is obliged to issue and publish a reference offer for this service. Such an offer must be based on the principles of transparency, non-discrimination and cost orientation and must provide for the conditions listed in Annex 3 to the ECA.[101]

25.71   The provisions of the Universal Service Directive regarding carrier selection and pre-selection[102] have been fully implemented. As a result, the STO is obliged to impose on SMP undertakings in the market of fixed public telephone service the obligation to enable their subscribers to access the services of any interconnected public telephone service provider both on a call-by-call basis and by means of pre-selection.[103] Based on a market analysis, the STO may also impose such an obligation on mobile network operators having SMP, if it is necessary to ensure effective competition.[104]

Regulatory Powers Applicable to All Market Participants

25.72   To implement article 5(1) sentence 2 (a) Access Directive, section 28 ECA directly imposes, on all public network operators controlling access to at least one

---

94   S 22(1) ECA.
95   Under s 22(3) ECA, the STO must publish a specific price calculation method, once mandated, in the manner consistent with art 13(4) Access Directive; see para 1.151 above.
96   See para 1.151 above.
97   S 22(2) ECA.
98   See paras 1.152 and 1.153 above.
99   'Lease of lines' is defined as the provision of transmission capacity between end points of the same network or different networks. It does not include switching functions operated by its users. A minimum set of leased lines is specified in the respective general authorisation for the provision of networks and services.
100   S 24(3) ECA.
101   The list is based on Annex VII to the Universal Service Directive; cf para 1.176 above.
102   See para 1.177 above.
103   S 27(1) ECA.
104   S 27(3) ECA.

network termination point identified by one or more numbers in the numbering plan, the obligation to mutually interconnect their networks, if any such operator requests the other one to do so, to ensure end-to-end communications between their users.[105] The interconnection of the public networks must be provided in a reasonable period of time, on a transparent and non-discriminatory basis and under reasonable contractual terms.

25.73   Operators providing conditional access to digital television and radio services, irrespective of the transmission means, are obliged to offer their services on fair, reasonable and non-discriminatory terms and must have the capability for cost-effective transcontrol.[106]

Transitional Provisions

25.74   The rights and obligations of the operators designated by the STO as having SMP in the telecommunications market prior to 31 December 2003 remain unaffected until the STO's new decisions determining SMP undertakings under the ECA become effective.[107]

REGULATION OF UNIVERSAL SERVICES AND USERS' RIGHTS: THE UNIVERSAL SERVICE DIRECTIVE

Regulation of Universal Service Obligations

Scope of universal service obligations

25.75   The list of the universal service obligations contained in section 50(2) ECA is based on articles 4–7 Universal Service Directive.[108] The ECA specifically includes in the scope of the universal service obligations the obligation to provide access to publicly available telephone services for disabled users, and adequate availability of public pay telephones accessible through barrier-free access and specially equipped public pay telephones.[109]

Designation of undertakings obliged to provide universal services

25.76   Section 50(4) ECA sets out the procedure for designating universal service providers and the fundamental principles and methods of such procedure in accordance with article 8 Universal Service Directive.[110] When designating universal

---

105   See also para 25.61 above.
106   S 25 ECA and STO's Measure No O-6/2004; see also para 1.155 above.
107   S 76(8) ECA.
108   See para 1.163 above.
109   Under the STO's Measure No O-4/2004, at least 25% of publicly accessible pay telephones operated by an universal service provider must be capable of being used by hearing-impaired users using special hearing tools and at least 25% of publicly accessible pay telephones must be accessible through barrier-free access. Further, universal service providers must provide hearing-impaired and speech-impaired users with terminals allowing access to publicly available telephone services and blind and partially sighted users with free enquiry services.
110   See para 1.164 above.

service providers, the STO must consider which undertaking needs the lowest expenditures to cover universal service costs.[111]

25.77   Currently, Slovak Telecom is the only operator designated as being obliged to provide universal services.

Regulation of retail tariffs users' expenditure and quality of service

25.78   The STO is obliged to monitor the evolution and level of prices for universal services,[112] and is authorised to impose on universal service providers the obligations corresponding to those described in articles 9(2) and 9(4) Universal Service Directive.[113] Universal service providers are prohibited from charging prices in such a way that users of the universal service must pay for facilities or services that are unnecessary or not required for the service requested.[114] The STO may impose on universal service providers the obligation to provide services enabling users to control their expenditures for the universal service. Such services may include selective call barring for outgoing calls (free of charge), pre-payment systems and phased payment of connection fees.[115]

25.79   The STO determines, by way of measure,[116] the quality of service parameters and performance targets in compliance with the relevant guidelines of the European Commission, considering the state of technology and economic conditions so as to ensure access by users to comprehensive, comparable and clear information. The quality of service parameters may include, inter alia, supply time required for initial connection, fault rate per access line, unsuccessful call ratio or call set up time. Each universal service provider is obliged to inform the STO, and publish the achieved results, in terms of quality of service parameters.[117]

Cost calculation and financing of universal services

25.80   A universal service provider is entitled to be compensated for the identified net cost of the universal service, if its income from such service is lower than the cost of providing the service. The net costs are determined by the STO based on the methods[118] compatible with the rules set out in article 12(1) Universal Service Directive.[119] In case of need, the STO may establish and maintain the special fund (so-called 'special account') for the purpose of compensating the net costs. Each public network/service provider whose annual revenue share in the domestic market of public networks or services is at least 0.2% is obliged to contribute to such a fund.[120]

---

111   S 50(4) ECA.
112   S 26(1) ECA.
113   See para 1.166 above.
114   S 52(1) ECA.
115   Cf S 52(2) ECA.
116   Currently, Measure No O-5/2004.
117   Under Measure No O-5/2004, a universal service provider must inform the STO of the achieved results two times a year and publish the information in the same periods in a nation-wide periodical.
118   The detailed procedure for calculating the net cost is set out in Annex No 2 to the Ministry's Regulation No 501/2004 Coll.
119   See para 1.169 above.
120   The amount of the contribution is determined by the STO for each provider separately based

Regulation of Retail Markets

Prerequisites for the regulation of retail markets

25.81   In accordance with article 17 Universal Service Directive,[121] the STO may take measures vis-à-vis SMP undertakings[122] in a given retail market[123] to protect end-users' interests and ensure effective competition only if regulation at wholesale level[124] does not achieve the above regulatory objectives.

Regulatory powers

25.82   Within its retail market regulation powers, the STO may, subject to the above prerequisites, impose on SMP undertakings the obligations listed in section 23(1) ECA, which correspond to those specified in article 17(2) Universal Service Directive.[125]

End User Rights

Contracts

25.83   Any public service provider is under an obligation to enter into a connection contract with any person requesting provision of the relevant public service,[126] unless there is a ground entitling the provider to refuse to enter into the contract.[127] Connection contracts consist of:

- the connection contract itself, which must at least provide a definition of the public service provided, the place of its provision and price;[128] the price may be agreed by making a reference to the applicable tariffs,
- general terms and conditions, which must also include the code of complaint handling procedure and the dispute resolution mechanism,[129] and
- tariffs.[130]

---

on the rules set out in Annex No 3 to the Ministry's Regulation No 501/2004 Coll; the amount is basically derived from the provider's annual domestic revenue share.

121 See para 1.172 above.

122 Slovak Telecom, a.s. has been designated as an operator having SMP in the market of publicly available telephone services provided via a public telecommunications network, and T-Mobile Slovensko, a.s. and Orange Slovensko, a.s. as operators with SMP in the market of publicly available telephone services provided via a public mobile telecommunications network; cf para 25.25 above.

123 Under s 23(1) ECA, the regulation of retail markets applies to the retail markets for publicly available telephone services only.

124 See paras 25.62–25.71 above.

125 See paras 1.174 and 1.175 above.

126 S 42(2)(a) ECA.

127 The provider may refuse to enter into a connection contract only if provision of the requested service is not technically feasible (not applicable to services falling within the universal service), or there is no guarantee that the applicant will comply with the contract, or the applicant does not agree with the general terms and conditions; cf S 42(1)(c) ECA.

128 S 43(2) ECA.

129 S 40(1) ECA provides for the minimum set of terms to be included in the general terms and conditions.

130 S 41(2) ECA provides for the minimum scope of the details to be specified in the tariffs.

25.84   The subscriber may rescind the connection contract without penalty upon the provider's notice of modifications to conditions in the contract; such notice must be given at least one month in advance of the proposed modifications.[131]

Transparency obligations

25.85   Each public service provider is obliged to publish its general terms and conditions and tariffs and any amendment thereto 15 days in advance.[132] If the STO so decides, public service providers must publish the comparable, adequate and up-to-date information on the quality of service level achieved.[133]

Other obligations

25.86   Public service providers are obliged to ensure that each user has uninterrupted and free access to all emergency call numbers, including the single European emergency call number '112', the possibility of dual tone multi-frequency operation and the possibility of calling line identification.[134] Public service providers are further obliged to handle all calls to the European telephone numbering space and provide, under the conditions compatible with article 28 Universal Service Directive,[135] that end-users from other EU Member States are able to access non-geographic numbers in the Slovak Republic.[136]

Transitional Provisions

25.87   Contractual relationships established between public network/service providers and users prior to 31 December 2003 are considered to be connection contracts under the ECA.[137]

DATA PROTECTION: IMPLEMENTATION OF THE E-PRIVACY DIRECTIVE

Confidentiality of Communications

25.88   Any communication and other data received, transmitted or stored in connection with the provision of services and traffic and location data and personal

---

131   S 43(4)(a) ECA.
132   S 40(1) ECA.
133   S 45(2) ECA.
134   S 39(2) ECA.
135   See para 1.187 above.
136   S 47(1)(c) ECA.
137   S 76(12) ECA.

data[138] are subject to secrecy.[139] Anyone who becomes privy to any information subject to secrecy, even if incidentally, is obliged to keep it confidential.[140]

25.89   Providers are obliged to take appropriate technical and organisational measures in order to safeguard the security of their networks/services.[141] In the case of a risk of security breach, the provider must inform subscribers of such a risk and any possible remedies, including cost implications.[142]

25.90   Any tapping, listening or storage of transmitted communications by persons other than the communicating users is prohibited,[143] except if such activities are consented to by users or conducted within the statutory authorisation of state authorities[144] or concern information relating to malicious calls or calls misusing the service.[145]

Traffic Data and Location Data

25.91   The ECA defines the terms 'traffic data'[146] and 'location data'[147] consistently with the E-Privacy Directive.

25.92   A provider may not store any traffic data without having obtained a user's consent and must delete or anonymise it immediately after transmission of a communication is terminated.[148] Traffic data necessary for the purposes of billing and interconnection payments may be stored only for the period during which the bill may be lawfully challenged or payment pursued.[149] Traffic data may be processed for marketing purposes only with a user's consent.[150]

25.93   Location data may be processed only if it is anonymised or a user's consent is obtained, to the extent and for the duration necessary for provision of a value added service.[151] Providers must inform users, prior to obtaining the consent, of the type of location data to be processed, the purposes and duration of the processing and whether the data will be transmitted to a third party. The user may withdraw

---

138   The rights and obligations relating to the protection of personal data, which are not specifically regulated by the ECA, are governed by Act No 428/2002 Coll on Personal Data Protection, as amended.
139   S 55(1) ECA.
140   S 55(2) ECA.
141   S 57(1) ECA.
142   S 57(6) ECA.
143   S 55(4) ECA.
144   S 88 Act No 141/1961 Coll on Criminal Procedure, as amended ('Code of Criminal Procedure'), permits listening and storage of communications in case of criminal proceedings concerning a serious criminal offence, bribery, misuse of powers by public authorities or other malicious criminal offences which must be prosecuted according to a promulgated international agreement. However, such listening and storage must be conducted strictly under the conditions set out in the said section of the Code of Criminal Procedure.
145   S 55(4) ECA.
146   S 59(1) ECA.
147   S 59(6) ECA.
148   S 59(2) ECA.
149   S 59(3) ECA.
150   S 59(5) ECA.
151   S 59(6) ECA.

the consent at any time.[152] The user's consent is not required for the provision of location data to the integrated rescue system.[153]

Itemised Billing

25.94   Upon a subscriber's request, a public service provider is obliged to provide the subscriber with itemised billing which gives details of each outgoing call.[154] The providers are not explicitly required to provide specific measures to protect the subscriber's privacy in connection with itemised billing. However, the data contained in itemised bills is subject to secrecy and must be protected by anyone who comes into contact with it.[155]

Calling and Connected Line Identification

25.95   Providers offering a calling line identification service must allow users to withhold their number on a per-call or per-line basis, using simple means and free of charge.[156] Further, users must have the facility to block the numbers of incoming calls[157] and reject incoming calls where the caller has withheld its identification.[158] Providers may temporarily suspend the above service, if a user so requests, to trace malicious or annoying calls and for emergency calls.

Automatic Call Forwarding

25.96   Every user must have the option to stop automatic call forwarding initiated by a third party, using simple means and free of charge.[159]

Directories of Subscribers

25.97   Each subscriber is entitled to verify, correct or withdraw his personal data included in a directory of subscribers.[160] If the subscriber so requests, the provider may not include the subscriber's data in the directory and provide it through a directory enquiry service.[161] The provider may not charge any fee to the subscriber for exclusion of his data from the directory. The data contained in the subscribers' directory may be used and processed exclusively for the purpose of providing the publicly available telephone service, unless the subscriber consents to using the data for other purposes. Each provider must adopt appropriate technical measures to exclude any possibility of copying of subscribers' directories issued in electronic form.[162]

---

152   S 59(6) ECA.
153   S 59(9) ECA.
154   S 42(2)(d) ECA.
155   See para 25.88 above.
156   S 62(1)(a) ECA.
157   S 62(1)(b) ECA.
158   S 62(1)(c) ECA.
159   S 63 ECA.
160   S 61(1) ECA.
161   S 61(3) ECA.
162   S 61(4) ECA.

Unsolicited Communications

25.98 Any direct marketing and advertisement communications may be conducted through automatic calling systems, faxes, e-mails or short messages only with a user's prior consent.[163] The consent may be withdrawn at any time.

---

163 S 65(2) ECA; S 3(6) Act No 147/2001 Coll on Advertising, as amended.

The Slovenian Market for Electronic Communications[1]

Srečo Jadek, Jure Levovnik and Ožbej Merc
Jadek & Pensa, Ljubljana

LEGAL STRUCTURE

Basic Policy

26.1 Slovenian electronic communications regulation is based on a single organic law (Electronic Communications Act, 'ECA')[2] that encompasses all the relevant issues dealt with by the EU Directives. This law forms the basis for a quite extensive executive regulation[3] that regulates certain issues individually and in more detail.

26.2 With an annual turnover of approximately €782 million in 2003, the Slovenian telecommunications market is one of the smallest in the EU, representing only 0.3 per cent of the total revenues in the EU. Electronic communications account for 3.2 per cent of Slovenian GDP. The general features of the Slovenian electronic communications market are quality service, low prices and high penetration. The market weaknesses are reflected primarily in the large differences in the market shares of operators, the small size of the market and the partial lack of interest in investment.[4]

In the market of fixed public telephone services, which is highly developed (49.5 connections per 100 residents and 98.7 connections per 100 households), 'Telekom Slovenije' is still the only provider. Competition is only present for international calls. 22 operators have been given the general authorisation to provide VoIP services. The market of mobile public radio services is also highly developed (90 connections per 100 residents) and there are currently three operators in this market. The leading operator has a 73% market share. The market of narrowband internet access is well developed (11.6 connections per 100 residents) and twelve operators are active in this market. The provision of broadband internet access is of very high quality and transmission rates are high. In the market of leased lines there are currently 18 providers.

---

1   Editing of this chapter closed on 1 June 2005.
2   Official Gazette of the Republic of Slovenia ('OG RS'), no 43/2004 and 86/2004.
3   Executive regulation means regulation by legislative instruments (mostly government regulations, minister's rules and regulator's general acts), which are based on the ECA.
4   See *APEK*, Annual report 2004, Ljubljana, February 2005, p 15, www.apek.si/.

Implementation of EU Directives

26.3   The Slovenian legislator enacted the ECA primarily with the purpose of implementing the EU Directives into Slovenian law. In general, the ECA consistently transposed the 2002 EU Regulatory Package.[5]

Legislation

26.4   The ECA entered into force on 1 May 2004 and replaced the previous Telecommunications Act.[6] Detailed regulation of certain issues is a matter of executive regulation (government regulations and minister's rules)[7] as well as of general acts of the Slovenian national regulatory authority (NRA).[8] Pursuant to the ECA, several executive legal acts have been adopted, concerning, *inter alia*, determination of relevant markets,[9] radio frequency bands allocation plan,[10] minimum set of leased lines,[11] use of the RDS system,[12] quality of universal services,[13] data transmission rates permitting functional internet access,[14] content and form of notification to the NRA,[15] transparency and the publication of information,[16] and radio frequencies that may be used without a decision on the assignment of radio frequencies.[17] Apart from that, a Regulation on right to the priority fixed telephone connection and a Regulation on the provision of non-discriminatory access to and use of public telephone services are currently in the procedure of adoption.

REGULATORY PRINCIPLES: IMPLEMENTATION OF THE FRAMEWORK DIRECTIVE

Scope of Regulation

26.5   The ECA follows the European model of creating a single legal framework for all transmission networks and, in that respect, replaced the term 'telecommunications' with the more neutral term 'electronic communications', which implicitly covers VoIP-services as well.

The definitions of 'electronic communications network', 'electronic communications service' and 'associated facilities'[18] are practically identical to those in the Framework Directive.

---

5   See para 26.4 below.
6   OG RS, no 30/2001, 110/2002 and 43/2004.
7   A regulation is based on law and may be adopted only by the government. Rules are based either on law or on a government regulation and may be adopted only by the competent minister. Both legislative instruments are designed for detailed regulation of certain issues.
8   A general act is a legal instrument by which the NRA may govern in greater detail issues arising in the implementation of individual provisions of the ECA (see art 117(4) ECA).
9   OG RS, no 77/2004.
10   OG RS, no 107/2004.
11   OG RS, no 96/2004.
12   OG RS, no 75/2004.
13   OG RS, no 110/2004.
14   OG RS, no 81/2004.
15   OG RS, no 81/2004.
16   OG RS, no 96/2004.
17   OG RS, no 45/2005.
18   Art 3(4) and (2) ECA.

National Regulatory Authorities: Organisation, Regulatory Objectives, Competencies

26.6   The only NRA in the field of electronic communications in Slovenia is the Post and Electronic Communications Agency ('APEK'), which is an autonomous legal entity under public law.

26.7   As regards the three main categories of APEK's objectives, as well as the secondary objectives and the measures for achieving them, the ECA is completely harmonised with the Framework Directive.[19] In addition, the ECA also obliges APEK to contribute within its competencies to the realisation of policies aimed at the promotion of cultural and linguistic diversity, as well as media pluralism.[20]

26.8   Whenever other state bodies are also competent regarding specific areas for which APEK is competent pursuant to the ECA, APEK and the other competent state bodies shall be obliged to cooperate and consult.[21]

The ECA also establishes specific rules for cooperation between APEK and the Slovenian competition regulator. APEK and the Competition Protection Office of the Republic of Slovenia shall provide each other with information necessary for the performance of their activities. They shall cooperate in analysing relevant markets and determining SMP, without interference with APEK's exclusive competence for making decisions in the field of electronic communications.[22]

26.9   With regard to the provision and publication of information, the ECA does not depart from the provisions of the Framework Directive. It does, however, define some purposes for which the information may be used by APEK, such as supervision of compliance with the provisions of the ECA, statistics, and market analysis.[23]

26.10   The public consultation procedure is regulated by the consumer rights chapter of the ECA.[24] The basic obligations of APEK and other state bodies with respect thereto are in complete accordance with the Framework Directive.[25] However, the ECA does not specify who is to be included among the 'interested public' that may cooperate in the consultation procedure.

26.11   The dispute resolution procedure extends not only to disputes between undertakings providing electronic communications networks or services but also to disputes between these undertakings and consumers.[26] The procedure may be initiated 'ex officio' or at the request of any of the parties to the dispute. In principle, the provisions of the General Administrative Procedure Act[27] shall apply. The decision shall be issued within 42 days after the initiation of the procedure, except in more complicated or extensive cases where the deadline for issuing a decision shall be four months. The decision shall be made available to the public.

The ECA also establishes rules for the resolution of cross-border disputes.[28]

---

19   Cf art 120(4), (5), (6) ECA and art 8 Framework Directive.
20   Art 120(2) ECA.
21   Art 123 ECA.
22   Art 124 ECA.
23   Art 126 ECA.
24   See art 95 ECA.
25   Cf art 6 Framework Directive.
26   Art 129(1) ECA.
27   OG RS, no 80/1999 with subsequent amendments.
28   Art 129(7) ECA; cf art 21 Framework Directive.

26.12   The parties to a dispute may, by written agreement, decide to resolve a specific or all possible disputes by mediation or arbitration.[29] For this purpose, the subjects in the electronic communications market (ie operators and users) may 'ad hoc' establish a special dispute resolution body. The arbitration procedure concludes with a decision that is legally binding and enforceable. There is no right of administrative appeal against the arbitration decision.

Right of Appeal against NRA's Decisions

26.13   Every decision or other individual act of APEK is adopted according to the General Administrative Procedure Act, unless provided otherwise.[30] There is no right of an administrative appeal against the decisions and other individual acts of APEK, which is why the decisions immediately become final in the administrative procedure.[31] The ECA does, however, provide for judicial protection against any final decision or individual act of APEK.[32] An action may be brought before the Administrative Court in Ljubljana. In spite of the fact that the procedures referring to the ECA shall be speedy and dealt with preferentially, which applies also to the appellate court,[33] this type of judicial protection is not always effective and the courts do not always have the required expertise.

26.14   The ECA does, however, provide for a right of administrative appeal against APEK's decisions concerning its supervision of the implementation of provisions of the ECA, general regulations and general acts, as well as its supervision of the execution of individual acts and measures.[34] The appeal is to be filed with the ministry in charge of electronic communications (Ministry of the Economy) within 15 days of the date of the decision. The decision of the ministry can be appealed in administrative proceedings before the Administrative Court in Ljubljana. As the ECA does not specify the natural or legal persons who are entitled to sue, the general rules of the Administrative Disputes Act[35] shall apply, according to which any person, who can show that his/her rights or legal interests have been aggrieved by the disputed decision, may sue.

The NRA's Obligations to Cooperate with the Commission

26.15   The ECA has fully implemented the provisions of the Framework Directive concerning the consolidation procedure.[36] The period for making comments to APEK according to article 7(3) Framework Directive shall correspond to the period for consultation of the interested public[37] and must not be shorter than 30 days.

---

29   The mediation and arbitration procedures are regulated in detail in arts 132–140 ECA.
30   See para 26.14 below.
31   Art 118(1) and (2) ECA.
32   Art 119 ECA. Individual acts of APEK are not only decisions, but also eg resolutions adopted in individual cases.
33   Art 119(3) ECA.
34   See art 146 ECA.
35   OG RS, no 50/1997 with subsequent amendments.
36   Cf art 7 Framework Directive and art 125 ECA.
37   See art 95 ECA.

26.16   As regards the veto procedure of the Commission and the possibility adopting provisional measures in certain exceptional circumstances, the ECA fully transposes the Framework Directive provisions as well.[38]

'Significant Market Power' as a Fundamental Prerequisite of Regulation

Definition of SMP

26.17   The ECA fully implements the definition of SMP from the Framework Directive.[39] In addition, it emphasises that two or more operators, operating in a market the structure of which is considered to be conducive to coordinated effects, may be treated as operators in a joint dominant position even in the absence of structural or other links between them.[40]

The criteria, which must, among others, be taken into account when assessing SMP, are in complete accordance with the Commission Guidelines on market analysis.[41] Besides, the ECA explicitly obliges APEK to act in accordance with EU legislation and to consistently take into account the Commission Guidelines on market analysis when assessing significant market power and using the above-mentioned criteria. In so doing, APEK shall cooperate with the Competition Protection Office.[42]

Definition of relevant markets

26.18   APEK defined relevant markets by adopting the General act on determination of relevant markets,[43] consistently taking into account the Commission Recommendation on relevant markets.[44] VoIP services have not been defined as a separate market and are covered by the existing voice telephony market.

Market analysis procedures must be carried out annually (or more often), in cooperation with the national competition authority, taking into account the Commission Guidelines on market analysis.[45]

If APEK adopts an act that differs from the recommendations of the European Commission it shall be obliged prior to doing so to implement public consultation and cooperation, and consultation with competent bodies of other member states of the EU and the European Commission.

26.19   As a part of the market analyses to be completed in 2005 pursuant to the ECA, APEK studied in detail the conditions in individual markets.[46] Based on the

---

38   Cf art 7(4), (5), (6) Framework Directive and art 125(4), (5), (6), (7) ECA.
39   Cf art 19(1)–(3) ECA and art 14 Framework Directive.
40   Art 19(2) ECA.
41   See art 19(4) and (5) ECA.
42   For details see also paras 1.72 and 1.73 above.
43   OG RS, no 77/2004.
44   See para 1.75 above.
45   See art 21(1), (2) ECA and para 1.72 above.
46   APEK began analysing the markets in 2004. The majority of analyses have not been performed yet (including analysis for market 12). Analysis of market 11 showed that the market is not competitive. The same applies to markets 15 and 16.

results obtained it will place certain obligations on operators with SMP, which shall result in increased competitiveness of the market.

On the basis of the previously valid Telecommunications Act, 'Telekom Slovenije' was designated as the operator with SMP in the market of fixed public telephone services and in the market of interconnection services through a fixed public telephone network. 'Si.mobil' and 'Mobitel' were assessed to have SMP in the market of mobile public radio services back in July 2003. In April 2004 APEK gave 'Telekom Slovenije' the status of SMP operator in the leased-line service segment, ordering it to publish prices for operator-leased lines within the sample offer for network interconnection.[47]

26.20   In accordance with the Framework Directive, APEK does not have any discretion in imposing regulatory obligations upon operators with SMP where it concludes that a certain market either is, or is not, effectively competitive.[48]

NRA's Regulatory Duties concerning Rights of Way, Co-location and Facility Sharing

Rights of way

26.21   The ECA regulates in detail the rights to install facilities on, over or under public or private property.[49] The construction, installation, operation and maintenance of public communications networks and associated infrastructure in accordance with regulations are in the public interest. Nevertheless, the public communications networks shall be planned so as to minimise encroachments on private property.

26.22   With respect to the rights of way, the ECA relates only to public electronic communications networks ('PECNs'), which means that only in cases of the construction, operation or maintenance of public communications networks may ownership rights and other real rights on real estate be deprived or restricted in the public interest.[50]

26.23   Rights of way shall be granted under the procedure and in the manner set out by the Spatial Planning Act[51] and by the Law of Property Code,[52] unless provided otherwise in the ECA. The matters concerning rights of way shall be regarded as 'urgent' within the meaning of article 104 Spatial Planning Act.

An undertaking operating public electronic communications networks and/or services ('operator') may either appear in the procedure as the expropriation beneficiary or propose the granting of a servitude.

26.24   A servitude encompasses several entitlements,[53] such as construction, installation and operation of electronic communications network and associated infrastructure, access to the network and infrastructure for purposes of operation

---

47   *APEK*, Annual report 2004, Ljubljana, February 2005, p 33, www.apek.si/.
48   Cf art 22(1), (5) ECA and art 16(3), (4) Framework Directive.
49   Arts 75–83 ECA.
50   Art 75(3) ECA.
51   OG RS, no 110/2002, 58/2003.
52   OG RS, no 87/2002.
53   See art 77 ECA.

and maintenance, and removal of natural obstacles during construction, installation, operation and maintenance of the network.

In order to establish a servitude, the interested operator must submit to the owner a proposed contract, which shall also contain a provision on appropriate monetary compensation. If the owner fails to agree within ten days of receipt of the proposed contract, the operator may propose that the competent administrative body (ie administrative unit)[54] decides on the establishment of the servitude. The parties may appeal against this decision to the Ministry of the Environment and Spatial Planning. After the decision becomes final, no further agreements are required.

Co-location and facility sharing

26.25   The ECA encourages co-location and facility sharing in accordance with the Framework Directive.[55] Where an operator of a public electronic communications network is deprived of access to useful alternatives and where no voluntary agreement is reached, APEK shall adopt a binding decision concerning the facility sharing.[56] The latter may be imposed only on the basis of a public consultation procedure, whereby all the interested parties may express their opinions.

REGULATION OF MARKET ENTRY: IMPLEMENTATION OF THE AUTHORISATION DIRECTIVE

The General Authorisation of Electronic Communications

26.26   Generally, no authorisation is required for the provision of electronic communications networks or services. An authorisation is required only for the use of radio spectrum and numbers.[57] However, a written notification, which must contain certain operator information, is required prior to the commencement of the provision of networks or services.[58]

Within seven days of the receipt of such a notification with all necessary data and evidence, APEK shall record the operator in the official records and at the same time send to the operator confirmation of receipt of notification and recording in the official records. Recording in official records shall not form a condition for the exercise of rights and obligations of operators under the ECA. The confirmation shall not be an administrative act and shall not in itself create rights and obligations under the ECA.[59]

The general authorisation does not affect the applicability of the provisions regarding operators having SMP or universal service providers. Such operators are determined through a decision by APEK.[60]

---

54   Administrative units are administrative bodies that perform tasks of the state administration on designated territories within the state.
55   Cf art 8 ECA and art 12(1) Framework Directive.
56   Art 8(4) ECA.
57   See paras 26.27 and 26.33 below.
58   For details see art 5 ECA.
59   Art 5(5) ECA.
60   See also paras 26.20 above and 26.51 below.

Rights of Use for Radio Frequencies

General authorisations and granting of individual rights

26.27   Notwithstanding the principle of general authorisation,[61] the use of radio frequencies is subject to the granting of individual rights.[62] A natural or legal person may use certain radio frequencies only on the basis of the prior authorisation (decision) of APEK. The decision shall be issued in accordance with APEK's General act on a plan of radio frequency usage.[63] In order to initiate the procedure, an application needs to be filed with APEK by the interested person.[64]

It shall not, however, be necessary to obtain such authorisation in cases where the relevant frequency is envisaged by the radio frequency utilisation plan (adopted by APEK in accordance with the Regulation on the radio frequency bands allocation plan)[65] for the purposes of national security, national defence or protection against natural and other disasters. The same applies to frequencies for which the competent minister prescribes that they may be used without prior decision of APEK.[66]

Admissible conditions

26.28   The decision of APEK must, inter alia, determine the conditions that must be fulfilled during the use of the radio frequencies. The set of possible conditions that may be imposed by APEK is in complete accordance with Annex B to the Authorisation Directive.[67]

26.29   The term of the assignment of a radio frequency may not exceed 15 years. There are also some exceptions to that rule providing for shorter maximum terms.[68] Extensions of the term, upon application by the rights holder, are permissible.

Licence holders are obliged to pay annual fees to APEK for the use of the radio frequencies assigned.[69] Except for the use of radio frequencies for performance of broadcasting, the use of radio frequencies that are assigned on the basis of a public tender is subject to an additional amount for the purpose of effective use of this scarce resource.

Limitation of number of rights of use to be granted

26.30   In cases where a person applies for radio frequencies for broadcasting and in cases where APEK establishes that effective use of a certain frequency might be

---

61   See para 26.26 above.
62   Art 35 ECA.
63   Art 36(1) ECA. As APEK has not yet adopted a new General act on a plan of radio frequency usage, the General act on a plan of radio frequency usage (OG RS, no 32/2002) shall remain applicable.
64   Art 37 ECA.
65   OG RS, no 107/2004.
66   Eg foreign radio amateurs may use without authorisation radio frequencies, which are allocated in Slovenia for radio amateur service and radio amateur satellite service, provided they have a valid radio amateur authorisation CEPT. See Rules on radio frequencies that may be used without a decision on the assignment of radio frequencies (OG RS, no 45/2005).
67   Art 49 ECA.
68   Art 50 ECA.
69   Art 56 ECA.

secured only by limiting the number of issued decisions, APEK shall adopt the decision on the basis of a public tender.[70]

If APEK considers that the interest in a particular radio frequency could exceed the availability and thereby prevent the efficient use thereof, it shall publish a public call to acquire the opinions of interested parties concerning the conditions of the use of such radio frequencies, particularly regarding the limitation of the number of holders of decisions on the assignment of radio frequencies. In cases where APEK, on the basis of the public consultation, establishes that certain frequencies will not be available to all interested persons, it shall, except in cases of broadcasting,[71] conduct a public tender procedure according to the provisions of the ECA. The public call, however, is obligatory if an interested party requests a public tender to be conducted. The public tender procedure shall be conducted by an impartial commission, appointed by the director of APEK.[72]

Frequency Trading

26.31   The ECA also establishes rules that allow for frequency trading. It provides that a licence holder may by way of legal transaction (ie contract) transfer his right to use the radio frequency to another natural or legal person that fulfils all the prescribed conditions.[73] The transfer is subject to prior consent of APEK.

Rights of Use for Numbers

26.32   All numbers to be used as a part of a public communications network are managed by APEK. It is APEK's responsibility to propose numbering plans, which are then adopted by the ministry in charge of electronic communications (Ministry of the Economy). The new numbering plan, which is currently in preparation, foresees separate area codes for non-geographic numbers for VoIP services. The use of geographic phone numbers, however, shall remain permissible for VoIP products.

26.33   Numbers are generally allocated through decisions of APEK in a regular administrative procedure, unless APEK establishes (using the same principles and procedures as in the case of radio frequencies) that a tender procedure is needed in order to ensure efficient use of certain numbers.[74] Only operators (ie persons under general authorisation) are entitled to apply for numbers and, in case of public tenders, only operators who will distribute the numbers to their users in a non-discriminatory, transparent and cost-based manner can apply.[75] Other persons are only entitled to apply for numbers if they can demonstrate that the numbers are needed in order to carry out activities which are in the public interest.[76]

26.34   The numbers allocated to an undertaking can be assigned to end-users of the undertaking or transferred to authorised dealers of the undertaking who can, in

---

70   Art 36(2) ECA. In the public tender procedure the interested parties shall submit bids in writing, the opening of which shall be public. The commission (see below) then evaluates the bids received and compiles a report presenting the evaluations of individual bids and stating which bid best meets the published selection criteria.
71   Art 36(3) ECA.
72   Art 39(2) ECA. The procedure is regulated in detail in arts 39–45 ECA.
73   Art 52 ECA.
74   See para 26.30 above.
75   Art 61 ECA.
76   Art 62(1) ECA.

turn, only assign such numbers to users of the same undertaking. The decision by which the numbers were allocated shall not be transferable and is issued for an indefinite period.[77]

26.35   The conditions that may be attached to rights of use for numbers correspond to those listed in Part C of the Annex to the Authorisation Directive.[78] No other conditions may be attached to rights of use for numbers.

26.36   All operators of publicly accessible telephone services (including mobile operators) must ensure number portability of geographic numbers at a precisely defined location and of non-geographic numbers at any location. This shall apply also to number transfer from PSTN to VoIP. Number portability from fixed to mobile networks or vice versa is not required. Only reasonable costs can be charged for requests for number transfers.[79] The obligations concerning number portability are imposed by law. An individual decision of APEK assigning numbers to the operators may, however, contain specific conditions regarding number portability.[80] On the other hand, carrier pre-selection obligations may only be imposed by the decision of APEK.[81]

The NRA's Enforcement Powers

26.37   If APEK establishes that an operator is in violation of the implementation of individual acts and/or measures adopted within the framework of the authorisations it has adopted under the ECA and the regulations pursuant thereto, it must notify the operator and request the violation to be remedied in a given period of time;[82] this period can be shorter than 30 days if it is a recurring violation.[83]

In case of violations APEK has the power to order proportionate and appropriate measures, to initiate misdemeanour proceedings, to initiate criminal proceedings, to recommend to the proper authorities adoption of other measures, to temporarily prohibit further performance of activities in case of serious and repeated violations, and to verify the accuracy of data supplied by the network or service providers.[84]

The procedure under ECA therefore properly implements the tiered procedure of article 10 Authorisation Directive.

26.38   Urgent interim measures (such as prohibition of the performance of activities, or seizure of items or documentation) are permissible under the conditions as set out by the article 10(6) Authorisation Directive and where a radio station transmits without a proper radio frequency decision.[85]

---

77   See arts 65 and 66 ECA.
78   See para 1.108 above.
79   Art 71 ECA.
80   Art 61(1) ECA.
81   See art 30 ECA.
82   The operator is also given the opportunity to state its view of the matter.
83   Art 141(2) ECA.
84   See arts 141 and 142 ECA.
85   Cf art 144 ECA.

Administrative Charges and Fees for Rights of Use

26.39 The general authorisation (notification)[86] carries with it the obligation for operators to pay administrative charges to APEK on an annual basis. The amount of the administrative charges depends on annual revenue of the operator and is intended to cover the operational costs of APEK, which are not related to the radio frequency operations and numbering operations of APEK.[87]

26.40 Operators who were granted the rights of use for radio frequencies or numbers are obliged to make additional payments to APEK. The level of the payments shall, in case of rights of use for radio frequencies, depend on the coverage, population density in the area of coverage, radio frequency, width of the radio frequency band, type of radio communication, or a combination thereof. In case of rights of use of numbers the level of payments shall depend on the quantity, length and type of numbers.

In addition, operators who have been granted the rights of use for radio frequencies or numbers through a public tender can be required to make additional payments directly into the budget of the Republic of Slovenia.[88]

Transitional Regulations for Existing Authorisations

26.41 In general, operators that were granted authorisations or have made notifications pursuant to the Telecommunications Act shall be deemed to have notified APEK[89] on the day of the entry into effect of the ECA.

The decisions on the allocation of radio frequencies issued pursuant to the Telecommunications Act shall apply until their expiry, and may be extended pursuant to the procedure laid down by the ECA. Decisions on the allocation of numbers issued pursuant to the Telecommunications Act shall remain valid and may be amended, revoked or expire under the conditions and in the manner laid down by the ECA.[90]

REGULATION OF NETWORK ACCESS AND INTERCONNECTION: IMPLEMENTATION OF THE ACCESS DIRECTIVE

Objectives and Scope of Access Regulation

26.42 The ECA very consistently transposed practically every provision of the Access Directive concerning access and interconnection.

26.43 The objectives of the access and interconnection regulation are in accordance with those set out in the Access Directive.[91] In principle, the basic obligations to facilitate the joint use of existing facilities of the communications network and to reach an agreement with other operators,[92] as well as the right and obligation to

---

86   See para 26.26 above.
87   Art 6 ECA.
88   See also para 26.29 above.
89   See para 26.26 above.
90   Art 160 ECA.
91   Art 2 ECA.
92   Art 8 ECA.

negotiate access and interconnection,[93] apply only to operators of public communications networks, regardless of whether they have SMP or not.[94]

Basic Regulatory Concepts

26.44   The definitions of access and interconnection[95] are identical to those established by the Access Directive.

The obligation of operators to negotiate amongst themselves agreements on technical and commercial arrangements refers not only to interconnection but also to access.[96] Only if, and to the extent that, no such agreement is reached, will APEK adopt a decision at the request of an interested party or 'ex officio' and pursuant to the provisions concerning its dispute resolution procedure.[97]

Access- and Interconnection-related Obligations with Respect to SMP Undertakings

26.45   With regard to access and interconnection, the ECA obliges APEK to impose on an SMP operator at least one of the following obligations: transparency; non-discrimination; accounting separation; access to, and use of, specific network facilities; price controls; and cost accounting.[98] It is completely up to APEK which obligations to impose. Imposition of the stated obligations is subject to a public consultation procedure and to consultation with the Slovenian competition authority. For the imposition of any other obligations that are not provided for in articles 23–30 ECA, prior consent of the European Commission is required.

As regards the above-mentioned access- and interconnection-related obligations, the ECA without exception consistently follows the provisions of the Access Directive.[99] With respect to price control, it is important to note that, according to the current Regulation on the methodology of formation of prices of public telecommunications services and networks ('Price Regulation'),[100] the SMP operators must obtain consent from APEK before they change their prices. However, according to the wording of the Price Regulation, this applies only to SMP operators of fixed public telephone networks and services and to SMP operators of leased lines.[101]

---

93   Art 9 ECA.
94   Cf art 4(1) Access Directive.
95   See art 3(24) and (18) ECA.
96   Art 9(1) ECA.
97   Art 9(4) ECA.
98   See arts 23–30 ECA.
99   Cf arts 23, 24, 25, 26, 27 ECA and arts 9, 10, 11, 12, 13 Access Directive.
100 OG RS, no 25/2002. The Government is currently preparing a regulation to repeal this regulation.
101 Art 1(1) Price Regulation.

Related Regulatory Powers with Respect to SMP Undertakings

26.46   Consistently with the Universal Service Directive, the ECA also empowers APEK to impose some other obligations, such as the provision of a minimum set of leased lines and the provision of carrier selection and carrier pre-selection.[102]

Regulatory Powers Applicable to All Market Participants

26.47   The ECA does not explicitly empower APEK to impose obligations on operators without SMP in terms of article 5(1) Access Directive. APEK may, however, by its own decision regulate technical and commercial issues of interconnection or access in which there is an absence of agreement between the parties.[103]

26.48   As regards digital radio and television broadcasting, the ECA is in complete accordance with the Access Directive.[104] APEK may also impose on an operator, regardless of its market power, an obligation to provide access to APIs and EPGs on fair, reasonable and non-discriminatory terms. APEK will prescribe by a general act the requirements for interoperability of digital television equipment used by consumers; such an act has not yet been adopted.

26.49   The provisions of ECA regarding the obligations relating to conditional access systems that may be imposed on an operator, regardless of its market power, and obligations concerning owners of industrial property rights, are in complete accordance with Access Directive and Annex I, Part I thereto.[105]

REGULATION OF UNIVERSAL SERVICES AND USERS' RIGHTS: THE UNIVERSAL SERVICE DIRECTIVE

Regulation of Universal Service Obligations

Scope of universal service obligations

26.50   The designated universal service provider must provide the minimum catalogue of universal services, which is identical to that under articles 4 to 7 Universal Service Directive.[106] Measures for disabled end users shall be defined by a government regulation,[107] which, however, has not been adopted yet.

The government may expand the catalogue of universal services if it establishes that such an expansion would be suitable due to development of electronic communications. The catalogue must be in line with the EU law.

Designation of undertakings obliged to provide universal services

26.51   One or more universal service providers are chosen in a tender procedure for five-year periods so that universal services are provided throughout the territory

---

102   Arts 28, 29, 30 ECA. See paras 1.173 et seq above. See also paras 26.56–26.58 below.
103   See para 26.44 above.
104   Cf art 113 ECA and arts 4(2), 5(1) sentence 2(b) Access Directive.
105   See art 114 ECA.
106   Cf art 11(2) ECA.
107   Art 11(2)4 ECA.

of Slovenia. If the tender procedure is not successful, the operator with SMP in the market of publicly accessible communications services at a fixed location is designated as the universal service provider; where there is no such operator, the operator having the greatest number of subscribers to publicly available telephone services at a fixed location is designated to be the universal service provider.[108]

In November 2004, APEK designated 'Telekom Slovenije' as the universal service provider for the entire Slovenian market.

Regulation of retail tariffs, users' expenditures and quality of service

26.52   APEK monitors the evolution and level of retail prices of universal services and may require that a universal service provider offers price options or bundled services for low income end-users or end-users with special needs, if it establishes that the prices are too high in comparison with the average monthly salary in Slovenia and that they are rising by more than five per cent faster than the living costs index per year.[109] The ministry shall determine the categories of end-users which are considered to be low-income end-users or end-users with special needs. APEK may require that a universal service provider offers itemised billing, selective call barring, pre-payment systems for the provision of access to the public telephone network and the use of publicly available telephone services and instalment plans for paying subscriptions to the public telephone network.[110] Prices must be set in such a manner that end-users are not required to pay for services which are not necessary or requested.[111]

26.53   Quality standards for universal services are defined by the Rules on the quality of universal services.[112] Universal service providers are required to publish data on universal services quality at least once a year.[113] If APEK suspects that the data published is not truthful, it may order 'ex officio' an independent audit or a review of the data on the quality of provision of universal service at the expense of the universal service provider concerned. If a universal service provider fails for three consecutive times to meet the quality requirements, APEK may initiate a procedure for a new universal service provider to be chosen.[114]

Cost calculation and financing of universal services

26.54   Universal service providers shall be entitled to compensation if the provision of the universal service causes them net costs.[115] The definition of net costs and the rules for calculation thereof follow those of the Universal Service Directive and are further defined by the General act on the net cost calculation method for the universal service,[116] in accordance with the Universal Service Directive.[117]

---

108   Art 13(1) and (2).
109   Art 14 ECA.
110   Art 14(6) ECA.
111   Art 14(5) ECA.
112   OG RS, no 110/2004.
113   Art 15(4) ECA.
114   Art 15(6) and (7).
115   Art 16(1) ECA. See also recitals 18 and 21 Universal Service Directive.
116   OG RS, no 81/2004.
117   See also paras 1.169 and 1.170 above.

Compensation for net costs of universal service provision shall be financed from the contributions of operators acting in the territory of the Republic of Slovenia which derive a revenue from public communications networks or services provision exceeding SIT 500 million (approximately €2 million).[118] The amounts of contributions are determined by APEK and must be paid directly to the universal service providers. Compensations for measures related to handicapped end-users or end-users with specific needs are financed by the ministry responsible for social affairs.

Regulation of Retail Markets

Prerequisites for the regulation of retail markets

26.55   Regulation of retail services is permissible only if, on the basis of market analyses, APEK determines that a relevant market intended for end users is insufficiently competitive and the obligations in articles 23 to 27 and 30 ECA would not achieve the objectives pursued by APEK.[119] Such regulation by APEK is not mandatory but at its discretion.

'Telekom Slovenije' was identified as the operator with SMP on retail markets.

Regulatory powers

26.56   Obligations that may be imposed by APEK with regard to regulation of retail services correspond to those set out in the Universal Service Directive.[120] The list of possible obligations is non-exhaustive.[121] No price and other controls have yet been imposed pursuant to the ECA.

26.57   APEK also imposes on the SMP operator in the leased lines market the obligation to provide the full minimum set of leased lines or only part thereof under equal, cost-oriented and transparent conditions, as defined by the EU legislation.[122]

26.58   APEK shall impose on SMP operators in the area of provision of connection to and use of the public telephone network at a fixed location the obligation to enable their subscribers to access the services of any interconnected operator of publicly available telephone services by means of carrier (pre-)selection.[123]

---

118   Art 17(1) ECA.
119   Art 28(2) ECA.
120   Cf art 28(2) ECA and art 17(2) Universal Service Directive.
121   See also para 1.174 above.
122   Art 29 ECA.
123   Art 30 ECA. Cf art 19 Universal Service Directive.

End User Rights

Contracts

26.59   Providers of public telephone networks are required to enter into contracts with end-users (not only with consumers) upon their request.[124] The contract must contain the so-called minimum terms as provided for in article 20(2) Universal Service Directive.[125]

End-users have to be informed at least 30 days in advance of proposed modifications in contractual obligations and can within another 30 days withdraw from their contract without notice and without penalties.[126]

Grounds on which operators can terminate contracts with end-users are limited to non-payment of end-user obligations and failure to perform other duties of end-users.[127]

Transparency obligations

26.60   Transparent information on tariffs and prices, access conditions and terms of use of publicly available telephone services must be published. Which information is to be published by the operators and which by APEK is defined in the General act on transparency and the publication of information.[128]

APEK may require operators of public communications services to publish comparable, adequate and up-to-date information on the quality of their services. Before publishing, operators must submit this information to APEK.[129]

Other obligations

26.61   Operators providing publicly available telephone services at fixed locations must adopt a plan of measures providing for the integrity of the public telephone network and for access to the public telephone network and services in case of network failure, war or natural disasters.[130]

End-users are entitled to the following additional rights:[131]

- the right to emergency calls free of charge (applicable also to VoIP),
- the right to be entered in the universal directory and to access the universal directory service and directory services in other member states,
- the right to receive call assistance,
- the right to have the bill for publicly accessible telephone services itemised, and
- the right of appeal against a decision or act of an operator regarding access to services or performance to an authority within the operator.

---

124   Art 85 ECA.
125   Cf art 85(1) ECA.
126   Art 85(3) ECA.
127   For details see art 94 ECA.
128   OG RS, no 96/2004.
129   Art 86(1) ECA.
130   Art 96 ECA. See also arts 97 et seq ECA.
131   See art 72 and arts 89 et seq ECA.

DATA PROTECTION: IMPLEMENTATION OF THE DIRECTIVE ON PRIVACY AND ELECTRONIC COMMUNICATIONS

Confidentiality of Communications

26.62   The ECA fully transposes article 4 E-Privacy Directive.[132] With regard to confidentiality, the operator and all persons participating in the provision of their activities shall be obliged to protect the confidentiality of communications even after ceasing to perform the activities in which they were obliged to protect such confidentiality. They may obtain information on communications only to the extent essential for the provision of specific public communications services, and may use or provide to others such information only for the provision of such services.[133] All forms of surveillance or interception of communications shall be prohibited, unless explicitly permitted.[134]

26.63   Generally, all exceptions to the prohibition on surveillance or interception of communications (lawful interception of communications upon receipt of a copy of the order of the competent body (ie court), conveyance of a message, provision of evidence of a commercial transaction) are regulated in accordance with the E-Privacy Directive.[135] Surveillance or interception shall, however, also be permitted if operators need to obtain information on the content of communications, or copy or store communications and related traffic data, whereby they shall be obliged to inform the user, and to erase the information on the content of communications or the communication as soon as technically feasible and no longer required for the provision of the specific public communications service.[136] Such exception seems to be too wide to provide a proper implementation of the E-Privacy Directive for two reasons: (1) the purposes of (the need for) obtaining such information are not further defined; and (2) only information to the user is required and not his consent, as explicitly provided for in article 5(1) E-Privacy Directive.

Recording of communications is permitted in accordance with article 5(2) E-Privacy Directive and also within organisations receiving emergency calls, for their registration, identification and resolution.[137]

26.64   Exceptions as to the storage of, and access to, the information stored in the terminal equipment of a subscriber or user are defined in complete accordance with the E-Privacy Directive.[138]

Traffic Data and Location Data

26.65   The definitions of location and traffic data are identical to those in the E-Privacy Directive.[139]

---

132   Cf art 102 ECA.
133   Art 103 ECA.
134   See para 26.63 below.
135   Cf art 103(5), (7) and art 5(1), (2) E-Privacy Directive
136   Art 103(4) ECA.
137   Cf art 103(7) ECA.
138   Cf art 5(3) E-Privacy Directive and art 103(8) and (9) ECA.
139   Cf art 3(17), (25) ECA and art 2(b), (c) E-Privacy Directive.

26.66   The conditions for the processing of traffic data, including the consent requirements, are set out in complete accordance with the E-Privacy Directive.[140] The same applies to location data other than traffic data.[141]

Itemised Billing

26.67   All end users of publicly available telephone services must have access to a level of itemised billing that enables them to verify and control their use and the sum charged. The basic level of itemised billing shall be sent free of charge to subscribers and on the issuing of each bill. All higher levels of itemised billing offered by the operator must be defined in the operator's general terms and conditions. The subscriber has the right to inform the operator that he or she does not wish to receive itemised bills.[142]

Calling and Connected Line Identification

26.68   The obligations of service providers are defined in complete accordance with article 8 E-Privacy Directive.[143] Operators providing public communications services shall be obliged in their general conditions to publish the possibility of presentation and prevention of calling and connected line identification.[144]

Operators shall be obliged to override the calling user's possibility of preventing calling line identification for emergency calls.[145]

If a subscriber requests in writing that the operator trace malicious or nuisance calls, the operator may temporarily record the origin of all calls ending in the network termination point of such subscriber, including those for which prevention of calling line identification has been requested.[146]

Automatic Call Forwarding

26.69   ECA explicitly provides for that subscribers must have the possibility, using simple means and free of charge, of stopping automatic call forwarding by a third party to the subscriber's terminal.[147]

Directories of Subscribers

26.70   As regards the rights of subscribers with respect to the inclusion of their personal data in directories, provisions of ECA are consistent with the E-Privacy Directive.[148] These provisions apply also to legal entities.[149]

---

140   Cf art 104 ECA and art 6 E-Privacy Directive.
141   Cf art 106 ECA and art 9 E-Privacy Directive.
142   Art 91 ECA.
143   See art 105(1), (3), (4), (5) and (6) ECA.
144   Art 105(9) ECA.
145   Art 105(2) in conjunction with art 105(1) ECA; cf art 10(b) E-Privacy Directive.
146   See art 105(7) ECA and art. 105(8) ECA. Cf art 10(a) E-Privacy Directive.
147   Art 108(1) ECA.
148   Cf art 111 ECA and art 12 E-Privacy Directive.
149   See the definition of a subscriber in art 3(20) ECA.

Unsolicited Communications

26.71   The ECA also contains provisions on unsolicited communications, which are entirely harmonised with the E-Privacy Directive.[150] The use of means for direct marketing using electronic communications other than automated calling systems for making calls to the subscribers' telephone numbers without human intervention, facsimile machines or electronic mail, shall be permitted only with the consent of the subscriber.

---

150   Cf art 109 ECA and art 13 E-Privacy Directive.

The Spanish Market For Electronic Communications[1]

Maite Díez and José Antonio de la Calle
Baker & McKenzie, Madrid

LEGAL STRUCTURE

Basic Policy

27.1 The second wave of liberalisation seems to have reached the shores of the Spanish telecommunications market just in time. Although the sector has gone through difficult times and its medium-term expectations are far from clear, the Spanish Telecommunications Market Commission (*Comisión del Mercado de las Telecomunicaciones* – 'CMT') believes that operators based in Spain are better prepared to benefit from the forthcoming economic tide than the majority of its EU counterparts. The reasons for this relative confidence appear to be twofold: on the one hand, expenditures by operators have been relatively less significant in Spain than in the rest of the EU; and, on the other hand, the potential growth of the telecommunications market is still higher in Spain than in economically comparable EU countries.[2] Moreover, the main players have already undertaken significant efforts to readjust their size and intend to grow by focusing only on their core business areas.[3]

27.2 In line with the above, the objectives pursued by the Spanish policymakers have also shifted. While the old set of rules was simply aimed at opening the telecommunications market for competition and promoting conditions to favour such competition among operators,[4] the new legislative package is meant to strengthen these objectives while introducing innovative corrective mechanisms, securing:

- the presence and viability of operators,

---

1   Editing of this chapter closed on 24 June 2005. The authors would like to express their gratitude to Kate White for her assistance in drafting this chapter and Norman Heckh for preparing the data protection section.

2   See the 2002 CMT Annual Report: www.cmt.es/cmt/centro_info/publicaciones/index.htm.

3   By way of an example of this trend, Spanish operators seem to be more interested in reaching business alliances with, for instance, content providers than acquiring stakes in such companies (see the 2003 CMT Annual Report at the above internet address).

4   By encouraging the development and the utilisation of new networks and IT services while supporting social and territorial cohesiveness through equal access to such networks and IT services.

- the protection of users' rights,
- minimum State intervention in the sector, and
- the Government's supervision of areas related to public services, the public domain and the safeguarding of competition.

Implementation of EU Directives

27.3 On 4 November 2003 (ie three months later than the specified period imposed by EU law), the Framework, Authorisation, Universal Service and Access Directives[5] were transposed into Spanish law by the Spanish Congress through a new comprehensive Telecommunications Act 32/2003 ('Telecoms Act').[6] The Telecoms Act superseded the General Telecommunications Act of 1998 ('Old Telecoms Act')[7] with the aim of implementing the new regulatory framework for electronic communications networks and services in Spain.

Legislation

27.4 Since the Telecoms Act has been drafted in very broad terms, the specific rights and obligations of the operators are described in detail in its implementing regulations, among which Royal Decrees 2296/2004 approving the regulation on electronic communications markets, access to networks and numbering ('Access and Numbering Regulation')[8] and 424/2005 approving the requirements to provide electronic communication services and universal services and to protect users ('Universal Service and Users Regulation')[9] are arguably the most significant.

27.5 Whereas the Access and Numbering Regulation deals, inter alia, with numbering resources, the assessment of electronic communications markets, the duties of operators with significant market power ('SMP') and the manner in which interconnection and access to electronic communications public networks may be obtained,[10] the Universal Service and Users Regulation focuses, among other things, on the universal service, the protection of personal data and the rights of end users of electronic communications services.

27.6 In addition to the Telecoms Act and its implementing regulations, the CMT frequently issues instructions (*resoluciones*) with regard to the matters subject to its control[11] to operators providing electronic communications services. These instructions – which are binding once they have been issued and, if applicable, published in the Spanish Official Journal – are often an excellent source of background regulatory information.

---

5   The Telecoms Act also transposed the sections of the E-Privacy Directive which were relevant to the electronic communications networks and services.
6   Telecommunications Act 32/2003 of 3 November 2003, Spanish Official Journal No 264 of 4 November 2003.
7   Telecommunications Act 11/1998 of 24 April 1998, Spanish Official Journal No 99 of 25 April 1998.
8   Royal Decree 2296/2004 of 10 December 2004, Spanish Official Journal No 314 of 30 December 2004.
9   Royal Decree 424/2005 of 15 April 2005, Spanish Official Journal N0 102 of 29 April 2005.
10   Art 1 Access and Numbering Regulation.
11   See paras 27.15 et seq below. CMT instructions may be accessed online at the following website: www.cmt.es/cmt/decisiones/materia.htm.

27.7   Apart from the instructions issued in connection with a particular matter, the CMT also issues guidelines of a general nature (*circulares*)[12] – which must always be published in the Spanish Official Journal – for the purposes of ensuring the diversity of operators in the market in accordance with article 1(2)(2)(f) Telecommunications Liberalisation Act.[13]

REGULATORY PRINCIPLES: IMPLEMENTATION OF THE FRAMEWORK DIRECTIVE

Scope of Regulation

27.8   The purpose of the Telecoms Act is to set out the principles governing the 'telecommunications'[14] business – which comprises the operation of networks and the provision of electronic communications services and their associated resources – in accordance with article 149(1)(21) Spanish Constitution.[15]

27.9   The following areas are excluded from the scope of the Telecoms Act and its implementing regulations:

- the regime applicable to broadcasting through electronic communications networks,
- the legal framework governing the media,[16] and
- the following activities already regulated under the 2002 Act on Information Society and Electronic Commerce[17] ('Electronic Commerce Act'):
    - information services transmitted through electronic communications networks and services,
    - the editorial management of such information, and
    - any other 'information society service',[18]

    provided that such activities do not entail, entirely or primarily, the transmission of signals through electronic communications.

---

12   The general guidelines issued by the CMT are publicly available at the following website: www.cmt.es/cmt/circulares/index.htm.

13   Act 12/1997 of 24 April 1997 on the Liberalisation of Telecommunications, Spanish Official Journal No 99 of 25 April 1997.

14   The term 'telecommunications' is defined in Annex II (Definitions) of the Telecoms Act as 'any transmission, emission or reception of signs, signals, writing, images, sounds or information of any nature by wire, radio electricity, optical media or other electromagnetic systems'.

15   Art 149(1)(21) Spanish Constitution provides that the national administration (as opposed to the 17 regional administrations into which Spain is divided) has exclusive powers over the general regime of communications, post offices and telecommunications, terrestrial and submarine cables and radio spectrum.

16   Art 149(1)(27) Spanish Constitution vests the National Administration with exclusive faculties in regulating the basic broadcasting framework (ie press, radio and television and, broadly speaking, any broadcasting media having an impact on Spanish society), notwithstanding the implementation and enforcement powers held by the Autonomous Communities.

17   Act 34/2002 of 11 July 2002 on Information Society and Electronic Commerce, Spanish Official Journal No 166 of 12 July 2002.

18   See para 27.10 below.

27.10   Pursuant to the Electronic Commerce Act, the term 'information society service' means 'any service normally provided for remuneration, at a distance, by electronic means and at the individual request of a recipient of services'. For the purposes of this definition:[19]

- 'at a distance' means that the service is provided without the parties being simultaneously present,
- 'by electronic means' means that the service is sent initially and received at its destination by means of electronic equipment for the processing (including digital compression) and storage of data, and entirely transmitted, conveyed and received by wire, by radio, by optical means or by other electromagnetic means, and
- 'at the individual request of a recipient of services' means that the service is provided through the transmission of data on individual request.

27.11   The terms 'electronic communications network', 'electronic communications service' and 'associated facilities', which are defined in Annex II to the Telecoms Act, follow word for word the definitions under article 2(a), (c) and (e) Framework Directive.[20]

National Regulatory Authorities: Organisation, Regulatory Objectives, Competencies

Overview

27.12   The Spanish Regulatory Authorities are the following:[21]

- the Government,
- the CMT,
- the newly created National Radio Spectrum Agency (*Agencia Estatal de Radiocomunicaciones* – 'AER'),
- the Ministry of Industry, Trade and Tourism (*Ministerio de Industria, Turismo y Comercio* – the 'Ministry'), and
- the Ministry of Economy.

The Government

27.13   The Government[22] is entitled to delegate the powers conferred by the Telecoms Act on the Ministry, the CMT, the AER and the Ministry of Economy at any time, as well as to provide them with the assets, personnel and financial resources that are deemed necessary or convenient so that they can achieve their objectives. Among the financial resources, the Government is particularly entitled to allocate charges in accordance with the terms laid down under the Telecoms Act.[23]

---

19   Cf Directive 98/48/EC of the European Parliament and of the Council of 20 July 1998 amending Directive 98/34/EC laying down a procedure for the provision of information in the field of technical standards and regulations, OJ L 217/18, 05.08.1998.
20   See paras 1.48 et seq above.
21   Art 46 Telecoms Act.
22   The Spanish Government website is the following: www.la-moncloa.es/.
23   See paras 27.89 et seq below.

The CMT

27.14   The CMT[24] is a 'public agency' (*organismo público*), as this term is defined in 10th additional provision, article 1, Act 6/1997 of 14 April 1997 (the 'Spanish Administration Act).[25] As such, the CMT has legal personality and full capacity to act.

27.15   The purposes of the CMT are essentially threefold:

- to establish and supervise the specific obligations that must be complied with by operators,
- to encourage competition in the markets of broadcasting services (in accordance with their specific regulations), and
- to settle disputes between operators, acting as an arbitration body in disputes between them at the request of any of the interested parties or, alternatively, on its own initiative (when this is justifiable in order to encourage and, if applicable, guarantee the access, interconnection and interoperability of the services).[26]

27.16   The CMT reports directly to the Ministry through the Ministry's Secretary of State for Telecommunications and the Information Society (*Secretaría de Estado de Telecomunicaciones y para la Sociedad de la Información* – 'SETSI'),[27] the SETSI serving as a link between the CMT and the Ministry.

27.17   In exercising its powers, the CMT is limited by the provisions of the Telecoms Act and its implementing provisions, the Act 30/1992 of 26 November 1992 (the 'Spanish Administrative Procedural Act')[28] and the Spanish Administration Act.

27.18   The major powers entrusted to the CMT are the following:

- to arbitrate in disputes arising between operators, when so agreed by the interested parties,[29]
- to allocate numbers to operators,[30]
- to exercise the functions regarding the universal service and its financing,[31]
- to settle conflicts that may arise between operators on matters of network access and interconnection, as well as those matters related to phone directories, the financing of the universal service and the shared use of infrastructures,
- to adopt the necessary measures to safeguard the diversity of service offers,

---

24   The CMT website is an excellent source of updated information on the Spanish telecommunications market: www.cmt.es.
25   Act 6/1997 of 14 April 1997 on the Structure and Management of the Spanish Administration (Spanish Official Journal No 90 of 15 April 1997).
26   Art 11(4) Telecoms Act.
27   The SETSI website is: www.setsi.mcyt.es.
28   Act 30/1992 of 26 November 1992 on the Legal Regime for Public Authorities and the Common Administrative Procedure, Spanish Official Journal No 285 of 27 November 1992.
29   Once the relevant arbitration proceedings have been initiated, the CMT may at any time – by the powers vested in it or upon request of the interested parties – adopt the preventative measures it deems appropriate to ensure the effectiveness of the arbitration award or decision made, should there be sufficient legal grounds for it.
30   See paras 27.66 et seq below.
31   See paras 27.129 et seq below.

access to electronic communications networks by operators, the interconnection and operation of networks (on the basis of the open network test), and operators' pricing and marketing policies,

- to define the relevant telecommunications markets,[32]
- to initiate inspections at its own initiative in those matters for which it has sanctioning powers, requesting the AER's involvement where deemed necessary, and
- to exercise the sanctioning powers in accordance with the terms set out in the Telecoms Act.[33]

27.19   The CMT is governed by a council composed of a chairman, a vice-chairman and seven directors appointed directly by the Government from among individuals of recognised professional experience in the telecommunications sector and other regulated markets.

27.20   The positions of chairman, vice-chairman and directors must be renewed every six years, and those that were originally appointed may be re-elected only once.

27.21   The CMT must draw up an annual report on the development of the telecommunications and broadcasting markets[34] that must be lodged with the Government for its subsequent submission to the Spanish Parliament.

27.22   The CMT's financial resources are essentially threefold:

- the assets and securities constituting its net worth,
- the earnings obtained from those charges collected in payment for the services rendered, as well as those resulting from the exercise of the powers and functions,[35] and
- the transfers of resources made available by the Ministry.

The AER

27.23   The AER has been created to manage the spectrum in accordance with the guidelines laid down by the Ministry. The AER – an 'autonomous agency' (*organismo autónomo*) pursuant to article 43(1)(a) Spanish Administration Act – is vested with separate legal personality and full capacity to act. In the exercise of its authority, the AER must act in accordance with the provisions laid down in the Spanish Administrative Procedural Act.

27.24   The AER reports, through the SETSI, to the Ministry, which is ultimately in charge of organising its overall strategy, while assessing and controlling the outcome of its activities.

---

32   See paras 27.36 et seq below.
33   In the proceedings initiated as a result of the complaint made by the Ministry, the CMT – prior to issuing a decision – must submit the case to the Ministry, which will issue a report on the case. The grounds for the CMT decision must be stated if they differ from the Ministry's report.
34   In practice, this annual report reflects all the activities of the CMT, its observations, comments and suggestions on the performance of the market, compliance with the terms of free competition and the measures to correct any deficiency detected.
35   See paras 27.89 et seq below.

27.25   In order to meet the regulatory objectives,[36] the major functions entrusted to AER are the following:

- advising on the planning, management and administration of the Spanish radio spectrum, as well as the processing and granting of 'administrative permits' (*títulos habilitantes*) for its use, except for those cases where the number of administrative permits is limited by the Ministry,[37]
- monitoring and inspecting the telecommunications sector,[38]
- allocating satellite orbit-spectrum resources, and
- managing the radio spectrum reservation fee and certain telecommunications charges.[39]

27.26   The AER's economic resources are listed in article 65(1) Spanish Administration Act:

- assets and securities constituting its net worth,
- products and earnings of the above assets and securities,
- resources made available by the Government through the national budget,
- transfers of resources made by other public entities,
- ordinary and extraordinary earnings,
- donations, contributions and similar resources, and
- any other resources that may eventually be transferred.

27.27   In addition to the above, the AER's economic resources include any other resources that – in accordance with the provisions of the Telecoms Act – are contributed by the CMT, as well as those charges related to the rendering of services entrusted to the AER.[40]

The Ministry

27.28   The Ministry is in charge of proposing to the Government the policies which, in its view, will strengthen the Spanish telecommunications market and of implementing these policies.[41] Moreover, the Ministry assumes the overall supervision and monitoring powers of the public service obligations to be complied with by the different electronic communications networks and services operators, without prejudice to the powers that the Telecoms Act bestows on the CMT with regard to the universal service. Furthermore, the powers which are not assigned to the CMT in accordance with the provisions of the Telecoms Act, and those faculties concerning the assessment of telecommunications equipment and the management of radio spectrum not expressly granted to the AER, are handled directly by the Ministry.[42]

---

36   See para 27.23 above.
37   See para 27.60 below.
38   The Ministry and the CMT may even entrust the AER with the power to carry out their own inspections.
39   The latter are also collected by the AER.
40   See para 27.25 above.
41   Much useful information regarding these policies may be found on SETSI's website: www.set-si.min.es.
42   Art 46(2) Telecoms Act.

Right of Appeal against NRA's Decisions

27.29   All provisions, decisions and instructions adopted by the CMT or the Ministry in the exercise of their respective public functions bring to a close the administrative proceedings and may be appealed before the Spanish administrative courts (*jurisdicción contencioso-administrativa*).

27.30   Moreover, the arbitration awards passed by the CMT in the exercise of its arbitration functions in accordance with the Arbitration Act 60/2003 (the 'Arbitration Act')[43] may be reviewed, annulled or enforced by the civil courts (*jurisdicción civil*) in accordance with the provisions established in the Arbitration Act.[44]

The NRA's Obligations to Cooperate with the Commission

27.31   Pursuant to article 10 Telecoms Act the CMT must take into account the Commission Guidelines on market analysis, as well as the Commission Recommendation on relevant markets.[45]

27.32   The CMT must also encourage the use of the technical standards and specifications identified in the document drafted by the European Commission for this purpose. These standards will be published in the Spanish Official Journal when their use has been declared mandatory to secure the interoperability of services and increase the freedom of choice of users. In the absence of the afore-mentioned regulations, the CMT must encourage the application of regulations, specifications or recommendations approved by European agencies or, in the absence of the latter, by international standardisation organisations.[46]

27.33   In addition to the above, the governmental procedures for fixing tolerable levels of radio emissions (ie not triggering public health hazards) must follow the limits and recommendations of the European Commission, which in any event must be respected by all other public authorities, at both regional and local levels.[47]

'Significant Market Power' as a Fundamental Prerequisite of Regulation

Definition of SMP

27.34   The Telecoms Act defines the term 'SMP operator' as an 'operator that, individually or jointly with other operators, enjoys a dominant position, ie a position of economic strength allowing it to act, to a notable extent, independently from competitors, clients and, ultimately, individual consumers'.[48]

27.35   Pursuant to article 3(3) Access and Numbering Regulation, the CMT may determine the existence of a 'collective dominant position' where – once it has

---

43   Arbitration Act 60/2003 of 23 December 2003, Spanish Official Journal No 309 of 26 December 2003.

44   The Telecoms Act actually refers to the Arbitration Act 36/1988 of 5 December 1988 (Spanish Official Journal No 293 of 7 December 1998), but this Act was superseded on 26 December 2003 by the new Arbitration Act 60/2003 of 23 December 2003.

45   See para 1.72 above.

46   Art 15 Telecoms Act.

47   Art 44(1)(a) Telecoms Act.

48   Cf Annex II Telecoms Act.

assessed the specific characteristics of a given market[49] – certain links favouring the market coordination between operators (but not necessarily corporate links) are deemed to exist.

Definition of relevant markets and SMP designation

27.36   The CMT is in charge of defining the relevant electronic communications networks and services markets[50] in accordance with certain faculties exercised prior to the entry into force of the Telecoms Act. The CMT must also assess their geographic scope, which is a key factor in determining the specific obligations (remedies) to be imposed on the relevant operators,[51] and take into account in its assessment both the Commission guidelines on market analysis and the Commission Recommendation on relevant markets.[52]

27.37   The purpose of the market analysis is to determine if the different markets are being developed within an environment of effective competition. Should this not be the case, the CMT will identify and disclose the SMP operators of the market in question. Where the CMT identifies that a specific market lacks an 'environment of effective competition', it may impose, maintain or amend certain specific obligations on SMP operators (eg specific duties on transparency, non-discrimination, access and interconnection, prices, and accounting).[53] When imposing such obligations, the CMT must give preference to measures related to access, interconnection, selection and pre-selection rather than those with greater impact on free competition. Furthermore, these specific obligations must be based on the nature of the identified issues, and must be proportionate and justifiable (eg they may only remain in force for the period of time deemed strictly necessary).

27.38   When imposing specific remedies, the particular conditions of newly expanding markets will have to be taken into consideration. Once effective competition in a given relevant market has been established, the CMT must withdraw those specific obligations that may have been imposed on SMP operators.

27.39   At the time of preparing this chapter, the CMT has not yet adopted a definitive position on which are the relevant markets to be considered in Spain. This does not mean that the CMT is not steadily working to reach such a position soon. As a matter of fact, five preliminary (but comprehensive) reports identifying and analysing certain electronic communications markets for purposes of assessing potential competition issues have already been published.[54] The services markets described in these reports are the following:

- retail direct access to the public telephony network from a fixed location,
- access to and traffic within data networks through a fixed permanent connection,

---

49   Eg market shares of the operators, level of transparency, degree of maturity.

50   Every two years, by means of a decision published in the Spanish Official Journal.

51   This analysis will be carried out subsequent to a report which will have to be drawn up by the SDC (at the time of preparing this chapter, the SDC report has not yet been issued).

52   See para 1.72 above.

53   The nature and scope of these specific obligations to be imposed on SMP operators are comprehensively described in the Regulation governing, among other things, the electronic communications networks and services, relevant markets and the obligations to be imposed on SMP operators.

54   These four preliminary reports, which are extremely detailed, are available online at the following CMT web page: www.cmt.es/cmt/centro_info/c_publica/index.htm.

- access to and traffic within data networks through a mobile connection,
- traffic from fixed locations, and
- transmission of radio and television signals.

27.40   Prior to the implementation of the 2002 EU Regulatory Package, the CMT adopted its resolution MTZ 2001/4975 of 4 October 2001, whereby the 'dominant operators' in Spain are currently Telefónica de España (in the fixed telephony, lease lines and interconnection markets), its wholly owned subsidiary Telefónica Móviles (in both the mobile and the mobile interconnection markets), and Amena and Vodafone (also in the mobile and the mobile interconnection markets). Pursuant to the 2nd transitional provision of the Access and Numbering Regulation, these relevant markets, the dominant operators therein and their respective obligations will be enforceable until new relevant markets have been defined.[55]

NRA's Regulatory Duties concerning Rights of Way, Co-location and Facility Sharing

Rights of way

RIGHTS OF WAY OVER PRIVATE PROPERTY

27.41   Operators awarded with an 'electronic communications authorisation'[56] enjoy generic rights of way to the extent that such rights are necessary to set up and maintain a public electronic communications network. An operator may only be granted a right of way over private property when – assessing its technical proposal – the competent authority[57] considers that two requirements are met:[58]

- necessity (the right of way must be deemed necessary for the installation of the relevant network), and
- absence of viable economic alternatives.

27.42   In practice, the approval of the relevant 'technical proposal' will include a reference to the right of way granted. Prior to the approval of this 'technical proposal', a report will be requested from the competent Autonomous Community (ie the regional government where the infrastructure is to be installed), which must be issued within a maximum period of 15 days following the date it was requested.[59]

27.43   Rights of way over private property will be effected either through:[60]

- the 'compulsory purchase' (*expropiación forzosa*) of such private property or by creating a legal burden on such private property, or

---

55   See paras 27.36 et seq above.
56   Cf paras 27.52 et seq below.
57   Generally the CMT but, in cases where the number of administrative licences has been limited, it will be the Ministry.
58   Art 26(1) Telecoms Act.
59   However, this period may be extended by up to two months at the request of the Autonomous Community concerned when the proposal affects a significant geographic area: art 27(3) Telecoms Act.
60   Art 27(1) Telecoms Act.

- the declaration of a compulsory 'easement of access' (*servidumbre forzosa de paso*) for the concerned electronic communications networks and services infrastructure.[61]

27.44   In either case the relevant operators will be treated as beneficiaries in the pertinent administrative proceedings.

27.45   In cases of expropriation of private property for the installation of public electronic networks where operators are subject to universal service obligations, a fast-track procedure established under the old Expropriation Act (*Ley de Expropiación Forzosa*)[62] will apply when so stated in the decision of the competent department of the Spanish Administration approving the technical proposal concerned.[63]

RIGHTS OF WAY OVER PUBLIC PROPERTY

27.46   Authorisations granting rights of way over public property must comply with any specific regulations applicable to the management of the public property concerned, and any regulations issued by the title holder on matters relating to the protection and management of such public property (eg local regulations issued by a town hall).

27.47   Once the generic rights of use have been granted, the operator needs to obtain specific authorisations from the town halls to use public domain resources located within their boundaries. These specific authorisations for using the public domain resources of the municipalities ('Municipality Licences') – which will be granted in accordance with the provisions of Royal Legislative Decree 2/2004 on the Income of Municipalities[64] – will take into account both the afore-mentioned 'technical proposal' and the applicable regulations of the local zoning plans.

27.48   In practice, the specific terms of these Municipality Licences are negotiated with the town halls, which frequently require ancillary burdens (eg, works not strictly necessary). In addition, Municipality Licences are subject to an annual tax payable to the relevant town hall and may be subject to a one-time tax on works (these taxes may be substantial).

27.49   Operators benefiting from the rights of way over private or public property must comply with the specific administrative regulations passed by the Administration which at any level (national, regional or local) has powers in the areas of environment, public health, public security, national defence, and/or town and territorial taxation. More particularly, when granting rights to use public or private property,[65] the relevant authorities may impose on the operator conditions relating to:

- compliance with environmental regulations,
- compliance with zoning plans and local zoning regulations,

---

61   A declaration which creates a 'legal burden' on the concerned plot of land.
62   Expropriation Act of 16 December 1954, Spanish Official Journal No 351 of 17 December 1954.
63   Art 27(4) Telecoms Act.
64   Royal Legislative Decree 2/2004 of 5 March 2004 on the Income of Municipalities, Spanish Official Journal No 63 of 13 March 2004.
65   In the absence of generic rights of use of public domain, it may be difficult to obtain from the town halls the Municipality Licences required to carry out any of the activities in the public domain of the town halls.

- the use and maintenance of the public domain, and
- co-location and facility sharing.[66]

Co-location and facility sharing

27.50   The Spanish national, regional or local authorities must promote co-location and facility sharing agreements between operators.[67]

27.51   For such purpose, the competent authority (at national, regional or local level), subsequent to a hearing with the concerned parties, may force existing operators and/or new entrants to share their infrastructure if such new entrants in the electronic communications networks and services market – being entitled to rights of way over public or private property – are unable to exercise their rights independently due to the lack of alternatives based on justifiable reasons.[68] In this case, the terms and conditions of the facility sharing shall be negotiated by the parties concerned. In the absence of an agreement, the terms for the facility sharing will be established by a resolution of the CMT, subsequent to a mandatory report issued by the afore-mentioned competent authority.[69]

REGULATION OF MARKET ENTRY: IMPLEMENTATION OF THE AUTHORISATION DIRECTIVE

The General Authorisation of Electronic Communications

27.52   The pre-existing regime of individual licences and general and provisional authorisations has been replaced by the all-inclusive electronic communications authorisation (the 'Telecoms Authorisation'). The rationale of this new framework is to reduce the administrative burden on prospective electronic communications networks and services and lowering barriers to market entry.

27.53   Under the new authorisation framework, a company intending to provide electronic communications services in Spain needs only to notify the CMT prior to starting up its business after a 15-day waiting period following the filing date (during which the CMT could only oppose the provision of the services on justified grounds).[70] Moreover, the restriction contained in the Old Telecoms Act, according to which non-EU companies could not generally have an interest exceeding 25% in the share capital of any company holding an 'individual licence',[71] has been removed. This means that any operator domiciled in the EU will be allowed to provide electronic communications services in Spain regardless of the country of origin of its shareholders.

27.54   Although the amount of bureaucratic intervention has been sensibly reduced, applying for a Telecoms Authorisation is still quite an onerous procedure

---

66   See paras 27.50 and 27.51 below.
67   Art 30(1) Telecoms Act.
68   Eg public health, public security or town and territorial planning.
69   If, as a result of the facility sharing set out in article 30 Telecoms Act, the shared use of radio emission stations (*instalaciones radioeléctricas emisoras*) belonging to public electronic communications networks is imposed, and this results in the obligation to reduce the emission power levels, further stations will be authorised, provided that they are deemed necessary to ensure the coverage in the service area.
70   Art 6 Telecoms Act.
71   Art 17(1) Old Telecoms Act.

that requires an authorised representative of the new entrant to file a standard application form and include the following documentation:

- articles of incorporation and by-laws/certificate of registration with the Companies' Registry,[72]
- power of attorney in favour of the individual signing the application duly apostilled, in the event that the power of attorney is notarised abroad, in accordance with The Hague Convention,[73] and
- technical document describing in Spanish the nature and features of the service and/or network to be deployed.

27.55   In addition, the following information must be included in the application:

- corporate name and corporate domicile of the applicant,
- telephone and fax number of a contact person within the company,[74]
- trade name of the applicant (where different from the corporate name),
- applicant's website, and
- legal representative and contact person, both domiciled in Spain.

27.56   Once the afore-mentioned 15-day period has elapsed without the CMT having opposed the provision of the services on justified grounds, the applicant will be deemed holder of a Telecoms Authorisation and must thereafter confirm to the CMT its intention to continue the provision of the relevant services once every three years.[75] If the operator fails to provide the CMT with this written confirmation, the Telecoms Authorisation will not be automatically cancelled, but the CMT will initiate administrative proceedings to terminate such Telecoms Authorisation.[76]

Rights of Use for Radio Frequencies

General authorisations and granting of individual rights

27.57   Except in those cases where the use of spectrum is limited on efficiency grounds[77] or, alternatively, where the requested radio frequencies are free to use pursuant to the national frequency allocation plan (*cuadro nacional de atribución de frecuencias* – 'CNAF'),[78] rights of use for radio frequencies are granted by the AER by means of an 'administrative concession' (*concesión administrativa*) or, depending on the specific use, an 'administrative authorisation' (*autorización administrativa*).

Admissible conditions

27.58   The Government is entitled to set out non-discriminatory, proportional and transparent conditions relating to the permits for using the radio spectrum, including those admissible conditions for guaranteeing the effective and efficient use of the limited frequencies.

---

72   For foreign operators, a sworn-translated version in Spanish of these documents will be required.

73   Again, for foreign operators a Spanish sworn-translated version of this document will be required.

74   This contact person may be domiciled abroad, ie not in Spain.

75   Art 5(2) Universal Service and Users Regulation.

76   Art 6 Universal Service and Users Regulation.

77   See para 27.60 below.

78   Art 45(1) Telecoms Act.

27.59   Prior to using the spectrum, applicants will have to undergo an inspection or accreditation of the installations in order to ensure that they comply with any applicable terms and regulations.[79]

Limitation of number of rights of use to be granted

27.60   When deemed necessary for guaranteeing the 'effective use' of the radio frequencies and subsequent to a hearing of 'interested parties',[80] the Ministry (and not the AER) is competent to limit the number of rights of spectrum use to be granted for the operation of electronic communications networks and services. In this case, public tenders will be initiated for the allocation of the relevant frequencies[81] (but not 'spectrum auctions', which are regarded sceptically by many who consider the legal nature of these auctions as contrary – or at least foreign – to Spanish administrative law principles). The public tender will be opened by the Ministry through an order approving the bidding terms and conditions and the call for bids related to the frequencies in question. This public tender must be decided within a period of eight months.

Charges for rights of use for radio frequencies

27.61   The reservation of the exclusive use of frequencies by operators is subject to a specific charge, ie the charge for the reservation of radio spectrum, which takes into consideration the 'fair market value' of the reserved frequency and the income that this may entail for the operator.[82]

27.62   For the purposes of assessing the 'fair market value' referred to above and possible returns for the operator arising from the reservation, the following parameters, among others, shall be taken into consideration:[83]

- the degree of use and demand of the various frequency bands in different geographic areas,
- the type of service for which the reserved frequency is intended, and in particular whether this entails public service obligations,
- the spectrum band or sub-band being reserved,
- the equipment and technology used, and
- the economic value generated by the use of the reserved frequencies.

27.63   These five parameters will be specified on an annual basis in the Spanish Budget Act, which will also include a formula for calculating the number of units reserved for the different radio spectrum services, the different types of radio spectrum services, and the minimum amount payable for reserving radio spectrum.

27.64   The amount of the charge will be paid on an annual basis. It shall initially be payable upon the date in which the right to use the relevant frequencies is

---

79   This preliminary inspection may be replaced in the future by a technical certificate.
80   Including consumers associations.
81   Art 44(2) Telecoms Act.
82   This charge must be paid by the individual or company holding the rights over the radio spectrum (as an exception, receiving-only stations that have not reserved a radio frequencies are not forced to pay the charge). The amount levied shall be deposited in the Public Treasury.

83   Annex I Telecoms Act.

granted, and then subsequently on the first day of every year. Non-payment of the charge may result in the suspension or loss of the right to use the relevant frequencies.

Frequency trading

27.65   Although frequency trading is not expressly authorised, the Telecoms Act leaves the door open for secondary legislation 'to authorise the transfer of certain rights of use of radio spectrum'.[84] In such event, the Telecoms Act provides that transferors of rights over spectrum frequencies (frequency traders) will continue to be liable vis-à-vis the Spanish administration. Moreover, any frequency trading will have to comply with the technical requirements established in the CNAF or set out by the European Union.[85]

Rights of Use for Numbers

General authorisations and granting of individual rights

27.66   National numbering plans and their implementing provisions identify the services allocated to the number ranges and, if applicable, the corresponding 'addresses' and 'names',[86] including any requirements related to the provision of such services. The content of these 'national numbering, addressing and naming plans' (*planes nacionales de numeración, direccionamiento y denominación* – 'Spanish Numbering Plans') will be proposed by the Ministry and subsequently approved by the Government depending on the specific needs.[87]

27.67   In order to comply with international standards or to guarantee the availability of numbers, addresses and names, the Ministry may amend the structure and/or management of national plans or, in the absence of Spanish Numbering Plans or specific plans for each service, set out measures for the use of numbering resources necessary for the provision of the services. For these purposes, the interests of the affected parties and the costs for operators and users resulting from the adaptation process must be taken into account.[88]

27.68   Pursuant to article 16(1) Telecoms Act, operators providing publicly available electronic communications services (ie undertakings holding a Telecoms Authorisation) are entitled to be awarded 'numbers'[89] and 'addresses'.[90]

27.69   As regards the allocation of rights of use for numbers, the Access and Numbering Regulation provides that operators managing 'public telephone networks' or providing 'publicly available telephone services'[91] must file a specific

---

84   Art 45(2) Telecoms Act.
85   Art 45(2) Telecoms Act.
86   The term 'name' is defined in Annex II to the Telecoms Act as a 'combination of characters (numbers, letters or symbols)'.
87   Arts 26, 27 and 32 Access and Numbering Regulation.
88   Art 17 Telecoms Act.
89   The term 'number' is defined in Annex II to the Telecoms Act as a 'series of decimal figures'.
90   The term 'address' is defined in Annex II to the Telecoms Act as a 'series or combination of figures and symbols identifying the specific termination points of a connection, used for routing purposes'.
91   Art 48 Access and Numbering Regulation.

application with the CMT including a description in Spanish language of certain topics (eg reasoned description of the requested numbers, foreseeable use of such numbers, preferred codes and blocks of numbers).[92] In general terms, once the afore-mentioned application has been filed, the CMT has a three-week period to allocate and grant the applicant an authorisation to use the requested set of numbers.[93]

Admissible conditions

27.70   The rights of use for numbers are subject to the following conditions:[94]

- the numbers must be used to provide the services described in the application in accordance with the Spanish Numbering Plan,
- the numbers must be controlled by the holder of the authorisation,[95]
- the holders of the right to use certain numbers must track and update a register describing the degree of use of each block of numbers and the transfers made to other operators as a result of the number portability rights of users, and
- the numbers must be used efficiently within 12 months from the authorisation date.

27.71   Operators providing publicly available telephone services or managing public telephone networks must guarantee, upon request, the portability of the numbers allocated to their customers[96] within four working days.[97] The costs resulting from updating the elements of the network and systems necessary for enabling a subscriber to retain a given number must be borne by each relevant operator.[98] Other costs associated with the number portability obligation will be jointly borne, on the basis of an appropriate agreement, by the operators concerned.[99]

27.72   Interconnection prices for implementing the number portability obligation must be cost-oriented. Moreover, any direct charges that are imposed by operators on subscribers may not, under any circumstances, deter them from benefiting from their right to number portability.

Limitation of number of rights of use to be granted

27.73   Pursuant to article 17(4) Telecoms Act, the Spanish Numbering Plans may establish competitive or comparative selection procedures for the allocation of

---

92   Art 52(2) Access and Numbering Regulation.
93   Art 56 Access and Numbering Regulation.
94   Art 59 Access and Numbering Regulation.
95   But sub-allocation of numbers may be authorised by the CMT, provided that the intended use of such numbers was described in the initial application.
96   In the Spanish fixed telephone market, 934,000 numbers were transferred up to April 2004. In the mobile telephone market, and despite the fact that compliance with portability obligations by mobile operators has been severely criticised by the CMT, the volume of mobile numbers exchanged between Spanish mobile operators reached 1.5 million in March 2004 according to the CMT.
97   Arts 18 Telecoms Act and 44(1) and (3) Access and Numbering Regulation.
98   Article 45(1) Access and Numbering Regulation.
99   In the absence of an agreement, the CMT will issue a binding decision.

numbering resources and names which are deemed to have an exceptional economic value. However, at the time of preparing this chapter, no such numbering selection procedure has yet taken place.

Charges for rights of use for numbers

27.74   The allocation of numbering blocks or numbers to operators is subject to a specific charge. The telephony numbering charge is payable on 1 January of each year, except for the initial period that will be payable upon the allocation of numbering resources to the operator. The amount to be charged must be the result of multiplying the amount of numbers allocated by the value given to each number.[100]

27.75   For the purposes of this charge, all the numbers are deemed to consist of nine digits (if numbers are allocated with less digits, the tax authorities consider that all the nine digits are being used for the purposes of calculating the amount payable).

27.76   Notwithstanding the above, in those exceptional cases provided for in the Spanish Numbering Plan and its implementing provisions, and on the basis of the special market value of certain numbers ('golden numbers'), the afore-mentioned annual taxable amount may be replaced by that resulting from the bidding procedure for the specific golden number.

The NRA's Enforcement Powers

27.77   Although one of the main purposes of the Telecoms Act and implementing regulations is to increase competition on the telecommunications market while minimising the intervention of the Spanish authorities, it is the opinion of many that the NRAs' enforcement powers, far from being minimised, have been increased compared to their pre-existing faculties. The rationale for these enhanced ex-post measures is, however, understandable, specially taking into account that the requirements to access the market, and hence the pre-existing ex-ante administrative control measures, have been substantially reduced.

27.78   The NRAs holding investigation powers are:[101]

- the AER, which is competent to control and inspect the use made by operators of the frequencies awarded to them,
- the CMT, in charge of inspecting those telecommunications activities in respect of which it has specific sanctioning powers in accordance with the Telecoms Act, and
- the Ministry, which has powers to inspect the telecommunications services and networks (as well as equipment, apparatus, installations and related civil infrastructure).

27.79   To undertake specific technical inspections, both the Ministry and the CMT may request the assistance of the AER in connection with matters within the scope of their respective powers. The officials of the AER, the Ministry and the

---

100   The value of each number, which may be different depending on the number of digits and the different services allocated to it, is fixed on an annual basis in the Spanish Budget Act.
101   Art 50(1) Telecoms Act.

specifically appointed personnel of the CMT are considered a 'public authority' in the exercise of their inspection functions, and may request the necessary support from the national security forces. In this respect, operators are forced to facilitate access of the inspection teams to their installations, documents and records (regardless of whether these are in electronic or written format) and permit that such inspection teams monitor anything which may affect their services and activities and/or the networks that they install or operate.[102]

27.80 The inspections may be undertaken by the AER, the Ministry and/or the CMT:[103]

- in any office, division or department of the individual or undertaking being inspected or of those individuals representing the latter,[104] and/or
- at the offices of the AER, the Ministry or the CMT.

27.81 The Telecoms Act divides infringements into three different categories: very serious infringements, serious infringements, and minor infringements.

27.82 Examples of actions undertaken by operators which are considered 'very serious infringements' are the following:[105]

- providing telecommunications services without having the necessary authorisation[106] or using non-authorised technical standards (depending on the merits of the specific case, this may be deemed a 'serious infringement'),
- using spectrum frequencies without the necessary authorisation,
- causing damaging interferences on purpose,
- installing, deploying or using non-authorised telecommunications equipment connected to public communications networks, provided that material damage is caused to such networks,[107] and
- not complying with instructions issued by the CMT in connection with the definition of relevant markets and the duties to be complied with by SMP operators.

27.83 Examples of 'serious infringements' under the Telecoms Act[108] are the following:

- providing telecommunications services without the necessary authorisation or using non-authorised technical standards,[109]
- installing non-authorised radio-electric stations, provided that prior authorisation was mandatory,
- causing damaging interferences without intending to do so,

102 Art 50(5) and (6) Telecoms Act.
103 Art 50(6) Telecoms Act.
104 In this case, the investigated undertaking's working day will be observed, unless otherwise agreed with the inspection team.
105 Art 53 Telecoms Act.
106 Which in practice would imply starting the provision of the electronic communication services: (i) not having applied for a Telecoms Authorisation at all; (ii) without waiting for the 15-day waiting period to elapse, or (ii) ignoring the formal opposition of the CMT.
107 Depending on the merits of the specific case, this may be considered a 'very serious infringement'.
108 Art 54 Telecoms Act.
109 Depending on the merits of the specific case, this may be considered a 'very serious infringement'.

- installing, deploying or using non-authorised telecommunications equipment connected to public communications networks, provided that material damage is caused to such networks,[110] and
- distributing, selling or showing non-authorised telecommunications equipment.

27.84   Finally, the following actions are examples of 'minor infringements':[111]

- emitting non-authorised radio-electric signals,
- causing interference, and
- not producing the mandatory tariff or prices information when required by the applicable legislation.

27.85   Sanctions imposed by either the Ministry or the CMT will depend on the gravity of the infringement.[112]

27.86   Not complying with instructions issued by the CMT in connection with the definition of relevant markets, the duties to be complied with by SMP operators, or the requirements to provide electronic communications services will generally trigger a penalty of up to five times the gross benefit connected to the breach. 'Very serious infringements' are sanctioned with a penalty up to five times the gross benefit triggered by the offence, with a limit of €2 million. 'Serious infringements' are sanctioned with a penalty up to twice the benefit triggered by the offence, with a limit of €500,000 and 'minor infringements' are sanctioned with a penalty up to €30,000.

27.87   In addition to the above, a fine of up to €60,000 may be imposed on the legal representatives of the infringing undertakings or, alternatively, on their directors.[113] The afore-mentioned infringements are subject to a statute of limitations of three years for very serious offences, two years for serious offences and six months for minor offences. This statute of limitations will be counted as from the date on which the infringement was committed.[114]

27.88   In the event of repeated infringements, the initial date for calculation will be the date on which the offending activity was suspended or, alternatively, the date when the last offending act was perpetrated. However, the infringement will be deemed to be still carried out if the equipment, apparatus or installations under consideration in the proceedings have not be placed at the disposal of the State, or if there is no reliable proof of it being impossible to use them.

Administrative Charges and Fees for Rights of Use

27.89   Operators may be subject to four different types of charges:[115]

- general operators charges (*tasa general de operadores*),

---

110 Depending on the merits of the specific case, this may be considered a 'very serious infringement'.
111 Art 55 Telecoms Act.
112 Art 56 Telecoms Act.
113 Art 56(4) Telecoms Act.
114 But the statute of limitations shall be suspended upon the initiation of sanctioning proceedings.
115 Cf Annex I Telecoms Act.

- charges for rights of use for numbers (*tasa por numeración telefónica*),[116]
- charges for rights of use for radio frequencies[117] (*tasa por reserva del dominio público radioeléctrico*), and
- administrative management charges (*tasas de telecomunicaciones*).

27.90   The purpose of these telecommunications charges is to cover:[118]

- the administrative costs incurred by the drafting and implementation of resulting EC law and administrative proceedings,
- the costs arising from the management, control and application of the regime laid down in the Telecoms Act,
- the management of notifications addressed to the NRAs, and
- the costs arising from international cooperation, harmonisation/standardisation, and analysis of the market.

27.91   Without prejudice to the foregoing, the purpose of the radio spectrum, numbering and electronic communications networks and services charges is to guarantee the necessary optimum use of these resources, bearing in mind the value of the asset that is to be used and its availability.

27.92   Moreover, these charges must be non-discriminatory, transparent, justified and proportional to their purpose.[119]

27.93   Without prejudice to the economic contribution that may be imposed on operators to finance the universal service,[120] electronic communications networks and services operators must pay an annual charge that may not exceed 0.2% of their gross operating revenues in Spain to finance the costs associated with the management, control, implementation and enforcement faculties of the SRAs and, more particularly, the administrative costs generated by the CMT (the actual percentage is fixed annually in the Spanish Budget Act).

27.94   The charge is payable on 31 December of each year. However, should an operator lose its authorisation to operate prior to this date, the charge will be payable upon the occurrence of such event.

27.95   The following administrative procedures and management actions undertaken by the Spanish authorities result in the right to levy a charge, ie the administrative management charge, to offset the costs incurred:

- issuing registration certificates related to a wide array of different telecommunications regulations (eg certificates for a technical project, installation certificates related to telecommunications infrastructures, or certificates of compliance with technical specifications for telecommunications equipment and apparatus),
- issuing technical reports assessing the conformity of telecommunications equipment and apparatus,
- keeping a register of telecommunication installers,
- undertaking compulsory technical inspections and verifications that are set out in the Telecoms Act and its implementing regulations, and

---

116   See paras 27.74 et seq above.
117   See paras 27.57 et seq above.
118   Art 49(2) Telecoms Act.
119   Art 49(3) Telecoms Act.
120   See paras 27.129 et seq below.

- processing licences or administrative concessions to use certain frequencies of the radio spectrum on an exclusive basis.

27.96   The individuals or companies subject to the administrative management charge will be those:

- applying for the corresponding technical assessment or entry in the register of telecommunication installers,
- receiving a team of inspectors acting within the scope of their faculties, and
- requesting licences or administrative concessions to use certain frequencies of the radio spectrum on an exclusive basis.

27.97   The specific amount of the charges will be laid down on an annual basis in the Spanish Budget Act, and the charge shall be payable upon the occurrence of one of the events described above.

27.98   The revenues generated by the charge shall be paid to the Public Treasury (or, if applicable, to the bank accounts authorised for this purpose by the CMT or the AER).

Transitional Regulations for Existing Authorisations

27.99   Authorisations granted within the framework of the Old Telecoms Act, ie the former administrative concessions, individual licences and general and provisional authorisations, are subject to a transitional regime characterised as follows:[121]

- existing Authorisations expired upon the entry into force of the Telecoms Act, but their holders are automatically authorised to provide electronic communications networks and services under the new regime (provided they comply with the requirements established in the Telecoms Act);
- the specific requirements applicable to existing Authorisations continued to be enforceable until the Telecoms Act entered into force; and
- in the event that a given existing Authorisation was granted to a limited number of operators (eg following a public tender procedure), the conditions applicable to the expired licence automatically become subject to an administrative concession.

REGULATION OF NETWORK ACCESS AND INTERCONNECTION: IMPLEMENTATION OF THE ACCESS DIRECTIVE

Objectives and Scope of Access Regulation

27.100   Pursuant to the Telecoms Act, operators of public electronic communications networks are entitled – and, when requested by other operators of public electronic communications networks, obliged – to negotiate interconnection agreements in order to provide publicly available electronic communications services and guarantee the provision of services and their interoperability.

27.101   As for electronic communications networks and services operators licensed in another EU member state that request access or interconnection in

---

121   1st Transitional Provision of the Telecoms Act.

Spain, they will not need to obtain the authorisation to provide electronic communications networks and services from the CMT when they are not operating electronic communications networks or rendering electronic communications services within the Spanish territory.

27.102 The CMT may intervene in relations between operators – of its own motion or at the request of the any of the interested parties – in order to encourage and, if applicable, guarantee access and interconnection to the networks and the interoperability of the services, as well as the fulfilment of a number of objectives described in article 3 Telecom Act.[122]

27.103 When obligations are imposed on an operator who wishes to access public electronic communications networks, the CMT may set out certain technical or operational conditions on the operator (or those who benefit from said access), when it is deemed necessary for guaranteeing the normal functioning of the network, in accordance with the applicable regulations.

27.104 In any event, the obligations and conditions imposed on operators must be objective, transparent, proportional and non-discriminatory.

Basic Regulatory Concepts

27.105 The definitions of 'access' and 'interconnection' in Annex II (Definitions) of the Telecoms Act follow closely their EU counterparts.[123]

27.106 The CMT is empowered to settle disputes concerning the obligations of interconnection and access resulting from the Telecoms Act and its implementing regulations. The CMT, subsequent to a hearing of the interested parties, will pass a final resolution on the matters of the dispute within a maximum period of four months from the date on which it intervened, without prejudice to any precautionary measures that may be adopted before a final resolution is taken.

27.107 In the event of a cross-border conflict arising in which one of the interested parties is domiciled in another EU member state, the CMT – upon request of one of the interested parties – will need to coordinate to reach a settlement with the other NRA concerned.

Access- and Interconnection-related Obligations with Respect to SMP Undertakings

Overview

27.108 The CMT may impose on SMP wholesale operators obligations regarding:[124]

● transparency, with regard to interconnection and access, whereby operators must make public certain information such as that concerning accounting, technical specifications, network characteristics, terms of supply and use, and

---

122 Art 3 Telecoms Act. Furthermore, the Ministry may act, within the scope of its competencies, to make sure that these objectives are met.

123 See paras 1.125 and 1.126 above.

124 Arts 6 et seq Access and Numbering Regulation.

prices. In particular, when obligations of non-discrimination are imposed on an operator, they may be required to make public a reference offer,

- non-discrimination, for the purposes of ensuring that they apply equivalent terms in circumstances similar to other operators,
- accounting separation, using the specified format and the technology,
- access to specific network resources and their use, and
- price control to avoid excessively high or low prices which conflict with the interests of end users (eg price/cost comparisons and cost accounting).

Transparency obligations and reference interconnection offers

27.109   Article 7(1) Access and Numbering Regulation sets out that SMP whole-sale operators must disclose access and interconnection-related information regarding accounting, network characteristics, terms of supply and use, and prices. Moreover, when non-discrimination duties have been imposed on the relevant SMP operator, the CMT may oblige it to publish a reference interconnection offer (*oferta de interconexión de referencia*) including, inter alia, a reference to the following topics:[125]

- localisation of the access points, including their associated numbering resources,
- available types of access, including a comprehensive description of its technical features and capabilities,
- technical requirements to be met by the networks or equipments to be interconnected,
- characteristics and requirements of carrier pre-selection, indirect access and number portability,
- service level agreements,
- general requirements to implement and maintain the requested access (eg technical tests and assessments to be performed), and
- tariffs applicable to each section of the reference interconnection offer.

27.110   The CMT is entitled to amend the reference interconnection offer proposed by the SMP operator concerned.[126]

Non-discrimination obligations

27.111   SMP wholesale operators may be subject to specific obligations for the purposes of ensuring that they apply equivalent terms in circumstances similar to operators rendering equivalent services and provide services and information of the same quality to third parties, which may use them for their own services or for the services of their subsidiaries or associate companies.

27.112   These obligations concern the quality of the services provided, the delivery dates and the terms of supply.[127]

Specific access obligations

27.113   If so decided by the CMT, SMP wholesale operators will be obliged to satisfy any reasonable requests for access to and use of their specific network and associated resources.

---

125   Art 7(2) Access and Numbering Regulation.
126   Art 7(3) Access and Numbering Regulation.
127   Art 8 Access and Numbering Regulation.

27.114   More particularly, examples of obligations that may be imposed are the following:[128]

- negotiate in good faith with third parties any requests for access to specific network and associated resources, including fully unbundled access to the local loop,
- refrain from denying access to specific network and associated resources previously made available, and
- provide specific wholesale services to be resold by third parties.

Price control obligations

27.115   Where the CMT considers that there is a lack of effective competition in a given wholesale market, it may impose certain price-control obligations on SMP operators to make sure that their prices are in line with the costs of the relevant services plus a reasonable return on the investments made. If challenged, the SMP operator will bear the burden of proof that the relevant prices are truly cost oriented.[129]

Accounting separation obligations

27.116   For the purpose of preventing SMP wholesale operators from 'squeezing' the margins of their competitors, they may be subject to separate accounting regarding the access and interconnection markets.[130] Where vertically integrated, the transfer wholesale prices between subsidiaries of the same group may be subject to public disclosure and a specific accounting method to be defined by the CMT.[131]

Related Regulatory Powers with Respect to SMP Undertakings

27.117   SMP fixed telephony operators must ensure that their subscribers have access to the services of any operator providing publicly available telephone services, either by indirect access or by carrier pre-selection.

27.118   Pursuant to article 17 Access and Numbering Regulation, SMP undertakings operating in the market for the total or partial supply of a minimum number of leased lines, as published in the OJEC in accordance with article 17 Universal Service Directive ('SMP Suppliers of Leased Lines'), will be subject to the principles of transparency, non-discrimination and cost-orientation of prices.

27.119   SMP suppliers of leased lines must publish on their website the following information:[132]

- technical characteristics of the leased lines,
- applicable fees (including the initial and subsequent subscription fees and others, if any), and
- conditions of the supply.

---

128 Art 10(1) Access and Numbering Regulation.
129 Art 11(1) Access and Numbering Regulation.
130 Art 9(1) Access and Numbering Regulation.
131 Art 9(2) Access and Numbering Regulation.
132 Art 17(1) Access and Numbering Regulation.

27.120   In addition, SMP suppliers of leased lines are forced to apply equivalent terms and conditions to any operators providing similar services.

27.121   Where the CMT requires a specific SMP supplier of leased lines to apply cost-oriented retail prices, then the supplier must ensure that its fees are cost-oriented by following the accounting requirements set out by the CMT.[133]

Regulatory Powers Applicable to All Market Participants

Obligations to ensure end-to-end connectivity

27.122   The CMT, insofar as it is necessary for guaranteeing end-to-end connection, may impose obligations on operators that control access to end-users, including, in justifiable cases, the obligation of interconnecting their networks when they have not done so.[134]

27.123   End- to-end connectivity is ensured by obliging operators of public electronic communications networks – at the request of other equivalent operators – to negotiate interconnection agreements in order to provide publicly available electronic communications services while securing the provision of services and their interoperability.[135]

27.124   Article 22(2) Access and Numbering Regulation provides that interconnection agreements must be negotiated within four months (unless both parties agree to extend such negotiation period). The CMT may participate in the negotiations, upon request of any of the parties or at its own initiative, where such intervention is considered justified.[136]

Access to digital radio and television broadcasting services

27.125   Although the regime applicable to broadcasting through electronic communications networks is expressly excluded from the new telecommunications regime (as it was from the pre-existing regulatory framework), article 24 Access and Numbering Regulation sets out the following requirements to be complied with by operators intending to provide 'conditional access' services to radio and television digital broadcasters:[137]

- technical capacity to allow total control over the broadcasting services on a national, regional and/or local level;
- supply radio and television digital broadcasters with reasonable and non-discriminatory technical equipment allowing them to enable the reception of their signal by their subscribers; and
- separate accounting.

---

133   Art 20 Access and Numbering Regulation.
134   Art 22 Access and Numbering Regulation.
135   Art 22 Access and Numbering Regulation.
136   Art 23(3) Access and Numbering Regulation.
137   The term 'Conditional Access System' is defined in Annex II to the Telecoms Act as 'any technical measure or mechanism which makes access in an intelligible form to a protected radio or television broadcasting service subject to the payment of a fee or another form of prior individual authorisation'.

27.126   In addition to the above, article 24(d) Access and Numbering Regulation provides that set-top boxes must be licensed by the holders of the industrial property rights to manufacturers on equivalent, reasonable and non-discriminatory terms, taking into account the status of the market and the technology.

Transitional Provisions

27.127   Pursuant to the 1st transitional provision of the Telecoms Act, the regulation implementing the Old Telecoms Act with regard to interconnection and access to the public networks and numbering resources[138] was not superseded until the Access and Numbering Regulation entered into force.

27.128   As for the existing relevant telecommunications markets, both the 1st Transitional Provision of the Telecoms Act and the 2nd Transitional Provision of the Access and Numbering Regulation set out that the current nomination of dominant operators in such relevant markets and the obligations imposed on them will be enforceable until new relevant markets and SMP operators are designated.[139]

REGULATION OF UNIVERSAL SERVICES AND USERS' RIGHTS: THE UNIVERSAL SERVICE DIRECTIVE

Regulation of Universal Service Obligations

Scope of universal service obligations

27.129   The scope of the universal services comprises the following obligations:[140]

- access to fixed public telephone lines for all end users that 'reasonably'[141] request such access,[142]
- availability to those telephone subscribers of a general directory – either in hard or soft copy, or both – which must be updated at least once a year,[143]
- availability of sufficient public pay telephones in the entire national territory to properly meet the needs of end users (in terms of geographic coverage, number of telephones, accessibility of these telephones by users with a disability, and the quality of services),[144] and

---

138   Royal Decree 1651/1998 of 24 July 1998 on interconnection and access to the public networks and numbering resources, Spanish Official Journal No 181 of 30 July 1989.
139   See paras 27.35 et seq above.
140   Arts 22 Telecoms Act and 27 et seq Universal Service and Users Regulation.
141   Pursuant to article 29(2) Universal Service and Users Regulation, requests of access for residential use will always be considered 'reasonable'.
142   This connection must offer the end user the possibility of making and receiving telephone calls, and allow fax and data communications at a speed which enables functional use of the internet (art 27(d) Universal Service and Users Regulation).
143   At least one general information service on subscriber numbers must be put at the disposal of the telephone end users, including those users using public pay telephones. Moreover, all subscribers with access to the public telephone service have the right to be registered in the afore-mentioned general directory, without prejudice to those regulations governing data protection and the right to privacy.
144   Emergency calls from public pay telephones must be made free of charge, using the number for emergency calls 112 or other Spanish emergency numbers.

- availability of sufficient fixed public telephone lines adapted to meet the needs of end-users with disabilities.

Designation of undertakings obliged to provide universal services

27.130   Pursuant to the 2nd transitional provision of the Universal Service and Users Regulation, Telefónica de España must guarantee the provision of universal service until 31 December 2007. Thereafter, the Ministry will designate one or more operators to guarantee the provision of the universal service ('Universal Service Operators'), so that the entire national territory enjoys proper coverage. For this purpose, when it transpires from a process of public consultation that several of the existing operators are interested in being designated as Universal Service Operators in a specific geographic area (exclusively or in competition with other operators), public tenders will be launched to provide the universal service for a definite duration within any given territory. The universal services that may be subject to public tender are the following:[145]

- access for all end users to fixed public telephone lines;
- implementation of a network of public pay telephones;
- commercialisation of a general directory ; and
- provision of 'directory inquiry services'.

27.131   Notwithstanding the above, any operator with SMP in the fixed public telephony market in a given geographic area may be appointed Universal Service Operator by the Ministry to guarantee the provision of any service pertaining to the universal service within its relevant geographic area for a limited period of time.[146]

Cost calculation and financing of universal services

27.132   The CMT is in charge of assessing if the obligation to render the universal service may imply an excessive cost for the relevant Universal Service Operator(s). Should this be the case, the net cost for the provision of the universal service will be calculated periodically in accordance with the Designation Regulation or, alternatively, according to the net savings that a competent operator would obtain if the obligation to render the universal service did not exist.[147] The Universal Service net cost of Telefónica de España (the Spanish incumbent and current universal service and SMP operator within the fixed telephone market) was valued by the CMT at €101.1 million during the 2002 fiscal year.[148]

27.133   Should the Universal Service net cost be deemed 'excessive' by the CMT, it will have to be financed by all or certain categories of operators (the 'Universal Service Supporters') through a transparent compensation mechanism.

27.134   The CMT will determine the contributions to be made by each Universal Service Supporter. These contributions will be deposited in the so-called 'universal service national fund', the purpose of which is to finance the universal service not only though the monetary assets originating from Universal Service Supporters but also via contributions made by any individual or legal entity willing to contribute to

---

145   Art 37 Universal Service and Users Regulation.
146   Art 38 Universal Service and Users Regulation.
147   Art 24 Telecoms Act.
148   See www.cmt.es/cmt/centro_info/publicaciones/revista/Marzo/Servicio_universal.htm.

the financing of any provision of the universal service (e g non-profit foundations). The CMT is responsible for the management of this national fund.[149] In its resolution of 25 March 2004, the CMT considered that the Universal Service net cost is not currently excessive and thus decided not to set up the universal service national fund for the time being.

End User Rights

27.135   Leaving aside the general rights granted by the Consumers and Users Act 26/1984[150] and other legislation enacted at regional level, consumers and end users of electronic communications networks and services enjoy, inter alia, the rights to:[151]

- receive compensation with regard to any damages sustained,
- receive truthful, efficient, sufficient, transparent and current information,
- get certain services disconnected at the end user's request,
- receive compensation for interruption of a service,
- enter into contracts with operators facilitating the connection or access to a public telephone network, as well as the minimum contents of these contracts,
- unilaterally terminate the contract in advance without being subject to any penalties in the event of proposals amending contractual terms,
- choose a method of payment from among those commonly used for business transactions in order to pay for the corresponding services,
- keep anonymous or cancel the data regarding their transactions when these data are no longer necessary for the purposes of transmitting a communication,[152]
- ensure that the data on their transactions are only used for commercial purposes (or for the provision of value added services in cases for which they have given their consent),
- receive non-itemised bills if they have so requested,
- process anonymous contact data, subject only to the prior consent of the customer (to the extent and for the period of time necessary for the provision, if applicable, of the value added services),[153]
- stop the automatic diversion of a call made at a given terminal by a third party,
- right to prevent, by means of a simple process and free of charge, outgoing call line identification,[154]
- prevent, by means of a simple procedure and free of charge, the identification

---

149   Its structure, organisation and control mechanisms, as well as the form and time periods for making the contributions, have not yet been determined by the Spanish legislator, who may also envisage a direct compensation mechanism between operators in the event that the universal service costs are so negligible that the mere existence of an universal service national fund to manage them is deemed unnecessary.

150   Consumers and Users Act 26/1984 of 19 July 1984, Spanish Official Journal No 176 of 24 July 1984.

151   Art 38 Telecoms Act.

152   Without prejudice to article 12 of the Electronic Commerce Act, according to which ENCS operators, providers of access to telecommunications networks and data hosting operators may store the traffic and connection data arisen from electronic communications for a maximum 12-month period.

153   Not applicable to 112 emergency services.

154   Not applicable to 112 emergency services. During a limited period of time, end users may not

of incoming calls (ensuring the possibility to reject those incoming calls for which the line may not be identified), and

• reject unsolicited automatic calls or faxes made for the purpose of direct sales.

Contracts

27.136   In addition to the above, individual consumers and end users are entitled to enter into contracts with fixed and mobile public telephony operators which must disclose certain minimum information (eg corporate name and registered and commercial address, client care telephone number, features of the service provided, quality levels, price and other economic terms, duration, termination events, information regarding personal data protection).[155]

Transparency obligations

27.137   Generally speaking, operators must file with the Ministry a copy of the standard terms and conditions to be used, including any amendments and updates[156] (the Ministry may then introduce clauses amending such standard terms and conditions to prevent any abusive practices). However, in the event that the standard terms and conditions are intended to be applied to public service-related communications, the relevant operator must request the prior authorisation to the SETSI.[157]

Consumer arbitration

27.138   Operators must always have a 'client care service or department' specialising in taking care of and solving any claims that customers may have.[158]

27.139   Customers may submit their complaints to the operator within a period of one month following the date when the event that triggered the complaint was known. Should the operator fail to respond or put an end to the alleged deficiency, the complainant is entitled to file a claim with the consumer arbitration boards (*juntas arbitrales de consumo*), which will become the deciding authority if both parties agree. If they do not agree, the customer is entitled to file a claim with the SETSI, which will issue a final decision within a period of six months. This decision brings to a close the administrative proceedings and may be appealed before the Spanish administrative courts (*jurisdicción contencioso-administrativa*).[159]

DATA PROTECTION: IMPLEMENTATION OF THE E-PRIVACY DIRECTIVE

Confidentiality of Communications

27.140   Operators providing publicly available electronic communications services or networks shall warrant the secrecy of communications pursuant to the Spanish

---

exercise this right where the recipient of the phone call has requested the identification of those calls deemed to be malicious or disturbing.

155 Art 105 Universal Service and Users Regulation.
156 Art 108(4) Universal Service and Users Regulation.
157 Art 108(1) Universal Service and Users Regulation.
158 Art 104(1) Universal Service and Users Regulation.
159 Art 104(2)–(4) Universal Service and Users Regulation.

Constitution and are obliged to take appropriate technical and organisational measures to safeguard the security of their services or networks, with the aim of warranting the levels of protection of personal data as required by the Universal Service and Users Regulation. Where there is a risk of security breach, subscribers must be informed of the risk and possible remedies, as well as cost implications.

27.141   Pursuant to article 83 of the Universal Service and Users Regulation, only such interceptions as set out under the Code of Criminal Procedure and the Organic Act governing the prior judicial control of the National Intelligence Centre may be conducted. The most important features of the Universal Service and Users Regulation are as follows:

- those subject to obligations: operators providing publicly available electronic communications services or networks,
- affected communications: any kind of electronic communication, including both telephony services and data transmission services,
- procedure: the interception must be allowed by law and requested by a judicial authority,
- interception measure: access to or transmission of the electronic communication and related information to competent authorities,
- information to be provided to the competent authority includes:
  - identification of the party subject to the interception;
  - identification of the other parties involved in the electronic communication;
  - basic services used;
  - supplementary services used;
  - indication of response;
  - cause of termination;
  - location information;
  - information exchanged through the control or signalling channel;
  - regarding its own subscribers: (i) identification of the physical or legal person involved in the communication; and (ii) address to which the provider sends its notifications;
  - regarding both subscribers and non- subscribers, where possible: (i) number of the service contracting party (both the directory number and any electronic communication identification of the subscriber); (ii) terminal identification number; (iii) account number allocated by the Internet service provider; and (iv) email address;
  - where possible, information on the geographic location of the originating or termination terminal; and
  - prior to the interception, the service provider must provide information on the services and characteristics of the telecommunications system, as well as the name and national identification code of the subscribers subject to interception;
- internal measures: the service provider must identify an internal unit entitled to receive interception orders as well as establish internal procedures to facilitate the interception. Additionally, the service provider must configure its equipment so as to facilitate the interception.
- costs incurred: the service provider is entitled to recoup from the relevant authority any amounts spent or use of communication channels, whether temporary or permanent, specifically established to facilitate the transmission of the intercepted electronic communication and related information. The amounts spent on specific interception equipment do not qualify as cost and

cannot be therefore recovered. In any event, to date, it is not clear what mechanism will be followed to recover the effective costs incurred by the operator.

27.142   As set out in article 22 Electronic Commerce Act, where service providers make use of data storage and recovery devices in terminal equipment (e g through the use of cookies), they shall notify the recipient of the services clearly and comprehensively of its use and purpose, offering them the possibility of rejecting the processing of their personal data by means of a straightforward process and free of charge. The foregoing shall not prevent the possible storage or access of data for the purpose of carrying out or facilitating the technical transmission of a communication via an electronic communications network, or insofar as it is necessary to render an information society service expressly requested by the service recipients.

Traffic Data and Location Data

27.143   Article 64 Universal Service and Users Regulation defines 'traffic data' as any data processed for the conduction of a communication through an electronic communications network or for billing purposes, and 'location data' as any data treated in an electronic communications network which indicates the geographical position of the terminal equipment of a publicly available electronic communications service user.

27.144   Operators must inform subscribers or users of the types of traffic data processed and the duration of such processing.

27.145   Traffic data related to subscribers and users processed for the purpose of transmitting communications must be erased or anonymised when it is no longer needed for that purpose. Traffic data necessary for the purpose of billing and interconnection payments may be retained only for the period during which the bill may be lawfully challenged and payment pursued, in accordance with the applicable law. Thereafter, operators must erase or anonymise the personal data.

27.146   Pursuant to article 65 of the Universal Service and Users Regulation, operators may process traffic data for the purposes of marketing electronic communications services or the provision of value added services, provided consent is obtained. To that end, operators shall inform subscribers with one month before the start of the marketing or the provision of value added services about the services for which the personal data will be processed, the type of traffic data processed and the duration of such processing. Such communication must be carried out through a mechanism that ensures its reception. Consent will be deemed to have been obtained for such purposes if no answer is received from the subscribers within such one-month term. Subscribers must be provided, free of charge, with an easy mechanism to opt out from such processing. Consent can in any event be withdrawn by the subscriber.

27.147   According to article 70 of the Universal Service and Users Regulation, location data related to users or subscribers of publicly available electronic communications services or networks may only be processed if it has been made anonymous or the previous and express consent has been obtained from the data subject, to the extent and for the duration necessary for the provision of a value added service. This consent may be withdrawn at any time.

Itemised Billing

27.148 As set out in article 66 of the Universal Service and Users Regulation, subscribers have the right to request operators not to provide itemised bills, in which case they will receive a bill for the total amount. If such right is not exercised, bills will be provided in an itemised manner. By resolution of the SETSI (not yet approved), the different types of presentation of itemised bills which subscribers may request (eg suppression of certain digits of the numbers called or of such numbers used through payment of credit cards) will be established.

Calling and Connected Line Identification

27.149 Article 75 of the Universal Service and Users Regulation sets out that operators offering calling line identification services must allow users to withhold their number on a per-call and per-line basis, using simple means and free of charge. Subscribers must also have the facility to block the numbers of incoming calls and to reject incoming calls automatically in cases where the caller has withheld the caller identification.

Automatic Call Forwarding

27.150 By article 82 of the Universal Service and Users Regulation such operators providing public telephony services must offer to their subscribers, by an easy mechanism and free of charge, the right to stop automatic call forwarding by a third party to its terminal equipment.

Directories of Subscribers

27.151 Pursuant to article 67 of the Universal Service and Users Regulation, operators shall inform their subscribers, in advance and free of charge, about the inclusion of their personal data in a subscribers' directory or communication to a third party for that purpose. Such information must be provided at least one month in advance, and the express consent of the subscriber is required.

Unsolicited Communications

27.152 Based on article 69 of the Universal Service and Users Regulation, automatic calls (including faxes) without human intervention for selling purposes are only allowed if subscribers have provided their express, prior and informed consent. Consent for non-requested calls conducted through different means is also required, although in this case it can be provided by an opt-out clause (unless the subscriber has chosen not to be included in subscribers' directories, in which case express consent is mandatory).

27.153 In addition, pursuant to article 21 Electronic Commerce Act, the transmission of publicity or promotional communications via electronic mail (email), or any other equivalent electronic communication medium, that has not been previously requested or expressly authorised by the addressees of the same shall be prohibited.

27.154 The provisions set out in the foregoing shall not apply where a previous contractual relationship exists, provided that the service provider has obtained the contact data from the recipient by lawful means, and used it to send commercial communications regarding products or services from their own company that are similar to those which were initially the subject matter of the contract with the client.

27.155   In any event, the service provider must offer the recipient of services the possibility of objecting to the processing of their data for promotional purposes by means of a straightforward process and free of charge, both at the time of collecting the data as well as at the moment of each separate commercial communication.

The Swedish Market for Electronic Communications[1]

Stefan Brandt and Sara Elgstrand Johansson
Baker & McKenzie Advokatbyrå KB

LEGAL STRUCTURE

Basic Policy

28.1 The basic policy objectives for the electronic communications sector in Sweden are that electronic communications shall be so efficient that they promote growth, increase Swedish competitiveness and contribute to enhanced productivity in society. Further, that individuals and authorities shall have the greatest possible access to efficient and secure electronic communications with the best possible choice, price and quality; that effective consumer protection is ensured; and that it promotes sustainable development towards a healthy environment.

28.2 Since 1993, when a comprehensive reform of the Swedish telecommunications market was undertaken, competition has increased and new markets have formed.[2] In addition, rapid technical development has brought increased convergence of previously separate forms of communications, such as voice and data communications. The high level of IT and mobile maturity, and easy entry into the Swedish market, have attracted a broad spectrum of players, from multinational telecom operators to computer companies and systems integrators.

28.3 During the last years, a few particularly notable events have occurred in the market for electronic communications: new legislation has been implemented; third generation mobile telephony has acquired its first customers; and internet services, including IP telephony, are steadily increasing.

Implementation of the EU Directives

28.4 The 2002 EU Regulatory Package was implemented in Sweden by the Electronic Communications Act[3] ('the 2003 Act'), replacing the Telecommunications Act[4] and the Radio Communications Act.[5] The Act was adopted on 5 June 2003 and entered into force on 25 July 2003.

---

1 Editing of this chapter closed on 27 May 2005.
2 Mobile services, internet access, internet services, IP telephony etc.
3 Lagen om elektronisk kommunikation (2003:389).
4 Telelagen (1993:597).
5 Radiolagen (1993:599).

Legislation

28.5   The primary sources of legislation are:

- the Electronic Communications Act;
- the Electronic Communications Ordinance,[6] and
- the Act on Implementation of the Electronic Communications Act.[7]

28.6   The 2003 Act is designed to consolidate the previous legislation, adapting it to the converging telecom, media and IT sectors and the harmonised EU rules. It is also intended to make the regulation of the electronic communications market more flexible and includes the tools that the national regulatory authority, the National Post and Telecom Agency ('PTS'), may use if a market definition and analysis demonstrates that a particular market is not effectively competitive. The new system allows for more adaptable regulation, as it is less time-consuming for the PTS to adjust a decision than for the Parliament to amend its legislation. The PTS shall be able to tailor obligations in decisions or regulations where necessary. Such obligations may only be imposed on a case-by-case basis.

28.7   In addition, although not strictly legally binding, statements, consultations and guidelines issued by the PTS are in practice very important when identifying rights and obligations in the Swedish telecommunication sector.

REGULATORY PRINCIPLES: IMPLEMENTATION OF THE FRAMEWORK DIRECTIVE

Scope of Regulation

28.8   The 2003 Act covers electronic communications networks and the communication services that are transmitted over the network. The Act regulates the technical infrastructure, but not the contents of the services. The terms 'electronic communications service' and 'electronic communications network' are identically defined[8] to those in the Framework Directive. The definition of 'associated facilities' is not identical, although it has the same meaning as in the Framework Directive.

National Regulatory Authorities: Organisation, Regulatory Objectives, Competencies

Powers and Duties

28.9   The PTS is the independent authority responsible for regulating the electronic communications[9] and post sectors. It is responsible, in particular, for the definition of relevant markets, identifying operators with significant market power (SMP) on the market and granting authorisations.

---

6   (2003:396).
7   (2003:390).
8   Ch 1 s 7 2003 Act.
9   Regulation (1997:401), Ch 7 s 1 2003 Act.

28.10   The PTS has enforcement powers[10] and is, inter alia, entitled to gain access to areas, premises and other spaces and has the power to require the provision of information in order to monitor compliance with the 2003 Act.[11]

Co-operation with other regulators

28.11   In accordance with the Framework Directive, the co-operation procedures between all authorities are strengthened by the new legislation.[12] According to the 2003 Act, the PTS's proposals for decisions, eg regarding measures which will have significant effect on a defined market as well as certain co-location, numbering or frequency matters, shall be consulted upon before a decision can be reached.[13] The consultations shall be made public.

28.12   In particular, the PTS liaises with the Competition Authority with regards to market analysis and SMP designation,[14] as the new system of competition rules outlined in the 2003 Act is supplemental to the competition legislation. The 2003 Act is intended to allow implementation of preventative measures in order to promote competition, irrespective of intervention under the competition legislation. Where the two systems collide, the regulatory authorities shall consult with each other in order to avoid over-regulation.

28.13   The Swedish Consumer Agency is responsible for consumer-related issues[15] and the Data Inspection Board is responsible for data protection issues,[16] to the extent such issues are not specifically regulated in the Electronic Communications Act. The PTS is responsible for consumer and privacy issues specifically regulated in the Electronic Communications Act. The Radio and TV authority is responsible for the Radio and TV Act and the Broadcasting Standards Act.[17] According to the preparatory works of the 2003 Act,[18] the co-operation and information exchange between the relevant authorities should be strengthened and, in certain cases, formalised through directions in the Government's instructions to the authorities. When the 2003 Act was implemented, it was determined that the organisational structure should be reviewed and analysed two years after the implementation of Act. Such review will thus be carried out during 2005.

Consultation Procedure

28.14   The 2003 Act[19] requires the PTS to undertake a public consultation process when proposing a decision to limit the number of licences to use radio transmitters, determine a market that differs from the Commission Recommendations on relevant markets, or a decision that otherwise has a significant impact on a specified market.

---

10   See para 28.57 below.
11   Ch 7 ss 1–9 2003 Act.
12   Preparatory works 2002/03:110.
13   Ch 8 s 10 2003 Act.
14   Ordinance (1997:401).
15   Consumer Authority Instruction Ordinance (1995:868).
16   Personal Data Ordinance (1998:1191).
17   Radio and TV Act (1996:844).
18   2002/03:110.
19   Ch 8 ss 10–14 2003 Act.

Dispute resolution

28.15   In accordance with the Framework Directive,[20] the PTS is empowered under the 2003 Act[21] to resolve disputes between operators.

28.16   The dispute resolution procedure applies to undertakings that provide electronic communications networks or services, and not to individuals. It is applicable to all obligations that may be issued on the grounds of the Act, or regulations, authorisations or decisions regarding obligations that emanate on the basis of the Act. The PTS is obliged to make a determination within four months from a request to resolve a dispute.

28.17   In addition to the Swedish public court system, the National Board for Consumer Complaints ('ARN')[22] provides consumer dispute resolution. Consumer disputes in relation to electronic communications may therefore be tried by ARN.[23] ARN is a public authority that functions almost like a court. Its main task is, upon application from consumers, to impartially resolve disputes between consumers and undertakings. Although the decisions of ARN are non-binding, the majority of undertakings nevertheless comply with them.

Right of Appeal against NRA's Decisions

28.18   Decisions of the PTS may be appealed to the general administrative court by any user or undertaking affected by a decision.[24]

28.19   The right to appeal is applicable to decisions concerning, inter alia, the grant of licences/authorisations, terms and conditions of licences, special obligations, obligations to notify and the revocation of licences.

28.20   According to the preparatory works of the 2003 Act[25] it would be unattainable to meet the Directives' demands on speedy and effective decision-making if every provisional decision in relation to SMP status may be appealed. Decisions proposing to designate SMP status on a particular operator, prior to a final decision being issued, on imposing obligations on such operator shall thus not be open for appeal[26] until the latter decision is appealed.

The NRA's Obligations to Co-operate with the Commission

28.21   The 2003 Act implements the consolidation procedure[27] and provides for increased requirements regarding the co-ordination of the PTS's decisions at EU

---

20   Art 20 Framework Directive.
21   Ch 7 s 10 2003 Act.
22   SFS (2004:1034), www.arn.se.
23   S 22.4, Preparatory works 2002/3:110.
24   Ch 8 s 19 2003 Act.
25   S 23, Preparatory works 2002/03:110.
26   Ch 8 s 20 2003 Act.
27   Art 7 Framework Directive; see para 1.60 above.

level. It is, inter alia, required to consult with other NRAs and with the Commission on certain decisions, take utmost account of the Commission's recommendations, provide information to the Commission, and notify the names of undertakings designated as having universal service obligations.[28]

28.22   National consolidation shall be undertaken by the PTS when it intends to take a regulatory measure that has significant impact on the market.[29] The 'veto procedure' has been implemented in accordance with Article 7 Framework Directive.

28.23   The Commission's power to specify and publish standards and specifications is recognised in chapter 2 section 3 of the 2003 Act. Undertakings are required to comply with the standards made compulsory and published by the Commission in the EU *Official Journal*.

'Significant Market Power' as a Fundamental Prerequisite of Regulation

Definition of SMP

28.24   In accordance with the Authorisation Directive,[30] a new SMP definition is introduced in the 2003 Act. SMP has the meaning of 'dominant position' as defined in established EU competition law practice. The 2003 Act[31] specifies that 'an undertaking shall be deemed to have significant market power in a relevant market if, either individually or together with others, it has a position of such financial strength that it can to a significant extent act independently of its competitors, its customers and ultimately the consumer'. SMP may refer to individual or collective dominance. Undertakings with SMP on one market may also be designated to have SMP on closely related markets where links between the two markets allow leveraging of market power.

28.25   The new definition may lead to less undertakings being determined to have SMP compared to the situation under the previous telecommunications act as an undertaking is normally required to possess a market share exceeding 40 per cent of the market in order to be considered dominant, in comparison to the previous requisite 25 per cent.[32]

Definition of relevant markets and SMP designation

28.26   The PTS shall annually determine product and service markets as well as national markets that may require the introduction of obligations under the Act. Decisions shall be made following a public consultation and take into account the Commission Recommendations on relevant markets as well as the Commission Guidelines on market analysis. The PTS shall define relevant markets and perform market analysis in consultation with the Competition authority.[33]

---

28   Ch 8 s 11 2003 Act.
29   Ch 8 s 10 2003 Act.
30   Art 14 Authorisation Directive.
31   Ch 8 s 7 2003 Act.
32   For details see para 1.70 above.
33   PTS-F 2003:2, s 20.2, Preparatory works 2002/3:110.

28.27   The markets defined shall continuously be analysed in order to determine whether effective competition prevails. If the PTS concludes that a determined market is not effectively competitive, undertakings with SMP shall be identified and appropriate regulatory obligations imposed.

28.28   In one of the first designation under the 2003 Act, the PTS designated TeliaSonera, the former incumbent, as having SMP in the market for access to the public telephone network at a fixed location for residential customers. Obligations of, inter alia, access, retail minus pricing, the publishing of a reference offer, transparency, non-discrimination and accounting separation have been imposed.[34]

28.29   TeliaSonera has also been designated as having SMP in the wholesale broadband access market and for wholesale unbundled access.[35] Obligations imposed include the provision of reasonable access, accounting separation, non-discrimination and price control. The PTS has further designated TeliaSonera as having SMP on the market for the minimum set of leased lines, for call origination for public telephone network provided at a fixed location, together with a number of other operators on the market for call termination on individual public telephone networks provided at a fixed location,[36] for wholesale terminating segments of leased lines as well as the market for transit services in the fixed public telephone network. TeliaSonera and a number of other SMP designated operators have appealed several of the PTS's decisions on imposing SMP obligations to the general administrative court.

28.30   The mobile operators TeliaSonera, Tele2 and Vodafone, Hi3G and Telenor/ Djuice have all been designated as having SMP in wholesale voice call termination on their individual markets. Obligations imposed include, inter alia, the provision of interconnection, non-discrimination and cost separation. All mobile operators have appealed the PTS's decision to the general administrative court.

28.31   The 2003 Act distinguishes between general regulatory powers and those with respect to SMP undertakings.

28.32   Obligations to be imposed on undertakings with SMP under the 2003 Act mirrors those in the Access and Universal Service Directive and include requirements regarding transparency, non-discrimination, cost-accounting, interconnection and other forms of access, price control or accounting separation.[37] At least one obligation must be imposed on undertakings that are found to have SMP on a relevant market.

28.33   The preparatory works of the 2003 Act[38] stipulates a restrictive approach to obligations on markets where the competition is satisfactory. Nevertheless, the PTS may, to the extent that it is necessary to ensure end-to-end connectivity, impose

---

34   PTS Decision 04–6943/23, b.
35   PTS Decision 04–6948/23, b.
36   In this market the following other operators have also been designated as having SMP: Tele2, Telenor, B2Bredband, Balder Tech, CallMedia Telecom CMT AB, Citylink AB, Consorte Sverige AB, Colt Telecom AB, Direct2Internet AB, Equant Sweden AB, First New Media Scandinavia, Infonet Bredband service, IP-Only, Quicknet AB, Rabbta AB, RIX Telecom AB, RSLCom Sweden AB, Song Networks AB, Tele2 Sverige AB, Telenor AB, TeliaSonera AB, Unicorn Telecom AB, Ventelo, Worldcom AB.
37   See para 28.67 below.
38   Preparatory works, s 20:1, 2002/3:110.

obligations on undertakings that control access to end-users.[39] Such obligations include, eg, the provision of interconnection to market related prices.

NRA's Regulatory Duties concerning Rights of Way, Co-location and Facility Sharing

Rights of way

28.34   Rights of way and access are regulated in the 2003 Act and in the Right of Way Act.[40] Access to property or rights of way may be granted through individual agreements or in accordance with the 2003 Act or the Right of Way Act. Expropriation issues are dealt with under the Expropriation Act.[41]

28.35   According to the Right of Way Act, rights can only be granted to publicly available networks. All undertakings with a general authorisation are eligible to apply for a right of way.

28.36   According to the preceding legislation, rights of way could only be granted with respect to real property. A legislative proposal[42] to amend the Rights of Way Act has been put forward in order to bring the legislation in line with the 2002 EU Regulatory Package. It is proposed that rights of way shall be extended to encompass personal property, which would include, inter alia, radio masts and other radio facilities.

Co-location and facility sharing

28.37   The 2003 Act stipulates that an operator may be obliged to grant rights or access[43] if required in order to protect the environment, public health, public security or in order to attain physical planning objectives. Decisions shall be taken on a case-by-case basis and take into consideration the applicable safety and planning rules in the Environment Code, the Planning and Building Act[44] and the Radiation Protection Act.[45] In order for the PTS to enforce facility sharing, it should be unambiguous that the building of, inter alia, a radio mast is difficult to accomplish due to any of the above stated reasons.

28.38   The PTS may therefore, upon application from an operator, require another operator to grant co-location to a radio mast if a local authority has denied the operator planning permission to build a mast and there are no alternative options to place the mast. The PTS shall consult with the parties involved before making such a decision.

---

39   See para 28.70 below.
40   SFS (1973:1144).
41   SFS (1972:719).
42   Preparatory works 2003/04:110.
43   For example, facility sharing, including physical co-location, and sharing of costs of applicable facility.
44   SFS (1987:10).
45   SFS (1988:220).

REGULATION OF MARKET ENTRY: IMPLEMENTATION OF THE AUTHORISATION DIRECTIVE

The General Authorisation of Electronic Communications

28.39   In accordance with the Authorisation Directive,[46] the requirement to apply for a licence to provide an electronic communications networks or service is abolished.[47] Any person or undertaking may do so, provided the conditions specified in the general authorisation are complied with.

28.40   Operators are required to notify[48] to the PTS prior to providing a network or a service. Notification is required for:

- operators who provide public communications networks of the kind that are typically provided against compensation. Typically, if an operator actively recruits customers on the market and offers connection on determined conditions, this will be considered a public communications network;[49] and
- Service Providers who provide publicly available electronic communications services.[50]

28.41   Company networks or Virtual Private Networks, as well as services only offered to a very limited and exclusive group of end-users are excluded from the notification requirement. Further, providers of internet telephony (VoIP) services are only required to notify if the services constitute means to making, and accepting calls, via one or several numbers within the national or international numbering plan. Calls are defined as real-time connections. If the delay in a network that uses internet protocols is not greater than that the user believes that the communication is in real time, the communication constitutes a call and the service must be notified to the PTS. The PTS has not defined 'delay', and it has been left for the courts and practice to determine.

28.42   The information required by the current notification form is:[51]

- information about the legal entity providing the network or service,
- information as to whether the notified entity will provide communication networks and/or electronic communications services and a short description of the intended business,
- the start date, and
- the annual turnover of the whole group and the turnover of the notified business. If the notified business has not yet commenced, the turnover shall be stated as nil.

28.43   The general authorisation is valid until the notified entity's business is terminated. The PTS requires the notified entity to inform immediately if the business is terminated.

---

46   Art 3 Authorisation Directive.
47   Except for radio frequencies and numbers, see paras 28.44 and 28.55 below.
48   Ch 2 s 1 2003 Act.
49   See para 28.8 above.
50   See para 28.8 above.
51   Form available at: www.pts.se.

Rights of Use for Radio Frequencies

General authorisations and granting of individual rights

28.44   The PTS shall allocate and assign frequencies on objective, transparent and proportionate conditions. Subject to limited exemptions, the right to use radio transmitters requires application for an individual authorisation. Under the 2003 Act, a licence shall be granted if the intended usage is considered efficient use of frequencies.[52] An application for a frequency authorisation may be rejected if the PTS has reason to believe that a radio transmitter be used in violation of authorisation conditions.

Admissible conditions

28.45   According to the 2003 Act, the grant of frequency rights can be subject to the conditions specified in Part B of the Annex to the Authorisation Directive, including, inter alia, network build-out obligations, geographical coverage and technical specifications. Conditions relating to usage rights may be specified for a limited period of time.

Limitation of number of rights of use to be granted

28.46   The number of rights of use for radio frequencies can be limited if it is necessary in order to ensure the efficient use of radio frequencies. The substantive and procedural rules regarding such limitations are set forth in chapter 3 section 7 of the 2003 Act and correspond with the provisions of the Authorisation Directive.[53]

28.47   The PTS may grant frequency usage rights on the basis of competitive or comparative selection procedures (auction or 'beauty contests').

28.48   A study conducted by consultants on behalf of the PTS published in April 2004 recommends the use of auctions as the preferred method of assigning scarce spectrum resources.[54] However, a final decision has not yet been taken on the principal method of assigning spectrum.

Frequency trading

28.49   Spectrum trading is allowed. Authorisations or parts of authorisations to use radio transmitters may be assigned to other undertakings, subject to the consent of the PTS.[55] Consent shall not be granted where there is reason to believe that the spectrum transfer will have a negative impact on competition.

Rights of Use for Numbers

General authorisations and granting of individual rights

28.50   The PTS is responsible for the regulation of the national numbering plan and its use.

---

52   Ch 3 s 6 2003 Act.
53   See para 1.101 above.
54   'Användning av auktioner för tilldelning av spektrum', April 2004.
55   Ch 3 s 23 2003 Act.

28.51   Numbers from the national numbering plan may only be used in accordance with an individual authorisation.[56] Numbering capacity is limited and so efficient use of resources is a prerequisite in order to safeguard access to numbers. Decisions on rights of use of numbers shall be taken within 21 calendar days after receipt of a completed application.

Admissible conditions

28.52   The PTS shall grant numbers on objective, transparent and non-discriminatory terms. Numbers may only be assigned to undertakings that provide or use electronic communications networks or services. It is not required, however, that an applicant has filed a notification with the PTS and thus is operating under a general authorisation.

28.53   Authorisations to use numbers may be subject to conditions regarding, inter alia, the type of service the number will be used for, actual and efficient use of the numbers, authorisation period and obligations that adhere to applicable international agreements concerning numbers.

Limitation of number of rights of use to be granted

28.54   In Sweden, the assignment of numbers has not previously been viewed as a procedure with economic implications. Numbers have been looked upon as a state-owned public resource that can be utilised according to needs. Through the 2003 Act, however, the PTS is empowered to assign numbers of exceptional economic value through a competitive or comparative selection procedure. The Act does not prescribe procedural rules, but allows the PTS to specify such rules through regulations.[57]

Number portability and number trading

28.55   Number portability was implemented for fixed networks in 1999 and for mobile networks in 2001. The 2003 Act specifies that undertakings providing public telephony services shall allow subscribers to keep their telephone number when changing service provider.[58] Although not specified in any regulation, the PTS's informal view is that service providers may only refuse to transfer a customer's number where the customer needs to buy out their minimum contract term by paying an early termination charge, but not in other cases of non-payment.

28.56   Number trading is permitted. Authorisations or parts of authorisations to use numbers may be assigned, subject to the consent of the PTS.[59]

The NRA's Enforcement Powers

28.57   In order to fulfil its duties as the supervisory authority over the electronic communications market, the PTS may require certain documents to be presented,

---

56   Ch 3 s 19 2003 Act.
57   Ch 3 s 19 2003 Act.
58   Ch 5 s 9 2003 Act.
59   Such consent shall not be granted if there is reason to believe that the transfer will have a negative impact on competition.

and gain access to grounds and premises, where activities covered by the 2003 Act are performed.[60] It is also competent to issue such orders, prohibitions and fines as are necessary to ensure that the Act is enforced. The PTS may further revoke authorisations, amend conditions and determine that a business shall cease, in part or completely.[61]

28.58   The PTS shall, as a general rule, firstly allow an undertaking that is required to verify compliance reasonable time to respond and state its views or voluntarily remedy any breaches within a certain deadline before taking action.

28.59   The Agency may, however, direct immediate compliance in the case of a breach representing an instantaneous and serious threat to public safety, health and security, or a breach which could in the Agency's opinion create serious economic or operational problems for undertakings or for end-users.

Administrative Charges and Fees for Rights of Use

28.60   The 2003 Act allows the PTS to impose administrative charges on undertakings providing a service or network under the general authorisation or to whom a right of use has been granted.[62]

28.61   The relevant fees are set out in the PTS's Regulation concerning fees according to the Electronic Communications Act.[63] The Regulation is amended annually.

28.62   The general authorisation (notification) fees vary, depending on whether or not the notified undertaking's annual turnover exceeds MSEK 5 (approx € 500,000). A notified undertaking with a business turnover below MSEK 5 shall pay an official notification fee to the PTS of SEK 1000 (approx € 100). Undertakings with a turnover of MSEK 5 or more are obliged to pay a yearly fee of 0.157 per cent of such annual turnover. In order for the PTS to charge the correct fee, it will send a form every year-end for the operators to fill out and return to the PTS. If no such information is provided, the annual turnover will be estimated by the Agency.

REGULATION OF NETWORK ACCESS AND INTERCONNECTION: IMPLEMENTATION OF THE ACCESS DIRECTIVE

Scope of Regulation

28.63   The Swedish provisions on interconnection and access apply to operators of public communications networks and authorised undertakings seeking interconnection or access to these networks or associated facilities.

Basic Regulatory Concepts

28.64   The 2003 Act constitutes a deregulation of interconnection obligations in comparison to the preceding legislation. The Telecommunications Act stipulated a

---

60   See para 28.9 above.
61   Ch 7 ss 1–7 2003 Act.
62   Ch 8 s 17 2003 Act.
63   (PTSF: 2005:1).

general interconnection obligation for those who provided telecommunications services that were subject to a notification duty, in particular fixed telephony and mobile telecommunications services. This interconnection obligation ceased under the new Act, and is replaced by a general obligation to *negotiate* interconnection.

28.65   It is anticipated that interconnection and other forms of access will be achieved primarily through voluntary agreements concluded on a commercial basis. If this fails, the 2003 Act provides powers, subject to certain pre-conditions, to introduce special obligations regarding interconnection and other forms of access.

28.66   Interconnection is defined as the physical and logical connection of public communications networks to make it possible for users to communicate with each other or to gain access to services that are provided in the network.[64] The preparatory works states that, as the term 'access' is not exhaustively defined in the Access Directive, the inclusion of a specific definition of the term in the 2003 Act would not make the application of the legislation easier. Access is therefore not defined within the Act.

Access- and Interconnection-related Obligations with Respect to SMP Undertakings

28.67   The PTS may impose such obligations identified in chapter 4 sections 4–9 of the 2003 Act on operators designated as having SMP. The provisions provide a framework of measures that the PTS may prescribe. Consequently, there is large discretion for determining how the obligations should be formulated and specified in the circumstances of each individual case, ie it is considered more beneficial if the power to determine these obligations is delegated to the relevant authority rather than comprehensively defined in the Act.

28.68   The primary special obligations the PTS may impose on SMP operators in a particular market are obligations to meet reasonable demands for access to and use of networks. These obligations may be paired with an obligation to publish a reference offer or certain specific information. Further, operators may be obliged, inter alia, to offer co-location, apply non-discriminatory terms and conditions, cost separation, price controls, and to observe a particular cost-accounting method.

Related Regulatory Powers with Respect to SMP Undertakings

28.69   The 2003 Act permits a number of other obligations to be imposed on operators with SMP in relevant markets which have an impact similar to access obligations. Such obligations include obligations to provide leased lines on whole-sale terms and carrier pre-selection.[65] If the PTS finds, as a result of a market analysis, that a relevant market for leased lines is not effectively competitive, it shall impose obligations to the specific leased lines market. It shall impose such obligations through individual decisions.

---

64   Art 2 Access Directive.
65   Ch 4 s 4 2003 Act

Regulatory Powers Applicable to All Market Participants

Obligations to ensure end-to-end connectivity

28.70   The PTS may impose obligations on an undertaking to the extent necessary to ensure end-to-end connectivity.[66] The measures that may be imposed by the PTS in order to ensure such connectivity are not specifically regulated in the 2003 Act. Rather, the preparatory works[67] stipulate that such measures may be determined by the PTS and courts on a case-by-case basis.

Access to digital radio and television broadcasting services

28.71   Swedish law is based on the principle of freedom of establishment in relation to radio and television. In order to control the use of frequencies, however, an absolute freedom of establishment is not possible.

28.72   Broadcasts to the public of radio and television programmes will continue to require a licence under the Radio and Television Act (1996:844) and the rules concerning retransmission duty, referred to as 'must carry', are specified in the Act. Investigation is ongoing regarding the networks to which the obligations shall apply.

28.73   According to the preparatory works,[68] there is no need for regulating Electronic Programming Guides ('EPG') and Application Programming Interfaces ('API') at present. EPG and API are therefore not regulated in the 2003 Act.

Transitional Provisions

28.74   All obligations regarding access and interconnection that were in force prior to the date of the implementation of the 2003 Act shall be maintained until such obligations have been reviewed and new determinations have been made on the basis of market analysis.

REGULATION OF UNIVERSAL SERVICES AND USERS' RIGHTS: THE UNIVERSAL SERVICE DIRECTIVE

Regulation of Universal Service Obligations

Scope of universal service obligations

28.75   The 2003 Act contains provisions prescribing that, if it is necessary in order to provide end-users with access to networks or services at affordable prices, the following universal services obligations may be imposed by the PTS on the appropriate undertaking:[69]

- connection to the public telephony network in a fixed network termination point;

---

66   Ch 4 s 3 2003 Act.
67   2002/3:110.
68   S 24:2, Preparatory works 2002/3:110.
69   Ch 5 s 1 2003 Act.

- access to such publicly available telephony services;
- the provision of at least one comprehensive directory to be provided to end-users either in printed or electronic form or both and to be updated at least once a year;
- the provision of comprehensive telephone directory enquiry service for end-users;
- the provision of public pay telephones, including the possibility to make emergency calls from public pay telephones using the single European emergency call number and other national emergency numbers free of charge; and
- the provision of services for disabled users on equal terms as other end users and take suitable measures to manage disabled users' needs for special needs.

28.76   The 2003 Act does not contain major modifications compared to the previous telecommunications legislation. The Act specifies that a fixed connection to the public telephone network provided as a universal service shall enable the end-user to call and receive local, national and international telephone calls, telefax and data communication with a minimum data bit rate that allows functional access to the internet. Such connection shall be offered to people with disabilities to the same extent and on the same terms as for other end-users.

28.77   Specifying the lowest data bit rate in the statutory text would, with regard to the dynamic developments that characterise the electronic communications sector, risk locking the application of law in an inappropriate manner, ie by specifying a data rate that would appear appropriate, but within a very short period of time would be outdated and considered too low. The term 'functional access' is thus not defined within the 2003 Act. It is left for the PTS to determine the speed by individual decisions. Today the PTS stipulates that 'functional internet access' means a data rate of at least 20 kbps.[70]

Designation of undertakings obliged to provide universal services

28.78   The 2003 Act is based on the assumption that the market will ensure the provision of universal services. The PTS may intervene only in case of a market failure. The Act specifies[71] that one or more undertakings may be designated to comply with universal service obligations including the provision of access at fixed locations, public pay phones, directory enquiry facilities and services for disabled users. It also sets out the procedure for designation of undertakings to comply with these obligations.[72]

28.79   In addition to the requirements that may be imposed on operators providing universal services, particular requirements are imposed on operators providing publicly available telephony services. This applies, inter alia, to sustainability and accessibility in the event of disasters and similar situations and an obligation to co-operate in forwarding emergency calls without interruption and without charge to the end-user.

---

70   S 29 a) Regulation 2003:396.
71   Ch 5 s 1 2003 Act.
72   See para 28.85 below.

Regulation of retail tariffs, users' expenditures and quality of service

28.80   The PTS may impose obligations on an operator to provide universal services and combine these with conditions concerning the achievement of particular performance goals. An obligation to provide a universal service can also be combined with, for instance, price adjustment in the form of common nationwide tariffs or a particular maximum price.[73] The PTS shall monitor[74] that the operators designated with universal service obligations comply with the stipulated performance goals. The relevant operator shall make available information concerning the performance of its service. The preparatory works of the 2003 Act stipulate that the PTS may determine the way, and the form, that such information shall be provided by the operator. The PTS may also, at the expense of the relevant operator, review the information that the operator has made public.[75] If the PTS finds that the performance goals have not been achieved, it may take necessary measures in order to require the operator to comply[76] with such goals.

Cost calculation and financing of universal services

28.81   The preparatory works of the 2003 Act conclude that the net cost of providing universal service in Sweden is small and does not merit a universal service funding mechanism.

28.82   Nevertheless, it will be possible for the Government or the PTS to satisfy public and private needs for access to electronic communications services or networks through procurement if the obligation to provide a universal service is considered unreasonable on the operator imposed with the obligation. This power applies where it is particularly appropriate in view of the costs of providing the service or network. The Act allows the PTS to determine, on a case-by-case basis, which financing procedure is the most appropriate.

Regulation of Retail Markets

Prerequisites for the regulation of retail markets

28.83   The basic principle is that regulation of retail services is permissible only if regulation at wholesale level does not achieve the regulatory objectives.[77]

28.84   The PTS has designated TeliaSonera as having SMP in the retail markets 1, 2 and 7.[78] The obligations imposed on TeliaSonera are, inter alia, to provide access, cost-oriented prices, apply non-discriminatory terms and conditions, accounting separation, reference offers and publication of information.[79]

---

73   Ch 5 s 4 2003 Act.
74   Ch 5 ss 1–2 and Ch 7 s 1 of the 2003 Act.
75   Preparatory works 2002/03:110.
76   Ch 7 s 1 2003 Act.
77   Article 17(1)(b) Universal Service Directive; Ch 8 ss 5–6 and preparatory works 2002/3:110.
78   The market for access to the public telephone network at a fixed location for residential customers, and access to the public telephone network at a fixed location for non-residential customers, and the minimum set of leased lines.
79   PTS Decision 04–6943/23, b.

Regulatory powers

28.85   The PTS monitors operators' compliance with the 2003 Act's provisions regarding universal service obligations.[80] The procedure for notifying breach and requiring compliance is set out in chapter 7 section 1 of the 2003 Act.

End User Rights

Contracts

28.86   Operators providing connection or access to the public telephony network shall do so in accordance with a contract containing a minimum level of information.[81] The minimum level shall apply not only to individuals but to 'other end-users' as well, ie legal entities. However, the obligation to specify in a contract how a dispute resolution procedure outside the general courts may be initiated is limited to consumer matters as ARN's[82] dispute resolution powers are specifically limited to disputes referred by consumers.

Transparency obligations

28.87   Transparency obligations regarding provisions of price tariffs, terms and quality of services are set out in the 2003 Act. Detailed obligations will be set out in regulations published by the PTS. Although such regulations have not yet been published, the PTS has developed an interactive guide for consumers to facilitate comparison of operators' rates.[83]

Other obligations

28.88   The PTS may impose obligations to the effect that operators providing publicly available telephony services at fixed locations shall ensure the availability of the public telephone network and publicly available telephone services at fixed locations in the event of a catastrophic network breakdown.

28.89   Operators shall further ensure that end-users are able to call the emergency services free of charge and, subject to the data protection legislation, meet all reasonable requests to make available subscriber information. The information shall be provided on fair, objective, cost-oriented and non-discriminatory terms.

28.90   A novelty introduced in the 2003 Act is that operators of public telephone networks, to the extent technically feasible, shall make caller location information available to the authorities handling emergencies.[84]

---

80   Ch 5 ss 1–14 and 7 s 1 2003 Act.
81   Ch 5 s 15 2003 Act.
82   See para 28.17 above.
83   Available at: http://hosting.ibitec.se/pts/.
84   Ch 5 s 7 2003 Act

DATA PROTECTION: IMPLEMENTATION OF THE E-PRIVACY DIRECTIVE

Confidentiality of Communications

28.91 Chapter 6 of the 2003 Act stipulates that operators that provide publicly available electronic communications services are obliged to take appropriate measures to ensure that the data they process are safeguarded.[85] This means that operators may need to take such measures in conjunction with the relevant network operators. Where there are special risks of security breach, subscribers must be informed about such risks.[86] If the service provider is not itself obliged to remedy the risk, subscribers must be informed of how, and at what approximate cost, the risk can be remedied.[87]

28.92 Chapter 6 section 17 of the 2003 Act contains a general prohibition on interception and surveillance of communications. It is an offence to gain access to, or process information from, an electronic communication in a publicly available telephony network or service without the consent of one of the users of the network or service.[88] This prohibition, however, excludes caching, ie storage solely for the effective transmission of the communication.

28.93 Electronic communication networks may only be used for storage, or access to information that is stored, in a subscriber's terminal equipment if the subscribers are informed about the purpose of the processing and provided with an opportunity to refuse the processing.[89]

Traffic Data and Location Data

28.94 Service providers shall inform subscribers of the type of traffic data that is processed and the duration of the processing.[90]

28.95 Traffic data that is processed and that refers to users that are physical persons or subscribers must be erased or anonymised when the data is no longer needed for the purpose of transmitting the communication.[91] Operators may process data for the purpose of invoicing or for services for which the data is required. In the latter circumstance, consent is necessary. Users shall be allowed to withdraw their consent at any time.

28.96 Traffic data necessary for the purpose of subscriber billing and interconnection payments may be retained only for the period during which the bill may be lawfully challenged and payment pursued.[92]

28.97 Location data may only be processed if it has been made anonymous or the user or subscriber has provided consent to the processing.[93] Prior to consent being provided, the service provider shall inform about the type of data that will be

---

85 Ch 6 s 3 2003 Act.
86 Ch 6 s 3 2003 Act.
87 Ch 6 s 3 2003 Act.
88 Ch 6 s 17 2003 Act.
89 Ch 6 s 18 2003 Act.
90 Ch 6 s 6 2003 Act.
91 Ch 6 s 5 2003 Act.
92 Ch 6 s 6 2003 Act.
93 Ch 6 s 9 2003 Act.

processed, the duration and purpose of the processing and whether the data will be forwarded or disclosed to a third party. Consent may be recalled by the user at any time.

Itemised Billing

28.98   Users have a right to request service providers not to provide itemised bills.[94]

Calling and Connected Line Identification

28.99   Service providers offering calling line identification services shall allow users to withhold their number on a per-call basis, using simple means and free of charge.[95] In addition, users shall also have the opportunity to block the numbers of incoming calls and to reject incoming calls automatically in cases where the caller has withheld the caller identification.

Automatic Call Forwarding

28.100   Service providers shall, on the request of and at no cost to the user, cease calls that have been automatically forwarded to the user as soon as practicable after the request.[96]

Directories of Subscribers

28.101   Subscribers shall be informed of the purposes of the publicly available subscriber directory or any other directory from which subscriber data can be obtained prior to any data is made available for inclusion in a directory, and without charge.

28.102   In order to process personal data concerning subscribers that are physical persons, consent from the subscribers is required. The subscribers shall also, without costs, be able to verify the data, including having erroneous data corrected or withdrawn as soon as practicable.[97]

Unsolicited Communications

28.103   Electronic unsolicited communications are regulated by the Swedish Market Practice Act.[98] The Act prohibits the sending of unsolicited commercial communications by fax or e-mail or other electronic messaging systems such as SMS and MMS unless the prior consent of the addressee has been obtained (opt-in system).

---

94   Ch 6 s 11 2003 Act.
95   Ch 6 s 12 2003 Act.
96   Ch 6 s 14 2003 Act.
97   Ch 6 s 16 2003 Act.
98   S 13b Market Practice Act (1995:450).

28.104   The only exception to this opt-in rule is in cases where contact details have been obtained in the context of a sale. Within such an existing customer relationship the undertaking that obtained the data may use it for the marketing of similar products and services as those already sold to the customer. Even then, the undertaking has to make clear, from the first time of collecting the data, that the data may be used for direct marketing. The addressee should be offered the right to object to such marketing. Moreover, each subsequent marketing message should include an easy way for the customer to stop further messages (opt-out).

28.105   The opt-in system is mandatory for any e-mail, SMS or fax addressed to natural persons for direct marketing.

28.106   The Act prohibits direct marketing messages by e-mail or SMS which conceal or disguise the identity of the sender and which do not include a valid address to which recipients can send a request to cease such messages.

The UK Market for Electronic Communications[1]

Peter Strivens, Helen Kemmitt and Keith Jones
Baker & McKenzie, London

LEGAL STRUCTURE

Basic Policy

Regulatory approach

29.1 More than 20 years since its privatisation British Telecommunications ('BT'), the former monopoly incumbent, still remains the dominant player in many markets, although it faces varying degrees of competition in different areas. Since becoming operational at the end of 2003, the new communications regulator, the Office of Communications[2] ('OFCOM'), has undertaken a strategic review of the telecommunications sector (the 'Strategic Review') with the aim of reassessing the regulatory framework. OFCOM has said that it believes that BT's combination of upstream market power and vertical integration provides it with the ability and incentive to discriminate against its downstream competitors, and it suspects that BT 'may have engaged in conduct which has had the effect of restricting competition'. It has said that a new approach is necessary based on real equality of access to those parts of the fixed telecoms network which BT's competitors cannot fairly replicate, and it has set out a number of proposed undertakings[3] which it has agreed with BT to try to address these concerns. These undertakings are in lieu of a market investigation reference to the Competition Commission.[4] The main elements of the undertakings are:

- BT is to supply a range of products in identified wholesale markets (including various wholesale line rental products) to all communications providers (including its own downstream operations) on the same timescales, terms and conditions (including price) and by the same systems and processes;
- BT is to establish a separate division which will control and operate the physical assets making up all of BT's local access and backhaul network. BT must also establish a new internal compliance board to monitor and report to

---

1   Editing of this chapter closed on 12 July 2005.
2   Established by Office of Communications Act 2002.
3   OFCOM: Notice under s 155(1) Enterprise Act 2002. Issued 30 June 2005.
4   See para 29.35 below.

OFCOM on compliance with these undertakings. BT has also agreed to a number of other organisational provisions which are aimed at guarding against 'inappropriate information flow'; and

- commitments from BT in respect of the design and provision of access to its next generation network.

Failure to comply with the undertakings could be enforced by OFCOM through the UK courts by way of injunction. There is also the potential for third parties affected by a breach to seek damages through the courts for any loss suffered.[5]

The proposed undertakings contain fairly detailed and technical requirements. They set out time limits by which BT must do certain things and limits of compensation which will be payable to other communications providers in certain circumstances, e g for the cost of reconfiguring their networks to interconnect with BT's new network.

29.2   There have also been some significant changes in approach to the use of spectrum. In 2001, the government commissioned an independent review of radio spectrum management issues. The objective of the review was to advise on the principles that should govern spectrum management and the changes required to ensure that all users are focussed on using spectrum in the most efficient way possible. The review made many recommendations but, in summary, concluded that the UK needed to radically change the way in which spectrum is allocated.[6]

29.3   OFCOM has subsequently undertaken its own review of spectrum management and has set out its intentions for the management of spectrum in its Spectrum Framework Review.[7] It is in the process of introducing measures which it hopes will result in a significant amount of de-regulation of spectrum. This will include reducing the number of restrictions both in terms of who can use spectrum and what it can be used for. This new approach is being implemented primarily through:

- spectrum trading,
- spectrum liberalisation, and
- prompt release of unused spectrum into the market allowing maximum flexibility as to subsequent use.

29.4   This has raised some controversial issues including the possibility of removing restrictions on licences to enable the holders to compete in the market for the provision of 3G services.[8]

Market conditions

29.5   Despite its continued dominance, BT's share of fixed voice volumes in both the residential and business markets continues to gradually decrease. BT's share of residential voice volumes stands at 63% and its share of business voice volumes is 40%. The introduction of a number of initiatives, such as carrier pre-selection and wholesale line rental may have started to have an effect on these figures. The

---

5   S 167 Enterprise Act.

6   Review of Radio Spectrum Management: An independent review for Department of Trade and Industry and HM Treasury by Professor Martin Cave, March 2002.

7   OFCOM: A Statement on Spectrum Trading – Implementation in 2004 and beyond – 6 August 2004.

8   OFCOM: Spectrum Framework Review: Implementation Plan: Consultation document: 13 January 2005.

number of carrier pre-selection lines now represents 15% of all BT exchange lines and 21% of all voice calls. Operators such as Carphone Warehouse with TalkTalk and Centrica's British Gas and OneTel have large customer bases.

29.6   Broadband take up in the UK has been an area of concern, although there are definite signs that this is now improving. The total number of broadband subscribers in the UK increased from 4.4 million in June 2004 to just over 6 million at the beginning of 2005. Only France and Germany have more subscribers.[9] At the retail level, BT's market share is slowly eroding. In September 2004, other ISPs using BT's wholesale products had managed to gain just under 40% of the retail broadband market. Tiscali, AOL and Wanadoo together have 25% of the total broadband market.

29.7   There are four GSM operators in the UK: Vodafone, Orange, O_2[10] and T-Mobile and there is an equal spread of market share between these operators. OFCOM has concluded that the market for mobile call origination is relatively competitive and that no operator has significant market power, save in call termination. (Previously, Vodafone and O_2 had been subject to additional regulatory restrictions.)

29.8   There are five holders of 3G licences in the UK, the four GSM operators and Hutchison 3G (UK) Limited ('3UK'). 3UK has announced that it has already hit the regulatory requirement of 80% population coverage for its services (imposed as a licence condition pursuant to the auction for the 3G licences). Orange and Vodafone both launched their 3G services in the final quarter of 2004.[11]

Implementation of EU Directives

29.9   The government implemented the 2002 EU Regulatory Framework through the Communications Act 2003. The Act also contained the government's proposals[12] for the reform of the communications industry, notably the transfer of powers to a new single regulatory body for the communications and media industries, OFCOM.

Legislation

29.10   The main pieces of UK legislation applicable to the telecommunications sector are:

- The Communications Act 2003 (the 'Communications Act'),
- The Wireless Telegraphy Acts 1949, 1967 and 1998 ('WTA'),[13]
- The Competition Act 1998 (the 'Competition Act'), and
- The Enterprise Act 2002 (the 'Enterprise Act').

---

9   Figures from Communications Committee Working Document Broadband Access in the EU dated 1 June 2005. Document reference: COCOM05–12 FINAL.

10   BT Cellnet was demerged from BT and floated in 1997 when it changed its name to mmO2. mmO2's UK brand is O_2.

11   Figures quoted are from OFCOM's January 2005 Quarterly Update of The Communications Market.

12   Communications White Paper – A New Future for Communications 12 December 2000 (Cm 5010).

13   The Government has been consulting on a consolidation of the Wireless Telegraphy Act and associated legislation.

29.11   The Communications Act[14] repealed major parts of the Telecommunications Act 1984 (the 'TAct'), previously the primary source of UK telecommunications law.

29.12   The management and administration of radio spectrum is primarily governed by the WTA. It is a criminal offence to establish or use any station for wireless telegraphy except under a licence or in accordance with an exemption.[15] The Communications Act made a number of changes to the WTA, notably the transfer of spectrum management from the Radiocommunications Agency (and thus in law the government) to OFCOM.[16] A number of other changes were made to the process for the granting of licences.

29.13   In addition to EU law, the main legislative instruments in the UK for dealing with abuse of a dominant position and anti-competitive behaviour are the Competition Act and the Enterprise Act.[17]

REGULATORY PRINCIPLES: IMPLEMENTATION OF THE FRAMEWORK DIRECTIVE

Scope of Regulation

29.14   The Communications Act applies to all providers of electronic communications networks, electronic communications services and associated facilities.

29.15   The definition of an electronic communications network[18] is broad and includes almost any network for the transmission of signals by electrical magnetic or electromagnetic energy. The person providing the network is the person exercising control of it as opposed to the actual service provider or operator. There is no requirement of ownership or exclusive rights to the network or any element of it. The definition includes private networks.

29.16   An electronic communications service[19] is a service consisting in, or having as its principal feature, the conveyance by means of an electronic communications network of signals, except in so far as it is a content service. The exclusion of content services means that, for example, providers of financial services over the internet, web hosting, and the provision of an Internet portal do not fall within the definition. OFCOM has said,[20] however, that this definition will be interpreted broadly. Services such as conference calls supported by conference bridges, and voice mail supported by voice mail services will be considered as electronic communications services even though the services involve doing something with the content of a service, as the services consist wholly or mainly in the conveyance of signals rather than the provision of a content service.

---

14   It is relatively common for OFCOM to issue guidelines. Sometimes it is required to do so under the Communications Act, for example on the proposed exercise of information gathering powers. It should be emphasised that such guidelines are non-binding. OFCOM is not allowed to fetter its discretion and it therefore must retain the ability to depart from any such guidelines where the circumstances warrant it.
15   S 1(1) WTA 1949.
16   Schedule 1 para1(1) Communications Act.
17   The Enterprise Act came fully into force on 20 June 2003.
18   S 32(1) Communications Act.
19   S 32(2) Communications Act.
20   OFCOM: Final Statement: Designation and Relevant Activity Guidelines for the purposes of administrative charging – 31 March 2005.

29.17   Associated facilities[21] are facilities that are available for use in association with the use of an electronic communications network or electronic communications services (whether or not provided by the person making the facility available).

29.18   There is an important distinction between private and public electronic communications services and publicly available telephone services. The level of regulation applicable to each is different, with the most onerous obligations being on providers of publicly available telephone services.

29.19   A public electronic communications service is a service that is available to members of the public. The Regulator has said[22] that it will consider that a service is available to the public if it is available to anyone who is willing to pay and to abide by the applicable terms and conditions. A public service is distinguishable from a bespoke service, which is restricted to a limited group of individual and identifiable customers. However, the *number* of customers who receive the service is not an indication of whether or not the service is publicly available. A public service may only have one customer because others have chosen not to take up the service. The important point is that others should not be prevented from taking it up.

29.20   The definition of publicly available telephone services is the same as that in the Universal Services Directive.[23] The main elements of this are:

- a service available to the public,
- for originating and receiving national and international calls,
- through a number or numbers in a national or international telephone numbering plan,
- with access to emergency organisations, and
- which may include additional services, eg directory enquiry facilities, operator assistance.[24]

29.21   This definition has raised a number of issues in particular for providers of new voice services at both national and EU levels. If it is interpreted narrowly the greater level of regulatory requirements applicable to publicly available telephone services can be avoided simply by not giving access to emergency services. An alternative, broader, definition is that a service provider will be a publicly available telephone service provider if the service is broadly equivalent to and intended to be a substitute for traditional telephone services. In interim advice,[25] OFCOM has said that it will not enforce those General Conditions of Entitlement which apply only to publicly available telephone service providers against new voice providers. Voice providers will, however, be expected to provide sufficient information at the point of sale *and* the point of use so that both consumers and users are fully aware of any limitations of the service. A final statement is expected from OFCOM in September 2005.

---

21   S 32(3) Communications Act.
22   Guidelines for the interconnection of public electronic communications networks – 23 May 2003. A statement issued by the Director General of Telecommunications.
23   Article 2(c) Universal Services Directive.
24   Implemented in General Conditions of Entitlement Part 2 condition 1.
25   OFCOM: New voice services – A consultation and interim guidance – 6 September 2004.

National Regulatory Authorities: Organisation, Regulatory Objectives, Competencies

Tasks and competencies

29.22   OFCOM replaced:

- the Broadcasting Standards Commission,
- the Director General of Telecommunications (the 'DG of Telecommunications'),
- the Independent Television Commission, and
- the Radio Authority.[26]

29.23   OFCOM also took over responsibility for the allocation, maintenance and supervision of the UK radio spectrum.[27]

29.24   In addition, the Independent Committee for the Supervision of Standards of Telephone Information Services (generally known as ICSTIS), an independent industry funded body regulates premium rate telephone calls.

29.25   OFCOM consists of a chairman, chief executive and various other members, totalling not more than six. It acts as a board and not, like the previous UK regulator, the DG of Telecommunications, as a single individual.

29.26   OFCOM's principal duties in carrying out its functions are:

- to further the interests of citizens in relation to communications matters; and
- to further the interests of consumers in relevant markets, where appropriate, by promoting competition.[28]

29.27   In addition, the Communications Act sets out a list of objectives which OFCOM is required to secure, including:

- the optimal use for wireless telegraphy of the electromagnetic spectrum, and
- the availability throughout the UK of a wide range of electronic communications services.[29]

29.28   OFCOM has a duty to act in accordance with the six Community requirements as set out in the Framework Directive.[30] Where there is a conflict between the different duties, the duties under the Community requirements will have priority.[31]

Powers

29.29   The government has retained a number of powers, including:

- to give directions to OFCOM in respect of network or spectrum functions for purposes of national security, securing compliance with international obligations or in the interests of public health, and

---

26   Office of Communications Act 2002 (Commencement No 3) and Communications Act 2003 (Commencement No 2) Order 2003 No 3142.
27   See para 29.12 above.
28   S 3(1) Communications Act.
29   S 3(2) Communications Act.
30   S 4(2)–(10) Communications Act.
31   S 3(6) Communications Act.

- changing the level of certain penalties if, for example, it is felt that the level is too low to provide a deterrent effect.

29.30   The Communications Act delegated extensive power to OFCOM to enact secondary legislation (for example in respect of the designation of universal service providers, the granting of recognised spectrum access and spectrum trading). The government felt that these powers were required because of the fast moving and unpredictable nature of the particular markets and the need to change provisions to reflect changes in circumstances.

29.31   The Office of Fair Trading ('OFT') is the national competition regulator in the UK. It is an independent statutory body with a board, which consists of a chairman and at least four other members.

29.32   The OFT and OFCOM have concurrent jurisdiction to enforce both national and EU competition law in respect of commercial activity connected with the communications sector.[32] Subject to a few minor exceptions, OFCOM has the same powers as the OFT for dealing with anti-competitive agreements or abuses of a dominant position. The main powers for dealing with such behaviour are under the Competition Act. There are two main prohibitions:

- Chapter I: a prohibition of anti-competitive agreements; and
- Chapter II: a prohibition on abuse of a dominant position in a market.

29.33   These provisions are more or less identical to articles 81 and 82,[33] the main difference being that the Competition Act concerns agreements and conduct that may affect trade *within the UK*, whereas articles 81 and 82 concern agreements and conduct where these may affect trade *between member states*. The Modernisation Regulation[34] requires conformity when applying national competition law to cases that would be covered by articles 81 and 82. In any event, the Competition Act[35] provides that there should generally be consistency with EU competition law on substantive issues. The OFT and OFCOM now have concurrent power to enforce articles 81 and 82 as well as national competition law.

29.34   The penalties for infringing the Chapter I and Chapter II prohibitions are severe and fines may be imposed of up to 10% of turnover for each year of the infringement (up to three years),[36] and disqualification for up to 15 years for directors of offending undertakings. There is also an express right for claims for damages to the Competition Appeal Tribunal ('CAT')[37] if a relevant competition authority concludes that there has been an infringement of UK or EC competition law.[38]

29.35   The OFT and OFCOM can both also make market investigation references to the Competition Commission under the Enterprise Act[39] where there are reasonable grounds for suspecting that any feature or combination of features of a

---

32   S 371(8) Communications Act.
33   See paras 2.1 et seq above.
34   Council Regulation (EC) No 1/2003 of 16 December 2002 on the implementation of the rules of competition laid down in Articles 81 and 82 of the EC Treaty (OJ L1, 4.1.03).
35   S 60 Competition Act.
36   The OFT looks at turnover in the relevant market when setting the fine.
37   The CAT replaced the Competition Commission Appeal Tribunals established as part of the Competition Commission by the Competition Act. It is a specialist independent body for appeals on matters relating to competition law.
38   The right to bring a similar claim in the courts still applies.
39   The Enterprise Act criminalises certain infringements of competition law, creating the

market in the UK for goods or services prevents, restricts or distorts competition. OFCOM may also, in certain circumstances, instead of making such a reference, accept undertakings from appropriate persons. As mentioned above, OFCOM is currently consulting on undertakings which it proposes to accept from BT.[40]

29.36   There are regulations in place to co-ordinate regulators' exercise of concurrent jurisdiction[41] and the OFT has issued guidelines on how complaints will be dealt with and how OFCOM, and other regulators with concurrent powers, will work with the OFT.[42]

29.37   The guidelines stipulate that the OFT and OFCOM must always inform the other before acting on a case in which they have concurrent powers. Generally, a case should be dealt with by whichever of the OFT or OFCOM is better or best placed to do so. In general, where the dispute concerns the communications sector, this will be OFCOM.

29.38   One of the major criticisms of the former regulator, the DG of Telecommunications, was his apparent reluctance to use powers under the Competition Act. It remains to be seen whether or not OFCOM will be more proactive in this area. To date, OFCOM has produced a series of non-infringement decisions, with often questionable reasoning.[43] Nevertheless, OFCOM issued its first statement of objections in its investigation into BT's residential broadband pricing,[44] and has followed that up with a second statement of objections, possibly leading to an infringement decision by the end of 2005 or early 2006.[45]

29.39   The OFT has taken a number of decisions where it has found a breach of competition law. However, it did not do so in relation to its margin squeeze investigation into BSkyB, the dominant pay-TV operator in the UK (despite issuing a statement of objections) on the basis that any squeeze was temporary and had no anti-competitive effects.

29.40   OFCOM also has specific information gathering powers under the Communications Act[46] for a wide range of purposes, including ascertaining whether a contravention of a condition has occurred, carrying out a market review and statistical purposes. Failure to comply with a request for information can lead to the imposition of a fine of up to £50,000 (approx €75,000) and/or criminal proceedings. OFCOM also has information gathering powers under the WTA.[47] The power to request information is subject to certain limitations. For example, requests must be

---

so-called 'cartel offence' (for dishonestly price fixing, bid-rigging or market sharing). If convicted, individuals may be jailed and/or disqualified from being a director.

40   Notice under s 155(1) Enterprise Act 2002 – 30 June 2005. Closing date for responses 12 August 2005.

41   Competition Act (Concurrency) Regulations 2004 No 1077.

42   Office of Fair Trading – Concurrent application to regulated industries, 2004.

43   OFCOM's Competition Act decisions in 2004/05 are: Complaint from Gamma Telecom Limited against BT Wholesale about reduced rates for Wholesale Calls from 1 December 2004, 17/06/2005; Pricing of BT Analyst; 28/10/2004; BT 0845 and 0870 retail price change, 20/08/2004; Investigation against BT about potential anti-competitive exclusionary behaviour, 12/07/2004; Suspected margin squeeze by Vodafone, O_2, Orange and T-Mobile, 27/05/2004; available at www.oft.gov.uk/Business/Competition+Act/Decisions/index.htm.

44   On 31 August 2004 – Case CW/613/04/03.

45   This investigation is related to the *Freeserve* and *Wanadoo UK* appeal cases, referred to in paras 29.52 and 29.53 below.

46   Ss 135 and 136 Communications Act.

47   S 13A WTA 1949, added by s 171 Communications Act.

proportionate to the uses to which the information is to be put; and persons to whom requests are made must be given OFCOM's reasons for requiring the information.[48]

29.41   OFCOM has issued a policy statement on how it will exercise its information gathering powers.[49] It has said that as a general rule it will seek all the information which it requires to investigate a potential breach of a condition using its statutory powers. It hopes, however, that the information that it requires for other purposes will be provided on a voluntary basis, although it will use its statutory powers if it considers it appropriate to do so.

Dispute resolution

29.42   OFCOM has specific duties as regards the resolution of disputes.[50] There is an important distinction between the resolution of disputes and the investigation of complaints. A dispute is the failure of commercial negotiation about a matter which falls within the scope of section 185 Communications Act, the provision of network access and/or other regulatory conditions imposed by OFCOM.

29.43   When a dispute is referred to OFCOM it must first decide whether or not it is appropriate for it to handle the dispute. OFCOM has said that:

* it will only accept a dispute where complainants submit clear information including information about the scope of the dispute, documentary evidence of commercial negotiations on all issues covered by the dispute, and a statement by an officer, preferably the Chief Executive Officer, that the company has used its best endeavours to resolve the dispute through commercial negotiation.
* it will be reluctant to resolve a dispute unless one party is dominant and/or failure to agree would result in detriment to competition or consumers.[51]

29.44   Where OFCOM decides to handle a dispute it will try to resolve it within four months.

29.45   OFCOM has separate powers to require information in connection with a dispute.[52] OFCOM has said that it intends to use these powers and will take enforcement action against companies that fail to respond to formal requests for information.

Right of Appeal against NRA's Decisions

29.46   Prior to the introduction of the Communications Act, the appeals process (including the body) which heard the appeal differed depending upon whether the decision being appealed was taken under the Competition Act or the TAct.

---

48   S 137 Communications Act.
49   It is required to issue a statement under s 145 Communications Act. OFCOM: Information gathering under s 145 Communications Act and s 13B WTA 1949 – 10 March 2005.
50   S 185 Communications Act.
51   OFCOM: Guidelines for the handling of competition complaints and complaints and disputes about breaches of conditions imposed under the EU Directives – July 2004.
52   S 191 Communications Act. These powers are in addition to the powers referred to in para 29.40 above.

Appeals/reviews of decisions taken under the TAct were to the normal courts whereas appeals of decisions taken under the Competition Act were to the CAT.

29.47 The Communications Act made the CAT the appellate body for communications sector matters in general. Decisions by OFT/OFCOM as to whether there has been an infringement of Chapter I and II prohibitions in the Competition Act (or articles 81 and 82) are still appealable to the CAT. To this has been added decisions made by OFCOM under Part 2 of the Communications Act (OFCOM's sectoral powers) and most decisions under the WTA.[53] This includes decisions taken pursuant to the exercise of powers to set, modify, revoke and enforce General and Specific Conditions, including access related conditions. Certain decisions are not appealable to the CAT, including, for example, the decision to designate an undertaking as a provider of a universal service and the making of regulations authorising spectrum trading.[54]

29.48 A peculiar mechanism exists for price control matters (ie matters relating to the imposition of any form of price control on a SMP service). These must be referred by the CAT to the Competition Commission for determination. The CAT must follow the determination of the Competition Commission[55] unless it decides that, applying the judicial review principles, the determination of the Competition Commission would fall to be set aside.

29.49 An appeal to the CAT can be on the grounds that the decision was based on an error of fact, was wrong in law or both or against the exercise of discretion by OFCOM or the government or another person. Appeals from decisions of the CAT are on points of law only and are to the Court of Appeal. Such appeals are only allowed with the permission of the CAT or Court of Appeal.[56]

29.50 The question of what is an appealable decision for the purposes of the Competition Act and the Communications Act looks set to be defined broadly. In *Freeserve*, Freeserve challenged the decision by the DG of Telecommunications to close the investigation into its complaint that BT had abused its position through, inter alia, pricing abuses. The DG argued that this decision was not an 'appealable decision' under the Competition Act, because he had decided to close the case rather than take a decision that the Competition Act had not been infringed. In a preliminary hearing,[57] the CAT ruled that the correspondence between the parties was, in effect, a decision that the Competition Act had not been infringed, and therefore that the CAT had jurisdiction to hear the appeal. This is important, as it frustrates any attempt by the regulator to control which of its 'decisions' are appealable and ensures there is examination of the merits of a decision.

29.51 A widely held criticism of the previous appeals system was that the courts were less well equipped than a specialist regulatory body to understand complex technical and economic issues and consequently were often reluctant to overturn the decision of a industry-specific regulator. Under the old appeals system no decision taken by the DG of Telecommunications was ever successfully challenged in the UK courts. There is growing evidence that the CAT may be a more effective appeals tribunal than the courts: the first case appealed to the CAT in the

---

53   S 192 Communications Act.
54   Although it has not been considered as to how this complies with the Framework Directive.
55   S 193 Communications Act.
56   S 196(4) Communications Act.
57   [2002] CAT 8.

telecommunications sector (the *Freeserve*[58] case) resulted in part of the DG's decision being struck down. (Enforcement of the proposed undertakings on BT and any claims for damages by third parties for failure to comply with the undertakings will be dealt with by the normal courts and *not* the CAT.)

29.52   There have been a number of recent cases where OFCOM has run into difficulties before the CAT. These include:

- *British Telecommunications plc v DG of Telecommunications*[59] concerning the meaning of 'interconnection' under the old regulatory framework.
- *Floe Telecom*[60] where the CAT quashed OFCOM's decision that Vodafone had not abused a dominant position for, inter alia, lack of reasoning.
- *Wanadoo UK*, where the CAT has expressed some doubt on the approach adopted by OFCOM,[61] although the case is currently adjourned while OFCOM takes a further decision on BT's pricing practices.

29.53   *Wanadoo UK* is also of interest in that the CAT has looked extremely closely at the procedures adopted by OFCOM, and the time taken to reach a decision.[62] Indeed, in *Floe Telecom*,[63] as in Freeserve, the CAT ordered OFCOM to come up with a decision within a specified period of time. OFCOM resisted this and sought leave to appeal. The CAT rejected its application.

29.54   The CAT has also noted the possibility of 'regulatory capture' and issued a judgment about the appropriateness of a regulator approaching a dominant operator to seek commitments and, moreover, not involving the complainant in such discussions.

'Significant Market Power' as a Fundamental Prerequisite of Regulation

Definition of SMP

29.55   The Communications Act provides that a person will have SMP in relation to a market 'if he enjoys a position which amounts to or is equivalent to dominance of the market'.[64] References to dominance must be construed in accordance with the Framework Directive and hence competition law. This can include joint dominance. In determining whether a combination of persons enjoys joint dominance the matters set out in Annex II of the Framework Directive must be taken into account. To date, there has not been a finding of joint dominance in any of the UK markets, although OFCOM has considered it specifically in respect of the market for wholesale access and call origination on mobile telephone networks.

Definition of relevant markets and SMP designation

29.56   Before SMP conditions can be imposed, OFCOM must follow a procedure which tracks the requirements of the Framework Directive. OFCOM has to identify

---

58   [2003] CAT 5.
59   [2004] CAT 8.
60   [2004] CAT 18.
61   See transcript of case management conference of 4 June 2004.
62   *Judgment (observations on procedure and binding commitments)* [2004] CAT 20.
63   [2005] CAT 14.
64   S 78 Communications Act.

the relevant markets and perform a market analysis to determine which operator (if any) has SMP in that market. It is also required to follow notification and consultation procedures tracking the equivalent requirements of the Framework Directive.[65]

29.57   The DG of Telecommunications started and OFCOM continued detailed reviews of a large number of markets.[66] They did not follow the Commission Recommendation on relevant markets precisely but identified a substantially larger number of wholesale markets. The European Commission has not objected to any of the conclusions although it has queried the reasoning at times. Consultations on market definitions, SMP and remedies have been carried out simultaneously rather than taking these in stages as in other countries.

29.58   Markets have been defined much more narrowly than was envisaged by the European Commission. An example of this is for wholesale services provided over fixed public narrowband networks: ten separate markets have been identified. These are:

- wholesale residential analogue exchange line services,
- wholesale residential ISDN 2 exchange line services,
- wholesale business analogue exchange line services,
- wholesale business ISDN 2 exchange line services,
- wholesale ISDN30 exchange line services,
- call origination on fixed public narrowband networks,
- local-tandem conveyance and transit on fixed public narrowband networks,
- inter-tandem conveyance and transit on fixed public narrowband networks,
- single transit on fixed public narrowband networks, and
- interconnection circuits.[67]

29.59   Currently, BT has SMP in most of the fixed line wholesale markets for the whole of the UK, excluding the City of Kingston-upon-Hull. (Kingston Communications, which is the fixed line incumbent operator within Kingston-upon-Hull, has also been found to have SMP in relation to a number of fixed line markets in that City.)[68] The exceptions to this are certain markets for international call services[69] and wholesale high bandwidth symmetric broadband origination.[70]

29.60   In addition, in the market for fixed geographical call termination[71] all providers of public electronic communications networks listed in the statement have been determined to have SMP in the provision of their own network fixed

---

65   Ss 79–89 Communications Act.

66   The DG of Telecommunications issued market review guidelines setting out the criteria for use in the assessment of SMP – June 2002.

67   DG of Telecommunications: Final Statement: Review of the fixed narrowband wholesale exchange line, call origination, conveyance and transit markets: 28 November 2003. BT has SMP in all markets included in this review.

68   The remedies proposed for Kingston Communications are broadly similar but not identical to those of BT. Kingston has not been considered further in this Chapter.

69   235 different routes have been identified, each as a separate market. BT has SMP in 108, C&W in 4 and 123 have been found to be competitive. DG Telecommunications Final Statement: Wholesale International Services markets – 18 November 2003.

70   OFCOM: Final Statement: Review of the retail leased lines, symmetric broadband origination and wholesale trunk segments markets – (Undated).

71   DG of Telecommunications Final Statement: Review of fixed geographic call termination markets – Identification and analysis of markets, determination of market power and setting of SMP conditions – 28 November 2003.

geographic call termination services. All those providers listed are required to provide network access (ie call termination to all other public electronic communications networks and to set fair and reasonable terms for the provision of call termination services). Additional obligations are imposed on BT.

29.61 In the case of mobile markets, the outcome of the market analysis is somewhat different. In the market for wholesale access and call origination on mobile networks, OFCOM has decided that no single firm has SMP and there is no evidence of collective dominance.[72] Previous regulation on O_2 and Vodafone has been withdrawn. In the market for wholesale voice call termination, OFCOM has determined that each mobile network operator has SMP in the market for the provision of wholesale voice call termination on its own network.[73]

29.62 The analysis of the mobile wholesale voice termination markets reflects the previous decisions made by the DG of Telecommunications and the Competition Commission (to which the DG's decision was referred for review). The rationale is that the relevant market for wholesale mobile call termination is each operator's subscriber base, as each mobile operator controls 100% of the subscriber base it has SMP in that market. 2G services provided by the four main mobile operators, Vodafone, Orange, O_2 and T-Mobile, are subject to an RPI-X[74] price charge control to last until 2006.[75] Slightly different price controls are imposed on Vodafone and O_2 on the one hand, and Orange and T-Mobile on the other reflecting the different cost profiles of the different organisations resulting from the fact that they operate, in part, on different parts of the radio spectrum.

29.63 Controls have also been imposed on the 2G activities of 3UK albeit not price controls (3UK has appealed the finding of SMP). OFCOM has taken the view that in the case of 3G services, it is too early to impose regulatory controls given their state of development. Accordingly no remedies have been imposed.

29.64 Once OFCOM has made a determination of SMP it must set such SMP conditions 'as it thinks appropriate'. This wording differs slightly from that of the Framework Directive: the directive provides that where an NRA identifies that a market is not effectively competitive it shall identify undertakings with SMP and shall impose appropriate obligations on that undertaking. The SMP conditions which OFCOM can impose are set out in the Communications Act and it is for OFCOM to decide which of these are appropriate. In current market conditions this difference is unlikely to be significant.

---

72 DG of Telecommunications Final Statement: Mobile access and call origination services market – Identification and analysis of market and determination on market power – 3 October 2003.

73 OFCOM: Statement on Wholesale Mobile Voice Call Termination – 1 June 2004.

74 The 'RPI-X' formula caps a selected basket of an operator's prices. These prices can then increase annually by the retail price index (RPI) minus the X factor, with the X being set by OFCOM.

75 OFCOM is currently consulting on its proposals to extend these price controls unchanged for a further 12 months to 31 March 2007.

NRA's Regulatory Duties concerning Rights of Way, Co-location and Facility Sharing

Rights of way

29.65 The Electronic Communications Code[76] (the 'Code') grants to holders of Code powers certain rights over land, which override private rights. The principal benefits are certain exemptions from the Town and Country planning regime as 'Permitted Developments' and the right to a streetworks licence under the New Roads and Street Works Act 1991 in order to carry out works in connection with the installation of electronic communications apparatus in streets.

29.66 The Code contains detailed provisions about how those with Code powers should negotiate with owners and occupiers of land (including Crown land) and allows an application for a court order in the event agreement cannot be reached. In practice, most rights are agreed by negotiation, without recourse to the courts.

29.67 Under the previous regime, Code powers were attached to individual licences. Now those wishing to benefit from Code powers have to apply on a stand alone basis. Applications must be made to OFCOM. There is an annual fee[77] which is fixed each year by OFCOM. Successful applicants also have to pay a one-off fee[78] on the granting of Code powers.

29.68 OFCOM can apply the Code to providers of electronic communications networks and providers of conduit systems available for use by providers of electronic communications networks. Conduit providers are entities who make available conduits (eg tunnels, pipes or subways) to electronic communications network providers. Code powers will not normally be granted to persons operating exclusively or mainly private networks. Transitional provisions provided that those to whom the Code applied immediately before the commencement of the new regime would still benefit from Code powers under the new regime.

29.69 Applications for Code powers must contain information on certain matters such as reasons for needing Code powers, description of the electronic communications network or conduit system which the applicant is intending to provide, evidence of willingness and ability to share infrastructure and evidence of an ability to put in place funds for liabilities before the exercise of Code powers.[79] OFCOM has said that for companies applying for Code powers it would expect to see letters from the directors certifying that they will put funds for liabilities in place before exercising their Code powers.

29.70 When considering applications for Code powers, OFCOM must consider certain statutory criteria,[80] including:

---

76 The Electronic Communications Code is set out in schedule 2 to the TAct, as amended by Schedule 3 to the Communications Act and The Electronic Communications Code (Conditions and Restrictions) Regulations, SI 2003/2553.
77 The annual fee is currently £3,000 (approx €4,500).
78 This is currently £10,000 (approx €15,000).
79 Under regulation 16 of the Electronic Communications Code (Conditions and Restrictions) 2003 (SI 2003/2553), persons benefiting from the Electronic Communications Code must put in place sufficient funds in order to meet certain liabilities. See policy statement on Funds for Liabilities, October 2003.
80 S 107(4) Communications Act.

- the benefit to the public of the relevant electronic communications network or conduit system, and
- the need to encourage sharing of the use of electronic communications apparatus.

29.71   OFCOM must maintain a register (which is available for public inspection on payment of a fee) of those with Code powers.[81]

29.72   Where a person to whom the Code applies is in contravention of the Code, OFCOM has powers to enforce penalties and suspend application of the Code.[82]

Co-location and facility sharing

29.73   When OFCOM is considering whether or not to grant Code powers it must have regard, inter alia, to the need to encourage sharing of the use of electronic communications apparatus.[83] OFCOM has said that grants of Code powers should be considered more favourably for those network operators which produce evidence of their ability or willingness to share infrastructure. This will be particularly the case where strong representations have been received from third parties against the grant of Code powers on the grounds of highway disruption or because of environmental impact. However, an inability or unwillingness to share should not in itself be regarded as a determining factor.[84]

29.74   Where providers of electronic communications networks and associated facilities with Code powers put up barriers to sharing and there is no viable alternative then OFCOM has the power to impose a condition to secure sharing under the access provisions referred to below.[85]

REGULATION OF MARKET ENTRY: IMPLEMENTATION OF THE AUTHORISATION DIRECTIVE

The General Authorisation of Electronic Communications

29.75   The previous UK regime of individual and class licences has been repealed and replaced with a system under which any person is generally authorised to provide electronic communications networks and/or electronic communications services without prior approval. OFCOM does have the power to designate certain types of communications networks and services and require that providers of these make a limited notification to OFCOM before commencing service.[86] It has, however, decided not to require any form of notification.

29.76   Licence conditions have been replaced by a combination of General Conditions of Entitlement[87] and Special Conditions of Entitlement. General Conditions are applicable to all providers of electronic communications networks

---

81   S 108 Communications Act.
82   S 110 Communications Act.
83   S 109 Communications Act.
84   The Granting of the Electronic Communications Code – A Statement, issued on 10 October 2003.
85   S 73(3) Communications Act.
86   S 34(1) Communications Act.
87   Notification setting general conditions under s 45 Communications Act.

and electronic communications services, or to all providers of a particular type. Each of the General Conditions specifies the type of operator to which it applies (public electronic communications networks, publicly available telephone services, etc). Specific Conditions are imposed by OFCOM on individual providers. Obligations imposed on providers who are determined to have SMP take the form of Special Conditions.

29.77   The Communications Act specifies the matters which can be covered by the General Conditions and by Specific Conditions.[88] The provisions in the Act do not exactly mirror the requirements set out in Annex A to the Authorisation Directive. Instead it sets out several general categories into which General Conditions must fall. For example, conditions can be set making such provision as OFCOM considers appropriate for protecting the interests of the end users of public electronic communications services, for requiring compliance with relevant international standards. Most of the General Conditions adopted to date are concerned with matters of consumer protection.

Rights of Use for Radio Frequencies

General authorisations and granting of individual rights

29.78   The WTA requires that radio equipment may only be used under the grant of a licence and the installation or use of radio equipment without a valid licence is an offence, except where regulations have been made to exempt specific types of apparatus from needing a licence to use it.[89]

29.79   The Wireless Telegraph (Exemption) Regulations 2003 ('2003 Regulations')[90] exempt various apparatus from the requirement for a licence. Subject to complying with interface requirements, any apparatus operating in the frequency bands 2400 to 2483.5 MHz, 5150 to 5350 MHz, 5470 to 5725 MHz (which are used for radio local area network services), or in the band 57.1 to 58.9 GHz[91] are exempt under the 2003 Regulations. In addition to exempting these bands, the 2003 Regulations exempt a range of devices from the licensing requirements, including land mobile-satellite service stations, mobile handsets and cordless telephones.

29.80   OFCOM is now required to exempt, by regulation, apparatus that is not likely to cause undue interference.[92] OFCOM has said that as technologies such as spectrally 'polite' radio become more widespread it may make greater use of licence exemption as a spectrum management tool.

29.81   Most types of licences are obtained by forwarding an application form to OFCOM. There is an overall time limit of six weeks for granting most licences. Licences will continue to be allocated in accordance with the national frequency plan.

---

88   Ss 51–77 Communications Act.
89   S 1(1) WTA 1949.
90   SI 2003/74.
91   For point-to-point radio relay systems.
92   S 166 Communications Act.

29.82   A licence either authorises the use of particular equipment or authorises the use of a particular block of spectrum. Those licences which authorise equipment may be standard (often referred to as 'pre-packaged') or may be customised to suit the particular need of users. Licences are not normally available for public inspection.

Admissible conditions

29.83   The WTA provides that licences granted by OFCOM may be issued subject to such terms, conditions and limitations as OFCOM thinks fit and these may include in particular terms, conditions and limitations as to the strength and type of signal and the times and use and sharing of such frequencies.[93] As for general conditions, the government did not replicate exactly the provisions of Annex B of the Authorisation Directive. The conditions which OFCOM can include in licences are potentially very wide.

29.84   Spectrum for 3G mobile telephony was auctioned in the UK in 2000. The successful bidders, being four existing 2G operators and one new entrant, paid a total of £22,477,400,000 (approx €33.8 billion) for the five licences. The licences include build-out obligations requiring that a telecommunications service is available to 80% of the UK population by the end of 2007.

29.85   3.4 GHz licences were auctioned in 2003. The licences only allow the licensee to offer fixed and not mobile services. OFCOM is currently, and controversially, consulting on removing this restriction in the interests of efficient spectrum management and competition which would allow competition with 3G services.

29.86   There have already been two auctions of 28 GHz licences in this band and 26 licences remain available for award. The licences have a number of restrictions including a 'purpose of use' and a 'use it or lose it' condition. The government has been considering removing these restrictions within new and existing licences.

Limitation of number of rights of use to be granted

29.87   OFCOM can, in order to secure the efficient use of spectrum, impose limitations on the use of particular frequencies. These limitations may be a limit on the number of licences to be granted in a particular frequency [94] or specify uses for which, on particular frequencies, OFCOM will grant licences. Where OFCOM decides to impose such limitations it must set out the criteria that it will apply in determining any limits imposed.[95]

29.88   OFCOM now has the responsibility for spectrum pricing. The WTA sets out two forms of spectrum pricing:

- Administrative incentive pricing,[96] in which fees are set by regulation on the basis of management criteria. For example, the price may be set to promote efficient use as well as to recover management costs.

---

93   S 1(2) WTA 1949.
94   Wireless Telegraphy (Limitation of Number of Licences) Order 2003 (SI 2003/1902).
95   S 164 Communications Act.
96   S 1 WTA 1998.

- Auctions,[97] in which fees are set directly by the market.

29.89   There have been a number of auctions in the UK, including the auction for 3G spectrum and broadband fixed wireless access in 2000. Auctions have in the past been conducted by the Radiocommunications Agency but responsibility for this has been passed to OFCOM under the new regime. OFCOM has said that it expects to continue to use market based methods such as auctions as its preferred mechanism for making primary assignments. These may be complex auctions for large assignments or single round auctions for smaller blocks of spectrum. Where auctions are not suitable other mechanisms such as first come first served will continue to be employed.

Frequency trading

29.90   Frequency trading was introduced in the UK but only in certain licence classes in December 2004.[98] OFCOM has said that it expects to extend the range of licence classes authorised to trade in each of the next three years. The licence classes for which trading have been introduced in 2004 include data networks (other than the UHF 1 Band) and fixed wireless access including broadband fixed wireless access (this includes licences in the 3.4GHz, 3.6 GHz and 28 GHz Bands). Licences in the 40 GHz Band will be tradable upon award. OFCOM is still considering the appropriate timing for the introduction of trading in 2G and 3G mobile spectrum.

29.91   OFCOM's consent is required for proposed trades and it can prevent a trade in certain circumstances,[99] for example, if the parties are attempting to escape licence obligations.

29.92   In parallel with the introduction of frequency trading, OFCOM has said that it will be willing to consider requests from licensees for a change in the use of their licence.

Recognised spectrum access

29.93   OFCOM has the power to make regulations to facilitate the introduction of a system of recognised spectrum access ('RSA'). This is similar to wireless telegraphy licensing, but it confers certain rights on the holder with respect to transmissions from outside the UK, such as transmissions from a satellite. A holder of RSA would be entitled to have their interests in the radio spectrum taken into account by OFCOM in the same way as a licence holder.[100] OFCOM has power to auction RSA rights where appropriate and they will be capable of being traded under the spectrum trading regime.[101]

---

97   S 3 WTA 1998.
98   The Wireless Telegraphy (Spectrum Trading) Regulations 2004 No 3154.
99   Regulation 9 – The Wireless Telegraphy (Spectrum Trading) Regulations 2004.
100 For further information see 'Introducing Recognised Spectrum Access', Radiocommunications Agency, July 2002.
101 S 159 Communications Act.

Rights of Use for Numbers

General authorisations and granting of individual rights

29.94   The term 'number' includes data of any description.[102] The government does not, however, feel that it is currently appropriate or necessary for OFCOM to regulate Internet-related providers, such as domain names, Internet addresses or identifiers based on domain names and Internet Protocol addresses. It has therefore specifically excluded Internet-related identifiers from regulation under the new regime.[103]

29.95   OFCOM has a duty[104] to publish a Numbering Plan which sets out the numbers which are available for allocation together with the restrictions which apply to their allocation and use. This exists alongside the National Numbering Scheme which is a record of all numbers allocated, available for allocation or protected.

29.96   Numbers are not owned by communications providers. They are either allocated to them by OFCOM or be acquired from a third party by way of a sub-allocation. Providers of both public electronic communications networks and services can be allocated telephone numbers. However, OFCOM has said that normally it would expect service providers to get their allocations from public electronic communications networks. Applicants are required to give information as to their services and the networks over which numbers will be used. If the service provider has not requested a sub-allocation from a network provider and has no arrangements with a network provider to provide a service, OFCOM may determine that the service provider is ineligible in that particular case.

29.97   There is currently no charge or fee for the right to use numbers.

Admissible conditions

29.98   It is OFCOM's duty to secure that what appears to them to be the best use is made of the numbers that are appropriate for use as telephone numbers, and to encourage efficiency and innovation for that purpose.[105]

29.99   The Communications Act sets out admissible conditions for the allocation and adoption of numbers.[106] OFCOM can also set conditions that apply to persons other than non-communications providers which relate to the allocation of numbers to such persons, the transfer of allocations to and from such persons and the use of numbers by such persons.[107]

29.100   The General Conditions of Entitlement also contain a number of provisions as regards the use of numbers including:

- the circumstances under which OFCOM may withdraw an allocation of numbers. For example, where a communications provider has not adopted allocated numbers within six months from the date of allocation, and

---

102   S 56(10) Communications Act.
103   See the Telephone Number Exclusion (Domain Names and Internet Addresses) Order 2003 No 3281.
104   S 56 Communications Act.
105   S 63 Communications Act.
106   S 58 Communications Act.
107   S 59 Communications Act.

- the provision of number portability. This is currently only required for subscribers of publicly available telephone services, for both geographic and non-geographic numbers.[108]

29.101 OFCOM has imposed directions on BT[109] to ensure that both carrier pre-selection and indirect access are available to their customers.[110]

29.102 The carrier pre-selection direction requires BT to provide carrier pre-selection at the request of any customer and to provide to carrier pre-selection providers relevant wholesale interconnection facilities on reasonable terms and conditions. It also sets out requirements as to the charges for the costs of the interconnection facilities.

29.103 The indirect access direction requires BT to provide indirect access on reasonable terms at the request of any customer and that relevant wholesale interconnection facilities are provided that will allow an alternative communications provider to provide Indirect Access services to its customers. It also sets out requirements as to the charges for the interconnection facilities.

Limitation of number of rights of use to be granted

29.104 The Communications Act contains a new right which expressly empowers OFCOM to auction numbers (including individual 'golden numbers') to the highest bidder.[111] It remains to be seen whether OFCOM will take up this option.

The NRA's Enforcement Powers

29.105 The Communications Act creates a broad framework for the enforcement of many of its provisions including new powers for OFCOM to impose penalties for contravention of General Conditions of Entitlement or Specific Conditions.[112] For contravention of a General or Specific Condition, any penalty imposed cannot exceed 10% of the turnover of the offender's relevant business for the relevant period, which is normally one year.[113] OFCOM has not yet imposed a penalty for breach of a condition. As set out above, OFCOM has wide powers to request information in connection with an alleged breach of condition.

29.106 The procedure for enforcing a General or Specific Condition[114] is:

- Stage one: OFCOM sends the offender a formal notification and gives the offender the opportunity to remedy the breach.
- Stage two: If the notification is not complied with, OFCOM can issue an enforcement notification.
- Stage three: As well as or instead of stage two, OFCOM may impose a penalty.
- Stage four: Where there has been a serious and repeated contravention of

---

108 General condition 18.
109 And Kingston Communications.
110 Final statement – Review of the fixed narrowband wholesale exchange line, call origination, conveyance and transit markets – 28 November 2003.
111 S 58(5) Communications Act.
112 S 96 Communications Act.
113 S 97(1) Communications Act.
114 Ss 94–101 Communications Act.

conditions and the imposition of penalties or notification notices has not succeeded in securing compliance, OFCOM can also give a direction suspending service provision. This direction can include a condition requiring the making of payments by way of compensation for loss and damage suffered by the offending operators' customers or in respect of annoyance, inconvenience or anxiety to which they have been put.[115]

- Stage five: A person who acts in contravention of a prohibition or restriction on service provision is guilty of an offence and will be liable on summary conviction to a fine not exceeding the statutory maximum and on conviction on indictment to a fine.

29.107   Any person who suffers loss or damage as a result of the action in failing to comply with the condition or enforcement notice can bring a separate action for loss.[116] These claims will be dealt with by the courts and not the CAT.

Administrative Charges and Fees for Rights of Use

29.108   OFCOM is required to ensure that its revenues fully cover its costs of regulation. These were previously covered by licence fees. Under the new regime, OFCOM has decided to retain a revenue measure with a degree of progression so that smaller operators pay a lower proportion of their revenue. An administrative charge applies to all designated providers of electronic communications networks, electronic communications services and associated facilities.[117] A communications provider will be designated if its gross annual turnover from 'relevant activities' provided either to end users or other telecommunications operators exceeds £5 million (approx €7.5 million).

29.109   Providers are divided into bands according to their turnover, and all providers within a band are charged the same administration charge calculated by applying a percentage tariff to the relevant turnover. The percentage tariff for the year 2005/06 is 0.0625%. There is a cap so as to ensure that the percentage tariff cannot be greater than 0.08%. Any provider with a turnover over £1 billion (approx €1.5 billion) pays a set percentage of its actual turnover.

29.110   Fees are normally payable for rights to use spectrum and the amount payable depends on the type of licence granted.

REGULATION OF NETWORK ACCESS AND INTERCONNECTION: IMPLEMENTATION OF THE ACCESS DIRECTIVE

Objectives and Scope of Access Regulation

29.111   Probably the main challenge for regulation in recent years in the UK has been to try to ensure some form of equality of access to BT's network at the wholesale level so that other operators and service providers can offer competitive products and services. OFCOM has recently acknowledged in the context of the Strategic Review that in the fixed line market, at least, past regulatory efforts to secure access at a wholesale level to BT's networks and facilities have had a limited

---

115   S 100 Communications Act.
116   S 104 Communications Act.
117   S 38(2) Communications Act.

effect in opening up the market (BT remains larger than most of its competitors put together) and have also led to a large range of detailed regulatory interventions. Accordingly, it has now proposed certain undertakings to be given by BT under the Enterprise Act, as discussed previously. These supplement the specific obligations imposed under the Communications Act, as discussed below.

29.112   OFCOM is now also having to deal with the implications for interconnection and access arrangements of BT's next generation network. BT's plans are to introduce a new single converged network to replace all its existing networks. Mass migration of its current customers is expected to start in 2006. This is a significant opportunity for OFCOM to ensure that the network of an incumbent operator accommodates competition from the outset.

The proposed undertakings to be given by BT address this by imposing a number of specific requirements on BT as regards the deployment of this new network. These include provisions intended to:

- ensure that other communications providers can purchase unbundled network access products on terms and conditions which allow those communications providers to 'compete effectively' with end-to-end services that BT provides over its network,
- ensure that BT builds its network in a manner to ensure that all other communications providers (including BT) can purchase access on the same terms and conditions (including price) by means of the same systems and processes, and
- prevent BT launching new retail products based on its new network before a suitable upstream wholesale SMP product is available for downstream competitors.

These requirements only apply to the provision of access in markets where BT has SMP.

Basic Regulatory Concepts

29.113   Under the Communications Act, OFCOM has powers to impose a wide variety of obligations to provide interconnection and access on all communications providers.

29.114   The definition of access in the Communications Act is wide[118] and includes interconnection. Guidelines[119] have set out examples of types of access. The term applies to any wholesale service that enables competitors to deliver their own services to customers. The wholesale product could be a network element, an end-to-end communications service or an interconnection service. Specific examples given include unbundled local loops, interconnection including partial private circuits, reseller products such as calls and access and virtual network services such as mobile virtual network operators.

29.115   OFCOM has said that it is preferable for requests for access to be resolved through commercial negotiation. The government did not feel that there are any restrictions in the UK that prevent persons from negotiating between themselves on

---

118 S 151(3) Communications Act.
119 Imposing Access Obligations under the New EU Directives – 13 September 2002.

technical and commercial arrangements for network access and as such there is no specific reference to this in the Communications Act.[120]

Access and Interconnection-related Obligations with Respect to SMP Undertakings

Overview

29.116   The Regulator has produced guidelines setting out in general terms in what circumstances and to what extent it will impose access obligations on operators with SMP.[121] The guidelines provide that:

29.116.1   Before OFCOM imposes an access obligation on an SMP operator it will undertake a regulatory option appraisal. This will take account of matters listed in the Access Directive and other relevant factors.

29.116.2   The access obligation imposed may be in the form of an obligation to meet all reasonable requests for products within the wholesale market in which the operator has SMP.

29.116.3   In addition to a general access obligation, OFCOM may also specify that a particular product or minimum set of products should be available within a particular wholesale market.

29.116.4   If another undertaking requires a new product, it should first submit a request to the SMP operator and both parties should negotiate in good faith. OFCOM's preference is that precise details of new products should first and foremost be refined through commercial negotiation. However, past experience has proved that this does not always work and there may be circumstances when OFCOM needs to get involved by, for example, chairing relevant meetings, specifying terms and timescales on which such products should be offered.

29.116.5   If the SMP operator can demonstrate that it will incur significant development costs in meeting a request for a new wholesale product, OFCOM may provide that the requesting operator should take on an appropriate level of risk, for example by committing to a level of demand at a price that would justify investment by the SMP operator.

29.116.6   The SMP operator should be required to supply an equivalent wholesale product when introducing innovative retail services.

29.117   In addition, the Communications Act[122] allows the imposition of obligations relating to transparency, non-discrimination, price control and regulatory accounting. The guidelines make it clear that OFCOM's intention in attaching other obligations to the supply of wholesale products is that those products should be available on terms which are consistent with those which would apply in a competitive market. If an SMP operator supplies a wholesale product but attaches conditions which will have a material adverse effect on competition, OFCOM will view this behaviour as a constructive refusal to supply.

29.118   The additional obligations include:

---

120   As required by Article 3(1) Access Directive.
121   Imposing Access Obligations under the New EU Directives – 13 September 2002.
122   S 87 Communications Act.

Transparency obligations

29.118.1 These include:

- A requirement to notify prices. This requires a SMP operator to give notice of any price changes typically 28 or 90 days in advance. The period varies in accordance with the perceived risk of abuse by the SMP operator.
- A requirement to notify technical information. This may overlap to some extent with the requirement to publish a reference offer. It is intended to be an additional obligation which in particular imposes a longer 90-day period on the SMP operator for announcing changes in technical specifications.
- An obligation to be transparent as to quality of service. This is a consequence of the fact that the requirement not to discriminate applies also to the quality of service. It imposes an obligation to publish key performance indicators showing that the same level of service applies both to its self provision and the provision to others.

Non-discrimination obligations

29.118.2 Where an access obligation has been imposed OFCOM will generally also impose a non-discrimination obligation. The requirement not to discriminate includes, in particular, a requirement not to discriminate in favour of a service provider's own business.[123] In many cases this is supported by an obligation to maintain cost accounts.

Price control obligations

29.118.3 In determining whether a charge control is needed in addition to a non-discrimination obligation, OFCOM has said that it will need to consider the specific conditions of the market.[124] In general, where markets are not competitive but where market power is diminishing it may be sufficient to rely on an imposition of a non-discrimination obligation and require that charges are based on a retail minus principle. In markets which are not competitive and there is little prospect of introducing competition it is generally appropriate to introduce price regulation in the form of cost based prices.

Accounting separation obligations

29.118.4 The main purpose of an accounting separation obligation is to ensure compliance with a non-discrimination obligation. The form and content of the accounting information typically provides for separate statements for a number of different activities in respect of a vertically integrated operator.

Reference offers

29.118.5 OFCOM has said that it will normally require that information on any new wholesale product is published in the form of a reference offer ('RO'). The

---

123 On 30 June 2005 OFCOM issued for consultation its proposals on how it may investigate potential contraventions of requirements not to unduly discriminate – Undue discrimination by SMP providers.

124 S 3.24 Imposing Access Obligations under the New EU Directives.

requirement to publish a RO specifies in some detail the specific provisions which must be included. These include technical characteristics and standard conditions of access, details of traffic and network management, details of maintenance and quality (including service level commitments) rules of allocation between the parties when supply is limited and standard terms and conditions. Where a RO must be published, service must be provided in accordance with it.

Related Regulatory Powers with Respect to SMP Undertakings

29.119   OFCOM has a duty to set, as it thinks appropriate, SMP conditions requiring the provision of carrier pre-selection and indirect access and the provision of leased lines.[125]

29.120   In addition to these general obligations OFCOM has imposed a number of specific remedies on BT requiring it to provide particular services. These services are generally services which have been the subject of previous disputes and have therefore been scrutinised by either OFCOM or its predecessor. Where there has been detailed regulatory action OFCOM has generally decided to preserve the outcome of the investigations. This has been done in some cases by imposing on BT a specific condition requiring the provision of the relevant service. The principal services dealt with in this way are as:

- *Wholesale Line Rental ('WLR')* - This is a service by which BT rents access lines on wholesale terms to competing operators. It means that competitors are able to provide a bundled lines and calls product. It allows competing operators to take on the full retail relationship with the customer and offer a 'single bill' to end-users for all basic communications services. BT's licence was changed in August 2002 to require it to provide WLR and BT has been providing a basic WLR product since September 2002. OFCOM has imposed an additional condition on BT to provide a fit for purpose WLR product in a number of specified markets.

- *ATM Interconnection* - This concerns the provision by BT of interconnection products which enable competing operators to interconnect at different points of the BT network, thus enabling them to use more of their own networks to provide broadband services.

- *Flat Rate Internet Access Call Origination ('FRIACO')* - FRIACO is the narrowband service by which BT provides to other operators dial up call origination to enable the customer to access the internet on a fixed rate without time based charging. FRIACO has been subject of intense regulatory scrutiny and the results of this are largely preserved in the condition which sets out BT's obligation to provide the wholesale product. The importance of FRIACO has decreased with the increasing popularity of broadband.

- *Partial Private Circuits ('PPCs')* - PPCs are wholesale private circuits provided by a dominant operator (normally BT) connecting the customer's premises to the point of interconnection between BT and another operator. It is intended to allow the competing operator to provide private circuits or other services using in part the BT network and in part its own. The directions reflect previous determinations by the DG of Telecommunications and include requirements on BT as regards migration of services from retail leased lines previously offered to PPCs, ordering procedures, service level agreements and prices.

---

125   Ss 90 and 92 Communications Act.

- *RBS Backhaul and LLU Backhaul* – A similar approach has been adopted for RBS Backhaul (which involves the provision of links to mobile phone companies connecting their radio based stations to their networks) and backhaul for local loop unbundling operators. In each case specific directions set out the specific products required, terms and conditions and pricing.

The proposed undertakings to be given by BT contain additional obligations on BT as regards the provision of a number of services including PPCs, carrier pre-selection, wholesale line rental and backhaul services including the provision of LLU. For example, for PPCs and carrier pre-selection, BT must provide sufficient transparency to other communications providers to enable them to identify differences between the matters that BT is required to list in its RO for the supply of these products and the comparable products that it supplies to itself.

Regulatory Powers Applicable to All Market Participants

Obligations to ensure end-to end-connectivity

29.121 The General Conditions[126] provide that all operators providing public electronic communications networks, if requested by an operator of another such network, must negotiate with a view to concluding an interconnection agreement within a reasonable period. This obligation is reciprocal.

29.122 The broad definition of public electronic communications networks means that a wide range of operators are entitled to benefit from, but are also subject to, the interconnection obligations. To qualify as a public electronic communications network, a network must provide publicly available services. To satisfy this test a network must be theoretically available to anyone who is willing to pay for it and abide by the applicable terms and conditions.

29.123 OFCOM maintains a list of operators which in its view are entitled to interconnection. The list is not mandatory and operators are able to negotiate interconnection without being on the list if they can satisfy other operators that they qualify. The purpose of the list is to give transparency and certainty and avoid the position when BT in effect has to determine whether other operators qualify. However, where a listed person fails to provide a public electronic communications network within a reasonable period OFCOM reserves the right to exclude it from the list.

29.124 In addition, OFCOM also has the power to impose certain access related conditions without a prior finding of SMP. OFCOM can impose obligations on operators to provide network access and service interoperability required (in its view) to secure efficiency on the part of communications operators, sustainable competition and the benefits for end users.[127] This includes requirements relating to facilities sharing and to ensure end-to-end connectivity. An example of the type of condition which could be imposed under these provisions is an obligation on each of Vodafone, O$_2$, T-Mobile and Orange to offer national roaming to 3UK.[128]

---

126 General condition 1.
127 Ss 73–75 Communications Act.
128 OFCOM has postponed its decision on whether to impose roaming pending a tendering exercise being run by 3UK to decide who should supply its 2G and GPRS roaming services

Access to digital radio and television broadcasting services

29.125   Electronic Programme Guides are specifically regulated. OFCOM has a duty to draw up a code giving guidance to providers of EPGs.[129] Any broadcaster operating an EPG must ensure compliance with the code. The code covers such things as the listing and promotion of the public service channels, with OFCOM having the power to require such a 'degree of prominence' as it considers appropriate for the listing of public service channels on the EPG, and the facilities for accessing those channels.

29.126   There are also specific provisions for conditional access systems. These are defined as any arrangement by means of which access to a programme service requires either subscription or authorisation.[130] In effect, this refers to the satellite and to the cable systems, the providers of which can charge broadcasters for carriage of content over their networks. The Communications Act contains provisions which allow OFCOM to regulate the price of access to conditional access systems, with the stated intention of maintaining competition between the providers and providing benefit for end users. OFCOM can also set conditions on a 'dominant' provider in relation to network access, use of relevant networks and availability of relevant facilities. It is currently proposed that the conditions be imposed only on Sky Subscriber Services Limited.

REGULATION OF UNIVERSAL SERVICES AND USERS' RIGHTS: THE UNIVERSAL SERVICE DIRECTIVE

Regulation of Universal Service Obligation

Scope of universal service obligations

29.127   The government, and not OFCOM, determines the specific universal service requirements.[131] OFCOM decides how these should be implemented.[132] The services which must be available include:[133]

- A connection to the public telephone network, able to support voice telephony, fax and data at rates sufficient to support functional Internet access.[134] The government has not set a specific connection speed in the legislation. Guidelines provide that a connection speed of 28.8 Kbit/s is a reasonable benchmark although this may need to be revised over time.
- The provision of at least one comprehensive directory and directory enquiry facility which must be updated once a year.
- The provision of public pay phones to meet the reasonable needs of end users including the ability to use the emergency call number free of charge.

---

from the fourth quarter of 2006. The national roaming condition which applied to O_2 and Vodafone under the previous regime still remains in force.

129   S 310 Communications Act.

130   S 75(3) Communications Act.

131   S 65 Communications Act.

132   As part of its Strategic Review, OFCOM has been looking at universal service and in particular whether it should be extended to mobile and broadband. Its conclusion is that currently an extension of the universal service obligation should not be recommended: Review of Universal Service Obligations: Statement and Further Consultation: 30 June 2005.

133   Electronic Communications (Universal Service) Order 2003 No 1904.

134   Article 4(2) Universal Services Directive.

- Billing and payment options to enable subscribers to monitor and control their expenditure and appropriate tariff options for those on low incomes or with special social needs.
- Special measures for end users with disabilities.

29.128   OFCOM can adopt such measures as it considers appropriate to secure compliance with the obligations set out above and designate which communications providers, if any, must provide such services.[135]

Designation of undertakings obliged to provide universal services

29.129   When deciding whether to designate an undertaking to provide universal services, OFCOM will look, inter alia, at the relative size of the undertaking's business, whether it provides service to at least 100,000 served premises, the financial stability of the undertaking and its relative capability to comply with any or all of the specific conditions.[136]

29.130   OFCOM has implemented the above requirements through:

- a number of specific conditions on BT as a universal service provider, and
- a number of General Conditions imposed on all publicly available telephone service providers. For example, General Condition 8 requires the provision of directory information and General Condition 18 requires the provision of certain facilities for end users with disabilities.

Regulation of retail tariffs, users' expenditures and quality of services

29.131   All the components of universal service must be offered at prices that are affordable to end-users and uniform throughout the UK, unless OFCOM has determined that there is clear justification for not doing so.[137] OFCOM has a duty to keep under review universal service tariffs and to monitor changes to the tariffs. The conditions imposed on BT provide that where an end user has requested service provided under a universal service obligation, it must not require the end user to pay for any other service that they may not have required, by means for example of bundling.

29.132   The universal service conditions provide that BT must publish information on, among other things, its provision of telephony services on request. This information must be published in accordance with the quality of service parameters, definitions and measurement methods referred to in Annex III to the Universal Service Directive and any other additional standards and/or requirements set by OFCOM. OFCOM has the power to require that such information is independently audited and that the costs of any such auditing are met by the provider.

29.133   At the beginning of 2005, OFCOM started a review of the obligations currently imposed on BT to ensure that it is continuing to meet the needs of consumers.

---

135   Ss 66–67 Communications Act.
136   DG of Telecommunications: Notification of proposals for the designation of universal services providers and setting of conditions – 12 March 2003.
137   Regulation 4 Universal Services Order.

Cost calculation and financing of universal services

29.134 The Communications Act does provide for the funding of universal services through cost sharing by communications providers.[138] OFCOM does not currently feel that the cost of providing such services represents an unfair burden on BT. It has, however, said that it recognises that in the future consideration may need to be given to its funding.

Regulation of Retail Markets

Prerequisites for the regulation of retail markets

29.135 OFCOM can set SMP conditions[139] in markets for end users of public electronic communications services in certain circumstances. These are that it has made a determination that a person has SMP in the market and OFCOM considers that it is unable by setting access related or SMP conditions in wholesale markets to fulfil its obligations under the Act in relation to that market.

29.136 OFCOM has determined that BT has SMP in the following retail markets:

* retail low bandwidth traditional interface leased lines up to and including 8 Mbits,[140] and
* fixed narrowband retail services which includes residential and business analogue and ISDN exchange lines services, local calls, national calls, calls to mobile, operator assisted calls and certain international calls on a route by route basis.

Regulatory powers

29.137 The types of conditions which can be imposed are similar to those mentioned above under wholesale controls.[141] These include:

* price control obligations,
* non-discrimination obligations,
* price publication and notification obligations, and
* cost accounting and accounting separation obligations.

29.138 OFCOM has applied a number of controls to the markets listed above, including charge controls. For retail leased lines a cost orientation and cost accounting system will apply but only if BT breaches a voluntary arrangement not to raise the combined prices of a basket of these services by more than RPI before June 2006.[142]

---

138 S 71 Communications Act.
139 S 91 Communications Act.
140 As part of the review OFCOM considered traditional retail leased lines at bandwidths above 8 Mbit/s, however it did not formally identify such markets as it considers that regulation at the wholesale level is sufficient to meet regulatory requirements.
141 S 91(3) Communications Act.
142 DG of Telecommunications: Final Statement: Review of the retail leased lines, symmetric broadband origination and wholesale trunk segments markets.

29.139   For fixed narrowband services, OFCOM has set a safeguard control of RPI-RPI on BT so that BT cannot raise its prices in absolute terms.[143] This control will last until July 2006. The control is applied to the spending patterns of the lowest 80% of residential customers and is based on a basket of services in a number of specified markets. OFCOM has said that it will relax this control to RPI+0 per cent when it is satisfied that a fit-for-purpose WLR product is available.[144]

End User Rights

Contracts

29.140   Providers of public electronic communications services to consumers must (on the request of the consumer) offer to enter into a contract or vary an existing contract.[145] A 'consumer' is defined as a natural person who uses the service for purposes outside his or her trade or profession. The information which must be contained in the contract mirrors that set out under the Universal Services Directive.[146]

29.141   Where the provider intends to modify a condition which is likely to be of material detriment to the consumer, the consumer must be given at least one month's notice of the change and informed of his right to terminate the contract without penalty if the proposed change is not acceptable. This is more limited than the Universal Services Directive[147] which provides that subscribers have a right to withdraw from their contracts without notice upon notice of proposed modifications in the contractual conditions.

29.142   Providers of public electronic communications services are also required to provide certain customers with basic codes of practice covering for example how the provider will handle complaints and comply with a Dispute Resolution Scheme.[148] The dispute resolution procedure must be independent, transparent, simple and free of charge.[149]

29.143   OFCOM has approved two schemes. These are:

- The Telecommunications Ombudsman Scheme (generally known as Otelo), and
- The Communication and Internet Services Adjudication Scheme (generally known as CISAS).

29.144   If a communications provider decides not to join either of the above schemes it is still obliged to have a scheme in place which will need to be approved by OFCOM.

---

143   An RPI-RPI price cap ensures that prices remain flat. RPI + 0% allows increases, but only in line with inflation.
144   DG of Telecommunications: Final Statement: Fixed Narrowband Retail Services Markets: 28 November 2003.
145   General condition 9.
146   Universal Services Directive Article 20.
147   Universal Services Directive Article 20(4).
148   General Condition number 14.
149   The requirement to comply with a dispute resolution scheme derives from article 34 of the Universal Service Directive.

Transparency obligations

29.145   Publicly available telephone service providers only are subject to transparency obligations under the General Conditions.[150] They must ensure, that clear and up to date information on matters such as prices and tariffs and standard conditions is published. The list of information which must be published conforms to the list set out in Annex II of the Universal Services Directive.

Other obligations

29.146   All communications providers who are public electronic communications services are subject to a number of other obligations through the General Conditions. They include the provision of up to date, comparable and adequate information on quality of service.

29.147   Providers of public electronic communications networks are required to provide tone dialling and calling line identification.

29.148   Publicly available telephone service providers are subject to an additional level of regulation. Obligations include:

- to provide basic level of itemised billing,
- additional measures for end users with disabilities,
- requirements as to approval of metering and billing systems, and
- number portability.

DATA PROTECTION: IMPLEMENTATION OF THE E-PRIVACY DIRECTIVE

Confidentiality of Communications

29.149   The E-Privacy Directive has been implemented by the Privacy and Electronic Communications (EC Directive) Regulations 2003[151] (the 'E-Privacy Regulations').

29.150   There is a prohibition on the use of an electronic communications network to store information or gain access to information stored in a user's computer terminal.[152] This includes cookies and other tracking devices. The prohibition does not apply if the user or subscriber:

- is provided with clear and comprehensive information about the purpose and use of the storage of, or access to, that particular information, and
- is given the opportunity to refuse storage or access.

29.151   These conditions regarding the provision of relevant information only apply the first time the cookie or other device is used and apply whether or not the

---

150   General condition number 10.
151   SI 2003/2426, as amended by the Privacy and Electronic Communications (EC Directive) (Amendment) Regulations 2004 (SI 2004/1039). Those in breach of the Regulations are liable to a fine of up to £5,000 (approx €7,500) in a magistrates' court, or unlimited if trial before jury.
152   Reg 6 E-Privacy Regulations.

information relates to personal data.[153] Where the use of a cookie-type device does involve the processing of personal data, service providers will also be required to comply with the provisions of the Data Protection Act.

29.152   Guidance Notes[154] provide that the mechanism by which the user/ subscriber[155] may exercise their right of refusal should be prominent, intelligible and readily available to all. Where the relevant information is contained in a privacy policy, the policy should be clearly signposted at least on those pages where a user may enter a website.

29.153   There is an exemption when either the sole purpose of the cookie or other device is the carrying out or facilitating the transmission of a communication over an electronic communications network; or where such storage or access is strictly necessary for the provision of an information society service[156] requested by the subscriber or user. The prohibition can also be overridden in the interests of national security.[157]

Traffic Data and Location Data[158]

29.154   Location data[159] relating to a user or subscriber of a public electronic communications network or service may only be processed:[160]

- where the user/subscriber cannot be identified by that data, or
- where necessary for the provision of a 'value added' service *and* the user/ subscriber has consented.

29.155   Prior to obtaining consent of the user/subscriber the communications provider must provide certain prescribed information to that user/subscriber set out in the E-Privacy Directive.[161]

---

153   Personal Data is defined in s 1 Data Protection Act. It is defined widely as data relating to living individuals who can be identified from those data, or from those data and other information, which is in the possession of, or is likely to come into the possession of, the data controller. It includes names and addresses but will also include e-mail addresses where the individual can be identified from the address.

154   Information Commissioner: Guidance to the Privacy and Electronic Communications (EC Directive) Regulations 2003.

155   Defined in Reg 2: 'User' means any individual using a public electronic communications service, 'Subscriber' means a person who is a party to a contract with a provider of public electronic communications services for the supply of such services.

156   The E-Privacy Regulations use the same definition of 'Information society services' as the E-Commerce Directive 2000/31/EC. The definition refers to 'any service normally provided for remuneration, at a distance, by means of electronic equipment for the processing (including digital compression) and storage of data, and at the individual request of a recipient of a service'.

157   Reg 28 E-Privacy Regulations.

158   Service providers and operators should also be aware of further obligations concerning the retention of data under the Anti-terrorism, Crime and Security Act 2001 and the voluntary code of practice under the Retention of Communications Data (Code of Practice) Order 2003 (SI 2003/3175) which requires that certain types of data be retained for up to 12 months.

159   Reg 2 E-Privacy Regulations. The definition of location data specifically refers to data relating to the latitude, longitude or altitude of the terminal equipment, the direction of travel of the user and the time the location information was recorded.

160   Reg 14 E-Privacy Regulations.

161   Reg 14(3) E-Privacy Regulations.

29.156 This consent may be withdrawn at any time and the opportunity to withdraw must be given by a simple means and free of charge, at every connection to the public communications network or each transmission of a communication.

29.157 Generally traffic data[162] must be erased or modified so that it no longer constitutes personal data when it is no longer required for the purpose of transmission of the communication.[163] There is an exception for traffic data relating to payment of charges. Traffic data may however be processed and stored for the provision of 'value added' services to that user or subscriber or for the marketing of electronic communications services if the subscriber or user has given his consent. The subscriber or user must be given certain prescribed information before he gives his consent.

Itemised Billing

29.158 All communications providers must provide a basic level of itemised billing[164] to all of their subscribers for the provision of publicly available telephone services, on request and at no extra charge or for a reasonable fee.[165]

29.159 In recognition of the fact that such bills may jeopardise the privacy of users, the Regulations state that providers of public electronic communications services shall, at the request of a subscriber, provide subscribers with bills that are not itemised.[166]

Calling and Connected Line Identification

29.160 The provisions of the E-Privacy Directive relating to calling and connected line identification are implemented by the E-Privacy-Regulations.[167] Communications providers must provide information to the public regarding the availability of such facilities.

Automatic Call Forwarding

29.161 A provider of electronic communications services must ensure that on the request of a subscriber any call forwarding is stopped, free of charge, without any avoidable delay.[168]

Directories of Subscribers

29.162 The General Conditions contain a number of provisions which oblige all communications providers to ensure that customers have access to directories,

---

162 Reg 2 E-Privacy Regulations. The definition of traffic data specifically includes data relating to the routing, duration or time of a communication.
163 Reg 7 E-Privacy Regulations. This also applies to corporate subscribers.
164 General condition 12.   .
165 This general obligation is subject to a number of limited exceptions for example it does not apply to publicly available telephone services provided on a prepaid basis.
166 Reg 9 E-Privacy Regulations.
167 Regs 10–13 E-Privacy Regulations.
168 Reg 17 E-Privacy Regulations.

directories enquiries and directory information. These are all subject to the provisions of relevant data protection legislation. The General Conditions include the following provisions:

29.162.1   All communications providers must ensure that any end user can access directory enquiry facilities containing directory information on all subscribers in the UK who have been assigned telephone numbers by the communications provider, subject to certain limitations including where a subscriber has exercised his right to have his directory information removed.[169]

29.162.2   Where a communications provider assigns telephone numbers to subscribers it must ensure that those subscribers are, on request, supplied with a directory containing directory information. The directory can be produced by the communications provider or a third party and must be updated on a regular basis, at least once a year.[170]

29.163   Personal data of an individual subscriber must not be included in a directory (whether in printed or electronic form) which is made available to the public, including by means of a directory inquiry service, unless the individual has, free of charge, been: informed by the collector of the personal data of the purposes of the directory; and given the opportunity to determine whether the personal data should be included in the directory.[171]

29.164   Corporate subscribers also have the right to request that their data will not be included in a directory.[172]

Unsolicited Communications

29.165   The use of personal data for direct marketing purposes is subject to a number of controls under the Data Protection Act. For example, a data subject has the right to prevent the processing of his personal data for direct marketing purposes at any time, even if he has previously given his consent.

29.166   The Privacy Regulations[173] extend controls on unsolicited direct marketing to all forms of electronic communications.

29.171   There are different provisions for individuals and corporate subscribers. Individual means a living individual but also includes an unincorporated body of such individuals. This include partnerships. There is also a distinction between those who are subscribers[174] and those who are just users.

29.172   E-mail: The definition of e-mail[175] is the same as that in the E-Privacy Directive, with a specific clarification that the definition includes SMS.

29.173   The Regulations set out a prior consent requirement for individual subscribers. This prohibition does not apply to corporate subscribers, and the

---

169 General Condition 8.1.
170 General Condition 8.2.
171 Reg 18(2) and (3) E-Privacy Regulations.
172 Reg 18(4) E-Privacy Regulations.
173 Prior to the introduction of the Privacy Regulations, the Telecommunications (Data Protection and Privacy) Regulations 1999 applied to the use of unsolicited communications for direct marketing purposes. These Regulations applied to unsolicited communications by phone and fax only.
174 See footnote 158 above.
175 Reg 2 E-Privacy Regulations. See Chapter 3 on the E-Privacy Directive.

definition of subscriber means that an e-mail to an individual's specific corporate e-mail address will not be caught by the prohibition, as the individual employee will not normally be a party to the contract for the provision of the e-mail service.

29.174   There is an exemption to this in the context of existing customer relationships.[176] This applies where e-mail addresses have been obtained in the course of 'a sale or negotiations for a sale of a product or service'.[177]

29.175   Automated calling systems: For both individuals and corporate subscribers there is a prohibition unless the subscriber has specifically consented.[178]

29.176   Unsolicited faxes:[179] There is a prohibition for individuals and for corporate subscribers who have specifically notified the caller that they do not want to receive such communications.[180]

29.177   Unsolicited calls: There is a prohibition for corporate subscribers or individuals who have previously notified the caller that such calls should not be made on that line.[181]

29.178   Those involved in direct marketing should also be aware of the British Code of Advertising, Sales Promotion and Direct Marketing.

---

176   As required by art 13 E-Privacy Directive.
177   Reg 22(3) E-Privacy Regulations. Art 13 of the Directive refers to in the context of a sale only.
178   Reg 19 E-Privacy Regulations.
179   For both faxes and calls, OFCOM must keep a register of numbers where the subscriber has registered a general objection to receiving unsolicited marketing calls and faxes on that number; both corporate and individual subscribers can register: regs 25 and 26 E-Privacy Regulations, as amended.
180   Reg 20 E-Privacy Regulations.
181   Reg 21 E-Privacy Regulations.

The Bulgarian Market for Electronic Communications[1]

Violetta Kunze and Lilia Kisseva
Djingov, Gouginski, Kyutchukov & Velichkov

LEGAL STRUCTURE

Basic Policy

30.1 Bulgaria applied to join the European Union (EU) and successfully completed negotiations with the European Commission last year. The accession agreement was signed on 25 April 2005 and the country is due to become a member of the EU by 1 January 2007. Bulgaria's articulate aspiration towards full EU membership and the improved market conditions in the country have determined the governmental and regulatory policy in the telecommunications sector.

30.2 The Bulgarian telecommunications sector has enjoyed substantial growth in the last few years. The market has been fully liberalised since 1 January 2003. The incumbent operator was successfully privatised in 2004 and currently more than a dozen landline operators are active in the country. There are three licensed, privately owned GSM operators and one NMT operator. Three UMTS licences have been recently awarded and the services are expected to be launched in 2006.

Legislation

30.3 The principal sources of Bulgarian telecommunication legislation comprise the laws passed by the Parliament, supported by secondary legislation. In particular, the Bulgarian telecommunications framework consists of:

- the Constitution of the Republic of Bulgaria[2] (the 'Constitution'),
- the Law on Telecommunications[3] ('TL'),
- the Law on Radio and Television[4] ('LRT'),

---

1   Editing of this chapter closed on 8 July 2005.
2   Promulgated in State Gazette Issue no 56 of 13 July 1991; subsequent amendment promulgated in State Gazette Issue no 85 of 26 September 2003.
3   Promulgated in State Gazette Issue no 88 of 7 October 2003, as subsequently amended and supplemented.
4   Promulgated in State Gazette Issue no 138 of 24 November 1998, as subsequently amended and supplemented.

- the Law on Electronic Document and Digital Signature[5] ('LEDDS'),
- the Law on Personal Data Protection[6] ('LPDP'),
- the Law on Protection of Competition[7] ('LPC'), and
- a number of pieces of secondary legislation adopted by the competent executive body or regulatory authority.[8]

30.4   The laws passed by Bulgarian Parliament enjoy superiority over any secondary legislation or rulings of the Communications Regulatory Commission ('CRC' or 'Regulator'), the national regulatory authority. The latter acts are designated to provide further clarity on the statutory provisions and to ensure the uniform implementation of law.

Implementation of EU Directives

30.5   With the adoption of the TL, Bulgaria 'made significant progress in aligning with the *telecommunications acquis*'.[9] The currently effective legislation implements the principles set out in the EU 1998–2000 Regulatory Package and reflects the Bulgarian commitments undertaken in the accession negotiations. Bulgarian legislation shall be further amended so that by 1 January 2007 it is in conformity with the *acquis communautaire* then in force.

REGULATORY PRINCIPLES

Scope of Regulation

30.6   Bulgarian legislation has not yet adopted the principle of technological neutrality set out in the New Regulatory Framework. The TL defines 'telecommunications' as 'conveyance, emission, transmission or receipt of signs, signals, written text, images, sound or messages of any type by wire, radio waves, optical or other electromagnetic medium'.[10] The scope of the telecommunications regulation includes broadcasting, except content, which is governed by the LRT.[11]

30.7   Implementing the traditional telecommunications definitions, the TL defines 'public telecommunications network' as a 'telecommunication network used fully or partially for the provision of public telecommunication services and/or for carrying

---

5   Promulgated in State Gazette Issue no 34 of 6 April 2001, as subsequently amended and supplemented.

6   Promulgated in State Gazette Issue no 1 of 4 January 2002, as subsequently amended and supplemented.

7   Promulgated in State Gazette Issue no 52 of 8 May 1998, as subsequently amended and supplemented.

8   Such as, among others, 'Licence Regulation', 'Interconnection Regulation', 'Leased Lines Regulation' and 'Universal Service Regulation'.

9   Strategy Paper and Report of the European Commission on the progress towards accession by Bulgaria, Romania and Turkey, 2003.

10   Art 1(2) TL.

11   Art 1(2) LRT defines 'radio and television broadcasting activities' as the creation of radio and television programmes for broadcasting by terrestrial transmitter, by cable, by satellite or by other means, in encoded or unencoded form, intended for immediate reception by an unlimited number of persons.

out of telecommunications to an unlimited number of users'[12] and 'telecommunications service' as 'provision of telecommunications in a commercial manner'.[13]

National Regulatory Authorities: Organisation, Regulatory Objectives, Competencies

Organisation and independence

30.8   The telecommunications sector is governed by the Council of Ministers (the government), the National Radio Frequency Spectrum Council and the Minister of Transport and Communications ('MTC'). The national regulatory authority in the telecommunications sector is the CRC, an independent specialised authority and a separate legal entity.

30.9   The audio-visual sector is regulated separately from the telecommunications sector by the CRC and the Council for Electronic Media ('CEM'), an independent specialised state authority and a separate legal entity. Whereas the CRC is the authority in charge of the technical parameters, the CEM regulates the audio-visual activity through registration or issuance of licences, and supervises broadcasters as to the content and manner of broadcasting of their programmes. Anti-competitive practices in the telecommunications and audio-visual sectors are controlled by the LPC, and the national regulatory authority is the Competition Protection Commission ('CPC').

30.10   The CRC consists of five members: the chairperson, who is appointed and dismissed by the government; the vice-chairperson; two members appointed by Parliament; and one member appointed by the President of the Republic. The CRC members serve for five years and for a maximum of two consecutive terms.

30.11   The independence of the CRC, being declared as a principle, is guaranteed by the appointment procedure and eligibility criteria for members and limitations imposed on them during and after their service.

Regulatory objectives and competencies

30.12   Article 19 TL establishes the objectives of the CRC as:

*   implementation of the telecommunications sector policy and the state radio frequency spectrum planning and allocation policy,
*   regulation and control of telecommunications activities, and
*   registration and control of digital signature certification services.

30.13   The powers conferred on the CRC include:

*   issuance, amendment, supplement, suspension, termination and revocation of licences,
*   development of a regulatory policy on using numbers, addresses and names in telecommunications activities,
*   development of the National Numbering Plan,
*   preparation of secondary legislation to be adopted by the MTC or the government,

---

12   Para 1(2) Additional Provisions TL.
13   Para 1(10) Additional Provisions TL.

- determination of the SMP operators and imposition of specific obligations on them,
- assignment of the provision of universal telecommunications services, and
- powers related to the management of the radio frequency spectrum.[14]

30.14   TL entitles the CRC to request from undertakings providing telecommunications activities any information necessary to perform its regulatory functions.[15]

Procedural Rules

30.15   The CRC shall publish an annual report on its activities in its information bulletin and post it on its website.[16] The CEM also issues an Information Bulletin, publishing among other issues the CEM's decisions and monitoring results.[17] The CEM shall also publish an annual report on its activity in the preceding year. The CRC shall conduct public hearings or consultations if it intends to issue general administrative acts,[18] as well as with respect to other issues of public significance for the development of the telecommunications sector.[19] Such consultation procedure is open to 'interested parties' only, legally defined to include 'state bodies, sector organisations of telecommunications operators, consumer organisations and telecommunications operators directly related to the draft measure'.[20] The CRC shall cooperate and exchange information with state bodies and institutions, municipal bodies and non-for-profit organisations in the process of drafting legislation.[21]

Dispute resolution powers

30.16   Currently the CRC is entitled to accept claims against public operators that have failed to fulfil their obligations regarding provision of access to and interconnection of networks, leased-line services and co-location, and to issue mandatory instructions against the defaulting operators.[22]

---

14   Art 27 TL. In implementation of these powers, the CRC has adopted Principles for Management and Allocation of the Radio Frequency Spectrum for Civil Needs and Regulatory Policy on Management of the Radio Frequency Spectrum Allocated for Civil Needs, promulated in State Gazette Issue no 53 of 28 June 2005.

15   Art 33(1) TL.

16   Art 38(3) TL.

17   Art 39(1) LRT.

18   Under Bulgarian law, administrative acts are divided into (i) individual administrative acts, and (ii) general administrative acts. The main difference between the two types of acts is that individual administrative acts grant rights or assign obligations, or affect the rights or obligations of individuals, for example an individual licence, whereas general administrative acts grant rights or assign obligations to an undefined scope of addressees, for example a general licence.

19   Art 36(1) TL.

20   Art 36(2) TL.

21   Art 33(2) TL.

22   Art 124, Art 136, Art 142 and Art 181 TL. See also the Procedures on Review and Rendering a Decision on Requests for Issuing of Mandatory Instructions for Provision of Co-location, issued by the CRC.

Right of Appeal against NRA's Decisions

30.17 Decisions made by the CRC can only be appealed to the Supreme Administrative Court[23] under the procedure of the Law on the Supreme Administrative Court[24] ('LSAC'). The Supreme Administrative Court resolves the cases in a three-member panel, and the decisions of such panel are subject to appeal before the five-member panel of the same court.

30.18 Penal rulings that may be issued by the CRC chairperson for the imposition of administrative sanctions under the TL[25] are subject to appeal before the regional court where the offence has been committed. The judgment of the regional court is subject to appeal before the district court, whereas the judgment of the latter court may be challenged before the Supreme Administrative Court, acting as a court of cassation.

30.19 The right to appeal is given to 'interested parties',[26] interpreted by legal theory and court practice to include the addressees of the decision and any other third party whose rights or obligations are affected by the decision. The law further states that the decisions made by regulatory authorities may be challenged by the Chief Prosecutor and the Deputy Chief Prosecutor to the Supreme Administrative Court.[27] The grounds for challenge must fall within the following categories: lack of power of the authority issuing the decision, failure to meet the requirements of form, material breach of procedural rules, or contradiction to the substantive provisions of the law and failure to pursue the purpose of the law.[28]

Obligation to Co-operate with the Commission

Currently the TL does not set out any obligations of the CRC to co-operate with the Commission.[29]

'Significant Market Power' as a Fundamental Prerequisite of Regulation

Definition of SMP

30.20 A SMP operator is defined as any public telecommunications operator that holds an individual licence, carries out telecommunications through:

* fixed telephone networks and provision of fixed voice telephony services,

---

23 Art 34(2) TL and Art 38(1) LRT.
24 Promulgated in State Gazette Issue no 122 of 19 December 1997, as subsequently amended and supplemented.
25 Art 246 TL.
26 Art 8 LSAC.
27 Art 8 LSAC.
28 Art 12 LSAC.
29 Pursuant to the Sector Policy of Telecommunications in the Republic of Bulgaria (adopted by Decision no 885 of the Council of Ministers of 10 November 2004, promulgated in State Gazette Issue no 104 of 26 November 2004, 'Updated Sector Policy'), the new Law on Electronic Communications or the amendments to the TL, to be adopted by 1 January 2007, shall govern among other issues the co-operation of the CRC at European level with the national regulatory authorities of EU member countries and the Commission.

- provision of leased-line services, or
- mobile telecom networks and provision of voice telephony services through them,

and possesses a share equal to or larger than 25 per cent of the respective telecommunications market coinciding with the territorial scope of the operator's licence.[30]

Particular SMP operators are determined by a justified decision of the CRC. The CRC may decide that an operator enjoys a significant market power even if that operator has a market share of less than 25 per cent on the respective market and, equally, that an operator with a market share over 25 per cent does not have SMP.

30.21   Public operators shall furnish the CRC with all the necessary documentation and information that is specified in the Methodology and in general relates to net income for the preceding year, the total volume of the respective market segment and respective share of the participants in that segment.[31] Particular criteria, formulae and procedures for determining the SMP operators are provided for in detail in the Methodology.

Definition of relevant markets and SMP designation

30.22   The relevant markets are service-based,[32] they are determined by law and do not reflect the definitions set out in the Commission Recommendation on relevant markets.

30.23   BTC AD, the incumbent operator, has been determined as the SMP operator on the markets of fixed voice telephony services and leased-line services by virtue of law. Mobiltel AD, Bulgaria's first mobile operator, is the SMP operator on the market of mobile services for the year 2003 with a market share of 82.7 per cent.[33]

30.24   Once the CRC determines that a certain operator has SMP on the respective market, the CRC has to assign to that operator through amendments to its individual licence specific obligations related to interconnection, provision of leased-line services, provision of special access, provision of unbundled access to the local loop and co-location.

---

30   Art 45(2) and Art 44(1) TL and Art 3 of the Methodology on the Requirements and Procedure for Determining the SMP Operators, promulgated in State Gazette Issue no 61 of 13 July 2004, drafted by the CRC in conjunction with the CPC ('Methodology').

31   Public operators shall deliver to the CRC by 30 April each year a report on their activities for the preceding year that includes information about net income, installed capacity and projected capacity, number of subscribers (number of lines, respectively), average income per subscriber, etc.

32   See para 30.20 above.

33   CRC Decision of 28 October 2004.

The CRC may also assign to the SMP operators the provision of the universal service obligation.[34]

NRA's Regulatory Duties concerning Rights of Way, Co-location and Facility Sharing

30.25 Any public operator[35] which carries out telecommunications through telecommunications networks shall enjoy a right of way if construction of new, or expansion or maintenance of existing, networks or facilities is needed.[36]

The public operator first has to establish whether the contemplated work might be accomplished on state or municipal property. The specific scope of the right of way shall then be determined by an order of the district governor (with respect to state property) or of the mayor (with respect to municipal property). When the right of way cannot be exercised within state- or municipal-owned real estate, public operators shall be granted the right of way over private real estate. The terms and conditions for exercising the right of way shall be subject to a written agreement between the operator and the private owners. If no such agreement is reached and there is no economically feasible technical alternative, the mayor of the municipality shall establish the right of way under the procedure set out in the Law on the Structure of Territory.[37]

30.26 In addition, public operators may also use publicly owned infrastructure (roads, railways, bridges, tunnels, etc) for construction, expansion and use of telecommunications networks.[38] In that case, the operator has to obtain a permit from the authorities or the legal entities that manage the respective part of the infrastructure. The procedure for exercising the right of use should be further specified in a regulation to be adopted by the MTC and the Minister of Regional Development and Public Works.

30.27 The operators are obliged to return, at their expense, the real estate to the condition for its designated or customary use. Furthermore, they are required to indemnify the owner for any damage caused to the real estate.[39]

REGULATION OF MARKET ENTRY

General Regulatory Approach

30.28 Depending on the means used for the provision of public telecommunications services, these can be provided:

---

34 Art 47 TL; the specific obligations that might be imposed by the CRC are discussed in more detail in paras 30.53–30.59 below.
35 Art 43(2) TL: a 'public operator' is 'any person who carries out telecommunications through a public telecommunications network and/or who carries out telecommunications through provision of telecommunications services on the grounds of an individual licence or a registration under a general licence'.
36 Art 174(1) TL.
37 Promulgated in State Gazette Issue no 1 of 2 January 2001, as subsequently amended and supplemented.
38 Art 176(1) TL.
39 Art 174(4) TL.

- freely, without any licensing or registration,
- based on an individual licence, or
- based on registration under a general licence.

30.29   Public telecommunications services that can be provided freely include:[40]

- access to the internet (the provision of 'access to the internet' is carried out on a free regime basis, as long as the internet service provider uses other operators' networks and does not build and maintain its own network),
- services provided using the public telecommunications networks of other telecommunications operators that are either licensed or registered under a general licence,
- telecommunications services provided using telecommunications networks for own needs and without using the radio frequency spectrum, and
- telecommunications services provided using radio equipment and radio equipment networks for own needs using the radio frequency spectrum for common use.[41]

Registration under a general licence is required for performing telecommunications services:

- via a telecommunications network or radio equipment using the radio frequency spectrum for common use determined by the CRC, and
- via a public telecommunications network without using scarce resource.[42]

Registration under a general licence is required also for providing access to satellite systems.

An individual licence is required:

- in the event that telecommunications services are provided by using individually allocated scarce resource,[43]
- for providing fixed voice telephony services and/or universal telecommunications service, and
- for providing leased lines, including international leased lines.[44]

Provision of voice over internet protocol (VoIP) falls within the definition of voice telephony services. Currently, under Bulgarian law an individual licence for the provision of fixed voice telephony services is required for the purposes of provision of VoIP services, provided that the service meets certain quality parameters, including one-way delay of signal of not more than 150 milliseconds.[45] However,

---

40   Art 48(1) TL.
41   The terms and conditions for carrying out telecommunications using radio equipment and radio equipment networks for own needs using radio frequency spectrum for common use are further specified in Regulation N 14 of 27 July 2004 on the Terms and Conditions for Carrying out Telecommunications Using Radio Equipment and Radio Equipment Networks for Own Needs Using Radio Frequency Spectrum for Common Use, promulgated in State Gazette Issue no 72 of 17 August 2004.
42   Art 49(1) TL.
43   Scarce resource is resource that is limited in nature or due to technical reasons, e g numbers from the National Numbering Plan, the radio frequency spectrum and the positions of geo-stationary orbit, allocated for Bulgaria by virtue of international treaties (para 1(18) Additional Provisions TL).
44   Art 49(2) TL.
45   See para 30.31, in particular at note 3, below.

such individual licences are issued without holding an auction or tender, upon application by the interested person and submission of a set of documents required by law.

The particular types of telecommunications services that are subject to registration under a general licence or to individual licensing are specified in detail in the 'Licence Regulation' adopted by the MTC.[46]

Individual Licences

30.30 Individual licences shall be granted according to the principles of objectivity, equal treatment and transparency.[47] The requirements for granting individual licences shall be the same with respect to all applicants for the same type of telecommunications service. Individual licences are granted for up to 20 years with a possibility of extension.[48]

30.31 Where scarce resource is not used, individual licences are granted without holding an auction or tender.[49] Where scarce resource is used, individual licences are granted after holding an auction or tender, except for cases enumerated in the TL.[50] Where an individual licence is granted without holding an auction or tender, the procedure is initiated upon application by the interested person. The CRC should decide on the application within six weeks of its submission; in certain cases provided for in the TL, the term may be extended.

The terms and procedure for issuance of individual licences without holding an auction or tender for specific telecommunications activities shall be set out in regulations adopted by the MTC.[51]

30.32 Where an individual licence is granted after holding an auction or tender, the procedure is initiated by the CRC ex officio or upon request by the interested party.[52] A tender is held when there is a need for a complex assessment, whereas an auction is held where the auction price offered is of material significance.[53]

---

46 Regulation N 13 of 22 December 2003 on Determining the Types of Telecommunications Services Subject to Individual Licence or to Registration under a General Licence, issued by the Minister of Transport and Communications, promulgated in State Gazette Issue no 2 of 9 January 2004, as subsequently amended and supplemented.
47 Art 50(2) TL.
48 Art 60 TL.
49 Art 54 TL.
50 Art 55 TL.
51 Such as Regulation N 12 of 5 May 2004 on the Terms and Procedure for Issuance of Individual Licences for the Provision of Fixed Voice Telephony Services, promulgated in State Gazette Issue no 46 of 28 May 2004, governing the terms and procedure for issuance without holding an auction or tender of individual licences for carrying out telecommunications through, among others, the provision of fixed voice telephony services.
52 Art 61(1) TL.
53 In practice, there have been tenders for issuance of individual licences for the construction, maintenance and operation of a public telecommunications network for radio broadcasting (or for television broadcasting respectively) with local coverage for specific towns. There has also been a tender for issuance of an individual licence for the construction, maintenance and operation of a public telecommunications network for terrestrial television and radio broadcasting with national coverage.

Individual licences are granted by a decision of the CRC, which represents an individual administrative act[54] and is subject to appeal before the Supreme Administrative Court.[55]

Pursuant to article 74 TL, individual licences for the same type of telecommunications services shall impose on operators requirements of the same character, unless the TL provides otherwise. The TL contains a set of conditions that should be obligatorily attached to individual licences.[56]

With respect to radio or television activity, the subject matter, the scope and the term of the individual licence for telecommunications activity using available and/or building, maintaining and using new terrestrial telecommunications networks granted by the CRC, may not deviate from those of the licence for radio or television activity granted by the CEM.[57]

General Licences

30.33   The CRC is obliged to make public the draft general licence and give third parties the opportunity to comment on it within a specified period, but not less than 30 days. The general licence enters into effect as of the date of publication in the State Gazette, unless the licence provides otherwise. The CRC may amend the general licence following the same procedure and if certain prerequisites specified in the TL are met. The CRC shall register eligible applicants wishing to perform telecommunications services under the general licence within 30 days from the date of filing the application for such registration, and after payment of the applicable registration fee.[58] The CRC issues a certificate of registration and it keeps a public registry of the registered entities. If the CRC fails to act on the application, the rights and obligations related to provision of the respective service should arise within 30 days as of the date of filing the application. General licences are not limited in time.

30.34   General licences shall include the conditions that are obligatorily attached to individual licences, as well as special conditions, depending on the type of the telecommunications service performed.[59] Persons registered under a general licence are obliged to comply with the conditions and requirements attached to the general licence.

Rights of Use for Radio Frequencies

30.35   Individual rights of use for radio frequencies are granted through the particular individual licence issued for the respective type of telecommunications activity. No radio frequency licences/permits are required in addition to the telecommunications services authorisation.

30.36   As the radio frequency spectrum is a scarce resource,[60] as a general rule, individual licences for carrying out telecommunications activities by using the radio

---

54   See para 30.15, note 3 above.
55   See paras 30.17 and 30.19 above.
56   Art 73(1) TL.
57   Art 52(2) TL.
58   See para 30.50 below.
59   Art 91 TL.
60   See para 30.29, note 4 above.

frequency spectrum are awarded on a competitive basis (after holding an auction or tender).[61] Holders of such individual licences pay annual fees for use of the radio frequency spectrum. Those fees are determined in the TL and in the Tariff for the Fees Collected by the CRC under the TL[62] (the 'Tariff').[63]

30.37   The Bulgarian regulatory regime does not allow for spectrum trading, and it is not intended to be introduced in the near future as this would require an amendment to the Constitution.

Rights of Use for Numbers

30.38   Modelling the regulatory policy on the use for numbers in the telecommunications falls within the competence of the CRC.[64] The Regulator develops the National Numbering Plan,[65] which sets out the allocation of numbers used in the public networks for identification, routing and charging.

30.39   The rules for allocation and the procedure for assigning, reserving and depriving of numbers are set out in detail in the 'Numbering Regulation' adopted by the MTC.[66] Numbers are also considered to be a scarce resource[67] and shall be allocated only to telecommunications operators with regard to the specific telecommunications activity they will carry out. Bulgarian legislation in force does not provide for the possibility of number trading.

30.40   Number portability with respect to mobile operators shall become effective on 1 January 2007, and with respect to the operators of public fixed networks on 1 January 2009. There is no timetable for introducing a fixed-to-mobile portability or vice versa.

30.41   The TL introduced obligations relating to carrier selection and pre-selection. Thus SMP operators providing fixed voice telephony services are required to secure the ability of any subscriber to choose an operator for long-distance and international calls on a call-by-call or a subscription basis.[68]

The NRA's Enforcement Powers

30.42   The CRC has far-reaching powers to exercise control over the market players' telecommunications activities. The TL establishes both procedural and substantive rules to ensure compliance with the conditions of the respective licences and the law.

---

61   See also para 30.31 above.
62   Promulgated in State Gazette Issue no 31 of 16 April 2004, as subsequently amended and supplemented.
63   See paras 30.49–30.51 below.
64   Art 27, item 10 TL. See also Regulatory Policy on Using Numbers, Addresses and Names in Telecommunications Activities, promulgated in State Gazette Issue 46 of 3 June 2005.
65   Promulgated in State Gazette Issue no 56 of 7 June 2002, as subsequently amended and supplemented.
66   Regulation N 16 of 13 October 2004 on the Rules for Allocation and the Procedure for Assigning, Reserving and Depriving of Numbers, Address and Names, promulgated in State Gazette Issue no 95 of 26 October 2004.
67   See para 30.29, note 4 above.
68   Art 158 TL.

30.43   The CRC may request from any undertaking performing telecommunications activities information to carry out its regulatory functions.[69] CRC officials are entitled to have free access to premises where telecommunications equipment is located, to check commercial and accounting documents of the respective undertaking related to the performed telecommunications activity, and to require information from third parties for counter-checks, etc.[70]

30.44   Where the CRC finds material or repeated breach of the terms of the TL or the conditions of the individual licence, and if the relevant undertaking does not remedy the breach after being notified of such breach and within a remedy period set, the CRC shall withdraw the individual licence.[71] The CRC shall further determine a time period, of not less than 1 year and not longer than 3 years, within which the undertaking may not apply for a new licence for the same activity.[72]

30.45   Further, the CRC may terminate or suspend the performance of some or all activities authorised by an individual licence if a threat to the national security and the defence of the country arises as a result of performance of one or more such activities and upon substantiated request of the competent authorities.[73]

30.46   Where the CRC finds that an operator registered under a general licence does not comply with the conditions and requirements of such general licence, and if the undertaking does not remedy the breach within 30 days as of being notified, the CRC may deregister it.[74]

30.47   Interim measures may be imposed by the CRC in the event of telecommunications activities performed in breach of the TL or the secondary legislation or the respective licence terms, including suspension of the telecommunications activity and closing of premises and/or equipment used for performing the breach.[75]

30.48   The CRC is empowered to impose financial sanctions for breaches of the TL. The types of infringement and the respective financial sanctions are determined by articles 233–346 TL.

Administrative Charges and Fees for Rights of Use

30.49   Administrative charges and fees payable by undertakings providing telecommunications services are determined in the TL and the Tariff.[76] The TL provides for licence fees and registration fees,[77] as well as fees for using scarce resource.[78]

30.50   Undertakings holding individual licences have to pay licence fees, which include an initial fee for the issuance of the licence, an annual fee and a fee for

---

69   Art 33(1) TL.
70   Art 229(1) TL.
71   Art 84(2) TL.
72   Art 84(3) TL.
73   Art 77(1), item 2 TL.
74   Art 92 TL.
75   Art 232 TL.
76   See para 30.36 above.
77   Art 220(1) TL.
78   Art 220(2) TL.

amendment and/or supplement of the licence.[79] Such undertakings also pay annual fees for use of scarce resource.[80] Undertakings registered under a general licence pay a registration fee.[81]

30.51   All administrative charges and fees imposed by the CRC shall be determined in accordance with the principles set out in the TL.[82] The amount, terms and methods of payment of fees are further specified in the Tariff.

REGULATION OF NETWORK ACCESS AND INTERCONNECTION

Objective and Scope of Access Regulation

30.52   The TL aims at securing open access to the networks of the public operators, as well as guaranteeing competitive access for new entrants to the end users. In the process of regulating access to and interconnection of the public telecommunications networks and associated facilities, the TL basically implements the Interconnection Directive and the ONP Voice Telephony Directive 1997.

Special Access and Unbundled Access to the Local Loop

30.53   'Special access to a public fixed telephone network' means the access to points of the network different from the network terminal points determined by the CRC for the purpose of providing telecommunication services.[83]

30.54   The TL transposes the requirements set out in Regulation 2887/2000 of 18 December 2000[84] with respect to unbundled access to the local loop with (physical) twisted metallic pair (circuit).[85]

30.55   The SMP operators on the market of fixed voice telephony services are obliged to provide special access to their network as well as unbundled access to the local loop upon a justified and technically feasible request by adhering to the principle of non-discrimination. They may refuse to provide access only if the requirements related to preserving the integrity of the network are not met by the entity making the request.

Special access by SMP operators shall be granted through a written agreement that has to be submitted for review to the CRC three weeks prior to the contemplated effective date. The CRC may issue mandatory instructions demanding such amendments as it deems necessary for procuring interoperability between the services in the interests of the end-users and/or for assuring effective competition.[86]

---

79   Art 221 TL.
80   Art 222 TL.
81   Art 223 TL.
82   Art 224(3) TL.
83   Art 125(1) TL.
84   Regulation (EC) No 2887/2000 of the European Parliament and the Council of 18 December 2000 on the unbundled access to local loops, OJ L 336/4, 30.12.2000; see also recital 12 sentence 2 Access Directive.
85   Art 125(2) TL.
86   Art 132 TL.

Interconnection

30.56   Public operators that provide transmission through their networks shall be vested with the right and imposed with the obligation to interconnect. The TL groups the operators that fall within that category as follows:[87]

- operators providing telecommunications services through fixed and/or mobile public telecommunications networks, which manage the facilities for access to one or more terminal points of the network, using numbers of the National Numbering Plan,
- operators providing leased-line services, except those that re-rent leased lines, and
- operators carrying out telecommunications through telecommunication networks, whose licences stipulate interconnection.

30.57   In general, public telecom operators shall interconnect their networks in a way that would allow the subscribers to one of the networks to use at least one of the following services rendered by the networks of the same or another operator:

- voice telephony services, permitting also facsimile and data transmission, and
- access to emergency calls.

End users may use any other services offered by the public operators and included in the respective interconnection agreement. By interconnecting, public operators provide the main network services 'origination' and 'termination', as well as any other additional services, which might be needed. The conditions and procedures for interconnection are further clarified in the 'Interconnection Regulation' adopted by the MTC.[88]

The SMP operators providing fixed voice telephony services are required to draft a Reference Interconnection Offer ('RIO'). The minimum contents of the RIO is statutorily determined.[89] The CRC shall approve the respective RIO within 45 days of its submission. The RIO shall be made available for public discussion, organised by the CRC, within a period of not less than 30 days.

Access to Leased Lines

30.58   The TL establishes the principle that leased-line services shall be made available to any person upon his request. In turn, only licensed operators may provide that service.[90] The conditions and procedures for provision of leased-line services are set out in detail in the 'Leased Lines Regulation' adopted by the MTC.[91]

The SMP operators providing leased-line services shall draft a Reference Offer for entering into a leased lines agreement. The minimum contents of such a Reference Offer is determined by article 140(4) TL. The CRC shall approve the respective Reference Offer within 45 days of its submission. The Reference Offer shall be made available for public discussion, organised by the CRC, within a period of not less than 30 days.

---

87   Art 114(1) TL.
88   Regulation N 10 on the Conditions and Procedures for Interconnection, promulgated in State Gazette Issue no 60 of 7 July 2004.
89   Art 119(2) TL.
90   See para 30.29 above.
91   Regulation on the Conditions and Procedures for the Provision of Leased-line Services, promulgated in State Gazette Issue no 10 of 6 February 2004.

SMP operators on the leased-line services market are obliged to provide a minimum package of standard leased lines with technical characteristics defined in the 'Leased Lines Regulation'. They may refuse to provide a 'leased line' included in the minimum package only if the requirements regarding preserving the integrity of the network, securing interoperability and personal data protection are not met by the entity making the request.

Co-location and Facility Sharing

30.59 The TL provides for the right of any public operator to request a shared use of premises and facilities used by any other public telecommunications operator.[92] The terms and conditions for such shared use should be agreed between the operators. The law obliges SMP operators providing fixed voice telephony services, and public operators with SMP on the leased-line services market, to grant a request for co-location unless technical or physical obstacles exist. Those SMP operators shall draft general conditions for co-location, which need to be approved by the CRC. The minimum contents of the general conditions for co-location is determined by article 179(2) TL.

Price Regulation

30.60 Wholesale prices are not subject to control by the CRC. They may only be challenged before the CPC on the basis of general competition law.

REGULATION OF UNIVERSAL SERVICES AND USERS' RIGHTS

Regulation of Universal Service Obligations

Scope of universal service obligations

30.61 Universal services are defined as services of specified quality to which all end users shall have access, independently of geographic location and at an affordable price.[93] Pursuant to article 93 TL, universal services include:

- initial connection at a fixed location to the public telephone network at an end point of such network, including access to publicly available voice telephony services at a fixed location, as such connection shall allow end-users to make and receive local, national and international telephone calls, as well as facsimile communications and data communications,
- access at a fixed location to voice telephony service through public pay phones, including the possibility to make emergency calls from public pay phones free of charge,
- the provision of a comprehensive directory for the numbers of end-users of fixed networks and of a comprehensive telephone directory enquiry service for the numbers of end-users of fixed and mobile networks,
- the possibility to make emergency calls free of charge, and

---

92   Art 177(1) TL.
93   Art 93(1) TL.

- access at a fixed location to voice telephony services under special conditions and/or procuring end devices, where appropriate, for disabled users.

30.62   The terms and procedure for ensuring the provision of the universal services and the quality that these should meet are set out in the Universal Service Regulation adopted by the MTC.[94]

Designation of Undertakings Obliged to Provide Universal Services

30.63   In order to ensure the provision of universal services on the entire national territory, the CRC shall designate one or more telecommunications operators which are obliged to provide some or all of the universal services.[95] SMP operators carrying out telecommunications services using a fixed telecommunications network and providing fixed voice telephony services are under an obligation to provide universal services.[96] With effect from 1 January 2005, the CRC shall hold a tender for designating operators, who are not SMP operators, to provide universal services.[97] Such tender is to be held upon request of the operators not designated as SMP operators. As of the date of this publication, such a tender has not yet been held.

Regulation of Retail Tariffs, Users' Expenditures and Quality of Service

30.64   Designated undertakings are obliged to determine affordable prices of the universal services on the basis of a methodology prepared by the CRC and adopted by the Council of Ministers. The prices of the universal services shall be made available to the public.

30.65   In order to allow subscribers to control their expenditures for universal services, designated undertakings shall allow subscribers (subject to technical feasibility) to monitor and restrict in due course the use of services which they would like to stop using.[98]

30.66   The quality parameters that universal services shall meet are set out in the Universal Service Regulation.[99]

30.67   The CRC has regulatory powers to monitor compliance with performance targets in relation to universal services.[100] If an undertaking materially or persistently breaches the provisions, including the universal service-related provisions, of the TL or its licence, or if an undertaking has no financial or technical capacity to perform its activity, the CRC may withdraw its licence after a prior written

---

94   Regulation N 15 of 2 September 2004 on the Terms and Procedure for Ensuring of the Universal Service and the Quality that it should Meet, promulgated in State Gazette Issue no 85 of 28 September 2004, effective as of 28 September 2004.
95   Art 94(1) TL.
96   Art 95(1) TL.
97   Art 95(2) TL.
98   Art 101 TL.
99   See para 30.62 above.
100   Art 102(2) TL.

notification of a specified term.[101] Also, subscribers may file claims to the designated operator or to the CRC regarding the provision of the universal services. Designated operators shall reply to any claims within 30 days of receipt thereof.[102]

Cost Calculation and Financing of Universal Services

30.68   The TL entitles the CRC to adopt rules for determining the net cost of universal service provision.[103] Designated undertakings wishing to receive compensation for the net cost of universal service provision shall prepare a system for determining the net cost based on the rules adopted. Such system is subject to approval by the CRC.

30.69   A designated undertaking may request compensation for the net cost of universal service provision where the provision of such service is found to constitute an 'unfair burden'[104] on it. Compensation of the net cost of the universal service provision is financed from a Fund for Guaranteeing the Universal Service Provision. Telecommunications operators providing voice telephony services contribute to the said fund.[105]

Regulation of Retail Markets

30.70   The principle that regulation of retail services is permissible only if regulation at wholesale level does not achieve the regulatory objectives has not been implemented yet into the national law.[106] Only the following prices, determined by SMP operators in the market of fixed telephone networks and fixed telephone services and provision of leased line services, are subject to regulation by the CRC:

- fixed voice telephony services,
- interconnection,
- provision of a minimum set of leased lines,
- specific access,
- unbundled access to the local loop, and
- co-location.[107]

The prices of said services may not be abusive or anti-competitive. Further, the prices may not create advantages for individual users of the same or similar service, or be below the cost of provision of the respective service.[108] SMP operators have to communicate the prices of the said services to the CRC prior to market launch. If the prices do not comply with the TL, the CRC may oblige designated undertakings to change the prices and, if the undertakings fail to do so, and after consultation

---

101   Art 84(1) TL.
102   Art 16(2) and (3) Universal Service Regulation.
103   Art 105 TL. See also Rules on Calculating the Net Cost of Public Operators of Universal Service Provision, promulgated in State Gazette Issue no 52 of 24 June 2005.
104   Cf art 104(2) TL.
105   Art 110 TL.
106   The Updated Sector Policy envisages the implementation of such principle by 1 January 2007 and the determination of SMP operators on the markets of interconnection and provision of leased lines, and fixed and mobile networks and services.
107   Art 215 TL.
108   Art 216(4) TL.

with the CPC, the CRC may set price caps for a period of up to six months.[109] SMP operators providing leased-line services shall determine prices that follow the principles of cost orientation and transparency, and make public tariffs and supply conditions in respect of the minimum set of leased lines.[110]

End User Rights

Contracts

30.71   When the execution of individual contracts only is not feasible in practice, public operators may use general terms and conditions to govern their relationships with end-users. Public operators that provide telecommunications services using fixed telephone networks and mobile networks are obliged to use general terms and conditions.[111]

30.72   The TL establishes minimum content requirements for general terms and conditions.[112]

30.73   The minimum content requirements apply also to individual contracts between end-users and public operators, where the service is provided solely on the basis of such contract.

30.74   General terms and conditions prepared by public operators are subject to approval by the CRC.[113] The CRC reviews the general terms and conditions as to conformity with the terms of the respective licence, and it is entitled to issue mandatory instructions and set a time period for corrections. Public operators shall publish their general terms and conditions after these have been approved by the CRC.

30.75   General terms and conditions can be modified upon initiative of the public operator following the procedure for initial approval thereof. In the second place, end-users may file with the CRC a request for modification of the general terms and conditions, and the CRC shall rule on such request following the procedure of the TL.[114] In the third place, the general terms and conditions may be modified upon the initiative of the CRC with a view to protecting the interests of end-users.[115]

Transparency Obligations

30.76   Public operators are obliged to provide telecommunications services to end-users in compliance with the principle of transparency. SMP operators have to publish prices, which are subject to regulation by the CRC. They are required to

---

109   Arts 217 and 218 TL.
110   Ch III Leased Lines Regulation.
111   Cf Art 146(3) TL; Art 147 TL.
112   Art 148 TL.
113   Art 149(1) TL; Art 151 TL: an opportunity for the CRC to prepare standard form general terms and conditions governing the relationships between end-users and public operators. In such case, public operators have to prepare their general terms and conditions following the pattern of such standard form general terms and conditions, and again submit these to the CRC for approval.
114   Art 150(3) and (4) TL.
115   Art 150(5) TL.

update and make publicly accessible their calculation system for determination of prices and to publish an annual analysis on the application of the principle of cost orientation of prices and of separate accounting for the services offered by them.[116]

Operator Assistance and Directory Inquiry Services

30.77   Telecommunications operators are obliged to provide assistance for ensuring telecommunications in the event of crisis or emergencies.[117] Obligations, requirements and restrictions related to the national defence and security shall be set out in the respective individual or general licences.

30.78   Subject to applicable data protection provisions, subscribers to publicly available telephone services have the right to have an entry in the publicly available directory free of charge.[118]

Obligations to Provide Additional Facilities

30.79   Operators of public mobile or fixed telephone networks providing voice telephony services shall make available to end-users, subject to technical feasibility, calling-line identification and connected-line identification.[119] Operators shall ensure that calling-line identification may not be deactivated for emergency calls.[120]

DATA PROTECTION AND PRIVACY

Confidentiality of Communications

30.80   Public telecommunications operators are obliged to take all necessary technical and organisational measures to ensure confidentiality of communications. The confidentiality obligations apply to the type of the service, the contents of the communications and all data related to the provision of the service.[121] Where there is a risk of security breach, subscribers must be informed of the risk and possible remedies, as well as cost implications.[122]

30.81   The TL contains a general prohibition on surveillance or interception or storage of communications designated for third parties.[123] Exceptions exist where the respective third party has given their consent or where such exception is provided for by law. Thus the TL obliges public telecommunications operators to ensure the possibility for interception and continuous surveillance of telecommunications related to national security and public order.[124] Such possibility shall be ensured through provision by the telecommunications operators of one or several interception interfaces and shall be effected only under the procedure of the Law on

---

116   Art 217(4) TL.
117   Art 183 TL.
118   Art 205(1) TL.
119   Art 204(1) TL.
120   Art 204(4) TL.
121   Art 195(1) TL.
122   Art 195(2) TL.
123   Art 196 TL.
124   Art 186 TL.

the Special Intelligence Means.[125] The requirements regarding interception interfaces shall be co-ordinated between the telecommunications operators and the competent authorities and included in the respective operator's telecommunications licence.[126]

30.82   Currently the TL does not contain any provisions in relation to the storage of or access to information on the terminal equipment of a subscriber/user (eg through cookies).[127]

Traffic Data and Location Data

30.83   Traffic data is defined as data necessary for the provision of telecommunications services, including inter alia calling and connected line identification, geographical position of a mobile end user, beginning and end of the call, type of the telecommunications service used and data necessary for the billing of the call.[128] Bulgarian telecommunications law does not provide for a separate definition of location data.

30.84   Public telecommunications operators may collect, process and use traffic data and data necessary for the purposes of subscriber billing. Traffic data processed for the purposes of transmitting communications must be erased or made anonymous after termination of the communications, unless such data is needed for transmitting new communications or in cases provided for by law.[129] Storage of data necessary for the purposes of subscriber billing is permissible only for the period during which the bill may be lawfully challenged or payment pursued.[130]

Itemised Billing

30.85   Providers of universal services related to fixed voice telephony shall provide to subscribers itemised bills for the services rendered, including information on the duration and value of the calls made.[131]

---

125   Promulgated in State Gazette Issue no 95 of 21 October 1997, as subsequently amended and supplemented.
126   The conditions and the procedure for coordination of the requirements towards interception interfaces and other related issues are set forth in Regulation N I-107 of 9 June 2004 on the Conditions and the Procedure for Coordination of the Requirements towards Interception Interfaces and Other Issues Related Thereto, promulgated in State Gazette Issue no 53 of 22 June 2004.
127   Pursuant to the Updated Sector Policy the legal framework ensuring a possibility for subscribers/users to refuse the use or installation on their terminal equipment of cookies for the purposes of facilitating the use of electronic services (such as advertisements, bank operations, etc) should be elaborated by 1 January 2007.
128   Art 197(2)(1) TL.
129   Art 199(1) TL.
130   Art 199(2) TL.
131   Art 13(1) and (2) Universal Service Regulation.

Calling and Connected Line Identification

30.86   Subject to technical feasibility, service providers shall ensure calling and connected line identification functions of the network.[132] Service providers offering calling line identification services must allow users to eliminate the presentation of calling line identification on a per-call or per-line basis, using simple means and free of charge.[133] An exception from this service exists in respect of calls to the emergency services.

Automatic Call Forwarding

30.87   Subject to technical feasibility of the terminal equipment, users to whom calls have been automatically forwarded as a result of third party actions have the right, without charge, to request that such forwarding be ceased.[134]

Directories of Subscribers

30.88   Subscribers are entitled to refuse part or all of their entry in a publicly available directory free of charge.[135] The terms and procedure for issuance of directories including the processing of related data shall be set out in a regulation to be adopted by the MTC.[136]

Unsolicited Communications

30.89   Telecommunications operators carrying out telecommunications activities through a mobile or fixed telephone network and providing voice telephony shall make, or make their networks available for the making of, calls or provision of fax messages, designated for direct advertisement, only with the explicit written consent of their subscribers.[137] Telecommunications operators also have to comply with the general provisions of the LPDP. The LPDP establishes an opt-out system, whereby any data subject is entitled to forbid a personal data administrator from providing fully or partially his or her processed personal data to third parties for the purposes of trade information, advertisement or market survey.[138]

---

132   Art 204(1) TL.
133   Art 204(3) TL.
134   Art 204(5) TL.
135   Art 205(3) TL.
136   Pursuant to the Updated Sector Policy such subsidiary legislation is to be adopted by mid-2005 and is to govern the right of subscribers to be informed in advance of the purposes of the directory and search functions embedded in electronic versions of the directory, as well as the right of subscribers to have personal data included in the directory with their consent.
137   Art 204(6) TL.
138   Art 28(1), item 4 LPDP.

The Norwegian Market for Electronic Communications[1]

Knut Glad, Espen Sandvik, Nicolai Stenersen and Margarethe Stoltz
Arntzen de Besche Advokatfirma AS

LEGAL STRUCTURE

Basic Policy

31.1 The overall market conditions in Norway are characterised by an increasing degree of liberalisation, mainly through the implementation of EU legislation. However, the now listed and partly privatised incumbent telecom operator, Telenor, still has a large share of the various telecom markets.

31.2 The main objective of Norwegian telecommunications law, as stated in the Electronic Communications Act ('E-Com Act'),[2] is 'to secure good, reasonably priced and future-oriented electronic communications services for the users throughout the country through efficient use of society's resources by facilitating sustainable competition, as well as stimulating industrial development and innovation'.[3]

Implementation of EU Directives

31.3 Norway is not a member of the EU. As a member of the EFTA,[4] Norway is however a contracting party to the EEA[5] Treaty.

31.4 The EEA Treaty imposed an obligation on the contacting parties to implement the then existing EC legislation by 1 January 1993. In addition, Article 102 EEA Treaty provides a system for the implementation of all subsequent EC directives covered by the EEA Treaty. In practice, this means that all EC Directives will be implemented.

31.5 As a result, Norway has implemented the Regulatory Package, mainly by enacting the new E-Com Act and sub-ordinate legislation hereto.

---

1   Editing of this chapter closed on 27 May 2005.
2   LOV-2003–07-04–83.
3   § 1–1 E-Com Act.
4   European Free Trade Association, currently consisting of Iceland, Liechtenstein, Switzerland and Norway.
5   European Economic Area.

Legislation

31.6   The main statutory instrument in the telecommunications sector is the E-Com Act of 4 July 2003. The E-Com Act is supplemented by various regulations, the most significant one being the Regulation on Electronic Communication Networks and Electronic Communications Services of 16 February 2004 ('E-Com Regulation').[6]

REGULATORY PRINCIPLES

Scope of Regulation

31.7   The E-Com Act applies to all types of activity connected to the transmission of electronic communications (transmission of sound, text, pictures or other data using electromagnetic signals in free space or by cable in a system for signal transmission) and associated infrastructure, services, equipment and installations.[7] Moreover, management and use of the electromagnetic frequency spectrum, and use of numbers, names and addresses are covered. The same applies to all radiation of electromagnetic waves from electronic communications and all inadvertent radiation of electromagnetic waves that may interfere with electronic communications. The E-Com Act does not, however, regulate content.

31.8   An 'electronic communications network' is defined as an 'electronic communications system that includes radio equipment, switches, other connection and routing equipment, associated equipment or functions'.[8] 'Electronic communications service' is defined as a 'service that wholly or primarily comprises arrangement of electronic communications and that is normally provided for a fee'.[9] 'Associated facilities' is not defined in the E-Com Act.

31.9   The Norwegian Post and Telecommunications Authority regards VoIP to be covered by the definition of electronic communication service, provided that the VoIP service offers all-to-all communication (rendering it possible both to originate and terminate calls in other networks).[10] All regulations applicable to electronic communication services is as a result also applicable to VoIP services. The NPT has announced that temporary exemptions from the E-Com Act may be granted, based on individual applications from VoIP providers.

National Regulatory Authorities: Organisation, Regulatory Objectives, Competencies

31.10   The Norwegian Post and Telecommunications Authority ('NPT') is an autonomous administrative agency, subordinate to the Norwegian Ministry of Transport and Communications. The NPT is responsible for the monitoring of the postal and telecommunication markets in Norway. Further, the NPT has been empowered to pass subordinate legislation supplementing the E-Com-Act. The

---

6   FOR-2004–02-16–401.
7   § 1–2 E-Com Act.
8   § 1–5 no. 2 E-Com Act.
9   § 1–5 no. 4 E-Com Act.
10   NPT guidelines 15 April 2005.

NPT also manages spectrum and national numbering resources and regulates the placing on the market of radio and communications equipment.

31.11   The NPT cooperates with the Norwegian Competition Authority in respect of issues governed by the Norwegian Competition Act.[11] This cooperation is regulated in an agreement between said administrative bodies.[12]

31.12   Neither the NPT nor the Competition Authority can be instructed by the Ministry or other governmental bodies on how to handle individual cases.[13]

31.13   Both the NPT and the Competition Authority may demand certain information from the telecom operators. The NPT has extensive powers to demand information regarding amongst others quality of services, terms and conditions, contingency plans in the event of bankruptcy, and specifications for interfaces.[14] The Competition Authority may demand any information that it believes is significant in relation to the enforcement of the Competition Act.[15]

31.14   The Civil Services Act[16] applies to any decision adopted by the NPT. Before the NPT makes individual decisions regarding issues that may have an influence on the telecom market, all interested parties shall be heard.[17] Before deciding on issues that may affect trade between the EEA countries[18] the NPT shall consult with the EFTA Surveillance Authority ('ESA').

31.15   In disputes between telecom providers, the NPT may act as a mediator,[19] and in certain cases also adjudicate.[20]

Right of Appeal against NRA's Decisions

31.16   Decisions made by the NPT may be appealed to the Ministry of Transport and Communications.[21] Decisions made by either the NPT or the Ministry may also be tried by the courts of law.[22] However, the discretionary elements of the decisions are not subject to the court's review. The Ombudsman for Public Administration[23] may also consider the decisions of the NPT, but is only empowered to make non-binding statements.

The NRA's Obligations to Cooperate with the Commission

31.17   The NPT is obliged to cooperate with ESA rather than the Commission, as Norway is a member of the EEA rather than the EU. There is however close contact and co-operation between ESA and the Commission.

---

11   LOV-2004–03-05–12.
12   Agreement of 28 February 2005.
13   § 10–2 (2) E-Com Act.
14   § 10–3 E-Com Act.
15   § 24 Competition Act.
16   LOV-1967–02-10.
17   § 9–2 E-Com Act.
18   Including all EU Member States.
19   § 11–1 E-Com Act.
20   § 11–2 E-Com Act.
21   § 11–6 E-Com Act.
22   § 11–1 (2) E-Com Act.
23   The Parliamentary Ombudsman is appointed by the Parliament and investigates complaints from citizens concerning injustice or maladministration on the part of public administration

31.18 The NPT is obliged to consult with ESA before concluding on any matter that may have a cross-border effect between the EEA countries.[24] [25]

31.19 If ESA concludes that a draft decision from the NPT regarding definitions of new markets or appointment or withdrawal of a SMP position may affect the trade between the EEA nations or establish a trade barriers violating the EEA agreement, or ESA is in serious doubt as to whether the draft decision is in accordance with EEA law, it may instruct the NPT to withdraw the proposal.[26]

31.20 In matters relating to the definition of relevant product and service markets and geographical markets, and in matters regarding analysis and assessment of significant market power,[27] the NPT's decision has to be in accordance with ESA's recommendations.[28]

'Significant Market Power' as a Fundamental Prerequisite to Regulation

Definition of SMP

31.21 The Norwegian law definition of Significant Market Power (SMP) is the same as in article 14(2) Framework Directive.[29] SMP in one market is relevant when considering possible SMP in a closely related market.[30]

Definition of relevant markets and SMP designation

31.22 The NPT is responsible for defining relevant product and services markets.[31] Consideration must be given to ESA's recommendations.[32]

31.23 A total of 18 product markets have so far[33] been identified by the NPT, none of these deviate from the Commission Recommendation on relevant markets.[34]

31.24 The NPT is also responsible for identifying providers having SMP. This identification shall be conducted in cooperation with ESA, and according to ESA's recommendations.[35] So far, no provider has been identified as having SMP. It is expected that the process of identifying SMP undertakings will be concluded during the second half of 2005.

31.25 A wide range of different obligations may be imposed on SMP undertakings. Some of the remedies cannot be imposed unless ESA has been consulted.[36]

---

24 See fn 18 above.
25 § 9–3 E-Com Act.
26 § 9–3 (2) E-Com Act.
27 See paras 31.21 et seq below.
28 § 3–2 E-Com Act.
29 § 3–1(1) E-Com Act.
30 § 3–1(2) E-Com Act.
31 § 3–2 E-Com Act.
32 ESA recommendation 14 July 2004 (No 194/04/COL).
33 May 2005.
34 See para 1.72 above.
35 § 3–2 E-Com Act.
36 § 9–3 E-Com Act and § 3–4(3) E-Com Act.

Such obligations are imposed by the NPT at its own discretion. The NPT does not have any express obligation to impose obligations on SMP undertakings. The NPT may also impose obligations on undertakings not having SMP, but only in relation to interconnection obligations[37] and co-location obligations.[38]

NRA's Regulatory Duties concerning Rights of Way, Co-location and Facility Sharing

Rights of way

31.26   As a starting point, rights of way must be obtained by means of voluntary agreements with the landowners. If it is not possible to reach an agreement with a landowner, the E-Com Act and the Compulsory Acquisition Act[39] may in certain cases entitle the telecom provider to be granted right of way for telecom purposes.[40] Compulsory acquisition requires payment of compensation to the landowner.[41] The Ministry of Transport and Communications is empowered to grant the right to undertake a compulsory acquisition.[42]

31.27   If the construction of telecommunication facilities falls within the scope of the Norwegian Planning and Construction Act,[43] notification or application must be filed with the local planning authorities in advance.

Co-location and facility sharing

31.28   The NPT may impose obligations on providers of electronic communication networks in relation to facility sharing. Such obligations may be imposed if considerations of effective use of resources, considerations of health, the environment, safety or other social considerations suggest that duplication of infrastructure should be avoided.[44]

31.29   Facility sharing may be imposed by the NPT on providers that have been granted rights of way through compulsory acquisition.[45] Further, the NPT may impose on providers with SMP an obligation to accept reasonable requests for co-location or other shared utilisation of infrastructure within the market where the provider has SMP. Such orders may only be given if this is needed in order to promote sustainable competition.[46]

REGULATION OF MARKET ENTRY

General Regulatory Approach

31.30   Prior to the implementation of the EU Regulatory Package, SMP providers of public telecom networks and services were subject to individual licensing. The

---

37   § 4–2(2) E-Com Act.
38   § 4–4 E-Com Act.
39   LOV-1959–10-23–3.
40   § 12–3 E-Com Act and § 2(9) Compulsory Acquisition Act.
41   § 2(9) Compulsory Acquisition Act.
42   § 5 Compulsory Acquisition Act.
43   LOV-1985–06-14–77.
44   § 4–4 E-Com Act.
45   See para 31.26 above.
46   § 4–4 (3) E-Com Act.

E-Com Act introduced a general authorisation regime which means that individual licences are now only required for the use of numbers and certain radio frequencies.

31.31   The general authorisation is subject to various conditions,[47] which reflect most of those admissible according to Annex A Access Directive.[48]

31.32   Notification is required for:[49]

'the establishment, operation and provision of access to electronic communication networks which are being used for provision of public electronic communication services, public telephony services and public transmission capacity'.

The notification procedure involves the filing of a notification form and an interface form with the NPT. The activities subject to notification may begin once notification has been filed.[50] Confirmation of registration is not given unless requested, but the operators that have been registered are listed on the NPT website.[51]

Rights of Use for Radio Frequencies

General regulatory approach

31.33   A national frequency plan has been established by the NPT.[52] The plan forms the basis for awards of both general authorisations and individual licences.

31.34   The Regulation on Allowed Use of Frequencies of 20 December 2000 ('Frequency Regulation')[53] establishes a general authorisation for the use of frequencies below 9 kHz and above 400 GHz.[54] Certain frequencies between 9 kHz and 400 GHz are also covered by the general authorisation, but only for designated types of use (ie use for remote controls and radio controls for toys), and on conditions relating to technical requirements.

31.35   Frequencies not covered by the general authorisation may not be used without an individual licence from the Ministry.[55] An application may be declined if this is justified in light of objectives such as efficient use of resources through sustainable competition, free movement of services and harmonised use of frequencies.[56]

---

47   Ch 2 E-Com Act.
48   See paras 1.96 et seq above.
49   § 2–1 E-Com Act and §1–2 E-Com Regulation.
50   § 1–2 E-Com Regulation.
51   www.npt.no.
52   § 6–1 E-Com Act (frequency plan published on www.npt.no).
53   FOR-2000–12-20–1399. Work on a replacement regulation is ongoing.
54   § 5 Frequency Regulation.
55   § 6–2(1) E-Com Act.
56   § 6–2 E-Com Act.

Admissible conditions

31.36 The conditions that may be attached to a licence[57] reflect the conditions allowed for in Part B of the Annex to the Authorisation Directive.[58] The conditions must be objectively justified, non-discriminatory, proportionate and transparent.[59]

Limitation of number of rights of use to be granted

31.37 The number of licences for use of the spectrum may be limited by the NPT, but only if this is required in order to protect the interests of the users and to ensure sustainable competition.[60] Before the number of licences can be limited, a public hearing must be held.[61] The decision must be in writing, and the reasons for the decision must be stated. Those interested must be allowed to apply for the licences, and the awards must be based on criteria that are objective, transparent, non-discriminatory and proportionate.

So far, awards have been based on both beauty contests (eg 3G) and auctions (all recent awards). The award process is decided by the NPT on a case-by-case basis.

Frequency trading

31.38 The NPT may regulate the transfer of spectrum licences.[62] No regulations have yet been provided. To date, a spectrum licence may not be transferred, unless a right of transfer follows from either the licence itself,[63] or from a subsequent decision by the NPT.[64] Transfers must be notified to the NPT.[65]

Rights of Use for Numbers

General regulatory approach

31.39 The NPT is authorised to establish numbering plans.[66]

31.40 It is not possible to obtain ownership of numbers. Rights of use for numbers are awarded through individual licences from the NPT.[67]

31.41 When considering number applications, the NPT must take into account certain factors such as availability, future needs, the needs of the applicant, and the applicant's exploitation ratio for previously awarded numbers.[68]

---

57 § 6–3 E-Com Act.
58 See para 1.103 above.
59 Ot.prp no 58 2002–2003, item 9.4.2.
60 § 6–4 E-Com Act.
61 § 9–2 E-Com Act.
62 § 6–5(4) E-Com Act.
63 § 6–3(6) E-Com Act.
64 § 6–5 E-Com Act.
65 § 6–5 E-Com Act.
66 § 7–1 E-Com Act and § 4 Number Regulation (FOR-2004–02-16–426).
67 § 7–1(2) E-Com Act and § 5 Number Regulation.
68 § 8 Number Regulation.

Admissible conditions

31.42   The conditions that may be attached to the right of use are listed in the Number Regulation.[69] These conditions reflect those listed in Part C of the Annex to the Authorisation Directive, items 1, 2, 3, 5 and 9.

31.43   The right of use for a number from the number plan may not be assigned without the consent of the NPT.[70]

31.44   Most five- and eight-digit telephone numbers are covered by obligations relating to number portability in the form of provider portability at cost-oriented prices.[71] These obligations do not include an obligation to offer geographic portability (portability of fixed line numbers between different geographical locations) or portability between service types (ie between fixed line and mobile operators).

31.45   Undertakings with SMP in the market for access to public telephony in fixed networks are obliged to offer call-by-call carrier pre-selection by use of a prefix.[72] Such undertakings must normally also offer fixed carrier pre-selection.[73]

Limitation of number of rights of use to be granted

31.46   No procedures for limiting the number of rights of use to be granted are found in the E-Com Act. It is thus left to the NPT's own discretion to find the most expedient way of doing this. When deciding whether limitations shall be made, the NPT must take into consideration the factors listed in the Number Regulation § 8, including future needs for numbering resources.

The NRA's Enforcement Powers

31.47   The NPT shall supervise that the conditions attached to general authorisations and individual licences are complied with.[74]

31.48   The factual basis for the exercising of the NPT's supervisory powers is found in the undertakings' obligation to either make public or submit to the NPT information regarding quality of the service.[75] Besides, the NPT gathers information from sample surveys, the taking of measurements, and other control activities.[76] The NPT is entitled to access premises without pre-warning if this is needed to gather relevant documentation.[77]

31.49   If an operator has not met the applicable conditions, the NPT shall notify the undertaking in question. Instructions to remedy the defect may be imposed one month after notification, if the breach has not been corrected within this deadline.[78] No deadline is required in relation to undertakings that have previously been in

---

69   § 9 Number Regulation.
70   § 10 Number Regulation.
71   § 7–3 E-Com Act and § 3–5 to 3–7 E-Com Regulation.
72   § 3–1 E-Com Regulation.
73   § 3–2 E-Com Regulation.
74   § 10–1 E-Com Act.
75   § 10–3 E-Com Act.
76   § 10–1 E-Com Act.
77   § 10–1 E-Com Act.
78   § 10–6(3) E-Com Act.

breach of their obligations, nor in relation to technical deficiencies concerning equipment and installations.[79] Prior to the said one-month deadline, sanctions may also be imposed if an immediate and serious threat to security or health is found.[80]

31.50   Continued breach gives rise to sanctions such as financial penalties,[81] revocation of licence,[82] and closing down of networks.[83]

Administrative Charges and Fees for Rights of Use

31.51   Annual fees for operators registered in accordance with the notification procedure are calculated in accordance with provisions of the fee regulation.[84]

31.52   The fees are calculated and collected by the NPT. The total, annual fees to be collected by the NPT are fixed by the Parliament in the state budget.[85] This total is divided on the respective types of operators and licences according to a distribution key found in the Fee regulation, which allocates percentages of the total fee to the various registrations and licences. For instance, 45.5 per cent of the total fees shall be taken from spectrum licence holders.[86] The fees for use of numbers are, however, fixed.

Transitional Regulations for Existing Authorisations

31.53   Existing SMP licences will remain in force until it has been examined whether the companies in question have SMP and whether there is a need to impose any obligations on them in the present market.[87]

31.54   Previously awarded spectrum and number licences will be upheld under the new Act.[88]

REGULATION OF NETWORK ACCESS AND INTERCONNECTION

Objectives and Scope of Access Regulation

31.55   The objective of the E-Com Act's access-specific regulation is to promote sustainable competition, and facilitate national and international competition in the market.[89]

31.56   Access obligations are mainly placed on SMP operators, but apply to some extent also to other providers of electronic communication networks and services.

---

79   § 10–6(3) E-Com Act.
80   § 10–9 E-Com Act.
81   § 10–7 E-Com Act.
82   § 10–8 E-Com Act.
83   § 10–9 E-Com Act.
84   FOR 2005–02-21 no 168.
85   § 1(1) Fee Regulation.
86   § 1(2) Fee Regulation.
87   § 13–2 E-Com Act.
88   § 13–2 E-Com Act.
89   § 3–4(2) E-Com Act.

The obligations are not in all cases limited to public networks, but it is assumed that they will have a very limited application on private networks. The access regulations do not regulate content requirements.

Basic Regulatory Concepts

31.57   The access related powers vested in the NPT are seen in its ability to enact statutory regulations supplementing the E-Com Act, as well as its ability to impose obligations on operators in individual cases. No express obligation to actually use these powers is found in the E-Com Act, except for the obligation to supervise the market.[90] It is however assumed that general principles of administrative law place obligations on the NPT to use its powers as required in order to meet the objectives of the E-Com Act.

31.58   The powers of the NPT must be exercised in observance of the requirements of transparency, proportionality, non-discrimination and objectivity.[91] Further, the NPT must observe requirements imposed by administrative law concerning decision making procedures,[92] and apply the reasonability test attached to most access obligations.[93] Certain actions cannot be taken unless consolidation and consultation procedures have been observed.[94]

31.59   'Access' is not defined, but must be understood in light of the definition of article 2(b) Access Directive.[95] In addition, certain statutory provisions clarify the scope of the obligations related to the notion of access.[96]

'Interconnection' is defined as a 'function that provides for handling traffic between providers so that end users may communicate with each other and have access to public electronic communication services independent of the provider connection'.[97]

31.60   Interconnection is dealt with separately from access in the E-Com Act, even though it is considered to be a specific type of access.

31.61   The principle of freedom of access[98] is not explicitly stated in the E-Com Act. However, no obstacles to voluntary interconnection negotiations are found, and no authorisation is required in order to request access or interconnection. The priority of commercial negotiations principle[99] has not been clearly expressed either. Given the requirement of Access Directive, it is assumed this principle must be observed as a guideline anyway.[100]

---

90   § 10–1 E-Com Act.
91   Ot.prp no 58, 2002–2003, items 6.4 and 9.2.
92   § 9–1 E-Com Act.
93   Eg § 4–1(1) E-Com Act.
94   § 9–2 and § 9–3 E-Com Act.
95   See para 1.125 above.
96   § 2–2 E-Com Regulation.
97   § 1–5 E-Com Act.
98   Cf para 1.127 above.
99   Cf para 1.128 above.
100 Cf the comments to § 4–2 in the preparatory works, Ot.prp nr 58, 2002–2003.

Access- and Interconnection-related Obligations with Respect to SMP Undertakings

General regulatory approach

31.62   Some obligations incumbent on SMP undertakings apply by law, whereas others have to be imposed by the NPT on a case-by-case basis. Both types of obligations have their legal basis in the E-Com Act and the E-Com Regulation. In addition, the NPT may in 'special cases' impose obligations in addition to those explicitly described in the E-Com Act.[101] The Act does not in itself place any limitations on the type of measures that can be imposed on SMP undertakings in such 'special cases'. This cannot, however, be understood to mean that the NPT has unlimited discretion to impose obligations. General principles of proportionality and objectivity must be observed. The use of such measures also requires that the consultation procedure be followed.[102]

Transparency obligations

31.63   The NPT may impose on SMP operators the publication of 'specified information'.[103] A non-exhaustive list states that such information encompasses accountancy data, technical specifications, and prices. Obligations to prepare and publish standard terms and conditions for offers on electronic communication networks and services may also be imposed. Such standard offers shall always be prepared in relation to access to the local loop.[104]

Non-discrimination obligations

31.64   The NPT may impose non-discrimination obligations in relation to access and interconnection in individual cases.[105] Such obligations also apply automatically by application of law in certain cases.[106] These obligations are subject to a reasonability test.

Specific access obligations

31.65   The NPT may impose on SMP operators an obligation to accept all reasonable requests for entering into or amending agreements for access to electronic communication networks and services.[107] A non-inclusive list of the relevant types of access encompasses bit stream access, access to the mobile network for virtual operators and for operators with limited coverage, and re-sale of subscriptions.[108] The NPT may also on certain conditions impose co-location obligations,[109] as well as access obligations in relation to information and support systems.

---

101   § 3–4(2) E-Com Act.
102   § 9–3 E-Com Act.
103   § 4–6 E-Com Act.
104   The transparency requirements are further elaborated in the § 2–5 and § 2–6 E-Com Act, see also § 4–8(4) and § 4–12(2) E-Com Act.
105   § 4–7 E-Com Act.
106   Chapter 2 E-Com Regulation.
107   § 4–1 E-Com Act.
108   § 2–2 E-Com Regulation.

31.66 These obligations are additional to the interconnection obligations that apply also to non-SMP operators.[110]

31.67 The rights of access now apply even to virtual mobile operators.[111]

Price control obligations

31.68

The NPT may regulate prices for access and interconnection if this is needed in order to prevent operators from exploiting their market position to the detriment of end-users by keeping a disproportionately high price level or by establishing a price squeeze on competing operators.[112] Methods for price regulation and accountancy may be imposed. The preparatory works refer to various methods that may be used for price regulation purposes, but leaves the choice of method to the NPT on a case-by-case basis. No regulations supplementing the Act in this respect have yet been adopted.

Accounting separation obligations

31.69 The NPT may impose accounting separation between the respective business sectors of a telecom company, or between specific activities connected to access and interconnection.[113]

Related Regulatory Powers with Respect to SMP Undertakings

31.70 In addition to the access and interconnection obligations described above, SMP operators in the market for access to public telephony services in the fixed network that control access to end-users must offer its customers call by call carrier selection and carrier pre-selection at cost oriented prices.[114]

31.71 Further, undertakings with SMP on of the leased lines market shall offer such leased lines to other operators.[115] The offer must be on non-discriminatory terms and at cost-oriented prices.

Regulatory Powers Applicable to All Market Participants

Obligations to ensure end-to-end connectivity

31.72 Access and/or interconnection obligations may be imposed on all operators regardless of their market position, if this is necessary to ensure end-to-end

---

109 § 4–4 E-Com Act.
110 See paras 31.72–31.74 below.
111 Ot.prp no 58, 2002–2003 item 7.2.
112 § 4–9 E-Com Act.
113 § 4–8 E-Com Act.
114 § 4–11 E-Com Act.
115 § 4–12 E-Com Act and § 2–3 E-Com Regulation.

communication.[116] Such instructions may not be imposed unless hearing and consultation procedures have been observed.[117]

31.73   Providers of access to electronic communication networks are obliged to conduct interconnecting negotiations with other operators, if requested.[118] This obligation applies by law and does not need to be specifically imposed by the NPT.

31.74   Undertakings given a right to expropriation[119] may be ordered to grant co-location to other operators without similar rights.[120] The NPT may also impose obligations concerning the joint use of infrastructure even if not requested by any undertaking, when justifiable on grounds of efficient use, health, environment, security or others.[121] The said obligations may not be imposed without conducting a public hearing.[122]

Access to digital radio and television broadcasting services

31.75   Providers of access control services for radio and television broadcasting services shall accept all reasonable requests for access from content suppliers. The criteria for access shall be objective, reasonable, non-discriminatory and publicly available.[123] The NPT may grant exemptions from such obligations for operators that do not have SMP, but only if the general access to such services is not reduced from such exemption.

REGULATION OF UNIVERSAL SERVICES AND USERS' RIGHTS

Regulation of Universal Service Obligations

Scope of universal service obligations and designation of undertakings

31.76   In order to secure the provision of universal service obligations the NPT has the power to either enter into a contract with or impose an obligation through an administrative decision on one or more providers of electronic communications networks and services.[124]

31.77   The services covered are:

- provision of public telephone services and digital electronic communications networks,
- provision of public pay telephones,
- provision of number information services,
- provision of telephone directories, and
- provision of special services for disabled persons and other end users with special needs.

---

116   § 4–1(4) and § 4–2(2) E-Com Act.
117   § 9–2 and § 9–3 E-Com Act.
118   § 4–2(1) E-Com Act.
119   § 13–3 E-Com Act.
120   § 4–4 (1) E-Com Act.
121   § 4–4 (2) E-Com Act.
122   §9–2 E-Com Act.
123   § 4–3 (1) and § 4–8 (2) E-Com Act and chapter 4 E-Com Regulation.
124   § 5–1 E-Com Act.

31.78   Currently, the above-mentioned universal service obligations have been imposed through the licence granted to Telenor ASA.

Regulation of retail tariffs, users' expenditures and quality of service

31.79   Providers obliged to provide universal services may not charge the customer for extra costs incurred in connection with providing network access. The obligation to provide customers with access to public telephony services applies to all places with permanent all-year residences or business activity.[125]

31.80   In order to monitor the provision of universal services, the NPT may request that the provider issues a yearly report regarding the services offered and the quality of these.[126]

31.81   Breach of the universal service obligations may result in fines, and in theory even imprisonment up to six months. The size of the fines is decided by the NPT.[127]

Cost calculation and financing of universal services

31.82   Providers of universal services may request that their extra costs are covered through a financing fund, if these costs constitute an unreasonable burden.

31.83   The NPT is given power to decide whether the costs should be regarded as an unreasonable burden and to impose duties on all providers to contribute to such financing.[128]

Regulation of Retail Markets

Prerequisites for the regulation of retail markets

31.84   Regulation of end-user services[129] may only take place if regulation of access and interconnection[130] does not achieve the desired objectives.[131]

31.85   The NPT has not yet decided which operators are considered as having SMP in the retail markets, but it a preliminary analysis which has been sent on a hearing suggests that Telenor has SMP in all wholesale markets.

Regulatory powers

31.86   The NPT may regulate the retail markets by prohibiting SMP operators from, inter alia, excessive pricing, predatory pricing, price discrimination and unreasonable product bundling.[132] The types of obligations that may be imposed

---

125   § 5–1 E-Com Regulation.
126   § 5–9 E-Com Regulation.
127   § 12–4 E-Com Act.
128   § 5–2 E-Com Act and § 5–7 and § 5–8 E-Com Regulation.
129   § 4–10 E-Com Act.
130   § 4–9 E-Com Act.
131   See paras 31.62–31.67 above.
132   § 4–10 E-Com Act

are such amongst others maximum prices, cost orientated prices, and geographical levelling. The scope of these measures is not clearly limited in the Act, but it is assumed that they are subject to the requirements of objectivity and proportionality.[133]

31.87   Operators with SMP on all or parts of[134] of the leased lines market, are obliged to offer leased lines to other operators and users.[135] The terms and conditions for such offers shall be prepared and made public, unless the NPT finds this to be unreasonable.[136] The prices offered shall be cost-oriented and non-discriminative.[137]

End User Rights

Contracts

31.88   Providers of electronic communication networks used for public communication services and providers of public communication services are obliged to offer end-users to enter into subscription agreements.[138] The minimum contents for such offers include, inter alia, price and duration, procedures for complaint, and remedies in case of defective services.[139]

Transparency obligations

31.89   The NPT may impose on providers of electronic communication services to end users obligations to publish the terms and conditions for such services.[140] This obligation includes information on prices.[141]

DATA PROTECTION AND PRIVACY

Confidentiality of Communications

31.90   In order to ensure the confidentiality of the communications, operators providing publicly available electronic communications services are obliged to take requisite safety measures to safeguard the communications in their own electronic communications network and services, if necessary in co-operation with the network operator. Where there is a risk of security breach, the operator must notify the subscribers.[142]

31.91   It is prohibited to use an electronic communications network to store information or to gain access to information stored in a user's communication

---

133   Ot.prp no 58, 2002–2003, item 6.4.
134   § 2–3 E-Com Regulation.
135   § 4–12 E-Com Act.
136   § 4–12 E-Com Act.
137   § 2–3 E-Com Regulation.
138   § 1–8 E-Com Regulation.
139   § 1–8 E-Com Regulation.
140   § 2–4 E-Com Act.
141   § 2–4 E-Com Act.
142   §§ 2–7 and 2–9 E-Com Act.

equipment, without providing clear information to the user about, ie the purpose of the processing and offering the user a possibility to oppose to the processing. An exception lies for technical storage or access for the sole purpose of transmitting or facilitate the transmitting the communication or providing services after the explicit request of the user.[143]

31.92 Without prejudice to the principle of confidentiality, the prosecuting authority, the police and other authority can after request and in accordance with law receive information about unlisted telephone numbers or other information concerning a subscriber, and also information about the electronic communication address. The same applies for a testimony in a court of law.[144]

Traffic Data and Location Data

31.93 'Traffic data' is defined as any data necessary in order to transfer communication in an electronic communications network or for the billing of such transfer.[145] 'Localisation data' is defined as data processed in an electronic communications network and which indicate the geographical placing of the terminal equipment employed by the user of a public electronic communications service.[146]

31.94 Service providers can process traffic data only for the purpose of transmitting the communication and for invoicing purposes.[147] Any other processing of traffic data, hereunder processing for marketing purposes, requires the consent of the subscriber to whom the traffic data relate.[148] The consent must be freely given, specific and informed, and the service provider must inform subscribers of the types of data processed, the duration and purpose of such processing, and whether the data is meant to be transferred to a provider of a additional service more than a public telephone service. A user must be able to withdraw the consent at any time.[149]

31.95 Traffic data processed for the purpose of transmitting communications or invoicing must be erased or anonymised when it is no longer needed for that purpose.[150]

31.96 Location data other than traffic data (ie not included in the definition of 'traffic data') may only be processed if it has been made anonymous.[151] This does not apply to the processing of data where the subscriber has consented and the processing relates to the delivery of an additional service more than a public telephone service. The processing must be restricted to the extent and for the duration necessary for the delivery of the service.[152]

---

143 § 7–3 E-Com Regulations.
144 § 2–9 E-Com Act.
145 § 7–1 E-Com Regulations.
146 § 7–2 E-Com Regulations.
147 § 2–7 E-Com Act cf § 7–1 E-Com Regulations.
148 § 2–7 E-Com Act and § 7–1 E-Com Regulations.
149 § 7–4 E-Com Regulations, cf. Personal Data Act.
150 § 2–7 E-Com Act.
151 § 7–2 E-Com Regulations.
152 § 7–2 E-Com Regulations.

Itemised Billing

31.97   The service provider shall, unless otherwise agreed, provide the subscriber with non-itemised bills. At the request of the subscriber, the service provider is required to provide itemised bills.[153]

Calling and Connected Line Identification

31.98   Service providers offering calling line identification services must allow calling end-users to withhold the display of their own number on a per-call and per-line basis. End-users must also be able to reject incoming calls where the caller has withheld the caller identification. The services must be offered free of charge. The service may be temporarily eliminated after the request of an end-user who believes to be exposed to insulting telephone calls. The service also does not apply for calls to emergency services. The service provider must store the identification details of the calling end-user and present these to the police for the purpose of investigations.[154]

Automatic Call Forwarding

31.99   A provider of a public telephone service shall free of charge give the user/subscriber the possibility to request that third parties' calls are not auto-matically forwarded to the user's/subscriber's terminal equipment.[155]

Directories of Subscribers

31.100   The provider of a public telephone service making subscribers' data available for inclusion in a publicly available printed or electronic directory shall inform the subscriber in advance and free of charge of the purposes of the directory and the possible use of the data based on search functions in the electronic directory. Subscribers must have the opportunity, free of charge, to verify, correct or withdraw the data. The subscriber also has the right to refuse that his data are made available.[156]

Unsolicited Communications

31.101   The Norwegian Marketing Control Act[157] ('Marketing Control Act') and the E-Commerce and Other Information Society Services Act ('E-Commerce Act')[158] contain provisions concerning communications for marketing purposes,[159] and the two provisions supplement each other.

---

153   § 1–9 E-Com Regulations.
154   § 6–1 E-Com Regulations.
155   § 6–4 E-Com Regulations.
156   § 6–2 E-Com Regulations.
157   LOV-1972–06-16–47.
158   LOV-2003–05-23–35.
159   § 2b Marketing Control Act and § 9 E-Commerce Act.

31.102 It is not permitted to send commercial communications to physical persons by means of electronic communications methods permitting individual communication, such as e-mail, telefax or automatic calling systems, unless the following requirements are fulfilled:

- the sender has obtained the prior consent of the receiver (opt-in), unless
  - the marketing is sent by email in an existing customer relationship where the business party has received the email address of the customer in relation to sales. In such a case, the marketing can only relate to the business party's own goods, services or other performances equivalent to those that the customer relationship is based on, or
  - the receiver is contacted orally by telephone
- the person on whose behalf the communication is sent is clearly identified
- the communication is clearly identifiable as communication containing marketing as soon as it is received.

31.103 Any promotional offers, games or competitions must be clearly identified, and any conditions related to the offers must be easily accessible and presented clearly for the receiver.

31.104 If possible, the receiver should be provided with price information. If the price of a product or service is provided in connection with the marketing, the sender is obliged to inform the receiver of all fees and delivery charges. If the receiver is a consumer, the sender must also inform the person concerned of the total costs to be paid.

31.105 The receiver must be given the possibility to opt-out, free of charge, from receiving such communications.

31.106 Processing of personal data for direct marketing purposes must take place in accordance with the Norwegian Personal Data Act.

The Romanian Market for Electronic Communications[1]

Horatiu Dumitru, Senior Associate and Bogdan-Petru Mihai, Associate
Musat & Asociatii, Attorneys-at-law, Bucharest

LEGAL STRUCTURE

Basic Policy

32.1   As part of the harmonisation of the national legal framework with the *acquis communautaire*, and considering the liberalisation of the Romanian communications market from 1 January 2003, pursuant to the dissolution of the monopoly held by Romtelecom (the national fixed telephony operator), a new legal framework for electronic communications was created, basically consisting of two primary laws: Emergency Government Ordinance no 79/2002 on the communications framework ('EGO no 79/2002'),[2] which completely repealed the previous regulation,[3] and Government Ordinance no 34/2002 on access to and interconnection of the electronic communication networks and related infrastructure ('GO no 34/2002').[4] The main new features introduced by EGO no 79/2002 are the independent regulatory authority established in the electronic communications field, the licensing regime for activities regarding electronic communication services and networks, and the definition of specific rules governing competition on the electronic communication networks and services market.

32.2   The Romanian telecommunications market is characterised by diverse market segments, such as large corporate customers with integrated data/voice requirements, a number of increasingly demanding data products, and domestic customers seeking inexpensive voice and broadband services. However, at the current time, the bulk of the Romanian fixed telephony market is owned by a single telecommunication services provider, namely Romtelecom.

---

1   Editing of this chapter closed on 8 July 2005.
2   Government Emergency Ordinance no 79 of 13 June 2002 on the general regulatory framework for communications, published in the Official Gazette Part I no 457 of 27/06/2002.
3   Telecommunications Law no 74/1996.
4   Government Ordinance no 34/2002 on the access to and interconnection of the electronic communication networks and related infrastructure published in the Official Gazette Part I no 88 of 02/02/2002.

32.3   The overall policy objectives of the National Regulatory Authority for Communications ('NRAC') are to encourage competition in the electronic communications sector, to promote end users' interests, and to consolidate its own administrative capacity in view of the contemplated accession of Romania to the European Union in 2007.

Implementation of EU Directives

32.4   For the implementation of the new enactments, secondary legislation was adopted at an accelerated pace, so that, by the beginning of 2003, Romania was among the first countries in Europe that had entirely transposed the new *acquis communautaire* in the electronic communication field.

Legislation

32.5   The main regulations adopted by the Romanian government related to the telecommunications market are:

- EGO no 79/2002,
- GO no 34/2002,
- GD no 744/2003,[5]
- GD no 180/2002,[6] and
- Law no 510/2004.[7]

32.6   The role of the regulations and decisions issued by the NRAC is to implement and to organise the implementation of its statutory obligations, providing the legal basis for the provision of telecommunication services in Romania.

REGULATORY PRINCIPLES

Scope of Regulation

32.7   The scope of applicability of the new legal framework for 'electronic communications' is broader than the scope of the old 'telecommunications' law. EGO no 79/2002 governs signal transport through wire, radio, optic fibres or other electromagnetic means.[8] The VoIP services are generally comprised in this definition.

However, VoIP services are not specifically regulated by any Romanian legal provision.

---

5   Government Decision no 744/2003 on the organisation and functioning of the Ministry of Communications and Information Technology published in the Official Gazette Part I no 494 of 09/07/2003.

6   Government Decision no 180/2002 on the setting up of the General Inspectorate for Communications and Information Technology through the reorganisation of the Autonomous Regie 'General Inspectorate of Communications' published in the Official Gazette Part I no 158 of 05/03/2002.

7   Law no 510/2004 on the reorganisation and functioning of the General Inspectorate for Communications and Information Technology published in the Official Gazette Part I no 1082 of 22/11/2004.

8   Art 1 EGO no 79/2002 .

National Regulatory Authorities: Organisation, Regulatory Objectives, Competencies

32.8   Under EGO no 79/2002, the NRAC was established as a public institution subordinated to the Government, entirely financed from extra-budgetary revenues[9] and tasked to put into operation the national policy in the electronic communications field.

32.9   The NRAC is bound to maintain its operational and financial independence from both networks and services providers and equipment manufacturers.

32.10   The most important powers and duties of the NRAC are:[10]

- implementing the sector-specific policies and strategies,
- assigning the numbering resources for electronic communication services and managing the same at national level,
- drafting and adopting the national technical norms and standards, and adopting the technical regulations that make the application of the international standards binding at national level,
- regulating activities within the electronic communication and numbering resources sector, by adopting and implementing general and individual decisions, and
- acting as arbitrator and ruling authority in settling disputes between network and service providers, in order to ensure free competition and protection of users' interests.

32.11   Certain regulatory powers are retained by the Ministry of Communications and Information Technology ('MCTI') which, in its capacity as the specialised body of the central public administration in the field of communications and information technology, has the following main powers:[11]

- defining the strategic and tactical sector objectives, meant to ensure the planning, elaboration and implementation of the electronic communication policy, and evaluation and control of this policy fulfilment,
- ensuring its participation in the process of elaborating the enactments and institutional framework necessary for the electronic communication sector organisation and functioning, as well as the implementation of the normative and methodological framework related to the sector policy, and the supervision and control of such policy observance,
- ensuring representation in the country and abroad, and
- ensuring supervision and control of the implementation and observance of the regulations in the electronic communications sector, as well as the unitary implementing and observance of the legal regulations by the institutions and the entities under its subordination and coordination.

32.12   The General Inspectorate for Communications and Information Technology ('IGCTI') is organised as a public institution with legal status and subordinated to the MCTI. It is entirely financed from extra-budgetary revenues, and its main object of activity consists of the supervision and control of activities within

---

9   Art 37 EGO no 79/2002.
10   Art 46 EGO no 79/2002.
11   Art 3 GD no 744/2003.

the communications sector mainly in relation to the management of radio frequencies, as well as the implementation at national level of the computer systems providing public services through electronic means. Its powers include the following:[12]

- management of the radio frequency bands assigned for non-governmental use,
- assignment for individual use of the radio frequencies in the bands set out in the national allocation table, and keeping permanent records of their use,
- control of the fulfilment of the obligations relating to radio frequency use, and
- issuance of certificates confirming the compliance of radio equipment and electronic communication terminals.

32.13   According to art 54 EGO no 79/2002, the NRAC may request from the service providers any information necessary in the exercise of its prerogatives, mentioning the legal ground and the purpose for such solicitation and may also establish terms in which such information must be provided.

The NRAC may also decide to commence an investigation, ex officio, or when it receives a complaint or any such request from any person.

32.14   In case of disputes between providers of electronic communication networks or services in connection with any obligations imposed by law, the interested party will notify the NRAC accordingly, in order to settle such litigation. The NRAC's president, in his position of arbitrator and decision-making body, will settle the dispute through conciliation between the litigation parties.

32.15   Conciliation is an optional procedure aiming at the amicable settlement of the dispute. Therefore, where the parties reach an understanding, the conciliation is finalised by a settlement concluded between them. If the parties do not wish to use such a procedure or, although they have chosen this procedure, the dispute is not settled within 30 days from the NRAC's notification, the dispute will then be settled through a classic court process.

32.16   Every time the NRAC intends to adopt measures, for the application of EGO no 79/2002 or the special legislation in the field of electronic communications, which may have a significant impact on the relevant market, it must observe the consultation procedure provided by EGO no 79/2002.[13]

32.17   The procedural rules provide that the NRAC is obliged to publish the issue subject to consultation on its own website. Within at least 30 days or, in case of measures to be urgently adopted, at least 10 days after the date of their publication on the internet, any interested person may submit written comments.[14]

32.18   A measure subject to the consultation procedure may not be adopted before the expiration of a 10-day period following the deadline for the comments submission. The NRAC must publish a synopsis of the comments so gathered, no later than the date of publication on the NRAC's website of the decision approving the relevant measure. The published material will also contain the NRAC's position with respect to the comments received on the issue.

---

12   Art 3 Law no 510/2004
13   Art 50 EGO 79/2002
14   Art 50(2) EGO 79/2002

Right of Appeal against NRA's Decisions

32.19   According to the provisions of article 38 EGO no 79/2002, the decisions taken by the NRAC may be appealed to the Administrative Division of the Bucharest Court of Appeal, by the affected party, within 30 days from their publication or communication, as the case may be, without following the prior administrative procedure set out in the Law no 554/2004 on the disputes with the public administration.

'Significant Market Power' as a Fundamental Prerequisite of Regulation

Definition of SMP

32.20   The 'Significant Market Power' definition in EGO no 79/2002 is a word-for-word implementation of the definition provided in the Framework Directive.[15]

Definition of relevant markets and SMP designation

32.21   The relevant markets are identified by the NRAC based on the provisions of the Regulation for identification of the relevant markets issued by the NRAC.[16] Actually, the Regulation follows the indications given by the provisions of the Commission Recommendation on relevant markets.

32.22   The NRAC and the Competition Council, following analysis of the relevant product market, have divided the electronic communications sector into the following categories:

- public electronic communications networks, publicly available electronic communications services, and electronic communications services provided for own needs,
- retail markets/wholesale markets,
- provision of electronic communications networks and services/provision of associated facilities,
- provision at fixed locations/provision at non-fixed locations,
- publicly available telephony services/other services, and
- services provided to consumers, and services provided to other end users.

32.23   Currently, the following specific relevant markets for products have actually been identified by the NRAC:[17]

- the market for access to the fixed public telephone network for call origination, termination, and transit, comprising the access to fixed public telephone networks for origination at fixed locations, termination at fixed locations, and commuted transit of the calls for publicly available telephony services and for dial-up, ISDN and fax services;
- the market for access to the mobile public telephone network operated by Cosmorom SA for call termination, comprising access to this network for call termination to non-fixed locations for publicly available telephony services originating in other networks;

---

15   Art 33 EGO 79/2002.
16   This Regulation was published in the Official Gazette Part I no 916 of 16/12/2002.
17   NRAC Decision no 136/2002 modified by NRAC Decision no 174/2003.

- access market to the mobile public telephone network operated by Mobifon SA for call termination, comprising access to this network for call termination to non-fixed locations for publicly available telephony services originating in other networks;
- access market to the mobile public telephone network operated by Orange Romania SA for call termination, comprising access to this network for call termination to non-fixed locations for publicly available telephony services originating in other networks;
- access market to the mobile public telephone network operated by Telemobil SA for call termination, comprising access to this network for call termination to non-fixed locations for publicly available telephony services originating in other networks;
- the market for the provision of unconditioned total or shared access to the local loop consisting of a pair of twisted metallic wires, for the purpose of provision of broadband electronic communications services and publicly available telephony services at fixed locations;
- the market for the provision of 'bit stream' access to the local loop made of a pair of twisted metallic wires, optical fibre or coaxial cable and to the radio local loop, for the purpose of providing broadband electronic communications services;[18]
- the market for the provision of leased lines-terminal segments services; and
- the market for the provision of leased lines-trunk segments services.

32.24   Orange, Telemobil, Mobifon and Cosmorom have been designated as having SMP on their own specific markets as specified above, while Romtelecom has been designated as having SMP on all other relevant markets, being at this moment one of the major players on the Romanian telecommunications market.

NRA's Regulatory Duties concerning Rights of Way, Co-location and Facility Sharing

Rights of way

32.25   The providers of electronic communications networks authorised pursuant to article 4 EGO no 79/2002 shall have the right to install, maintain, replace, or move any elements of the electronic communications networks, on, above, in, or under the state-owned or on local administration owned real-estate, to the extent that exercising this right is compatible with the public use or interest of that specific real-estate:

- performing such right of way-related activities does not contravene the specific requirements concerning the town planning, protection of environment, health or public order;
- the conditions for exercising this right have been established by agreement between the parties or, in the absence of such agreement, by a court decision.[19]

---

18   This identified market is a wholesale market subject to the provisions under GO no 34/2002, as well as their interconnection, approved, with amendments and completions, by Law no 527/2002.

19   Arts 22–23 EGO no 79/2002.

32.26   The providers of public electronic communications networks authorised pursuant to EGO no 79/2002 shall have the right to perform such right of way-related activities, in or under the private property real-estate, only to the extent that:

- the related real-estate would not be affected or would be insignificantly affected by such activities,
- these activities do not contravene the specific requirements concerning the town planning, protection of environment, health or public order, or
- the conditions for exercising this right have been established by agreement between the parties or, in the absence of such agreement, by a court decision.[20]

Co-location and facility sharing

32.27   The NRAC may, in accordance with the provisions of the law, impose obligations on operators to allow access to, and use of, specific elements of the network and of the associated infrastructure, particularly in situations where it considers that the refusal of access or imposition of terms and conditions with a similar effect would result in hindering the development of a competitive market at the retail level, or in harming end-users' interests.[21]

32.28   The NRAC may impose, on a provider of electronic communications networks performing rights of way activities under public or private property, the obligation to allow other providers to use the facilities of the network elements which have been installed, built, or restored by the first provider, in order for these providers to perform such activities themselves.[22]

REGULATION OF MARKET ENTRY: IMPLEMENTATION OF THE AUTHORISATION DIRECTIVE

General Regulatory Approach

32.29   At least seven days before starting the activity, any person intending to provide electronic communications networks or services shall transmit to the NRAC a notification of this intention, for the purpose of establishing an official record of the provider.[23]

32.30   Article 4 of EGO no 79/2002 provides that the NRAC shall establish and update the standard notification form, which shall contain the information that any person intending to provide electronic communications networks or services shall communicate in order to benefit from the general authorisation. This information shall be grouped under the following categories:

- data necessary to identify and efficiently communicate with the provider,
- description of the types of networks or services that the relevant person intends to provide, and
- estimated date for starting the activity.

---

20   Art 24 EGO no 79/2002.
21   Art 44 EGO no 79/2002.
22   Art 25 EGO no 79/2002.
23   Art 4 EGO no 79/2002.

32.31   The persons who submitted the notification within the term and in compliance with the conditions set out above shall be authorised automatically, based on the provisions of EGO no 79/2002, to provide the types of networks or services indicated in the notification, having all the rights and obligations under the general authorisation that shall be elaborated, updated, modified and repealed.

32.32   If a person's right to provide electronic communication networks or services has been revoked, such person cannot benefit from the general authorisation for the same type of network or service, for a five-year period after the revocation of the right.[24]

Rights of Use for Radio Frequencies

General regulatory approach

32.33   The use of radio frequencies shall only be allowed upon obtaining a licence granted under such conditions as to ensure their efficient use.

32.34   IGCTI may designate certain categories of frequencies that can be used freely, subject to the general authorisation regime concerning the access and the conditions of use, in cases where this is technically possible and especially when the harmful interference risk is low.[25] IGCTI has already issued a Decision[26] regarding the free use of certain frequencies.

32.35   Where applicable, the granting of the right of use for radio frequencies shall comply with the procedure and the conditions harmonised at European level, should such procedures and conditions have been established by international agreements and by observing the provisions under the international agreements to which Romania is a party.

Admissible conditions

32.36   The licence for the use of radio-electric frequencies is the administrative document whereby the NRAC grants to an authorised provider the right to use one or several radio frequencies in order to provide electronic communications networks or services, in compliance with certain technical parameters and for a limited period of time ('usage right').

32.37   The licence for the use of radio frequencies establishes the conditions subject to which the holder may exercise the usage right.[27] These conditions may target the following:

- the designation of the type of network or service or of the technology for which the right of use has been granted,
- the effective, rational and efficient use of the frequencies, including, where appropriate, territory coverage requirements, and

24   Art 4 EGO no 79/2002.
25   Art 13 EGO no 79/2002.
26   IGCTI's Decision 62/2005 on the free use of frequencies.
27   Art 19 EGO no 79/2002.

- technical and operational requirements necessary for the avoidance of harm-ful interferences, where such conditions are different from those included in the general authorisation.[28]

Limitation of number of rights of use to be granted

32.38   The number of licences for the use of radio-electric frequencies to be granted may be limited only when necessary in order to ensure an efficient use of the radio frequency spectrum.[29]

32.39   The holder of the licence for the use of radio-electric frequencies is bound to pay annually to IGCTI a spectrum usage tariff established by the MCTI.

32.40   There have been no auctions for spectrum, but considering the power of the existing major market players, such auctions might take place although the regula-tors have issued no official statements yet. According to the law, such auctions will be supervised by the MCTI. Article 6 of 403/2003[30] provides that the terms and conditions for such spectrum auction are to be established individually for the specific auctioned spectrum by order of the MCTI.

Frequency trading

32.41   The licence for use of radio-electric frequencies and the licence for use of numbering resources may be transferred to a third party authorised in accordance with EGO 79/2002, but only with the prior approval of the MCTI or the NRAC, and only subject to undertaking all obligations deriving from these licences, as well as to observing the transfer conditions set out therein.[31]

Rights of Use for Numbers

General regulatory approach

32.42   The National Numbering Plan[32] ('PNN') establishes the structure and the destination of the numbering resources used in Romania for the telephony services provided through public fixed electronic communications networks and for the telephony services provided through public mobile electronic communications networks.

32.43   The licence for the use of numbering resources is the administrative document whereby the NRAC grants to an authorised provider the right to use certain numbers, in order to provide electronic communications services for a limited period of time.

32.44   There are no categories of numbers that can be used freely, subject to the general authorisation regime.

---

28   Art 5 EGO no 79/2002.
29   Art 16 EGO no 79/2002.
30   MCTI Order 403/2003 on the solicitation and issuance procedure for radio-electric frequency licences.
31   Arts 19–20 EGO 79/2002.
32   NRAC's Decision 140/2002 for the regulation of the National Numbering Plan.

Admissible conditions

32.45   The NRAC may also compel the holders of licences for the use of numbering resources to pay a tariff for the usage of these resources. The licence for the use of numbering resources establishes the conditions on which the holder may exercise the right of use. These conditions shall be objectively justified in relation to the service concerned and shall be non-discriminatory, proportionate, and transparent.[33] They may target the following:

- the designation of the service for which the right of use has been granted, including any requirements related to the provision of that service,
- the effective, rational, and efficient use of numbering resources,
- requirements concerning number portability, and
- obligations related to the services for public directories of subscribers.

32.46   The holder of the licence for the use of radio-electric frequencies is bound to pay annually to IGCTI a spectrum usage tariff established by the MCTI. The NRAC may require the holders of licences to pay a tariff for the use of numbering resources.

Limitation of number of rights of use to be granted

32.47   The licences for the use of numbering resources are granted through an open, transparent, and non-discriminatory procedure, within at most three weeks after receipt of an application in this respect, except for licences that are granted through a competitive or comparative selection procedure, for which the term is at most six weeks.

32.48   The competitive and comparative procedure is applicable for numbering resources which have an important economical value. This procedure is mainly an auction in which the bidders are evaluated based on the offerings they make as well as on their infrastructure capacity.

NRA's Enforcement Powers

32.49   The NRAC is empowered to monitor compliance with the provisions of EGO no 79/2002 and with the specific legislation in the field of electronic communications, as well as with the obligations set out in the general authorisation and in the licences, except for monitoring compliance with the obligations concerning the use of radio frequencies for which the responsible authority is IGCTI together with the MCTI.

32.50   In case of serious and repeated breaches, or if the respective provider has failed to comply with the measures taken by the NRAC,

- the NRAC may suspend or revoke the provider's right to provide electronic communications networks or services on the basis of the general authorisation or the licence for the use of numbering resources, as the case may be, or
- the MCTI may suspend or revoke the respective provider's licence for the use of radio frequencies.

32.51   There are no specific provisions within the law that regulate the first-time failure by a service provider to comply with the regulations.

---

33   Art 18 EGO no 79/2002.

Administrative Charges and Fees for Rights of Use

32.52   Under the general authorisation, service providers must pay an annual monitoring tariff which is calculated as an equivalent of 0.5 per cent of the service provider's annual turnover.[34]

32.53   The tariffs for the use of spectrum frequencies are established by IGCTI, and vary from an annual rate of €2,000 for an analogue cellular telephony system NMT 450 for one nation-wide allocated channel to €300,000 for a digital cellular telephony system CDMA 450 for one nation-wide allocated channel.

32.54   The failure to pay within the due time the monitoring tariff set out by the NRAC, or the spectrum usage tariff or the numbering resources usage tariff, results in penalties being applied for each day of delay, calculated in accordance with the legal provisions applicable to penalties due for the late payment of budgetary duties.[35]

32.55   If the provider fails to pay the tariff and penalties within 90 days from the date when the payment becomes outstanding, the NRAC or the MCTI, as the case may be, may suspend and/or revoke its right to provide electronic communications networks or services based on the general authorisation, or the licence for the use of radio frequencies or numbering resources.

REGULATION OF NETWORK ACCESS AND INTERCONNECTION: IMPLEMENTATION OF THE ACCESS DIRECTIVE

Objectives and Scope of Access Regulation

32.56   The access regulations of GO no 34/2002 established the regulatory framework for the relationships between network operators and service providers, and network operators with regard to the access to public electronic communications networks and to the associated infrastructure, as well as to their interconnection.

32.57   The objectives of the NRAC and other regulatory bodies established under the legislative framework are to maximise the end-users' benefits, thus ensuring their ability to choose the best offer of electronic communications services in terms of quality, diversity and price. For this purpose, the NRAC elaborates principles and procedures, imposes specific conditions in order to foster the timely and effective implementation of the access and interconnection agreements, so as to promote competition and to ensure service interoperability.

The ANRC approach observes the following principles:

- focus on the wholesale markets for the provision of fixed telephone networks and services, where the end of monopoly – on 1 January 2003 – required prompt intervention from the ANRC;
- prioritise the regulatory measures according to the actual needs of the market; and
- rapid settlement of the essential issues, within short review periods, based on the market development.

---

34   Art 47 EGO 79/2002.
35   Art 22 Order no 164/21/05.2003 for the approval of the tariff procedure and of the List containing the tariffs for spectrum utilisation annually due to IGCTI.

Basic Regulatory Concepts

32.58   The terms 'access' and 'interconnection' are defined in Romanian legislation according to the definitions provided by the 2002 EU Regulatory Package.[36]

32.59   In order to ensure provision and interoperability of publicly available electronic communications services, any operator of a public communications network has:

- the right to negotiate an interconnection agreement with any other operator of a public communications network for the purpose of providing publicly available electronic communications services, including electronic communications services available to users via another public communications network interconnected with the network of any of the two operators, and
- the obligation, when requested by a third party legally authorised, to negotiate an interconnection agreement with the requesting party, for the purpose of providing publicly available electronic communications services, including electronic communications services available to users via another public communications network interconnected with the network of any of the parties.[37]

Access- and Interconnection-related Obligations with Respect to SMP Undertakings

32.60   If, as a result of a market analysis carried out under the conditions set out by the legal provisions in force, an operator is designated as having SMP in a relevant market, the regulatory authority shall impose on that operator one or more of the obligations set out in GO no 34/2002, as appropriate.

32.61   If, as a result of a market analysis carried out under the conditions set out by the legal provisions in force, the regulatory authority establishes that a relevant market is effectively competitive, it shall withdraw or modify, as appropriate, the obligations imposed in accordance with the provisions of GO no 34/2002. With at least 30 days' notice prior to withdrawal of any obligations imposed on a specific operator, the regulatory authority shall bring this intention to the knowledge of those having concluded access or interconnection agreements with that operator, in order to allow them to find alternative providers or to renegotiate the agreement concluded.[38]

32.62   The NRAC may impose obligations for transparency in relation to the interconnection of communications networks or to the access to these networks or to the associated infrastructure. These obligations may consist in making public specified information, such as technical specifications, network characteristics, terms and conditions for supply and use, accounting information, and tariffs.[39]

32.63   In situations where a market analysis indicates a lack of effective competition, meaning that the operator concerned might sustain prices at an excessively high level, or apply a price squeeze, to the detriment of end-users, the regulatory authority may impose obligations relating to cost recovery and price controls, including obligations for cost orientation of prices and obligations concerning cost

---

36   Art 2 GO no 34/2002.
37   Art 4 GO no 34/2002.
38   Art 8 GO no 34/2002.
39   Art 12 GO no 34/2002.

accounting systems, for the provision of specific types of access or interconnection. Such obligations may also be imposed on those operators having SMP in a relevant market. When imposing such obligations, the regulatory authority shall take into account the investment made by the operator concerned and shall allow him a reasonable rate of return on the capital invested, taking into account the risks associated with this investment.

32.64   The NRAC has issued several decisions imposing requirements on SMP operators in their respective markets,[40] such as:[41]

- transparency,
- non-discrimination,
- keeping separate accounting records, and
- justification of tariffs on the basis of cost.

32.65   These above-mentioned obligations are mandatory in an equal manner and usually these obligations have been imposed by the NRAC on all operators having SMP in their relevant markets. The NRAC actually controls the tariffs used by the operators having SMP, by imposing such cost-based tariffs which are calculated using models initially approved by the NRAC.

Regulatory Powers Applicable to All Market Participants

32.66   The NRAC shall take all the necessary measures in order to encourage and, where appropriate, ensure, in accordance with the provisions of GO no 34/2002, access and interconnection under adequate conditions, as well as interoperability of services, in keeping with the principles of economic efficiency, promoting competition, and maximising end-users' benefit.

32.67   Thus, without prejudice to measures that may be taken with regard to SMP undertakings, the measures imposed by the NRAC on operators regardless of their market position or legal persons other than the operators, in specific cases, may in particular consist of the imposition of the following obligations:

- obligations on legal persons other than the operators (we have no knowledge of such legal persons at the current time) that control access to end-users, including, if such is the case, the obligation to interconnect their networks, if the imposition of these obligations is necessary to ensure end-to-end connectivity, and
- obligation on operators to provide access to elements of the associated infrastructure under fair, reasonable, and non-discriminatory conditions, if the imposition of these obligations is necessary to ensure the access of end-users to digital radio and television broadcasting services.[42]

---

40   See para 32.23 above.
41   NRAC Decisions 123, 124,125, 126 /2003.
42   Art 5 GO no 34/2002.

REGULATION OF UNIVERSAL SERVICES AND USERS' RIGHTS: THE UNIVERSAL SERVICE DIRECTIVE

Regulation of Universal Service Obligations

Scope of universal service obligations

32.68   According to the provisions of article 3(1) of Law no 304/2003 on the Universal Service and Users' Rights Relating to the Electronic Communications Networks and Services ('Law no 304'),[43] the right of access to universal service represents the right of all end-users on the Romanian territory to benefit from the provision of services in the area of universal service, at a specified quality level, regardless of their geographical location, and, considering the specific conditions, at affordable prices.

32.69   According to art 3 Law no 304/2003, universal services include:

- provision of access to the public telephone network, at a fixed point,
- provision of directory enquiry and directories of subscribers services, and
- provision of public pay telephones.

Designation of undertakings obliged to provide universal services

32.70   Based on the policy and strategy established by the MCTI, the NRAC has the obligation to ensure the right of access to universal service on the entire territory of Romania. The NRAC will start by designating one or more universal service providers, which will make one or more services available in the area of universal service, within certain areas or on the entire territory of Romania. Basically, following the provisions of Decision no 1074/2004,[44] the NRAC may designate, ex officio or by auction, the universal service providers for specific areas such as telecentres or public pay telephones. These designation procedures are complex in nature and are mainly cost-oriented procedures. In order to award the winning offer, the tender commission shall mainly apply the criterion of the most advantageous financial offer, as regards the volume of the net cost.

32.71   Currently, according to the NRAC's Decision no 1345/2004, only Orange Romania SA has been designated for a three-year period, following a public tender, as a universal service provider in the electronic communications sector with a view to providing access to the public telephone network, at a fixed location, by means of telecentres, in 5 Romanian cities.

Regulation of retail tariffs, users' expenditures and quality of service

32.72   The NRAC shall monitor the evolution and level of tariffs of the services, which are within the scope of the universal service, provided by the universal service providers, in particular in relation to the general level of prices and consumer income.[45] The NRAC may compel universal service providers to apply common

---

43   Published in the Official Journal on 31 July 2003.
44   Decision 1074/2004 on the implementation of universal service in the electronic communications sector.
45   Art 9 Law no 304/2003.

tariffs, possibly by reference to a geographically established average, throughout the national territory, in the light of specific conditions, or to comply with certain tariff ceilings or tariff increase control formulae.[46]

32.73   The NRAC may compel universal service providers to provide tariff options or packages to consumers which depart from those provided under normal commercial conditions, in order to ensure the ability of people with low incomes or special social needs to benefit from publicly available telephone services.[47] The MCTI may establish the categories of persons who will benefit from the tariff options or packages offered.

32.74   The NRAC may impose modifications or withdraw certain tariffs or tariff schemes, whilst respecting the consultation procedure.[48]

32.75   The NRAC sets out the quality parameters for the provision of universal services, and the methods for evaluation of compliance with these parameters. Universal service providers shall have the obligation to transmit to the NRAC, and to publish, adequate and up-to-date information concerning compliance with the quality parameters for the provision of services within the scope of the universal service which they are obliged to provide.

32.76   The NRAC may impose on the universal service providers the obligation to meet certain performance targets concerning the quality of the services within the scope of the universal service which they are obliged to provide.[49]

32.77   The NRAC shall monitor compliance with the quality standards imposed on the universal service providers. For this purpose, the NRAC may order verification of data concerning compliance with the performance targets by an independent audit, paid for by the universal service provider concerned, in order to ensure the accuracy and comparability of the data made available by this provider.[50]

Cost calculation and financing of universal services

32.78   Where the NRAC estimates that the provision of universal services may represent an unfair burden on the universal service providers, it shall determine the net cost of the provision of these services.

For that purpose, the NRAC may resort to the following methods:

- calculate the net cost of the obligations to provide universal services, or
- make use of the net cost identified following the procedure for the designation of the universal service provider as provided by Decision no 1074/2004.

32.79   The NRAC shall determine the mechanism to compensate the net cost of the provision of the services within the scope of the universal service, whilst respecting the principles of transparency, minimal competition distortion, non-discrimination and proportionality. For that purpose, the NRAC shall identify the providers of electronic communications networks and the providers of electronic communications services having the obligation to contribute to compensation, the

---

46   NRAC may impose specific tariffs on all universal service providers in a specific area, by using an average of the tariffs used by all the universal operators in that area: art 9(2) Law 304/2003.
47   Art 9(3) Law no 304/2003.
48   Art 9(5) Law no 304/2003.
49   Art 11 Law no 304/2003.
50   Art 11 Law no 304/2003.

amount of the contributions due, the manner and due date of payment, as well as any other elements necessary for the functioning of this mechanism.[51] As far as we know, no such compensation has taken place yet.

End User Rights

Contracts

32.80   The contracts between end-users and providers of electronic communications services shall be concluded in writing and shall contain, as a minimum, clauses regarding:[52]

- the identification data of the provider,
- the services provided, the service quality levels offered, as well as the time for the initial connection,
- the types of maintenance and repair services offered,
- the prices and tariffs for each product or service covered by the contract, the way in which they are applied, as well as the means by which up-to-date information on the tariffs for the provision of the electronic communications services and of the maintenance and repair services may be obtained,
- the duration of the contract, the conditions for renewal and termination of the contract, as well as the conditions under which service suspension operates,
- the applicable compensations for damages and the procedure for granting them which apply if contracted service quality levels or the other contractual clauses are not met, and
- the method of initiating the procedure for settlement of disputes.[53]

There is no specific obligation for certain providers to enter into contracts with end-users.

Transparency obligations

32.81   The providers of public telephone networks and the providers of publicly available telephone services shall have the obligation to make available to the public clear, detailed and up-to-date information on the applicable prices and tariffs, as well as on the other conditions concerning the possibility of access to and use of publicly available telephone services, in order to ensure that end-users are able to make informed choices.[54]

---

51   Art 12 Law no 304/2003.
52   Art 19 Law no 304/2003.
53   The parties will establish this method at their own free will, by choosing the competent court for solving their contractual disputes. The law only stipulates for the obligation of introducing such a clause into this kind of agreement.
54   Art 20 Law no 304/2003.

DATA PROTECTION AND PRIVACY

Confidentiality of Communications[55]

32.82   The main Romanian piece of legislation that regulates data protection in electronic communications is Law no 506/2004 on the administering of personal data in the electronic communications sector ('Law no 506/2004'), which fully transposes the E-Privacy Directive.[56]

32.83   Providers of publicly available electronic communications services are required to take the appropriate technical and organisational measures for ensuring the security of the services provided. The providers of electronic communications services are bound to take the necessary security measures along with the provider of the public network of electronic communications in order to ensure the security of their respective network.

32.84   The measures taken must ensure a security level proportional to the actual risk, considering the cutting-edge technological resources and the implementation costs of such measures.[57]

32.85   In case there is a risk determined by a breach in the network security, the provider of a publicly available electronic communications service is bound to:

●   inform subscribers about such a risk, as well as any possible consequences,
●   inform subscribers about any possible remedies, and
●   inform subscribers about the estimate costs for clearing the risk.

32.86   The listening, tapping, storage and any other kinds of interception or surveillance of communications conveyed by means of publicly available electronic communications services and the related traffic data are prohibited, except for the following cases:

●   where it is performed by the users concerned;
●   where the users concerned have given their prior written consent with regard to the performance of such operations; or
●   where it is performed by competent authorities, under legal terms.[58]

32.87   However, the following are permitted:

●   the technical storage necessary for the conveyance of a communication without prejudice to the principle of confidentiality; and
●   the possibility of making authorised recordings of communications and related traffic data, under legal terms, when carried out in the course of lawful business practice for the purpose of providing evidence of a commercial transaction or of any other business communication.[59]

---

55   Pursuant to the law, 'communication' means 'any information exchanged or conveyed between a finite number of participants by means of a publicly available electronic communications service …'.
56   Published in the Official Gazette Part 1, 25 November 2004.
57   Art 3 Law no 506/2004.
58   Art 4 Law no 506/2004.
59   Art 4 Law no 506/2004

Traffic Data and Location Data

32.88   The definitions of 'traffic data' and 'location data' are identical to those in the E-Privacy Directive.[60]

32.89   Traffic data relating to subscribers and users, processed and stored by the providers of publicly available electronic communications services, must be erased or made anonymous when they are no longer needed for conveying a communication.

32.90   The processing of traffic data for the purpose of billing subscribers is permitted within a maximum period of three years from the maturity date of the financial obligation.

32.91   The providers of publicly available electronic communications services may process the traffic data related to subscribers and users for the purpose of merchandising its services or for the provision of value added services,[61] to the extent and over the duration necessary for merchandising and for providing the service, provided that the subscriber or user to whom the data relates has given his/her consent in advance. The user or the subscriber may withdraw at any time its consent for the processing of traffic data.[62]

32.92   In all the above-mentioned cases, the provider of the publicly available electronic communications service must inform the subscriber or user of the types of traffic data that are processed and of the duration of such processing.

32.93   Processing of traffic data must be restricted to persons acting under the authority of providers of publicly available electronic communications services with responsibility for traffic billing or management, customer service, fraud detection, merchandising electronic communications services or providing value added services, and must be restricted to what is necessary for the purposes of such activities.[63]

32.94   The processing of location data, other than traffic data, relating to users or subscribers of public communications networks or publicly available electronic communications services, can be processed, when it is possible, and only in one of the following cases:

- such data are made anonymous;
- with the express prior consent of the user or subscriber to which such data refer, to the extent and for the duration necessary for the provision of a value added service; or
- where the value added service with a location function has as its purpose the unidirectional and undifferentiated transmission of some information to its users.[64]

---

60   Art 2(b) Law no 506/2004.
61   Pursuant to Law no 506/2004 a 'value added service' means 'any service which requires the processing of traffic data or location for other purposes than the transmission of a communication or the billing of the equivalent for such an operation'.
62   Art 5 Law no 506/2004.
63   Art 5 Law no 506/2004.
64   Art 8 Law no 506/2004.

Itemised Billing

32.95   Users do not automatically receive itemised bills. The service providers issue itemised bills upon request from various users. There are no legal provisions regarding the obligation to pay for itemised bills. However, in practice, the operators issue itemised bills free of charge.

Calling and Connected Line Identification

32.96   Service providers offering calling line identification services must allow users to withhold their number on a per-call and per-line basis, using simple means and free of charge.[65] The police and other authorities may request the service provider to cease the provision of a withholding identity service for specific users.

Automatic Call Forwarding

32.97   Users to whom calls have been automatically forwarded as a result of third party actions have the right, without charge, to request that these be ceased as soon as practicable after receipt of the request.[66]

Directories of Subscribers

32.98   The universal service operator and any other person or undertaking making subscribers' data available for inclusion in a directory must inform all subscribers in advance of the purposes of the directory and any further usage possibilities based on search functions embedded in electronic versions of the directory. Subscribers will have the opportunity, free of charge, to determine whether and to what extent their personal data is included in the directory and be given the opportunity to verify, correct or withdraw the data.[67]

Unsolicited Communications

32.99   The use of automated calling systems without human intervention (automatic calling machines), facsimile machines (fax) or electronic mail or any other method using the publicly available electronic communications services, for the purposes of direct marketing may only be allowed in respect of subscribers who have given their prior consent for such communications.

32.100   However, where a natural or legal person obtains from its customers their electronic contact details for electronic mail, in the context of the sale of a product or a service, it may use those details for direct marketing of its own similar products or services, provided that customers clearly and distinctly are given the opportunity to object, free of charge and in an easy manner, to such use of electronic contact details when they are collected and on the occasion of each message where the customer has not initially refused such use.[68]

---

65   Art 7 Law no 506/2004.
66   Art 10(1) Law no 506/2004.
67   Art 11 Law no 506/2004.
68   Art 12 Law no 506/2004.

The Russian Market for Electronic Communications[1]

Dr Max B Gutbrod, Sergei Nosov and Edward Bekeschenko LLM
Baker & McKenzie, Moscow

LEGAL STRUCTURE

Basic Policy

33.1 During recent years, the telecommunications market in Russia has undergone significant changes and has become one of the most rapidly growing markets in the world. This is a result of liberalisation, development of the infrastructure in the telecommunications industry, and the continuous growth of the Russian economy in general since 1998. According to official information the telecommunications market expanded by 40% in 2004 alone.[2]

33.2 Whilst the telecommunications sector of the Soviet Union was state owned, since early 1990 many of the Soviet enterprises in all sectors in Russia have been privatised and new operators (the entities that have entered the telecommunications market and begun business as private companies) have become active on the market.

33.3 As a rule, the new operators are showing faster growth, especially in new sectors of the telecommunications market, such as mobile and satellite communications, broadband access, cable TV, etc. In contrast, the traditional operators, whilst sometimes also strong in the new sectors, are concentrated on providing such services as fixed line communications, long-distance calls etc. Some of the traditional operators, in fact, remain monopolists (eg Rostelecom), though talk about this situation has intensified since the beginning of 2005.

33.4 The number of customers using mobile phones has grown in the last few years by around 80% per year, which is the largest growth rate in the telecommunications sector in Russia. At present, market penetration in the biggest cities such as Moscow and St. Petersburg is very high, and operators are now turning to Russia's regions to obtain new customers. GSM continues to be the most popular standard used by the mobile providers, but other standards such as IMT-MC-450 are also in use. To date, no licences have been issued for providing services based on 3G technology. Currently, the first licences are expected to be issued by the end of 2005.

---

1   Editing of this chapter closed on 13 June 2005. The authors thank Ilya Petukhov, Ekaterina Solomatina, Olga Frolova, and Nadia Urazaeva for their assistance.
2   www.minsvyaz.ru/news.shtml?n_id=2501.

33.5   There has also been significant development in other telecom services. In the first quarter of 2004 the total number of fixed phone lines increased in the cities by almost 30% and, in the countryside, the number more than doubled year-on-year. 92 traditional operators and 2700 new operators provide local phone call services.

33.6   According to information provided by the Ministry of Information Technologies and Communications ('MITC'), the revenue collected by the traditional operators in the first quarter of 2004 increased by 30.6% and, by the new operators, by 51.9%.

Implementation of EU Directives – WTO Context

33.7   Although, from time to time, the idea of Russia joining the EU has enjoyed some support in Russia, it is unrealistic that any movement in this direction will happen in the next 10 to 20 years, so that its telecommunications legislation will not need to be adapted to the laws of the EU for that reason, and there are doubts as to whether EU telecommunications legislation would be appropriate for Russia's current stage of development. Also, since the EU-Russia summit on 10 May 2005, the idea of approaching EU and Russian legislation gradually has gained support, and it is likely that harmonising telecommunications legislation will be a part of this discussion. On the other hand, since accession to the WTO is high on Russia's list of priorities, WTO requirements for changes in telecommunications laws will affect further development of the relevant Russian laws.

33.8   After years of lack of progress with the WTO negotiations under the Yeltsin Administration, in the second half of 2000 the Putin Administration made WTO accession one of its priorities. Negotiations, therefore, continued with some degree of intensity and seemed to gain momentum due to the generally improved climate in relations between Russia and the West, and negotiations are believed to be at the decisive and final phase. Russia has been implementing laws that are necessary for WTO accession.

Legislation

33.9   On 7 July 2003, the President of the Russian Federation signed a new law 'On Communications' (the 'Communications Law').[3] This new law replaced the old Communications Law of 16 February 1995 ('Communications Law 1995') which was in effect more than eight years and, when first enacted, was considered to be fairly progressive.

33.10   The Communications Law contains more specific provisions than the Communications Law 1995, thus making regulation of the Russian telecommunications market more transparent and stable.

33.11   On 4 December 2003, the Russian Government approved a plan to draft government regulations to implement the Communications Law.[4] The plan specifies a number of regulations which are to be enacted by the end of 2005.[5]

---

3   RF Law No 126-FZ, amended on 23 December 2003, in force from 1 January 2004. Certain provisions came into force from 1 January 2005.
4   Government Resolution No 1776-r of 4 December 2003.
5   At the moment a significant number of regulations have been adopted: Government Resolution No 68 of 11 February 2005 'On Approval of Rules on state registration of ownership and

33.12 Until the new regulations are in force, the regulations which were enacted pursuant to the Communications Law 1995 will remain in force, provided that they do not contradict the provisions of the Communications Law.

REGULATORY PRINCIPLES

Scope of Regulation

33.13 The Communications Law has adopted a very wide and technology-neutral approach.[6] However, the terms used in sub-laws very clearly differentiate between telecommunication, radio and cellular communications, data transfer and telematics services.[7]

National Regulatory Authorities (NRA): Organisation, Regulatory Objectives, Competencies

33.14 State regulations on the provision of services and other communications activities shall be approved by the President, the Government and the Ministry of Information Technologies and Communications ('MITC') as the federal governmental authority for communications.[8]

33.15 The MITC is a state body responsible for the preparation of drafts of federal laws, presidential decrees and government resolutions in the area of communications and information technology. The MITC is entitled to issue its own regulations, such as setting out requirements for the use of numbering capacity, regulations for the use of radio frequencies, rules for providing communications services to subscribers, etc.[9]

33.16 The MITC coordinates and exercises control over the activities of the state agencies in the sphere of telecommunications, namely the Federal Service for Supervision in the Area of Communications (*Rossvyaznadzor* – 'FSS') and Federal Agency of Communications (*Rossvyaz* – 'FAC').

33.17 The FSS is responsible for exercising control in the area of communications, monitoring use of the frequency spectrum, registration of radio electronic equipment and issuance of licences in the area of communications.[10]

33.18 The FAC is responsible for the coordination of international and federal programs in the area of information technologies and communications, the allocation of frequencies and numbering capacity to operators, the registration of

---

other rights to cable lines', Government Resolution No 110 of 2 March 2005 'On Approval of Rules on state supervision over activity in the sphere of telecommunication', Government Resolution No 161 of 28 March 2005 'On Approval of Rules on telecommunications networks interconnection and interaction'; Government Resolution No 242 of 21 April 2005 'On Approval of Rules on tariffs for universal telecommunications services', Government Resolution No 328 of 25 May 2005 'On Approval of Rules on provision of mobile communications services'.

6   Arts 1 and 3 Communications Law.
7   See, for example, Government Resolution No 87 of 18 February 2005 On Approval of the List of Services Subject to Licensing and the Lists of Licensing Conditions..
8   Presidential Decrees No 314 of 9 March 2004 and No 649 of 20 May 2004.
9   Government Resolution No 311 of 26 June 2004.
10   Government Resolution No 318 of 30 June 2004.

frequency allocations, certifying compliance of equipment, and organising the operation, development and modernisation of the federal communications and national information and telecommunications infrastructure.[11]

33.19   MITC also organises the work of the State Frequency Commission ('SFC'). The SFC consists of representatives of different ministers and state bodies. The main purpose of the SFC is to coordinate the use of the frequency spectrum by different state bodies, and frequency spectrum allocation. The SFC is responsible for development of the concept of allocation and use of the frequency spectrum, providing scientific and technical research in the area of use of the frequency spectrum, frequency spectrum demilitarisation/conversion, determination of technical policy for use of the frequency spectrum and also with regard to electromagnetic compatibility.[12]

MITC and subordinated state agencies interact with the Federal Anti-monopoly Service ('FAS'), a competition regulator acting directly under the Government. FAS in its turn is entitled to prohibit MITC and subordinated state agencies from adopting acts or performing actions which may result in the restriction of competition. FAS is also entitled to provide MITC with recommendations aimed at ensuring competition. State agencies are usually independent, but they all interact with each other. State agencies act under a particular ministry (such as FSS and FAC) or the Government (such as FAS).

Right of Appeal against NRA's Decisions

33.20   Any decision of MITC, FSS or FAC may be appealed before the courts. If a decision violates a right of a legal entity, a claim can be filed with an Arbitrazh (state commercial) court, and if a decision violates the rights of an individual a claim can be filed with a court of general jurisdiction (general court). A claim is to be filed within three months after the claimant knows or should have known of the decision violating the claimant's rights.[13]

33.21   A judgment should be rendered by the Arbitrazh Court within two months after filing of the claim. The judgment may be appealed within one month to the court of appeal.[14]

33.22   In a general court, judgment should be rendered within 10 days. The judgment may be further challenged within 10 days in a higher court.[15]

33.23   In practice, the hearing of a case may take much longer than the time stipulated by procedural law.

33.24   Court procedures are very formalistic. The claimant has to prove the fact that the NRA's decision violates his rights. The respective regulatory authority must prove that the decision was issued in compliance with the law.

33.25   Sub-laws adopted by MITC can also be challenged: by legal entities in an Arbitrazh court and by individuals in a general court. After filing a claim, judgment should be rendered within one month in a general court or within two months in an Arbitrazh court. There is no statute of limitation for the challenging of a sub-law.

---

11   Government Resolution No 320 of 30 June 2004.
12   Government Resolution No 336 of 2 July 2004.
13   Art 256 Code of Civil Procedure; art 197 Code of Arbitrazh Procedure.
14   Art 200 Code of Arbitrazh Procedure.
15   Art 257 Code of Civil Procedure.

'Dominance' as a Fundamental Prerequisite of Regulation

33.26   Dominance under Russian legislation exists if a business entity holds 65% of the market. It may also be deemed to exist if a company holds more than 35% of the market, depending on the market shares of competitors, stability of the market share, and similar criteria. Dominance may refer to individual or collective dominance.[16]

33.27   The Communications Law seeks to ensure effective and fair competition in the telecommunications services market. Moreover, the prices for telecommunications services provided by companies enjoying dominance are subject to state regulation.

Although there is a comprehensive set of regulations for anti-competitive behaviour, there are still many 'grey areas' in the procedure for their implementation. To date, practical measures for de-monopolisation of the telecommunications sector have been insufficient. Also, the authorities have tacitly tolerated several existing or newly created monopolies, including the abuse of their dominant position in the market. Markets are defined by individual decision of state authorities in accordance with law. The following markets have been identified to date: the market of telecommunication services, the market of intercity and international electric communication, and the market of postal services.

NRA's Regulatory Duties concerning Rights of Way, Co-location and Facility Sharing

Rights of way

33.28   The RF Land Code ('Land Code') provides for a specific category of lands designated for communications purposes.[17] In order to carry out activities in the areas of communications, radio and television broadcasting, such rights to land plots may be granted for the location of infrastructure facilities, including radio relay, aerial, and underground cable communications lines and relevant restricted zones, amplification stations, land-based satellite communications facilities and infrastructure.[18]

33.29   The state or a municipality can allocate state land plots for communications purposes by way of granting ownership rights, or a right of perpetual use, or a lease to the operator. Such titles and rights are subject to state registration. A lease agreement signed for a term of less than one year does not, however, require state registration.

33.30   As regards privately owned land, the Land Code provides for easements as an instrument of private law that are to be established by agreement between two parties.[19] Easements are also subject to state registration. The parties may also agree on other use rights that can be granted to the operator by a private owner. The Russian legislation does not provide any specific regulation for the case where a private owner refuses to enter into such an agreement.

---

16   Art 4 Federal Law 'On Competition and Restriction of Monopoly Activities on Commodity Markets', No 948–1 of 22 March 1991.
17   Art 87 Land Code.
18   Art 87 Land Code.
19   Arts 274, 277 Civil Code.

33.31   The ownership of real estate such as buildings, masts, and other constructions must be registered in the Unified State Register of Rights to Immovable Property of Rights. Aerial and underground communication cables and related equipment are also subject to registration as immovable property.[20]

Co-location and facility sharing

33.32   The Communications Law entitles communications operators to place their cable lines in cable line equipment (cable vaults) belonging to another person/entity. Expenses of the owner of the cable equipment (cable vaults) shall be covered by the communications operator.[21]

REGULATION OF MARKET ENTRY

General Regulatory Approach

33.33   Communications services can only be provided on the basis of a licence. The 'List of Communications Services Requiring a Licence in the Sphere of Communications and the Licensing Conditions' is established in Government Resolution No 87.[22] The FSS is the federal authority currently responsible for the issuance of licences, ie for the following communications services subject to mandatory licensing:

- provision of local telephone communications services, provision of international and domestic long-distance communications services,
- provision of telegraph communications services,
- provision of paging communications services,
- provision of radio, cellular, or satellite communications services,
- provision of lease of communications channel services,
- provision of communications services via data transmission networks (including or not including voice transmission), and
- provision of telematics services.

Licensing Procedures

33.34   A licence may be obtained upon application. If the communications service requires the use of radio frequency, numbering capacity or other limited resources, the licence may be obtained only through a competitive procedure (auction or tender).[23]

33.35   The application form must contain basic information about the applicant, the term, and the territory where the licensee intends to provide communications services. A copy of the company Charter, certificate of registration as a legal entity or private entrepreneur, certificate of registration as a taxpayer, network configuration chart, a short description of the services to be provided, and confirmation of payment of the state fee (300 roubles, approx €9) for consideration of the application are to be submitted.

---

20   Art 1 Rules on state registration of ownership and other rights to cable lines.
21   Art 6(5) Communications Law.
22   Government Resolution No 87 of 18 February 2005 On Approval of the List of Services Subject to Licensing and the Lists of Licensing Conditions.
23   Art 31(1) Communications Law.

33.36 If the applicant intends to provide TV, radio, local, long-distance or international telecommunications services, a description of the network, of the communications devices, and the business plan shall additionally be attached to the application.

33.37 If an application is made for a licence to provide communications services requiring the use of a radio frequency, the decision of the SFC on frequency allocation (the radio frequency use permit) must be attached.

33.38 A decision on whether to issue the licence shall be taken by the FSS within 30 days after filing the application.

33.39 The applicant shall pay a state fee for issuance of the licence. The amount of the fee varies from a multiple of 20 to 90 times the minimum wage. At the moment it is equivalent to €60–€260. The fee shall be multiplied by the number of regions where the services will be provided.

33.40 The territory for which the licence is valid shall be specified in the licence. There are no restrictions on the number or type of communications licences that a single licensee may hold. In the past, licences were only granted for internal connections; since 13 June 2005, international licences have reportedly been granted.

33.41 Licences are issued for a term of between three and 25 years. An application to extend the term of a licence must be submitted no less than two months, and no earlier than six months, prior to its expiration date. The licence may be prolonged for the term of its issuance or for a longer term, but not for more than for 25 years.

33.42 The Communications Law does not allow the transfer of a licence or any rights that are based on the licence to another person. The licence can be re-issued by the FSS only to a legal successor of the licensee, for which purpose the legal successor must provide documents evidencing transfer of the relevant communications networks and devices for provision of communications services to it. If the licence was for the use of a radio frequency, the radio frequency use permit needs to be re-issued prior to re-issuing the licence.[24]

Admissible Conditions

33.43 The grounds for refusal to issue a licence to provide communications services are limited to the following:

- non-compliance of the documents attached to the application form with the requirements of the Communications Law,
- failure to provide a document required by the Communications Law,
- providing documents that contain incorrect information,
- non-compliance of the activity for which the licence is requested with the applicable standards and regulations,
- failure to win the tender for providing a communications licence,
- termination of the permit for use of the frequency spectrum, or
- the impossibility of implementing the communications service for which the licence is requested.[25]

---

24   Art 35 Communications Law.
25   Art 34 Communications Law.

33.44   The refusal of the FSS to issue a licence may be challenged by the applicant before the courts.[26]

Termination of Licences

33.45   The FSS has a right to terminate a licence without applying to the courts if the operator is liquidated, has applied for termination of the licence, or fails to pay the licence fee within three months following the date of issuance of the licence.

33.46   The licence may be suspended if the FSS discovers a breach of statute, or conditions of the licence by the operator, or non-performance of the services for more than three months.[27]

33.47   The FAC may file a claim for termination of an operator's licence to court if:

- it is discovered that the operator has provided incorrect information when applying for the licence,
- the licence was suspended and the operator did not take the necessary steps to eliminate grounds for the suspension of the licence,
- the operator did not comply with conditions and obligations undertaken during an auction/tender.

Rights of Use for Radio Frequencies

General regulatory approach

33.48   According to the Communications Law,[28] the procedures for frequency allocation and for the national frequency allocation have to be transparent. Allocation of the frequency spectrum is to be made in accordance with the Frequency Allocation Table, which has to be reviewed at least once every four years.

33.49   The FAC is in charge of establishing the procedure for allocation of frequency ranges, bands and channels. The decision on frequency allocation shall be taken within 120 days following the date when an application is made. Radio frequency ranges, bands and channels are allocated on the basis of a decision by the FAC and for a term of up to 10 years.[29]

33.50   The Communications Law does not allow transfer of the right of radio frequency use to another operator.

33.51   The use of the frequency spectrum is subject to a one-time fee for allocation of a radio frequency, and an annual fee for use of the radio frequency depending on the service provided: from approximately 70 roubles to 18,000 roubles (€2 to €600) in the Central Circuit.[30]

33.52   The compulsory change by the SFC of the frequency band or the channel is allowed only in order to prevent a threat to human life or health, to ensure state

---

26   See paras 33.20 et seq above.
27   Art 37(1) Communications Law.
28   Art 22(4) Communications Law.
29   Art 24(2) Communications Law.
30   www.rfc-cfa.ru/main.phtml?p=tarif&l=ru.

security or to secure compliance of the Russian Federation with the terms and conditions of international treaties to which the latter is a party. Such change of the frequency bands or the channels can be challenged by the frequency spectrum's user before the courts.[31]

Admissible conditions

33.53   The allocation of rights of use for frequencies is subject to the following conditions:

- the frequency band should correspond to the Frequency Allocation Table,
- parameters of the electronic equipment must correspond with the national electromagnetic compatibility standards and regulations,
- electronic equipment of the applicant needs to have past electromagnetic compatibility analysis,
- the applicant shall submit all the necessary documents and certificates for the electronic equipment,
- the activity in the area of communications for which the allocation of the frequency spectrum was requested shall comply with the applicable standards and regulations, and
- the results of the international procedure for coordination of radio frequency use need to be positive.

33.54   Where the FAC discovers violations of the terms and conditions set out by the FAC in its decision for allocation of the frequency spectrum, the permit for the frequency spectrum use can be suspended for a period required for correction of such violation, but shall not exceed 90 days.[32]

33.55   The permit for the use of a radio frequency spectrum can be terminated by the FAC without applying to the general courts in the following cases:

- an operator filed an application for termination of the permit for frequency spectrum use,
- the licence for providing communications services with the use of spectrum, ie mobile communications services, has been cancelled,
- the term for which the spectrum was allocated has expired and the operator failed to file an application to extend such term 30 days prior to the expiry date of the permission,
- the electronic equipment was used by the operator for illegal purposes,
- the operator has failed to comply with the terms and conditions set out by the FAC in its decision for allocation of the frequency spectrum,
- the operator has failed to make payments for spectrum use for more than 30 days after the due date,
- the operator to whom the permit for frequency spectrum use was provided has been liquidated, and
- the operator has failed to remedy the violations of the terms and conditions set out by the FAC in its decision for allocation of the frequency spectrum.[33]

---

31   Art 24(6) Communications Law.
32   Art 24(10) Communications Law.
33   Art 24(11) Communications Law.

Limitation of rights of use to be granted

33.56   Under the Communications Law,[34] providing licences to communications operators via a competitive bidding process such as an auction or tender shall take place if the communications services involving the use of radio frequencies are to be provided in a territory where the available frequency spectrum limits the number of possible operators, or where the capabilities of the network, such as numbering capacity, are insufficient. Auctions and tenders shall be organised by FAC.[35] A number of such auctions and tenders have taken place, with the sums paid in the auctions being relatively low.

Rights of Use for Numbers

General regulatory approach

33.57   Under the Communications Law, allocation of numbering capacity falls within the exclusive competence of the state.[36] Allocation of numbering capacity shall be undertaken by the FAC upon the application of an operator within 60 days after the application is filed.[37]

33.58   The operators are required to pay a state fee for the allocation of numbering capacity. The amount of such payment for allocation of numbers is set out in the RF Tax Code.

33.59   Rights of use for numbers already granted may be withdrawn in the following cases:

- an operator files an application for the withdrawal of numbering capacity,
- the communications licence issued to an operator has expired,
- the numbering capacity has been used by an operator with violations of the numbering system and plan,
- the allocated numbering capacity has not been used for two years since allocation,
- the operator fails to fulfil the obligations undertaken by such operator during the tender procedure, and
- the operator fails to pay the duty for the allocation of numbering capacity within 90 days after such allocation was made.

33.60   The operator shall be notified of the forthcoming withdrawal of the numbering capacity as well as about the reasons for doing so 30 days prior to the date of such withdrawal.[38]

33.61   The Communications Law establishes the right of an end-user to keep its number on changing their address or changing the mobile operator.[39] However, at the present time this right cannot be implemented for technical reasons.

---

34   Art 31 Communications Law.
35   Government Resolution No 320 of 30 June 2004.
36   Art 26(1) Communications Law.
37   Art 26(5) Communications Law.
38   Art 26(2) Communications Law.
39   Art 45(2) Communications Law.

Admissible conditions

33.62 Operators are obliged to start using the allocated numbering capacity within two years after allocation.[40] Operators shall bear all expenses caused by allocation or changes of numbering capacity.

33.63 Information about allocation of the numbering capacity to a particular operator is not considered as confidential.

33.64 Numbering capacity cannot be transferred from one operator to another without the prior permission of the FAC. Numbering capacity can be transferred to a legal successor upon the latter's written request without additional payment of duty for allocation of numbering capacity.[41]

Limitation of number of rights of use to be granted

33.65 If the total number of allocated numbers in a particular region is more than 90%, further allocation shall be made through a tender.[42]

The NRA's Enforcement Powers

33.66 The FSS has the right to suspend the operation of a licence, to terminate a licence in some cases without filing a claim, and to file a claim for termination of the licence if the operator fails to comply with the terms and conditions of the licence.[43] The FSS is obliged to send a notice prior to the suspension, describing the violation and establishing a timeframe to rectify it.

33.67 The FSS has the right to inspect the work of operators. Scheduled inspections of the same entity or person shall be conducted no more than once in two years. An inspection should not take more than one month. However, the FSS has the right to make an unscheduled inspection if it receives information on a violation of the law, licensing conditions, or technological process by the operator, or in case of emergency.[44]

33.68 The Chief State Inspector of the FSS, his deputies and FSS inspectors have the right to make written protocols on administrative offences with regard to violations of communications law, to make investigations, assessments, calculations and measurements, to suspend the operation of communications equipment and networks, and to request necessary documents and information.[45] The Chief State Inspector of the FSS, his deputies and senior inspectors may also impose administrative penalties for violation of the law and make compulsory orders to eliminate violations.[46]

---

40 Art 26(2), (6) Communications Law.
41 Art 26(8) Communications Law.
42 Art 26(5) Communications Law.
43 See para 33.46 above.
44 Arts 10–16 Procedure for Implementing State Control in the Sphere of Communications
45 Art 7 'Rules on state supervision over activity in the sphere of telecommunication' Approved by Government Resolution No 110 of 2 March 2005.
46 Art 8 'Rules on state supervision over activity in the sphere of telecommunication' Approved by Government Resolution No 110 of 2 March 2005.

Administrative Charges and Fees for Rights of Use

33.69   All operators are obliged to pay 1.2% of the difference between their profits from telecommunications services and their profits from interconnection services and services on traffic transit to the reserve of universal telecommunications services. [47]

33.70   State fees for allocation of numbering capacity are fixed in Article 333.33 Tax Code. For example, the payment for allocation of a single phone number is 10 roubles (approx €0,30).

33.71   Operators will be obliged to pay a fee for using a radio frequency, but the scale of this fee has not yet been determined.

REGULATION OF NETWORK ACCESS AND INTERCONNECTION

Objectives and Scope of Access Regulation

33.72   The purpose of the regulation of access and interconnection is to ensure adequate access to telecommunications services throughout the Russian Federation, to promote sustainable competition, to ensure growth of the telecommunications infrastructure, and to protect end-users' rights.

33.73   The access- and interconnection-related provisions of the Communications Law differentiate between the following types of communications networks:

- public switched telephone network. This comprises all communications networks under the jurisdiction of the Russian Federation, except for dedicated networks, closed networks and special purpose networks.[48]
- dedicated networks ('non-public networks'). These are networks operated by individuals and legal entities with no access to the public switched telephone network.[49]
- closed networks. These are networks established to meet the industrial and special needs of the federal executive authorities, and are supervised and operated by them.[50]
- special purpose networks. These networks are designated for government needs, state defence and security purposes.[51]

Basic Regulatory Concepts

33.74   The Communications Law uses a single term for access and interconnection.[52] The meaning of the term used is very close to the term 'access' used in the Access Directive.[53]

33.75   Each operator has the right to interconnect its network to the public switched telephone network, subject to certain conditions. Interconnection of

---

47   Government Resolution On Approval or Rules for Collection and Consumption of the Reserve of the Universal Telecommunication Services.
48   Art 13 Communications Law.
49   Art 14 Communications Law.
50   Art 15 Communications Law.
51   Art 16 Communications Law.
52   Art 18 Communications Law.
53   See para 1.125 above.

communications networks and their interaction shall be governed by interconnection agreements between the operators. The prices for interconnection and transit of traffic should be set by the connecting operators reasonably and in good faith. Disputes between operators regarding interconnection agreements shall be resolved by the courts, but there is no established court practice yet. The court would have to examine whether the operator acted reasonably and in good faith.

The Communications Law for the first time provides a definition of an operator holding a key position in the public switched telephone network (the 'Incumbent Operator'), and also establishes for such Incumbent Operators special conditions for connecting telecommunications networks of other operators and the transit of their traffic.

Access- and Interconnection-related Obligations with Respect to Incumbent Operators

33.76   According to the Communications Law, Incumbent Operators are those who, alone or together with associated entities, control at least 25% of the PSTN capacity in a particular region that has the same area code or within the entire Russian Federation or, alternatively, operators that have the ability to handle at least 25% of the transit of traffic.[54] The definition of dominance[55] is independent from the definition of control.

33.77   The Register of Incumbent Operators is managed by FSS.

33.78   Incumbent Operators are obliged to establish equal terms for connection to the public switched telephone network of other operators, as well as for transit of their traffic.[56]Furthermore, Incumbent Operators must provide such other operators with connection services and transit of traffic services under the same terms and at the same level of quality as they do for their own divisions and/or affiliates. No Incumbent Operator may refuse to enter into interconnection agreements with other operators, unless providing the interconnection would contradict the terms of a specific operator's licence and/or the law regulating the formation and functioning of the public switched telephone network.

33.79   The procedure for interconnection of communication networks of operators with the communication network of the Incumbent Operator is determined by the access and interconnection rules approved by the Russian Government.[57]

33.80   An Incumbent Operator cannot refuse to conclude an access and interconnection contract and must establish equal terms and conditions for access, interconnection and traffic transit for all operators.[58] The prices of the Incumbent Operator for interconnection and traffic transit are subject to state regulation. There is no practice on pricing available yet.

33.81   Should an Incumbent Operator refuse to sign a contract for access and interconnection, the interested operator may file a claim with the courts in order to force the signing of an agreement and to receive compensation for damage

---

54   Art 2 Communications Law.
55   See para 33.26 above.
56   Art 19 Communications Law.
57   Government Resolution No 161 of 28 March 2005 On Approval of the Rules on Telecommunications Networks Interconnection and Interaction.
58   Art 19 Communications Law.

sustained. An Incumbent Operator may refuse to sign such a contract only if such access would violate the licensing conditions or regulations which set out the rules of construction and functioning of the Russian Federation telecommunications network.

33.82 Should the MITC notify an Incumbent Operator that its terms and conditions for interconnection do not comply with the interconnection rules, the Incumbent Operator shall rectify such violation within 30 days after such notification.

REGULATION OF UNIVERSAL SERVICES AND USERS' RIGHTS

Regulation of Universal Service Obligations

33.83 The concept of universal communications services was first introduced by the Communications Law to target those categories of the population that presently have difficulty in taking advantage of communications resources. Universal services under the Communications Law include payphone services, as well as services for data transmission and internet access through collective-use stations.[59]

33.84 The time in which a user should be able to reach a coin- or card-operated telephone by foot should not exceed one hour. Each populated locality should have at least one such payphone offering free access to emergency medical and other related services. Localities with 500 or more inhabitants should have at least one collective-access internet station.[60]

33.85 According to the Communications Law, the provision of universal services to any user of communications services in the Russian Federation within a pre-determined period, at a standard level of quality and at affordable prices, will be obligatory for universal service operators.[61] Rates for universal services are subject to state regulation.[62]

33.86 The regional authorities will arrange a tender among the communications companies for the right to provide universal services in certain geographical areas. The company that offers the best terms of service will be awarded the contract. If the tender fails for whatever reason, the obligation to provide universal services in a particular geographical area shall be imposed by the RF Government (upon recommendation of MITC) on the Incumbent Operator, which has no right to decline such obligation.[63]

33.87 After the first six months of universal service coverage, and every six months thereafter, the universal service provider shall submit service volume data and cost data to FAC to compensate for losses from universal services. Universal service providers are to be reimbursed out of a Universal Services Fund to which all operators of the public switched telephone network will be required to make contributions of 1.2%.[64]

---

59   Art 57 Communications Law.
60   Art 57 Communications Law.
61   Art 2 Communications Law.
62   Government Resolution No 242 of 21 April 2005 On Approval of Rules for the State Regulation of Tariffs for Universal Telecommunication Services
63   Art 58 Communications Law.
64   See para 33.69 above.

33.88   The maximum amount of compensation for losses from universal services shall be determined as the balance between the income and the economically justified expenses of the operator resulting from providing universal services, on the one hand, and the income and expenses of the operator which the operator would have if the obligation to provide universal services did not apply to such operator, on the other hand.

Regulation of Retail Markets

33.89   Under the Communications Law, subscribers will have the option of choosing between two schemes of charging for local connections – either subscription or time-based billing.

33.90   The Communications Law preserves communications service discounts for selected categories of individuals, who will, however, have to pay initially for their use of such services in full and only then claim reimbursement from the respective government budget account. Under the old legislation, such citizens enjoyed access to services at privileged rates, while the operators had to be recompensed later from the government budget accounts and often incurred substantial losses as a result. Now, users will have to obtain their own refunds on a case-by-case basis.[65]

End User Rights

33.91   The principal legal acts regulating the rights of telecommunications service users include the Russian Civil Code, the Communications Law and, in respect of consumer rights, also the Law 'On Consumer Rights Protection',[66] the Rules for the Provision of Telephone Services[67] (the 'Rules') and Rules on Provision of Mobile Communications Services.[68]

33.92   The contract between a provider of telecommunications services and an individual is a public contract,[69] ie for communication services rendered to individuals, the operator does not have the right to give preference to one person over another with regard to entering into the contract, or the right to refuse to enter into the contract whenever the operator is capable of providing the required service(s).[70]

33.93   The Rules formulate a Model Telecommunication Services Contract, which is fairly short and makes reference to a list of services and the payment terms only. The Rules also require operators to make available to users, whenever a contract is being negotiated, certain information (regarding tariffs, procedures for reviewing claims, directory enquiry services, repair services, etc). Such data are provided by way of information, ie there is no requirement concerning their incorporation into the contract.

33.94   A telecommunication operator is obliged to furnish consumers with information concerning available services in order to enable the latter to make the right

---

65   Art 47 Communications Law.
66   RF Law No 212-FZ 'On Consumer Rights Protection' dated 7 February 1992.
67   Government Resolution No 1235 of 26 September 1997.
68   Government Resolution No 328 of 25 May 2005.
69   Art 45 Communications Law.
70   Art 426 Russian Civil Code.

choice, including, inter alia, information regarding any obligatory standards exist-ing in respect of such services.[71] The Communications Law provides individuals with certain guarantees, including the right of a subscriber to retain its number whenever the subscriber changes its address, the right to receive at least 60 days' prior notice if its number is to be replaced, compulsory renewal of the existing contract with a new owner of the premises to which telephone services is provided, and round-the-clock access, free of charge, to emergency telephone numbers.[72]

33.95   Tariffs payable for publicly available telecommunications services are sub-ject to government regulation.[73] The tariffs of an operator must be the same for all users.[74]

33.96   Telecommunications operators are obliged to provide users with services of such quality as may be required by statute or relevant technical standard, and in accordance with the quality requirements established by contract, specification or specimen.[75]

33.97   An operator is liable for the published quality of its services, for failure to comply with the timing of the provision of services or the timing of actions to deal with defects, and for misinformation regarding the services provided.[76] Whenever the rights of a consumer are breached, the latter is entitled to certain remedies: the right to demand performance of the contract according to its terms; to reduce the cost of a particular service; to dissolve the contract; to assign the contract to a third party; or to claim a penalty and request compensation for damage.[77]

33.98   A breach of a telecommunications services contract initiates the obligatory procedure for pre-trial settlement of a dispute: the user must first send to the operator a letter before action setting out all its demands, and may only take the matter to court if such demands are turned down or ignored.[78]

DATA PROTECTION AND PRIVACY

Confidentiality of Communications

33.99   The right to privacy of correspondence, telephone conversations, and postal, telegraph and other messages is guaranteed by the RF Constitution.[79] This guarantee is restated in the Communications Law, namely, the guarantee of the confidentiality of correspondence, telephone conversations, telegraph and other communications transmitted along telecommunications networks.[80]

---

71   Para 69 Rules.
72   Art 45 Communications Law.
73   Art 28 Communications Law.
74   Art 426 Civil Code, para 80 Rules.
75   Art 4 Consumer Rights Protection Law.
76   Para 113 Rules.
77   Paras 113–114 Rules.
78   Art 55 Communications Law.
79   Art 23(2) Constitution of the Russian Federation of 12 December 1993.
80   Art 63(1) Communications Law.

33.100   The Communications Law also imposes on operators an obligation to ensure the privacy of communications.[81] Operators providing electronic communications services are obliged to take the measures necessary to secure the privacy of telecommunications.

33.101   Information concerning such communications that is transmitted by telecommunications networks may be disclosed only to the sender or the recipient, or their authorised representatives.[82] Review of the information transmitted by telecommunications networks by any person other than the sender and recipient may be done only on the basis of a court order.

33.102   Special state organisations may be granted the right to intercept and review information sent by means of electronic communications and to make interception of telephone communications for the purpose of investigation. Such interception or review may be conducted only after a court order has been obtained.

33.103   In those cases prescribed by federal law, communications operators are obliged to supply to the criminal investigation authorities information on the users of communications services or services rendered, as well as other information necessary for the discharge their investigatory functions.[83]

Itemised Billing

33.104   The Government Resolution 'On Approval of Rules on provision of mobile communications services'[84] provides for subscribers to mobile communications services to be able to request in writing the issue of a detailed bill showing the date, time and duration of all effected connections, as well the subscribers' numbers.

Calling and Connected Line Identification

33.105   No obligations are imposed on service providers in relation to calling line identification and connected line identification.

Directories of Subscribers

33.106   Information about subscribers and information relating to communications services provided to them in the possession of any communications operators is deemed to be confidential information and subject to protection. The following information is confidential and subject to legal protection:

- the name or nickname of individuals,
- the firm name of legal entities, the names of their head officers or employees,
- the address of a subscriber or the address of the installation of the end equipment,
- the subscription numbers and other data allowing identification of a subscriber or their end equipment, and

---

81   Art 63(2) Communications Law. Some breaches of confidentiality have been reported in the media.
82   Art 63(3) and (4) Communications Law.
83   Art 64(1) Communications Law
84   Art 37(d) Government Resolution No 328 of 25 May 2005 'On Approval of Rules on provision of mobile communications services'.

- information on charges for the services rendered, including on the subscriber's connections, traffic and payments.[85]

33.107   Subject to prior confirmation by the subscriber, operators are entitled to use some information available to them for information and referral services, namely the name of an individual and the subscriber's number, or the name (firm name) of legal entities, and the numbers and addresses of the installation of the end equipment they have indicated.

33.108   However, information on individuals cannot be used in databases to give reference or other information services by the communications operator or by a third party without the prior written consent of the subscribers.[86]

33.109   The submission of information on individual subscribers to third parties in other circumstances may also be effected only with the written consent of the subscriber, except as stipulated in federal laws.

Unsolicited Communications

33.110   The current legislation does not deal with unsolicited communications. However, there are two draft laws regulating unsolicited communications being elaborated, both providing an opt-in system for such communications.

---

85   Art 53(1) Communications Law.
86   Art 53(2) Communications Law.

The Swiss Market for Telecommunications[1]

Markus Berni and Corinne Casanova
Baker & McKenzie Zurich

LEGAL STRUCTURE

Basic Policy

34.1 On 1 January 1998 the Swiss telecommunications market was liberalised. As a result of the opening of the market, consumers have been enjoying a wider range of services; and prices, especially in the area of fixed line telephony, have been decreasing. Mobile telephony and broadband services have been boosted as well. In 2004 the penetration rate for mobile telephony subscriptions in Switzerland was 85%, compared to 15% at the end of 1997. Prices for mobile telephony have remained relatively high.

34.2 Despite the high number of telecommunications providers,[2] the former monopolist, Swisscom, today still dominates many markets, mainly those linked to the provision of fixed line services, but also mobile telephony.[3] Thus, competition has decreased again. So far, Swisscom has retained total control of local loops.

34.3 From the beginning, the regulatory regime of the Swiss telecommunications legislation was less interventionist than in many EU member states, in that the provision of telecommunications services generally required merely a notice to the regulator and no licence; a licence was required only by operators controlling significant portions of the infrastructure used for providing telecommunications services. Moreover, the interconnection regime was based from the beginning on the paradigm of self-regulation through negotiations. Under the new telecommunications legislation, a licence is now only required by operators who use radio frequencies and by operators providing services under the universal service obligation.

Implementation of EU Directives

34.4 Switzerland is not a member of the EU and is not a contracting party to the EEA Treaty. Initially, the liberalisation of services was part of the second package

---

1 Editing of this chapter closed on 30 June 2005.
2 In August 2003 there were 115 providers in possession of a licence for the operation of a public network and 110 providers of voice telephony services.
3 With a market share of approximately 62% in 2004.

of bilateral agreements between Switzerland and the EU. However, due to the complexity of the matter, the parties agreed to suspend negotiations on the services dossier. Therefore, the Draft LTC does not (yet) include all of the principles set out in the 2002 EU Regulatory Package, although the intention of the drafters clearly was to adapt Swiss legislation to the EU regulatory framework. In particular, the Swiss drafters did not introduce ex-ante provisions which allow the regulatory authority to define the relevant markets and to define the providers which have a dominant position ex officio and to impose certain obligations on these providers. Under the Draft LTC, the relations between the telecommunications providers will continue to be governed by the parties themselves. The regulatory authority may only fix the conditions for interconnection where the parties cannot reach an agreement.

Legislation

34.5   The Federal Telecommunications Act of 30 April 1997 ('LTC 1997')[4] is currently being revised. After taking note of the public consultation procedure, the Swiss Federal Government submitted a draft to the Swiss Federal Parliament in November 2003. In October 2004 an amended version of the draft ('Draft LTC')[5] was adopted by the first chamber (National Council). The second chamber (Council of States) adopted the Draft LTC in mid-June 2005; at this point in time, the two chambers had not yet agreed on the scope of access to be provided by providers of telecommunications services with a dominant position in the market. The National Council had laid down that bitstream access would have to be granted for two years, after which time the alternative providers would have to set up their own infrastructure. The Council of States, on the other hand, took the position that bitstream access has to be granted indefinitely and, after a transitional period of three years, the Federal Government would be authorised to make the granting of bitstream access subject to conditions in order to encourage investments in infrastructure. Hence, as at the time of writing, the issue of bitstream access is still open. The revised LTC is expected to enter into force during 2006 at the earliest.

34.6   The transmission of radio and television programmes is covered by the Federal Act regarding Radio and Television ('LRTV') of 21 June 1991. At present, the LRTV is also subject to revision. The draft ('draft LRTV')[6] has already been debated in both chambers and will probably enter into force in 2006.

34.7   The Federal Government has adopted several ordinances based on the LTC 1997. An amended version of the Ordinance on Telecommunications Services came into effect on 1 April 2003.[7] The Ordinance as amended already deals with some of the measures to be implemented in the new LTC, such as the unbundling of the local loops (full access), bitstream access and shared line access. The approach chosen by the Federal Government to open up access by means of amendment to the ordinance, before the actual Federal Telecommunications Act has been amended, is politically controversial. Through the (new) obligations of access the alternative providers will no longer be dependent on the former monopolist, and

---

4   RS (Systematic Compilation of Swiss Law (an official source), available at: www.admin.ch) 784.10.
5   Initial version published in the Federal Gazette no 49 of 16 December 2003, p 8007.
6   Initial version published in the Federal Gazette no 8 of 4 March 2003, p 1779.
7   RS 784.101.1; RO (Official Compilation of Swiss Law, available at: www.admin.ch) 2003 544.

consumers will benefit from a bigger range of services. The other ordinances[8] will be amended once the Draft LTC has been adopted.

REGULATORY PRINCIPLES

Scope of Regulation

34.8   The LTC applies to the transmission of information by means of telecommunications techniques, with the exception of the broadcasting or re-broadcasting of programmes within the meaning of the LRTV.[9] 'Information' includes signs, signals, characters, images, sounds and any other form of representation addressed to human or other living beings or to machines. 'Transmission by means of telecommunications techniques' has the meaning of sending or receiving of information, by wire, cable or radio, by means of electrical, magnetic or optical signals or other electromagnetic signals.

34.9   Although the concepts and terminology of the Draft LTC are in the spirit of the EU legislation, the terms 'electronic communications network', 'electronic communications service' and 'associated facilities' as such are not defined in Swiss law. The Draft LTC uses the term 'telecommunication services' which does not include radio and television broadcasting regulated in the LRTV. However, the Draft LRTV does not prevent the increasing harmonisation of telecommunication and broadcast (convergence), and thus the scope of application of the LTC will be in accordance with the one of the 2002 EU Regulatory Package.[10]

National Regulatory Authorities: Organisation, Regulatory Objectives, Competencies

34.10   In comparison to the NRAs within the EU, the Swiss regulatory authorities only possess a few, clearly defined regulatory instruments with little administrative discretion. The regulatory objectives result from the aim of the LTC, which is to ensure that a range of cost-effective, high quality and nationally and internationally competitive telecommunications services is available to private individuals and the business community.[11]

34.11   The Federal Communications Commission ('ComCom') is an independent regulatory authority which consists of five to seven members nominated by the Federal Government. The members must be independent specialists. They inform the public of their activities, and each year produce a report for the Federal Government.[12] According to the Draft LTC, ComCom determines the types of

---

8   Such as, among others, 'Ordinance regarding Frequency Management' (RS 784.102.1), 'Ordinance regarding Address Elements in Telecommunications' (RS 784.104), 'Ordinance regarding Telecommunications Facilities and Equipment' (RS 784.101.2), 'Ordinance regarding Telecommunications Fees' (RS 784.106).

9   Art 2 LTC 1997.

10   Message (explanations from the Federal Government) of 12 November 2003 to the revision of the LTC, published in the Federal Gazette no 49 of 16 December 2003, p 7951; message of 18 December 2002 to the revision of the LRTV, published in the Federal Gazette no 8 of 4 March 2003, p 1569.

11   Art 1(1) LTC 1997 and Draft LTC.

12   Arts 56 and 57 LTC 1997 and Draft LTC.

access to be provided by the market-dominant providers and lays down the details thereto.[13] Furthermore, ComCom grants the licences for the provision of the universal service.[14] It approves national numbering plans[15] and the national frequency allocation plan,[16] and supervises the application of number portability and the free choice of suppliers.[17]

34.12   The Federal Office of Communication ('OFCOM') is the supervisory and administrative authority responsible for all telecommunication, radio and television broadcasting matters. It prepares the decisions of the Swiss Government and the commercial transactions of ComCom, makes the necessary applications and implements its decisions. Under the Draft LTC, OFCOM is responsible for the registration of the telecommunications providers[18] and the supervision of all legal provisions and licences.

34.13   If ComCom is asked to intervene in relations between service providers and the issue of market dominance is raised, OFCOM has to consult the Swiss Competition Commission – an independent federal authority whose task is to protect competition using the instruments provided by the Act on Cartels – to determine whether a provider has a dominant position on the market. The Competition Commission may publish its opinion.[19]

34.14   Moreover, in the area of licences for radio frequencies, ComCom has to consult the Competition Commission if there is doubt whether the granting of a licence eliminates effective competition or constitutes a serious obstacle to effective competition.[20]

34.15   All persons subject to the LTC are required to provide the competent authorities with the necessary information to implement the LTC.[21]

34.16   Both ComCom and OFCOM have specific dispute resolution powers. If telecommunications providers cannot reach an agreement on their respective access to local loops, bitstream access, interconnection or leased lines within three months, ComCom, upon request of one of the parties and of OFCOM, determines the conditions of access. It can also grant interim legal protection.[22]

34.17   OFCOM and ComCom have no dispute resolution powers relating to disputes involving customers. The Draft LTC introduces a conciliation procedure for the settlement of disputes between customers and providers of telecommunications services.[23]

Right of Appeal against the NRA's Decisions

34.18   Decisions taken by ComCom are open to administrative appeal before the Federal Supreme Court. Decisions taken by OFCOM are open to appeal before the

---

13   Art 11(2) Draft LTC.
14   Art 14(1) Draft LTC.
15   Art 28(3) LTC 1997 and Draft LTC.
16   Art 25(2) LTC 1997 and Draft LTC.
17   Art 28(4) LTC 1997 and Draft LTC.
18   Art 4(1) Draft LTC.
19   Art 11(4) Draft LTC; see also para 34.55 below.
20   Art 23(4) LTC 1997 and Draft LTC; see also para 34.37 below.
21   Art 59(1) Draft LTC.
22   Art 11(4) Draft LTC.
23   See para 34.72 below.

Appeals Board established by the Federal Government in accordance with articles 71a to 71c Law on Administrative Procedure.[24] The appellate procedure is governed by the Law on Administrative Procedure and by the Law on Judicial Organisation,[25] save as otherwise provided by the LTC.[26]

34.19   The right of appeal is given to everybody who is affected by the decision in question and whose interest in the annulment or modification of the decision is worthy of protection.[27] Before the Federal Supreme Court, the Federal Department of Environment, Transport, Energy and Communications also has the right to appeal the decision.[28]

34.20   Disputes between operators relating to a negotiated agreement concerning access, interconnection, etc or a valid decision concerning such matter can be brought before the ordinary civil courts.[29]

'Dominant Position in the Market' as a Fundamental Prerequisite of Regulation

Definition of 'dominant position in the market'

34.21   The term 'significant market power' as such is not mentioned in the LTC and is not defined in the Federal Act on Cartels.[30] The latter distinguishes between the concepts of 'market power'[31] and 'dominant position in the market',[32] the LTC refers to 'dominant position in the market'.[33] Nonetheless, the definition of 'dominant position in the market' under Swiss law is very similar to the EU definition of SMP as given in article 14(2) Framework Directive.

34.22   Under Swiss competition law, 'enterprises having a dominant position in the market' means one or more enterprises being able, as regards supply or demand, to behave in a substantially independent manner with regard to the other participants (competitors, offerors or offerees) in the market.[34]

34.23   Under the Draft LTC, providers of telecommunications services having a dominant position must provide access to their installations and services, such as unbundled access to local loops, bitstream access, interconnection and leased lines, to other providers without discrimination and according to the principle of a transparent and cost-related price policy.[35]

Definition of relevant markets

34.24   Under Swiss law the definition of 'relevant market' is the same as under Community law. The relevant market comprises all telecommunication services and

---

24   RS 172.021.
25   RS 173.110.
26   Arts 61 and 63 LTC 1997 and Draft LTC.
27   Art 103 Law on Judicial Organisation, Art. 48 Law on Administrative Procedure.
28   Art 103(1)(b) Law on Judicial Organisation.
29   Art 11(6) Draft LTC.
30   RS 251.
31   Art 2(1) Act on Cartels.
32   Art 4(2) Act on Cartels.
33   Art 11(1) Draft LTC.
34   Art 4(2) Act on Cartels.
35   Art 11(1) Draft LTC; see para 34.58 below for more details.

installations which the demand side of the market (provider desiring access to local loops, etc) considers to be interchangeable. The geographic market comprises the area in which the demand side of the market requests these services. Depending on the range of the telecommunication service or installation, it may be a regional, national or international market.[36] According to the Competition Commission, the broadcasting of TV programmes via satellite is no substitute for reception via cable.[37]

34.25   Swisscom is still the market leader in both fixed line and mobile telephony. As regards the latter, its market share in 2004 amounted to 62%. In the fixed line market, there has been almost no competition concerning the local loops and leased lines.[38] The situation will hopefully improve with the entry into force of the new LTC.[39] Providers which cannot reach an agreement with Swisscom regarding access to Swisscom's installations and services will have broader and enhanced possibilities of applying to ComCom for a decision on the conditions of access.

NRA's Regulatory Duties concerning Rights of Way, Co-location and Facility Sharing

Rights of way

34.26   Owners of land in public use[40] have a duty to permit providers of telecommunications services the use of this land for the installation and operation of lines and public call boxes, provided those installations do not interfere with the public use of the land. In return, the providers have a duty to consider, and take into account, the use made of the land up to the moment they want to use the land for the placement of any infrastructure. Moreover, the providers have a duty to remove their lines if the landowner decides to use his land in a manner which conflicts with the position of a line. In order to minimise disruption, however, the providers have a duty to coordinate the necessary work. Provided public use is not disrupted, no compensation is payable for the use of land by a telecommunication services provider, except that the owner of public land may levy a cost-covering fee. All costs relating to the construction of infrastructure are to be paid by the network owner.[41]

34.27   Furthermore, in order to ensure that private land, and land owned by a State or Municipality but which is not in public use, is also available for telecommunication purposes, the Department may grant the right to expropriate to a telecommunications services provider. In such cases, full compensation for the total value of the expropriated land must be paid.[42]

Co-location and facility sharing

34.28   In addition, in order to protect public interests such as zone planning concerns, protection of landmarks and the environment in general, and to prevent

---

36   This definition can be found on the OFCOM website (www.bakom.ch).
37   RPW 2002/1, pp 118 et seq, available at www.weko.admin.ch.
38   See message to the revision of the LTC, p 7957.
39   See para 34.7 above.
40   Ie roads, footpaths, squares, waterways, lakes and banks.
41   Art 35 LTC 1997 and Draft LTC and art 36 Ordinance on Telecommunications Services (RS 784.101.1).
42   Art 36(1) LTC 1997 and Draft LTC and Federal Law on Expropriation (RS 711).

technical difficulties, telecommunications service providers may be required by OFCOM to allow third persons co-use of their telecommunication facilities in return for fair compensation, unless the facility lacks sufficient capacity. 'Fair compensation' means the relevant pro rata share of the full costs.[43] For the same reasons, OFCOM may oblige providers to install and use telecommunication installations and other facilities jointly.[44]

34.29 Ownership of telecommunication lines remains with the provider who built or acquired the lines, even if they are located over land owned by others. Land owners are liable for any damage they cause to telecommunication lines on their land, but only to the extent that such damage is caused wilfully or as a result of gross negligence.[45]

REGULATION OF MARKET ENTRY

General Regulatory Approach

34.30 With the entry into force of the new LTC the licence system for telecommunications services[46] will be abolished. The former licences are replaced by a general obligation of notification[47] which corresponds to the European system of 'general authorisation'. However, licences are still required for the provision of universal services[48] and the use of radio frequencies.[49]

34.31 All providers of telecommunications services must notify OFCOM in order to become registered.[50] Furthermore, they need to comply with the following requirements:

- have the necessary technical capacities,
- undertake to comply with the applicable legislation, in particular the LTC and its implementing provisions, and
- comply with the provisions of industrial law and the provisions on working conditions applicable in the sector.[51]

Subject to any international obligations to the contrary, ComCom may prohibit the provision of telecommunications services in Switzerland to undertakings incorporated under foreign law, unless a reciprocal right is granted.[52]

34.32 OFCOM can levy an administrative charge to cover its expenses for the registration and supervision of the telecommunication service providers.[53]

---

43 Art 36(2) Draft LTC and Art 39 Ordinance on Telecommunications Services.
44 Art 36(3) Draft LTC.
45 Art 37 Draft LTC.
46 Arts 4 et seq LTC 1997.
47 Art 4(1) Draft LTC.
48 See para 34.61 below.
49 See para 34.36 below.
50 Art 4(1) Draft LTC.
51 Art 6 Draft LTC.
52 Art 5 Draft LTC.
53 See para 34.51 below.

34.33   The Federal Government can ask telecommunications service providers to publish information on the quality of their services[54] and it can adopt regulations in order to prevent misuse of value added services.[55]

34.34   Moreover, providers of telecommunications services still have to submit a request for the allocation of address elements.[56]

34.35   In respect of the universal service obligation, the system of granting individual licences is maintained.[57]

Rights of Use for Radio Frequencies

34.36   A special regime, distinct from the notification procedure, applies to the use of radio frequencies. Anyone intending to use the radio frequency spectrum up to 3000 GHz must obtain a licence.[58] A licence is granted only if, having regard to the national plan for their allocation, enough frequencies are available.[59] The national frequency allocation plan is the most important instrument for planning the radio frequency resource. It is based on the CEPT and ITU guidelines and consists of several sections: first, the actual plan itself (classified according to frequency ranges) and, secondly, the requirements for radio interfaces plus the other rules and restrictions on use of the corresponding frequency range. The plan highlights the distinction made between civil, non-civil (eg military) or shared, as well as between primary and secondary band allocations.[60] Pursuant to the Ordinance on Frequency Management and Radio Licences,[61] there are three different classes of frequency:

- exclusive frequencies to be allocated to one single licence holder per application territory (class 1),
- joint frequencies to be allocated to a limited number of licence holders per application territory (class 2), and
- collective frequencies to be allocated to an indefinite number of licence holders per application territory (class 3).

The allocation has to take into account the degree of call and transmission security required.[62] The frequency allocation plan is drawn up by OFCOM and approved by ComCom,[63] which is also the authority granting the individual licences.[64]

34.37   Additionally, the granting of a licence is subject to the condition that it does not eliminate effective competition or constitute a serious obstacle to effective competition, unless an exception can be justified on grounds of economic efficiency.

---

54   Art 12a Draft LTC.
55   Art 12b Draft LTC.
56   See para 34.41 below.
57   Art 14(1) Draft LTC; see para 34.61 below for more details.
58   Art 22(1) LTC 1997 and Draft LTC, art 7(1) Ordinance on Frequency Management and Radio Licences (RS 784.102.1).
59   Art 23(3) LTC 1997 and Draft LTC.
60   The plan can be consulted on the OFCOM website: www.bakom.ch.
61   Which will also be modified after the revision of the LTC and LRTV.
62   Art 6 Ordinance on Frequency Management and Radio Licences.
63   Art 3(2) Ordinance on Frequency Management and Radio Licences, art 25 LTC 1997 and Draft LTC.
64   Art 24a Draft LTC.

In case of doubt, ComCom has to consult the Competition Commission.[65] The applicant, furthermore, has to meet the same requirements as the providers of telecommunications services,[66] i e it must have the necessary technical capacities and undertake to comply with the applicable legislation, its implementing provisions and licence conditions. Again, ComCom may refuse to grant a licence to undertakings incorporated under foreign law if no reciprocal rights are granted.[67]

34.38 Radiocommunications licences are granted on the basis of an open invitation to tender if the frequencies are requested to provide telecommunications services and there are not enough frequencies available to meet all applicants' present and future needs.[68] OFCOM is responsible for frequency management.[69] The procedure is conducted in accordance with the principles of objectivity, non-discrimination and transparency.[70] A licence fee is to be charged.[71]

34.39 The Swiss regulatory regime does not allow for spectrum trading.

Rights of Use for Numbers

34.40 The administration and allocation of numbers and address elements is the responsibility of OFCOM; however, the national numbering plans must be approved by ComCom.[72] In March 2002 a new numbering plan[73] came into effect. The most important consequence of this plan is that the area code now also has to be dialled for local calls.

34.41 OFCOM grants number blocks to providers of telecommunications services. The providers therefore have to submit a request to OFCOM stating their range of services, the geographical extent of their network and their plan to use these numbers for a minimum period of three years.[74] There is no competitive or comparative selection procedure. The providers then pass on the numbers granted to them to their clients. The grant of individual numbers to natural and legal persons is possible if they intend to use the number for the identification of a certain specified service.[75]

34.42 The LTC 1997 already contained obligations for telecommunications service providers relating to number portability and carrier selection.[76] Number portability with respect to fixed line telephony and mobile telephony was implemented by all providers in March 2000; however, number portability between fixed line and mobile telephony has not yet been introduced.[77] As to carrier selection, operators providing fixed line telephone services are required to secure the ability of any subscriber to choose another carrier (call-by-call and pre-selection) for national and

---

65 Art 23(4) LTC 1997 and Draft LTC.
66 See para 34.31 above.
67 Art 23(1) and (2) LTC 1997 and Draft LTC.
68 Art 24(1) LTC 1997 and Draft LTC.
69 Art 25(1) LTC 1997 and Draft LTC.
70 Art. 24 (2) LTC 1997 and Draft LTC.
71 See para 34.50 below.
72 Art 28(1) and (3) LTC 1997 and Draft LTC.
73 RS 784.101.113/2.2 Numbering Plan E.164/2002.
74 Arts 20 and 21 Ordinance on Address Elements in the Telecommunications Area (RS 784.104).
75 Arts 24b et seq Ordinance on Address Elements in the Telecommunications Area.
76 Art 28(3) LTC 1997 and Draft LTC.
77 SR 784.101.112/1 p 3.

international calls. In the area of mobile telephony, so far only call-by-call selection is possible until the technology allows the safe introduction of carrier pre-selection on the mobile network.[78]

34.43   The management, allocation and revocation of numbers and address elements are subject to an administrative charge.[79]

34.44   The new LTC allows for introduction by the Federal Government of an alternative dispute resolution procedure between the holders of address elements and third parties.[80]

The NRA's Enforcement Powers

34.45   OFCOM and ComCom are vested with extensive powers to exercise control regarding compliance with the applicable legal provisions. Several penal provisions contained within the LTC itself add to these enforcement powers.

34.46   First of all, all persons subject to the LTC are under an obligation to disclose information for the implementation of the law to the competent author- ity.[81] In particular, OFCOM, as the supervisory body, ensures compliance with international telecommunications law, the LTC, its implementing provisions and the licence conditions.[82]

34.47   Where OFCOM detects a breach of law, it can pronounce sanctions such as:

- call on the responsible person to remedy the infringement or take measures to prevent any repetition of it; the responsible person must inform OFCOM of the measures taken,
- require the responsible person to surrender to the Confederation any revenue generated during the infringement,
- impose charges on the licence, or
- restrict, suspend, revoke or withdraw the licence; or restrict, suspend or prohibit the activity of the responsible person.[83]

If the licence was granted by ComCom, the latter will take the corresponding measures at the request of OFCOM. The competent authority can order interim measures.[84] Moreover, OFCOM can impose administrative sanctions (fine of up to 10% of the average turnover generated in Switzerland during the last three business years) if an undertaking contravenes the applicable law, the licence conditions or a decision having the force of law.[85]

34.48   The LTC also provides a number of penalties for illegal conduct, such as falsification or misuse of information, interference in telecommunications or broad- casting, use of frequency spectrum without licence, acting contrary to the licence conditions, supply of telecommunications installations which do not comply with

---

78   Document for the implementation and operation of Carrier Selection, prepared by the Working Group on Carrier Selection, p 27, available on the OFCOM website: www.bakom.ch.
79   Art 40(1)(f) Draft LTC; see para 34.51 below.
80   Art 28(2bis) Draft LTC.
81   Art 59(1) Draft LTC.
82   Art 58(1) Draft LTC.
83   Art 58(2) and (3) Draft LTC.
84   Art 58(4) and (5) Draft LTC.
85   Art 60 Draft LTC.

the regulations in force, or intentional or negligent infringement of the law or of any decision taken thereunder and notified to the person with an indication of penalties available under the LTC etc. Such offences are prosecuted and heard by the Department in accordance with the provisions of the Federal Law on Administrative Penalty Rules.[86] The Department may delegate these tasks to OFCOM.[87]

Administrative Charges and Fees for Rights of Use

34.49 All providers of telecommunications services are charged a fee which is used exclusively to finance outstanding costs of the universal service and the costs for administering the financing mechanism.[88] Providers whose turnover resulting from telecommunications services offered does not reach a specified amount may be exempted from the payment.[89]

34.50 Radio licences are subject to a fee. The amount of the fee is calculated on the basis of:

- the frequency range allocated, the class of frequency and the value of the frequencies,
- the bandwidth allocated,
- the territorial scope, and
- the timescale.

In relation to the granting of frequencies by tender, the licence fee shall correspond to the amount of the bid, less administrative expenses for the invitation to tender and the allocation of the radio licence. ComCom may fix a minimum bid. Authorities, public bodies, public transport undertakings, diplomatic authorities and private bodies performing duties of public interest may be exempted from payment of the licence fee, provided that they do not supply telecommunications services and that they make rational use of frequencies.[90]

34.51 In addition, the competent authority always levies an administrative charge to cover its expenses, e g for:

- the registration and supervision of telecommunications service providers,
- the management, allocation and revocation of address elements (including numbers),
- the allocation, supervision, modification and revocation of universal service licences and radio licences,
- the decision on access, the provision of directories, interoperability, leased lines and facility sharing.[91]

The exact amount of the administrative charges to be paid by the telecommunications service providers are fixed by the Department.[92]

---

86   RS 313.0.
87   Arts 49–55 LTC 1997 and Draft LTC.
88   See para 34.67 above.
89   Art 38 Draft LTC.
90   Art 39 LTC 1997 and Draft LTC.
91   Art 40 Draft LTC; see paras 34.32 and 34.43 above and para 34.65 below.
92   Art 41(2) LTC 1997 and Draft LTC.

REGULATION OF NETWORK ACCESS AND INTERCONNECTION

Objectives and Scope of Access Regulation

34.52   Following the EU terminology, the Draft LTC introduces the general term of 'access', whereas 'interconnection' is a particular case of access. At the same time the obligations of providers with a dominant position in the market are stated more precisely and are being enhanced. Notwithstanding this, the Draft LTC renounces the introduction of ex-ante provisions[93] in order to avoid a regime which would be seen as excessive interventionism.

34.53   Access obligations only apply to telecommunications service providers with a dominant position in the market. Article 11 Draft LTC is supposed to cover all questions relating to the access to installations and services of such providers.

34.54   'Access' is defined as the provision of facilities and/or services to another provider of telecommunications services in order to provide such services.[94] 'Interconnection' means setting up access through connection of the facilities and services of two telecommunication service providers in order to enable a logical interaction of the connected parts and services by means of telecommunication as well as the access to services of third parties.[95]

Basic Regulatory Concepts

34.55   Under the revised LTC the commercial negotiations between the parties still prevail over regulatory intervention. The regulators may only intervene if the providers themselves cannot reach an agreement on the issue. If the providers fail to do so within three months, ComCom has to fix the access conditions upon request of one of the parties and of OFCOM. If, at this point, it is unclear whether a provider has a dominant position in the market, OFCOM has to consult the Federal Competition Commission.[96] In order for the latter to be able to respond within the four weeks required,[97] under the regime of the LTC 1997 the two authorities have drawn up a questionnaire to be handed in by the parties by which they request a decision on the conditions of access. The questionnaire gathers information on the affected providers, markets and services. It enquires about turnovers, market shares, conditions of demand, market entry requirements, etc.[98]

34.56   Additionally, ComCom is given the competence to determine the types of access to be provided by providers having a dominant position in the market, and lays down the details thereto in an ordinance.[99] Furthermore, it fixes the details regarding the accounting and financing information to be furnished by the parties

---

93   See para 34.4 above.
94   Art 3(d^bis) Draft LTC.
95   Art 3(e) Draft LTC.
96   Art 11(4) Draft LTC.
97   Art 56 Ordinance regarding Telecommunications Services.
98   The questionnaire can be found on the OFCOM website: www.bakom.ch under 'Telecom Services', 'Interconnection'. It is available in German and French only.
99   Art 11(2) Draft LTC.

in the framework of the procedure set out in the preceding paragraph.[100] OFCOM, on the other hand, is entitled to a copy of all access agreements agreed between telecommunications service providers.[101]

34.57 Although the principle of freedom of access is not explicitly stated in the LTC, there are no obstacles for registered providers desiring to conclude voluntary access agreements.

Access- and Interconnection-related Obligations with Respect to Undertakings with a Dominant Position

34.58 Under the new LTC, undertakings deemed to have a dominant position in the market have a clearly defined legal obligation to provide access to their facilities and services to other providers. The provision of access includes the unbundled access to local loops, bitstream access, interconnection and leased lines. The details regarding these specific access obligations will be fixed by ComCom,[102] however, the Federal Government will first lay down the basic principles for each type of access,[103] so that the discretion of ComCom is rather limited. Access has to be provided according to the principles of non-discrimination, transparency and a cost-based price policy. Conditions and prices for each of the access services have to be stated separately and unbundled from all other services.[104] Hence, no applicant may be disadvantaged compared to other business units, subsidiaries and partners of the undertaking with a dominant position in the market.[105] Upon request the technical and commercial conditions of the agreement as well as the calculation basis have to be disclosed.[106] Prices are to be fixed according to the relevant costs of access, the long run incremental costs (LRIC), a constant mark-up[107] and a return on investment customary in the industry.[108]

34.59 Besides the obligation to provide access and to do so at cost-based prices, no other specific obligations can be imposed on undertakings with a dominant position in the market.

Regulatory Powers Applicable to All Market Participants

34.60 End-to-end connectivity is guaranteed, based on the fact that a universal service provider must ensure the ability of communication between all users of these services. Such providers also have a duty to interconnect even though they do not have a dominant position in the market.[109] Under the Draft LTC the Federal

---

100 Art 11(5) Draft LTC.
101 Art 11(3) Draft LTC.
102 Art 11(2) Draft LTC.
103 Art 11(1) last sentence. The Federal Government will therefore amend the Ordinance on Telecommunications Services.
104 Art 11(1) Draft LTC.
105 Art 40 Ordinance on Telecommunications Services.
106 Art 44 Ordinance on Telecommunications Services.
107 Constant surcharge based on a proportional share of the joint and common costs.
108 Art 45 Ordinance on Telecommunications Services.
109 Art 21a(3) Draft LTC.

Government is given the possibility to extend the obligation of interoperability to other telecommunications services which are accessible to the public and satisfy a common need.[110]

REGULATION OF UNIVERSAL SERVICES AND USERS' RIGHTS

Regulation of Universal Service Obligations

Scope of universal service obligations

34.61   The holder of a licence to provide a universal service has to provide the following services at a level which corresponds to the technological 'state of the art':

- a public telephone service, ie transmission of speech in real time by means of telecommunications techniques, including transmission of data employing transfer rates compatible with the channels for transmitting speech; as well as access to the network and additional services,
- access to emergency call services,
- public call boxes in sufficient numbers, and
- access to the Swiss directories of subscribers to the public telephone service.[111]

Moreover, these services must be ensured nationwide in such a way that disabled people are offered comparable terms and conditions with respect to quality, quantity and prices as those without disabilities.[112]

Designation of undertakings obliged to provide universal services

34.62   ComCom periodically grants one or several licences to provide a universal service. These licences are granted on the basis of an open invitation to tender. The procedure is conducted in accordance with the principles of objectivity, non-discrimination and transparency. If it is clear from the start that the invitation to tender cannot take place under conditions of competition or if there are no feasible applicants, ComCom can oblige one or several providers to provide universal services.[113]

34.63   Applicants wishing to obtain a licence have to meet the following requirements:

- have the necessary technical capacities,
- furnish convincing evidence that the service, in particular in the financial respect, can be offered and operated for the entire duration of the licence, and state what financial contribution will be required,
- undertake to comply with the applicable legislation, in particular the LTC and its implementing provisions and the licence conditions, and

---

110 Art 21a Draft LTC.
111 The Federal Government may oblige one holder of a licence to provide a universal service to set up a directory of all customers which have access to the universal service.
112 Art 16 LTC 1997 and Draft LTC.
113 Art 14 Draft LTC.

- guarantee to comply with the provisions of industrial law and the provisions on working conditions applicable in the sector.[114]

34.64   Under the LTC 1997, Swisscom was required to provide the universal service for the whole national territory for five years from the entry into force of the act.[115] At the expiry of this period at the end of 2002, a public invitation to tender took place and Swisscom was again granted the only licence to provide a universal service for the whole country for another five years.

34.65   ComCom can levy an administrative charge for the allocation, supervision etc of universal service licences.[116]

Regulation of retail tariffs, users' expenditures and quality of service

34.66   The legislation provides for certain quality standards and price caps to be established by the Federal Government. In particular, the universal service must be available nationwide at a certain quality, and prices must not depend upon distance.[117] The Federal Government has clarified these objectives in the Ordinance on Telecommunications Services. Since 1 January 2003 price caps have been set for the following services:

- connection to the network,
- domestic traffic to fixed line terminals,
- surcharge for the use of public call boxes, and
- use of the transcription service.[118] [119]

Quality is examined within the licence territory based on various criteria, including the waiting period for the installation of a station, voice transmission quality, repair time, the time for connection build-up, reaction time for operator assistance, number of public call boxes ready for use, etc.[120]

Cost calculation and financing of universal services

34.67   If it is clear before the granting of the licence that, even with cost-effective management, it will be impossible to cover the costs for the provision of a universal service in a given area, the licence holder will be entitled to a financial compensation.[121] The financing of this compensation can be ascertained through contributions by all telecommunications service providers.[122] Such contribution duty, however, has not been introduced so far.

---

114   Art 15 LTC 1997 and Draft LTC.
115   Art 66(1) LTC 1997.
116   Art 40(1)(d) Draft LTC; see also para 34.51 above.
117   Art 17 LTC 1997 and Draft LTC.
118   Service for deaf people, including round-the-clock emergency call service.
119   Art 26 Ordinance on Telecommunications Services.
120   Art 25 Ordinance on Telecommunications Services.
121   Art 19(1) Draft LTC.
122   Art 38 Draft LTC; see para 34.49 above.

Regulation of Retail Markets

34.68 Swisscom still dominates the retail market, especially with respect to fixed line telephone services.[123] However, with the introduction of more precise obligations of access imposed on the providers with a dominant position on the market,[124] the competition in this field is expected to become more effective and the end consumer should be in a position to choose from a new, wider and more advantageous range of services.

34.69 Retail services as such are not directly regulated under Swiss Telecommunication Law. These services are only indirectly regulated within the fields of access,[125] universal service,[126] address elements,[127] and through the supervision of individual telecommunications service providers exercised by OFCOM.[128]

34.70 In addition, anti-competitive behaviour may be sanctioned under the Federal Act on Cartels.[129]

End User Rights

Contracts

34.71 The LTC does not deal with contracts between providers and end users at all. Only the content of contracts between holders of a licence to provide a universal service and the end users is regulated to some extent, in that these licence holders are obliged to provide a certain range of services to the end users.[130] Besides that, all service contracts are governed by general contract law. The general tort law applies in the case of civil liability.

34.72 The Draft LTC introduces a conciliation procedure for the settlement of disputes between end users and providers of telecommunications services. The costs of the proceedings are borne by the telecommunications service provider and the final decision does not bind the parties. The Federal Government still has to finalise the details of the conciliation procedure.[131]

Transparency obligations

34.73 Through the telecommunication statistics drawn up and published by OFCOM every year, the end user has access to information on terms and price tariffs of the services offered by the telecommunications service providers.[132]

---

123 See para 34.2 above.
124 Art 11 Draft LTC; see para 34.58 above.
125 See para 34.58 above.
126 See para 34.61 above.
127 See para 34.40 above.
128 See para 34.46 above.
129 RS 251.
130 See para 34.61 above.
131 Art 12c Draft LTC.
132 Arts 73 et seq Ordinance on Telecommunications Services.

Moreover, the Draft LTC stipulates the possibility for the Federal Government to oblige providers of telecommunications services to publish information on the quality of their services offered.[133]

DATA PROTECTION

Confidentiality of Communications

34.74   Under the Federal Constitution, protection of the secrecy of telecommunication is a constitutional right.[134] Consequently, the LTC imposes a duty on all telecommunication service providers not to disclose to third parties any information relating to subscribers' communications or give anyone else an opportunity to do so.[135] The providers of telecommunications services have to inform their clients about the risks involved in using their services and are under a duty to provide requisite means to eliminate these risks.[136]

34.75   Exceptions to the prohibition on the interception or surveillance of communications are dealt with in the Federal Act concerning the surveillance of post and telecommunication communication.[137] A special federal authority is entrusted with the implementation of this act. For an order of surveillance, the following conditions have to be met:

- certain facts lead to the strong suspicion that the person to be kept under surveillance has committed one of the criminal offences listed in the act or has participated therein,
- the surveillance is justified by the gravity of the criminal offence, and
- other means of investigation have been unsuccessful, or the investigation would be unpromising or unreasonably complicated if there was no surveillance.[138]

Any order of surveillance has to be approved by the competent judicial (as the case may be, federal or cantonal) authority.[139]

34.76   The processing of data on terminal equipment of third persons (eg the installation and use of cookies, web-bugs, hidden identifiers, etc) by means of telecommunication is only allowed for the provision of telecommunications services and their billing, or if the users have been informed about the processing and the fact that they may object to the processing.[140]

Traffic Data and Location Data

34.77   The terms 'traffic data' and 'location data' are not defined in Swiss telecommunications legislation. However, there are a few provisions dealing with the protection of such data.

---

133   Art 12a Draft LTC.
134   Art 13 Federal Constitution (RS 101).
135   Art 43 LTC 1997 and Draft LTC.
136   Art 64 Ordinance on Telecommunications Services.
137   Art 44 LTC 1997 and Draft LTC; RS 780.1.
138   Art 3 Act concerning the surveillance of post and telecommunication communication.
139   Art 7 Act concerning the surveillance of post and telecommunication communication.
140   Art 45c Draft LTC.

34.78   ComCom and OFCOM are allowed to process personal data as well as personal profiles if this is necessary for the fulfilment of their obligations under telecommunications legislation. They are obliged to take such measures as to ensure the protection and security of the data being processed and transferred.[141] Moreover, both OFCOM and ComCom can transfer to other Swiss authorities data, including personal data especially worthy of protection and personal profiles resulting from administrative procedures, needed by these authorities for the execution of their legal obligations. Subject to any international obligations to the contrary, the transfer of such data to foreign surveillance authorities is restricted to cases where the requested data is used exclusively for the surveillance of providers of telecommunications services and for market analysis.[142]

34.79   Data on the location of mobile telephone users may only be processed by the telecommunications service providers for the purpose of:

- the provision of services and their billing, or
- for other services if the clients have given their consent, or
- in an anonymous manner.[143]

Itemised Billing

34.80   Customers are entitled to receive all relevant data relating to a particular invoice, including the numbers called, date, time and duration of connection, and the relevant charge.[144] Customers may request to generally receive itemised invoices. There is no duty to provide this information free of charge.

Calling and Connected Line Identification

34.81   Where technically feasible, providers of telecommunication services have to ensure to their clients the possibility of eliminating their own number on the equipment of the person called on a per call or on a permanent basis, using simple means and free of charge. Under the same conditions, the person called must be offered the possibility to reject incoming calls where the presentation of the number is eliminated.[145]

34.82   A customer who can establish that he/she is the target of abusive calls is entitled to be informed of the number and the name and address of customers from whose equipment such calls were made.[146]

---

141   Art 13a Draft LTC.
142   Art 13b Draft LTC.
143   Art 45b Draft LTC.
144   Art 45(1) LTC 1997.
145   Art 61 Ordinance on Telecommunications Services.
146   Art 45(2) LTC 1997 and Draft LTC.

Automatic Call Forwarding

34.83   Where technically feasible, providers of telecommunications services have to offer to their subscribers the possibility to stop automatic call forwarding to their terminal by third persons. This service has to be offered using simple means and free of charge.[147]

Directories of Subscribers

34.84   All telecommunications service providers providing access to the public telephone service have to keep a directory of their customers.[148] Moreover, the holder of a licence to provide a universal service may be obliged to keep a universal directory of all customers benefiting from universal services.[149] However, customers have the right to refuse to have their address elements entered in a directory.[150] The directories are published (in paper and online). The provider of an electronic directory must take the necessary measures to prevent the copying of directories into countries which have a lower level of data protection than Switzerland. It also must ascertain by technical and organisational measures that the directory entries cannot be changed or deleted.[151]

34.85   The Federal Government fixes the minimum content of an entry.[152] Name and surname or company name, the complete address and call number of the subscriber have to be published.[153]

Unsolicited Communications

34.86   The customer's directory entry may contain a sign showing that he or she would not like to receive advertising material from third parties, and that his or her data must not be passed on for advertising purposes.[154] Furthermore, all providers are under a duty to combat unfair mass advertising as defined in the Federal Act on unfair competition.[155]

---

147   Art 63 Ordinance on Telecommunications Services.
148   Art 29 Ordinance on Telecommunications Services.
149   Art 16(1)(d) Draft LTC.
150   Art 12d(1) Draft LTC.
151   Art 65(3) and (4) Ordinance on Telecommunications Services.
152   Art 12d(2) Draft LTC.
153   Art 29(2) Ordinance on Telecommunications Services.
154   Arts 29(1) and (2) and 65(1) Ordinance on Telecommunications Services.
155   Art 45a Draft LTC; RS 241.

The Turkish Market for Electronic Communications[1]

Dr. Mehmet Komurcu & Serdar Akcasu
Birsel Law Offices, Istanbul

LEGAL STRUCTURE

Basic Policy

35.1 The Turkish telecommunications sector has been undergoing three important developments at the same time: liberalisation of the telecommunications market; privatisation of the state-owned de facto monopoly Turk Telekomunikasyon A.S ('TT'); and initiation of membership negotiations with the EU. The successful conclusion of these developments will determine to a large extent the future structure and regulatory framework of the Turkish telecoms market.

35.2 Turkey achieved full liberalisation of the telecommunications sector by opening its markets with effect from 1 January 2004. This also brought an end to the monopoly rights of the state-owned incumbent operator, TT, on the public and private fixed telecommunications infrastructure and basic telecommunications services, including domestic and international public voice telephony.

35.3 TT is the 13th largest telecom company in the world with its 21.5 million lines. TT presently dominates all fixed telecommunications services to its retail customers throughout Turkey. Following liberalisation of the telecommunications market, 43 companies have obtained licences to provide long-distance telephony services.

35.4 However, Turkey needs more time to establish a fully liberalised market by achieving full competition and to harmonise its legal and regulatory system with that of the EU. Assuming Turkey proceeds on a steady course toward EU accession, it has to adopt and implement further national telecommunications legislation incorporating the EU Regulatory Package.

Implementation of EU Directives

35.5 In line with its desire to accede to the European Union, Turkey has launched an intense program for the harmonisation of Turkish law with that of the EU. In

---

1 Editing of this chapter closed on 14 July 2005.

this context, the current regulatory framework has been progressively made compliant with the 2002 EU Regulatory Package.

35.6 Even though Turkey has gone some way towards harmonisation of its regulatory framework with the EU Directives to achieve liberalisation and competition, further efforts are essential to complete the national telecommunications regulatory framework and ensure effective implementation and enforcement.[2] In particular, the EU identified in its 2004 report on Turkey's Progress Towards Accession that there are still fundamental areas remaining to be addressed and that legislation in various areas, including leased lines, carrier selection and pre-selection, number portability, local loop unbundling, and universal service, is lacking.[3]

Legislation

35.7 As part of Turkey's efforts to harmonise its telecommunications regulatory framework with the EU Directives, a number of amendments have been made to the main piece of telecoms legislation, the Telephony and Telegraph Law ('Law No 406'),[4] and a number of new items of secondary legislation have been passed. Most recently, a draft 'Electronic Communications Act' ('Draft ECA') and a 'Universal Service Obligation Act' ('USO Law') have been prepared. Both laws include provisions parallel to the EU regime and aim at providing the legal basis for continued market liberalisation. The USO Law was passed by the Turkish Parliament on 16 June 2005.[5] The Draft ECA is expected to be enacted and enter into force by the end of 2005. The USO Law and Draft ECA address, inter alia, universal service provision and empower the Telecommunications Authority ('TA') to impose obligations on operators with respect to number portability and carrier selection.

35.8 While Law No 406 constitutes the 'backbone' of the telecommunications sector, it does not comprehensively address the important regulatory issues necessary for the supply of telecommunications services and the establishment and operation of the telecommunications infrastructure. In order to fill this gap, a number of secondary legislative acts have been passed to regulate important regulatory aspects, such as authorisation, interconnection and access, tariffs, numbering and licensing.

35.9 Law No 406 sets out a number of general principles, such as universal access, non-discriminatory treatment, and the provision of minimum services that are to be taken into consideration in the provision of telecoms services and/or the operation of infrastructure.

35.10 Another important piece of legislation is Law No 2813 (the 'Wireless Law').[6] It sets out the principles and methods for controlling the installation and operation of wireless systems and devices. The Wireless Law also sets out the duties of the TA in respect of both telephony and wireless systems.

---

2   Commission of the European Communities, 2004 Regular Report on Turkey's Progress Towards Accession, COM(2004) 656 final, 06.10.2004, p 128.

3   Commission of the European Communities, 2004 regular report on Turkey's Progress Towards Accession, p 128.

4   Law No 406 of 4 February 1924, Official Gazette, 21 February 1924 no 59.

5   Law No 5369 of 16 June 2005.

6   Wireless Law No 2813 of 5 April 1983, Official Gazette, 7 April 1983 no 18011.

35.11   The TA decisions play a very important role in the operation of the Turkish telecoms sector. Due to its independence, the TA's decisions cannot be quashed by the ultimate policy maker (Ministry of Transport).

REGULATORY PRINCIPLES

Scope of Regulation

35.12   Law No 406 regulates the provision of telecommunication services and the installation and operation of telecommunication infrastructure. Article 1 Law No 406 defines the term 'telecommunications' to mean the transmission, emission and reception of all kinds of sign, symbol, voice and image as well as all kinds of data which can be converted into electric signals through cable, wireless, optical, electric, magnetic, electro-magnetic, electro-chemical, electro-mechanic and other transmission systems. 'Telecommunication service' is defined as the provision of all or some of the activities included in the definition of telecommunications.

35.13   In order to bring the existing legal system in line with the EU Directives, the Draft ECA has adopted the approach of the 2002 EU Regulatory Package and defined in article 3 the two key terms 'electronic communications network' and 'electronic communications service'. The definitions of these terms are identical to those in the Framework Directive.

35.14   Neither Law No 406 nor the Draft ECA provides a definition for 'associated facilities'.

National Regulatory Authorities: Organisation, Regulatory Objectives, Competencies

35.15   The Ministry of Transport is the policy-making body for the telecommunications sector. The Telecommunications High Council is established as the superior policy-advisory body to the Ministry of Transport, and the main duty of the Telecommunications High Council is to advise the Ministry of Transport in the field of wireless communications.

35.16   The Ministry of Transport carries out formulation of the telecommunication policy with support from the national regulator, the TA. The TA was established in August 2000. The TA's responsibility is to regulate and supervise the Turkish telecommunications sector. The Telecommunications Board is the decision-making body of the TA and consists of a chairman and six members.

35.17   The TA's main powers and duties can be classified as consisting of regulatory functions, policy-making functions, supervisory functions, dispute resolution functions, and functions in relation to the market.

35.18   One of the main functions of the TA is to issue a wide range of secondary legislation. The TA is empowered to prepare and enact the secondary legislation necessary for transforming the current legislative environment to that of a fully liberalised telecommunication sector. The TA has so far enacted various regulations regarding access and interconnection,[7] roaming,[8] authorisations,[9] unbundling of

---

7   Regulation on Access and Interconnection dated 23 May 2003.
8   Regulation on Principles and Procedures regarding National Roaming dated 8 March 2002.

local loop,[10] co-location,[11] numbering and numbering fees,[12] Significant Market Power,[13] user rights,[14] and quality of services.[15] However, the regulations concerning rights of way and number portability have not yet been enacted, although they were included in the TA's 2005 Work Plan.

35.19   The primary policy-making authority in the telecommunications sector is the Ministry of Transport. However, in accordance with article 7 Wireless Law, the TA is obliged to prepare necessary plans in the field of wireless communication and telecommunications and to submit such plans to the Ministry.

35.20   The TA also has supervisory powers to ensure operators' compliance with the principal requirements and rules. The TA's powers in this respect include: tracking and controlling implementations performed under applicable legislation; monitoring compliance with the related legislation by operators, subscribers, users and all real persons and legal entities active in the Turkish telecommunication sector;[16] imposing sanctions prescribed by laws when necessary;[17] monitoring and determining unauthorised transmissions and interference; and inspecting the application of the provisions and conditions of the concession agreements executed between the TA and the operators granting telecommunications services and telecommunication licences signed/obtained by the operators.

35.21   Under article 10 Law No 406, the TA has certain dispute resolution powers. If two operators fail to agree on the terms of an interconnection agreement, the TA initiates, upon application by the party requesting interconnection, conciliation procedures between the parties of the interconnection agreement in accordance with principles it shall determine in the public interest, and it may take other reasonable measures that it deems necessary in the public interest.

35.22   The TA is empowered to determine the general criteria to be applied to tariffs. Moreover, one of the main duties of the TA is to carry out planning and allocation of scarce resources such as frequencies or numbers.

35.23   Furthermore, according to the Law on Protection of Competition, the Competition Authority is empowered to investigate anti-competitive collusive behaviours and abuses of dominance, and examine proposed mergers which may have a detrimental effect on competition. While the TA and the Competition Authority are independent of each other, they are required by the Draft ECA to seek each other's opinion in relation to actions within their respective areas. In particular, the Competition Authority is required to obtain the opinion of the TA, and to take into consideration regulations issued by the TA, before performing any action in respect of the telecoms sector.[18] Moreover, article 7 Wireless Law gives power to the TA to investigate matters involving competition issues in the telecommunications sector.

---

9   Authorisation Regulation for Telecommunication Services and Infrastructure dated 26 August 2004.

10   Communiqué on Local Loop Unbundling dated 20 July 2004.

11   Communiqué on Co-location and Facility Sharing dated 31 December 2003.

12   Communiqué on Numbering Fees dated 23 September 2004.

13   Communiqué on Principles regarding determination of Significant Market Power Operators dated 3 June 2003.

14   Regulation on User Rights dated 22 December 2004.

15   Regulation on Quality of Service dated 3 March 2005.

16   Art 7 Wireless Law.

17   See paras 35.51 et seq below.

18   Art 7 Wireless Law.

35.24   Co-operation between the two bodies is further guaranteed in a protocol.[19] The purpose of the protocol is to clarify overlapping responsibilities, to enhance co-operation between the two authorities, and to prevent possible disputes.

35.25   Conversely, the TA is obliged to request a written opinion from the Competition Authority before reaching a decision on whether a telecommunications service operator has a dominant position in the market; and granting a permit (ie a concession agreement or general authorisation). Moreover, the TA may apply, if necessary, to the Competition Board in order to ensure that standard reference tariffs or interconnection-roaming agreements do not impede free competition in the provision of telecommunication services and the operation of infrastructure.[20]

Right of Appeal against the NRA's Decisions

35.26   The existing telecommunications legislation does not include specific provisions regarding the ability to challenge the decisions of the TA. However, concerned parties may object to the TA's decisions and request the TA to reconsider its decisions in accordance with provisions of general administrative law. Action against decisions of the TA may also be brought directly before the administrative courts. In general, concerned parties are reluctant to follow the procedure of applying to the TA, and prefer to challenge such decisions before the court.

'Significant Market Power' as a Fundamental Prerequisite of Regulation

Definition of SMP

35.27   The principles and procedures to determine SMP undertakings in a relevant telecoms market are regulated in the Communiqué on SMP Operators.[21] The concept of SMP is defined in article 4 Communiqué on SMP Operators as 'any position enjoyed in a relevant telecoms market by one or more enterprises by virtue of which those enterprises have the power to affect economic parameters such as the price of services supplied to other operators and users, the amount of supply and demand, the market conditions, the main telecoms network elements used for supplying telecoms services and the control of access to users'. It is also stated in article 6 Communiqué on SMP Operators that the TA will annually designate the operators that are in SMP position and publish their list in the Official Gazette.

35.28   An SMP operator in a relevant market may also have SMP in a closely related market if the activities of the operator lead to a rise in its market power in the related market, due to similarity in the nature of the two markets.

35.29   When designating the SMP operators, the TA shall take the following criteria into consideration:

- market share,
- power to determine market conditions,

---

19   Cooperation Protocol between the Competition Authority and the Telecommunication Authority dated 16 September 2002.
20   Art 10 Law No 406.
21   Communiqué on Principles regarding determination of Significant Market Power Operators dated 3 June 2003.

- relation between quantity of sales and size of the market,
- power to control the tools of access to the end user,
- power of access to financial resources, and
- experience in supplying the products and services in the market.

Definition of relevant markets and SMP designation

35.30   A relevant telecoms market is defined as a market for a specific telecommunications service that is present in the whole or part of the country, and includes other telecoms services with a high degree of substitutability for that specific service.[22]

35.31   The incumbent fixed-line telephony operator, TT, was designated by the TA in 2004 as the operator having a de facto monopoly in all telephony services composed of national and international voice transmission over the telecommunication network and all telecommunication infrastructure, until other operators reach competitive market shares as a result of the full liberalisation of the market. The TA also designated in 2003 the biggest mobile operator, Turkcell, as an SMP operator in the mobile telecommunications service market and the mobile call termination service market. Telsim, which is the second biggest GSM operator, was also declared in 2003 as an SMP operator in the call termination market.

35.32   There are several obligations imposed on SMPs, regarding co-location, interconnection, unbundling, and account separation.

NRA's Regulatory Duties concerning Rights of Way, Co-location and Facility Sharing

Rights of way

35.33   Law No 406 provides for operators to use public lands and roads to install transmission equipment and cables. However, since there is currently no right of way regulation, the procedure for granting rights of way is not specifically regulated.

35.34   However, Law No 2942 concerning State Expropriation allows the relevant state authorities to expropriate private real property at the request of the telecommunications operators where necessary to install telecom facilities. The expropriation option becomes applicable if the operators cannot reach an agreement with the landowner, and operators' application to the relevant state authority approves expropriation. In such a case, the relevant state entity performs the required expropriation on behalf of the operator; ownership of the expropriated immovable property remains with the state, and the operator is granted a right to use the relevant property.

Co-location and facility sharing

35.35   In accordance with article 6 Communiqué on Co-location and Facility Sharing, TT and SMP operators are obliged to provide co-location at their

---

22   Art 4 Communiqué on SMP.

premises. Moreover, article 15 Regulation on Access and Interconnection empowers the TA to impose on SMP undertakings a cost-based obligation to provide co-location. This obligation may be removed if the SMP undertakings can prove that physical co-location is not necessary. In such situations, an alternative cost-based obligation may be imposed on SMP undertakings to provide co-location using a different method on equal economic, technical and operational conditions such as virtual co-location, remote co-location, or co-location on modified terms and conditions.

35.36   The TA may impose, on operators who are entitled to install facilities on or under public or private land, an obligation to share the facilities and/or property with other operators at reasonable prices.[23] The TA may issue case-specific regulations, setting out the provisions to be applied in dividing the costs of the facility and/or property among the parties.

REGULATION OF MARKET ENTRY

General Regulatory Approach

35.37   Operators of fixed and mobile networks need to obtain a permission to provide telecommunications services and/or for the establishment and operation of telecom infrastructure.

35.38   In accordance with the Authorisation Ordinance on Telecommunications Services and Infrastructure ('Authorisation Ordinance'),[24] five types of authorisations and licences may be granted:

- *Authorisation Agreement* is an agreement between the TA and the state-owned telecommunications operators. TA currently has authorisation agreements with Turk Telecom and state-owned satellite company, Turksat A.S., for the provision, respectively, of all kinds of telecoms services and the operation of telecoms infrastructure and satellite services. The authorisation agreements are valid as long as the majority shares of the relevant operator are held by the state.[25]
- *Concession Agreement* is an agreement between the TA and a private telecommunications network operator for telecoms services for the provision and/or the establishment or operation of telecommunications infrastructure by a limited number of operators on a national basis, including GSM mobile telephone services.
- *Type 1 Telecoms Licence* is granted for telecoms services to be provided and/or telecoms infrastructure to be established or operated by a limited number of operators on a regional or local basis.
- *Type 2 Telecoms Licence* is granted for telecoms services and/or telecoms infrastructure which do not need to be provided by a limited number of

---

23   Art 11 Regulation on Access and Interconnection.
24   Authorisation Ordinance on Telecommunications Services and Infrastructure dated 20 August 2004.
25   According to Turkish law, public services may be provided either by public legal entities or by private corporate bodies. If a specific service is to be provided by a public legal entity, then the scope and principles of this supply are governed by an Authorisation Agreement. However, if a private corporate body is to provide the service, then a concession agreement is the necessary contractual basis for the supply of services.

operators (ie can be provided by everyone who fulfils relevant requirements), and which fall within one of the following categories:[26]
- satellite communications services,
- satellite platform services,
- GMPCS mobile telephony,
- data transmission over terrestrial lines,
- cable TV,
- provision of telephone directories, and
- long-distance telephony services.
- *General Authorisation* is granted for telecoms services which do not need to be provided by a limited number of operators (ie can be provided by everyone who fulfils relevant requirements), and do not fall within the categories of a Type 2 Telecoms Licence. An individual licence/authorisation is not issued; instead, these services can be provided following application and registration of the service provider with the TA.[27]

35.39 Operators are required to make separate applications for each category of authorisation. The maximum term of authorisation agreements, concession agreements and Type 1 and Type 2 telecoms licences is 25 years.[28] The operator may apply to the TA for renewal of the licence before the expiry of its term.

35.40 According to article 36 Authorisation Ordinance, TA may oblige authorised operators to comply with certain requirements such as number portability, carrier selection, access, interconnection and roaming and universal services.

35.41 Currently, 'Voice over Internet Protocol' (VoIP) services have not been introduced on the Turkish telecoms market.

Rights of Use for Radio Frequencies

35.42 According to article 7 (d) Wireless Law, the TA[29] is in charge of the planning, allocation and registration of national and international frequency planning and the provision of international frequency coordination.

35.43 Permissions to use spectrum are granted to operators by the TA, upon request. The number of rights to use frequencies can be limited by the TA in accordance with the National Frequency Plan. The TA may modify or revoke the frequencies allocated to an operator if necessary to achieve more efficient and effective use of frequencies. Spectrum trading and auctions for spectrums are not allowed.

35.44 Authorised operators are required to comply with regulations issued by the TA on frequency registration and allocation, and on numbering,[30] the National Frequency Plan and the National Numbering Plan.

Rights of Use for Numbers

35.45 The TA is responsible for the registration and allocation of the national telecommunications numbering resources. In this regard, a National Numbering

---

26 Also includes data networks, pagers, intelligent networks, payphones, telephone information services, and certain PAMR services.
27 Internet service providers are authorised by means of a general authorisation etc.
28 Art 9 Authorisation Ordinance.
29 The Department of Spectrum Management of the TA.
30 Regulation on Numbering dated 26 February 2004.

Plan has been prepared to define the system of numbers for providing information on routing, addressing, pricing and service type.

35.46   Operators are required to apply to the TA for the allocation of numbers. Companies that have applied to the TA to obtain a licence to provide telecommunications services or to establish and operate telecommunications infrastructure (ie companies that are newly entering the sector) are deemed also to have applied for the allocation of numbers. If the company that applies for number allocation is an active operator (ie if such company has already obtained a telecommunications licence), it is required to submit its application form to the TA at least six months before the planned activation date of the requested numbers. The TA will render its decision on completed applications within three weeks.[31]

35.47   Conditions for the allocation of numbers are set out in article 12 Numbering Regulation. In this context, the allocation of numbers will be considered in accordance with: compliance with the national numbering plan; availability; consistency with the geographical area of coverage; sufficiency of technical capacity for the number of the requested allocations; and availability of a market projection and investment plan for the operator supporting the request. The rights of use for numbers are granted on a 'first come first served' basis.

35.48   Allocation of the numbers is limited for the duration of the licences granted to the respective operators.

35.49   When it is deemed necessary, the TA may modify the national numbering plan. The TA is to obtain the opinion of the operators where amendments to the plan are made as a result of technological developments and new services.[32]

35.50   In accordance with article 26 Numbering Regulation, operators are obliged to comply with the relevant general regulations to be enacted by the TA. Even though the preparation of the number portability regulation is included in TA's 2005 Work Plan, no specific regulation has been enacted.

The NRA's Enforcement Powers

35.51   The TA is authorised to take the necessary measures to ensure compliance with legislation, authorisations and licences issued by it, and to impose administrative fines on operators in the event that an operator's activities are in breach of the relevant legislation, assignments and concession contracts, telecommunications licences or general provisions.[33] The TA may impose an administrative fine of up to 3% of the annual turnover in the previous calendar year, or may cancel, in cases of gross negligence, a concession agreement, licence or general authorisation. The TA also has the power to take necessary measures in order to protect national security, public order or the public interest.

35.52   The TA is empowered to impose fines on operators who fail to remedy the breach within a period determined by the TA.[34] In the case of failure to remedy the breach, the Telecommunications Board may impose an administrative fine, depending on the type of the breach, up to a maximum of either 0.5%, 1% or 2% of the

---

31   Art 10 and 11 Regulation on Numbering.
32   Art 24 Regulation on Numbering.
33   Art 2 Law No 406.
34   Art 2 Law No 406.

previous calendar year's turnover.[35] If more than one administrative fine is to be imposed due to various violations, all fines shall apply separately, but the total amount of fines cannot exceed 3% of the previous calendar year's turnover for cases of repeated or continued breach.

35.53 Article 7 Wireless Law empowers the TA to request information and documents from operators within the scope of its mandate. The TA may impose administrative fines if the operators fail to comply with such a request.[36]

Administrative Charges and Fees for Rights of Use

35.54 Operators are required to pay to the TA the sum of 0.35% of their annual turnover after deduction of taxes, duties, charges and VAT as a contribution to the TA's expenses.[37]

35.55 Additionally, operators need to pay the following fees in accordance with the Authorisation Ordinance:

- *Authorisation fee* (articles 8 and 35 (a) Authorisation Ordinance): The fee for a concession agreement or 1st type telecoms licence is to be specified in the tender and/or the concession agreement; the fee for a 2nd type telecoms licence or general authorisation is determined by the TA,
- *Permission and usage fees* (article 35 (b) Authorisation Ordinance): Operators are obliged to collect radio communication permission and usage fees payable paid to them by their subscribers in accordance with article 27 Wireless Law, and to convey these to the TA. Operators are also required to pay permission and usage fees to the TA for the frequencies they use for their own transmission purposes.

REGULATION OF NETWORK ACCESS AND INTERCONNECTION

Objectives and Scope Of Access Regulation

35.56 The objectives of the TA in regulating access and interconnection are to ensure: that users derive maximum benefit from the telecommunications services and networks in return for a reasonable price; the provision of efficiency and sustainable competition in the telecommunications sector; and incentives for investment in infrastructures to constitute a competitive environment insofar as it serves the long-term benefit of end-users.[38]

35.57 Under article 4 Regulation on Access and Interconnection[39] access is defined as the making available of telecommunications services or infrastructure to other operators including:

- access by all kinds of methods to elements of a fixed or mobile telecoms network and associated facilities, including unbundled access to the local loop and bit stream access,

---

35 Arts 10–18 Regulation on Administrative Fines.
36 Arts 5–7 Regulation on Administrative Fines.
37 Art 35 Authorisation Ordinance.
38 Art 1 Regulation on Access and Interconnection.
39 Regulation on Access and Interconnection dated 23 May 2003.

- access to physical infrastructure including buildings, ducts and masts,
- access to relevant software systems including operational support systems,
- access to number translation or systems having equivalent functionality,
- access to virtual network services, and
- interconnection between two telecoms networks.

35.58   Furthermore, interconnection is defined as the connection with each other of two telecommunications networks in order to provide telecommunication traffic between such networks.

Access- and Interconnection-related Obligations with Respect to SMP Undertakings

35.59   Operators identified by the TA as having SMP are obliged to provide interconnection.[40]

35.60   However, in accordance with article 10 Law No 406, TT is under an obligation and duty to provide interconnection in all circumstances. This obligation on TT stems from its de facto monopoly in the Turkish telecoms market with its nation-wide infrastructure.

35.61   In accordance with chapters 2, 3 and 4 of the Regulation on Access and Interconnection, the TA may impose on SMP operators the following obligations:

- interconnection-related obligations,
- non-discrimination obligations,
- unbundling obligations,
- obligations to provide co-location,
- accounting separation obligations,
- reporting and auditing obligations,
- obligations to prepare a reference access and interconnection offer, and
- obligations to apply cost-based pricing.

35.62   If operators fail to comply with the access and interconnection obligations, the TA may impose an administrative fine on such operators.[41]

35.63   Although the TA may impose obligations on SMP operators regarding number portability, carrier pre-selection and leased lines, no respective regulations has been enacted so far. However, the TA has imposed certain deadlines on TT to provide carrier selection.

Regulatory Powers Applicable to All Market Participants

Access obligations

35.64   In accordance with article 8 Regulation on Access and Interconnection, the TA may oblige operators to meet requests for access, where it considers that denial of an access request by a particular operator would hinder the emergence of a competitive market. Operators obliged to provide access are required to make access available to other operators on equal conditions and provide services and

---

40   Art 10 Regulation on Access and Interconnection.
41   See para 35.52 above.

information under the same conditions and quality as the operator provides for its own shareholders, partnerships and affiliates.

35.65   Access may only be restricted by an operator, by obtaining approval from the TA, if the denial is objectively justified by reasons of network security, network integrity or data protection or if interoperability of the networks cannot be assured technically.

Interconnection

35.66   All operators are entitled to request, and have a corresponding obligation to enter into, negotiations for interconnection. Agreements to be concluded for interconnection shall include the necessary technical provisions, conditions and tariffs. A certified copy of all such agreements, their annexes and amendments shall be submitted to the TA and be made publicly available.

35.67   If an interconnection agreement cannot be agreed within the maximum of three months from the date of the initial request, the TA, upon application by the requesting party, will initiate conciliation procedures and may take any other measure deemed to be reasonable and necessary in the public interest.[42] If the parties fail to reach an agreement within a period of six weeks, that is extendable by the TA for a further four weeks, the TA is authorised to set such terms, conditions and tariffs of such interconnection agreement as it deems fit. Such terms, conditions and tariffs shall remain in effect unless and until the parties agree otherwise.

35.68   The TA is empowered to determine operators which are obliged to provide interconnection, pursuant to article 10 Regulation on Access and Interconnection, irrespective of their market power. TT and operators which are responsible to provide interconnection as determined by the TA are defined as 'interconnection providers'.

35.69   Upon request by an operator, the TA may restrict an interconnection obligation if there are technically and commercially viable alternatives to the interconnection or if resources for providing interconnection are not available.

35.70   Interconnection providers are required to deal with interconnection requests based on the principles of equality, non-discrimination, transparency, cost-orientation, reasonable profit and under the same conditions and quality as provided for their own services.[43]

35.71   The TA shall publish, and amend from time to time, standard reference interconnection tariffs. Relevant operators may incorporate the terms and conditions of such tariffs into their interconnection agreements.

REGULATION OF UNIVERSAL SERVICES AND USERS' RIGHTS

Regulation of Universal Service Obligations

Scope of universal service obligations

35.72   As outlined in article 5 USO Law, universal service is to include basic internet access, communication for coastal protection, navigation safety and also

---

42   Art 10 Law No 406.
43   Art 10 Law No 406.

maritime passenger transport, fixed phone services, payphones, telegraph service, emergency calls and directories; however, the scope of universal service obligations may be re-evaluated by the Council of Ministers by considering the country's social, cultural, economic and technological conditions.

35.73   A universal service provider may be obliged to provide (some or all of) the above services.

Designation of undertakings obliged to provide universal services

35.74   The USO sets out that universal service providers are designated by the TA at a local and/or national level from among the operators who submitted a request to be considered for such designation. The TA has the authority to designate SMP operators as universal service providers for certain types of universal services, even in the absence of such a request. Currently, only TT has been designated as universal service provider.

Regulation of retail tariffs, users' expenditures and quality of service

35.75   Subject to certain guiding principles, operators may freely determine tariffs, which they shall receive in return for the provision of telecommunication services and/or for the operation of infrastructure, provided that they comply with the relevant legislation and their authorisation or concession agreement, telecommunication licence or general authorisation and the instructions of the TA.[44]

35.76   The TA is empowered to determine the methods of calculation and caps of tariffs, on reasonable and non-discriminatory terms. In calculating tariffs, the applicable regulations, communiqués and administrative rules needs to be taken into consideration, as well as the terms and conditions of concession agreements and telecommunication licences.

35.77   The guidelines for regulating tariffs are set out article 30 Law No 406. Accordingly, the main principles for determining tariffs are that the prices shall be fair and non-discriminatory, balanced, approximated to international standards, supportive of technological development and new investments, conscious of international agreements to which Turkey is a party, as well as reflecting the costs and avoiding cross-subsidisation. In the event that there are justifiable reasons, a cap may be applied to tariffs on condition that compensatory costs and a reasonable profit are recovered.

Cost calculation and financing of universal services

35.78   The USO Law establishes a brand new financing system for services within the scope of the universal service obligation. Accordingly, an allocation from the budget of the Ministry of Transport shall be reserved for each year to cover net cost losses that operators may suffer in the future due to provision of universal services. Net cost losses arising from the provision of universal services shall be covered by the Ministry. However, the TA and the operators are obliged to deposit annually a

---

44   Art 29 Law No 406.

contribution, calculated on a percentage basis as defined in the USO Law, in order to refund the payments made during the year by the Ministry of Transport for universal service purposes.[45]

End User Rights

35.79   The rights of end users in the telecommunications sector are regulated under the Regulation on Consumer Rights, which is enacted by the TA. According to article 16 of this Regulation, the terms of subscription contracts to be concluded with subscribers are to include, at least, the following information:[46]

- subject of the subscription agreement,
- names, titles and clear addresses of the parties,
- liabilities of the parties,
- term and renewal of the agreement,
- definition of the services, quality of service level and supply time for initial connection,
- tariff package chosen by the subscriber at the date of the agreement, and
- dispute resolution procedure.

35.80   Furthermore, the subscription contracts in relation to telecommunications services to be executed between the operators and the subscribers are subject to review by the TA. The TA may at any time request the operators to amend the general terms and conditions of standard subscription contracts. Certain administrative fines may be imposed on operators who conclude subscription contracts with subscribers without obtaining the approval of the TA.[47]

35.81   In addition, the issues related to the protection of end-user rights are regulated in Section V of the Draft ECA in parallel terms to Chapter IV of the Universal Service Directive.

DATA PROTECTION AND PRIVACY

35.82   The Regulation on Protection and Processing of Personal Data in the Telecommunications Sector[48] sets out the rules concerning the confidentiality of communications. Article 6 of this Regulation provides that operators are obliged to take appropriate technical and organisational measures to ensure the security of their services and to submit such measures to the approval of the TA. If there is a risk of security breach in relation to the services being rendered by such operators, subscribers must be informed without delay of the risk and possible remedies.[49]

---

45   Art 6 Draft Law on Universal Service.
46   The following are also included: kinds of support/repair types; date and location where the agreement is made; compensation and pay-back procedures if the service level stated in the agreement cannot be achieved due to the fault of the operator; conditions of default by the subscriber in the case of non-payment of the invoice; applicable tariffs and ways to obtain information on changes to tariffs; information about the necessary technical equipment for the service; and date of approval by the TA, if such standard subscription agreement requires the approval of the TA in accordance with article 17 Regulation on Consumer Rights
47   Art 16 Regulation on Administrative Fines.
48   Dated 6 February 2004.
49   Art 7 Regulation on Protection and Processing of Personal Data in the Telecommunications Sector.

Furthermore, operators are obliged to provide necessary devices and equipment required for the processing of personal data and the protection of confidentiality.

35.83   Article 8 of the Regulation provides that telecommunications are confidential, and surveillance, recording, interception and storage of telecommunications are prohibited in the absence of the consent of all of the parties to the telecommunication, except in circumstances as required by law or a court order.

Traffic Data and Location Data

35.84   After obtaining consent from the users, operators may process data for the purposes of marketing electronic communications services or the provision of value added services, to the extent and for the duration necessary for the provision of such services.[50]

35.85   Location data may, subject to the consent of the user, only be processed if it has been made anonymous, to the extent and for the duration necessary for the provision of a value added service.[51]

Itemised Billing

35.86   Users have the right to receive itemised or non-itemised bills as per their request.

Directories of Subscribers

35.87   Operators must inform all subscribers, free of charge, before including their data in a directory, of the purposes of such a subscribers' directory. Subscribers must have the opportunity, free of charge, to verify, correct or withdraw the data.[52]

---

50   Art 9 Regulation on Protection and Processing of Personal Data in the Telecommunications Sector.
51   Art 15 Regulation on Protection and Processing of Personal Data in the Telecommunications Sector.
52   Art 19 Regulation on Protection and Processing of Personal Data in the Telecommunications Sector.

The Ukrainian Market for Electronic Communications[1]

Olexander Martinenko, Anna Yegupova, Vitaliy Radchenko
Baker & McKenzie, Kiev

LEGAL STRUCTURE

Basic Policy

36.1   Since Ukraine's independence, significant changes have been incorporated into the regulatory framework of the Ukrainian telecommunications sector. Those changes initiated, to a large extent, the process of adjusting domestic legislation to the fundamental principles adopted by the European Union. All of the organisations involved in planning, building and operating public telecommunications networks in Ukraine were merged into the open joint stock company 'Ukrtelecom', currently the major Ukrainian telecommunications operator. The primary communications networks are to remain in the ownership of Ukrtelecom, which is prohibited by law from transferring them to other entities.[2] Following the adoption of the Telecommunications Law,[3] most regulatory functions were transferred from the Ministry of Transportation and Communications of Ukraine ('MTCU') to an independent authority – the National Commission for Communications Regulation ('NCCR'), established on 19 April 2005.[4]

36.2   Ukraine's telecommunications market is highly diversified. Most telecommunications companies in Ukraine are privately held entities with or without foreign investment. Since 2000, foreign investors have been authorised to hold up to 100% equity interest in Ukrainian telecommunication companies. Previously, the maximum share was 49%. At the same time, foreign investments in radio broadcasting or television companies remained restricted to 30% equity interest.

36.3   The overall regulatory objectives, as set out in the state communications policy for 2005[5] and applicable laws, are the development of Ukrainian communications legislation and its harmonisation with EU law, the provision of high-tech

---

1   Editing of this chapter closed on 8 July 2005.
2   Art 19 Law of Ukraine No 1869-III 'On Specific Aspects of the Privatisation of Open Joint Stock Company 'Ukrtelecom', dated 13 July 2000.
3   Law of Ukraine No 1280-IV 'On Telecommunications', dated 18 November 2003.
4   Presidential Decree No 664/2005 'On Composition of the National Commission for Communications Regulation', dated 19 April 2005.
5   Draft Law of Ukraine No 6147 'On the State Program of Economic and Social Development of Ukraine in 2005'.

communications services, participation by Ukraine in international fibre-optic lines construction projects, and the improvement of internet regulation and information security.

Implementation of EU Directives

36.4   Implementation of the EU regulatory framework, as predetermined by the Partnership and Co-operation Agreement between the European Communities and their Member States, and Ukraine,[6] has been addressed in a number of legislative acts.[7] Although the 2002 EU Regulatory Package has not yet been implemented into Ukrainian law in its entirety, its general rules relating to the regulatory framework, access to and interconnection of networks, universal services and data protection have been incorporated into the Telecommunications Law. In addition, the EU-Ukraine Action Plan under the European Neighbourhood Policy[8] provides for the adoption of regulations concerning licensing, interconnection, numbering and generally accessible telecommunications services.

36.5   The recent EU Adaptation Law,[9] aimed at the adoption of the *acquis communautaire*, prescribes the approximation of Ukrainian legislation with that of the EU in certain priority areas, including competition, technical rules, and standards. The government agency responsible for the approximation – the Coordination Council for the Adaptation of the Legislation of Ukraine to the Legislation of the European Union – examines proposed legislation in the areas falling within the scope of EU legislation as to its conformity with EU law. Those laws or regulations that are found to contradict EU law may be adopted for a fixed term only, provided there are compelling reasons for such adoption.

Legislation

36.6   Ukrainian telecommunications legislation consists of laws adopted by the Parliament and implementing regulations of competent state authorities, ie the NCCR and the MTCU. The Telecommunications Law establishes the competence of state authorities in regulating telecommunication activities, and determines the legal status of telecommunications operators, providers, and consumers of telecommunications services. The Telecommunications Law also regulates access to the telecommunications market, the interconnection of telecommunications networks, rights of way, privacy issues, authorisations, pricing policy, and dispute settlement. The Licensing Conditions Order[10] contains requirements relating to telecommunication services rendered by telecommunications operators under telecommunications licences. The Numbering Resources Order[11] regulates the allocation of

---

6   Signed on 14 June 1994.

7   Presidential Decree No 1072/2000 'Program of Ukraine's Integration into the European Union', dated 14 September 2000; Law of Ukraine No 1280-IV 'On Telecommunications', dated 18 November 2003 and Law of Ukraine No 228-IV 'On the Concept of the Nationwide Program of Adaptation of the Legislation of Ukraine to the Legislation of the European Union', dated 21 November 2002.

8   www.kmu.gov.ua/control/en/publish/article?art_id=12854890&cat_id=12853974.

9   Law of Ukraine No 1629-IV 'On the Nationwide Program of Adaptation of the Legislation of Ukraine to the Legislation of the European Union', dated 18 March 2004.

10   Order No 132 of the former State Committee for Communications and Informatisation of

numbering resources for telephone communications services. The Radio Frequencies Law[12] provides comprehensive rules for the allocation, assignment, interrelation and use of radio frequencies in Ukraine. The Resolution on Radio Frequencies Licensing[13] sets out a detailed procedure for the issuance of radio frequency licences for specific bandwidths.

36.7 Although the Telecommunications Law is relatively new, the market expectations are that it will undergo significant changes. Such changes will be aimed at bringing it in line with EU Directives/Regulations and at the further liberalisation of the telecommunications markets.

36.8 Decisions of the NCCR and the MTCU in individual cases, provided they are adopted within the authorities' competence, are binding on those to whom they are addressed. The MTCU is also charged with monitoring the application of telecommunications laws and submitting appropriate proposals to the Parliament.[14]

REGULATORY PRINCIPLES

Scope of Regulation

36.9 The scope of application of the Telecommunications Law extends to fixed-line and mobile telephone communications, the maintenance and exploitation of on-air and cable broadcasting and television networks, leasing of electronic communications channels, and communication services based on the internet protocol (IP telephony).[15] The regulatory regime of the Telecommunications Law does not apply to those telecommunications networks which do not interact with publicly available networks, except for the use of such networks under a state of emergency or in the event of war.[16]

36.10 The terms 'telecommunications' and 'electronic communications' are used interchangeably throughout the Telecommunications Law. The term 'telecommunications network' is defined as 'a complex of technical means of telecommunications and structures designed for routing, commuting, transmitting and/or receiving symbols, signals, written text, images and sounds or communications of any kind by radio, wire, optical or other electromagnetic systems between terminal equipment'.[17] 'Telecommunications service' is defined as 'a product of activities of a telecommunications operator and/or provider aimed at the satisfaction of consumer needs in the area of telecommunications'. VoIP services are fully covered by the definition of 'electronic communications'. There is no definition of 'associated

---

Ukraine ('SCCI') 'On the Approval of Licensing Conditions for Carrying Out the Business Activity of Providing International, Long-distance, Local Telephone Communication Services', dated 17 June 2004.

11 Order No 82 of the SCCI 'On the Approval of the Regulations on the Management of Numbering Resources of General-Purpose Telecommunication Networks of Ukraine', dated 25 April 2002.

12 Law of Ukraine No 1770-III 'On Radio Frequency Resource of Ukraine', dated 1 June 2000.

13 Resolution No 112 of the Cabinet of Ministers of Ukraine 'On the Procedure for the Issuance of Licences for the Use of the Radio Frequency Resource of Ukraine', dated 7 February 2001.

14 Presidential Decree No 1009/2004 'On Regulations on the Ministry of Transportation and Communications of Ukraine' ('Decree No. 1009/2004'), dated 27 August 2004.

15 Arts 1, 42(3), 42(3)(3) Telecommunications Law.

16 Art 5(2) Telecommunications Law.

17 Art 1 Telecommunications Law.

facilities'. Rather, article 1 Telecommunications Law defines 'technical means of telecommunications' to be 'equipment, stations and linear structures designed for the formation of telecommunications networks'.

National Regulatory Authorities: Organisation, Regulatory Objectives, Competencies

36.11   At present, there are two governmental authorities, independent of each other, that are in charge of the Ukrainian telecommunications sector: the NCCR and the MTCU. The MTCU develops legislative measures, technical rules and standards, while the NCCR is responsible for registration and licensing issues, allocation of numbering resources, tariff regulation and regulation of interconnection agreements.

36.12   The regulatory objectives for the NCCR, as determined in article 16 Telecommunications Law, are as follows:

- utmost satisfaction of consumer demand for telecommunications services,
- creation of favourable organisational and economic conditions for attracting investment,
- increase in the volume and quality of services, and
- development and modernisation of telecommunications networks, having regard to national security interests.

The regulatory objectives of the MTCU are set out in Decree No 1009/2004 as:

- participation in the shaping and realisation of state policies in the areas of telecommunications, allocation and use of radio frequency resources, and the Information Society,
- development and implementation of measures aimed at the improvement of quality, accessibility and sustained performance of public telecommunication networks,
- formation and implementation of the National Information Society Program, and
- creation of conditions for the integration of Ukrainian national telecommunication and information services to global information areas.

36.13   The NCCR is authorised to make filings with the Anti-Monopoly Committee of Ukraine ('AMC') with respect to competition law infringements.[18] Once a filing is made, the AMC will proceed with the case in accordance with the Competition Law.[19]

36.14   Both the NCCR and the MTCU have the power to obtain information from telecommunications companies.[20] In particular, companies are obliged to file periodical statistical reports with the NCCR[21] and to provide the MTCU with annual information on their telecommunications networks for defence purposes as prescribed by the Cabinet of Ministers.[22]

---

18   As prescribed by art 18(14) Telecommunications Law.
19   Law of Ukraine No 2210-III 'On the Protection of Economic Competition', dated 11 January 2001.
20   Art 39 Telecommunications Law.
21   Art 18 Telecommunications Law.
22   Art 39 Telecommunications Law.

36.15 The MTCU and the NCCR are obliged to co-operate with Ukrainian governmental authorities and with the NRAs of other countries.[23] In particular, the MTCU is obliged to participate in international co-operation in the areas of communications, the allocation of radio frequencies and information and to ensure the fulfilment of Ukraine's obligations arising out of its membership of international, European and regional organisations.[24]

36.16 The NCCR has the power to resolve interconnection disputes between telecommunications undertakings,[25] without prejudice to the right of either party to bring an action before the courts.[26]

Right of Appeal against NRA's Decisions

36.17 Any foreign or Ukrainian undertaking affected by a particular administrative act of the MTCU or the NCCR may bring a court action seeking to annul such act and/or to recover damages.[27] According to the applicable rules governing exclusive jurisdiction, disputes with central governmental authorities, such as the MTCU or the NCCR, are heard by the Kiev City Commercial Court.[28]

36.18 Generally, there are no legal restrictions on the enforcement of court decisions against state authorities. If the court decision renders a particular administrative act ineffective, such administrative act will be annulled within the prescribed period of time. However, an undertaking seeking to recover damages from a state authority may find it difficult due to the unavailability of the state budget funds for such a recovery.

'Monopolistic position' as a Fundamental Prerequisite of Regulation

Definition of a 'monopolistic position'

36.19 The telecommunications legislation does not define or use the term SMP. However, the concept of SMP has been expressed through the concept of a monopolistic operator, defined as an operator who occupies the monopolistic (dominant)[29] position on the market of specific telecommunications services on a nation-wide or regional basis.[30] Pursuant to the Competition Law, an undertaking is deemed to occupy a monopolistic position if it is the sole market-player on a relevant market, or it is not subject to significant competition due to the limited access available to other entities to the procurement of raw materials or sale of

---

23 Art 18(22) Telecommunications Law imposes the duty to cooperate with other states' telecommunications authorities upon the NCCR after the latter's establishment.

24 Art 4(34) Decree No 1009/2004. Ukraine is a member of International Telecommunication Union, INTELSAT, EUTELSAT, Intersputnik, CEPT, ICANN, and ETSI.

25 Art 18(19) Telecommunications Law.

26 Art 61 Telecommunications Law.

27 Explanation No 02–5/35 of the Presidium of the Supreme Commercial Court of Ukraine 'On Certain Practical Issues of Resolving Disputes Related to the Recognition of Acts of State or Other Authorities Ineffective', dated 26 January 2000.

28 Art 16 Commercial Procedural Code, dated 6 November 1991.

29 The terms 'monopolistic' and 'dominant' are used synonymously in Ukrainian law. For convenience, the term 'monopolistic' will be used throughout the rest of this chapter.

30 Art 1 Telecommunications Law.

goods/services, due to existing barriers to access on to the market by other entities, due to the privileges enjoyed by such undertaking, or other circumstances.[31]

36.20   An undertaking is presumed to enjoy a monopolistic position on a relevant market if its market share exceeds 35% of the relevant market, unless such undertaking proves that it is subject to significant competition. An undertaking may be deemed to enjoy a monopolistic market position if its market share is equal to or less than 35% but it is not subject to significant competition, in particular, due to a comparatively insignificant market share of its competitors.

36.21   Each of two or more entities is deemed to enjoy a monopolistic position on a respective market if there is no significant competition between them with respect to a particular product and they, jointly, are not subject to significant competition from other market players. Finally, each of several business entities is deemed to occupy a monopolistic position if the following conditions apply: the combined market share of no more than three business entities, to which the largest market shares on a relevant market belong, exceeds 50% of the relevant market; or the combined market share of no more than five business entities, to which the largest market shares on a relevant market belong, exceeds 70% of the relevant market; provided that such business entities are unable to prove that there is significant competition between them with respect to a specific product or they are subject to significant competition by the other market players.

36.22   The determination of whether a specific undertaking or group of entities is in a monopolistic position on a relevant market falls within the authority of the AMC. The AMC publishes the List of Entities that Occupy a Monopolistic Position on the National Market (the 'List').[32]

Definition of relevant markets

36.23   The relevant markets are identified by the AMC either on an ad hoc basis (eg within proceedings with respect to anti-competitive concerted actions) or in connection with defining monopolistic market players for the purposes of the List. So far, the following relevant markets have been identified in the List:

- lease of broadcasting channels,
- lease of radio-relay communications channels,
- lease of non-switched communications channels,
- local telephone communications services,
- inter-city telephone communications services,
- lease of technical means for, and channels of, wire broadcasting,
- local radio telecommunications services, and
- international telephone communications services.

36.24   Ukrtelecom has been designated as having a monopolistic position in the markets for local telephone communications services, inter-city telephone communications services, lease of non-switched communications channels, lease of technical means for, and channels of, wire broadcasting, local radio telecommunications services, and international telephone communications services.[33]

---

31   Art 12(1) Competition Law.
32   No 31–29/04–904, dated 12 March 1999.
33   The List has not been updated since 1999.

36.25   Closed Joint Stock Company 'Utel' has been designated as having a monopolistic position in the market for inter-city telephone communications services.

36.26   Concern RRT ('Radio Broadcasting, Radio Communications and Television Concern') has been designated as having a monopolistic position in the markets for lease of broadcasting channels and lease of radio-relay communication channels.

36.27   In addition to the general restrictions and obligations imposed on a monopolistic undertaking by the Competition Law, monopolistic operators are required to comply with certain telecommunications-specific restrictions and obligations. In particular, a monopolistic operator may not refuse interconnection with another telecommunications operator.[34] Furthermore, a monopolistic operator is required to provide the NRA with detailed information regarding the technical and commercial conditions for interconnection with its network, to be published by the NRA in a catalogue of interconnection offers on an annual basis.

36.28   The NCCR has the power to regulate the following matters with respect to monopolistic operators:

- technical, organisational and commercial conditions for interconnection,
- interconnection fees charged, and
- tariffs for the lease of communications channels charged by operators who occupy a monopolistic position in the markets for lease of communications channels.

36.29   Finally, the NRA may impose obligations on nation-wide monopolistic operators to develop and provide universal services in certain areas of Ukraine with low penetration of telecommunications services.

NRA's Regulatory Duties concerning Rights of Way, Co-location and Facility Sharing

36.30   Article 10(6) Telecommunications Law provides that holders of telecommunications licences have rights of way over the so-called 'lands reserved for communications purposes'[35] for laying out underground telecommunications networks and/or their repair. The tariffs for exercising such rights of way shall be as determined by the Cabinet of Ministers of Ukraine.

36.31   Rights of way over particular property, whether public or private, may be granted on the basis of an agreement with the property owner or, in the absence of such agreement, on the basis of a court decision.[36] Since most lands in Ukraine still remain in public ownership (whether national or municipal), in practice, rights of way are granted by decisions of the relevant local councils allocating particular land plots for specific purposes, e g for laying out telecommunications lines or installing masts.

---

34   Art 60(5) Telecommunications Law.
35   Land plots allocated for air and cable telephone and telegraph lines and satellite means of communications, art 75 Land Code of the Ukraine, dated 25 October 2001. Such land may be held in state, municipal, or private property.
36   Art 100 Land Code. Since easements/servitudes, including rights of way, are a relatively new concept in the Ukraine, there is as yet little guidance as to how a court should exercise such powers.

36.32 There are no relevant provisions concerning co-location and facility sharing in Ukrainian law.

REGULATION OF MARKET ENTRY

General Regulatory Approach

36.33   An undertaking wishing to provide telecommunication services must notify the NCCR at least a month in advance of the commencement of the services.[37] The NCCR is required to enter the undertaking into a register and to send confirmation to the telecommunications operator within one month after the receipt of the notice.

36.34   Furthermore, an undertaking wishing to provide the following telecommunications services is required to apply for and obtain a licence from the NCCR:

- local, inter-city, and international fixed line telecommunication services with the right to carry out technical maintenance and operation of telecommunications networks and to lease communications channels,
- mobile telecommunications services with the right to carry out technical maintenance and operation of telecommunications networks and to lease communications channels, and
- technical maintenance and operation of TV and radio air broadcasting networks, wire broadcasting networks and TV networks and leasing of broadcasting channels.

36.35   The NCCR must decide whether to issue or refuse a licence within 30 working days from the date of receipt of the application.[38] The NCCR must then notify the applicant of its decision within three working days.[39]

36.36   If the decision is favourable to the applicant, the NCCR shall inform the applicant of the amount of the official fees to be paid by the applicant for the issue of the licence and the procedure for payment and for the licence receipt.[40]

36.37   A decision refusing a licence may be appealed by the applicant to the courts.

36.38   A licence grants the right to an undertaking to provide particular telecommunications services within a certain territory and on certain licensing terms and conditions. In addition to the standard licensing terms and conditions set out by the NCCR[41] (applicable to all undertakings who provide a particular type of telecommunications services), a licence may provide for special terms and conditions established by the NCCR on a case-by-case basis. The NCCR may amend such special licensing terms and conditions on renewal of the licence.[42]

36.39   The duration of a licence is determined by the NCCR on a case-by-case basis, but may not be shorter than five years. A licence may be renewed by filing an

---

37   Art 42(1) Telecommunications Law.
38   Art 46(1) Telecommunications Law.
39   Art 46(2) Telecommunications Law.
40   Art 46(4) Telecommunications Law.
41   Order No 984 of the MTCU, dated 10 November 2004, and Order No 132 of the SCCI, dated 17 June 2004.
42   Art 49(5) Telecommunications Law.

application with the NCCR at least four months before its expiration. The NCCR may not refuse the renewal of a licence if the licensee has complied with the licensing terms and conditions, or if the failure to comply with the licensing terms and conditions was beyond the licensee's control.

36.40   The NCCR monitors the licensee's compliance with the licensing terms and conditions via regular and extraordinary audits. If an audit uncovers a violation of the licensing terms and conditions, the NCCR must issue an order obliging the licensee to remedy the violation or take a decision on the revocation of the licence.[43]

36.41   The NCCR may take a decision limiting the number of licences if there is a need to ensure the efficient use of networks and the use of limited resources.[44] If NCCR takes such a decision, licences must be issued on a competitive basis within four months after the competition announcement. The results of a competition may be appealed to the courts.

36.42   A licence may be revoked by the NCCR on the following grounds:[45]

- submission by a licensee of false information when applying for a licence,
- transfer of a licence to another undertaking or individual for the purpose of providing telecommunications services,
- failure of an operator/provider to remedy a violation of the licensing terms and conditions, and
- repeated violation of the licensing terms and conditions.[46]

Rights of Use for Radio Frequencies

General regulatory approach

36.43   Use of radio frequencies is governed by the Radio Frequencies Law. An undertaking intending to use radio frequencies must apply for a licence. The decision to issue or refuse a licence must be taken within 60 days from the date of the application. A licensee is required to pay official fees for the grant of a licence. In addition, a licensee is required to make monthly payments for the use of radio frequency resource.[47]

36.44   A licence is issued for the use of specific bands and channels of radio frequencies in specific regions or cities, for the purpose of providing certain telecommunication services. A licence is issued for a minimum period of five years and may be renewed by filing a renewal application at least four months prior to the expiration of the licence.[48]

36.45   The issue of a licence for the use of radio frequency resource is dependent, inter alia, on whether there are frequencies available in the respective radio frequency resource that are not in use by other operators or the military. The issuing process, as well as other technical issues involved in the licensing procedure, falls

---

43   Art 54(5) Telecommunications Law; see para 36.53 et seq below.
44   Art 47(1) Telecommunications Law.
45   Art 55 Telecommunications Law.
46   Other grounds for revocation include: application for revocation by the licensee, prevention of the NCCR officials from conducting an audit of the operator/provider, winding up of a corporate operator/provider or death of an individual operator/provider.
47   Arts 32, 49 and 57 Radio Frequencies Law.
48   Arts 31(4) and 37(1) Radio Frequencies Law.

within the competence of the Ukrainian Center for Radio Frequencies, a state-owned entity subordinated to the MTCU.

Admissible conditions

36.46   A number of special conditions are attached to a licence for the use of radio frequency resource:

- receipt by the licensee of a permit for the use of the respective radio emission device(s),
- use of certified equipment,
- the licensee's compliance with the health standards and requirements for the protection of the population from electromagnetic radiation, and
- a schedule for the commencement of the use of radio frequencies throughout different regions.[49]

Limitation of number of rights of use to be granted

36.47   A licence for the use of radio frequency resource shall be granted via tender if there are two or more applications for the same resource in the same region, if there is limited availability of radio frequencies, or if there is insufficient capacity on the communications services market.[50]

Frequency trading

36.48   Frequency trading is not allowed in Ukraine.[51]

Rights of Use for Numbers

General regulatory approach

36.49   An operator may obtain rights of use for numbers by filing an application with the NCCR. The NCCR must issue or refuse a permit for the use of numbers within one month from the application.[52] The permit is issued within three days of payment of the prescribed fee by the operator. The right of use for numbers is valid for the term of the licence, and may not be assigned by an operator to a third party.

36.50   The NCCR may withdraw all or some numbers from an operator if:

- the operator fails to commence the use of such numbers within the timeframe specified in the relevant permit,
- the numbers are being misused (eg are transferred to a third party), or

---

49   Art 36(2)(4) Radio Frequencies Law.
50   Order No 102 of the SCCI 'On the Approval of the Regulations on the Procedure for Organisation and Holding of Auctions for the Sale of Licences for the Use of Radio Frequencies in Ukraine', dated 6 July 1998.
51   If the frequency licence holder transfers the licence to another undertaking, through sale or otherwise, the licence will be revoked pursuant to art 38(1)(3) Radio Frequencies Law.
52   Art 70(2) Telecommunications Law.

- the relevant licence has expired, been revoked or invalidated.[53]

Admissible conditions

36.51   The following conditions can be attached to a permit for the use of numbers:

- conditions relating to the efficient use of the numbers in accordance with the requirements set out in the permit,
- conditions relating to the creation and maintenance of a comprehensive database of the numbers allocated to the operator, and
- conditions obliging the operator to submit annual information on the use of the numbers to the NCCR.[54]

Limitation of number of rights of use to be granted

36.52   Although the Telecommunications Law states that numbers are deemed to be a scarce resource, the applicable legislation fails to address the issue of the limitation of the number of rights of use to be granted.

The NRA's Enforcement Powers

36.53   The recently established NCCR will take over the regulatory powers of enforcing licensing conditions in accordance with the Telecommunications Law.[55] Meanwhile, the Control Procedure Order[56] sets out a procedure for the enforcement of licensing conditions and specifies the measures that the MTCU may take to ensure compliance. To that end, the MTCU is authorised to carry out periodical examinations of licence holders.

36.54   Under the Telecommunications Law, the NCCR will be authorised to have unrestricted access to the property and facilities of telecommunication operators and providers and to obtain, free of charge, any necessary information, clarifications and other materials from business entities on the telecommunication market.[57]

36.55   Where the NCCR finds that the undertaking does not comply with the licensing conditions, it shall issue an order to remedy any breaches within a prescribed time limit.[58] Failure to do so may result in the revocation of the relevant telecommunication licence.[59]

---

53   Art 70(4) Telecommunications Law.
54   Order No 82 of the SCCI 'On the Approval of the Regulations on the Management of the Numbering Resource of the Public Communications Networks of Ukraine', dated 25 April 2002.
55   Art 54(1) Telecommunications Law.
56   Joint Order No 15/27 of the State Committee of Ukraine for Regulatory Policy and Entrepreneurship and the Committee for Communications and Informatisation of Ukraine 'On the Approval of the Procedure for the Control of Compliance with Licensing Conditions of Carrying Out Certain Licensed Business Activities in the Area of Communications', dated 7 February 2002.
57   Art 19(3) Telecommunication Law.
58   Art 54(5) Telecommunications Law.
59   Art 55(1)(4) Telecommunications Law.

Administrative Charges and Fees for Rights of Use

36.56 The Cabinet of Ministers of Ukraine has established the following administrative fees for the right of use:

- one-time fees for the issue of telecommunication services licences, which vary from €50 to €1,400,000,[60]
- one-time charges for the allocation of numbers, number blocks or codes, which vary from €50 to €800,000,[61]
- one-time fees for the issue of licences for radio frequencies use, which vary from €10 to €220,000 per MHz in each region,[62] and
- monthly fees for radio frequencies use, which vary from €0.03 to €1,300 per MHz in each region.[63]

REGULATION OF INTERCONNECTION

Objectives and Scope of Interconnection Regulation

36.57 The objectives of the NCCR in regulating interconnection are:

- the regulation of technical, organisational, pricing and commercial conditions of interconnection with telecommunication operators who hold a monopolistic position on the telecommunication market, and
- ensuring effective competition, non-discrimination and fair conditions which are acceptable to the parties to interconnection agreements and are beneficial for end users.[64]

36.58 Interconnection-related provisions of Ukrainian telecommunication laws generally apply to operators (network providers) irrespective of their market position,[65] although monopolistic operators have stricter obligations regarding interconnection.[66]

Basic Regulatory Concepts

36.59 The NCCR regulates the manner of submission, consideration and approval of proposals of operators in relation to interconnection of telecommunications networks, sets requirements applicable to agreements on interconnection of telecommunications networks and may participate in the settlement of interconnection disputes.[67]

36.60 There is no definition of 'access' in Ukrainian law. 'Interconnection of telecommunications networks' is defined as 'the installation of physical and/or

---

60 Resolution No 773 of the Cabinet of Ministers of Ukraine, dated 16 June 2004.
61 Resolution No 839 of the Cabinet of Ministers of Ukraine, dated 5 July 2004.
62 Resolution No 140 of the Cabinet of Ministers of Ukraine, dated 14 February 2001.
63 Resolution No 77 of the Cabinet of Ministers of Ukraine, dated 31 January 2001.
64 Art 57 Telecommunications Law.
65 Chapter IX Telecommunications Law.
66 See para 36.61 below.
67 Arts 59, 60 and 61 Telecommunications Law.

logical connection between different telecommunications networks enabling users to exchange information directly or indirectly'.[68]

Obligations with Respect to Undertakings with a Monopolistic Position

36.61   Telecommunication operators holding a monopolistic position do not have the right to reject interconnection with a telecommunication network of another operator at the points which are indicated in the catalogue of interconnection offers,[69] except where the interconnecting telecommunication network does not comply with the standards prescribed by the Telecommunications Law.[70] Moreover, the NCCR shall fix tariffs for access to telecommunications networks of operators which hold a monopolistic position.[71] Price control, transparency and non-discrimination obligations may also be imposed on monopolistic operators.[72]

Obligations Applicable to All Market Participants

36.62   The following Telecommunications Law provisions apply to all network operators irrespective of their market position:

- material terms of interconnection agreements, such as technical conditions of interconnection and interconnection charges, should be the product of free negotiations between network operators,[73]
- interconnection charges should be based on the economic costs of providing interconnection,[74]
- interconnection disputes between operators are resolved by the NCCR on a timely basis and in a transparent manner,[75] and
- rulings of the NCCR on interconnection agreements may be appealed to the courts.[76]

36.63   Telecommunications operators are obliged, inter alia, to comply with technical requirements applicable to networks, to provide other operators with information required for the preparation of interconnection agreements, to ensure timely settlement under such agreements, to avoid creating obstacles to interconnection, and to exchange data on telecommunications services provided through interconnected networks.[77]

36.64   The Telecommunications Law provides for the settlement of disputes arising in connection with entry into, amendments to, and/or termination of interconnection agreements, by the NCCR upon an application from a party so such an agreement.[78] If any of the parties is not satisfied with the NCCR decision, such party may appeal to a competent court.

---

68   Art 1 Telecommunications Law.
69   See para 36.27 above.
70   Art 60(5) Telecommunications Law.
71   Art 57(4) Telecommunications Law.
72   Art 57(1)(4), 58, 57(1)(5) Telecommunications Law.
73   Art 57(1)(1) Telecommunications Law.
74   Art 57(1)(2) Telecommunications Law.
75   Art 57(1)(5) Telecommunications Law.
76   Art 57(1)(6) Telecommunications Law.
77   Art 58 Telecommunications Law.
78   Art 61(1) Telecommunications Law.

REGULATION OF UNIVERSAL SERVICES AND USERS' RIGHTS

Regulation of Universal Service Obligations

36.65   'Public (universal) telecommunication services' are defined as a minimum of telecommunication services, identified by the Telecommunications Law, that are available for all customers throughout Ukraine.[79] Universal services include a voice telephony service, which allows the making and receiving of local, long-distance and international calls, facsimile communications, free access to emergency services, and access to operator services; and public payphones capable of providing these services.[80]

36.66   The NCCR may impose obligations to provide a universal service on nation-wide monopolistic operators and on regional fixed-line operators in certain areas of Ukraine with low telecommunications services penetration.[81] The Telecommunications Law, however, fails to establish a universal service fund to provide financial support for the maintenance of universal services.

DATA PROTECTION AND PRIVACY

Confidentiality of Communications

36.67   Telecommunications network providers and service providers are required to take technical and organisational measures to ensure protection of telecommunication facilities, telecommunications networks, and information which is transmitted via these networks.[82]

36.68   Exceptions from the confidentiality of communications principle may be made exclusively by a court in accordance with the law, with the purpose of preventing crime or ascertaining the truth in the course of a criminal investigation, provided it is not possible to obtain information by any other means.[83]

36.69   As a general rule, the collection, storage, use and dissemination of confidential information about an individual without his or her consent is not permitted, except in cases determined by law, and only in the interests of national security, economic welfare and human rights.[84] Network and service providers must ensure, and are liable for, the confidentiality of user information.[85]

---

79   Art 1 Telecommunications Law.
80   Art 62 Telecommunications Law.
81   Art 64(5) Telecommunications Law.
82   Art 9(3) Telecommunications Law.
83   Art 31 Constitution of Ukraine, dated 28 June 1996.
84   Art 32 Constitution of Ukraine.
85   Art 34(1) Telecommunications Law.

Traffic Data and Location Data

36.70 There are no definitions of traffic data or location data in Ukrainian law. However, operators (network providers) are obliged to keep records on telecommunication services actually provided and may disclose information on users and services in certain limited cases determined by law.[86]

Itemised Billing

36.71 There are no itemised billing regulations in Ukrainian telecommunications laws.

Calling and Connected Line Identification

36.72 There are no legislative provisions concerning calling and connected line identification in Ukrainian law. Operators usually provide calling line and connected line identification services by default and free of charge. In practice, subscribers can order calling line identification restriction services.

Automatic Call Forwarding

36.73 There are no legislative provisions on automatic call forwarding in Ukraine.

Directories of Subscribers

36.74 Telephone directories, as well as their electronic versions and databases of referral and information services, may contain family name, first name, middle name, title, address and telephone number of a subscriber only if the subscriber agreed in the relevant telecommunication services contract that such information may be made publicly available. A subscriber has the right to have his complete or partial information withdrawn, free of charge, from electronic databases.[87]

Unsolicited Communications

36.75 Neither telecommunications nor competition laws of Ukraine regulate unsolicited communications. However, the Criminal Code[88] has been amended recently to protect internet users from spam, defined as intentional mass sending of electronic messages, committed without preliminary consent of the addressee, which resulted in malfunction or breaking down of computers, automated systems, computer networks or networks of electronic communications.[89]

36.76 The only way in which unsolicited communications can be permitted is where the prior consent of the addressee has been obtained. Opt-in/opt-out systems are not foreseen in Ukrainian law.

---

86 Eg as requested by competent Ukrainian authorities.
87 Art 34(2) Telecommunications Law.
88 Criminal Code of Ukraine, dated 5 April 2001.
89 Art 363[1] Criminal Code.

36.77   Self-regulation is usually adopted by network providers and service providers. With respect to unsolicited communications they usually refer to the documents of the Open Forum of Internet Service Providers,[90] which adopted the Terms of Network Use. Those terms regulate limitations on the distribution of unsolicited and unauthorised information (spam), prohibition on the dissemination of certain types of information, and a ban on unauthorised access and network attacks.

---

90   www.ofisp.org.

Index

All references are to paragraph number.